MW00782545

West's Law School
Advisory Board

JESSE H. CHOPER
Professor of Law,
University of California, Berkeley

DAVID P. CURRIE
Professor of Law, University of Chicago

YALE KAMISAR
Professor of Law, University of San Diego
Professor of Law, University of Michigan

MARY KAY KANE
Chancellor, Dean and Distinguished Professor of Law,
University of California,
Hastings College of the Law

LARRY D. KRAMER
Dean and Professor of Law, Stanford Law School

JONATHAN R. MACEY
Professor of Law, Yale Law School

WAYNE R. LaFAVE
Professor of Law, University of Illinois

ARTHUR R. MILLER
Professor of Law, Harvard University

GRANT S. NELSON
Professor of Law,
University of California, Los Angeles

JAMES J. WHITE
Professor of Law, University of Michigan

CASES AND MATERIALS ON
APPELLATE PRACTICE AND PROCEDURE
Second Edition

By

Robert J. Martineau
Distinguished Research Professor of Law (Emeritus)
University of Cincinnati

Kent Sinclair
Professor of Law and Director of Advocacy Training
University of Virginia

Michael E. Solimine
Donald P. Klekamp Professor of Law
University of Cincinnati

Randy J. Holland
Justice
Supreme Court of Delaware

AMERICAN CASEBOOK SERIES®

Mat #40238958

Thomson/West have created this publication to provide you with accurate and authoritative information concerning the subject matter covered. However, this publication was not necessarily prepared
by persons licensed to practice law in a particular jurisdiction. Thomson/West are not engaged in
rendering legal or other professional advice, and this publication is not a substitute for the advice of
an attorney. If you require legal or other expert advice, you should seek the services of a competent
attorney or other professional.

American Casebook Series and West Group are trademarks
registered in the U.S. Patent and Trademark Office.

COPYRIGHT © 1987 WEST PUBLISHING CO.
© 2005 Thomson/West
        610 Opperman Drive
        P.O. Box 64526
        St. Paul, MN 55164–0526
        1–800–328–9352

Printed in the United States of America

ISBN 0–314–15246–6

 TEXT IS PRINTED ON 10% POST
CONSUMER RECYCLED PAPER

*To our wives, Connie, Katy, Pat, and Ilona,
who have never lost their appeal.*

*

Foreword

The first edition of this book, published in 1986, was a direct result of the 1985 report *Appellate Litigation Skills Training—The Role of the Law Schools*. This report was issued by the American Bar Association's Appellate Judges Conference and prepared its committee on Appellate Skills Training. (It is reprinted at 54 University of Cincinnati Law Review 129.) The report pointed out the dramatic disparity between the greatly increased attention given in law schools to trial litigation—both substantive knowledge and skills training—and the almost total ignoring of litigation at the appellate level aside from first year appellate advocacy programs and student run moot court competitions. One of the reasons cited for the dearth of regular law school courses on appellate practice and procedure was the fact that there was no published casebook on the subject. If a regular or adjunct faculty member wanted to teach appellate practice and procedure, the faculty member had to put together a set of materials, usually a daunting task especially for an adjunct. This led Professor Martineau, who was a member of the Committee on Appellate Skills Training and the principal author of the report, to convert the mimeographed materials he had been using to teach a course on appellate practice and procedure into the first edition of this casebook. That book did lead to an increase in the number of law schools offering an appellate practice and procedure course but even today appellate litigation receives little attention in the law schools compared to litigation at the trial level.

There are a number of explanations for this continuing lack of attention but one of the principal ones is the common perception of law students and professors and lawyers is that a lawyer is far more likely to try a case in a trial court than write a brief and make an oral argument in an appellate court. The facts are, however, quite to the contrary, as the following statistics demonstrate.

In the fiscal year ending September 30, 2003 there were in the federal district courts a total of 12,948 trials, 6,103 of which were jury trials and only 2,603 of which were in civil cases. In the federal courts of appeals, however, there were 27,009 appeals decided on the merits after the filing of brief, with oral arguments occurring in 8,791 of them. Thus a lawyer handling a case in federal court is:

1. over twice as likely to take or defend an appeal and file a brief in a court of appeal than to try a case in a district court;

2. over twice as likely to argue a case orally in a court of appeal than to conduct a jury trial in a district court;

3. almost one and one half times as likely to argue a appeal orally in a court of appeal than to conduct a jury trial in a district court.

One would think that in light of these statistics law faculties and students would embrace appellate litigation including both substantive knowledge and skills training, with the same fervor as litigation at the trial level. To date this has not been the case and the quality of the performance of lawyers in appellate courts continues to be a cause of concern to appellate judges. If this situation is to improve it is clear that a second edition of this casebook is necessary. Much has changed in appellate litigation in the past 18 years and there has been 18 years of experience in using the first edition in the classroom. This second edition both incorporates those changes and reflects the use of the book in class.

A course in appellate practice and procedure using this book can be structured in a variety of ways. The course can be a traditional course with regular classes going through the book in a semester followed by a written examination. The course could also be divided into two semesters, with the first semester covering the substantive material on appellate courts and procedure with the second semester covering brief writing and oral argument with the students doing both. Another alternative, which Professor Martineau and Justice Holland have used, is to cover all of the casebook in the first part of the semester with each student then being assigned an actual case pending in a local appellate court. After reviewing the record and the briefs and attending the oral argument the student writes a paper applying the materials in the casebook to the case. The principal benefit of this format is that the students are exposed all of the elements of handling an actual appeal form the filing of the notice of appeal to the oral argument, the key factor being working with a real record. This course could be expanded to a second semester in which the students are assigned a real record and then write briefs and make oral arguments. The best type of case for the course, whether one or two semesters, is a civil trial in which there is a transcript of testimony.

Appellate litigation can and should be just as an important part of the law school curriculum as trial litigation. It is our hope that this second edition can help bring that about.

The authors wish to express their sincere appreciation to the following persons, without whose assistance this book could not have become a reality. To Connie Miller of the Word Processing Department at the University of Cincinnati College of Law who not only provided Professors Martineau and Solimine with her word processing skills but who was responsible for combining all of the chapters into a final text; Peggy Scheimann for research assistance provided to Professors Martineau and Solimine; Sarah Bausch for preparing the Table of Secondary Authorities; Sharon E. Hutchinson for secretarial assistance provided to Professor Sinclair; and Mary Katherine Pritchett for secretarial assistance to Justice Holland.

ROBERT J. MARTINEAU
KENT SINCLAIR
MICHAEL E. SOLIMINE
RANDY J. HOLLAND

May, 2005

Acknowledgements

In addition to acknowledgements provided by special request at the foot of the first page on which copyrighted material appears, acknowledgement is also given for the kind permission of the copyright holders to reprint excerpts from the following materials:

Calvert, Appellate Court Judgments or Strange Things Happen on the Way to Judgment, 6 Texas Tech L.Rev. 915 (1975)

Goldman, The Appellate Settlement Conference: An Effective Procedural Reform, 32 State Court Journal 3 (Winter, 1978)

R. Leflar, Internal Operating Procedures of Appellate Courts (1976)

Leflar, Quality in Judicial Opinions, 3 Pace L.Rev. 579 (1983)

Martineau, The Appellate Process in Civil Cases: A Proposed Model, 63 Marquette L.Rev. 163 (1979)

Marvell, Is There an Appeal from the Caseload Deluge, 24 Judges' Journal 34 (Summer, 1985)

McConkie, Decision-making in State Supreme Courts, 59 Judicature 337 (1976)

R. Pound, Appellate Procedure in Civil Cases (1941)

Rubin and Ganucheau, Appellate Delay and Cost—An Ancient and Common Disease: Is it Intractable?, 42 Maryland L.Rev. 752 (1983)

Smith, The Selective Publications of Opinions: One Court's Experience, 32 Arkansas Law Review 26 (1978)

Wright, The Doubtful Omniscience of Appellate Courts, 41 Minnesota Law Review 751 (1957)

*

Summary of Contents

———

*

Table of Contents

Table of Cases

The principal cases are in bold type. Cases cited or discussed in the text are roman type. References are to pages. Cases cited in principal cases and within other quoted materials are not included.

*

Table of Secondary Authorities

CASES AND MATERIALS ON
APPELLATE PRACTICE AND PROCEDURE
Second Edition

*

Chapter 1

THE NATURE AND FUNCTION
OF APPELLATE COURTS

SECTION A. WHY APPELLATE REVIEW

PARKER, IMPROVING APPELLATE METHODS

25 N.Y.U.L.Rev. 1 (1950).*

The judicial function in its essence is the application of the rules and standards of organized society to the settlement of controversies, and for there to be any proper administration of justice these rules and standards must be applied, not only impartially, but also objectively and uniformly throughout the territory of the state. This requires that decisions of trial courts be subjected to review by a panel of judges who are removed from the heat engendered by the trial and are consequently in a position to take a more objective view of the questions there raised to maintain uniformity of decisions throughout the territory.

*obj. &
uniformity*

R. POUND, APPELLATE PROCEDURE IN CIVIL CASES

3 (1941).

Ulpian tells us that appeals are needful because they correct the unfairness or unskillfulness of those who adjudicate. But review does more than correct unfairnesses and mistakes. That determinations may be reviewed is a preventive of unfairness and a stimulus not to make mistakes. The possibility of review by an independent tribunal, especially by a bench of judges as distinguished from a single administrative official, is not the least of the checks which the law imposes upon its tribunals of first instance. That hasty, unfair or erroneous action may be reversed by a court of review holds back the impulsive, impels caution, constrains fairness and moves tribunals to keep to the best of their ability in the straight path.

* © Copyright 1950 New York University
Law Review.

1

F. COFFIN, THE WAYS OF A JUDGE
16–17 (1980).*

The opportunity to take one's case to "a higher court" as a matter of right is one of the foundation stones of both our state and federal court systems. It fits in with our most seasoned folk wisdom that a human being vested with the responsibility of passing judgment is never so wise, so pure, so alert as to make a "second opinion" redundant. Furthermore, with courts in every city throughout the fifty states, often differing in their views of the law, there must be a way for some court or courts higher than the others to settle what the law is or should be.

Probably most Americans, if they think at all about the matter, assume that every country and legal system of any sophistication has a right of appeal serving the same functions. A look at how the appellate idea has fared in other countries from remotest times to the present is both illuminating and disquieting. It tells us that there is nothing new under the sun, including the idea of appeal. It also tells us that by no means has the idea been deemed vital by all civilizations; there are great voids in history when even the most law-conscious countries seemingly made little provision for effective appeals. Then the idea painfully emerges once again; the wheel is reinvented. And where judicial review of lower court decisions is provided for, the purposes to be served may have been—and may be—quite different from those served by our appellate review.

WILNER, CIVIL APPEALS: ARE THEY USEFUL IN THE ADMINISTRATION OF JUSTICE?
56 Geo.L.J. 417, 448–50 (1968).**

In an age which has seen the growth of entirely new fields of law, a rapidly growing fusion of law and equity, and a nearly thorough overhaul of civil procedure, the permanence of civil appeals has remained remarkably unchallenged. Few of the technological and normative girders sustaining our legal edifice can rival the appellate procedure in importance or effect. Yet, it has successfully avoided any inquiry into its utility or theory. With but rare exceptions, legal writing concerned with appeals, voluminous as it is both in the judicial and extra-judicial sectors, is of a technical nature, addressed to the mechanics of practice and procedure. Basically, there continues in this country a general, matter-of-course acceptance of the right of a non-prevailing party to civil litigation to have one or more appeals.

* * *

With the exception of cases raising constitutional issues or involving primacy of administrative adjudication, judicial review in the area of civil appeals should be abolished.

* © Copyright 1980 by Frank M. Coffin. Reprinted by permission of Houghton Mifflin Company.

** Reprinted with the permission of the publisher, © 1968 The Georgetown Law Journal Association.

unless before then

For the most part, appeals are regarded as meliorators of nisi prius decisions or, on a broader level, as the ordering force in the law—the guarantor of certainty and uniformity. Nevertheless, experience affords no basis for the conviction that the appellate process results in specific decisions which are particularly sure to be "just" or consonant with "law" (except in the tautological sense that the judgment of the reviewing court *is* the "law"). Neither is there any support for crediting appeals with achieving integrated guiding principles.

The "correctness" of the legal principle applied in a given case by an appellate court is no more objectively determinable than the claimed "error" of the court below. In the ultimate, the authority of the reviewing process rests on nothing but a formal, whether constitutional or statutory, fiat. Nothing essential would be withheld if, by the same formal process, final authority were to be bestowed upon the original judicial forum. This reasoning is reflected by the uniform trend of decisions holding that due process does not require the granting of judicial review.

Neither do ideals of certainty and uniformity dictate the indispensability of an appellate process to insure freedom from errors of law in the administration of justice. Uniformity of decision is not a virtue in itself; it is meaningful only as fostering equality and is, essentially, an antithesis to arbitrary discrimination. Equal protection of the law has uniformly been recognized not to require uniformity of legal decisions. No statistical evidence is necessary to suggest that both uniformity and certainty are just as jeopardized by an erroneous finding of fact as by an incorrect application of a principle. Yet, despite our heightened awareness of the importance of fact determinations, neither equality nor certainty are urged as grounds for their regular reviewability in jury or non-jury cases.

From the viewpoint of uniformity and certainty, appeals are to some extent self-defeating. The clarification of a doubtful specific in an appellate decision necessarily involves the reification of multiple theoretical considerations, a process which potentially converts the thus clarified specific into a spectrum of totally new uncertainties.

Appeals are predicated upon a number of doubtful premises. Among these are: (1) that there is a clear distinction between fact and law; (2) that appellate review is an efficient method for assuring just results; (3) that legal principles enunciated by reviewing tribunals are scientific pronouncements, partaking of the qualities of determinism, objectivity, and causality; and (4) that there exists an identifiable line of demarcation between issues which are legal and those which are social, economic, or political.

Judicial review is internally contradictory. The process presupposes the independent existence of "correct" principles of law which are not, however, ascertainable until the exhaustion of laborious and involved procedures encompassing a hierarchy of tribunals. While review procedure assumes that trial judges are capable of "error," it generally does not permit an examination of their activity until the final judgment.

When the judgment is reviewed, the guidance afforded is usually limited to that phase of the matter which is found to be affected with error, leaving the proceeding open to the possibility of further error upon remand. There is also the anomaly that while courts of appeal will at times utilize a case as an occasion for announcing a new doctrine, though not requested by either party to do so, they continue to insist that only an "actual case or controversy" is an acceptable instrument for generating legal principles.

Appellate procedures should likewise be scrutinized in the context of the current crisis of confidence in the administration of justice. Our unquestioning acceptance of judicial review in civil matters contributes to that crisis, for the resultant proliferation of pronouncements bewilders the legal profession and utterly baffles the public. Since many appellate opinions are by divided courts and constitute reversals of precedent, appellate courts themselves are a factor in engendering a sense of frustration in the public by conveying an impression of arbitrariness and factitiousness. A not insignificant by-product of the review process is a detraction from the authority of the trial court—the only judicial forum with which the public comes into personal contact and in which citizens may participate as litigants, jurors, experts, or witnesses.

The continued adherence to our review procedure is ineffective in meeting the overriding problem facing our system of administering justice—the making of readily *accessible* law in a truly *authoritative* manner, at a point of time when its normative function will be most truly felt. In place of appeals, which at best are mere ex post facto declarations of legal norms, methods should be devised for making authoritative legal information available as a guide to conduct. No administration of justice can rest on an assumed knowledge of law without making the means for obtaining such knowledge readily available. To the extent to which they are truly serviceable, legal rules should be authoritatively set forth by appropriately constituted public bodies unrelated to the making of decisions in actual court cases. Such formulations will have the advantages of continuity, orderliness, and expertise—qualities not found in the necessarily haphazard functioning of appellate courts. A reform of this magnitude will, however, make great demands upon the legal profession, for greater accessibility of the law and of legal processes will likewise require a rethinking of the function of the bar, a utilization of all its resources, and a thorough restructuring and reallocation of its administrative and adjudicative responsibilities.

Notes and Questions

1. What are the purposes of appellate review as expressed by Judges Parker and Coffin and Dean Pound? How different are these purposes? Are they real differences or just semantic?

2. Will the purposes of appellate review differ depending upon the perspective of the observer? Should the purposes differ depending upon whether the observer is a judge, litigant, lawyer, public official, or an average citizen?

3.   If the need for appellate review is so obvious, should it be considered a requirement of due process? The Supreme Court has answered in the negative both as to civil cases (National Union of M.C. & S. v. Arnold, 348 U.S. 37, 75 S.Ct. 92, 99 L.Ed. 46 (1954); M.L.B. v. S.L.J., 519 U.S. 102, 117 S.Ct. 555, 136 L.Ed.2d 473 (1996)) and to criminal cases (Ross v. Moffitt, 417 U.S. 600, 94 S.Ct. 2437, 41 L.Ed.2d 341 (1974)).

4.   Does Wilner provide any substantial basis for questioning the necessity of a system of appellate review? Is it significant that in two states, Virginia and West Virginia, there is no right to appellate review, it being in the discretion of the appellate court? See Lilly & Scalia, Appellate Justice: A Crisis in Virginia?, 57 Virginia L.Rev. 3 (1971). For a limited period of time in the 19th century, the state of Georgia had no system of appellate review. See Lamar, A Unique and Unfamiliar Chapter in Our American Legal History, 10 A.B.A.J. 513 (1924). See also Bilder, The Origin of the Appeal in America, 48 Hastings L.J. 913 (1997).

5.   For a provocative discussion questioning many of the standard arguments in favor of an appeal as of right, see Dalton, Taking the Right to Appeal (More of Less) Seriously, 95 Yale L.J. 62 (1985). Dalton references, among other things, the relatively low rate of appeal and the high rate of affirmance. See also Lay, A Proposal for Discretionary Review in Federal Courts of Appeals, 34 Sw. L.J. 1151 (1981); Parker & Chapman, Accepting Reality: The Time for Adopting Discretionary Review in the Courts of Appeals Has Arrived, 50 SMU L. Rev. 573 (1997). For a rejoinder to Dalton, emphasizing the need to hold trial judges accountable, see Carrington, The Function of the Civil Appeal: A Late–Century View, 38 S. Car. L. Rev. 411 (1987). See also R. Posner, Economic Analysis of Law 643–45 (5th ed. 1998); Drahozal, Judicial Incentives and the Appeals Process, 51 SMU L. Rev. 469 (1998); Shavell, The Appeals Process as a Means of Error Correction, 24 J. Legal Stud. 379 (1995).

6.   Data from various sources indicates that about twenty percent of appealable decisions from U.S. District Courts are appealed. C. Krafka, et al., Stalking the Increase in the Rate of Federal Civil Appeals 8–9 (Fed. Jud. Ctr. 1995); R. Posner, The Federal Courts: Challenge and Reform 113–21 (1996). Is that higher or lower than the rate that you might expect? Would you expect a higher appeal rate for cases that are tried as opposed to cases that are resolved in a pretrial motion? Eisenberg, Appeals Rates and Outcomes in Tried and Nontried Cases: Further Exploration of Anti–Plaintiff Appellate Outcomes, 1 J. Empirical Legal Stud. 659 (2004) (showing higher appeal rates for former as opposed to latter).

7.   There is a small empirical literature on the decision of litigants, and their attorneys, to appeal a case. See S. Barclay, An Appealing Act: Why People Appeal in Civil Cases (1999); Rathjen, Lawyers and the Appellate Choice: An Analysis of Factors Affecting the Decision to Appeal, 6 Am. Pol. Q. 387 (1978); Songer, Cameron & Segal, An Empirical Test of the Rational–Actor Theory of Litigation, 57 J. Pol. 1119 (1995).

8.   For a broad ranging discussion of the extent of appellate review in other legal systems, see Shapiro, Appeal, 14 Law & Soc'y Rev. 629 (1980).

SECTION B.   THE FUNCTIONS
OF APPELLATE REVIEW

1.   ERROR CORRECTION

P. CARRINGTON, D. MEADOR, AND M. ROSENBERG,
JUSTICE ON APPEAL

2 (1976).

In the received tradition, the functions of appellate adjudication are two-fold. One is to "review for correctness." It is probably true for most legal systems, and is emphatically true for this country's, that appellate courts serve as the instrument of accountability for those who make the basic decisions in trial courts and administrative agencies. The traditional appeal calls for an examination of the rulings below to assure that they are correct, or at least within the range of error the law for sufficient reasons allows the primary decision-maker. The availability of the appellate process assures the decision-makers at the first level that their correct judgments will not be, or appear to be, the unconnected actions of isolated individuals, but will have the concerted support of the legal system; and it assures litigants that the decision in their case is not prey to the failings of whichever mortal happened to render it, but bears the institutional imprimatur and approval of the whole social order as represented by its legal system. Thus, the review for correctness serves to reinforce the dignity, authority, and acceptability of the trial, and to control the adverse effects of any personal shortcomings of the basic decision-makers.

KNABB v. SCHERER

Court of Appeals of Ohio, 1933.
45 Ohio App. 535, 187 N.E. 574.

HAMILTON, PRESIDING JUDGE.

Plaintiff in error, Harry G. Knabb, who was plaintiff below, brought an action as administrator of the estate of Harry Knabb, Jr., for wrongful death, claimed to have been occasioned through the negligence of the defendant, Arthur F. Scherer. The deceased, a son of the plaintiff administrator, was a boy of eight years of age.

The case was submitted to the jury, which returned a verdict for the defendant. The plaintiff prosecutes error, and alleges several errors in the charge of the court.

The first error complained of in the charge is that the court committed error in injecting into the case the question of inevitable and unavoidable accident. On this question, the trial court charged the jury by this brief statement: "Of course, if the injury or death was caused by inevitable or unavoidable accident, there could be no recovery on the part of the plaintiff."

This was error, as this court held in the case of Avra, Admx., v. Karshner, 32 Ohio App. 492, 168 N.E. 237. The Karshner Case is directly in point, and, in substance, involves practically the same language. This court said in the opinion in the Karshner Case, at page 496 of 32 Ohio App., 168 N.E. 237, 238: "If the negligence of the defendants was proven to have proximately caused the injury, and no contributory negligence was shown, plaintiff would be entitled to recover. If plaintiff failed to prove that the negligence of the defendants proximately caused the injury, plaintiff could not recover. In such cases, there is no place for the question of unavoidable accident."

Moreover, in the case under consideration the court did not define what was meant by "inevitable or unavoidable accident." This charge could not have been other than misleading to the jury.

misleading

The trial court further stated one of the issues to be: "Was such negligence on the part of the defendant the sole and proximate cause of the injury?" On this point the court, in Avra v. Karshner, supra, stated: "The law is that in order for a plaintiff to recover the negligence of the defendant must be the proximate cause of the accident and injury. The use by the court of the words 'sole and proximate cause' placed a greater burden on the plaintiff than the law required." The giving of this charge was erroneous.

It is claimed that the court erred in submitting to the jury the question whether or not the place where the accident occurred was a closely built up section. The accident happened in a school zone, for which there is a special law, which was submitted to the jury, and the trial court did submit to the jury the question as to whether or not the accident happened in a closely built up section. Since the law with reference to a school zone is as strict in its control and operation of motor vehicles as the law with reference to closely built up sections of a municipality, no prejudice could have resulted. Moreover, there was some dispute in the evidence as to the built up condition. Under such circumstances, the court may submit that question to the jury. It is only where there is no dispute that the trial court is justified in charging the jury as to whether the section is closely built up or not. We find no prejudice in this instruction.

It is claimed the court erred in giving defendant's special charge, which is as follows:

"Plaintiff's decedent, Harry Knabb, Jr., being a boy eight years of age at the time of the accident, was required to exercise that degree of care for his protection which boys of the same age and similar experience are accustomed to exercising under the same or similar circumstances. If plaintiff's decedent failed to exercise such degree of care, for his own safety, then plaintiff's decedent would be guilty of negligence, and, if you find from the evidence, that plaintiff's decedent was guilty of the slightest degree of negligence, which directly and proximately caused his injuries and subsequent death, then your verdict must be for the defendant, notwithstanding the fact that you also find that the defendant himself was guilty of negligence."

It is contended that where the court used the language, "that degree of care for his protection which boys of the same age and similar experience are accustomed to exercising," it should have included the word "education." We know of no rule of law which requires the use of the word "education." The rule is that the attention of the jury should be called to the minority of the decedent, to the fact that he is only required to use that degree of care which youth of his age are accustomed to exercise.

It is complained that in the special charge the use of the word "slightest" was improper. The charge states: "If you find from the evidence, that plaintiff's decedent was guilty of the slightest degree of negligence, which directly and proximately caused his injuries and subsequent death, then your verdict must be for the defendant, notwithstanding the fact that you also find that the defendant himself was guilty of negligence." It is claimed that the word "slightest" should modify ["caused"] rather than "negligence." While the statement is awkward, standing alone it would not require a reversal. "Slightest degree" should modify ["proximately" or "caused,"] rather than "negligence."

This same application of the word "slightest" appears in the general charge, and is complained of by plaintiff in error. What we have said with reference to the special charge applies to the general charge.

Further, in the general charge, the court uses this language: "And if the plaintiff has in making out or putting in his case produced such testimony that from it an inference fairly arises that the plaintiff's decedent was guilty of negligence, then the burden of proof is upon the plaintiff to remove that inference, and if the plaintiff does not remove such inference, and does not produce evidence tending to remove that inference, then the plaintiff cannot recover."

This was error. In the case of Smith v. Lopa, 123 Ohio St. 213, 174 N.E. 735, the Supreme Court holds in the syllabus that it is only necessary to "produce evidence sufficient to equal or dispel the inference or presumption. But in such case the plaintiff is not obliged to remove the inference or presumption by a preponderance of the evidence."

The statement as given in the charge would call for a preponderance of the evidence, and leaves the inference that more than sufficient to counterbalance or dispel the inference is needed.

It is argued in the brief that these errors, which counsel refer to as minor errors, may be passed over under the substantial justice statute (Gen.Code, § 11364). The substantial justice statute is to be applied where there has been a fair trial, and not as a means of avoiding the requirements of the law. The law is that the jury shall judge the evidence under the law as given it by the court, and none other. Where these rules of law are erroneously given to the jury as its guidance, no substantial justice would follow the party prejudiced. The numerous errors referred to could not be overlooked under the substantial justice section of the Code. They were prejudicial to the plaintiff in the case, preventing a fair trial.

reversed due to errors

The judgment will be reversed for the errors in the charge.

Judgment reversed.

CUSHING and ROSS, JJ., concur.

Notes and Questions

1. How can it be determined from the opinion of a court whether it views its role solely as one of error correction? Does the opinion in the principal case give any indication of how the court viewed its role?

2. What authority does the court rely upon for its decision on each of the issues presented? If the court does not cite any clear precedent for its decision when it holds the trial court committed error, how can it be said that the trial court erred? Was the trial court wrong just because the appellate court says so?

3. You may have noted that in the principal case, the party bringing the appeal is referred to as the "plaintiff in error." As the English system developed in the early Eighteenth Century there were two principal procedures for seeking an appeal, one called a "writ of error" and the other, simply, an "appeal." In the writ procedure the party who lost the trial proceeding commenced what amounted to a new lawsuit to challenge the outcome of the first proceeding. The party initiating the writ procedure was the "plaintiff in error." As the American courts began to refine the fundamental concepts of appeal, review of actions at law was commonly by some version of the writ procedure, while equity suits were simply appealed–and a "de novo" hearing was given to the equity decree on appeal. Myriad technicalities and traps developed for both forms of appellate review procedure. Reform efforts in the early 20th century led to a combining of the two concepts of an appeal such that a new lawsuit is no longer involved, yet "de novo" review is not provided except on certain categories of issues, such as pure questions of law. Today, the "writ" of error has transformed into a requirement for the losing party to have made objection in the trial court and be in a position to point out errors in that proceeding to the appellate court. See generally R. Martineau, Modern Appellate Practice—Federal and State Civil Appeals 3–8 (1983) and R. Pound, Appellate Procedure in Civil Cases, 300–01, 319–20, 328–60, 375–76 (1941).

4. The court in the principal case states in the last paragraph of the opinion that the errors in the instructions were prejudicial to the plaintiff. On what basis did the court come to that conclusion? The court also refers to the substantial justice statute but refuses to rely on it as a basis for ignoring the errors in the instructions. This type of statute is common in many jurisdictions, state as well as federal. The following is typical: 28 U.S.C.A. § 2111 provides that on an appeal "the court shall give judgment after an examination of the record without regard to errors or defects which do not affect the substantial rights of the parties." Does this mean that a reviewing court should never base its decision on procedural grounds? Observe in the remaining chapters the extent to which this principle is observed.

2. LAW DEVELOPMENT

P. CARRINGTON, D. MEADOR, AND M. ROSENBERG, JUSTICE ON APPEAL
2–3 (1976).

The second function in the traditional tandem is sometimes described as "institutional" review. Trial courts working independently have no self-regulating capacity to promote uniformity among their decisions. Without appellate review, such great divergences in practices and variations in results would arise between trial courts in the same system that they would jeopardize the belief that legal principles are a vital force in their decisions or provide a basis for predicting the application of official power. Accordingly, appellate courts are needed to announce, clarify, and harmonize the rules of decision employed by the legal system in which they serve. Until recent decades, it was customary to conceal, even from ourselves, the creative and political aspects of this function; we were given to proclaiming that judges do not make law. Today, such comment is seldom heard; it is widely understood that the judges who enunciate legal principles are engaged in a creative activity which can have significant social, economic, and political consequences. On the other hand, it is still true that rampant judicial free-wheeling in law-declaring may threaten the democratic ideal that representative government is designed to foster. Few would deny that there are appropriate limits to the judges' assumption of responsibility for the full range of social, economic and political ills which might conceivably be subjected to the judicial power.

Recognizing traditional duality in the functions of appellate adjudication is unquestionably helpful to understanding. It serves to illumine the contrast in both the concerns and the affects of appellate justice. On the one hand, appellate justice is preoccupied with the impact of decisions on particular litigants, but on the other it is concerned with the general principles which govern the affairs of persons other than those who are party to the cases decided. While appellate justice has impact on the realities of situations, it also affects the appearances and symbols which pervade the government. An appellate system which is unduly preoccupied with one of these functions to the neglect of the other, is inadequate to advance the purposes which appellate courts should serve.

WILLIAMS v. DETROIT
Supreme Court of Michigan, 1961.
364 Mich. 231, 111 N.W.2d 1.

[Plaintiff's decedent was employed by a moving company hired by the City of Detroit to remove furniture from a city owned building it was abandoning. He was fatally injured after falling into an open elevator shaft. Plaintiff's negligence claim against the city was dismissed on the defense of governmental immunity.]

Carr, Justice.

* * *

Justice Edwards has written for reversal of the judgment entered by the trial court. He prefaces the opinion that he has served with the declaration that:

> "From this date forward the judicial doctrine of governmental immunity from ordinary torts no longer exists in Michigan."

* * *

) judicial law making

The radical departure from existing law in this State contemplated by Justice Edwards, and those of like mind with him, obviously involves the exercise of legislative authority. The fact that the change to be made is prospective only is significant in this respect. In other words, it is proposed that the Court shall declare what the law will be in the future rather than what it is in the present and has been in the past.

* * *

The query immediately arises whether the people have in the Constitution that they have adopted, and by which they have created departments and agencies of government for the performance of governmental functions in the public interest, delegated to this Court any such authority as it is now suggested the Court should exercise.

It is conceded that the legislature of the State, under the powers vested in it by the people, may modify the doctrine of governmental immunity as it has done in certain respects in the past, and may abolish it. The exercise of such authority is wholly legislative in character. It has not been vested in the judiciary. On the contrary, the people expressly declared in Article IV, § 1, of the present State Constitution that:

> "The powers of government are divided into 3 departments: The legislative, executive and judicial."

And section 2 of the same article renders crystal clear the intent of the fundamental law of the State. It declares:

> "No person belonging to 1 department shall exercise the powers properly belonging to another, except in the cases expressly provided in this constitution."

The admission of the obvious fact that a change in the policy of governmental immunity from liability in cases of the nature here involved is within the scope of legislative authority carries with it the further admission that such action is not within the scope of judicial powers.

) ≠ within scope of jud. p.

Justice Edwards declares in his opinion that some members of this Court have in prior cases expressed dissatisfaction with the doctrine of immunity in the performance of sovereign functions of government, and that the legislature has failed to take action. It must be assumed that the legislature did not consider that it would be for the best interests of the

State of Michigan to abolish the doctrine or to further modify it in material respects. The expressions of dissatisfaction that have been made from time to time impose no obligation for legislative action. * * *

This Court has repeatedly held that in the absence of statute imposing liability a municipal corporation is not liable for the negligence of its agents, representatives or employees engaged in the performance of a governmental function.

* * *

The authority of the legislature to act with reference to the matter under consideration here has not been challenged. Justice Edwards in his opinion expressly recognizes it and also admits the power of the legislature to provide for governmental tort immunity notwithstanding a decree or judgment of this Court abrogating it. He speaks also of a trend toward abolition of governmental immunity from liability for torts committed in the performance of governmental functions, suggesting that such trend has been begun ''by this Court and the legislature.'' Other than cases involving so-called proprietary functions as distinguished from governmental, attention is not directed to any instance in which this Court has heretofore undertaken to modify in any particular the doctrine of governmental immunity as involved in the instant case. Rather, as before suggested, the right of the legislature to act has been repeatedly recognized. Jurisdiction cannot be vested in both the legislative and judicial departments of the State government. Clearly in the legislative field the law-making department alone is empowered to act.

* * *

We have cited herein a number of decisions from various States in support of the general principle that in dealing with the doctrine of governmental immunity from damages for tortious acts committed in carrying out governmental functions the legislature alone is clothed with authority to modify, extend or abrogate such doctrine. Additional quotations from such decisions to those above included herein would be merely cumulative and would extend this opinion to an unnecessary length. Unquestionably the overwhelming weight of authority supports the rule that has heretofore obtained in Michigan. Abrogation of that rule by this Court is in excess of the powers vested in the judiciary of the State by the Constitution adopted by the people acting in their sovereign capacity. The practical situation presented is that if the legislature deems it necessary so to do it may act to modify, or even abrogate entirely, the doctrine of governmental immunity. It is also true that the people acting under the initiative provisions of the State Constitution may accomplish a like result by legislation or by Constitutional amendment.

The decision of the trial court was right and should be affirmed.

DETHMERS, C.J., and KELLY, J., concurred with CARR, J.

BLACK, JUSTICE (concurring in affirmance).

* * *

Once again 2 widely divided opinions are presented by familiarly grouped extremities of the Court. JUSTICES CARR, KELLY and DETHMERS, looking on _stare decisis_ as set and cured legal concrete, stand as before against any doctrine of judicial self-correction. JUSTICE EDWARDS and his votaries, misconceiving and so misapplying what the Supreme Court affirmed in the Sunburst case (Great Northern Ry. Co. v. Sunburst Oil & Refining Co.) 287 U.S. 358, 53 S.Ct. 145, 77 L.Ed. 360, would in this distinct field of municipal law discriminate grossly against all similarly situated plaintiffs whose luck is that of having lost to one of their class the race to a long overdue judicial decision. Conversely, these last mentioned Brethren would discriminate against the present defendant (Detroit) in favor of all other similarly situated municipal defendants who, by luck or calculated delay, have succeeded in preventing their plaintiff adversaries from winning the same race.

* * *

I differ _toto caelo_ with both opinions, tendering instead the view that any majority determination to cast aside the rule of municipal immunity should be effected either by _wholly_ prospective decision or _wholly_ retrospective decision. For reasons to be stated, I favor the former; hence this vote to affirm.

FIRST: THE OPINION PROPOSED BY MR. JUSTICE CARR

Little time need be spent in determining whether the strict doctrine of municipal immunity from tort liability should be repudiated. All this is old straw. The question is not "Should we?"; it is "How may the body be interred judicially with nondiscriminatory last rites?" No longer does any eminent scholar or jurist attempt justification thereof. All unite in recommendation of corrective legislation. * * * the doctrine looks in vain around our conference table for a defender of its once alleged merit. The elder Brethren say only that the rule _stare decisis_ is—by our constitutional schedule—fortified to the impregnable and that this Court upon oath must continue to apply it until the legislature wills otherwise.

* * *

So we enter again upon a perennial controversy: Whether a judge should let others "long dead and unaware of the problems of the age in which he lives, do his thinking for him." (Mr. Justice Douglas; "Stare Decisis"; 49 Columbia Law Review, 735, 736). My answer to this question was written in City of Dearborn v. Bacila, 353 Mich. 99, 112, 90 N.W.2d 863, 870:

* * *

"Mr. Justice Holmes, commenting on 'The Path of the Law', leads the thought-way here. He said (Collected Legal Papers, Oliver Wendell Holmes, p. 187):

" 'It is revolting to have no better reason for a rule of law than that so it was laid down in the time of Henry IV. It is still more revolting if the grounds upon which it was laid down have vanished long since, and the rule simply persists from blind imitation of the past.'

* * *

"The late and distinguished Judge Frank (of the 2nd federal judicial circuit) follows the path of Holmes this way:

" 'Especially are professional or other groups of specialists addicted to set ways. Even the natural scientists, presumably inspired by the spirit of intellectual adventuring, are by no means free of stick-in-the-mudism. * * * Partly it involves pride: Judges, like doctors and others, are reluctant to admit they made mistakes. *Then, too, there is plain old-fashioned animal laziness. It's a nuisance to revise what you have once settled.* Out of such laziness comes what Holmes called "one of the misfortunes of the law," that "ideas become encysted in phrases and thereafter for a long time cease to provoke further analysis." ' Courts On Trial, by Jerome Frank, Princeton University Press, 1950, pp. 272, 273."

Surely, with the passage of years, today's question is become a game of quasi-legal basketball with legislators and judges tossing the sphere back and forth with neither making visible effort to loop it for decisive result. It is time one branch or the other act affirmatively and, since the legislature with over-borrowed time has done nothing, this Court should force the issue as other courts have done and are now doing. Then and then only may the people expect what all have a right to expect, that is, prompt if prodded legislation which lifts from the individual the total burden arising from what is now court-licensed negligence and yet reasonably protects the municipality from unbearable diversions of municipal tax revenues. The only alternative is inertia and cozy complacence in our lofty quarters as "the rule of law" burns slowly to utter public disrespect.

What indeed are judges to do as inexcusable injustice continues unremittingly before their very eyes; injustice occasioned by the over-protracted life of a rule made at common law by judges who knew naught of modern elevators and like appliances which, being negligently constructed or maintained by public authority, cause repetitious sufferings—as here—of totally innocent victims? Are judges powerless to act, as year after year goes by with primarily responsible legislators standing by, totally disinterested or politely amused at the plight of the courts?

The right answer is the same as given by life's teachings; teachings which are no stranger to the law. Action of any kind is always better than total inaction. Sins of cold-blooded omission invariably average out to greater error than sins of warm-hearted commission. As Dante tells us, the two will be weighed in different scales when the great day of Final Judgment arrives in our Highest Court.

Such is the ground from which previous like declarations have been made. "*Stare decisis* is usually the wise policy" [355 Mich. 103, 94

N.W.2d 427]; yet it "is not inflexible." "Whether it shall be followed or departed from is a question entirely within the discretion of the court, which is again called upon to consider a question once decided." "This Court, unlike the House of Lords, has from the beginning rejected a doctrine of disability at self-correction." "It is a persuasive but not necessarily controlling factor and, in the language of text-amended American Jurisprudence, 'must give way to overriding considerations under cogent circumstances.' " Quotations from separate opinion of Park v. Employment Security Comm., supra, 355 Mich. at pages 145–150, 94 N.W.2d at page 429.

* * *

It proves, too, the accuracy of Justice Cardozo's wisdom when he wrote "The Growth of the Law" (pp. 132, 133, 134):

> "Some months ago the New York Law Journal published letters of its readers, some in praise, some in criticism, of a decision recently announced. The critics, or some of them, went upon the theory that the rule of *stare decisis* was imbedded in the constitution, and that judges, when they departed from it, were usurpers, though the precedent ignored was as mouldy as the grave from which counsel had brought it forth to face the light of a new age. *Stare decisis* is not in the constitution, but I should be half ready to put it there, and to add thereto the requirement of mechanical and literal reproduction, if only it were true that legislation is a sufficient agency of growth. * * * Substitute statute for decision, and you shift the center of authority, but add no quota of inspired wisdom. If legislation is to take the place of the creative action of the courts, a legislative committee must stand back of us at every session, a sort of supercourt itself. No guarantee is given us that a choice thus made will be wiser than our own, yet its form will give it a rigidity that will make retreat or compromise impossible. We shall be exchanging a process of trial and error at the hands of judges who make it the business of their lives for a process of trial and error at the hands of a legislative committee who will give it such spare moments as they can find amid multifarious demands."

* * *

SECOND: THE OPINION PROPOSED BY MR. JUSTICE EDWARDS

* * *

The Supreme Court did not, in cited Sunburst, affirm what JUSTICE EDWARDS (miscalling it "the Sunburst doctrine") proposes for this case of Williams, that is, an overruling decision *effective for the case at bar* plus causes arising in the future. What was affirmed, in Sunburst, was a wholly prospective decision of the supreme court of Montana [Citations omitted.] *with the parties before the Court held firmly bound to the earlier rule.* As avowed earlier in this opinion, I would on pinpointed authority of the Sunburst case do the same here.

Sunburst opinion U. S. Sup. Ct.

* * *

What is the proper course here, five members of the Court having determined to override this common law rule of immunity? The Sunburst case answers directly. So, on another occasion that same year (1932), did the great author of the Supreme Court's unanimous Sunburst opinion:

> "For such cases and others where a retroactive declaration is for any reason inexpedient, I find myself driven more and more to the belief that courts should be competent to follow the practice proposed by Mr. Wigmore in his suggestive little book 'The Problems of Law' and since espoused by others; *they should apply the outworn rule to the case that is then at hand,* and couple their judgment with the declaration that they will feel free to apply another rule to transactions consummated in the future." * * *

The only defense offered in the books, for decisions of overrulement effective for the case at hand plus future causes of action, is that otherwise there will be no incentive for appeals which, even though successful in overturning an outmoded rule, will result in no benefit to the appellant. See, for exposition of such defense, Molitor v. Kaneland Community Unit Dist. No. 302, 18 Ill.2d 11, 163 N.E.2d 89, 97.

With the dictum and its supporters I disagree. * * * Such counsel usually find that one intentionally risked loaf, when cast with timed care upon picked legal waters, is likely to bring multiple and worthy results even though the appellant—expendable or not expendable—is set down without day.

Conclusion

All distinguished writers recommend corrective legislation, enacted with the adjusted detail carefully drawn statutes only can provide. So do I. But what is an appellate court to do when the legislative process remains comatose, year after year and decade after decade, the court meanwhile bearing the onus of what was done judicially during the dim yesterdays and maintained to this day by the self-stultifying fetish of *stare decisis?* Must the court continue to proclaim its impotence as legislators shrug their responsibility with a nod of *risus sardonicus* toward the error-guilty judicial branch? My answer is that this Court may relieve itself of past error by confessing and adjudging that error, and that it may at the same time force what all students of the problem have rightly sought for lo these many years; a statute relieving the injured citizen from the total burden of municipal negligence and still controlling the result so that municipal functions may be carried on without serious financial risk.

* * *

I return, then, to the original thrust of this review of reviews: How should the Court go about elimination of its error of yesteryear? To do nothing is unthinkable. To reward one plaintiff and deny like rights to others of that plaintiff's class is equally abhorrent to judges who stand for equal justice under law. There is one way only of right, and that is to pursue what was done in Montana and affirmed in Sunburst.

* * *

I vote to affirm, without costs and with accompanying declaration that like causes of action arising hereafter will, unless and until the legislature rises and ordains otherwise, be treated in the courts of Michigan as typical negligence cases.

EDWARDS, JUSTICE.

From this date forward the judicial doctrine of governmental immunity from ordinary torts no longer exists in Michigan. In this case, we overrule preceding court-made law to the contrary. We eliminate from the case law of Michigan an ancient rule inherited from the days of absolute monarchy which has been productive of great injustice in our courts. By so doing, we join a major trend in this country toward the righting of an age-old wrong. * * * In the Richards case, the desirability of legislative attention to this problem was pointed out (348 Mich. at page 520, 83 N.W.2d at page 658):

> "The clear-cut remedy to the problem of governmental immunity undoubtedly lies with State legislation of the nature and character of that adopted within recent years by the Federal government through congress. Court action to achieve the same goal by repudiation of this long-established common-law doctrine is hampered by unnumbered precedents and the doctrine of *stare decisis*. It cannot come as can legislative change after ample public discussion and with full warning to those bodies upon whom liability would be thrust to take such measures of an insurance nature as they might deem desirable."

Four years have passed since then without legislative action. The legislature has, of course, every right to say to us, "The courts created this problem. The courts can solve it."

Since our consideration of immunity in the Richards case, a number of State supreme courts have acted in this field. Supreme courts in Florida, Illinois and California have squarely rejected the doctrine of governmental immunity. [Citations omitted.]

In the most recent of these cases, the California supreme court said:

> " 'After a re-evaluation of the rule of governmental immunity from tort liability we have concluded that it must be discarded as mistaken and unjust.' * * * The rule of governmental immunity for tort is an anachronism, without rational basis, and has existed only by the force of inertia. * * * Only the vestigial remains of such governmental immunity have survived; its requiem has long been

foreshadowed. * * * in holding that the doctrine of governmental immunity for torts for which its agents are liable has no place in our law we make no startling break with the past but merely take the final step that carries to its conclusion an established legislative and judicial trend." Muskopf v. Corning Hospital District, 11 Cal.Rptr. 89, 90, 92, 95, 359 P.2d 457, 458, 460, 463.

[handwritten margin note: can a common law trend be overturned by judges?]

It is interesting to note that in Michigan, too, we here complete a trend begun both by this Court and the legislature.

The legislature has specifically imposed liability upon political subdivisions for keeping streets and highways reasonably fit and safe for travel. C.L.S.1956, § 242.1 (Stat.Ann.1958 Rev. § 9.591).

It has much more recently exempted from the immunity rule negligence actions against political subdivisions of the State pertaining to motor vehicles. C.L.1948, §§ 691.151, 691.152 (Stat.Ann.1960 Rev. §§ 9.1708[1], 9.1708[2]).

In the court of claims act, it has applied the same exemption from the judicial immunity rule to the State itself as to torts arising from motor-vehicle or aircraft accidents. P.A.1960, No. 33, amending C.L. 1948, § 691.141 (Stat.Ann.1959 Cum.Supp. § 27.3548[41]).

Moving somewhat in the same direction, this Court has adopted the expedient of refusing the immunity rule to governmental units where the activity engaged in was of a revenue-producing or "proprietary" nature. [Citations omitted.]

These trends would, of course, avail the present plaintiff nothing. If the doctrine of governmental immunity from torts is to continue as it has existed in Michigan, she plainly cannot maintain her suit.

* * *

The chief legal argument pertains to the desirability of rigid application herein of the doctrine of *stare decisis*. As to the fundamental nature of this doctrine, we entertain no doubt. The common law, as we know it in this country and Great Britain, is founded upon the following of case precedent. By this rule, our society preserves the best of the wisdom and morality of past ages.

But *stare decisis* in its most rigorous form does not prevent the courts from correcting their own errors, or from establishing new rules of case law when facts and circumstances of modern life have rendered an old rule unworkable and unjust.

* * *

One of the opinions in this case while agreeing with our fundamental holding that the immunity rule as applied below represents historic injustice and should be overruled prospectively, criticizes the fact that we seek to follow the precedent set in Parker v. Port Huron Hospital, supra, and to apply the overruling likewise to this case in which the decision is being made.

The choice in this regard is, of course, difficult—but it is deliberate. We have pointed out that any date or point of change involves the application of the old (and unjust) rule to some, and its alteration as to others. This Court has overruled prior precedent many times in the past. In each such instance the Court must take into account the total situation confronting it and seek a just and realistic solution of the problems occasioned by the change.

* * *

It is evident that there is no single rule of thumb which can be used to accomplish the maximum of justice in each varying set of circumstances. The involvement of vested property rights, the magnitude of the impact of decision on public bodies taken without warning or a showing of substantial reliance on the old rule may influence the result.

In no instance which we have discovered, however, has this Court's decision taken the benefit of the change from the party whose case occasioned it—even though retroactivity may have been limited to a greater or lesser degree.

The reasons for denying general retroactivity in this case we have already discussed. The reasons for including the case which occasioned the change lies in the court's basic interest in preserving the vitality of the common law. The parties and lawyers who are certain of defeat for a lawsuit may well be deterred from bringing the appeal which would best illustrate the need for alteration of a rule. Nor (assuming some prosperous law offices might undertake such litigation as a matter of public service or long range self-interest), should we limit the presentation of precedent-making cases to a particular classification of attorneys.

* * *

There is, of course, ample precedent not only in Michigan but elsewhere for prospective overruling with the new rule applied to the case in which decision is made. [Citations omitted.]

Finally it is suggested that the Sunburst case (Great Northern → *Sunburst* Railway Co. v. Sunburst Oil and Refining Company, supra) is authority for rejecting Mrs. Williams' plea for damages for her husband's death. We believe that the opinion of Mr. Justice Cardozo for the United States Supreme Court has much broader significance than mere ratification of the Montana Supreme Court's decision to change a rule wholly prospectively. Levy, Realistic Jurisprudence and Prospective Overruling, 109 U.Penn.L.Rev. 1 (1960). The question, as to whether or not the Montana Court could have applied the otherwise prospective ruling to the case at bar (as we seek to do here) was not presented, discussed or decided. But the thrust of the Cardozo opinion may be found in the following quotation which we read as affirming the power of a state supreme court in overruling prior precedent to apply the most practical and most just solution it has available under the circumstances presented by that case.

"This is a case where a court has refused to make its ruling retroactive, and the novel stand is taken that the Constitution of the United States is infringed by the refusal.

"We think the Federal Constitution has no voice upon the subject. A state in defining the limits of adherence to precedent may make a choice for itself between the principle of forward operation and that of relation backward. It may say that decisions of its highest court, though later overruled, are law none the less for intermediate transactions. * * * On the other hand, it may hold to the ancient dogma that the law declared by its courts had a Platonic or ideal existence before the act of declaration, in which event the discredited declaration will be viewed as if it had never been, and the reconsidered declaration as law from the beginning."

* * *

For reasons set forth above this case should be:

Reversed and remanded for trial.

SMITH, KAVANAGH and SOURIS, JJ., concurred with EDWARDS, J.

Notes and Questions

1. How many members of the supreme court participated in the decision in the principal case? Does the number seem unusual? When an appellate court is evenly divided, the judgment appealed from is automatically treated as affirmed. Why? Does this explain the fact that almost all appellate panels are composed of an odd number of judges? Compare Hartnett, Ties in the Supreme Court, 44 Wm. & Mary L. Rev. 744 (2002).

2. Did the doctrine of *stare decisis* require the result reached by Justice Carr? If Justice Black was in favor of changing the law, why did he vote to affirm the judgment of the trial court?

3. Why does the dissent of Justice Edwards begin by stating that the doctrine of sovereign immunity no longer exists in Michigan when the decision affirmed a judgment based on the doctrine?

4. Why is this case considered a law development case rather than one of error correction? If the trial court did not commit an error, how can its judgment be reversed?

5. Is there an answer to Justice Carr's argument that if the legislature can change the common law then the power to change it must be legislative in character and thus, under the separation of powers doctrine, one that cannot be exercised by the courts?

6. What is the significance of legislative activity in the field of governmental immunity? In Muskopf v. Corning Hospital District, 55 Cal.2d 211, 11 Cal.Rptr. 89, 359 P.2d 457 (1961) the California Supreme Court, in an opinion by Justice Traynor, pointed to both legislative and judicial exceptions to governmental immunity as being so illogical as to cause serious inequality. It also read the legislature's abolition of immunity in some areas as not implying affirmance of it in other areas. It concluded that the court

was thus free to decide whether to abolish it in those other areas. Is that the appropriate interpretation to give to legislative action or inaction?

7. A disagreement over whether a decision to override prior law should be applied to the parties before the court or only in future cases resulted the affirmance of the judgment in the principal case. What are the various possibilities for retrospective or prospective application of a ruling? Which one should a court follow? One approach was taken by the Massachusetts Supreme Judicial Court in Colby v. Carney Hospital, 356 Mass. 527, 254 N.E.2d 407 (1969). In that case the court referred to an earlier opinion in which it had stated that the defense of charitable immunity should be overruled only prospectively and preferably by legislative action. The court further noted that only three or four states still adhered to the doctrine. After commenting that no legislative action seemed likely in the near future, it said "[w]e take this occasion to give adequate warning that the next time we are squarely confronted by a legal question respecting the charitable immunity doctrine it is our intention to abolish it." 356 Mass. at 528, 254 N.E.2d at 408. Is it proper for a court to make such a statement? What is its legal effect? What rule should the trial courts apply until the court does render a decision that is binding precedent?

8. One of the most thoughtful writers on the role of appellate courts in making law was Roger Traynor, long time member of the California Supreme Court and a professor of law before and after his judicial service. Many of his thoughts on judicial law making were stated in his article Transatlantic Reflections on Leeways and Limits of Appellate Courts, 1980 Utah L.Rev. 255.

9. For an excellent collection of articles by federal and state judges on judicial activism and restraint see D. O'Brien, ed., Judges and Judging: Views from the Bench (1997).

LANDGRAVER v. EMANUEL LUTHERAN CHARITY BOARD

Supreme Court of Oregon, 1955.
203 Or. 489, 280 P.2d 301.

TOOZE, JUSTICE.

This is an action for damages for personal injuries caused by alleged negligence brought by Larry Landgraver, as plaintiff, against Emanuel Lutheran Charity Board, Inc., a corporation, as defendant. Judgment on the pleadings was entered in favor of defendant. Plaintiff appeals.

The judgment on the pleadings was granted by the trial court upon the theory that a charitable institution, such as the defendant, was immune to tort liability.

The parties are agreed that the defendant is a charitable corporation, organized under the appropriate laws of this state, and that its funds and income are perpetuated in trust to carry on the charitable purposes for which it was created.

The parties also agree that under the existing law of this state, as announced in prior decisions of this court, the defendant is immune to the tort liability sought to be fastened upon it by the instant litigation. But the plaintiff insists that, in the light of modern conditions, we should reexamine the question of tort liability as it applies to charitable institutions, and adopt a new rule holding them liable for damages for their negligent acts. That presents the only matter before us for decision.

We have, therefore, re-examined the question. Some courts of high repute, including the Supreme Court of our sister state of Washington, have also done the same thing, and in many instances have, in the light of changed conditions, overturned the rule of immunity, expressly overruling their prior decisions in which the doctrine was recognized. This was true with the Supreme Court of Washington: Pierce v. Yakima Valley Memorial Hospital Ass'n, 43 Wash.2d 162, 260 P.2d 765. For a complete discussion of the doctrine of immunity to tort liability enjoyed by charitable institutions, and of the trend of recent court decisions, see Note 25 A.L.R.2d 29. Many sound reasons are given for abrogating the rule of immunity, particularly as it applies to charitable corporations engaged in big business, such as hospitals. Not the least of those reasons is the availability of insurance in this modern age to cover the risks.

The rule of immunity as applied to charitable organizations was established in this state as a matter of public policy. The term "public policy" is not susceptible to an exact or precise definition. Generally, it is said to be that principle of law which holds that no one can lawfully do that which has a tendency to be injurious to the public or against the public good, 72 C.J.S., Policy, p. 209. It varies with the times, and the public policy at one time may not be the public policy of another time. In Turney v. J.H. Tillman Co., 112 Or. 122, 132, 228 P. 933, 936, we said:

> "By reason of the fact that the habits, opinions, and wants of the people vary with the times so public policy may change with them. So because these habits, opinions, and wants are different in different places, what may be against public policy in one state or country may not be so in another. 13 C.J. 427, § 363."

Primarily, it is the function of the legislature to establish the public policy of the state; it is the duty of the courts to recognize it like any other matter of public law. However, cases may arise covering a field where no direct legislation exists. In such cases, it is for the courts to ascertain and declare what is the public policy of the state. Many factors enter into that consideration. The state's public history, its constitution, its legislation upon kindred subjects, its court decisions, and, in some cases, the constant practices of state officials, are all matters to be considered. But once the court has ascertained and declared that public policy, it becomes the law of the state, and is as binding as a legislative enactment. [Citations omitted.]

From the beginning, the overriding public policy of this state, as evidenced by many legislative acts, has been to protect the assets of charitable institutions from use for any purpose other than that for which they were organized. The legislation of the state exempting such institutions from taxation is one example of the legislative policy.

Exempting charitable organizations from tort liability is but another phase of that same public policy. This court did not establish that policy in this state; it simply declared what it was in the light of the general public policy established by the legislature. Since its first opportunity to discuss the policy as it concerned the question of immunity from tort liability in the case of Hill v. President, etc., of Tualatin Academy, 1912, 61 Or. 190, 121 P. 901, this court has been consistent in approving the doctrine of immunity in general, although it has discussed some exceptions: [Citations omitted.] In the Gregory case, our prior decisions were reviewed; we also recognized the attacks made in that litigation upon the doctrine that a hospital is exempt from liability for its negligence. But in the final analysis, we refused to repudiate the rule. We also suggested that a change in the rule, if a change was to be made, was a matter for legislative determination, and not one for the court.

Over the years the legislature has taken no action to overturn the doctrine. By its silence, we may well infer its approval. But, however that may be, there was no occasion for it to act specifically if it was satisfied with the rule. The doctrine had become the firmly established law of this state; a part of the general public policy of the state relating to charitable institutions, and as established by the legislature.

The legislature had the right to assume that the rule would not be changed unless it itself acted.

We are divided in this court as to the proper course that should be → *divided court* taken. Whatever a divided court may decide today may be changed tomorrow, if there happens to be a change in the personnel of the court, or a change of opinion on the part of members of the court as now constituted. The matter is of the highest importance to every charitable institution in Oregon, including hospitals, churches, private schools, organizations such as the Y.M.C.A., Salvation Army, and other charities, *legislative* as well as to the public at large. In such circumstances, it seems clear *determin* that any change in the public policy of this state should be a matter *public policy* solely for legislative determination.

Judgment affirmed.

LUSK, JUSTICE (specially concurring).

I concur in the judgment of affirmance but solely on the ground that the plaintiff was a patient in the hospital operated by the defendant. I find no legislation in this state touching the subject. The immunity is purely court made and is said to be a part of the public policy of Oregon. But public policy "is a very unruly horse, and when you once get astride it you never know where it will carry you." Burrough, J., in Richardson v. Mellish, 2 Bing 229, 252. The opinion of the court in the case at bar expresses a policy of total immunity for charitable corporations from tort liability. I think that this is wrong and that the dissenting opinion of Mr. Justice Brand demonstrates that it is wrong. I am unwilling to be carried so far as to concur in a holding, for example, that a person injured on a public thoroughfare as the result of the negligent operation of an ambulance by the employee of a charitable corporation operating a hospital is without redress against the corporation. That, of course, is not this case. But the language of the opinion could be invoked to support such a ruling. We have held that a patient in a hospital cannot recover against the institution for a tortious injury suffered at the hands of its employees. That is as far, in my judgment, as the public policy goes. That, likewise, is the extent of the immunity (where immunity prevails) under the weight of authority in this country. 3 Scott on Trusts 2151; A.L.I. Restatement, Trusts, p. 1240. I would limit the decision strictly to the issue presented by the pleadings in this case.

BRAND, JUSTICE (dissenting).

I am authorized to state that MR. CHIEF JUSTICE WARNER joins in the following dissent.

* * *

For a second time this court has been requested to reconsider its holdings on the question of liability of charitable corporations. Briefs by the plaintiff and by a considerable group of lawyers, as amici curiae, urge upon us that the rule of immunity is archaic, unjust, unworkable, and contrary to the modern trend of authority. We are cited to an exhaustive annotation of 170 pages in 25 A.L.R.2d, 29 to 200, which was published in 1952, more than seven years after the date of our last decision on the subject. The annotation was made "Because of recent developments in the law on the subject * * *." Since our last decision adhering to the immunity doctrine, persuasive judicial opinions have been written. A decent respect for the able presentation of the issue and for recent authority suggests a consideration of the reasoning which supports or opposes charitable immunity. The early British decisions which gave rise to the theory of immunity have been overruled, but the doctrine of immunity persists in a number of American jurisdictions.

It will be observed that nine of the cases cited were decided since the date of our last decision on the subject, and that in five jurisdictions the courts have reconsidered the issue, overruled previous decisions and held charities liable for tort and that, since our last decision.

The gradual erosion of the rule of immunity has been demonstrated in the decisions of many jurisdictions which have in the past been listed as supporting immunity on the grounds of public policy or on the trust fund theory. Decisions in 15 jurisdictions which have denied recovery to beneficiaries, have nevertheless held that charities are liable in damages for negligent injury of strangers. The cases are listed in 25 A.L.R.2d pages 91 to 93, § 23.

The view that immunity does not extend to a tort committed against a servant of the charity has been supported in eight jurisdictions. 25 A.L.R.2d pages 89 to 90, § 22. In eight jurisdictions decisions have been rendered tending to indicate an abandonment of the immunity theory in its entirety, and holding that a charitable institution is liable for a tort committed against a paying patient, as distinguished from one who receives treatment without cost. 25 A.L.R.2d 106, 107.

* * *

The courts have repeatedly pointed out that the early cases which followed the rule of nonliability were considered under conditions which no longer prevail. The later decisions which still adhere to the ancient doctrine are strangely lacking in any supporting argument, except that which is drawn from the doctrine of stare decisis. The courts have taken judicial notice that charity hospitals and like institutions have become big business. They are not merely the invested wealth of some benevolent donor. They are supported in part by community drives for funds. They pay reasonable salaries, and, to a preponderant extent, their charges approach the limit of what the traffic will bear. * * * These are great, good, and necessary institutions, but in their modern management, business and charity are inextricably merged. One court has recently said that these institutions are nonprofit rather than charitable in character. Silva v. Providence Hospital of Oakland, supra, 14 Cal.2d 762, 97 P.2d 798.

It has been pointed out that the so-called public policy which protects charities from liability is "diametrically opposed" by the declared public policy of practically all of the states.

"* * * As examples practically every state in the Union has enacted a workmen's compensation law; occupational disease disability laws making employers liable to workmen if the injury or illness arises out of and in the course of their employment regardless of any question of negligence; employment security acts designed to take care of individuals during periods of enforced idleness, and even in cases of voluntary strikes under certain circumstances thus relieving the unfortunates of the burdens of misfortune and shifting such burdens to the shoulders of the public at large. In addition to these laws Federal legislation has encompassed the entire field of welfare and social security.

"We believe that these legislative declarations of public policy which relieves the individual from the burden of his misfortunes and makes the general public bear the load levying taxes directly or indirectly to carry out such policy, completely repudiate the rule of nonliability of charitable institutions for the torts of their servants based on public policy." Ray v. Tucson Medical Center, supra, 72 Ariz. 22, 230 P.2d 220, at page 229.

* * *

Since the decisions on both sides of this question are based upon broad conceptions of public policy as determined by the courts, it is proper to consider the nature of public policy and the function of the courts with respect to it. A learned article by Professor Lester W. Freezer contains a splendid exposition of public policy, as it applies to these cases. He demonstrates the profound changes which have taken place in the administration of charities. He comments on the private right of a negligently injured person to compensation, but he deals chiefly with the public interest in the case of such an injured person. That interest is, first, that he be rehabilitated, to the end that he shall not become a public charge, and, second, that he shall again be rendered capable of contributing to the economic life of the community. The author continues:

interests:
1. rehab
2. contrib.
to community

" * * * If the institution, through negligent injury to him, prevents the fulfillment of either of these objects, it has in that case and to that extent defeated the purpose for which it was created. Laying aside the loss and suffering of the individual, the institution whose negligent servant injures an inmate so that his economic value to society is reduced, has failed in its duty to society and to the members of society who have established and maintained it.

"This thought, that the charity which has negligently injured a beneficiary, defeats its purpose, has been suggested in some judicial opinions, but this type of reasoning is usually based upon considerations referring to the individual welfare of the beneficiary involved. The judiciary has, so far as may be inferred from the cases discovered in this study, generally failed to recognize the obligation which charity, according to the theory of modern sociology, owes to society, and which it shifts to other shoulders if it be immune from liability for negligent injury to its beneficiaries. * * * "

* * *

From Ray v. Tucson Medical Center, supra, we quote the following:

"Realizing that public policy is, in its very nature, always fluctuating, varying with customs growing out of changing social, political and economic conditions and recognizing the radical changes that have taken place in each of these fields of activity during the past two decades, we believe it not only proper but necessary that we reconsider the rule laid down in those cases.

* * *

"The declaration of 'public policy' is primarily a legislative function. The courts unquestionably have authority to declare a public policy which already exists and to base its decisions upon that ground. But in the absence of a legislative declaration of what that public policy is, before courts are justified in declaring its existence such public policy should be so thoroughly established as a state of public mind, so united and so definite and fixed that its existence is not subject to any substantial doubt. Sheehan v. North Country Community Hospital, 273 N.Y. 163, 7 N.E.2d 28, 29, 109 A.L.R. 1197. It is equally true that when the reason for the existence of a declared public policy no longer obtains that the courts should without hesitation declare that such public policy no longer exists." Ray v. Tucson Medical Center, 230 P.2d at pages 222 and 229.

The most recent decision to which our attention has been called is Noel v. Menninger Foundation, 175 Kan. 751, 276 P.2d 934, 943. The case was decided by the Supreme Court of Kansas in March 1954. In that case, the lower court followed earlier decisions of the Kansas Supreme Court and denied recovery to an injured patient. As in the case at bar, the plaintiff asked the Supreme Court of Kansas to reconsider its former holdings in the light of social conditions and tendencies now prevailing. The court reviewed the modern tendencies which demonstrate a public policy favoring recovery. It then overruled its previous decisions and held against the immunity doctrine generally. The court held that the legislature and not the courts create and grant immunity from liability for wrong-doing, and it even went so far as to say that "To exempt charitable and nonprofit corporations from liability for their torts is plainly contrary to our constitutional guaranties, Bill of Rights, § 18." The court quoted further, and with approval, the following:

> " 'The declaration of public policy is primarily a legislative function though courts have authority to declare a public policy which already exists and to base its decisions upon that ground, but in absence of a legislative declaration before courts are justified in declaring existence of public policy it should be so thoroughly established as a state of public mind so united and so definite and fixed that its existence is not subject to any substantial doubt. (Headnote 7.)' " Noel v. Menninger Foundation, 175 Kan. 751, 267 P.2d 934, at page 941.

In Iowa the Supreme Court reconsidered its previous decisions based upon matters of public policy and said:

> "Public policy simply means that policy recognized by the state in determining what acts are unlawful or undesirable as being injurious to the public or contrary to the public good. It is not quiescent but active. A policy adopted today as being in the public good, unlike the Ten Commandments, is not necessarily an ever enduring thing. As times and prospectives change, so changes the policy. * * * " Haynes v. Presbyterian Hospital Ass'n., 241 Iowa 1269, 45 N.W.2d 151, 153.

> "The fact that the courts may have at an early date, in response to what appeared good as a matter of policy created an immunity, does not appear to us as sound for continuing the same, when under all legal theories, it is basically unsound and especially so, when the reasons upon which it was built, no longer exist." 45 N.W.2d at page 154.

The court then said:

> "It is our considered judgment that incorporated charity should respond as do private individuals, business corporations, and others, when it does good in the wrong way. * * * " Haynes v. Presbyterian Hospital Ass'n, 241 Iowa 1269, 45 N.W.2d 151 at page 154.

Previous decisions overruled.

* * *

For the foregoing reasons we dissent from the opinion of the majority.

Notes and Questions

The principal case raises the question of the respective roles of the legislature and the courts in declaring public policy. Is it proper for a court to declare public policy when the legislature is available to do so? If not, doesn't that mean public policy will never change except by legislative action? See Brachtenbach, Public Policy in Judicial Decisions, 21 Gonzaga L.Rev. 1 (1985/86). What does the concurring opinion mean when it refers to public policy as an "unruly horse"? Should public policy in one state be determined by public policies in other states?

YOECKEL v. SAMONIG

Supreme Court of Wisconsin, 1956.
272 Wis. 430, 75 N.W.2d 925.

This action was commenced on July 3, 1954, by Norma Yoeckel against Sam Samonig to recover for the invasion of plaintiff's right of privacy. The material allegations of the complaint are as follows:

"2. That the defendant is by occupation a tavern keeper and operator and whose place of business is known as 'Sad Sam's Tavern', which is located in the Town of Delafield, Waukesha County, Wisconsin and the residence of the defendant is unknown to the plaintiff.

"3. That on or about June 30, 1954 in the evening of said day the plaintiff was a patron in the establishment operated by the defendant. That the plaintiff, while said patron of the defendant, entered into the ladies rest room of said establishment.

"That while the plaintiff was in the ladies rest room the defendant entered into said room with a camera and flash camera equipment and invaded the plaintiff's privacy while she was in said rest room and photographed the said plaintiff.

"That thereafter the plaintiff demanded that the defendant give to her the photograph he had taken of her while in the ladies rest room and the defendant refused and neglected so to do.

"That the plaintiff, upon returning to the dining area of the establishment observed the defendant displaying and showing to other patrons in his establishment pictures that he had taken of ladies in the ladies rest room. The plaintiff does not know whether or not the picture taken of her was so demonstrated and shown to other patrons, both men and women.

"4. That as a result of the invading of her privacy and of the taking of the picture while occupying the ladies rest room the plaintiff has suffered great mental anguish, embarrassment and humiliation, all to her damage in the sum of Five Thousand ($5,000.00) Dollars.''

Defendant demurred to the complaint on the ground that it does not state facts sufficient to constitute a cause of action. The demurrer was sustained and judgment dismissing the complaint was entered on May 18, 1955. Plaintiff appeals.

GEHL, JUSTICE.

The parties agree that plaintiff seeks to plead a cause of action based upon defendant's violation of her right of privacy, sometimes defined as the right to be let alone. As appears from the Annotations at 138 A.L.R. 22 and at 168 A.L.R. 446, the right has been recognized and enforced in some jurisdictions and denied in others. In the only cases in which this court has been called upon to consider the question we refused to recognize the right. In Judevine v. Benzies–Montanye Fuel & Warehouse Co., 1936, 222 Wis. 512, 527, 269 N.W. 295, 302, 106 A.L.R. 1443, recovery was sought on that ground among others. It was alleged that defendant had distributed hand bills through the city of plaintiffs residence purporting to advertise for sale to the highest bidder an account for merchandise sold to him by the defendant. It is apparent from the opinion that the court made a careful study of the subject. It held that no cause of action was stated and said:

> "We are of opinion, especially in view of the fact that truth is held no defense to the action where it has been recognized as it is to actions for injury to reputation through libel and slander, that if a right of action for violation of the right of privacy by such acts as are here involved is to be created, it is more fitting that it be created by the Legislature by declaring unlawful such acts as it deems an unwarranted infringement of that right."

In State ex rel. Distenfeld v. Neelen, 1949, 255 Wis. 214, 38 N.W.2d 703, the petitioner sought a writ prohibiting certain officials of the city of Milwaukee from reading before a meeting of the common council testimony given by him at a John Doe proceeding previously held and closed. He alleged that he had testified at the John Doe proceeding on assurance that his testimony was secret, that his right of privacy was about to be invaded and that he would be held up to public contempt, ridicule and disgrace by having his testimony read as threatened. The court held that Judevine v. Benzies–Montanye Fuel & Warehouse Co., supra, is authority for the ruling that petitioner's cause of action for invasion of the right of privacy did not exist, and denied the application for a writ.

The rulings in these cases must be accepted as a refusal to recognize a right of action for violation of one's right of privacy and as an expression that if the right is to be created it be done by the legislature. The legislature has refused to create it. Apparently in response to the court's suggestion made in Judevine v. Benzies–Montanye Fuel & Warehouse Co. supra, there was introduced at the 1951 session, bill No. 215 S.

legislative bill proposed to create me cause of action

It contained a short provision which would have created the broad enactment that:

> "The legal right of privacy is recognized in this state and an invasion thereof shall give rise to an equitable action to prevent and restrain such invasion as well as an action to recover damages for injuries sustained by reason thereof."

Two substitute amendments to the bill were introduced.

The amended bill, if passed, would have recognized the right of privacy in only extremely limited situations. It would have made it unlawful, (1) for one to use the picture or likeness of any living person without his consent (an act which it appears is sought to be charged in the complaint in the instant action), (2) for a creditor to advertise unpaid commercial accounts in a manner which discloses the identity of the debtor and with intent to embarrass the debtor as a means of making collection or of punishing non-payment (the precise conduct considered in Judevine v. Benzies–Montanye Fuel & Warehouse Co. supra, and which we also refused to characterize as wrong), and (3) for one to maliciously or fraudulently represent another by impersonation or other means without the other person's authority. The proposal, limited as it was to a scope so narrow, was rejected by the legislature.

Included in the legislative record of the treatment of the proposal found in the Legislative Reference Library is a note in which specific reference to the two cases to which we have referred is made. This would indicate that at some stage of the proceedings some one interested in the proposal had the cases in mind and that they sought to supply, by legislative act, that which we had indicated we were without power to accomplish by judicial act.

At the 1953 session another bill containing the same provisions and written in the identical language as is found in the second substitute amendment to the bill introduced at the 1951 session was introduced. The bill was again defeated. It does not appear that a further effort to create the liability was made at the 1955 session of the legislature.

right ≠ exist legislature ≠ pass bill

In view of what we said and held in the two cases referred to with respect to our lack of power to create a right for the violation of which recovery was there sought, as it is in this case, and particularly because of the refusal of the legislature at two sessions to recognize even a limited right to protection against invasion of the right of privacy, we are compelled to hold again that the right does not exist in this state.

We agree with what was recently said by the Nebraska court in Brunson v. Ranks Army Store, 1955, 161 Neb. 519, 73 N.W.2d 803, 806:

> "Our research develops no Nebraska case holding that this court has in any form or manner adopted the doctrine of the right of privacy, and there is no precedent in this state establishing the doctrine. Nor has the Legislature of this state conferred such a right of action by statute. We submit that if such a right is deemed necessary or desirable, such right should be provided for by action of

our Legislature and not by judicial legislation on the part of our courts. This is especially true in view of the nature of the right under discussion, under which right not even the truth of the allegations is a defense."

Judgment affirmed.

Notes and Questions

1. In the preceding cases the question was whether the courts should abolish a judicially created immunity. In the principal case the issue is whether an entirely new cause of action should be created. Is there a significant difference?

2. What effect should be given to the refusal of the legislature to enact a bill? Compare the judicial response in the principal case to those in prior cases. Is the failure of a bill to pass the legislature always attributable to the fact that a majority of the legislature was opposed to it on the merits? If not, should the failure be given any effect? Does it make a difference if in fact there was a vote on the bill and a majority voted against it?

3. The Wisconsin legislature ultimately recognized a right to privacy in 1977. See Wis.Stat.Ann. § 895.50 (West 1997).

3. DOING JUSTICE

R. MARTINEAU, MODERN APPELLATE PRACTICE— FEDERAL AND STATE CIVIL APPEALS
§ 1.10 (1983).

The functions of error correction and law development have uniformity as their ultimate objective. Appellate judges, however, neither can nor should forget that their decisions are not rendered in the abstract but directly and immediately affect the parties before them. On the other hand they also cannot forget that their decisions should not be good for one case and one case only, and irrelevant to all other cases. Precedent and stare decisis are essential features of a common law legal system, and appellate courts no more than trial courts can ignore the requirements of the law in deciding individual cases. Judge Albert Tate, Jr., of the United States Court of Appeals for the Fifth Circuit expressed the principle in the following terms:

> The result that seems "just" for the present case must be a principled one that will afford just results in similar conflicts of interest. This judge has an initial human concern that the litigants receive common sense justice, but he also realizes that the discipline of legal doctrine governs his determination of the cause.

Doing justice, if it means having the most deserving party prevail, cannot be divorced from doing justice in the context of the entire legal system. Obviously the legal system does not exist for the purpose of doing injustice. But justice is not done by ignoring the applicable substantive and procedural law to achieve a particular result in an individual case.

HOPKINS, THE ROLE OF AN INTERMEDIATE APPELLATE COURT

41 Brooklyn L.Rev. 459, 473–75 (1975).*

A function of the intermediate appellate court, sometimes overlooked, is its authority—at least in New York—to reverse or modify in the interests of justice. The power apparently also exists in some other jurisdictions. In New York, the power is a concomitant of the link between the Appellate Division and the Supreme Court, of which it is a part, and is related to the right to exercise an independent source of discretion by the Appellate Division.

Once a reversal or modification is made by the Appellate Division in the interests of justice, the determination is not reviewable by the Court of Appeals. In the highest court, the determination is treated as if it were an exercise of discretion by the Appellate Division and, thus, without the jurisdiction of the Court of Appeals. Hence, the power of the intermediate court seems virtually unlimited.

In practice, however, this potential threat to the rule of precedent as an arbitrary power to set aside judgments in the court of original jurisdiction has not been realized. First, it has been sparingly used; most reversals or modifications are made on the ground of prejudicial error. Second, whenever used, it is usually the response to an egregious error overshadowing the case and which, by the omissions of counsel, was not properly challenged in the lower court. Thus, the rule of precedent is not impaired, but rather, applied in that particular case. It is within this area that the power of the intermediate court to review in the interests of justice finds its greatest expression.

A second area of use is more amorphous and, perhaps for that reason, has limited application. For want of a better description, I call it "the appeal to conscience." It is the case in which the result is so incongruous in light of the facts, or where there is such a disturbing lack of evidence on a critical point, that the impression is induced that justice has not been done. Sometimes, the record indicates that the result stemmed from the absolute failure of counsel or the striking contrast between the relative ability and experience of opposing counsel. Sometimes an element in the case, though properly in evidence, appears to have assumed a disproportionate weight in the decision.

It is in this last category that the reviewing court should be most cautious. The atmosphere of a trial cannot be transmitted into the record or into the argument by counsel before the appellate court. The seeming omission or neglect of counsel may have been more a choice of strategy dictated by the pressure of circumstances not hinted in the record, rather than ineptitude. The incongruity in result may also be

* © Brooklyn Law School, Brooklyn Law Review.

explained by the jury's appraisal of the demeanor of witnesses in giving their testimony. Or, the jury may in fact have disregarded that element in the case which was improperly stressed by the prevailing party.

The chance of injustice caused however ironically by a reversal in the interests of justice is lessened by the collegial form of the reviewing court. The impression that the case went awry must be shared by a majority of the court. Though a majority does not guarantee the justice of the reversal, it reduces the possibility of a wild or completely baseless conclusion by the intermediate court that an unjust result was reached in the trial court.

Hence, the power to reverse in the interest of justice is more in the nature of a safety valve, seldom used when the system is working satisfactorily, rather than a short circuit which disrupts the system. It guards against the unusual case wrongly decided which might escape correction were the appellate court not empowered to act unrestrained by the fetters of the doctrine that only errors preserved by timely objection or appropriate exception may be reviewed on appeal.

WRIGHT, THE DOUBTFUL OMNISCIENCE OF APPELLATE COURTS

41 Minnesota L.Rev. 751, 778–81, 787 (1957).

For a good many years my colleague, Leon Green, has been pointing out that:

> Probably the strangest chapter in American legal history is how in the short period of the last fifty or seventy-five years, the same period during which trial courts were losing most of their power, the appellate courts have drawn unto themselves practically all the power of the judicial system.

In a recent statement of his views Dean Green has observed, with much justification:

> The trial judge is not much more than a trial examiner, while the jury simply satisfies the public and professional craving for ceremonial—the necessity for dealing with simple matters as though they were freighted with great significance.

The principal means by which appellate courts have obtained such complete control of litigation has been the transmutation of specific circumstances into questions of law. Subtle rules about presumptions and burden of proof, elaborate concepts of causation and consideration and the rest, have been devised in such a way that unless the appellate judge handling the case is a dullard, some doctrine is always at hand to achieve the ends of justice, as they appear to the appellate court.

It is easier to summarize what we have seen than it is to evaluate it. The four specific examples considered in this paper should be enough to persuade anyone that appellate power is rapidly on the increase. The appraisal by trial judge and jury of the damages suffered by an injured person is now subject to review by appellate courts; a decade ago it could not have been reviewed. The determination by the judge that the verdict is not contrary to the clear weight of the evidence is now said, by at least one appellate court, to be within its power to reverse; heretofore the precedents have been uniform that such a determination was not subject to reversal. Many appellate courts now believe that they need not give any weight to findings of fact of a trial judge sitting without a jury where these findings are based on documentary evidence; both the language and intent of Federal Rule 52(a), adopted by the Supreme Court only 19 years ago, are explicit that such findings can only be set aside when clearly erroneous. Finally discretionary decisions by the trial judge on interlocutory procedural matters may now be vacated in the exercise of a supervisory power of appellate courts, contrary to what the Supreme Court said as recently as 1956. Thus the centralization of legal power in the appellate courts, which Dean Green detected more than a quarter century ago, proceeds at an accelerating pace.

But now we must venture some views as to whether this development is good or bad for the cause of justice to which all are devoted. It would be irresponsible even to suggest that these changes have taken place merely because appellate courts are power-mad. The obvious truth, which must be readily admitted by anyone familiar with appellate judges, is that these recent developments in the law, these departures from what had seemed fairly clear lines of precedent, have come only because the judges who have voted for them sincerely believe that they are needed and justified by the highest public interests.

This leads us to the philosophical question which underlies all these specific issues: what is the proper function of an appellate court? Everyone agrees, so far as I know, that one function of an appellate court is to discover and declare—or to make—the law. From the earliest times appellate courts have been empowered to reverse for errors of law, to announce the rules which are to be applied, and to ensure uniformity in the rules applied by various inferior tribunals.

The controversial question is whether appellate courts have a second function, that of ensuring that justice is done in a particular case. In each of the situations considered the motivating force in the appellate court's mind has been the desire to "do justice." Thus the appellate court is unwilling to let an award of damages stand which seems to it so excessive as to be unjust, it refuses to put its approval on a verdict which it deems contrary to the clear weight of the evidence, it will not affirm a judgment based on findings it thinks wrong when it is as well able to interpret documentary evidence and make the finding in question as was the trial court, and it will not let a trial judge's mistaken conception of what is an "exceptional condition" result in exposing parties to the delay and expense of reference to a master.

If it is the function of appellate courts to do justice in individual cases, then each of the developments we have canvassed was sound and desirable, since each has made it easier for the appellate court to enforce its concept of justice in a particular case. The notion that appellate courts should undertake to "do justice" is so attractive on its face that it is difficult to disagree with it. And it enjoys the weighty support of such famous students of the judicial process as Roscoe Pound, Edson Sunderland, Wirt Blume and James Wm. Moore. Nevertheless, with deference to these great men, I think we should refrain from agreeing that appellate courts are to do justice until we have seen the price we must pay for this concept.

The principal consequences of broadening appellate review are two. Such a course impairs the confidence of litigants and the public in the decisions of the trial courts, and it multiplies the number of appeals. Until recently if a defendant thought an award of damages was excessive, he nevertheless had no choice but to pay it, for no appellate court would listen to his attack on it. Now, in similar circumstances, he will appeal. Until recently if a lawyer was dissatisfied when his case was referred to a master, he appeared before the master nevertheless, for an attempted appeal from the order of reference would have been dismissed out of hand. Now he files a petition for a writ of mandamus. We may be sure that the broadened scope of appellate review we have seen will mean an increase in the number of appeals. Is this desirable? We need not worry too much that an increase in appeals will mean overwork for appellate judges; they, after all, have invited the increase. But we should worry about the consequences of more numerous appeals for the litigants and the public. Appeals are always expensive and time-consuming. When they are successful, and lead to a new trial, they add to the burden on already-crowded trial courts. Interlocutory review, as by writ of mandamus, delays the case interminably while the lawyers go off to the appellate court to argue the propriety of the challenged order by the trial judge. It is literally marvelous that, at a time when the entire profession is seeking ways to minimize congestion and delay in the courts, we should set on a course which inevitably must increase congestion and delay.

But we have courts in order to do justice. If better justice can be obtained by broadening the scope of appellate review, then even congestion, delay and expense are not too high a price to pay. Do we really get better justice by augmenting the power of the appellate courts? In some fairly obvious senses I feel quite sure that we do not. If in two similar cases the person rich enough to afford an appeal gets a reversal, however just, while the person of insufficient means to risk an appeal is forced to live with the judgment of the trial court, has justice really been improved? And what of the injured person who settles his claim for less than the amount awarded him by the jury and approved by the trial court rather than wait a year or more until an appellate court has agreed that the verdict is not excessive? Broader appellate review has led to injustice for him.

Further, it may well be, as Blackstone says, that "next to doing right, the great object in the administration of public justice should be to give public satisfaction." It is hard to believe that there has been any great public dissatisfaction with the restricted appellate review which was traditional in this country. Very early in our history Chief Justice Ellsworth observed:

> But, surely, it cannot be deemed a denial of justice, that a man shall not be permitted to try his case two or three times over.

Yet increased review is likely to lead to quite tangible public dissatisfaction. Every time a trial judge is reversed, every time the belief is reiterated that appellate courts are better qualified than trial judges to decide what justice requires, the confidence of litigants and the public in the trial courts will be further impaired. Under any feasible or conceivable system, our trial courts must always have the last word in the great bulk of cases. I doubt whether there will be much satisfaction with the judgments of trial courts among a public which is educated to believe that only appellate judges are trustworthy ministers of justice.

Finally, to come to the very heart of the issue, is there any reason to suppose that the result an appellate court reaches on the kinds of issues discussed is more likely to be "just" than was the opposite result reached by the trial court? Judge Chase's observation, quoted earlier, is in point here:

> Though trial judges may at times be mistaken as to facts, appellate judges are not always omniscient.

* * *

There is no way to know for sure whether trial courts or appellate courts are more often right. But in the absence of a clear showing that broadened appellate review leads to better justice, a showing which I think has not been made and probably cannot be made, the cost of increased appellate review, in terms of time and expense to the parties, in terms of lessened confidence in the trial judge, and in terms of positive injustice to those who cannot appeal, seems to me clearly exorbitant.

I do not wish to speak critically of the appellate courts which have recently announced broader powers of appellate review. Only the most insensitive observer could fail to sympathize with their problem. When a judge upholds the constitutionality of a statute he believes unwise, he has at least all the tradition of deference to a coordinate and popularly responsible branch of government to sustain him in his self-restraint. But there is no such tradition to bolster self-restraint when he is passing on the work of his constitutional inferiors within the judiciary. It must be hard, indeed, for a judge to approve a judgment below he considers to be unjust when he knows that he has the power to set it aside and achieve justice as he sees it. Our hope must be that in those hard moments the judge will remember Justice Jackson's caution that "we are not final because we are infallible, but we are infallible only because we are final," and that, remembering, he may believe that the best way to do justice in the long run is to confine to a minimum appellate tampering with the work of the trial courts.

Notes and Questions

1.   Should an appellate court ever reverse simply because it believes the equities of the case are on the side of the appellant rather than the appellee? If so, what is the precedential effect of the decision?

2.   Given the vagaries of the trial process as affected by the rules of evidence, relative competence of counsel, the jury system, availability of witnesses, and the fact that appellate judges read only a cold record, can an appellate court ever know with confidence whose side justice is on?

3.   Does doing justice mean that the failure of the appellant to comply with rules of procedure should always be ignored, when to enforce them would require a decision against the appellant? Doesn't justice mean playing by the rules? Judge Learned Hand tells the story of one day driving Justice Oliver Wendell Holmes, Jr. to the Supreme Court chambers to attend a conference of the Court. As Holmes was walking away, Hand said "Do justice." Holmes replied: "That is not my job. My job is to play the game according to the rules." L. Hand, The Spirit of Liberty 306–07 (I. Dilliard, ed. 3rd ed. 1960). For further discussion, see Chapter 8, section B, infra.

4.   THE JUDGE'S VIEWPOINT

In the foregoing three subsections, the functions of the appellate court were presented. Another way to approach the same issue is to look at how appellate judges view themselves and their function. This is the subject of the following comment by Judge Albert Tate, Jr. of the Fifth Circuit:

> Based principally upon twenty-six years of appellate experience, most judges, most of the time, view their function and are principally motivated in their decision making by three principal characteristics or drives. First and foremost, the judge is motivated to achieve the humanly fair or socially useful result, subject to the limitations of judicial review and the demands of consistency with legal doctrine—sometimes flexibly interpreted. Second, the judge is concerned that the opinion is technically sound and fairly applies relevant constitutional, statutory, and jurisprudential authority that fairly distinguishes the authority relied upon by the losing party. Third in listing—but not necessarily in importance or weight—the appellate judge is concerned about the implications for application of the rationale of the opinion to different factual situations that may arise in the future. This factor is of special concern in the 10–15% borderline decisions in which the court has respectable discretion in the selection of rationales or results.

> Obviously, these considerations have different weight according to the nature of the appeal before the court. Different fields of law inherently call for different values. Real estate or tax law calls more for doctrinal stability and precise rules, despite inequities that may result. While in tort law, where human equities may have more play, there is more doctrinal flexibility. In criminal constitutional law, where the facts might call for affirming the conviction of an obvious-

ly guilty defendant, the doctrinal considerations may require placing a higher value upon upholding rather than weakening constitutional safeguards designed to protect all individuals (as well as this guilty defendant) from the misuse of the power of the state.

Tate, Federal Appellate Advocacy in the 1980's, 5 Am.J.Trial Adv. 63, 65 (1981).* For a fuller discussion see F. Coffin, The Ways of a Judge 195–249 (1980). For the views of four authorities on the appellate process as to what makes a good appellate judge see Aldisert, Erickson, Leflar, and Roberts, What Makes A Good Appellate Judge? Four Views, 22 Judges J. 14 (Spring 1983). For a discussion of the freedom judges have to decide a case a particular way, see Simonett, The Use of the Term "Result–Oriented" to Characterize Appellate Decisions, 10 William Mitchell L.Rev. 187 (1984).

Notes and Questions

1. Judges frequently emphasize the need for collegiality on appellate courts. E.g., Edwards, The Effects of Collegiality on Judicial Decision Making, 151 U. Pa. L. Rev. 1639 (2003). Since, with rare exceptions, trial judges sit alone, and appellate courts are multimember, does this suggest that the qualities that constitute a good trial judge are not necessarily the same as those that make up a good appellate judge? What are those qualities? In answering that, consider that many appellate judges started as trial judges. R. Posner, The Federal Courts: Challenge and Reform 350 (1996) (39% of federal appellate judges were promoted from the district court). See also Slotnick, Federal Trial and Appellate Judges: How Do They Differ?, 36 W. Pol. Q. 570 (1983).

2. If the orientation and abilities of trial and appeals judge differ, in various respects, what do you make of the widespread practice, in the federal system, of federal district judges sitting by designation on the Courts of Appeals? In recent years up to 20 percent of panels in some circuits have such a judge on the panel. The reasons usually advanced for this practice are to increase the number of judges hearing appeals, to deal with rising caseloads, as well as to mutually educate judges on different levels. See Brudney & Ditslear, Designated Diffidence: District Court Judges on the Courts of Appeals, 35 Law & Soc'y Rev. 565 (2001); Saphire & Solimine, Diluting Justice on Appeal? An Examination of the Use of District Judges Sitting by Designation on the United States Courts of Appeals, 28 U. Mich. J.L. Ref. 351 (1995).

* Reprinted with permission copyright © 1981, *American Journal of Trial Advocacy*, Cumberland School of Law of Samford University, Birmingham, Alabama, 35229. All rights reserved.

SECTION C.   THE RELATIONSHIP BETWEEN STRUCTURE AND FUNCTION

D. MEADOR & J. BERNSTEIN, APPELLATE COURTS IN THE UNITED STATES
18–29 (1994).

ORGANIZATION OF THE INTERMEDIATE APPELLATE LEVEL

The intermediate judicial tier, located between the trial courts and the court of last resort, can be organized in one of three ways: by establishing a single, jurisdiction-wide court (the single-court design); by establishing two or more co-equal courts in different geographical areas within the jurisdiction (the geographical design); or by establishing two or more co-equal courts with authority over different categories of cases (the subject-matter design). Each has advantages and disadvantages.

The Single–Court Design. A majority of the states with three-tiered judicial systems (but not the federal judiciary) maintain only one intermediate court. That tribunal hears appeals from trial courts throughout the state. If the volume of appeals is sufficiently low, the court can sit en banc on every appeal. However, this is usually not the case, so most of the statewide intermediate courts function through rotating three-judge panels. Functioning through panels is deemed acceptable in an intermediate court because such a court, unlike a court of last resort, is not responsible for the definitive enunciation of the state's law.

A court that sits in panels can consist of as many judges as are necessary to deal with the volume of business. Statewide appellate courts usually have from six to a dozen judges. A few have substantially more; the largest are the New Jersey Appellate Division with twenty-eight and the Michigan Court of Appeals with twenty-four. A few have only three.

The two major advantages of this style of organization are efficiency and doctrinal coherence. Efficiency is fostered because the appellate business of the state can be centrally managed and the work distributed evenly among the judges. Three-judge panels can sit anywhere in the state, in accordance with appellate demands, or the court can always sit at one convenient location, whichever arrangement better suits the needs of the day. Having a single set of statewide appellate procedural rules facilitates the task of lawyers whose practice spans different parts of the state.

Doctrinal coherence is promoted because it is easier to avoid inconsistencies in decisions and to maintain uniformity in the law when all of the judges in the intermediate tier are under one management. Internal procedures can be devised to foster consistency in a way that would not be possible with separate courts. Moreover, collegiality can be heightened and the likelihood of decisional harmony increased when all of the state's intermediate appellate judges associate together on the same court.

The single-court form of organization becomes less workable as the territory and population of the jurisdiction increase. Large, populous jurisdictions tend to adopt a dispersed, geographical plan of intermediate appellate organization.

The Geographical Design. Under this scheme, the jurisdiction is divided territorially into regions usually designated as numbered judicial districts or circuits (or sometimes as named divisions), and an appellate court is established in each. Nine states and the federal system have adopted this plan.

In the states with the regional plan of appellate organization, the number of intermediate courts ranges from two in Arizona to twelve in Ohio and fourteen in Texas. The other states have from three to six intermediate courts. The number of judges on each regional court ranges from three to a dozen or more. They typically sit in three-judge panels. Each of these courts has authority over appeals from the trial courts located in its territorial region. In a few states with a single statewide intermediate court, designated three-judge panels sit regularly in particular regions (*e.g.*, Oklahoma, Washington, Wisconsin), thus approaching a de facto geographical design.

In the federal system, spanning the entire United States, there are twelve geographical circuits. Eleven are denominated numerically as the First through the Eleventh; the other is the District of Columbia Circuit. In each circuit there is a United States Court of Appeals. These courts range in size from six judges in the First Circuit to twenty-eight in the Ninth. They regularly function through rotating three-judge panels, though they have authority to sit en banc. Each circuit court hears appeals from the federal trial courts (called district courts) located in its circuit and also entertains appeals from certain federal administrative agencies. Each of these courts has its headquarters at a central location, but panels often sit in other places within the circuit.

The federal circuits vary greatly in their territorial expanse. Among the numbered circuits, the smallest is the First, which covers Maine, New Hampshire, Massachusetts, Rhode Island, and Puerto Rico, and the largest is the Ninth, which embraces seven far western states plus Alaska, Hawaii, and other Pacific islands. The District of Columbia includes on the District of Columbia. . . .

The advantages of the geographical arrangement are that it makes the appellate courts more conveniently accessible to lawyers and litigants throughout a large territorial area and takes into account varying regional interests by having a forum whose judges are drawn from the region. Geographical organization may also facilitate case management where the totality of appellate business throughout the jurisdiction might overwhelm a single intermediate court. A disadvantage of this arrangement is that it creates the possibility for inconsistencies in the decisional law, with one regional court deciding an issue differently from the way it is decided in another regional court. . . .

The Subject–Matter Design. Under both the single-court and geographical designs the traditional practice is that each court and all panels on it may hear and decide appeals of all kinds, spanning the entire corpus of the law. In contrast, under the subject-matter plan, an appellate court or panel is allotted only a portion of the appellate business, defined by types of cases; its jurisdiction over those cases is exclusive of all other appellate courts or panels (except the court of last resort sitting above it). This scheme of appellate organization has been developed to a high degree in Germany, and it is also found in other countries that follow the civil-law tradition.

The best American example of subject-matter organization is the United States Court of Appeals for the Federal Circuit, established by Congress in 1982. The court is headquartered in Washington, D.C., and is coequal with the twelve geographically organized federal intermediate appellate courts, but its authority, unlike that of the regional courts, is not confined territorially. Rather, it is nationwide in scope and is defined by the subject matter of the cases or by the origin of the appeals. The Federal Circuit has jurisdiction over appeals from federal district courts throughout the country in patent cases and in certain suits to recover damages from the government. In addition, it has jurisdiction over all appeals from certain other forums, including the Court of International Trade, the Court of Federal Claims, the Merit Systems Protection Board, and some administrative agencies. Even though it does not hear appeals spanning the entire range of legal issues, its jurisdiction is quite varied.

The subject-matter plan of appellate organization has not gained wide popularity in the states. It can be found in Pennsylvania, where the Commonwealth Court has jurisdiction over appeals in cases involving local government units and from state administrative agencies, while the Superior Court takes appeals in all other civil cases and in criminal cases. Alabama and Tennessee maintain separate intermediate courts for civil and criminal cases. As previously mentioned, Texas and Oklahoma have separate civil and criminal courts of last resort.

Subject-matter courts are inconsistent with the American Bar Association's standards on court organization, which assert that every appellate court should have jurisdiction over the entire range of appellate business. Many lawyers and judges agree with that view. Their apprehension about subject-matter organization seems to stem from their confusing it with specialization.

A subject-matter court need not be specialized. Appellate specialization occurs if a court entertains appeals in only one relative narrow category of case. For example, a court could properly be called specialized if its jurisdiction were restricted to deciding patent appeals or workers' compensation cases. The illustration most often cited in the federal system, usually with horror, is the Commerce Court, which existed for a few years just before the First World War. Its jurisdiction was confined to reviewing orders of the Interstate Commerce Commission. It exhibited or at least suggested to observers, the dangers thought to accompany specialization: risk of capture by those with special interests in the court's work (there, the railroads), tendencies of the judges to lose contact with the general body of jurisprudence and develop esoteric legal views, and difficulty in attracting able lawyers to the bench. However, the U.S. Court of Appeals for the Federal Circuit shows that those dangers can be avoided while at the same time designated categories of cases are routed to a single court; the key to success is the variety of business given the court.

An appellate court with a caseload consisting solely of criminal matters is generally disfavored in the American legal world. In addition to some of the reasons against specialization just mentioned, it is thought that because of the peculiar human element in criminal matters and their special social importance, it is preferable to have criminal appeals decided by a court with at least some judges who also decide appeals in other legal fields. Thus the scheme found in Texas, Oklahoma, Alabama, and Tennessee does not enjoy wide acceptance.

The subject-matter style of appellate organization has several advantages. It avoids conflicting decisions on the same legal issue–one of the major problems of co-equal regional courts–because only one court decides any given type of case. It also provides the optimum means of achieving coherent development of legal doctrine; a given group of judges dealing over time with a body of law within its exclusive jurisdiction develops a knowledge of the subject and its nuances that judges dealing only occasionally with the issues cannot attain. This familiarity enhances efficiency and productivity because the judges do not need to re-educate themselves each time a particular legal issues comes before them. Continuity of decision makers also helps lawyers to predict the likely outcome of appeals and thus retards the filing of hopeless ones.

The only disadvantages of subject-matter organization in the intermediate tier are encountered if a court's jurisdiction is defined too narrowly, thus making it a specialized court. The dangers of specialization can be avoided by giving the court authority over a varied array of case types.

RELATIONSHIPS BETWEEN THE TWO APPELLATE LEVELS

When a judicial structure is expanded vertically by inserting an intermediate appellate tier–whether of the single-court, geographical, or subject-matter variety–it is necessary to decide how the appellate functions are to be allocated. The two appellate levels will be sharing the work formerly done by one. A legislature creating such a bifurcated structure must decide which level will do what and should design procedures to ensure that the functions of each level are performed without unnecessary delay and duplication.

An intermediate court is in an odd position. It looks in two directions simultaneously–down to the trial courts and up to the court of last resort. It is clothed with authority to reverse the trial courts, but it in turn can be reversed by the top court. Its insertion into the judicial pyramid creates a potential for complications, added expense to litigants, and delay in the ultimate resolution of controversies. The challenge for judicial architects is to fit the new tier into the existing pyramid in a way that maximizes its potential advantages while avoiding its possible dysfunctional effects. Below we sketch the array of jurisdictional and procedural arrangements that can be employed to fit the middle tier into the judicial structure.

Discretionary Second Review in the Court of Last Resort

While it is widely believed that every losing litigant should have the opportunity as a matter of right to a review, it is also believed that one review is sufficient to protect a litigant's interest in an error-free trial proceeding. Two reviews, absent special justification in a particular case, are seen as wasteful of judicial resources, imposing undue expense on litigants, and unnecessary to protect the rights of the parties.

The specter of double appeals has always haunted the creation of intermediate appellate courts. As a result, in three-tiered judicial systems it is generally provided that an appeal may be taken as a matter of right to the intermediate court but that any further review in the supreme court is at the discretion of that court. Thus double appeals can occur only with the top court's permission. This is the arrangement in the federal system and in many state systems.

Under that arrangement the top court is freed from reviewing the mass of appeals and can therefore devote its energies to deciding cases of significance to the legal order and the public interest. The intermediate court is a buffer, a breakwater against which the tidal waves of appeals spend themselves, leaving the top court protected in quieter waters to deliberate on specially important questions. Another way of putting the matter is to say that the supreme court is concerned primarily with the development of the law, while the intermediate court is concerned primarily with the application of existing law.

This division of responsibility rests on the premise that all appellate work can be sorted into the two categories of error correcting and lawmaking (or law declaring, as some prefer). In performing its lawmaking responsibility, also known as institutional review, a supreme court chooses the cases it will consider and decide from among the petitions filed with it. Error correcting is assigned to intermediate courts, which receive appeals directly from the trial courts and typically have no discretion to decline to decide any case.

It is assumed that a court reviewing for correctness applies established rules of law to determine whether the trial court committed error. But the function of error correction is not always neatly separable from that of lawmaking. The task of deciding cases inevitably involves some measure of law declaring, as the appellate court must articulate the legal precept being applied even when that precept has not previously been articulated in precisely the same way. In the course of applying established rules to varying factual situations, the intermediate court may at times unavoidably affect the development of the law. Moreover, in cases of first impression, for which there is no established rule, the court must formulate one. However, the intermediate court does not have the last say if review in the supreme court is sought and granted. In practice, though, the finite capacity of a court of last resort prevents its reviewing more than a small percentage of intermediate court decisions, thus leaving the latter as the final ruling in a great many cases.

Although some lawmaking by the intermediate court is inescapable, that court must follow the law as enunciated by its court of last resort. Its primary mission is to apply the existing law of the jurisdiction as best it can interpret it, not to make new law. Invoking that principle in a 1973, opinion, the Florida Supreme Court chastised one of the state's intermediate courts for holding that the doctrine of contributory negligence would no longer be followed and that the doctrine of comparative negligence would replace it, saying that only the supreme court could make such a change. Yet the court then proceeded in that same opinion to reach the identical result that the intermediate court had reached, thus evidencing that the latter's view of Florida law had been correct. The point being made, however, was that it was for the supreme court, not the intermediate court, to say so.

Sometimes language or trends in the supreme court's opinions, particularly if accompanied by a recent, significant change in its membership, reveal that a prior decision would no longer be adhered to. In such situations some intermediate courts have not considered themselves bound by the prior decision, on the reasoning that it no longer represented the law of the jurisdiction. To take such a position, however, risks introducing uncertainty into the law, and most intermediate appellate judges would probably say (as would trial judges) that supreme court decisions, even though thought to be unsound, outmoded, and doomed to oblivion, must be followed until overruled by the supreme court itself.

An intermediate court can, of course, write an opinion criticizing an existing common-law rule and suggesting that it be modified or abandoned for reasons stated. Such a step calls the problem to the attention of the top court and the legislature, either of which can appropriately address the matter. In this way intermediate courts can make useful contributions to the development of legal doctrine even though they lack definitive authority in that regard.

The supreme court's discretion to review or not review an intermediate court's decision is typically unlimited by statute or constitution. However, top courts with that sort of discretionary jurisdiction–usually referred to as "certiorari jurisdiction"–have adopted rules that in varying degrees of particularity describe the situations in which the court is likely to take a case. The situations listed in these rules often include the following: when the intermediate court's decision conflicts with a decision of another intermediate court or conflicts with a decision of the supreme court, when the case involves an issue of law that has not been but should be authoritatively resolved, and when the court below has so far departed from the normal course of judicial procedure as to call for an exercise of the top court's supervisory authority. The U.S. Supreme Court has a rule of this sort, and it has served as a model for many of the state supreme courts' rules.

This kind of rule serves the purpose of letting the bar and public know that the court does not exercise its discretion idiosyncratically or arbitrarily, but rather acts in accordance with some rational criteria. It also gives guidance to lawyers as to the kinds of cases the court is interested in reviewing, thus working to discourage hopeless petitions. In addition, the rule provides a structure for the judges themselves, some standards under which they can discuss petitions and perhaps achieve a more consistent pattern of grants and denials. These rules, however, usually contain a good deal of general language so that they do not operate to restrain the judges unduly.

———

The American Bar Association has promulgated Standards Relating to Court Organization (1990), and associated Commentary, which discuss many of the same issues addressed by Meador and Bernstein. In particular, section 1.13 of those Standards deals with appellate courts. That section has numerous recommendations on how the highest appellate court, and intermediate appellate courts (if there are any in a particular state) should be structured. Among other things, the section recommends that there should be only one appeal as of right to the intermediate appellate court, if there is one, and only discretionary appeals thereafter to the highest court. Exceptions to this model are permitted, one of which would be capital cases, where there could be an appeal as of right at both stages. At the intermediate stage, three-judge appellate panels (as opposed to two-judge panels) are recommended, and standards "should be established for the timely disposition and clearance of appellate cases." The Commentary further addresses some of these issues. For example, it discusses whether intermediate appellate courts should be established (and staffed by judges) on a regional basis within a state, or in a single, centrally located tribunal, but does not take a stand on those issues. In contrast, the Standards and Commentary argue against the establishment of appellate courts of *specialized* subject-matter jurisdiction. The Commentary concedes that "many specialized appellate courts have performed honorable and effective judicial service", but contends that the "appellate court function of developing the law cannot be performed in a coherent and consistent way if jurisdictional divisions compel the law's fabric to be made in a decisional patchwork."

———

Notes and Questions

1. Why should there be a division in function between the intermediate appellate court and the supreme court? Does this mean that the intermediate appellate court should never play a law development role? The role of state intermediate appellate courts is addressed in an excellent collection of articles that were presented at a national symposium: Caught in the Middle:

The Role of State Intermediate Appellate Courts, 35 Ind. L. Rev. 329–555 (2002).

2. Is an intermediate appellate court always bound to follow the precedent of a superior court? No matter how old the precedent is? In some jurisdictions the intermediate appellate court is authorized to certify questions or the entire case to the supreme court. See, e.g., 28 U.S.C.A. § 1254(3) and Wis.Stat.Ann. § 808.05(2) (West Supp.1994). The United States Court rejected the concept of anticipatory overruling in Rodriguez de Quijas v. Shearson/American Express, Inc., 490 U.S. 477, 109 S.Ct. 1917, 104 L.Ed.2d 526 (1989).

3. An intermediate court of appeal in a two-tiered appellate system frequently functions to alleviate the error correction workload in the court of last resort. As the volume of cases at all appellate levels continues to increase, however, the intermediate appellate courts have assumed an ever-expanding role in developing the law, serving as a *de facto* court of last resort in the majority of cases. The federal system and many state systems have followed this pattern. See, e.g., George & Solimine, Supreme Court Monitoring of the United States Court of Appeals En Banc, 9 Sup. Ct. Eco. Rev. 171 (2001).

4. Vertical *stare decisis* refers to the principle that a lower court is bound by decisions of a higher court, while horizontal *stare decisis* requires a court to follow its own precedents. Horizontal *stare decisis* has special application for intermediate appellate courts that sit in panels. At one time, the Michigan Court of Appeals, an intermediate court sitting in panels, considered itself bound only by precedents of the Michigan Supreme Court and not by its own prior panel decisions. Wise, The Legal Culture of Troglodytes: Conflicts Between Panels of the Court of Appeals, 37 Wayne L. Rev. 313 (1991). Then the Michigan Supreme Court entered an administrative order requiring intermediate court panels to adhere to prior published opinions of other panels. Through a variety of measures, most states make the decision of a prior panel the decision of the intermediate appellate court. In these states, the decision of the prior panel is fully binding on all subsequent panels until overruled by the intermediate appellate court sitting *en banc* or by the state's highest court.

5. In the federal court system, the circuit courts of appeals are not bound by decisions from another circuit, although those opinions may be considered persuasive authority. Conversely, most federal courts of appeals provide for decisions of a prior panel to be recognized as binding precedent on subsequent panels until changed by an *en banc* decision in that circuit or by the United States Supreme Court. George, The Dynamics and Determinants of the Decision to Grant En Banc Review, 74 Wash. L. Rev. 213 (1999). Despite this norm, what if a second panel does not follow a decision of a prior panel? Should a third subsequent panel, faced with this situation, follow the first or second panel? See McMellon v. United States, 387 F.3d 329, 332–34 (4th Cir. 2004) (en banc) (earliest panel decision should be followed).

6. Federal Rule of Appellate Procedure 35(a) states that en banc rehearings are "not favored and ordinarily will not be ordered unless:

(1) en banc consideration is necessary to secure or maintain uniformity of the court's decisions; or

(2) the proceeding involves a question of exceptional importance."

How should these criteria be applied? In particular, what is an issue of "exceptional importance"? Should it be enough that the en banc court disagrees with the decision of the three-judge panel? If not, what more should be required? Might each circuit have legitimately different views about what cases are exceptionally important for *that* circuit? For discussion of these issues, see Solimine, Ideology and En Banc Review, 67 N.C. L. Rev. 29 (1988).

7. The Commentary on the ABA Standards refers to the possibility of two-judge, rather than three-judge, appellate panels. Are the former more or less likely to properly undertake the appellate function, as opposed to three (or more) judges? For evidence from English courts using two-judge appellate panels showing a very low rate of reversal, see R. Martineau, Appellate Justice in England and the United States: A Comparative Analysis 168–69, 173–74 (1990).

8. Texas and Oklahoma each have *two* courts of last resort. Although the intermediate court of appeals in both Texas and Oklahoma review civil and criminal matters, that responsibility is divided at the highest appellate level. The highest appellate court for civil cases in Oklahoma and Texas is dominated the supreme court and its criminal counterpart in each of those states is called the court of criminal appeals.

9. For a thorough discussion of the pros and cons of specialized appellate courts, see R. Posner, The Federal Courts: Challenge and Reform 244–70 (1996). For an analysis of a specialized federal appellate court, see Dreyfuss, The Federal Circuit: A Continuing Experiment in Specialization, 54 Case W. Res. L. Rev. 769 (2004).

10. Depending on the facts of a particular case, and the structure of the appellate court system at issue, litigants (and their attorneys) may be in effect able to shop for a favorable appellate forum. See Mullins & Mullins, You Better Shop Around: Appellate Forum Shopping, 25 Litigation 32 (Summer 1999).

RULES OF THE SUPREME COURT OF THE UNITED STATES (2003)

Rule 10. Consideration Governing Review on Certiorari

Review on a writ of certiorari is not a matter of right, but a judicial discretion. A petition for a writ of certiorari will be granted only for compelling reasons. The following, although neither controlling nor fully measuring the Court's discretion, indicate the character of the reasons the Court considers:

(a) a United States court of appeals has entered a decision in conflict with the decision of another United States court of appeals on the same important matter; has decided an important federal question in a way that conflicts with a decision by a state court of last resort; or has so far departed from the accepted and usual course of judicial proceedings, or sanctioned such a departure by a lower court, as to call for an exercise of this Court's supervisory power;

(b) a state court of last resort has decided an important federal question in a way that conflicts with the decision of another state court of last resort or of a United States court of appeals;

(c) a state court or a United States court of appeals has decided an important question of federal law that has not been, but should be, settled by this Court, or has decided an important federal question in a way that conflicts with relevant decisions of this Court.

A petition for a writ of certiorari is rarely granted when the asserted error consists of erroneous factual findings or the misapplication of a properly state rule of law.

RULES OF PRACTICE OF THE SUPREME COURT OF OHIO (2004)

Rule III. Determination of Jurisdiction on Claimed Appeals of Right and Discretionary Appeals.

Section 1. Memorandum in Support of Jurisdiction

(A) In a claimed appeal of right or a discretionary appeal, the appellant shall file a memorandum in support of jurisdiction with the notice of appeal. . . .

(B) A memorandum in support of jurisdiction shall contain all of the following:

. . .

(2) A thorough explanation of why a substantial constitutional question is involved, why the case is of public or great general interest, or, in a felony case, why leave to appeal should be granted. . . .

Notes and Questions

1.   The Rules of the United States Supreme Court, and those of state supreme courts with discretionary jurisdiction, vest considerable discretion in those courts to decide what cases to hear. The existence of a conflict in decisions in courts below is usually easy enough to identify. To what extent do criteria like an "important question of federal law," or a case "of public or great general interest," provide principled and predictable guidance for judges and attorneys? To what extent do such broad criteria invite high court judges to follow their own personal or policy preferences in setting their own agenda? There is a considerable literature discussing the normative and empirical issues raised by such criteria. See, e.g., S. Estreicher & J. Sexton, Redefining the Supreme Court's Role: A Theory of Managing the Federal Judicial Process (1986), H.W. Perry, Deciding to Decide: Agenda Setting in the United States Supreme Court (1991); Cross, The Justices of Strategy, 48 Duke L.J. 511 (1998); Hartnett, Questioning Certiorari: Some Reflections Seventy–Five Years After the Judges' Bill, 100 Colum. L. Rev. 1643 (2000).

2. The United States Supreme Court rarely explains why it is granting or denying certiorari in a particular case, at that time or, in the former case, in the decision on the merits. When, if ever, should a denial of certiorari be read by lower courts as approval for the decision from which review is sought? Justices occasionally write opinions concurring in or dissenting from the denial of certiorari. Should they? See Singleton v. C.I.R., 439 U.S. 940, 99 S.Ct. 335, 58 L.Ed.2d 335 (1978) (opinion of Stevens, J., respecting denial certiorari) (answering the question "no"). For general discussion see Hellman, Error Correction, Lawmaking, and the Supreme Court's Exercise of Discretionary Review, 44 U. Pitt. L. Rev. 795 (1983); Linzer, the Meaning of Certiorari Denials, 79 Colum. L. Rev. 1227 (1979).

3. The long-standing practice of the United States Supreme Court is that only four votes out of nine are needed to grant certiorari. Lieman, The Rule of Four, 57 Colum. L. Rev. 975 (1957); Stevens, The Life Span of a Judge–Made Rule, 58 N.Y.U. L. Rev. 1 (1983). In these circumstances, are the remaining five Justices under an obligation to decide the case on the merits? Why should a counter-majoritarian rule be followed? When, if ever, should the Justices be able to dismiss a writ of certiorari as improvidentally granted and, if so, what should be the required number of Justices to so hold? For a spirited debate on these issues, see Rogers v. Missouri Pacific RR. Co. 352 U.S. 500, 77 S.Ct. 443, 1 L.Ed.2d 493 (1957) (opinions of Justices Brennan, Frankfurter, and Harlan). See also Revesz & Karlan, Non–Majority Rules and the Supreme Court, 136 U. Pa. L. Rev. 1067 (1988).

4. Despite increasing caseloads in lower appellate courts, the United States Supreme Court, in the last decade of the twentieth century began deciding fewer cases on the merits. During much of the Warren and Burger Court eras, the Court was routinely deciding almost 150 cases each Term. As late as the early 1990s the Court was deciding about 100 cases per Term. But that number has steadily dropped, and since that time the Court has only been deciding about 75 or 80 cases per Term. Various explanations have been offered to explain the decline, including the almost total elimination of the Court's mandatory appellate jurisdiction; changes in the ideological makeup of the judges on the lower federal courts; and the policy preferences of some Justices that fewer decided cases are better than more. For discussion, see Cordray & Cordray, The Supreme Court's Plenary Docket, 58 Wash. & Lee L. Rev. 737 (2001); Hellman, The Shrunken Docket of the Rehnquist Court, 1996 Sup. Ct. Rev. 403; Solimine, Supreme Court Monitoring of State Courts in the Twenty–First Century, 35 Ind. L. Rev. 335 (2002).

SECTION D. THE CRISIS OF VOLUME

1. 1960–1985

TATE, FEDERAL APPELLATE ADVOCACY
IN THE 1980'S

5 Am.J/Trial Adv. 63, 66–69 (1981).*

The Appellate Environment of the 1980's

The overriding difference in the appellate milieu from earlier decades can be summarized in one word: volume. Into the unhurried and contemplative atmosphere of the appellate courts has intruded a counter-contemplative need for hurry. The perfect decision, too long delayed, may result in a denial of justice. Further, the time spent on a single appeal, prevents the judge from attending to the many other appeals that arrive at the same time. Some of these appeals may be quickly disposed of, if only the judge is able to give attention to them. The delay as to one appeal has a multiplier effect in hindering prompt decision of many other appeals. Even with the much greater use of research staff, in the last analysis the deciding judge must personally review the briefs of counsel, as well as the cited authority. The judge must personally decide upon the rationale and wording adopted, as part of the non-delegable judicial duty of deciding the appeal. For present purposes, however, the exponential recent increases in volume is primarily noted for its effects upon the preparation of brief and oral argument by appellate counsel.

It is easy to accept the abstract notion that greatly increased volume has qualitative as well as quantitative effects upon the appellate judicial process. Concrete and specific illustration may enable counsel to visualize the appellate environment in which human judges will consider the brief and oral arguments prepared for those judges. The phenomenon I will describe is the ever increasing volume of ever more complex issues flooding the appellate courts because of the law explosion of the Seventies and Eighties.

As an example of this increased workload, we can look to the United States Fifth Circuit Court of Appeals. In general, each judge will have the following work this next year. Each judge will sit on 7 three-judge panels and 3 en bane rehearings consuming a total of 40 days. The judge serves as a member of a three-judge screening panel that screens about 350 appeals, about 50% of which result in written opinions. The judge serves upon a three-judge administrative panel deciding about 60 administrative matters (most of them requiring little time, however). The judge will also consider about 350 applications for rehearing en bane, vote on polls requested in about 60 of them, which result in en bane

* Reprinted with permission copyright ©
1981, *American Journal of Trial Advocacy*,
Cumberland School of Law of Samford University, Birmingham, Alabama, 35229. All
rights reserved.

rehearings granted in about 20. In addition to writing the formal opinions generated by this work, the judge must study and concur in or dissent from the opinions written by other judges on the panel. After taking into consideration the time spent on the bench or in en banc or administrative conferences, a judge comes perilously close to writing one formal opinion a day and concurring in or dissenting from two others, in addition to performing the various administrative and other chores that attach to a member of the court. In addition, in order to keep current with controlling precedent, the judge must read more than 7,000 pages of slip opinions of the other members of court, as well as the 2,000–plus pages of advance sheets of the United States Supreme Court opinions.

I dwell this much on the appellate judge's environment of volume because of the obvious implications for an appellate lawyer. In perspective, the brief in a particular appeal is a minute part of a mass of reading the judge must do. If the brief is turgid, if it is long-winded in making its points, if the issues it raises are unnecessarily numerous (and from experience an appellate judge senses many arguments of error indicate a grasping at weak straws in the absence of even one strong contention), the brief is less likely to direct the judge's attention to the points the advocate wishes to make. For the most effective contribution to the judge's decision of an appeal, it is essential that the appellate advocate make careful selection of issues, authorities and relevant facts to be cited, describe them accurately (including their weaknesses) with appropriate citation, and be concise and lucid in presentation of the argument. Otherwise, the appellate judge may use the brief only for a cursory check of the result reached by a proposed opinion, virtually as if counsel had filed no brief at all.

* * *

* * * the subject matter of the appellate caseload is infinitely more complex than it was two decades ago. Then, the appellate courts were faced with accretion of legislation at a minor pace and with deciding appeals on the basis of a relatively stable body of accepted precedent and authority. Then, innovation was necessary only on the fringe areas in the leeways of precedent, in order to accommodate the old jurisprudence and legislation to the then-slowly changing conditions of society. From the point of view of an appellate judge, innovative judicial response requires much more time to formulate the appropriate resolution than does routine legal research—time for research of the broad historical and social background and context, time to study and choose from the permissible alternatives, time to contemplate the future implications.

MARVELL, IS THERE AN APPEAL FROM THE CASELOAD DELUGE?
24 Judges' J. 34–37, 52–53 (Summer, 1985).

In recent years both civil and criminal appeals have increased rapidly—much faster than trial court caseloads, the number of judgeships, or any other factor one might associate with appellate volume. This article summarizes the results of a research project that explored the extent and causes of appellate caseload growth. The first part outlines caseload trends during the past century, and the second part documents the growth of appeals during the decade between 1973 and 1983, for which considerable information is available in most states.

Finally, and most importantly, it examines the factors that might be expected to affect the burgeoning number of appeals. Does appellate volume vary with trial court volume or with the number of trial judges?

* * * Do appeals increase when a new intermediate court is created or when the jurisdiction of an existing one is expanded? Does eliminating the requirement for printed briefs or records lead to more appeals? Do appellate settlement conferences attract more appeals? The answers to these and similar questions should help appellate judges predict whether, and roughly by how much, their caseloads will increase when changes are made in the courts.

HISTORICAL TRENDS

Long-term appellate caseload statistics, compiled from widely scattered reports and articles, show a clear nationwide pattern. Appellate caseloads grew during the 19th and early 20th centuries, reaching a high plateau in the 1920s. In the 1930s and 1940s appeals plummeted, dropping by 50 to 75 percent, even in fast-growing states like California. The nadir was reached just after World War II, with caseloads rising gradually for two decades thereafter. In the mid–1960s they began to skyrocket. First, criminal appeals shot up following the expansion of criminal procedural rights, especially a 1963 ruling that indigent defendants must be provided counsel on appeal. Within a few years civil appeals also shot up, although no causes can be singled out for this increase. This rapid caseload growth has continued unabated to the present day.

These trends are reflected in structural changes in the appellate court system during the past century. Between 1870 and 1915, 13 states created permanent intermediate appellate courts to relieve supreme courts. The next intermediate courts were not created until 1957 in Florida and 1963 in Michigan. During the past 20 years, states have established intermediate courts at the rate of one per year, and these courts are now operating in 36 states.

RECENT APPELLATE FILING STATISTICS

Appellate court caseload statistics improved sufficiently by the 1970s to permit detailed analysis of caseload trends. Statistics for total appeals between 1973 and 1983, obtained for 43 states, show that the number of appeals increased by 112 percent (see Table 1). The number of criminal and civil appeals in the states with available statistics increased by similar amounts. Criminal appeals nationwide remained at about 45 percent of the total appellate volume throughout the decade, although the portion changed greatly in individual states.

Table 1

**INCREASES IN APPEALS AND ASSOCIATED FACTORS,
1973–83**

Total Appeals (43 states, including D.C.)	112%	
Population		11%
Real personal income		16%
Appellate judgeships		36%
Trial judgeships		24%
Criminal Appeals (38 states)	107%	
Criminal trial filings (28 states)		52%
FBI Crime Index		39%
Prison commitments (except D.C.)		113%
Civil Appeals (38 states)	114%	
Civil trial filings (33 states)		43%

The appeals counted here are initial appeals of right from trial courts or administrative agencies. This definition permits a caseload measure that is comparable from state to state and that best represents the judges' workloads. To avoid double-counting, appeals do not include transfers from one appellate court to another. However, I did include initial appeals filed in supreme courts in states where intermediate courts do not receive all appeals. Appeals do not include original writs or discretionary jurisdiction cases.

Table 1 compares the growth of appeals to the growth of comparable social trends in states with appellate data. The appellate growth rate is more than 10 times that of the population, seven times that of real personal income, and three times that of appellate court judgeships. The average number of appeals per judgeship grew from 85 to 133 between 1973 and 1983. Criminal appeals grew faster than the FBI Crime Index but not quite as fast as prison commitments, which increased greatly in the past five years.

Table 2

TEN YEAR APPEALS GROWTH, 1973–83

Alabama	156%	Nebraska	68%
Alaska	305%	Nevada	159%
Arizona	145%	New Hampshire	144%
California	89%	New Jersey	62%
Colorado	108%	New Mexico	86%
Connecticut	265%	New York	87%
Delaware	67%	Ohio	95%
Dist. of Col.	57%	Oklahoma	85%
Florida	186%	Oregon	212%
Hawaii	201%	Pennsylvania	94%
Idaho	72%	Rhode Island	110%
Illinois	129%	South Dakota	156%
Iowa	68%	Tennessee	62%
Kansas	108%	Texas	140%
Kentucky	186%	Utah	116%
Louisiana	139%	Vermont	137%
Maine	161%	Virginia	60%
Maryland	53%	Washington	96%
Massachusetts	154%	Wyoming	103%
Michigan	167%		
Minnesota	172%		
Mississippi	38%		
Missouri	97%		
Montana	187%		

Comparisons with trial court caseloads are more difficult because statistics are less often available and are less accurate. Civil trial filing statistics since 1973 were obtained in 33 of the 43 states with appellate data; these filings increased by 43 percent during the decade, less than half the growth rate for civil appeals. Criminal trial court filings, which are limited to felonies (and some misdemeanors in several states), grew 52 percent, again less than half as much as appeals.

One would expect appeals to be associated primarily with the number of cases decided by the trial courts, for with few exceptions only these cases can be appealed. Unfortunately, there is no adequate measure of trial court decisions. The only statistic available is the number of trials, which have increased much more slowly than trial court filings and show very little relationship to appellate volume. But no conclusions can be drawn because there are widespread problems with trial statistics, which often reflect disparate judgments by numerous local court officials as to what constitutes a trial.

The growth rate for appeals differs greatly from state to state, as can be seen in Table 2, which gives the ten-year growth for states with available statistics. Appellate caseloads also grew exceptionally fast in Alaska, Connecticut, Florida, Hawaii, Michigan, Montana, and Oregon.

FACTORS BEHIND GROWTH IN APPEALS

Although appeals have grown faster than most other factors listed in Table 1, those factors account for much of the appellate growth because they work together to push appellate volume upward. This process was explored using a statistical analysis that differentiates the impact of various factors by comparing changes from year to year in the states. Separate analyses were run for criminal and civil appeals. This research, like all statistical analyses, does not reach precise results, but provides ranges in which the actual answer is likely to fall.

Some factors explored are broad background factors, such as trial court filings and judgeships; these are used largely as control variables for the second stage, which analyzes the impact of specific changes in court structure and operation on appellate caseloads.

* * *

On the civil side, three dominant background factors are economic conditions, trial court filings, and the number of trial court judgeships (see Table 4). There is no obvious reason for the much greater association between trial and appellate filings in civil cases than in criminal cases. Economic conditions have a tremendous impact on civil case filings at both the trial and appellate level. Trial filings tend to rise about two years after the economy improves and appeals increase about three or four years after an economic upswing.

COURT FEATURES THAT AFFECT APPELLATE VOLUME

What happens to appellate volume when changes are made in appellate court procedures or structure? Their effects are measured by comparing caseloads within states before and after a particular change was made, while adjusting for the other factors discussed here.

Intermediate courts. Earlier research suggested that intermediate courts attract more appeals. The findings here, however, are that intermediate courts have little or no impact on the volume of filings. The use of intermediate courts is measured by the percentage of filings that go to those courts: this takes into consideration the great variety of dual appellate systems. After taking into account other changes—appellate jurisdiction, for example, is often expanded when intermediate courts are created—neither the creation nor expansion of intermediate courts was found to lead to more than a slight increase in filings.

Backlog: Whether delay affects appellate volume is the topic of many conflicting arguments. Delay might reduce criminal appeals because, for example, a defendant in prison with a two-year sentence gains little by appealing to a court with a two-year backlog. On the other hand, defendants on bail might wish to delay their prison commitment, but there are few defendants on bail pending appeal in most states. In civil cases, long delays may lead some defendants to appeal so they can delay payment of judgments; but other litigants may decide not to appeal because relief would take too long.

Delay is measured by a "backlog index," which is the number of cases pending divided by the number of dispositions that year. This index estimates the length of time, in years, required to dispose of pending cases at the current disposition rate. The research found that there are a few more appeals, especially civil appeals, when delay is greater, but the impact is almost negligible. The various ways delay effects incentives to appeal seem to cancel each other out.

New rules and criminal codes: The research explored the impact of new trial court rules and new criminal codes. One might expect these to create interpretation problems and, thus, more issues to appeal. But there was no evidence of this in the research.

Appellate briefs and records: Appellate courts have been modernizing procedures by eliminating requirements for printed briefs, printed records, and narrative transcripts. One might speculate that these changes attract appeals by making them less expensive and time consuming. Our analysis, however, showed that this had little impact on the volume of civil or criminal appeals. Appeals did increase slightly when printed records were no longer necessary, but the impact was very slight.

Interest differential: A civil defendant who loses at trial can delay paying the adverse judgment by appealing. The interest paid on the judgment pending appeal is sometimes less and sometimes more than prevailing interest rates. When less, there is more economic incentive to appeal. Nevertheless, the research found virtually no relationship between the volume of civil appeals and the gap between the statutory interest rates and rates for three-month treasury bills.

Appellate court prehearing settlement conferences: Many of the courts studied have initiated conferences to persuade attorneys to settle cases. Some commentators claim that any settlements resulting from the conferences are outnumbered by new appeals from parties seeking to take advantage of the settlement opportunities. The research supports this contention: civil appeals increased moderately when settlement conferences were used.

POLICY CONSEQUENCES

These findings cannot provide exact forecasts of overall appellate volume, but they can help predict the impact of specific changes by analyzing which changes may be related to increased, reduced, or not appreciably affected appellate volumes. One clear conclusion is that more trial judges lead to more appeals. In fact, using the elasticity ratios in Tables 3 and 4, it can be predicted that a 10 percent increase in trial judgeships will lead to 4 to 12 percent more criminal appeals and 1 to 7 percent more civil appeals than would otherwise be filed.

In a similar manner, one can estimate that a 10 percent increase in a state's FBI Crime Index will mean roughly 8 percent more criminal appeals the following year. Ten percent more trial court civil filings in each of two years will probably translate to roughly 5 percent more civil appeals, while a similar change in real personal income will mean roughly 8 percent more appeals four years later. Finally, the analysis shows that settlement conferences in civil cases attract roughly 30 civil appeals per million population, which is almost a 10 percent increase in the average state.

It is also important to know that some changes have little impact on appellate volume. This is true of most of the factors studied, including creation or expansion of intermediate courts, the amount of backlog, modernization of appellate procedure, and increased interest rate on appeal. Judges and legislatures can make changes in these areas without fear that they will noticeably affect appellate volume.

Notes and Questions

1. Is there any reason for the appellate lawyer to be concerned about the caseload of appellate courts? How should it affect litigation strategy at the following stages? The initial decision to file suit? Issues to be raised in the trial court? Whether to file a post trial motion? Whether to appeal? Whether to settle? Issues to be raised on appeal? The type of brief to file? Whether to seek oral argument? Whether to seek rehearing? Whether to seek review in a higher court?

2. What are the factors that will affect these decisions? See generally R. Martineau, Modern Appellate Practice—Federal and State Civil Appeals Ch. 2, Decision to Appeal (1983).

3. For additional reading on the effect of volume on the appellate process see Weisberger, Appellate Courts: The Challenge of Inundation, 31 American U.L.Rev. 237 (1982); S. Wasby, T. Marvell & A. Aikman, Volume and Delay in State Appellate Courts: Problems and Responses (1979); Mills, Caseload Explosion: The Appellate Response, 16 John Marshall L.Rev. 1 (1982); Marvell, Appellate Capacity and Caseload Growth, 16 Akron L.Rev. 43 (1982).

Note

Even more dramatic than the growth in appeals in state courts was the growth in the caseloads of the United States courts of appeal.

From 1961 through 1983 the number of appeals filed grew from 4,204 in 1961 to 29,630 in 1983, an increase of 705%. These statistics are found in Table B–1 in the Annual Reports of the Director of the Administrative Office of the U.S. Courts. During the same period the number of judges increased from 68 to 132. There have been a host of books, reports, and articles written on the effect of the increase in the number of appeals to the federal courts of appeals. These include R. Posner, The Federal Courts: Crisis and Reform (1985); P. Carrington, D. Meador & M. Rosenberg, Justice on Appeal (1976); Commission on Revision of the Federal Court Appellate System, Structure and Internal Procedures: Recommendations for Change (1975); Martineau, Frivolous Appeals: The Uncertain Federal Response, 1984 Duke L.J. 845; Rubin and Ganucheau, Appellate Delay and Cost—An Ancient and Common Disease: Is It Intractable?, 42 Md.L.Rev. 752 (1983).

2. 1986–2003

MARVELL AND MOODY, THE EFFECTIVENESS OF MEASURES TO INCREASE APPELLATE COURT EFFICIENCY AND DECISION OUTPUT

21 U. Mich. J.L. Ref. 415, 441–42 (1988).*

Appellate court caseloads have increased greatly since World War II, doubling approximately every ten years. Because states created appellate judgeships only one-third as fast as caseloads grew, the judges have faced heavy demands to increase productivity. Most state appellate courts successfully expanded decision output to match the appeals "explosion"; decision growth averaged 116% over the ten-year period from 1974 to 1984, only slightly less than the 123% growth for filings over the corresponding period. Output per judge increased, on average, from fifty-three to eight-eight decisions in the 1974–1984 period for the forty-five states with available information.

The plight of the appellate courts has resulted in an enormous body of literature recommending procedures for increasing judicial resources and judicial productivity. The literature, however, has not provided more than educated guesses about which procedures work best. This Article attempts to fill this void by evaluating the changes that state appellate courts have made to increase decision output. The changes fall into seven categories: (1) adding judges or temporarily assigning trial and retired judges; (2) hiring law clerks and staff attorneys; (3) curtailing opinion practices by deciding cases with unpublished opinions, with unsigned opinions, or without opinions; (4) creating or expanding inter-mediate courts; (5) reducing the number of judges who participate in each division; (6) curtailing oral arguments; and (7) using summary judgment procedures. These categories encompass virtually all of the major changes that appellate courts have made to increase productivity in the past two decades. Although questions of productivity and efficiency are never the sole criteria for determining how appellate courts should adapt to rising caseloads, knowledge about which changes actually do increase productivity and efficiency, and by how much, should be valuable information when making such decisions.

This Article will examine the effectiveness of measures employed to increase appellate court productivity. * * * The Article, although not advocating the adoption of the discussed efficiency measures, concludes that the failure to enact any type of efficiency measure will cause appellate courts to fall behind in the handling of their caseloads. * * *

The volume of decisions by state appellate courts has grown dramatically, as has the judges' productivity. Exploring the reasons for this

* Copyright © 1988, University of Michigan, Journal of Law Reform, University of Michigan Law School, Thomas B. Marvell and Carlisle B. Moody. Reprinted by permission. All rights reserved.

growth is difficult because numerous interacting factors influence output and productivity. This research uses the only feasible research design for such a task, the multiple time-series design.

The analysis found that changes intended to increase appellate court productivity usually have that effect, although the impact is often not substantial. Importantly, the study found that adding judges ordinarily produces a corresponding increase in the number of appeals decided (provided, of course, that filings also increase). Supreme courts, however, may exhibit slight "declining returns to scale." Assigning temporary judges to appellate courts also helps increase the volume of appeals decided.

The most effective procedural changes are those that reduce the burden of writing and publishing opinions. Deciding cases without opinion greatly increases court output, and reducing the number of opinions published has a lesser, but still substantial, impact. Issuing unsigned memorandum or per curium opinions, rather than full signed opinions, has but a slight impact.

Reducing the number of cases argued also has a moderate impact on productivity. In conducting our research, we were not able to gather information concerning the actual length of oral arguments, but we determined that rule changes that reduce time limits for arguments have no impact.

The fact that curtailing opinion writing and publication, and limiting arguments increase appellate court efficiency does not, of course, automatically lead to a recommendation that these practices be adopted. Many have argued that such changes reduce the quality of justice provided by the courts. The present research looks only at the impact of changes on the number of cases decided per judge. Before judges or others can apply these findings, they must factor in their feelings about the potential impact on the quality of appellate justice.

The act of creating intermediate courts, or expanding their jurisdiction, in itself increases the productivity of the entire appellate system. This occurs even after controlling for contemporaneous changes, such as adding judges, using three-judge panels, and routing minor appeals to the appellate courts rather than to general jurisdiction trial courts.

Changes found to have very little or no impact include reducing panel size, adopting summary procedures, and adding staff attorneys. Adding law clerks has a small impact. Appellate courts commonly make these changes in the belief that they will help them cope with the rising caseloads. The research here suggests otherwise, and judges are advised to consider other changes, especially reducing arguments and full opinions, when desiring to increase productivity. There are, however, reasons for making changes other than productivity concerns–changes that are beyond the scope of this research. For example, law clerks and staff attorneys may well increase the quality of information used by judges when making decisions.

When all is said and done, the greatest determinant of the number of decisions is the number of filings. Caseload pressures are by far the most important stimulus increasing productivity, and the great increase in decision output and productivity of appellate courts in recent decades is largely due to an equally great increase in appeals filed. The implication is that when caseloads rise, judges either work harder or reduce the amount of attention given each case in ways not measured here, such as by spending less time reading briefs and transcripts. On the other hand, filing growth does not lead to a one-to-one growth in decisions; for example, a ten percent filing increase typically stimulates about six percent more decisions. Therefore, unless more judges are added or efficiency measures adopted, the average appellate court will soon fall hopelessly behind.

BAKER AND HAUPTLY, TAKING ANOTHER MEASURE OF THE "CRISIS OF VOLUME" IN THE U.S. COURTS OF APPEALS

51 Wash. & Lee L. Rev. 97, 100–112 (1994).*

In 1990, the Federal Courts Study Committee began its discussion of the problems facing the U.S. Courts of Appeals with the tag line we use in our title: "However people may view other aspects of the federal judiciary, few deny that its appellate courts are in a 'crisis of volume' that has transformed them from the institutions they were even a generation ago." This was the most comprehensive and most recent effort in a long line of studies, committees, and commissions that have focused on the intermediate federal courts, to undertake an assessment of their status, to evaluate the threats from their workload, and to make recommendations for their survival and reform.

Everyone, would-be-reformers and defenders-of-the-status-quo alike, and anyone who has examined the available statistics, must admit the obvious: the caseloads of the U.S. Courts of Appeals have grown dramatically over the last four decades. There has been a pronounced disagreement over the effects of this docket growth and what, if anything, should be done about it. We hope to contribute to this debate by demonstrating a new methodology to quantify and then to compare over the time the aggregate delay that has occurred in the U.S. Courts of Appeals as a result of docket growth.

* * *

In November 1998, Congress created the Federal Courts Study Committee as an ad hoc committee within the Judicial Conference of the United States. Appointed by Chief Justice Rehnquist, the fifteen-person Study Committee included representatives of the three federal branches, state government officials, practitioners, and academics. The Study Com-

* Copyright © 1994, Washington & Lee Law Review, Washington & Lee University School of Law; Thomas E. Baker and Den- nis J. Hauptly. Reprinted by permission. All rights reserved.

mittee members were thus broadly representative of the individuals and entities who share a compelling interest in the work of the federal courts. The Study Committee surveyed members of the federal judiciary and solicited the views of citizens' groups, bar organizations, research groups, academics, civil rights groups, and others. Numerous public outreach meetings were held and regional hearings focused on published proposals, leading up to the final report.

Congress gave the Study Committee a fifteen month deadline with which to examine the problems facing the federal courts and to develop a long-range plan for the judicial branch. In the explicit charge to the Study Committee, Congress asked for an evaluation of the structure and administration of the United States Courts of Appeals. That section of the Study Committee's final report begins with a supposition that provides the point of departure for our Article: The federal appellate courts are faced with a "crisis of volume" that will continue and that will eventually require some "fundamental change." The Study Committee's black-letter recommendation reads: "Fundamental structure alternatives deserve the careful attention of Congress, the courts, bar associations, and scholars over the next five years."

In the spirit of the Federal Courts Study Committee's entreaty for "careful attention" of these issues, we will attempt to examine the assumption/conclusion reached in most of these previous studies, and repeated by the Study Committee itself: The U.S. Courts of Appeals are undergoing a "crisis in volume."

The Data

Everyone knows that the federal appellate caseload has increased enormously over the last four decades, and everyone knows that the increases in the numbers of circuit judgeships have not kept pace with the docket growth in the U.S. Courts of Appeals. At the same time, as we will elaborate below, the individual appellate litigant today still gets a reasonably timely resolution of the case on appeal. Indeed, in absolute terms, considered per appeal, today it takes only slightly longer to resolve each appeal than it took forty years ago. Our thesis, however, is that this is too narrow a focus. Focusing only on the time period for each individual appeal gives, at best, an incomplete measure of the systemic effect felt from the "crisis of volume." We believe that the traditional method of assembling and reporting data subtly masks the systemic effects of the increases in the volume of appeals. The traditional and familiar "months-per-appeal" statistic disaggregates, and consequently fragments and marginalizes, the delay caused by the caseload growth. Delay technically is not understated, statistically speaking, but it is less normatively understood when presented and considered in the time-per-appeal format.

The alternative way we assemble the data demonstrates that, while the records and briefs are being filed in roughly as timely a fashion as forty years ago, the circuit judges are taking significantly much longer periods to decide cases after the appeal is submitted. Most importantly, we conclude that the traditional focus on the admittedly slight incremental increases in individual case delay overlooks the aggregate effect of relatively slight incremental delays, which can be fully appreciated only when the delay-per-appeal is multiplied and generalized across the huge national appellate docket.

Long-term trends in the time intervals on appeal, measured per appeal and in the national aggregate for all the regional Court of Appeals, provide some added sense of the impact of caseload on the federal appellate system as a whole. Quantitative comparisons in the length of time it now takes to hear and decide an appeal indicate how severely the volume of appeals is stressing the system. Consider this table (footnotes have been omitted):

MEDIAN TIME INTERVALS ON APPEAL (months)

	FILING RECORD TO LAST BRIEF	LAST BRIEF TO HEARING/ SUBMISSION	HEARING/ SUBMISSION TO DECISION/ FINAL ORDER	FILING RECORD TO FINAL DISPOSITION
1950	3.7	0.7	1.5	7.1
1960	3.6	0.8	1.5	6.8
1970	3.5	1.8	1.6	8.2
1980	2.8	2.9	1.6	8.9
1990*	4.5	3.1	2.5/1.1	10.1

* The figures for 1990 were complied somewhat differently, as explained in the footnotes to the entries.

A Preliminary Analysis

What comparisons over time can be deduced from this table? It is quite remarkable that collectively the Courts of Appeals remain virtually current despite sustained off-the-chart levels of growth in their caseload. In 1950, there were 65 authorized circuit judgeships, 2,830 appeals were filed, and 2,355 appeals were terminated (36 per authorized judgeship.) In 1990, there were 156 authorized circuit judgeships; 40,898 appeals were filed; and 38,520 appeals were terminated (246.9 per authorized judgeship). Despite this huge increase in workload, the total time from filing to disposition increased only ninety days. While this is roughly a 40% increase in delay, in absolute terms, few would argue that this much of an increase amounts to a "justice-delayed-is-justice-denied" problem.

The ability to keep relatively current despite the huge docket growth might be explained in several ways, all of which seem to ring true, at least partly. First, an excess of federal appellate capacity at the beginning of this forty-year period likely allowed the Courts of Appeals to absorb greater and greater numbers of appeals for many years. Second, Congress in fact did add large cohorts of circuit judges to increase the national appellate capacity over the last four decades. Third, the various and sundry intramural reforms, procedural shortcuts fashioned by the circuit judges out of a sense of docket desperation, have allowed the Courts of Appeals to resolve many more appeals without expending as much judicial resources.

These hypotheses raise important questions. We might ask what has been the cost of increasing the national appellate capacity? If appeals are being decided today in a qualitatively different way from the way appeals were decided in 1950, does the difference so diminish the appellate process as to compromise federal appellate ideals? If not, can intramural reforms be refined further to achieve still greater economies of appeal so that appellate capacity can continue to expand to help meet projected increased demands without resulting in further delays and without creating more and more judgeships?

In beginning to answer these questions, let us take another look at the figures in the table, because a somewhat different picture emerges when we compare the forty-year changes between the appellate interval under the primary control of the litigants (from the filing of the notice of appeal to the filing of the last brief) with the appellate interval under the primary control of the judges (from the filing of the last brief to final disposition). This comparison indicates the magnitude of the cumulative effect of the increases in caseload volume felt on the federal appellate court system qua system. The resulting image depicts a system under severe stress.

The first column of the table shows an interval of 3.7 months for the appellate interval between the filing of the record on appeal to the filing of the last brief for the year 1950. The figures are reported differently over time, because during this forty-year period most of the Courts of Appeals stopped using formal records on appeals and substituted record excerpts and joint appendices. The 1990 figure is less than a month more, 4.5 months, but it is measured from the filing of the notice of appeal to the filing of the last brief. This small increase might even be explained, at least in party, by the fact that the notice of appeal procedurally and necessarily is always filed first in time. This column describes a four-decade-long trend line that for all intents and purposes is flat. The appellate interval under the control of the attorneys, adjusting for the reporting discontinuity that has been noted, therefore did not grow appreciably longer over the last forty years. This was to be expected, because the effect of caseload volume would not be filed at all by the individual advocate preparing a single appeal. Thus, as would be expected, there has been no appreciable increase in this appellate interval over the period.

Over the same period, however, examine closely what has happened to the two appellate intervals under the control of the judges, as depicted in the next two columns. Look at the sum of the second column (the interval between the last brief and the hearing or submission) plus the third column (the interval between the hearing or submission and the decision or final order). Those two appellate intervals added together comprise the period during which an appeal is lodged with the judges, that is, how long it takes the Court of Appeals to perform its appellate review function. In 1950, the median time an appeal was lodged with the court was 2.2 months. By 1990, the median time had more than doubled to a figure of 5.6 months in argued cases and 4.2 month in nonargument summary calendar cases.

It is important to keep in mind that over this same forty-year period the Courts of Appeals implemented numerous procedural shortcuts, various intramural reforms–such as the nonargument summary calendar and the decision without opinion–intended to help cope with dramatic caseload growth. The Courts of Appeals designed these reforms to process many more appeals more efficiently and faster than the more traditional procedures and, therefore, presumably should be understood as having had the expected cumulative effect of reducing these appellate time intervals. At least, that is the justification most often offered for implementing and continuing these appellate procedural shortcuts.

On the contrary, the data show that there as been a significant quantitative increase in the appellate time intervals it takes the Courts of Appeals to hear and decide an appeal. The Courts of Appeals took 255% longer to decide an orally argued appeal in 1990 (5.6 months) than they took to decide an appeal in 1950 (2.2 months). Even an appeal on the nonargument summary calendar, the most significant of the appellate efficiency reforms of the last forty years, took 190% longer (4.2 months) in 1990 than an appeal took in 1950 (2.2 months). And it should be remembered that back in 1950 an oral argument and a written opinion were afforded in every federal appeal as of right.

An Alternative Analysis

Of course, the argument can be made that overall the Courts of Appeals continue to perform at capacity and their capacity is adequate and their efficiency is sufficient. It might be observed that the Courts of Appeals continue to terminate approximately the same number of appeals each year as are filed, although the precise numbers demonstrate some worrisome slippage. In 1950, there were 475 more appeals filed than terminated (2,830—2,355 = 475); in 1990, there were 2,378 more appeals filed than were terminated (40,898—38,520 = 2,378). The 1990 "backlog" thus was larger than the total number of appeals terminated by all the Courts of Appeals in 1950. One way to measure whether an intermediate court of appeals is keeping up with its caseload is to calculate the court's "clearance rate," which is the number of appeals filed in a given year divided by the number of terminations in the same year. Because these two sets of appeals are not identical–since appeals terminated in one year may have been filed in a previous year–a multiple year clearance rate is a more useful gauge of how well the court is keeping up with the volume of appeals being filed. A clearance rate of 100% or higher indicates that the court is holding its own or reducing the backlog. A clearance of less than 100% indicates that the backlog is worsening.

Three-year clearance rate calculations for the U.S. Courts of Appeals and for available state intermediate courts covering the years 1989, 1990, and 1991 yield the rankings in the following table:

COURT	3 YEAR CLEARANCE RATE	COURT	3 YEAR CLEARANCE RATE
New York	118.50	Kansas	96.80
California	110.00	North Carolina	96.50
Idaho	105.30	ALL STATES	96.10
Connecticut	104.00	Hawaii	95.80
Iowa	103.30	Illinois	95.80
Pennsylvania	101.40	ALL CIRCUITS	95.60
Florida	101.30	Tennessee	94.90
Colorado	101.00	Missouri	94.60
D.C. Circuit	100.00	Arkansas	94.60
1st Circuit	100.00	Alaska	93.80
6th Circuit	100.00	5th Circuit	92.60
10th Circuit	100.00	Maryland	92.60
Minnesota	99.60	11th Circuit	90.70
Ohio	99.50	Oklahoma	90.20
2nd Circuit	98.40	South Carolina	89.90
Alabama	97.70	7th Circuit	89.30
Louisiana	97.60	Kentucky	88.80
Wisconsin	97.60	Oregon	88.00
New Jersey	97.60	9th Circuit	87.80
3rd Circuit	97.10	Arizona	85.80
8th Circuit	97.10	Michigan	84.60
New Mexico	97.10	Washington	84.20
4th Circuit	96.90	Georgia	76.20
Texas	96.90		

This table reveals that while eight state intermediate court systems actually are reducing their appellate backlogs, not one of the U.S. Courts of Appeals that has a backlog of filings actually is reducing it. Furthermore, the federal intermediate appellate court system, considered as a system, is not even performing above average, when compared to the three-year clearance rates of the state intermediate appellate courts for which data is available. Indeed, only four of the regional U.S. Courts of Appeals are currently "holding their own" against their filing increases. The Courts of Appeals for the D.C. Circuit, First Circuit, Sixth Circuit, and Tenth Circuit, like Alice in Through the Looking Glass, are running as fast as they can to stay in the same place. All the others are falling behind.

Alternatively, it might be argued, perhaps even more soundly, that going back to the first table the per-appeal intervals of 5.6 months in argued cases and 4.2 months in nonargued cases—representing additional delays of "only" 3.4 months and 2.0 months respectively over the forty-year period—are not very large when considered relatively or absolutely. There are two levels of response to this argument.

First, it should be pointed out that these are median figures and that they are for all the Courts of Appeals. Mathematically speaking, therefore, there are equal numbers of appeals in the federal appellate system being decided in longer and in shorter appellate time intervals; some particular appeals take more time than others; and some particular Courts of Appeals take more time than other Courts of Appeals. This may be a statistical way of saying nothing more than that things actually could be better or worse than these figures suggest and, because it is difficult to know, we should not make too much out of median statistics. Our expressed purpose here is to make the most of these statistics, but not too much.

Second, there is a more interesting way to consider the increases in the appellate intervals systemically, which takes into account the increase in the volume of appeals during the last four decades. While somewhat novel, we believe this system is more revealing of the effect of the "crisis of volume." Our method is to multiply the length of the median appellate intervals by the total number of appeals decided during the year to compute a figure of the aggregate median appellate time interval. This new methodology yields an aggregate measure of how long all the Courts of Appeals took to decide all the federal appeals for that year. Then we will compare this systemic aggregate measure of decision time for the years 1950 and 1990. This will allow a comparison of roughly how long the Courts of Appeals took to hear and decide a full year's worth of federal appeals before and after what has been called the "crisis of volume." The mean number, of course, would be preferable, even ideal, for this computational comparison. Unfortunately, the mean appellate intervals are not compiled and reported and, therefore, are not available. Presumably, the median figures are at least some rough approximation of what the mean figures would be. At least that is the explicit assumption we make here.

In 1950, the Courts of Appeals decided 2,355 appeals with a median appellate interval of 2.2 months, for a national aggregate of 5,181 months of appellate decision time for that year. In 1990, the Courts of Appeals decided 21,006 appeals on the merits; screening the appeals for different appellate procedural tracks complicates the mathematics somewhat, but the national aggregate for that year was 88,456 months of appellate decision time.

This increase in the national aggregate decision time for the appellate year represents an increase of one full order of magnitude in the total number of months it took the circuit judges to decide a year's worth of federal appeals. Measured in years, the 1990 aggregate is just over 17 times the 1950 aggregate, an increase from four centuries to more than seven millennia, an added difference of biblical proportions. Keep in mind that these national aggregations of appellate delay are annual figures. This is the total for each calendar year. Beyond peradventure, these numbers must be considered significant, relatively, or absolutely.

The comparison makes the current situation seem even worse when considered in reverse. In 1990, the Courts of Appeals decided 21,006 cases on the merits and took 88,456 months of judge time in the aggregate to decide them. If the Courts of Appeals of 1990, with all their "new-fangled" appellate procedures, added resources and more personnel, were as efficient as the 1950 Courts of Appeals (2.2 months appellate interval), the same caseload would have been decided in 46,213 months of judge time, closer to half the time they actually took. In addition, every appeal could have been orally argued and decided with a published opinion. Finally, it should be remembered, the appellate interval within the control of the attorneys has not changed appreciably over the same period of comparison. Either the 1990 Courts of Appeals are half as efficient today as they were back in 1950 or the "crisis of volume" has them doubled over.

Because these aggregate appellate time intervals, which are median computations, are spread over so large a number of appeals they are actually experienced and then accounted for in fragments. The magnitude of their cumulative increase, by and large, has escaped the notice of court watchers. The conclusion to be drawn from these computations and comparisons over time may be stated succinctly. The increases in the median judicial time intervals for individual appeals demonstrate that appellate justice is being delayed on the appeal as of right (1950: 2.2 months for all appeals; 1990: 5.6 months in argued appeals and 4.2 months in nonargued appeals). But this is only the tip of the iceberg. The national aggregate computations provide some estimate of the overall systemic delay caused by the docket growth. In other words, these figures are some indication of the magnitude of the overall effect felt by the federal appellate court system from the increases in the number of appeals. This provides a new and different vantage on what the "crisis of volume" has wrought.

The often-repeated observation in the debate over what to do about the growth in the federal appellate docket identifies only three logical possibilities: adding appellate resources, reducing appellate procedures, or accepting longer delays. Over the last forty years, there has been enormous growth on the supply side, as new judgeships were created, more law clerks were added, new technologies were implemented, et cetera. Over the same period, federal appellate procedures have been streamlined and efficiencies have been pursued at every stage of the consideration of an appeal, so that most observers have concluded that little marginal gain is to be expected from further intramural reforms.

Despite all these additions to appellate capacity and all these new efficiencies, longer and longer delays have occurred. This Essay has attempted to quantify the magnitude of the growing delay. On an individual or per appeal basis, the increase in the delay certainly is noteworthy. Considered in the national aggregate, the increase in the systemic delay simply is staggering. Furthermore, there is no sign that the growth in the federal appellate docket is slowing. Any discussion of what to do about the continuing growth in the appellate caseload, therefore, must be informed by a fuller appreciation for the relationship between increases in appellate filings and the resultant appellate delay experienced in the federal intermediate appellate court system qua system.

Some Concluding Observations

Certainly, everything about the Courts of Appeals is bigger in the 1990s. Of course, there are more judges deciding more appeals. But it is most noteworthy that the time it takes the Courts of Appeals to hear and decide all the cases on their annual docket is appreciably longer than it was one generation ago. 1950 represents a typical year before the deluge of appeals and before the intramural reforms of appellate procedures. 1990 represents the aftermath of the crisis of volume. That the aggregate increase is so huge is even more significant given the wholesale reforms of appellate practice and procedure implemented by the Courts of Appeals over the same period. The trend lines for this period are charted in the Appendix following this Article.

The comparative computations these two years yield, most assuredly, would be wholly unacceptable in other areas of federal public policy performance. For example, suppose that in 1950 it took two days for the Post Office to deliver a letter mailed from Lubbock, Texas to Washington, D.C. Suppose that forty years later, in 1990, faced with larger volumes of mail but afforded more personnel and greater resources, including new technology and other economies of scale, it took the Postal Service four or five or even six days to deliver the same letter and then it was delivered to a post office box rather than to the person's home. Who would find that acceptable? Could any responsible person comfortably accept that trend or allow it to continue? Would Congress sit idly by? While our analogy uses letters and days, the comparisons of aggregate appellate time intervals, after all, deal with appeals in federal litigation and months. The matters involved are more weighty and the added delay is much more pronounced.

Most of the previous studies, committees, and commissions have expressed varying degrees of concern, often expressed as a grave concern, for the problems facing the U.S. Courts of Appeals. Many fear, however, that their warnings resemble those of the Greek seer Cassandra, whose curse was that her prophecies would be accurate but always ignored. These commentators have expressed their warnings both qualitatively and quantitatively.

Some have expressed concerns that the pressures of caseload over the last four decades have resulted in intramural "reforms" that already have misshaped the quality of federal appellate procedure almost unrecognizably. They worry that the federal appellate tradition and ideals already have been severely compromised by these responses to docket growth. Others have expressed an even more profound worry about quantitative predictions, expressing a concern for an uncertain and not too distant future that threatens to worsen the "crisis of volume" until the existing federal appellate structure collapses under the weight of caseloads and judgeships. They also worry that if we do nothing we run a grave risk of irrevocably losing our federal appellate tradition and ideals; they insist we must plan and prepare alternative structures for the inevitable transfiguration of the intermediate federal court.

Along with Chief Justice Rehnquist, we confidently predict that "change will come" for the U.S. Courts of Appeals. We hope that this Article will contribute to a better understanding of the problems facing the federal appellate courts and, in turn, that our effort will aid the thoughtful search for solutions.

APPENDIX

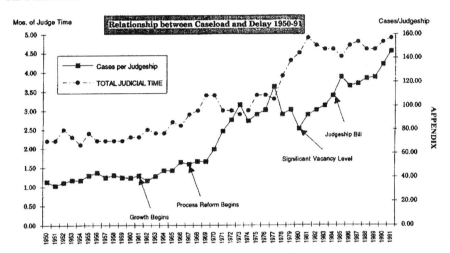

GIZZI, EXAMINING THE CRISIS OF VOLUME IN THE U.S. COURTS OF APPEALS *

77 Judicature 96 (1993).**

Caseload statistics and judicial perceptions deflect exaggerated notions of an overwhelming number of federal appeals court cases.

However people may view other aspects of the federal judiciary, few deny that its appellate courts are in a "crisis of volume" that has transformed them from the institutions they were even a generation ago. Further and more fundamental change to the appellate courts would seem inevitable unless there is a halt to the climb in appellate workload. While it is impossible to read the future, we see little reason to anticipate such a halt. * * * *

Are the federal courts of appeals at a critical juncture? Students of the federal courts are forced to contemplate this question in light of the dramatic increases in appellate filings over the past 30 years. Since as

* Some tables in the original are omitted, along with all footnotes relating to the tables, and the remaining tables are reformatted and renumbered. [Ed. Footnote]

** Copyright © 1993, Prof. Michael C. Gizzi, Ph.D., Mesa State College, Colorado. Reprinted by permission. All rights reserved.

early as 1974, claims have been made that caseload pressures have resulted in a "crisis of volume" threatening the very nature of the federal intermediate appellate courts. Cries of a caseload crisis were amplified by the Federal Courts Study Committee after it completed a 15–month study of problems facing the federal courts and, in particular, those of the courts of appeals.

The exact nature of this crisis is not altogether clear, however. While the committee's report claimed that "few deny" that the federal appellate courts are experiencing a crisis of volume, prominent committee members voiced the "fear that the alleged 'caseload crisis' has not been adequately demonstrated," and that although there are "sobering statistics concerning the growth of the federal judiciary and ever-increasing appellate caseload pressures, these numbers in and of themselves provide little guidance for determining the capacity of the system or the breaking point at which 'crisis' must set in." To better understand the problems facing the federal courts of appeals, this article takes a fresh look at several dimensions of the alleged crisis of volume.

There is no question that the courts of appeals have experienced a tremendous growth in filings in the past 50 years (see Table 1 and Figure 1). While 2,730 appeals were filed in 1945, there were 47,013 new appeals in 1992. This growth in caseload has been met by adding judges, increasing judicial productivity, introducing modern case management techniques, and streamlining the adjudicatory process for specific classes of cases. These changes, along with the belief that filings will continue to grow, provide the basis of claims of the crisis of volume. A decade ago, Eighth Circuit Chief Judge Donald P. Lay wrote that although the use of innovative processes has allowed the federal courts of appeals to "deal admirably with the case crunch," the judges of the various circuits have found that "they are now working to the very limit of their human capacities." More recently, the Federal Courts Study Committee warned that "within as few as five years the nation could have to decide whether or not to abandon the present circuit structure." Still, it is not clear that the courts of appeals are really in as bad a condition as a crisis of volume thesis would suggest.

Table 1 Measurements of growth in the U.S. courts of appeals, 1945–1992

	Total filings	Percent change	Number of judgeships	Filings per judgeship	Percent change
1945	2,730	n/a	59	46	n/a
1950	2,830	4%	65	44	–6%
1955	3,695	31	65	57	31
1960	3,899	6	68	57	1
1965	6,766	4	78	87	51
1970	11,662	72	97	120	39
1975	16,685	43	97	172	43
1980	23,200	39	132	176	2

	Total filings	Percent change	Number of judgeships	Filings per judgeship	Percent change
1985	33,360	44	132	253	44
1990	40,898	23	156	262	4
1992	47,013	15	167	281	7

Figure 1 Total filings in the U.S. Courts of Appeals, 1945-1992

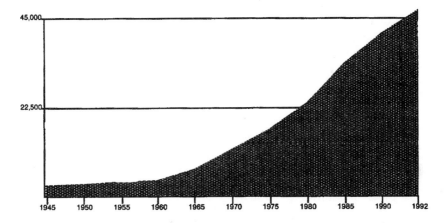

PATHOLOGIES

A "crisis of volume" conjures up an image of a court system slowed to a snail's pace, burdened by an excessive caseload, and on the verge of collapsing under its own weight. Crisis, of course, is a subjective, loaded term. While it is difficult to measure the empirical existence of a crisis, it is possible to approach the issue indirectly by asking what pathologies the appeals courts would suffer if a crisis existed. For if there is a crisis, something disturbing must be going on. Thus, the crisis of volume can be examined by comparing the pathologies of the crisis with the actual practices and conditions found in the courts of appeals.

It is highly plausible that a court system experiencing a crisis of volume would exhibit several deleterious consequences of its caseload pressures. First, a court in crisis probably would not be able to keep up with the workload. One result of having more cases to dispose should be an increase in disposition time or court delay. Related to the inability to keep up with the workload is the likelihood that the courts would spend less time on individual cases. Courts seeking greater efficiency might attempt to truncate their procedures and give less important cases abbreviated treatment.

A second set of problems a court system in crisis would be likely to face is a decrease in the quality of its work. A crisis of volume suggests that judges do not have enough time to properly assess cases on the merits. They might not be able to give the necessary time required to fully consider cases and to produce decisions of the quality expected from them in the past. The judges may become overworked and not have adequate time to devote to preparing for oral argument, to reading the lower court's record, or to writing opinions. Because of the demands on their time, judges may be forced to delegate more of their work to law clerks and central staff attorneys, placing substantial responsibility in less experienced and non-democratically accountable officials. The concerns raised about keeping up with the workload may force judges to forego writing opinions for publication in cases that merit it.

Finally, as a consequence of the increased volume and the addition of more judges to accommodate that volume, it is likely that unpredictability and inconsistency would be injected into the law, resulting in conflicts interpreting the law among the various panels of an individual circuit and between circuits.

POINTS OF ANALYSIS

While the preceding discussion represents only a crude outline of the likely pathologies of a court system experiencing a crisis of volume, it provides one perspective for evaluating current conditions in the courts of appeals. This article examines two types of data. For the first set of questions, dealing with the ability of the appeals courts to keep up with their workload, case management statistics published by the Administrative Office of U.S. Courts are used. This data can help determine the degree to which these courts have been able to keep up with their workload and offers an objective assessment of the crisis.

Questions of whether the courts of appeals have experienced a decrease in the quality of their work, however, are of a different nature. These questions are much more subjective, and little insight is uncovered by examining case management statistics alone. Fortunately, a data set exists that specifically addresses these issues: a 1989 survey of 154 U.S. circuit judges commissioned by the Federal Courts Study Committee. This data provides information about the judges' perceptions of their workload that is valuable in assessing the crisis of volume. * * *

Three brief comments about the survey data are in order. First, while there are limitations to survey data because of problems of validity relating to judges' responses about their work, the data is still useful. It is possible that judges may be influenced by a sensitivity as to how others might view their work. Judges may be reluctant to admit that they are overworked or that they rely on staff to do work they believe they should do themselves. At the same time, however, the confidentiality of the judges' identities was ensured by the anonymous questionnaires. Moreover, there is no more reason to assume that judges will not be completely honest with their responses than to assume they will be reluctant to do so. Given the unique status of the survey respondents they are federal judges and the rare opportunity to examine their perceptions, the possible limitations of the survey data do not outweigh their potential value in this examination.

A second concern is that of the 154 survey respondents, 41 are senior judges. Because senior judges do not carry the same workloads as active judges, some might question their inclusion in the survey. The senior judges' responses are retained in the analysis for two reasons. First, although it is true that senior judges do not have the same workloads as active judges, many continue to carry a substantial percentage of a full workload. Of the 41 senior judges polled, 63 percent claimed to carry between 50 and 100 percent of a full-time workload. Moreover, when survey questions are examined without the senior judges, the responses are substantially the same as when all 154 judges are included. Removing the senior judges only reduces the sample size. Thus, more doubt may be cast on the data by removing the senior judges from the analysis than by retaining them.

Finally, when examining case management statistics and perceptual survey data, multiple interpretations of data always can be made. The interpretation given to data may reflect the initial perspective one has about the questions under study. Thus, for example, one who believes the courts of appeals are at the verge of a system breakdown may be likely to perceive survey responses showing 25 percent of judges believe they are "overworked" as indicative of the grave problems facing the courts of appeals. On the other hand, one unconvinced of the actual existence of a volume crisis may read that same data very differently. It is not the intent of this article, nor is it possible, to have the final word about the crisis of volume. Rather, this article is intended to add to the already existing dialogue among academics, judges, and practitioners about the issues and problems facing the federal courts of appeals.

OBJECTIVE MEASURES

If the federal courts of appeals are experiencing a crisis of volume, case management statistics should reflect some aspects of excessive volume. An inquiry into the median disposition times and the backlog of pending cases should reveal one of the most visible symptoms of a court system in crisis: delay. If a crisis exists, the courts should be burdened by the volume of their workload, and their efficiency, in terms of the ability to dispose cases timely, should be diminished. Case management statistics presenting the median time for the disposition of cases, however, indicate that the courts of appeals are current with their caseload, with a median disposition time slightly more than 10 months. Moreover, since 1980 the median disposition times have actually shortened slightly.

Table 2 reports the median disposition times for the courts of appeals from 1968 to 1992. There has been surprisingly little change in median disposition times since 1968. Median times ranged from a low of 9.8 months in 1968 to a high of 11.5 months in 1982. Because the Administrative Office changed how it reported median disposition times in 1980, the data since then is worth a closer examination. Disposition times reached a decade-high median of 11.5 months in 1982 and then began a slow decline to close the decade at 10.1 months in 1990. By 1992, the median disposition times rebounded slightly, to 10.6 months. Interestingly, disposition times actually decreased by slightly less than one month since 1980, while filings more than doubled during the same period (Table 1). These findings contradict what should be one of the most visible signs of a crisis of volume. The data implies not a workload crisis, but a court system that has managed to remain fairly current with its work despite substantial increases in filings.

Table 2 Median disposition times in the U.S. courts of appeals, 1968–1992

	Median time (months) from filing notice of appeal to disposition	Median time (months) from filing complete record to disposition
1968	9.8	7.8
1970	10.2	8.2
1972	8.6	6.6
1974	8.8	6.8
1976	11.0	9.0
1978	10.0	8.0
1980	10.8	8.9
1982	11.5	
1984	10.8	
1986	10.3	
1988	10.1	
1990	10.1	
1992	10.6	

One possible cause for this phenomenon may be found in both the increase of judicial resources since 1980 and the increase in terminations per judge. As Table 1 shows, 132 judges in 1980 each were responsible for disposing 176 filings, while in 1992, 167 judges each disposed 281 cases. Increased delay probably has been avoided by adding judges and increasing their productivity. This lack of delay casts some doubt on an important aspect of the crisis of volume thesis.

The median disposition time findings are further supported by data examining the backlog of pending cases. Table 3 reports the inventory control index, a measure of how long it would take for a court to dispose all pending cases at its current termination rate. The index is useful in examining the courts of appeals over time because an increase in the index shows that the courts are falling behind in their work, while a decrease shows they are becoming current. Since 1965, the inventory control index has stayed fairly constant, generally fluctuating between 9 and 10 months. The national index reached its highest point in 1980, at 11.5 months. It dropped to 9.5 months by 1985, increased to 10.0 months by 1990, and then dropped once more to 9.8 months in 1992. Like the disposition times already discussed, the inventory control index indicates a court system that has consistently been reasonably current with its work. While 10 months' delay may not be viewed favorably by some, the consistency of the courts of appeals in its speed of disposing the caseload does not support claims of a crisis of volume.

Table 3 Inventory control index, 1965–1992

	Index score (in months)	Number of judges
1965	9.9	78
1970	9.9	97
1975	9.1	97
1980	11.5	132
1985	9.5	156
1990	10.0	156
1992	9.8	167

Among the possible consequences of a crisis of volume is the likelihood that courts would find means to truncate the appellate process, giving abbreviated treatment to less important cases. Modern techniques of judicial administration offer several means by which a court could accomplish this objective. Appellate court settlement programs could be implemented, cases could be decided based only on the submission of the briefs, dispensing with oral hearings, or summary orders could be issued instead of written opinions in cases. In addition, judges could delegate the screening of certain types of cases such as prisoner habeas corpus petitions or social security appeals to staff attorneys or law clerks, preserving judicial resources for the most important cases. Staff attorneys could also draft motions and summary orders. These methods all allow judges to increase their productivity and dispose greater numbers of cases. Administrative Office statistics allow consideration of one aspect of the need to truncate the appellate process, namely dispensing with oral argument and resolving cases on the submission of briefs. By comparing the percentage of cases disposed after a full oral hearing with those resolved based solely on the submission of briefs, it is possible to test this pathology of the crisis of volume.

Figure 2 demonstrates a significant shift in the percentage of cases resolved after a full oral hearing, a traditional part of the federal appellate process. As late as 1980, more than 70 percent of cases received a full oral hearing. By 1992, that percentage had dropped to 43.9 percent. This represents a substantial change in the federal appellate process, and it is the one objective measure considered here that supports the crisis of volume thesis. One way the courts of appeals have dealt with caseload growth has been by limiting the cases that receive full oral hearings. By deciding cases based solely on the appellate briefs, the courts have saved time needed to accommodate larger workloads without imposing additional delay.

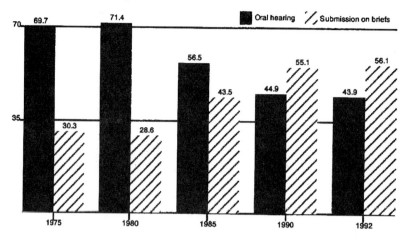

Figure 2 Cases disposed after oral hearing versus submission on the briefs, 1975-1992

Note: Statistics unavailable before 1975.

Source: Flanagan, *Appellate Court Caseloads*, Table 24; 1990 and 1992 statistics derived from Administrative Office of United States Courts, *Annual Report of the Director*, 1992, 1990, Table B-4.

This finding supports one aspect of the crisis of volume by suggesting that one consequence of increased workload has been a decrease in the percentage of cases receiving full oral hearing. The data does not indicate whether there are differences in the quality of decisions in cases disposed without oral argument. The answer to questions like this give the best indication of the crisis of volume. Case management statistics cannot resolve whether a crisis of volume exists because if one does, it is one primarily concerned with the quality of the work produced by the courts of appeals, not with delay and backlog. Objective case management statistics suggest that the courts of appeals are functioning efficiently. By turning to issues regarding the quality of the appellate process, more about the crisis of volume may be uncovered. It is necessary to consider the crisis of volume from the perspective of the judges themselves.

JUDICIAL PERCEPTIONS

To explore the effects of caseload growth on appeals court judges, the responses to the Federal Courts Study Committee survey are examined here by dividing the judges into groups of low, medium, and high workload based on the average per-judge workload for each circuit. By controlling for the judicial workload, it is possible to understand better how judges on busy courts differ in their perspectives from judges on courts with less demanding workloads.

If the courts of appeals are in a crisis of volume, the judges should feel demoralized and overworked by the volume of their work. The judges were asked two pertinent questions that are worth examining initially. Table 4 presents the judges' views about their current work-load. The responses show that a quarter of all judges believe their workload is "overwhelming." A majority of judges thought the workload was "heavy, but what they were used to" before becoming a judge. Twenty-three judges (15.2 percent) thought the workload was "busy, but not overwhelming," and one judge each felt it was either "fairly relaxed" or "no problem." There were no statistically significant nor substantive differences between workload groups. The responses suggest that the majority of judges believe their workloads are heavy, but not overly so.

Table 4 The current workload is:

	RESPONSES OF ALL JUDGES
Overwhelming	26%
Heavy, but what I was used to before I became a judge	58%
Busy, but not burdensome	15%
Fairly relaxed or no problem	1%

Table 5 reports the results to a similar question, "Do caseload pressures have an adverse effect on how you work?" The results were similar to those found in the previous question. A fifth of the judges answered "never or almost never." A majority of judges said they "sometimes" experienced such adverse effects, while a quarter said they "often or usually" experienced adverse effects of caseload pressure on their work. When examined by the workload of the court, there was a statistically significant difference between low-workload judges and medium-and high-workload judges. Forty percent of low-workload judges said they "never or almost never" experienced adverse effects of caseload pressure, while only 13 percent of medium-workload and nearly 20 percent of high-workload judges agreed. Low-workload judges were least likely to say their work was adversely affected "often or usually," with only one judge (4.5 percent) responding, while approximately 25 percent of the medium-and high-workload judges gave the same response.

Table 5 Do caseload pressures have an adverse effect on how you work?

	CIRCUIT WORKLOAD			Response of all judges
	Low	Medium	High	
Never or almost never	41%	13%	20%	20%
Sometimes	55%	63%	55%	55%
Often or usually	5%	24%	26%	24%

The responses indicate that while close to 8 out of 10 judges were adversely affected by caseload pressures at least sometimes, only a quarter of the judges said that such occurrences happened "often or usually." In a crisis of volume, we might expect the percentage of judges who are often adversely affected by caseload pressures to be much higher than the 25 percent response found here. From the responses to these two questions alone, it seems that if there is a crisis of volume, it is one perceived by a distinct minority of judges.

The crisis of volume may manifest itself, however, in less obvious ways than the judges' outright recognition of a problem. Several more survey questions exploring more specific aspects of the problems that should be found in a crisis of volume are worth considering. One of the consequences that a court system in a caseload crisis would be likely to face is a need for judges to delegate more work to non-judicial staff. In the courts of appeals, judges have law clerks and central staff attorneys to assist them. The survey asked how often the judges rely on law clerks and central staff to do things that they believe should be done by themselves. Table 6 reports the responses to the question regarding law clerks. Responses were fairly evenly divided, with 35 percent of the judges saying they "never or almost never" rely on their law clerks to do things they believe they should do themselves, 33 percent saying "sometimes," and 32 percent responding "often or usually." While more than 60 percent of the judges say they "sometimes" rely on law clerks to do what are more appropriately judicial tasks, only 30 percent said they believe that reliance on law clerks for judicial tasks occurs often or usually. Low-workload judges were most likely to say "never or almost never," and they were least likely to say "often or usually." There were only slight differences between medium-and high-workload judges, with 32.8 percent of medium-workload judges responding "often or usually" compared with 32.0 percent of high-workload judges.

Table 6 How often do you rely on your law clerks to do things you believe you should do yourself?

	CIRCUIT WORKLOAD			
	Low	**Medium**	**High**	**Response of all judges**
Never or almost never	41%	33%	36%	35%
Sometimes	46%	29%	32%	33%
Often or usually	14%	33%	32%	32%

When the same question is asked substituting central staff for law clerks, however, the responses are strikingly different ... A majority of the judges (67.8 percent) said they "never or almost never" rely on central staff to do things they believe they should do themselves. Exactly 25 percent of the judges said they "sometimes" rely on central staff, and only 11 judges (7.2 percent) said they "often or usually" rely on central staff. No statistically significant differences were found when the responses were examined by the judges' workload.

Judges were more likely to say they relied on law clerks to do work they believed they should do themselves than they were to say the same about central staff attorneys. But even so, only 30 percent of the judges thought they often relied on their law clerks to do what is more appropriately judicial work. The remainder of the judges said they sometimes or rarely rely on their clerks. The apparent differences in perceptions about central staff is somewhat surprising because staff attorneys are a newer addition to the courts of appeals, and they have a less traditional place in the federal appellate process. Perhaps the apparent lack of concern about central staff can be explained by their being viewed by judges as having more experience in the federal courts than law clerks. Still, the responses to both questions seem to provide weak evidence for the crisis of volume.

As described above, one way that a court system could accommodate increased volume is by reducing the amount of process given to each case. As the data presented in Figure 2 demonstrate, there has been a substantial reduction in the percentage of cases that receive a full oral hearing. A subjective assessment of the reduction of oral argument can be examined by asking the judges, "How frequently do you feel that you are forced to forego argument in cases that could benefit from it?" (Table 7). More than three-fourths of the judges indicated "never or almost never," while 19 percent of the judges said "sometimes," and just six judges (3.9 percent) said "often or usually." There were virtually no differences between judges when controlled for workload. The data suggests that at least from the judges' perspective, the decreased reliance on oral argument has not had deleterious effects in the quality of justice.

Table 7 How frequently do you feel that you are forced to forego argument in cases that could benefit from it?

	RESPONSES OF ALL JUDGES
Never or almost never	77%
Sometimes	19%
Often or usually	4%

While foregoing argument in cases that merit it is not regarded as a problem by most judges, another issue related to oral argument is worth considering. Table 8 addresses the question, "How frequently do you feel that you do not have enough time to prepare for oral argument?" One likely result of a crisis of volume, even if judges believe they do not have to forego argument in cases that merit it, is the reality of not having enough time to prepare for oral argument in the cases that do receive it. The sheer numbers of cases assigned to individual judges might make it difficult to prepare for oral argument in all cases, by fully reading the record of the lower court and the briefs of the parties.

Sixty-three judges (40.9 percent) answered "never or almost never." Another 56 judges (36.4 percent) said they sometimes do not have enough time to prepare for oral argument. Thirty-five judges (22.7 percent) said they "often or usually" do not have enough time for preparation. The responses suggest that judges do have some difficulty finding adequate time to prepare for oral argument. While the workload breakdowns of the responses were not statistically significant, there are visible differences between low-workload judges and medium-and high-workload judges responding that they either "never or almost never" do not have enough time, or they "often or usually" do not have enough time. Low-workload judges were most likely to say they "never do not have enough time," with 56.5 percent of the judges responding. Only 40 percent of medium-workload judges and 39.2 percent of high-workload judges gave the same answer. The low-workload judges were least likely to say that they often do not have enough time, with only two judges (8.7 percent) responding. This is in comparison with medium-and high-workload judges, of whom 23.6 and 21.6 percent agreed. The responses to these questions do show some signs of a problem in the courts of appeals, but not to the degree that one would expect to find in a crisis of volume.

Table 8 How frequently do you feel that you do not have enough time to prepare for oral argument?

	CIRCUIT WORKLOAD			
	Low	Medium	High	Response of all judges
Never or almost never	57%	40%	39%	41%
Sometimes	35%	36%	39%	36%
Often or usually	9%	24%	22%	23%

Two final questions deal with writing opinions. Under a crisis of volume, it is likely that judges would be forced to limit the cases that receive full published opinions. Table 9 reports the answers to the question that asks whether judges are forced to forego writing opinions for publication in cases that merit it, or if they are otherwise forced to reduce the amount of time they spend on a written opinion. The responses suggest that while foregoing writing is sometimes a problem for judges, it is not of crisis proportion. In fact, close to 60 percent of the judges say they "never or almost never" are forced to forego writing opinions. Fewer than 30 percent of the judges said that they "sometimes" are forced to forego writing, and only 12.5 percent said they "often or usually" do so. Examined by the workload of the judge's court, there is a statistically significant difference in responses between low-workload judges and medium-and high-workload judges. More than 80 percent of low-workload judges said they "never or almost never" forego writing, while only 58.2 percent of medium-workload judges and 59.2 percent of high-workload judges gave the same response. Only four low-workload judges said they "sometimes" forego writing, compared with

32.7 percent of medium-workload judges and 26.5 percent of high-workload judges.

Table 9 How frequently are you required to forego writing opinions for publication in cases you believe should be decided by published opinion or otherwise reduce the amount of time you spend on a written opinion?

<u>**CIRCUIT WORKLOAD**</u>

	Low	Medium	High	Response of all judges
Never or almost never	83%	58%	59%	59%
Sometimes	17%	33%	27%	29%
Often or usually	9%	14%	13%	11%

Finally, Table 10 reports the responses to the question, "Do you have sufficient time for the drafting of opinions?" Here, a fifth of the judges said that they "always" have sufficient time, slightly more than a majority said they "often" have sufficient time, and a fourth said they "never or almost never" have sufficient time. There were virtually no differences in responses by workload. All in all, the responses resemble those from most of the other questions: the majority of judges generally do not seem to perceive there is a problem.

Table 10 I feel that I have sufficient time for the drafting of opinions:

Always	20%
Often	53%
Almost never or never	27%

EVALUATING THE CRISIS

On both objective and subjective dimensions examined, the deleterious consequences expected to be found did not materialize. Case management statistics show the courts of appeals to be fairly current in their work, and the survey responses reveal that the majority of judges do not believe that the workload is overwhelming or that they are forced to jeopardize the appellate process to accommodate the volume of cases.

Given the mixed measures uncovered about the crisis, it is probable that claims of impending doom might be exaggerations of problems that may only have the potential to reach crisis proportion. As one scholar of the federal courts of appeals recently noted, "Crisis is a much overused word. Burgeoning caseloads are nothing new, nor is the sense that the system is on the verge of a breakdown." There may indeed be reason for concern about the methods that the courts of appeals are using to accommodate the demands of their workload. There is genuine disagreement about the consequences of the growth of the size of the courts of appeals, the increases in staff, and the modifications made to the appellate process. Taken as a whole, these changes probably do represent a transformation of the federal intermediate appellate courts, at least to the degree that the courts of appeals barely resemble their counterparts of 1940 or even 1960.

But such a transformation does not necessarily constitute a crisis. As the data considered here have shown, little empirical evidence supports the claim that the courts of appeals are in a crisis of volume. The survey data show that the great majority of judges do not have perceptions about their workload that are suggestive of a crisis of volume. It is important to recognize, however, that just because the courts of appeals are not in a crisis of volume does not mean that they may not face serious problems. While not examined here, it is quite possible that the unpredictability and inconsistency that result from having too many judges and too many decisions may be an important issue that needs to be confronted.

In addressing the future of the courts of appeals, it is important not to ignore the minority of judges who do exhibit signs of a crisis in their perceptions. While the majority of judges surveyed do not believe their courts are in a crisis of volume, there is a core of approximately 30 to 40 judges, a distinct minority (about 25 percent) of the appellate judiciary, who do think they are overworked, and whose responses generally support claims of a crisis of volume. This core of judges who believe they are overworked or otherwise exhibit signs of the stress of a crisis of volume generally come from the largest and busiest circuits in the courts of appeals, and most of them have been circuit judges since at least 1983. Table 11 reports the circuits these judges are from. It is very probable that if asked, these judges would say that the courts of appeals are indeed in a crisis of volume. It is also possible that they are the judges who are most vocal in their concerns. The views expressed by these judges should not be taken lightly, as they may be a warning beacon for the future. At the same time, their concerns only represent a distinct minority of all judges. Consider, for example, the Ninth Circuit with 28 judges, the nation's largest. While eight of the "overworked" judges are from this circuit, they only represented 29 percent of the total Ninth Circuit judges who responded to the survey. * * * *

Table 11 The overworked judges: Where they are from?

Circuit	Number of Overworked judges	% of respondents in circuit	% of total active and senior judges in circuit	Circuit workload
Ninth	8	29	21	Medium

Third	8	57	40	Medium
Fifth	7	39	33	High
Sixth	4	40	19	High
Fourth	4	36	31	High
Eleventh	3	25	19	High
Others	7	19	18	Small and Medium

The Federal Courts Study Committee expressed concern in its final report that if caseloads continue to rise in numbers as they have in the past 30 years, more drastic changes will be necessary to accommodate this growth than is possible from merely tinkering with the amount of process given to cases and forcing judges to become even more productive. Major structural reforms might be needed to refashion the courts of appeals to meet the demands of the caseload. While the committee's concerns are prudent, this analysis questions whether the courts of appeals are currently experiencing a crisis of volume, exhibiting all the consequences of excessive caseloads.

These findings are consistent with the perspectives expressed at a recent conference of federal circuit judges. When asked to give their perceptions of various structural reforms for the courts of appeals, the vast majority of judges indicated they would not support any changes, nor did they seem to perceive themselves as being in the midst of a crisis of volume. On the other hand, the fact that a fourth of the federal circuit judiciary believes there is something seriously wrong with the courts of appeals should not be taken lightly. Policy makers and students of judicial administration should consider both of these points when assessing where to go from here.

Notes

In a large study tracking 16 years worth of federal appeals from 1977 through 1993 researchers with the Federal Judicial Center concluded that claims of a broadscale increase in caseloads were overstated and imprecise, and that "the disproportionate increase is largely accounted for by growth of appeals in just three types of cases." Krafka, Cecil & Lombard, Stalking the Increase in the rate of Federal Civil Appeals, 18 Justice Sys. J. 233, 244–25 (1996) (concluding that civil rights, prisoner cases and Social Security benefits cases accounted for the bulk of the caseload growth observed in the federal appellate courts during that entire period). Among the highest appeal rates these authors found were 15% for appeal of Social Security dispositions at the trial level, 24% for appeal of decisions in prisoner civil rights and habeas petitions, over 30% for non-civil rights prisoner petitions, and 24% for all non-prisoner civil rights actions. Id. at 254–55. Taking the prisoner cases, Social Security appeals and civil rights cases out of the statistics, the authors found the growth of filings to be very modest. Id. at 245.

NATIONAL CENTER FOR STATE COURTS, EXAMINING THE WORK OF STATE COURTS 2003, at 63–67 (2004)*

Appellate courts, whether at the intermediate or highest level, provide review of decisions of lower courts and, as the final arbiters of disputes, shape and define the law. In most states, appellate courts are required to review decisions in criminal cases when the defendant is sentenced to death. Appellate courts are also responsible for disciplining attorneys and judges for serious violations of ethics and conduct.

Most states divide their appellate system into two levels: an intermediate appellate court (IAC), which renders a first level of trial court review, and a court of last resort (COLR), which handles the most critical and important matters and appeals from the IACs. Only eleven states and the District of Columbia function without an IAC, while two states, Oklahoma and Texas, have more than one COLR.

Many of the analyses included here make a distinction between mandatory and discretionary caseloads in appellate court. As the terms imply, mandatory jurisdiction over cases means that an appellate court is obligated by its state constitution or statutes to consider the merits of a case. Discretionary jurisdiction means the court decides whether it will grant review of a case.

Appellate court filings show a slight increase for the first time since 1998

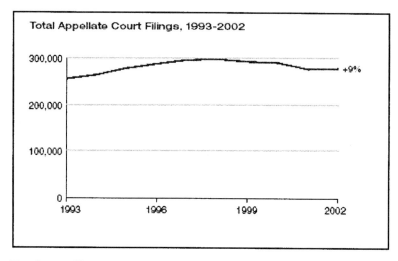

Total appellate court caseloads include original proceedings and appeals over which the appellate courts have mandatory or discretionary jurisdiction. This trend shows annual filing data for state appellate courts for the last 10 years.

* Copyright © 1994, National Center for State Courts, B. Ostrom, N. Kaudler, and   R. La Fountain, copyright. Reprinted by permission. All rights reserved.

Between 1993 and 1998 the number of appellate court filings increased 17 percent, from 254,000 to 297,000. Over the next five years, filings declined 6 percent to 278,000.

Intermediate appellate courts handle most mandatory appeals

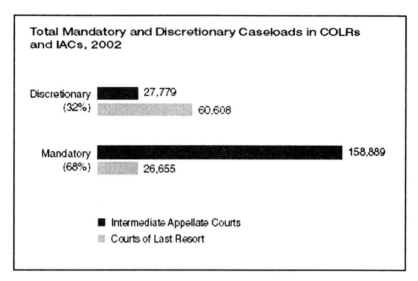

Intermediate appellate courts provide first-level review, while courts of last resort are the final arbiters of disputes. This structure results in intermediate appellate courts handling the majority of appeals. Where there is no intermediate appellate court, a state supreme court conducts first and final appellate review.

The caseloads in IACs and COLRs are reported here as filings of mandatory appeals and discretionary petitions. Mandatory appeals in IACs outnumbered those in COLRs by a margin of 6 to 1. Conversely, there are more than two discretionary petitions filed in COLRs for every one filed in IACs.

Appellate court filing rates vary widely across the states

States in [the following] table are divided into those with and without an intermediate appellate court and then ranked according to their number of appeals per 100,000 population. Caseloads are shown as percentages composed of mandatory appeals and discretionary petitions.

When adjusted for population, Louisiana (population rank 24) reported the highest number of appeals (283 per 100,000 population) and North Carolina (population rank 11) reported the lowest (38 per 100,000 population).

Proportions of mandatory and discretionary caseloads very dramatically, but several states show 100 percent mandatory or discretionary jurisdiction. These populations were based upon the number of cases reported in each category rather than actual mandated jurisdiction.

Hence, a 100 percent designation in one category could simply mean that there were no cases filed in the other category in 2002.

Total Appellate Caseloads by State, 2002

States	Appeals for 100,000 Population	Total Appeals	Mandatory Appeals	Discretionary Appeals	Population Rank
With an Intermediate Appellate Court					
Louisiana	283	12,706	29%	71%	24
Alabama	141	6,325	82	18	23
Florida	140	23,379	83	17	4
Puerto Rico	132	5,079	33	67	27
Pennsylvania	131	16,178	83	17	6
New Jersey	123	10,546	72	28	9
Oregon	120	4,213	83	17	28
Alaska	114	736	74	26	48
Ohio	113	12,952	88	12	7
Nebraska	106	1,830	82	18	39
Texas	103	22,413	86	14	2
Kansas	99	2,678	67	33	33
Illinois	95	11,985	78	22	5
Michigan	94	9,429	44	56	8
Washington	94	5,692	70	30	15
Idaho	93	1,248	85	15	40
Kentucky	92	3,783	78	22	26
Hawaii	92	1,146	94	6	43
Arizona	91	4,951	76	24	19
Colorado	90	4,041	69	31	22
California	89	31,296	45	55	1
Virginia	88	6,440	11	89	12
New York	86	16,386	76	24	3
Arkansas	83	2,256	74	26	34
Wisconsin	83	4,522	75	25	20
Missouri	80	4,519	88	14	17
New Mexico	78	1,440	58	42	37
Iowa	73	2,137	100	0	31
South Carolina	70	2,856	59	41	25
Tennessee	65	3,784	61	39	16
Maryland	63	3,453	63	37	18
Georgia	60	5,132	68	32	10
Minnesota	59	2,942	74	26	21
Massachusetts	57	3,694	60	40	13
Utah	55	1,264	100	0	35
Indiana	52	3,185	77	23	14
Connecticut	49	1,693	71	29	30
Mississippi	49	1,401	78	22	32
North Carolina	38	3,157	55	45	11
Without an Intermediate Appellate Court					
District of Columbia	266	1,520	96	4	51
West Virginia	147	2,653	0	100	38
Delaware	89	715	100	0	46
Montana	88	798	73	27	45
Vermont	86	530	97	3	50
Nevada	79	1,723	100	0	36
Rhode Island	70	754	45	55	44

States	Appeals for 100,000 Population	Total Appeals	Mandatory Appeals	Discretionary Appeals	Population Rank
New Hampshire	64	813	0	100	42
South Dakota	60	457	84	16	47
North Dakota	57	363	94	6	49
Maine	57	738	76	24	41

Notes: Oklahoma and Wyoming were unable to provide data for 2002. States in bold are the nation's 10 most populous.

State appellate courts issued over 38,000 opinions

Most appeals are resolved by opinions, memoranda/orders, or pre-argument dismissals. While opinions can be rendered through a variety of means, the data here capture only two: signed opinions and *per curiam* affirmed opinions. In 2002, 17 courts of last resort issued almost 3,700 such opinions while 24 intermediate courts issued over 34,500.

During 2002, these courts also issued more than 23,000 memoranda/orders and dismissed approximately 27,000 cases.

Manner of Disposition in 17 Courts of Last Report and 24 Intermediate Appellate Courts, 2002

State	Number of Justices	Total Dispositions	Opinions Signed	Per Curiam	Memos/ Orders	Non–Opinion Pre-Argument	Dispositions Transferred	Other
Courts of Law Resort								
With an Intermediate Appellate Court								
Florida	7	2,977	95	213	2,669			
Nevada	7	2,454	38	61	1,767	588	1,015	46
Iowa	8	2,180	180	11		928		57
District of Columbia	9	1,836	339	571	865		7	
Colorado	7	1,415	121		1,287		118	119
Washington	9	1,328	129		892	70		18
Puerto Rico	7	1,240	92	44	129	957		13
Indiana	5	1,103	195	18	190	687		141
Hawaii	5	847	191			257	258	
Without an Intermediate Appellate Court								
Rhode Island	5	818	75	105	70	290		278
Montana	7	792	343		239	210		
Delaware	5	713	71	19	546	77		
Vermont	5	603	68		388	147		
Alaska	5	516	182	68		95		171
South Dakota	5	428	164		167	64		33
Oregon	7	371	60	40	251			20
North Dakota	5	345	189			71		85
Intermediate Appellate Courts								
Ohio	68	10,627	6,992			3,389		246
Pennsylvania Superior Ct.	15	8,152	5,315			2,835	2	
Michigan	28	7,647	212	102	3,636	1,793		1,904
New Jersey	34	7,280	431	3,560	250	3,039		
Pennsylvania Commonw. Ct.	9	4,753	1,746			2,722	117	168
Washington	22	4,306	1,846		264	1,593	11	592
Oregon	10	3,844	393	118	1,483	1,660		190
Missouri	32	3,661	1,686		103	1,200	92	580
Wisconsin	16	3,486	761	523	867			1,335
Georgia	12	3,389	1,401		643	567	69	709
Massachusetts	22	2,869	363		1,071	618	76	741

State	Number of Justices	Total Dispositions	Signed	Per Curium	Memos/ Orders	Pre- Argument	Transferred	Other
Alabama Ct. of Criminal Appeals	5	2,748	122		1,673	578		375
Colorado	16	2,463	291		1,330	834	8	
Maryland	13	2,381	144	1,179		500	41	517
Minnesota	16	2,007	1,324	3	61	609		10
Kansas	10	1,742	1,246		292		204	
Tennessee Ct. of Appeals	12	1,504	843		422	4		235
Alabama Ct. of Civil Appeals	5	1,306	323		574	358	51	
Tennessee Ct. of Criminal Appeals	12	1,304	89		288	17		109
Connecticut	9	1,271	637			262	129	243
Iowa	9	1,231	1,144	70		14		3
Arkansas	12	1,200	629			43	80	448
New Mexico	10	855	152		541	145	8	9
Alaska	3	302	55		172	31		44

Memoranda/orders are the most common disposition in state courts of last resort

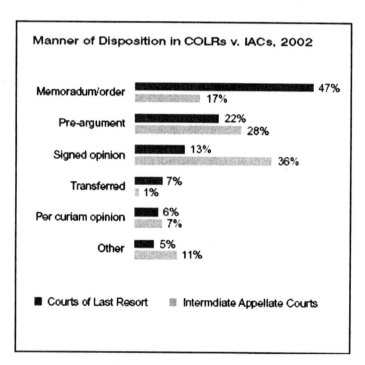

The most common disposition in intermediate appellate courts are signed opinions and pre-argument dismissals. Together, these two actions comprise about two-thirds of all dispositions in IACs. Opinions typically include statements of fact, points of law, rationale, and dicta, while a pre-argument dismissal is based on a review of briefs rather than oral arguments.

Nearly one-half of cases in appellate courts of last resort are resolved by a memorandum/order, which is a simple order based on a unanimous opinion. Pre-argument dismissals and signed opinions are the next most common at 22 percent and 13 percent, respectively.

The remaining appeals are disposed of by *per curiam* opinions (usually a short opinion issued in the name of the court rather than specific justices), transfers to another court, or some other method.

ADMINISTRATIVE OFFICE OF U.S. COURTS, FEDERAL COURT MANAGEMENT STATISTICS (2004)

U.S. COURT OF APPEALS – JUDICIAL CASELOAD PROFILE

NATIONAL TOTALS				12-Month Period Ending September 30					
				2003	2002	2001	2000	1999	1998
OVERALL CASELOAD STATISTICS	Appeals Filed		Total	60,847	57,555	57,464	54,697	54,693	53,805
			Prisoner	17,691	18,272	18,343	17,252	17,191	17,422
			Other	21,200	21,925	24,540	23,501	23,971	22,055
			Criminal	11,968	11,569	11,281	10,707	10,251	10,535
			Administrative	9,988	5,789	3,300	3,237	3,280	3,793
		% Change in Total Filings	Over Last Year	5.7					
			Over Earlier Years		5.9	11.2	11.3		13.1
	Appeals Terminated		Total	56,396	57,586	57,422	56,512	54,088	52,002
			Consolidations & Cross Appeals	2,108	2,721	2,797	2,740	2,651	2,986
			Procedural	27,279	26,107	25,785	26,256	24,710	24,106
		On the Merits	Total	27,009	27,758	28,840	27,516	26,727	24,910
			Prisoner	5,259	5,341	5,287	5,328	4,995	4,956
			Other	11,807	13,065	14,363	13,497	12,893	11,463
			Criminal	8,078	7,978	7,873	7,236	7,385	6,830
			Administrative	1,865	1,374	1,317	1,455	1,453	1,661
			Percent by Active Judges	78.0	77.1	79.0	76.9	79.0	77.2
	Pending Appeals			44,600	40,965	40,303	40,410	42,271	41,649
ACTIONS PER ACTIVE JUDGE*	Terminations on the Merits			459	485	498	458	432	410
	Procedural Terminations			185	191	176	168	151	156
	Written Decisions		Total	154	165	168	156	150	142
			Signed	51	51	54	51	53	50
			Unsigned	98	106	106	97	89	81
			Without Comment	5	8	8	8	8	11

*Includes only judges active during the entire 12 month period.

U.S. COURT OF APPEALS JUDICIAL CASELOAD PROFILE

			12-MONTH PERIOD ENDING SEPTEMBER 30						2003 Numerical Standing
NATIONAL TOTALS			2003	2002	2001	2000	1999	1998	
Number of Judgeships/Number of Panels			167/55.7	167/55.7	167/55.7	165/55.7	167/55.7	167/55.7	
Number of Sitting Senior Judges			92	90	87	81	81	80	
Number of Vacant Judgeships Months			282.7	355.7	331.0	278.9	227.7	247.4	
ACTIONS PER PANEL	Appeals Filed	Total	1,093	1,034	1,032	983	983	967	
		Prisoner	318	328	330	310	309	313	
		Other	381	394	440	423	431	397	
		Criminal	215	208	203	192	184	189	
		Administrative	179	104	59	58	59	68	
	Appeals Terminated	Total	1,018	1,017	1,032	1,015	972	934	
		Consolidations & Cross Appeals	38	49	51	49	48	54	
		Procedural	490	469	463	472	444	433	
		On the Merits — Total	485	499	518	494	480	447	
		On the Merits — Prisoner	94	96	95	96	90	89	
		On the Merits — Other	212	235	258	242	231	205	
		On the Merits — Criminal	145	143	141	130	133	123	
		On the Merits — Administrative	34	25	24	26	26	30	
	Pending Appeals		801	736	724	726	759	748	
Median Time	Median Time From Filing Notice of Appeal to Disposition		10.5	10.7	10.9	11.6	12.0	11.6	
Other Caseload Per Judgeship	Applications for Interlocutory Appeals		2	1	2	2	1	1	
	Pro Se Mandamus Petitions		**	**	**	**	1	6	
	Petitions for Rehearing		39	58	54	56	55	56	

Notes and Questions

1. Compare the caseloads of both state and federal appellate courts pre–1985 and those of today. Have the courts been able to keep up with their workloads? In later sections on internal operating procedures, oral argument, and opinion writing consider whether the techniques adopted to increase productivity have hurt the quality of justice rendered by appellate courts, and how they will affect litigants and the attorney taking an appeal.

2. Baker and Hauptly clearly disagree with Gizzi on whether the increase in the median time for the disposition of appeals in the federal courts of appeals is affecting the quality of justice. Who is correct?

3. Since 2000 the number of appeals in the federal system has continued to increase while in the state courts they have not only leveled off but have gone down. Are there any identifiable reasons for this disparity?

Chapter 2

PRESERVING ISSUES
FOR APPEAL

INTRODUCTION

Throughout the appellate process there are constant reminders of the close relationship between what happens in the trial court and in the appellate court. Nowhere is this more graphically demonstrated than in the relationship between those issues that are presented to the trial court for decision and matters that the appellate court will consider. The rules that govern this relationship—and important exceptions—are the focus of this chapter.

SECTION A. THE GENERAL RULE
REQUIRING ERROR
PRESERVATION

MARTINEAU, CONSIDERING NEW ISSUES
ON APPEAL: THE GENERAL RULE
AND THE GORILLA RULE

40 Vand. L. Rev. 1023, 1026–1030 (1987).*

HISTORICAL DEVELOPMENT AND RATIONALE

The rule against considering new issues on appeal is as old as appellate review. Appellate review as we know it today originated in the English legal system in proceedings against a jury or judge for a false verdict or a false judgment. A review of a finding of fact leading to a verdict was obtained through an attaint, which involved a new trial before a jury of twenty-four persons. This group of twenty-four reviewed the action of the original jury of twelve, and, if it found that the original jury had rendered a false verdict, the jury could be punished by imprisonment. The jury of twenty-four also could render a new verdict in favor

jury punished by imprisonment

* Copyright © 1987, Vanderbilt Law Review, Vanderbilt University. Reprinted by permission. All rights reserved.

of the party oppressed by the original verdict, but the proceeding was primarily a means of punishing the original jury.

A similar proceeding developed for challenging the actions of the trial judge by accusing the judge of rendering a false judgment. This semi-criminal procedure, which was a new proceeding against the judge personally, evolved into the writ of error, the principal common-law procedure for appellate review of trial court proceedings. Both the title of the writ and its nature were predicated on the concept that its purpose was to determine whether the trial judge had erred. Unlike the appeal in equity proceedings, the writ of error did not provide an opportunity for the higher court to substitute its judgment for that of the trial court with regard to which party should prevail on the merits.

Under the writ of error review procedure the only issues that could be presented to the appellate court were those that had been raised and decided in the trial court. The entire purpose of the proceeding was to test the correctness of the judge's actions. The purpose was not to test whether the proper party had won, but only whether the judge had made an error. Logic and fairness dictated, of course, that the judge could not have committed an error only by doing something he was asked not to do or refusing to do something one of the parties requested.

The division of responsibility between judge and jury and the significance of the record were related factors supporting the restrictive nature of appellate review. A trial judge's authority was limited to questions of law, while the jury served as fact-finder. Because it would be an interference with the right to a jury trial to review a jury's factual determination, the appellate court's authority was limited to legal questions decided by the trial judge. Furthermore, the appellate court could not rule on any question not reflected in the record because the record was the only way to determine the basis of the judge's ruling. At the time, the record consisted only of formal documents filed in court and the official record of the actions of the jury and the judge. Because there was no way to record verbatim what occurred at trial, a procedure developed whereby a party could challenge a court's action that otherwise would not be reflected in the record (e.g., a ruling or an objection to evidence or a request for an instruction). Under this procedure, a party could ask the judge or a third party to record in writing the action or inaction of the judge and the fact that the party took exception to the judge's ruling. This became known as the bill of exceptions and was sent to the appellate court along with the record. In effect, the bill of exceptions was the complaint against the trial judge. Thus, a matter had to be presented to and ruled on by the trial judge before the issue could be raised in the appellate court, both because of the nature of the writ of error procedure and the practicalities of recording the lower court proceeding.

A totally different type of review developed in equity. This procedure was termed an appeal, and the review was do novo. The appellate court could review the entire case, both law and facts, and render any type of judgment it thought justice demanded, without regard to whether the issue upon which the appellate court based its judgment had been presented to the lower court.

American appellate procedure followed the writ of error model rather than the appeal in equity, much to the chagrin of Roscoe Pound and Edison Sunderland, the principal academic commentators on the appellate process during the first half of the twentieth century. To Pound and Sunderland, this meant that appellate review in America focused on a search for error rather than a search for justice, which resulted in an overemphasis on the content of the record. According to Pound, most of the effort to reform the American appellate process in the period between 1900 and World War II was directed at changing the focus from the procedure to the merits (i.e., doing justice between the parties). This trend certainly has continued since that time. The most obvious examples of this effort are statutes authorizing appellate courts to render any judgment that justice dictates.

search for error v. search for justice

THE MODERN JUSTIFICATION

The significance of error as the basis for appellate review is almost as strong today as it was in seventeenth-century England, notwithstanding the long-term effort to have the appellate court focus on the correct result rather than correcting error. The effect of history on court procedures, of course, is felt long after the reason for the procedure's development has disappeared. The staying power and current viability of the essential elements of the writ of error procedure suggest, however, that the procedure has a functional basis in addition to an historical premise.

In *Pfeifer v. Jones & Laughlin Steel Corp.* Judge Ruggero Aldisert of the Court of Appeals for the Third Circuit stated succinctly the rationale for the general rule in modern appellate practice. The major question in *Pfeifer* was the proper method of measuring damages involving future lost wages. The appellant argued that the trial court had applied the Pennsylvania state court's formula rather than the federal standard. The Third Circuit held that the appellant had not <u>preserved properly</u> the issue of whether the trial court had applied the state rather than the federal rule, and was limited to arguing the proper elements of damages under the federal rule. The court stated that in order to establish reversible error, the appellant must identify the error to the trial court and suggest a legally appropriate course of action. The court observed that the reasons for this requirement go to the heart of the common law tradition and the adversary system. It affords an opportunity for correction and avoidance in the trial court in various ways: it gives the adversary the opportunity either to avoid the challenged action or to present a reasoned defense of the trial court's action; and it provides the trial court with the alternative of altering or modifying a decision or of ordering a more fully developed record for review.

Fed. R. Civ. P.
46

The court pointed out that the philosophy behind the requirement is embodied in Federal Rule of Civil Procedure 46, which requires that a party make known to the trial court the action it requests or opposes and give the reasons therefore.

While recognizing the common-law tradition behind the general rule, this approach justifies the rule against considering new issues on appeal in terms of "correction and avoidance" by either the adversary or the trial court. The rationale is that if the party who objects to the trial court's action is forced to state its objection and to offer an alternative, the adversary or the trial court or both can decide whether to agree with the objecting party, offer a third alternative, or set out in the record the factual or legal basis for the trial court's action. If the adversary or the court accepts the objecting party's proposal, there is no error insofar as that party is concerned and thus no basis for appeal. If the adversary or the trial court follows a course of action that differs both from the action originally objected to and the objecting party's alternative proposal, the objecting party may be satisfied and once again not pursue an appeal. If the trial court proceeds as originally planned notwithstanding the objection, both the adversary and the trial court can ensure that the record supports the factual and legal basis for the action, thus making it easier for the adversary to defend the action on appeal and less likely that the appellate court will find the trial court's action reversible error.

1. HISTORICAL DEVELOPMENT

SUNDERLAND, IMPROVEMENT OF APPELLATE PROCEDURE

26 Iowa L. Rev. 3, 7–12 (1940).*

One of the most extensive fields of legal procedure is that which deals with appellate review. No part of the law is more deeply incrusted with the relics of ancient customs and institutions. None has been more completely removed from the influence of lay opinion, and consequently none has been more highly technical. It is a field which abounds in rationalized explanations for unnecessary processes and useless restrictions, and it is possibly for that reason that appellate practice is in so chaotic a condition in the United States. The subject of Appeal and Error occupies more space in *Corpus Juris* than any other except Corporations.
* * *

When we look at the remedies offered by our system of appeals, we are immediately struck by the survival of one of the most irrational features of the ancient common law—namely, the proceeding in error. The Iowa Code, for example, provides that upon appeal in ordinary actions the court shall hear and try the case only on the legal errors

* Copyright © 1940, University of Iowa (Iowa Law Review). Reprinted by permission. All rights reserved.

law v. equity

presented, while in equitable actions the supreme court shall try the case anew.

There was nothing known to the common law which was, or could properly be called, a true appeal from one court to another, and this was so in England until the Judicature Act of 1873. All questions of fact were decided by juries, and a review of the facts could be had by what was called the attaint. This was the common-law predecessor of the new trial, but it took place before a superior jury of twenty-four who reviewed the action of the twelve. It was primarily a proceeding against the jury rather than against the verdict. The attainted jury was punished by imprisonment and fined for its false verdict, although the false verdict was at the same time, and as a useful incident, replaced by the true verdict of the higher jury.

Questions of law, on the other hand, were decided by the judges, and a proceeding very much like the attaint was developed to reach false judgments. In the 1200's complaints against judgments took the form of semi-criminal proceedings against the judges, and Holdsworth tells us that even to the present day the writ of error is deemed to commence a new suit for no better reason than because six hundred years ago it really was a new proceeding directed against the judge and was based upon a new cause of action arising out of the wrongful act committed by him in rendering his false judgment. To this day, also, we employ formal assignments of error because six hundred years ago the judge was held to be entitled to know what were the charges against him, and the assignments of error are still regarded in many of our states as the appellant's pleading in the court of errors, just as they were regarded six hundred years ago.

formal assignments of labor

The amazing thing about the common-law proceeding in error was that it did not operate as a review of the merits of the judgment. The question never arose as to whether the judgment was just or unjust, nor did the proceeding ever involve an inquiry as to what the true judgment ought to be. The sole question was, Did the judge commit an error? Such error might be great or small, its consequences might be serious or trifling, but an error was an error and the judgment must fall. The persistence with which the scope of judicial review in common-law actions was confined to the identification of errors was due to the institution of trial by jury. Errors brought up by bills of exception did not immediately control the judgment, but only affected the minds of the jury. The extent and character of that influence could not, however, be shown to the reviewing court. They could tell if an error had been made in admitting or excluding evidence or in any other matter involved in the trial before the jury, but they could not be sure what effect it may have had upon the verdict. In such a situation there was nothing to do but send the case back for a new trial, so that another verdict could be obtained free from the error which had vitiated the first one. The remand of cases for new trials was therefore a necessary incident in the use of juries. As long as the jury had the exclusive right to weigh the evidence and find the facts, no error which was related in any material

trial by jury

respect to either of those functions could be cured in any other way. The judges of the higher court could not undertake to adjust the verdict so as to eliminate the error, without depriving the parties of their right to trial by jury. * * *

The Continental notion of a unified tribunal, capable of dealing at the same time with the law and the facts, was adopted in England in the courts of chancery, so that in reviewing equity cases there was no need for resorting to the clumsy and ineffective procedure in error. If the upper court had the power to determine the merits of the case, it became less important to know whether an error had been committed than to know how it could be rectified. In a proceeding in error the entire aim of the review was to affirm or deny the existence of the error; in a true appeal that problem became merely preliminary to the really basic question of what the right decree should be. The appeal in equity, however, fell short of being a true rehearing, for new questions could not be considered. This was doubtless due to the tenacious influence of the concept of a proceeding in error, which contemplated as a sole function of an appellate court the review of matters already passed upon below.

2 restrictions on the scope of review →

There were thus two distinct restrictions on the scope of review, one excluding the presentation of new evidence or of new points not raised below, which applied both to appeals in equity and to proceedings in error at law; the other prohibiting the review of facts, which applied only to proceedings in error. As far as the rules of practice, both at law and in equity, excluded new evidence or the raising of new points in the appellate court, this was a mere survival of the ancient common-law theory of an accusation against the judge. It was an inherited tradition and nothing more. It was often defended on the ground that it would be unfair to the trial judge to reverse his judgment on a point which had never been brought to his attention. This was based on the medieval theory that the judge was interested in the review as the real defendant in the accusation of error. It entirely overlooked the immensely greater interest which the appellant had in obtaining a correct judgment, and it ignored the interest of the state in the just and effective operation of its courts. The rule was often defended on the ground that it would be unfair to the appellee to raise new points against him in the appellate court, but this was obviously an excuse and not a reason, for the restriction was administered as an inflexible rule of jurisdiction and not as a rule of convenience subject to special circumstances.

As far, on the other hand, as the rules of practice in law cases prohibited the review of matters of fact and prevented the adjustment of the judgment on account of errors which might have affected the opinions of the jury, they rested, not on traditional practice merely, but upon the institution of the civil jury. When waiver of juries in common-law actions was authorized in England by statute in 1854, the way should have been open for the review of facts in cases tried without a jury, but so insidious was the power of inherited tradition that the very act which authorized the waiver provided that the finding of the judge in an action at law unlike his finding in an action in equity, should have the same effect as the verdict of a jury, thus destroying the possibility of a true appeal.

The Judicature Act finally emancipated the English courts from this irrational limitation upon the effectiveness of an appeal in law actions, and English appellate courts now review questions of fact as freely in law actions where no jury is employed as in suits in equity, and they show no hesitancy in considering new questions or even of admitting new evidence, as long as the parties are protected from prejudice and the ends of justice are served.

The United States unfortunately inherited the proceeding in error as it came down from the Middle Ages, with its dual restriction against reviewing facts and raising new points on appeal, and these ancient doctrines still persist in many of our states. * * *

This narrow conception of the function of a court of review in an action at law has frequently been held to have the compulsory sanction of those constitutions which grant only appellate power to their highest courts. It is said that such power can be exercised only as to matters which have already been passed upon, and if new points were to be considered, that would be the exercise of original jurisdiction. But the argument begs the question. What, it may be asked, is being reviewed? The judgment or the rulings which became merged in it? Obviously it is the judgment with which the appellant is dissatisfied, and the correctness of that judgment is equally under review whether new points or old points are being considered. The argument confuses appellate power with the manner of its exercise and would place upon modern courts a constitutional restriction against using any data for testing the justice of a judgment which was not available to courts of error in the Middle Ages.

Notes and Questions

1. What are the historical reasons given by Professor Sunderland for the requirement that an issue must first be raised in the trial court before it can be raised on appeal? Are any of these reasons valid today?

2. What was the distinction between a writ of error and an appeal? Was there a difference in the scope of review under each? In reading the remainder of this chapter, note whether courts still recognize any difference.

3. While criminal proceedings present issues beyond the scope of the present Casebook, it bears noting that waivers of the right to appeal—in conjunction with plea bargains—present difficult issues with respect to administration of the justice system, particularly in connection with efforts by defendants to obtain review of sentences imposed after such a "waiver" is given. See generally Calhoun, Waiver of the Right to Appeal, 23 Hastings Const. L. Q. 127 (1995) and Hillier, Commentary by Federal Defenders on the August 1997 Proposed Amendment to F.R. Crim. P. 11(c), 11 Federal Sentencing Rptr. 48 (1998). General suggestions for counsel in criminal cases, including military justice proceedings, can be found in Ham, Making the Appellate Record, 2003 Army Lawyer 1 (2003).

2. MODERN JUSTIFICATIONS FOR THE RULE

The preceding readings explained the historical basis for the rule requiring that an issue must be raised in the trial court before it can be argued in the appellate court. The cases in this Chapter demonstrate the extent to which the rule is still prevalent and the exceptions to it.

PFEIFER v. JONES & LAUGHLIN STEEL CORP.

United States Court of Appeals, Third Circuit, 1982.
678 F.2d 453.

ALDISERT, CIRCUIT JUDGE.

Jones & Laughlin Steel Corporation appeals from a judgment in favor of plaintiff Howard E. Pfeifer in a third-party negligence action under the Longshoremen's and Harbor Workers' Compensation Act. The major question presented is whether the district court erred in applying the "total offset method" as a federal rule of damages, wherein the discount factor used to reduce future earnings to present worth is presumed offset by future inflation. We find no error and affirm.

Pfeifer was employed by appellant Jones & Laughlin (J & L) as a landing helper on its coal barges. On January 13, 1978, he slipped and fell because of ice and snow that had accumulated on the gunnel of a barge on which he was working. He struck a barge rail and landed on his tailbone, and a heavy electric motor that he was carrying fell in his lap. He has not returned to work since the accident. He has been examined by a number of physicians, several of whom testified at the trial, and he has undergone extensive physical therapy.

The district court found that appellant was negligent and that its negligence was the proximate cause of Pfeifer's accident and resulting injury. It determined further that Pfeifer was completely disabled from the date of the accident until July 1, 1979, and that thereafter he was capable of doing "light work" and lifting weights of up to twenty-five pounds, but that he could not work on the river. Appellant has not offered Pfeifer a job of any type since his injury, and the parties have not discussed the availability of a light duty position. * * *

In measuring damages, it declined to consider future wage increases or to discount the award to present value, citing Kaczkowski v. Bolubasz, 491 Pa. 561, 421 A.2d 1027 (1980). The court multiplied Pfeiffer's 1978 annual wage by his work life expectancy, deducted the amount of compensation Pfeiffer had received under LHWCA, and subtracted his projected earnings at minimum wage from July 1, 1979, until his sixty-fifth birthday, taking judicial notice that the federal minimum wage at the time of the accident was $2.90 per hour. * * *

Appellant * argues that the district court erred in its calculation of damages by applying the rule announced in Kaczkowski. It contends that damages in an LHWCA case must be computed according to a uniform federal standard; and that federal law requires that a lump sum award for lost future earnings be reduced to present value, a practice effectively

Fed. standard abolished by Kaczkowski

abolished in Pennsylvania by the decision in *Kaczkowski*. To meet this contention, we must explore the developing law of damages in state and federal decisions in light of controlling legal precepts and prevailing economic conditions.

But first we must make the preliminary determination of what precise aspect of the damage issue has been preserved for appeal. Our examination of the record persuades us that appellant has not preserved for review its contention that the court erred in applying Pennsylvania law because it felt obliged to apply state law, rather than federal law. It was the plaintiff's position at trial that federal law controlled damages and that inflation was a valid consideration under federal law. Appellant did not seem to challenge this position except to suggest that evidence of inflation had to be introduced by expert testimony and that future earnings had to be reduced to present worth:

preservation of appeal of damages

> MR. MURDOCH: We're here today under a Federal statute under Federal law and I don't think that the finding of the Pennsylvania Supreme Court in the recent case regarding not reducing damages to present worth is applicable in this particular case.

> THE COURT: We may have to have a little argument on that at some point.

> MR. MURDOCH: Yes, sir.

> MR. LIBENSON: Under Federal law, you can add inflation.

> MR. MURDOCH: If we have expert testimony.

> THE COURT: That's a little bit down the road and we'll wait on that.

Standing alone, the court's damages discussion in its opinion, id. at 492–93a, may be considered ambiguous; without more, it could be argued that the court was of the view that although this was a federal claim brought in a federal court in Pennsylvania it was required to apply the state law of damages. But when the opinion is read in conjunction with the earlier dialogue between the court and counsel, we are persuaded that the court applied federal law and that the dispute between the parties at trial was limited to the proper federal measure of damages. We conclude that appellant has preserved for review only the question of the proper elements in the federal law of damages under the circumstances of this case.[1] It is to this analysis that we now turn. * * *

Analylsis

The judgment of the district court will be affirmed.

---

1. For a reviewing court to determine that there is reversible error, three critical prerequisites must be implicated in the judicial error-correcting process. It is necessary that there be (a) specific acts or omissions by the trial court constituting legal error, (b) properly suggested as error to the trial court, and (c) if uncorrected on that level, then properly presented for review to the appellate court. For there to be *reversible* error, it is mandatory for the appellant properly to identify the error to the trial court and to suggest a legally appropriate course of action. The reasons for this requirement go to the heart of the common law tradition and the adversary * * *

Notes and Questions

1. What are the justifications given by the court for enforcing the general rule on raising issues in the trial court? Are they valid? Are they different from the historical reasons stated by Professor Sunderland? Should it make any difference that the issue was raised in the trial court in a motion for new trial rather than during the trial?

2. Does enforcement of the general rule interfere with the ability of the appellate court to do justice between the parties? Can enforcement of the rule ever be justified if it means that the person who should win on the merits does not? Does the answer depend on whose viewpoint the question is considered from, the appellant's, the appellee's, the trial court's or the appellate court's?

3. A detailed analysis of the requirements of one state is set forth in Allbee & Kincaid, Error Preservation in Civil Litigation: A Primer for the Iowa Practitioner, 35 Drake L. Rev. 1 (1985–86).

4. For "checklists" and various suggestions for the general process of preserving error for appeal, see Walbolt & Landy, Pointers on Preserving the Record, 25 Litigation 31 (Winter 1999); Zagel, What to Do When a Judge Makes a Mistake, 27 Litigation 3 (Fall 2000).

3. OBJECTIONS, CURATIVE INSTRUCTIONS, AND MISTRIAL MOTIONS

An aggrieved party's reaction to improper evidence, rulings or conduct may take three forms: (1) a timely, specific objection, (2) a request for an instruction to disregard, and (3) a motion for a mistrial. Each of these methods furthers the policies of preventing and correcting errors and conserving judicial resources, but in different ways and to varying degrees.

An objection serves as a preemptive measure. Because it informs the judge and opposing counsel of the potential for error, an objection conserves judicial resources by prompting the prevention of foreseeable, harmful events.

The other two methods of complaint are corrective measures. An instruction to disregard attempts to cure any harm or prejudice resulting from events that have already occurred. Where the prejudice is curable, an instruction eliminates the need for a mistrial, thereby conserving the resources associated with beginning the trial process anew. Like an instruction to disregard, a mistrial serves a corrective function. However, the class of events that require a mistrial is smaller than that for which a sustained objection or an instruction to disregard will suffice to prevent or correct the harm. A grant of a motion for mistrial should be reserved for those cases in which an objection could not have prevented, and an instruction to disregard could not cure, the prejudice stemming from an event at trial—i.e., where an instruction would not leave the jury in an acceptable state to continue the trial. Therefore, a mistrial conserves the resources that would be expended in completing the trial as well as those required for an appeal should a conviction occur.

Because the objection, the request for an instruction to the jury, and the motion for mistrial seek judicial remedies of decreasing desirability for events of decreasing frequency, the traditional and preferred procedure for a party to voice its complaint has been to seek them in sequence—that is, (1) to object when it is possible, (2) to request an instruction to disregard if the prejudicial event has occurred, and (3) to move for a mistrial if a party thinks an instruction to disregard was not sufficient. However, this normal sequence may not be essential to preserve complaints for appellate review. The essential requirement is a timely, specific request that the trial court refuses. See, e.g., Tex. R. APP. P. 33.1(a).

In most instances, an objection will prevent the occurrence of the prejudicial event, and the failure to make a timely, specific objection precludes appellate review. If an objectionable event occurs before a party could reasonably have foreseen it, the omission of objection will not prevent appellate review. The reasons are clear. It is not possible to make a timely objection to an unforeseeable occurrence, and an objection after an event occurs cannot fulfill the purpose of the objection, which is to prevent the occurrence of the event.

Similarly, the request for an instruction that the jury disregard an objectionable occurrence is essential only when the such an instruction could have had the desired effect, which is to enable the continuation of the trial by a impartial jury. The party who fails to request an instruction to disregard will have forfeited appellate review of that class of events that could have been "cured" by such an instruction. But if an instruction could not have had such an effect, the only suitable remedy is a mistrial, and a motion for a mistrial is the only essential prerequisite to presenting the issue on appeal.

Escalating Steps. In keeping with the fundamental principle that a contemporaneous objection is required at trial to properly preserve an error for appellate review, the proper course to be pursued when improper events take place at trial is normally to make an objection. The escalating steps are illustrated in the following dichotomy:

• an objection that is sustained followed by action or inaction of the trial judge as to a curative instruction; and

• an objection that is overruled.

Objection Sustained

In the first scenario, the cases are legion in holding that if an appellant objects and the objection is sustained but he does not move for a curative instruction or request a mistrial, he has received what he asked for and cannot be heard to complain on appeal. Thus when objection is timely made to improper remarks of opposing counsel, the judge should rule on the objection, give a curative charge to the jury, and instruct offending counsel to desist from improper remarks.

Where a curative instruction is given and the objecting party does not contemporaneously challenge the sufficiency of the corrective charge or move for mistrial, it is commonly held that no issue is preserved for review. Thus if a judge gives a curative charge, and initial objecting party is not satisfied with instruction, a further objection and request for further instruction should be made at that time; if objecting party fails to make this additional objection, asserted error is not preserved for review on appeal.

Objection Overruled

In the second scenario, a plethora of cases articulate the rule that once an objection has been overruled, it is not necessary to make a motion for mistrial or new trial to preserve an error for appellate review. As expressed by some courts, when the trial judge overrules a party's objections, it will be futile to move for a mistrial based upon the same objection. So long as the judge had an opportunity to rule on an issue, and did so, it is not incumbent upon counsel to harass the judge by parading the issue before him again by asking for a mistrial.

Moving Immediately for Mistrial. Many courts would hold that—faced with incurable harm—a party is entitled to move immediately for a mistrial and, if denied one, that the party will be heard on the issue upon appeal However, if a party's first action is to move for mistrial the scope of appellate review may well be limited to the question whether the trial court erred in not taking the most serious action of ending the trial; in other words, an event that could have been prevented by timely objection or cured by instruction to the jury will not lead an appellate court to reverse a judgment on an appeal by the party who did not request these lesser remedies in the trial court. Limited as this scope of appellate review may be, such an appellate review is available to such a party.

Mistrial is the appropriate remedy when the objectionable events are dramatic and incurable, such as emotionally inflammatory material so powerful that curative instructions are not likely to prevent the jury from being unfairly prejudiced against the party.

Notes and Questions

1. A party cannot use an objection which has been sustained as the basis for an appeal. Beverly Enterprises, Inc. v. Spragg, 695 N.E.2d 1019, 1022 (Ind. Ct. App. 1998). If a party believes that she has been prejudiced despite the trial court's favorable ruling on the objection, her remedy would have been to ask for an admonition to the jury, or for mistrial.

2. Where a party noted his objection to opposing counsel's opening statement remarks, and persisted in his objection despite the trial court's proposed remedy of giving a series of supposed curative instructions, continuing to object until cut-off by the trial judge, signaling the end of discussion on that issue at this trial, that was all that is required to preserve the issue for our consideration. Lai v. Sagle, 373 Md. 306, 818 A.2d 237 (Md. App. 2003).

3. In Howard v. State of Mississippi, 853 So.2d 781 (2003) on appeal of a capital murder conviction and death sentence, the Mississippi Supreme

Court said: "Howard contends that the trial judge made improper facial expressions of disbelief and disapproval during defense counsel's opening statement and closing argument. No objection was made by either Howard or his two attorneys nor is there any indication whatsoever in the record to indicate as much. This assignment of error is without merit." See Annotation, Gestures, Facial Expressions, or Other Nonverbal Communications of Trial Judge in Criminal Case as Ground for Relief, 45 A.L.R.5th 531 (1997).

4.   While it is not uncommon for an aggrieved party to object at the trial level, and move for a jury instruction in an effort to remedy an objectionable event, it has been held in some jurisdictions that a party may move for a mistrial immediately upon the happening of some forms of objectionable events, at least where the misconduct or other even is so dramatic that a curative instruction from the trial court would not have been able to salvage the situation in any event. Young v. The State of Texas, 137 S.W.3d 65 (Tex. Ct. Crim. App. 2004).

5.   In Kaplan v. O'Kane, 2003 Pa. Super 402, 835 A.2d 735 (Pa. Super. 2003), it was held that delaying a motion for mistrial from the time of the objectionable event to a post-trial motion waived the error in a civil case. Reviewing case law, the court noted that while the waiver principle was harsh, however difficult some strategic decisions are for trial counsel, a party is bound by his or her counsel's actions and if an issue is waived on strategic grounds or by inadvertence, it is waived. Failure to preserve an issue on appeal "will be excused when a strong, public interest outweighs the need to protect the judicial system from improperly preserved issues," particularly in criminal cases. However, such an exception does not apply to "fairly routine civil cases".

6.   A similar result followed in Urrutia v. Jewell, 257 Ga.App. 869, 572 S.E.2d 405 (Ga. App. 2002), where an investor sued a business associate and others alleging material misrepresentation, fraud, and diversion of funds. Plaintiff's counsel characterized defendant as "a convicted perjurer." Defendant objected, and moved for a mistrial. After denying the motion, the trial court crafted an instruction to restrict the purpose for which the jury could consider the defendant's prior convictions:

> Now, there were statements made by [plaintiff's counsel] in his opening about Mr. Urrutia being convicted of perjury. The documents do not indicate that he has been convicted or pled guilty to the offense of perjury, and I'm going to strike that from the evidence. You should not consider that statement or any other statements about Mr. Urrutia having previously been convicted of perjury.

After the curative instruction, however, the defendant failed to object or renew his motion for mistrial. This inaction resulted in waiver of the issue.

7.   Bowers v. Watkins Carolina Express, Inc., 259 S.C. 371, 376, 192 S.E.2d 190 (1972) held that where motions for mistrial or new trial would be futile they are not necessary to preserve a timely objection for review. By the same logic it would be both futile and nonsensical for counsel to request curative instructions from a trial court which has already ruled an argument to be proper.

8.   Where, in closing argument, opposing counsel makes an objectionable and prejudicial statement, some jurisdictions require the aggrieved party to seek an admonishment of opposing counsel by the court. In those jurisdictions, not only must a party object to alleged misconduct, he or she must also request an appropriate remedy, often an admonishment. However, if counsel is not satisfied with the admonishment or it is obvious that the admonishment will not be sufficient to cure the error, counsel may then move for a mistrial. Jackson v. State of Indiana, 758 N.E.2d 1030 (Ind. App. 2001).

9.   When the trial court sustains an objection and instructs the jury to disregard but denies a motion for a mistrial, the issue is whether the trial court erred in denying the mistrial. Its resolution depends on whether the court's instruction to disregard cured the prejudicial effect, if any, of the improper material. Generally, an instruction to disregard impermissible argument cures any prejudicial effect. In assessing the curative effect of the court's instruction to disregard, the correct inquiry is whether, in light of the record as a whole, the argument was extreme, manifestly improper, injected new and harmful facts into the case, or violated a mandatory statutory provision and was thus so inflammatory that the instruction to disregard was ineffective. If the instruction cured any prejudicial effect caused by the improper argument, a reviewing court should find that the trial court did not err. Only if the reviewing court determines the instruction was ineffective does the court go on to determine whether, in light of the record as a whole, the argument had a substantial and injurious effect or influence on the jury's verdict. See Faulkner v. State, 940 S.W.2d 308, 312 (Tex. App. 1997).

10.   In some states, objecting (sustained) and moving for a mistrial will not preserve the issue for appeal, if counsel have not also moved for a curative instruction. See Horn v. State, 2004 WL 726783 (Tex. App. 2004).

4.   OBJECTIONS AND "EXCEPTIONS"

KONCHESKY v. S.J. GROVES AND SONS CO.

Supreme Court of Appeals of West Virginia, 1964.
148 W.Va. 411, 135 S.E.2d 299.

BERRY, JUDGE.

This action was instituted in the Circuit Court of Monongalia County by the plaintiffs, Joe Konchesky and Anna Konchesky, against S.J. Groves and Sons, Inc., a Corporation, and two other defendants, to recover damages to property owned by the plaintiffs, alleged to have been caused as the result of blasting operations at the Morgantown Airport in Monongalia County, West Virginia, in an area known as "the Mileground", located near the City of Morgantown. The buildings owned by the plaintiffs were located quite some distance from the airport and the damage in question was allegedly caused by vibration as a result of the blasting. * * *

The case proceeded to trial against the defendant Groves and at the completion of the plaintiffs' evidence upon motion of the defendant for a directed verdict, which was resisted by the plaintiffs, the trial court sustained said motion and the jury returned a verdict in favor of the defendant and judgment was entered thereon September 29, 1962. The order recording the directed verdict and the judgment did not contain specific objection by the plaintiff to such action by the court, although the record indicates that said order was entered on the same day after the attorney for the plaintiffs resisted the motion. This argument, which is contained in the record, clearly indicates objection on behalf of the plaintiffs as to the granting thereof. * * *

The trial court directed the verdict to be returned in favor of the defendant because damages had not been properly proved by the plaintiffs during the trial so as to warrant recovery.

The errors assigned in this Court by the appellants, the plaintiffs below, can be consolidated into one assignment, that is, that the trial court erred in directing a verdict in favor of the defendant on the grounds that it was contrary to the law and evidence. The appellee, defendant below, cross assigned error in this Court asserting that the appeal was improvidently granted because of the failure of the plaintiffs below to request that a specific objection be inserted in the final order of September 29, 1962, wherein judgment was entered against them.

It will be necessary to consider the cross assignment of error by the appellee first, because if it prevails it would then be necessary to dismiss the appeal as improvidently awarded, and the assignment of error by the appellants would not be reached.

It is true that it has always been necessary for a party to object or except in some manner to the ruling of a trial court, in order to give said court an opportunity to rule on such objection before this Court will consider such matter on appeal. * * *

This matter is now governed by *Rule* 46 of the West Virginia Rules of Civil Procedure, which reads as follows:

"Formal exceptions to rulings or orders of the court are unnecessary; but for all purposes for which an exception has heretofore been necessary it is sufficient that a party at the time the ruling or order of the court is made or sought, makes known to the court the action which he desires the court to take or his objection to the action of the court and his grounds therefor; and, if a party has no opportunity to object to a ruling or order at the time it is made, the absence of an objection does not thereafter prejudice him."

It will be noted that this Rule clearly shows that formal exceptions are unnecessary, but parties must still make it clear that they object to the ruling or order of the court in order to preserve such matter for appeal. Exceptions to the action of the trial court may now be made by the parties under this Rule by making it known to the court the action which is desired of the court or by an objection being made to the action taken by the court and the grounds therefor; and, if a party has no opportunity to object to the ruling or order at the time it is made, the absence of an objection is not prejudicial on appeal. Rule 46 of the West Virginia Rules of Civil Procedure is in the identical language as Rule 46 of the Federal Rules of Civil Procedure governing such matters, and the authorities construing Federal Rule 46 hold that although exceptions are unnecessary by this Rule, it is still necessary for objections to be made.

However, this Rule provides that it is sufficient if a party against whom a ruling is made opposes the action taken by the court at the time and indicates the action which he desires, or, if such party did not have an opportunity to object at the time any ruling or order was made by the trial court on a motion of the opposing party, no objection or exception is required, and an appellate court may consider the alleged error even though no formal objection or exception was made or taken. Hasselbrink v. Speelman, 6 Cir., 246 F.2d 34. Of course, the safest procedure to avoid the argument that has arisen in this case is to insist upon an unmistakable objection or exception on behalf of the losing party to be placed in every order deciding a point on which the parties have disagreed if such party has the opportunity to do so.

It will therefore be seen that under the circumstances involved in the case at bar, wherein the record clearly indicates that a full discussion on the motion to direct a verdict was had in which the attorney for the appellants, plaintiffs below, stated his grounds in objection to said motion and to the ruling of the court in sustaining said motion, there was no necessity for a formal objection to be contained in the order of the court sustaining the motion and rendering judgment on the verdict directed by the court. Under this interpretation of the Rule in question, which is supported by the authorities construing the Federal Rule and which is in the same language and copied into the West Virginia Rule, it is considered that an objection had been made and the court had an opportunity to make a correct ruling on the legal question involved, and the reason for such objections to be made, as indicated in the prior decided cases relative to such matters, is preserved. For these reasons, the cross assignment of error by the appellee, defendant below, is not well taken and the appeal was properly granted.

Affirmed.

Notes and Questions

1. Does the court distinguish between an objection and an exception? What is an exception? A bill of exceptions? See. R. Martineau, Modern Appellate Practice: Federal and State Civil Appeals § 3.17 (1983). Almost all states today have abolished the requirement to except to the rulings of a trial judge. See, e.g., Ohio Civil Rule 46: "Exceptions unnecessary. An exception at any stage or step of the case or matter is unnecessary to lay a foundation for review whenever a matter has been called to the attention of the court by objection, motion, or otherwise and the court has ruled thereon."

2.   An exception in addition to an original objection is still required in some states. In Ralph v. Ohio Casualty Ins. Co., 320 Pa.Super. 262, 467 A.2d 29 (1983) the plaintiff appealed without first filing exceptions in the trial court. The appellate court refused to consider the issues raised, citing its own prior decisions holding that a party who wishes to preserve issues for appellate review must file exceptions to the trial court's decision and have the exceptions passed on by the trial court *en banc*. See also Commonwealth v. Fisher, 545 Pa. 233, 681 A.2d 130 (1996)(declining review of issues not excepted to at the trial court level). What purpose is served by requiring an exception in addition to the original objection? Is there any difference between requiring an exception and a new trial motion?

3.   Is waiver for lack of specificity a two-way street? In State Ex Rel. McLeod v. C & L Corp., Inc., 280 S.C. 519, 313 S.E.2d 334 (1984), the appellant filed 149 exceptions, to which the appellee lodged a blanket objection. One of the exceptions was vague and failed to put the court and parties on notice, but the court stated that the appellee's failure to object specifically to it allowed appellant to have it considered on appeal. The court complained that the failure to object to the exception was "flagrant" and burdened the court just as much as the improper exception.

4.   What if the trial court itself compounds the procedural error? In Storti v. Minnesota Mutual Life Ins. Co., 331 Pa.Super. 26, 479 A.2d 1061 (1984), the order from which the appeal was taken failed to contain, among other things, language suggesting that exceptions must be filed to preserve the right to appeal. Under the circumstances the court excused the appellant's failure to file exceptions. Assuming the order's other deficiencies were minor, would it have been the attorney's responsibility to know and comply with the rules concerning exceptions whatever the order said or failed to say?

5.   A good overview of strategies for preserving error in civil cases is found in Bennett, Preserving Issues for Appeal: How to Make a Record at Trial, 1997 Trial Lawyer's Guide 1 (1997). Judicial perspectives on the preservation of error are illustrated in Tacha, How to Try a Case in Order to Effectively Appeal, 31 N. Mex. L. Rev. 219 (2001).

SECTION B.   PRESERVING ERROR IN SPECIFIC STEPS OF THE LITIGATION PROCESS

Federal Rule of Evidence 103 requires a party opposing the admission of evidence to make a timely objection "stating the specific ground of objection, if the specific ground was not apparent from the context." Ordinarily, a district court's evidentiary determinations are reviewed under an abuse of discretion standard. Where a party fails to preserve an objection, the appellate courts review only for "plain error." See Rule 103(d).

Not only will sitting on one's hands waive all but plain error— failing to make the precise objection that suits the situation may also result in an ability to make arguments on appeal. See United States v.

Evans, 883 F.2d 496, 499 (6th Cir. 1989) (concluding that the plain error rule applies when a "party objects to [an evidentiary determination] on specific grounds in the trial court, but on appeal the party asserts new grounds challenging [that decision]"); United States v. Gomez–Norena, 908 F.2d 497, 500 (9th Cir. 1990) ("a party fails to preserve an evidentiary issue for appeal not only by failing to make a specific objection, but also by making the wrong objection.")

1. PRETRIAL MOTIONS IN LIMINE AND RENEWAL OF OB-
    JECTIONS

Motions in limine are generally used to ensure evenhanded and expeditious management of trials by eliminating evidence that is clearly inadmissible for any purpose. The court has the power to exclude evidence in limine only when evidence is clearly inadmissible on all potential grounds. Unless evidence meets this high standard, most courts hold that evidentiary rulings should be deferred until trial so that questions of foundation, relevancy and potential prejudice may be resolved in proper context.

Denial of a motion in limine does not necessarily mean that all evidence contemplated by the motion will be admitted at trial. Denial merely means that without the context of trial, the court is unable to determine whether the evidence in question should be excluded. The court will entertain objections on individual proffers as they arise at trial, even though the proffer falls within the scope of a denied motion in limine. Indeed, it was traditionally held that even if nothing unexpected happens at trial, the district judge is free, in the exercise of sound judicial discretion, to alter a previous in limine ruling.

WILSON v. WILLIAMS

United States Court of Appeals for the Seventh Circuit, 1999 (en banc).
182 F.3d 562.

Easterbrook, Circuit Judge.

We heard this case en banc to decide whether an objection at trial always is necessary after a pretrial ruling that evidence will be admitted. We conclude that a definitive ruling in limine preserves an issue for appellate review, without the need for later objection—but this is just a presumption, subject to variation by the trial judge, who may indicate that further consideration is in order. Moreover, issues about how the evidence is used, as opposed to yes-or-no questions about admissibility, frequently require attention at trial, so that failure to object means forfeiture. This latter principle determines the outcome of today's case.

Jackie Wilson alleges in this suit under 42 U.S.C. § 1983 that James Williams, a guard at the Cook County Jail, attacked him without provocation and inflicted serious injuries. Williams contends that Wilson was the aggressor and that the force used in defense was reasonable under the circumstances. The district court granted summary judgment to Williams, but we reversed and held that the conflicting stories must be presented to a jury. After a trial ended in a verdict for Williams, we reversed because of errors in the jury instructions. The second jury likewise sided with Williams, and this time the panel affirmed.

Two police officers stopped the car in which Jackie and his brother Andrew were riding. Andrew grabbed one officer's service revolver and shot both with it, killing them; Jackie, who stole the second officer's gun, is culpable as an accomplice under the felony-murder doctrine because the deaths occurred during the commission of another felony (not only the thefts of the guns but also a plan to use the guns in helping a friend break out of prison). Andrew was convicted of both murders, and Jackie of one. Both Wilsons are serving terms of life imprisonment without possibility of parole, and both filed § 1983 suits contending that they were beaten (in separate incidents) while in custody before their convictions. Andrew recovered a substantial judgment, Wilson v. Chicago, 120 F.3d 681 (7th Cir. 1997), though he had trouble receiving a fair trial because the defendants harped on the nature of the crime he had committed. See Wilson v. Chicago, 6 F.3d 1233 (7th Cir. 1993) (reversing an initial jury verdict in defendants' favor because the district judge failed to control inappropriate use of Andrew's criminal history).

Before the second trial of his civil suit began, Jackie Wilson asked the district judge to prevent Williams from informing the jury that he had been convicted of killing a police officer. Wilson recognized that his criminal history could be used to impeach him. Although the convictions could not be used automatically under Fed. R. Evid. 609(a)(1), he remained subject to impeachment if application of Fed. R. Evid. 403 made it appropriate. Cf. Fed. R. Evid. 609(a)(2); Green v. Bock Laundry Machine Co., 490 U.S. 504, 104 L. Ed. 2d 557, 109 S. Ct. 1981 (1989). Wilson's crimes called into question his willingness to be an honest witness. His life sentence meant that the threat of a perjury prosecution could not deter him from lying, and his lack of assets meant that malicious prosecution or abuse-of-process litigation likewise held no terror for him. But Wilson sought to keep the identity of his crime from the jury's knowledge, lest the "cop killer" label inflame the jury against him. Old Chief v. United States, 519 U.S. 172, 136 L. Ed. 2d 574, 117 S. Ct. 644 (1997), shows that Wilson's was a reasonable request. Nonetheless, the judge denied the motion in limine, and when the trial began Wilson tried to make the best of his situation. His lawyer told the jury during his opening statement why Wilson was in custody and tried to use this to Wilson's advantage by arguing that Williams attacked Wilson because of the nature of Wilson's crime. Although Wilson's lawyer used the nature of the crime circumspectly, Williams's counsel had no reservations about the subject and invited the jury to rule against Wilson on emotional grounds. Practically the first words of counsel's opening statement were: I'd like to reintroduce the litigant, Jackie Wilson, cop killer, murdered a Chicago police officer who was on duty, Officer O'Brien. He also robbed Officer O'Brien. He was convicted of that. He also robbed Officer O'Brien's partner, Officer Fahey. He was also convicted of that. And, yes, that is the crime he was waiting trial on back in 1988 in the Cook County Jail. Throughout the trial, Williams's lawyer did not miss an opportunity to remind the jury that Wilson had committed a despicable offense, and therefore must be a despicable person who should not collect a dime. Defense counsel was not satisfied with a suggestion that the jury should consider the conviction in connection with Wilson's credibility as a witness. The nature of the crime colored the trial. "Cop killer" was the refrain; defense counsel was inflammatory throughout; neutral language such as "criminally accountable because he participated in a robbery during which his brother Andrew shot two men" did not pass counsel's lips.

Wilson did not object to defendant's telling the jury that he had been convicted of killing a police officer; by the time defense counsel stood up Wilson was hardly in a position to object, having provided that information himself. But he did argue on appeal that the judge should have granted the motion in limine and put the subject off limits to both sides. The majority of the panel concluded that failure to object at trial forfeited any opportunity to raise the issue on appeal; that the anticipatory use of the information affirmatively waived any entitlement to its exclusion; and that any error was harmless. The dissenting judge concluded that objection at trial was unnecessary, given the ruling in limine, and that the error was prejudicial. Although this may seem impossible, the court en banc concludes that both the majority and the dissent were fundamentally correct, and we affirm for a combination of the reasons given by both the majority and the dissent.

First in sequence is the question whether an objection at trial was necessary, given the district court's pretrial ruling that Williams would be allowed to inform the jury that Wilson had been convicted, not simply of murder, but of killing a police officer. As the panel recognized, this court's precedents are in conflict. On the one hand, United States v. York, 933 F.2d 1343, 1360 (7th Cir. 1991), holds that an objection at trial is necessary no matter how definitive the pretrial ruling may be. On the other hand, United States v. Madoch, 149 F.3d 596, 600 (7th Cir. 1998), holds that although conditional rulings require further action at trial, definitive ones do not. Most cases in this circuit reach a conclusion similar to that of *Madoch*. An amendment to Fed. R. Evid. 103 that would resolve this disagreement, and provide that objection at trial is not necessary if the pretrial ruling is definitive, is wending its way through the long process under the Rules Enabling Act. See 181 F.R.D. 133 (1998). As it stands, however, Rule 103 is silent on the subject; we must formulate our own approach rather than appeal to authority or decide whether the pending amendment is the best solution.

One good example of a conditional ruling is a judge's statement that, if a litigant testifies, then the adverse party will be entitled to cross-examine in such-and-such a way. Until the condition has been satisfied by the testimony, the ruling has no effect. It is impossible to determine on appeal whether the ruling made a difference unless the witness does testify and the unfavorable evidence is admitted; what is more, there is a risk that the witness did not plan to testify even if the ruling had been favorable, but sought only to create an issue for appeal. In circumstances like this, the litigant must satisfy the condition in order to present the claim on appeal. Luce v. United States, 469 U.S. 38, 83 L. Ed. 2d 443, 105 S. Ct. 460 (1984). Similarly, if the judge's pretrial ruling is tentative—if, for example, the judge says that certain evidence will be admitted unless it would be unduly prejudicial given the way the trial develops—then later events may lead to reconsideration, and the litigant adversely affected by the ruling must raise the subject later so that the judge may decide whether intervening events affect the ruling. An appeal in such a case without an objection at trial would bushwhack both the judge and the opponent. Objections alert the judge at critical junctures so that errors may be averted. When a judge has made a conditional, contingent, or tentative ruling, it remains possible to avert error by revisiting the subject.

Definitive rulings, however, do not invite reconsideration. When the judge makes a decision that does not depend on how the trial proceeds, then an objection will not serve the function of ensuring focused consideration at the time when decision is best made. A judge who rules definitively before trial sends the message that the right time has come and gone. An objection is unnecessary to prevent error, and it may do little other than slow down the trial. Sometimes an objection or offer of proof will alert the jury to the very thing that should be concealed. Suppose the judge had ruled that the identity of Wilson's victim was not to be brought out at trial. Would Williams have been required to do so anyway, letting the cat out of the bag, in order to preserve the claim of error for appeal? Motions in limine are designed to avoid the delay and occasional prejudice caused by objections and offers of proof at trial; they are more useful if they can serve these purposes, which they do only if objections (and offers of proof) can be foregone safely.

Treating a definitive ruling as sufficient to preserve the litigant's position for appeal also avoids laying a trap for unwary counselors. Many lawyers suppose that it is enough to raise an issue once and receive a definitive ruling. They may believe that raising the question again may annoy the judge. Rules of procedure should be as tolerant as is practical of lawyers' suppositions and omissions. When the function of an objection has been served via a motion and ruling before trial, requiring repetition at trial does little to advance the goals of vindicating rights and avoiding errors, but may create an opportunity for rights to be lost by inadvertence. Instead of laying snares, we adopt an approach that tolerates human failings. Lawyers can concentrate their mental energies on subjects that are more pressing or have yet to be dealt with, without the need to harp on issues that have been resolved.

Conclusive pretrial rulings on evidence serve another useful end: they permit the parties to adjust their trial strategy in light of the court's decisions. Wilson wanted to keep the occupation of his victim out of the case, but if this could not be accomplished he wanted to introduce the evidence himself, if only to draw its sting. Sensible adaptations could not be accomplished if Wilson had to wait until Williams offered the evidence, and then raise an objection, acting in the jury's eyes as if he had something to hide. Waiting, objecting, and only then trying to make something of the subject not only would divest Wilson of the initiative but also would deprive him of an alternative theory of the case.

Trial-time adaptations are benefits of pretrial rulings on evidence, so it follows that adaptations do not waive positions already staked out. Wilson did not surrender his objection by making the best he could of his situation after the judge's adverse ruling. See Judd v. Rodman, 105 F.3d 1339 (11th Cir. 1997). Although some courts have held that a litigant who loses an evidentiary ruling and then offers the evidence himself has waived any opportunity to complain about the decision in limine, see United States v. Williams, 939 F.2d 721, 723 (9th Cir. 1991); Gill v. Thomas, 83 F.3d 537, 540 (1st Cir. 1996), this approach gives up one of the principal benefits of the pretrial-ruling procedure, and we therefore do not follow it. Our conclusion that preemptive use of evidence does not waive an established objection is compatible with United States v. DePriest, 6 F.3d 1201, 1209 (7th Cir. 1993), which held that a defendant gives up his objection by making use of the evidence before the district judge renders a definitive ruling. Until a conditional or tentative decision has been made definitive, it is subject to reconsideration, and the party must preserve his position at trial. But once the ruling is definitive, the function of the objection requirement has been served, and both parties are entitled to formulate trial strategies that make the best use of the evidence that the judge has decided to admit or exclude. We overrule York to the extent it holds that an objection at trial is invariably required to preserve for appeal arguments that were fully presented to the district court before trial.

A vital qualification is implicit in this way of putting the conclusion. Only arguments that were actually presented to the district court before trial are preserved for appeal—and then only if the district judge came to a definitive conclusion. A judge who expresses a tentative or conditional ruling can by that step require the parties to raise the issue again at trial. District judges thus are fully in charge of the process; they can require or excuse further exchanges on a subject by the way they express their rulings. A judge would do well to explain in the decision proper (or in the final pretrial conference) whether the conclusion is definitive, and whether consideration at trial is required, appropriate, or forbidden; the majority of the panel sensibly pointed out advantages to such a procedure; but if the judge does not elaborate, then we assume that an apparently unconditional ruling is conclusive.

Even if the ruling is unconditional, however, it resolves only the arguments actually presented. That much is clear from Fed. R. Evid. 103(a)(1), which requires a litigant to state a specific ground for an objection to evidence; grounds not presented cannot be raised later, else both judge and adversary are sandbagged (and preventable errors occur). There's a corollary to this point: a pretrial objection to and ruling on a particular use of evidence does not preserve an objection to a different and inappropriate use. Thus if the judge decides before trial that particular evidence can be used for impeachment, then there is no need to object at trial to this use; but a completely different use of the evidence is not covered by the ruling, and therefore fresh attention at trial (prompted by an objection) is essential if the error prevention function of the contemporaneous objection rule is to be achieved.

This is where Wilson's appeal founders. The district judge, asked before trial to forbid all reference to the occupation of the murder victims, said no. This meant at a minimum that Wilson could be cross-examined about the conviction when he testified on his own behalf. It also implied that Williams could present the testimony of another guard, Officer Cavallone, that Wilson stated during a trip to the infirmary after the altercation: "You should have killed me when you had the chance. I already killed two Chicago police officers. My attorney is going to have a field day with this. I have no respect for the law. And the next thing we are going to do is take care of the blue shirts [guards] inside the jail." Williams offered this statement to corroborate his view that Wilson had a hostile and aggressive attitude, and either initiated the altercation or planned to invent a story for his attorney to have a "field day" with. Wilson denies saying any such thing to Cavallone, and he wanted the line "I already killed two Chicago police officers" redacted. The judge did not require this step. But beyond permitting Cavallone to testify to the full version of the statement, and permitting the use of the conviction to call Wilson's credibility as a witness into question, the ruling in limine did not sanction any particular use of evidence. In particular, the judge did not give Williams's counsel permission to introduce Wilson as a "cop killer," to describe the details of the crime, to seek sympathy for Wilson's victims, or to imply that people who commit heinous offenses are fair game in prison—all of which Williams's lawyer did, and without objection. The pretrial ruling did not say or imply that such uses (or misuses) of the evidence would be allowed. We reversed the verdict for defendants in the first trial of Andrew Wilson's § 1983 action precisely because defense counsel harped on the details of the murders and sought an emotional rather than reasoned evaluation of the facts. The defense strategy in Jackie Wilson's second trial was similar to that in Andrew Wilson's first—but the big difference is that Andrew Wilson's lawyers objected, and Jackie Wilson's did not. Misuse of evidence that has a proper use cannot be argued on appeal without a specific objection. See Fed. R. Evid. 103(a)(1).

A pretrial ruling is definitive only with respect to subjects it covers. Details of usage were not raised or resolved before trial. If the only problem were that Williams's counsel once said "cop killer" rather than a more neutral formulation, or repeated the statement when using the conviction for impeachment, we would be reluctant to say that objection has been forfeited. Misuse of evidence is a matter of degree, and litigants receive the benefit of the doubt in grey areas. But defense counsel strummed on "cop killer" as if it were a guitar rather than a bit of evidence; whatever line there was between proper and improper use was overstepped; objection never came, so forfeiture occurred and the plain-error standard governs. Fed. R. Evid. 103(d).

Plain error means an error that not only is clear in retrospect but also causes a miscarriage of justice. United States v. Olano, 507 U.S. 725, 736, 123 L. Ed. 2d 508, 113 S. Ct. 1770 (1993). Wilson has not persuaded us that justice miscarried in his trial because of the way Williams used Wilson's crime. Blatant efforts to manipulate jurors' emotions and persuade them to ignore the facts and instructions often backfire. Wilson may have withheld objection in the hope that jurors would deem that Williams had overplayed his hand. Moreover, Wilson might have thought that Williams's efforts to hammer away on the cop-killer theme showed animus, and thus made Wilson's accusation against Williams more credible. Wilson had a weak case on damages, and success on liability depended on the resolution of a credibility contest. How the balance of advantage from the overuse of the cop-killer theme plays out in such a trial is difficult to say. The effects are not so inevitably baleful to the truth-finding function of trial that the problem must be deemed "plain error."

At last, in what must appear to be an afterthought, we tackle the issue that has been preserved: whether the district judge should have ruled before trial that the nature of Wilson's crime is inadmissible. As the Supreme Court observed in Old Chief, the precise identity of a crime often creates a potential for prejudice that overwhelms its constructive value. Any legitimate use of the conviction by the defense would have been served by informing the jury that Wilson has been convicted of murder and sentenced to life imprisonment. The judge thus abused his discretion in denying the motion outright. But at oral argument before the court en banc, Wilson's lawyer disclaimed any contention that the district judge should have barred Cavallone from testifying that Wilson said "I already killed two Chicago police officers." With this statement in evidence, the district judge's error with respect to the Old Chief issue is harmless. Williams's harping on the subject, and his implication that "cop killers" are not entitled to damages when guards behave as vigilantes, could not be thought harmless, but the lack of objection means that the misuse of the evidence has not been preserved for appellate review. As a result, the judgment is affirmed.

MANION, CIRCUIT JUDGE, concurring in part, dissenting in part, and concurring in judgment.

I agree with the court that the judgment be affirmed. But I am concerned with the court's attempt to construct a rule distinguishing a definitive and a conditional ruling on a motion in limine. * * * The court concludes a motion in limine is definitive when the judge's ruling is not tentative and does not depend on a condition being satisfied. Inevitably this invites satellite litigation over whether a ruling is definitive or conditional.

A pre-trial motion in limine serves two valuable purposes. The first is to allow the court and the parties to argue evidentiary issues in detail, avoiding significant delay after a jury has been impaneled. Thereby, when the issue presents itself during trial, counsel need do no more than renew the motion in limine (or the objection thereto). If, as the trial evidence develops, the district court is of the same opinion as before trial, the judge merely has to incorporate his reasoning in denying (or granting) the motion in limine. This is neither time-consuming nor difficult. The second benefit of the motion is to alert the district court to evidentiary issues which are potentially prejudicial in their nature. Rule 103(c) of the Federal Rules of Evidence already recognizes this concern, and directs district courts to conduct proceedings "so as to prevent inadmissible evidence from being suggested to the jury by any means, such as making statements or offers of proof . . . in the hearing of the jury." A motion in limine allows counsel to apprise the district court of these potential issues, so that when (and if) they arise during the proceedings, the district court will be positioned to excuse the jury or call a sidebar if necessary. And if the factual basis of the motion in limine was accurate, and the judge sees no need to revisit the issue, the attorneys and court may simply incorporate the motion in limine material by reference, without alerting the jury to their substance. Or, if necessary, opposing counsel can make an offer of proof when the jury isn't present. Neither of these purposes are substantially advanced by the court's definitive/conditional test.

I also have concerns over how this court will be able to assess whether a definitive evidentiary ruling made in advance of trial would be sufficiently prejudicial to warrant reversal. When counsel on appeal argues that the case would have been tried in a completely different fashion but for an erroneous ruling on a motion in limine, will we have to envision an entirely different trial, and anticipate what the result would have been, in order to determine whether the error was harmless? One alternative, to grant an automatic reversal, would no doubt stop district courts from granting definitive motions in limine.

I echo the sentiments of Judge Diane P. Wood in concluding that even now, the prudent practice will be to renew all objections at trial, thus avoiding equivocation over whether the ruling in place will suffice. I also share the concerns of Judge Coffey regarding the practicality of this rule. Very little will change before the district courts, but I expect that this court will face appeals over whether a "definitive" ruling covered evidence entered without objection. I also question establishing a presumptive rule, that motions in limine are definitive, when most motions will fall under the conditional exception. In my view, the bright line rule always requiring an objection or offer of proof is the most efficient, most straightforward, and most fair rule that we can adopt.

DIANE P. WOOD, Circuit Judge, with whom RIPPLE, Circuit Judge, joins, dissenting in part.

While I agree with the en banc majority on the larger issues of law that this case presents, I am unable to concur with its finding that the errors that infected this trial do not require reversal. I therefore dissent from the disposition of Wilson's appeal.

At the outset, I wish to make clear the points on which I am entirely in agreement with the majority. First, I agree that in a case where the district judge has ruled on a motion in limine, further objection at trial is necessary if the ruling was in any sense conditional, but it is not necessary to the extent the ruling was definitive. Second, I also agree that, in applying this rule to definitive rulings, it is important to respect the limits of the ruling. If there is an expansion, modification, or other alteration in the predicate upon which the district court based its earlier definitive ruling, counsel must make a separate objection at trial to the altered use in order to preserve that new point on appeal. The boundary between what has been decided definitively and what is new will sometimes be difficult to discern, as Wilson's case illustrates. The court holds today that his lawyer's motion in limine preserved his right to appeal the district court's decision to allow into evidence the fact that his victim was a Chicago police officer, but it did not preserve his right to appeal defense counsel's incessant harping on that fact. In some cases, it may be difficult for counsel to know when permissible use is transformed into abusive misuse. Only case-by-case development will throw light on where that line lies, and prudent counsel should certainly err on the side of renewing objections at trial, lest the affected party forfeit valid arguments for appeal.

I also agree with the majority that a party faced with a definitive ruling on a motion in limine does not forfeit the right to object to evidence when she tries to make the best of a bad situation. Wilson's lawyer therefore had the right to introduce the fact that he was not only a convicted murderer, but a convicted murderer of a Chicago police officer. This also justified Wilson's effort to make strategic use of that damning information, by suggesting that the identity of his victim might have inspired Williams's allegedly unprovoked attack on him.

The place where I part company with the majority is in its application of these rules. To begin with, it is important to remember that there are two separate potential sources of reversible error in this case: the introduction of evidence concerning the victims of Wilson's crimes and the misuse of this evidence. With respect to the latter, because Wilson's failure to object to the improper use of the victim identity evidence led him to forfeit this point, the question is how his appeal fares under the plain error standard of review of Fed. R. Evid. 103(d). A review of this transcript leaves no doubt that the error is clear in retrospect, and I do not understand the majority to assert otherwise. That leaves the question whether this was an error that "seriously affected the fairness, integrity, or public reputation of judicial proceedings," and thereby caused a miscarriage of justice. See United States v. Olano, 507 U.S. 725, 736, 123 L. Ed. 2d 508, 113 S. Ct. 1770 (1993) (internal quotations deleted). In a brisk paragraph, the majority concludes that it did not, based solely on the fact that Wilson succeeded in finding a strategic use for the offensive information. Ante at 10. But this conclusion loses sight of the very point that lies behind the finding of forfeiture: far more was going on here than the simple act of making sure the jury knew what Wilson had done. Instead, defense counsel openly, repeatedly, and blatantly urged the jury to find against Wilson because of what lay in his past. The misuse of the evidence was so extreme and so pervasive that, even though Wilson forfeited his objection, I would find plain error and reverse on this ground.

The First Circuit has held: "Merely making an unsuccessful motion in limine to exclude evidence is insufficient to preserve a claim of error; the protesting party ordinarily must revivify his opposition at the time the evidence is offered." United States v. Joost, 133 F.3d 125, 129 (1st Cir. 1998). The Second Circuit, writing on the in limine issue, has stated: "When the district court denied [the defendant's] in limine motion to exclude all evidence of [the death of an individual to whom he sold heroin], it did not thereby relieve ... counsel of the obligation to object whenever specific inflammatory statements were made at trial." United States v. Birbal, 62 F.3d 456, 465 (2nd Cir. 1995). The Tenth Circuit has noted: "A party whose motion in limine has been overruled must nevertheless object when the error he sought to prevent by his motion occurs at trial." McEwen v. City of Norman, Okla., 926 F.2d 1539, 1544 (10th Cir. 1991). A number of other circuits have reached similar conclusions: " '[A] party whose motion in limine has been overruled must object when the error he sought to prevent with his motion is about to occur at trial.' " Hendrix v. Raybestos–Manhattan, Inc., 776 F.2d 1492, 1504 (11th Cir. 1985). See also Hale v. Firestone Tire & Rubber Co., 756 F.2d 1322, 1333 (8th Cir. 1985); Collins v. Wayne Corp., 621 F.2d 777, 785 (5th Cir. 1980) ("An objection is required to preserve error in the admission of testimony or the allowance of cross-examination even when a party has unsuccessfully moved in limine to suppress that testimony or cross-examination."). The confusion generally surrounding preservation of appeal rights with respect to motions in limine mandates that, absent clear authority in a given jurisdiction, counsel treat all rulings, no matter how couched, as preserved only through objection or offer of proof made at trial. Obviously, with respect to preliminary motions in limine, no other conclusion is possible. Michael H. Graham, Rulings on Admissibility of Evidence Outside the Hearing of the Jury—Motions in Limine, 17 Crim. L. Bull. 60, 68 (1981). See also Johnny K. Richardson, Comment, Use of Motions in Limine in Civil Proceedings, 45 Mo. L. Rev. 130, 138 (1980). The highly respected evidentiary commentator, Jack B. Weinstein, has stated: "If a party has raised an objection before trial by means of a motion in limine that the court has denied, most courts hold that the objection must be renewed at trial for the objection to be preserved for appeal." Weinstein's Federal Evidence § 103.11[2][b] at 103–16 (1997 ed.) (emphasis added). See also 1 Michael H. Graham, Handbook of Federal Evidence § 103.8 at 50 (4th ed. 1996) ("To preserve error for appeal, counsel most often will be required to and thus to be safe should either renew the objection or make an offer of proof at trial." (emphasis added)). Such actions on the part of trial counsel only serve to create a more complete and accurate record for the reviewing courts in our never-ending search for justice.

The author of the proposed majority en banc, without any reasoning, has cast aside York and refuses to recognize the extent of the broad based support the circuit courts' majority view expressed in York has received throughout the country and, on the other hand, attempts to bolster his argument by bootstrapping and pointing out that the Advisory Committee on the Rules of Evidence is currently amending Fed. R. Evid. 103 to provide that the renewal of the objection at trial is not necessary. This type of bolstering is of little value, for it is impossible to predict when or whether the Advisory Committee's proposals, if ever, will be approved by the United States Supreme Court and/or the U.S. Congress. On the other hand, if the suggested rule does become law, then this Circuit, along with the other six circuits which have endorsed and continue to follow the view adopted in York and have obviously found it most helpful in conducting well-orchestrated trials, will be free to adjust their decisions in the future. The rule-making process can often be derailed when the well-educated, reasoned minds of the Supreme Court weigh in, and what are predicted to be quick changes can be short-circuited.

The new majority opinion goes on to argue that attorneys may be hesitant to continue raising objections at trial for fear that they will "annoy the judge." I query the majority whether an attorney would similarly be "annoying" the judge when asking him to explain his ruling and whether it is "qualified" or "definitive"? In deference to the drafters of the amended rules, including those who may not have had the benefit of trial experience, even if Wilson's counsel had believed that the judge had issued a "definitive" in limine ruling, any qualified trial counsel would be well advised to ask the presiding judge for a clarification concerning whether he should restate his in limine motion prior to the introduction of evidence at trial. Repeating the objection gives the trial judge an opportunity to review his earlier ruling based upon the totality of the evidence received up to that point and flags it for the attention of the appellate tribunal. Furthermore, "counsel has a duty to object, and even at the risk of incurring the displeasure of the trial court, to insist upon his objection." United States v. Warner, 855 F.2d 372, 374 (7th Cir. 1988) (citation and internal quotations omitted). In fact, the same Committee that has recommended the change in the evidentiary rules even alludes to such a requirement in its commentary, in an attempt to protect itself: "the amendment imposes the obligation on counsel to clarify whether an in limine or other evidentiary ruling is definitive when there is doubt on that point." It is a shame that Wilson's counsel was not aware of his obligation to properly and timely object in this case—had he done so, a discussion of this issue would have been unnecessary.

———

Rule 103. Rulings on Evidence

(a) Effect of erroneous ruling. Error may not be predicated upon a ruling which admits or excludes evidence unless a substantial right of the party is affected, and

(1) Objection. In case the ruling is one admitting evidence, a timely objection or motion to strike appears of record, stating the specific ground of objection, if the specific ground was not apparent from the context; or

(2) Offer of proof. In case the ruling is one excluding evidence, the substance of the evidence was made known to the court by offer or was apparent from the context within which questions were asked.

Once the court makes a definitive ruling on the record admitting or excluding evidence, either at or before trial, a party need not renew an objection or offer of proof to preserve a claim of error for appeal.

(b) Record of offer and ruling. The court may add any other or further statement which shows the character of the evidence, the form in which it was offered, the objection made, and the ruling thereon. It may direct the making of an offer in question and answer form.

(c) Hearing of jury. In jury cases, proceedings shall be conducted, to the extent practicable, so as to prevent inadmissible evidence from being suggested to the jury by any means, such as making statements or offers of proof or asking questions in the hearing of the jury.

(d) Plain error. Nothing in this rule precludes taking notice of plain errors affecting substantial rights although they were not brought to the attention of the court.

Notes of Advisory Committee on 2000 amendments. The amendment applies to all rulings on evidence whether they occur at or before trial, including so-called "in limine" rulings. One of the most difficult questions arising from in limine and other evidentiary rulings is whether a losing party must renew an objection or offer of proof when the evidence is or would be offered at trial, in order to preserve a claim of error on appeal. Courts have taken differing approaches to this question. Some courts have held that a renewal at the time the evidence is to be offered at trial is always required. See, e.g., Collins v. Wayne Corp., 621 F.2d 777 (5th Cir. 1980). Some courts have taken a more flexible approach, holding that renewal is not required if the issue decided is one that (1) was fairly presented to the trial court for an initial ruling, (2) may be decided as a final matter before the evidence is actually offered, and (3) was ruled on definitively by the trial judge. See, e.g., Rosenfeld v. Basquiat, 78 F.3d 84 (2d Cir. 1996) (admissibility of former testimony under the Dead Man's Statute; renewal not required). Other courts have distinguished between objections to evidence, which must be renewed when evidence is offered, and offers of proof, which need not be renewed after a definitive determination is made that the evidence is inadmissible. See, e.g., Fusco v. General Motors Corp., 11

F.3d 259 (1st Cir. 1993). Another court, aware of this Committee's proposed amendment, has adopted its approach. Wilson v. Williams, 182 F.3d 562 (7th Cir. 1999) (en banc). Differing views on this question create uncertainty for litigants and unnecessary work for the appellate courts.

The amendment provides that a claim of error with respect to a definitive ruling is preserved for review when the party has otherwise satisfied the objection or offer of proof requirements of Rule 103(a). When the ruling is definitive, a renewed objection or offer of proof at the time the evidence is to be offered is more a formalism than a necessity. See Fed.R.Civ.P. 46 (formal exceptions unnecessary); Fed.R.Cr.P. 51 (same); United States v. Mejia–Alarcon, 995 F.2d 982, 986 (10th Cir. 1993) ("Requiring a party to renew an objection when the district court has issued a definitive ruling on a matter that can be fairly decided before trial would be in the nature of a formal exception and therefore unnecessary."). On the other hand, when the trial court appears to have reserved its ruling or to have indicated that the ruling is provisional, it makes sense to require the party to bring the issue to the court's attention subsequently. See, e.g., United States v. Vest, 116 F.3d 1179, 1188 (7th Cir. 1997) (where the trial court ruled in limine that testimony from defense witnesses could not be admitted, but allowed the defendant to seek leave at trial to call the witnesses should their testimony turn out to be relevant, the defendant's failure to seek such leave at trial meant that it was "too late to reopen the issue now on appeal"); United States v. Valenti, 60 F.3d 941 (2d Cir. 1995) (failure to proffer evidence at trial waives any claim of error where the trial judge had stated that he would reserve judgment on the in limine motion until he had heard the trial evidence).

The amendment imposes the obligation on counsel to clarify whether an in limine or other evidentiary ruling is definitive when there is doubt on that point. See, e.g., Walden v. Georgia–Pacific Corp., 126 F.3d 506, 520 (3d Cir. 1997) (although "the district court told plaintiffs' counsel not to reargue every ruling, it did not countermand its clear opening statement that all of its rulings were tentative, and counsel never requested clarification, as he might have done.").

Even where the court's ruling is definitive, nothing in the amendment prohibits the court from revisiting its decision when the evidence is to be offered. If the court changes its initial ruling, or if the opposing party violates the terms of the initial ruling, objection must be made when the evidence is offered to preserve the claim of error for appeal. The error, if any, in such a situation occurs only when the evidence is offered and admitted. United States Aviation Underwriters, Inc. v. Olympia Wings, Inc., 896 F.2d 949, 956 (5th Cir. 1990) ("objection is required to preserve error when an opponent, or the court itself violates a motion in limine that was granted"); United States v. Roenigk, 810 F.2d 809 (8th Cir. 1987) (claim of error was not preserved where the defendant failed to object at trial to secure the benefit of a favorable advance ruling).

A definitive advance ruling is reviewed in light of the facts and circumstances before the trial court at the time of the ruling. If the relevant facts and circumstances change materially after the advance ruling has been made, those facts and circumstances cannot be relied upon on appeal unless they have been brought to the attention of the trial court by way of a renewed, and timely, objection, offer of proof, or motion to strike. See Old Chief v. United States, 519 U.S. 172, 182, n. 6 (1997) ("It is important that a reviewing court evaluate the trial court's decision from its perspective when it had to rule and not indulge in review by hindsight."). Similarly, if the court decides in an advance ruling that proffered evidence is admissible subject to the eventual introduction by the proponent of a foundation for the evidence, and that foundation is never provided, the opponent cannot claim error based on the failure to establish the foundation unless the opponent calls that failure to the court's attention by a timely motion to strike or other suitable motion. See Huddleston v. United States, 485 U.S. 681, 690, n. 7 (1988) ("It is, of course, not the responsibility of the judge sua sponte to ensure that the foundation evidence is offered; the objector must move to strike the evidence if at the close of the trial the offeror has failed to satisfy the condition.").

Nothing in the amendment is intended to affect the provisions of Fed.R.Civ.P. 72(a) or 28 U.S.C. § 636(b)(1) pertaining to nondispositive pretrial rulings by magistrate judges in proceedings that are not before a magistrate judge by consent of the parties. Fed.R.Civ.P. 72(a) provides that a party who fails to file a written objection to a magistrate judge's nondispositive order within ten days of receiving a copy "may not thereafter assign as error a defect" in the order. 28 U.S.C. § 36(b)(1) provides that any party "may serve and file written objections to such proposed findings and recommendations as provided by rules of court" within ten days of receiving a copy of the order. Several courts have held that a party must comply with this statutory provision in order to preserve a claim of error. See, e.g., Wells v. Shriners Hospital, 109 F.3d 198, 200 (4th Cir. 1997)("[i]n this circuit, as in others, a party 'may' file objections within ten days or he may not, as he chooses, but he 'shall' do so if he wishes further consideration."). When Fed.R.Civ.P. 72(a) or 28 U.S.C. § 636(b)(1) is operative, its requirement must be satisfied in order for a party to preserve a claim of error on appeal, even where Evidence Rule 103(a) would not require a subsequent objection or offer of proof.

Nothing in the amendment is intended to affect the rule set forth in Luce v. United States, 469 U.S. 38 (1984), and its progeny. The amendment provides that an objection or offer of proof need not be renewed to preserve a claim of error with respect to a definitive pretrial ruling. Luce answers affirmatively a separate question: whether a criminal defendant must testify at trial in order to preserve a claim of error predicated upon a trial court's decision to admit the defendant's prior convictions for impeachment. The Luce principle has been extended by many lower courts to other situations. See United States v. DiMatteo, 759 F.2d 831

(11th Cir. 1985) (applying Luce where the defendant's witness would be impeached with evidence offered under Rule 608). See also United States v. Goldman, 41 F.3d 785, 788 (1st Cir. 1994) ("Although Luce involved impeachment by conviction under Rule 609, the reasons given by the Supreme Court for requiring the defendant to testify apply with full force to the kind of Rule 403 and 404 objections that are advanced by Goldman in this case."); Palmieri v. DeFaria, 88 F.3d 136 (2d Cir. 1996) (where the plaintiff decided to take an adverse judgment rather than challenge an advance ruling by putting on evidence at trial, the in limine ruling would not be reviewed on appeal); United States v. Ortiz, 857 F.2d 900 (2d Cir. 1988) (where uncharged misconduct is ruled admissible if the defendant pursues a certain defense, the defendant must actually pursue that defense at trial in order to preserve a claim of error on appeal); United States v. Bond, 87 F.3d 695 (5th Cir. 1996) (where the trial court rules in limine that the defendant would waive his fifth amendment privilege were he to testify, the defendant must take the stand and testify in order to challenge that ruling on appeal).

The amendment does not purport to answer whether a party who objects to evidence that the court finds admissible in a definitive ruling, and who then offers the evidence to "remove the sting" of its anticipated prejudicial effect, thereby waives the right to appeal the trial court's ruling. See, e.g., United States v. Fisher, 106 F.3d 622 (5th Cir. 1997) (where the trial judge ruled in limine that the government could use a prior conviction to impeach the defendant if he testified, the defendant did not waive his right to appeal by introducing the conviction on direct examination); Judd v. Rodman, 105 F.3d 1339 (11th Cir. 1997) (an objection made in limine is sufficient to preserve a claim of error when the movant, as a matter of trial strategy, presents the objectionable evidence herself on direct examination to minimize its prejudicial effect); Gill v. Thomas, 83 F.3d 537, 540 (1st Cir. 1996) ("by offering the misdemeanor evidence himself, Gill waived his opportunity to object and thus did not preserve the issue for appeal"); United States v. Williams, 939 F.2d 721 (9th Cir. 1991) (objection to impeachment evidence was waived where the defendant was impeached on direct examination).

Notes and Questions

1.   As set forth in F.R.Evid. 103 and the advisory commentary quoted above, in federal practice, a motion in limine, authoritatively decided, preserves the arguments that were advanced in limine, but not other arguments against admission of the same evidence. A case in point: a sexual harassment plaintiff moved in limine to exclude proof that while she worked on the subject premises she wore a tongue-ring and had other body piercings. She argued—pre-trial—that proof of the piercings was irrelevant and violated the prejudice provisions of Rule 403 of the Rules of Evidence. The court denied the motion, and the defense was allowed to offer evidence that plaintiff stuck out her tongue in a fashion the individual defendant understood to be sexually provocative. On appeal plaintiff argued that this evidence violated the sex victim's protective provisions of Rule 412 of the Rules of Evidence, being a comment upon her sexual character or tendencies. The

court held that the in limine motion relying on other evidentiary principles was not sufficient to preserve the argument that the tongue-ring evidence violated the rape/sexual assault "shield" provisions of Rule 412. See Ferencich v. Merritt, 79 Fed. Appx. 408 (10th Cir. 2003).

2. Under Fed. R. Crim. P. 12, a defendant must raise all "defenses and objections based on defects in the institution of the prosecution before trial." Fed. R. Crim. P. 12(b)(1). Failure to properly raise such an objection "shall constitute waiver thereof, but the court for cause shown may grant relief from the waiver." Fed. R. Crim. P. 12(f). In United States v. Pitt, 193 F.3d 751, 760 (3rd Cir. 1999), the court commented that "the necessity for the pretrial motion to dismiss is obvious unless the evidence supporting the claim of outrageous government conduct is not known to the defendant prior to trial." Several states have similar rules. See, e.g., Tex. Code Crim. Proc. Ann. Art. 1.14(b).

3. In Colgate–Palmolive Company v. The Procter & Gamble Company, (03 Civ. 9348 (LLS)) (S.D. N.Y. 2004) the trial judge explained the effect of his in limine rulings:

> These rulings on the parties' in limine motions are provisional and may be altered if the circumstances at trial differ from the context and impressions conveyed by the in limine briefs, or if I determine they are erroneous. Evidence excluded by these rulings may be relevant and admissible in contexts other than those considered on the in limine applications.

Given this form of ruling, what reliance can trial counsel place on an in limine motion disposition?

4. Where in limine motions to preclude proof are denied "without prejudice to renewing them at trial" and the opponent of such proof fails to either renew the motion in limine or make specific objections to the proof when it is offered at the trial itself, the objections are waived. See United States v. Funaro, 222 F.R.D. 41 (D. Conn. 2004).

5. While some states follow the federal approach to in limine motions, others hold that merely filing a motion in limine which is denied by the trial judge does not preserve any claim for appellate review unless the objector obtains "the express acquiescence of the trial court that an objection at trial was not necessary." See, e.g., McGowan v. State, 2003 WL 22928607 (Ala. 2003).

6. Consider the following trap. In a state jurisdiction where if a motion in limine is denied, the losing party need not renew objection when evidence is offered at trial to preserve the objection (see McClarity v. State, 234 Ga.App. 348, 506 S.E.2d 392 (1998)) criminal defense counsel moved to exclude proof that certain conduct in the case was "gang signals." After hearing argument, the trial court told defense counsel, "I'm not going to grant the motion in limine at this time.... If we get to the point it doesn't tie up, then we'll have to take it up at that point." When such "gang" proof was offered at trial, however, defendant did not object. On appeal it was held that "[b]ecause the trial court reserved ruling on the motion in limine, [defendant] was required to object when the evidence was offered in order to

preserve the issue for appellate review." See Squires v. State, 265 Ga.App. 673, 595 S.E.2d 547 (Ga. App. 2004).

7. In Anderson v. State of Arkansas, 354 Ark. 102, 118 S.W.3d 574 (2003) the Arkansas court reviewed a proceeding in which the trial judge *granted* a pretrial motion in limine holding that convictions more than ten years old could not be used for impeachment. At trial, however, older convictions were raised in questions by the adversary. The appellate court found appeal for this violation of the in limine motion "procedurally barred" because the party benefitted by the pretrial motion did not object and demand a ruling at the time of the questioning which violated the in limine ruling.

2. OBJECTIONS AT THE TRIAL

Trial counsel have the burden of preserving the record for appeal by objecting to the opponent's proof, and any other conduct of the participants, as well as making the trial court's rulings a part of the record. An appellate court cannot discharge its review function without a record of what transpired at trial. The party who wishes to assert that the judgment of the trial court should be reversed, i.e., the appellant or cross-appellant, has the burden of demonstrating on the record that an error occurred at trial. Because all litigants are potential appellants, the trial attorneys for all parties must be diligent in preserving the record of the trial court proceedings prior to the entry of the final trial court judgment.

A "general objection" to the proof will often be found inadequate to preserve the issue for appellate review. Appellate courts expect trial counsel to make specific and timely objections so that the trial judge can have an opportunity to address the issue in the first instance. Federal Rule of Evidence 103(a) provides that "[e]rror may not be predicated upon a ruling which ... excludes evidence unless a substantial right of the party is affected, and ... (2) ... the substance of the evidence was made known to the court by offer or was apparent from the context within which questions were asked."

Notes and Questions

1. It is the general rule that issues must be raised in lower courts in order to be preserved as potential grounds of decision in higher courts. This principle does not, however, demand the incantation of particular words. It only requires that the lower court be fairly put on notice as to the substance of the issue. See Nelson v. Adams USA, Inc., 529 U.S. 460, 120 S.Ct. 1579, 146 L.Ed.2d 530 (2000).

2. Specificity in making an objection is important. In People v. Gurule, 28 Cal.4th 557, 51 P.3d 224 (2002), the California Supreme Court considered a claim of prosecutorial misconduct by a prosecutor who made comments in opening statement disclosing to the jury that defendant had previously been convicted of murder. In the defense opening statement, a few minutes later, defendant's attorney said that the prosecutor's opening statement "almost sounds like a closing argument." On appeal, defendant argued that this

protest by defense counsel served as an objection and placed the trial court on notice that a curative admonition was necessary. The state Supreme Court disagreed, noting "in addition to coming well after the allegedly offending statement, defense counsel's comment was ambiguous and could not reasonably have indicated to the trial court that he was objecting to the prosecutor's earlier remark."

3.   While it creates perverse incentives, some states have the rule that litigants are not required to state the specific ground for an objection unless requested to do so by the trial court. See, e.g., Md. Rules 2–517; 3–517; 4–323. Under that forgiving aspect of the system, if a trial judge overrules an objection, all grounds for the objection may be raised on appeal. However, in such a system, if counsel state with particularity the grounds for an objection, either voluntarily or at the trial judge's request, the litigant may raise on appeal only those grounds actually presented to the trial judge. All other grounds for the objection, including those appearing for the first time in a party's appellate brief, are deemed waived. See Anderson v. Litzenberg, 115 Md.App. 549, 568–70, 694 A.2d 150, 159–60 (1997)(discussing at length the requirements for objections and preserving issues for appeal). Does this suggest that in such states counsel should make only generalized objections unless ordered by the trial court to be more specific?

4.   Where objected to testimony is cumulative of other testimony that has not been objected to, the error that occurred is harmless. United States v. Sotelo, 97 F.3d 782, 798 (5th Cir. 1996).

IN RE POWERS

Court of Civil Appeals of Alabama, 1988.
523 So.2d 1079.

PER CURIAM.

The circuit court adjudged the attorney to be in contempt of court and fined him $100. The attorney appeals to this court, contending that his conduct was insufficient to constitute contempt. We agree and reverse.

The attorney represented a party in a child custody action. His client was being cross-examined by opposing counsel concerning whether certain facts were introduced at a 1970's juvenile hearing. The attorney entered a hearsay objection to the testimony being elicited. The objection was overruled and the witness was allowed to answer. Opposing counsel asked another question along the same lines and another specific objection was entered and overruled. Specific objections were made and were overruled to a third question of a similar nature. After a fourth question on the subject and objections thereto, the court informed the attorney that he would allow the particular line of questioning and he could have continuing exceptions. The following dialogue transpired:

"MR. POWERS: Judge, I feel like to protect the record I have to make my objections.

"THE COURT: No, you don't. If the Court overrules and says you may have a continuing objection—

"MR. POWERS: If the Court rules that I cannot object—

"THE COURT: No. I'm just telling you we'll have a general objection and I'll overrule, and you'll have that tied to any question he asks regarding this affidavit. Now, that's the Court's ruling.

"THE COURT: I'm going to give you a general objection. Now, I've already explained that to you, and I'm going to give you a continuing exception to the Court's overruling your objection and you don't have to do it each time that he asks a question on cross examination regarding testimony in that juvenile court proceeding. You've opened the door and he's going into it.

"MR. POWERS: I object to it being received and I except to the characterization that it came in. And I state to the Court that the Supreme Court of this state has said in numerous cases that the Court cannot give a

general objection in cases, that it must be made to each individual question.

"THE COURT: Give me that citation on that so I'll have that knowledge.

"MR. POWERS: I don't have it with me, judge.

"THE COURT: Well, you will if you're going to continue to do it in spite of the Court's ruling. I want you to cite me some law so I can go by it.

"MR. POWERS: I can state to the Court that a party has a right to make an objection to any question that comes in, and it is the Court's duty to rule on it. And the Court cannot limit me in making my objection.

"THE COURT: You've got a true assertion of the law, in my opinion, but once we have a line of questions regarding a particular question, I can give you a general objection. The courts have never said, in my opinion, that I cannot.

"MR. POWERS: Judge, if you tell me that I cannot make an objection, then I'll obey the Court's ruling.

"THE COURT: I'm not going to make such a ridiculous ruling, Mr. Powers. I just said you have a general objection to those questions. I overruled and you have an exception.

"MR. POWERS: I've excepted to each question, Judge.

"THE COURT: Mr. Powers, I'm telling you one other time. It's the Court's belief that the law says I can give] you an objection, and if you can show me a law where I cannot do it, I will certainly abide by that law. But until you do, that will be the Court's ruling that he is cross examining this witness and you may have a general objection to each of those questions regarding the testimony in the juvenile court, and I'll overrule same and you may have your exception.

"And if you continue to go on I'll find you in contempt of court.

"MR. POWERS: Judge, may I say this? You have not ordered me not to make an objection. And if you order me not to make an objection to any question regarding that, then I won't do it. But until you tell me I can't do it, I have to keep on doing it. If you're telling me I can't I won't.

"THE COURT: I'm telling you what you have. You have a general objection to those questions, and you have my overruling to the objection and your exception. You have that as the Court's ruling in the record.

"So you shouldn't raise objections every time because I've already given you that.

"MR. POWERS: Judge, I'm not trying to be—if you're telling me I can't do it—

"THE COURT: I'm not going to tell you you can't do it, but I'll tell you if you continue on in spite of the Court's ruling, I will have to consider finding you in contempt of Court."

Thereafter, the attorney objected three times, raising the hearsay issue as to three questions on that subject. At the conclusion of the trial the court held the attorney in contempt of court and imposed a fine. The contempt order provided in part:

"The Court told Attorney Powers that he would have a continuing objection and exception to questions of this nature and it would not be necessary that he continue to interpose objection to each question of like nature.

"Attorney Powers stated to the Court that under the Court's decisions it would be necessary that he interpose objection to each question; that the Court could not grant a continuing ruling and exception.

"The Court stated to Attorney Powers that the Court was of the opinion that such continuing objection and ruling could be granted and if he had some law to the contrary, the Court would like to have same as the Court desired to abide by the law.

"The Court stated to Attorney Powers that without law to the contrary, if he continued to object to the same line of question which the Court had granted to him a continuing objection and exception that the Court would find him in contempt of Court.

"Such conduct of Attorney Powers obstructed the orderly procedure of the Court in the trial of the case."

The attorney contends that his conduct was not sufficient to sustain a contempt punishment pursuant to section 12–1–8(1), Code 1975. He asserts that his conduct was not disrespectful, insolent, discourteous, or calculated to impede the orderly progress of the proceeding.

We have not been cited to, and our extensive research has not located, any Alabama case which either permits or prohibits a trial court from authorizing continuing objections and exceptions to a line of questions upon the same subject although such a procedure is extensively, if not universally, utilized by the trial courts of this state. We approve that procedure and declare that, where the trial court indicates a continuing adverse ruling and grants to an attorney a continuous objection, which contains all grounds which he has previously interposed to the lead questions, the attorney is thereby relieved from making a formal objection after each future question concerning the same general train of factual material and, thereafter, the attorney can properly raise on appeal the propriety of the adverse ruling upon his specific "continuing objections" to those questions. The closest parallel decision which we located is Liberty National Life Insurance Co. v. Beasley, 466 So. 2d 935 (Ala. 1985), which decided that a party who suffers an adverse ruling on a motion in limine to exclude evidence is not required to object and to assign specific grounds to the introduction of the proffered evidence during the trial if he has obtained the express acquiescence of the trial court that such subsequent objection and assignment of grounds to evidence offered at trial are not necessary.

While we have made the law more definite concerning "continuing objections," we cannot find that the attorney's actions were sufficient to constitute contempt of court in view of the apparent lack of any prior case upon that subject. While his action constituted an error in judgment in this respect, it did not rise to the level of contemptuous conduct. An error in judgment without clear and convincing evidence of bad faith intent is insufficient for a finding of contempt. In re Carter, 412 So. 2d 811 (Ala. Civ. App. 1982). The record does not reveal that the attorney had such bad faith in this case.

Additionally and perhaps more importantly, while the trial court's order which adjudged the attorney to be in contempt of court recited that the trial court told the attorney that he could have a "continuing objection and exception" to questions, in actuality the record discloses that the trial court informed the attorney twice that he had a "continuing exception" and eight different times that he had a "general objection" to that line of questions. "A general objection to evidence is one which does not definitely and specifically state the ground upon which it is based so that the court may intelligently rule on it." C. Gamble, McElroy's Alabama Evidence '426.01(7) (3d ed. 1977). There is a great legal difference between authorizing an attorney's "continuing objections" to a line of questions and authorizing only "general objections" to such questions. A general objection ordinarily waives its appellate review while a specific objection is normally a condition precedent to appellate review. A general objection does not include the ground of hearsay and, without a specific objection as to hearsay, that ground cannot be reviewed on appeal. Donaldson v. State Department of Industrial Relations, 439 So. 2d 1301, 1304 (Ala. Civ. App. 1983). Therefore, the attorney could not have preserved the hearsay evidentiary issue as a ground of review under the grant by the trial court of only a "general objection" to him. The attorney interposed only specific objections, including hearsay, to the three questions which were objected to after the threat of contempt was made. He thereby maintained the record in such condition that appellate issues as to his specific objections could be raised and reviewed on appeal and the attorney should not have been adjudged to be in contempt of court for doing so. Under those circumstances, he had the absolute right and the professional duty to specifically object to the questions.

The adjudication that the attorney was in contempt of court and the fine imposed upon him are reversed and that judgment is hereby set aside by our holding that the attorney was not in contempt of court.

All the judges concur.

Notes and Questions

1. For a discussion of "continuing," "standing" or "running" objections—where a single ruling is "deemed" to reject an argument and where the objector is supposedly to be treated as having objected to any "similar" proof and the court is "deemed" to have overruled that objection, see Parker, Running Objections: A Practical Tool for Trial Lawyers, 58 Texas B. J. 668 (1995).

2. A "continuing objection" is an objection that is deemed to apply to later evidentiary stages that raise the same issue. The problem often becomes, therefore, defining the matter subject to the objection. Objecting to all references to "the meeting on January 12th" may be clear. Objection to any reference to "misleading statements" would not be.

3. Continuing objections serve only to obviate repeated objections to evidence admitted within the scope of the court's specific evidentiary ruling. See, e.g., United States v. Ladd, 885 F.2d 954, 958 (1st Cir. 1989) (party may argue violation of Rule 403 in appeal because it posited a continuing objection on the basis of that particular rule); United States v. Verrusio, 803 F.2d 885, 893 (7th Cir. 1986) (continuing objection on hearsay grounds would preserve appeal of admission of subsequent hearsay statements); United States v. Marshall, 762 F.2d 419, 425 (5th Cir. 1985) (overruling of timely specific objection amounted to continuing objection, thereby preserving error for "subsequent evidence admitted within the scope of the ruling"); United States v. Gillette, 189 F.2d 449, 453 (2d Cir.) (party may not rely on continuing objection lodged on one evidentiary ground to argue a different ground on appeal); see generally J. Strong, McCormick on Evidence, § 52, at 132 (implying that a continuing objection extends to all similar evidence subject to the same objection).

4. The purpose of a asking the trial court to grant a continuing objection is simply to provide the court with an opportunity and reason to reconsider its prior evidentiary ruling. The request signals both the importance and the number of items to which a particular evidentiary argument pertains. See Daskarolis v. Firestone Tire and Rubber Co., 651 F.2d 937, 940 (4th Cir. 1981). See also United States v. Rivera–Santiago, 872 F.2d 1073, 1083 (1st Cir.) (absent a continuing objection, parties can expect court to reconsider earlier ruling only by making repeated objections on same grounds). Cf. Squyres v. Hilliary, 599 F.2d 918, 921 (10th Cir. 1979) (continuing objection serves to warn court of future evidentiary problems).

5. Some states provide by rule for the process of a continuing objection. See, e.g., Maryland Rule 4–323(b), which provides:

(b) Continuing objections to evidence.—At the request of a party or on its own initiative, the court may grant a continuing objection to a line of questions by an opposing party. For purposes of review by the trial court or on appeal, the continuing objection is effective only as to the questions clearly within its scope.

6. "A continuing objection to 'all inadmissible evidence' is not an adequate method of preserving error for appeal. This is similar to what the defendant has attempted here. Although allowing continuing specific objections to preserve error may facilitate more orderly and efficient proceedings, the defendant here has attempted to impose a blanket objection to all spousal communications. This left to the trial court the task of thoroughly evaluating every question and answer to determine their evidentiary propriety. In other words, the defense counsel has, in effect, unloaded upon the trial court the responsibility of detecting inadmissible evidence and has circumvented his responsibility to articulate and adequately support specific objections. This is an abuse of the continuing objection which in this instance constitutes a waiver of the issue." Kindred v. State, 540 N.E.2d 1161 (Ind. 1989).

7. In Hogan v. State of Nebraska, 402 F.Supp. 812 (D. Neb. 1975) the trial court granted a continuing objection to various categories of testimony and exhibits. However, when a key exhibit was offered, defense counsel said "I have no objections to the Exhibit #3." In that situation it was later held that the trial court could conclude that counsel was waiving all objections, including the continuing objection.

8. Courts occasional caution that granting a "continuing objection" in advance of trial is risky business. In United States v. Fortenberry, 919 F.2d 923 (5th Cir. 1990) the court said: "[W]e are troubled that the continuing objection was granted at a pretrial hearing. In general, evidentiary rulings depend in large part on the context in which the evidence is offered. Granting a continuing objection to evidence before the trial begins, thus precluding a re-evaluation of admissibility in context, seems ill advised; and we strongly caution both the district courts against granting and counsel against accepting pretrial continuing objections."

9. Continuing objections are not appropriate to preserve claims that particular evidence is so prejudicial that its impermissible effect outweighs its probative value. See United States v. McVeigh, 153 F.3d 1166, 1199–1200 (10th Cir. 1998)(continuing objections generally are considered inappropriate for preserving error on appeal under Rule 403).

3. CLOSING ARGUMENT

Closing argument is often viewed as an opportunity for uninterrupted summation of the evidence and theories, and—traditionally—few objections were made during closing argument. Case law in recent decades has made it clear, however, that failure to object in a timely fashion to improper comments by the adversary counsel during closing argument is also a waiver of those objections. "Timely" objection may require interruption of the adversary's argument, though in some situations it is satisfactory to wait until the argument has ended, then approach the bench for a ruling and an instruction to the jury concerning the improper argument.

Notes and Questions

1. In the civil context, a motion for mistrial was timely when the motion was made after all four opening statements had been presented and the jury had been excused from the courtroom. See White v. Consol Freightways Corp. of Del., 766 So.2d 1228, 1233 (Fla. Ct. App. 2000). Under those facts, it was held that the purpose of the contemporaneous objection rule had been satisfied. Furthermore, by delaying the motion for mistrial until the jurors had left the courtroom, the appellants' counsel avoided further emphasis of the objectionable comments.

2. Objection to counsel's closing argument was timely when made after the opposing attorney completed the argument and the jury was excused, but jury instructions had not been given. Cole v. State of Florida, 866 So.2d 761 (Fla. App. 2004). A motion for mistrial made immediately following the closing argument while the jury was on recess and prior to the jury being given instructions and retiring for deliberations, satisfied the purpose of the contemporaneous objection rule.

3. In People v. Bell, 343 Ill.App.3d 110, 796 N.E.2d 1114 (2003) the intermediate appellate court noted that the Illinois procedures with respect to alleged prejudicial comments in opening statements and closing argument require the aggrieved party to object at trial and also make a specific objection in a written posttrial motion. Where there is no follow-up with a posttrial motion, the objector has forfeited objections to those statements.

4. JURY INSTRUCTIONS

A significant number of appeals relate to alleged errors in jury instructions. Alleged errors in jury instructions are perhaps the most fertile ground for finding reversible error in American law. Federal Rule of Civil Procedure 51 was amended in 2003 to take into account a large volume of case law on preservation of error claims with respect to instructions, and these doctrines are spelled out in the advisory commentary accompanying the rule:

FEDERAL RULE OF CIVIL PROCEDURE 51

Instructions to Jury; Objections; Preserving a Claim of Error

(a) Requests.

(1) A party may, at the close of the evidence or at an earlier reasonable time that the court directs, file and furnish to every other party written requests that the court instruct the jury on the law as set forth in the requests.

(2) After the close of the evidence, a party may:

(A) file requests for instructions on issues that could not reasonably have been anticipated at an earlier time for requests set under Rule 51(a)(1), and

(B) with the court's permission file untimely requests for instructions on any issue.

(b) Instructions. The court:

(1) must inform the parties of its proposed instructions and proposed action on the requests before instructing the jury and before final jury arguments;

(2) must give the parties an opportunity to object on the record and out of the jury's hearing to the proposed instructions and actions on requests before the instructions and arguments are delivered; and

(3) may instruct the jury at any time after trial begins and before the jury is discharged.

(c) Objections.

(1) A party who objects to an instruction or the failure to give an instruction must do so on the record, stating distinctly the matter objected to and the grounds of the objection.

(2) An objection is timely if:

(A) a party that has been informed of an instruction or action on a request before the jury is instructed and before final jury arguments, as provided by Rule 51(b)(1), objects at the opportunity for objection required by Rule 51(b)(2); or

(B) a party that has not been informed of an instruction or action on a request before the time for objection provided under Rule 51(b)(2) objects promptly after learning that the instruction or request will be, or has been, given or refused.

(d) Assigning Error; Plain Error.

(1) A party may assign as error:

(A) an error in an instruction actually given if that party made a proper objection under Rule 51(c), or

(B) a failure to give an instruction if that party made a proper request under Rule 51(a), and—unless the court made a definitive ruling on the record rejecting the request—also made a proper objection under Rule 51(c).

(2) A court may consider a plain error in the instructions affecting substantial rights that has not been preserved as required by Rule 51(d)(1)(A)or (B).

Notes of Advisory Committee on 2003 amendments. Rule 51 is revised to capture many of the interpretations that have emerged in practice. The revisions in text will make uniform the conclusions reached by a majority of decisions on each point. Additions also are made to cover some practices that cannot now be anchored in the text of Rule 51.

Scope. Rule 51 governs instructions to the trial jury on the law that governs the verdict. A variety of other instructions cannot practicably be brought within Rule 51. Among these instructions are preliminary instructions to a venire, and cautionary or limiting instructions delivered in immediate response to events at trial. * * *

Objections. Subdivision (c) states the right to object to an instruction or the failure to give an instruction. It carries forward the formula of present Rule 51 requiring that the objection state distinctly the matter objected to and the grounds of the objection, and makes explicit the requirement that the objection be made on the record. The provisions on the time to object make clear that it is timely to object promptly after learning of an instruction or action on a request when the court has not provided advance information as required by subdivision (b)(1). The need to repeat a request by way of objection is continued by new subdivision (d)(1)(B) except where the court made a definitive ruling on the record.

Preserving a claim of error and plain error. Many cases hold that a proper request for a jury instruction is not alone enough to preserve the right to appeal failure to give the instruction. The request must be renewed by objection. This doctrine is appropriate when the court may not have sufficiently focused on the request, or may believe that the request has been granted in substance although in different words. But this doctrine may also prove a trap for the unwary who fail to add an objection after the court has made it clear that the request has been considered and rejected on the merits. Subdivision (d)(1)(B) establishes authority to review the failure to grant a timely request, despite a failure to add an objection, when the court has made a definitive ruling on the record rejecting the request.

Many circuits have recognized that an error not preserved under Rule 51 may be reviewed in exceptional circumstances. The language adopted to capture these decisions in subdivision (d)(2) is borrowed from Criminal Rule 52.

Although the language is the same, the context of civil litigation often differs from the context of criminal prosecution; actual application of the plain-error standard takes account of the differences. The Supreme Court has summarized application of Criminal Rule 52 as involving four elements: (1) there must be an error; (2) the error must be plain; (3) the error must affect substantial rights; and (4) the error must seriously affect the fairness, integrity, or public reputation of judicial proceedings. Johnson v. U.S., 520 U.S. 461, 466–467, 469–470 [137 L.Ed.2d 718, 726–727, 728–729] (1997). (The Johnson case quoted the fourth element from its decision in a civil action, U.S. v. Atkinson, 297 U.S. 157, 160 [80 L.Ed. 555, 557] (1936): "In exceptional circumstances, especially in criminal cases, appellate courts, in the public interest, may, of their own motion, notice errors to which no exception has been taken, if the errors are obvious, or if they otherwise substantially affect the fairness, integrity, or public reputation of judicial proceedings.")

The court's duty to give correct jury instructions in a civil action is shaped by at least four factors.

The factor most directly implied by a "plain" error rule is the obviousness of the mistake.

The importance of the error is a second major factor.

The costs of correcting an error reflect a third factor that is affected by a variety of circumstances.

In a case that seems close to the fundamental error line, account also may be taken of the impact a verdict may have on nonparties.

ALLEN v. TONG

Court of Appeals of New Mexico, 2003.
133 N.M. 594, 66 P.3d 963.

SUTIN, JUDGE.

Plaintiff Phillip Allen, also known as Phillip Lindberg, appeals from an adverse jury verdict on his medical malpractice claims against Defendant Dr. Rolando M. Tong. Plaintiff asserts: the district court erred by refusing Plaintiff's tendered [version of a Uniform Jury Instruction "UJI"] and by submitting [an alternative] instruction that was prejudicially confusing and not in conformity with UJI requirements. * * * We affirm.

BACKGROUND

On September 29, 1994, Bobbi Lindberg (Lindberg) took her then fifteen-year-old son, Phillip (Plaintiff), to the emergency room at Rehobeth McKinley Hospital, because Plaintiff had a swollen, tender testicle, and he was in pain and vomiting. An emergency room physician, Dr. Beamsley, took Plaintiff's history, examined him, and took a Doppler reading of Plaintiff's pulse in both testicles. Dr. Beamsley called Defendant, who was the on-call surgeon, and described Plaintiff's condition. Dr. Beamsley told Defendant that he felt Plaintiff had testicular torsion and also stated that the condition was a surgical emergency.

Defendant received this call from Dr. Beamsley at about 6:40 a.m. After the call, Defendant took a shower, shaved, got dressed, and then went to the hospital. Defendant thought he arrived at the hospital before 8 a.m. Plaintiff contends Defendant did not arrive until about 9:20 a.m. It would usually take Defendant anywhere from two to five minutes to drive from his home to the hospital. When Defendant arrived at the hospital, he reviewed Plaintiff's chart, spoke with Plaintiff, collected medical history from him, and proceeded with a physical examination and a Doppler examination to check for a pulse in each of Plaintiff's testicles. Through differential diagnosis, Defendant believed that the diagnosis was fifty-fifty between testicular torsion and epididymitis and he ordered a scan. Defendant agreed that a safe time to wait to operate and explore was about six hours from the onset of symptoms. The physician who administered the scan, Dr. Biunno, diagnosed epididymitis.

Dr. Tong did not see Plaintiff again on September 29 until 5 p.m. Plaintiff had been on pain medication during the day and was in a lot less pain when Defendant saw him at 5 p.m. Defendant performed another Doppler exam and could not hear a pulse in the left testicle. Lindberg testified that Defendant told her he was not going to take Plaintiff to surgery because Plaintiff had an infection, epididymitis. Defendant kept Plaintiff in the hospital and on intravenous antibiotics for the night.

In the morning of September 30, Plaintiff had no pain and was hungry. His pain medication was discontinued and he ate some breakfast and most of his lunch. Defendant examined Plaintiff between 11 a.m. and noon that day. Plaintiff had no pain and wanted to go home. During his examination of Plaintiff, Defendant found that the left testicle was larger and he could not hear a pulse on the Doppler. Defendant attributed these circumstances to the infection. He discharged Plaintiff, having determined that Plaintiff was no longer in severe pain and was able to hold down a meal.

Lindberg took Plaintiff back to the hospital the night of September 30 because Plaintiff's testicle had become greatly enlarged and discolored. The next morning, another surgeon, Dr. Voss, examined Plaintiff, conducted surgery, and found testicular torsion. Dr. Voss determined that it was too late to save the testicle and removed it. Plaintiff sued Defendant and others relating to the loss of his left testicle.

Plaintiff presented expert medical testimony indicating that Defendant's actions fell below accepted medical practice standards because Defendant should have recognized the probability of testicular torsion and therefore should have conducted surgery in time to confirm the existence of the condition and likely save the testicle. Defendant presented expert medical testimony indicating that his conduct did not fall below those standards.

In regard to instructing the jury, Plaintiff contends that many acts and omissions of Defendant constituted medical malpractice, including: the delay in arriving at the hospital; Defendant's failure to properly consider each of many circumstances, such as Plaintiff's age, his normal urinalysis, the onset of severe pain, nausea and vomiting, the testicle swollen to twice its size, the absence of pain when urinating; and Plaintiff's prior painful episodes; Defendant's failure to realize the critical significance of delay in regard to surgically acting to save a testicle when testicular torsion is indicated; Defendant's failure to examine Plaintiff while Plaintiff was standing, rather than lying down; Defendant's mistaken judgment that the Doppler was not operating properly; Defendant's failure to properly consider Doppler readings; Defendant's release of Plaintiff with a swollen testicle and the positive Doppler results for torsion; Defendant's having ordered unnecessary and improper tests, resulting in harmful delay; and Defendant's failure to perform the required simple surgical procedure of untwisting the testicle and tacking the torsion to the scrotum early on, based on the possibility of testicular torsion.

The parties submitted requested jury instructions prior to trial, including their proposed 302B instructions (we refer to the tendered and given UJI 13–302B as the "302B instruction"). Plaintiff's tendered 302B instruction consisted of nineteen individual acts and omissions, each of which, Plaintiff contended, would constitute a breach of duty on Defendant's part. As his 302B instruction, Defendant tendered the form UJI 13–302B with no blanks filled in. The district court held a pretrial conference on the requested instructions, at which Plaintiff's nineteen-part 302B instruction was discussed; however, Plaintiff has not supplied a transcript of that conference, and we are unable to determine what was discussed. Following that conference, both parties submitted revised 302B instructions. Plaintiff reduced his 302B instruction to five individually listed acts and omissions each of which, Plaintiff contended, constituted a breach of duty on Defendant's part. Defendant submitted a two-contention instruction. At the direction of the district court, the parties then fashioned a 302B instruction that was given to the jury.

The jury returned a defense verdict. Plaintiff filed a motion for a new trial based on instruction error * * * The motion was deemed denied due to the passage of thirty days. See Rule 1–059(D) NMRA 2003.

DISCUSSION

The Asserted Instruction Error

Plaintiff asserts that the nineteen acts and omissions set out in his pretrial requested 302B instruction were all supported by evidence. This assertion also applies to his condensed five-part instruction later tendered. Plaintiff argues that each of the separately listed acts and omissions in his original instruction had a proper place in that instruction and that it was error to refuse it. Plaintiff further asserts that the court also erred in not giving his five-part 302B instruction as it was written. Plaintiff also argues that the instruction given by the district court exceeded the UJI 13–302B guideline and was prejudicially ambiguous, in that it was compound and confusing.

We first set out the requested 302B instructions. We next discuss what is required under UJI 13–302B. Following that, we set out what occurred in the conference settling the revised 302B instruction. We conclude that the court did not err in requiring refinement of Plaintiff's tendered instructions, and that Plaintiff failed to preserve error as to the instruction given to the jury.

The Requested 302B Instructions

Plaintiff's original nineteen-part 302B instruction read:

To establish the claim of negligence on the part of defendant, the plaintiff has the burden of proving at least one of the following contentions:

1. Defendant failed to properly consider [Plaintiff's] age, normal urinalysis, sudden onset of severe pain, nausea and vomiting on the way to and at the E.R., the swelling of the left testicle to twice its normal size, and the absence of pain when urinating in ruling out

testicular torsion as being the cause of [Plaintiff's] condition when admitted to the hospital.

2.   Defendant failed to go [to] the hospital on September 29, 1994, to treat [Plaintiff] within a reasonable time after being notified that [Plaintiff] had been diagnosed with testicular torsion in his left testicle.

3.   Defendant ignored [Plaintiff's] history that a few weeks before he had developed a sudden painful testicle that went away quickly.

4.   Defendant did not properly consider the emergency room doctor's finding of testicular torsion on admission based on no pulse to the left testicle shown by Doppler examination.

5.   Defendant did not properly consider his own Doppler findings of no pulse on the left testicle.

6.   Defendant wasted valuable time by ordering a scan, thereby reducing the chance of saving [Plaintiff's] testicle.

7.   Defendant failed to resolve the inconsistency that he thought existed between the nuclear scan as against the two Dopplers.

8.   Defendant failed to resolve the perceived inconsistency between the scan showing epididymitis and the clinical indications of testicular torsion.

9.   Defendant diagnosed epididymtis [sic] based upon the use of a nuclear scan not designed for this purpose.

10.   Defendant failed to read the actual report of the radiologist or to consult with her to resolve the apparent inconsistencies between the scan and his clinical findings and history.

11.   Defendant failed to perform surgery on [Plaintiff] to verify his suspicion that [Plaintiff] had testicular torsion.

12.   Defendant examined [Plaintiff] laying down instead of standing, causing him to miss important information about the position of the testicles within the scrotum.

13.   Defendant discharged [Plaintiff] on September 30, 1994, with his left testicle swollen larger than on admission in the face of having conducted two more Doppler examinations which, like the two on the day before showed no pulse in the left testicle, thereby further reducing the chances of saving the testicle.

14.   Defendant failed to monitor [Plaintiff's] left testicle after the scan results were reported to confirm or dispute the erroneous scan diagnosis of epididymitis.

15.   Defendant, after the nuclear scan was performed, ignored two further doppler examinations indicating no pulse to the left testicle and ignored other classical indications of a torsed testicle, leading directly to the loss of [Plaintiff's] left testicle.

16.   Defendant did not attempt at anytime to manually detorse [Plaintiff's] left testicle.

17. From the time of his admission on September 29, 1994 at 6:30 a.m. until [Plaintiff] was discharged on September 30, 1994 in the early afternoon, Defendant failed to try to consult with another general surgeon available in the call-up area or with a urologist to resolve what Defendant perceived to be inconsistent or equivocal test results and clinical findings, some of which indicated surgical emergency.

18. Defendant failed to take into account the effect that the pain medication administered to [Plaintiff] would have on his clinical findings.

19. Defendant failed to recognize that the marked swelling in the left testicle reduced the pulse to the right testicle on Doppler.

The plaintiff also contends and has the burden of proving, that such negligence was a proximate cause of the injuries and damages.

Plaintiff's revised five-part 302B instruction read:

To establish the claim of negligence on the part of defendant, the plaintiff has the burden of proving at least one of the following contentions:

1. Defendant failed to properly consider [Plaintiff's] symptoms, history, laboratory results, and Doppler and nuclear scan results in diagnosing testicular torsion as against epididymitis;

2. Defendant took too long to get to the hospital after being notified of a surgical emergency, thereby reducing the chances of saving [Plaintiff's] testicle;

3. Defendant failed to perform surgery on [Plaintiff] to diagnose testicular torsion as against epididymitis;

4. Defendant examined [Plaintiff] laying down instead of standing, causing him to miss important information about the position of the testicles within the scrotum;

5. Defendant sent [Plaintiff] home from the hospital with testicular torsion which he knew or should have known existed, contributing to the loss of the testicle;

The plaintiff also contends and has the burden of proving, that such negligence was a proximate cause of the injuries.

Defendant's two-part 302B instruction read:

To establish the claim of negligence on the part of Defendant, the Plaintiff has the burden of proving at least one of the following contentions:

1. [Defendant] failed to diagnose torsion.

2. [Defendant] failed to operate on Plaintiff in a timely manner.

The Plaintiff also contends and has the burden of proving that such medical negligence was a proximate cause of the injuries and damages.

The court's 302B instruction given to the jury read:

To establish the claim of negligence on the part of defendant, the plaintiff has the burden of proving at least one of the following contentions:

1. Defendant failed to properly consider [Plaintiff's] symptoms, history, laboratory results, and Doppler and nuclear scan results and examined him laying down instead of standing up in diagnosing testicular torsion as against epididymitis; or

2. Defendant failed to operate on [Plaintiff] in a timely manner and sent him home from the hospital with testicular torsion which he knew or should have known existed.

The plaintiff also contends and has the burden of proving, that such negligence was a proximate cause of the injuries.

UJI 13–302B and Its Use

UJI 13–302A NMRA 2003 is titled "Statement of theories for recovery," and its purpose is "to introduce by name the theory or theories of recovery relied upon by plaintiff." The theory for recovery of "negligence" is given in an example. * * * UJI 13–302B thrusts upon the district court the obligation to wade through a party's tendered factual contentions and to determine if those contentions properly fit within the purpose and wording of UJI 13–302B and its directions for use. The district court is required to assure that each separately numbered contention contains "a statement of facts which, standing alone, established a breach of duty."

Settlement of the 302B Instruction

The district court and counsel discussed the 302B instruction in a conference that was held after the conclusion of the evidence and after the parties rested their cases. The initial discussion was in reference to Plaintiff's earlier tendered nineteen-part instruction. The 302B instruction was not "decided on," and the court stated, "I've got it crossed out." Defendant then tendered a 302B instruction. Plaintiff also tendered a 302B instruction with "a new set [of instructions] that I made that's complete with a praecipe." Referring to his 302B instruction, Plaintiff's counsel continued: "I tried to track what we agreed upon and all of that.... I reduced it down to five things instead of [19]."

Defendant then spelled out his objections to Plaintiff's revised, five-part instruction, stating, among other things, that the factual statements in paragraph 1 were merely the factual bases for the factual contention in paragraph 3, and that the former was really incorporated in the latter. In addition, Defendant argued that paragraphs 2, 4, and 5 were improper because of the lack of expert testimony of a causal link between those facts and any resulting harm to Plaintiff. Defendant also stated that there was no expert testimony that the contention in paragraph 5 constituted malpractice. Defendant argued in support of his own tendered 302B instruction, stating that Plaintiff's evidence supported the two contentions Defendant set out, which were (1) failure to diagnose torsion, and (2) failure to operate in a timely manner.

Plaintiff's counsel stated, "I have summarized in brief form the five paragraphs [that are] our specific factual basis for the claims which the rules specifically allow us to do." Plaintiff's counsel and the court then discussed some of Plaintiff's contentions. The court said:

> Let me ask you this: I agree that a majority of these things are probably supportable by the evidence. My concern is some of these really go toward damages, the egregiousness of it. I'm worried that somebody standing on their own is not going to be upheld by a review in court. I don't think they're going to utilize this as being able to support a medical malpractice, except for 3. You know, I'm just real worried about that. Whereas, the instruction that has been tendered by the Defendant, to me it is more comprehensive. I don't know if you need to get into all of the details. Like I said, I think they go to damages. Convince me otherwise.

After further discussion about the contentions, the court refused paragraph 2 of Plaintiff's five-part instruction because of lack of expert testimony. The court and Plaintiff's counsel then discussed the possibility of moving language and combining contentions. In the midst of this discussion, after Plaintiff's counsel appears to have conceded that one of the contentions was "in a way subsumed" within another, Plaintiff's counsel stated, "I'm not withdrawing our objection simply because I think we're entitled to list our specific factual contentions." The appellate record does not indicate which objection was referenced. Also during this discussion, the court stated:

> Again, I'm still very concerned that when we're in court they're going to look at this, and it's just one of these, because that's what the instruction says, to establish a claim of negligence on the part of the Defendant, the Plaintiff has the burden of proving at least one. I'm not really sure that any one of these can stand on their own.

Following which this exchange occurred:

> [PLAINTIFF'S COUNSEL]: Okay. Let me make sure that I understand, Your Honor, what you have told me I need to do. I take No. 4 and combine it with No. 1.
>
> THE COURT: Yes.
>
> [DEFENDANT'S COUNSEL]: Just throw in that—the laying down portion. And then No. 2 is out.
>
> THE COURT: Two is out. That definitely is out.
>
> [PLAINTIFF'S COUNSEL]: And No. 3 is okay.
>
> THE COURT: I think you can mesh five and three together, actually, because that's where it starts, Defendant failed to perform surgery in a timely fashion, and he sent him home. I would be happy with that. Then I think you have encompassed the either/or of the preliminary statement, to establish a claim of negligence, has the burden of proving at least one of the following. I think any one, either one of those would stand on its own then.

[PLAINTIFF'S COUNSEL]: So by saying Defendant—on No. 5, Defendant failed to operate on [Plaintiff] in a timely manner, and sent him home from the hospital, et cetera, and leave out No. 3?

THE COURT: Yes, that would be right.

[DEFENDANT'S COUNSEL]: And sent him home from the hospital, period?

THE COURT: Right.

[PLAINTIFF'S COUNSEL]: I think we need to put with testicular torsion which he knew or should have known existed, contributing to the loss of the testicle.

THE COURT: I said period. Okay, I'm going to let you put it in.

[DEFENDANT'S COUNSEL]: What all is going to go in there?

THE COURT: [Defendant] failed to operate on [Plaintiff] in a timely manner, and thereafter sent [him] home from the hospital with testicular torsion which he knew or should have known existed, period.

Then both of you agree on that very last sentence, I'll put "agreed." Next we have—

[DEFENDANT'S COUNSEL]: Judge, we did tender our 302(B) and you should have that for the record.

THE COURT: I have it right here. Actually, I have them all here to go into the record.

The entire discussion of the 302B instruction then ended as follows:

[PLAINTIFF'S COUNSEL]: So what we have left, Your Honor, let me make sure before I start drafting things here: No. 1 and 4 are going to be combined, and No. 5 is going to be given as the second factual contention with the changes that you've already indicated?

THE COURT: Yes, with respect to No. 5. Three and five are kind of together.

[PLAINTIFF'S COUNSEL]: Yes.

THE COURT: Okay.

The record reflects a definite "give and take" to arrive at a 302B instruction. What we glean from this conference settling the 302B instruction is that the court wanted paragraph 2 of the five-part instruction eliminated for failure of evidence, and wanted the remaining four paragraphs combined, resulting in a two-part instruction. The court, therefore, moved counsel toward and ultimately gave an instruction substantially containing the specific factual contentions in Plaintiff's five-part instruction except those relating to how long it took Defendant to get to the hospital. The court apparently thought that the four specific factual contentions, those in paragraphs 1, 3, 4, and 5, could not separately stand alone, but that, in combinations, paragraph 1 with 4, and paragraph 3 with 5, they could stand alone as two separate factual contentions. It is also apparent that the court was attempting to break the basic factual contentions of negligence into failures to (1) diagnose a probability of testicular torsion, and (2) timely act to confirm the existence of testicular torsion and to correct the condition. As the 302B instruction was ultimately customized, with its conjunctions, Plaintiff was required to prove one or the other of two sets of facts, instead of having the benefit of being required to prove only one of nineteen, or perhaps five, separate factual contentions.

Plaintiff complains that the given 302B instruction prejudicially lessened his chances of proving a breach of duty by Defendant. Plaintiff insists he was entitled to submit his nineteen-part instruction and to have the jury consider each of the nineteen parts as an independent basis on which to find a breach of duty. He also asserts that it was error for the court to require him to prove combinations of the five factual contentions in his revised 302B instruction in the combinations that appeared in the 302B instruction given by the court.

Preservation of Error

Defendant contends that Plaintiff failed to preserve the error he asserts. Defendant argues that Plaintiff waived any objection to the court's refusal to give the nineteen-part instruction because Plaintiff has not produced a record of the discussions regarding that instruction, and also because Defendant submitted a revised, two-part instruction as a part of a new set of jury instructions in place of Plaintiff's original instruction. Defendant further argues that Plaintiff agreed to change the five-part instruction by combining the factual contentions into two basic contentions. Defendant also argues that, while Plaintiff did state he was not withdrawing his objection that he was entitled to list his specific factual contentions, Plaintiff failed to identify any specific objection to the instruction ultimately given to the jury.

The basic tension in building an appropriate UJI 13–302B instruction has always been whether, and if so, to what extent, specific detail is to be stated, or whether broader, more ultimate, factual contentions should be listed. UJI 13–302B purposely leaves room for discussion about what acts and omissions should be listed, and what wording will clearly convey to a jury a plaintiff's factual contentions showing a breach of duty. "The goal is clarity." App. 1, ch. 11 (instructions).

It appears that both the court and Plaintiff were appropriately headed in the direction of moving away from the detailed facts in the nineteen-part instruction to broader, more ultimate factual contentions as contained in the five-part instruction and then, finally, to the instruction given to the jury. For example, paragraphs 1 and 3 of Plaintiff's nineteen-part instruction listed Defendant's failure "to properly consider [Plaintiff's] age, normal urinalysis, sudden onset of severe pain, nausea and vomiting on the way to and at the E.R., the swelling of the left testicle to twice its normal size," and stated that "Defendant ignored [Plaintiff's] history that a few weeks before he had developed a sudden painful testicle that went away quickly." Paragraph 1 of Plaintiff's revised five-part instruction omitted these specific facts. Instead, it attempted to list broader facts, such as, Defendant failed "to properly consider [Plaintiff's] symptoms, history, [and] laboratory results." For another example, paragraphs 6, 13, and 16, among several others, of Plaintiff's nineteen-part instruction detailed specific facts that Plaintiff contends led to a reduced chance of saving the testicle. Paragraphs 1, 2, and 5 of Plaintiff's five-part instruction attempt consolidation of those details into three broader contentions showing a reduction in chance of successful treatment. Finally, detail as to what Defendant should have done or failed to do to assure a proper diagnosis, and detail relating to Defendant's failure to timely operate, were combined to form the two-part instruction given to the jury.

UJI 13–302B provides guidance on what is to be stated as a factual contention which, standing alone, could prove breach of duty. To be listed, the acts and omissions must pass certain tests. Substantial evidence must exist to support the contention. UJI 13–302B. An asserted act or omission may fail due to the lack of medical testimony required to prove that it fell below the standard of care in the medical community. See Pharmaseal Labs., Inc. v. Goffe, 90 N.M. 753, 758, 568 P.2d 589, 594 (1977) ("Negligence of a doctor in a procedure which is peculiarly within the knowledge of doctors, and in which a layman would be presumed to be uninformed, would demand medical testimony as to the standard of care."). Further, the contention is not viable if required evidence of causation linking the act or omission to the injury is missing. See Cervantes v. Forbis, 73 N.M. 445, 448, 389 P.2d 210, 213 (1964) ("Expert testimony is generally required to establish causal connection."). A tendered 302B instruction that passes these tests is to be worded in a way that fairly and clearly describes the act or omission that, if proven, establishes a breach of duty. See Mireles v. Broderick, 117 N.M. 445, 451, 872 P.2d 863, 869 (1994) ("When draft language gives rise to concern, the trial court is nonetheless under a duty to instruct the jury succinctly and accurately on the issue of law presented.").

Plaintiff stated he was not withdrawing an earlier objection apparently related to his right to list specific factual contentions. This appears to refer to some objection made earlier in regard to the court's concern about Plaintiff's nineteen-part instruction. However, the district court did not err by requiring Plaintiff to substantially trim and consolidate his nineteen proffered contentions. The instruction contained factual statements that were too detailed, were repetitive, and that, standing alone, would not establish a breach of a duty. Many of the statements contained facts to be argued to the jury, not to be placed in a 302B instruction. Thus, the court did not err in requiring Plaintiff to submit another instruction. See id. at 452, 872 P.2d at 870 ("The trial court may submit the instruction as tendered or change the instruction, with or without consultation with counsel, to suit his or her particular proclivity and style. Only legal or factual insufficiency will justify rejection.").

Plaintiff's evidence of breach of duty was: Defendant's delay in coming to the hospital; the existence of facts tending to indicate testicular torsion; Defendant's alleged failures to properly evaluate symptoms and tests, to read reports, and to conduct a proper physical examination; and Defendant's having caused or permitted critical time to pass due to his own faulty clinical judgment and diagnosis, unnecessary tests; and his having sent Plaintiff home. Plaintiff attempted to condense these evidentiary facts in his five-part instruction.

Plaintiff's five-part instruction came much closer to the letter and spirit of UJI 13–302B. However, that instruction still did not clearly and succinctly set out the factual contentions underlying Plaintiff's negligence claim. The crux of Plaintiff's claim of negligence is contained in paragraph 2 of the given 302B instruction, namely, that "Defendant failed to operate on [Plaintiff] in a timely manner and sent him home from the hospital with testicular torsion which he knew or should have known existed." All of the more specific, evidentiary detail constituted support for the factual statements in this contention. The experts' testimony and the facts as to Defendant's specific actions and failures to act could potentially show that Defendant should have diagnosed the probability of torsion, should have known to conduct timely exploratory surgery, and should not have sent Plaintiff home without conducting that surgery.

The court, therefore, did not err in rejecting Plaintiff's five-part instruction as written and by working with Plaintiff on a restated 302B instruction. The five-part instruction needed refinement before its presentation to the jury. The court obviously wanted the instruction to more clearly and succinctly set out Plaintiff's factual contentions establishing negligence. Yet, it is equally obvious that the court also wanted to accommodate Plaintiff by incorporating in the instruction wording used in his five-part instruction.

It appears from the last of the discussion between the court and Plaintiff's counsel that Plaintiff's counsel was in charge of drafting appropriate language. Where the court and Plaintiff went wrong was that the instruction given to the jury was defective. The two contentions listed in the given 302B instruction need not, and should not, have been separated by the word "or." See UJI 13–302, Examples A and B (listing factual contentions without "or"). Further, because of the use of the conjunction "and" in each of the two contentions in the given instruction, the jury was instructed that it had to find the existence of each fact stated in order to conclude Defendant was negligent. Thus, in the first paragraph, to prove that Defendant failed to diagnose testicular torsion as opposed to epididymitis, it appears Plaintiff had to prove not only that Defendant failed to properly consider Plaintiff's symptoms, but also failed to consider history, laboratory and other test results, and to conduct a proper physical examination. In addition, the parties did not follow the example in Appendix 1 to Chapter 11 which sets out UJI 13–302B with a general contention of failure to use the skill and care required in a particular area of practice, followed by a brief description of the failure.

During the conference settling the 302B instruction, Plaintiff stated he was not withdrawing an earlier objection that is not contained in the record on appeal and that was apparently related to his right to list specific factual contentions. However, it appears from the record of the conference that although he preferred listing several factual contentions, Plaintiff felt he could accept the instruction as given by the court. Not only does it appear from the record that Plaintiff drafted the 302B instruction given to the jury, Plaintiff has not provided any record showing, nor does he assert on appeal, that he objected to any particular aspect of that instruction. He did not attack the instruction as inaccurate, deficient, or confusing. He did not attempt to explain to the court why it was inaccurate or deficient or why his five-part instruction was more appropriate. He nowhere suggests that he was not afforded a reasonable opportunity to object.

Rule 1–051(I) NMRA 2003 reads:

> For the preservation of any error in the charge, objection must be made to any instruction given, whether in UJI Civil or not; or, in case of a failure to instruct on any point of law, a correct instruction must be tendered, before retirement of the jury. Reasonable opportunity shall be afforded counsel so to object or tender instructions.

The principal purposes behind the rule requiring preservation are to ensure that the district court and opposing counsel are alerted to the error in order to provide the court an opportunity to correct a potential mistake and to provide opposing counsel an opportunity to respond to any objection. McLelland v. United Wis. Life Ins. Co., 1999 NMCA 55, P 24, 127 N.M. 303, 980 P.2d 86; Gracia v. Bittner, 120 N.M. 191, 195, 900 P.2d 351, 355 (Ct. App. 1995). Rule 12–216(A) NMRA 2003 governing our scope of review requires, for preservation of a question for review, that "a ruling or decision by the district court was fairly invoked."

Plaintiff objected to neither the wording, nor the structure of the given instruction, and never suggested better or different wording or structure. He thereby failed to preserve error for review. See Sonntag v. Shaw, 2001 NMSC 15, P 17, 130 N.M. 238, 22 P.3d 1188 ("If a party wishes to preserve for appellate review the trial court's decision to provide the jury with one instruction rather than another, that party must draw the court's attention to a specific flaw in the given instruction."); Lewis v. Rodriguez, 107 N.M. 430, 435, 759 P.2d 1012, 1017 (Ct. App. 1988) (holding error not preserved where party failed to alert court to error in given instruction that was constructed from both parties' tendered instructions); Echols v. N.C. Ribble Co., 85 N.M. 240, 246, 511 P.2d 566, 572 (Ct. App. 1973) ("Objections must be explicit. Objections in general terms are not sufficient. The trial court must be advised of the specific error so [it] may have an opportunity to correct it.").

In sum, we see no basis on which to hold that the district court erred under the circumstances. Plaintiff's tendered 302B instructions were unacceptable as written and Plaintiff's counsel and the court settled the 302B instruction through discussion in an uncoercive, bona fide give-and-take process. During this discussion, Plaintiff had the opportunity to present wording and structure satisfactory to Plaintiff and to object to the wording and structure of the instruction given to the jury. We do not believe the circumstances are so exceptional as to require reversal based on fundamental error.

Notes and Questions

Some courts take the position that error in issuing jury instructions is not preserved for appeal purposes by mere tender of alternative instruction without objecting to some specific error in trial court's charge or explaining why the proffered instruction better states law. Other courts have made it clear that the objection requirement is satisfied even where a party does not object to instructions but proposes alternative instructions and affirmatively makes the trial judge aware that the party does not agree with court's instructions; both requirements must be met, so that proposing alternative instructions but not making court aware of any specific concern with proposed instructions fails to preserve objections for review. Benigni v. Hemet, 879 F.2d 473 (9th Cir. 1988); Mattson v. Brown University, 925 F.2d 529 (1st Cir. 1991).

ABUAN v. LEVEL 3 COMMUNICATIONS, INC.

United States Court of Appeals for the Tenth Circuit, 2003.
353 F.3d 1158.

SEYMOUR, CIRCUIT JUDGE.

The jury found in favor of Mr. Abuan on his age discrimination and retaliation claims, and determined the age discrimination to be willful. It awarded Mr. Abuan $300,000 in back pay, $5,000,000 in compensatory damages, and $5,000,000 in punitive damages. In a post trial order, the district court held the jury's award of $300,000 in back pay to be against the weight of the evidence and remitted the amount to $56,252.25, remitted the liquidated damages under the ADEA to the same amount, and applied the $300,000 cap on punitive and compensatory damages imposed by the Civil Rights Act of 1991, 42 U.S.C. § 1981a(b)(3), in the case of a defendant who, as here, has more than 500 employees. The result was a total award of $412,504.50. The district court subsequently awarded Mr. Abuan front pay for two years in the amount of $245,160.
* * *

JURY INSTRUCTIONS

Level 3 argues that the district court erred in failing to give the jury two instructions, one describing the conduct qualifying as an adverse employment action and one telling the jury the legal standard applicable to conflicting testimony on Mr. Abuan's performance. Mr. Abuan counters that Level 3 neither objected at the conference on jury instructions nor timely proffered the instructions it claims were erroneously omitted, and that the omission does not constitute plain error.

> "No party may assign as error ... the failure to give an instruction unless that party objects thereto before the jury retires to consider its verdict, stating distinctly the matter objected to and the grounds of the objection."

Fed. R. Civ. P. 51. In this circuit, to comply with Rule 51 a party must both proffer an instruction and make a timely objection to the refusal to give a requested instruction. Giron v. Corr. Corp. of America, 191 F.3d 1281, 1288–89 (10th Cir. 1999). A party does not "satisfy the requirements for Rule 51 by merely submitting to the court a proposed instruction that differs from the instruction ultimately given to the jury." Id. at 1289.

The record does contain Level 3's second submission of proposed jury instructions, see Aplt. App. vol. I, doc. 5, which includes the proposed instructions at issue. The record is clear, however, that Level 3 did not proffer these instructions at the instruction conference or object at that time to the district court's failure to include them. Level 3 maintains this failure does not constitute a waiver because it had previously raised the issues in a motion for summary judgment and the district court rejected its position. In so doing, Level 3 attempts to invoke the "futility" exception to Rule 51 , under which a "litigant is excused from complying with the strict objection requirement of Rule 51 if the district court is aware of the party's position and it is plain that further objection would be futile, where [the] litigant's position [was] clearly made to the district court." Ecolab Inc. v. Paraclipse, Inc., 285 F.3d 1362, 1370 (Fed. Cir. 2002) (quoting 9 James Wm. Moore et al., Moore's Federal Practice ¶ 51.12[2][a], at 51–40.2 to 51–41 (3d Ed. 1997), and Citing 9A Charles Allen Wright & Arthur R. Miller, Federal Practice & Procedure § 2553, at 441 (2d Ed. 1986)).

This court applied the futility exception in Asbill v. Housing Authority of the Choctaw Nation of Oklahoma, 726 F.2d 1499 (10th Cir. 1984). In that case, although the party had not voiced during the instruction conference the specific objection he was raising on appeal, we did not consider the matter waived. In so holding, we pointed out that the party did not raise the issue at the conference out of knowledge that the court had previously rejected its position at least four times before and during trial. Id. at 1502 n.3. We concluded under these circumstances that the party's position had been made clear to the court and further objection would have been futile.

The record in this case reveals no such circumstances. Level 3 contends it made known to the court in its summary judgment materials its position that the two instructions were required. In those pleadings, Level 3 asserted Mr. Abuan had failed to establish a prima facie case of Title VII retaliation because he did not present any evidence he had suffered an adverse employment action. In denying summary judgment, the district court pointed to evidence that Mr. Abuan was demoted when he was assigned to report to Mr. Bourne and when he was assigned to perform menial clerical duties, and concluded that genuine issues of material fact precluded the grant of summary judgment for Level 3. The summary judgment proceedings thus dealt only with whether Level 3's treatment of Mr. Abuan was or was not adverse employment action as a matter of law. As such, they did not clearly inform the court of Level 3's position that its jury instruction defining "adverse employment action" was necessary. The court's ruling denying summary judgment cannot, in these circumstances, be construed as making plain its position rejecting the need for such an instruction.

In support of its summary judgment motion Level 3 also argued that where poor job performance is the reason cited by the defendant for its actions, the plaintiff cannot rebut that as a legitimate, nondiscriminatory reason with only evidence of his own belief that his work was satisfactory. For, "it is the manager's perception of the employee's performance that is relevant, not plaintiffs subjective evaluation of her own relative performance." Aplt. Supp. App., doc. 1, at 17. In so doing, Level 3 claimed a plaintiff's mere conjecture that an employer's explanation is a pretext for intentional discrimination is an insufficient basis for denial of summary judgment. The district court rejected this argument, stating its belief that fact issues existed as to whether "Mr. Abuan's reassignments during three years at Level 3 constituted demotions motivated by discriminatory animus." Aplt. App. vol. I, doc. 8, at 100. Level 3's assertion that the evidence of pretext was insufficient as a matter of law cannot be construed as giving the court clear notice of its position that an instruction on evaluating evidence of Mr. Abuan's performance was necessary. And, of course, the court's denial of summary judgment is not a plain indication that it would not give a jury instruction on the issue. Accordingly, we conclude that the futility exception, a " 'rarely' applied 'narrow exception' to Rule 51" should not be employed in this case. Cadena v. The Pacesetter Corp., 224 F.3d 1203, 1212 (10th Cir. 2000).

We therefore review only for plain error the court's failure to give the two instructions at issue.

Level 3's proposed instruction on evaluating Mr. Abuan's performance states, ungrammatically, as follows: "In order to find that plaintiff was discriminated against because of an unfavorable personnel evaluation, you must consider only plaintiff's managers' perception of the employee's performance. Neither plaintiff's self-evaluation of his own performance nor any evaluations of plaintiff's performance by his co-employees." Aplt. App. vol. I, doc. 5, at 62.

The proposed instruction is drawn from Furr, 82 F.3d at 988, but it misstates the holding in that case. Furr addressed only the "plaintiff's subjective evaluation" of his own performance relative to that of other employees who were not eliminated in the RIF. Id. Furr does not support the notion that evidence from Mr. Abuan's co-workers as to his performance is irrelevant. Level 3 is correct to assert that the ultimate issue

before the jury was Mr. Abuan's supervisors' appraisal of his performance. Mr. Abuan's co-workers' assessment of his work, however, is
clearly probative of pretext. Yet under Level 3's proposed instruction
most evidence of pretext would become irrelevant once a defendant has
stated that its action was based on its own evaluation of the plaintiff's
performance. This result is legally insupportable.

Because this instruction was an incorrect statement of the applicable law, the failure to give it was not error at all.

Notes and Questions

1.   On the doctrine excusing objection where an argument has clearly
been presented to the trial court previously—and rejected—see Ecolab Inc. v.
Paraclipse, Inc., 285 F.3d 1362 (Fed. Cir. 2002) where the court cited
authority for the proposition that failure to object may be disregarded if the
party's position has been made clear to the trial judge and it is plain that a
further objection would be unavailing. This is known as the "futility"
exception.

2.   In Dresser Industries, Inc. v. Gradall Co., 965 F.2d 1442, 1450 (7th
Cir. 1992), a party in a contract dispute did not object to a jury instruction
defining a contract term but was nonetheless allowed to challenge the
instruction on appeal, because the party had fully briefed the argument on
summary judgment and the district court had rejected the same argument in
denying summary judgment. A further objection would have been futile.
Similarly, in Hamman v. Southwestern Gas Pipeline, Inc., 821 F.2d 299, 303
(5th Cir. 1987), the Fifth Circuit held that a party had not waived its
challenge to a jury instruction, where the party's position on the same legal
issue had been clearly stated in the party's trial brief, and had been rejected
by the district court. Again, the court of appeals found that further objection
would have been futile.

3.   According to Moore's Federal Practice, "federal courts of appeal in
all jurisdictions recognize this [futility] exception." 9 James Wm. Moore et
al., Moore's Federal Practice, § 51.12[2][a], at 51–41 (3d ed. 1997). This,
however, may not be true in the Eighth Circuit. In Starks v. Rent-a-Center,
58 F.3d 358, 362 (8th Cir. 1995), the court did not excuse a party's failure to
object to a jury instruction, even though the trial judge repeatedly indicated
that he preferred that counsel not repeat arguments already presented,
because "in this circuit, ... concern that the trial judge would prefer no
objection or the view that the objection would be futile does not relieve the
parties from making an objection to preserve errors for review." See also
Jones Truck Lines, Inc. v. Full Serv. Leasing Corp., 83 F.3d 253, 256 (8th
Cir. 1996).

4.   In International House of Pancakes v. Twin City Fire Insurance Co.,
19 Fed. Appx. 686 (9th Cir. 2001) the plaintiff IHOP's view of the law had
seemingly been rejected by the trial court in trial rulings on objections made
in chambers, and had been set forth by IHOP in pretrial briefs and proposed
jury instructions. On the last day of trial, the court asked counsel for both
IHOP and the fire insurance company whether they had reviewed the
revised jury instructions. The following conversation ensued:

The Court: Have you seen these new instructions?

[Counsel for Twin City]: Which one ... ?

The Court: All of the instructions?

[Counsel for IHOP]: We have seen them, Your Honor.

The Court: Are they satisfactory?

[Counsel for IHOP]: They are, Your Honor.

At this time not only did IHOP have an opportunity to object to the jury instructions, but, rather then stating its disagreement with the instructions for the record, IHOP expressly accepted the court's instructions. Although the appellate courts do not require a formal objection where such an objection would be futile, it does not follow that the objecting party can specifically acquiesce to the formulation of the instructions and then argue that an objection would be a futile formality. It was held that by agreeing that the instructions were "satisfactory," IHOP expressly waived its right to appeal the formulation of those jury instructions.

5.   In Jarvis v. Ford Motor Co. , 283 F.3d 33 (2nd Cir. 2002), a products liability case in which the guardian of a minor sued an auto maker for negligence and strict liability, the appellate court held that a party has an obligation to do more than state a "general objection" to planned instructions. The Court said: "Fed. R. Civ. P. 51 requires more than the disclosure of a 'fundamental position' desiring one jury charge over another. The federal rules instead require that Ford 'state distinctly the matter objected to and the grounds of the objection." The court found that Ford had waived its objection and that to excuse it from the well-established rules of waiver "would permit precisely the sort of 'sandbagging' that the rules are designed to prevent, while undermining the ideal of judicial economy that the rules are meant to serve."

6.   In Dupre v. Fru–Con Engineering Inc., 112 F.3d 329 (5th Cir. 1997) the trial court granted an age discrimination defendant's motion to exclude proof of its alleged discrimination against a different individual. At trial the court gave an instruction directing the jury not to consider the treatment of the other individual. The district court conducted extensive discussions off the record in chambers concerning the jury instructions. After these discussions, the judge and the attorneys returned to the courtroom, where the court informed the parties that it would go through the instructions and "if we come to [an instruction] that anybody has an objection about, ... you can certainly make your record on that objection." When the instruction about discrimination against the other individual was read, plaintiff's counsel made a "general objection" and stated, "[T]his instruction should not be given to the jury at all." On appeal it was held that this general objection was insufficient to preserve the specific objections to the instruction. The argument that Rule 51 does not require that objections and the grounds therefor be on the record was rejected.

7.   Ordinarily, the legal correctness of a jury charge is subject to plenary review. United States v. Newcomb, 6 F.3d 1129, 1132 (6th Cir. 1993). However, where a party, even a criminal defendant, has failed to preserve challenges to the jury instructions in the trial court, they are assessed on review for plain error. No reversible error exists in jury instruc-

tions unless "viewed as a whole [they] were confusing, misleading or prejudicial." Innes v. Howell Corp. 76 F.3d 702, 714 (6th Cir. 1996).

5. POST–TRIAL MOTIONS

WELLS v. DAIRYLAND MUTUAL INS. CO.

Supreme Court of Wisconsin, 1957.
274 Wis. 505, 80 N.W.2d 380.

Action by the plaintiff Lee R. Wells, special administrator of the estate of Julius Meyers, deceased, against the defendant Dairyland Mutual Insurance Company to recover damages for the fatal injuring and resulting death of plaintiff's decedent in an automobile accident.

Meyers, while crossing a public street in the city of Sparta as a pedestrian on September 5, 1954, was struck by a taxicab operated by Vernon F. Tucker, an employee of the Sparta Cab Company, to which company the defendant had issued a policy of automobile public liability insurance. Meyers was rendered unconscious and remained in a coma until his death five days later. Tucker died before trial from a cause disassociated with the accident.

The action was tried to a court and jury. The jury returned a special verdict whereby Tucker was found causally negligent as to speed, lookout, and management and control; Meyers was found causally negligent as to failure to yield the right of way and lookout; and the total aggregate negligence was apportioned 70 per cent to Tucker and 30 per cent to Meyers. The trial court answered the damage question in the verdict, finding the plaintiff special administrator's damages to be $856.60. Judgment was rendered upon the verdict in favor of the plaintiff under date of April 23, 1956, for 70 per cent of such found damages and costs. The defendant has appealed from such judgment.

CURRIE, JUSTICE.

The issues raised on this appeal are: * * *

(3) If defendant is not entitled to a dismissal on the merits, should a new trial be directed because of duplicity in the verdict?

* * *

Lastly, we must pass upon the contention advanced that the defendant should be awarded a new trial because of the error of the trial court in submitting a duplicitous verdict as to Tucker's negligence. There is no question but under the decisions of this court that defendant would be entitled to such new trial if it has not waived its right to raise such issue on this appeal.

We find that counsel for the defendant did properly object on the record to the form of the verdict before argument to the jury, which objection specifically pointed out to the trial court the manner in which the verdict was duplicitous. However, we do not consider that the error of a duplicitous verdict was properly called to the trial court's attention after verdict.

In addition to moving after verdict for judgment notwithstanding the verdict, and for the court to change certain answers, and upon the verdict as so changed for a judgment of dismissal, defendant did move in the alternative for a new trial. The alternative motion for a new trial specified five grounds in support thereof, none of which specifically referred to a duplicitous verdict. We do not deem that merely alleging, as did defendant, in such a motion that the verdict is contrary to the evidence and contrary to law is sufficient in itself to properly raise the issue of duplicitous verdict before the trial court. No memorandum opinion passing on the motions after verdict was filed by the learned trial judge, and the order for judgment throws no light on whether the issue of duplicitous verdict was briefed or argued by defendant's counsel after verdict on the question of granting a new trial for error. In fact, the record before us is entirely silent on this point.

As to those errors which must be raised by a motion for new trial as a condition precedent to having this court pass thereon as a matter of right, and not discretion, we are constrained to hold that the burden is upon the party alleging error in this court to affirmatively establish by the record before us that such error was specifically called to the trial court's attention in considering the motion for new trial. Where the motion for new trial is couched in such general terms as not to do this, but the claimed error was specifically pointed out in a brief filed, or oral argument made, in support of the motion, one way of meeting such burden would be to have the bill of exceptions recite such fact.

Is the submission to the jury of a duplicitous verdict the type of error which must he properly raised in the trial court after verdict in order to have this court award a new trial therefor as a matter of right, and not discretion? Viewed from the standpoint of which result would most accord with our conception of the proper administration of justice, the answer must be that it is. Appeals to this court are expensive and time-consuming. A procedural device which affords an opportunity to a trial court to correct its own errors by directing a new trial, without the necessity of an appeal to this court to reach the same result, would seem to be in the public interest. During the course of a trial the trial judge often is required to "shoot from the hip" in making his rulings without the benefit of briefs or time to make an independent research of the authorities. A very different situation prevails when the trial judge has before him after verdict a motion for new trial grounded upon alleged error. Time will then permit the preparation and filing of briefs by counsel, and for the judge to do independent research of his own.

We consider most apropos the following quotation from 39 Am.Jur., New Trial, p. 42, sec. 17, appearing in Mr. Justice Gehl's opinion in Ferry v. State, 1954, 266 Wis. 508, 511, 63 N.W.2d 741, 742:

> " 'While the primary object of a motion for a new trial is to secure re-examination of issues of fact, it serves also to bring to the notice

of the trial court errors which may have been committed in the course of the trial, and enables the court to correct such errors without subjecting the parties to the expense and inconvenience of prosecuting review proceedings. In many jurisdictions a motion for a new trial is a condition precedent to a right to have the case reviewed in an appellate court. In other words, under the practice in most jurisdictions, it was the duty of counsel to give the trial court an opportunity, by motion for a new trial, to correct whatever errors it may have made in respect of matters which may properly be made the grounds of such a motion.' 39 Am.Jur., New Trial, p. 42, sec. 17.''

When we approach the problem from the standpoint of attempting to find a controlling principle laid down in the past decisions of this court we discover a chaotic inconsistency which cries out for rectification.

In Plankinton v. Gorman, 1896, 93 Wis. 560, 562, 67 N.W. 1128, 1129, Mr. Justice Marshall, speaking for the court, declared: "A motion for a new trial is only necessary to preserve for review errors committed by the jury. Errors committed by the court are reviewable without such motion." This same principle was expressly approved in the following subsequent cases: If this principle were held to govern the instant appeal, there would be no necessity for the defendant to have moved after verdict in the circuit court for a new trial grounded upon the error in submitting a duplicitous verdict.

However, we find that such principle laid down in Plankinton v. Gorman, supra, has been quite frequently departed from by this court. The giving of an erroneous instruction to a jury is an error committed by the court and not the jury. Nevertheless, we have held that such error cannot be raised on appeal in the absence of a motion after verdict in the trial court pointing out such error. Failure to submit a requested question in a special verdict is also error committed by the court. Nevertheless, we recently held that failure to move for a new trial because of such refusal constituted a waiver of the right to raise the issue on appeal. Huffman v. Reinke, 1955, 268 Wis. 489, 491, 67 N.W.2d 871.

If failure to submit a requested question in a special verdict cannot be raised on appeal without first having moved for a new trial after verdict in the trial court on such ground, there would seem to be no logical basis for invoking a different rule with respect to submitting a duplicitous verdict which included questions which should not have been submitted.

We think that the time has come to repudiate the *cliché*, that errors by the court are reviewable without necessity of first grounding a motion for new trial thereon, because we consider it to be highly erroneous. We deem the correct rule to be that no error of the court should be reviewable *as a matter of right* on appeal without first moving in the trial court for a new trial bottomed on such error, if the error is of a category that a trial court could correct by granting a new trial. Sec. 251.09, Stats., authorizes this court *in its discretion* to grant a new trial whenever we deem that there has been a miscarriage of justice. The exercise of such power is not dependent on whether the aggrieved party protected his rights by objection or motion in the trial court. While this power is sparingly exercised by this court, we do not hesitate to employ it in hardship cases to prevent a miscarriage of justice.

We decline to exercise our power to direct a new trial in the interests of justice in the instant case for the simple reason that we are not convinced that there has been any miscarriage of justice here, in spite of the duplicitous verdict returned. This is because we consider that there is strong likelihood that the jury might have made the same apportionment of negligence between Tucker and Meyers if the lookout question had been omitted from the verdict.

Judgment affirmed.

Notes and Questions

1. Did the decision in the principal case change the law in Wisconsin as to the necessity for raising an issue in a new trial motion? Does the decision make it any less imperative for counsel to file a motion for a new trial and raise all the questions that may possibly be argued on appeal?

2. Compare the procedure followed in the principal case with that found in Dilliplaine v. Lehigh Valley Trust Co. Section D, infra, where counsel specifically raised the error in a posttrial motion but not at trial. Does one requirement have any more validity than the other?

3. An additional requirement was imposed in Cherry v. Willer, 317 Pa.Super. 58, 463 A.2d 1082 (1983), in which the court stated that "boiler-plate" posttrial motions were insufficient to preserve specific issues for review. Compare the more lenient approach in Nave v. Rainbo Tire Service, Inc., 123 Ill.App.3d 585, 78 Ill.Dec. 501, 462 N.E.2d 620 (1984), in which the court, after noting the general rule of waiver of any issue not presented in a posttrial motion, stated that the issue of improper argument by counsel would be considered on review because of objection made at trial. The court explained that the rule on posttrial motions stated an admonition to the parties, not a limitation on the appellate court's jurisdiction. Are these cases reconcilable?

4. A new trial motion is no longer required in Wisconsin to permit a party as a matter of right to raise an issue in the appellate court. Wis. Stat.Ann. 809.10(4) (West 1983). See R. Martineau & R. Malmgren, Wisconsin Appellate Practice § 604 (1978).

5. The requirement of a new trial motion has been abolished in most jurisdictions, including the federal courts. See R. Martineau, Modern Appellate Practice—Federal and State Civil Appeals § 3.10 (1983). The reasons for the elimination of the requirement were stated by the Indiana Civil Code Study Commission, quoted in 4 W. Harvey, Indiana Practice 119–20 (1971):

Following are some of the important reasons for eliminating the motion to correct errors (replacing the prior motion for a new trial) as a condition to an appeal:

First: It will assure consideration of cases upon the merits, rather than solution on technical grounds which must be blamed only on the lawyer taking the appeal or the very uncertainty of the technical law involved.

Second: The motion to correct error seldom is effective below. It is common knowledge that not more than 2% or 3% of all case's are reversed when the motion is made. It, therefore, wastes everybody's time.

Third: The transcript of evidence seldom, if ever, is available to aid a party in determining whether or not prejudicial error was committed. Consequently, a lawyer cannot fairly present the issues for correction within the time provided, and out of caution he is forced to raise issues which may prove not to be reversible error.

Fourth: The expenses of reproducing the motion for a new trial,' rather than emphasizing the actual events in the record where error was committed are costly, and time consuming.

Fifth: Past experience has shown a tendency upon the part of courts on appeal to develop technical language for assigning error on appeal especially when such error must go through a series of restatements in motions, briefs and arguments.

Sixth In criminal cases the technical limitation that all errors be raised within a relatively short period of time after the trial and before the transcript is prepared is almost unbelievable in this day when the rights of those accused of crimes are so well recognized.

Seventh: The real effect of requiring a motion for a new trial is to consume time and promote delay. The delay involved often is such that, if generally known, it would lead to more radical innovations. *Compare, e.g.,* Indianapolis Life Ins. Co. v. Lundquist, 222 Ind. 359, 53 N.E.2d 338 (1944).

Eighth: If the trial judge is permitted to serve as a court of appeal, his decision on questions of law raised by the motion to correct error is made without the benefit of briefs which represent the final step in the appeal process. Briefs cannot be artfully drawn without the transcript and the record which usually are not available in the time and place where the motion is made below.

Ninth: Judges on appeal often admit that failure to raise error properly below is an effective means of allowing them to dispose of the cases. If the case is without merit, or if it is poorly presented, the proper remedy is by means of the court's power to deal with counsel, and in all cases with the merits.

Tenth: In view of the over-all ineffectiveness of the motion to correct error (formerly motion for a new trial), it presents, in final analysis, a technical obstacle in the way of consideration of a case upon its merits. Parties who feel that relief can be obtained below are free to seek it. As a mandatory rule it presents an unreasonable cost to the time of professors, students and lawyers in getting to the merits on an appeal.

Eleventh: The old rule followed in Indiana has long since been rejected in the federal courts and other jurisdictions where effort has been made to eliminate delay and cost in judicial administration.

Reasons in support of alternative Rule 59(g) and in support of the old rule requiring a motion to correct error as a condition to appeal are not convincing. The new rule meets the argument that the judge below should be allowed to correct his errors, since the parties have the option of presenting a motion to correct errors and the judge may do so on his own motion. However, the Commission was divided upon the question, and therefore seeks assistance of the bar and public.

Are these reasons persuasive?

6. For a review of the confusion in Indiana over whether more than one posttrial motion was required see Grove, The Requirement of a Second Motion to Correct Errors as a Prerequisite to Appeal, 10 Ind.L.Rev. 462 (1977).

7. For a discussion of Federal Rule 50 and the interplay of motions for new trial and motions for judgment as a matter of law, see Arenson v. Southern Univ. Law Center, 43 F.3d 194 (5th Cir. 1995) and Note, The Fifth Circuit Adopts a "Use it or lose it" System for Rule 50(c) Conditional Rulings on Judgments as a Matter of Law and New Trials, 70 Tulane L. Rev. 371 (1995).

8. Where the issue to be raised on appeal deals with the irregularity of a verdict, or problems of excessive or inadequate damages in a verdict, a post-verdict motion before the trial court is often seen as a prerequisite for preserving the issue for appellate review. See Rivera–Torres v. Velez, 341 F.3d 86 (1st Cir. 2003) in which private and municipal defendants failed to move for a new trial after the jury delivered its verdict, or file a post-trial motion to reduce or set aside the verdict as excessive. The First Circuit held: "We have long held that defendants who fail to preserve challenges to the jury verdict below forfeit review of those claims on appeal. We generally will not review a party's contention that the damages award is excessive or insufficient where the party has failed to allow the district court to rule on the matter." (Citing cases where appellate review of allegedly excessive or inadequate damages was denied where trial court was not given the opportunity to exercise its discretion on the matter).

SECTION C.   PRESERVING ERROR DURING THE APPEAL ITSELF

It is not enough that the appealing party has clearly preserved a point of error at the trial level. There are opportunities for waiver of arguments during the appeal itself. Failure to initiate the appeal in a timely fashion, and perfect it, present examples of waiver of rights otherwise preserved. See Chapter 5.

During the appeal itself, waiver may occur by failure to generate an adequate record, failure to brief certain points adequately, and in other ways.

1. THE RECORD

Spillios v. Green, 137 Ariz. 443, 671 P.2d 421 (App.1983). In this wrongful death case, defendants husband and wife appealed from an adverse judgment awarding damages against them. Appellants contended that they had not been allowed to argue that the negligence of the husband of the deceased was imputable to the deceased. The court found no error, noting that even though the record showed an objection by the appellants it did not contain the trial court's ruling on the objection. The court stated: "If lawyers want to preserve the record for appellate review, they must make sure that their arguments to the trial judge are being transcribed by the court reporter and that any ruling is in the record." (137 Ariz. at 446, 671 P.2d at 424). Thus both the objection and the trial court's ruling on the objection must appear in the record before the appellate court will consider the issue to have been preserved properly. The federal rule is to the same effect. I.B.M. Corp. v. Edelstein, 526 F.2d 37, 45 (2d Cir. 1975).

Notes and Questions

1. Why should it be necessary for the ruling as well as the objection to appear on the record? What if it is clear from the record that the trial court acted as though the objection had been overruled, even though the record does not show an express ruling? Should it be the responsibility of counsel or the trial judge to make sure the ruling does appear on the record? Should it make a difference whether the trial court actually did not rule on the objection or merely that the ruling was not shown on the record?

2. For a more complete consideration of the record and the procedure for supplementing the record, see Chapter 7, infra.

2. THE BRIEF

ROCA v. E.I. Du PONT DeNEMOURS AND COMPANY

Supreme Court of Delaware, 2004.
842 A.2d 1238.

HOLLAND, JUSTICE.

This is an appeal from a final judgment entered by the Superior Court. In October 2001, the plaintiff-appellant, Carl Roca, filed a complaint in the Superior Court. The defendant-appellees are E.I. du Pont de Nemours and Company, General Motors Corporation, DaimlerChrysler Corporation and Rhone–Poulenc, Inc., as successor-in-interest to Stauffer Chemical Company. Roca alleged inter alia that he contracted mesothelioma, a deadly lung cancer, as a result of exposure to asbestos dust and fibers while working for independent contractors on the premises of the defendants-appellees.

The defendants filed motions for summary judgment on a number of issues. Following briefing and oral argument, the Superior Court granted the defendants' motions in a bench ruling on July 1, 2002 and in a memorandum opinion dated September 3, 2002. These rulings were entered by the Superior Court on November 7, 2002, as a stipulated final judgment in favor of all defendant-appellees.

In this appeal, Roca's opening brief raised only two issues as the basis for his challenge to the Superior Court's complete dismissal of his complaint: first, "The Trial Court Abused Its Discretion and Erred As A Matter Of Law In Determining That Plaintiff Was Not An 'Other' Pursuant To Chapter 15 Of The Restatement Of Torts (2nd)"; and second, "The Trial Court Abused Its Discretion And Erred As A Matter Of Law In Finding That Defendants Did Not Retain Control Of Their Premises And Did Not Assume [The Duty Of] Job Site Safety."

We have concluded that neither of the two claims expressly raised by Roca in his opening brief are meritorious. We have also determined that the final judgments entered by the Superior Court should be affirmed on the basis of and for the reasons stated by the Superior Court in it memorandum Opinion dated September 3, 2003. Roca, however, asserts that there is a third issue before this Court that must be decided. Section 343 and Oral Argument

During the oral arguments before this Court, Roca contended that the Superior Court erred by denying his claim that was made pursuant to Section 343 of the Restatement (Second) of Torts ("Section 343"). Following oral arguments, this Court directed Roca tofile an opening memorandum that:

1.   Clearly identifies that portion of the Superior Court's ruling which explicitly or implicitly rejected appellant's Section 343 argument; and

2.   Explains why the Superior Court's decision on that issue constituted reversible error.

Roca's response to this Court's request did not identify the portion of the Superior Court's opinion that explicitly or implicitly rejects his purported claim under Section 343 of the Restatement. The defendants' response to this Court asserts that Roca's "Opening Memorandum does not do so for the simple reason that no such portion exists. That is, the [Superior] Court did not reject a § 343 claim because [Roca] never made such a claim."

Section 343 and Superior Court

Roca contends that, as a result of his factual allegations about the defendants' knowledge of asbestos hazards in paragraphs 17 and 18 of his complaint, the Superior Court should have recognized that he was asserting a legal claim under Section 343 of the Restatement. Roca also contends that he presented "lengthy arguments" below on a premises owner's duty to warn invitees, and that this put the Superior Court on notice of a Section 343 claim.

The record reflects, however, that when the Superior Court asked Roca to identify the legal theories under which he intended to proceed Roca expressly identified Sections 413, 416, 422 and 427 of the Restatement, but not Section 343. The defendants' submit that: "in over 332 pages of briefing to the [Superior] Court, not once did Plaintiff mention § 343. Roca's original four answering briefs in opposition to defendants' respective summary judgment motions contained: 77 pages for General Motors; 75 pages for Chrysler; 106 pages for du Pont; and 74 pages for Rhone–Poulenc." According to the defendants, "Roca also made no reference whatsoever to invitees or Section 343 at oral argument before the Superior Court on either June 20, 2002 or July 1, 2002."

The Superior Court's memorandum opinion indicates that it did not believe there was a Section 343 claim before it. Citing the Third Circuit's decision in Monk v. Virgin Islands Water & Power Authority, [53 F.3d 1381 (3d Cir. 1995)], the Superior Court stated: "employers need not be held liable under the peculiar risk provisions of Chapter 15 because other remedies exist under the Restatement, such as the right of the contractor's employees, like other invitees, to sue for certain defects on the land under Restatement § 343." Roca did not file a motion for reargument, pursuant to Superior Court Rule 59(e).

The defendants submit that the first time Roca specifically raised Section 343 as a theory of recovery was in a letter to the Superior Court dated September 17, 2002.

> In light of Your Honor's reference to § 343, is the written opinion of September 3, 2002 combined with Your Honor's oral ruling at the close of argument on the Defendants' Motions meant to be a complete dismissal as to all of Plaintiff's claims against Defendants DuPont, GM, Chrysler, and Rhone–Poulenc?

> If that is the case, Plaintiff respectfully requests that Your Honor sign the attached Order of Judgment evidencing the fact that the Court has entered a final judgment so that Plaintiff may move forward with his appeal.

That letter was written after Roca had received the Superior Court's September 3, 2002 memorandum opinion and after the period for reargument had expired. Thereafter, Roca stipulated to the entry of a final judgment. Section 343 and this Appeal.

Assuming arguendo that Roca did assert a Section 343 claim before the Superior Court and further assuming arguendo that the Superior Court rejected that claim, this Court determined that a question remained about whether Roca waived the Section 343 issue in his present appeal. This Court asked the parties to address the following question: "Did Carl Roca waive his purported claim under Restatement (Second) of Torts Section 343 by not citing that section as a basis for relief in his opening brief on appeal to this Court?"

In Murphy v. State,[632 A.2d 1150 (Del. 1993)] this Court noted that an appellant is entitled to frame the issues on appeal. We also stated that "[t] he failure to raise a legal issue in the text of the opening brief generally constitutes a waiver of that claim on appeal." The defendants argue that because Roca "omitted from his opening brief any challenge to the Superior Court's finding or failure to decide a claim under section 343, that issue has been waived."

Roca argues that he raised Section 343 as an issue for review, and claims that he "specifically cited Section 343 on page 37 of his opening brief." An examination of that page, however, reflects that Roca did not cite to Section 343, but rather cited Niblett v. Pennsylvania R.R. Co., [52 Del. 380, 158 A.2d 580, 2 Storey 380 (Del. Super. 1960)] in which the Superior Court cited Section 343 among a number of other authorities. The fact that Roca did not cite to Section 343 in his opening brief is emphasized by the fact that, although Roca's Table of Citations references Restatement Sections 411 , 413, 416 and 527, it includes no reference to Section 343.

Roca also asserts that he raised Section 343 on pages thirty-six through forty of his opening brief. The defendants acknowledge that selected sentences of the text on these pages refer to the duty of premises owners to invitees. The defendants assert, however, that those references to duty don't mention Section 343 but are interspersed among general discussions on the other expressly identified sections of the Restatement with regard to the issue of control of contractors and assumption of a duty for safety by an owner.

Section 343 Waived On Appeal

It is well established that "to assure consideration of an issue by the court, the appellant must both raise it in [the Summary of the Argument] and pursue it in the Argument portion of the brief."[9] The rules of this Court specifically require an appellant to set forth the issues raised on appeal and to present an argument in support of those issues in their opening brief. If an appellant fails to comply with these requirements on a particular issue, the appellant has abandoned that issue on appeal irrespective of how well the issue was preserved at trial.

We have concluded that Roca failed to comply with Supreme Court Rule 14(b)(iv) when he omitted any reference to Section 343 in the summary of argument section of his opening brief. Rule 14(b)(iv) expressly requires that an appellant's opening brief contain a summary of argument section "stating in separate numbered paragraphs the legal propositions upon which each side relies." We have also concluded that Roca failed to raise Section 343 as a basis for relief in the argument section of his opening brief. Supreme Court Rule 14(b)(vi) requires that "[t] he argument ... be divided under appropriate headings distinctly setting forth the separate issues presented for review...."

---

9. Charles A. Wright, et al., Federal   (1999 and Supp. 2003).
Practice and Procedure § 3974.1, at 504–08

Most importantly, however, Rule 14(b)(vi)(2) provides that "[t] he merits of any argument that is not raised in the body of the opening brief [is] deemed waived and will not be considered by the Court on appeal." Roca presented only two arguments in his opening brief, neither of which refers to Section 343 either in the headings or in the body of those arguments on the merits. Thus, nowhere in his opening brief does Roca either identify or present an argument on the issue of Section 343 in the manner that is required by the Rules of this Court.

This Court has held that the appealing party's opening brief must fully state the grounds for appeal, as well as the arguments and supporting authorities on each issue or claim of reversible error.[12] "[C]asual mention of an issue in a brief is cursory treatment insufficient to preserve the issue for appeal"[13] and a fortiori no specific mention of a legal issue is insufficient. The "failure of a party appellant to present and argue a legal issue in the text of an opening brief constitutes a waiver of that claim on appeal."[14] Accordingly, we hold that, assuming arguendo that Roca preserved the Section 343 issue in the Superior Court, Roca abandoned and waived that issue in his appeal to this Court by raising it for the first time at oral argument.[15]

CONCLUSION

The judgments of the Superior court are affirmed.

Notes and Questions

1.   Justice Scalia (then Circuit Judge) wrote: "We will not resolve [an] issue on the basis of briefing and argument by counsel which literally consisted of no more than the assertion of violation of due process rights, with no discussion of case law supporting that proposition or of the statutory text and legislative history relevant to the central question of the exclusiveness of entitlements * * * The premise of our adversarial system is that appellate courts do not sit as self-directed boards of legal inquiry and research, but essentially as arbiters of legal questions presented and argued by the parties before them. Thus, Rule 28(a) (4) of the Federal Rules of Appellate Procedure requires that the appellant's brief contain "the contentions of the appellant with respect to the issues presented, and the reasons therefor, with citations to the authorities, statutes and parts of the record

12. Turnbull v. Fink, 644 A.2d 1322, 1324 (Del. 1994). See also Willhauck v. Halpin, 953 F.2d 689, 700 (1st Cir. 1991) (quoting United States v. Zannino, 895 F.2d 1, 17 (1st Cir. 1990)). ("[I] ssues adverted to in a perfunctory manner, unaccompanied by some effort at developed argumentation, are deemed waived.... It is not enough merely to mention a possible argument in the most skeletal way, leaving the court to do counsel's work ... Judges are not expected to be mindreaders. Consequently, a litigant has an obligation to spell out its arguments squarely and distinctly, or else forever hold its peace.").

13. Kost v. Kozakiewicz, 1 F.3d 176, 182 (3d Cir. 1993).

14. Id.; see also Central States, Southeast and Southwest Areas Pension Fund v. Midwest Motor Exp., Inc., 181 F.3d 799, 808 (7th Cir. 1999); Smith v. Marsh, 194 F.3d 1045, 1052 (9th Cir. 1999); King v. Town of Hanover, 116 F.3d 965, 970 (1st 1997); Matter of Texas Mortg. Servs. Corp., 761 F.2d 1068, 1073–74 (5th Cir. 1985).

15. Cannon v. Teamsters and Chauffeurs Union, 657 F.2d 173, 177–78 (7th Cir. 1981) (issue raised by appellant at oral argument had been waived because appellant failed to argue the issue in its brief).

relied on." Failure to enforce this requirement will ultimately deprive us in substantial measure of that assistance of counsel which the system assumes—a deficiency that we can perhaps supply by other means, but not without altering the character of our institution. Of course not all legal arguments bearing upon the issue in question will always be identified by counsel, and we are not precluded from supplementing the contentions of counsel through our own deliberation and research. But where counsel has made no attempt to address the issue, we will not remedy the defect, especially where, as here, "important questions of far-reaching significance" are involved. We therefore decline to entertain appellant's asserted but unanalyzed constitutional claim." Carducci v. Regan, 714 F.2d 171 (D.C. Cir. 1983).

2. One of the basic rules of effective appellate advocacy is that the number of issues raised in a brief should be limited to one or two, but never more than three. R. Martineau, Modern Appellate Practice—Federal and State Civil Appeals § 11.24 (1983). Does this put the attorney in a "Catch 22" situation—do not raise too many issues in the brief, but if you fail to raise an issue you waive it?

3. Contrast the principal case with Plymouth Fertilizer Co., Inc. v. Selby, 67 N.C.App. 681, 313 S.E.2d 885 (1984). In that case the court stated that the defendant had so ignored the rules of appellate procedure as to render his appeal subject to dismissal. Nevertheless, in the interests of justice and expediency the court entertained the appeal. (Does it help to know that the court further found that in the bench trial below the judge had made findings of fact unsupported by the evidence; failed to make findings on critical issues raised by the evidence; and reached conclusions of law that perhaps no construction of the evidence would support?)

4. Should a reviewing court ignore other deficiencies in the briefs submitted? In Terre Haute First Nat. Bank v. Stewart, 455 N.E.2d 362 (Ind.App.1983), the trial court had given judgment on the evidence for defendant as to certain of plaintiff's contentions of negligence. On appeal the court stated that when the appellant did not direct the court to specific evidence in support of its contentions, it would not search the record to find evidence to support them. Does this approach square with the courts' oft-stated desire to avoid manifest injustice?

5. In addition to requiring that an issue be raised in the brief, courts have imposed a number of requirements as to how the issue is raised and discussed in the brief. These include: an appellant claiming error in the refusal of the trial court to give a proposed jury instruction must include in the brief or the petition for review the proposed instruction, the instruction actually given, the objection to the instruction, and the ruling on the instruction, Thomas v. French, 99 Wa.2d 95, 659 P.2d 1097 (1983); a party must cite to the transcript showing a request to the trial court and its denial, Spillios v. Green, 137 Ariz. 443, 671 P.2d 421 (App.1983); a party must support an issue by a cogent argument, New England Whalers Hockey Club v. Nair, 1 Conn.App. 680, 474 A.2d 810 (1984); a citation limited to a legal encyclopedia is not sufficient, Randall v. Salvation Army, 100 Nev. 466, 686 P.2d 241 (1984); a party must set forth argument separately and not

combine them under one catchall point heading, Re Parlow, 192 N.J.Super. 247, 469 A.2d 940 (1983).

6. Most appellate rules specify in detail the manner in which issues must be set forth in the briefs and supported by references to the record and argument. These requirements are discussed in Chapter 8, infra.

7. Some courts require some type of preliminary statement to be filed with the court and the opposing party providing some information about the case, including the issues to be recorded. Courts differ on the effect of failure to include an issue in the preliminary statement. A court held that any issue not included in the preliminary statement of issues required by its rules is waived in Barrett v. Central Vermont Railway, Inc., 2 Conn.App. 530, 480 A.2d 589 (1984). Contra is 10th Circuit Rule 8(b). What is the purpose of the preliminary statement?

8. Once a claim is properly presented, a party can make any argument in support of that claim. Parties are not limited to the precise arguments they made at trial or in an intermediate court of appeals. See Harris Trust v. Solomon Smith Barney, Inc., 530 U.S. 238, 120 S.Ct. 2180, 147 L.Ed.2d 187 (2000).

9. Arguments presented only in a footnote of an opening brief; not argued in the opening brief; or raised only in the reply brief are generally not deemed to be properly preserved for appeal.

10. Courts of appeal comment periodically that a "passing reference" in a party's papers may not be sufficient. The appellant needs to spell out an argument in a fashion which "frames and develops an issue sufficient to invoke appellate review." Murrell v. Shalala, 43 F.3d 1388, 1389 n.2 (10th Cir. 1994) (refusing to consider perfunctory complaints about ruling not distinctly designated as issue for review).

11. Fed.R.App.P. 28(a)(9)(A) requires that the argument section of appellant's brief contain "appellant's contentions and the reasons for them, with citations to the authorities and parts of the claim does not comply with that rule." An appellant who fails to comply with this requirement fails to preserve the arguments that could otherwise have been raised. See Lunderstadt v. Colafella, 885 F.2d 66, 78 (3d Cir. 1989). See also United States v. Voigt, 89 F.3d 1050, 1064 n.4 (3d Cir. 1996) ("[B]riefs must contain statements of all issues presented for appeal, together with supporting arguments.")

3. THE APPENDIX

HILL v. PORTER MEMORIAL HOSPITAL

United States Court of Appeals for the Seventh Circuit, 1996.
90 F.3d 220.

MANION, CIRCUIT JUDGE.

While at work Robert Hill fell from a loading dock onto railroad tracks crushing his face and jaw. He was rushed to a hospital where one day later he suffered respiratory arrest. Further complications, including lack of oxygen to Hill's brain during the respiratory arrest, produced a coma and he eventually died. Hill's widow sued claiming medical malpractice. The defendants asserted Hill's respiratory arrest and death were due to preexisting blocked arteries. A jury found for the defense, and Mrs. Hill appeals, claiming error on a number of evidentiary and other rulings. We affirm the district court's decision on the merits and sanction Mrs. Hill's counsel for failing to include the district court's orders in the appendix as required under Rule 30. * * *

On appeal Mrs. Hill raises a myriad of arguments.[2] * * *

We turn now to an important matter of legal practice before this court. Circuit Rule 30 requires that a party's appendix contain any relevant portion of the district court's findings, opinions, or orders that the appellant refers to as part of the appeal. Ready access to essential parts of the record is absolutely necessary to accurately and expeditiously assess and resolve any case. By omitting key documents, Mrs. Hill's appendix was entirely inadequate.

In this appeal, Mrs. Hill challenges many of the magistrate judge's evidentiary rulings. Pursuant to Circuit Rule 30(c), her counsel certified that all materials required by subsections (a) and (b) of that rule were included in the appendix. This certification was false. Mrs. Hill's appendix did not include complete copies of district court orders: (1) granting defendants' motion to strike the expert testimony of Drs. Cranberg and Rothenberg; (2) denying plaintiff's motion to reconsider this order; (3) denying plaintiff's motion to strike and bar contentions, witnesses, and exhibits of defendants Zelaya, Swarner, and Whetsel; (4) denying in part plaintiff's motion to strike additional contentions, witnesses, and exhibits of defendants; (5) denying plaintiff's motion to bar expert testimony of Drs. Rosen, Fahey, and Geremia; and (6) denying plaintiff's motion to bar all treating physicians and staff from providing expert testimony. The appendix excluded key pages from some of the magistrate judge's orders (sometimes including only the first page of the order) and totally excluded other relevant rulings. Importantly, the appendix did not include the transcript pages at which the magistrate judge explained the reasoning for his rulings, as required by Circuit Rule 30(a). These are the precise orders and rulings that are the subject of Mrs. Hill's appeal.

In its response brief, the hospital pointed out these errors and called for this court to summarily affirm the district court's judgment as we did in Mortell v. Mortell Co., 887 F.2d 1322, 1327 (7th Cir. 1989), where the appellant likewise filed a false certificate of compliance with Circuit Rule 30. Mrs. Hill's counsel ignored this request in their reply brief. They did so at their own peril.

On March 20, 1996, this court ordered Mrs. Hill to show cause why the district court's judgment should not be summarily affirmed as a sanction for filing a false Rule 30(c) certification. Mrs. Hill's counsel

---

2. The statement of facts in Mrs. Hill's principal brief is improperly argumentative as it treats contested testimony of her witnesses as "facts." This violates both Circuit Rule 28(d)(1) and our admonition in Avitia v. Metropolitan Club of Chicago, Inc., 49 F.3d 1219, 1224 (7th Cir. 1995).

apologized and stated that they did not intend to omit the magistrate judge's various orders and rulings. They also pleaded ignorance, let slip that this was the first appeal they had initiated in this court, and attached the missing documents. When questioned at oral argument about the deficient appendix, Mrs. Hill's counsel offered no convincing explanation for the false certification under Rule 30, partial inclusion of certain documents, and total exclusion of others.

We have repeatedly stated that Circuit Rule 30 mandates parties provide us with a district court's reasoning for its decision. United States v. Gomez, 24 F.3d 924, 929–30 (7th Cir.) (failure of appellant to include trial court's opinion or transcript of oral reasons in appendix warranted order to show cause why attorneys signing brief should not be subject to professional discipline for violation of Circuit Rule 30(a), citing United States v. Smith, 953 F.2d 1060, 1068 (7th Cir. 1992) (order to show cause for violation of circuit rule), and In re Mix, 901 F.2d 1431, 1433 (7th Cir. 1990) (same)). The purpose of Fed. R. App. P. 30 and Circuit Rule 30 is for this court to have all necessary documents before it as it considers the parties' arguments and renders its decision. Transgression of these rules is not a "nit-picky" violation. Failure to supply necessary documents goes to the heart of this court's decision-making process. We cannot consider arguments that the lower court was incorrect and should be reversed if the written orders and transcript pages containing the appealed decisions are not before us.

This is not a new rule. "For more than 35 years, this court has declined to entertain appeals when the appellant does not file a required appendix." Urso v. United States, 72 F.3d 59, 61 (7th Cir. 1995) (failure to provide district court's explanation for refusal to award attorneys' fees to taxpayer prevented appellate review of that issue, citing numerous decisions, including *Gomez* and *Mortell*). See also Morrison v. Texas Co., 289 F.2d 382, 384 (7th Cir. 1961) (court has power to dismiss appeal or affirm judgment due to appellant's disregard of appendix rule by failing to delineate relevant portions of district court record from which appeal was taken); Potomac Ins. Co. v. Stanley, 281 F.2d 775, 778 (7th Cir. 1960) (failure to include in appendix all parts of record and transcript necessary to present any error justifies refusal to consider same).[4] "In an era of swollen appellate dockets, courts are entitled to insist on meticulous compliance with rules sensibly designed to make appellate briefs as valuable an aid to the decisional process as they can be." Avitia v.

4. This case is factually distinguishable from GCIU Employer Retirement Fund v. Chicago Tribune, 66 F.3d 862 (7th Cir. 1995), and Glass v. Dachel, 2 F.3d 733 (7th Cir. 1993), which Mrs. Hill relies upon in her response to the order to show cause. In GCIU, the appellant did not include in the appendix a one-page order in which the district court entered final judgment, but did include the district court's opinion granting summary judgment. In Glass, the appellant included in the appendix the dis-trict court's opinion denying appellant summary judgment and the short order granting appellee summary judgment, but did not attach the opinion granting appellee summary judgment. In GCIU and Glass this court accepted the appellants' explanation of inadvertent omission of a few pages. In this case numerous orders and portions of the transcript were excluded, including documentation of the lower court's reasoning.

Metropolitan Club of Chicago, Inc., 49 F.3d 1219, 1224 (7th Cir. 1995). Given this well-established law, ignorance of Rule 30 and its consequences is no excuse for Mrs. Hill's counsel's conduct.

We are especially struck that Mrs. Hill's counsel did not reply when opposing counsel pointed out the deficient appendix. Only an order to show cause focused their attention on this obvious problem. Counsel paying attention to the prosecution of an appeal, as they should, would never ignore a request from opposing counsel for summary affirmance. Cf. United States v. Smith, 953 F.2d at 1067–68 ("We cannot fathom why a lawyer, alerted to [Circuit Rule 30], would fail to correct the shortcoming and instead certify that he has complied in full."). At that juncture Mrs. Hill's counsel should have moved to correct the appendix rather than disregard the issue. For all of these reasons we have no trouble concluding that Mrs. Hill's counsel violated Circuit Rule 30. The question is the proper sanction for this violation.

The serious nature of Mrs. Hill's counsel's conduct makes this case a candidate for summary affirmance under *Mortell*. This and other courts have failed to entertain an appeal, or summarily affirmed a district court's decision, on solely this ground. See Guentchev v. I.N.S., 77 F.3d 1036, 1039 (7th Cir. 1996) (collecting cases). Yet summary affirmance would be no real sanction in this case because we affirm the judgment on the merits. Further, in this case at least, to summarily affirm would punish Mrs. Hill for her attorneys' misfeasance. Summary affirmance would impact the attorneys only indirectly, assuming they had a compensation arrangement contingent on winning the case.

This court recently considered this issue in *Guentchev*. Counsel for a resident alien petitioned for judicial review of a Board of Immigration Appeals' decision denying his claim for asylum. Id. at 1037. We explained in that case in detail how even if Circuit Rule 30(a), which requires in an appendix "any relevant portions of the ... findings or opinion," is misunderstood, subsection (b) of the rule directs counsel to include copies of any opinions or orders or findings of fact and conclusions of law rendered by the administrative law judge in the case. Id. at 1038–39. Because the appellant in Guentchev did not include the immigration judge's opinion in the appendix to his brief, we issued an order to show cause why his counsel should not be reprimanded or otherwise disciplined for noncompliance with Fed. R. App. P. 30(a) and Circuit Rules 30(b) and (c). Id. at 1039.

As Circuit Rule 30(b)(3) directed appellant's counsel in *Guentchev* to include the immigration law judge's opinion, so Rule 30(b)(2) mandated that Mrs. Hill's counsel include "copies of any opinions or orders in the case rendered by magistrate judges or bankruptcy judges that address the issues sought to be raised." Mrs. Hill's counsel failed to do so with no satisfactory explanation. We have already ordered her counsel to show cause and found the response lacking. Because we will affirm on the merits, vitiating the teeth of summary affirmance, and because the attorneys rather than their client deserve a reprimand for this transgression, discipline of a monetary fine is better tailored to the nature of the violation. Considering counsel's unexcusable omission of necessary documents, the impact of the deficient appendix on this court's work, as well as the ostrich-like approach to the violation, pursuant to Fed. R. App. P. 46(c) we fine attorneys for plaintiff-appellant $1,000 payable to the court for violation of Fed. R. App. P. 30 and Circuit Rule 30.

For the above-mentioned reasons, the district court's judgment is affirmed and sanctions are assessed as discussed above.

AFFIRMED with SANCTIONS.

Notes and Questions

1. The abstract of record in Illinois, and some federal circuits (e.g., the Ninth Circuit) is the counterpart of the appendix in other jurisdictions. See Goodman v. Motor Products Corp. 22 Ill.App.2d 378, 161 N.E.2d 31 (Ill. App. 1959)("There is nothing in the abstracts to show that plaintiff's attorney objected to any of the instructions which were given by the court. In order to assign as error the giving of an instruction, there must first be an objection made in the trial court to the giving of such instruction. The abstract should indicate who tendered the instructions that were given or refused. It has recently been stated that the abstract is the pleading of the party in a court of review and what is sought to be reviewed must be contained in that pleading.")

2. When the appellant has failed to include the matter in the appendix should it make a difference that the brief has a citation to the place in the original record where the issue sought to be raised on appeal was presented to and ruled upon in the trial court?

3. Under some appellate rules the appendix is treated as a substitute for the original record, while in others it is not. See Chapter 8, infra. Should this make a difference when a matter is included in the record but not the appendix?

4. In some jurisdictions the original record is forwarded to the appellate court while in others it is retained in the trial court. Should this affect the decision on the necessity for including some relevant portion of the record in the appendix?

4. ORAL ARGUMENT

R. Martineau, Modern Appellate Practice—Federal and State Civil Appeals § 3.15 (1983).

> "The relationship between preserving an issue in the brief and oral argument is twofold. The first is a consequence of the rule that an issue not in the brief is considered waived. Necessarily if the issue is considered as waived, it is not subject for oral argument.

> "The second is that courts do not treat as waived an issue raised in the brief but not argued orally. Courts usually prefer to have oral argument limited to one or two main points even if more points are included in the brief. Appellate attorneys have to expect, however, that the court will not give those issues presented in the brief but

not covered in oral argument the same careful examination as those covered in both. Appellate attorneys, therefore, should usually include in the brief only those few issues important enough to be argued orally."

Notes and Questions

1. A few courts do not follow the general rule and treat as abandoned any issue not argued orally nor expressly reserved at oral argument. See, e.g., Stevens v. Ford Motor Co., Inc., 226 Va. 415, 309 S.E.2d 319 (1983).

2. Why would a court treat raising an issue in the brief differently from doing so in the oral argument? Is it in the interest of the court, the appellant, or both?

3. In a discussion of the relationship between waiver at oral argument and the appellate courts' power of sua sponte review of issues, Miller, Sua Sponte Appellate Rulings: When Courts Deprive Litigants of an Opportunity to Be Heard, 39 San Diego L. Rev. 1253 (2002), points out that a classic case of the harshness of waiver—with a result even the court handing down the decision viewed as unjust on the merits—is Judge Posner's opinion in Hartmann v. Prudential Insurance Co. of America, 9 F.3d 1207, 1214 (7th Cir. 1993), in which the Seventh Circuit applied the waiver rule against orphans whose stepmother killed their father after bribing an insurance agent to defraud the orphans. The orphans sued for fraud and equitable reformation of the policies. There was no question of guilt—the wife and insurance agent were convicted of mail fraud in connection with the murder. The Seventh Circuit held that the court could not grant reformation of the contract, but that fraud damages were theoretically available. In oral argument, however, the plaintiffs' lawyer said—incorrectly—that reformation was required before damages were available. Because the plaintiffs' lawyer did not argue the correct grounds, the Seventh Circuit applied waiver and refused to reach the correct result sua sponte. In discussing the applicable policies, Judge Posner wrote:

> We are not happy with this result. This is a sympathetic case for the plaintiffs. But we cannot have a rule that in a sympathetic case an appellant can serve us up a muddle in the hope that we or our law clerks will find somewhere in it a reversible error. One consequence of such an approach would be that prudent appellees would have to brief issues not raised or pressed by appellants lest the appellate court fasten on such a (non)issue and use it to upend the judgment of the trial court. So briefs would be even longer than they are, and their focus even more diffuse. Another consequence would be to diminish the responsibility of lawyers and to reduce competition among them, since the court would tend to side with the weaker counsel even more than it does anyway, at least when his was the more appealing case. Our system unlike that of the Continent is not geared to having judges take over the function of lawyers, even when the result would be to rescue clients from their lawyers' mistakes. The remedy, if any, for the questionable tactical decisions apparently made by the plaintiffs' counsel in this case lies elsewhere.

After explaining why the adversary process of our system of litigation requires waiver, Judge Posner acknowledged that courts sometimes have not followed that model, but explained why those cases were different:

> It is true that courts sometimes relieve parties from the consequences of their waivers, even if the case does not fall within one of the established exceptions such as those for issues of jurisdiction or comity. We did that in a recent case where the defendant had waived an issue in the district court, but it was a pure issue of law fully briefed in our court and we could find "no reason to defer its resolution to another case. There will be no better time to resolve the issue than now." This is not such a case. Nor is it a case ... where a court decides to reexamine a precedent so deeply entrenched in the law that a litigant might not think to challenge it.

Judge Posner concluded that the plaintiffs were not entitled to relief from the waiver rule in *Hartmann* because the lawyer had told the appellate court he was not advancing what later proved to be the correct theory, "but the court's independent research and reflection persuade the court that the lawyer is wrong." The plaintiffs were bound by their lawyers' mistake because: "If reversal on such grounds is proper, we no longer have an adversary system of justice in the federal courts." Miller argues that *"Hartmann* cries out for a different result. If there were ever a case where a strict application of waiver in private litigation seems inappropriate on its facts, it would seem to be a case involving orphans (whose father's killing was arranged by their stepmother) suing an insurance company whose agent had been bribed. The Hartmann judges seemed to share this view, but felt bound by doctrine. What else could they have done?" 39 San Diego L. Rev. at 1269–70.

SECTION D.   EXCEPTIONS TO THE PRESERVATION REQUIREMENT

1.   PLAIN OR FUNDAMENTAL ERROR

DILLIPLAINE v. LEHIGH VALLEY TRUST COMPANY

Supreme Court of Pennsylvania, 1974.
457 Pa. 255, 322 A.2d 114.

ROBERTS, JUSTICE.

On April 23, 1966, automobiles driven by Wayne F. Dilliplaine and James A. Burdette collided. Subsequently Burdette died of causes unrelated to the accident. Dilliplaine then brought this trespass action against the executor of Burdette's estate, Lehigh Valley Trust Company, for injuries suffered in the accident.

The jury found for defendant and Dilliplaine's motion for a new trial was denied. The Superior Court affirmed. We granted the petition for allowance of appeal. The sole issue is whether the trial court erred by instructing the jury that the deceased was presumed to have exercised due care at the time the accident occurred.

Appellant Dilliplaine frankly concedes that he neither offered a point for charge nor took specific exception to the due care instruction actually given. In his motion for a new trial and again on appeal, he argued that in giving the presumption of due care instruction the trial judge committed basic and fundamental error.

Appellant espouses the theory that an appellate court must consider trial errors claimed to be basic and fundamental despite the absence of any objection or specific exception at trial. This theory has been applied primarily to asserted infirmities in a trial court's instructions to the jury.

We believe that two practical problems with basic and fundamental error make it an unworkable appellate procedure. Initially, appellate court recognition of alleged errors not called to the trial court's attention has a deleterious effect on the trial and appellate process. Also, despite its repeated articulation, the theory has never developed into a principled test, but has remained essentially a vehicle for reversal when the predilections of a majority of an appellate court are offended.

Appellate court consideration of issues not raised in the trial court results in the trial becoming merely a dress rehearsal. This process removes the professional necessity for trial counsel to be prepared to litigate the case fully at trial and to create a record adequate for appellate review. The ill-prepared advocate's hope is that an appellate court will come to his aid after the fact and afford him relief despite his failure at trial to object to an alleged error. The diligent and prepared trial lawyer—and his client—are penalized when an entire case is retried because an appellate court reverses on the basis of an error opposing counsel failed to call to the trial court's attention. Failure to interpose a timely objection at trial denies the trial court the chance to hear argument on the issue and an opportunity to correct error. It also tends to postpone unnecessarily disposition of other cases not yet tried for the first time. See Pa.R.C.P. 214(d), 12 P.S. Appendix.

The notion of basic and fundamental error not only erodes the finality of the trial court holdings, but also encourages unnecessary appeals and thereby further burdens the decisional capacity of our appellate courts. Trial counsel, though he may not have claimed error at trial, is inspired after trial and an adverse verdict by the thought that an appellate court may seize upon a previously unclaimed error and afford relief on a ground not called to the trial court's attention.

Perhaps at an earlier stage of our jurisprudential development this practice could be justified. Today, however, there is no excuse for and appellate courts should not encourage less than alert professional representation at trial. Virtually all active practitioners at our bar have had a formal legal education at a law school accredited by the American Bar Association. The Pennsylvania Bar Institute, Pennsylvania Trial Lawyers Association, and local bar associations as well as the American Bar Association and the American Law Institute provide programs of continuing legal education for members of the bar.

Requiring a timely specific objection to be taken in the trial court will ensure that the trial judge has a chance to correct alleged trial errors. This opportunity to correct alleged errors at trial advances the orderly and efficient use of our judicial resources. First, appellate courts will not be required to expend time and energy reviewing points on which no trial ruling has been made. Second, the trial court may promptly correct the asserted error. With the issue properly presented, the trial court is more likely to reach a satisfactory result, thus obviating the need for appellate review on this issue. Or if a new trial is necessary, it may be granted by the trial court without subjecting both the litigants and the courts to the expense and delay inherent in appellate review. Third, appellate courts will be free to more expeditiously dispose of the issues properly preserved for appeal. Finally, the exception requirement will remove the advantage formerly enjoyed by the unprepared trial lawyer who looked to the appellate court to compensate for his trial omissions.

The other major weakness of the basic and fundamental error theory is its ad hoc nature. The theory has been formulated in terms of what a particular majority of an appellate court considers basic or fundamental. Such a test is unworkable when neither the test itself nor the case law applying it develop a predictable, neutrally-applied standard.

We conclude that basic and fundamental error has no place in our modern system of jurisprudence. This doctrine, which may in the past have been acceptable, has become an impediment to the efficient administration of our judicial system. Basic and fundamental error will therefore no longer be recognized as a ground for consideration on appeal of allegedly erroneous jury instructions; a specific exception must be taken.

Because appellant failed to specifically object to the trial court's instruction on presumption of due care, we will not consider this allegation of error. The order of the Superior Court is affirmed.

MANDERINO, J., joins the Opinion of the Court and filed a concurring opinion.

O'BRIEN, J., concurs in the result.

POMEROY, J., filed a concurring and dissenting opinion in which EAGEN, J., joined.

MANDERINO, JUSTICE (concurring).

I join in the majority opinion by Mr. Justice Roberts holding that the rule of basic and fundamental error is a rule without specific standards and should be abolished. The abolition of the rule, I should like to add, does not leave an aggrieved party without a remedy.

Issues not raised in the trial court because of ineffective assistance of counsel may be reviewable on appeal in a criminal case. Commonwealth ex rel. Washington v. Maroney, 427 P. 599, 235 A.2d 349 (1967), sets forth specific standards which are applicable in determining whether counsel was effective in a criminal case.

An aggrieved party in a civil case, involving only private litigants unlike a defendant in a criminal case, does not have a constitutional right to the effective assistance of counsel. The remedy in a civil case, in which chosen counsel is negligent, is an action for malpractice.

POMEROY, JUSTICE (concurring and dissenting).

While I concur in the result reached by the majority in the case before us, I cannot agree that the time has come to discard the doctrine of basic and fundamental error as it applies to erroneous jury instructions. However limited its scope and rare the occasions for its application, I believe the doctrine has a useful role to play in protecting the constitutional rights of litigants in our courts.

The doctrine of basic and fundamental error has been long established in this and other jurisdictions. The doctrine is not confined to errors in jury instructions but can embrace any trial error which deprives a litigant of his fundamental right to a fair and impartial trial. This right is an integral part of due process of law, guaranteed to all litigants by the Fifth and Fourteenth Amendments. Obviously it is only an unusual trial error that will amount to a denial of due process, and in my view, the doctrine should be available to remedy only those trial errors so contrary to fundamental fairness as to reach the dimensions of a constitutional violation.

I am not persuaded that the doctrine of basic and fundamental error encourages careless or cynical disregard of orderly trial procedure by trial lawyers. The very uncertainty, indeed the unlikelihood, of the doctrine's application argues against any such consequence. Attorneys have everything to gain and nothing to lose from timely objection to errors at trial. We have applied the doctrine so sparingly that surely it is a rare lawyer indeed who would risk a charge of malpractice or incompetence on the speculation that an appellate court will find a particular error to be basic and fundamental.

The majority suggests that, whatever justification may once have existed for the fundamental error concept, it may now be safely discarded in view of the high quality of formal education which most trial attorneys receive today, and the various opportunities for continuing legal education. This complacency is not shared by other observers of the workings of our legal system. As Chief Justice Warren E. Burger has remarked but recently:

> "Many judges in general jurisdiction trial courts have stated to me that fewer than 25 percent of the lawyers appearing before them are genuinely qualified; other judges go as high as 75 percent. I draw this from conversations extending over the past twelve to fifteen years at judicial meetings and seminars, with literally hundreds of judges and experienced lawyers. It would be safer to pick a middle ground and accept as a working hypothesis that from one-third to one-half of the lawyers who appear in the serious cases are not really qualified to render fully adequate representation." W.E. Burger, The Special Skills of Advocacy: Are Specialized Training and

Certification of Advocates Essential to Our System of Justice? 42 Ford.L.Rev. 227, 234 (1973).

While in Pennsylvania we have what I consider a generally high degree of competence in the trial bar, the fact remains that there has been in recent decades, here as elsewhere, phenomenal change in both substantive and procedural law, accompanied by a tremendous increase in the volume of litigation. As Chief Justice Burger suggests, there is evidence that, at the same time, the quality of trial advocacy in our nation's courts has been declining. We must strive to reverse this trend, to be sure, but I do not think we should do so at the expense of litigants who are not to blame for their attorneys' shortcomings. There are other, more direct and less costly ways of raising standards of trial advocacy than discarding the doctrine of basic and fundamental error.

Nor do I believe that the fundamental error doctrine adds significantly to admittedly overcrowded appellate dockets. It is the nature of humankind to be ever hopeful in the face of the most discouraging odds, and I fear that as long as there are appellate courts there will be litigants pursuing frivolous appeals. This is particularly true in the area of criminal law, where most defendants receive legal representation at no personal cost, and where all state remedies must be exhausted to pave the way for possible relief in the federal courts. A truly egregious criminal trial error which we decline to consider on appeal because not preserved below is almost certain to resurface in a post-conviction proceeding in the form of a charge of ineffectiveness of counsel. Considerations of judicial economy argue in favor of dealing with errors of this sort on direct appeal from the judgment of sentence. See, e.g., Commonwealth v. Hallowell, supra.

Finally, it bears emphasizing that the rule now being discarded has existed not for the benefit of lazy and incompetent lawyers, but for the protection of litigants who may have been denied the essential elements of a fair and impartial trial. The considerations of judicial convenience and efficiency cited by the majority, important as they are, should give way in the rare situation where basic rights of this sort are in the balance. Cf. Niederman v. Brodsky, 436 Pa. 401, 412, 261 A.2d 84 (1970). I believe that, in repudiating the doctrine as it applies to erroneous jury instructions, the majority has taken a step which is both unnecessary and unwise.

EAGEN, J., joins in this opinion.

Notes and Questions

1.   What are the objections of the majority to the plain or fundamental error rule? Does the concurring opinion suggest a viable remedy? Is the dissenting opinion correct in suggesting that the failure to consider a fundamental issue may deny due process? Are the considerations different in a criminal proceeding than in a civil case? The position of the dissent was followed in Matter of Will of Maynard, 64 N.C.App. 211, 307 S.E.2d 416 (1983). Rejecting this approach is Mayrose v. Fendrich, 347 N.W.2d 585 (S.D.

1984). The effect of the principal case is discussed in Note, The Demise of the Doctrine of Basic and Fundamental Error in Pennsylvania and the New Role of Strict Issue Preservation, 23 Duq. L. Rev. 395 (1985).

2.   The rule in the principal case is not followed in most appellate courts. They will consider an issue not raised in the trial court if it involves a plain or fundamental error, but only a few have set out criteria for doing so. The Fifth Circuit in Rojas v. Richardson, 703 F.2d 186, 190 (5th Cir. 1983) quoted Justice Stone in United States v. Atkinson, 297 U.S. 157, 160, 56 S.Ct. 391, 392, 80 L.Ed. 555, 557 (1936) to the effect that appellate courts should notice errors which are "obvious, or * * * otherwise seriously affect the fairness, integrity, or public reputation of public proceedings." Based on this principle, the court reversed a judgment and remanded for a new trial a case in which the plaintiff's attorney had referred to the defendant as an "illegal alien." The defendant's attorney failed to object but later appealed, relying primarily on the prejudice caused by the remark. The court found that the remarks were prejudicial because they were a blatant appeal to racial and ethnic bias. Fundamental error was defined in Fallin v. Maplewood-North St. Paul Dist. Co. No. 622, 348 N.W.2d 811 (Minn.App.1984), reversed on other grounds 362 N.W.2d 318 (Minn.1985), as an error that destroys the substantial correctness of an instruction, causes a miscarriage of justice, or results in substantial prejudice. Is this any different than the general rule than an appellate court will not reverse for a harmless error?

3.   "Special verdicts" and the use of "jury interrogatories" provide a fertile ground for appeal, especially when conflicting inferences can be drawn from different questions answered by a jury. For a complete survey of the doctrines governing appellate review of special verdicts see Comment, Jury Interrogatories and the Preservation of Error in Federal Cases: Should the Plain–Error Doctrine Apply?, 30 St. Mary's L. J. 1163 (1999).

4.   The leading explication of the doctrine in the criminal context is United States v. Olano, 507 U.S. 725, 113 S.Ct. 1770, 123 L.Ed.2d 508 (1993), where the Supreme Court noted that Criminal Rule 52(b) defines a single category of forfeited-but-reversible error: "Although it is possible to read the Rule in the disjunctive, as creating two separate categories—'plain errors' and 'defects affecting substantial rights'—that reading is surely wrong." Id. at 732. The Court declared that the authority created by Rule 52(b) is circumscribed. There must be an "error" that is "plain" and that "affect[s] substantial rights." The Court held that the three limits on the doctrine of plain error are (1) that there indeed must be an "error," such as "deviation from a legal rule;" (20 the error must be "plain." The Court stated that "plain" is synonymous with "clear" or, equivalently, "obvious." ... At a minimum, court of appeals cannot correct an error pursuant to Rule 52(b) unless the error is clear under current law. (3) The third and final limitation on appellate authority under Rule 52(b) is that the plain error "affec[t] substantial rights." This is the same language employed in Rule 52(a), and in most cases it means that the error must have been prejudicial: It must have affected the outcome of the district court proceedings. Id. at 733–34. See also United States v. Promise, 255 F.3d 150, 154 (4th Cir. 2001) (en banc). For an overview of the plain error doctrine in criminal cases, see Sanders, Unpreserved Issues in Criminal Cases, 76 Florida Bar J. 51 (2002).

5.   As a final sort of catch-all, many appellants in criminal cases argue that "the cumulative effect" of a district court's evidentiary errors resulted in the denial of a fair trial. Several appellate courts have responded, however, that a "cumulative-error analysis should evaluate only the effect of matter[s] determined to be in error, not the cumulative effect of non-errors." See United States v. Rivera, 900 F.2d 1462, 1471 (10th Cir. 1990); see also Campbell v. United States, 364 F.3d 727, 736 (6th Cir. 2004). Thus where an appellate court determines that the trial court did not err in its evidentiary rulings, there can be no "cumulative error."

2. FAILURE TO STATE A CLAIM

DALE v. LATTIMORE

Court of Appeals of North Carolina, 1971.
12 N.C.App. 348, 183 S.E.2d 417.

MORRIS, JUDGE.

Defendant first contends that the complaint fails to state a cause of action and moves this Court *ore tenus* that the cause be dismissed. It appears from the record that the complaint was filed 12 March 1969, and that a demurrer was filed 30 April 1969. Order was entered overruling the demurrer on 10 July 1969. The record does not reveal an objection and exception to the entry of that order, nor does the record reveal that a motion to dismiss under Rule 12(b)(6) (failure to state a claim upon which relief can be granted) was made by defendant at trial.

We have before us, then, the question of whether a motion to dismiss an action for failure of the complaint to state a claim upon which relief can be granted can be interposed on appeal.

It is true that under the former procedure, defendant, by answering the complaint, did not waive the right to demur for failure of the complaint to state a cause of action, or for its statement of a defective cause of action. Demurrer *ore tenus* on this ground could be interposed at any time before final judgment, even in the Supreme Court on appeal. Under the former procedure, the appellate court could take cognizance of the complaint's deficiency *ex mero motu*. 6 Strong, N.C. Index 2d, Pleadings, § 26.

G.S. § 1A–1, Rule 7(c) abolished demurrers, and with them the concept of "a defective statement of a good cause of action." G.S. § 1A–1, Rule 12(b)(6) permits a motion to dismiss upon the ground that the complaint states a defective claim or cause of action but not upon the ground that the complaint contains a defective statement of a good cause of action, relief for that defect being available under other sections of Rule 12. Sutton v. Duke, 277 N.C. 94, 176 S.E.2d 161 (1970).

G.S. § 1A–1, Rule 12(b), provides that certain defenses may, at the option of the pleader, be made by motion. Among the seven listed is: "(6) Failure to state a claim upon which relief can be granted." The rule further provides: "A motion making any of these defenses shall be made before pleading if a further pleading is permitted. The consequences of failure to make such a motion shall be as provided in sections (g) and (h).''

The pertinent provision of section (g) is that if a party does make a motion under this rule but fails to include a defense or objection available to him and permitted to be raised by motion by this rule, he cannot thereafter make a motion based on the defense or objection omitted, ''except a motion as provided in section (h)(2) hereof on any of the grounds there stated.''

Section (h)(2) provides: ''A defense of failure to state a claim upon which relief can be granted, a defense of failure to join a necessary party, and an objection of failure to state a legal defense to a claim may be made in any pleading permitted or ordered under Rule 7(a), or by motion for judgment on the pleadings, or at the trial on the merits.''

Unquestionably, a motion to dismiss for failure to state a claim upon which relief may be granted, under Rule 12(b)(6), can be made as late as trial upon the merits. However, we are of the opinion that, as a general rule, the motion comes too late on appeal. The verbiage of G.S. § 1A–1, Rule 12(h) and Rule 12(h) of the Federal Rules is identical except the Federal Rule refers to ''a party indispensible under Rule 19'' and G.S. § 1A–1, Rule 12(h) refers to ''a necessary party''. The Rules of Civil Procedure in the federal courts are substantially identical, and the application thereof over the years by the federal courts may often serve as a guide in our interpretations. In Black, Sivalls & Bryson v. Shondell, 174 F.2d 587 (8th Cir. 1949), the action was brought in a Missouri state court but removed to federal district court because the requisite amount was involved, and there was diversity of citizenship. Plaintiffs sued for damages for breach of express and implied warranty in the sale of five oil storage tanks manufactured by defendant and sold to plaintiffs. The jury returned a verdict for plaintiffs and defendant appealed. Defendant had not moved for dismissal for failure of the complaint to state a claim upon which relief could be granted nor had it moved for directed verdict at the close of the evidence. After the verdict was returned and judgment entered, it moved for judgment notwithstanding the verdict or in the alternative for a new trial. On appeal one of defendant's contentions was that the complaint did not state a claim upon which relief could be granted. As to that, the Court said:

> ''Under Rule 12, Rules of Civil Procedure, 28 U.S.C.A., a defendant waives all defenses and objections which he does not present either by motion or in his answer except that the defense of failure to state a claim upon which relief may be granted may also be made by a later pleading if one is permitted or by motion for judgment on the pleadings or at the trial on the merits. The record shows no such defense presented by defendant in a motion or answer and it must be deemed to have waived the defense that the petition did not state a claim upon which relief may be granted. The motion which defendant made for judgment notwithstanding the verdict was on the grounds that 'the plaintiff's petition and the evidence discloses

that there was no privity of contract between the plaintiff and the defendant' and that 'it is uncontroverted in the evidence that the five tanks delivered by defendant complied with the terms specified in the [written] order' given by Midwest to defendant. It was made after the trial and not on the trial and did not preserve the defense of failure of the petition to state a claim. The defendant is therefore in the position of having waived that defense and may not urge it here."

We hold that where there has been a trial, a party cannot on appeal interpose the defense that the complaint fails to state a claim upon which relief can be granted.

We are aware, of course, that Rule 12(h)(3) provides that "Whenever it appears by suggestion of the parties or otherwise that the court lacks jurisdiction of the subject matter, the court shall dismiss the action." This rule is identical to Federal Rule 12(h)(3). Unquestionably lack of jurisdiction of the subject matter may always be raised by a party, or the court may raise such defect on its own initiative. See 2A Moore's Federal Practice ¶ 12.23, at 2460 (2d ed. 1968), where it is said: "Such lack of jurisdiction can never be waived by the parties or such jurisdiction conferred on a court by consent of the parties, except where a valid statute, such as the Bankruptcy Act, may allow jurisdiction to be so conferred." However, the failure of the complaint to state a claim upon which relief can be granted does not constitute a lack of jurisdiction of the subject matter. Jurisdiction of the court over the subject matter is not defeated by the possibility that the allegations of the complaint may fail to state a cause of action upon which plaintiff can recover.

"For it is well settled that the failure to state a proper cause of action calls for a judgment on the merits and not for a dismissal for want of jurisdiction. Whether the complaint states a cause of action on which relief could be granted is a question of law and just as issues of fact it must be decided after and not before the court has assumed jurisdiction over the controversy. If the court does later exercise its jurisdiction to determine that the allegations in the complaint do not state a ground for relief, then dismissal of the case would be on the merits, not for want of jurisdiction." Bell v. Hood, 327 U.S. 678, 682, 66 S.Ct. 773, 776, 90 L.Ed. 939, 943 (1946). See also North Carolina State ex rel. Utilities Commission v. Youngblood Truck Lines, 243 N.C. 442, 91 S.E.2d 212 (1956).

Appellant grouped 95 exceptions in his record on appeal. He brings forward and argues only 10 of them. The others are deemed abandoned. Rule 28, Rules of Practice in the Court of Appeals of North Carolina.

We have carefully studied and considered all of defendant's assignments of error. It is true that the record reveals technical procedural error. However, in view of the entire record, we do not deem the procedural errors sufficiently prejudicial to warrant a new trial, nor do we feel that a new trial would produce a different result.

Affirmed.

BROCK and HEDRICK, JJ., concur.

Notes and Questions

1. Some courts still treat a failure to state a claim as raising a jurisdictional issue. In Interest of B.K., 121 Ill.App.3d 662, 77 Ill.Dec. 184, 460 N.E.2d 43 (1984). Can this be justified only if fact pleading is still required?

2. See generally Martineau, Subject Matter Jurisdiction as a New Issue on Appeal: Reining in an Unruly Horse, 1988 BYU L. Rev. 1.

3. OTHER GROUNDS

Appellate courts have allowed appellants to raise a whole range of issues that were not initially presented to or considered by the trial court. Some of these exceptions arise from the nature of the question raised and others from the manner in which it is raised. The broadest statement of the authority of an appellate court to consider questions not raised below was made by the Supreme Court in Singleton v. Wulff, 428 U.S. 106, 121, 96 S.Ct. 2868, 2877, 49 L.Ed.2d 826, 837 (1976): "The matter of what questions may be taken up and resolved for the first time on appeal is one left primarily to the discretion of the court of appeals, to be exercised on the facts of the individual cases." Does this mean that an appellate court is free to consider any issue presented to it even though it was not raised below? If the only standard is one of discretion, would it ever be an abuse of discretion for an appellate court to consider an issue if it thought it might affect the result of the case?

Some of the types of issues that have been argued to be argued on appeal notwithstanding their not being presented to the trial court include:

a. Issue not raised below but briefed and argued by both sides: Haney v. Mizell Memorial Hospital, 744 F.2d 1467 (11th Cir. 1984); Nauss v. Pinkes, 2 Conn.App. 400, 480 A.2d 568 (1984).

b. Effect of subsequent relevant decision of a court whose decisions are binding on trial court: Selected Risks Ins. Co. v. Bruno, 718 F.2d 67 (3d Cir. 1983).

c. Immunity of a state under Eleventh Amendment: Ohio v. Madeline Marie Nursing Homes, 694 F.2d 449 (6th Cir. 1982).

d. Legal issue that does not require the development of additional facts: Alaska Chapter, Associated General Contractors, Inc. v. Pierce, 694 F.2d 1162 (9th Cir. 1982).

e. Issue of great public concern: Dean Witter Reynolds, Inc. v. Fernandez, 741 F.2d 355 (11th Cir. 1984); New Jersey Dept. of Education v. Hufstedler, 724 F.2d 34 (3d Cir. 1983).

MARTINEAU, CONSIDERING NEW ISSUES ON APPEAL: THE GENERAL RULE AND THE GORILLA RULE*

40 Vand. L. Rev. 1023—1061 (1987).**

I. INTRODUCTION

One aspect of the appellate process that most bedevils judges and lawyers occurs when a party attempts to raise an issue in the appellate court that it did not present to the trial court. This question creates problems for the following reasons: (1) the general rule against considering new issues on appeal; (2) the perception that it is unfair to the appellant if the new issue is not considered, yet it is unfair to the appellee if the new issue is considered; and (3) the failure or inability of appellate courts to articulate any principled basis for determining when and under what circumstances a new issue will be considered. As a result, it is almost impossible to predict in a particular case whether or not the appellate court will consider a new issue raised by the appellant. This uncertainty reduces the value of being the successful party in the trial court and adds to the already overwhelming caseload of American appellate courts by encouraging appeals. Further, in many appeals, which would have been taken in any event, it can add two issues: whether or not to consider the new issue, as well as the merits of the issue itself.

* * * The purpose of this Article is to reexamine the general rule against considering new issues on appeal, explore the many exceptions to it, and analyze whether courts should continue to apply the rule. The Article will also examine whether exceptions to the general rule should exist and, if so, which exceptions should be recognized and under what circumstances.

To present the issue clearly, the Article will focus on those issues in a civil case that (1) the appellant knew or should have known about; (2) could have been raised in the trial court but were not raised, only because of the act or omission of the complaining party; (3) may constitute reversible error; (4) are sought to be raised by appellant over the objection of the appellee. With these limitations, other factors such as constitutional requirements applicable only to criminal cases, inability to raise the issue earlier for reasons not attributable to the appellant, new theory to support the judgment, specificity, harmless error, and acquiescence of appellee are beyond the scope of this Article. In essence, this Article will consider the question of waiver by the appellant.

II. THE GENERAL RULE

A. Historical Development and Rationale

[Professor Martineau's introduction to the historical role of error review is set forth in Section A of this Chapter].

---

* A well known riddle asks: "Where does an eight-hundred pound gorilla sleep?" The response is: "Anywhere it wants." J. Sarnoff, I Know! A Riddle Book 53 (1976). The judicial application of this rule would be: "When will an appellate court consider a new issue?" The response is: "Any time it wants."

** Copyright © 1987, Vanderbilt Law Review, Vanderbilt University. Reprinted by permission. All rights reserved.

The validity of [the modern approach to the requirement of error preservation] should be examined from the viewpoints of the private and public interests involved in the court proceeding. The private interests are those of the litigants in the particular case. From the perspective of the party who is affected adversely by the trial court action, common sense dictates that the party should be compelled to "speak up now or forever hold your peace" if the party realizes or should realize at the time the action is taken that the effect will be adverse to its interests. In various legal contexts, this principle is characterized as waiver, clean hands, and invited error. At the heart of these doctrines is the essential point that a person should not benefit from his own inaction or, stated obversely, a person has an obligation to assert his rights at the first opportunity or within a specified time. The various rules of procedure that require a matter to be raised in a particular document, by a particular time, or in a particular way, with the failure to do so resulting in a forfeiture of the right or claim are merely expressions of the same principle. Implicit in the general rule against considering new issues on appeal is the recognition that courts must come to a conclusion if they are to perform their function of resolving disputes; but to reach conclusions, courts must enforce rules of procedure. It is not unreasonable to expect that persons who avail themselves of a forum should follow that forum's rules of procedure, and not be heard to complain about an adverse effect from their failure to do so.

From the viewpoint of the adversary whose interests are advanced by the trial court's action, requiring the objecting party to speak up at the time the action occurs is not only highly desirable but a matter of simple fairness. If the adverse party is aware of the objection the party can, as Judge Aldisert has pointed out, urge that the action not be taken, an alternative be adopted, or make as complete a record as possible to support the action. If no objection is made, the adverse party may think that the other party agrees with the action or for tactical reasons decides not to raise an objection. In either case the adverse party may fail to develop a record that would support the action taken or forgo taking some step that would avoid the alleged error. The failure to object is particularly important with regard to the development of the record. The party seeking to have the trial court act is unlikely to attempt to put the basis for the request in the record when there is no objection from the other party. That is just "gilding the lily" insofar as the trial court proceedings are concerned. Competent trial counsel always are conscious of the hazards of trying to prove that which does not have to be proven and of appearing to waste the court's time in so doing.

The public interests to consider include those of the trial and appellate courts and other present and future litigants who look to the courts to resolve disputes. It is difficult to see any positive effect on the trial court other than the time saved initially when no objection is made. Three results can flow from considering a new issue on appeal. First, the appellate court will consider the new issue to be reversible error requiring either the entry of a new judgment or, more likely, further proceedings in the trial court. Second, the appellate court will not find reversible error, in which case the trial court's original judgment will stand (unless some other reversible error is found). Third, the appellate court will find reversible error not only on the new issue but on some other properly preserved issue that requires further proceedings in the trial court. From the viewpoint of the trial court, the effect of considering the new issue may be neutral at best, requiring no additional time on its part. At worst the new issue may require substantial additional proceedings in the trial court and possibly a new trial, which is the most likely result of reversible error. Furthermore, the appellate court is unlikely to consider the new issue unless the court perceives some likelihood that reversible error exists.

Invariably, there is a negative effect on the appellate court when new issues are raised on appeal. Each time an appellant asks the appellate court to consider an issue not raised in the trial court, the appellate court must devote time to deciding whether to consider the issue and, if it decides to do so, must then spend additional time examining its merits. Inevitably, the more an appellate court is willing to consider new issues, the more likely it is that additional appeals will be taken. A losing party who will not appeal if the party knows that the appellate court will not consider new issues may do so if it thinks that the appellate court may consider the issue. The same principle applies in a case in which other issues are properly preserved on appeal. The losing party may decide to raise an issue overlooked in the trial court just in case the other issues are found to be without merit. The work of the appellate court is increased in either instance.

Litigants in other present and future cases necessarily are affected whenever an appellate court devotes time to a new issue or a trial court is compelled to spend time on a case that has been reversed and remanded by the appellate court as a result of considering the new issue. Any additional time spent on one case necessarily delays the consideration of cases involving other litigants. The only advantage to other litigants occurs if they also seek to raise a new issue in the appellate court.

In Dilliplaine v. Lehigh Valley Trust Co. [set forth in Section D of this Chapter] the Pennsylvania Supreme Court analyzed the reasons for the enforcement of the general rule against considering new issues on appeals. In *Dilliplaine* the appellant attempted to challenge an instruction given by the trial court even though the appellant had neither requested a different instruction nor objected when the instruction was given. The appellant argued that the appellate court should ignore the general rule because the giving of the instruction by the trial court was plain or fundamental error. The court acknowledged previously allowing new issues to be raised under the plain or fundamental error exception to the general rule. In eliminating the exception, however, the court pointed to the exception's harmful effects on both the trial and appellate processes. The court's analysis, which examined the effects on the adversary, the trial and appellate courts, and other litigants, is similar to that outlined in the preceding paragraphs. The court also criticized the practice of allowing exceptions to the general rule. In looking at its own experience with the plain and fundamental error exception, the court concluded that another major weakness of the exception was its ad hoc nature. Despite the court's repeated use of the exception, the court indicated:

> [T]he theory [of the exception] has never developed into a principled test, but has remained essentially a vehicle for reversal when the predilections of a majority of an appellate court are offended. * * * The theory has been formulated in terms of what a particular majority of an appellate court considers basic or fundamental. Such a test is unworkable when neither the test itself nor the case law applying it develop a predictable, neutrally-applied standard.

This statement, remarkable in its candor, acknowledges that appellate courts ignore a basic requirement of the appellate process when they make exceptions to procedural rules for reasons they describe as "plain," "basic," "fundamental error," or "in the interests of justice." Appellate judges must recognize that they cannot render decisions that apply only to the facts of one case. Precedent and stare decisis are essential features of a common-law system. Appellate courts undercut the entire system when they ignore the precedential value of cases. Judge Albert Tate, Jr. made this point in the following terms:

> The result that seems "just" for the present case must be a principled one that will afford just results in similar conflicts of interest.... [A] judge has an initial human concern that the litigants receive common-sense justice, but he also realizes that the discipline of legal doctrine governs his determination of the cause.

When courts deviate from this principle, they inject a degree of uncertainty into the law that is inimical to the system of justice, weakening the predictability that is such an important part of any system of appellate review. Without predictability, the appellate process becomes little more than an exercise by which the appellant attempts to persuade the appellate court that the result reached by the trial court was not the "right" result. This system of appellate review makes every appeal a de novo proceeding in which the parties try the issue on the merits. Such an unpredictable system is inconsistent with the premises of appellate review in this country. To act in some cases as though it were consistent is to change the premises of the system on an ad hoc basis with no clearly established criteria for doing so.

III. EXCEPTIONS TO THE GENERAL RULE

A. Criteria

A court usually does not give a rationale when it decides whether to consider a new issue on appeal in contravention of the general rule. Instead, the court merely cites the general rule if it refuses to consider the new issue. If the court chooses to consider the issue, it points to some earlier case in which the same type of issue was considered for the first time on appeal and then proceeds to decide the issue. On a few occasions, however, courts have identified certain previously developed criteria for allowing exceptions to the general rule and have attempted to determine whether the new issue satisfies these criteria. In United States v. Krynicki, [689 F.2d 289 (1st Cir. 1982)], for example, the First Circuit listed the following factors as determinative: (1) is the issue purely legal, not requiring the introduction of additional facts?; (2) is the proper resolution of the issue beyond doubt?; (3) is the issue certain to arise in other cases?; and (4) will declining to consider the issue result in a miscarriage of justice? These criteria are helpful in analyzing individual exceptions to the general rule because they can be examined in light of the various interests affected by the general rule.

The first criterion creates an exception for purely legal issues that do not require the development of additional facts. The issue considered in *Krynicki* is typical. The court was asked in that case to decide an issue of statutory construction—does the Speedy Trial Act require an indictment within thirty days of the initial arrest, even though the charges stemming from that arrest are no longer pending? The trial court dismissed the indictment because it was not made within thirty days of the original arrest. On appeal the government argued for the first time that the original charges still had to be pending when the indictment was handed down for the thirty-day period to apply. The Court of Appeals for the First Circuit concluded that the appellee would not have been able to introduce any facts bearing on the question at trial because its resolution was dependent solely on the language of the statute and its legislative history. Thus, the court's consideration of the issue for the first time on appeal did not prejudice the appellee.

Courts have characterized many issues as purely legal, thus allowing them to be raised for the first time on appeal. These issues include questions of the applicability of a constitutional provision, statute, or legal doctrine concededly or arguably applicable but not mentioned in the lower court. According to the *Krynicki* court, the assumption behind this exception is that facts are irrelevant to the resolution of the question or all of the relevant facts are in the record. This being true, the courts reason that the opposing party would not have introduced any additional evidence had the issue been raised in the trial court, and thus the opposing party is not prejudiced when the new issue is considered on appeal.

This series of assumptions is of questionable validity. To suggest that an appellate court can look at the record and conclude that no additional, relevant evidence could have been introduced on a completely new legal issue had the parties known it would be decisive in the case simply flies in the face of what we know about the trial process. No case is tried so completely and competently that an appellate court can confidently say that the trial would have gone exactly the same way if a new, determinative, legal issue had been raised in the trial court. The presumption should be to the contrary. It does not require a great deal of imagination to predict the reaction of the trial judge who questions the relevance of evidence sought to be introduced that may not be relevant to any issue before the trial court, but may be relevant to a new issue that the opposing party may decide to raise in the appellate court.

Royal Indemnity Co. v. Blakely, [372 Mass. 86, 360 N.E.2d 864 (1977)], is one of the few cases in which an appellate court has given a thoughtful response to an appellant's attempt to raise a new, purely legal, issue on appeal. In Blakely the Massachusetts Supreme Judicial Court refused to consider the question of the applicability of a statute requiring uninsured motorist coverage to the limitations on coverage in an insurance policy. The appellee argued that it would be prejudiced by the new issue because it had no opportunity to produce evidence on the legality of the limitations. The appellee did not state explicitly, however, what kind of evidence it would have offered on the issue. The court suggested that evidence could have been introduced on the interpretation of the statute by the administering state agency. The court pointed out that courts often look to administrative statutory interpretations in construing a statute.

Forcing the appellee to show prejudice from consideration of a new issue places the appellee in an almost impossible position because it asks the appellee to speculate on what might have been different had the issue been raised in the trial court. The appellee cannot state with any confidence what might have been different and thus cannot be certain how it would have benefited had it been aware of the issue in the trial court. By allowing the issue to be raised for the first time on appeal, appellate courts ignore the most obvious prejudice to the appellee: the taking away of a judgment in the appellee's favor. Defeat rather than victory is the ultimate prejudice. The response to this reasoning is that the appellee is losing nothing to which it is entitled because the result would have been adverse to the appellee anyway had the issue been raised in the trial court. This argument is faulty, however, in its assumption that the appellate court is able to know where justice lies between the parties in some absolute sense and can ensure that the "right" party prevails by considering a new issue.

The reality of the judicial process renders this assumption untenable. What an appellate court knows about a case, particularly regarding the equities between the parties, is limited to what is shown in the record. The record in turn is limited to the trial court proceedings, which are a function of the pleadings, the abilities of counsel, the rulings of the trial court, the availability of witnesses and other evidence, the identity of the trial judge, the composition of the jury, the rules of evidence, the rules of procedure, and the substantive laws of the jurisdiction. No one would argue that the system is a system of perfect justice. In the words of Justice Holmes, the best that appellate judges can do is to ensure that the game is played by the rules.[50] Yet an appellate court ignores a rule

50. L. Hand, The Spirit of Liberty 306–07 (I. Dilliard 3d ed. 1960).

long considered basic to the adversary process in an effort to come to the "right" result when it decides a case on a legal issue not raised in the trial court.

Considering a new legal issue on appeal unless the appellee can show prejudice also ignores the practicalities of appellate practice. In the usual case the appellant will raise the new issue in its initial brief. Consequently, the appellee will learn of the new issue for the first time when it receives the appellant's brief. The appellee has thirty days at most in which to file its own brief in which the appellee must address those issues raised by the appellant that were considered in the trial court, the question of whether the new issue should be considered by the appellate court, and the merits of that issue. The appellee also must address whether considering the new issue is permitted under any exception to the general rule. If consideration is permitted, the appellee must attempt to show prejudice. Thus, the appellee has but a few short days in which to develop theories and arguments and conduct research on an issue that it otherwise would have had months or years to develop had the issue been raised in the trial court. Clearly, this is procedural prejudice. Yet appellate courts again and again consider new legal issues with a mere recitation of the rubric that the new issue is purely legal, no new facts are required to decide the issue, and the appellee has not shown that it will be prejudiced if the new issue is considered.

When appellate courts follow this course of action they either do not understand, or chose to ignore, the implication of their actions. When the "purely legal" criterion is measured against the modern rationale for the general rule, a conclusory statement that the issue is purely legal and its resolution would not require the development of additional facts ignores the likelihood that both the appellee and the trial court would have had other options in addition to the opportunity to develop fully a record to support the action. These options include the decision not to take the action in question or take some other action to avoid the objection. Of course, these options are not available if the objection is not raised until the case reaches the appellate court.

The second criterion listed in *Krynicki* for considering a new issue on appeal is that the proper resolution of the question must be beyond doubt. The *Krynicki* court found that "preliminary examination of this legal issue by the trial court would not benefit either the court or the parties appreciably" because the government's argument was so compelling. This reasoning ignores both the assistance to the appellate court of having statutes or other legal principles first construed by the trial court where its effects are felt directly, as well as the opportunity for the opposing party or the trial court to take some alternative action or no action to avoid the alleged error. Presumably, the likelihood that the trial court would have persisted in its course of action after the error was pointed out is highly unlikely if the action taken by the trial court was so clearly an error. This criterion essentially is characterized as the plain, basic, or fundamental error exception.

The third criterion does not relate so much to the issue's impact on the case in which it is raised but its impact on future cases. In *Krynicki* the court held that declining to reach the issue "will neither promote judicial economy, nor aid in the administration of the criminal justice system" because the issue was certain to arise in other cases. This is a strange reason to consider an issue in a particular case as an exception to the general rule. The only other type of case in which the courts hear an issue not properly before the court on the ground that the issue is certain to arise in future cases is when the mootness of the case otherwise would prevent its consideration. The justification for the mootness exception is closely akin to the doctrine of necessity. Considering an issue in a moot case is the only way the issue will be considered. This crucial factor, however, is not present when the only reason the issue is not properly before the appellate court is because the issue was not presented to the trial court. In fact, the assumption is just the opposite. There is every likelihood that the issue will be raised properly in future cases; thus, the court will be able to rule on the issue without making an exception to the general rule. The court can state its views on the issue in the present case without making an exception to the general rule if the court wishes to do so. A common procedure is for the court to decide expressly that the issue is not properly before the court but to state what its position will be in future cases. While pure dictum is not binding in future cases, such a statement provides guidance to attorneys and lower courts. This practice is followed most often when the court wishes to take the opportunity to indicate that it finds no merit to the issue being raised.

The *Krynicki* court identified the last criterion—causing a miscarriage of justice—is the most important. In the *Krynicki* opinion and other cases that follow the same approach, the phrase "miscarriage of justice" is not defined. What the courts apparently mean is that the issue would have resulted in reversible error if it had been properly raised; failure to consider the issue will cause the affirmance of a judgment infected by reversible error; to affirm such a judgment would be a miscarriage of justice; to avoid a miscarriage of justice the court will consider the new issue.

The logic of this reasoning has the virtue of simplicity to recommend it, but little else. Under this reasoning, an appellate court should allow any reversible error to be raised as an exception to the general rule because a miscarriage of justice will result if any reversible error is ignored. This means that the only issues an appellate court should not allow to be raised as an exception to the general rule are issues that do not constitute reversible error. If an issue would not constitute reversible error, however, there is no harm to either the appellee or the public interests by considering the issue because the judgment that is appealed still will stand. Consequently, the miscarriage of justice criterion is simply another way of saying that the general rule is not the general rule but, rather, is a rule that should never be followed, at least in any case in which it would affect the result.

In *Krynicki* it is unclear whether the four criteria on which the analysis is based are intended to be cumulative or in the alternative. In *Krynicki* the particular issue satisfied all four criteria, but the court did not indicate whether the result would have been different had it not. The first of the four criteria requires that the issue be a legal issue requiring no further factual development. Presumably, the court would not consider the issue or at least would remand the case for further development of the record if the factual record was not complete. The latter procedure would give the opposing party an opportunity to present any facts it thought would support its position. While this procedure would reduce the unfairness to the appellee, it would not allow the trial court or the appellee, absent remand, to take an alternative action or no action at all in order to avoid the claimed error. The requirement that the issue be purely legal would appear to be a sine qua non of exceptions to the general rule.

Requiring that the resolution of the issue be so clear as to leave no doubt as to the result appears to be cumulative with the requirement that the issue be purely legal. As with the first criterion, the rationale for the second criterion is that having the trial court consider the issue would not aid in its resolution. The second could not exist independently of the first because if all of the facts necessary for resolution of the issue were not in the record, its proper resolution could not be clear.

Whether or not the issue is likely to arise in future cases does not appear to be so much a requirement that supplements the first two criteria but is simply an added reason to consider the issue. It is highly unlikely that an issue would be unique to the pending case and not likely to arise in the future. Even if this were the situation, it hardly would be a reason to refuse to consider the issue if the first two conditions were satisfied.

The requirement that refusal to consider the issue would result in a miscarriage of justice is clearly cumulative with the first and second criteria. The likelihood of the issue arising in future cases and the miscarriage of justice criteria could, however, be considered to be in the alternative. The resolution of the issue to give guidance in future cases may be sufficient reason to consider the issue even if for some reason the issue would not constitute reversible error in the pending case. By the same token, avoiding a miscarriage of justice in the present case would be a sufficient basis for considering the issue even if it were doubtful that the issue would arise again.

In summary, it would appear that of the four requirements set forth in *Krynicki*, an issue would have to satisfy both the first and the second as well as one or both of the third and fourth criteria, but not all four, in order to allow an exception to the general rule. In other words, an exception to the general rule against considering new issues on appeal is justified under *Krynicki* if the following criteria are satisfied: (1) the new issue is purely legal and does not require the introduction of additional facts; (2) the proper resolution of the issue is beyond doubt; and (3) either the issue is certain to arise in future cases or failure to consider the issue will result in a miscarriage of justice in the present case.

Most courts faced with the question of whether to allow an exception to the general rule do not make an analysis similar to that in *Krynicki*. Far more common is for a court to consider an issue solely on the basis of its substantive nature (e.g., legal issue, constitutional issue, jurisdictional issue, eleventh amendment) or its impact on the proceedings (plain error or miscarriage of justice). Some cases have attempted to qualify the issue under one of the criteria set forth in *Krynicki* without examining the other criteria. For instance, in Singleton v. Wulff, [428 U.S. 106 (1976)], the Supreme Court listed two types of cases in which a court of appeals could exercise its discretion to resolve an issue not raised in the trial court. The Court cited those cases in which the issue was not in doubt or where injustice may otherwise result. The Court, however, merely was citing these instances as examples of when it would be appropriate for a court of appeals to exercise its discretion to hear and decide a new issue. The attitude of the court is summarized best by its statement, "[W]e announce no general rule." Singleton would have been a particularly appropriate case for the Court to have established general guidelines for consideration of a new issue on appeal. The Court reversed an appellate decision that relied on an issue not considered in the trial court. The Court, however, held only that under the circumstances of the case, consideration of the new issue was improper. The Court gave little guidance other than to cite two types of cases in which considering a new issue would be proper. * * *

B. Analysis of the Principal Exceptions

1. Subject Matter Jurisdiction

The most universally recognized exception to the general rule is subject matter jurisdiction. The exception applies to the subject matter jurisdiction of both the trial court and the appellate court. Subject matter jurisdiction is considered so central to the legal process that it can be raised at any time by either party, or by the court on its own motion. If an appellate court is not satisfied that it has jurisdiction over an appeal, the court must dismiss the appeal. Because subject matter jurisdiction cannot be waived, this objection differs from most other jurisdictional objections such as lack of personal jurisdiction and expiration of the statute of limitations.

The requirement that a court have subject matter jurisdiction—something that cannot be conferred by the parties either by failure to object or by express consent—is a fundamental doctrine of civil procedure to which there are no exceptions. While there may be some debate over exactly what is an issue of subject matter jurisdiction, once an issue is fairly within the scope of the term, the court must be satisfied that it has jurisdiction or dismiss the proceeding. Concerns over how, when, or by whom the issue of subject matter jurisdiction is raised are irrelevant. The various interests to consider in analyzing the validity of the general rule and its exceptions do not even begin to come into play. Put simply, the general rule presupposes subject matter jurisdiction. Thus, allowing the issue of subject matter jurisdiction to be raised at any time is not an exception to the general rule but a precondition before the general rule can become applicable.

2.   *Quasi–Jurisdictional Issues*

a.   Eleventh Amendment

Some courts also allow certain issues relating to the exercise of jurisdiction to be raised at any time. The immunity from suit granted to states by the eleventh amendment is one issue that is treated most like subject matter jurisdiction. Recent cases have held that when the state's attorney does not interpose the eleventh amendment as a bar to a lawsuit against the state in the trial court, the issue can be raised on appeal. The rationale for these decisions is that the immunity granted by the eleventh amendment can be waived only by the state legislature, not by the state's attorney's failure to raise the defense. This position was first enunciated by the Supreme Court in Ford Motor Co. v. Department of Treasury, [323 U.S. 459 (1945)]. The Court stated: "The Eleventh Amendment declares a policy and sets forth an explicit limitation on federal judicial power of such compelling force that this court will consider the issue arising under this amendment in this case even though urged for the first time in this court." * * *

Viewed only as an immunity issue, the closest analogies to the state's immunity from suit under the eleventh amendment are the sovereign immunity of governments and the absolute and qualified immunity of public officials. The ordinary waiver doctrine applies to both the sovereign immunity of governments and the immunity of public officials. The waiver doctrine similarly should apply to eleventh amendment immunity. As a result, the issue of immunity under the eleventh amendment should not be an exception to the general rule against considering new issues on appeal.

b.   Constitutionality of a State Statute

Whether or not a federal court should abstain from ruling on the constitutionality of a state statute when its decision may depend upon the state court's interpretation of the statute is another issue that the Supreme Court and some lower federal courts have held is an exception to the general rule. The underlying reason for the courts' reluctance to act on the constitutional issue, and to allow the statutory question to be raised in violation of the general rule, arises from the principle that a court should not rule on a constitutional issue unless it is absolutely necessary to do so. Arguing on appeal that the appellate court should not decide an issue when no similar objection had been presented to the trial court is not the same as asking the appellate court to decide an issue not raised in the trial court. There is no rule that requires an appellate court to decide every issue decided by the trial court. This same principle is used to permit a court to consider a new statutory issue not raised below if it will permit avoidance of the constitutional issue.

To allow the statutory issue to be considered in these circumstances can be viewed as an exception to the general rule because the appellate court is not required to consider a new issue. As with subject matter jurisdiction, however, the "no constitutional decision unless absolutely necessary" principle operates totally outside the general rule. This principle arises not from a concern for the party raising the issue but from basic considerations of federalism and restraint in the use of judicial power. Unlike the general rule, this principle does not have its basis in the adversary system or in concern for the rights of the litigants to the proceeding. Whether or not a court should follow this principle in a particular case depends upon considerations totally independent of the general rule. Consequently, it should not be considered as an exception to the general rule.

3. *Questions of Law*

The exception to the general rule for pure questions of law is discussed in section III, part A.

4. *"Plain," "Basic," or "Fundamental Error"*

Other than subject matter jurisdiction and a pure legal issue, the exception to the general rule most often used by appellate courts is when the trial court makes an error that is described as plain, basic, or fundamental. One of the most common errors within this classification involves instructions to a jury—either the failure to give an instruction or the giving of an improper instruction. This Article will use jury instructions as the basis for an analysis of the exception to the general rule for plain, basic, or fundamental error.

The first step in this analysis is to define plain error. One of the major problems in analyzing the general rule and its exceptions is that courts seldom define their terms. Instead, courts do little more than make conclusory statements. Nowhere is this more blatant than when courts deal with the plain error exception. Recently the Court of Appeals for the Fifth Circuit attempted to define plain error by quoting a statement by Justice Stone in United States v. Atkinson, [297 U.S. 157, 160 (1936)]. Stone stated that appellate courts should "notice errors to which no exception has been taken, if the errors are obvious, or if they otherwise seriously affect the fairness, integrity or public reputation of judicial proceedings."The Minnesota Supreme Court has defined plain error as error that destroys the substantial correctness of an instruction, causes a miscarriage of justice, or results in substantial prejudice.[110]

An examination of the development of Justice Stone's definition of plain error demonstrates how a narrowly drawn exception to the general rule can be expanded into a roving commission for appellate judges to seek out and correct error wherever it can be found. Justice Stone's full statement of the exception reads as follows: "In exceptional circumstances, especially in criminal cases, appellate courts, in the public

---

110.   Lindstrom v. Yellow Taxi Co., 298 Minn. 224, 229, 214 N.W.2d 672, 676 (1974).

interest, may, of their own motion, notice errors to which no exception has been taken, if the errors are obvious, or if they otherwise seriously affect the fairness, integrity or public reputation of judicial proceedings." Justice Stone was stating a rule with particular application to criminal cases in which the court was acting in the public interest and on its own motion. Only if a court ignores these crucial qualifiers can the exception be expanded to apply to a civil case in which the appellant is seeking to have the appellate court consider a new issue solely to protect its private interests. Justice Stone obviously was concerned with something more than just an erroneous instruction or the failure to give an instruction. This conclusion is made abundantly clear by the circumstances of the case in which the statement was made.

Atkinson involved the question of whether there was statutory authority for a Veterans Administration regulation permitting government insurance policies to define total disability as including the loss of hearing in both ears. The Court held that the government could not raise the issue on appeal, having failed to object to the jury instructions on the issue in the trial court. The Court gave the general rule as its reason for not allowing the new issue to be raised, citing fairness to the court and the parties as well as the public interest in bringing to an end litigation after a fair opportunity has been provided to present all issues of fact and law. Only after discussing the general rule did Justice Stone define plain error. Stone concluded that the question presented in Atkinson did not fall within the exception. Consequently, Justice Stone's statement of the plain error exception was mere dictum.

In his statement of the exception, Justice Stone cited two previous opinions that he authored. The earlier of the two was a criminal case in which the issue was whether the defendant's objection to a question by the trial judge asking the jury on how it was divided and thus unable to reach a verdict was sufficiently particularized. The Court held that particularization was not necessary to allow review of the action because it involved the proper relation of the trial court to the jury and could not be remedied by a modification of the charge to the jury after the harm had been done. The second case also involved an objection which, it was argued, was not sufficiently particularized to allow the objection to be considered as raising the issue in the trial court. In this case the error was the trial court's failure to prevent or correct misconduct by counsel. The appellate court emphasized the trial court's responsibility to prevent appeals to passion and prejudice independent of an objection. This last point is especially significant because Justice Stone framed the rule in terms of what an appellate court may notice on its own motion, or sua sponte, and not when the court may consider a new issue raised by a party. Although it bears some similarity to allowing a party to raise a new issue, sua sponte consideration involves substantially different considerations. For this reason, the two questions have always received separate treatment.

Justice Stone's essential point was that in some circumstances the responsibility of the court to protect the integrity of judicial proceedings transcends the adversary process. The Court held that an attorney's appeal to a jury's racial or ethnic prejudice is one of those circumstances. The courts have the same responsibility to preserve the integrity of the judicial process as they do to ensure they have jurisdiction; these are not matters that can be waived by the parties. Thus they both fall into the same category and should not be considered as exceptions to the general rule.

The plain error exception has received a full analysis in only one case, *Dilliplaine v. Lehigh Valley Trust Co.* [set forth in Section C of this Chapter]. In *Dilliplaine* the Pennsylvania Supreme Court decided to abandon its long held recognition of the plain error exception. The court's reasons for abandoning the exception were based on the exception's adverse effect on the various interests involved, namely the litigants, their attorneys, the trial court, and the appellate court. The court also recognized the ad hoc nature of the exception and that neutral standards for the rule never had been developed. Thus, the court acknowledged that the exception was used whenever a majority of the court felt in any given case that an error meriting reversal had been committed. The alleged error in *Dilliplaine* was the trial court's instruction relating to due care in an automobile accident case. The opinion of Justice Pomeroy, who concurred in the result in the case but dissented from the abolition of the plain error exception, is instructive. In Pomeroy's view the plain error rule applies to

> any trial error which deprives a litigant of his fundamental right to a fair and impartial trial. This right is an integral part of due process of law, guaranteed to all litigants by the Fifth and Fourteenth Amendments. Obviously it is only an unusual trial error that will amount to a denial of due process, and in my view, the doctrine should be available to remedy only those trial errors so contrary to fundamental fairness as to reach the dimensions of a constitutional violation.

The cases cited by Justice Pomeroy in support of his position were criminal cases. There is no question that in criminal cases the requirements of due process outweigh principles of waiver, particularly in view of the opportunity to raise constitutional issues in post conviction proceedings. One court specifically has refused to apply the plain error rule to civil cases, describing it as a rule of criminal procedure inapplicable to civil cases. This approach is valid because due process in civil cases requires only notice and an opportunity to be heard; in contrast, far more extensive protection is required in criminal proceedings. Waiver of both substantive and procedural questions are part and parcel of civil procedure. Questions of due process simply do not arise if the requirements of minimal notice and opportunity to be heard have been met.

In applying these standards to jury instructions in a civil case, a court should not permit an objection to jury instructions to be raised for the first time on appeal under the plain error exception if a litigant has failed to request or object to an instruction in the trial court. Neither due process nor the integrity of the judicial process is involved when a party who is participating in a jury trial has an opportunity to request or object to an instruction but does not through no fault of the court. The party had ample opportunity to protect its rights, but simply failed to do so.

The provisions of Federal Rule of Procedure 51 and its state counterparts demonstrate the impatience of the drafters of civil procedure rules with tardy requests for, or objections to, jury instructions. Rule 51 expressly provides that a party cannot assign as error the giving or failing to give an instruction unless an objection is made, including giving the grounds for the objection. This rule is not qualified so as to exempt a really "bad" instruction or the failure to give an obvious instruction. There is, in short, no plain error exception to this rule, and the courts should not create one.

IV. "WE ANNOUNCE NO GENERAL RULE"

The ultimate goal of a system of appellate review is uniformity. Uniformity in this context means that persons in similar circumstances are treated similarly. In Singleton v. Wulff the Supreme Court stated that one way to test the validity of allowing appellate courts to permit exceptions to the general rule is to examine whether appellate courts consistently apply the various types of exceptions. If courts consistently recognize certain exceptions to the general rule, the general rule can be said to incorporate these exceptions. Therefore, litigants, attorneys, and judges will share the same expectations regarding considerations of new issues on appeal.[137] Attorneys and their clients will not be surprised or

---

137. Even the original gorilla rule is not without its exceptions.

THE FAR SIDE   By GARY LARSON

"Look. I'm sorry ... If you *weighed* 500 pounds, we'd certainly accommodate you — but it's simply a fact that a 400-pound gorilla does *not* sleep anywhere he wants to."

THE FAR SIDE, by Gary Lason, Copyright, 1986, Universal Press Syndicate, Reprinted with permission. All rights reserved.

disappointed when the court considers or refuses to consider a new issue, which enhances uniformity and predictability.

The principal difficulty with this idealized description of appellate courts' application of exceptions to the general rule is that it is exactly the opposite of how these exceptions are currently applied by appellate courts. Inconsistency is the hallmark of the various exceptions. For every case that can be found in which an exception to the general rule is allowed, another exists in which the court refused to permit the exception and enforced the general rule. This is a situation in which the rule is sometimes honored and sometimes breached, with no discernible basis for predicting when one or the other will occur. The best description of the current status of all of the exceptions to the general rule was given by the *Dilliplaine* court in describing the plain error rule in Pennsylvania—the exceptions are nothing more than vehicles for reversal when the predilections of a majority of an appellate court are offended. This is ad hoc decision making at its worst.

Inconsistency in the recognition and application of exceptions to the general rule is easily demonstrated. An examination of cases in state appellate courts clearly shows that for every exception to the general rule one court has permitted, another court has refused to permit a similar exception. An extensive list of these cases is set forth in Appendix I, [40 Vand. L. Rev. At 1062 et seq.].The list ranges from subject matter jurisdiction to objections to the admission of evidence and covers virtually every aspect of the trial court proceedings.

Inconsistency also exists in the federal courts, but in a slightly different way. The principal problem is not so much that one circuit will allow an exception and another will not (although that problem does exist), but that the various circuits are creating an ever expanding list of exceptions with little or no regard to prior case law, previously developed criteria, or limitations imposed in earlier cases. The statement in Singleton that "[w]e announce no general rule," while intended to describe the lack of any specific limitations on exceptions to the general rule means, in effect, that the general rule is no longer a general rule.

If the courts attempted to develop objective criteria for determining when an exception should be recognized and simply differed on the application of the criteria, inconsistency in the recognition of exceptions to the general rule would not be a matter of great concern. The cases indicate, however, that very few courts have attempted to develop objective criteria. In the overwhelming majority of cases the court merely decides whether or not to recognize an exception, giving no rationale for its action. If the court refuses to consider the new issue it merely recites the general rule. If the court does consider the new issue, it simply states the exception to the rule (with or without citing authority for allowing the exception). The question is resolved in conclusory terms with little or no analysis to support whatever decision is made. As a result, the dominant characteristic of the application of the general rule and its exceptions is inconsistency.

V.   A PROPOSED SOLUTION

The rationale behind the general rule against considering new issues on appeal provides compelling reasons for its continued vitality. A few instances exist, however, when the general rule should not be enforced. One instance is when the issue involves subject matter jurisdiction, which is properly not an exception to the general rule but a precondition to appellate review that a court should raise on its own motion. The same applies to those cases in which principles of federalism or constitutional adjudication are involved or when the integrity of the judicial process is threatened.

Besides those situations in which the general rule is not applicable, there are other types of issues that can be raised for the first time in the appellate court without doing violence to the rationale of the general rule. The Federal Rules of Civil Procedure recognize two avenues for a party to seek relief from a judgment: a motion filed in the court that issued the judgment or a separate action. Under Rule 60(b) a party can seek relief from a judgment for any of six reasons. Some of the reasons would not be exceptions to the general rule by their nature because they involve matters about which the appellant could not have known at the time of trial. The others provide a well developed body of law for permitting exceptions to the general rule, including mistake, inadvertence, surprise, excusable neglect, void judgment, misconduct of a party, or the reasons for which a court in a separate action will grant relief from a judgment. It makes sense to permit an issue not originally raised in the trial court to be raised on appeal if, under the law of the jurisdiction, the issue could be a basis for relief from the judgment long after the judgment is final.

One of the requirements for allowing this type of issue to be raised on appeal would be that the matter upon which relief is sought was not known and could not reasonably have been known in time to have been raised at trial. Without this requirement, this exception would allow the party seeking to raise the issue to lie in wait during trial proceedings, hoping for a favorable result there and, if unsuccessful, to raise the previously known defect in the appellate court. This is essentially equity's "clean hands" doctrine applied to the raising of new issues and is applicable to the Rule 60(b) type of motion.

Allowing the new issue to be raised under these circumstances would permit the appellate court to rectify the error at the earliest possible time. This procedure would avoid the waste and embarrassment of having the appellate court affirm the judgment only to have the judgment subsequently set aside on grounds already in the record. If the grounds are not in the record as it comes to the appellate court, the new issue should not be heard. Allowing the new issue to be raised in this instance would require the court to remand the case for the purpose of an evidentiary hearing. This procedure could be used too easily as a delay tactic and may not even be necessary because the judgment may be reversed on grounds properly preserved in the trial court.

VI. Conclusion

The rule preventing an appellate court from considering an issue not raised in the trial is as old as the common-law system of appellate review. Even though the historical reasons for its original development are no longer valid, the rule today finds strong support in the balancing of the interests of the litigants and their attorneys as well as the institutional interests of the judicial system. Making adherence to the general rule a matter of discretion in the appellate court has resulted in the effective abolition of the general rule. The general rule has been replaced by a system in which the question of whether an appellate court will consider a new issue is decided solely on the basis of whether a majority of the court considers the new issue necessary to decide the case in accordance with their view of the relative equities of the parties. The only consistent feature of the current system is its inconsistency. If courts are free to disregard the general rule whenever they wish to do so, in effect there is no general rule. The current situation is destructive of the adversary system, causes substantial harm to the interests that the general rule is designed to protect, and is an open invitation to the appellate judges to "do justice" on ad hoc rather than principled bases.

To restore predictability to this crucial area of the judicial process, appellate courts should consider only those new issues that are reflected in the record and would provide a basis for relief pursuant to a rule similar to Federal Rule of Procedure 60(b) or a separate action. If appellate courts were limited by this standard, the occasions on which appellate courts would consider a new issue would be sharply reduced. This standard would help restore predictability to the appellate process and serve the interests the general rule was designed to protect.

There is no question but that appellate courts, like gorillas, are subject to few restraints except those that are self-imposed. It can only be hoped that unlike gorillas, appellate judges will recognize the necessity for self-restraint in the exercise of their awesome powers.

Notes and Questions

1. A thorough illustrative table showing the parallel situations where appellate courts have both allowed and disallowed consideration of new issues—in a wide variety of subject matters and procedural postures—is presented as appendix to Professor Martineau's article, and may be viewed at 40 Vand. L. Rev. 1062 et seq.

2. Some aspects of Professor Martineau's article excerpted above are updated in Miller, Sua Sponte Appellate Rulings: When Courts Deprive Litigants of an Opportunity to Be Heard, 39 San Diego L. Rev. 1253 (2002)(arguing that deciding cases on points not preserved and presented to the appellate tribunal violates Due Process, and suggesting that an appellate

court which recognizes such an issue should ask the parties for supplemental briefs on the topic and/or remand the matter for any proceedings in the lower court necessary to present the issue properly). Application of the principles discussed by Professor Martineau in criminal cases is explored in Carter, A Restatement of Exceptions to the Preservation of Error Requirement in Criminal Cases, 46 Kan. L. Rev. 947 (1998). For general treatment of these topics see also Campbell, Extent to Which Courts of Review Will Consider Questions Not Properly Raised and Preserved (pts I–III), 7 Wis. L. Rev. 91, 160 (1932), 8 Wis. L. Rev. 147 (1933); Vestal, Sua Sponte Consideration in Appellate Review, 27 Fordham L. Rev. 477 (1958–59); Comment, Jury Interrogatories and the Preservation of Error in Federal Civil Cases: Should the Plain–Error Doctrine Apply?, 30 St. Mary's L.J. 1163 (1999); Annotation, What Issues Will the Supreme Court Consider, Though Not, or Not Properly, Raised by the Parties, 42 L.Ed.2d 946 (1976).

3. Consider Note, Pushing Aside the General Rule in Order to Raise New Issues On Appeal, 64 Ind. L. J. 985 (1989), where an alternative to Professor Martineau's proposal for an approach patterned on Rule 60(b) is offered, in the form of a model rule:

> A new issue should be heard on appeal only when the party raising the issue can show:
>
> > (1) that there was no intentional choice to fail to raise the issue in the trial court below; and
> >
> > (2) no further factual development of the record is necessary; and
> >
> > (3) opposing party will not be prejudiced by his or her inability to present evidence or arguments on the new issue; or
> >
> > (4) that there was no opportunity to object to or to raise the issue below in the trial court.

Under this proposal, if both (2) and (3) above are not met, but the court still deems it necessary to hear the new issue (such as where the issue is one of great public interest),the court would hear the issue only if the case is remanded to ensure full factual development and to ensure the opposing party is not prejudiced.

How does this approach differ from that of Professor Martineau? Which offers better guidance to the courts, and which best serves the policy goals?

4. One context that has given rise to many issues concerning appellate review of events that were not raised at the trial level is allegedly prejudicial comments made during closing argument—a stage where, traditionally, counsel are reluctant to interrupt an adversary. Klein, Allowing Improper Argument of Counsel to Be Raised for the First Time on Appeal as Fundamental Error, 26 Fla. St. U. L. Rev. 971 (1998).

SECTION E. *SUA SPONTE* CONSIDERATION

The preceding section was concerned with the type of issue a party to the appeal can raise in the appellate court even though the issue has not been raised in the trial court. In this section the focus is on an issue neither of the parties raised in the trial court or in the appellate court, but that the appellate court may nonetheless review and find dispositive of the case. This is called *sua sponte* consideration or considering an issue on the court's own motion. The most dramatic and well-known example of this was Erie v. Tompkins, 304 U.S. 64, 58 S.Ct. 817, 82 L.Ed. 1188 (1938), which is the subject of study in almost every course in civil procedure. The opening sentence of the opinion of Justice Brandeis states: "The question for decision is whether the oft-challenged doctrine of *Swift v. Tyson* shall now be disapproved." (304 U.S. at 69, 58 S.Ct. at 818, 82 L.Ed. at 1189). Only by reading the dissenting opinion of Justice Butler is it revealed that the question of overruling *Swift v. Tyson* was not only not raised in the trial court, but it was also not briefed or argued in the Supreme Court. The first time the attorneys in the case knew that the Court was considering disavowing *Swift v. Tyson* was when they read the opinion in which the Court did so. Justice Butler even complained that "[a]gainst the protest of those joining in this opinion, the court declines to assign the case for reargument." (304 U.S. at 88, 58 S.Ct. at 827, 82 L.Ed. at 1200) Does this suggest what the proper procedure should be when the appellate court thinks that the controlling issue was not previously discussed by the parties to the case? Should it make a difference that the court is performing its law development function rather than error correction?

1. SUBJECT MATTER JURISDICTION

MANSFIELD, C. & L.M. RY. CO. v. SWAN

Supreme Court of the United States, 1884.
111 U.S. 379, 4 S.Ct. 510, 28 L.Ed. 462.

MATTHEWS, J.

His was an action at law originally brought in the court of common pleas of Fulton county, Ohio, by John Swan, S.C. Rose, F.M. Hutchinson, and Robert McMann, as partners under the name of Swan, Rose & Co., against the plaintiffs in error. The object of the suit was the recovery of damages for alleged breaches of a contract for the construction of the railroad of the defendants below. It was commenced June 10, 1874. Afterwards, on October 28, 1879, the cause being at issue, the defendants below filed a petition for its removal to the circuit court of the United States. They aver therein that one of the petitioners is a corporation created by the laws of Ohio alone, and the other, a corporation consolidated under the laws of Michigan and Ohio, the constituent corporations having been organized under the laws of those states respectively, and that they are, consequently, citizens, one of Ohio, and one of both Michigan and Ohio. It is also alleged, in the petition for removal, "that the plaintiffs, John Swan and Frank M. Hutchinson, at the time of the commencement of this suit, were, and still are, citizens of the state of Pennsylvania; that the said Robert H. McMann was then (according to your petitioners' recollection) a citizen of the state of Ohio, but that he is not now a citizen of that state, but where he now resides or whereof he is now a citizen (except that he is a citizen of one of the states or territories comprising the United States) your petitioners are unable to state; that he went into bankruptcy in the bankruptcy court held at Cleveland, in the state of Ohio, several years since, and since the alleged claim of the plaintiffs arose, but your petitioners cannot now state whether he has now an assignee in bankruptcy or not, but they are informed and believe that he has not; that the said Stephen C. Rose, at the time of the commencement of this suit, was a citizen of the state of Michigan; that he died therein during the pendency of this suit, and the said Lester E. Rose is the administrator of the estate of the said Stephen C. Rose in the state of Michigan, he holding such office under and by virtue of the laws of that state only, the said Lester E. Rose being a citizen of the state of Michigan when so appointed and now, but that he is not a necessary party as plaintiff in this suit, for the reason that the suit being prosecuted by the plaintiffs as partners under the firm name and style of Swan, Rose & Co., and for the collection of an alleged debt or claim due to them as such partners, and which arose wholly out of their dealings as partners, if it exists at all, upon the death of the said Stephen C. Rose the cause of action survived to the other partners." The petition, being accompanied with a satisfactory bond, was allowed, and an order made for the removal of the cause. The plaintiffs below afterwards, on December 13, 1879, moved to remand the cause on the ground, among others, that the circuit court had no jurisdiction, because the "real and substantial controversy in the cause is between real and substantial parties who are citizens of the same state and not of different states." But the motion was denied. Subsequently a trial took place upon the merits, which resulted in a verdict and judgment in favor of the plaintiffs, the defendants in error, for $238,116.18 against the defendants jointly, and the further sum of $116,468.32 against one of them. Many exceptions to the rulings of the court during the trial were taken, and are embodied in a bill of exceptions, on which errors have been assigned, and the writ of error is prosecuted by the defendants below to reverse this judgment.

An examination of the record, however, discloses that the circuit court had no jurisdiction to try the action, and as, for this reason, we are constrained to reverse the judgment, we have not deemed it within our province to consider any other questions involved in it. It appears from the petition for removal, and not otherwise by the record elsewhere, that, at the time the action was first brought in the state court, one of the plaintiffs, and a necessary party, McMann, was a citizen of Ohio, the same state of which the defendants were citizens. It does not affirmatively appear that at the time of the removal he was a citizen of any other state. The averment is that he was not then a citizen of Ohio, and that his actual citizenship was unknown, except that he was a citizen of one of the states or territories. It is consistent with this statement that he was not a citizen of any state. He may have been a citizen of a territory; and, if so, the requisite citizenship would not exist. New Orleans v. Winter, 1 Wheat. 91. According to the decision in Gibson v. Bruce, 108

U.S. 561, S.C. 2 Sup.Ct.Rep. 873, the difference of citizenship on which the right of removal depends must have existed at the time when the suit was begun, as well as at the time of the removal; and, according to the uniform decisions of this court, the jurisdiction of the circuit court fails, unless the necessary citizenship affirmatively appears in the pleadings or elsewhere in the record. It was error, therefore, in the circuit court to assume jurisdiction in the case, and not to remand it, on the motion of the plaintiffs below.

It is true that the plaintiffs below, against whose objection the error was committed, do not complain of being prejudiced by it, and it seems to be an anomaly and a hardship that the party at whose instance it was committed should be permitted to derive an advantage from it; but the rule, springing from the nature and limits of the judicial power of the United States, is inflexible and without exception which requires this court, of its own motion, to deny its own jurisdiction, and, in the exercise of its appellate power, that of all other courts of the United States, in all cases where such jurisdiction does not affirmatively appear in the record on which, in the exercise of that power, it is called to act. On every writ of error or appeal the first and fundamental question is that of jurisdiction, first, of this court, and then of the court from which the record comes. This question the court is bound to ask and answer for itself, even when not otherwise suggested, and without respect to the relation of the parties to it. This rule was adopted in Capron v. Van Noorden, 2 Cranch, 126, decided in 1804, where a judgment was reversed on the application of the party against whom it had been rendered in the circuit court, for want of the allegation of his own citizenship, which he ought to have made to establish the jurisdiction which he had invoked. This case was cited with approval by CHIEF JUSTICE MARSHALL in Brown v. Keene, 8 Pet. 112.

In Jackson v. Ashton, 8 Pet. 148, the court itself raised and insisted on the point of jurisdiction in the circuit court; and, in that case, it was expressly ruled that because it did not appear that the circuit court had jurisdiction, this court, on appeal, had no jurisdiction except for the purpose of reversing the decree appealed from on that ground. And in the most recent utterance of this court upon the point in Bors v. Preston, ante, 407, it was said by MR. JUSTICE HARLAN: "In cases of which the circuit courts may take cognizance only by reason of the citizenship of the parties, this court, as its decisions indicate, has, except under special circumstance, declined to express any opinion upon the merits, on appeal or writ of error, where the record does not affirmatively show jurisdiction in the court below; this, because the courts of the Union, being courts of limited jurisdiction, the presumption is, in every stage of the cause, that it is without their jurisdiction unless the contrary appears from the record." The reason of the rule, and the necessity of its application, are stronger and more obvious, when, as in the present case, the failure of the jurisdiction of the circuit court arises, not merely because the record omits the averments necessary to its existence, but because it recites facts which contradict it.

In the Dred Scott Case, 19 How. 393B400, it was decided that a judgment of the circuit court, upon the sufficiency of a plea in abatement, denying its jurisdiction, was open for review upon a writ of error sued out by the party in whose favor the plea had been overruled. And in this view MR. JUSTICE CURTIS, in his dissenting opinion, concurred; and we adopt from that opinion the following statement of the law on the point: "It is true," he said, (19 How. 566,) "as a general rule, that the court will not allow a party to rely on anything as cause for reversing a judgment which was for his advantage. In this we follow an ancient rule of the common law. But so careful was that law of the preservation of the course of its courts that it made an exception out of that general rule, and allowed a party to assign for error that which was for his advantage, if it were a departure by the court itself from its settled course of procedure. The cases on this subject are collected in Bac.Abr. "Error," H, 4. And this court followed this practice in Capron v. Van Noorden, 2 Cranch, 126, where the plaintiff below procured the reversal of a judgment for the defendant on the ground that the plaintiff's allegations of citizenship had not shown jurisdiction. But it is not necessary to determine whether the defendant can be allowed to assign want of jurisdiction as an error in a judgment in his own favor. The true question is not what either of the parties may be allowed to do, but whether this court will affirm or reverse a judgment of the circuit court on the merits, when it appears on the record, by a plea to the jurisdiction, that it is a case to which the judicial power of the United States does not extend. The course of the court is, when no motion is made by either party, on its own motion, to reverse such a judgment for want of jurisdiction, not only in cases where it is shown negatively, by a plea to the jurisdiction, that jurisdiction does not exist, but even when it does not appear, affirmatively, that it does exist. Pequignot v. Pennsylvania R. Co. 16 How. 104. It acts upon the principle that the judicial power of the United States must not be exerted in a case to which it does not extend, even if both parties desire to have it exerted. Cutler v. Rae, 7 How. 729. I consider, therefore, that when there was a plea to the jurisdiction of the circuit court in a case brought here by a writ of error, the first duty of this court is, *sua sponte*, if not moved to it by either party, to examine the sufficiency of that plea, and thus to take care that neither the circuit court nor this court shall use the judicial power of the United States in a case to which the constitution and laws of the United States have not extended that power."

This is precisely applicable to the present case, for the motion of the plaintiffs below to remand the cause was equivalent to a special plea to the jurisdiction of the court; but the doctrine applies equally in every case where the jurisdiction does not appear from the record. * * *

The judgment of the circuit court is accordingly reversed, with costs against the plaintiffs in error, and the cause is remanded to the circuit court, with directions to render a judgment against them for costs in that court, and to remand the cause to the court of common pleas of Fulton county, Ohio; and it is so ordered.

Notes and Questions

1. The rule that jurisdiction of the trial court may be raised at any time is a familiar one. Federal Rule of Civil Procedure 12(h)(3) expressly provides that, unlike other defenses, the court must dismiss a case whenever it appears it does not have jurisdiction of the subject matter. Should the same rule apply at the appellate level? Holding to the contrary of the principal case was Musico v. Champion Credit Corp., 764 F.2d 102 (2d Cir. 1985)(waiver of arguments challenging diversity). But see MOREL v. INS, 144 F.3d 248, 251 (3d Cir. 1998) ("[A federal] court, including an appellate court, will raise lack of subject-matter jurisdiction on its own motion.").

2. Because subject-matter jurisdiction is "an Art. III as well as a statutory requirement ... no action of the parties can confer subject-matter jurisdiction upon a federal court." Insurance Corp. of Ir., Ltd. v. Compagnie des Bauxites de Guinee, 456 U.S. 694, 702, 102 S.Ct. 2099, 72 L.Ed.2d 492 (1982).

3. "Dismissal for lack of subject-matter jurisdiction is proper only when the claim is so insubstantial, implausible, foreclosed by prior decisions ... or otherwise completely devoid of merit as not to involve a federal controversy." Steel Co. v. Citizens for a Better Env't, 523 U.S. 83, 89, 118 S.Ct. 1003, 140 L.Ed.2d 210 (1998); see Bell v. Hood, 327 U.S. 678, 682–83, 66 S.Ct. 773, 90 L.Ed. 939 (1946).

4. Courts generally lack the ability to raise an affirmative defense sua sponte. See Hutcherson v. Lauderdale County, 326 F.3d 747 (6th Cir. 2003). Nevertheless, the Supreme Court has indicated that a court may take the initiative to assert the res judicata defense sua sponte in "special circumstances." Arizona v. California, 530 U.S. 392, 412, 120 S.Ct. 2304, 147 L.Ed.2d 374 (2000).

5. Should it make a difference whether the question is over the trial court's subject matter jurisdiction or the jurisdiction of the appellate court over the appeal? The overwhelming authority is that it does not. In Bethlehem Township v. Emrick, 77 Pa.Cmwlth. 327, 465 A.2d 1085 (1983), however, the court in an action to quiet title noted that the appeal properly lay with the other intermediate appellate court in Pennsylvania, but since the appellees failed to object to the court's jurisdiction, the court had the discretion to decide the appeal. Did it make a difference that the appeal was simply taken to the wrong appellate court rather than that no appellate court had jurisdiction?

2. STANDING

Many states consider standing to be an affirmative defense that, once waived, no longer bars an appellate court from acting. See, e.g., Bennett v. Napolitano, 206 Ariz. 520, 81 P.3d 311 (2003) (comparing cases where standing is challenged, and where it has gone without objection). In the federal system, however, Article III of the Constitution limits the federal courts to consideration of claims by persons with standing. Even without an Article III analogue, several states take a similar view, and allow standing challenges to be asserted for the first time on appeal. See Starks v. State, 74 Ark.App. 366, 49 S.W.3d 122 (Ark. App. 2001).[1]

As a result, in both federal and state courts, whether the issue is raised below, or even contested on appeal, the appellate courts often express a duty to consider and resolve standing issues as a prerequisite to the power to adjudicate the merits of an appeal.

BENDER v. WILLIAMSPORT AREA SCHOOL DIST.

Supreme Court of the United States, 1986.
475 U.S. 534, 106 S.Ct. 1326, 89 L.Ed.2d 501.

JUSTICE STEVENS delivered the opinion of the Court.

This case raises an important question of federal appellate jurisdiction that was not considered by the Court of Appeals: Whether one member of a School Board has standing to appeal from a declaratory judgment against the Board. We conclude that although the School Board itself had a sufficient stake in the outcome of the litigation to appeal, an individual Board member cannot invoke the Board's interest in the case to confer standing upon himself.

1. Garriga v. Sanitation Dist. No. 1, NO. 2001–CA–002593–MR, NO. 2002–CA–001192–MR (Ky. Ct. App. 2003, unpublished) discusses Fort Trumbull Conservancy, LLC v. Alves, 262 Conn. 480, 815 A.2d 1188, 1193–94 (Conn. 2003). Texas Association of Business v. Texas Air Control Board, 852 S.W.2d 440, 443–47, 36 Tex. Sup. Ct. J. 607 (Tex. 1993), and arrives at the conclusion that most state courts in America have found that standing is a jurisdictional issue which can be raised at any stage of an action. See, e.g., United States v. Hays, 515 U.S. 737, 742, 115 S.Ct. 2431, 132 L.Ed.2d 635 (1995) (the question of standing is not subject to waiver); Gunaji v. Macias, 2001 NMSC 28, 130 N.M. 734, 31 P.3d 1008, 1013–14 (N.M. 2001) (lack of standing is a potential jurisdictional defect, which may not be waived and may be raised at any stage of the proceedings, even sua sponte by the appellate court); Hood River County v. Stevenson, 177 Ore. App. 78, 33 P.3d 325, 326–27 (Or.App. 2001) (standing is an essential feature of justiciability that can be raised at any stage in the action); Transcontinental Gas Pipe Line Corp. v. Calco Enterprises, 132 N.C.App. 237, 511 S.E.2d 671, 675 (N.C.App. 1999) (standing is an aspect of subject-matter jurisdiction and as such it can be raised at anytime, even on appeal); Buckeye Foods v. Cuyahoga County Board of Revision, 78 Ohio St.3d 459, 1997 Ohio 199, 678 N.E.2d 917 (Ohio 1997) (the issue of standing, inasmuch as it is jurisdictional in nature, may be raised at any time during the pendency of the proceedings); Newman v. Newman, 235 Conn. 82, 663 A.2d 980, 990 (Conn. 1995) (lack of standing is a subject-matter jurisdictional defect that cannot be waived); Texas Air, 852 S.W.2d at 445 (standing is a component of subject-matter jurisdiction and as such it cannot be waived and may be raised for the first time on appeal); State v. Baltimore, 242 Neb. 562, 495 N.W.2d 921, 926 (Neb. 1993) (because the requirement of standing is fundamental to a court's exercising jurisdiction, a litigant or a court before which a case is pending can raise the question of standing at any time during the proceeding); Bennett v. Board of Trustees for University of Northern Colorado, 782 P.2d 1214, 1216 (Colo.App. 1989) (standing is a jurisdictional issue which can be raised at any stage of an action, including the appeal); Pace Construction Co. v. Missouri Highway & Transportation Commission, 759 S.W.2d 272, 274 (Mo.App. 1988) (lack of standing cannot be waived); State by McClure v. Sports & Health Club, Inc., 370 N.W.2d 844, 850 (Minn. 1985) (an objection to want of standing goes to the existence of a cause of action, is jurisdictional, and may be raised at any time); Smith v. Allstate Insurance Co., 483 A.2d 344, 346 (Me. 1984) (standing may be raised by the court on its own motion for the first time on appeal); Stewart v. Board of County Commissioners of Big Horn County, 175 Mont. 197, 573 P.2d 184, 188 (Mont. 1977) (objections to standing cannot be waived and may be raised by the court sua sponte). See also 59 Am.Jur.2d, Parties, § 34 (2002).

[In a case where high school students raised freedom of religion claims in challenging a refusal of permission to meet on school property, the] final order entered by the District Court was a ruling "in favor of the plaintiffs and against the defendants on plaintiffs' freedom of speech claim." No injunction was entered, and no relief was granted against any defendant in his individual capacity. The District Court, in effect, merely held that the Board's attorney was incorrect in his legal advice.

The School District did not challenge the judgment of the District Court in any way. It made no motion for a stay and took no appeal. Instead, it decided to comply with the judgment and to allow Petros to conduct the meetings it had requested.

However, John C. Youngman, Jr., who was then still a member of the Board, did file a timely notice of appeal.

III

In the Court of Appeals no one raised any question about Mr. Youngman's standing to appeal. * * *The importance of the question presented by the students' petition for certiorari persuaded us that the case merited plenary review. After granting certiorari, however, we noticed that neither the Board nor any of the defendants except Mr. Youngman opposed the students' position and that only Mr. Youngman had challenged the District Court's judgment by invoking the jurisdiction of the Court of Appeals. We therefore find it necessary to answer the question whether Mr. Youngman had a sufficient stake in the outcome of the litigation to support appellate jurisdiction. The parties and the *amici* have identified three different capacities in which Mr. Youngman may have had standing to appeal—as an individual, as a member of the Board, and as a parent.

IV

Before considering each of the standing theories, it is appropriate to restate certain basic principles that limit the power of every federal court. Federal courts are not courts of general jurisdiction; they have only the power that is authorized by Article III of the Constitution and the statutes enacted by Congress pursuant thereto. See, e.g., Marbury v. Madison, 1 Cranch (5 U.S.) 137, 173B180, 2 L.Ed. 60 (1803). For that reason, every federal appellate court has a special obligation to "satisfy itself not only of its own jurisdiction, but also that of the lower courts in a cause under review," even though the parties are prepared to concede it. Mitchell v. Maurer, 293 U.S. 237, 244, 55 S.Ct. 162, 165, 79 L.Ed. 338 (1934). See Juidice v. Vail, 430 U.S. 327, 331B332, 97 S.Ct. 1211, 1215, 51 L.Ed.2d 376 (1977) (standing). "And if the record discloses that the lower court was without jurisdiction this court will notice the defect, although the parties make no contention concerning it. [When the lower federal court] lack[s] jurisdiction, we have jurisdiction on appeal, not of the merits but merely for the purpose of correcting the error of the lower court in entertaining the suit." United States v. Corrick, 298 U.S. 435, 440, 56 S.Ct. 829, 831, 80 L.Ed. 1263 (1936).

This obligation to notice defects in a court of appeals' subject-matter jurisdiction assumes a special importance when a constitutional question is presented. In such cases we have strictly adhered to the standing requirements to ensure that our deliberations will have the benefit of adversary presentation and a full development of the relevant facts. Thus, as we emphasized in Valley Forge Christian College v. Americans United for Separation of Church and State, Inc., 454 U.S. 464, 472, 102 S.Ct. 752, 758-59, 70 L.Ed.2d 700 (1982):

> "[A]t an irreducible minimum, Art. III requires the party who invokes the court's authority to 'show that he personally has suffered some actual or threatened injury as a result of the putatively illegal conduct of the defendant,' Gladstone, Realtors v. Village of Bellwood, 441 U.S. 91, 99 [99 S.Ct. 1601, 1608, 60 L.Ed.2d 66] (1979), and that the injury 'fairly can be traced to the challenged action' and 'is likely to be redressed by a favorable decision,' Simon v. Eastern Kentucky Welfare Rights Org., 426 U.S. 26, 38, 41 [96 S.Ct. 1917, 1924, 1925, 48 L.Ed.2d 450] (1976). * * *

> "The requirement of 'actual injury redressable by the court,' Simon [v. Eastern Kentucky Welfare Rights Org., 426 U.S. 26], at 39 [96 S.Ct. 1917, at 1924, 48 L.Ed.2d 450] [1976], serves several of the 'implicit policies embodied in Article III,' Flast [v. Cohen, 392 U.S. 83,] 96 [88 S.Ct. 1942, 1950, 20 L.Ed.2d 947] [(1968)]. It tends to assure that the legal questions presented to the court will be resolved, not in the rarified atmosphere of a debating society, but in a concrete factual context conducive to a realistic appreciation of the consequences of judicial action. The 'standing' requirement serves other purposes. Because it assures an actual factual setting in which the litigant asserts a claim of injury in fact, a court may decide the case with some confidence that its decision will not pave the way for lawsuits which have some, but not all, of the facts of the case actually decided by the court."

V

The first paragraph of the complaint alleged that the action was brought against the defendants "in their individual and official capacities." There is, however, nothing else in the complaint, or in the record on which the District Court's judgment was based, to support the suggestion that relief was sought against any School Board member in his or her *individual* capacity. Certainly the District Court's judgment granted no such relief. Accordingly, to paraphrase our holding in Brandon v. Holt, 469 U.S. 464, ___, 105 S.Ct. 873, 877, 83 L.Ed.2d 878 (1985), "[t]he course of proceedings * * * make it abundantly clear that the action against [Mr. Youngman] was in his official capacity and only in that capacity." Since the judgment against Mr. Youngman was not in his individual capacity, he had no standing to appeal in that capacity. [Discussion omitted].

We therefore hold that because the Court of Appeals was without jurisdiction to hear the appeal, it was without authority to decide the merits. Accordingly, the judgment of the Court of Appeals is vacated, and the case is remanded with instructions to dismiss the appeal for want of jurisdiction.

It is so ordered.

[Concurring and dissenting opinions of JUSTICE MARSHALL, CHIEF JUSTICE BURGER, JUSTICE WHITE, JUSTICE REHNQUIST and JUSTICE POWELL are omitted].

Notes and Questions

1.   Is standing a question of subject matter jurisdiction? Or is it more like the question of failure to state a claim upon which relief can be granted? For a state case with a similar analysis to that in the principal case see Nichols v. Rockland, 324 A.2d 295 (Me.1974).

2.   Is there a difference between standing to bring the original action and standing to prosecute the appeal? See Chapter 4, infra, on Parties.

3.   CONSTITUTIONAL ISSUES

BAYER v. JOHNSON

Supreme Court of South Dakota, 1984.
349 N.W.2d 447.

FOSHEIM, CHIEF JUSTICE.

This is an administrative appeal from a decision of the South Dakota Secretary of Revenue (Secretary) which denied Barry E. Bayer's application for a refund of sales tax paid under protest. The circuit court affirmed the Secretary. We reverse.

Appellant candidly states he is engaged in the bookmaking business and the facts seem essentially undisputed. SDCL 10B45B5.2, by reference, subjects bookmaking to the retail sales and service tax. Mr. Bayer holds a retail occupational sales tax license for a service business in the area of amusements.

It is also undisputed that as a provider of services, a bookmaker is taxed pursuant to SDCL 10B45B4, which reads:

> There is hereby imposed a tax at the same rate as that imposed upon sales of tangible personal property in this state upon the *gross receipts* of any person from the engaging or continuing in the practice of any business in which a service is rendered. Any service as defined by § 10B45B4.1 shall be taxable, unless the service is specifically exempt from the provisions of this chapter. [emphasis added]

"Gross receipts" means

> the amount received in money, credits, property, or other money's worth in consideration of sales at retail within this state, without

any deduction on account of the cost of the property sold, the cost of materials used, the cost of labor or services purchased, amounts paid for interest or discounts, or any other expenses whatsoever, *nor shall any deduction be allowed for losses * * *.* [emphasis added]

SDCL 10B45B1(2). "Sales at retail" includes sale of services. SDCL 10B45B1(5).

The dispute concerns how much of the money received by a bookmaker in a bookmaking transaction is to be considered gross receipts. The Secretary claims the entire amount of a lost wager paid by a bettor to a bookmaker is includable in gross receipts, without any offset for losses of the bookmaker. It is the position of appellant that only the "vigorish," or service fee, is subject to the tax.

We perceive no way this issue can be decided without giving tacit approval to that which is constitutionally forbidden. Article III, Section 25 of our state constitution clearly provides: "The Legislature shall not authorize any game of chance, lottery or gift enterprise, under any pretense or for any purpose whatever * * *." A "game of chance" is a contest wherein chance predominates over skill.

While the record reveals no evidence of appellant's bookmaking methods, he did establish usual bookmaking practices by the testimony of an expert witness. According to this witness, a bookmaker receives wagers from players, or customers, the outcome of which depends upon the happening of an uncertain event. The occurrence of the event determines which party, the player or the bookmaker, must pay the other an amount specified at the time the wager was placed. Appellant's witness identified races and athletic events as frequent subjects of bookmaking. The outcome of such events in no way depends upon the skill of the bettors. The wagering is therefore a contest in which chance predominates over skill. Bookmaking is accordingly a "game of chance" which the legislature is constitutionally prohibited from authorizing. * * *

In licensing bookmaking as a service subject to a retail service tax, the legislature is effectively authorizing a game of chance and treating it as a legitimate source of revenue. Requiring service tax licenses and exacting tribute, blind to the activity, is an implicit, if not formal recognition. It cannot be reconciled with Article III, Section 25 of our constitution.

This conclusion can come as no surprise. We recently reaffirmed our long-standing position that, regarding matters of gambling, it is the duty of the courts to pierce any disguise of legitimacy and to ascertain the real activities involved.

The Secretary seems to justify the tax by arguing that Congress has imposed a tax on income derived from illegal sources, Federal practice is not analogous. Unlike the South Dakota Constitution, the United States Constitution is silent about whether the Congress may authorize games of chance.

Neither party has challenged the constitutionality of the tax statute involved. We have consistently held that the constitutionality of a statute cannot be raised for the first time on appeal. This position has arisen, however, in response to parties who urge it on appeal but who failed to raise the question with the trial court. We have never decided whether this court *sua sponte* will examine a patent constitutional dilemma not raised by either party.

There is good authority that where the appellate court has jurisdiction on other grounds it may decide a constitutional question on its own motion. City of St. Louis v. Butler Co., 358 Mo. 1221, 219 S.W.2d 372 (1949); 4 C.J.S. *Appeal & Error* § 240 (1957). This is especially true when the constitutional question is decisive of the appeal, In re Clark's Estate, 105 Mont. 401, 74 P.2d 401, 114 A.L.R. 496 (1937), or when the point is one of law and not dependent on facts that might have been presented below had the point been there raised. Stierle v. Rohmeyer, 218 Wis. 149, 260 N.W. 647 (1935).

State officials, including supreme court justices, are by constitutional mandate required to take an oath or affirmation to support the constitution of this state. S.D. Const. Art. XXI, § 3. Courts, above all, must jealously protect the integrity of the constitution. In the case of In re Clark's Estate, supra, the Montana Supreme Court supported its consideration of a state constitutional issue not raised by the parties with this reference to the oath:

> In the case of Marbury v. Madison, 1 Cranch 137, 179, 2 L.Ed. 60, Chief Justice Marshall, after reviewing various provisions of the Federal Constitution, said: "From these, and many other selections which might be made, it is apparent, that the framers of the constitution contemplated that instrument, as a rule for the government of courts, as well as of the legislature. Why otherwise does it direct the judges to take an oath to support it? This oath certainly applies, in an especial manner, to their conduct in their official character. How immoral to impose it on them, if they were to be used as the instruments, and the knowing instruments, for violating what they swear to support! * * * Why does a judge swear to discharge his duties agreeably to the constitution of the United States, if that constitution forms no rule for his government? If it is closed upon him, and cannot be inspected by him? If such be the real estate of things, this is worse than solemn mockery. To prescribe, or to take this oath, becomes equally a crime."

Id. 105 Mont. at 411B412, 74 P.2d at 406. We would be less than supportive if we failed to meet that which is constitutionally offensive.

In 1970 the people of South Dakota amended Article III, Section 25 of our constitution by adding a proviso authorizing games of chance by public-spirited organizations. If it be the will of the people to license, tax and thus authorize privately operated games of chance, that likewise requires further amendment. It cannot be done by the legislature.

Reversed.

All the Justices concur.

Notes and Questions

1. Does *Marbury v. Madison* provide the basis for an appellate court to decide a case on a constitutional issue not raised by the parties?

2. Many state courts hold that constitutional issues should not, or cannot, be addressed if the parties have not raised them below. For an opinion contrary to the principal case, see Tetterton v. Long Manufacturing Co., Inc., 67 N.C.App. 628, 313 S.E.2d 250 (1984) (constitutionality of statute of limitations).

3. Should the plain or fundamental error rule apply to *sua sponte* consideration? For an affirmative answer see Jordan v. General Growth Dev. Corp., 675 S.W.2d 901 (Mo.App.1984).

4. Other matters that have been considered by courts on their own motion include the applicability of a statute of limitations, Stevens v. Tennessee Valley Authority, 712 F.2d 1047 (6th Cir. 1983); mootness, New Jersey Turnp. Auth. v. Jersey Central Power and Light, 772 F.2d 25 (3d Cir. 1985); res judicata, Diggs v. Hood, 772 F.2d 190 (5th Cir. 1985); improper comments by the trial judge, Gardiner v. A.H. Robins Co., Inc., 747 F.2d 1180 (8th Cir. 1984).

5. Another approach is for the appellate court not to decide the case on the new issue that the court itself raised, but to remand the case for further consideration, as was done in Gubernick v. Philadelphia, 85 Pa.Cmwlth. 397, 481 A.2d 1255 (1984) Are there other alternatives?

6. For a good synthesis of the issues raised by the process of sua sponte raising of issues, see Milani & Smith, Playing God: A Critical Look at Sua Sponte Decisions by Appellate Courts, 69 Tenn. L. Rev. 245 (2002). The authors report that an appellate judge, who shall remain anonymous, told one of them: "We don't know enough about them. You're playing God then because you haven't had the benefit of the lawyers, the judge below, or the clients, or the evidence. You're just playing God without a record, and you have to assume a certain competence in your counsel.... I'm loath to do it. I have done it, I guess I really don't like to do it because it's too dangerous. There's nothing worse than a lawyer being beaten by an assumption that simply is incorrect and wasn't raised." The authors suggest that sua sponte consideration of issues denies the parties Due Process, is inconsistent with the adversary system, and leads to mistakes (because issues are not briefed and properly presented in light of all the available evidence).

7. For excellent general discussions of *sua sponte* review see: Tate, Sua Sponte Consideration on Appeal, 9 Trial Judges J. 68 (1970); Vestal, Sua Sponte Consideration in Appellate Review, 27 Fordham L. REV. 477 (1959); Annotation, What Issues Will the Supreme Court Consider, Though Not, or Not Properly, Raised by the Parties, 42 L.Ed.2d 946 (1976). See also Miller, Sua Sponte Appellate Rulings: When Courts Deprive Litigants of an Opportunity to be Heard, 39 San Diego L. Rev. 1253 (2002).

8. Probably the most bizarre example of *sua sponte* consideration is Marshall v. Gibson, 19 Ohio St.3d 10, 482 N.E.2d 583 (1985) in which the Ohio Supreme Court reversed a judgment in favor of the defendants because the defendants had been improperly denied a requested instruction on comparative negligence. This issue was not raised in the appellate court or

the supreme court by either party. The missing instruction could have benefitted the defendants only if the jury had found them negligent, which it didn't.

SECTION F. ASSIGNMENTS OF ERROR

In the early part of the 20th Century most American courts required appellants to identify the specific errors which the party claimed were a basis for reversal, in a formal notice called an "assignment of error." This list was a separate paper, or a section of the notice of appeal, or a part of the appellant's opening brief, or an entry in any appendix or other record excerpts prepared for the appeal. Error which an attorney dutifully "preserved" by making timely objection can be lost under an assignment of error system if the mistake is not set forth in the formal assignment specification.

A substantial number of states still require a listing of assignments of error, sometimes call a bill of exceptions. See Nebraska Ct. R. 5 (2004). In Virginia, for example, the assignment of error list is normally the very last page of the appendix of record documents prepared for an appeal, and is reprinted early in the appellant's brief. In Connecticut, the governing section, Conn. Super. Ct. § 23–50 (2003) provides:

Sec. 23–50. Writs of Error

In every writ of error there must be a special assignment of errors, in which the precise matters of error in the proceedings in the superior court relied upon as grounds of relief must be set forth. No others will be heard or considered by the judicial authority.

Where the practice of listing assignments of error is still followed, rules of appellate procedure often make requirements for tying sections of the brief and the supporting appendix of record entries to individual "assignment." For example, Louisiana Sup. Ct. R. X (2004) prescribes with respect to applications for a hearing that counsel prepare:

3. A memorandum, not exceeding 25 pages in length, containing:

(a) A concise statement of the case summarizing the nature of the case and prior proceedings;

(b) An assignment of errors in the opinion, judgment, ruling or order complained of;

(c) A summary of the argument which should be a succinct but accurate and clear condensation of the argument actually made within the body of the memorandum; it should not be a mere repetition of the headings under which the argument is arranged.

(d) An argument of each assignment of error on the facts and law ...

The same state's unified appellate rules direct that the record be prepared in such a way as to tie together the assignments of error and the supporting portions of the transcripts and exhibits:

RULE 2–1. PREPARATION OF RECORD

[The record shall contain:]

(2) judgment or order (interlocutory and final); and, in criminal cases, all orders, including the verdict, judgment and sentence;

(3) petition (motion) and order for appeal, and bond (if any);

(4) assignments of error in criminal cases in numerical order, and the trial judge's per curiams (if any), each of which should follow the respective assignment of error. (If the evidence necessary to form a basis for an assignment of error has been transcribed elsewhere in the record, such as in a full transcript of the proceedings, it may be incorporated by reference to the appropriate volume and page of the record, so as to avoid unnecessary duplication in the record)

Louisiana Cts. App. Unif. R. 2–1 (2004). In such a system it is normal that a "written designation of the assignments of error to be urged on appeal in a criminal case shall be filed with this court on or before the date of filing of the appellant's brief with this court." Louisiana La. Cts. App. Internal Rule 15.

Several states using this process today attempt to alert counsel that generalized claims of error are insufficient. Virginia Sup. Ct. R. 5:17 provides:

(c) Form and Content. Under a separate heading entitled "Assignments of Error," the petition shall list the specific errors in the rulings below upon which the appellant intends to rely. Only errors assigned in the petition for appeal will be noticed by this Court. Where appeal is taken from a judgment of the Court of Appeals, only assignments of error relating to questions presented in, or to actions taken by, the Court of Appeals may be included in the petition for appeal to this Court. An assignment of error which merely states that the judgment or award is contrary to the law and the evidence is not sufficient. If the petition for appeal does not contain assignments of error, the appeal will be dismissed.

Under another separate heading entitled "Questions Presented," the petition shall list the questions upon which the appellant intends to submit argument, with a clear and exact reference to the particular assignment of error to which each question relates.

Washington State's Rule of Appellate Procedure 10.3 is similar.

The expected functions of the assignment of error are illustrated in the detailed provisions for this listing that are specified in the current North Carolina App. Proc. Rules, Art. II, Rule 10 (2004):

Rule 10. Assigning error on appeal.

(a) Function in limiting scope of review.

Except as otherwise provided herein, the scope of review on appeal is confined to a consideration of those assignments of error set out in the record on appeal in accordance with this Rule 10.

Provided, that upon any appeal duly taken from a final judgment any party to the appeal may present for review, by properly making them the basis of assignments of error, the questions whether the judgment is supported by the verdict or by the findings of fact and conclusions of law, whether the court had jurisdiction of the subject matter, and whether a criminal charge is sufficient in law.

(b) Preserving questions for appellate review.

(1) General.

In order to preserve a question for appellate review, a party must have presented to the trial court a timely request, objection or motion, stating the specific grounds for the ruling the party desired the court to make if the specific grounds were not apparent from the context. It is also necessary for the complaining party to obtain a ruling upon the party's request, objection or motion. Any such question which was properly preserved for review by action of counsel taken during the course of proceedings in the trial tribunal by objection noted or which by rule or law was deemed preserved or taken without any such action, may be made the basis of an assignment of error in the record on appeal.

(2) Jury instructions; findings and conclusions of judge.

A party may not assign as error any portion of the jury charge or omission therefrom unless he objects thereto before the jury retires to consider its verdict, stating distinctly that to which he objects and the grounds of his objection; provided, that opportunity was given to the party to make the objection out of the hearing of the jury, and, on request of any party, out of the presence of the jury.

(3) Sufficiency of the evidence.

A defendant in a criminal case may not assign as error the insufficiency of the evidence to prove the crime charged unless he moves to dismiss the action, or for judgment as in case of nonsuit, at trial. If a defendant makes such a motion after the State has presented all its evidence and has rested its case and that motion is denied and the defendant then introduces evidence, his motion for dismissal or judgment in case of nonsuit made at the close of State's evidence is waived. Such a waiver precludes the defendant from urging the denial of such motion as a ground for appeal.

A defendant may make a motion to dismiss the action or judgment as in case of nonsuit at the conclusion of all the evidence, irrespective of whether he made an earlier such motion. If the motion at the close of all the evidence is denied, the defendant may urge as ground for appeal the denial of his motion made at the conclusion of all the evidence. However, if a defendant fails to move to dismiss the action or for judgment as in case of nonsuit at the close of all the evidence, he may not challenge on appeal the sufficiency of the evidence to prove the crime charged.

If a defendant's motion to dismiss the action or for judgment as in case of nonsuit is allowed, or shall be sustained on appeal, it shall have the force and effect of a verdict of "not guilty" as to such defendant.

(c) Assignments of error.

(1) Form; Record references.

A listing of the assignments of error upon which an appeal is predicated shall be stated at the conclusion of the record on appeal, in short form without argument, and shall be separately numbered. Each assignment of error shall, so far as practicable, be confined to a single issue of law; and shall state plainly, concisely and without argumentation the legal basis upon which error is assigned. An assignment of error is sufficient if it directs the attention of the appellate court to the particular error about which the question is made, with clear and specific record or transcript references. Questions made as to several issues or findings relating to one ground of recovery or defense may be combined in one assignment of error, if separate record or transcript references are made.

(2) Jury instructions.

Where a question concerns instructions given to the jury, the party shall identify the specific portion of the jury charge in question by setting it within brackets or by any other clear means of reference in the record on appeal. A question of the failure to give particular instructions to the jury, or to make a particular finding of fact or conclusion of law which finding or conclusion was not specifically requested of the trial judge, shall identify the omitted instruction, finding or conclusion by setting out its substance in the record on appeal immediately following the instructions given, or findings or conclusions made.

(3) Sufficiency of evidence.

In civil cases, questions that the evidence is legally or factually insufficient to support a particular issue or finding, and challenges directed against any conclusions of law of the trial court based upon such issues or findings, may be combined under a single assignment of error raising both contentions if the record references and the argument under the point sufficiently direct the court's attention to the nature of the question made regarding each such issue or finding or legal conclusion based thereon.

(4) Assigning plain error.

In criminal cases, a question which was not preserved by objection noted at trial and which is not deemed preserved by rule or law without any such action, nevertheless may be made the basis of an assignment of error where the judicial action questioned is specifically and distinctly contended to amount to plain error.

(d) Cross-assignments of error by appellee.

Without taking an appeal an appellee may cross-assign as error any action or omission of the trial court which was properly preserved for appellate review and which deprived the appellee of an alternative basis in law for supporting the judgment, order, or other determination from which appeal has been taken.

Portions of the record or transcript of proceedings necessary to an understanding of such cross-assignments of error may be included in the record on appeal by agreement of the parties under Rule 11(a), may be included by the appellee in a proposed alternative record on appeal under Rule 11(b), or may be designated for inclusion in the verbatim transcript of proceedings, if one is filed under Rule 9(c)(2).

Where assignments of error are used, they become the organizing feature of the briefing in most states. In Oregon, for example, Rule of Appellate Procedure 5.45 tells counsel how to format assignments of error and what they should contain:

Rule 5.45 ASSIGNMENTS OF ERROR AND ARGUMENT

(1) A question or issue to be decided on appeal shall be raised in the form of an assignment of error, as prescribed in this rule. Assignments of error are required in all opening briefs of appellants and cross-appellants. No matter claimed as error will be considered on appeal unless the claimed error was preserved in the lower court and is assigned as error in the opening brief in accordance with this rule, provided that the appellate court may consider an error of law apparent on the face of the record.

(2) Each assignment of error shall be separately stated under a numbered heading. The arrangement and form of assignments of error, together with reference to pages of the record, should conform to the illustrations [set forth below].

(3) Each assignment of error shall identify precisely the legal, procedural, factual, or other ruling that is being challenged.

(4) (a) Each assignment of error shall demonstrate that the question or issue presented by the assignment of error timely and properly was raised and preserved in the lower court. Under the subheading "Preservation of Error":

    (I) Each assignment of error, as appropriate, must specify the stage in the proceedings when the question or issue presented by the assignment of error was raised in the lower court, the method or manner of raising it, and the way in which it was resolved or passed on by the lower court.

    (II) Each assignment of error must set out pertinent quotations of the record where the question or issue was raised and the challenged ruling was made, together with reference to the pages of the transcript or other portions of the record quoted or to the excerpt of record if the material quoted is set out in the excerpt of record. When the portions of the record relied on under this subparagraph are lengthy, they shall be included in the excerpt of record instead of the body of the brief.

(b) An assignment of error for a claimed error apparent on the face of the record shall comply with the requirements for assignments of error generally by identifying the precise ruling, specifying the state of the proceedings when the ruling was made, and setting forth pertinent quotations of the record where the challenged ruling was made.

(c) The court may decline to consider any assignment of error that requires the court to search the record to find the error or to determine if the error properly was raised and preserved.

(5) Under the subheading "Standard of Review," each assignment of error shall identify the applicable standard or standards of review, supported by citation to the statute, case law, or other legal authority for each standard of review.

(6) Each assignment of error shall be followed by the argument. If several assignments of error present essentially the same legal question, the argument in support of them may be combined so far as practicable. The argument in support of a claimed error apparent on the face of the record shall demonstrate that the error is of the kind that may be addressed by the court without the error having been preserved in the record.

Subsequent filings track the initial assignments of error:

Oregon R. App. Proc. 5.55 RESPONDENT'S BRIEF

(1) The respondent's brief shall follow the form prescribed for the appellant's opening brief, omitting repetition of the verbatim parts of the record in appellant's assignments of error. It shall contain a concise answer to each of the appellant's assignments of error preceding respondent's own argument as to each.

Illustrative samples for assignments of error are provide by the Oregon Rules of Appellate Procedure. Appendix C illustrates permissible "short form" assignments in a criminal case:

The trial court erred when, over objection, it categorized defendant as a criminal history category C offender.

The trial court erred when, over objection, it imposed a condition of probation that requires defendant to undergo drug evaluation and treatment.

The trial court erred when, over objection, it imposed a condition of probation that prohibits defendant from contacting defendant's children.

The trial court erred when, over objection, it imposed a disputed amount of restitution.

The traditional format for assignments of error is also illustrated in Appendix J to the Oregon Appellate Rules:

Model Complete Assignment of Error;
Other Partial Assignments of Error

Illustration 1

(Model Complete Assignment of Error)

FIRST ASSIGNMENT OF ERROR

The trial court erred in declining to give defendant's requested menacing instruction on the ground that menacing is not a lesser-included offense of robbery in the first and second degrees.

A.   Preservation of Error

At the close of the evidence, defendant submitted a requested instruction on menacing. (ER-_____.) By way of memorandum in support of the requested instruction, defendant argued to the trial court that menacing is necessarily included in the statutory definition of robbery in the first degree (the crime with which defendant was charged) and that the record contained evidence from which a jury could find defendant guilty of the lesser charge and not guilty of the greater charge. (ER-_____.) The trial court declined to give the instruction, stating:

> I'm not going to give the requested instruction on menacing. Menacing is not expressly included in the charging instrument and, in my view, is not a statutorily lesser-included offense of the crime of robbery because it does not share all of the same elements as robbery. The prosecutor could have charged defendant with menacing, but didn't. And without a match on the elements of the two offenses, a lesser-included instruction isn't proper."

(Tr 142.)

B.   Standard of Review

The court reviews the trial court's decision either to give or to decline to give a requested jury instruction pursuant to a combination of standards of review. Regarding review of the record to support such an instruction, the court review[s] the evidence in the light most favorable to the establishment of facts that would require those instructions." State v. Boyce, 120 Or.App. 299, 302, 852 P.2d 276 (1993). Whether the language of the statute defining the lesser offense is necessarily included in the greater offense is a pure question of law, one that the court decides without any particular deference to its resolution below. See State v. Cunningham, 320 Or. 47, 57, 880 P.2d 431 (1994); State v. Moses, 165 Or.App. 317, 319, 997 P.2d 251 (2000).

ARGUMENT

[Other Partial Forms for Assignments of Error)

Illustration 2

The court erred in denying (or allowing) the following motion:

[Show that the error was preserved, including setting forth verbatim the motion and the ruling of the court.]

Illustration 3

The court on examination of witness _____ erred in sustaining (or failing to sustain) objection to the following question:[Show that the error was preserved, including setting forth verbatim the question, the objection made, the answer given, if any, offer of proof, if any, and the ruling of the court.]

Illustration 4

The court erred in denying (or sustaining) the motion for dismissal or direct verdict: [Show that the error was preserved, including setting forth verbatim the motion and the ruling of the court.]

Illustration 5

The court erred in giving the following instruction:

[Show that the error was preserved, including setting forth verbatim the instruction (or citing to the excerpt of record, if the instruction is set forth verbatim in the excerpt of record), and the exception made to the instruction.]

Illustration 6

The court erred in holding ORS _____ (or Oregon Laws 19_____, chapter _____, section _____) unconstitutional (or constitutional).

[Show that the error was preserved, including setting forth verbatim the statutory provision and the manner in which constitutionality was challenged.]

Most states have abolished a separate listing of errors "assigned." They require parties to *preserve* error with proper objections, but they treat the listing of issues in the appellant=s brief as a sufficient means to distill the claims of reversible error advanced by the appellant. The provision of the Alabama Rules of Appellate Procedure is not atypical:

Rule 20. Assignment of error not required.

Assignments of error are not required. Statement of the issues presented on appeal in the appellant's brief as required by Rule 28 shall be sufficient.

Many states have rules or statutes like this, simply declaring that assignments of error are not necessary. See, e.g., Mississippi R. App. P. 28. Florida R. App. P. 9.040(e) (2004) is to the same effect, but goes even farther by forbidding the style of listing assignments of error ("Assignments of error are neither required nor permitted").

Thus in the most modern American jurisdictions, there are provisions to the effect that "[n]o written assignment of error shall be necessary, but the judgment may be reversed or modified for any error appearing in the record to the prejudice of an appellant or cross-appellant." Arkansas Code Annot. § 16–67–319. Note, however, that even in those states (and in the federal courts, where no assignment of error is expected) the appellate courts often refer to an appellant's grounds for reversal as "assignments of error" in a generic sense, not tied to a particular filing or way of summarizing the issues. See, e.g., Dixon v. State, 327 Ark. 105, 937 S.W.2d 642 (1997).

Assignments of error at succeeding levels of appellate review are generally narrower than the prior level: from among all the issues "preserved" at the trial level, the appellant states those that will be pursued in the initial appeal. From an adverse appellate ruling, the subset of issues argued in the initial appeal which will be argued at the next level of appeal is selected. While there are exceptions, generally points not raised at one level are waived, and may not be resurrected later.

An illustration of this narrowing effect of multiple levels of appeal is a case that proceeded through the Ohio courts, Powell v. Collins, 332 F.3d 376 (6th Cir. 2003), in which the defendant was convicted of murdering a seven-year-old girl by throwing her out of an upper-story apartment window when his attempt to rape her was discovered by others.

Direct Appeal. Following his convictions, Petitioner took a direct appeal to the First Appellate District Court in Ohio, where he was represented by one of his trial co-counsel as well as a new second counsel. There, he raised the following eleven assignments of error:

(1) The trial court erred to the prejudice of the defendant-appellant by instructing the jury on both counts of the aggravated murder indictment and entering convictions for both aggravated murder counts of the indictment.

(2) The trial court erred to the prejudice of the defendant-appellant in denying the motion for acquittal as to count V of the indictment made by the defendant-appellant at the close of all the evidence.

(3) The trial court erred to the prejudice of the defendant-appellant by denying the motions for acquittal on counts III and IV of the indictment made by defendant-appellant.

(4) The trial court erred to the prejudice of the defendant-appellant in denying the defendant-appellant's motion for acquittal on the two (2) counts of kidnapping.

(5) The trial court erred to the prejudice of the defendant-appellant in denying the defendant-appellant's motion to continue the mitigation hearing.

(6) The trial court erred to the prejudice of the defendant-appellant in failing to properly instruct the jury at the mitigation phase regarding the issue of merger of aggravating circumstances.

(7) The recommendation of the death sentence by the jury and the finding by the court that aggravating circumstances outweighed mitigating factors were against the manifest weight of the evidence.

(8) The trial court erred to the prejudice of the defendant-appellant in denying the motion of the defendant-appellant for a motion to have the defendant referred for further psychiatric testing.

(9) The court erred to the prejudice of defendant-appellant in denying the motion of the defendant-appellant for the appointment of a psychiatrist and psychologist pursuant to Ohio Revised Code, Section 2929.024.

(10) The trial court erred to the substantial prejudice of the defendant-appellant by admitting into evidence inflammatory photographs of the victim.

(11) The trial court erred to the prejudice of the defendant-appellant in denying the defendant-appellant's motion to dismiss at the close of the state's case.

On August, 17, 1988, the Ohio Court of Appeals affirmed the trial court's judgment. Specifically, the court of appeals found that these assignments of error were not meritorious; that the aggravating circumstances outweighed the mitigating factors beyond a reasonable doubt; and that the death sentence was neither excessive nor disproportionate to the penalty imposed in similar cases and was the appropriate penalty.

Petitioner sought leave to appeal with the Ohio Supreme Court, presenting the following seven issues:

(1) The failure to grant a short continuance of the mitigation hearing effectively denies the great latitude in the preparation of evidence of the mitigating factors guaranteed by Ohio Revised Code § 2929.024 and Ohio Revised Code § 2929.03(D)(1).

(2) The trial court erred in overruling the appellant's pre-trial motions to hire a psychiatrist to assist in the preparation of the defense after the appellant demonstrated to the court that his sanity at the time of the offense was to be a significant factor at trial.

(3) Reasonable expert assistance is denied the appellant when the court fails to follow the recommendations of its own appointed expert.

(4) The finding of guilt by the jury of attempted rape, in violation of Ohio Revised Code § 2907.02, is against the manifest weight of the evidence.

(5) The finding of guilty by a jury of attempted rape and kidnapping, both of which are aggravated circumstances, is in violation of Ohio Revised Code § 2941.25(A), since both attempted rape and kidnapping are crimes of similar import for which only one (1) conviction can be obtained.

(6) The finding of guilty by the jury of two (2) counts of kidnapping is against the weight of the evidence.

(7) The trial court and the court of appeals incorrectly weighed the aggravating circumstances and the mitigating factors, and therefore the sentence of death is against the manifest weight of the evidence.

On March 14, 1990, the Ohio Supreme Court affirmed the court of appeal's decision and set Petitioner's execution date as June 12, 1990. On March 27, 1990, Petitioner filed a motion for reconsideration with the supreme court, wherein he raised the following single issue:

Whether the Appellant was denied due process of law by the Court failing to grant a continuance of the penalty hearing to secure additional evidence related to a mitigating factor. The Ohio Supreme Court denied this motion on April 18, 1990. Petitioner was granted a motion for stay of the execution pending review of his petition for a writ of certiorari in the United States Supreme Court. Petitioner sought review of two questions before the United States Supreme Court:

(1) Is Ake v. Oklahoma, 470 U.S. 68, 105 S.Ct. 1087, 84 L.Ed.2d 53 (1985), and the Sixth, Eighth and Fourteenth Amendments to the United States Constitution satisfied by the Trial Court appointing as the sole expert to assist the defense in the sentencing phase a psychologist who admits that further expert assistance is necessary to render competent opinion?

(2) May a state preclude a capital defendant from presenting mitigating evidence in the penalty phase by denying a continuance which defense counsel has demonstrated through psychological testimony is necessary in order to develop that mitigating evidence?

The Supreme Court denied Petitioner's application for a writ of certiorari.

Note, however, that in state and federal post conviction proceedings, the number of claims may expand again, subject to narrowing as various levels of appellate review are provided concerning the collateral attacks on the conviction. In the example case above, the state post-conviction petition raised 35 alleged errors, and the subsequent federal habeas corpus petition had some 13 assigned errors of allegedly constitutional dimension, some with "subparts" representing different factual theories purporting to show parallel deprivations of a single constitutional right. The process continues, and appellate review of the federal habeas proceeding normally reviews that portion of the issues raised in the initial review which the petitioner both preserves and deems feasible to argue on appeal at that stage.

Chapter 3

APPEALABILITY

SECTION A.   THE FINAL JUDGMENT RULE

28 U.S.C.A. § 1291. Final decisions of district courts

The courts of appeals (other than the United States Court of Appeals for the Federal Circuit) shall have jurisdiction of appeals from all final decisions of the district courts of the United States, the United States District Court for the District of the Canal Zone, the District Court of Guam, and the District Court of the Virgin Islands, except where a direct review may be had in the Supreme Court.

MARTINEAU, DEFINING FINALITY AND APPEALABILITY BY COURT RULE: RIGHT PROBLEM, WRONG SOLUTION

54 U. Pitt. L. Rev. 717, 726–29 (1993).*

final judgment rule 1789

The final judgment rule and the problems it causes were introduced to the federal legal system by three sections of the statute that established the federal court system, the Judiciary Act of 1789. Each of the three sections granted jurisdiction to appellate courts over appeals from only a final decree in admiralty and a final judgment or decree at either law or equity, making no exception for any type of interlocutory order.

The legislative history of the 1789 Act is silent as to both the choice of language limiting the right to appeal to final judgments and the decision to apply that requirement to equitable as well as legal proceedings. The final judgment requirement, however, was by 1789 a basic feature of Anglo–American jurisprudence. The common law courts of England required a final disposition of an entire controversy before a writ of error, the principal means of appellate review, would lie. On the equity side of the English court system, however, the courts of chancery allowed free resort to interlocutory review. That the Americans borrowed the final judgment rule from the English writ of error procedure is a virtual certainty. The uncertainty lies in determining why drafters of

England

* Copyright © 1993, University of Pitts-burgh Law Review, University of Pitts-burgh School of Law. Reprinted by permission. All rights reserved.

largely left to conjecture

the Judiciary Act adopted it and decided to apply it to equity as well as law. Some commentators have declared that the drafters' motive "must be left largely to conjecture."

rule's impact to prevent delays & fractured appeals

The earliest references to the statutory requirement by the Supreme Court were mere acknowledgments of the rule, the Court stating simply that the words of the Act allowed a writ of error only in the case of a final judgment. It was some forty years before the Supreme Court extolled the wisdom of the final judgment rule, and elaborated upon its deemed purpose of preventing delays. In 1830 Justice Story praised the Act for discouraging excessive appeals, saying that it was important to the administration of justice to allow appeals only from final judgments because if cases were fragmented by successive appeals "[i]t would occasion very great delays and oppressive expenses." Likewise, Chief Justice Marshall also surmised that Congress intended the final judgment rule to be a mechanism to avoid "all the delays and expense incident to a repeated revision" of fragmented appeals of a single issue. Chief Justice Taney made similar comments in *Forgay v. Conrad.*[69] One commentator noted, perhaps ironically, that the timing of these proclamations coincided with a time when appellate courts were becoming greatly overworked and congested.

Fed. Ct. of Appeals est. → 1891

In 1891, the Evarts Act established the federal courts of appeals. In granting jurisdiction to those courts, Congress empowered them to review "by appeal or by writ of error final decision[s] in the district court." The language restricting appellate review was thereby changed from a limitation of appeals to those sought from "judgments or decrees" as provided in the original Judiciary Act, to appeals from "decison[s]." That change was not perceived as a substantive one. The Supreme Court declared that both phrases had the same meaning in regulating appellate jurisdiction. Eventually the final judgment rule was

Final Judgment rule → 28 USC 1291

embodied in 28 U.S.C. § 1291, which provides that "the courts of appeals ... shall have jurisdiction of appeals from all final decisions of the district courts." Surprisingly, the Court for a long time did not develop a general definition of final judgment. It was not until the court's opinion in *Catlin v. United States,*[77] a 1945 decision, that the Court defined a final judgment as one that ends the litigation on the merits, leaving only execution to be completed.

↳ defined final judgment

CRICK, THE FINAL JUDGMENT
AS A BASIS FOR APPEAL
41 Yale L.J. 539–40, 548–50, 552–54, 557–58, 560–63 (1932).*

In connection with the mechanics of an appeal two principal problems arise. First, we have the question of the method by which a review may be obtained, and second, the problem of at what stage of the

69. 47 U.S. (6 How.) 201, 12 L.Ed. 404 (1848).

77. 324 U.S. 229, 233 (1945).

* Reprinted by permission of The Yale Law Journal Company and Fred B. Rothman & Company.

proceeding in the trial court an appeal can be taken. The two are not unconnected, but it is with the second that this paper will mainly be concerned. Decisions of the trial court from which counsel will wish to appeal may occur, of course, in many stages of the case. It may be a ruling relating to service of process or an order with regard to the pleadings. Hope for a reversal may be based upon some ruling handed down in a preliminary hearing or during the course of the trial, or it may be some decision made during the process of enforcement of the judgment to which objection is made. A fundamental question necessarily arises, therefore, as to just when the appeal may be taken. The extremes of the proposition are that either each ruling or decision is appealable, or on the other hand, that only when the last or final judgment is rendered can a review be had. In the United States it is agreed that we have taken the second of the two extremes, and all the books concur in the general proposition that appeal can be taken only from a final judgment. The policy behind this rule is said to be that it is the only way in which the appellate court can prevent itself from being swamped with appeals. The following quotation is typical of many of the cases:

appeal can be taken only from final judgment → workload

"The apparent object of this statutory restriction on the right of appeal is to prevent the protraction of litigation to an indefinite period by reiterated applications for an exercise of the revisory powers of the appellate tribunal. If, for alleged error in any interlocutory proceeding, a case could be brought here for revision, a multiplicity of appeals would create vexatious delay, and might eventually result in a ruinous accumulation of costs."

But, say the same authorities, there is a regrettable difficulty involved in the application of the rule. What is a final judgment, and does final always mean final? The treatment of the subject usually takes the form of a statement of the rule in one sentence, followed by many definitions of what constitutes a final judgment (of which the reader may take his choice, depending, presumably, upon what result he wishes to reach), the whole enlivened by variations and refinements set out in voluminous footnotes. That all has not been well we may gather from no less an authority than the United States Supreme Court when it says with admirable restraint, "Probably no question of equity practice has been the subject of more frequent discussion in this court than the finality of decrees. * * * The cases, it must be conceded, are not altogether harmonious."

In the present paper the writer proposes to examine this problem of at what point in the case an appeal should be allowed. Did the rule requiring a final judgment arise, as stated above, in the effort to avoid excessive appeals? Does it in fact accomplish that result, and is it suited to the needs and requirements of our modern system of courts?

* * *

When we pass to the American scene we are at once confronted with confusion. The almost complete lack of historical research in American legal history makes it difficult, if not impossible, to trace with any

Two main trends →

① ②

accuracy the breaking up of the old English system of dual appeals into the conglomerate mass which constitutes our modern appellate procedure. However, two main trends seem to have characterized the process.

First, there has been a general tendency to take the common law rule that error lay only after final judgment and to apply it to equity procedure. Second, hampered by this restriction in both law and equity, the courts have gone through elaborate logical exercises in order to escape from the strict application of the restriction, so that, as Coke said, "for the most part, every particular case which has been ruled in the said books may well stand upon a several and particular reason."

Taking up first the adoption of the common law rule into equity, we find that this was accomplished by statute very early in the judicial history of a number of jurisdictions. Thus, the first federal judiciary act of 1789 provided for appeals from "final judgments or decrees" only.

* * *

Another factor which may have had some effect was the failure to keep distinct the practice of law and equity, particularly on appeal. Very commonly one appellate court was established to hear appeals in both law and equity, and in some states, at least, the common law writ of error was the method of appeal in equity cases as well as at law. Such a situation could only result in the confusion of the appellate practice in those jurisdictions.

We may believe further, perhaps, that there was some reluctance on the part of the courts of appeal of those early days to decide questions of comparatively little importance, such as those generally brought up on interlocutory appeals. This had doubtless been a factor at all times in the development of the rule and when congestion of dockets began to be felt it was reinforced by a stronger element, namely, the fear that if interlocutory appeals were heard it would result in the court being swamped with appeals. * * *

The basic principle, then, in practically all jurisdictions in this country is that only final judgments are appealable.[64] When we have said this, however, we have not told the whole story.

In simple actions such as those which composed most of the litigation before the original common law courts, when the case is begun and

---

64. In practically all jurisdictions today the subject is regulated by statute, and in most instances the rule has been modified to some extent.

Many jurisdictions allow interlocutory appeals from certain enumerated decisions or in particular kinds of actions. This is true of the procedure in the federal courts. [Citations omitted.]

In addition to such specific exceptions to the general rule, the statutes in a few jurisdictions gave a certain amount of discretion either to the trial or to the appellate court as an alternative to appeal from the final judgment only. [Citations omitted.]

Still another type of act allows appeal where the decision in the lower court "determines the action" or "prevents a judgment or decree". [Citations omitted.]

Some of these jurisdictions also allow appeals where the decision complained of "affects a substantial right". [Citations omitted.]

Other variations permit a review where the decision "adjudicates the principles of the case".

finished in a short time, the limitation of appeal to the last or final judgment works with a fair degree of convenience, but when confronted with a long and complicated case such as often characterized the old chancery litigation, it breaks down completely. Rights of the parties may be gravely jeopardized or destroyed if it is necessary to wait until the entire case has been disposed of below. If we take, for instance, an action for partition, we find there are generally many orders and decrees made during the course of the proceedings. It is often necessary to decide whether to admit or exclude parties; decrees must be made for appraisement, sale, confirmation of sale, and distribution of proceeds. Again, where there is a petition for and granting of a receivership for a business, the case may be under the control of the court for years, and obviously an appeal only from the decree winding up the case is worthless.

long v. short litigation

As a result of this situation a number of escapes from the restriction have grown up. In addition to statutory modification in some states, the principal method seems to have been the use of extraordinary remedies in the shape of writs of mandamus, prohibition, certiorari, and habeas corpus.

statutory exceptions & writ exceptions

Extraordinary remedies have long been recognized by appellate tribunals as means of controlling and superintending the work of the trial courts. As one court has put it, "the writs already named form a veritable arsenal of legal weapons by means of which all ordinary excesses or defaults on the part of inferior courts which call for the exercise of such power can be corrected and controlled."

writs described

* * *

I have noted heretofore that it is generally thought that the rule requiring final judgments before appeals can be taken was invoked in order to prevent congestion in the appellate court. If we assume that no restriction at all would result in a multiplicity of appeals, and if we assume further that restriction is always desirable, it still remains to be seen whether attempting to restrict them by a rule requiring final judgments is at all successful. It is true that to some extent it prevents a case from being presented for review in fragments but, on the other hand, it has caused protracted and repeated litigation over the question of what judgments and orders are final. As Professor Sunderland has put it:

remains to be seen if successful

> "There is one thing to be said in favor of no restrictions at all,— it will save an immense amount of useless litigation over the question whether parties may or may not appeal particular cases. Every restriction to ward off appeals creates litigation over the force and effect of the restriction itself. Machinery to save labor may become so complex as to waste more labor than it saves."

It would not be surprising if this be true of the final judgment rule. What is sought to be accomplished is to label a definite point in a given case as "final," and to allow appeals only when that point has been reached. This procedure necessarily involves a satisfactory definition of "final" which will be recognizable with a minimum of uncertainty, and which, when applied to the case at hand will yield information as to whether that final stage has been reached. The difficulty lies just at this point. In law, as in any other field, the value of any definition in so far as it aids in classifying or describing specific facts or cases, varies inversely to its degree of generality. Yet when we say that only final judgments are appealable we are assuming that all the law, the entire *corpus juris,* can be brought under a single definition, which, when applied to a given case, will disclose automatically whether the desired stage in its progress has been reached.

These considerations, then, should prepare us for the large volume of litigation over the question of what constitutes a final judgment, and we should not be surprised at the spectacle of a labor saving device which causes more labor than it saves. We are really seeking to determine whether this is the sort of decision which the appellate court wishes to hear, but we spend our time arguing the question of whether the decision is a final judgment. As the number of cases increase, generalizations which were used in past times must be reformulated, or cast aside for new ones which are yet more vague or which contain words capable of more than one meaning. Thus we create machines within machines in order to exclude or include given sets of cases as the situation may require. And since so many different kinds of cases are included in these generalizations, learned counsel are able to parade a vast army of decisions for the edification of the court, although the subject matter involved in them is entirely different from the case which is being argued.

* * *

Up to this point, therefore, I have sought to show that, assuming restriction of appeals to be desirable in all cases, the concept of the final judgment is wholly unsatisfactory as a method of accomplishing that result. However, it would seem that restriction, even if it be desirable as an ultimate goal, should not be exercised blindly. The needs of the appellate court must be considered, of course, but they are not the only parties interested in the appeal. Since courts are organized primarily to serve litigants, their needs cannot be ignored, nor can we put the trial court entirely out of view. Since the appellate courts have the last word, however, and since they write the opinions, we have tended to view the problem mainly from the point of view of their special difficulty, that is, the danger of excessive appeals.

Looking at the matter from the standpoint of the trial court, we see that when an appeal is sought from a given decision, as for instance, when a demurrer to a complaint has been overruled, or a motion to dismiss denied, there exists what might be termed a conflict of interest between the trial and appellate courts. It is to the advantage of the trial court to have the question of whether the plaintiff has a cause of action determined at once by the appellate court, for if he has not, a trial will be unnecessary. On the other hand, the appellate court will prefer, especially if its calendar is crowded, not to pass upon the question until the trial is had and judgment rendered, thus obviating the possibility of more than one appeal. Since there are physical limitations to the amount of work which can be done by each court, the rules of appeal should be a compromise between the needs of each. The rule requiring a final judgment before appeal, however, if rigidly adhered to, relieves only the strain upon the reviewing court, and the trial court is left to dispose of its docket as best it can. Perhaps the relief which could be afforded by a more flexible method of determining when appeals should be allowed would be small, but there is at least opportunity for intelligent experimentation. There is no particular reason why the decisions which may be appealed should be the same yesterday, today and forever, but rather the courts might use the process to control to at least a limited extent the amount of business done by each.

Now as to the litigants, it is rather obvious that to allow or disallow appeals upon the basis of whether or not the final judgment has been rendered is to ignore wholly the needs created by the particular situation. If in a partition suit there is a decree for the sale of property of which defendant claims to be the sole owner, he will not look kindly upon a decision on appeal which says that he may not obtain a review of the case until the sale has been made and the proceeds distributed, Again, when alimony *pendente lite* has been granted in a divorce suit, are we to determine whether an appeal shall be allowed upon the arbitrary basis of whether or not it is a final judgment, or shall we take into consideration the fact that to refuse an appeal will deprive the husband of any review at all, since an appeal from the final decree is likely to be worthless so far as the money already paid out is concerned.

In other words, it should be recognized that all cases are not alike; that the need for an appeal may not arise at the same stage in a partition case or a divorce suit that it does in replevin or in an action on a promissory note.

Aside from these considerations, moreover, there is a further danger involved. Statutes generally provide a set time within which the appeal may be taken, and if it is not brought within that time the right to a review is lost. Now where there is some doubt as to just which decree is the final one, the litigant is compelled to choose between the horns of a dilemma. If he appeals from one decree he may be thrown out of court because it is not final, while if he waits until a subsequent time to appeal he may be told that the first decree was the final one and thus he has lost his chance of appeal. Illustrating this was a case decided in the Supreme Court of Alabama in 1923. There certain equities of the case were decided in favor of the plaintiff, with reference to a register to state an account. An appeal was taken from the decree rendered after the accounting, but more than six months after the first decree. The court held that the first decree was the final one, and the statutory time having elapsed, plaintiff had lost his right to appeal.

As a consequence of the foregoing, the final judgment would seem to be a wholly inadequate criterion to determine whether an appeal should be allowed from a given decision. Favored by appellate courts because it seems to restrict appeals, it would appear upon analysis to cause about as much labor as it saves, because it requires repeated litigation over the question of what is or is not a final judgment. Faced with this situation, and with the fact that it has no relation to the problems of the trial court nor to the needs of the parties in a particular case, we should be prepared to examine the possibilities of discarding the rule as an instrument for controlling appeals, in favor of some method more elastic and more capable of meeting the difficulties raised by our modern judicial system.

Notes and Questions

1. What is the final judgment rule? When is a judgment final?

2. In order to understand the development of the final judgment rule, the concept of the judicial unit is crucial. It was explained in Sears, Roebuck & Co. v. Mackey, 351 U.S. 427, 431–32, 76 S.Ct. 895, 897–98, 100 L.Ed. 1297, 1304 (1956) in the following terms:

> Before the adoption of the Federal Rules of Civil Procedure in 1939, such a situation was generally regarded as leaving the appellate court without jurisdiction of an attempted appeal. It was thought that, although the judgment was a final decision on the respective claims in Counts I and II, it obviously was not a final decision of the whole case, and there was no authority for treating anything less than the whole case as a judicial unit for purposes of appeal.[3] This construction of the judicial unit was developed from the common law which had dealt with litigation generally less complicated than much of that of today.

What is the relationship between the judicial unit and 28 U.S.C.A. § 1291?

3. What are the historical reasons for the development of the final judgment rule?

4. According to Crick, what were the principal justifications for the final judgment rule in the 1930's? Whose interest should be looked at in assessing the validity of the final judgment rule?

5. Is Crick correct in suggesting that the trial court would prefer to have some questions, such as whether the plaintiff has a valid cause of action, be appealed as soon as the trial court has ruled on the question rather than to wait until after there has been a trial on the merits?

---

3. United States v. Girault, 11 How. 22, 13 L.Ed. 587; Metcalfe's Case, 11 Co. Rep. 38a, 77 Eng.Rep. 1193. The rule generally followed in the federal courts was that, in a case involving a single plaintiff and a single defendant, a judgment was not appealable if it disposed of some, but less than all, of the claims presented. See Collins v. Miller, 252 U.S. 364, 40 S.Ct. 347, 64 L.Ed. 616; Sheppy v. Stevens, 2 Cir., 200 F. 946. In cases involving multiple parties where the alleged liability was joint, a judgment was not appealable unless it terminated the action as to all the defendants. See Hohorst v. Hamburg–American Packet Co., 148 U.S. 262, 13 S.Ct. 590, 37 L.Ed. 443. But if, in a multiple party case, a judgment finally disposed of a claim that was recognized to be separate and distinct from the others, that judgment, under some circumstances, was appealable. See Republic of China v. American Express Co., 2 Cir., 190 F.2d 334.

6. One aspect of "finality" is whether the trial court has decided all of the issues in the pending case. For an interesting discussion of whether a judgment that imposes a liability judgment for damages, and awards pre-judgment interest but does not fix either the starting date or the rate for computing prejudgment interest has decided all of the issues in the case, making for appealable, see SEC v. Carrillo, 325 F.3d 1268 (11th Cir. 2003) (no).

7. Some courts have allowed the parties to "stipulate" to a final judgment. For example, while the denial of summary judgment is not a final and appealable disposition, where the parties stipulate that the proof–at trial–will be identical to that already presented to the court, and in effect ask the court to enter judgment in lieu of further proceedings on the same evidentiary record, this procedure is occasionally accepted as a means to an appealable judgment. See, e.g., Regula v. Delta Family–Care Disability Survivorship Plan, 266 F.3d 1130 (9th Cir. 2001) (discussing other cases).

8. Another maneuver plaintiffs have used in an effort to produce an appealable order where only some of the claims have been adjudicated is to voluntarily dismiss the remaining claims, such that all of the claims plaintiff has "pressed" have been decided. Case law has generally deemed a dismissal *without prejudice* of other claims to be insufficient to permit appeal of the decision relating to the non-withdrawn claims. See American States Ins. Co. v. Dastar Corp., 318 F.3d 881 (9th Cir. 2003) (2–1 decision, where the parties agreed to a stipulated dismissal of the unadjudicated claims and the trial court endorsed the stipulation as a means to afford the parties appellate relief). Dismissal of the other claims *with prejudice* would normally be sufficient. In one review of the law, the Second Circuit determined that a *conditional dismissal with prejudice* was enough to allow appeal of the claims which had been ruled upon. Thus, where some claims are decided by the trial court, and the plaintiff agrees to a dismissal of the remaining claims which will be with prejudice if the appeal on the decided claims is unsuccessful (the condition) the court will allow the appeal. Under this arrangement, a plaintiff who appeals and loses, will be forever barred from bringing the claims that were decided, and the claims that were conditionally dismissed. However, if the plaintiff succeeds on the appeal of the decided claims, further proceedings on the remaining claims could be instituted. See Purdy v. Zeldes, 337 F.3d 253 (2d Cir. 2003); Cochran, Gaining Appellate Review by "Manufacturing" A Final Judgment Through Voluntary Dismissal of Peripheral Claims, 48 Mercer L. Rev. 979 (1997).

SECTION B. EXCEPTIONS

1. THE "COLLATERAL ORDER" DOCTRINE

COHEN v. BENEFICIAL IND. LOAN CORP.

Supreme Court of the United States, 1949.
337 U.S. 541, 69 S.Ct. 1221, 93 L.Ed. 1528.

Mr. Justice Jackson delivered the opinion of the Court.

The ultimate question here is whether a federal court, having jurisdiction of a stockholder's derivative action only because the parties are of diverse citizenship, must apply a statute of the forum state which makes the plaintiff, if unsuccessful, liable for all expenses, including attorney's fees, of the defense and requires security for their payment as a condition of prosecuting the action.

Petitioners' decedent as plaintiff, brought in the United States District Court for New Jersey an action in the right of the Beneficial Industrial Loan Corporation, a Delaware corporation doing business in New Jersey. The defendants were the corporation and certain of its managers and directors. The complaint alleged generally that since 1929 the individual defendants engaged in a continuing and successful conspiracy to enrich themselves at the expense of the corporation. Specific charges of mismanagement and fraud extended over a period of eighteen years and the assets allegedly wasted or diverted thereby were said to exceed $100,000,000. The stockholder had demanded that the corporation institute proceedings for its recovery but, by their control of the corporation, the individual defendants prevented it from doing so. This stockholder, therefore, sought to assert the right of the corporation. One of 16,000 stockholders, he owned 100 of its more than two million shares, so that his holdings, together with 150 shares held by the intervenor, approximated 0.0125% of the outstanding stock and had a market value that had never exceeded $9,000.

The action was brought in 1943, and various proceedings had been taken therein when, in 1945, New Jersey enacted the statute which is here involved. Its general effect is to make a plaintiff having so small an interest liable for all expenses and attorney's fees of the defense if he fails to make good his complaint and to entitle the corporation to indemnity before the case can be prosecuted. These conditions are made applicable to pending actions. The corporate defendant therefore moved to require security, pointed to its by-laws by which it might be required to indemnify the individual defendants, and averred that a bond of $125,000 would be appropriate.

The District Court was of the opinion that the state enactment is not applicable to such an action when pending in a federal court, 7 F.R.D. 352. The Court of Appeals was of a contrary opinion and reversed, 3 Cir., 170 F.2d 44, and we granted certiorari. 336 U.S. 917, 69 S.Ct. 639.

APPEALABILITY

At the threshold we are met with the question whether the District Court's order refusing to apply the statute was an appealable one. Title 28 U.S.C. § 1291, 28 U.S.C.A. § 1291, provides, as did its predecessors, for appeal only "from all final decisions of the district courts," except when direct appeal to this Court is provided. Section 1292 allows appeals also from certain interlocutory orders, decrees and judgments, not material to this case except as they indicate the purpose to allow appeals from orders other than final judgments when they have a final and irreparable effect on the rights of the parties. It is obvious that, if Congress had allowed appeals only from those final judgments which terminate an action, this order would not be appealable.

The effect of the statute is to disallow appeal from any decision which is tentative, informal or incomplete. Appeal gives the upper court a power of review, not one of intervention. So long as the matter remains open, unfinished or inconclusive, there may be no intrusion by appeal. But the District Court's action upon this application was concluded and closed and its decision final in that sense before the appeal was taken.

review not intervention

Nor does the statute permit appeals, even from fully consummated decisions, where they are but steps towards final judgment in which they will merge. The purpose is to combine in one review all stages of the proceeding that effectively may be reviewed and corrected if and when final judgment results. But this order of the District Court did not make any step toward final disposition of the merits of the case and will not be merged in final judgment. When that time comes, it will be too late effectively to review the present order and the rights conferred by the statute, if it is applicable, will have been lost, probably irreparably. We conclude that the matters embraced in the decision appealed from are not of such an interlocutory nature as to affect, or to be affected by, decision of the merits of this case.

holding

This decision appears to fall in that small class which finally determine claims of right separable from, and collateral to, rights asserted in the action, too important to be denied review and too independent of the cause itself to require that appellate consideration be deferred until the whole case is adjudicated. The Court has long given this provision of the statute this practical rather than a technical construction. [Citations omitted.]

We hold this order appealable because it is a final disposition of a claimed right which is not an ingredient of the cause of action and does not require consideration with it. But we do not mean that every order fixing security is subject to appeal. Here it is the right to security that presents a serious and unsettled question. If the right were admitted or clear and the order involved only an exercise of discretion as to the amount of security, a matter the statute makes subject to reconsideration from time to time, appealability would present a different question.

holding

reasoning

Since this order may be reviewed on appeal, the petition in No. 512, whereby the corporation asserts the right to compel security by mandamus, is dismissed.

* * *

The judgment of the Court of Appeals is affirmed.

Affirmed.

[The dissenting opinion, in part, by JUSTICE DOUGLAS, with whom JUSTICE FRANKFURTER concurred, and the dissenting opinion of JUSTICE RUTLEDGE, are omitted.]

COOPERS & LYBRAND v. LIVESAY

Supreme Court of the United States, 1978.
437 U.S. 463, 98 S.Ct. 2454, 57 L.Ed.2d 351.

Mr. Justice Stevens delivered the opinion of the Court.

The question in this case is whether a district court's determination that an action may not be maintained as a class action pursuant to Fed. Rule Civ.Proc. 23 is a "final decision" within the meaning of 28 U.S.C. § 1291 and therefore appealable as a matter of right. Because there is a conflict in the Circuits over this issue, we granted certiorari and now hold that such an order is not appealable under § 1291.

Petitioner, Coopers & Lybrand, is an accounting firm that certified the financial statements in a prospectus issued in connection with a 1972 public offering of securities in Punta Gorda Isles for an aggregate price of over $18 million. Respondents purchased securities in reliance on that prospectus. In its next annual report to shareholders, Punta Gorda restated the earnings that had been reported in the prospectus for 1970 and 1971 by writing down its net income for each year by over $1 million. Thereafter, respondents sold their Punta Gorda securities and sustained a loss of $2,650 on their investment.

Respondents filed this action on behalf of themselves and a class of similarly situated purchasers. They alleged that petitioner and other defendants had violated various sections of the Securities Act of 1933 and the Securities Exchange Act of 1934. The District Court first certified, and then, after further proceedings, decertified the class.

Respondents did not request the District Court to certify its order for interlocutory review under 28 U.S.C. § 1292(b).[5] Rather, they filed a notice of appeal pursuant to § 1291.[6] The Court of Appeals regarded its appellate jurisdiction as depending on whether the decertification order had sounded the "death knell" of the action. After examining the amount of respondents' claims in relation to their financial resources and the probable cost of the litigation, the court concluded that they would not pursue their claims individually.[7] The Court of Appeals

---

5. Section 1292(b) provides:

"When a district judge, in making in a civil action an order not otherwise appealable under this section, shall be of the opinion that such order involves a controlling question of law as to which there is substantial ground for difference of opinion and that an immediate appeal from the order may materially advance the ultimate termination of the litigation he shall so state in writing in such order. The Court of Appeals may thereupon, in its discretion, permit an appeal to be taken from such order, if application is made to it within ten days after the entry of the order: *Provided, however,* 'That applica-

tion for an appeal hereunder shall not stay proceedings in the district court unless the district judge or the Court of Appeals or a judge thereof shall so order.''

6. Respondents also petitioned for a writ of mandamus directing the District Court to recertify the class. Since the Court of Appeals accepted appellate jurisdiction, it dismissed the petition for a writ of mandamus.

7. "Plaintiffs, both of whom are employed, have an aggregate yearly gross income of $26,000. Their total net worth is approximately $75,000, but only $4,000 of

therefore held that it had jurisdiction to hear the appeal and, on the merits, reversed the order decertifying the class. Livesay v. Punta Gorda Isles, Inc., 550 F.2d 1106.

Federal appellate jurisdiction generally depends on the existence of a decision by the District Court that "ends the litigation on the merits and leaves nothing for the court to do but execute the judgment." Catlin v. United States, 324 U.S. 229, 233, 65 S.Ct. 631, 633, 89 LEd. 911.[8] An order refusing to certify, or decertifying, a class does not of itsown force terminate the entire litigation because the plaintiff is free to proceed on his individual claim. Such an order is appealable, therefore, only if it comes within an appropriate exception to the final-judgment rule. In this case respondents rely on the "collateral order" exception articulated by this Court in Cohen v. Beneficial Industrial Loan Corp., 337 U.S. 541, 69 S.Ct. 1221, 93 L.Ed. 1528, and on the "death knell" doctrine adopted by several Circuits to determine the appealability of orders denying class certification.

I

In *Cohen,* the District Court refused to order the plaintiff in a stockholder's derivative action to post the security for costs required by a New Jersey statute. The defendant sought immediate review of the question whether the state statute applied to derivative suits in federal court. This Court noted that the purpose of the finality requirement "is to combine in one review all stages of the proceeding that effectively may be reviewed and corrected if and when final judgment results." Id., at 546, 69 S.Ct., at 1225. Because immediate review of the District Court's

this sum is in cash. The remainder consists of equity in their home and investments.

"As of December 1974 plaintiffs had already incurred expenses in excess of $1,200 in connection with this lawsuit. Plaintiffs' new counsel has estimated expenses of this lawsuit to be $15,000. The nature of this case will require extensive discovery, much of which must take place in Florida, where most defendants reside. Moreover, the allegations regarding the prospectus and financial statements will likely require expert testimony at trial.

"After considering all the relevant information in the record, we are convinced that plaintiffs have sustained their burden of showing that they will not pursue their individual claim if the decertification order stands. Although plaintiffs' total net worth could absorb the cost of this litigation, 'it [takes] no great understanding of the mysteries of high finance to make obvious the futility *of* spending a thousand dollars to get a thousand dollars—or even less.' Douglas, Protective Committees in Railroad Reorganizations, 47 Harv.L.Rev. 565, 567 (1934). We conclude we have jurisdiction *to* hear the appeal." Livesay v. Punta Gorda Isles, Inc., 550 F.2d 1106, 1109—1110.

8. For a unanimous Court in Cobbledick v. United States, 309 U.S. 323, 325, 60 S.Ct. 540, 541, 84 LEd. 783, Mr. Justice Frankfurter wrote:

"Since the right to a judgment from more than one court is a matter of grace and not a necessary ingredient of justice, Congress from the very beginning has, by forbidding piece-meal disposition on appeal of what for practical purposes is a single controversy, set itself against enfeebling judicial administration. Thereby is avoided the obstruction to just claims that would come from permitting the harassment and cost of a succession of separate appeals from the various rulings to which a litigation may give rise, from its initiation to entry of judgment. To be effective, judicial administration must not be leaden-footed. Its momentum would be arrested by permitting separate reviews of the component elements in a unified cause."

order was consistent with this purpose, the Court held it appealable as a "final decision" under § 1291. The ruling had "settled conclusively the corporation's claim that it was entitled by state law to require the shareholder to post security for costs * * * [and] concerned a collateral matter that could not be reviewed effectively on appeal from the final judgment."[9]

To come within the "small class" of decisions excepted from the final-judgment rule by *Cohen*, the order must conclusively determine the disputed question, resolve an important issue completely separate from the merits of the action, and be effectively unreviewable on appeal from a final judgment.[10] Abney v. United States, 431 U.S. 651, 658, 97 S.Ct. 2034, 2039, 52 L.Ed.2d 651; United States v. MacDonald, 435 U.S. 850, 855, 98 S.Ct. 1547, 1549, 56 L.Ed.2d 18. An order passing on a request for class certification does not fall in that category. First, such an order is subject to revision in the District Court. Fed.Rule Civ.Proc. 23(c)(1).[11] Second, the class determination generally involves considerations that are "enmeshed in the factual and legal issues comprising the plaintiff's cause of action." Mercantile Nat. Bank v. Langdeau, 371 U.S. 555, 558, 83 S.Ct. 520, 522, 9 L.Ed.2d 523.[12] Finally, an order denying class certification is subject to effective review after final judgment at the behest of the named plaintiff or intervening class members. United Airlines, Inc. v. McDonald, 432 U.S. 385, 97 S.Ct. 2464, 53 L.Ed.2d 423. For these reasons, as the Courts of Appeals have consistently recognized, the collateral-order doctrine is not applicable to the kind of order involved in this case.

II

Several Circuits, including the Court of Appeals in this case, have held that an order denying class certification is appealable if it is likely to sound the "death knell" of the litigation. The "death knell" doctrine assumes that without the incentive of a possible group recovery the individual plaintiff may find it economically imprudent to pursue his lawsuit to a final judgment and then seek appellate review of an adverse class determination. Without questioning this assumption, we hold that

9. Eisen v. Carlisle & Jacquelin, 417 U.S. 156, 171, 94 S.Ct. 2140, 2149, 40 L.Ed.2d 732.

10. As the Court summarized the rule in *Cohen:*

"This decision appears to fall in that small class which finally determine claims of right separable from, and collateral to, rights asserted in the action, too important to be denied review and too independent of the cause itself to require that appellate consideration be deferred until the whole case is adjudicated." 337 U.S., at 546, 69 S.Ct., at 1225.

11. The Rule provides that an order involving class status may be "altered or amended before the decision on the mer-

its." Thus, a district court's order denying or granting class status is inherently tentative.

12. "Evaluation of many of the questions entering into determination of class action questions is intimately involved with the merits of the claims. The typicality of the representative's claims or defenses, the adequacy of the representative, and the presence of common questions of law or fact are obvious examples. The more complex determinations required in Rule 23(b)(3) class actions entail even greater entanglement with the merits * * *." 15 C. Wright, A. Miller, & E. Cooper, Federal Practice and Procedure § 3911, p. 485 n. 45 (1976).

orders relating to class certification are not independently appealable under § 1291 prior to judgment.

In addressing the question whether the "death knell" doctrine supports mandatory appellate jurisdiction of orders refusing to certify class actions, the parties have devoted a portion of their argument to the desirability of the small-claim class action. Petitioner's opposition to the doctrine is based in part on criticism of the class action as a vexatious kind of litigation. Respondents, on the other hand, argue that the class action serves a vital public interest and, therefore, special rules of appellate review are necessary to ensure that district judges are subject to adequate supervision and control. Such policy arguments, though proper for legislative consideration, are irrelevant to the issue we must decide.

There are special rules relating to class actions and, to that extent, they are a special kind of litigation. Those rules do not, however, contain any unique provisions governing appeals. The appealability of any order entered in a class action is determined by the same standards that govern appealability in other types of litigation. Thus, if the "death knell" doctrine has merit, it would apply equally to the many interlocutory orders in ordinary litigation—rulings on discovery, on venue, on summary judgment—that may have such tactical economic significance that a defeat is tantamount to a "death knell" for the entire case.

Though a refusal to certify a class is inherently interlocutory, it may induce a plaintiff to abandon his individual claim. On the other hand, the litigation will often survive an adverse class determination. What effect the economic disincentives created by an interlocutory order may have on the fate of any litigation will depend on a variety of factors.[15] Under the "death knell" doctrine, appealability turns on the court's perception of that impact in the individual case. Thus, if the court believes that the plaintiff has adequate incentive to continue, the order is considered interlocutory; but if the court concludes that the ruling, as a practical matter, makes further litigation improbable, it is considered an appealable final decision.

The finality requirement in § 1291 evinces a legislative judgment that "[r]estricting appellate review to 'final decisions' prevents the debilitating effect on judicial administration caused by piecemeal appeal disposition of what is, in practical consequence, but a single controversy." Eisen v. Carlisle & Jacquelin, 417 U.S. 156, 170, 94 S.Ct. 2140, 2149, 40 L.Ed.2d 732. Although a rigid insistence on technical finality would sometimes conflict with the purposes of the statute, Cohen v. Beneficial Industrial Loan Corp., 337 U.S. 541, 69 S.Ct. 1221, 93 L.Ed. 1528, even adherents of the "death knell" doctrine acknowledge that a refusal to certify a class does not fall in that limited category of orders

---

15. E.g., the plaintiff's resources; the size of his claim and his subjective willingness to finance prosecution of the claim; the probable cost of the litigation and the possi-bility of joining others who will share that cost; and the prospect of prevailing on the merits and reversing an order denying class certification.

which, though nonfinal, may be appealed without undermining the policies served by the general rule. It is undisputed that allowing an appeal from such an order in the ordinary case would run "directly contrary to the policy of the final judgment rule embodied in 28 U.S.C. § 1291 and the sound reasons for it * * *." Yet several Courts of Appeals have sought to identify on a case-by-case basis those few interlocutory orders which, when viewed from the standpoint of economic prudence, may induce a plaintiff to abandon the litigation. These orders, then, become appealable as a matter of right.

In administering the "death knell" rule, the courts have used two quite different methods of identifying an appealable class ruling. Some courts have determined their jurisdiction by simply comparing the claims of the named plaintiffs with an arbitrarily selected jurisdictional amount; others have undertaken a thorough study of the possible impact of the class order on the fate of the litigation before determining their jurisdiction. Especially when consideration is given to the consequences of applying these tests to pretrial orders entered in non-class-action litigation, it becomes apparent that neither provides an acceptable basis for the exercise of appellate jurisdiction.

The formulation of an appealability rule that turns on the amount of the plaintiff's claim is plainly a legislative, not a judicial, function. While Congress could grant an appeal of right to those whose claims fall below a specific amount in controversy, it has not done so. Rather, it has made "finality" the test of appealability. Without a legislative prescription, an amount-in-controversy rule is necessarily an arbitrary measure of finality because it ignores the variables that inform a litigant's decision to proceed, or not to proceed, in the face of an adverse class ruling. Moreover, if the jurisdictional amount is to be measured by the aggregated claims of the named plaintiffs, appellate jurisdiction may turn on the joinder decisions of counsel rather than the finality of the order.

While slightly less arbitrary, the alternative approach to the "death knell" rule would have a serious debilitating effect on the administration of justice. It requires class-action plaintiffs to build a record in the trial court that contains evidence of those factors deemed relevant to the "death knell" issue and district judges to make appropriate findings. And one Court of Appeals has even required that the factual inquiry be extended to all members of the class because the policy against interlocutory appeals can be easily circumvented by joining "only those whose individual claims would not warrant the cost of separate litigation"; to avoid this possibility, the named plaintiff is required to prove that no member of the purported class has a claim that warrants individual litigation.

A threshold inquiry of this kind may, it is true, identify some orders that would truly end the litigation prior to final judgment; allowing an immediate appeal from those orders may enhance the quality of justice afforded a few litigants. But this incremental benefit is outweighed by the impact of such an individualized jurisdictional inquiry on the judicial system's overall capacity to administer justice.

The potential waste of judicial resources is plain. The district court must take evidence, entertain argument, and make findings; and the court of appeals must review that record and those findings simply to determine whether a discretionary class determination is subject to appellate review. And if the record provides an inadequate basis for this determination, a remand for further factual development may be required. Moreover, even if the court makes a "death knell" finding and reviews the class-designation order on the merits, there is no assurance that the trial process will not again be disrupted by interlocutory review. For even if a ruling that the plaintiff does not adequately represent the class is reversed on appeal, the district court may still refuse to certify the class on the ground that, for example, common questions of law or fact do not predominate. Under the "death knell" theory, plaintiff would again be entitled to an appeal as a matter of right pursuant to § 1291. And since other kinds of interlocutory orders may also create the risk of a premature demise, the potential for multiple appeals in every complex case is apparent and serious.

Perhaps the principal vice of the "death knell" doctrine is that it authorizes *indiscriminate* interlocutory review of decisions made by the trial judge. The Interlocutory Appeals Act of 1958, 28 U.S.C. § 1292(b), was enacted to meet the recognized need for prompt review of certain nonfinal orders. However, Congress carefully confined the availability of such review. Non-final orders could never be appealed as a matter of right. Moreover, the discretionary power to permit an interlocutory appeal is not, in the first instance, vested in the courts of appeals.[24] A party seeking review of a nonfinal order must first obtain the consent of the trial judge. This screening procedure serves the dual purpose of ensuring that such review will be confined to appropriate cases and avoiding time-consuming jurisdictional determinations in the court of appeals.[25] Finally, even if the district judge certifies the order under § 1292(b), the appellant still "has the burden of persuading the court of

24. Thus, Congress rejected the notion that the courts of appeals should be free to entertain interlocutory appeals whenever, in their discretion, it appeared necessary to avoid unfairness in the particular case. H.R.Rep. No. 1667, 85th Cong., 2d Sess., 4–6 (1958); Note, Interlocutory Appeals in the Federal Courts under 28 U.S.C. § 1292(b), 88 Harv.L.Rev. 607, 610 (1975).

25. *H.R.Rep. No. 1667,* supra, at 5–6:

"We also recognize that such savings may be nullified in practice by indulgent extension of the amendment to inappropriate cases or by enforced consideration in Courts of Appeals of many ill-founded applications for review. The problem, therefore, is to provide a procedural screen through which only the desired cases may pass, and to avoid the wastage

of a multitude of fruitless applications to invoke the amendment contrary to its purpose. * * *

"* * * Requirement that the Trial Court certify the case as appropriate for appeal serves the double purpose of providing the Appellate Court with the best informed opinion that immediate review is of value, and at once protects appellate dockets against a flood of petitions in inappropriate cases. * * * [A]voidance of ill-founded applications in the Courts of Appeals for piecemeal review is of particular concern. If the consequence of change is to be crowded appellate dockets as well as any substantial number of unjustified delays in the Trial Court, the benefits to be expected from the amendment may well be outweighed by the lost

appeals that exceptional circumstances justify a departure from the basic policy of postponing appellate review until after the entry of a final judgment." Fisons, Ltd. v. United States, 458 F.2d 1241, 1248 (CA 7 1972). The appellate court may deny the appeal for any reason, including docket congestion. By permitting appeals of right from class-designation orders after jurisdictional determinations that turn on questions of fact, the "death knell" doctrine circumvents these restrictions.[27]

Additional considerations reinforce our conclusion that the "death knell" doctrine does not support appellate jurisdiction of prejudgment orders denying class certification. First, the doctrine operates only in favor of plaintiffs even though the class issue—whether to certify, and if so, how large the class should be—will often be of critical importance to defendants as well. Certification of a large class may so increase the defendant's potential damages liability and litigation costs that he may find it economically prudent to settle and to abandon a meritorious defense. Yet the Courts of Appeals have correctly concluded that orders granting class certification are interlocutory. Whatever similarities or differences there are between plaintiffs and defendants in this context involve questions of policy for Congress.[28] Moreover, allowing appeals of right from nonfinal orders that turn on the facts of a particular case thrusts appellate courts indiscriminately into the trial process and thus defeats one vital purpose of the final-judgment rule—"that of maintaining the appropriate relationship between the respective courts. * * * This goal, in the absence of most compelling reasons to the contrary, is very much worth preserving."

Accordingly, we hold that the fact that an interlocutory order may induce a party to abandon his claim before final judgment is not a sufficient reason for considering it a "final decision" within the meaning of § 1291.[30] The judgment of the Court of Appeals is reversed with directions to dismiss the appeal.

It is so ordered.

motion of preparation, consideration, and rejection of unwarranted applications for its benefits."

27. Several Courts of Appeals have heard appeals from discretionary class determinations pursuant to § 1292(b). [Citations omitted.]

As Judge Friendly has noted:

"[T]he best solution is to hold that appeals from the grant or denial of class action designation can be taken only under the procedure for interlocutory appeals provided by 28 U.S.C. § 1292(b). * * * Since the need for review of class action orders turns on the facts of the particular case, this procedure is preferable to attempts to formulate standards which are necessarily so vague as to give rise to undesirable jurisdictional litigation with concomitant expense and delay." Parkinson v. April Industries, Inc., 520 F.2d 650, 660 (CA2 1975) (concurring opinion).

28. "The Congress is in a position to weigh the competing interests of the dockets of the trial and appellate courts, to consider the practicability of savings in time and expense, and to give proper weight to the effect on litigants. * * * This Court * * * is not authorized to approve or declare judicial modification. It is the responsibility of all courts to see that no unauthorized extension or reduction of jurisdiction, direct or indirect, occurs in the federal system. * * * Any such *ad hoc* decisions disorganize practice by encouraging attempts to secure or oppose appeals with a consequent waste of time and money. The choices fall in the legislative domain." Baltimore Contractors v. Bodinger, 348 U.S. 176, 181–182, 75 S.Ct. 249, 252–53, 99 L.Ed. 233.

30. Respondents also suggest that the Court's decision in Gillespie v. United States Steel Corp., 379 U.S. 148, 85 S.Ct. 308, 13 L.Ed.2d 199, supports appealability

DIGITAL EQUIPMENT CORP. v. DESKTOP DIRECT

Supreme Court of the United States, 1994.
511 U.S. 863, 114 S.Ct. 1992, 128 L.Ed.2d 842.

JUSTICE SOUTER delivered the opinion of the Court.

Section 1291 of the Judicial Code confines appeals as of right to those from "final decisions of the district courts." 28 U.S.C. § 1291. This case raises the question whether an order vacating a dismissal predicated on the parties' settlement agreement is final as a collateral order even without a district court's resolution of the underlying cause of action. See Cohen v. Beneficial Loan Corp., 337 U.S. 541, 546 (1949). We hold that an order denying effect to a settlement agreement does not come within the narrow ambit of collateral orders.

I

Respondent, Desktop Direct, Inc. (Desktop) sells computers and like equipment under the trade name "Desktop Direct." Petitioner, Digital Equipment Corporation is engaged in a similar business and in late 1991 began using that trade name to market a new service it called "Desktop Direct from Digital." In response, Desktop filed this action in the United States District Court for the District of Utah, charging Digital with unlawful use of the Desktop Direct name. Desktop sent Digital a copy of the complaint, and negotiations between officers of the two corporations ensued. Under a confidential settlement reached on March 25, 1992, Digital agreed to pay Desktop a sum of money for the right to use the "Desktop Direct" trade name and corresponding trademark, and for waiver of all damages and dismissal of the suit. That same day, Desktop filed a notice of dismissal in the District Court.

Several months later, Desktop moved to vacate the dismissal and rescind the settlement agreement, alleging misrepresentation of material facts during settlement negotiations. The District Court granted the motion, concluding "that a fact finder could determine that [Digital] failed to disclose material facts to [Desktop] during settlement negotiations which would have resulted in rejection of the settlement offer."

of a class-designation order as a matter of right. We disagree. In *Gillespie,* the Court upheld an exercise of appellate jurisdiction of what it considered a marginally final order that disposed of an unsettled issue of national significance because review of that issue unquestionably "implemented the same policy Congress sought to promote in § 1292(b)," id., at 154, 85 S.Ct. at 312, and the arguable finality issue had not been presented to this Court until argument on the merits, thereby ensuring that none of the policies of judicial economy served by the finality requirement would be achieved were the case sent back with the important issue undecided. In this case, in contrast, respondents sought review of an inherently nonfinal order that tentatively resolved a question that turns on the facts of the individual case; and, as noted above, the indiscriminate allowance of appeals from such discretionary orders is plainly inconsistent with the policies promoted by § 1292(b). If *Gillespie* were extended beyond the unique facts of that case, § 1291 would be stripped of all significance.

After the District Court declined to reconsider that ruling or stay its order vacating dismissal, Digital appealed.

The Court of Appeals for the Tenth Circuit dismissed the appeal for lack of jurisdiction, holding that the District Court order was not appealable under § 1291, because it neither "ended the litigation on the merits" nor "[fell] within the long-recognized 'collateral order' exception to the final judgment requirement." 993 F. 2d 755, 757 (1993). Applying the three-pronged test for determining when "collateral order" appeal is allowed, see *Cohen*, supra; Coopers & Lybrand v. Livesay, 437 U.S. 463 (1978), the Court of Appeals concluded that any benefits claimed under the settlement agreement were insufficiently "important" to warrant the immediate appeal as of right. Although Digital claimed what it styled a "right not to go to trial," the court reasoned that any such privately negotiated right as Digital sought to vindicate was different in kind from an immunity rooted in an explicit constitutional or statutory provision or "compelling public policy rationale," the denial of which has been held to be immediately appealable. 993 F. 2d at 758–60.

The Tenth Circuit recognized that it was thus deviating from the rule followed in some other Courts of Appeals* * *. We granted certiorari to resolve this conflict and now affirm.

II

A

The collateral order doctrine is best understood not as an exception to the "final decision" rule laid down by Congress in § 1291, but as a "practical construction" of it, *Cohen*, supra, 337 U.S., at 546, 69 S.Ct., at 1225–1226; see, e.g., *Coopers & Lybrand*, supra, 437 U.S., at 468, 98 S.Ct., at 2457–2458. We have repeatedly held that the statute entitles a party to appeal not only from a district court decision that "ends the litigation on the merits and leaves nothing more for the court to do but execute the judgment," Catlin v. United States, 324 U.S. 229, 233, 65 S.Ct. 631, 633, 89 L.Ed. 911 (1945), but also from a narrow class of decisions that do not terminate the litigation, but must, in the interest of "achieving a healthy legal system," cf. Cobbledick v. United States, 309 U.S. 323, 326, 60 S.Ct. 540, 541, 84 L.Ed. 783 (1940), nonetheless be treated as "final." The latter category comprises only those district court decisions that are conclusive, that resolve important questions completely separate from the merits, and that would render such important questions effectively unreviewable on appeal from final judgment in the underlying action. See generally *Coopers & Lybrand*, supra. Immediate appeals from such orders, we have explained, do not go against the grain of § 1291, with its object of efficient administration of justice in the federal courts, see generally Richardson–Merrell, Inc. v. Koller, 472 U.S. 424, 105 S.Ct. 2757, 86 L.Ed.2d 340 (1985).

But we have also repeatedly stressed that the "narrow" exception should stay that way and never be allowed to swallow the general rule, that a party is entitled to a single appeal, to be deferred until final judgment has been entered, in which claims of district court error at any stage of the litigation may be ventilated, see United States v. Hollywood Motor Car Co., 458 U.S. 263, 270, 102 S.Ct. 3081, 3085, 73 L.Ed.2d 754 (1982). We have accordingly described the conditions for collateral order appeal as stringent, see, e.g., Midland Asphalt Corp. v. United States, 489 U.S. 794, 799, 109 S.Ct. 1494, 1498, 103 L.Ed.2d 879 (1989), and have warned that the issue of appealability under § 1291 is to be determined for the entire category to which a claim belongs, without regard to the chance that the litigation at hand might be speeded, or a "particular injustice[e]" averted, Van Cauwenberghe v. Biard, 486 U.S. 517, 529, 108 S.Ct. 1945, 1953, 100 L.Ed.2d 517 (1988), by a prompt appellate court decision. See also *Richardson-Merrell*, supra, 472 U.S., at 439, 105 S.Ct., at 2764 (this Court "has expressly rejected efforts to reduce the finality requirement of § 1291 to a case-by-case [appealability] determination"); Carroll v. United States, 354 U.S. 394, 405, 77 S.Ct. 1332, 1339, 1 L.Ed.2d 1442 (1957).

B

Here, the Court of Appeals accepted Digital's claim that the order vacating dismissal (and so rescinding the settlement agreement) was the "final word on the subject addressed," 993 F. 2d, at 757 (citation omitted) and held the second *Cohen* condition, separability, to be satisfied, as well. Neither conclusion is beyond question, but each is best left untouched here, both because Desktop has made no serious effort to defend the Court of Appeals judgment on those points and because the failure to meet the third condition of the *Cohen* test, that the decision on an "important" question be "effectively unreviewable" upon final judgment, would in itself suffice to foreclose immediate appeal under § 1291. Turning to these dispositive factors, we conclude, despite Digital's position that it holds a "right not to stand trial" requiring protection by way of immediate appeal, that rights under private settlement agreements can be adequately vindicated on appeal from final judgement.

C

The roots of Digital's argument that the settlement with Desktop gave it a "right not to stand trial altogether" (and that such a right per se satisfies the third *Cohen* requirement) are readily traced to Abney v. United States, 431 U.S. 651 (1977), where we held that § 1291 entitles a criminal defendant to appeal an adverse ruling on a double jeopardy claim, without waiting for the conclusion of his trial. After holding the second Cohen requirement satisfied by the distinction between the former jeopardy claim and the question of guilt to be resolved at trial, we emphasized that the Fifth Amendment not only secures the right to be free from multiple punishments, but by its very terms embodies the broader principle, " 'deeply ingrained ... in the Anglo–American system of jurisprudence,' " that it is intolerable for " 'the State, with all its resources ... [to] make repeated attempts to convict an individual [defendant], thereby subjecting him to embarrassment, expense and ordeal and compelling him to live in a continuing state of anxiety and insecurity.' " 431 U.S., at 661–662 (quoting Green v. United States, 355 U.S. 184, 187–188 (1957)). We found that immediate appeal was the only way to give "full protection" to this constitutional right "not to face trial at all." 431 U.S. at 662, and n. 7; see also Helstoski v. Meanor, 442 U.S. 500 (1979) (decision denying immunity under the Speech and Debate Clause would be appealable under § 1291).

Abney's rationale was applied in Nixon v. Fitzgerald, 457 U.S. 731, 742 (1982), where we held to be similarly appealable an order denying the petitioner absolute immunity from suit for civil damages arising from actions taken while petitioner was President of the United States. Seeing this immunity as a "functionally mandated incident of the President's unique office, rooted in the ... separation of powers and supported by our history," id., at 749, we stressed that it served "compelling public ends," id., at 758, and would be irretrievably lost if the former President were not allowed an immediate appeal to vindicate this right to be free from the rigors of trial, see id., at 752, n. 32.

Next, in Mitchell v. Forsyth, 472 U.S. 511 (1985), we held that similar considerations supported appeal under § 1291 from decisions denying government officials qualified immunity from damages suits. An "essential attribute," id. at 525, of this freedom from suit for past conduct not violative of clearly established law, we explained, is the "entitlement not to stand trial or face the other burdens of litigation," id., at 526, one which would be "effectively lost if a case [were] erroneously permitted to go to trial." Ibid. Echoing the reasoning of Nixon v. Fitzgerald, supra (and Harlow v. Fitzgerald, 457 U.S. 800 (1982)), we explained that requiring an official with a colorable immunity claim to defend a suit for damages would be "peculiarly disruptive of effective government," and would work the very "distraction ... from ... duty, inhibition of discretionary action, and deterrence of able people from public service" that qualified immunity was meant to avoid. See 472 U.S., at 526 (internal quotation marks omitted); see also Puerto Rico Aqueduct & Sewer Authority v. Metcalf & Eddy, Inc., 506 U.S. 139 (1993) (State's Eleventh Amendment immunity from suit in federal court may be vindicated by immediate appeal under § 1291).

D

Digital puts this case on all fours with *Mitchell*. It maintains that it obtained dual rights under the settlement agreement with Desktop, not only a broad defense to liability but the "right not to stand trial," the latter being just like the qualified immunity held immediately appealable in *Mitchell*. As in *Mitchell*, that right must be enforceable on collateral order appeal, Digital asserts, or an adverse trial ruling will destroy it forever.

While Digital's argument may exert some pull on a narrow analysis, it does not hold up under the broad scrutiny to which all claims of immediate appealability under § 1291 must be subjected. To be sure,

Abney and *Mitchell* are fairly cited for the proposition that orders denying certain immunities are strong candidates for prompt appeal under § 1291. But Digital's larger contention, that a party's ability to characterize a district court's decision as denying an irreparable "right not to stand trial" altogether is sufficient as well as necessary for a collateral order appeal, is neither an accurate distillation of our case law nor an appealing prospect for adding to it.

Even as they have recognized the need for immediate appeals under § 1291 to vindicate rights that would be "irretrievably lost," *Richardson-Merrell*, 472 U.S., at 431, if review were confined to final judgments only, our cases have been at least as emphatic in recognizing that the jurisdiction of the courts of appeals should not, and cannot, depend on a party's agility in so characterizing the right asserted. This must be so because the strong bias of § 1291 against piecemeal appeals almost never operates without some cost. A fully litigated case can no more be untried than the law's proverbial bell can be unrung, and almost every pretrial or trial order might be called "effectively unreviewable" in the sense that relief from error can never extend to rewriting history. Thus, erroneous evidentiary rulings, grants or denials of attorney disqualification, see, e.g., *Richardson-Merrell*, supra, and restrictions on the rights of intervening parties, see Stringfellow v. Concerned Neighbors in Action, 480 U.S. 370 (1987), may burden litigants in ways that are only imperfectly reparable by appellate reversal of a final district court judgment, cf. Carroll, 354 U.S., at 406; Parr v. United States, 351 U.S. 513, 519–520 (1956); and other errors, real enough, will not seem serious enough to warrant reversal at all, when reviewed after a long trial on the merits, see Stringfellow, supra. In still other cases, see Coopers & Lybrand v. Livesay, 437 U.S. 463 (1978), an erroneous district court decision will, as a practical matter, sound the "death knell" for many plaintiffs' claims that might have gone forward if prompt error correction had been an option. But if immediate appellate review were available every such time, Congress's final decision rule would end up a pretty puny one, and so the mere identification of some interest that would be "irretrievably lost" has never sufficed to meet the third *Cohen* requirement. See generally Lauro Lines, s.r.l. v. Chasser, 490 U.S. 495, 499 (1989) ("It is always true, however, that 'there is value ... in triumphing before trial, rather than after it' ") (quoting United States v. MacDonald, 435 U.S., 850, 860, n. 7 (1978)); *Richardson-Merrell, supra,* at 436.

Nor does limiting the focus to whether the interest asserted may be called a "right not to stand trial" offer much protection against the urge to push the § 1291 limits. We have, after all, acknowledged that virtually every right that could be enforced appropriately by pretrial dismissal might loosely be described as conferring a "right not to stand trial," see, e.g., Midland Asphalt, 489 U.S., at 501; Van Cauwenberghe v. Biard, 486 U.S. 517, 524 (1988). Allowing immediate appeals to vindicate every such right would move § 1291 aside for claims that the district court lacks personal jurisdiction, see *Van Cauwenberghe,* that the statute of limitations has run, see 15B C. Wright, A. Miller, & E. Cooper, Federal Practice and Procedure § 3918.5, and n. 65, p. 521 (1992), that the movant has been denied his Sixth Amendment right to speedy trial, see MacDonald, supra, that an action is barred on claim preclusion principles, that no material fact is in dispute and the moving party is entitled to judgment as a matter of law, or merely that the complaint fails to state a claim. Such motions can be made in virtually every case, see generally *MacDonald*, supra, at 862; United States v. Hollywood Motor Car Co., 458 U.S., at 270, and it would be no consolation that a party's meritless summary judgment motion or res judicata claim was rejected on immediate appeal; the damage to the efficient and congressionally mandated allocation of judicial responsibility would be done, and any improper purpose the appellant might have had in saddling its opponent with cost and delay would be accomplished. Cf. *Richardson-Merrell*, 472 U.S., at 434 (appeals from "entirely proper" decisions impose the same costs as do appeals from "injudicious" ones). Thus, precisely because candor forces us to acknowledge that there is no single, "obviously correct way to characterize" an asserted right, Lauro Lines, 490 U.S., at 500, we have held that § 1291 requires courts of appeals to view claims of a "right not to be tried" with skepticism, if not a jaundiced eye. Cf. *Van Cauwenberghe*, supra, at 524–525.

In *Midland Asphalt*, for example, we had no trouble in dispatching a defendant's claim of entitlement to an immediate appeal from an order denying dismissal for alleged violation of Federal Rule of Criminal Procedure 6(e), forbidding disclosure of secret grand jury information. Noting " 'a crucial distinction between a right not to be tried and a right whose remedy requires the dismissal of charges,' " 489 U.S. at 801, quoting *Hollywood Motor Car*, 458 U.S., at 269, we observed that Rule 6(e) "contains no hint," 489 U.S., at 802, of an immunity from trial, and we contrasted that Rule with the Fifth Amendment's express provision that "no person shall to held to answer" for a serious crime absent grand jury indictment. Only such an "explicit statutory or constitutional guarantee that trial will not occur," we suggested, id., at 801, could be grounds for an immediate appeal of right under § 1291.[3]

The characterization issue surfaced again (and more ominously for Digital, see infra, in *Lauro Lines s.r.l. v. Chasser*, supra, where a defendant sought to appeal under § 1291 from an order denying effect to a contractual provision that a Neapolitan court would be the forum for trying all disputes arising from the parties' cruise-ship agreement. While we realized of course that the value of the forum-selection clause would

---

3. That reasoning echoed our decision one Term earlier in Van Cauwenberghe v. Biard, 486 U.S. 517, 100 L. Ed. 2d 517, 108 S. Ct. 1945 (1988), where we unanimously rejected the contention that a defendant brought to the United States under an extradition treaty could appeal immediately under § 1291 from a decision denying a motion to dismiss based on the principle of "specialty," which he asserted immunized him from service of civil process in the United States. Even if such an immunity might supply a basis for vacating a judgment on appeal, we held, the right "should be characterized as the right not to be subject to a binding judgment of the court," and so understood, it could therefore "be effectively vindicated following final judgment." Id., at 526–527.

be diminished if the defendant could be tried before appealing, we saw the contractual right to limit trial to an Italian forum as "different in kind" from the entitlement to "avoid suit altogether" that *Abney* and *Mitchell* held could be "adequately vindicated" only on immediate appeal. 490 U.S., at 501.

E

As Digital reads the cases, the only things standing in the way of an appeal to perfect its claimed rights under the settlement agreement are the lone statement in *Midland Asphalt*, to the effect that only explicit statutory and constitutional immunities may be appealed immediately under § 1291, and language (said to be stray) repeated in many of our collateral order decisions, suggesting that the "importance" of the right asserted is an independent condition of appealability. See Brief for Petitioner 28–34. The first, Digital explains, cannot be reconciled with Mitchell's holding, that denial of qualified immunity (which we would be hard-pressed to call "explicitly ... guaranteed" by a particular constitutional or statutory provision) is a collateral order under § 1291; as between *Mitchell* and the *Midland Asphalt* dictum, Digital says, the dictum must give way. As for the second obstacle, Digital adamantly maintains that "importance" has no place in a doctrine justified as supplying a gloss on Congress's "final decision" language.

1

These arguments miss the mark. First, even if *Mitchell* could not be squared fully with the literal words of the *Midland Asphalt* sentence, (but cf. *Lauro Lines*, 490 U.S., at 499, noting that *Midland Asphalt* was a criminal case and *Mitchell* was not), that would be only because the qualified immunity right is inexplicit, not because it lacks a good pedigree in public law. Indeed, the insight that explicitness may not be needed for jurisdiction consistent with § 1291 only leaves Digital with the unenviable task of explaining why other rights that might fairly be said to include an (implicit) "right to avoid trial" aspect are less in need of protection by immediate review, or more readily vindicated on appeal from final judgment, than the (claimed) privately negotiated right to be free from suit. It is far from clear, for example, why § 1291 should bless a party who bargained for the right to avoid trial, but not a party who "purchased" the right by having once prevailed at trial and now pleads res judicata, see In re Corrugated Container Antitrust Litigation v. Willamette Industries, Inc., 694 F. 2d 1041 (CA5 1983); or a party who seeks shelter under the statute of limitations, see, e.g., United States, v. Weiss, 7 F. 3d 1088 (CA2 1993), which is usually understood to secure the same sort of "repose" that Digital seeks to vindicate here, see Brief for Petitioner 25; or a party not even subject to a claim on which relief could be granted. See also *Cobbledick,* 309 U.S., at 325 ("Bearing the discomfiture and cost of a prosecution for crime even by an innocent person is one of the painful obligations of citizenship"); Firestone Tire & Rubber Co. v. Risjord, 449 U.S. 368, 378 (1981) ("Potential harm" should be compared to "the harm resulting from other interlocutory orders that may be erroneous . . .") (citation omitted).

Digital answers that the status under § 1291 of these other (seemingly analogous) rights should not give us pause, because the text and structure of this particular settlement with Desktop confer what no res judicata claimant could ever have, an express right not to stand trial. n5 But we cannot attach much significance one way or another to the supposed clarity of the agreement's terms in this case. To ground a ruling here on whether this settlement agreement in terms confers the prized "right not to stand trial" (a point Desktop by no means concedes) would flout our own frequent admonitions, see, e.g., *Van Cauwenberghe*, 486 U.S., at 529, that availability of collateral order appeal must be determined at a higher level of generality. Indeed, just because it would be the rare settlement agreement that could not be construed to include (at least an implicit) freedom-from-trial "aspect," we decide this case on the assumption that if Digital prevailed here, any district court order denying effect to a settlement agreement could be appealed immediately. (And even if form were held to matter, settlement agreements would all include "immunity from suit" language a good deal plainer than what Digital relies on here, see Tr. of Oral Arg. 44). See also *Van Cauwenberghe*, supra, at 524 ("For purposes of determining appealability, . . . we will assume, but not decide, that petitioner has presented a substantial claim" on the merits).

2

The more fundamental response, however, to the claim that an agreement's provision for immunity from trial can distinguish it from other arguable rights to be trial-free is simply that such a right by agreement does not rise to the level of importance needed for recognition under § 1291. This, indeed, is the bone of the fiercest contention in the case. In disparaging any distinction between an order denying a claim grounded on an explicit constitutional guarantee of immunity from trial and an order at odds with an equally explicit right by private agreement of the parties, Digital stresses that the relative "importance" of these rights, heavily relied upon by the Court of Appeals, is a rogue factor. No decision of this Court, Digital maintains, has held an order unappealable as "unimportant" when it has otherwise met the three Cohen requirements, and whether a decided issue is thought "important," it says, should have no bearing on whether it is "final" under § 1291.

If "finality" were as narrow a concept as Digital maintains, however, the Court would have had little reason to go beyond the first factor in *Cohen*, see also United States v. 243.22 Acres of Land in Babylon, Suffolk Cty., 129 F. 2d 678, 680 (CA2 1942) (Frank, J.) (" 'Final' is not a clear one-purpose word"). And if "importance" were truly aberrational, we would not find it featured so prominently in the Cohen opinion itself, which describes the "small class" of immediately appealable prejudgment decisions in terms of rights that are "too important to be denied review" right away, see 337 U.S., at 546. To be sure, Digital may validly question whether "importance" is a factor "beyond" the three Cohen conditions or whether it is best considered, as we have sometimes suggested it should be, in connection with the second, "separability," requirement, see, e.g., *Coopers & Lybrand*, 437 U.S., at 468; *Lauro Lines*, 490 U.S., at 498, but neither enquiry could lead to the conclusion that "importance" is itself unimportant. To the contrary, the third Cohen question, whether a right is "adequately vindicable" or "effectively reviewable," simply cannot be answered without a judgment about the value of the interests that would be lost through rigorous application of a final judgment requirement. See generally *Van Cauwenberghe*, supra, at 524 (" 'The substance of the rights entailed, rather than the advantage to a litigant in winning his claim sooner' " is dispositive), quoting MacDonald, 435 U.S., at 860, n. 7; *Lauro Lines*, supra, at 502–503 (SCALIA, J., concurring).

While there is no need to decide here that a privately conferred right could never supply the basis of a collateral order appeal, there are surely sound reasons for treating such rights differently from those originating in the Constitution or statutes. When a policy is embodied in a constitutional or statutory provision entitling a party to immunity from suit (a rare form of protection), there is little room for the judiciary to gainsay its "importance." Including a provision in a private contract, by contrast, is barely a prima facie indication that the right secured is "important" to the benefitted party (contracts being replete with boilerplate), let alone that its value exceeds that of other rights not embodied in agreements (e.g., the right to be free from a second suit based on a claim that has already been litigated), or that it qualifies as "important" in Cohen's sense, as being weightier than the societal interests advanced by the ordinary operation of final judgment principles. Where statutory and constitutional rights are concerned, "irretrievable loss" can hardly be trivial, and the collateral order doctrine might therefore be understood as reflecting the familiar principle of statutory construction that, when possible, courts should construe statutes (here § 1291) to foster harmony with other statutory and constitutional law, see, e.g., Ruckelshaus v. Monsanto Co., 467 U.S. 986, 1018 (1984); United States ex rel. Milwaukee Social Democratic Publishing Co. v. Burleson, 255 U.S. 407, 437–438 (1921) (Holmes, J., dissenting). But it is one thing to say that the policy of § 1291 to avoid piecemeal litigation should be reconciled with policies embodied in other statutes or the Constitution, and quite another to suggest that this public policy may be trumped routinely by the expectations or clever drafting of private parties.[7]

---

7. This is not to say that rights originating in a private agreement may never be important enough to warrant immediate appeal. To the contrary, Congress only recently enacted a statute, 102 Stat. 4671, see 9 U.S.C. § 16 (1988 ed., Supp. IV), essentially providing for immediate appeal when a district court rejects a party's assertion that, under the Arbitration Act, a case be-

longs before a commercial arbitrator and not in court, a measure predicted to have a "sweeping impact," 15B C. Wright, A. Miller, & E. Cooper 17 § 3914., Federal Practice and Procedure p. 11 (1992); see generally, id., pp. 7–38. That courts must give full effect to this express congressional judgment that particular policies require that private rights be vindicable immediate-

Indeed, we do not take issue with the Tenth Circuit's observation that this case shares more in common with *Lauro Lines* than with *Mitchell*. It is hard to see how, for purposes of § 1291, the supposedly explicit "right not to be tried" element of the settlement agreement in this case differs from the unarguably explicit, privately negotiated "right not to be tried in any forum other than Naples, Italy," in that one. There, no less than here (if Digital reads the settlement agreement correctly), one private party secured from another a promise not to bring suit for reasons that presumably included avoiding the burden, expense, and perhaps embarrassment of a certain class of trials (all but Neapolitan ones or, here, all prompted by Desktop). Cf. *Lauro Lines*, 490 U.S. 495 (1976) (asserted right was "surely as effectively vindicable" on final judgment appeal as was the right in *Van Cauwenberghe*).[8] The losing argument in *Lauro Lines* should be a losing argument here.

Nor are we swayed by Digital's last-ditch effort to come within *Cohen*'s sense of "importance" by trying to show that settlement-agreement "immunities" merit first-class treatment for purposes of collateral order appeal, because they advance the public policy favoring voluntary resolution of disputes. It defies common sense to maintain that parties' readiness to settle will be significantly dampened (or the corresponding public interest impaired) by a rule that a district court's decision to let allegedly barred litigation go forward may be challenged as a matter of right only on appeal from a judgment for the plaintiff's favor.

III

A

Even, finally, if the term "importance" were to be exorcised from the *Cohen* analysis altogether, Digital's rights would remain "adequately vindicable" or "effectively reviewable" on final judgment to an extent that other immunities, like the right to be free from a second trial on a criminal charge, are not. As noted already, experience suggests that freedom from trial is rarely the sine qua non (or "the essence," see *Van Cauwenberghe*, 486 U.S., at 525) of a negotiated settlement agreement. Avoiding the burden of a trial is no doubt a welcome incident of out-of-court dispute resolution (just as it is for parties who prevail on pretrial motions), but in the run of the mill cases this boon will rarely compare

ly, however, by no means suggests that they should now be more ready to make similar judgments for themselves. Congress has expressed no parallel sentiment, to the effect that settlement-agreement rights are, as a matter of federal policy, similarly "too important" to be denied immediate review.

8. To be fair, the Lauro Lines opinion does contain language that, taken alone, might lend succor to petitioner's claim, see 490 U.S., at 501 ("An entitlement to avoid suit is different in kind from an entitlement to be sued only in a particular forum"), but

the opinion is not easily read as endorsing Digital's claim that a privately negotiated right not to stand trial would be immediately appealable. To the contrary, Lauro Lines expressly adopted (at least for criminal appeals) Midland Asphalt's limitation that " '[a] right not to be tried in the sense relevant to the Cohen exception rests upon an explicit statutory or constitutional guarantee,' " 490 U.S., at 499, quoting 489 U.S., at 801, and stated that the collateral order doctrine operates "similarly" in civil cases, ibid.

with the " 'embarrassment' " and " 'anxiety' " averted by a successful double jeopardy claimant, see *Abney*, 431 U.S., at 661–662, or the " 'distraction from ... duty,' " *Mitchell*, 472 U.S., at 526, avoided by qualified immunity. Judged within the four corners of the settlement agreement, avoiding trial probably pales in comparison with the benefit of limiting exposure to liability (an interest that is fully vindicable on appeal from final judgment). In the rare case where a party had a special reason, apart from the generic desire to triumph early, for having bargained for an immunity from trial, e.g., an unusual interest in preventing disclosure of particular information, it may seek protection from the district court.

The case for adequate vindication without immediate appeal is strengthened, moreover, by recognizing that a settling party has a source of recompense unknown to trial immunity claimants dependent on public law alone. The essence of Digital's claim here is that Desktop, for valuable consideration, promised not to sue, and we have been given no reason to doubt that Utah law provides for the enforcement of that promise in the same way that other rights arising from private agreements are enforced, through an action for breach of contract. See, e.g., VanDyke v. Mountain Coin Machine Distributors, Inc., 758 P. 2d 962 (Utah App. 1988) (upholding compensatory and punitive damages award against party pursuing suit in the face of settlement agreement); see generally 5A A. Corbin, Corbin on Contracts § 1251 (1964); cf. Yockey v. Horn, 880 F. 2d 945, 947 (CA7 1989) (awarding damages for breach of settlement agreement promise not to "participate in any litigation" against plaintiff); see also *Richardson-Merrell*, 472 U.S. at 435, and n. 2 (existence of alternative fora for vindicating asserted rights is relevant to appealability under § 1291). . . .

B

In preserving the strict limitations on review as of right under § 1291, our holding should cause no dismay, for the law is not without its safety valve to deal with cases where the contest over a settlement's enforceability raises serious legal questions taking the case out of the ordinary run. While Digital's insistence that the District Court applied a fundamentally wrong legal standard in vacating the dismissal order here may not be considered in deciding appealability under § 1291, it plainly is relevant to the availability of the discretionary interlocutory appeal from particular district court orders "involving a controlling question of law as to which there is substantial ground for difference of opinion," provided for in § 1292(b) of Title 28. Indeed, because we suppose that a defendant's claimed entitlement to a privately negotiated "immunity from suit" could in some instances raise "a controlling question of law ... [which] ... may materially advance the ultimate termination of the litigation," the discretionary appeal provision (allowing courts to consider the merits of individual claims) would seem a better vehicle for vindicating serious contractual interpretation claims than the blunt, categorical instrument of § 1291 collateral order appeal. See *Van Cau-*

wenberghe, 486 U.S., at 529–530; *Coopers & Lybrand*, 437 U.S., at 474–475.[9]

IV

The words of § 1291 have long been construed to recognize that certain categories of pre-judgment decisions exist for which it is both justifiable and necessary to depart from the general rule, that "the whole case and every matter in controversy in it [must be] decided in a single appeal." *McLish v. Roff*, 141 U.S. 661, 665–666 (1891). But denying effect to the sort of (asserted) contractual right at issue here is far removed from those immediately appealable decisions involving rights more deeply rooted in public policy, and the rights Digital asserts may, in the main, be vindicated through means less disruptive to the orderly administration of justice than immediate, mandatory appeal. We accordingly hold that a refusal to enforce a settlement agreement claimed to shelter a party from suit altogether does not supply the basis for immediate appeal under § 1291. The judgment of the Court of Appeals is therefore Affirmed.

CUNNINGHAM v. HAMILTON COUNTY

Supreme Court of the United States, 1999.
527 U.S. 198, 119 S.Ct. 1915, 144 L.Ed.2d 184.

JUSTICE THOMAS delivered the opinion of the Court.

[Petitioner was an attorney representing a client in a federal civil rights action filed against respondent county and others. After several failures to heed a magistrate judge's orders pertaining to discovery, the court imposed monetary sanctions pursuant to Fed. R. Civ. P. 37(a)(4). Petitioner was disqualified as counsel on the ground that she was a material witness in the case. Though proceedings in the trial court were continuing, petitioner immediately appealed the sanction ruling. The court of appeals dismissed petitioner's appeal for lack of jurisdiction, holding that "a non-participating attorney, like a participating attorney, ordinarily must wait until final disposition of the underlying case before filing an appeal."]

Federal courts of appeals ordinarily have jurisdiction over appeals from "final decisions of the district courts." 28 U.S.C. § 1291. This case presents the question whether an order imposing sanctions on an attorney pursuant to Federal Rule of Civil Procedure 37(a)(4) is a final decision. We hold that it is not, even where, as here, the attorney no longer represents a party in the case.

9. We recognize that § 1292 is not a panacea, both because it depends to a degree on the indulgence of the court from which review is sought and because the discretion to decline to hear an appeal is broad, see, e.g., Coopers & Lybrand, 437 U.S., at 475, (serious docket congestion may be adequate reason to support denial of certified appeal). On the other hand, we find nothing in the text or purposes of either statute to justify the concern, expressed here by Digital, that a party's request to appeal under § 1292(b) might operate, practically or legally, to prejudice its claimed right to immediate appeal under § 1291.

* * * *

The Federal Courts of Appeals disagree over whether an order of Rule 37(a) sanctions against an attorney is immediately appealable under § 1291. Compare, e.g., Eastern Maico Distributors, Inc. v. Maico–Fahrzeugfabrik, G.m.b.h., 658 F.2d 944, 946–951 (CA3 1981) (order not immediately appealable), with Telluride Management Solutions, Inc. v. Telluride Investment Group, 55 F.3d 463, 465 (CA9 1995) (order immediately appealable). We granted a writ of certiorari, limited to this question, and now affirm.

II

Section 1291 of the Judicial Code generally vests courts of appeals with jurisdiction over appeals from "final decisions" of the district courts. It descends from the Judiciary Act of 1789 where "the First Congress established the principle that only 'final judgments and decrees' of the federal district courts may be reviewed on appeal." Midland Asphalt Corp. v. United States, 489 U.S. 794, 798 (1989) (quoting 1 Stat. 84); see generally Crick, The Final Judgment as a Basis for Appeal, 41 Yale L. J. 539, 548–51 (1932) (discussing history of final judgment rule in the United States). In accord with this historical understanding, we have repeatedly interpreted § 1291 to mean that an appeal ordinarily will not lie until after final judgment has been entered in a case. As we explained in *Firestone Tire & Rubber Co. v. Risjord*, 449 U.S. 368, 101 S.Ct. 669, 66 L.Ed.2d 571 (1981), the final judgment rule serves several salutary purposes:

> "It emphasizes the deference that appellate courts owe to the trial judge as the individual initially called upon to decide the many questions of law and fact that occur in the course of a trial. Permitting piecemeal appeals would undermine the independence of the district judge, as well as the special role that individual plays in our judicial system. In addition, the rule is in accordance with the sensible policy of avoid[ing] the obstruction to just claims that would come from permitting the harassment and cost of a succession of separate appeals from the various rulings to which a litigation may give rise, from its initiation to entry of judgment. The rule also serves the important purpose of promoting efficient judicial administration." . . .

The Rule 37 sanction imposed on petitioner neither ended the litigation nor left the court only to execute its judgment. Thus, it ordinarily would not be considered a final decision under § 1291. See, e.g., Midland Asphalt Corp., supra, at 798; Richardson–Merrell, supra, at 430. However, we have interpreted the term "final decision" in § 1291 to permit jurisdiction over appeals from a small category of orders that do not terminate the litigation. E.g., Quackenbush, supra, at 711–715; Puerto Rico Aqueduct and Sewer Authority v. Metcalf & Eddy, Inc., 506 U.S. 139, 142–147 (1993); Mitchell v. Forsyth, 472 U.S. 511, 524–30 (1985); Cohen, 337 U.S. at 545–547. "That small category includes only decisions that are conclusive, that resolve important questions separate from the merits, and that are effectively unreviewable on appeal from the final judgment in the underlying action." Swint, 514 U.S. at 42.[4]

Respondent conceded that the sanctions order was conclusive, so at least one of the collateral order doctrine's conditions is presumed to have been satisfied. We do not think, however, that appellate review of a sanctions order can remain completely separate from the merits. See Van Cauwenberghe, supra, 486 U.S. at 527–530; Coopers & Lybrand v. Livesay, 437 U.S. 463, 469 (1978). In *Van Cauwenberghe*, for example, we held that the denial of a motion to dismiss on the ground of forum non conveniens was not a final decision. We reasoned that consideration of the factors underlying that decision such as "the relative ease of access to sources of proof" and "the availability of witnesses" required trial courts to "scrutinize the substance of the dispute between the parties to evaluate what proof is required, and determine whether the pieces of evidence cited by the parties are critical, or even relevant, to the plaintiff's cause of action and to any potential defenses to the action." 486 U.S. at 528. Similarly, in Coopers & Lybrand, we held that a determination that an action may not be maintained as a class action also was not a final decision, noting that such a determination was enmeshed in the legal and factual aspects of the case. 437 U.S. at 469.

Much like the orders at issue in *Van Cauwenberghe* and *Coopers & Lybrand*, a Rule 37(a) sanctions order often will be inextricably intertwined with the merits of the action. An evaluation of the appropriateness of sanctions may require the reviewing court to inquire into the importance of the information sought or the adequacy or truthfulness of a response. See, e.g., Thomas E. Hoar, Inc. v. Sara Lee Corp., 882 F.2d 682, 687 (2nd Cir. 1989) (adequacy of responses); Outley v. New York, 837 F.2d 587, 590–91 (2nd Cir. 1988) (importance of incomplete answers to interrogatories); Evanson v. Union Oil Company of Cal., 619 F.2d 72, 74 (Temp. Emerg. Ct. App. 1980) (truthfulness of responses). Some of the sanctions in this case were based on the fact that petitioner provided partial responses and objections to some of the defendants' discovery requests. To evaluate whether those sanctions were appropriate, an appellate court would have to assess the completeness of petitioner's responses. See Fed. Rule Civ. Proc. 37(a)(3) ("For purposes of this subdivision an evasive or incomplete disclosure, answer, or response is to

---

4. Most of our collateral order decisions have considered whether an order directed at a party to the litigation is immediately appealable. E.g., Coopers & Lybrand v. Livesay, 437 U.S. 463, 468–69 (1978). Petitioner, of course, was an attorney representing the plaintiff in the case. It is nevertheless clear that a decision does not automatically become final merely because it is directed at someone other than a plaintiff or defendant. See Richardson–Merrell Inc. v. Koller, 472 U.S. 424, 434–35 (1985) (rejecting, as outside collateral order doctrine, immediate appeal of

order disqualifying counsel). For example, we have repeatedly held that a witness subject to a discovery order, but not held in contempt, generally may not appeal the order. See, e.g., United States Catholic Conference v. Abortion Rights Mobilization, Inc., 487 U.S. 72, 76 (1988); United States v. Ryan, 402 U.S. 530, 533–34 (1971); Cobbledick v. United States, 309 U.S. 323, 327–30 (1940); Webster Coal & Coke Co. v. Cassatt , 207 U.S. 181, 186–87 (1907); Alexander v. United States, 201 U.S. 117, 121 (1906).

be treated as a failure to disclose, answer, or respond"). Such an inquiry would differ only marginally from an inquiry into the merits and counsels against application of the collateral order doctrine. Perhaps not every discovery sanction will be inextricably intertwined with the merits, but we have consistently eschewed a case-by-case approach to deciding whether an order is sufficiently collateral. See, e.g., Digital Equipment Corp., 511 U.S. at 868; Richardson–Merrell, 472 U.S. at 439.

Even if the merits were completely divorced from the sanctions issue, the collateral order doctrine requires that the order be effectively unreviewable on appeal from a final judgment. Petitioner claims that this is the case. In support, she relies on a line of decisions holding that one who is not a party to a judgment generally may not appeal from it. See, e.g., Karcher v. May, 484 U.S. 72, 77 (1987). She also posits that contempt orders imposed on witnesses who disobey discovery orders are immediately appealable and argues that the sanctions order in this case should be treated no differently.

Petitioner's argument suffers from at least two flaws. It ignores the identity of interests between the attorney and client. Unlike witnesses, whose interests may differ substantially from the parties', attorneys assume an ethical obligation to serve their clients' interests. Evans v. Jeff D., 475 U.S. 717, 728 (1986). This obligation remains even where the attorney might have a personal interest in seeking vindication from the sanctions order. See *Richardson-Merrell*, supra, 472 U.S. at 434–435. In *Richardson-Merrell*, we held that an order disqualifying an attorney was not an immediately appealable final decision. 472 U.S. at 429–440; see also Flanagan v. United States, 465 U.S. 259, 263–69(1984) (order disqualifying attorney in criminal case not a "final decision" under § 1291). We explained that "an attorney who is disqualified for misconduct may well have a personal interest in pursuing an immediate appeal, an interest which need not coincide with the interests of the client. As a matter of professional ethics, however, the decision to appeal should turn entirely on the client's interest." Richardson–Merrell, supra, at 435 (citing ABA Model Rules of Professional Conduct 1.7(b), 2.1 (1985)). This principle has the same force when an order of discovery sanctions is imposed on the attorney alone. See In re Coordinated Pretrial Proceedings in Petroleum Products Antitrust Litigation, 747 F.2d 1303, 1305 (CA9 1984) (opinion of Kennedy, J.). The effective congruence of interests between clients and attorneys counsels against treating attorneys like other nonparties for purposes of appeal. Cf. United States Catholic Conference v. Abortion Rights Mobilization, Inc., 487 U.S. 72, 78 (1988).

Petitioner's argument also overlooks the significant differences between a finding of contempt and a Rule 37(a) sanctions order. "Civil contempt is designed to force the contemn or to comply with an order of the court." Willy v. Coastal Corp., 503 U.S. 131, 139 (1992). In contrast, a Rule 37(a) sanctions order lacks any prospective effect and is not designed to compel compliance. Judge Adams captured the essential distinction between the two types of orders when he noted that an order such as civil contempt "is not simply to deter harassment and delay, but to effect some discovery conduct. A non-party's interest in resisting a discovery order is immediate and usually separate from the parties' interests in delay. Before final judgment is reached, the non-party either will have surrendered the materials sought or will have suffered incarceration or steadily mounting fines imposed to compel the discovery. If the discovery is held unwarranted on appeal only after the case is resolved, the non-party's injury may not be possible to repair. Under Rule 37(a), no similar situation exists. The objective of the Rule is the prevention of delay and costs to other litigants caused by the filing of groundless motions. An attorney sanctioned for such conduct by and large suffers no inordinate injury from a deferral of appellate consideration of the sanction. He need not in the meantime surrender any rights or suffer undue coercion." Eastern Maico Distributors, 658 F.2d at 949–950 (citation and footnote omitted).

To permit an immediate appeal from such a sanctions order would undermine the very purposes of Rule 37(a), which was designed to protect courts and opposing parties from delaying or harassing tactics during the discovery process. Immediate appeals of such orders would undermine trial judges' discretion to structure a sanction in the most effective manner. They might choose not to sanction an attorney, despite abusive conduct, in order to avoid further delays in their proceedings. Not only would such an approach ignore the deference owed by appellate courts to trial judges charged with managing the discovery process, see Firestone Tire & Rubber Co., 449 U.S. at 374, it also could forestall resolution of the case as each new sanction would give rise to a new appeal. The result might well be the very sorts of piecemeal appeals and concomitant delays that the final judgment rule was designed to prevent.

Petitioner finally argues that, even if an attorney ordinarily may not immediately appeal a sanction order, special considerations apply when the attorney no longer represents a party in the case. Like the Sixth Circuit, we do not think that the appealability of a Rule 37 sanction imposed on an attorney should turn on the attorney's continued participation. Such a rule could not be easily administered. For example, it may be unclear precisely when representation terminates, and questions likely would arise over when the 30–day period for appeal would begin to run under Federal Rule of Appellate Procedure 4. The rule also could be subject to abuse if attorneys and clients strategically terminated their representation in order to trigger a right to appeal with a view to delaying the proceedings in the underlying case. While we recognize that our application of the final judgment rule in this setting may require nonparticipating attorneys to monitor the progress of the litigation after their work has ended, the efficiency interests served by limiting immediate appeals far outweigh any nominal monitoring costs borne by attorneys. For these reasons, an attorney's continued participation in a case does not affect whether a sanctions order is "final" for purposes of § 1291.

We candidly recognize the hardship that a sanctions order may sometimes impose on an attorney. Should these hardships be deemed to outweigh the desirability of restricting appeals to "final decisions," solutions other than an expansive interpretation of § 1291's "final decision" requirement remain available. Congress may amend the Judicial Code to provide explicitly for immediate appellate review of such orders. See, e.g., 28 U.S.C. §§ 1292(a)(1)-(3). Recent amendments to the Judicial Code also have authorized this Court to prescribe rules providing for the immediate appeal of certain orders, see §§ 1292(e), 2072(c), and "Congress' designation of the rulemaking process as the way to define or refine when a district court ruling is 'final' and when an interlocutory order is appealable warrants the Judiciary's full respect." Swint, 514 U.S. at 48 (footnote omitted). Finally, in a particular case, a district court can reduce any hardship by reserving until the end of the trial decisions such as whether to impose the sanction, how great a sanction to impose, or when to order collection.

For the foregoing reasons, we conclude that a sanctions order imposed on an attorney is not a "final decision" under § 1291 and, therefore, affirm the judgment of the Court of Appeals.

It is so ordered.

JUSTICE KENNEDY, concurring.

This case comes to our argument docket, of course, so that we may resolve a split of authority in the Circuits on a jurisdictional issue, not because there is any division of opinion over the propriety of the underlying conduct. Cases involving sanctions against attorneys all too often implicate allegations that, when true, bring the law into great disrepute. Delays and abuses in discovery are the source of widespread injustice; and were we to hold sanctions orders against attorneys to be appealable as collateral orders, we would risk compounding the problem for the reasons suggested by JUSTICE THOMAS in his opinion for the Court. Trial courts must have the capacity to ensure prompt compliance with their orders, especially when attorneys attempt to abuse the discovery process to gain a tactical advantage.

It should be noted, however, that an attorney ordered to pay sanctions is not without a remedy in every case. If the trial court declines to stay enforcement of the order and the result is an exceptional hardship itself likely to cause an injustice, a petition for writ of mandamus might bring the issue before the Court of Appeals to determine if the trial court abused its discretion in issuing the order or denying the stay. See Richardson–Merrell, Inc. v. Koller, 472 U.S. 424, 435 (1985). In addition, if a contempt order is entered and there is no congruence of interests between the person subject to the order and a party to the underlying litigation, the order may be appealable. See In re Coordinated Pretrial Proceedings in Petroleum Products Antitrust Litigation, 747 F.2d 1303, 1305–06 (CA9 1984). In United States Catholic Conference v. Abortion Rights Mobilization, Inc., 487 U.S. 72, 76 (1988), a case involving a nonparty witness, we said: "The right of a nonparty to appeal an adjudication of contempt cannot be questioned. The order finding a nonparty witness in contempt is appealable notwithstanding the absence of a final judgment in the underlying action."

The case before us, however, involves an order for sanctions and nothing more. I join the opinion of the Court and its holding that the order is not appealable under the collateral order doctrine.

Notes and Questions

1. Prior to *Digital*, the argument was made that the collateral order doctrine was an illegitimate judge-made exception to the finality requirement of section 1291, not justified by ordinary methods of statutory construction. Redish, The Pragmatic Approach to Appealability in the Federal Courts, 75 Colum. L. Rev. 89, 125–26 (1975). Compare Sell v. United States, 539 U.S. 166, 123 S.Ct. 2174, 156 L.Ed.2d 197 (2003) (Scalia, J., dissenting) (asserting that the "so-called 'collateral order' doctrine" was "invented" by the Court as a "narrow exception to the statutory command" of section 1291). Perhaps in response, the Court in *Digital* held that the doctrine "is best understood not as an exception to the 'final decision' rule laid down by Congress in § 1219, but as a 'practical construction' of it" (quoting *Cohen*). Does that adequately answer the legitimacy argument? How does one glean the *Cohen* criteria from the language of section 1291? What weight should be given to fact that Congress has proved capable of legislating exceptions to section 1291 (e.g., section 1292)?

2. Why should the issue being appealed be "completely separate from the merits of the action"? How persuasive is the Court's statement in *Coopers & Lybrand* that the class certification's determination is "enmeshed" with the "factual and legal issues comprising the plaintiff's cause of action"? Class certification decisions are usually thought to be analytically separate from the merits. E.g., Eisen v. Carlisle & Jacquelin, 417 U.S. 156, 178, 94 S.Ct. 2140, 40 L.Ed.2d 732 (1974).

3. As the *Digital* case illustrates, a frequently litigated issue under the collateral order doctrine is whether the trial court's decision is an "important" issue which is "effectively unreviewable" upon final judgment. With respect to that prong of the test consider Sell v. United States, 539 U.S. 166, 123 S.Ct. 2174, 156 L.Ed.2d 197 (2003). There, the majority held that an appeal of a court order of involuntary anti-psychotic medication to enable a criminal defendant to be tried was a collateral order. With regard to the "effectively unreviewable" prong, the Court stated that by "the time of trial Sell will have undergone forced medication–the very harm that he seeks to avoid. He cannot undo the harm even if he is acquitted. Indeed, if he is acquitted, there will be no appeal through which he might obtain review." Justice Scalia, joined by Justices O'Connor and Thomas, dissented on that point. He argued that Sell could appeal the order after a conviction. At that point, he conceded, Sell would "not receive the *type* of remedy he would prefer–a predeprivation injunction rather than the postdeprivation vacation of conviction. ...But *that* ground for interlocutory appeal is emphatically rejected by our cases." (In a footnote, Justice Scalia agreed that the order is unreviewable after final judgment if the defendant is acquitted. "But," he added, "the 'unreviewability' leg of our collateral order doctrine–which, as it is framed, requires that the interlocutory order be 'effectively unreviewable

on appeal from a final judgment' [quoting *Coopers & Lybrand*]–it is not satisfied by the possibility that the aggrieved party will have no occasion to appeal.") He concluded that the majority's "analysis effects a breathtaking expansion of appellate jurisdiction over interlocutory orders." Is Justice Scalia right to be concerned?

4. A particularly controversial application of the collateral order doctrine has been to appeals of denials of the qualified immunity defense in civil rights cases for damages, discussed in *Digital*. In 1982 the Supreme Court held that such a defense was available to public officials if their conduct did not violate "clearly established statutory or constitutional rights of which a reasonable person would have known." Harlow v. Fitzgerald, 457 U.S. 800, 102 S.Ct. 2727, 73 L.Ed.2d 396 (1982). Not long thereafter, the Court held in Mitchell v. Forsyth, 472 U.S. 511, 105 S.Ct. 2806, 86 L.Ed.2d 411 (1985) that a trial court's denial of a motion for summary judgment based on the qualified immunity defense was immediately appealable as a collateral order. The majority, over two dissents, held that the *Cohen* criteria were met since, among other things, the defense is a "purely legal and . . . conceptually distinct from the merits of the plaintiff's claim." Also, the unreviewability prong was met since qualified immunity is "an entitlement not to stand trial or face the other burdens of litigation." How convincing is the Court's application of the criteria, especially the assertion that the defense is distinct from an examination of the underlying merits of the case? For a careful, and critical, discussion of *Mitchell*, see 15A C. Wright, A. Miller & E. Cooper, Federal Practice and Procedure § 3914.10 (2d ed. 1992). Should your analysis be impacted by empirical evidence indicating that in approximately 70% of such cases the trial court decision is reversed? Solimine, Revitalizing Interlocutory Appeals in the Federal Courts, 58 Geo. Wash. L. Rev. 1165, 1189–90 (1990).

In any event, the Court placed limits on the scope of the *Mitchell* holding in Johnson v. Jones, 515 U.S. 304, 115 S.Ct. 2151, 132 L.Ed.2d 238 (1995). There, the Court held that appeals in qualified immunity cases were limited to those cases where the facts concerning that defense were undisputed, an assumption, the Court explained, that undergirded *Mitchell*. Not long after *Johnson*, however, the Court tacked in the other direction, holding in Behrens v. Pelletier, 516 U.S. 299, 116 S.Ct. 834, 133 L.Ed.2d 773 (1996) that there may be more than one such appeal in a single case. There, the defendant asserted the defense in a Rule 12(b)(6) motion, which motion was denied and affirmed upon appeal. The defendant renewed the defense in a summary judgment motion, which again was denied. The Court held that an immediate appeal of the latter motion was permissible. To what extent do the piecemeal appeals permitted by *Mitchell* and *Behrens* undermine the efficient litigation of cases at the trial level? Or vest too much power in defendants in these cases? Or lead to "what seems like an ever-increasing flow of interlocutory appeals" in civil rights cases involving qualified immunity? Finsel v. Cruppenink, 326 F.3d 903, 904 (7th Cir. 2003).

5. The *Digital* opinion makes much of the juridical source of the right involved in the order sought to be immediately appealed. Thus, the Court distinguishes rights originating in the Constitution or statutes from those based on contracts. How strong is that distinction? Does it provide a principled basis to measure the "importance" of an issue for *Cohen* pur-

poses? Note that, given the downplaying of the mere financial burden of proceeding with the case as a factor in *Coopers & Lybrand, Digital* and other cases, it seems doubtful that the result in *Cohen* itself would be the same: the harm visited on the plaintiff in that case by the requirement of posting a bond was arguably merely financial, not legal in any meaningful sense of the term. Martineau, Defining Finality and Appealability by Court Rule: Right Problem, Wrong Solution, 54 U. Pitt. L. Rev. 717, 743 (1993).

6.　As the *Cunningham* case illustrates, trial court rulings on discovery issues—commonplace in civil litigation—are rarely immediately appealable. Thornburg, Interlocutory Review of Discovery Orders: An Idea Whose Time Has Come, 44 Sw. L.J. 1045 (1990). A significant exception to that generalization, also addressed in *Cunningham*, are appeals from contempt orders. But that route is not without potential hardship, either, not the least of which is the possibility of suffering contempt sanctions, in addition of course to losing the underlying appeal. 15B C. Wright, A. Miller & E. Cooper, Federal Practice and Procedure § 3914.23 (2d ed. 1992). It has been suggested that appeals of discovery issues appropriately "go through the contempt process, which by raising the stakes helps the court winnow strong claims from delaying tactics that, like other interlocutory appeals, threaten to complicate and prolong litigation unduly." Burden–Meeks v. Welch, 319 F.3d 897, 900 (7th Cir. 2003) (Easterbrook, J.).

To what extent should it make a difference that the contempt sanction falls on a non-party from whom discovery is sought, as opposed to a party? As summarized by the court in *Burden-Meeks*, courts do recognize a distinction: "parties must wait until the end of the case or a finding of criminal contempt, while non-parties may appeal from a finding of civil contempt." Why is there such a distinction?

7.　As alluded to in *Digital*, lower courts continue to struggle with applying the collateral order criteria to a wide variety of issues, including (to name but a few) denials of motions raising personal jurisdiction, subject matter jurisdiction, statute of limitations, various types of immunities, to compel arbitration, and a host of other defenses. For discussions of the abundant cases, both in the Supreme Court and the lower courts, see 15A & 15B C. Wright, A. Miller & E. Cooper, Federal Practice and Procedure § 3911–3919 (2d ed. 1992); Anderson, The Collateral Order Doctrine: A New 'Serbonian Bog' and Four Proposals for Reform, 46 Drake L. Rev. 539 (1998); Pate, Interlocutory Appeals, 25 Litigation 42 (Winter 1999).

2.　MULTIPLE CLAIMS OR PARTIES

FEDERAL RULE OF CIVIL PROCEDURE 54

Judgments; Costs

* * *

(b) Judgment Upon Multiple Claims or Involving Multiple Parties. When more than one claim for relief is presented in an action, whether as a claim, counterclaim, cross-claim, or third-party claim, or when multiple parties are involved, the court may direct the entry of a final judgment as to one or more but fewer than all of the claims or parties only upon an express determination that there is no just reason for delay and upon an express direction for the entry of judgment. In the absence of such determination and direction, any order or other form of decision, however designated, which adjudicates fewer than all the claims or the rights and liabilities of fewer than all the parties shall not terminate the action as to any of the claims or parties, and the order or other form of decision is subject to revision at any time before the entry of judgment adjudicating all the claims and the rights and liabilities of all the parties.

SEARS, ROEBUCK & CO. v. MACKEY

Supreme Court of the United States, 1956.
351 U.S. 427, 76 S.Ct. 895, 100 L.Ed. 1297.

Mr. Justice Burton delivered the opinion of the Court.

This action, presenting multiple claims for relief, was brought by Mackey and another in the United States District Court for the Northern District of Illinois, Eastern Division, in 1953. The court expressly directed that judgment be entered for the defendant, Sears, Roebuck & Co., on two, but less than all, of the claims presented. It also expressly determined that there was no just reason for delay in making the entry. After Mackey's notice of appeal from that judgment to the Court of Appeals for the Seventh Circuit, Sears, Roebuck & Co. moved to dismiss the appeal for lack of appellate jurisdiction. The Court of Appeals upheld its jurisdiction and denied the motion, relying upon 28 U.S.C. § 1291, 28 U.S.C.A. § 1291 and Rule 54(b) of the Federal Rules of Civil Procedure, as amended in 1946, 28 U.S.C.A. 218 F.2d 295. Because of the importance of the issue in determining appellate jurisdiction and because of a conflict of judicial views on the subject, we granted certiorari. 348 U.S. 970, 75 S.Ct. 535, 99 L.Ed. 755. For the reasons hereafter stated, we sustain the Court of Appeals and its appellate jurisdiction.

Although we are here concerned with the present appealability of the judgment of the District Court and not with its merits, we must examine the claims stated in the complaint so as to consider adequately the issue of appealability.

The complaint contains six counts. We disregard the fifth because it has been abandoned and the sixth because it duplicates others. The claims stated in Counts I and II are material and have been dismissed without leave to amend. The claim contained in Count III and that in amended Count IV are at issue on the answers filed by Sears, Roebuck & Co. The appeal before us is from a judgment striking out Counts I and II without disturbing Counts III and IV, and the question presented is whether such a judgment is presently appealable when the District Court, pursuant to amended Rule 54(b), has made "an express determination that there is no just reason for delay" and has given "an express direction for the entry of judgment."

In Count I, Mackey, a citizen of Illinois, and Time Saver Tools, Inc., an Illinois corporation owned by Mackey, are the original plaintiffs and the respondents here. Sears, Roebuck & Co., a New York corporation doing business in Illinois, is the original defendant and the petitioner here. Mackey charges Sears with conduct violating the Sherman Antitrust Act in a manner prejudicial to three of Mackey's commercial ventures causing him $190,000 damages, for which he seeks $570,000 as treble damages. His first charge is unlawful destruction by Sears, since 1949, of the market for nursery lamps manufactured by General Metalcraft Company, a corporation wholly owned by Mackey. Mackey claims that this caused him a loss of $150,000. His second charge is unlawful interference by Sears, in 1952, with Mackey's contract to sell, on commission, certain tools and other products of the Vascoloy–Ramet Corporation, causing Mackey to lose $15,000. His third charge is unlawful destruction by Sears, in 1952, of the market for a new type of carbide-tipped lathe bit and for other articles manufactured by Time Saver Tools, Inc., resulting in a loss to Mackey of $25,000. Mackey combines such charges with allegations that Sears has used its great size to monopolize commerce and restrain competition in these fields. He asks for damages and equitable relief.

In Count II, Mackey claims federal jurisdiction by virtue of diversity of citizenship. He incorporates the allegations of Count I as to the Metalcraft transactions and asks for $250,000 damages for Sears' wilful destruction of the business of Metalcraft, plus $50,000 for Mackey's loss on obligations guaranteed by him.

In Count III, Mackey seeks $75,000 in a common-law proceeding against Sears for unlawfully inducing a breach of his Vascoloy commission contract.

In Count IV, Time Saver seeks $200,000 in a common-law proceeding against Sears for unlawfully destroying Time Saver's business by unfair competition and patent infringement.

The jurisdiction of the Court of Appeals to entertain Mackey's appeal from the District Court's judgment depends upon 28 U.S.C. § 1291, 28 U.S.C.A. § 1291, which provides that "The courts of appeals shall have jurisdiction of appeals from *all final decisions* of the district courts of the United States * * *." (Emphasis supplied.)

If Mackey's complaint had contained only Count I, there is no doubt that a judgment striking out that count and thus dismissing, in its entirety, the claim there stated would be both a final and an appealable decision within the meaning of § 1291. Similarly, if his complaint had contained Counts I, II, III and IV, there is no doubt that a judgment striking out all four would be a final and appealable decision within the meaning of § 1291. The controversy before us arises solely because, in this multiple claims action, the District Court has dismissed the claims stated in Counts I and II, but has left unadjudicated those stated in Counts III and IV.

With the Federal Rules of Civil Procedure, there came an increased opportunity for the liberal joinder of claims in multiple claims actions. This, in turn, demonstrated a need for relaxing the restrictions upon what should be treated as a judicial unit for purposes of appellate jurisdiction. Sound judicial administration did not require relaxation of the standard of finality in the disposition of the individual adjudicated claims for the purpose of their appealability. It did, however, demonstrate that, at least in multiple claims actions, some final decisions, on less than all of the claims, should be appealable without waiting for a final decision on *all* of the claims. Largely to meet this need, in 1939, Rule 54(b) was promulgated in its original form through joint action of Congress and this Court. It read as follows:

> "(b) Judgment at Various Stages. When more than one claim for relief is presented in an action, the court at any stage, upon a determination of the issues material to a particular claim and all counterclaims arising out of the transaction or occurrence which is the subject matter of the claim, may enter a judgment disposing of such claim. The judgment shall terminate the action with respect to the claim so disposed of and the action shall proceed as to the remaining claims. In case a separate judgment is so entered, the court by order may stay its enforcement until the entering of a subsequent judgment or judgments and may prescribe such conditions as are necessary to secure the benefit thereof to the party in whose favor the judgment is entered."

It gave limited relief. The courts interpreted it as not relaxing the requirement of a "final decision" on each individual claim as the basis for an appeal, but as authorizing a limited relaxation of the former general practice that, in multiple claims actions, *all* the claims had to be finally decided before an appeal could be entertained from a final decision upon any of them. Thus, original Rule 54(b) modified the single judicial unit theory but left unimpaired the statutory concept of finality prescribed by § 1291. However, it was soon found to be inherently difficult to determine by any automatic standard of unity which of several multiple claims were sufficiently separable from others to qualify for this relaxation of the unitary principle in favor of their appealability. The result was that the jurisdictional time for taking an appeal from a final decision on less than all of the claims in a multiple claims action in some instances expired earlier than was foreseen by the losing party. It thus became prudent to take immediate appeals in all cases of doubtful appealability and the volume of appellate proceedings was undesirably increased.

Largely to overcome this difficulty, Rule 54(b) was amended, in 1946, to take effect in 1948.[7] Since then it has read as follows:

7. " * * * situations arose where district courts made a piecemeal disposition of an action and entered what the parties thought amounted to a judgment, although a trial remained to be had on other claims similar or identical with those disposed of. In the interim the parties did not know their ultimate rights, and accordingly took

"(b) Judgment Upon Multiple Claims. *When more than one claim for relief is presented in an action,* whether as a claim, counterclaim, cross-claim, or third-party claim, *the court may direct the entry of a final judgment upon one or more but less than all of the claims only upon an express determination that there is no just reason for delay and upon an express direction for the entry of judgment.* In the absence of such determination and direction, any order or other form of decision, however designated, which adjudicates less than all the claims shall not terminate the action as to any of the claims, and the order or other form of decision is subject to revision at any time before the entry of judgment adjudicating all the claims." (Emphasis supplied.)

In this form, it does not relax the finality required of each decision, as an individual claim, to render it appealable, but it does provide a practical means of permitting an appeal to be taken from one or more final decisions on individual claims, in multiple claims actions, without waiting for final decisions to be rendered on *all* the claims in the case. The amended rule does not apply to a single claim action nor to a multiple claims action in which all of the claims have been finally decided. It is limited expressly to multiple claims actions in which "one or more but less than all" of the multiple claims have been finally decided and are found otherwise to be ready for appeal.

To meet the demonstrated need for flexibility, the District Court is used as a "dispatcher." It is permitted to determine, in the first instance, the appropriate *time when each "final decision"* upon "one or more but less than all" of the claims in a multiple claims action is ready for appeal. This arrangement already has lent welcome certainty to the appellate procedure. Its "negative effect" has met with uniform approval. The effect so referred to is the rule's specific requirement that for "one or more but less than all" multiple claims to become appealable, the District Court must make both "an express determination that there is no just reason for delay" and "an express direction for the entry of judgment." A party adversely affected by a final decision thus knows that his time for appeal will *not* run against him until this certification has been made.

In the instant case, the District Court made this certification, but Sears, Roebuck & Co. nevertheless moved to dismiss the appeal for lack of appellate jurisdiction under § 1291. The grounds for such a motion ordinarily might be (1) that the judgment of the District Court was not a decision upon a "claim for relief", (2) that the decision was not a "final decision" in the sense of an ultimate disposition of an individual claim entered in the course of a multiple claims action, or (3) that the District Court abused its discretion in certifying the order.

an appeal, thus putting the finality of the partial judgment in question." Report of Advisory Committee on Proposed Amendments to Rules of Civil Procedure 70–71 (June 1946).

In the case before us, there is no doubt that each of the claims dismissed is a "claim for relief" within the meaning of Rule 54(b), or that their dismissal constitutes a "final decision" on individual claims. Also, it cannot well be argued that the claims stated in Counts I and II are so inherently inseparable from, or closely related to, those stated in Counts III and IV that the District Court has abused its discretion in certifying that there exists no just reason for delay. They certainly *can* be decided independently of each other.

Petitioner contends that amended Rule 54(b) attempts to make an unauthorized extension of § 1291. We disagree. It could readily be argued here that the claims stated in Counts I and II are sufficiently independent of those stated in Counts III and IV to satisfy the requirements of Rule 54(b) even in its original form. If that were so, the decision dismissing them would also be appealable under the amended rule. It is nowhere contended today that a decision that would have been appealable under the original rule is not also appealable under the amended rule, provided the District Court makes the required certification.

While it thus might be possible to hold that in this case the Court of Appeals had jurisdiction under original Rule 54(b), there at least would be room for argument on the issue of whether the decided claims were separate and independent from those still pending in the District Court.[9] Thus the instant case affords an excellent illustration of the value of the amended rule which was designed to overcome that difficulty. Assuming that the requirements of the original rule are not met in this case, we nevertheless are enabled to recognize the present appellate jurisdiction of the Court of Appeals under the amended rule. The District Court *cannot,* in the exercise of its discretion, treat as "final" that which is not "final" within the meaning of § 1291. But the District Court *may,* by the exercise of its discretion in the interest of sound judicial administration, release for appeal final decisions upon one or more, but less than all, claims in multiple claims actions. The timing of such a release is, with good reason, vested by the rule primarily in the discretion of the District Court as the one most likely to be familiar with the case and with any justifiable reasons for delay. With equally good reason, any abuse of that discretion remains reviewable by the Court of Appeals.

Rule 54(b), in its original form, thus may be said to have modified the single judicial unit practice which had been developed by court decisions. The validity of that rule is no longer questioned. In fact, it was applied by this Court in Reeves v. Beardall, 316 U.S. 283, 62 S.Ct. 1085, 86 L.Ed. 1478, without its validity being questioned.

9. In the instant case, the claim dismissed by striking out Count I is based on the Sherman Act, 15 U.S.C.A. §§ 1–7, 15 note, while Counts III and IV do not rely on, or even refer to, that Act. They are largely predicated on common-law rights. The basis of liability in Count I is independent of that on which the claims in Counts III and IV depend. But the claim in Count I does rest in part on some of the facts that are involved in Counts III and IV. The claim stated in Count II is clearly independent of those in Counts III and IV.

Rule 54(b), in its amended form, is a comparable exercise of the rulemaking authority of this Court. It does not supersede any statute controlling appellate jurisdiction. It scrupulously recognizes the statutory requirement of a "final decision" under § 1291 as a basic requirement for an appeal to the Court of Appeals. It merely administers that requirement in a practical manner in multiple claims actions and does so by rule instead of by judicial decision. By its negative effect, it operates to restrict in a valid manner the number of appeals in multiple claims actions.

We reach a like conclusion as to the validity of the amended rule where the District Court acts affirmatively and thus assists in properly timing the release of final decisions in multiple claims actions. The amended rule adapts the single judicial unit theory so that it better meets the current needs of judicial administration. Just as Rule 54(b), in its original form, resulted in the release of some decisions on claims in multiple claims actions before they otherwise would have been released, so amended Rule 54(b) now makes possible the release of more of such decisions subject to judicial supervision. The amended rule preserves the historic federal policy against piecemeal appeals in many cases more effectively than did the original rule.

Accordingly, the appellate jurisdiction of the Court of Appeals is sustained, and its judgment denying the motion to dismiss the appeal for lack of appellate jurisdiction is affirmed.

Affirmed.

CURTISS-WRIGHT CORP. v. GENERAL ELECTRIC CO.

Supreme Court of the United States, 1980.
446 U.S. 1, 100 S.Ct. 1460, 64 L.Ed.2d 1.

MR. CHIEF JUSTICE BURGER delivered the opinion of the Court.

Federal Rule of Civil Procedure 54 (b) allows a district court dealing with multiple claims or multiple parties to direct the entry of final judgment as to fewer than all of the claims or parties; to do so, the court must make an express determination that there is no just reason for delay. We granted certiorari in order to examine the use of this procedural device. 444 U.S. 823 (1979).

From 1968 to 1972, respondent General Electric Co. entered into a series of 21 contracts with petitioner Curtiss–Wright Corp. for the manufacture of components designed for use in nuclear powered naval vessels. These contracts had a total value of $215 million.

In 1976, Curtiss–Wright brought a diversity action in the United States District Court for the District of New Jersey, seeking damages and reformation with regard to the 21 contracts. The complaint asserted claims based on alleged fraud, misrepresentation, and breach of contract by General Electric. It also sought $19 million from General Electric on the outstanding balance due on the contracts already performed.

General Electric counterclaimed for $1.9 million in costs allegedly incurred as the result of "extraordinary efforts" provided to Curtiss–Wright during performance of the contracts which enabled Curtiss–Wright to avoid a contract default. General Electric also sought, by way of counterclaim, to recover $52 million by which Curtiss–Wright was allegedly unjustly enriched as a result of these "extraordinary efforts."

The facts underlying most of these claims and counterclaims are in dispute. As to Curtiss–Wright's claims for the $19 million balance due, however, the sole dispute concerns the application of a release clause contained in each of the 21 agreements, which states that "Seller ... [agrees] as a condition precedent to final payment, that the Buyer and the Government ... are released from all liabilities, obligations and claims arising under or by virtue of this order." App. 103a. When Curtiss–Wright moved for summary judgment on the balance due, General Electric contended that so long as Curtiss–Wright's other claims remained pending, this provision constituted a bar to recovery of the undisputed balance.

The District Court rejected this contention and granted summary judgment for Curtiss–Wright on this otherwise undisputed claim. Applying New York law by which the parties had agreed to be bound, the District Court held that Curtiss–Wright was entitled to payment of the balance due notwithstanding the release clause. The court also ruled that Curtiss–Wright was entitled to prejudgment interest at the New York statutory rate of 6% per annum.

Curtiss–Wright then moved for a certification of the District Court's orders as final judgments under Federal Rule of Civil Procedure 54 (b).... The court expressly directed entry of final judgment for Curtiss–Wright and made the determination that there was "no just reason for delay" pursuant to Rule 54 (b).

The District Court also provided a written statement of reasons supporting its decision to certify the judgment as final. It acknowledged that Rule 54 (b) certification was not to be granted as a matter of course, and that this remedy should be reserved for the infrequent harsh case because of the overload in appellate courts which would otherwise result from appeals of an interlocutory nature. The essential inquiry was stated to be "whether, after balancing the competing factors, finality of judgment should be ordered to advance the interests of sound judicial administration and justice to the litigants."

The District Court then went on to identify the relevant factors in the case before it. It found that certification would not result in unnecessary appellate review; that the claims finally adjudicated were separate, distinct, and independent of any of the other claims or counterclaims involved; that review of these adjudicated claims would not be mooted by any future developments in the case; and that the nature of the claims was such that no appellate court would have to decide the same issues more than once even if there were subsequent appeals.

Turning to considerations of justice to the litigants, the District Court found that Curtiss–Wright would suffer severe daily financial loss from nonpayment of the $19 million judgment because current interest rates were higher than the statutory prejudgment rate, a situation compounded by the large amount of money involved. The court observed that the complex nature of the remaining claims could, without certification, mean a delay that "would span many months, if not years."

The court found that solvency of the parties was not a significant factor, since each appeared to be financially sound. Although the presence of General Electric's counterclaims and the consequent possibility of a setoff recovery were factors which weighed against certification, the court, in balancing these factors, determined that they were outweighed by the other factors in the case. Accordingly, it granted Rule 54 (b) certification. It also granted General Electric's motion for a stay without bond pending appeal.

A divided panel of the United States Court of Appeals for the Third Circuit held that the case was controlled by its decision in Allis–Chalmers Corp. v. Philadelphia Electric Co., 521 F.2d 360 (1975), where the court had stated:

> "In the absence of unusual or harsh circumstances, we believe that the presence of a counterclaim, which could result in a set-off against any amounts due and owing to the plaintiff, weighs heavily against the grant of 54 (b) certification." Id., at 366 (footnote omitted).

In *Allis-Chalmers*, the Court defined unusual or harsh circumstances as those factors "involving considerations of solvency, economic duress, etc." Id., at 366, n. 14.

In the Third Circuit's view, the question was which of the parties should have the benefit of the amount of the balance due pending final resolution of the litigation. The court held that *Allis-Chalmers* dictated "that the matter remain in status quo when non-frivolous counterclaims are pending, and in the absence of unusual or harsh circumstances." 597 F.2d 35, 36 (1979) (per curiam). The Court of Appeals acknowledged that Curtiss–Wright's inability to have use of the money from the judgment might seem harsh, but noted that the same could be said for General Electric if it were forced to pay Curtiss–Wright now but later prevailed on its counterclaims. Ibid.

The Court of Appeals concluded that the District Court had abused its discretion by granting Rule 54 (b) certification in this situation and dismissed the case for want of an appealable order; it also directed the District Court to vacate its Rule 54 (b) determination of finality. Curtiss–Wright's petition for rehearing and suggestion for rehearing en banc were denied. 599 F.2d 1259 (1979). Four judges dissented from that denial, observing that the case was in conflict with United Bank of Pueblo v. Hartford Accident & Indemnity Co., 529 F.2d 490 (CA10 1976). We reverse.

II

Nearly a quarter of a century ago, in Sears, Roebuck & Co. v. Mackey, 351 U.S. 427 (1956), this Court outlined the steps to be followed in making determinations under Rule 54 (b). A district court must first determine that it is dealing with a "final judgment." It must be a "judgment" in the sense that it is a decision upon a cognizable claim for relief, and it must be "final" in the sense that it is "an ultimate disposition of an individual claim entered in the course of a multiple claims action." 351 U.S., at 436.

Once having found finality, the district court must go on to determine whether there is any just reason for delay. Not all final judgments on individual claims should be immediately appealable, even if they are in some sense separable from the remaining unresolved claims. The function of the district court under the Rule is to act as a "dispatcher." Id., at 435. It is left to the sound judicial discretion of the district court to determine the "appropriate time" when each final decision in a multiple claims action is ready for appeal. Ibid. This discretion is to be exercised "in the interest of sound judicial administration." Id., at 437.

Thus, in deciding whether there are no just reasons to delay the appeal of individual final judgments in a setting such as this, a district court must take into account judicial administrative interests as well as the equities involved. Consideration of the former is necessary to assure that application of the Rule effectively "preserves the historic federal policy against piecemeal appeals." Id., at 438. It was therefore proper for the District Judge here to consider such factors as whether the claims under review were separable from the others remaining to be adjudicated and whether the nature of the claims already determined was such that no appellate court would have to decide the same issues more than once even if there were subsequent appeals.[2]

Here the District Judge saw no sound reason to delay appellate resolution of the undisputed claims already adjudicated. The contrary conclusion of the Court of Appeals was strongly influenced by the existence of nonfrivolous counterclaims. The mere presence of such claims, however, does not render a Rule 54 (b) certification inappropriate. If it did, Rule 54 (b) would lose much of its utility. In Cold Metal Process Co. v. United Engineering & Foundry Co., 351 U.S. 445 (1956), this Court explained that counterclaims, whether compulsory or permissive, present no special problems for Rule 54 (b) determinations; counterclaims are not to be evaluated differently from other claims. 351 U.S., at 452. Like other claims, their significance for Rule 54 (b) purposes turns on their interrelationship with the claims on which certification is sought. Here, the District Judge determined that General Electric's counterclaims were severable from the claims which had been deter-

---

2. §§ 21, 22, 25 of the Act of September 24, 1789, 1 Stat. 73, 83–85. For a discussion of the historical background, English and American, of the finality concept, see Crick, The Final Judgment as a Basis for Appeal, 41 Yale L. J. 539.

mined in terms of both the factual and the legal issues involved. The Court of Appeals did not conclude otherwise.

What the Court of Appeals found objectionable about the District Judge's exercise of discretion was the assessment of the equities involved. The Court of Appeals concluded that the possibility of a setoff required that the status quo be maintained unless petitioner could show harsh or unusual circumstances; it held that such a showing had not been made in the District Court.

This holding reflects a misinterpretation of the standard of review for Rule 54 (b) certifications and a misperception of the appellate function in such cases. The Court of Appeals relied on a statement of the Advisory Committee on the Rules of Civil Procedure, and its error derives from reading a description in the commentary as a standard of construction. When Rule 54 (b) was amended in 1946, the Notes of the Advisory Committee which accompanied the suggested amendment indicated that the entire lawsuit was generally the appropriate unit for appellate review, "and that this rule needed only the exercise of a discretionary power to afford a remedy in the infrequent harsh case to provide a simple, definite, workable rule." 28 U. S. C. App., p. 484; 5 F.R.D. 433, 473 (1946). However accurate it may be as a description of cases qualifying for Rule 54 (b) treatment, the phrase "infrequent harsh case" in isolation is neither workable nor entirely reliable as a benchmark for appellate review. There is no indication it was ever intended by the drafters to function as such.

In *Sears*, the Court stated that the decision to certify was with good reason left to the sound judicial discretion of the district court. At the same time, the Court noted that "[with] equally good reason, any *abuse* of that discretion remains reviewable by the Court of Appeals." 351 U.S., at 437 (emphasis added). The Court indicated that the standard against which a district court's exercise of discretion is to be judged is the "interest of sound judicial administration." Ibid. Admittedly this presents issues not always easily resolved, but the proper role of the court of appeals is not to reweigh the equities or reassess the facts but to make sure that the conclusions derived from those weighings and assessments are juridically sound and supported by the record.

There are thus two aspects to the proper function of a reviewing court in Rule 54 (b) cases. The court of appeals must, of course, scrutinize the district court's evaluation of such factors as the interrelationship of the claims so as to prevent piecemeal appeals in cases which should be reviewed only as single units. But once such juridical concerns have been met, the discretionary judgment of the district court should be given substantial deference, for that court is "the one most likely to be familiar with the case and with any justifiable reasons for delay." *Sears*, supra, at 437. The reviewing court should disturb the trial court's assessment of the equities only if it can say that the judge's conclusion was clearly unreasonable.

Plainly, sound judicial administration does not require that Rule 54 (b) requests be granted routinely. That is implicit in commending them to the sound discretion of a district court. Because this discretion "is, with good reason, vested by the rule primarily" in the district courts, *Sears*, supra, at 437, and because the number of possible situations is large, we are reluctant either to fix or sanction narrow guidelines for the district courts to follow. We are satisfied, however, that on the record here the District Court's assessment of the equities was reasonable.

One of the equities which the District Judge considered was the difference between the statutory and market rates of interest. Respondent correctly points out that adjustment of the statutory prejudgment interest rate is a matter within the province of the legislature, but that fact does not make the existing differential irrelevant for Rule 54 (b) purposes. If the judgment is otherwise certifiable, the fact that a litigant who has successfully reduced his claim to judgment stands to lose money because of the difference in interest rates is surely not a "just reason for delay."

The difference between the prejudgment and market interest rates was not the only factor considered by the District Court. The court also noted that the debts in issue were liquidated and large, and that absent Rule 54 (b) certification they would not be paid for "many months, if not years" because the rest of the litigation could be expected to continue for that period of time. The District Judge had noted earlier in his opinion on the merits of the release clause issue that respondent General Electric contested neither the amount of the debt nor the fact that it must eventually be paid. App. 164a–172a. The only contest was over the effect of the release clause on the timing of the payment, an isolated and strictly legal issue on which summary judgment had been entered against respondent.

The question before the District Court thus came down to which of the parties should get the benefit of the difference between the prejudgment and market rates of interest on debts admittedly owing and adjudged to be due while unrelated claims were litigated. The central factor weighing in favor of General Electric was that its pending counterclaims created the possibility of a setoff against the amount it owed petitioner. This possibility was surely not an insignificant factor, especially since the counterclaims had survived a motion to dismiss for failure to state a claim. Id., at 173a–174a. But the District Court took this into account when it determined that both litigants appeared to be in financially sound condition, and that Curtiss–Wright would be able to satisfy a judgment on the counterclaims should any be entered.

The Court of Appeals concluded that this was not enough, and suggested that the presence of such factors as economic duress and insolvency would be necessary to qualify the judgment for Rule 54 (b) certification. 597 F.2d, at 36. But if Curtiss–Wright were under a threat of insolvency, that factor alone would weigh against qualifying; that very threat would cast doubt upon Curtiss–Wright's capacity to produce all or part of the $19 million should General Electric prevail on some of its counterclaims. Such a showing would thus in fact be self-defeating.

Nor is General Electric's solvency a dispositive factor; if its financial position were such that a delay in entry of judgment on Curtiss–Wright's claims would impair Curtiss–Wright's ability to collect on the judgment, that would weigh in favor of certification. But the fact that General Electric is capable of paying either now or later is not a "just reason for delay." At most, as the District Court found, the fact that neither party is or will become insolvent renders that factor neutral in a proper weighing of the equities involved.

The question in cases such as this is likely to be close, but the task of weighing and balancing the contending factors is peculiarly one for the trial judge, who can explore all the facets of a case. As we have noted, that assessment merits substantial deference on review. Here, the District Court's assessment of the equities between the parties was based on an intimate knowledge of the case and is a reasonable one. The District Court having found no other reason justifying delay, we conclude that it did not abuse its discretion in granting petitioner's motion for certification under Rule 54 (b).[3]

Accordingly, the judgment of the Court of Appeals is vacated, and the case is remanded for proceedings consistent with this opinion.

It is so ordered.

QUINN v. CITY OF BOSTON

United States Court of Appeals for the First Circuit, 2003.
325 F.3d 18.

SELYA, Circuit Judge.

For over a quarter of a century, the hiring of firefighters in the City of Boston (the City) has taken place in the albedo of a federal court consent decree designed to remedy the effects of past discrimination against African–Americans and Hispanics. On April 11, 2001, five candidates for employment (the Candidates) brought suit in the federal district court alleging that the City had discriminated against them on the basis of race when hiring new firefighters in the fall of 2000. The City defended its hiring practices as compliant with, and compelled by,

---

3. We note that the Federal Rule of Civil Procedure 62 (h) allows a court certifying a judgment under Rule 54 (b) to stay its enforcement until the entering of a subsequent judgment or judgments. Rule 62 (h) also states that the court "may prescribe such conditions as are necessary to secure the benefit thereof to the party in whose favor the judgment is entered." Under this Rule, we assume it would be within the power of the District Court to protect all parties by having the losing party deposit the amount of the judgment with the court, directing the Clerk to purchase high yield government obligations and to hold them pending the outcome of the case. In this way, valid considerations of economic duress and solvency, which do not affect the juridical considerations involved in a Rule 54 (b) determination, can be provided for without preventing Rule 54 (b) certification.

In the instant case, after certifying the judgment as final under Rule 54(b), the District Court granted respondent's motion for a stay of judgment without bond, but only pending resolution of the appeal.

the terms of the consent decree. The district court granted summary judgment in the defendants' favor. The Candidates appeal. * * *

The Candidates (other than Kendrick, who joined the litigation at a later date) then sued the City. They argued that the City impermissibly had used preferences based on race and ethnicity to rank minorities ahead of them on the eligibility list. In the Candidates' view, this constituted discrimination in violation of the Fourteenth Amendment to the United States Constitution and 42 U.S.C. § 1983 (count 1), Mass. Gen. Laws ch. 151B, § 4 (count 2), and 42 U.S.C. § 2000e et seq. (count 3). The Candidates also attacked another aspect of the hiring process; they argued that requiring them to submit to medical examinations without a conditional offer of employment violated both federal and state law (counts 4–6). The district court granted the motion of the Boston Chapter of the NAACP to intervene as a party defendant. See Fed. R. Civ. P. 24.

The Candidates moved for summary judgment on the first three counts of their complaint or, in the alternative, for a preliminary injunction forbidding the City from filling at least five firefighter positions pending a resolution of the action. They maintained, among other things, that the City should not have applied the Beecher decree to the November 2000 hiring cycle because, by that time, the City had achieved parity in the firefighter force (and, therefore, had met the benchmark for release from the strictures of the decree). The defendants did not controvert the material facts, but, rather, opposed this motion as a matter of law and cross-moved for summary judgment. The district court denied the Candidates' motion and granted summary judgment for the defendants on counts 1 through 3. This appeal followed. Counts 4 through 6 remain pending before the district court.

II. APPELLATE JURISDICTION

It is too familiar a proposition to require citation of authority that a federal court may not act beyond the scope of its jurisdiction. As a logical corollary, parties cannot confer subject matter jurisdiction on a federal court by waiver or consent. See Prou v. United States, 199 F.3d 37, 42 (1st Cir. 1999). Consequently, when a court senses a potential lack of subject matter jurisdiction, it ought to inquire further regardless of whether the parties have raised the issue. BIW Deceived v. Local S6, 132 F.3d 824, 828 (1st Cir. 1997). We must conduct such an inquiry here.

In the usual case, an appeal must await the entry of a final judgment, commonly regarded as a judgment that fully disposes of all claims asserted in the action. See Curtiss–Wright Corp. v. Gen. Elec. Co., 446 U.S. 1, 8, 64 L. Ed. 2d 1, 100 S. Ct. 1460 (1980); Spiegel v. Trustees of Tufts Coll., 843 F.2d 38, 42 (1st Cir. 1988); see also 28 U.S.C. § 1291. There are, however, exceptions to the classic final judgment rule. One such exception, embodied in Rule 54(b) of the Federal Rules of Civil Procedure, allows the immediate entry of a partial final judgment as to fewer than all the claims in a multi-claim action "upon an express determination that there is no just reason for delay." The district court made such a determination here and directed that a separate and final judgment enter as to counts 1 through 3.

Despite this explicit direction, a jurisdictional problem looms. The law is firmly established in this circuit that a rote recital of Rule 54(b)'s talismanic phrase is not enough, in and of itself, to trump the wonted application of the final judgment rule. See Spiegel, 843 F.2d at 42 (endorsing the "long-settled and prudential policy against the scatter-shot disposition of litigation"). To warrant recourse to the special procedure envisioned by Rule 54(b), the district court typically must make an individualized assessment of the desirability and effect of an immediate appeal. Id. at 42–43. Thus, if a district court wishes to enter a partial final judgment on the ground that there is no just reason for delay, it should not only make that explicit determination but should also make specific findings and set forth its reasoning. See id.

We have warned that the parties have an obligation to bring this requirement to the district court's attention. See id. at 44 n.5. In this instance, the parties did not fulfill this obligation, and the court neither made the requisite findings nor explicated the reasons underlying its Rule 54(b) certification.

Although this deviation from preferred practice is troubling, it is not necessarily fatal. We have noted that there are "infrequent instances" in which the record, on its face, makes it sufficiently apparent that the circumstances support an appeal from a partial judgment. Id. at 43 n.4. This is such a case.

Counts 1 through 3 of the complaint deal with the obligations and protections afforded by the Beecher decree. In contrast, counts 4 through 6 have very little to do with the decree (and nothing to do with race or ethnicity). Moreover, one of the principal parties—the NAACP—has no knowledge about (and, for aught that appears, no interest in) the claims still pending in the lower court. Given the discrete nature of the two sets of claims, the summary judgment decision appears to be "final in the sense that it is an ultimate disposition of . . . individual claims entered in the course of a multiple claims action." *Curtiss-Wright*, 446 U.S. at 7 (internal quotation marks omitted).

Equally as important, the proof needed to establish the allegations of counts 1 through 3 is materially different from the proof needed to establish the allegations of counts 4 through 6. By the same token, the legal issues are separate and distinct. Moreover, if the Candidates prevail on one or more of the first three counts and obtain satisfactory relief, counts 4 through 6 may well be rendered moot. This concatenation of circumstances means that, in all probability, there will be no significant duplication of effort in litigating one set of claims to a conclusion and then addressing the remaining set of claims. Such a lack of overlap strongly supports the finding of no just reason for delay (and, thus, the entry of a partial final judgment under Rule 54(b)). See, e.g., Maldonado-

Denis v. Castillo–Rodriguez, 23 F.3d 576, 580 (1st Cir. 1994); Feinstein v. Resolution Trust Corp., 942 F.2d 34, 40 (1st Cir. 1991).

The most important factor counseling in favor of allowing an immediate appeal in this case is the public interest. As a practical matter, a final resolution of the issues raised in counts 1 through 3 will have a broad impact on the future of all applicants for firefighter positions in the City of Boston. This is a vital concern, as hiring is ongoing. The district court recognized this consideration when it agreed to render an expedited decision on counts 1 through 3. See *Quinn*, 204 F. Supp. 2d at 157 n.3. In short, the nature of the issue calls out for immediate resolution: time is of the essence if for no other reason than that race-based hiring preferences inevitably shift some of the burden of remediation to innocent persons, Wygant v. Jackson Bd. of Educ., 476 U.S. 267, 280–81, 90 L. Ed. 2d 260, 106 S. Ct. 1842 (1986) (plurality op.), and thus should not remain in place for any longer than necessary to alleviate the effects of past discrimination. See Regents of the Univ. of Cal. v. Bakke, 438 U.S. 265, 308, 57 L. Ed. 2d 750, 98 S. Ct. 2733 (1978) (plurality op.) (cautioning that such "remedial action [must] . . . work the least harm possible").

To sum up, the "findings" requirement that we have superimposed on Rule 54(b) is important, but it is not to be applied woodenly. When the record and the interests of justice permit, we have on occasion relaxed the requirement. See, e.g., *Maldonado-Denis*, 23 F.3d at 580–81; *Feinstein*, 942 F.2d at 40. Given the factors enumerated above—especially the substantial public interest that attaches to an expeditious resolution of whether the Beecher decree should continue to constrain the BFD's hiring practices—we conclude that this is one of the rare cases in which, despite the absence of detailed district court findings, the conditions for the use of Rule 54(b) effectively have been met. Accordingly, we have jurisdiction over the Candidates' appeal.

Notes and Questions

1. As was recognized by the opinion in the *Mackey* case, the Supreme Court in exercising its rulemaking power cannot enlarge the jurisdiction of a federal court, a matter solely within the power of Congress. Is the opinion of Justice Burton persuasive that the jurisdiction of the courts of appeals was not enlarged by Rule 54(b)? If the court of appeals would not have had jurisdiction over the appeal but for Rule 54(b), is this not conclusive that it is Rule 54(b) that created the jurisdiction over the appeal?

2. How malleable are the criteria the trial court must apply under Rule 54(b)? As illustrated by *Curtiss-Wright*, why do appellate courts emphasize the discretion to be afforded trial judges in applying the criteria? Note that most exceptions to the final judgment rule do not require input from the trial court, much less give that input deference at the appellate level. Why is Rule 54(b) different in this regard? Note also that appellate courts are reluctant to give deference when the trial court has not explained its reasons for certifying an appeal. E.g., Ebrahimi v. City of Huntsville Bd. of Educ., 114 F.3d 162, 166 (11th Cir. 1997).

3. INJUNCTIONS

28 U.S.C.A. § 1292. Interlocutory decisions

(a) The courts of appeals shall have jurisdiction of appeals from:

(1) Interlocutory orders of the district courts of the United States, * * * or of the judges thereof, granting, continuing, modifying, refusing or dissolving injunctions, or refusing to dissolve or modify injunctions, except where a direct review may be had in the Supreme Court * * *.

CARSON v. AMERICAN BRANDS, INC.

Supreme Court of the United States, 1981.
450 U.S. 79, 101 S.Ct. 993, 67 L.Ed.2d 59.

JUSTICE BRENNAN delivered the opinion of the Court.

The question presented in this Title VII class action is whether an interlocutory order of the District Court denying a joint motion of the parties to enter a consent decree containing injunctive relief is an appealable order.

I

Petitioners, representing a class of present and former black seasonal employees and applicants for employment at the Richmond Leaf Department of the American Tobacco Co., brought this suit in the United States District Court for the Eastern District of Virginia under 42 U.S.C. § 1981 and Title VII of the Civil Rights Act of 1964, 42 U.S.C. § 2000e et seq. Alleging that respondents had discriminated against them in hiring, promotion, transfer, and training opportunities, petitioners sought a declaratory judgment, preliminary and permanent injunctive relief, and money damages.

After extensive discovery had been conducted and the plaintiff class had been certified, the parties negotiated a settlement and jointly moved the District Court to approve and enter their proposed consent decree. See Fed.Rule Civ.Proc. 23(e).[3] The decree would have required respondents to give hiring and seniority preferences to black employees and to fill one-third of all supervisory positions in the Richmond Leaf Department with qualified blacks. While agreeing to the terms of the decree, respondents "expressly den[ied] any violation of * * * any * * * equal employment law, regulation, or order." App. 25a.

The District Court denied the motion to enter the proposed decree. 446 F.Supp. 780 (1977). Concluding that preferential treatment on the basis of race violated Title VII and the Constitution absent a showing of past or present discrimination, and that the facts submitted in support of the decree demonstrated no "vestiges of racial discrimination," id., at

---

3. Rule 23(e) provides:

"A class action shall not be dismissed or compromised without the approval of the court, and notice of the proposed dismiss- al or compromise shall be given to all members of the class in such manner as the court directs."

790, the court held that the proposed decree illegally granted racial preferences to the petitioner class. It further declared that even if present or past discrimination had been shown, the decree would be illegal in that it would extend relief to *all* present and future black employees of the Richmond Leaf Department, not just to *actual* victims of the alleged discrimination. Id., at 789.

The United States Court of Appeals for the Fourth Circuit, sitting en banc, dismissed petitioners' appeal for want of jurisdiction. 606 F.2d 420 (1979). It held that the District Court's refusal to enter the consent decree was neither a "collateral order" under 28 U.S.C. § 1291, nor an interlocutory order "refusing" an "injunctio[n]" under 28 U.S.C. § 1292(a)(1). Three judges dissented, concluding that the order refusing to approve the consent decree was appealable under 28 U.S.C. § 1292(a)(1).

Noting a conflict in the Circuits, we granted certiorari. 447 U.S. 920, 100 S.Ct. 3009, 65 L.Ed.2d 1111 (1980). We hold that the order is appealable under 28 U.S.C. § 1292(a)(1), and accordingly reverse the Court of Appeals.[7]

II

The first Judiciary Act of 1789, 1 Stat. 73, established the general principle that only *final* decisions of the federal district courts would be reviewable on appeal. 28 U.S.C. § 1291. Because rigid application of this principle was found to create undue hardship in some cases, however, Congress created certain exceptions to it. See Baltimore Contractors, Inc. v. Bodinger, supra, 348 U.S., at 180–181, 75 S.Ct., at 252–253. One of these exceptions, 28 U.S.C. § 1292(a)(1), permits appeal as of right from "[i]nterlocutory orders of the district courts * * * granting, continuing, modifying, *refusing* or dissolving *injunctions* * * *." (Emphasis added.)[8]

Although the District Court's order declining to enter the proposed consent decree did not in terms "refus[e]" an "injunctio[n]," it nonetheless had the practical effect of doing so. [Citations omitted.] This is because the proposed decree would have permanently enjoined respondents from discriminating against black employees at the Richmond Leaf Department, and would have directed changes in seniority and benefit systems, established hiring goals for qualified blacks in certain supervisory positions, and granted job-bidding preferences for seasonal employ-

---

7. We therefore need not decide whether the order is also appealable under 28 U.S.C. § 1291.

8. This statutory exception was first established by the Evarts Act of 1891, § 7, 26 Stat. 828, which authorized interlocutory appeals "where * * * an injunction shall be granted or continued by interlocutory order or decree." In 1895, that Act was amended to extend the right of appeal to orders of

the district courts refusing requests for injunctions. 28 Stat. 666. Although the reference to orders refusing injunctions was dropped from the statute in 1900 for reasons not relevant here, 31 Stat. 660, the reference was reinstated in § 129 of the Judicial Code of 1911, 36 Stat. 1134, and has since remained part of the statute.

ees. Indeed, prospective relief was at the very core of the disapproved settlement.[9]

For an interlocutory order to be immediately appealable under § 1292(a)(1), however, a litigant must show more than that the order has the practical effect of refusing an injunction. Because § 1292(a)(1) was intended to carve out only a limited exception to the final-judgment rule, we have construed the statute narrowly to ensure that appeal as of right under § 1292(a)(1) will be available only in circumstances where an appeal will further the statutory purpose of "permit[ting] litigants to effectually challenge interlocutory orders of serious, perhaps irreparable, consequence." Baltimore Contractors, Inc. v. Bodinger, supra, at 181, 75 S.Ct., at 252. Unless a litigant can show that an interlocutory order of the district court might have a "serious, perhaps irreparable, consequence," and that the order can be "effectually challenged" only by immediate appeal, the general congressional policy against piecemeal review will preclude interlocutory appeal.

In Switzerland Cheese Assn., Inc. v. E. Horne's Market, Inc., 385 U.S. 23, 87 S.Ct. 193, 17 L.Ed.2d 23 (1966), for example, petitioners contended that the District Court's denial of their motion for summary judgment was appealable under § 1292(a)(1) simply because its practical effect was to deny them the permanent injunction sought in their summary-judgment motion. Although the District Court order seemed to fit within the statutory language of § 1292(a)(1), petitioners' contention was rejected because they did not show that the order might cause them irreparable consequences if not immediately reviewed. The motion for summary judgment sought permanent and not preliminary injunctive relief and petitioners did not argue that a denial of summary judgment would cause them irreparable harm *pendente lite*. Since permanent injunctive relief might have been obtained after trial,[10] the interlocutory order lacked the "serious, perhaps irreparable, consequence" that is a prerequisite to appealability under § 1292(a)(1).

Similarly, in Gardner v. Westinghouse Broadcasting Co., 437 U.S. 478, 98 S.Ct. 2451, 57 L.Ed.2d 364 (1978), petitioner in a Title VII sex discrimination suit sought a permanent injunction against her prospective employer on behalf of herself and her putative class. After the

---

9. Neither the parties nor the Court of Appeals dispute that the predominant effect of the proposed decree would have been injunctive. The parties entitled the major part of the decree. "Injunctive Relief for the Class," and expressly agreed that respondents would be "*permanently enjoined* from discriminating against black employees at the facilities of the Richmond Leaf Department." App. 26a, 27a (emphasis added). The Court of Appeals, in construing the effect of the District Court's action, similarly characterized the relief contained in the proposed decree as "injunctive." 606 F.2d, at 423.

10. The District Court denied petitioners' motion for summary judgment because it found disputed issues of material fact, not because it disagreed with petitioners' legal arguments. Thus, not only was the court free to grant the requested injunctive relief in full after conducting a trial on the merits, but it was also not precluded from granting a motion for preliminary injunction during the pendency of the litigation if petitioners were to allege that further delay would cause them irreparable harm.

District Court denied petitioner's motion for class certification, petitioner filed an appeal under § 1292(a)(1). She contended that since her complaint had requested injunctive relief, the court's order denying class certification had the effect of limiting the breadth of the available relief, and therefore of "refus[ing] a substantial portion of the injunctive relief requested in the complaint." 437 U.S., at 480, 98 S.Ct., at 2453.

As in *Switzerland Cheese,* petitioner in *Gardner* had not filed a motion for a preliminary injunction and had not alleged that a denial of her motion would cause irreparable harm. The District Court order thus had "no direct or irreparable impact on the merits of the controversy." 437 U.S., at 482, 98 S.Ct., at 2454. Because the denial of class certification was conditional, Fed.Rule Civ.Proc. 23(c)(1), and because it could be effectively reviewed on appeal from final judgment, petitioner could still obtain the full permanent injunctive relief she requested and a delayed review of the District Court order would therefore cause no serious or irreparable harm. As *Gardner* stated:

> "The order denying class certification in this case did not have any such 'irreparable' effect. It could be reviewed both prior to and after final judgment; it did not affect the merits of petitioner's own claim; and it did not pass on the legal sufficiency of any claims for injunctive relief." 437 U.S., at 480–481, 98 S.Ct., at 2453–2454 (footnotes omitted).[11]

III

In the instant case, unless the District Court order denying the motion to enter the consent decree is immediately appealable, petitioners will lose their opportunity to "effectually challenge" an interlocutory order that denies them injunctive relief and that plainly has a "serious, perhaps irreparable, consequence." First, petitioners might lose their opportunity to settle their case on the negotiated terms. As United States v. Armour & Co., 402 U.S. 673, 681, 91 S.Ct. 1752, 1757, 29 L.Ed.2d 256 (1971), stated:

> "Consent decrees are entered into by parties to a case after careful negotiation has produced agreement on their precise terms. The parties waive their right to litigate the issues involved in the case and thus save themselves the time, expense, and inevitable risk of litigation. Naturally, the agreement reached normally embodies a compromise; in exchange for the saving of cost and elimination of

11. By contrast, General Electric Co. v. Marvel Rare Metals Co., 287 U.S. 430, 53 S.Ct. 202, 77 L.Ed. 408 (1932), a case in which respondents sought to appeal the District Court's dismissal of their counterclaim for injunctive relief on jurisdictional grounds, concluded that the District Court's order *did* have a serious, perhaps irreparable, consequence and that it could not be effectually challenged unless an appeal were immediately taken. The Court noted that the District Court "necessarily decided that upon the facts alleged in the counterclaim defendants were not entitled to an injunction," id., at 433, 53 S.Ct., at 204, and that this decision resolved "the very question that, among others, would have been presented to the court upon formal application for an interlocutory injunction." Ibid.

risk, the parties each give up something they might have won had they proceeded with the litigation."

Settlement agreements may thus be predicated on an express or implied condition that the parties would, by their agreement, be able to avoid the costs and uncertainties of litigation. In this case, that condition of settlement has been radically affected by the District Court. By refusing to enter the proposed consent decree, the District Court effectively ordered the parties to proceed to trial and to have their respective rights and liabilities established within limits laid down by that court.[12] Because a party to a pending settlement might be legally justified in withdrawing its consent to the agreement once trial is held and final judgment entered,[13] the District Court's order might thus have the "serious, perhaps irreparable, consequence" of denying the parties their right to compromise their dispute on mutually agreeable terms.[14]

---

12. By refusing to enter the proposed consent decree, the District Court made clear that it would not enter any decree containing remedial relief provisions that did not rest solidly on evidence of discrimination and that were not expressly limited to actual victims of discrimination. 446 F.Supp., at 788–790. In ruling so broadly, the court did more than postpone consideration of the merits of petitioners' injunctive claim. It effectively foreclosed such consideration. Having stated that it could perceive no "vestiges of racial discrimination" on the facts presented, id., at 790, and that even if it could, no relief could be granted to future employees and others who were not "actual victims" of discrimination, id., at 789, the court made clear that nothing short of an admission of discrimination by respondents plus a complete restructuring of the class relief would induce it to approve remedial injunctive provisions.

13. Indeed, although there has yet been no trial, respondents are even now claiming a right to withdraw their consent to the settlement agreement. After the Court of Appeals dismissed petitioners' appeal and returned jurisdiction to the District Court, respondents filed a motion for a pretrial conference in which they stated: "In support of this motion the defendants assert that they do not now consent to the entry of the proposed Decree * * *." App. 67a. Neither the District Court nor the Court of Appeals has yet considered whether respondents' statement constitutes a formal motion to withdraw consent or whether such a withdrawal would be legally permissible at this point in the litigation, and we therefore do not decide those issues.

14. Furthermore, such an order would also undermine one of the policies underlying Title VII. In enacting Title VII, Con-

gress expressed a strong preference for encouraging voluntary settlement of employment discrimination claims. As explained in Alexander v. Gardner–Denver Co., 415 U.S. 36, 44, 94 S.Ct. 1011, 1017, 39 L.Ed.2d 147 (1974):

"Congress enacted Title VII * * * to assure equality of employment opportunities by eliminating those practices and devices that discriminate on the basis of race, color, religion, sex, or national origin. * * * Cooperation and voluntary compliance were selected as the preferred means for achieving this goal."

Moreover, postjudgment review of a district court's refusal to enter a proposed consent decree raises additional problems. Not only might review come after the prevailing party has sought to withdraw its consent to the agreement, but even if the parties continued to support their decree, the court of appeals might be placed in the difficult position of having to choose between ordering the agreed-upon relief or affirming the relief granted by the trial court even when such relief rested on different facts or different judgments with respect to the parties' ultimate liability.

In addition, delaying appellate review until after final judgment would adversely affect the court of appeals' ability fairly to evaluate the propriety of the district court's order. Courts judge the fairness of a proposed compromise by weighing the plaintiff's likelihood of success on the merits against the amount and form of the relief offered in the settlement. See Protective Comm. for Independent Stockholders v. Anderson, 390 U.S. 414, 424–425, 88 S.Ct. 1157, 1163–1164, 20 L.Ed.2d 1 (1968). They do not decide the

There is a second "serious, perhaps irreparable, consequence" of the District Court order that justifies our conclusion that the order is immediately appealable under § 1292(a)(1). In seeking entry of the proposed consent decree, petitioners sought an immediate restructuring of respondents' transfer and promotional policies. They asserted in their complaint that they would suffer irreparable injury unless they obtained that injunctive relief at the earliest opportunity.[15] Because petitioners cannot obtain that relief until the proposed consent decree is entered, any further delay in reviewing the propriety of the District Court's refusal to enter the decree might cause them serious or irreparable harm.[16]

In sum, in refusing to approve the parties' negotiated consent decree, the District Court denied petitioners the opportunity to compromise their claim and to obtain the injunctive benefits of the settlement agreement they negotiated. These constitute "serious, perhaps irreparable, consequences" that petitioners can "effectually challenge" only by an immediate appeal. It follows that the order is an order "refusing" an "injunctio[n]" and is therefore appealable under § 1292(a)(1).

Reversed.

Notes and Questions

1. What tests are established in the principal case for determining appealability under section 1292(a)(1)?

2. What was the irreparable harm found by the Court to the petitioners? Is this harm truly irreparable?

3. Could it be argued that the result in this case was determined more by the subject matter of the appeal rather than by the extent of the irreparable harm to the petitioners? The Second Circuit in New York v. Dairylea Cooperative, Inc., 698 F.2d 567 (2d Cir. 1983) refused to review the denial of a proposed settlement even though the settlement included an injunction. The court stated that allowing the appeal, if taken to the extreme, would permit the appeal of every disapproval of a proposed settlement. Can this case be reconciled with the principal case?

merits of the case or resolve unsettled legal questions. Since the likely outcome of a trial is best evaluated in light of the state of facts and perceptions that existed when the proposed consent decree was considered, appellate review would be more effective if held prior to the trial court's factfinding rather than after final judgment when the rights and liabilities of the parties have been established.

15. In the "Relief" section of their complaint, petitioners alleged:

"Plaintiffs and the class they represent have suffered and will continue to suffer irreparable injury by the policies, practices, customs and usages of the defendants complained of herein until the same are enjoined by this Court. Plaintiffs have no plain, adequate or complete remedy at law to redress the wrongs alleged herein and this suit for a preliminary and permanent injunction and declaratory judgment is their only means of securing adequate relief.

16. For example, petitioners might be denied specific job opportunities and the training and competitive advantages that would come with those opportunities.

ASSOCIATION OF COMMUNITY ORGANIZATIONS FOR REFORM NOW (ACORN) v. ILLINOIS STATE BOARD OF ELECTIONS

United States Court of Appeals, Seventh Circuit, 1996.
75 F.3d 304.

POSNER, CHIEF JUDGE.

The plaintiffs have moved to dismiss the defendants' appeal from an order of the district court on the ground that it is not an appealable order. The motion raises questions concerning federal appellate jurisdiction in the context of a major constitutional litigation. The plaintiffs had brought suit to enforce the federal "motor voter" law (National Voter Registration Act of 1993, 42 U.S.C. §§ 1973gg *et seq.*) against the governor and other officials of the State of Illinois, which had refused to comply with the law on the ground that it was unconstitutional. We upheld the constitutionality of the law and affirmed so much of the district court's injunction as commanded the defendants to obey it. *Association of Community Organizations for Reform v. Edgar,* 56 F.3d 791 (7th Cir. 1995). That was last June. The district judge then scheduled monthly status hearings to monitor the defendants' compliance with the injunction. The state board of elections submitted a plan of compliance to which the plaintiffs raised three objections at the August status hearing. The judge directed the parties to brief these objections and after they did so he issued a "memorandum opinion and order" on September 6 addressing the issues. The first two objections were to regulations that the board of elections had promulgated concerning verification of the addresses of new registrants and challenged-voter forms; the third was to the plans' failure to provide for oral assistance in Spanish to prospective registrants. The judge held the regulations "invalid" as inconsistent with the motor-voter law, and with regard to the issue of oral assistance he directed the defendants "to come prepared to [address the issue] at the next status hearing." He did not, however, issue any order that purported to enjoin the regulations.

The defendants argue that the order is a final decision and therefore appealable under 28 U.S.C. § 1291. One of the plaintiffs, the United States, agrees that the order is appealable but believes that it is appealable not as a final decision but as an order modifying an injunction. 28 U.S.C. § 1292(a)(1). The order in fact seems to fall between two stools. It is not final in any ordinary sense of the word, since compliance proceedings continue before the district court with regard to Spanish-language assistance and no doubt other issues as well. And it does not purport to modify the injunction. It interprets the injunction, but interpretations of injunctions as distinct from modifications of them are not appealable, provided they really are interpretive, and do not change the meaning of—that is, modify—the original injunction. Motorola, Inc. v. Computer Displays Int'l, Inc., 739 F.2d 1149, 1155 (7th Cir. 1984); In re Ingram Towing Co., 59 F.3d 513, 516 (5th Cir. 1995); Mikel v. Gourley, 951 F.2d 166, 168–69 (8th Cir. 1991). Yet there is a felt need, reflected in the submission by the United States, for prompt definitive resolution of legal disputes arising in what may be a protracted postjudgment proceeding to bring Illinois into compliance with the motor-voter law.

The position of the United States is untenable. To modify an injunction is to change it. The injunction has not been changed. It commanded Illinois to comply with the motor-voter law; it still commands that. An injunction that merely commands compliance with a statute (in order to attach the sanction of contempt to continued noncompliance) is as vague as the statute, and invites interpretation. Whether a requirement of verifying a new voter's address violates the statute and consequently the injunction as well is an archetypal issue of interpretation and the resolution of it clarifies, it does not modify, the injunction. Cf. Major v. Orthopedic Equipment Co., 561 F.2d 1112 (4th Cir. 1977). A misinterpretation would be a modification, because it would change the meaning of the original injunction. Wilder v. Bernstein, 49 F.3d 69, 72 (2d Cir. 1995). But in a case such as this, where the injunction is vague (though not so vague as to be unenforceable by contempt proceedings and thus a nullity), supplementary rulings particularizing its requirements are unlikely to be challengeable as misinterpretations.

Had the judge couched his rulings as supplementary injunctions, they would be appealable even if they did no more than make explicit what had been implicit in the original, vague injunction. Injunctions are appealable under section 1292(a)(1) whether they are primary or supplementary. Eli Lilly & Co. v. Medtronic, Inc., 915 F.2d 670, 673 (Fed.Cir. 1990). The statute makes no distinction.

The defendants' position on appealability, as opposed to that of the United States, depends on the uncertain meaning of "final decision" in postjudgment proceedings. The injunction that we modified and affirmed in our previous decision was a final judgment—so when are subsequent orders "final"? The simplest and most sensible approach, one that we have expressly endorsed, most recently in Resolution Trust Corp. v. Ruggiero, 994 F.2d 1221, 1224–25 (7th Cir. 1993), is to treat the postjudgment proceeding as a free-standing litigation, in effect treating the final judgment as the first rather than the last order in the case. Our decision last June kicked off a postjudgment proceeding that will end, unless the parties reach an agreement, with a judicial order setting forth the steps that Illinois must take to comply with the injunction that it obey the motor-voter law. That order will be appealable as a final decision under section 1291; interim orders will be appealable only if they meet the criteria for the appealability of interlocutory orders. The order issued by the district judge in September is clearly one of the interlocutory orders. It is not appealable, because it does not fit into the pigeonhole for orders modifying injunctions or into any of the other pigeonholes for interlocutory appeals. See *Major v. Orthopedic Equipment Co.,* supra, 561 F.2d at 1115.

We do not want to be besieged by successive appeals in injunctive proceedings. The position of the defendants, if accepted, would make virtually all postjudgment orders immediately appealable. If the board of elections wants to stick to its guns, it can refuse to submit a compliance plan that omits the regulations that the district judge believes invalid. Although an order to submit a plan of compliance, like a discovery order, is not an injunction, Mercer v. Magnant, 40 F.3d 893, 896 (7th Cir. 1994), the refusal to obey such an order might be punishable as a contempt, and if so the refuser could then obtain appellate review of the order by appealing from the judge's imposition of a sanction for contempt. Cobbledick v. United States, 309 U.S. 323, 328, 60 S.Ct. 540, 542–43, 84 L.Ed. 783 (1940); In re Establishment Inspection of Skil Corp., 846 F.2d 1127, 1129 (7th Cir. 1988). Were there any doubt about the mandatory character of the judge's order, he could embody it in a mandatory injunction, which would be appealable without the interim steps of defiance and sanction. Such severe measures are unlikely here despite the judge's evident exasperation with what he regards as the state's foot-dragging. Comity has its claims. Far more likely would it be for the judge to devise his own plan of compliance and order the state to put it into effect. At that point there would be a final decision from which the state would be entitled to appeal.

The United States points out, sensibly as it seems to us, that the dispute over appealability would have been avoided had the district judge, instead of issuing "orders" invalidating state regulations, simply directed the state to submit a compliance plan and then rejected it as noncomplying in various particulars. There would be no basis for arguing that the rejection was an appealable order. But this is, from a practical standpoint, what the judge did; and the fact that he used inapt words ought not convert an unappealable ruling into an appealable order.

The appeal is therefore

DISMISSED.

Notes and Questions

1. Given the plain language of section 1292(a)(1), why isn't the order under review in *ACORN* an appealable modification of an injunction?

2. How many times can a trial court decision on a request for an injunction, or modification of an existing injunction, be appealed?

3. Although an order denying a preliminary injunction is immediately appealable as an interlocutory decision under 28 U.S.C. § 1292(a)(1), an immediate appeal nonetheless *is not mandated* by the statute. A party may forgo an interlocutory appeal and present the issue for appeal after final judgment. Interlocutory orders therefore may be stored up and raised at the end of the case. Retired Chicago Police Association v. City of Chicago, 7 F.3d 584 (7th Cir. 1993). See also 15A C. Wright, A. Miller & E. Cooper, Federal Practice and Procedure § 3911 (2d ed. 1992) for more on storing up interlocutory issues for appeal after final judgment.

4. CONTROLLING QUESTION OF LAW

28 U.S.C.A. § 1292(b). When a district judge, in making a civil action an order not otherwise appealable under this section, shall be of the opinion that such order involves a controlling question of law as to which there is substantial ground for difference of opinion and that an immediate appeal from the order may materially advance the ultimate termination of the litigation, he shall so state in writing in such order. The Court of Appeals may thereupon, in its discretion, permit an appeal to be taken from such order, if application is made to it within ten days after the entry of the order: *Provided, however,* That application for an appeal hereunder shall not stay proceedings in the district court unless the district judge or the Court of Appeals or a judge thereof shall so order.

<h2 style="text-align:center">AHRENHOLZ v. BOARD OF TRUSTEES OF
THE UNIVERSITY OF ILLINOIS</h2>

United States Court of Appeals, Seventh Circuit, 2000.
219 F.3d 674.

POSNER, CHIEF JUDGE.

Since the beginning of 1999, this court has received 31 petitions for interlocutory appeal under 28 U.S.C. § 1292(b) and has granted only six of them. The majority have been denied or dismissed for jurisdictional reasons but seven have been denied even though the district judge had certified that the order sought to be appealed "involves a controlling question of law as to which there is substantial ground for difference of opinion and that an immediate appeal from the order may materially advance the ultimate termination of the litigation," which is the statutory standard. Although the standard is the same for the district court and for us, some disagreement in its application is to be expected. In several cases, however, including this one, we have been unsure whether the district court was using the correct standard. Because on the one hand merely the filing of a section 1292(b) petition tends to delay the litigation in the district court even though the filing does not cause the litigation to be stayed, and on the other hand the denial of the petition may cause the litigation to be unnecessarily protracted, we think it may be useful to remind the district judges of this circuit of the importance of the careful application of the statutory test.

There are four statutory criteria for the grant of a section 1292(b) petition to guide the district court: there must be a question of *law*, it must be *controlling*, it must be *contestable*, and its resolution must promise to *speed up* the litigation. There is also a nonstatutory requirement: the petition must be filed in the district court within a *reasonable time* after the order sought to be appealed. Richardson Electronics, Ltd. v. Panache Broadcasting of Pennsylvania, Inc., 202 F.3d 957, 958 (7th Cir.2000). (The statute requires the petition to be filed in *this* court within 10 days of the district court's 1292(b) order, but there is no statutory deadline for the filing of the petition in the district court.)

Unless *all* these criteria are satisfied, the district court may not and should not certify its order to us for an immediate appeal under section 1292(b). To do so in such circumstances is merely to waste our time and delay the litigation in the district court, since the proceeding in that court normally grinds to a halt as soon as the judge certifies an order in the case for an immediate appeal.

The criteria, unfortunately, are not as crystalline as they might be, as shown by this case, a suit against university officials by a former employee of a public university, contending that the defendants effected his termination in retaliation for his exercise of his First Amendment right of free speech. The district judge denied summary judgment on the ground that the plaintiff had established a prima facie case of retaliation. He then certified this denial for an immediate appeal under section 1292(b). He recited the statutory standard but did not explain how its criteria were satisfied, except the last—that if the defendants were entitled to summary judgment, granting summary judgment now would bring the suit to an immediate end. The criteria are conjunctive, not disjunctive. "The federal scheme does not provide for an immediate appeal solely on the ground that such an appeal may advance the proceedings in the district court." Harriscom Svenska AB v. Harris Corp., 947 F.2d 627, 631 (2d Cir. 1991). The defendants' petition to us for permission to take an immediate appeal does not deign to discuss the statutory criteria; it merely reargues the case for summary judgment.

Formally, an appeal from the grant or denial of summary judgment presents a question of law (namely whether the opponent of the motion has raised a genuine issue of material fact), which if dispositive is controlling; and often there is room for a difference of opinion. So it might seem that the statutory criteria for an immediate appeal would be satisfied in every case in which summary judgment was denied on a nonobvious ground. But that cannot be right. Section 1292(b) was not intended to make denials of summary judgment routinely appealable, see Williamson v. UNUM Life Ins. Co., 160 F.3d 1247, 1251 (9th Cir. 1998); *Harriscom Svenska AB v. Harris Corp.*, supra, 947 F.2d at 631; Chappell & Co. v. Frankel, 367 F.2d 197, 200 n. 4 (2d Cir. 1966), which is the implication of the district court's certification and of the defendants' petition in this court. A denial of summary judgment is a paradigmatic example of an interlocutory order that normally is not appealable.

We think "question of law" as used in section 1292(b) has reference to a question of the meaning of a statutory or constitutional provision, regulation, or common law doctrine rather than to whether the party opposing summary judgment had raised a genuine issue of material fact. See, besides the cases cited in the previous paragraph, In re Hamilton, 122 F.3d 13 (7th Cir. 1997); S.B.L. by T.B. v. Evans, 80 F.3d 307, 311 (8th Cir. 1996); Palandjian v. Pahlavi, 782 F.2d 313 (1st Cir. 1986) (per curiam). We also think, here recurring to our recent order denying permission to take a section 1292(b) appeal in Downey v. State Farm Fire & Casualty Co., No. 00–8009 (7th Cir. May 18, 2000), that the question of the meaning of a contract, though technically a question of law when there is no other evidence but the written contract itself, is not what the framers of section 1292(b) had in mind either. Cf. *Williamson v. UNUM Life Ins. Co.*, supra, 160 F.3d at 1251; *Harriscom Svenska AB v. Harris Corp., supra*, 947 F.2d at 631; United States Rubber Co. v. Wright, 359 F.2d 784 (9th Cir. 1966) (per curiam). We think they used "question of law" in much the same way a lay person might, as referring to a "pure" question of law rather than merely to an issue that might be free from a factual contest. The idea was that if a case turned on a pure question of law, something the court of appeals could decide quickly and cleanly without having to study the record, the court should be enabled to do so without having to wait till the end of the case. (Similar considerations have shaped the scope of interlocutory appeal from orders denying immunity defenses. See Johnson v. Jones, 515 U.S. 304, 317, 115 S.Ct. 2151, 132 L.Ed.2d 238 (1995).) But to decide whether summary judgment was properly granted requires hunting through the record compiled in the summary judgment proceeding to see whether there may be a genuine issue of material fact lurking there; and to decide a question of contract interpretation may require immersion in what may be a long, detailed, and obscure contract, as in *Downey*, which involved a contract of flood insurance.

It is equally important, however, to emphasize the duty of the district court and of our court as well to allow an immediate appeal to be taken when the statutory criteria are met, as in our recent case of United Airlines, Inc. v. Mesa Airlines, Inc., 219 F.3d 605 (7th Cir.2000), where we took a section 1292(b) appeal to decide whether federal law preempts state business-tort law in suits between air carriers over routes and rates of service. That was an abstract issue of law, timely sought to be appealed under section 1292(b), resolution of which could (because it was indeed a *controlling* issue) head off protracted, costly litigation. And because it was an abstract issue of law, it was suitable for determination by an appellate court without a trial record.

To summarize, district judges should use section 1292(b) when it should be used, avoid it when it should be avoided, and remember that "question of law" means an abstract legal issue rather than an issue of whether summary judgment should be granted. The present case, like *Downey*, is unsuitable for appeal under section 1292(b) because it does not present an abstract legal issue, and the petition for permission to take such an appeal is therefore

DENIED.

Notes and Questions

1. As suggested in the principal case, section 1292(b) appeals are used relatively infrequently. Data from all of the circuits indicates that only about one-third of such appeals certified by district courts are accepted by the courts of appeals. Solimine, Revitalizing Interlocutory Appeals in the Federal Courts, 58 Geo. Wash. L. Rev. 1165, 1176 (1990). And of course district courts do not always grant requests by litigants to certify section 1292(b) appeals in the first instance. Is the apparent grudging attitude toward the

use of section 1292(b) appeals justified by the language of the statute? By sound principles of appellate review? In this regard, consider the apparently laudatory references to section 1292(b) in *Coopers & Lybrand* and *Digital*. Does that suggest that the Supreme Court thinks that section 1292(b) appeals should be used more often as a useful safety valve to counter the burdens of strict adherence to the final judgment rule?

2. One of the reasons that section 1292(b) has not enjoyed wider use is that some courts insist that it should only be used for "big cases." These cases hold that section 1292(b) "was not intended for use in ordinary suits for personal injuries or wrongful death that can be tried and disposed of on their merits in a few days." Kraus v. Board of County Rd. Comm'rs, 364 F.2d 919, 922 (6th Cir. 1966). Is this a proper interpretation of the statute? Would the floodgates of appeals open if some version of the "big case" requirement were not followed? Compare Solimine, Revitalizing Interlocutory Appeals in the Federal Courts, 58 Geo. Wash. L. Rev. 1165, 1193–96 (1990) (arguing that "big case" requirement is not mandated by the statutory text or the legislative history). More recent cases are more skeptical of the requirement or simply don't mention it at all. E.g., In re Cement Antitrust Litig., 673 F.2d 1020, 1026 (9th Cir. 1982); 16 C. Wright, A. Miller & E. Cooper, Federal Practice and Procedure § 3929 (2d ed. 1996).

3. The principal case is a rare example of an appellate court explaining its disposition of a request to certify a section 1292(b) appeal. For another example, see McFarlin v. Conseco Services, LLC, 381 F.3d 1251 (11th Cir. 2004). Most times, appellate courts dispose of such requests in short unpublished orders by motion panels, or briefly note without elaboration that a section 1292(b) application was accepted, in a published opinion on the merits. Should longer explanations be the norm?

5. ATTORNEY FEES

The award of attorney fees and the relationship of the award to the final judgment rule is another area that has created confusion. In Liberty Mutual Ins. Co. v. Wetzel, 424 U.S. 737, 96 S.Ct. 1202, 47 L.Ed.2d 435 (1976) it was held that when attorneys fees are part of the original relief sought, the judgment is not final until the attorney fees are established. In Boeing Co. v. Van Gemert, 444 U.S. 472, 100 S.Ct. 745, 62 L.Ed.2d 676 (1980) the Court held that when the ultimate liability of the defendant has been included in a judgment and subsequently an allocation of attorney fees is made, the principal final judgment and the attorney fees award are appealable separately. In White v. New Hampshire Dept. of Employment Security, 455 U.S. 445, 102 S.Ct. 1162, 71 L.Ed.2d 325 (1982) the Supreme Court held that a post-judgment request for an award of attorney's fees under the Civil Rights Attorney's Fees Awards Act was not a "motion to alter or amend the judgment," subject to the 10–day timeliness standard of Rule 59(e) of the Federal Rules of Civil Procedure. Numerous issues were recognized in the case law. See Green, From Here to Attorney's Fees: Certainty, Efficiency, and Fairness in the Journey to the Appellate Courts, 69 Cornell L.Rev. 207 (1984).

BUDINICH v. BECTON DICKINSON & CO.

Supreme Court of the United States, 1988.
486 U.S. 196, 108 S.Ct. 1717, 100 L.Ed.2d 178.

JUSTICE SCALIA delivered the opinion of the Court.

Petitioner brought this action in Colorado state court to recover employment compensation allegedly due. Respondent removed the case to the United States District Court for the District of Colorado on the basis of diversity of citizenship. 28 U. S. C. §§ 1332, 1441. A jury awarded petitioner a verdict of $5,000 (considerably less than had been sought), and judgment was entered on March 26, 1984. Petitioner timely filed new-trial motions, challenging various rulings by the District Court, and a motion for attorney's fees. (Colorado law provides that in a suit to collect compensation due from employment "the judgment ... shall include a reasonable attorney fee in favor of the winning party, to be taxed as part of the costs of the action." Colo. Rev. Stat. 8–4–114 (1986).) On May 14, 1984, the District Court denied the new-trial motions, found that petitioner was entitled to attorney's fees, and requested further briefing and documentation before determining their amount. The District Court issued its final order concerning the attorney's fees on August 1, 1984. On August 29, petitioner filed notice of appeal to the Court of Appeals for the Tenth Circuit, covering all the District Court's post-trial orders.

Respondent filed a motion to dismiss the appeal, arguing that the judgment was final and immediately appealable when the order denying the new-trial motions was entered May 14, 1984, and that the notice of appeal was not filed within 30 days of that order as required by Federal Rules of Appellate Procedure 4(a)(1) and (4). The Court of Appeals granted the motion to dismiss as to all issues except the award of attorney's fees, which it affirmed. We granted certiorari, 484 U.S. 895 (1987), to resolve a conflict in the Courts of Appeals.

It is common ground in this case that if the District Court's decision on the merits was appealable before its determination of attorney's fees, then the merits appeal was untimely. See Fed. Rules App. Proc. 4(a)(1), (4), (6); Fed. Rules Civ. Proc. 54(a), 58. Petitioner contends that Colorado law governs this question and that "[u]nder Colorado law a claim is not final and appealable until attorneys fees are fully determined." Brief for Petitioner 13. We do not agree that Colorado law governs.

Although state law generally supplies the rules of decision in federal diversity cases, see 28 U. S. C. § 1652; Erie R. Co. v. Tompkins, 304 U.S. 64, 78 (1938), it does not control the resolution of issues governed by federal statute, see U.S. Const., Art. VI, cl. 2 (Supremacy Clause); 28 U. S. C. § 1652; Prima Paint Corp. v. Flood & Conklin Mfg. Co., 388 U.S. 395, 404–405 (1967). Under 28 U. S. C. § 1291, "all final decisions of the district courts" are appealable to the courts of appeals. In using the phrase "final decisions" Congress obviously did not mean to borrow or incorporate state law. "Final decisions" is not a term like "property," which naturally suggests a reference to state-law concepts, cf. Board of Regents v. Roth, 408 U.S. 564, 577 (1972); and the context of its use in § 1291 makes such a reference doubly implausible, since that provision applies to all federal litigation and not just diversity cases. Nor is it possible to accept petitioner's contention that § 1291 does not apply to diversity cases because that would violate the Tenth Amendment to the Constitution. We have held that enactments "rationally capable of classification" as procedural rules are necessary and proper for carrying into execution the power to establish federal courts vested in Congress by Article III, § 1. Hanna v. Plumer, 380 U.S. 460, 472 (1965); see also Burlington Northern R. Co. v. Woods, 480 U.S. 1, 5, and n. 3 (1987). A statute mandating when an appeal may be taken from one federal court to another certainly meets this test. Cf. Cohen v. Beneficial Industrial Loan Corp., 337 U.S. 541 (1949) (treating appealability as an issue of federal law in a case brought under diversity jurisdiction).

The question before us, therefore, is whether a decision on the merits is a "final decision" as a matter of federal law under § 1291 when the recoverability or amount of attorney's fees for the litigation remains to be determined. "A 'final decision' generally is one which ends the litigation on the merits and leaves nothing for the court to do but execute the judgment." Catlin v. United States, 324 U.S. 229, 233 (1945). A question remaining to be decided after an order ending litigation on the merits does not prevent finality if its resolution will not alter the order or moot or revise decisions embodied in the order. See, e. g., Brown Shoe Co. v. United States, 370 U.S. 294, 308–309 (1962); Dickinson v. Petroleum Conversion Corp., 338 U.S. 507, 513–516 (1950). We have all but held that an attorney's fees determination fits this description. In White v. New Hampshire Dept. of Employment Security, 455 U.S. 445 (1982), we held that a request for attorney's fees under 42 U. S. C. § 1988 is not a motion "to alter or amend the judgment" within the meaning of Federal Rule of Civil Procedure 59(e) because it does not seek "reconsideration of matters properly encompassed in a decision on the merits." 455 U.S., at 451. This holding was based on our conclusion that "a request for attorney's fees under § 1988 raises legal issues collateral to" and "separate from" the decision on the merits. Id., at 451–452. We went so far as to observe in dicta that "[t]he collateral character of the fee issue establishes that an outstanding fee question does not bar recognition of a merits judgment as 'final' and 'appealable.' " Id., at 452–453, n. 14. See also Sprague v. Ticonic National Bank, 307 U.S. 161, 170 (1939) (observing that a petition for attorney's fees in equity is "an independent proceeding supplemental to the original proceeding and not a request for a modification of the original decree").

The foregoing discussion is ultimately question-begging, however, since it assumes that the order to which the fee issue was collateral was an order ending litigation on the merits. If one were to regard the demand for attorney's fees as itself part of the merits, the analysis would not apply. The merits would then not have been concluded, and § 1291 finality would not exist. See Liberty Mutual Insurance Co. v. Wetzel, 424 U.S. 737, 740–742 (1976). As a general matter, at least, we think it indisputable that a claim for attorney's fees is not part of the merits of the action to which the fees pertain. Such an award does not remedy the injury giving rise to the action, and indeed is often available to the party defending against the action. At common law, attorney's fees were regarded as an element of "costs" awarded to the prevailing party, see 10 C. Wright, A. Miller, & M. Kane, Federal Practice and Procedure: Civil § 2665 (1983), which are not generally treated as part of the merits judgment, cf. Fed. Rule Civ. Proc. 58 ("Entry of the judgment shall not be delayed for the taxing of costs"). Many federal statutes providing for attorney's fees continue to specify that they are to be taxed and collected as "costs," see Marek v. Chesny, 473 U.S. 1, 43–48 (1985) (BRENNAN, J., dissenting) (citing 63 such statutes)—as does, in fact, the Colorado statute at issue here.

Petitioner contends, however, that the general status of attorney's fees for § 1291 purposes must be altered when the statutory or decisional law authorizing them makes plain (as he asserts Colorado law does) that they are to be part of the merits judgment. This proposition is not without some support. Some Courts of Appeals have held that the statutes creating liability for attorney's fees can cause them to be part of the merits relief for purposes of § 1291. See, e. g., Holmes v. J. Ray McDermott & Co., 682 F. 2d, at 1146; McQurter v. Atlanta, 724 F. 2d 881, 882 (CA11 1984) (per curiam). This Court itself implicitly acknowledged the possibility of such an approach in Boeing Co. v. Van Gemert, 444 U.S. 472 (1980), where, in holding that a judgment on the merits was final and immediately appealable apart from the question of attorney's fees, we expressly distinguished cases in which the plaintiff had specifically requested attorney's fees as part of the prayer in his complaint. Id., at 479–480, n. 5. Now that we are squarely confronted with the question, however, we conclude that the § 1291 effect of an unresolved issue of attorney's fees for the litigation at hand should not turn upon the characterization of those fees by the statute or decisional law that authorizes them.

We have said elsewhere that "[t]he considerations that determine finality are not abstractions but have reference to very real interests— not merely those of the immediate parties, but, more particularly, those that pertain to the smooth functioning of our judicial system." Republic Natural Gas Co. v. Oklahoma, 334 U.S. 62, 69 (1948). Indeed, in the context of the finality provision governing appealability of matters from state courts to this Court, 28 U. S. C. § 1257, we have been willing in effect to split the "merits," regarding a claim for an accounting to be sufficiently "dissociated" from a related claim for delivery of physical property that "[i]n effect, such a controversy is a multiple litigation allowing review of the adjudication which is concluded because it is independent of, and unaffected by, another litigation with which it happens to be entangled." Radio Station WOW, Inc. v. Johnson, 326 U.S. 120, 126 (1945). This practical approach to the matter suggests that what is of importance here is not preservation of conceptual consistency in the status of a particular fee authorization as "merits" or "nonmerits," but rather preservation of operational consistency and predictability in the overall application of § 1291. This requires, we think, a uniform rule that an unresolved issue of attorney's fees for the litigation in question does not prevent judgment on the merits from being final.

For all practical purposes an appeal of merits-without-attorney's-fees when there is a statute deeming the attorney's fees to be part of the merits is no more harmful to the trial process than an appeal of merits-without-attorney's-fees when there is no such statute. That "deeming" does not render the appeal more disruptive of ongoing proceedings, more likely to eliminate a trial judge's opportunity for reconsideration, more susceptible to being mooted by settlement, or in any way (except nominally) a more piecemeal enterprise. In short, no interest pertinent to § 1291 is served by according different treatment to attorney's fees deemed part of the merits recovery; and a significant interest is disserved. The time of appealability, having jurisdictional consequences, should above all be clear. We are not inclined to adopt a disposition that requires the merits or nonmerits status of each attorney's fee provision to be clearly established before the time to appeal can be clearly known. Courts and litigants are best served by the bright-line rule, which accords with traditional understanding, that a decision on the merits is a "final decision" for purposes of § 1291 whether or not there remains for adjudication a request for attorney's fees attributable to the case.

Finally, petitioner argues that even if the Court of Appeals properly decided the question of appealability, the decision constitutes a significant change in the law and therefore should only be applied prospectively. Regardless of whether today's decision works a change, our cases hold that "[a] court lacks discretion to consider the merits of a case over which it is without jurisdiction, and thus, by definition, a jurisdictional ruling may never be made prospective only." Firestone Tire & Rubber Co. v. Risjord, 449 U.S. 368, 379–380 (1981). Since the Court of Appeals properly held petitioner's notice of appeal from the decision on the merits to be untimely, and since the taking of an appeal within the prescribed time is mandatory and jurisdictional, see Fed. Rules App. Proc. 2, 3(a), 4(a)(1), 26(b); United States v. Robinson, 361 U.S. 220, 229 (1960); Farley Transportation Co. v. Santa Fe Trail Transportation Co., 778 F. 2d 1365, 1368–1370 (CA9 1985), the Court of Appeals was without jurisdiction to review the decision on the merits.

* * *

The Tenth Circuit correctly concluded that federal law governed the question of appealability and that petitioner's judgment on the merits was final and appealable when entered. Accordingly, its judgment is

Affirmed.

Rule 54, which deals with judgments, has been significantly amended since *Budinich*. It now provides in subsection (d):

(d) Costs; Attorneys' Fees.

(1) *Costs Other than Attorneys' Fees.* Except when express provision therefor is made either in a statute of the United States or in these rules, costs other than attorneys' fees shall be allowed as of course to the prevailing party unless the court otherwise directs; but costs against the United States, its officers, and agencies shall be imposed only to the extent permitted by law. Such costs may be taxed by the clerk on one day's notice. On motion served within 5 days thereafter, the action of the clerk may be reviewed by the court.

(2) *Attorneys' Fees.*

(A) Claims for attorneys' fees and related nontaxable expenses shall be made by motion unless the substantive law governing the action provides for the recovery of such fees as an element of damages to be proved at trial.

(B) Unless otherwise provided by statute or order of the court, the motion must be filed no later than 14 days after entry of judgment; must specify the judgment and the statute, rule, or other grounds entitling the moving party to the award; and must state the amount or provide a fair estimate of the amount sought. If directed by the court, the motion shall also disclose the terms of any agreement with respect to fees to be paid for the services for which claim is made.

(C) On request of a party or class member, the court shall afford an opportunity for adversary submissions with respect to the motion in accordance with Rule 43(e) or Rule 78. The court may determine issues of liability for fees before receiving submissions bearing on issues of evaluation of services for which liability is imposed by the court. The court shall find the facts and state its conclusions of law as provided in Rule 52(a).

(D) By local rule the court may establish special procedures by which issues relating to such fees may be resolved without extensive evidentiary hearings. In addition, the court may refer issues relating to the value of services to a special master under Rule 53 without regard to the provisions of Rule 53(a)(1) and may refer a motion for attorneys' fees to a magistrate judge under Rule 72(b) as if it were a dispositive pretrial matter.

(E) The provisions of subparagraphs (A) through (D) do not apply to claims for fees and expenses as sanctions for violations of these rules or under 28 U.S.C. § 1927.

The 1993 Advisory Committee notes to this section state in part:

Subparagraph (B) provides a deadline for motions for attorneys' fees—14 days after final judgment unless the court or a statute specifies some other time. One purpose of this provision is to assure that the opposing party is informed of the claim before the time for appeal has elapsed. Prior law did not prescribe any specific time limit on claims for attorneys' fees. White v. New Hampshire Dep't of Employment Sec., 455 U.S. 445 (1982). In many nonjury cases the court will want to consider attorneys' fee issues immediately after rendering its judgment on the merits of the case. Note that the time for making claims is specifically stated in some legislation, such as the Equal Access to Justice Act, 28 U.S.C. § 2412 (d)(1)(B) (30–day filing period). Prompt filing affords an opportunity for the court to resolve fee disputes shortly after trial, while the services performed are freshly in mind. It also enables the court in appropriate circumstances to make its ruling on a fee request in time for any appellate review of a dispute over fees to proceed at the same time as review on the merits of the case.

Filing a motion for fees under this subdivision does not affect the finality or the appealability of a judgment, though revised Rule 58 provides a mechanism by which prior to appeal the court can suspend the finality to resolve a motion for fees. If an appeal on the merits of the case is taken, the court may rule on the claim for fees, may defer its ruling on the motion, or may deny the motion without prejudice, directing under subdivision (d)(2)(B) a new period for filing after the appeal has been resolved. A notice of appeal does not extend the time for filing a fee claim based on the initial judgment, but the court under subdivision (d)(2)(B) may effectively extend the period by permitting claims to be filed after resolution of the appeal. A new period for filing will automatically begin if a new judgment is entered following a reversal or remand by the appellate court or the granting of a motion under Rule 59.

The rule does not require that the motion be supported at the time of filing with the evidentiary material bearing on the fees. This material must of course be submitted in due course, according to such schedule as the court may direct in light of the circumstances of the case. What is required is the filing of a motion sufficient to alert the adversary and the court that there is a claim for fees and the amount of such fees (or a fair estimate).

* * *

Notes of Advisory Committee on 2002 amendments. Subdivision (d)(2)(C) is amended to delete the requirement that judgment on a motion for attorney fees be set forth in a separate document. This change complements the amendment of Rule 58(a)(1), which deletes the separate document requirement for an order disposing of a motion for attorney fees under Rule 54. These changes are made to support amendment of Rule 4 of the Federal Rules of Appellate Procedure. It continues to be important that a district court make clear its meaning when it intends an order to be the final disposition of a motion for attorney fees.

The requirement in subdivision (d)(2)(B) that a motion for attorney fees be not only filed but also served no later than 14 days after entry of judgment is changed to require filing only, to establish a parallel with Rules 50, 52, and 59. Service continues to be required under Rule 5(a).

Rule 58 has also been amended several times in recent years. As pertinent to fee applications, it now provides:

Rule 58. Entry of Judgment

(a) Separate Document.

(1) Every judgment and amended judgment must be set forth on a separate document, but a separate document is not required for an order disposing of a motion:

> (A) for judgment under Rule 50(b);
>
> (B) to amend or make additional findings of fact under Rule 52(b);
>
> (C) for attorney fees under Rule 54;
>
> (D) for a new trial, or to alter or amend the judgment, under Rule 59; or
>
> (E) for relief under Rule 60.

* * *

(c) Cost or Fee Awards.

(1) Entry of judgment may not be delayed, nor the time for appeal extended, in order to tax costs or award fees, except as provided in Rule 58(c)(2).

(2) When a timely motion for attorney fees is made under Rule 54(d)(2), the court may act before a notice of appeal has been filed and has become effective to order that the motion have the same effect under Federal Rule of Appellate Procedure 4(a)(4) as a timely motion under Rule 59.

The Advisory Committee Notes to this rule contain the following observations:

> Ordinarily the pendency or post-judgment filing of a claim for attorney's fees will not affect the time for appeal from the underlying judgment. See Budinich v. Becton Dickinson & Co., 486 U.S. 196 (1988). Particularly if the claim for fees involves substantial issues or is likely to be affected by the appellate decision, the district court may prefer to defer consideration of the claim for fees until after the appeal is resolved. However, in many cases it may be more efficient to decide fee questions before an appeal is taken so that appeals relating to the fee award can be heard at the same time as appeals relating to the merits of the case. This revision permits, but does not require, the court to delay the finality of the judgment for appellate purposes under revised Fed. R. App. P. 4(a) until the fee dispute is decided. To accomplish this result requires entry of an order by the district court before the time a notice of appeal becomes effective for appellate purposes. If the order is entered, the motion for attorney's

fees is treated in the same manner as a timely motion under Rule 59.

Notes of Advisory Committee on 2002 amendments. * * * The new all-purpose definition of the entry of judgment must be applied with common sense to other questions that may turn on the time when judgment is entered. If the 150–day provision in Rule 58(b)(2)(B)—designed to integrate the time for post-judgment motions with appeal time—serves no purpose, or would defeat the purpose of another rule, it should be disregarded. In theory, for example, the separate document requirement continues to apply to an interlocutory order that is appealable as a final decision under collateral-order doctrine. Appealability under collateral-order doctrine should not be complicated by failure to enter the order as a judgment on a separate document–there is little reason to force trial judges to speculate about the potential appealability of every order, and there is no means to ensure that the trial judge will always reach the same conclusion as the court of appeals.

Recall that Rule 4(a)(4) of the appellate rules provides:

(4) *Effect of a Motion on a Notice of Appeal.*

(A) If a party timely files in the district court any of the following motions under the Federal Rules of Civil Procedure, the time to file an appeal runs for all parties from the entry of the order disposing of the last such remaining motion:

(i) for judgment under Rule 50(b);

(ii) to amend or make additional factual findings under Rule 52(b), whether or not granting the motion would alter the judgment;

(iii) for attorney's fees under Rule 54 if the district court extends the time to appeal under Rule 58;

(iv) to alter or amend the judgment under Rule 59;

(v) for a new trial under Rule 59; or

(vi) for relief under Rule 60 if the motion is filed no later than 10 days after the judgment is entered.

(B)

(i) If a party files a notice of appeal after the court announces or enters a judgment—but before it disposes of any motion listed in Rule 4(a)(4)(A)—the notice becomes effective to appeal a judgment or order, in whole or in part, when the order disposing of the last such remaining motion is entered.

(ii) A party intending to challenge an order disposing of any motion listed in Rule 4(a)(4)(A), or a judgment altered or amended upon such a motion, must file a notice of appeal, or an amended notice of appeal—in compliance with Rule

3(c)—within the time prescribed by this Rule measured from the entry of the order disposing of the last such remaining motion.

(iii) No additional fee is required to file an amended notice.

* * *

(7) *Entry Defined.*

(A) A judgment or order is entered for purposes of this Rule 4(a):

(i) if Federal Rule of Civil Procedure 58(a)(1) does not require a separate document, when the judgment or order is entered in the civil docket under Federal Rule of Civil Procedure 79(a); * * *

In part, the Advisory Committee Note on appellate Rule 4 reads:

To conform to a recent Supreme Court decision, however—Budinich v. Becton Dickinson and Co., 486 U.S. 196 (1988)—the amendment excludes motions for attorney's fees from the class of motions that extend the filing time unless a district court, acting under Rule 58, enters an order extending the time for appeal. This amendment is to be read in conjunction with the amendment of Fed. R. Civ. P. 58.

6. INTERLOCUTORY APPEAL AND RULEMAKING: THE EXAMPLE OF RULE 23(f)

28 U.S.C. § 2072. Rules of procedure and evidence; power to prescribe

(a) The Supreme Court shall have the power to prescribe general rules of practice and procedure and rules of evidence for cases in the United States district courts (including proceedings before magistrate judges thereof) and courts of appeals

* * *

(c) Such rules may define when a ruling of a district court is final for the purposes of appeal under section 1291 of this title.

28 U.S.C. § 1292

(e) The Supreme Court may prescribe rules, in accordance with section 2072 of this title, to provide for an appeal of an interlocutory decision to the courts of appeals that is not otherwise provided for under subsection (a), (b), (c), or (d).

Rule 23

(f) Appeals. A court of appeals may in its discretion permit an appeal from an order of a district court granting or denying class action certification under this rule if application is made to it within ten days after entry of the order. An appeal does not stay proceedings in the district court unless the district judge or the court of appeals so orders.

BLAIR v. EQUIFAX CHECK SERVICES, INC.

United States Court of Appeals for the Seventh Circuit, 1999.
181 F.3d 832.

EASTERBROOK, CIRCUIT JUDGE.

In 1992, at the suggestion of the Federal Courts Study Committee, Congress authorized the Supreme Court to issue rules that expand the set of allowable interlocutory appeals. 28 U.S.C. § 1292(e). An earlier grant of jurisdictional rulemaking power–28 U.S.C. § 2072(c), which permits the Court to "define when a ruling of a district court is final for the purposes of appeal under section 1291"—had gone unused, in part because it invites the question whether a particular rule truly "defines" or instead expands appellate jurisdiction. Section 1292(e) expressly authorizes expansions. So far, it has been employed once. Last year the Supreme Court promulgated Fed.R.Civ.P. 23(f), which reads:

> A court of appeals may in its discretion permit an appeal from an order of a district court granting or denying class action certification under this rule if application is made to it within ten days after entry of the order. An appeal does not stay proceedings in the district court unless the district judge or the court of appeals so orders.

This rule became effective on December 1, 1998, and we have for consideration the first application filed in this circuit (and, so far as we can tell, the nation) under the new rule. A motions panel directed the parties to file briefs discussing the standard the court should employ to decide whether to accept appeals under this rule.

The Committee Note accompanying Rule 23(f) remarks: "The court of appeals is given unfettered discretion whether to permit the appeal, akin to the discretion exercised by the Supreme Court in acting on a petition for certiorari. . . . Permission to appeal may be granted or denied on the basis of any consideration that the court of appeals finds persuasive." (The parties call this an "Advisory Committee Note," following old usage, but its title was changed more than a decade ago to "Committee Note." It speaks not only for the responsible advisory committee but also for the Standing Committee on Rules of Practice and Procedure, which coordinates and superintends the several bodies of federal rules.) Although Rule 10 of the Supreme Court's Rules identifies some of the considerations that inform the grant of certiorari, they are "neither controlling nor fully measuring the Court's discretion". Likewise it would be a mistake for us to draw up a list that determines how the power under Rule 23(f) will be exercised. Neither a bright-line approach nor a catalog of factors would serve well—especially at the outset, when courts necessarily must experiment with the new class of appeals.

Instead of inventing standards, we keep in mind the reasons Rule 23(f) came into being. These are three. For some cases the denial of class status sounds the death knell of the litigation, because the representative plaintiff's claim is too small to justify the expense of litigation. Coopers & Lybrand v. Livesay, 437 U.S. 463, 98 S.Ct. 2454, 57 L.Ed.2d 351 (1978), held that an order declining to certify a class is not appealable, even if that decision dooms the suit as a practical matter. Rule 23(f) gives appellate courts discretion to entertain appeals in "death knell" cases—though we must be wary lest the mind hear a bell that is not tolling. Many class suits are prosecuted by law firms with portfolios of litigation, and these attorneys act as champions for the class even if the representative plaintiff would find it uneconomical to carry on with the case. E.g., Rand v. Monsanto Co., 926 F.2d 596 (7th Cir. 1991). These law firms may carry on in the hope of prevailing for a single plaintiff and then winning class certification (and the reward of larger fees) on appeal, extending the victory to the whole class. A companion appeal, briefed in tandem with this one, presented just such a case. After class certification was denied, the plaintiff sought permission to appeal under Rule 23(f); although the remaining plaintiff has only a small stake, counsel pursued the case in the district court while we decided whether to entertain the appeal, and before the subject could be argued here the district judge granted summary judgment for the defendant. That plaintiff now has appealed on the merits and will seek to revive the class to boot. Many other cases proceed similarly; *Coopers & Lybrand* did not wipe out the small-stakes class action. But when denial of class status seems likely to be fatal, and when the plaintiff has a solid argument in opposition to the district court's decision, then a favorable exercise of appellate discretion is indicated.

Second, just as a denial of class status can doom the plaintiff, so a grant of class status can put considerable pressure on the defendant to settle, even when the plaintiff's probability of success on the merits is slight. Many corporate executives are unwilling to bet their company that they are in the right in big-stakes litigation, and a grant of class status can propel the stakes of a case into the stratosphere. In re Rhone–Poulenc Rorer Inc., 51 F.3d 1293 (7th Cir. 1995), observes not only that class actions can have this effect on risk-averse corporate executives (and corporate counsel) but also that some plaintiffs or even some district judges may be tempted to use the class device to wring settlements from defendants whose legal positions are justified but unpopular. Empirical studies of securities class actions imply that this is common. Janet Cooper Alexander, *Do the Merits Matter? A Study of Settlements in Securities Class Actions*, 43 Stan.L.Rev. 497 (1991); Reinier Kraakman, Hyun Park & Steven Shavell, *When are Shareholder Suits in Shareholder Interests?*, 82 Geo. L.J. 1733 (1994); Roberta Romano, *The Shareholder Suit: Litigation Without Foundation?*, 7 J.L. Econ. & Org. 55 (1991). Class certifications also have induced judges to remake some substantive doctrine in order to render the litigation manageable. See Hal S. Scott, *The Impact of Class Actions on Rule 10b–5*, 38 U.Chi.L.Rev. 337 (1971). This interaction of procedure with the merits justifies an earlier appellate look. By the end of the case it will be too late—if indeed the case has an ending that is subject to appellate review.

So, in a mirror image of the death-knell situation, when the stakes are large and the risk of a settlement or other disposition that does not reflect the merits of the claim is substantial, an appeal under Rule 23(f) is in order. Again the appellant must demonstrate that the district court's ruling on class certification is questionable—and must do this taking into account the discretion the district judge possesses in implementing Rule 23, and the correspondingly deferential standard of appellate review. However dramatic the effect of the grant or denial of class status in undercutting the plaintiff's claim or inducing the defendant to capitulate, if the ruling is impervious to revision there's no point to an interlocutory appeal.

Third, an appeal may facilitate the development of the law. Because a large proportion of class actions settles or is resolved in a way that overtakes procedural matters, some fundamental issues about class actions are poorly developed. Recent proposals to amend Rule 23 were designed in part to clear up some of these questions. Instead, the Advisory Committee and the Standing Committee elected to wait, anticipating that appeals under Rule 23(f) would resolve some questions and illuminate others. When an appellant can establish that such an issue is presented, Rule 23(f) permits the court of appeals to intervene. When the justification for interlocutory review is contributing to development of the law, it is less important to show that the district judge's decision is shaky. Law may develop through affirmances as well as through reversals. Some questions have not received appellate treatment because they are trivial; these are poor candidates for the use of Rule 23(f). But the more fundamental the question and the greater the likelihood that it will escape effective disposition at the end of the case, the more appropriate is an appeal under Rule 23(f). More than this it is impossible to say.

Judges have been stingy in accepting interlocutory appeals by certification under 28 U.S.C. § 1292(b), because that procedure interrupts the progress of a case and prolongs its disposition. That bogey is a principal reason why interlocutory appeals are so disfavored in the federal system. Disputes about class certification cannot be divorced from the merits—indeed, one of the fundamental unanswered questions is whether judges should be influenced by their tentative view of the merits when deciding whether to certify a class—and so this argument against interlocutory appeals carries some weight under Rule 23(f). But it has less weight than under § 1292(b), because Rule 23(f) is drafted to avoid delay. Filing a request for permission to appeal does not stop the litigation unless the district court or the court of appeals issues a stay—and a stay would depend on a demonstration that the probability of error in the class certification decision is high enough that the costs of pressing ahead in the district court exceed the costs of waiting. (This is the same kind of question that a court asks when deciding whether to issue a preliminary injunction or a stay of an administrative decision. See Illinois Bell Telephone Co. v. WorldCom Technologies, Inc., 157 F.3d 500 (7th Cir. 1998); American Hospital Supply Corp. v. Hospital Products Ltd., 780 F.2d 589, 593–94 (7th Cir. 1986).) We did not stay either of the two cases in which permission to appeal was sought; both continued in the district court and, as we related above, one already has been decided on the merits. Because stays will be infrequent, interlocutory appeals under Rule 23(f) should not unduly retard the pace of litigation.

* * * This situation fits our third category of appropriate interlocutory appeals. Equifax contends that it is entitled to be rid of multiple overlapping class actions. Questions concerning the relation among multiple suits may evade review at the end of the case, for by then the issue will be the relation among (potentially inconsistent) judgments, and not the management of pending litigation. That neither side can point to any precedent in support of its position implies that this is one of the issues that has evaded appellate resolution, and the issue is important enough to justify review now.

IN RE: SUMITOMO COPPER LITIGATION

United States Court of Appeals for the Second Circuit, 2001.
262 F.3d 134.

JOHN M. WALKER, JR., CHIEF JUDGE:

This case presents the issue of the circumstances under which leave will be granted to permit an interlocutory appeal from a district court's decision on class certification pursuant to the recently enacted Rule 23(f) of the Federal Rules of Civil Procedure ("Rule 23(f)"). * * *

The Seventh Circuit, the first to consider the question, identified two categories of cases appropriate for review under Rule 23(f). See Blair v. Equifax Check Servs., Inc., 181 F.3d 832, 834-35 (7th Cir. 1999). The first category comprises the so-called "death knell" cases and their counterparts—namely cases in which the class certification order effectively terminates the litigation either because the denial of certification makes the pursuit of individual claims prohibitively expensive or because the grant of certification forces the defendants to settle. See id. Noting that the reviewing court "must be wary lest the mind hear a bell that is not tolling," the Seventh Circuit concluded that under circumstances in which the certification order would effectively terminate the litigation the party seeking leave to appeal had to further demonstrate, at a minimum, that "the district court's ruling on class certification is questionable ... taking into account the discretion the district judge possesses in implementing Rule 23, and the correspondingly deferential standard of appellate review." Id. at 834–35.

The second category of cases are those in which the class certification order implicates an unresolved legal issue concerning class actions. See id. at 835. Observing that "the more fundamental the [legal] question and the greater the likelihood that it will escape effective disposition at the end of the case, the more appropriate is an appeal under Rule 23(f)," the Seventh Circuit concluded that the party seeking leave in such a case had to demonstrate, at minimum, that an immediate appeal would contribute to the development of the law of class actions.

Id.; see also Richardson Elec., Ltd. v. Panache Broad. of Pa., Inc., 202 F.3d 957, 958 (7th Cir. 2000) (noting that immediate appeal is warranted where it "would advance the development of the law governing class actions").

The certification order at issue in *Blair* implicated an unresolved legal issue, namely whether the district court erred in certifying the class when, in a separate overlapping class action suit, the defendant had agreed to settle on the condition that further class action suits would be prohibited. See *Blair*, 181 F.3d at 836–38. Noting that there were no prior cases addressing the issue, the court concluded that it was one that had "evaded appellate resolution [and was] important enough to justify [immediate] review." Id. at 838. The Seventh Circuit granted the petition, turned to the merits of the appeal, and affirmed the class certification order. See id. at 838–39.

After the decision in *Blair*, the First and Eleventh Circuits weighed in, agreeing with the Seventh Circuit's standard for discretionary review, but somewhat refining the grounds that would warrant such review. The First Circuit noted that, with respect to the second category of cases, the legal issue had to be "important to the particular litigation as well as important in itself and likely to escape effective review if left hanging until the end of the case." Waste Mgmt. Holdings, Inc. v. Mowbray, 208 F.3d 288, 294 (1st Cir. 2000). The *Mowbray* court also allowed for the possibility that under certain circumstances, review should be granted even where the petition did not satisfy the requirements of either Blair category. Id. This was the case with the *Mowbray* petition itself, as to which the First Circuit granted the appeal because the merits of the appeal had, pursuant to court order, "already ... been briefed with exquisite care" and the disposition of the appeal would enable more effective management of the suit by "clarifying some imprecision in the case law." Id. at 295.

In Prado–Steiman v. Bush, 221 F.3d 1266, 1275 (11th Cir. 2000), the Eleventh Circuit held that in a case where the class certification order effectively terminated the litigation, the "mere[] demonstration that the district court's ruling is questionable ... will be insufficient to support a Rule 23(f) petition in the absence of [some indication that the district court abused its discretion]." But the court also found that its "authority to accept Rule 23(f) petitions is highly discretionary, and the ... list of factors [enunciated] is not intended to be exhaustive; there may well be special circumstances that lead us to grant or deny a Rule 23(f) petition even where some or all of the relevant factors point to a different result." Id at 1276. Thus, while the petition in Prado–Steiman failed to meet the requirements under either Blair category, the Eleventh Circuit allowed the appeal because the certification order implicated public interests of "tremendous importance." Id. at 1277–78.

In line with our sister circuits, we hold that petitioners seeking leave to appeal pursuant to Rule 23(f) must demonstrate either (1) that the certification order will effectively terminate the litigation and there has been a substantial showing that the district court's decision is questionable, or (2) that the certification order implicates a legal question about which there is a compelling need for immediate resolution.

Our determination of whether the district court's decision is sufficiently questionable to warrant interlocutory review will be tempered by our longstanding view that the district court is often in the best position to assess the propriety of the class and has the ability, pursuant to Rule 23(c)(4)(B), to alter or modify the class, create subclasses, and decertify the class whenever warranted. Cf. Robidoux v. Celani, 987 F.2d 931, 935 (2d Cir. 1993) (discussing the broad discretion afforded the district court in class certification questions); Caridad v. Metro–North Commuter R.R., 191 F.3d 283, 291–92 (2d Cir. 1999) (noting that this Court is more deferential to the district court whenever class certification is granted), cert. denied, 529 U.S. 1107, 146 L. Ed. 2d 791, 120 S. Ct. 1959 (2000). As noted by the court in *Prado-Steiman*, interlocutory review is particularly appropriate "when it promises to spare the parties and the district court the expense and burden of litigating the matter to final judgment only to have it inevitably reversed by this Court on appeal after final judgment." *Prado-Steiman*, 221 F.3d at 1274–75. On the other hand, issues that would result at most in a modification of a certification order or whose ultimate resolution will depend on further factual development will be unlikely candidates for Rule 23(f) appeal. Similarly, we agree with the other circuits that have discussed Rule 23(f) that a novel legal question will not compel immediate review unless it is of fundamental importance to the development of the law of class actions and it is likely to escape effective review after entry of final judgment. See *Mowbray*, 208 F.3d at 294; *Blair*, 181 F.3d at 835. Views expressed by the district court at the time of class certification, although not required, would be relevant to our determination of whether interlocutory appeal is warranted. See Fed. R. Civ. P. 23(f) committee notes.

We anticipate, therefore, that the standards of Rule 23(f) will rarely be met. This approach will prevent the needless erosion of the final judgment rule and the policy values it ensures, including efficiency and deference. See, e.g., Aluminum Co. of Am. v. Beazer E., Inc., 124 F.3d 551, 561 (3d Cir. 1997) (final judgment rule "minimizes the possibility of piecemeal appeals, accords due deference to trial court judges, and promotes the conservation of judicial resources"). In so holding, however, we leave open the possibility that a petition failing to satisfy either of the foregoing requirements may nevertheless be granted where it presents special circumstances that militate in favor of an immediate appeal. See *Prado-Steiman*, 221 F.3d at 1276; *Mowbray*, 208 F.3d at 294 ("We do not foreclose the possibility that special circumstances may lead us either to deny ... or grant leave to appeal."); *Blair*, 181 F.3d at 834 (refusing to adopt a "bright-line" or "catalog of factors" approach).

Finally, we note that parties should not view Rule 23(f) as a vehicle to delay proceedings in the district court. While the rule gives both the district court and the court of appeals discretion to stay the proceedings, we hold that a stay will not issue unless the likelihood of error on the part of the district court tips the balance of hardships in favor of the party seeking the stay. ...The instant case does not meet any of the requirements of Rule 23(f) set forth above. ...

Notes and Questions

1. Congress amended the Rules Enabling Act, 28 U.S.C. § 2072, and 28 U.S.C. § 1292, in 1990 and 1992, respectively, to permit exceptions to section 1291 to be made by the promulgation of rules, rather than statutory amendment. Although such a change had been discussed before, the primary impetus for the amendments was the recommendation of the Federal Courts Study Committee in 1990. See Report of the Federal Courts Study Committee 89, 95–96 (1990). The Committee felt that efforts to define appealable orders (such as the collateral order doctrine) had been unsatisfactory and could be better handled by rule-making. Similar reasons animated the 1992 amendment to § 1292. Are these reasons convincing? Is rulemaking superior to, say, amending § 1291 or 1292? For an extensive (and skeptical) discussion of these issues, see Martineau, Defining Finality and Appealability by Court Rule: Right Problem, Wrong Solution, 54 U. Pitt. L. Rev. 717, 722–26 (1993) (concluding that "The almost casual manner in which an informal suggestion concerning the final judgment rule produced two separate congressional enactments authorizing changes in a cornerstone of federal appellate practice since 1789 defies rational explanation.") For a more favorable assessment, see Rowe, Defining Finality and Appealability by Court Rule: A Comment on Martineau's "Right Problem, Wrong Solution," 54 U. Pitt. L. Rev. 795 (1993).

2. The promulgation of Rule 23(f) in the 1990s was not without controversy.

> Persons who commented on the proposed rule split predictably into supporters and opponents. Supporters argued that class certification is "the whole ballgame" and is an important issue that deserves an immediate appeal. Other supporters contended that § 1292(b) and mandamus have proven inadequate to provide interlocutory review, and that the proposed rule would be a useful safety valve as courts began to implement the other proposed changes to Rule 23. Still other supporters argued that the presence of a realistic interlocutory appeal opportunity would encourage more careful district court decision making, and deter the use of certification as a tool to coerce settlements of class actions.

> In contrast, opponents of the proposed rule argued that defendants would abuse it and plaintiffs would rarely use it. They also suggested that § 1292(b) and mandamus have been adequate to provide a route of interlocutory appeal. The text of the proposal, they contended, offered no guidelines for the courts and disregarded the views of the trial judge. The upshot, they concluded, would be an increase in litigation expenses and further delays in resolving class actions.

Solimine & Hines, Deciding to Decide: Class Action Certification and Interlocutory Review by the United States Courts of Appeals Under Rule 23(f), 41 Wm. & Mary L. Rev. 1531, 1565–66 (2000).* (Ironically, or not, the attorney-

* Copyright © 2000, William & Mary Law Review. Reprinted by permission. All rights reserved.

famed securities litigation lawyer Melvyn Weiss–who represented the plaintiffs in *Coopers & Lybrand*, opposed the promulgation of Rule 23(f).) Consider whether the Advisory Committee Note to Rule 23(f), and the actual application of the Rule, have responded to the concerns of the critics.

3. How useful and appropriate are the factors found in the Advisory Committee Note to Rule 23(f) in guiding the discretion vested in the appellate courts by Rule 23(f)? In this regard, consider whether those factors resemble, or depart from, the death-knell doctrine, criticized by the Court in *Coopers & Lybrand*. For discussion, see Solimine & Hines, supra; Mullenix, Some Joy in Whoville: Rule 23(f), A Good Rulemaking, 69 Tenn. L. Rev. 97 (2001); Comment, Appealability of Class Certification Orders Under Federal Rule of Civil Procedure 23(f): Toward a Principled Approach, 96 Nw. U. L. Rev. 755 (2002).

4. How might other aspects of federal appellate practice be modified by rulemaking? Consider one suggestion to change qualified immunity appeals by limiting (or overruling) *Mitchell v. Forsyth*, or to permit only one such appeal in a single piece of litigation (i.e., by overruling *Behrens v. Pelletier*). Anderson, The Collateral Order Doctrine: A New 'Serbonian Bog' and Four Proposals for Reform, 46 Drake L. Rev. 539, 611–14 (1998).

7. PENDENT APPELLATE JURISDICTION

SWINT v. CHAMBERS COUNTY COMMISSION

United States Supreme Court, 1995.
514 U.S. 35, 115 S.Ct. 1203, 131 L.Ed.2d 60.

Justice Ginsburg delivered the opinion of the Court.

In the wake of successive police raids on a nightclub in Chambers County, Alabama, two of the club's owners joined by an employee and a patron (petitioners here) sued the Chambers County Commission (respondent here), the City of Wadley, and three individual police officers. Petitioners sought damages and other relief, pursuant to 42 U.S.C. § 1983, for alleged civil rights violations. We granted certiorari to review the decision of the United States Court of Appeals for the Eleventh Circuit, which held that the Chambers County Commission qualified for summary judgment because the sheriff who authorized the raids was a state executive officer and not an agent of the County Commission. We do not reach that issue, however, because we conclude that the Eleventh Circuit lacked jurisdiction to rule on the County.

The Eleventh Circuit unquestionably had jurisdiction to review the denial of the individual police officer defendants' motions for summary judgment based on their alleged qualified immunity from suit. But the Circuit Court did not thereby gain authority to review the denial of the Chambers County Commission's motion for summary judgment. The Commission's appeal, we hold, does not fit within the "collateral order" doctrine, nor is there "pendent party" appellate authority to take up the Commission's case. We therefore vacate the relevant portion of the

Eleventh Circuit's judgment and remand for proceedings consistent with this opinion.

I

On December 14, 1990, and again on March 29, 1991, law enforcement officers from Chambers County and the City of Wadley, Alabama, raided the Capri Club in Chambers County as part of a narcotics operation. The raids were conducted without a search warrant or an arrest warrant. Petitioners filed suit, alleging, among other claims for relief, violations of their federal civil rights. Petitioners named as defendants the County Commission; the City of Wadley; and three individual defendants, Chambers County Sheriff James C. Morgan, Wadley Police Chief Freddie Morgan, and Wadley Police Officer Gregory Dendinger.

The five defendants moved for summary judgment on varying grounds. The three individual defendants asserted qualified immunity from suit on petitioners' federal claims. See Anderson v. Creighton, 483 U.S. 635, 639 (1987) (governmental officials are immune from suit for civil damages unless their conduct is unreasonable in light of clearly established law). Without addressing the question whether Wadley Police Chief Freddie Morgan, who participated in the raids, was a policymaker for the municipality, the City argued that a respondeat superior theory could not be used to hold it liable under § 1983. See Monell v. New York City Dept. of Social Services, 436 U.S. 658, 694 (1978) (a local government may not be sued under § 1983 for injury inflicted solely by its nonpolicymaking employees or agents). The Chambers County Commission argued that County Sheriff James C. Morgan, who authorized the raids, was not a policymaker for the County.

The United States District Court for the Middle District of Alabama denied the motions for summary judgment. The District Court agreed that § 1983 liability could not be imposed on the City for an injury inflicted by a nonpolicymaking employee; that court denied the City's summary judgment motion, however, because the City had failed to argue that Wadley Police Chief Freddie Morgan was not its policymaker for law enforcement. Regarding the County Commission's motion, the District Court was "persuaded by the Plaintiffs that Sheriff [James C.] Morgan may have been the final decision-maker for the County in ferreting out crime, although he is a State of Alabama employee." App. to Pet. for Cert. A–67. The District Court later denied the defendants' motions for reconsideration, but indicated its intent to revisit, before jury deliberations, the question whether Sheriff Morgan was a policymaker for the County:

"The Chambers County Defendants correctly point out that whether Sheriff James Morgan was the final policy maker is a question of law that this Court can decide. What this Court decided in its [prior order] was that the Plaintiffs had come forward with sufficient evidence to persuade this Court that Sheriff Morgan may be the final policy maker for the County. The parties will have an opportunity to convince this Court that Sheriff Morgan was or was not the final policy maker for the County, and the Court will make a ruling as a matter of law on that issue before the case goes to the jury." Id., at A–72.

Invoking the rule that an order denying qualified immunity is appealable before trial, Mitchell v. Forsyth, 472 U.S. 511, 530 (1985), the individual defendants immediately appealed. The City of Wadley and the Chambers County Commission also appealed, arguing, first, that the denial of their summary judgment motions—like the denial of the individual defendants' summary judgment motions—was immediately appealable as a collateral order satisfying the test announced in Cohen v. Beneficial Industrial Loan Corp., 337 U.S. 541, 546 (1949) (decisions that are conclusive, that resolve important questions apart from the merits of the underlying action, and that are effectively unreviewable on appeal from final judgment may be appealed immediately). Alternatively, the City and County Commission urged the Eleventh Circuit Court of Appeals to exercise "pendent appellate jurisdiction," a power that court had asserted in earlier cases. Stressing the Eleventh Circuit's undisputed jurisdiction over the individual defendants' qualified immunity pleas, the City and County Commission maintained that, in the interest of judicial economy, the court should resolve, simultaneously, the City's and Commission's appeals.

The Eleventh Circuit affirmed in part and reversed in part the District Court's order denying summary judgment for the individual defendants. 5 F.3d 1435, 1448 (1993), modified, 11 F.3d 1030, 1031–32 (1994). Next, the Eleventh Circuit held that the District Court's rejections of the County Commission's and City's summary judgment motions were not immediately appealable as collateral orders. 5 F.3d at 1449, 1452. Nevertheless, the Circuit Court decided to exercise pendent appellate jurisdiction over the County Commission's appeal. Id., at 1449–1450. Holding that Sheriff James C. Morgan was not a policymaker for the County in the area of law enforcement, the Eleventh Circuit reversed the District Court's order denying the County Commission's motion for summary judgment. Id., at 1450–1451. The Eleventh Circuit declined to exercise pendent appellate jurisdiction over the City's appeal because the District Court had not yet decided whether Wadley Police Chief Freddie Morgan was a policymaker for the City. Id., at 1451–1452.

We granted certiorari to review the Court of Appeals' decision that Sheriff Morgan is not a policymaker for Chambers County. We then instructed the parties to file supplemental briefs addressing this question: Given the Eleventh Circuit's jurisdiction to review immediately the District Court's refusal to grant summary judgment for the individual defendants in response to their pleas of qualified immunity, did the Circuit Court also have jurisdiction to review at once the denial of the County Commission's summary judgment motion? We now hold that the Eleventh Circuit should have dismissed the County Commission's appeal for want of jurisdiction.

II

We inquire first whether the denial of the County Commission's summary judgment motion was appealable as a collateral order. The answer, as the Court of Appeals recognized, is a firm "No." * * *.

The District Court planned to reconsider its ruling on the County Commission's summary judgment motion before the case went to the jury. That court had initially determined only that "Sheriff Morgan *may have been* the final policy maker for the County." App. to Pet. for Cert. A–67 (emphasis added). The ruling thus fails the *Cohen* test, which "disallows appeal from any decision which is tentative, informal or incomplete." 337 U.S. at 546; see Coopers & Lybrand v. Livesay, 437 U.S. 463, 469 (1978) (order denying class certification held not appealable under collateral order doctrine, in part because such an order is "subject to revision in the District Court") * * *.

III

Although the Court of Appeals recognized that the District Court's order denying the County Commission's summary judgment motion was not appealable as a collateral order, the Circuit Court reviewed that ruling by assuming jurisdiction pendent to its undisputed jurisdiction to review the denial of the individual defendants' summary judgment motions. Describing this "pendent appellate jurisdiction" as discretionary, the Eleventh Circuit concluded that judicial economy warranted its exercise in the instant case: "If the County Commission is correct about the merits in its appeal," the court explained, "reviewing the district court's order would put an end to the entire case against the County...." 5 F.3d at 1450.

Petitioners join respondent Chambers County Commission in urging that the Eleventh Circuit had pendent appellate jurisdiction to review the District Court's order denying the Commission's summary judgment motion. Both sides emphasize that § 1291's final decision requirement is designed to prevent parties from interrupting litigation by pursuing piecemeal appeals. Once litigation has already been interrupted by an authorized pretrial appeal, petitioners and the County Commission reason, there is no cause to resist the economy that pendent appellate jurisdiction promotes. See Supplemental Brief for Petitioners 16–17; Supplemental Brief for Respondent 5, 9. Respondent County Commission invites us to adopt a " 'liberal' " construction of § 1291, and petitioners urge an interpretation sufficiently "practical" and "flexible" to accommodate pendent appellate review as exercised by the Eleventh Circuit. See Supplemental Brief for Respondent 4; Supplemental Brief for Petitioners 14.

These arguments drift away from the statutory instructions Congress has given to control the timing of appellate proceedings. The main rule on review of "final decisions," 28 U.S.C. § 1291, is followed by prescriptions for appeals from "interlocutory decisions," 28 U.S.C. § 1292. Section 1292(a) lists three categories of immediately appealable interlocutory decisions. Of prime significance to the jurisdictional issue before us, Congress, in 1958, augmented the § 1292 catalogue of immediately appealable orders; Congress added a provision, § 1292(b), according the district courts circumscribed authority to certify for immediate appeal interlocutory orders deemed pivotal and debatable * * *.

Congress thus chose to confer on district courts first line discretion to allow interlocutory appeals. If courts of appeals had discretion to append to a Cohen-authorized appeal from a collateral order further rulings of a kind neither independently appealable nor certified by the district court, then the two-tiered arrangement § 1292(b) mandates would be severely undermined.

Two relatively recent additions to the Judicial Code also counsel resistance to expansion of appellate jurisdiction in the manner endorsed by the Eleventh Circuit. The Rules Enabling Act, 28 U.S.C. § 2071 et seq., gives this Court "the power to prescribe general rules of practice and procedure ... for cases in the United States district courts ... and courts of appeals." § 2072(a). In 1990, Congress added § 2072(c), which authorizes us to prescribe rules "defining when a ruling of a district court is final for the purposes of appeal under section 1291." Two years later, Congress added § 1292(e), which allows us to "prescribe rules, in accordance with section 2072 ... to provide for an appeal of an interlocutory decision to the courts of appeals that is not otherwise provided for under [§ 1292] subsection (a), (b), (c), or (d)."

Congress thus has empowered this Court to clarify when a decision qualifies as "final" for appellate review purposes, and to expand the list of orders appealable on an interlocutory basis. The procedure Congress ordered for such changes, however, is not expansion by court decision, but by rulemaking under § 2072. Our rulemaking authority is constrained by §§ 2073 and 2074, which require, among other things, that meetings of bench-bar committees established to recommend rules ordinarily be open to the public, § 2073(c)(1), and that any proposed rule be submitted to Congress before the rule takes effect. § 2074(a). Congress' designation of the rulemaking process as the way to define or refine when a district court ruling is "final" and when an interlocutory order is appealable warrants the Judiciary's full respect.[16]

Two decisions of this Court securely support the conclusion that the Eleventh Circuit lacked jurisdiction instantly to review the denial of the County Commission's summary judgment motion: Abney v. United States, 431 U.S. 651 (1977), and United States v. Stanley, 483 U.S. 669 (1987). In *Abney*, we permitted appeal before trial of an order denying a

---

16. In the instant case, the Eleventh Circuit asserted not merely pendent appellate jurisdiction, but pendent party appellate jurisdiction: The court appended to its jurisdiction to review the denial of the individual defendants' qualified immunity motions jurisdiction to review the denial of the Commission's summary judgment motion. We note that in 1990, Congress endeavored to clarify and codify instances appropriate for the exercise of pendent or "supplemental" jurisdiction in district courts. 28 U.S.C. S 1367 (1988 ed., Supp. V); see § 1367(a) (providing for "supplemental jurisdiction" over "claims that involve the joinder or intervention of additional parties").

motion to dismiss an indictment on double jeopardy grounds. Immediate appeal of that ruling, we held, fit within the *Cohen* collateral order doctrine. 431 U.S. at 662. But we further held that the Court of Appeals lacked authority to review simultaneously the trial court's rejection of the defendant's challenge to the sufficiency of the indictment. Id., at 662–663. We explained:

> "Our conclusion that a defendant may seek immediate appellate review of a district court's rejection of his double jeopardy claim is based on the special considerations permeating claims of that nature which justify a departure from the normal rule of finality. Quite obviously, such considerations do not extend beyond the claim of formal jeopardy and encompass other claims presented to, and rejected by, the district court in passing on the accused's motion to dismiss. Rather, such claims are appealable if, and only if, they too fall within Cohen's collateral-order exception to the final-judgment rule. Any other rule would encourage criminal defendants to seek review of, or assert, frivolous double jeopardy claims in order to bring more serious, but otherwise nonappealable questions to the attention of the courts of appeals prior to conviction and sentence." Id., at 663 (citation omitted).

Petitioners suggest that *Abney* should control in criminal cases only. Supplemental Brief for Petitioners 11. But the concern expressed in *Abney*—that a rule loosely allowing pendent appellate jurisdiction would encourage parties to parlay *Cohen*-type collateral orders into multi-issue interlocutory appeal tickets—bears on civil cases as well.

In *Stanley*, we similarly refused to allow expansion of the scope of an interlocutory appeal. That civil case involved an order certified by the trial court, and accepted by the appellate court, for immediate review pursuant to § 1292(b). Immediate appellate review, we held, was limited to the certified order; issues presented by other, noncertified orders could not be considered simultaneously. 483 U.S. at 676–677.

The parties are correct that we have not universally required courts of appeals to confine review to the precise decision independently subject to appeal. See, e.g., Thornburgh v. American College of Obstetricians and Gynecologists, 476 U.S. 747, 755–57 (1986) (court of appeals reviewing district court's ruling on preliminary injunction request properly reviewed merits as well); Eisen v. Carlisle & Jacquelin, 417 U.S. 156, 172–73 (1974) (court of appeals reviewing district court's order allocating costs of class notification also had jurisdiction to review ruling on methods of notification); Chicago, R. I. & P. R. Co. v. Stude, 346 U.S. 574, 578 (1954) (court of appeals reviewing order granting motion to dismiss properly reviewed order denying opposing party's motion to remand); Deckert v. Independence Shares Corp., 311 U.S. 282, 287 (1940) (court of appeals reviewing order granting preliminary injunction also had jurisdiction to review order denying motions to dismiss). Cf. Schlagenhauf v. Holder, 379 U.S. 104, 110–111 (1964) (court of appeals exercising mandamus power should have reviewed not only whether district court had authority to order mental and physical examinations of defendant in personal injury case, but also whether there was good cause for the ordered examinations).

We need not definitively or preemptively settle here whether or when it may be proper for a court of appeals with jurisdiction over one ruling to review, conjunctively, related rulings that are not themselves independently appealable. The parties do not contend that the District Court's decision to deny the Chambers County Commission's summary judgment motion was inextricably intertwined with that court's decision to deny the individual defendants' qualified immunity motions, or that review of the former decision was necessary to ensure meaningful review of the latter. Cf. Kanji, The Proper Scope of Pendent Appellate Jurisdiction in the Collateral Order Context, 100 Yale L. J. 511, 530 (1990) ("Only where essential to the resolution of properly appealed collateral orders should courts extend their *Cohen* jurisdiction to rulings that would not otherwise qualify for expedited consideration."). Nor could the parties so argue. The individual defendants' qualified immunity turns on whether they violated clearly established federal law; the County Commission's liability turns on the allocation of law enforcement power in Alabama.

* * *

The Eleventh Circuit's authority immediately to review the District Court's denial of the individual police officer defendants' summary judgment motions did not include authority to review at once the unrelated question of the County Commission's liability. The District Court's preliminary ruling regarding the County did not qualify as a "collateral order," and there is no "pendent party" appellate jurisdiction of the kind the Eleventh Circuit purported to exercise. We therefore vacate the relevant portion of the Eleventh Circuit's judgment, and remand for proceedings consistent with this opinion.

It is so ordered.

LIMONE v. CONDON

United States Court of Appeals for the First Circuit, 2004.
372 F.3d 39.

SELYA, CIRCUIT JUDGE.

[Three individuals were allegedly framed and convicted 34 years ago by an FBI agent and a Boston Detective. Two died in prison. The third was released and the Massachusetts state courts overturned his conviction. The individual, and the estates of the two deceased convicts, brought a *Bivens* claim against the FBI agent and a claim under 42 U.S.C.S. § 1983 against the detective. The defendants pled qualified immunity, but the trial court denied immunity.]

The appellants exhort us to reverse that decree or, alternatively, to exercise pendent appellate jurisdiction over another (potentially dispositive) issue. We conclude that at this stage of the proceedings (i) the district court appropriately rejected the appellants' qualified immunity defenses, and (ii) the scope of these interlocutory appeals should not be broadened to encompass an unrelated issue. Consequently, we affirm the denial of qualified immunity and remand for further development of the facts. * * *

The amended complaints allege that the former FBI agent, Dennis Condon, and the former Boston detective, Frank L. Walsh, framed Limone, Greco, and Tameleo, assisted the Commonwealth of Massachusetts in wrongly convicting them on a charge of first-degree murder, participated in a coverup, and allowed the three innocent men to languish in prison for years. In relevant part, the complaints assert Bivens claims against Condon, see Bivens v. Six Unknown Named Agents of the FBN, 403 U.S. 388, 397, 29 L. Ed. 2d 619, 91 S. Ct. 1999 (1971), and section 1983 claims against Walsh, see 42 U.S.C. § 1983 (2000). The central theme of these claims is the accusation that Condon and Walsh, inter alios, violated the Constitution by developing one Joseph "Baron" Barboza as a witness for the prosecution in spite of their knowledge that Barboza would perjure himself and falsely implicate three innocent men in Deegan's murder.

Condon and Walsh (appellants here) moved to dismiss both amended complaints based on the doctrine of qualified immunity. They simultaneously moved to dismiss the suits brought on behalf of Greco and Tameleo on the ground that those plaintiffs had failed to satisfy the favorable termination requirement (described infra Part III) laid down by the Supreme Court in Heck v. Humphrey, 512 U.S. 477, 486–87, 129 L. Ed. 2d 383, 114 S. Ct. 2364 (1994). The district court rebuffed these initiatives. As to qualified immunity, the court found it inconceivable that, at the time of the relevant events, "a reasonable law enforcement officer would have thought it permissible to frame somebody for a crime he or she did not commit." As to Heck, the court found the favorable termination requirement satisfied vis-a-vis the Greco and Tameleo plaintiffs on a theory of constructive reversal and, alternatively, on a theory of estoppel. These timely appeals ensued.

II. THE QUALIFIED IMMUNITY DEFENSE

Condon and Walsh have appealed from the district court's order denying their motions to dismiss based on qualified immunity. An interlocutory appeal lies from such an order where, as here, qualified immunity turns on abstract legal questions. Stella v. Kelley, 63 F.3d 71, 74 (1st Cir. 1995). We review the district court's order de novo, directing dismissal of the complaints "only if it is clear that no relief could be granted under any set of facts that could be proved consistent with the allegations." Hishon v. King & Spalding, 467 U.S. 69, 73, 81 L. Ed. 2d 59, 104 S. Ct. 2229 (1984). * * *

Although these appeals involve claims based on two different legal theories—Bivens and section 1983—the analytical framework is, for our purposes, identical. See Wilson v. Layne, 526 U.S. 603, 609, 143 L. Ed. 2d 818, 119 S. Ct. 1692 (1999). Drawing on Supreme Court precedent, see, e.g., Saucier v. Katz, 533 U.S. 194, 200–02, 150 L. Ed. 2d 272, 121 S. Ct. 2151 (2001), we have developed a three-part algorithm for assessing whether a federal or state actor is entitled to qualified immunity. We consider (i) whether the plaintiff's allegations, if true, establish a constitutional violation; (ii) whether the constitutional right at issue was clearly established at the time of the putative violation; and (iii) whether a reasonable officer, situated similarly to the defendant, would have understood the challenged act or omission to contravene the discerned constitutional right. *Savard,* 338 F.3d at 27. More often than not, proper development of the law of qualified immunity is advanced if courts treat these three questions sequentially. See *Saucier,* 533 U.S. at 201; Fabiano v. Hopkins, 352 F.3d 447, 453 (1st Cir. 2003).

A

The threshold question in a qualified immunity appeal centers on the current state of the law. On a motion to dismiss, this question asks whether the facts alleged, viewed in the light most favorable to the complaining party, show that the officer's conduct violated some constitutional right. Siegert v. Gilley, 500 U.S. 226, 232–33, 114 L. Ed. 2d 277, 111 S. Ct. 1789 (1991); Santana v. Calderon, 342 F.3d 18, 23 (1st Cir. 2003). We turn directly to that question.

The amended complaints paint a sordid picture. Although the misdeeds described therein are many and varied, the plaintiffs' claims may be distilled into two basic allegations: first, that the appellants purposefully suborned false testimony from a key witness; and second, that the appellants suppressed exculpatory evidence in an effort both to cover up their own malefactions and to shield the actual murderers (one of whom was being groomed as an FBI informant). The complaints weave these allegations together. From that platform, the plaintiffs asseverate that an individual's right not to be convicted by these tawdry means—his right not to be framed by the government—is beyond doubt.

This is easy pickings. Although constitutional interpretation occasionally can prove recondite, some truths are self-evident. This is one such: if any concept is fundamental to our American system of justice, it is that those charged with upholding the law are prohibited from deliberately fabricating evidence and framing individuals for crimes they did not commit. See, e.g., Devereaux v. Abbey, 263 F.3d 1070, 1074–75 (9th Cir. 2001) (en banc). Actions taken in contravention of this prohibition necessarily violate due process (indeed, we are unsure what due process entails if not protection against deliberate framing under color of official sanction). Thus, we resist the temptation to expound needlessly upon the first element in the qualified immunity catechism and simply pronounce that requirement satisfied.

B

The second question in the algorithm asks whether the state of the law at the time of the putative violation afforded the defendant fair warning that his or her conduct was unconstitutional. See Hope v. Pelzer, 536 U.S. 730, 741, 153 L. Ed. 2d 666, 122 S. Ct. 2508 (2002). In the circumstances of this case, that question requires us to determine whether the right not to be framed by law enforcement agents was clearly established in 1967—the year in which the appellants are alleged to have started twisting their investigation to target the plaintiffs. We think that it was. * * *

C

Since the relevant right and rule were clearly established and the contours of the right were sufficiently well-defined at the critical time (1967), we must proceed to the third and final step in the qualified immunity pavane. This part of the inquiry considers whether it would have been clear to an objectively reasonable official, situated similarly to a particular appellant, that the actions taken or omitted contravened the clearly established right. See *Saucier,* 533 U.S. at 202; *Hatch,* 274 F.3d at 20; see also *Anderson,* 483 U.S. at 639 (emphasizing that the standard is an objective one). While the first two parts of the inquiry deal with abstract legal rules, the final step depends on the facts of a given case. *Hatch,* 274 F.3d at 24.

On an appeal from an order denying a motion to dismiss—a situation in which the court of appeals is required to credit the allegations of the complaint—the first two steps will frequently go a long way toward resolving the third. This case aptly illustrates that point. Given the facts that are set out in the amended complaints, we have scant difficulty in concluding that it should have been transparently clear to a reasonable officer situated similarly to either Condon or Walsh that his actions violated the constitutional rights of Limone, Greco, and Tameleo. * * *

Both complaints allege that Condon was reliably informed that Deegan had been executed by a crew that included Joseph Barboza, Vincent Flemmi, Roy French, Ronald Cassesso, and Joseph Martin; that he knew, based on conversations with Barboza, that Barboza would commit perjury by swearing not only that Flemmi had no involvement in the murder but also that three innocent men (Limone, Greco, and Tameleo) had helped to perpetrate the crime; that he nonetheless developed Barboza as a witness and turned him over to the Suffolk County district attorney, knowing that Barboza's false testimony would be used to prosecute Limone, Greco, and Tameleo for a crime they did not commit; that he failed to disclose exculpatory evidence before, during, and after the trial; and that he interceded on Barboza's behalf in a subsequent murder prosecution with a view toward ensuring Barboza's continued silence and covering up his own misdeeds. It is plain beyond hope of contradiction that a reasonable officer, confronted with the same circumstances, would have understood that this behavior infracted the plaintiffs' constitutional rights. * * *

In sum, we share the district court's view that, by 1967, "[no] reasonable law enforcement officer would have thought it permissible to frame somebody for a crime he or she did not commit." *Limone,* 271 F. Supp. 2d at 365–66. Taking the facts alleged in the amended complaints as true, we hold that neither appellant is entitled to qualified immunity at this juncture. We add, of course, that this ruling does not preclude the appellants from reasserting that defense, on a more fully developed record, either at summary judgment or at trial.

III. THE FAVORABLE TERMINATION DEFENSE

Our work here is not done. Limone succeeded in having his conviction set aside in 2001, and the district attorney subsequently declined further prosecution. Greco and Tameleo died in prison before they could secure similar remediation. In their motions to dismiss, the appellants argued that the lack of favorable terminations precludes the Greco and Tameleo plaintiffs from pursuing their claims for damages. See Heck v. Humphrey, 512 U.S. 477, 486–87, 129 L. Ed. 2d 383, 114 S. Ct. 2364 (1994) (holding that a plaintiff, in order to recover damages for an allegedly unconstitutional conviction, must show a favorable termination of the underlying conviction); Figueroa v. Rivera, 147 F.3d 77, 80 (1st Cir. 1998) (same). The district court rejected this defense, holding that the Greco and Tameleo plaintiffs could ride piggyback on the vacation of Limone's conviction to satisfy the favorable termination requirement under a theory of "constructive reversal," or in the alternative, that any failure to secure favorable termination was excused by allegations of "government wrongdoing that effectively denied access to post-conviction remedies."

The appellants ask us to review this determination here and now. That request runs headlong into the general rule that only final judgments and orders are immediately appealable in civil cases. See Espinal–Dominguez v. Puerto Rico, 352 F.3d 490, 495 (1st Cir. 2003) (citing 28 U.S.C. § 1291). This rule admits of exceptions, however, and one judge-made exception allows for interlocutory review of an order rejecting a qualified immunity defense so long as the order turns on a purely legal question. See, e.g., *Stella,* 63 F.3d at 73–74. The appellants assert that we may use this exception as a vehicle to review the Heck issue as well. We demur.

Federal courts long have recognized that interlocutory review of a denial of qualified immunity "does not in and of itself confer jurisdiction over other contested issues in the case." Roque–Rodriguez v. Lema Moya, 926 F.2d 103, 105 (1st Cir. 1991). To overcome this obstacle, the appellants invite us to embrace the seldom-used doctrine of pendent appellate jurisdiction. See Swint v. Chambers County Comm'n, 514 U.S. 35, 50–51, 131 L. Ed. 2d 60, 115 S. Ct. 1203 (1995); Nieves-Marquez v. Puerto Rico, 353 F.3d 108, 123 (1st Cir. 2003). We decline the invitation.

The Supreme Court repeatedly has cautioned that exceptions to the final judgment rule should be narrowly construed. See, e.g., Digital Equip. Corp. v. Desktop Direct, Inc., 511 U.S. 863, 868, 128 L. Ed. 2d 842, 114 S. Ct. 1992 (1994). In an effort to avoid needless encroachments on the final judgment rule, we have been quite sparing in our endorsement of pendent appellate jurisdiction. See Fletcher v. Town of Clinton, 196 F.3d 41, 55 (1st Cir. 1999) (noting that the exercise of pendent appellate jurisdiction is "discouraged"); *Roque-Rodriguez*, 926 F.2d at 105 n.2 (classifying this restraint as "self-imposed"). Thus, we have required that, at a bare minimum, a party promoting the exercise of pendent appellate jurisdiction demonstrate either that the pendent issue is inextricably intertwined with the issue conferring the right of appeal or that review of the pendent issue is essential to ensure meaningful review of the linchpin issue. See, e.g., *Nieves-Marquez*, 353 F.3d at 123; Suboh v. Dist. Attorney's Office, 298 F.3d 81, 97 (1st Cir. 2002); see also Clinton v. Jones, 520 U.S. 681, 707 n.41, 137 L. Ed. 2d 945, 117 S. Ct. 1636 (1997). Because these two considerations were limned by the Court in *Swint*, 514 U.S. at 51, we sometimes refer to them as the *Swint* criteria.

Here, the linchpin issue and the pendent issue cannot fairly be described as intertwined, let alone inextricably intertwined. Whereas the former (qualified immunity) focuses principally on the appellants' conduct leading up to the plaintiffs' convictions, the latter (favorable termination) entails an examination of post-conviction events. The fact that we already have conducted an exhaustive review of the district court's qualified immunity ruling without needing to touch upon the favorable termination issue, see supra Part II, makes manifest this lack of imbrication. By the same token, it conclusively proves that the exercise of pendent appellate jurisdiction is not essential to our ability to conduct meaningful review of the linchpin issue. On that score alone, this case is an unfit candidate for the invocation of pendent appellate jurisdiction.

The appellants strive to parry this thrust by arguing that failure to satisfy the *Swint* criteria should bar the exercise of pendent appellate jurisdiction only when the party appealing the linchpin issue and the party appealing the pendent issue are different. They posit that where, as here, the same parties seek review of both issues, pendent appellate jurisdiction may be justified on the basis of fairness and efficiency concerns. See, e.g., Jungquist v. Sheikh Sultan Bin Khalifa Al Nahyan, 325 U.S. App. D.C. 117, 115 F.3d 1020, 1026–27 (D.C. Cir. 1997) (exercising pendent appellate jurisdiction on that basis when the same parties sought review of both issues); Gilda Marx, Inc. v. Wildwood Exercise, Inc., 318 U.S. App. D.C. 109, 85 F.3d 675, 679 & n.4 (D.C. Cir. 1996) (declining to read fulfillment of the *Swint* criteria as an absolute condition precedent to the exercise of pendent appellate jurisdiction). They tell us that exercising pendent appellate jurisdiction in the instant case would allow for the early resolution of a potentially dispositive issue, thus catering to fairness and efficiency concerns.

We think that the appellants' position ignores reality. There is no sound reason why the identity of the parties should have decretory significance in deciding whether to exercise pendent appellate jurisdiction. This court has used the *Swint* criteria as the benchmark for pendent appellate jurisdiction in all sorts of cases, including cases in which the party appealing the pendent issue was also appealing the linchpin issue. See, e.g., *Nieves-Marquez*, 353 F.3d at 123; *Suboh*, 298 F.3d at 97. So too the Second Circuit. See Rein v. Socialist People's Libyan Arab Jamahiriya, 162 F.3d 748, 757 (2d Cir. 1998) (stating that "pendent issues raised by the party that has the right to bring an interlocutory appeal are at least as great a threat to the final-order scheme as are pendent issues raised by other parties"). Several other courts of appeals have likewise endorsed a universal application of the *Swint* criteria. See id. at 758 (collecting cases). Consequently, we hold explicitly that when a party who has the right to bring an interlocutory appeal on one issue attempts simultaneously to raise a second issue that ordinarily would be barred by the final judgment rule, we will not exercise appellate jurisdiction over the pendent issue unless one of the *Swint* criteria is satisfied.

Given this paradigm, instances demanding the exercise of pendent appellate jurisdiction are likely to be few and far between. This is not one of them. We conclude, therefore, that it would be ultracrepidarian— and wrong—for us to exercise pendent appellate jurisdiction over the favorable termination issue just for the *Heck* of it.

* * *

Affirmed.

Notes and Questions

1. After *Swint*, when, if ever, should pendent appellate jurisdiction be used? As Judge Posner has put it, the *Swint* case made lower courts "skittish" about applying this "controversial and embattled doctrine," Greenwell v. Aztar Indiana Ganning Corp., 268 F.3d 486, 491 (7th Cir. 2001), but in the same case he acknowledged that "the doctrine clearly still lives," as numerous examples can attest. See, e.g., Clinton v. Jones, 520 U.S. 681, 707 n.41, 117 S.Ct. 1636, 137 L.Ed.2d 945 (1997) (pendent to collateral order appeal); Meredith v. Oregon, 321 F.3d 807, 811–12 (9th Cir. 2003) (pendent to appeal under § 1292(a)(1)); Greenwell, supra (pendent to Rule 54(b)); Montaño v. City of Chicago, 375 F.3d 593, 599–600 (7th Cir. 2004) (pendent to collateral order appeal).

2. For further discussion of pendent appellate jurisdiction, see 16 C. Wright, A. Miller & E. Cooper, Federal Practice & Procedure § 3937 (2d ed. 1996); Steinman, The Scope of Appellate Jurisdiction: Pendent Appellate Jurisdiction Before and After *Swint*, 49 Hastings L.J. 1337 (1998).

8. STAY ORDERS

"Stay orders" are those where a trial court grants a motion to stay further proceedings before it, often in lieu of the litigants proceeding to arbitration or with related litigation in another forum. Are the grants or denials of such motions immediately appealable? For affirmative answers, see Moses H. Cone Memorial Hosp. v. Mercury Const. Corp., 460 U.S. 1, 103 S.Ct. 927, 74 L.Ed.2d 765 (1983) (also holding that grant of stay fell under the collateral order doctrine); Gulfstream Aerospace Corp.

v. Mayacamas Corp., 485 U.S. 271, 108 S.Ct. 1133, 99 L.Ed.2d 296 (1988) (motion to stay in lieu of pending litigation elsewhere is immediately appealable).

Questions of appealability of stay orders under the Federal Arbitration Act can present their own complications, as the next case illustrates.

GREEN TREE FINANCIAL CORP.— ALABAMA v. RANDOLPH

Supreme Court of the United States, 2000.
531 U.S. 79, 121 S.Ct. 513, 148 L.Ed.2d 373.

CHIEF JUSTICE REHNQUIST delivered the opinion of the Court.

In this case we first address whether an order compelling arbitration and dismissing a party's underlying claims is a "final decision with respect to an arbitration" within the meaning of § 16(a)(3) of the Federal Arbitration Act, 9 U.S.C. § 16(a)(3), and thus is immediately appealable pursuant to that Act. Because we decide that question in the affirmative, we also address the question whether an arbitration agreement that does not mention arbitration costs and fees is unenforceable because it fails to affirmatively protect a party from potentially steep arbitration costs. We conclude that an arbitration agreement's silence with respect to such matters does not render the agreement unenforceable.

I

Respondent Larketta Randolph purchased a mobile home from Better Cents Home Builders, Inc., in Opelika, Alabama. She financed this purchase through petitioners Green Tree Financial Corporation and its wholly owned subsidiary, Green Tree Financial Corp.-Alabama. Petitioners' Manufactured Home Retail Installment Contract and Security Agreement required that Randolph buy Vendor's Single Interest insurance, which protects the vendor or lienholder against the costs of repossession in the event of default. The agreement also provided that all disputes arising from, or relating to, the contract, whether arising under case law or statutory law, would be resolved by binding arbitration.

Randolph later sued petitioners, alleging that they violated the Truth in Lending Act (TILA), 15 U.S.C. § 1601 et seq., by failing to disclose as a finance charge the Vendor's Single Interest insurance requirement. She later amended her complaint to add a claim that petitioners violated the Equal Credit Opportunity Act, 15 U.S.C. §§ 1691–1691f, by requiring her to arbitrate her statutory causes of action. She brought this action on behalf of a similarly situated class. In lieu of an answer, petitioners filed a motion to compel arbitration, to stay the action, or, in the alternative, to dismiss. The District Court granted petitioners' motion to compel arbitration, denied the motion to stay, and dismissed Randolph's claims with prejudice. The District Court also denied her request to certify a class. She requested reconsideration, asserting that she lacked the resources to arbitrate, and as a result, would have to forgo her claims against petitioners. The District Court denied reconsideration. Randolph appealed.

The Court of Appeals for the Eleventh Circuit first held that it had jurisdiction to review the District Court's order because that order was a final decision. The Court of Appeals looked to § 16 of the Federal Arbitration Act (FAA), 9 U.S.C. § 16, which governs appeal from a district court's arbitration order, and specifically § 16(a)(3), which allows appeal from "a final decision with respect to an arbitration that is subject to this title." The court determined that a final, appealable order within the meaning of the FAA is one that disposes of all the issues framed by the litigation, leaving nothing to be done but execute the order. The Court of Appeals found the District Court's order within that definition.

The court then determined that the arbitration agreement failed to provide the minimum guarantees that respondent could vindicate her statutory rights under the TILA. Critical to this determination was the court's observation that the arbitration agreement was silent with respect to payment of filing fees, arbitrators' costs, and other arbitration expenses. On that basis, the court held that the agreement to arbitrate posed a risk that respondent's ability to vindicate her statutory rights would be undone by "steep" arbitration costs, and therefore was unenforceable. We granted certiorari, and we now affirm the Court of Appeals with respect to the first conclusion, and reverse it with respect to the second.

II

Section 16 of the Federal Arbitration Act, enacted in 1988, governs appellate review of arbitration orders. 9 U.S.C. § 16. It provides:

"(a) An appeal may be taken from—

"(1) an order—

"(A) refusing a stay of any action under section 3 of this title,

"(B) denying a petition under section 4 of this title to order arbitration to proceed,

"(C) denying an application under section 206 of this title to compel arbitration,

"(D) confirming or denying confirmation of an award or partial award, or

"(E) modifying, correcting, or vacating an award;

"(2) an interlocutory order granting, continuing, or modifying an injunction against an arbitration that is subject to this title; or

"(3) a final decision with respect to an arbitration that is subject to this title.

"(b) Except as otherwise provided in section 1292(b) of title 28, an appeal may not be taken from an interlocutory order—

"(1) granting a stay of any action under section 3 of this title;

"(2) directing arbitration to proceed under section 4 of this title;

"(3) compelling arbitration under section 206 of this title; or

"(4) refusing to enjoin an arbitration that is subject to this title."

The District Court's order directed that arbitration proceed and dismissed respondent's claims for relief. The question before us, then, is whether that order can be appealed as "a final decision with respect to an arbitration" within the meaning of § 16(a)(3). Petitioners urge us to hold that it cannot. They rely, in part, on the FAA's policy favoring arbitration agreements and its goal of "mov[ing] the parties to an arbitrable dispute out of court and into arbitration as quickly and easily as possible." Moses H. Cone Memorial Hospital v. Mercury Constr. Corp., 460 U.S. 1, 22, 103 S.Ct. 927, 74 L.Ed.2d 765 (1983); id., at 24, 103 S.Ct. 927. In accordance with that purpose, petitioners point out, § 16 generally permits immediate appeal of orders hostile to arbitration, whether the orders are final or interlocutory, but bars appeal of interlocutory orders favorable to arbitration.

Section 16(a)(3), however, preserves immediate appeal of any "final decision with respect to an arbitration," regardless of whether the decision is favorable or hostile to arbitration. And as petitioners and respondent agree, the term "final decision" has a well-developed and longstanding meaning. It is a decision that " 'ends the litigation on the merits and leaves nothing more for the court to do but execute the judgment.' " Digital Equipment Corp. v. Desktop Direct, Inc., 511 U.S. 863, 867, 114 S.Ct. 1992, 128 L.Ed.2d 842 (1994), and Coopers & Lybrand v. Livesay, 437 U.S. 463, 467, 98 S.Ct. 2454, 57 L.Ed.2d 351 (1978) (both quoting Catlin v. United States, 324 U.S. 229, 233, 65 S.Ct. 631, 89 L.Ed. 911 (1945)). See also St. Louis, I.M. & S.R. Co. v. Southern Express Co., 108 U.S. 24, 28–29, 2 S.Ct. 6, 27 L.Ed. 638 (1883). Because the FAA does not define "a final decision with respect to an arbitration" or otherwise suggest that the ordinary meaning of "final decision" should not apply, we accord the term its well-established meaning. See Evans v. United States, 504 U.S. 255, 259–260, 112 S.Ct. 1881, 119 L.Ed.2d 57 (1992).

The District Court's order directed that the dispute be resolved by arbitration and dismissed respondent's claims with prejudice, leaving the court nothing to do but execute the judgment. That order plainly disposed of the entire case on the merits and left no part of it pending before the court. The FAA does permit parties to arbitration agreements to bring a separate proceeding in a district court to enter judgment on an arbitration award once it is made (or to vacate or modify it), but the existence of that remedy does not vitiate the finality of the District Court's resolution of the claims in the instant proceeding. 9 U.S.C. §§ 9, 10, 11. The District Court's order was therefore "a final decision with respect to an arbitration" within the meaning of § 16(a)(3), and an appeal may be taken.[2] See Sears, Roebuck & Co. v. Mackey, 351 U.S. 427, 431, 76 S.Ct. 895, 100 L.Ed. 1297 (1956) (explaining that had the District Court dismissed all the claims in an action, its decision would be final and appealable); *Catlin, supra,* at 236, 65 S.Ct. 631 (noting that had petitioners' motion to dismiss been granted and a judgment of dismissal entered, "clearly there would have been an end of the litigation and appeal would lie . . .").

Petitioners contend that the phrase "final decision" does not include an order compelling arbitration and dismissing the other claims in the action, when that order occurs in an "embedded" proceeding, such as this one. "Embedded" proceedings are simply those actions involving both a request for arbitration and other claims for relief. "Independent" proceedings, by contrast, are actions in which a request to order arbitration is the sole issue before the court. Those Courts of Appeals attaching significance to this distinction hold that an order compelling arbitration in an "independent" proceeding is final within the meaning of § 16(a)(3), but that such an order in an "embedded" proceeding is not, even if the district court dismisses the remaining claims. Petitioners contend that the distinction between independent and embedded proceedings and its consequences for finality were so firmly established at the time of § 16's enactment that we should assume Congress meant to incorporate them into § 16(a)(3).

We disagree. It does not appear that, at the time of § 16(a)(3)'s enactment, the rules of finality were firmly established in cases like this one, where the District Court both ordered arbitration and dismissed the remaining claims. We also note that at that time, Courts of Appeals did not have a uniform approach to finality with respect to orders directing arbitration in "embedded" proceedings. The term "final decision," by contrast, enjoys a consistent and longstanding interpretation. Certainly the plain language of the statutory text does not suggest that Congress intended to incorporate the rather complex independent/embedded distinction, and its consequences for finality, into § 16(a)(3). We therefore conclude that where, as here, the District Court has ordered the parties to proceed to arbitration, and dismissed all the claims before it, that decision is "final" within the meaning of § 16(a)(3), and therefore appealable.

III

We now turn to the question whether Randolph's agreement to arbitrate is unenforceable because it says nothing about the costs of arbitration, and thus fails to provide her protection from potentially substantial costs of pursuing her federal statutory claims in the arbitral forum. [The Court held the agreement to be enforceable.]

---

2. Had the District Court entered a stay instead of a dismissal in this case, that order would not be appealable. 9 U.S.C. § 16(b)(1). The question whether the District Court should have taken that course is not before us, and we do not address it.

The judgment of the Court of Appeals is affirmed in part and reversed in part.

It is so ordered.

JUSTICE GINSBURG, with whom JUSTICE STEVENS and JUSTICE SOUTER join, and with whom JUSTICE BREYER joins as to Parts I and III, concurring in part and dissenting in part.

I

I join Part II of the Court's opinion, which holds that the District Court's order, dismissing all the claims before it, was a "final," and therefore immediately appealable, decision. On the matter the Court airs in Part III, . . . allocation of the costs of arbitration—I would not rule definitively. Instead, I would vacate the Eleventh Circuit's decision, which dispositively declared the arbitration clause unenforceable, and remand the case for closer consideration of the arbitral forum's accessibility. * * *

Notes and Questions

1. The 1988 Amendment to the FAA is a rare example of a legislative body speaking directly to the issue of interlocutory appeals. How would you evaluate their work?

2. After *Green Tree*, when are stay orders (as opposed to dismissals) immediately appealable? What criteria should a trial judge consider when deciding whether to stay or dismiss? See Bergeron, District Courts as Gatekeepers? A New Vision of Appellate Jurisdiction Over Orders Compelling Arbitration, 51 Emory L.J. 1365 (2002).

SECTION C. STATE SYSTEMS

WEST'S ANN.CAL.CIV.PROC.CODE § 904.1

Superior Courts; Appealable Judgments and Orders

An appeal may be taken from a superior court in the following cases:

(a) From a judgment, except (1) an interlocutory judgment, other than as provided in subdivisions (h) *and* (i) * * *, (2) a judgment of contempt which is made final and conclusive by Section 1222, * * * (3) a judgment on appeal from a municipal court or a justice court or a small claims court, or (4) a judgment granting or denying a petition for issuance of a writ of mandamus or prohibition directed to a municipal court or a justice court or the judge or judges thereof which relates to a matter pending in a municipal or justice court. However, an appellate court may, in its discretion, review a judgment granting or denying a petition for issuance of a writ of mandamus or prohibition upon petition for an extraordinary writ.

(b) From an order made after a judgment made appealable by subdivision (a).

(c) From an order granting a motion to quash service of summons or granting a motion to stay or dismiss the action on the ground of inconvenient forum.

(d) From an order granting a new trial or denying a motion for judgment notwithstanding the verdict.

(e) From an order discharging or refusing to discharge an attachment or granting a right to attach order.

(f) From an order granting or dissolving an injunction, or refusing to grant or dissolve an injunction.

(g) From an order appointing a receiver.

(h) From an interlocutory judgment, order, or decree, hereafter made or entered in an action to redeem real or personal property from a mortgage thereof, or a lien thereon, determining the right to redeem and directing an accounting.

(i) From an interlocutory judgment in an action for partition determining the rights and interests of the respective parties and directing partition to be made.

(j) From an order or decree made appealable by the provisions of the Probate Code.

N.Y.–McKINNEY'S CIV. PRACTICE LAW AND RULES 5701

Appeals to Appellate Division from Supreme and County Courts

(a) **Appeals as of right**. An appeal may be taken to the appellate division as of right in an action, originating in the supreme court or a county court:

1. from any final or interlocutory judgment except one entered subsequent to an order of the appellate division which disposes of all the issues in the action; or

2. from an order not specified in subdivision (b), where the motion it decided was made upon notice and it:

(i) grants, refuses, continues or modifies a provisional remedy; or

(ii) settles, grants or refuses an application to resettle a transcript or statement on appeal; or

(iii) grants or refuses a new trial; except where specific questions of fact arising upon the issues in an action triable by the court have been tried by a jury, pursuant to an order for that purpose, and the order grants or refuses a new trial upon the merits; or

(iv) involves some part of the merits; or

(v) affects a substantial right; or

(vi) in effect determines the action and prevents a judgment from which an appeal might be taken; or

(vii) determines a statutory provision of the state to be unconstitutional, and the determination appears from the reasons given for the decision or is necessarily implied in the decision; or

3. from an order, where the motion it decided was made upon notice, refusing to vacate or modify a prior order, if the prior order would have been appealable as of right under paragraph two had it decided a motion made upon notice.

(b) **Orders not appealable as of right**. An order is not appealable to the appellate division as of right where it:

1. is made in a proceeding against a body or officer pursuant to article 78; or

2. requires or refuses to require a more definite statement in a pleading; or

3. orders or refuses to order that scandalous or prejudicial matter be stricken from a pleading.

(c) **Appeals by permission**. An appeal may be taken to the appellate division from any order which is not appealable as of right in an action originating in the supreme court or a county court by permission of the judge who made the order granted before application to a justice of the appellate division; or by permission of a justice of the appellate division in the department to which the appeal could be taken, upon refusal by the judge who made the order or upon direct application.

WIS.STAT.ANN. § 808.03

Appeals to the Court of Appeals

(1) **Appeals as of right**. A final judgment or a final order of a circuit court * * * may be appealed as a matter of right to the court of appeals unless otherwise expressly provided by law. A final judgment or final order is a judgment or order entered in accordance with s. 806.06(1)(b) or 807.11(2) or a disposition recorded in docket entries in traffic regulation cases and municipal ordinance violation cases prosecuted in circuit court which disposes of the entire matter in litigation as to one or more of the parties, whether rendered in an action or special proceeding.

Note

The statutes on appeals of California, New York, and Wisconsin indicate that the states run the gamut of appealability from allowing an appeal of right only from a final judgment (Wisconsin) to almost every kind of interlocutory order (New York) to following the federal model (California). The following cases illustrate some of the different types of responses of state courts in deciding what is appealable and when.

NORTH EAST INDEPENDENT SCHOOL DISTRICT v. ALDRIDGE

Supreme Court of Texas, 1966.
400 S.W.2d 893.

CALVERT, CHIEF JUSTICE.

Guy Aldridge appealed from a trial court judgment awarding a recovery from him by North East Independent School District of damages in the sum of $30,000.00. The Court of Civil Appeals dismissed the appeal upon a holding that the trial court's judgment was not a final judgment. 392 S.W.2d 607. We reverse the judgment of the Court of Civil Appeals and order the appeal reinstated.

School District's suit was based upon an alleged breach of a written contract between it and Aldridge. By the terms of the contract Aldridge agreed to sell and School District agreed to buy a tract of 20.963 acres of land at a price of $3,500.00 per acre, and Aldridge obligated himself to construct a sewer line along a section of the southern boundary and streets along the northern and western boundaries of the tract. The petition alleged that School District had fully performed its amended answer included a plea in abatement, a general denial, a plea that the contract was in reality made by School District with King–O–Hills Development Company for which he acted only as agent in executing the contract, and, with permission of the court, a cross-action against King–O–Hills Development Company to recover any sum which he might be adjudged liable to pay to School District. At a later date he filed a supplemental answer in which he pleaded that School District was estopped to assert its claim against him. King–O–Hills was duly cited and filed its answer to the cross-action. The record indicates that on June 5, 1964, the case was set for trial on the jury calendar for the month of October, 1964.

School District moved for summary judgment on its claim against Aldridge for the damages sued for, or, alternatively, on the issue of Aldridge's personal liability for damages for breach of the contract. Aldridge filed an answer to the motion in which he asserted that there was an issue of fact concerning his personal liability inasmuch as School District knew that in executing the contract he was acting only as agent for King–O–Hills Company, and also an issue of fact concerning the amount of the damages. On July 8, 2964, the trial court granted School District's motion on its alternative prayer and rendered judgment that Aldridge was personally liable for damages for breach of the contract. The judgment also directed that "this cause proceed to trial upon the sole remaining issue of the amount of damages to which the plaintiff is entitled."

On October 5, 1964, the attorneys for School District and the attorney for Aldridge entered into a written stipulation that the damages suffered by school District as a result of the failure to construct the sewer line and streets amounted to $30,000.00. Thereupon, the court rendered judgment that North East School District recover of and from Guy Aldridge the sum of $30,000.00 with interest and costs. The judgment was approved as to form by the attorneys for both parties. There is no mention in the judgment of the third-party defendant, King–O–Hills Company, and no disposition is made therein of the cross-action by Aldridge against such defendant. It was because of the failure of the judgment to dispose of the cross-action that the Court of Civil Appeals held that it was not a final judgment. It is that holding which we are called upon to review.

The finality of judgments for appealability has been a recurring and nagging problem throughout the judicial history of this State. We have steadfastly adhered through the years to the rule, with certain exceptions not applicable here, that an appeal may be prosecuted only from a final judgment and that to be final a judgment must dispose of all issues and parties in a case. Gulf, C. & S.F. Ry. Co. v. Forth Worth & N.O. Ry. Co., 68 Tex. 98, 2 S.W. 199, 3 S.W. 564 (1886); Davis v. McCray Refrigerator Sales Corp., 136 Tex. 296, 150 S.W.2d 377 (1941). The rule is deceiving in its apparent simplicity and vexing in its application.

In Linn v. Arambould, 55 Tex. 611 (881), this Court reviewed many of the earlier decisions and announced rules for determining finality which no doubt were thought adequate to settle all future questions in the area. If so, the thought died aborning. In one of the rules announced, the Court said that to be final "the judgment must in substance show *intrinsically, and not inferentially*, that the matters in the record had been determined in favor of one of the litigants, or the rights of the parties in litigation had been adjudicated." 55 Tex. 619. That rule has long since passed into limbo. It was too simple. By its application most judgments easily became black or white–final or interlocutory; but all to often judgments which were obviously *intended* to be final were being held interlocutory because of careless draftsmanship. The rule had to be changed to accommodate oversight or carelessness.

In 1896 this Court decided Rackley v. Fowlkes, 89 Tex. 613, 36 S.W. 77. No question of finality of a judgment was involved; only a question of res judicata. In a prior suit the plaintiff sought to recover title to land and rents from the land. The trial court's judgment awarded recovery of title to the land but did not mention the issue of rents. The plaintiff then filed a second suit for rents. This Court held that the defendant's plea of res judicata should have been sustained in the absence of a showing by the plaintiff that in his first suit he withdrew his count for rents or the court refused to decide it. The holding was bottomed upon a rule stated by the Court, as follows (36 S.W. 78):

> "The proposition seems to be sound in principle and well supported by authority that where the pleadings and judgment in evidence show that the pleadings upon which the trial was had put in issue plaintiff's right to recover upon two causes of action, and the judgment awards him a recovery upon one, but is silent as to the

other, such judgment is prima facie an adjudication that he was not entitled to recover upon such other cause."

The Court arrived at the rule by indulging "the presumption that the [trial] court performed the duty devolved upon it upon the submission of the cause by disposing of every issue presented by the pleadings so as to render its judgment final and conclusive of the litigation* * *." Taking no notice of the rule announced in *Linn v. Arambould*, or of the distinction between rules governing finality of judgments and those relating to res judicata, the Court in Davies v. Thomson, 92 Tex. 391, 49 S.W. 215 (1899), applied the rule quoted from *Rackley v. Fowlkes* in holding that a judgment which awarded plaintiffs relief they sought in one particular would "be construed" to deny relief they sought in another particular. *Davies v. Thomson* has been followed by our latest decisions on the subject. *See* Gamble v. Banneyer, 137 Tex. 7, 151 S.W.2d 586 (1941); Vance v. Wilson, Tex.Sup., 382 S.W.2d 107 (1964).

The decision in *Davies v. Thomson* obviously did not necessarily settle the issue of finality of a judgment which granted relief to a plaintiff but failed to dispose expressly of a cross-action or counterclaim by the defendant against the plaintiff. The Courts of Civil Appeals were badly divided in their rulings on the finality of judgments of that character. The issue was settled by this Court in favor of finality in Trammell v. Rosen, 106 Tex. 132, 157 S.W. 1161 (1913). The Court dealt a final blow in that case to the rule announced in *Linn v. Arambould* by indicating, in effect, that it was a dictum. For the first time the Court spoke of the disposition of issues by implication and by necessary implication; but it did so only in referring to holdings of various Courts of Civil Appeals. It should be noted that the Court did *not* hold that the defendants' cross-action in Trammell v. Rosen was disposed of by *necessary implication*, or even by *implication*. Instead, the Court stated that the "principle" which controlled *Rackley v. Fowlkes* and *Davies v. Thomson* was "applicable in great measure to this case." 157 S.W. 1163. That "principle" was, of course, that a *presumption would be indulged* that the court's judgment disposed "of every issue presented by the pleadings so as to render its judgment final and conclusive of the litigation;" and, in the absence of a showing that a claim for relief had been withdrawn or that the court refused to decide it, that the judgment would be "construed" to deny all relief not expressly granted. The Court need not have gone quite so far in *Trammell v. Rosen*. Instead of holding that the judgment would be construed as *denying all relief sought* in the pleadings and not expressly granted, the Court needed to hold only that the judgment would be construed as *disposing of all issues* made by the pleadings in the case. Whether the judgment was construed as *denying* all relief not expressly granted or as *dismissing* all claims for relief not expressly granted was immaterial to the holding of finality. The distinction becomes important when the subsequent opinion of the Commission of Appeals in Burton Lingo Co. v. First Baptist Church of Abilene, Tex.Com.App., 222 S.W. 203 (1920), is considered.

In *Burton Lingo Co. v. First Baptist Church of Abilene*, Burton Lingo Co. sued a number of defendants, including a contractor and the sureties on his bond, on an account for materials furnished the contractor. A joint answer was filed on behalf of the contractor and the sureties. Bankruptcy was pleaded as a defense on behalf of the contractor, and the sureties pleaded their suretyship, and by cross-action sought a recovery over against the contractor. At the conclusion of the evidence the trial court instructed a verdict against the plaintiff on its claim against the contractor, and in favor of the plaintiff against the sureties. No instruction was given with respect to the sureties' cross-action. The trial court's judgment decreed that the plaintiff recover the amount of its account from the sureties, but it neither disposed of nor mentioned the sureties' cross-action against the contractor. The sureties appealed. The Court of Civil Appeals held that the judgment was not a final judgment and dismissed the appeal. 198 S.W. 1013. The Commission of Appeals called attention to the fact that a joint answer had been filed on behalf of the contractor and the sureties and observed that the record did not show that the sureties had objected to the failure of the trial court to instruct a verdict in their favor on their cross-action, or that they had complained of the failure of the trial court to award them a recovery on their cross-action at the time the judgment was rendered, in their motion for new trial, or in their appeal to the Court of Civil Appeals. Under these circumstances, said the court, "It is not unreasonable to presume in favor of the finality of the judgment that the sureties elected to waive and abandon their cross-action, or that a dismissal or discontinuance was had with reference thereto." 222 S.W. 204. Here, as in *Trammell v. Rosen*, the Court was presuming that the trial court made disposition of the cross-action *in a particular manner*, when all that was necessary to a holding of finality was a presumption that the claim *had been disposed of*, as in *Rackley v. Fowlkes* and *Davies v. Thomson*.

Notice should be taken of the holding in Davis v. McCray Refrigerator Sales Corp., 136 Tex. 296, 150 S.W.2d 377 (1941). In that case the defendant filed a plea in abatement and a cross-action against the plaintiff. The trial court entered a judgment sustaining the plea in abatement and dismissing the suit. No disposition was made of the cross-action. The plaintiff appealed. This Court held that the judgment dismissing the plaintiff's suit did not by *necessary implication* dispose of the defendant's cross-action against the plaintiff and was not final. The rationale of the decision is found in the Court's statement that had the trial court intended to retain the cross-action for further consideration, it would have entered the very judgment which it did enter. The effect of the holding is to engraft an exception upon the general rule formulated by the decisions preceding *Davis*. The exception may be stated thusly: It will not be presumed that a judgment dismissing a plaintiff's suit on nonsuit, plea to the jurisdiction, plea in abatement, for want of prosecution, etc., also disposed of the issues in an independent cross-action.

There are a great number of decisions by Courts of Civil Appeals and by the Commissions of Appeals dealing with finality of judgments in various fact situations. It would serve no good purpose to review them here. Analysis of the decisions we have discussed is sufficient to lead us to the statement of a rule for determining, in most instances, whether judgments in which parties and issues made by the pleadings are not disposed of in express language are, nevertheless, final for appeal purposes. When a judgment not intrinsically interlocutory in character, is rendered and entered in a case regularly set for a conventional trial on the merits, no order for a separate trial of issues having been entered pursuant to Rule 174, Texas Rules of Civil Procedure, it will be presumed for appeal purposes that the Court intended to, and did, dispose of all parties legally before it and of all issues made by the pleadings between such parties. A claim duly severed under Rule 41 is a "case" within the meaning of the foregoing rule. The rule will be subject to the exception created by *Davis v. McCray Refrigerator Sales Corporation*; but it will apply to separate claims of the plaintiff, cross-actions and counterclaims by defendants against the plaintiff, cross-actions by defendants against other defendants and cross-actions by defendants against third-party defendants. Of course, the problem can be eliminated entirely by a careful drafting of judgments to conform to the pleadings or by inclusion in judgments of a simple statement that all relief not expressly granted in denied.

The rule announced disposes of the question to be decided in this case unless the statement contained in the court's summary judgment is regarded as an order for a separate trial of the issue of damages. As heretofore noted, that judgment decreed that Aldridge was personally liable to School District for damages caused by breach of the contract, and then directed that "this cause proceed to trial upon the sole remaining issue of the amount of the damages to which the plaintiff is entitled." We are not disposed to regard the quoted order as one entered under Rule 174 for trial of the separate issue of the amount of damages. The order speaks of the "cause" proceeding to trial of a particular issue; it does not speak of a separate trial of an issue as a preliminary matter or as independent of final trial of the cause. It indicates that at that stage of the proceedings the court overlooked the fact that under the pleadings there were other issues and parties to be disposed of when the case was reached for trial on the October, 1964, jury docket.

Under the rule announced, the presumption is that the judgment entered on October 7, 1964, disposed of Aldridge's cross-action against King–O–Hills Development Company; and in the absence of a contrary showing in the record, we hold that the judgment entered on that date was a final judgment.

The proper judgment to be rendered by this Court is one reversing the judgment of the Court of Civil Appeals, and ordering the cause reinstated on the docket of that court for consideration of the appeal on its merits. *See* Bay v. Mecom, Tex. Sup., 393 S.W.2d 819 (1965); Trammell v. Rosen, 106 Tex. 132, 157 S.W. 1161 (1913). It is so ordered.

Smith, J., concurs in the result.

Notes and Questions

1. The principal case is representative of the situation in most states, indicating that state courts have had as much trouble with the final judgment rule as have the federal courts.

2. Does the court in the principal case identify the cause of the problems with the final judgment rule in Texas? Can any court opinion, rule, or statute cure the problem?

3. Compare the result in this case with what it would be under federal procedure. Would it be the same?

4. Most states have adopted a provision similar to Fed.R.Civ.P. 54(b) for cases in which there are multiple parties or claims. Problems similar to those that arise under the federal rule also arise under the state rules. In Bonner v. Krause, 69 Or.App. 1, 684 P.2d 10 (1984), the court held an order dismissing a complaint against one of several defendants was not appealable because, although the trial judge had certified that there was no just reason to delay entry of judgment, the judge not only failed to give reasons to support immediate entry of judgment but did not direct entry of a judgment based on the order. According to Norvell v. Cuyahoga County Hospital, 11 Ohio App.3d 70, 463 N.E.2d 111 (1983), an order that struck some damage allegations but permitting consideration of others based on the same cause of action could not be certified under 54(b) type rule.

HOBERMAN v. LAKE OF ISLES, INC.

Supreme Court of Errors of Connecticut, 1952.
138 Conn. 573, 87 A.2d 137.

INGIS, ASSOCIATE JUSTICE.

This action was brought to foreclose a mortgage. The answer denied the execution of the mortgage and alleged that the loan purporting to be secured had not been made. Judgment was entered for the defendants. Thereafter, the plaintiff filed his motion for a new trial pursuant to Practice Book, § 229. The court found that material testimony relating to the execution of the mortgage given by the defendant Girden on the trial of the case was false. It concluded that for that reason the judgment must be opened and a new trial had in order to avoid injustice or judicial error and entered an order granting the motion. From that order this appeal has been taken. The only questions raised or argued on the appeal related to the propriety of the order. The appeal, however necessarily raises another and more fundamental question, namely, whether the order is one from which an appeal lies.

Section 8003 of the General Statutes authorizes an appeal only from a final judgment or from a decision granting a motion to set aside a verdict. The jurisdiction of this court is therefore limited to appeals which are within either of those two categories. Since it is a matter of jurisdiction, this court may and should upon its own motion reject any purported appeal which is not within the statute even though the question has not been raised by a motion to erase.

The present appeal is clearly not one from a decision granting a motion to set aside a verdict. The sole question, therefore, is whether the order granting the motion for a new trial is a final judgment under the statute. In determining whether a decision of a trial court is a final judgment, we have uniformly applied the test laid down in Banca Commerciale Italiana Trust Co. v Westchester Artistic Works, Inc., 108 Conn. 304, 307, 142 A. 838, 839: "The test lies, not in the nature of the judgment, but in its effect as concluding the rights of some or all of the parties. If such rights are concluded, so that further proceedings after the entry of the order or decree of the court cannot effect them, then the judgment is a final judgment form which an appeal lies." In *State v. Kemp*, 124 Conn. 639, 643, 1 A.2d 761, 762, we said: "We did not sue the word 'rights' in [the Banca] opinion in an inclusive sense. There are many rulings in the course of an action by which rights are determined which are interlocutory in their nature and reviewable only upon an appeal taken from a judgment later rendered."

Proceedings upon a motion to open a judgment and for a new trial are interlocutory. The rule requires such a motion to be filed within six days after the rendition of the judgment. It contemplates that action on the motion shall be taken while the court has power to modify its judgment, that is, during the term in which the judgment is rendered or while the court has the power by virtue of the fact that the motion is pending. The granting of the motion does not determine any of the substantive rights of the parties. *See* Magill v. Lyman, 6 Conn. 59, 61. It determines merely that the parties must retry the issues in order to obtain a final adjudication of those rights. After the retrial is had and judgment is entered, on appeal from that judgment the granting of the motion for a new trial may be assigned as error.

The effect of the granting of such a motion is analogous to that of an order of the Superior Court remanding a case to a workmen's compensation commissioner to hear further evidence, correct the finding and enter a new award. Such an order, we have held, is not appealable to this court. Burdick v. United States Finishing Co., 128 Conn. 284, 22 A.2d 629. An order restoring to the docket a case which was previously withdrawn provides an even closer analogy. Such an order deprives the defendant of the equivalent of a judgment in his favor and compels him to relitigate the issue. Yet we have held that the granting of a motion to restore is not a final judgment from which an appeal lies.

In *Ferguson v. Sabo*, supra, 115 Conn. 623, 162 A. 844, we said that the granting of a motion to open a judgment of strict foreclosure after title had become absolute is not a final judgment permitted an appeal. Directly in point is Ostroski v. Ostroski, 135 Conn. 509, 66 A.2d 599. In that case it is held that an order opening a divorce judgment is not appealable. The opinion, 135 Conn. at page 510, 66 A.2d at page 600, says: "The opening of the judgment in this case left the issues undisposed of, and upon a rehearing the plaintiff may still prove that he is entitled to a divorce. He is not precluded from asserting on a rehearing every right he has to the legal relief he claims." If the word "foreclosure" is substituted for "divorce," this quotation is a complete and accurate statement of the situation in the present case. The question presented in the *Ostroski* case was the same as that now before us. The decision in that case concludes the matter.

So far as the right of appeal is concerned, there is a distinction between an order granting a motion for a new trial and a judgment entered upon a petition for a new trial, which may be instituted at any time within three years after a judgment is rendered. *See General Statutes*, § 8322. The latter is appealable. The difference is in at least two essential particulars. In the first place, a petition for a new trial is instituted by writ and complaint served upon the adverse party in the same manner as in any other new action. Although the action so started is collateral to the action in which the new trial is sought, it nevertheless is a distinct suit in itself. The judgment rendered therein is, therefore, the termination of the suit. It is the final judgment in the action. *See* State v. Kemp, 124 Conn. 639, 644, 1 A.2d 761. On the other hand, a motion for a new trial is filed in a case already pending and is merely a step in the procedure leading to the final judgment in that case. In the second place, claimed errors committed in rendering judgment on a petition for a new trial are not reviewable on an appeal from the judgment rendered in the action in which a new trial is sought. This consideration is given as the basis of the decision in both the Palverari case and the Husted case. The same is not true of a decision by the trial court on the less formal motion for a new trial. As I pointed out above, errors claimed in connection therewith may be assigned on the appeal from the judgment in the case in which the motion was made.

The order for a new trial from which this appeal was taken was purely interlocutory. It was entered at a time when the trial court still had control over and power to modify the judgment which it had rendered. The order did not finally concluded any of the rights of the parties which were in litigation. It, therefore, is not a final judgment from which an appeal lies. This court is without jurisdiction and the appeal must be dismissed. When an appeal is dismissed for lack of jurisdiction no costs are taxable.

The appeal is dismissed without taxable costs to either party.

In this opinion the other judges concurred.

Notes and Questions

1. Was it necessary for the court in the principal case to discuss the appealability of grants or denials of new trials? If not, why did the court discuss it?

2. What is the different between a petition for a new trial and a motion for a new trial? Why should one be appealable and the other not?

LIPSON v. LIPSON

Supreme Court of Delaware, 2001.
799 A.2d 345.

HOLLAND, JUSTICE.

The appellant, Robert Lipson ("Husband"), filed a notice of appeal with this Court on March 5, 2001. The Husband seeks to appeal five separate orders of the Family Court dated April 5, 1999, September 1, 2000, November 30, 2000, January 3, 2001, and February 8, 2001. The orders addressed the following issues: (i) interim unallocated alimony and child support (April 5, 1999); (ii) ancillary relief, alimony, and fees (September 1, 2000); (iii) reargument relating to the September 1, 2000 order (November 30, 2000); (iv) disposition of a Rule 60(a) motion (November 30, 2000); and (v) attorney's fees (February 8, 2001).

MOTION TO DISMISS

The appellee, Joan Lipson ("Wife"), has filed a motion to dismiss the appeal on the grounds that the Husband's appeal was not timely filed as to any of the Family Court's orders except the order dated February 8, 2001. The Wife contends, among other things, that the Family Court in its November 30, 2000 decision disposing of the motion for reargument, stated that the decision was "a final order effective December 11, 2000." The Wife therefore argues that the Husband was required to file his notice of appeal within 30 days of December 11, 2000.

The Husband has filed a response to the Wife's motion to dismiss. The Husband contends that, notwithstanding the Family Court's statement that the November 30, 2000 order would become final as of December 11, 2000, the ancillary matters before the Family Court could not be considered final for purposes of appeal until the Family Court entered its decision on the related issue of attorney's fees, which did not occur until February 8, 2001.

The Court has carefully considered the parties' respective positions. The Family Court's statement that its order would become final as of a date certain is not dispositive of whether that decision was the Family Court's "final act" for purposes of appeal. We have determined that the motion to dismiss should be denied. The Clerk has been directed to issue a briefing schedule.

DIVORCE AND ANCILLARY RELIEF

When a party files a petition for divorce or annulment in the Family Court, in addition to a prayer for divorce or annulment, the relief prayed for may include prayers for other relief that may be available under Title 13 "including, without limitation, prayers for interim relief (§ 1509), alimony (§ 1512), property disposition (§ 1513), resumption of prior name (§ 1514), costs and attorneys' fees (§ 1515), support for a child (subchapter I, Chapter 5) and custody and/or child visitation (subchapter

11, Chapter 7)." "The right of a party to petition for ancillary relief, is not an assertion of a separate cause of action, 'but is a prayer that the [Family] [C]ourt, in its discretion, exercise one of its incidental powers possessed solely by reason of its jurisdiction over the matrimonial cause.'"

For purposes of appeal, however, the final order granting a divorce decree and a final order regarding ancillary relief are severable. The language of Section 1518(a) states:

> A decree granting ... a petition for divorce ... is final when entered, subject to the right of appeal. An appeal that does not challenge the decree of divorce ... but challenges only rulings with respect to relief awarded under other sections of this chapter, or other matters incidental or collateral to such decree, shall not delay the finality of the decree of divorce ... and the parties may remarry while the appeal is pending.

When the Family Court retains jurisdiction to consider requests for ancillary relief, following the entry of a divorce decree, each *final* ruling on a request for a specific type of ancillary relief is directly and separately appealable to this Court. *See, e.g.,* Ann Marie H. v. Joseph J. H., Del.Supr., 456 A.2d 1233 (1983) (alimony and attorneys fees); Jerry L.C. v. Lucille H. C., Del.Supr., 448 A.2d 223 (1982) (division of marital property). All rulings that are made within the context of a particular ancillary proceeding are not necessarily final, however, and, therefore, appealable as a matter of right, e.g., an award of interim alimony is clearly not a final ruling on an ancillary application for alimony. An appeal from an interlocutory ruling, which is made within the course of deciding a particular request for ancillary relief, is subject to the requirements of Supreme Court Rule 42.

FINAL JUDGMENT RULE

An aggrieved party can appeal to this Court, as a matter of right, only after a final judgment is entered by the trial court. Del. Const. art. IV, § 11(1)(a); Harrison v. Ramunno, Del.Supr., 730 A.2d 653 (1999). "A 'final decision' is generally defined as one that ends the litigation on the merits and leaves nothing for the trial court to do but execute the judgment." Catlin v. United States, 324 U.S. 229, 233, 65 S.Ct. 631, 89 L.Ed. 911 (1945). The proper application of the final judgment rule has been the subject of frequent litigation in federal and state courts.

FEDERAL FINALITY AND ATTORNEY'S FEES

In this case, the question presented is whether a decision on the merits of an application for the ancillary relief of alimony constituted a separately appealable final judgment, notwithstanding the fact that a related application for an award of attorney's fees remained undecided. At one time, the United States Supreme Court suggested the answer to the question of finality on the merits in federal courts, prior to ruling on a related request for attorney's fees, would "turn upon the characterization of those [attorney's] fees by the statute or decisional law that authorizes them." Budinich v. Becton Dickinson and Co., 486 U.S. 196, 108 S.Ct. 1717, 100 L.Ed.2d 178 (1988); see also White v. New Hampshire Dep't of Employment Security, 455 U.S. 445, 102 S.Ct. 1162, 71 L.Ed.2d 325 (1982); Boeing Co. v. Van Gemert, 444 U.S. 472, 100 S.Ct. 745, 62 L.Ed.2d 676 (1980). Several years later, after those distinctions caused more confusion than certainty, the United States Supreme Court adopted "a uniform rule that an unresolved issue of attorney's fees does not prevent a judgment on the merits from being final." Budinich v. Becton Dickinson and Co., 486 U.S. at 201, 108 S.Ct. 1717; *see* Robert J. Martineau, *Defining Finality and Appealability by Court Rule: Right Problem, Wrong Solution,* 54 U. Pitt. L.Rev. 1717, 1744 (1993) (critically assessing the holding in *Budinich*).

Delaware Finality and Attorney's Fees

In this case, the ancillary relief at issue was for alimony and for an award of attorney's fees related to the application for alimony. The appellant filed this appeal after the issue of attorney's fees had been decided. This Court has held that an order is deemed final and appealable if the decision is the trial court's last act in disposing of all justiciable matters within its jurisdiction.

Section 1515 provides that the Family Court may "from time to time" award either party attorney's fees for maintaining or defending a divorce or *any* ancillary proceeding under Chapter 15 of Title 13. In most cases, an application for any type of ancillary relief in conjunction with a divorce proceeding is accompanied by a related application for attorney's fees. Consequently, this Court has consistently held, and hereby reaffirmed, that a judgment on the merits of any request for ancillary relief is not final until an outstanding related application for an award of attorney's fees has been decided.

There are, however, two independent methods of seeking appellate review by this Court of a decision on the merits of a particular application for ancillary relief, before the issue of attorney's fees has been decided by the trial court. First, the party seeking to immediately appeal a ruling on the merits of an application for ancillary relief can seek interlocutory review, pursuant to Delaware Supreme Court Rule 42. Second, and alternatively, the party seeking immediate review of an ancillary ruling can request the trial judge to certify the otherwise interlocutory ancillary decision on the merits as a final judgment, pursuant to Family Court Rule 54(c).

Conclusion

In this case, the Family Court's final act, for the purpose of appealing the merits of the Wife's application for the ancillary relief of alimony, was the issuance of its February 8, 2001 decision on attorney's fees. The Wife's contention that the Husband was required to file separate appeals from each of the Family Court's ancillary decisions on alimony and attorney's fees is inconsistent with this Court's policy of avoiding piecemeal litigation. We hold that the Husband's notice of appeal was timely filed after the entry of the final judgment of the Family Court on the issue of attorney's fees related to the award of alimony.

The Husband has properly invoked the jurisdiction of this Court to review any or all interlocutory rulings made by the Family Court that preceded the entry of its final judgment on the issue of attorney's fees, e.g. interim alimony and alimony. Any of these interlocutory rulings will be properly raised if they are fairly presented in the appellant's opening brief. The Wife's motion to dismiss is denied.

GOLDSTON v. AMERICAN MOTORS CORPORATION

Supreme Court of North Carolina, 1990.
326 N.C. 723, 392 S.E.2d 735.

MARTIN, JUSTICE.

Our decision does not require an extensive recital of the facts. In brief, on 7 February 1982 the plaintiff, an East Carolina University coed, was rendered a quadriplegic when the 1979 Jeep CJ–7 Golden Eagle in which she was riding flipped over on the sand dunes of Radio Island. She filed suit on 18 May 1984 against American Motors Corporation ("AMC"), and two of its subsidiaries, American Motors Sales Corporation and American Motors (Canada), Inc. for negligent design of the factory-mounted roll bar, negligent construction, negligent marketing, negligent failure to warn and negligent failure to recall. Her lawsuit further alleged breach of warranties by AMC, its subsidiaries and East Carolina Honda–Volvo. Two years later, R. Ben Hogan of the Alabama Bar was admitted pro hac vice to represent plaintiff along with her present counsel, Norman Williams, Michael Mauney and Charles Darsie. Hogan is nationally known for his active involvement in product liability litigation and specifically in liability actions arising from accidents involving AMC or Jeep vehicles.

In 1988 Hogan was contacted by Rahn Huffstutler, a former AMC attorney and engineer who had assisted AMC in the defense of similar product liability suits. Upon his departure from AMC, Huffstutler had retained several confidential and protected documents. Huffstutler met with Hogan on various occasions to discuss the probable use of the documents at trial and the potential use of Huffstutler as an expert witness for plaintiff. Upon learning of these meetings, AMC moved to enjoin Huffstutler from disclosing the confidential and privileged information obtained during his employment with AMC. The Court of Common Pleas of Ohio (Huffstutler's residence) granted AMC's prayer for permanent injunctive relief and that decision was upheld by the Ohio Supreme Court.

At the same time, AMC moved to have Hogan disqualified as counsel in each of the Jeep cases in which he was involved across the country. Because of his involvement in this case, a series of hearings was conducted in the trial court between October 1988 and April 1989 to determine the extent of Hogan's contacts with Huffstutler. Judge Manning conditionally denied the motion by defendants to disqualify Hogan upon the express requirement that Hogan file an affidavit verifying that his contacts with Huffstutler were limited to those admitted by him during the hearings. Upon reviewing the submitted affidavit which enumerated substantially greater contacts than previously disclosed, Judge Farmer, in accordance with Judge Manning's order, ruled that Hogan must be disqualified from any further representation of plaintiff.

Plaintiff appealed the ruling and the Court of Appeals dismissed the appeal. Plaintiff then filed a notice of appeal and a petition for discretionary review with this Court. We dismissed the appeal but allowed the petition limited to the sole issue of the appealability of the trial court's interlocutory order. The issue before us is whether plaintiff has a substantial right to counsel of her own choosing and, if so, whether plaintiff may immediately appeal when her chosen counsel is disqualified.

Generally, there is no right of immediate appeal from interlocutory orders and judgments. The North Carolina General Statutes set out the exceptions under which interlocutory orders are immediately appealable. Relevant here are the following statutes:

N.C.G.S. § 1–277(a) provides:

An appeal may be taken from every judicial order or determination of a judge of a superior or district court, upon or involving a matter of law or legal inference, whether made in or out of session, which affects a substantial right claimed in any action or proceeding. . . .

N.C.G.S. § 7A–27(d) provides:

From any interlocutory order or judgment of a superior court or district court in a civil action or proceeding which affects a substantial right . . . appeal lies of right directly to the Court of Appeals.

This Court, speaking through Justice Huskins, said: "Ordinarily, an appeal from an interlocutory order will be dismissed as fragmentary and premature unless the order affects some substantial right and will work injury to appellant if not corrected before appeal from final judgment." Stanback v. Stanback, 287 N.C. 448, 453, 215 S.E.2d 30, 34 (1975). Therefore plaintiff is not entitled to appeal from the interlocutory order disqualifying her counsel unless the order deprived her of a "substantial right which [s]he would lose absent a review prior to final determination." Robins & Weill v. Mason, 70 N.C.App. 537, 540, 320 S.E.2d 693, 696, *cert. denied*, 312 N.C. 495, 322 S.E.2d 559 (1984). Essentially a two-part test has developed—the right itself must be substantial and the deprivation of that substantial right must potentially work injury to plaintiff if not corrected before appeal from final judgment. *See* Wachovia Realty Investments v. Housing, Inc., 292 N.C. 93, 232 S.E.2d 667 (1977).

"Normally, a litigant has a fundamental right to select the attorney who will represent him in his lawsuit." Hagins v. Redevelopment Commission, 275 N.C. 90, 102, 165 S.E.2d 490, 498 (1969). This is a basic premise of the adversary system in judicial proceedings. We hold that plaintiff had a substantial right to have R. Ben Hogan represent her in her lawsuit against AMC. We are mindful of the apparent disharmony with the decision in Leonard v. Johns–Manville Corp., 57 N.C.App. 553, 291 S.E.2d 828, *cert. denied,* 306 N.C. 558, 294 S.E.2d 371 (1982). There the Court of Appeals denied the appeal on the basis that the trial court's interlocutory order denying a motion for admission of counsel pro hac vice did not involve a substantial right and was not immediately appealable as a matter of right. In *Leonard,* the subject matter of the appeal was to have been whether the trial court erred in its determination that the out-of-state counsel failed to meet the conditions precedent for admission pro hac vice set forth in N.C.G.S. § 84–4.1. "[P]arties do not have a right to be represented in the courts of North Carolina by counsel who are not duly licensed to practice in this state. Admission of counsel in North Carolina pro hac vice is not a right but a discretionary privilege." 57 N.C.App. at 555, 291 S.E.2d at 829. In the case at bar, R. Ben Hogan had been properly admitted pro hac vice under the statute and was actively involved in plaintiff's lawsuit for several years. The distinction is thus: once the attorney was admitted under the statute, plaintiff acquired a substantial right to the continuation of representation by that attorney—just as with any other attorney duly admitted to practice law in the State of North Carolina. We also note that the trial court did not summarily remove Hogan pursuant to N.C.G.S. § 84–4.1. The order removing Hogan as counsel affected a substantial right of the plaintiff.

Depriving plaintiff of her counsel of choice, who is an alleged expert in cases of this nature, certainly exposed her to potential injury unless corrected before trial and appeal from final judgment. Plaintiff is faced with an extremely difficult task of showing harm in the event that she should receive a favorable verdict. How does one prove the actual amount of damages sustained in the loss of representation by counsel with the years of experience and know-how which Mr. Hogan allegedly has developed through his practice of suing major manufacturers of jeeps and related vehicles for tort liability? Thus, when the trial court's order disqualifying counsel was entered, plaintiff correctly moved to appeal that decision immediately before proceeding with further discovery and the trial.

We are cognizant of the United States Supreme Court decision in Richardson–Merrell, Inc. v. Koller, 472 U.S. 424, 105 S.Ct. 2757, 86 L.Ed.2d 340 (1985), which held that appellate courts do not have jurisdiction to review on appeal an order disqualifying counsel in a civil case because it is not a collateral order subject to immediate appeal under 28 U.S.C.A. § 1291. The federal statute grants the courts of appeals jurisdiction of appeals from all "final decisions of the district courts," except where a direct appeal lies to the United States Supreme

Court. The United States Supreme Court has consistently held that the finality requirement means that a party may not appeal until there has been a decision on the merits. Firestone Tire & Rubber Co. v. Risjord, 449 U.S. 368, 101 S.Ct. 669, 66 L.Ed.2d 571 (1981) (citations omitted). The narrow exception to this rule is called the "collateral order doctrine." For a case to fall within this doctrine and be immediately appealable, it must: (1) conclusively determine the disputed question; (2) resolve an important issue completely separate from the merits of the action; and (3) be effectively unreviewable on appeal from a final judgment. Coopers & Lybrand v. Livesay, 437 U.S. 463, 98 S.Ct. 2454, 57 L.Ed.2d 351 (1978).

Richardson-Merrell is inapposite because the issue before us is controlled by our interpretation of the North Carolina statutes. Our statutes setting forth the appeals process do not include the same jurisdictional "finality" requirement as does the federal statute. As a result, our Court has taken a different approach and developed the *Wachovia* two-prong test. As we have previously stated, for an interlocutory order to be immediately appealable, it must: (1) affect a substantial right and (2) work injury if not corrected before final judgment. *Wachovia,* 292 N.C. 93, 232 S.E.2d 667. Here, these requirements have been met by plaintiff.

The trial court's order is appealable, and the Court of Appeals was in error in dismissing plaintiff's appeal without first passing on the merits thereof. The cause is remanded to the Court of Appeals for a decision on the merits.

REVERSED AND REMANDED.

Notes and Questions

1. The rules on appealability and finality are frequently different between state and federal courts. Those same rules are also not uniform in all state courts.

2. The *Lipson* and *Goldston* cases illustrate the differences between finality in state and federal courts. Are the approaches in these two state cases easier to apply than the federal approach to finality on attorney's fees and attorney disqualification? Interestingly, Delaware follows the federal construction of the collateral order doctrine regarding attorney disqualification. *See* Acierno v. Hayward, 859 A.2d 617 (Del. 2004).

3. Consider how one state has modified its interlocutory appeals regime in light of experience. Ohio appellate courts have only the constitutional authority to hear appeals of "judgments or final orders." Ohio Const., art. IV, § 3(B)(2). A statute defined "final orders" to include, among other things, an order affecting a "substantial right" made in a "special proceeding." The Ohio Supreme Court in Amato v. General Motors Corp., 67 Ohio St.2d 253, 423 N.E.2d 452 (1981) held that interlocutory orders could be immediately appealed under this language, if a balancing test was met. The test weighed the "harm to the 'prompt and orderly disposition of litigation,' and the consequent waste of judicial resources, resulting from the allowance

of an appeal, with the need for immediate review because appeal after final judgment is not practicable."

The *Amato* decision resulted in a torrent of cases addressing whether particular interlocutory orders satisfied the balancing test. Dissatisfaction with the balancing test led the Court in Polikoff v. Adam, 67 Ohio St.3d 100, 616 N.E.2d 213 (1993), to replace that test with one that focused more closely on the statutory language, considering, inter alia, whether the special proceeding was one that was essentially as independent judicial inquiry created by statute, as opposed to one recognized at common law or equity. In 1998 the Ohio legislature amended the Ohio statute to provide definitions of "substantial right" and a "special proceeding," Ohio Rev. Code § 2505.02(A)-(B), in ways that in part codified the *Polikoff* analysis. The codification has not settled all questions of what interlocutory orders are appealable. E.g., Stevens v. Ackman, 91 Ohio St.3d 182, 743 N.E.2d 901 (2001) (denial of summary judgment in wrongful death case on basis of statutory immunity not a "special proceeding" and hence not immediately appealable).

SECTION D. PROPOSED ALTERNATIVES

MARTINEAU, DEFINING FINALITY AND APPEALABILITY BY COURT RULE: RIGHT PROBLEM, WRONG SOLUTION

54 U.Pitt.L.Rev. 717, 770–78, 782–87 (1993).*

To resolve the dilemma posed by continued adherence to the final judgment rule and the numerous exceptions or proposed exceptions to it by statute, court rule, or judicial decision, an understanding of the three elements of appealability and the relationship between them is necessary. These three elements are the right to appeal, the jurisdiction of the appellate court, and the timing of the appeal.

These three elements are incorporated in the final judgment rule as follows: (1) a person aggrieved by an order or judgment of a trial court has the right to appeal the order or judgment to an appellate court; (2) the appellate court has jurisdiction over and must review the merits of the order or judgment; and (3) the aggrieved person must wait until the trial court has disposed of the entire case before it can take an appeal. Two corollaries of the final judgment rule are that an aggrieved person may not appeal an interlocutory order before the end of the case, and that the appellate court does not have jurisdiction over an interlocutory appeal. The final judgment rule thus exists in a world of absolutes: right or no right to appeal, mandatory or no jurisdiction over an appeal, and appeal only after a final judgment.

When an exception to the final judgment rule is made or proposed, almost invariably (section 1292(b) being the exception to the contrary) the exception is in absolute terms and affects all three elements—

* Copyright © 1993, University of Pittsburgh Law Review, University of Pittsburgh School of Law. Reprinted by permission. All rights reserved.

extending the right to appeal and thus mandatory jurisdiction to one or more classes of interlocutory orders before the entry of the final judgment. If there is the right to appeal an interlocutory order, the appeal must be taken and reviewed immediately. Neither the taking of the appeal nor the review of it can be delayed until the final judgment is entered. Further, the extension is absolute in terms of type or class of the order made appealable. Thus, if an interlocutory order falls within the definition of the exception, it is appealable immediately without regard to the effect of the order in the particular case. The harm the particular appellant will suffer if the appeal is delayed until the final judgment is entered is ignored. Similarly ignored is the harm to the appellee from an immediate appeal and the effect on the trial court, the appellate court, and other litigants in both courts. Further, no consideration is given to whether an immediate appeal may expedite or delay the termination of the litigation, or serve some public purpose. The result is that when an exception to the final judgment rule is made, the exception is likely to produce just what the final judgment rule was designed to prevent—multiple appeals in a single case.

The final judgment rule, which had its origins in the practicalities of the English common law courts having only one record in each case, has continued in existence because in most cases it serves the purposes of some or most litigants and prospective litigants, their lawyers, the trial court, the appellate court, and ultimately the public. The general purpose of the rule is to aid in the resolution of disputes as expeditiously and inexpensively as possible. The rule by its terms, however, does not recognize the reality that in some cases the appeal of an interlocutory order will serve some of these same interests better than strict adherence to the final judgment rule. The constant tension between strict adherence to the final judgment rule and the occasional need for an immediate appeal of an interlocutory order has produced the present confused situation in which the final judgment rule is riddled with exceptions. Each exception almost always requires an immediate appeal of an interlocutory order that falls within the exception, and the appellate court has jurisdiction over the interlocutory order only if appealed immediately and not on appeal from the final judgment. In many cases the exceptions are not necessary to avoid unduly harsh effects of the rule, while often the exceptions do not reach all cases in which strict enforcement of the rule is unduly harsh. For example, 28 U.S.C. § 1292(a)(1) by its terms allows the immediate appeal of any order that grants or denies a request for injunctive relief without regard to the harm or lack of harm to the litigants of a delayed appeal. The result is constant pressure on the courts and legislative bodies to create new exceptions or to enlarge or narrow exceptions previously made.

The two proposals of the [Federal Courts Study] Committee, like most other proposals to modify the final judgment rule, continue this flawed approach in that they are concerned only with appeals of right, either from final judgments or interlocutory orders, and thus either confer mandatory jurisdiction or deny jurisdiction in the appellate court.

Thus these two proposals will not accomplish the goals stated by the FCS Committee in its report—to reduce litigation on issues of finality and appealability, to avoid dismissal of appeals as premature, and in particular, to avoid instances in which an appeal of an order not truly final but immediately appealable is held to be untimely because the appeal was not taken until after the final judgment was entered. The first proposal to permit a rule to define "final" for purposes of appeal, and enacted into law as section 315 of the 1990 Act, can only expand the definition of "final" to include rulings that are not truly final but become final only because the rule says so. This expansion will result because the Court has consistently defined "final" as used in section 1291 to include two types of rulings: one, the traditional final judgment rule, that is a judgment that disposes of the entire matter in litigation leaving only execution to be done, and two, an order that affects a right that will be irretrievably lost absent an immediate appeal. It is highly unlikely that the rulemakers would seek to eliminate either type of order from its definition of "final." If the rulemakers do anything, consequently, they will add to the list. The second proposal, to list interlocutory orders appealable of right, was enacted into law by section 101 of the 1992 act. By its terms the amendment expands rather than contracts appealability because it permits additions but not deletions from section 1292.

Sixty years ago Crick pointed out the misplaced focus of litigation over what type of judicial action is final and thus appealable. The FCS Committee and Congress have recognized the same problem and were correct in so doing. The source of the litigation, however, is neither definitional nor whether the definition is found in a statute or a rule. Reducing the litigation, consequently, cannot result from giving the rulemakers authority to define "final" or to list certain classes of interlocutory orders appealable of right. The litigation arises, rather, from efforts to avoid the effect of the final judgment rule in a particular case by making certain types of interlocutory orders appealable of right, either because of perceived harm from delaying the appeal until the final judgment is entered or perceived advantages of an immediate appeal of an interlocutory order.

There are two techniques to permit an interlocutory appeal of right. One is to change the definition of "final" to include the particular type of interlocutory order. The other is to make an exception to the final judgment rule to permit the immediate appeal of the class of orders into which the particular interlocutory order falls. These are, of course, the two recommendations of the FCS Committee incorporated into the 1990 and 1992 acts of Congress that prompted this article. Either technique, however, increases rather than decreases litigation over issues of finality or appealability. A litigant aggrieved by an order clearly interlocutory under the classic definition of "final" but potentially falling within the expanded definition of "final" or within the definition of the immediately appealable interlocutory order will take an immediate appeal of the order for one of two reasons. One is because the litigant wants an early review of the order. The second is the litigant's fear that the order will be classified on appeal of the true final judgment as having been appealable immediately when entered but not on appeal from the final judgment, thus losing the right to appellate review of the order.

The collateral order doctrine is a classic example of what happens when a court attempts to loosen the definition of "final." The Supreme Court in *Cohen* gave a clear, three point test for a collateral order, and this test was subsequently restated but not substantively redefined in *Coopers & Lybrand*. These well stated criteria, however, did not reduce litigation. Instead, the criteria have increased litigation because each order that an aggrieved party claims or fears meets the criteria and is thus immediately appealable must be tested by a court of appeals against each of the three criteria, thus multiplying rather than reducing litigation. The same process will occur if the Supreme Court attempts to exercise its new authority to define by rule "final" for purposes of appeal, thus defeating rather than achieving the stated goals of the FCS Committee. Similarly, each statute or rule designating a class of interlocutory orders as immediately appealable has produced litigation over whether a particular order falls within the class.

The Carrington proposal that was the basis for a bill introduced and the subject of a congressional hearing in 1987 is even more problematic than expanding the definition of "final" or the collateral order rule. The proposal combined general language on protecting substantial rights that cannot be effectively enforced on an appeal from a final judgment with the right to an immediate appeal, but it did not provide a basis for predicting in advance whether a court of appeals would find an immediate appeal was necessary. The result can only compound the problems created by the final judgment rule and the present exceptions to it.

An additional problem created by the listing power is the potential for an ever expanding list. The English rules committee has a similar power, stated in terms of classifying orders as final or interlocutory. Orders classified as final are appealable of right and those classified as interlocutory are appealable only in the discretion of the Court of Appeal. The FCS Committee has classified in its rule a total of eight specific types of interlocutory orders as final and thus appealable of right. The FCS Committee also has a broader definition of final that includes orders clearly interlocutory. The Restatement of Interlocutory Appeals in *Law and Contemporary Problems* devotes thirty sections and 152 pages to listing various types of orders that have been held to be final or interlocutory, with many falling into the latter category. It is highly unlikely that the federal rulemakers would be substantially less restrictive. The best evidence of their tendencies are the amendments to Federal Rules of Appellate Procedure 3 and 4 made since 1979. In every instance, the rulemakers have relaxed rather than tightened the procedural requirements for taking an appeal.

An even more fundamental objection to an appealable interlocutory list has been made by Crick, Cooper, Redish, and several student authors. These commentators have pointed out that it is virtually impossible to identify in advance classes or types of interlocutory orders that should be appealable immediately. The type of order that should be appealable immediately will vary from period to period and from case to case, depending upon all of the variables that make one case different from another. It is impossible to predict when in a particular case the relative interests of the parties, the prospects for early termination of the case, or the public significance of the case will dictate the advisability of an earlier rather than later review of an interlocutory order. Thus, attempting to classify interlocutory orders for appeal purposes whether by statute, rule, or judicial decision, can be nothing other than an exercise in futility.

The principal reason advanced by Professor Rowe for authorizing the rulemakers to define "final" and to list certain interlocutory orders as immediately appealable is that the rulemaking process is more responsive to the needs of the courts and those who use them than Congress and the legislative process. Recent criticisms of the rulemaking process at the federal level suggest that while the process may have been responsive once, it is no longer. The process has become more public and thus more political and more time consuming. It is unlikely, consequently, that the rulemaking process will be better able than legislative process to deal with issues of finality and appealability to accomplish the goals stated by the FCS Committee.

As previously discussed, the approach proposed by Crick, Resnik, Dalton, and several judges is at the opposite end of the spectrum—to eliminate completely the right to appeal, and to make all judgments and orders, both final and interlocutory, appealable only in the discretion of the court of appeals. This proposal, of course, would eliminate the confusion over what a final judgment is as well as what classes of interlocutory orders should be appealable immediately. The drawbacks, however, far outweigh the advantages. First and foremost, the proposal would eliminate the right to appeal a final judgment. This right has been a basic part of the American judicial process since colonial times and has been part of the federal judicial system since it was established in 1789. As Judge Frank Coffin has said, the "[opportunity] to take one's case to 'a higher court' as a matter of right is one of the foundation stones of both our state and federal court systems." To do away with this right other than for the most compelling reasons cannot be justified. Eliminating confusion over the final judgment rule and its exceptions is certainly a desirable goal, but it does not call for eliminating the right of appeal if there is a less drastic solution available. Also inappropriate are the suggestions that the courts use their statutory construction powers to expand the meaning of "final" by adopting a "practical" rather than technical definition, use the supervisory writ of mandamus or prohibition to review interlocutory orders not otherwise immediately appealable, or expand the definition of "controlling questions of law" as used in section 1292(b). The final judgment rule is, after all, a policy adopted by Congress to govern the right to appeal. When Congress has felt the need to relax the rule, it has done so. Perhaps it has not acted often enough to satisfy some, and certainly not in such a way as to permit the courts to avoid demonstrable irreparable harm in particular cases. The remedy, however, should be to persuade Congress to allow the courts to prevent irreparable harm or to protect some other important interest, but at the same time to protect both the right to appeal and the final judgment rule. Persuading Congress to allow the rulemakers to accomplish the same objectives merely converts a one step process into a two step process.

Only one proposal satisfies all of these objectives—that contained in section 3.12 of the *ABA Standards Relating to Appellate Courts*[345] and as advocated by Judge Frank, Professor Cooper and a student author. Under the proposal, the right to appeal and the final judgment rule remain intact—there is a right to appeal in every case, but only when the entire case is concluded. At the same time, however, a party aggrieved by an interlocutory order who believes that delaying review of the order until the final judgment would prevent the review from being effective can seek immediate review. A court of appeals would have the discretion to refuse to hear the appeal if it finds that irreparable harm will not occur or that some important interest will not be served if the appeal is not heard immediately. The discretionary appeal thus provides the relief valve in those cases in which strict adherence to the final judgment rule would not serve the best interests of the parties or the public, but with an individualized balancing of interests made on a case by case basis. Just as important, jurisdiction of the appellate court is never an issue, because the court has discretionary jurisdiction over any interlocutory order. No interlocutory appeal will ever be dismissed as premature, and no interlocutory order will ever be unreviewable on appeal from the final judgment because there was an earlier appeal of right.

Several objections can be raised to this proposal. One is that, notwithstanding the opportunity for discretionary review, the courts would still create judicial exceptions to the final judgment rule by defining final in a "practical" manner so as to allow appeals of right from certain types of interlocutory orders. Another is that the courts of appeals would be inundated with applications for leave to appeal interlocutory orders, thus increasing rather than decreasing their workloads. The U.S. Judicial Conference in 1952 made a similar objection in rejecting Judge Frank's proposal. The Conference stated that giving the courts discretion to hear an immediate appeal from any interlocutory order would encourage "fragmentary and frivolous appeals" and lead to delay. A third objection is that the courts of appeals, so burdened with appeals from final judgments, would refuse to hear any interlocutory appeal, no matter how clear a case of irreparable harm was made.

Fortunately, the validity of these objections does not have to be judged on the basis of sheer speculation. Wisconsin adopted the ABA

345. [ABA Comm'n on Standards, of Judicial Admin.] ABA STANDARDS RELATING TO   APPELLATE   COURTS,   § 3.12,   [at   25 (1977)]. . . .

proposal almost word for word in 1978 and thus has had more than thirteen years experience under it.[351] An examination of that experience can demonstrate how the proposal actually works, and whether any of the potential objections to it are valid.

Before the adoption of the ABA proposal in 1978, Wisconsin's law on finality and appealability was similar to current federal law—there was a right to appeal a final judgment, but by virtue of statutory and judicial exceptions, many interlocutory orders could also be appealed of right. Ascertaining what types of interlocutory orders could be appealed, however, was not always easy. To remedy this problem, and as part of the establishment of an intermediate appellate court and a general revision of the statutes and rules governing appeals, Wisconsin adopted the ABA proposal.

* * *

Just as important to an evaluation of the ABA–Wisconsin approach is how the discretionary appeal works in practice. * * *

Cases in which a petition to appeal has been granted have involved issues such as double jeopardy, appointment of counsel in a civil contempt action, jurisdiction over a minor by a juvenile court, a claim that a delinquency petition was untimely, subject matter jurisdiction in an insurance dispute, choice of law, refusal to submit to a blood test as civil contempt, an order compelling testimony of a minor in a child abuse prosecution, constitutionality of judicial substitution statutes, postponement of hearing on a petition to vacate a street, statutory construction, disqualification of a party's attorney, change of venue, discovery, a party's obligation under an installment contract, and the right to bail.

The statistics show several things. One, as compared to appeals of right, the petitions for leave to appeal are a relatively small number, averaging about one petition to appeal for every nine appeals of right. By

---

351. Wis.Stat.Ann. § 808.03 (West Supp.1992). The statute provides for appeals to the court of appeals:

(1) **Appeals as of right.** A final judgment or a final order of a circuit court may be appealed as a matter of right to the court of appeals unless otherwise expressly provided by law. A final judgment or final order is a judgment or order entered in accordance with s. 806.06(1)(b) or 807.11(2) or a disposition recorded in docket entries in ch. 799 cases or traffic regulation or municipal ordinance violation cases prosecuted in circuit court which disposes of the entire matter in litigation as to one or more of the parties, whether rendered in an action or special proceeding.

(2) **Appeals by permission.** A judgment or order not appealable as a matter of right under sub. (1) may be appealed to the court of appeals in advance of a final judgment or order upon leave granted by the court if it determines that an appeal will:

(a) Materially advance the termination of the litigation or clarify further proceedings in the litigation;

(b) Protect the petitioner from substantial or irreparable injury; or

(c) Clarify an issue of general importance in the administration of justice.

Id.

Section 808.03 differs in three respects from the ABA proposal. One is that the section defines "final." The second is that a judgment is final and appealable if it is final as to less than all the parties. The third is that the harm to a party in subsection (2)(b) need be substantial or irreparable, rather than substantial and irreparable. . . .

the same token, the Wisconsin Court of Appeals grants approximately one-third of the petitions, indicating neither an unduly strict nor unduly generous attitude toward interlocutory appeals. The same conclusion can be drawn from the wide range of interlocutory orders that have been reviewed on the merits.

The frivolous appeals that were a concern of the 1952 U.S. Judicial Conference do not appear to be a problem in Wisconsin. In addition, federal courts of appeals have express statutory and rule power as well as inherent power to deal with frivolous appeals, and increasingly have been willing to use that power. Delay also does not appear to be a problem in Wisconsin. Under Wisconsin procedure, a request for an interlocutory appeal must be filed within ten days of entry of the order, and while the request is pending it has no effect on the proceedings in the trial court. Unlike the situation in 1952, federal courts of appeals now utilize motion and administrative panels assisted by staff attorneys to rule on petitions to appeal and various motions. These panels usually act on a petition or motion after review and recommendation by a staff attorney. With this type of process, the additional workload on the judges of the courts of appeals should be marginal, and would be more than offset by the reduction in time spent on questions of finality and appealability. It is significant that the Judicial Conference took its position only three years after the collateral order doctrine had been established in Cohen and before the courts of appeals began using the doctrine as an easy way to avoid the final judgment rule. Further, the courts of appeals had not yet had experience with discretionary appeals under section 1292(b), which was not enacted until 1958.

* * *

The ABA–Wisconsin approach, on the other hand, recognizes what Judge Frank and commentators such as Crick, Redish, and Cooper as well as student commentators have long recognized—that it is impossible to predict in advance those classes of cases in which an appeal before final judgment should be permitted. Crick pointed out that the nature of the harm and its immediacy will vary from case to case. He further decried the time and effort devoted to determining whether a particular order met the definition of "final." His solution to eliminate the right to appeal and to make all appeals discretionary with the appellate court, however, is overly drastic and unnecessary. The ABA–Wisconsin approach is far superior because it maintains both the right to appeal and the final judgment rule, but allows a court of appeals the flexibility to weigh the relative benefits and harm to the opposing parties and the public interests of allowing an immediate appeal of an interlocutory order versus delaying the appeal until the final judgment is entered.

In addition to allowing a discretionary appeal to avoid irreparable harm, the ABA–Wisconsin approach has two additional criteria, either of which will authorize a discretionary appeal. One criterion permits a discretionary appeal if it will materially advance termination of the litigation or clarify further proceedings. The other criterion permits an early appeal to clarify an issue of general importance in the administration of justice. Essentially the first criterion is, like the irreparable harm test, focused on the parties to the litigation. The criterion also encompasses the interests of the trial court and the other litigants in the court. Advancing the termination of one case not only benefits the parties to that case but also parties to other cases then pending or which may be filed in the same court, because the speed with which one case is terminated determines when the trial court can devote its time to other cases. The primary focus of the second criterion, on the other hand, is not the parties to the lawsuit or litigants generally, but some broader public interest. The case could involve a bond issue, an election dispute, separation of powers, the environment, a procedural or evidentiary rule, national defense, or the like. The ABA–Wisconsin system thus allows significant flexibility while strictly adhering to the final judgment rule.

Notes and Questions

1.   What are the different philosophies of appealability represented by the different proposals discussed? What is the basis on which one approach should be chosen over others?

2.   Based on the readings in this chapter, is it practical to attempt to regulate appealability by statute, rule, or judicial opinion?

3.   For further discussion of these issues, see Glynn, Discontent and Indiscretion: Discretionary Review of Interlocutory Orders, 77 Notre Dame L. Rev. 175 (2001); Note, Replacing the Crazy Quilt of Interlocutory Appeals Jurisprudence with Discretionary Review, 44 Duke L.J. 200 (1994).

Chapter 4

PARTIES AND NON–PARTIES
TO THE APPEAL

SECTION A.   PARTIES IN THE TRIAL
COURT AND ON APPEAL

The simple scenario is this: any party who has lost at least part of the case in the trial court can seek to appeal. This Chapter explores several facets of what that simple model actually means in practice. It is also important to recognize that there are actually several different forms of participation in an appeal. It turns out that the consequences of the decision to participate in one form or another in an appeal—or to stand aside—are not intuitively obvious.

Being "a party" in a litigation normally means being a named plaintiff or a named defendant, and thus an active participant. "Named" in this context means that a party is identified in the caption of the plaintiff's pleading. Named plaintiffs are those who have joined to commence the suit, thus subjecting themselves to the jurisdiction of the court in seeking an adjudication of rights and responsibilities. Party defendants are those listed in the pleadings as the defendants and who have actually been served with process—thus making them subject to the power and jurisdiction of the court where the action is pending.

Parties must comply with discovery obligations and all of the court system's procedural statutes and rules, and they are subject to the binding effects of the eventual judgment. Once a final judgment is entered, any party to the case who is "aggrieved" by the outcome may seek an appeal.

1.   THE "GENERAL RULE"

It is often said that only parties to the case in the trial court can appeal to a higher tribunal. It turns out that there are exceptions, but as a general rule this proposition is surely correct.

UNITED STATES v. LTV CORP.

United States Court of Appeals, District of Columbia Circuit, 1984.
746 F.2d 51.

On Motions to Dismiss

Per Curiam.

The LTV Corporation ("LTV") and Republic Steel Corporation ("Republic") announced plans for a merger in September of 1983 whereby LTV would acquire all the assets of Republic. In February 1984, the Justice Department, having concluded an investigation of the proposed merger, indicated that it would seek to have the transaction enjoined as violative of the federal antitrust laws. The two companies and the Justice Department then entered into negotiations, the upshot of which was that LTV and Republic agreed to modify the transaction to avoid the Department's antitrust concerns. In accordance with the negotiated settlement, on March 21, 1984, the United States filed in United States District Court for the District of Columbia both a civil antitrust complaint challenging the acquisition of Republic by LTV as a violation of Section 7 of the Clayton Act, 15 U.S.C. § 18, and a proposed consent decree. Notice of the proposed settlement was issued in compliance with the Antitrust Procedures and Penalties Act, 15 U.S.C. § 16(b)–(h) ("APPA") ("the Tunney Act").

During the ensuing months, several companies participated in APPA proceedings designed to elicit comments on the proposed settlement. Appellant Wheeling–Pittsburgh Steel Corporation ("Wheeling") moved to participate in those proceedings. In particular, Wheeling sought to examine government materials with respect to the Justice Department's change in position as to the legality of the merger. The district court permitted Wheeling to participate in the proceedings, but denied Wheeling's request to compel discovery from the United States. Wheeling did not appeal this ruling. In expressing its interest in participating in the APPA proceedings, Wheeling clearly indicated to the district court that it did not intend to move for status as an intervenor under Fed.R.Civ.P. 24.[3]

On August 2, 1984, the district court issued a memorandum opinion which concluded that entry of the proposed final judgment was in the public interest, and the court accordingly entered final judgment approving the merger. Wheeling did not, however, move to intervene for purposes of appeal from the judgment. Instead, Wheeling filed a notice of appeal from the judgment on August 31, 1984. The United States and LTV now move to dismiss Wheeling's appeal on the ground that Wheel-

---

3. See Motion of Wheeling–Pittsburgh Steel Corporation to Participate in Proceedings and to Compel Compliance with the Antitrust Procedures and Penalties Act at 3 (April 6, 1984) "Wheeling does not seek the status of an intervenor under the Federal Rules of Civil Procedure, nor is this a request to participate as an *amicus curiae*."); Transcript of hearing of May 1, 1984, at 11 ("THE COURT: Are you petitioning to intervene? MR. FERGUSON [counsel for Wheeling]: No sir, we are not.").

ing was not a party to the proceedings below. We hold that, because Wheeling never sought to and did not become a party below, its appeal must be dismissed.

"It has long been settled that one who is not a party to a record and judgment is not entitled to appeal therefrom." United States v. Seigel, 168 F.2d 143, 144 (D.C. Cir. 1948); see also Fed.R.App.P. 3(c) ("The notice of appeal shall specify the *party* or *parties* taking the appeal.") (emphasis added). Parties to the record include the original parties and those who have become parties by intervention, substitution, or third-party practice. In this case, Wheeling's only avenue for becoming a party in the district court was by intervention.

Wheeling did not automatically acquire party status simply by being permitted to comment on the proposed final judgment or by filing its notice of appeal. In Moten v. Bricklayers, Masons & Plasterers, 543 F.2d 224 (D.C. Cir. 1976), for example, a black local union brought suit, alleging discrimination by a white local and an international union. An employers' association appeared at hearings on a proposed settlement of the suit, but never sought to become a party. See id. at 227. Because the association had not sought intervention as a party, this court held that "they stand in a relationship analogous to that of an amicus curiae.... As amicus curiae may not appeal from a final judgment, the appeal ... must be dismissed for want of jurisdiction." Id.

Wheeling does not contend that it ever became a party to the government antitrust lawsuit. Nor does Wheeling dispute the general rule that an appellant must be a party to the proceedings in order to file an appeal. Rather, Wheeling asserts that this general rule contains numerous exceptions, and requires only that the appellant be privy to the record and be aggrieved by the order appealed from. Wheeling also contends that in any event the APPA changes the operation of the rule against nonparty appeals in cases to which that Act applies.

There are indeed exceptions to the general rule but none is relevant to this appeal. The examples Wheeling cites involve appeals from orders which effectively bound a non-party despite its lack of party status in the trial court.[5] The final judgment in this case, however, does not foreclose

---

5. Wheeling relies on two types of cases. The first involved non-party appeals from consent judgments and other final judgments in shareholder's derivative suits and class actions. See, e.g., Tryforos v. Icarian Dev. Co., 518 F.2d 1258 (7th Cir. 1975), cert. denied, 423 U.S. 1091, 96 S.Ct. 887, 47 L.Ed.2d 103 (1976); Research Corp. v. Asgrow Seed Co., 425 F.2d 1059 (7th Cir. 1970); Cohen v. Young, 127 F.2d 721 (6th Cir. 1942). However, judgments in such cases bind shareholders and non-party class members who have received notice of the pendency of the actions. See, e.g., Nathan v. Rowan, 651 F.2d 1223, 1226 (6th Cir. 1981); Fowler v. Birmingham News Co., 608 F.2d 1055, 1058 (5th Cir. 1979). In *Research Corp.*, supra, for example, the court noted that, because judgments rendered in class actions bind non-party class members "[i]f a class member intervenes or even appears in response to a notice * * * and objects to the dismissal or compromise, he has a right to appeal. * * *" 425 F.2d at 1060 (citations omitted).

The other set of cases Wheeling relies upon involved collateral disputes which arose subsequent to the entry of an antitrust decree. See, e.g., United States v. ASCAP, 442 F.2d 601 (2d Cir. 1971) (appeal by non-party to original judgment from injunction against prosecution of collateral chal-

other means of challenging the proposed merger, such as a private antitrust suit. Moreover, Wheeling points to no examples of non-parties permitted to appeal from the entry of a consent judgment under the Tunney Act.

More generally, Wheeling cites a leading treatise for the proposition that the rule requiring an appellant to be a party to the proceedings below is not formalistic, but functional, requiring only that the appellant be "privy to the record" and be "aggrieved by the order appealed from." 9 Moore's *Federal Practice* ¶ 203.06 at 3–20 (1980). This comment, however, in context relates to the exceptions just discussed.[6] Moreover, even on a functional analysis, the general rule against non-party appeals serves a useful purpose in cases like this. Under the rule, those who object to the entry of a consent judgment must seek to intervene in the proceedings (either before or after entry of the judgment) as a condition of taking an appeal. To gain status as an intervenor, the would-be appellant must first establish that participation by the intervenor would aid the court in making its public interest determination under the APPA.[7] Courts of appeals may, of course, review district court orders on intervention in such cases under an abuse of discretion standard.[8] Under this procedure, the responsibility for determining when intervention by one who objects to the entry of a consent judgment should be permitted falls, as it should, to the trial court in the first instance.[9]

lenge to original judgment); United States v. United Fruit Co., 410 F.2d 553 (5th Cir.) (appeal by non-party to original judgment from order sealing documents discovered in course of original proceedings), cert. denied, 396 U.S. 820, 90 S.Ct. 59, 24 L.Ed.2d 71 (1969). The appellants in these cases were also effectively bound by the original judgment.

Finally, Wheeling cites Matter of Penn Cent. Transp. Co., 596 F.2d 1155 (3d Cir.), cert. denied, 444 U.S. 835, 100 S.Ct. 68, 62 L.Ed.2d 45 (1979). That case, a bankruptcy proceeding, referred to an exception to the requirement of party status: "Failure to seek intervenor status would not, however, be fatal to this appeal if appellants had a right to be heard in the proceedings below." Id. at 1160. The court, however, was speaking of persons who have the right to be heard precisely because they are essential parties to the bankruptcy proceedings. Id. at 1159 (citing 11 U.S.C. § 205(c)(13)) ("The debtor, any creditor or stockholder, * * * shall have the right to be heard on all questions arising in the proceedings. * * *").

6. See cases discussed supra at note 5. Moore's treatise cites other exceptions to the general rule.

7. See e.g., United States v. Hartford–Empire Co., 573 F.2d 1, 2 (6th Cir. 1978)

("A private party generally will not be permitted to intervene in government antitrust litigation absent some strong showing that the government is not vigorously and faithfully representing the public interest."); accord, United States v. Associated Milk Producers, Inc., 534 F.2d 113 (8th Cir.), cert. denied, 429 U.S. 940, 97 S.Ct. 355, 50 L.Ed.2d 309 (1976); United States v. G. Heileman Brewing Co., 563 F.Supp. 642, 649 (D.Del.1983); United States v. The Stroh Brewing Co., 1982–2 Trade Cas. (CCH) ¶ 64,804 at 71,960 (D.D.C. June 4, 1982).

8. See e.g., United States v. Am. Cyanamid Co., 719 F.2d 558, 563 (2d Cir. 1983) (indicating that district court decision whether leave to intervene permissively should be granted can only be overturned if it constitutes abuse of discretion), cert. denied, ___ U.S. ___, 104 S.Ct. 1596, 80 L.Ed.2d 127 (1984); United States v. Am. Tel. & Tel. Co., 642 F.2d 1285, 1290 (D.C. Cir. 1980) (same).

9. This procedure will not, as Wheeling suggests, foreclose all appellate review of antitrust consent judgments. Objectors to a consent judgment may seek to intervene in the proceedings for the limited purpose of appeal. See e.g., United States v. Western Elec. Co., Inc., 578 F.Supp. 677, 678 (D.D.C. 1983); United States v. Am. Tel. & Tel. Co.,

The language and the legislative history of the APPA do not alter our view. Nothing in the language of the Act indicates that Congress intended to change the general rule.[10] Indeed, the procedure authorized by the Act, which grants the district courts discretion in determining who may intervene in proceedings under the Act, is entirely consistent with the general rule under the Federal Rules of Civil Procedure. Moreover, given that an important purpose of the Act was to preserve the consent judgment as a method of resolving government antitrust cases, it would be anomalous to conclude that Congress intended to permit persons who had not even attempted to intervene in the proceedings to appeal, and thereby disrupt, the entry of a final consent judgment.

Finally, Wheeling suggests that the court should apply any adverse ruling in this case prospectively, inasmuch as, in Wheeling's view, it had no basis on which to anticipate this result. Yet Wheeling does not dispute that the general rule requires it first to seek to become a party to the proceedings before taking an appeal. Nor does Wheeling cite any precedent in this or any other court recognizing an exception from the general rule in APPA cases.[12] Moreover, Wheeling was given an opportunity to seek to intervene in the proceedings below, an offer which it specifically declined. These circumstances do not justify disregarding the general principle that prospective applications of rules are only rarely granted.[13]

For these reasons, it is ORDERED by the court that the appeal of Wheeling–Pittsburgh Steel Corporation is dismissed.

552 F.Supp. 131 (D.D.C.1982), aff'd sub nom. Maryland v. United States, 460 U.S. 1001, 103 S.Ct. 1240, 75 L.Ed.2d 472 (1983) (summary affirmance).

10. The Act provides, in relevant part, 15 U.S.C. § 16(f):

[T]he court may * * * authorize full or limited participation in proceedings before the court by interested persons or agencies, including appearances amicus curiae, intervention as a party pursuant to the Federal Rules of Civil Procedure, examination of witnesses or documentary materials, or participation in any other manner and extent which serves the public interest as the court may deem appropriate.

12. The district court in United States v. Am. Tel. & Tel. Co., 552 F.Supp. 131 (D.D.C.1982) aff'd sub nom. Maryland v. United States, 460 U.S. 1001, 103 S.Ct. 1240, 75 L.Ed.2d 472 (1983) (summary affirmance) followed the intervention procedure in an APPA case, allowing those who objected to a consent decree to become parties for the limited purposes of an appeal. Moreover, in the district court in this case, another participant in the comment proceedings, Cyclops Corporation, unsuccessfully sought intervention for purposes of taking an appeal.

13. See Railroad Yardmasters of America v. Harris, 721 F.2d 1332, 1347 (D.C.Cir. 1983) (Wald, J., dissenting) ("Even when a court applies a new rule of law prospectively only, it generally applies the rule to the case before it.") (citing cases); Johnson v. Lehman, 679 F.2d 918, 920 (D.C.Cir. 1982) (prospective applications of rules reserved for instances of "manifest injustice") (citing cases).

MICROSYSTEMS SOFTWARE, INC.
v. SCANDINAVIA ONLINE AB

United States Court of Appeals, First Circuit, 2000.
226 F.3d 35.

SELYA, CIRCUIT JUDGE.

This appeal trails in the wake of a permanent injunction entered by the United States District Court for the District of Massachusetts that restrained the named defendants—Eddy L.O. Jansson, Matthew Skala, and the companies that host their respective web pages (Scandinavia Online AB and Islandnet.com)—and "their agents, employees, and all persons in active concert or participation" with them from publishing or otherwise using a bypass code known as "cp4break.zip" or "cphack.exe." The named defendants stipulated to the entry of the injunction, but three nonparties—Waldo Jaquith, Lindsay Haisley, and Bennett Haselton—now attempt to appeal. They claim to have copied the proscribed code from the named defendants' web pages and assert that the injunction impermissibly interferes with their right to continue posting it on their "mirror sites."

Although this proceeding takes place against the futuristic backdrop of cyberspace, its resolution lies in traditional principles of standing. Application of those principles requires us to terminate the attempted appeal. Consequently, we have no occasion to reach the tangled issues of copyright and First Amendment law that simmer beneath the surface of the appellants' plaints.

I. BACKGROUND

The plaintiffs, Microsystems Software, Inc. and Mattel, Inc. (collectively, Microsystems), developed and distributed "Cyber Patrol"—a blocking device coveted by parents who wish to prevent their children from roaming into salacious Internet venues. This software program contains a secret list of objectionable web sites and, once installed, prevents computer users from accessing those sites.

It is said that every action produces an equal, yet opposite, reaction. So it was here: shortly after Microsystems introduced Cyber Patrol, Jansson and Skala reverse-engineered it and wrote a bypass code that enabled users not only to thwart the program but also to gain access to the list of blocked sites.[1] They then posted the bypass code on their own web sites and gave blanket permission for others to copy it. The appellants took advantage of this offer.

Microsystems was not pleased. [I]t brought suit seeking injunctive relief against the defendants and "those persons in active concert or

---

1. "Reverse engineering" involves gaining access to the functional elements of a software program. Methods of reverse engineering include observing the program in operation, performing a static or dynamic examination of the individual computer in-structions contained within the program, and using a program known as a disassembler to translate the binary machine-readable object code that runs on the computer into the human-readable words and symbols known as source code.

participation with them." Microsystems complained that it was suffering irreparable injury because "multiple individuals throughout the United States and the world ... have downloaded, copied and created 'mirror' Web sites" revealing the bypass code. When the district court issued a temporary restraining order two days later, Microsystems e-mailed copies of it, along with sundry supporting documents, to various persons (including the appellants). Its cover letter stated in pertinent part:

> On March 17, 2000, United States District Judge Edward Harrington entered a temporary restraining order ... prohibiting any further publication of "CP4break.sip" or "cphack.exe" or any derivative thereof, which likely violate United States copyright laws ... It has come to our attention that your Web hosting service or Web site is publishing one or both of those prohibited files. This letter and the enclosed Word documents and *uni files will place you on notice of Judge Harrington's order.

Microsystems also served the appellants with subpoenas directing them to disclose information concerning the identity of "each and every person who produced, received, viewed, downloaded or accessed [the bypass code] or any derivative thereof from your Web site or Web site hosting service."

The appellants promptly removed the bypass code from their web sites. They then filed special appearances in the pending case and, without submitting to the court's jurisdiction, moved to quash the subpoenas. They also proffered oppositions to the pending motion for preliminary injunction. Notably, however, they did not move to intervene.

On March 24, the district court granted the motion to quash. Three days later, the court held a hearing on the motion for preliminary injunction. At that session, Microsystems advised the court that it had reached an accord with the named defendants and proffered a proposed final decree that purported to prohibit the defendants and those persons "in active concert" with them from posting the bypass code. Notwithstanding the appellants' nonparty status, the district court allowed them to argue in opposition to the entry of the injunction and to file a supplemental memorandum. The appellants submitted this memorandum on March 28. Later that day, the court entered the permanent injunction, accompanying it with findings of fact and conclusions of law.

Microsystems lost no time in furnishing the appellants with notice of the injunction. The appellants unsuccessfully sought a stay—the district court denied it, declaring that they had "no standing to pursue any appeal ... in view of the fact that they had never intervened in the case"—and simultaneously filed a notice of appeal.

II. ANALYSIS

The existence vel non of appellate standing calls for a quintessentially legal judgment, to be made without deference to the trial court's view. See In re Cusumano, 162 F.3d 708, 713 (1st Cir. 1998). Because standing is a sine qua non to the prosecution of a suit in a federal court, the absence of standing sounds the death knell for a case. See Sea Shore Corp. v. Sullivan, 158 F.3d 51, 54 (1st Cir. 1998). The same holds true for appeals: if the putative appellants lack standing to appeal, the only role for the appellate court is to memorialize that fact and simultaneously terminate the proceeding. See Warth v. Seldin, 422 U.S. 490, 498–99, 45 L. Ed. 2d 343, 95 S. Ct. 2197 (1975); United States v. AVX Corp., 962 F.2d 108, 113 (1st Cir. 1992).

As a general rule, only parties to a civil action are permitted to appeal from a final judgment. See Marino v. Ortiz, 484 U.S. 301, 304, 98 L. Ed. 2d 629, 108 S. Ct. 586 (1988) (per curiam). The Supreme Court, in its most recent pronouncement on the subject, has described this rule as "well settled." Id. History confirms the accuracy of that description. See, e.g., Karcher v. May, 484 U.S. 72, 77, 98 L. Ed. 2d 327, 108 S. Ct. 388 (1987); United States ex rel. Louisiana v. Jack, 244 U.S. 397, 402, 61 L. Ed. 1222, 37 S. Ct. 605 (1917); Ex parte Leaf Tobacco Bd. of Trade, 222 U.S. 578, 581, 56 L. Ed. 323, 32 S. Ct. 833 (1911) (per curiam); Ex parte Cockcroft, 104 U.S. (14 Otto) 578, 578–79, 26 L. Ed. 856 (1882); Ex parte Cutting, 94 U.S. (4 Otto) 14, 20–21, 24 L. Ed. 49 (1877); Dopp v. HTP Corp., 947 F.2d 506, 512 (1st Cir. 1991).

For purposes of the "only a party may appeal" rule, the term "party" includes not only those who are parties in the case when judgment is entered, but also those who properly become parties (as, say, by intervention). See *Marino,* 484 U.S. at 304. The term sometimes encompasses those who "have acted or been recognized as parties," but by some oversight were not formally made parties. *Ex parte Cutting,* 94 U.S. at 20–21; see also Sangre de Cristo Community Mental Health Serv. v. United States (In re Vargas), 723 F.2d 1461, 1464 (10th Cir. 1983). Finally, the term also extends, in limited circumstances, to those who were parties "to some earlier judgment called into question by the appeal." *Dopp,* 947 F.2d at 512. The appellants plainly do not qualify as parties under any of these definitions.

Of course, exceptions exist to virtually every rule, and courts, from time to time, have endeavored to craft exceptions to the rule that only parties may appeal from an adverse judgment. By and large, the Supreme Court has been inhospitable to these endeavors. *Marino* illustrates the point. In the underlying case, the Second Circuit had dismissed an appeal taken by nonparties, but suggested in dictum that there were several exceptions to the rule that only parties may appeal from an adverse judgment. See Hispanic Soc'y of New York City Police Dep't v. New York City Police Dep't, 806 F.2d 1147, 1152 (2d Cir. 1986). Although the *Marino* Court subsequently affirmed the judgment, it took pains to add a caveat:

> The Court of Appeals suggested that there may be exceptions to this general rule, primarily "when the nonparty has an interest that is affected by the trial court's judgment." 806 F.2d at 1152. We think

the better practice is for such a nonparty to seek intervention for purposes of appeal.

484 U.S. at 304.

We believe that this message is reasonably clear. While there is an exception to the "only a party may appeal" rule that allows a nonparty to appeal the denial of a motion to intervene, see id., the situation differs when intervention is readily available. In that event, courts are powerless to extend a right of appeal to a nonparty who abjures intervention. See Felzen v. Andreas, 134 F.3d 873, 874 (7th Cir. 1998), aff'd sub nom. by an equally divided Court, California Pub. Employees' Retirement Sys. v. Felzen, 525 U.S. 315, 142 L. Ed. 2d 766, 119 S. Ct. 720 (1999).[3]

The appellants labor to convince us that, *Marino* notwithstanding, we ought to recognize a long string of exceptions to the rule mandating party status as a prerequisite to an appeal. We are not persuaded. *Marino*, as we read it, teaches that if any exceptions to the rule exist, those exceptions are few and far between.

Turning from the general to the specific, we address the appellants' principal arguments. First, they venerate our statement that "when a lower court specifically directs an order at a non-party or enjoins it from a course of conduct," the nonparty may enjoy a right to appeal. *Dopp*, 947 F.2d at 512 (dictum). They then note that the injunction in this case purports to bind not only the named defendants but also "those persons in active concert or participation" with them. Using this phrase as a springboard, they jump to the conclusion that the injunction was specifically directed at them, and claim that it therefore fits within the *Dopp* dictum. We reject this construct.

To state the obvious, a dictum is not a holding—and the *Dopp* dictum may be no more than mere buzznacking. We need not probe that point too deeply, however, because, even if we assume for argument's sake that the *Dopp* dictum has some force, the resultant exception, narrow in all events, see id. (describing exception as "isthmian"), would not apply at all in this case. The boilerplate terminology contained in the instant injunction merely parrots the language of Federal Rule of Civil Procedure 65(d).[4] So phrased, the injunction in no way attains the degree of specificity necessary to open the gates to the potential exception that Dopp envisioned. Cf. Keith v. Volpe, 118 F.3d 1386, 1391 n.7 (9th Cir. 1997) (holding that a nonparty who was haled into court to respond to a show-cause order had appellate standing in a subsequent appeal of that order).

---

3. An affirmance by an equally divided court denies precedential force to the opinion in question. See Rutledge v. United States, 517 U.S. 292, 304, 134 L. Ed. 2d 419, 116 S. Ct. 1241 (1996). It does not, however, tarnish earlier opinions.

4. That rule provides in pertinent part that all orders granting injunctive relief shall bind "the parties to the action, their officers, agents, servants, employees, and attorneys, and ... those persons in active concert or participation with them who receive actual notice...." Fed. R. Civ. P. 65(d) .

In a related vein, the appellants assert that the lower court's findings of fact propel them into a safe harbor. In particular, they note the court's finding that "multiple individuals throughout Massachusetts and the United States downloaded, copied and created 'mirror' sites on the internet, which replicated the Bypass Code," and that "many ... did so for the avowed purpose of seeking to prevent [the district court] from awarding meaningful relief." This finding, they say, specifically directs the injunction at them. But this line of argumentation elevates hope over reason. The description "multiple individuals throughout the United States" is breathtakingly broad. There is nothing in the record that limits its application to the appellants or that aims the court's ukase in their direction.

The appellants next attempt to lure us into weighing the equities of the case, asseverating that it is unfair to force them into a judicial proceeding and then prevent them from prosecuting an appeal. We have two rejoinders, either of which is fully dispositive of the matter.

First and foremost, the appellants' asseveration is a doctrinal misfit. Although it draws some sustenance from the case law, see, e.g., Commodity Futures Trading Comm'n v. Topworth Int'l, Ltd., 205 F.3d 1107, 1113 (9th Cir. 2000), the asseveration overlooks the abecedarian principle that a court that lacks adjudicatory power has no authority over a case. See Steel Co. v. Citizens for a Better Environment, 523 U.S. 83, 94, 118 S. Ct. 1003, 140 L. Ed. 2d 210 (1998); Ex parte McCardle, 74 U.S. (7 Wall.) 506, 514, 19 L. Ed. 264 (1868). Since standing is jurisdictional in nature, that principle dictates that where, as here, the putative appellants lack standing, the court lacks power to assay and reconcile the equities of the case. See *Felzen*, 134 F.3d at 877–78. Consequently, equitable considerations are immaterial to our determination of the standing issue.

Second—and equally devastating to the appellants' position—the equities do not favor permitting them to appeal. After entering the proceedings in a successful effort to quash the subpoenas that had been served upon them, the appellants did not quit the field victorious, but, rather, elected to expand their role and contest the merits of the case before the district court. At the same time, they made a strategic choice not to intervene in the proceedings. By intervening, see Fed. R. Civ. P. 24, the appellants could have become parties, entitled to both that status's benefits (including the right to appeal an unfavorable judgment) and its burdens.

In our view, the decision to forgo intervention works a forfeiture of any claim to appellate standing. Those who aspire to litigate issues cannot have it both ways: they cannot evade potential liability by declining to seek party status and still expect to be treated as parties for the purpose of testing the validity of an ensuing decree.[6] Cf. United

---

6. To be sure, the appellants complain that they were put between a rock and a hard place because intervention would have forced them to waive their jurisdictional defenses and submit to the district court's jurisdiction. But this seems to be another

States v. Tierney, 760 F.2d 382, 388 (1st Cir. 1985) ("Having one's cake and eating it, too, is not in fashion in this circuit.").

Moving ahead, the appellants maintain that they should be permitted to appeal because they have an interest that is affected by the district court's judgment and they were permitted to vindicate that interest by participating in the proceedings below. Some courts have recognized exceptions to the "only a party may appeal" rule in analogous cases. See, e.g., Kaplan v. Rand, 192 F.3d 60, 66–67 (2d Cir. 1999). To the extent that these cases are authority for the appellants' position, we respectfully decline to follow them. A mere interest in the outcome of litigation will not suffice to confer standing upon a nonparty. See *Marino,* 484 U.S. at 304; *Felzen,* 134 F.3d at 874; J.A. Shults v. Champion Int'l Corp., 35 F.3d 1056, 1060 (6th Cir. 1994); see also Guthrie v. Evans, 815 F.2d 626, 627 (11th Cir. 1987). As we have said, "the fact that an order has an indirect or incidental effect on a non-party does not confer standing to appeal. If the rule were otherwise, Pandora's jar would be open, and strangers to a litigated case could pop in and out of the proceedings virtually at will." *Dopp,* 947 F.2d at 512.

By the same token, mere participation in the proceedings below will not suffice to confer standing upon a nonparty. After all, the officers who became the nonparty appellants in Hispanic Society participated in the proceedings before the district court, see 806 F.2d at 1152, but the Supreme Court found that they lacked standing to appeal, see *Marino,* 484 U.S. at 304; see also Croyden Assocs. v. Alleco, Inc., 969 F.2d 675, 679 (8th Cir. 1992) (noting that the Marino Court did not perceive the Marino appellants' participation in the proceedings below as warranting an exception to the general rule). Thus, we reject the appellants' claim that participation below, even if coupled with an indirect interest in the judgment sought to be appealed, confers standing.

Ably represented, the appellants take yet another tack. They remonstrate that if they are not permitted to appeal at this juncture, they will forfeit any opportunity to contest the injunction on the merits. In their view, this would deprive them of due process.

This argument has a certain superficial allure, because "the validity and terms of an injunction [ordinarily] are not reviewable in contempt proceedings." G. & C. Merriam Co. v. Webster Dictionary Co., 639 F.2d 29, 34 (1st Cir. 1980). This rule applies both to those who were parties to the underlying case, see, e.g., NLRB v. Union Nacional de Trabajadores, 611 F.2d 926, 928 n.1 (1st Cir. 1979), and to nonparties in active concert

way of saying that they made a calculated decision that the injunction sought by Microsystems would not aggrieve them enough to warrant taking whatever risks were attendant to intervention. There is nothing remotely unfair about being put in that position. Litigation strategies almost always involve balancing of risk and reward, and the fundamental rationale behind the "no intervention, no appeal" rule counsels in favor of holding the appellants to the predictable consequences of their strategic choice. See *Dopp,* 947 F.2d at 512; Kenny v. Quigg, 820 F.2d 665, 667 (4th Cir. 1987).

or participation with the enjoined party, see, e.g., NBA Props., Inc. v. Gold, 895 F.2d 30, 33–34 (1st Cir. 1990).

The attractiveness of the appellants' argument diminishes rather rapidly, however, when one recalls that the appellants filed two memoranda with the district court and contested the merits of the injunction at a hearing. More importantly, they had every opportunity to intervene and purposefully declined to do so. In these circumstances, whatever predicament they envision is of their own construction.

Even if more were needed—and we doubt that it is—the adjudicative framework surrounding contempt proceedings fully protects nonparties' constitutional rights. If contempt proceedings are in fact undertaken, the forum court will resolve the fact-specific question of whether the cited nonparty was in active concert or participation with the named defendant. If so, the named defendant will be deemed the nonparty's agent, and the nonparty's right to due process will have been satisfied vicariously. See *Merriam*, 639 F.2d at 35; Alemite Mfg. Corp. v. Staff, 42 F.2d 832, 832–33 (2d Cir. 1930) (L. Hand, J.). If, however, the party prosecuting the contempt proceeding fails to show active concert or participation, a finding of contempt will not lie. See Zenith Radio Corp. v. Hazeltine Research, Inc., 395 U.S. 100, 112, 23 L. Ed. 2d 129, 89 S. Ct. 1562 (1969); *Merriam*, 639 F.2d at 35.

We explain briefly why, in either of these events, due process is not at risk. Contempt proceedings operate to ensure that nonparties have had their day in court. In order to hold a nonparty in contempt, a court first must determine that she was in active concert or participation with the party specifically enjoined (typically, the named defendant). See *Merriam*, 639 F.2d at 35; *Alemite*, 42 F.2d at 832–33. This means, of course, that the nonparty must be legally identified with that defendant, or, at least, deemed to have aided and abetted that defendant in the enjoined conduct. See *Merriam*, 639 F.2d at 35; *Alemite*, 42 F.2d at 832–33. The existence of such a linkage makes it fair to bind the nonparty, even if she has not had a separate opportunity to contest the original injunction, because her close alliance with the enjoined defendant adequately assures that her interests were sufficiently represented. See *NBA Props.*, 895 F.2d at 33; *Merriam*, 639 F.2d at 37; cf. Regal Knitwear Co. v. NLRB, 324 U.S. 9, 14, 89 L. Ed. 661, 65 S. Ct. 478 (1945) ("Defendants may not nullify a decree by carrying out prohibited acts through aiders and abettors, although they were not parties to the original proceeding.").

The coin, however, has a flip side. A nonparty who has acted independently of the enjoined defendant will not be bound by the injunction, and, if she has had no opportunity to contest its validity, cannot be found in contempt without a separate adjudication. See id.; see also *Alemite*, 42 F.2d at 832 (declaring that a decree which purports to enjoin nonparties who are neither abettors nor legally identified with the defendant "is pro tanto brutum fulmen," and may safely be ignored).

This tried and true dichotomy safeguards the rights of those who truly are strangers to an injunctive decree. It does not offend due process.

III.   CONCLUSION

To summarize, we hold that nonparties who have had the opportunity to seek intervention, but have eschewed that course, lack standing to appeal. See *Marino*, 484 U.S. at 304; *Dopp*, 947 F.2d at 512. While there may be isolated exceptions to this rule—a matter on which we take no view—the instant appeal falls comfortably within the mainstream. Because the appellants lack standing, we can go no further.

Appeal dismissed. Costs in favor of plaintiffs-appellees.

Notes and Questions

1.   Is the rule that requires a person to be a party simply a technical procedural requirement or is there a substantive basis for it? Did the court in the principal cases consider it one or the other or both? What would be the harm in allowing any person who felt affected by the judgment in the trial court to appeal from the judgment without the necessity of intervention?

2.   Modern usage refers simply to parties. Another traditional term for this status was "party to the record." Party status includes the named plaintiffs and defendants. If not initially named as a party, how does a person become a party to the record? Amendment of the pleadings to add a person as a named party is a common development in modern litigation. If no existing party sponsors an amendment of the prior pleadings, must the person seeking party status always do so formally by filing a motion to intervene, for example, or are there less formal ways to do so? Can a person be bound by a judgment and still not be permitted to take an appeal?

3.   The principal cases would appear to require intervention in the trial court before an appeal can be taken by a person not formally a party. There are, however, exceptions. In United States v. Chagra, 701 F.2d 354, 359–60 (5th Cir. 1983), the court held that a newspaper and a reporter, though not parties to a criminal case, could appeal an order closing a pretrial bail reduction hearing. The court listed some exceptions to the general rule:

> Thus, a non-party may appeal orders for discovery if he has no other effective means of obtaining review. Similarly, non-parties have been allowed to appeal orders granting or denying further disclosure of documents already in the possession of a court or grand jury. Non-party creditors who assert rights in receivership proceedings may appeal orders affecting their legitimate interests. If an injunction extends to non-parties, they may appeal from it. Similarly, a non-party may generally appeal an order holding him in civil contempt. Attorneys and experts, though non-parties, may sometimes appeal orders relating to their fees. Finally, unindicted co-conspirators may appeal an order refusing to strike their names from the indictment.

> The courts differ on whether the media, though not parties to a case, may appeal closure orders or must seek other avenues of review. Some, including ours, have allowed such appeals. Others allow an appeal

after one of the media has "intervened" in the underlying action for the purpose of challenging the closure order. * * *

Other courts, noting that non-parties may not generally appeal, hold that closure orders are reviewable only on petition for writs of prohibition or mandamus.[14] In the District of Columbia, a motion filed by the press objecting to a closure order is treated as initiating a separate miscellaneous civil proceeding. Taking yet another approach, the court in State v. Bianchi, 92 Wash.2d 91, 92–93, 593 P.2d 1330, 1331 (1979) (en banc), indicated that closure orders could be challenged by a separate action for declaratory judgment, mandamus, or prohibition.

The rule previously adopted by this circuit compels our adherence. This appeal is, therefore, properly before us.

4. On the basis of the principal cases and the exceptions noted in *U.S. v. Chagra,* do the non-parties who are allowed to appeal without intervening as a party have a common status that would permit the formulation of a general rule on when a non-party can appeal?

5. A non-party who seeks to intervene in order to appeal must ensure that the applicable rule for seeking intervention is followed. In Newberg v. Board of Public Education, 330 Pa.Super. 65, 478 A.2d 1352 (1984) the court rejected an appeal by persons who had participated as *amicus curiae* in the trial court and who sought to intervene in the trial almost a month *after* the appealable judgment was entered. The court held that the intervention rule required a petition for leave to intervene to be filed during the pendency of the action, thus a petition filed after final adjudication was too late.

6. The fact that a person has been permitted to intervene as a party in the trial court does not mean, however, the person necessarily has the necessary personal interest to take an appeal. In Diamond v. Charles, 476 U.S. 54, 106 S.Ct. 1697, 90 L.Ed.2d 48 (1986) the Court dismissed for want of jurisdiction an appeal by a doctor from a judgment declaring unconstitutional several sections of the Illinois abortion law. The doctor has been permitted to intervene in the trial court in support of the disputed sections. The Illinois attorney general, who had defended the statute in the trial court, did not appeal but filed a letter with Court indicating it agreed with the doctor. Even though Supreme Court rules provided that a party in the lower court is also a party in the Supreme Court and thus the State continued as a party to the case, the Court drew a distinction between status as a party and status as an appellant. The Court held that because the doctor did not have the requisite personal interest in the outcome to have standing to appeal, and the State did not appeal, thus there was no proper appellant and the appeal had to be dismissed.

7. Similar difficulties can arise when the parties to a litigation settle the case and interested third-persons wish to obtain appellate review of the issues. See, e.g., Backus v. Independent Wireless One Corp., 75 Fed. Appx. 820 (2nd Cir. 2003)("Because the parties have settled their dispute, the [citizens] must show that they have Article III standing before we can consider this appeal. . . . [The] ability to ride 'piggyback' on [another party's]

---

14. Indeed, the great majority of cases involving challenges to closure and similar orders have been reviewed pursuant to some sort of extraordinary writ.

undoubted standing exists only if the [other party] is in fact an appellant before the Court; in the absence of the [other party] in that capacity, there is no case for [an intervenor] to join.'').

2. PARTIES ADDED DURING THE LITIGATION (AMEND-MENT AND THIRD PARTY STATUS)

In the American justice system, plaintiffs shape the case at the outset, based on information known at the time of the initial filing. There are several ways in which parties may be added to the action after it begins. Amendment of the pleadings (Rule 15 of the Federal Rules of Civil Procedure) is a common means. New parties can be added to the case by seeking leave of court to amend the complaint, and then serving the process upon the newly-added defendant. Sometimes the statute of limitations will prevent plaintiff from adding a new party, but under Federal Rule 15(c) and state law equivalents, it is often the case that the pendency of the action as originally framed will be sufficient to "toll" (stop) the running of the limitations period as to the persons added as defendants later. The statute of limitations is an affirmative defense, so the general procedure is that a plaintiff who has leave to amend to add the new party files the amended complaint and arranges for its service, and the newly-added party becomes a party to the case. Whether the new party makes a motion based on limitations grounds will depend on the defense analysis of the arguments concerning the definition of the claim, "accrual" of the cause of action, any "tolling" events (such as disability of a party, or absence from the jurisdiction) and other arguments applicable in the particular context.

Defendants, also, can expand the parties before the court by *impleading* defendants as third-parties. In any situation where the third-party may be liable to the defendant for all or part of that defendant's potential liability to the plaintiff, the third-party may be sued. Upon service of process, the "third-party defendant" becomes formally a party to the case, and can assert rights against the defendant who has brought the third party in, and against the original plaintiff to the case.

Upon the entry of an appealable order (See Chapter 3), parties added late in the case, whether by plaintiff or by the defendant, can appeal if they are aggrieved by the outcome.

3. PARTIES DROPPED OR DISMISSED DURING THE LITIGA-TION

Plaintiffs sometimes voluntarily discontinue a case against a defendant, or some defendants in a multi-defendant case. The court may involuntarily dismiss a party as well, such as through the granting of a motion for summary judgment.

Generally, if plaintiff has moved to dismiss the claim against a party, the plaintiff cannot thereafter attempt to appeal with respect to that party.

4. INTERVENTION

Intervention is the process by which a non-party may seek to join a pending lawsuit by becoming a party. Depending on how the interests and goals of the participants are aligned under the existing pleadings, an intervenor may join the plaintiff(s) in pressing a claim, or may intervene as a defendant. If intervention is granted by the trial court, the intervenor becomes a full-fledged party, with responsibilities for preparing the case for disposition, and the normal rights to make motions, offer proof, examine witnesses, argue the case, and appeal an adverse ruling.

Intervention almost always occurs early enough in the trial-level proceedings to permit the intervenor to participate appropriately in the preparations, and to allow pre-existing parties to obtain discovery and exercise motion opportunities against the intervenor. Case law (including that set forth below) suggests that one key factor in whether to allow intervention is whether the applicant has waited "too long" to assert an interest in participating in the case.

However, intervention late in the case—including intervention after a case is settled, or even intervention after a trial is held and final judgment is entered—has occasionally been permitted. Intervention "on appeal" is also not unknown, though it is very rare.

There are interesting differences in the forms of intervention sought, and in the appealability of a motion for leave to intervene that is denied. Many would-be intervenors who have been denied leave to participate have lost their right to seek review of the ruling by failing to seek an immediate appeal. The trap works like this: the stronger the party's claimed "right" to intervene, the more likely it is that failure to seek an immediate appeal (while the rest of the trial court proceedings are ongoing) will be deemed a waiver of rights.

Finally, there is a continuum of levels of possible participation to consider. A party seeking intervention wants to have the rights to fully participate, not only at trial, but on appeal (briefing, motion practice and oral argument to the extent permitted). However, denial of intervention is not the end of the matter, because a party who fails to attain full party status, may be able to "have a say" in the appeal, by becoming an amicus.

5. WHO IS "NAMED" AS A PARTY TO THE APPEAL

As is explored more completely in Chapter 5 of this Casebook ("Initiating and Perfecting an Appeal") the only persons who are parties on appeal are those who get named as parties in a properly filed notice of appeal, or who are allowed to be added to the appeal later by permission of the appellate court (such as by intervention as discussed in this Chapter).

Thus, for example, if there are seven defendants held liable in a trial-level proceeding, and only one appeals, there is only one appellant and the other six defendants are not parties to the appeal even if they are situated exactly as is the appealing defendant.

There have been numerous kinds of problems with the "naming" of parties to appeal, normally done in the notice of appeal itself, and sometimes accomplished in associated documents. There are also problems of failure to name people who were meant to be named or, on the other hand, attempts to name people the appellant cannot name for one reason or another (e.g., plaintiff voluntarily dismissed a party during trial-level proceedings, and cannot "resurrect" the defendant on appeal). There are also problems with pro se parties purporting to name other appellants on behalf of whom to proceed, including family members and personal businesses. These matters are also explored in Chapter 5.

To make the most general point here: there may be numerous persons who *were* parties in the trial court, and who have standing to appeal as aggrieved persons, but who do not purport to be named in the notice of appeal, and thus are not parties on appeal. Put another way, no litigant is "automatically" a party to an appeal.

SECTION B. PERSONS AGGRIEVED BY THE JUDGMENT

1. GENERALLY

The general lay of the land is summarized by the United States Supreme Court in Deposit Guaranty Nat'l Bank v. Roper, 445 U.S. 326, 333 (1980):

> Ordinarily, only a party aggrieved by a judgment or order of a district court may exercise the statutory right to appeal therefrom. A party who receives all that he has sought generally is not aggrieved by the judgment affording the relief and cannot appeal from it.

Some states have statutes providing that a party must be aggrieved by a minimum dollar amount for money or property cases in order to appeal. These figures are typically quite low, such as $200, or even $50. Thus if a party wins most of the relief sought in the trial court, a very minor discrepancy between the amount sought and recovered would not permit appeal.

Each party seeking to appeal must be "aggrieved." Thus in a litigation against Microsoft Corporation involving "ergonomic keyboards" for computers, featuring v-shaped designs with separate right- and left-hand clusters of keys, the trial court dismissed the claims of patent infringement against Microsoft on the ground that the plaintiff keyboard producer did not have a valid patent to enforce. Microsoft's counterclaims were then "dismissed without prejudice." When the keyboard manufacturer appealed, Microsoft attempted to obtain appellate review concerning its cross-claims by filing a notice of a cross-appeal. (The cross-appeal process is explored in Chapter 5 of this casebook). The

Court of Appeals held that since the adversary's patent had been held invalid, there was no greater relief Microsoft could obtain, and hence that it was not aggrieved sufficiently to permit a cross-appeal. Typeright Keyboard Corp. v. Microsoft Corporation, 374 F.3d 1151 (Fed. Cir. 2004).

WATSON v. CITY OF NEWARK

United States Court of Appeals, Third Circuit, 1984.
746 F.2d 1008.

GIBBONS, CIRCUIT JUDGE.

Ronald E. Watson, Ronald Anderson and Dixie D. Wilson are employees of the City of Newark, Delaware, who claim that their right to political expression is unconstitutionally denied to them by Section 1104 of the Charter of the City of Newark, as amended. These employees specifically complain about the following language:

> No person who holds any paid appointive city position shall make, solicit or receive, or be in any manner concerned in the making, soliciting or receiving of any assessment, subscription or contribution to any candidate for public office in the city government; nor shall any such person take any part in any political campaigns for said offices.

The employees desire to express their views as to the issues in City Council and Mayoral campaigns and to endorse candidates for city office both publicly and privately. * * *

The City of Newark has not issued guidelines to the employees describing what kind of conduct is prohibited by the aforementioned City Charter provision Section 1104. Deposition of Peter S. Marshall, p. 26. * * *

The employees filed this civil action for declaratory and injunctive relief on March 17, 1983, in the United States District Court for the District of Delaware to enjoin deprivation of their civil rights. The City of Newark filed its Answer and subsequently filed a Motion to Dismiss and Motion for Declaratory Judgment. At the hearing * * * the court determined that the case should be treated as having been presented on Cross–Motions for Summary Judgment. On March 22, 1984, the employees filed a Motion for Preliminary Injunction to enjoin enforcement of Section 1104 prior to City elections scheduled for April 10, 1984.

On March 28, 1984, the district court denied defendants' Motion for Summary Judgment and granted plaintiffs' Motion for Summary Judgment. The court enjoined defendants, their employees and agents, from enforcing Section 1104 of the Charter of the City of Newark insofar as it prohibits any person who holds any paid appointive city position from taking part in any political campaigns for City government offices. The court's ruling was based on its conclusion that "the challenged portion of Section 1104 is impermissibly vague and can be construed to apply to protected expression."

In *dictum*, however, the court opined against the employees' argument that the First Amendment does not allow restrictions on the political rights of employees of nonpartisan cities. Employees had argued that the United States Supreme Court's decisions in earlier "Hatch Act" cases, United States Civil Service Commission v. National Ass'n of Letter Carriers, 413 U.S. 548 (1973) and Broadrick v. Oklahoma, 413 U.S. 601 (1973) had upheld only narrowly drawn restrictions upon *partisan* political activities of governmental employees. The district court, in *dictum*, declined to give weight to this partisan/nonpartisan distinction.

This "ruling",[2] employees claim, has given the City of Newark the green light to trample on their rights by allowing Newark to resurrect restrictions on political activity by City employees in the City's nonpartisan elections. Appellants claim that the City has already evidenced a present, firm intention to reimpose limits upon the extent to which its employees may participate in nonpartisan City politics. For example, appellants submit, the letter from the City Solicitor, Thomas G. Hughes, to the district court in opposition to plaintiffs' fee application, indicates that the City intends to "effectively limit" political activity by its employees as much as possible:

> The Court ... held that municipalities can limit political activity of its employees even if the City is a nonpartisan City and that the "partisan/nonpartisan" issue is not a valid distinction which voids the teaching of the *Broaderick* [sic] and *Letter Carriers* decisions....
>
> Thus insofar as Newark is concerned, Newark lost a battle but won the war. Newark believes the decision vindicates its power to enact rules or ordinances which effectively limit the extent to which its employees may participate in Newark City politics so long as the rules or ordinances are "reasonable" in striking a balance between the First Amendment and the City's rights.

Based on the foregoing, the employees contend that Newark intends to continue its "war against its employees' participation in political activity." Accordingly, they appeal the district court's *dictum* that the City of Newark may constitutionally restrict the political participation of its employees in nonpartisan City elections.

II

An appellant must be privy to the record and *must be aggrieved by the order appealed from.*

Generally, a party who receives all of the relief which he sought is not aggrieved by the judgment affording the relief and cannot appeal from it. Id. In this case the appellants received all of the relief which

---

2. Employees claim that the district court "held" or "ruled" against them on their argument that the first amendment does not allow restrictions on the political rights of employees of nonpartisan cities. Appellants' brief at 4. The referenced passage of the district court memorandum opinion (App. 100–101) is better characterized as "dictum" not necessary to the result in the instant case.

they sought, and were in no way aggrieved by the district court order—an order which granted a final judgment enjoining the defendants from enforcing Section 1104 of the Charter of the City of Newark. Accordingly, appellants may not appeal from this favorable disposition. See also Liberty Mutual Insurance Co. v. Wetzel, 424 U.S. 737 (1976); Perez v. Ledesma, 401 U.S. 82, 87 n. 3 (1971) (successful party cannot appeal from its victory); Electrical Fittings Corp. v. Thomas & Betts Co., 307 U.S. 241, 242 (1939); New York Telephone Co. v. Maltbie, 291 U.S. 645, 646 (1934) (telephone company obtained permanent injunction against enforcement of challenged rate order but unsuccessfully sought to appeal portions of the decree fixing the value of its property and the rate of return to be allowed); In re First Colonial Corp. of America, 693 F.2d 447, 449–450 n. 5 (5th Cir. 1982) ("One may not appeal an issue upon which one prevailed absent exceptional circumstances."); In re Arthur Treacher's Franchisee Litigation, 689 F.2d 1137, 1149 n. 16 (3d Cir. 1982) (plaintiff who had obtained a preliminary injunction could not cross-appeal to secure review of a sentence in the district court opinion. A party successful in the district court has no right to appeal for the purpose of obtaining review of findings that are not necessary to support the favorable order); Williams v. Frey, 551 F.2d 932, 934 (3d Cir. 1977) (a representative of a plaintiff class could not appeal denial of the defendants' motion to modify the judgment, since he was not injured by the denial); In re Glenn W. Turner Enterprises Litigation, 521 F.2d 775, 781 (3d Cir. 1975) (parties aggrieved by various interlocutory pretrial orders directed at the handling of a class action could not "piggy-back an appeal" by joining an appeal by a party subject to an interlocutory injunction order that did not affect other parties).

Therefore, we will dismiss this appeal for lack of standing. Of course the doors of the courthouse always remain open to appellants should the City of Newark enact new regulations that, in appellants' opinion, constitute unconstitutional restriction upon their first amendment rights.

Appeal dismissed.

Notes and Questions

1. In the principal case the court said that the appellants could not appeal because they did not have standing. Would it be more accurate to say that they could not appeal because they were appealing from the trial court's opinion rather than from the judgment? For two informative cases in which the Supreme Court dismissed appeals because the appellant was not aggrieved by the decision, see Diamond v. Charles, 476 U.S. 54, 106 S.Ct. 1697, 90 L.Ed.2d 48 (1986)(a pediatrician who wanted to uphold the constitutionality of an abortion statute was not himself threatened with punishment) and Bender v. Williamsport Area School Dist., 475 U.S. 534, 106 S.Ct. 1326, 89 L.Ed.2d 501 (1986) (printed Chapter 2, Section E, supra.).

2. In a case in which a plaintiff seeks to recover $100,000 in damages and is awarded $99,000, can it be said that the plaintiff is aggrieved by the judgment and thus can appeal from it? The general rule is that a person who

receives less than the full relief sought is aggrieved by the judgment, notwithstanding a judgment in the person's favor. Aetna Casualty & Surety Co. v. Cunningham, 224 F.2d 478, 480 (5th Cir. 1955). The other extreme would be if the judgment were for only one cent, and the question was whether the defendant could appeal from it. Why would the plaintiff appeal in the first instance, or the defendant appeal in the latter? Could there be reasons other than the amount of the judgment that could cause a party to appeal a judgment that could have been either more or less favorable? Could there be reasons other than the amount of the judgment that could cause a party to appeal a judgment that could have been either more or less favorable? Could both the plaintiff and defendant be aggrieved by the same judgment and appeal from it? Isn't this why cross appeals are permitted?

3.   Ordinarily when a plaintiff voluntarily dismisses a suit, it cannot appeal. It can appeal however, when the dismissal follows the granting of the defendant's motion to dismiss for failure to state ultimate facts upon which relief can be granted. Paddack v. Mcdonald, 294 Or. 667, 661 P.2d 545 (1983). Similarly, the plaintiff can appeal a voluntary dismissal granted on the condition of the payment of attorney fees to the defendants. Cauley v. Wilson, 754 F.2d 769 (7th Cir. 1985). See annotation, 75 A.L.R.Fed. 505 (1985).

4.   Even if a party prevails in the trial court, it may appeal an adverse ruling if the matter cannot be litigated in subsequent litigation. In Trust–House Forte, Inc. v. 795 Fifth Ave. Corp., 756 F.2d 255 (2d Cir. 1985) the defendant, who was successful in having a suit dismissed on the ground that a condition precedent to the action had not been satisfied, was allowed to appeal an intermediate ruling that the defendant could not raise a waiver defense, the court reasoning that the ruling would be binding in any later litigation.

5.   Cases involving multiple parties also create problems as to who is an aggrieved party and therefore who can appeal. When several defendants settle with the plaintiff, the defendants can still appeal trial court actions relating to the apportionment of liability among the defendants. Thompson v. Philadelphia, 320 Pa.Super. 124, 466 A.2d 1349 (1983). A defendant can appeal the summary judgment granted to co-defendant if the defendant asserts a right of contribution, R.E. Thomas Erectors, Inc. v. Brunswick Pulp & Paper Co., 171 Ga.App. 903, 321 S.E.2d 412 (1984).

6.   An appeal by a third party defendant of the judgment against it operates as an appeal of the original judgment and thus the third party defendant can challenge the validity of the judgment against the original defendant. Gino's Pizza v. Kaplan, 193 Conn. 135, 475 A.2d 305 (1984); Kicklighter v. Nails by Jannee, Inc., 616 F.2d 734 (5th Cir. 1980).

7.   The traditional rule was that a ''receiver'' (a person appointed by the court or statute to hold property pending final resolution of a dispute) could not appeal. As a mere ''stakeholder'' the receiver was not ''interested'' in the disposition, and could not appeal. See In Re Fidelity Assur. Ass'n, 247 Wis. 619, 20 N.W.2d 638 (Wisc. 1945). In bankruptcy law today, however, the trustee is empowered to bring all manner of claims, and may appeal any ruling—even though in an important sense the trustee is a mere holder of the property who is responsible for maximizing the assets for the benefit of

the creditors. The bankruptcy trustee's power is far-reaching. In Martin–Trigona v. Shiff, 702 F.2d 380 (2d Cir. 1983) trustees in bankruptcy were allowed to appeal the grant of a habeas corpus petition releasing the debtor from imprisonment ordered after the debtor had been found in civil contempt. The court held that the trustees were the real parties in interest because the orders the debtor refused to obey which caused his being held in contempt related to his refusal to testify in connection with the administration of his bankrupt estate.

2. LEAVING A PARTY EXPOSED TO OTHER CLAIMS

Cases sometimes arise where a party receives judgment on one of several claims, perhaps even the "main" claim, and other issues are shunted aside. If the claim that *was decided* affords complete relief, the prevailing party will not be aggrieved. However, if there is exposure to additional claims or difficulties, the victorious party may be entitled to seek an appeal in which the failure to rule in its favor on additional grounds is a viable issue.

AMAZON, INC. v. DIRT CAMP, INC.

United States Court of Appeals, Tenth Circuit, 2001.
273 F.3d 1271.

BALDOCK, CIRCUIT JUDGE.

Professional mountain bike rider Missy Giove assigned publicity rights in her name and likeness to Plaintiff Amazon, Inc., a Colorado corporation with its principal place of business in New York. Defendant Cannondale Corp., a Delaware corporation with its principal place of business in Connecticut, manufactures and sells high performance bicycles and equipment. Since 1994, Cannondale has co-sponsored a mountain bike team, of which Ms. Giove was a member from 1994 to 1998. * * * A contract * * * licensed Cannondale, as a team sponsor, use of the publicity rights.

During the summer and early fall of 1998, while Ms. Giove was still a member of the team, Cannondale designed, published, and distributed its 1999 products catalog. The catalog included several photographs of Ms. Giove. Subsequently, [the] contract expired on December 31, 1998. Cannondale continued to distribute the 1999 catalog . * * * Amazon filed a complaint in federal district court alleging that Cannondale's continued distribution of the 1999 catalog improperly used Ms. Giove's name and likeness in violation of the Lanham Act and Colorado state unfair competition and publicity law. According to the complaint, federal jurisdiction was founded on the Lanham Act claim under 28 U.S.C. §§ 1331 and 1338(a), and 15 U.S.C. § 1125(a), with supplemental jurisdiction over the state law claims under 28 U.S.C. § 1367. Amazon's complaint also alleged that the district court had diversity jurisdiction. * * * Amazon's first amended complaint added several defendants, including Dirt Camp, Inc. ("Dirt Camp"), which runs instructional mountain biking camps. Dirt Camp's advertisement in Cannondale's 1999 catalog included Ms. Giove's name and photograph. * * *

Cannondale subsequently moved for summary judgment on all claims pursuant to Fed. R. Civ. P. 56. The district court granted summary judgment in favor of Cannondale and Dirt Camp on the Lanham Act claim. The district court dismissed the state law claims without prejudice, declining to exercise supplemental jurisdiction pursuant to 28 U.S.C. § 1367(c)(3). Cannondale now appeals, arguing that the district court had diversity jurisdiction over the state law claims, and should have addressed the merits rather than dismissing the claims.[3] * * *

Although neither party challenges our appellate jurisdiction, we have an independent duty to examine our own jurisdiction. See Skrzypczak v. Kauger, 92 F.3d 1050, 1052 (10th Cir. 1996) (citing FW/PBS, Inc. v. City of Dallas, 493 U.S. 215, 231 (1990)).

A party generally cannot appeal from a judgment in its favor. On the surface at least, Cannondale apparently prevailed below. The district court granted summary judgment in favor of Cannondale on the federal claim, and dismissed the state law claims without prejudice. Exceptions to this general rule exist, however. For example, a prevailing party "is aggrieved and ordinarily can appeal a decision granting in part and denying in part the remedy requested." Forney v. Apfel, 524 U.S. 266, 271 (1998) (a party denied the preferred relief of reversal may appeal even though prevailing on the alternative relief of remand); Jarvis v. Nobel/Sysco Food Systems, 985 F.2d 1419, 1424 (10th Cir. 1993) ("Where a judgment gives the successful party only part of that which he seeks and denies him the balance, with the result that injustice has been done him, he may appeal from the entire judgment.")

Applying this rationale, we have specifically held that "when a district court denies summary judgment on the merits, and then exercises its discretion to decline pendent jurisdiction, the moving party is a 'party aggrieved by the judgment.'" Jarvis, 985 F.2d at 1425 (finding that prevailing party below and on primary appeal had standing to pursue cross-appeal to avoid future litigation costs) (quoting Deposit Guaranty Nat'l Bank v. Roper, 445 U.S. 326, 333–34 (1980) (a prevailing party may appeal "so long as that party retains a stake in the appeal")).

Here, Cannondale sought final disposition on the merits as to all claims, but the district court granted summary judgment only on the federal claim. The court dismissed without prejudice the state law claims. As a result, Cannondale received only a part of what it sought. This disposition left Cannondale open to precisely what happened in this case, a second litigation. Cannondale was sufficiently aggrieved by this result, and consequently has standing to appeal. See Jarvis, 985 F.2d at 1425 ("In this case, a successful appeal by Nobel would eliminate any

---

3. After the district court dismissed the state law claims without prejudice, Amazon filed a complaint against Cannondale in Colorado state court asserting the dismissed state law publicity claim. * * *

possible re-filing ... in state court[, and because] avoiding a state court suit would substantially reduce Nobel's future litigation costs, we find that Nobel has the requisite stake in this appeal."); Disher v. Information Res., Inc., 873 F.2d 136, 138–39 (7th Cir. 1989) (defendant prevailing on summary judgment on all but two claims may appeal dismissal without prejudice because the decision is not entirely in the defendant's favor by exposing the defendant to further litigation).

Accordingly, we have jurisdiction over this appeal under 28 U.S.C. § 1291.

---

3. OTHER WAYS A "WINNER" CAN BE AGGRIEVED

ENVIRONMENTAL PROT. INFORMATION CNTR. v. PACIFIC LUMBER CO.

United States Court of Appeals, Ninth Circuit, 2001.
257 F.3d 1071.

WALLACE, CIRCUIT JUDGE.

[In a suit by an environmental group against a lumber company about treatment of an endangered species of coho salmon, the district judge initially granted an injunction based on findings concerning the environmental risks that reflected negatively upon the defendant, but then dissolved the injunction and dismissed the action in the lumber company's favor. Seeking to expunge the trial judge's comments, the lumber company appealed. The Ninth Circuit explained the range of situations where a prevailing party may seek appellate relief.]

A.

At the center of this standing controversy are the familiar concepts that courts "review judgments, not statements in opinions," California v. Rooney, 483 U.S. 307, 311 (1987), and that interlocutory orders entered prior to the judgment merge into the judgment. See, e.g., Amer. Ironworks & Erectors Inc. v. N. Amer. Const. Co., 248 F.3d 892, 897 (9th Cir. 2001); Madison Square Garden Boxing, Inc. v. Shavers, 562 F.2d 141, 144 (2d Cir. 1977) ("With the entry of the final judgment, the life of the preliminary injunction came to an end, and it no longer had a binding effect on any one."). As a result, "ordinarily, only a party aggrieved by a judgment or order of a district court may exercise the statutory right to appeal therefrom. A party who receives all that he has sought generally is not aggrieved by the judgment affording the relief and cannot appeal from it." Deposit Guar. Nat'l Bank v. Roper, 445 U.S. 326, 333(1980), see also Elec. Fittings Corp. v. Thomas & Betts Co., 307 U.S. 241, 242 (1939). This rule "is one of federal appellate practice, however, derived from the statutes granting appellate jurisdiction and the historic practices of the appellate courts; it does not have its source in the jurisdictional limitations of Art. III." Roper, 445 U.S. at 333–34.

As a result, three established prudential routes have developed by which a winning party may be deemed "aggrieved" by a favorable judgment, and thus be deemed to have standing on appeal.

First, the Supreme Court has held that a party may seek reformation of a favorable decree—but not review of its merits—that contains discussion of issues "immaterial to the disposition of the cause." *Electrical Fittings*, 307 U.S. at 242. We have, however, strictly interpreted "decree" to mean "judgment." In United States v. Good Samaritan Church, 29 F.3d 487 (9th Cir. 1994), we dismissed an appeal "because the appellants won the case below. They lost on the issue which they want us to review, but the decision on that issue has no effect on them." Id. at 488. We explained,

> If the alter ego determination from the summary judgment order [the issue lost by appellants] had found its way into the judgment then review might be appropriate to "direct reformation of the decree." But the judgment in favor of the [appellants] dismissed the government's case without prejudice. That is all it did.... All the judgment said was that the government's "complaint is dismissed without prejudice." There was no declaratory judgment language ... used, no injunctive relief, and nothing to establish any rights or liabilities on the basis of the alter ego determination.

Here, the judgment states only, "it is ordered and adjudged that the motion for summary judgment and/or motion to dismiss as moot filed by defendants [Pacific Lumber] is granted and this action brought by plaintiffs is dismissed in its entirety." Thus, as in Good Samaritan, there is nothing for us to reform in the judgment, and we are unable to hold that Pacific Lumber is "aggrieved" by the judgment under the rationale of *Electrical Fittings*. See also *In re DES Litig.*, 7 F.3d 20, 25 (2d Cir. 1993) (holding Electrical Fittings to be inapplicable because the superfluous "rulings on personal jurisdiction and choice of law do not appear on the face of the judgment").

Second, the Supreme Court has recognized that a winning party will be considered aggrieved by a favorable judgment if future economic loss will result to the party on account of adverse collateral rulings. This route to prudential standing is powerful because it allows for review of the merits—if the parties retain a stake in the controversy satisfying Article III—of the adverse collateral order. See *Roper*, 445 U.S. at 334 & n. 6 (reviewing denial of class certification because class action would spread costs of the litigation). It is rare that a winning party will be able to use this method successfully for gaining review of an adverse collateral order because future economic loss does not include the costs of relitigating the same issue at a later date. See Asarco, Inc. v. Sec. of Labor, 206 F.3d 720, 723–24 (6th Cir. 2000) (holding that winning party failed to meet requirement of future economic loss). Pacific Lumber has not alleged any cognizable future economic loss arising from the collateral adverse orders. In addition, because there is no longer an Article III case or controversy, the primary benefit of meeting this requirement—

review on the merits of the adverse collateral order—is unavailable to Pacific Lumber.

Finally, a prevailing party will meet the prudential standing requirement "if the adverse [collateral]ruling can serve as the basis for collateral estoppel in subsequent litigation." *Ruvalcaba v. City of Los Angeles*, 167 F.3d 514, 520 (9th Cir. 1999). The March 15 order and extraneous statements in the May 5 order will not have collateral estoppel effects under our case law because "determinations which are immaterial to the judgment below have no preclusive effect on subsequent litigation." *Good Samaritan*, 29 F.3d at 489. We agree with the D.C. Circuit that this "argument from collateral estoppel consequences has elements of circularity. As collateral estoppel does not apply to an unappealable determination, simply holding a ruling unappealable eliminates any prospect of preclusion." *Sea-Land Serv.*, 137 F.3d at 648. Here, however, the March 15 order and portions of the May 5 order have no collateral estoppel effect, not only because they are immaterial to the judgment, but also because they were entered without jurisdiction.

B.

Although this appeal does not qualify for prudential standing in the most used settings (reformation of judgment, future economic loss or collateral estoppel), our review is not completed. Thus, although we are unable to deem Pacific Lumber "aggrieved" by the judgment under any of the preceding established rationales, we consider next whether the circumstances of this case render Pacific Lumber "aggrieved" for other reasons. See *Roper*, 445 U.S. at 334 ("In an appropriate case, appeal may be permitted from an adverse ruling collateral to the judgment on the merits at the behest of the party who has prevailed on the merits. . . .").

Article III of the Constitution prohibits federal courts from taking further action on the merits in moot cases. *Liner v. Jafco, Inc.*, 375 U.S. 301, 306 n. 3 (1964). The Supreme Court has repeatedly emphasized that "without jurisdiction the court cannot proceed at all in any cause. Jurisdiction is power to declare the law, and when it ceases to exist, the only function remaining to the court is that of announcing the fact and dismissing the cause." *Steel Co.*, 523 U.S. at 94. Relying on these principles, the Third Circuit, in *New Jersey v. Heldor Indus. Inc.*, 989 F.2d 702 (3d Cir. 1993), determined that a party who had received a favorable judgment had standing to request vacatur of an opinion entered after the lower court had lost jurisdiction. In that case, a bankruptcy judge had invested considerable energy into resolving a fairly complicated question. *Id.* at 705. Before the judge rendered his opinion on the matter, however, the parties agreed to a settlement, mooting the question. The bankruptcy judge decided to issue the opinion anyway with a footnote stating that the parties had actually settled the question. *Id.* at 704. The Third Circuit vacated the opinion because the bankruptcy judge had "opined and ruled upon an objection that was known to him to have been withdrawn prior to the issuance of his opinion and order." *Id.* at 703.

This holding was reached over a dissent which argued that since the appellant had received all that it sought—approval of the settlement—from the bankruptcy judge, it had no prudential standing to appeal. Id. at 710 (Nygaard, J., dissenting). Nevertheless, it is now the position of the Third Circuit. The parties have not cited, nor have we found, another federal case ruling on this precise issue. The question before us is whether we should follow the Third Circuit or create an intercircuit conflict. Our court has provided us with the analysis to be followed: unless there are valid and persuasive reasons to hold otherwise, we should not create an intercircuit conflict. That is, the presumption is not to create an intercircuit conflict. See United States v. Chavez–Vernaza, 844 F.2d 1368, 1374 (9th Cir. 1987). There is no reason to reject this analysis or not to follow the Third Circuit on the legal issue involved.

We, like the majority in *Heldor*, hold that the district court's decision to flout the dictates of Article III and render an opinion in spite of knowing the cause was moot did render Pacific Lumber an "aggrieved party." While it is true that all dicta "have no preclusive effect," Abbs v. Sullivan, 963 F.2d 918, 924 (7th Cir. 1992), dicta entered after a court has lost jurisdiction over a party inflicts a wrong on that party of a different order than that which exists in the usual case of extraneous judicial pronouncement. See *Heldor*, 989 F.2d at 709 n. 10 ("We do not believe it will suffice merely to describe the bankruptcy judge's action . . . as 'dictum' and do nothing more. That action declared a major public law . . . unconstitutional in the course of rejecting a non-existent objection.").

We therefore remand and order the district court to vacate its March 15 order and reform the May 5 order in accordance with this opinion.

Notes and Questions

1. As might be expected, when the *government* is the winner in some sense, but seeks to appeal, it may well be found to have grounds to be viewed as "aggrieved". See, e.g., Viraj Group v. United States, 343 F.3d 1371 (Fed. Cir. 2003)(after the lower court ruled *in favor of a government agency*, the United States was permitted to appeal. While exclaiming that "this appeal comes to us in a strange posture: The government has appealed from the court's decision affirming the government agency's determination; in other words, the winner has appealed because its determination was affirmed by the trial court only on the basis of reasoning with which it disagrees," the Federal Circuit allowed the appeal, finding that no other avenue for appellate review had been available to the government to challenge the doctrines being applied.

2. Generally, a party has no standing to appeal from a judgment to which he or she consented. Thus unless a consent decree is altered in the process of being implemented by the trial court, a party to the agreement is not aggrieved and cannot appeal. See Reynolds v. Roberts, 202 F.3d 1303 (11th Cir. 2000), citing 5 Am. Jur. *Appellate Review* § 5 (1995).

3.   A winning party normally cannot appeal an adverse ruling against a co-party. Consider the dilemma of the Colt firearms company in a case where it was held *not liable* after a four-week jury trial in which seven plaintiffs injured or killed by handguns sued 25 handgun manufacturers under a theory that defendants' negligence in marketing and distributing handguns proximately caused the harm plaintiffs suffered. A "special verdict" (numbered written findings by the jury) found that Colt was one of the 15 defendants *who were negligent*, but was *not* one of the nine defendants found to have proximately caused plaintiffs' injuries. Thus, Colt's was held not liable for plaintiffs' harm. Absent review on appeal, the judgment will become final as to Colt. Colt asked the appellate court for permission to participate in the appeal to challenge the negligence findings because "plaintiffs in other potential actions may well attempt to argue that these findings somehow support such an argument." The plaintiffs opposed Colt's participation, noting that prevailing parties generally lack standing to appeal from a favorable judgment, even when it was awarded on grounds other than those urged by the prevailing party. Further, Colt was not able to point to "present injury stemming from an adverse ruling of the district court that might confer standing to appeal." How should the appellate court rule on such a request? To assess this issue fairly, is it necessary to figure out whether collateral estoppel doctrines ("issue preclusion") will be available to future plaintiffs to make some use of the jury's finding in this case (so-called "offensive" collateral estoppel, which is permitted in some circumstances in the most but not all courts)? See generally Hamilton v. Beretta U.S.A. Corp., 2000 WL 1160600 (2nd Cir. 2000)(denying Colt the right to participate in the appeal, but not discussing whether the finding could be used against Colt in a future case).

SECTION C.   STANDING TO APPEAL

1.   THE CONSTANT DUTY TO CONSIDER STANDING

All courts require that parties appearing before them have a justiciable interest, often called "standing" to warrant consideration by the court. In the federal courts, access to the judicial system is conditioned by the Constitution to cases and controversies, which requires that a litigant have personal standing to sue.

"In essence the question of standing is whether the litigant is entitled to have the court decide the merits of the dispute or of particular issues." Trump Hotels & Casino Resorts, Inc. v. Mirage Resorts Inc., 140 F.3d 478, 484 (3d Cir. 1998) (quoting Warth v. Seldin, 422 U.S. 490, 498 (1975)). "Standing 'subsumes a blend of constitutional requirements and prudential considerations.' " Id. See Valley Forge Christian College v. Americans United for Separation of Church and State, Inc., 454 U.S. 464, 471 (1982)). "Obviously, satisfying the Article III 'case or controversy' requirement is the 'irreducible constitutional minimum' of standing." Lujan v. Defenders of Wildlife, 504 U.S. 555, 560 (1992).

In *Lujan,* one of the most widely cited decisions ever issued by the United States Supreme Court, the standing requirements imposed by the Constitution were summarized.

Article III constitutional standing contains three elements: (1) the Plaintiff must have suffered an injury in fact—an invasion of a legally protected interest which is (a) concrete and particularized and (b) actual or imminent, not conjectural or hypothetical; (2) there must be a causal connection between the injury and the conduct complained of—the injury has to be fairly traceable to the challenged action of the defendant and not the result of independent action of some third party not before the court; and (3) it must be likely, as opposed to merely speculative, that the injury will be redressed by a favorable decision.

Lujan, 504 U.S. at 560–61. See Miller v. Nissan Motor Acceptance Corp., 362 F.3d 209 (3rd Cir. 2004).

In addition to the foregoing "immutable requirements of Article III," the federal judiciary has also distilled a set of prudential principles that bear on the question of standing. See Bennett v. Spear, 520 U.S. 154, 117 S.Ct. 1154, 137 L.Ed.2d 281 (1997). These principles are:

(1) the Plaintiff generally must assert his own legal rights and interests, and cannot rest his claim to relief on the legal rights or interests of third parties; (2) even when the Plaintiff has alleged redressable injury sufficient to meet the requirements of Article III, the federal courts will not adjudicate abstract questions of wide public significance which amount to generalized grievances shared and most appropriately addressed in the representative branches; and (3) the Plaintiff's complaint must fall within the zone of interests to be protected or regulated by the statute or constitutional guarantee in question.

Valley Forge Christian College, 454 U.S. at 474–75.

It is generally held that Article III constitutional standing is a threshold issue that must be addressed *before* considering issues of prudential standing. See, e.g. Joint Stock Society v. Udv North America, Inc., 266 F.3d 164, 175 (3d Cir. 2001). It will be seen in cases set forth in this Chapter that one or both sets of requirements are applied when considering the right to pursue a claim at trial, and on appeal.

Not Waivable—Always At Issue. Under Article III, "standing . . . is jurisdictional and not subject to waiver." Lewis v. Casey, 518 U.S. 343, 349 n.1, 116 S.Ct. 2174, 135 L.Ed.2d 606 (1996). It is well-established that any party, and even the court sua sponte, can raise the issue of standing for the first time at any stage of the litigation, including on appeal. Nat'l Org. of Women, Inc. v. Scheidler, 510 U.S. 249, 255, 114 S.Ct. 798, 127 L.Ed.2d 99 (1994) (issue of standing raised by defendant for the first time on appeal); FW/PBS, Inc. v. City of Dallas, 493 U.S. 215, 230, 110 S.Ct. 596, 107 L.Ed.2d 603 (1990) (issue of standing raised sua sponte on appeal to the Supreme Court). When standing is challenged on appeal after a final judgment on the merits, the appellate court determines standing based on an examination of the whole record.

Appellate vs. Trial Court Standing. Though similar and overlapping, the doctrines of appellate standing and trial standing are not identical. Wolff v. Cash 4 Titles, 351 F.3d 1348 (11th Cir. 2003) "The primary limitation on [a litigant's] appellate standing is the adverseness requirement which is one of the rules of standing particular to the appellate setting. Only a litigant 'who is aggrieved by the judgment or order may appeal.'" Knight v. Alabama, 14 F.3d 1534, 1555–56 (11th Cir. 1994). Thus, it is entirely possible that named defendants in a trial proceeding, who would doubtless have appellate standing for the purposes of challenging some final rulings by the trial court, could lack standing to appeal other trial court rulings that do not affect their interests.

Fuzzy but Critical. There are more standing decisions rendered in federal courts each year than on any other constitutional or procedural topic: thousands of reported cases. Neither this vast body of decisions nor the Supreme Court's own jurisprudence on the topic is unified. In *Valley Forge Christian College* the Court said: "We need not mince words when we say that the concept of 'Art. III standing' has not been defined with complete consistency ... But of one thing we may be sure: Those who do not possess Art. III standing may not litigate as suitors in the courts of the United States." 454 U.S. at 475.

There is, therefore, tremendous room for "lawyering" (argumentation based on the facts and procedural circumstances in each case) as to whether a particular party, in a specific case, should be *deemed* to have standing.

Notes and Questions

1. The Supreme Court has held that because the constitutional aspects of standing involve the issue whether there is a controversy over which *the court* has jurisdiction, so long as there is *one* appellant with standing, the court may proceed to hear the appeal. Thus in federal courts at least the doctrine is: So long as one appellant has standing, the proceeding may go forward without any consideration of the standing of co-appellants. Tilley v. TJX Cos., 345 F.3d 34 (1st Cir. 2003), applying Watt v. Energy Action Educ. Found., 454 U.S. 151, 160, 102 S.Ct. 205, 70 L.Ed.2d 309 (1981); Arlington Heights v. Metro. Hous. Dev. Corp., 429 U.S. 252, 264, 97 S.Ct. 555, 50 L.Ed.2d 450 (1977).

2. Citizenship, or taxpayer status, is generally not sufficient to give one standing to participate in an appeal, even where the would-be active participant(s) believe that an elected governmental unit is making a mistake in the litigation. Even when the governmental unit settles a case, and thus there will be no adversary on appeal, standing is generally lacking for a taxpayer and resident to appeal. See Connecticut Yankee Atomic Power Co. v. Town of Haddam, 68 Fed.Appx. 249 (2nd Cir. 2003). In some states, such as Wisconsin, taxpayer standing has been extended situations where there is any form of pecuniary loss, which need not be in a substantial amount. "Even a loss or potential loss which is infinitesimally small with respect to each individual taxpayer will suffice to sustain a taxpayer suit." Hart v. Ament, 176 Wis.2d 694, 696, 500 N.W.2d 312, 313 (1993). This doctrine can

be especially broad where constitutional challenges are involved. See Appleton v. Menasha, 142 Wis.2d 870, 419 N.W.2d 249 (1988). Note, however, that for many purposes even the Wisconsin courts have "followed the approach of federal law on standing and concluded the plaintiff must have suffered some actual or threatened injury from the allegedly illegal action and there must be a logical nexus between the status of the plaintiff and the claim sought to be adjudicated." Chenequa Land Conservancy, Inc. v. Hartland, , 275 Wis.2d 533, 685 N.W.2d 573, 579 (2004).

3. Competitors of one or more of the parties in a pending case have been held on occasion to have standing to appeal a judgment involving their business rivals. The United States Supreme Court has upheld "competitor standing" even though the economic injury was latent. See Ass'n of Data Processing Serv. Orts. v. Camp, 397 U.S. 150, 152, 90 S.Ct. 827, 25 L.Ed.2d 184 (1970) (sellers of data processing services had standing to test ruling allowing national banks to sell data processing services because competition "might entail some future loss of profits" in that respondent bank was already preparing to perform such services for two of plaintiffs' clients); Arnold Tours, Inc. v. Camp, 400 U.S. 45, 45–46, 91 S.Ct. 158, 27 L.Ed.2d 179 (1970) (travel agents had "competitor standing" to challenge ruling allowing national banks to provide travel services); Investment Co. Inst. v. Camp, 401 U.S. 617, 620–21, 91 S.Ct. 1091, 28 L.Ed.2d 367 (1971) (investment companies had "competitor standing" to test regulatory ruling authorizing national banks to operate collective investment funds). *But see* New World Radio, Inc. v. FCC, 294 F.3d 164 (D.C. Cir. 2002)(rival broadcaster lacked standing to appeal under the Supreme Court's "competitor standing" doctrine because it was not currently operating in the same market as the party involved in the litigation. Speculation about future direct competition was not enough to confer standing). *Compare* FCC v. Sanders Brothers Radio Station, 309 U.S. 470, 477, 60 S.Ct. 693, 84 L.Ed. 869 (1940) (a competing broadcast station has "aggrieved" party standing to challenge the grant of a license to another "on the ground that the resulting competition may work economic injury to him").

4. Note that standing to appeal generally requires a showing of injury from the implementation of the trial court's judgment, not injury from economic forces or competition generally. "Although the determination of an injury may not always be simple, standing to appeal is recognized if the appellant can show an adverse effect of the judgment, and denied if no adverse effect can be shown." Ass'n of Banks in Ins. v. Duryee, 270 F.3d 397 (6th Cir. 2001), quoting See 15A Charles A. Wright, Arthur R. Miller & Edward H. Cooper, Federal Practice and Procedure: § 3902 (2d ed. 1992).

5. Numerous special rules apply in bankruptcy. In general, the debtor is *dis*-empowered to take appeals with respect to the bankruptcy estate—the rights thereto having been transferred by operation of law to the trustee in bankruptcy. Conversely, it is said that the trustee always has standing to appeal any issue with respect to the proceedings. See, e.g., Stanley v. McCormick, 215 F.3d 929 (9th Cir. 2000).

6. For a thoughtful and thorough survey of standing to appeal, drawing parallels between plaintiffs and appellants, between trial-level defendants and appellate-level appellees, and between standing to sue and standing to

appeal, exploring where the analogies between trial-level and appellate standing break down, see Steinman, Shining a Light in a Dim Corner: Standing to Appeal and the Right to Defend a Judgment in the Federal Courts, 38 Ga. L. Rev. 813 (2004). Professor Steinman concludes: "The law of standing to appeal and defend appeals in many ways tracks the law of standing to sue and to defend in the trial court. A somewhat fluid mix of constitutional, prudential, and practice-based doctrines appears to govern each, and considerations of injury, causation, and redressability are crucial to each. The nature and source of the injury claimed on appeal differ from those claimed in district court but, in each context, the plaintiff or appellant, as the case may be, typically stands to gain relative to his pre-existing condition, should the court rule for him. The defendant or appellee, as the case may be, typically stands to suffer relative to his pre-existing condition, if the court rules against him." Id. at 922.

2. DIRECT AND "ASSOCIATIONAL" STANDING

PENNSYLVANIA PSYCHIATRIC SOC. v. GREEN SPRINGS HEALTH SERV.

United States Court of Appeals, Third Circuit, 2002.
280 F.3d 278.

SCIRICA, CIRCUIT JUDGE.

[The plaintiff medical society sued various managed health care organizations ("MCO's") on behalf of member doctors and patients, alleging that defendants were impairing healthcare quality by not authorizing needed treatments and by excessively burdening reimbursement for care rendered. The "principal issue" in the case was whether the association had sufficient "associational and third-party standing" to pursue the litigation.]

On appeal, we must accept as true all material allegations of the complaint and draw all reasonable inferences in a light most favorable to plaintiff. Maio v. Aetna, Inc., 221 F.3d 472, 481–82 (3d Cir. 2000). " 'The issue is not whether a plaintiff will ultimately prevail but whether the claimant is entitled to offer evidence to support the claims.' " In re Burlington Coat Factory Sec. Litig., 114 F.3d 1410, 1420 (3d Cir. 1997) (quoting Scheuer v. Rhodes, 416 U.S. 232, 236 (1974)). [Since the district court threw the case out], we may affirm the district court only if we believe that the association would be entitled to no relief under any set of facts consistent with its allegations. Allegheny Gen. Hosp. v. Philip Morris, Inc., 228 F.3d 429, 434–35 (3d Cir. 2000).

A.

To satisfy the "case or controversy" standing requirement under Article III, § 2 of the United States Constitution, a plaintiff must establish that it has suffered a cognizable injury that is causally related to the alleged conduct of the defendant and is redressable by judicial action. Friends of the Earth, Inc. v. Laidlaw Envtl. Servs. (TOC), Inc., 528 U.S. 167, 180–81 (2000) (discussing Lujan v. Defenders of Wildlife,

504 U.S. 555, 560–61 (1992)). Associations may satisfy these elements by asserting claims that arise from injuries they directly sustain. See, e.g., Babbitt v. United Farm Workers Nat'l Union, 442 U.S. 289, 299 n.11 (1979). Absent injury to itself, an association may pursue claims solely as a representative of its members. See, e.g., New York State Club Ass'n, Inc. v. City of New York, 487 U.S. 1 (1988); Pub. Interest Research Group of N.J., Inc. v. Magnesium Elektron, Inc., 123 F.3d 111 (3d Cir. 1997). By permitting associational standing, we "recognize that the primary reason people join an organization is often to create an effective vehicle for vindicating interests that they share with others." Int'l Union, United Auto., Aerospace & Agric. Implement Workers v. Brock, 477 U.S. 274, 290 (1986); see also Joint Anti–Fascist Refugee Comm. v. McGrath, 341 U.S. 123, 187 (1951) (Jackson, J., concurring) (noting purpose of joining an association "often is to permit the association . . . to vindicate the interests of all").

The Supreme Court has enunciated a three-prong test for associational standing. An association must demonstrate that "(a) its members would otherwise have standing to sue in their own right; (b) the interests it seeks to protect are germane to the organization's purpose; and (c) neither the claim asserted nor the relief requested requires the participation of individual members in the lawsuit." Hunt v. Wash. State Apple Adver. Comm'n, 432 U.S. 333, 343 (1977) (permitting state agency that represented apple industry to challenge North Carolina statute); see also Laidlaw Envtl. Servs., 528 U.S. at 181. The need for some individual participation, however, does not necessarily bar associational standing under this third criterion. Hospital Council, 949 F.2d at 89–90.

In this case, the MCOs concede the Pennsylvania Psychiatric Society satisfies *Hunt*'s first and second prongs. But echoing defendants' objections, the District Court found the psychiatrists' claims would require a level of individual participation that precludes associational standing. As noted, the Society has not appealed the dismissal of its damages claims. This is noteworthy because damages claims usually require significant individual participation, which fatally undercuts a request for associational standing. On this point, the Supreme Court has explained that

> "whether an association has standing to invoke the court's remedial powers on behalf of its members depends in substantial measure on the nature of the relief sought. If in a proper case the association seeks a declaration, injunction, or some other form of prospective relief, it can reasonably be supposed that the remedy, if granted, will inure to the benefit of those members of the association actually injured. Indeed, in all cases in which we have expressly recognized standing in associations to represent their members, the relief sought has been of this kind."

Hunt, 432 U.S. at 343 (quoting Warth v. Seldin, 422 U.S. 490, 515 (1975)). Because claims for monetary relief usually require individual participation, courts have held associations cannot generally raise these claims on behalf of their members. E.g., Air Transp. Ass'n v. Reno, 80

F.3d 477, 484–85 (D.C. Cir. 1996) (collecting cases); Sanner v. Bd. of Trade, 62 F.3d 918, 923 (7th Cir. 1995) (same). Specifically, the Supreme Court has counseled "that an association's action for damages running solely to its members would be barred for want of the association's standing to sue." United Food & Commercial Workers Union Local 751 v. Brown Group, Inc., 517 U.S. 544, 546 (1996) (relying on *Hunt*, 432 U.S. at 343). Had the Society continued to press its claims for damages on appeal, dismissal under Rule 12(b)(6) would be entirely appropriate.

The sole associational standing question remains whether, taking the allegations as true, the Pennsylvania Psychiatric Society's requests for declaratory and injunctive relief will require an inappropriate level of individual participation.[3] We first addressed this question in Hospital Council of Western Pennsylvania v. City of Pittsburgh, where an association alleged that certain city and counties threatened to discriminate against nonprofit hospitals on taxation, zoning, and contract matters if the hospitals refused to make voluntary payments in lieu of taxes. 949 F.2d 83. Interpreting Hunt's third prong through the prism of earlier Supreme Court jurisprudence, we rejected the city's argument that some individual participation violated this requirement. Id. at 89. Explaining the circumstances on which this conclusion rested, we concluded:

> The claims asserted by the Council would require some participation by some Council members. This case, unlike many prior association-al standing cases, does not involve a challenge to a statute, regulation, or ordinance, but instead involves a challenge to alleged practices that would probably have to be proved by evidence regarding the manner in which the defendants treated individual member hospitals. Adjudication of such claims would likely require that member hospitals provide discovery, and trial testimony by officers and employees of member hospitals might be needed as well. Nevertheless, since participation by "each [allegedly] injured party" would not be necessary, we see no ground for denying associational standing.

Id. at 89–90.

* * * The MCOs argue the medical coverage decisions on psychiatric care and substance abuse services, which form the basis of the organization's allegations, are fact-intensive inquiries. For this reason, they assert the examination of medical care determinations will demand significant individual participation. To buttress this point, defendants note they offer subscribers various health care plans that in turn provide varying benefits. Consequently, they argue, demonstrating any single

---

3. Individual participation by an association's membership may be unnecessary when the relief sought is prospective (i.e., an injunction or declaratory judgment). See Brock, 477 U.S. at 287–88; Ark. Med. Soc'y, Inc. v. Reynolds, 6 F.3d 519, 528 (8th Cir. 1993); Action Alliance of Senior Citizens v. Snider, 1994 WL 384990 (E.D. Pa. July 18, 1994) ("Participation of individual members is rarely necessary when injunctive relief rather than individual damages is sought. Hospital Council, 949 F.2d at 89. This particularly true where ... a broad based change in procedure rather than individualized injunctive relief is sought.").

coverage decision violated their obligations will entail a case-by-case examination of a patient's condition along with the corresponding available benefits. In support, defendants rely on Rent Stabilization Association v. Dinkins, where an association of landowners alleged rent regulations constituted an unconstitutional taking of their property. 5 F.3d 591 (2d Cir. 1993). There, the Court of Appeals for the Second Circuit held that the extensive individual testimony required to adjudicate the claims would violate *Hunt.* Id. at 596; see also Reid v. Dep't of Commerce, 793 F.2d 277, 279–80 (Fed. Cir. 1986) (holding that a union lacked standing to assert back pay claims for its members because each claim depended on member's individual circumstances). The court reasoned the claims foreclosed standing because it

> would have to engage in an ad hoc factual inquiry for each landlord who alleges that he has suffered a taking. [The court] would have to determine the landlord's particular return based on a host of individualized financial data, and [the court] would have to investigate the reasons for any failure to obtain an adequate return, because the Constitution certainly cannot be read to guarantee a profit to an inefficient or incompetent landlord.

Rent Stabilization, 5 F.3d at 596. But the Court of Appeals for the Second Circuit has not rejected associational standing where only limited individual participation by some members would be required. See N.Y. State Nat'l Org. for Women v. Terry, 886 F.2d 1339, 1349 (2d Cir. 1989) (association warranted standing although evidence from some individual members necessary). We agree that conferring associational standing would be improper for claims requiring a fact-intensive-individual inquiry.

The District Court reviewed the Pennsylvania Psychiatric Society's allegations—overly restrictive treatment authorizations; care determinations based on criteria besides medical necessity; creation of improper obstacles to physician credentialing; imposition of overly-burdensome administrative requirements; failure to pay psychiatrists for rendered services; direct interference with psychiatrist-patient relations—and found each assertion would necessitate significant individual participation. If this were true, the organization would not satisfy the associational standing requirements.[6]

But the Pennsylvania Psychiatric Society maintains that the heart of its complaint involves systemic policy violations that will make extensive individual participation unnecessary. In effect, the Society contends the methods the MCOs employ for making decisions—e.g., authorizing or denying mental health services, credentialing physicians, and reimbursement—represent breaches of contract as well as tortious conduct. Therefore, insofar as its allegations concern how the MCOs render these decisions, the Society's complaint "involves challenges to alleged prac-

---

6. Likewise, if the Pennsylvania Psychiatric Society continued to press damages claims on behalf of its members, it would not meet the requirements for associational standing. See discussion above.

tices," Hospital Council, 949 F.2d at 89, that may be established with sample testimony, which may not involve specific, factually intensive, individual medical care determinations. If the Pennsylvania Psychiatric Society can establish these claims with limited individual participation, it would satisfy the requirements for associational standing. While we question whether the Society can accomplish this, at this stage of the proceedings on a motion to dismiss for lack of standing, we review the sufficiency of the pleadings and "must accept as true all material allegations of the complaint and must construe the complaint in favor of the plaintiff." Trump Hotels & Casino Resorts, Inc. v. Mirage Resorts Inc., 140 F.3d 478, 483 (3d Cir. 1998) (citing Warth, 422 U.S. at 501). For this reason, we believe the Society's suit should not be dismissed before it is given the opportunity to establish the alleged violations without significant individual participation. * * * Therefore, we conclude that the District Court erred in dismissing the matter on this basis. * * *

B.

In addition to advancing the rights of its member psychiatrists, the Pennsylvania Psychiatric Society seeks to assert the claims of its members' patients who are also allegedly injured by defendants' practices. Because the patients are not members of, or otherwise directly associated with, the Pennsylvania Psychiatric Society, the Society does not have associational standing to assert their claims. Nonetheless, the Society maintains it may bring the patients' claims under the doctrine of third-party standing.[7]

In particular, the Society contends its member psychiatrists have third-party standing to assert the claims of their patients, and the Society has standing to bring the claims of its members, including their third-party claims. Defendants have challenged both of these steps. Therefore, we must decide, first, whether the member psychiatrists have third-party standing to bring the claims of their patients, and second, whether the Pennsylvania Psychiatric Society has associational standing to assert these members' third-party claims.

Apart from the constitutional requirements for standing, courts have imposed a set of prudential limitations on the exercise of federal jurisdiction over third-party claims. Bennett v. Spear, 520 U.S. 154, 162 (1997) ("The federal judiciary has also adhered to a set of prudential principles that bear on the question of standing."); Warth, 422 U.S. at 498; Powell v. Ridge, 189 F.3d 387, 404 (3d Cir. 1999). The restrictions against third-party standing do not stem from the Article III "case or controversy" requirement, but rather from prudential concerns, Amato v. Wilentz, 952 F.2d 742, 748 (3d Cir. 1991), which prevent courts from "deciding questions of broad social import where no individual rights

7. Third-party standing is also commonly known as jus tertii standing. City of Chicago v. Morales, 527 U.S. 41, 56 n.22 (1999); The Pitt News, 215 F.3d at 362 n.6; see also Henry Monaghan, Third Party Standing, 84 Colum. L. Rev. 277, 278 n.6 (1984) (explaining jus tertii standing).

would be vindicated and ... limit access to the federal courts to those litigants best suited to assert a particular claim." Gladstone, Realtors v. Vill. of Bellwood, 441 U.S. 91, 99–100 (1979); see also Sec'y of State v. Joseph H. Munson Co., 467 U.S. 947, 955 (1984).

It is a well-established tenet of standing that a "litigant must assert his or her own legal rights and interests, and cannot rest a claim to relief on the legal rights or interests of third parties." Powers v. Ohio, 499 U.S. 400, 410 (1991); see also Valley Forge Christian Coll. v. Ams. United for Separation of Church and State, Inc., 454 U.S. 464, 474–75 (1982). This principle is based on the assumption that "third parties themselves usually will be the best proponents of their own rights," Singleton v. Wulff, 428 U.S. 106, 114 (1976) (plurality opinion), which serves to foster judicial restraint and ensure the clear presentation of issues. See Munson, 467 U.S. at 955.

Yet the prohibition is not invariable and our jurisprudence recognizes third-party standing under certain circumstances.[10] Campbell v. Louisiana, 523 U.S. 392, 397–98 (1998); see also Hodel v. Irving, 481 U.S. 704, 711 (1987) (acknowledging general rule that party must assert own interests is "subject to exceptions"). In particular, if a course of conduct "prevents a third-party from entering into a relationship with the litigant (typically a contractual relationship), to which relationship the third party has a legal entitlement," third-party standing may be appropriate. United States Dep't of Labor v. Triplett, 494 U.S. 715, 720 (1990); see also Munson, 467 U.S. at 954–58 (fundraiser had third-party standing to challenge statute limiting fees charitable organizations could pay because law infringed on organizations' right to hire fundraiser for a higher fee).

The Supreme Court has found that the principles animating these prudential concerns are not subverted if the third party is hindered from asserting its own rights and shares an identity of interests with the plaintiff. See Craig, 429 U.S. at 193–94; Singleton, 428 U.S. at 114–15; Eisenstadt v. Baird, 405 U.S. 438, 443–46 (1972). More specifically, third-party standing requires the satisfaction of three preconditions: 1) the plaintiff must suffer injury; 2) the plaintiff and the third party must have a "close relationship"; and 3) the third party must face some obstacles that prevent it from pursuing its own claims. Campbell, 523 U.S. at 397; Powers, 499 U.S. at 411; The Pitt News, 215 F.3d at 362. It remains for courts to balance these factors to determine if third-party standing is warranted. Amato, 952 F.2d at 750.

---

10. For instance, doctors may be able to assert the rights of patients; lawyers may be able to assert the rights of clients; vendors may be able to assert the rights of customers; and candidates for public office may be able to assert the rights of voters. See, e.g., Caplin & Drysdale, Chartered v. United States, 491 U.S. 617 (1989) (holding lawyer could bring Sixth Amendment lawsuit on behalf of criminal defendant); Singleton, 428 U.S. 106 (conferring standing on physicians on behalf of patients to challenge a statute that excluded funding for abortions from Medicaid benefits); Craig, 429 U.S. 190 (allowing vendor to challenge statute that prohibited males under age of twenty-one from buying beer); Mancuso v. Taft, 476 F.2d 187 (1st Cir. 1973) (permitting candidate for public office to raise voters' rights).

a.

Although the Pennsylvania Psychiatric Society itself has not suffered direct injury, it is uncontested that it properly pleaded that defendants' policies and procedures have economically injured its member psychiatrists and undermined their ability to provide quality health care. Thus, while the Society does not itself stand in an appropriate relationship to the patients' claims to directly assert them, its members may have third-party standing to do so.[11] And because plaintiff seeks to establish standing on the basis of its members' standing to bring these claims, the members are the appropriate focus of inquiry for these purposes.

b.

We next turn to whether the psychiatrists and their patients have a sufficiently "close relationship" which will permit the physicians to effectively advance their patients' claims. To meet this standard, this relationship must permit the psychiatrists to operate " 'fully, or very nearly, as effective a proponent' " of their patients' rights as the patients themselves.[12] Powers, 499 U.S. at 413 (quoting Singleton, 428 U.S. at 115).

The patients' relationships with their psychiatrists fulfills this requirement. In *Singleton v. Wulff*, 428 U.S. 106, the Supreme Court granted physicians third-party standing on behalf of their patients to challenge a statute prohibiting Medicaid funding for certain abortions. Because of the inherent closeness of the doctor-patient relationship, the plurality found the physicians could efficaciously advocate their patients' interests. Id. at 117 (noting "abortion decision is one in which the physician is intimately involved"). The relationship forged between psychiatrists and their patients is equally compelling.

Psychiatrists clearly have the kind of relationship with their patients which lends itself to advancing claims on their behalf. This intimate relationship and the resulting mental health treatment ensures psychiatrists can effectively assert their patients' rights. Because the Pennsylvania Psychiatric Society alleges the MCOs prevent patients from receiving necessary mental health services and psychiatrists from providing them, its member psychiatrists would be well-suited to litigate these claims for both parties, as their interests are clearly aligned. See

11. The District Court held—and the dissent argues—that the Pennsylvania Psychiatric Society could not raise these claims because it did not itself suffer injury. Injury to the Society, however, is not relevant to the issue of the psychiatrists' standing to bring the patients' claims. Because of the Society's posture, that is the initial question to be resolved. Only after it is determined that the member psychiatrists would have third-party standing over these claims do we assess whether the Society can bring its members' third-party claims. It is in the latter context that injury to appellant itself is a potential requirement, which we discuss below.

12. Courts have generally recognized physicians' authority to pursue the claims of their patients. Am. Coll. of Obstetricians & Gynecologists v. Thornburgh, 737 F.2d 283, 290 & n.6 (3d Cir. 1984) (collecting cases where physicians allowed to assert patients' claims); see also Planned Parenthood v. Farmer, 220 F.3d 127, 147 & n.10 (3d Cir. 2000).

Amato, 952 F.2d at 751 (noting doctor-patient relationship provides strong likelihood of effective advocacy by a physician on behalf of his patients). Accordingly, we believe the psychiatrist-patient relationship would satisfy the second criterion for third-party standing.

c.

Finally, we examine whether the mental health patients face obstacles to pursuing litigation themselves. This criterion does not require an absolute bar from suit, but "some hindrance to the third party's ability to protect his or her own interests," Powers, 499 U.S. at 411. In other words, a party need not face insurmountable hurdles to warrant third-party standing.[14] Id. at 415 (holding excluded juror's limited incentive to bring discrimination suit satisfied obstacle requirement for criminal defendant to merit third-party standing); Singleton, 428 U.S. at 117 (recognizing lawsuit's invasion of patient's privacy and "imminent mootness" of pregnancy sufficiently impeded patient from bringing suit herself). The District Court found the patients' mental health problems did not significantly hinder them from suing. We disagree.

The stigma associated with receiving mental health services presents a considerable deterrent to litigation. * * *. Therefore, we believe the patients' fear of stigmatization, coupled with their potential incapacity to pursue legal remedies, operates as a powerful deterrent to bringing suit.

Because the third-party claims asserted by the Pennsylvania Psychiatric Society do not implicate any constitutional rights of the psychiatrists' patients, the MCOs contend that granting third-party standing is unwarranted. While successful third-party standing claims have involved alleged violations of third parties' constitutional rights, Singleton and its progeny have not stipulated that constitutional claims are a prerequisite. It is true that the rule against third-party standing "normally bars litigants from asserting the rights or legal interests of others in order to obtain relief from injury to themselves." Warth, 422 U.S. at 509. Furthermore, the Supreme Court has noted that courts must consider "the relationship of the litigant to the person whose rights are being asserted; the ability of the person to advance his own rights; and the impact of the litigation on third-party interests." Caplin & Drysdale, 491 U.S. at 623 n.3. But the Court has not held that a constitutional claim must also be alleged, see, e.g., Powers, 499 U.S. at 410–11, and absent further guidance, we will not impose this requirement. For these reasons, we hold the Pennsylvania Psychiatric Society's member psychiatrists would have third-party standing to assert the claims of their patients.

---

14. One treatise insists that "cases do not demand an absolute impossibility of suit in order to fall within the impediment exception. At the other end of the spectrum, a practical disincentive to sue may suffice, although a mere disincentive is less persuasive than a concrete impediment." 15 James Wm. Moore et al., Moore's Federal Practice § 101.51[3][c].

2.

The Pennsylvania Psychiatric Society contends it has standing to bring these third-party claims just as it has standing to bring its members' other claims under the doctrine of associational standing. Defendants maintain the patients' claims are too attenuated from the Society to permit derivative standing.

We decline to adopt a per se rule barring such derivative claims. The Supreme Court did not delineate in *Hunt* which types of claims associations could bring on behalf of their members, but rather simply held that "an association has standing to bring suit on behalf of its members" when the requisite elements are established. *Hunt*, 432 U.S. at 343.

The limitations on derivative standing, therefore, are to be determined by applying the test for associational standing specified in *Hunt*. Our holding that the Pennsylvania Psychiatric Society has alleged facts sufficient to establish the third-party standing of its members to bring their patients' claims implies the satisfaction of only the first requirement of the *Hunt* test—that "its members would otherwise have standing" to bring these claims. A third-party claim must also meet the requirements that "the interests it seeks to protect are germane to the organization's purpose" and that "neither the claim asserted nor the relief requested requires the participation of individual members in the lawsuit." Id. These factors inform the analysis whether an association stands in the correct relationship to a claim to allow it to assert that claim on behalf of others.

Other courts of appeals have adopted this approach in finding standing in similar cases. In Fraternal Order of Police v. United States, 152 F.3d 998, 1002 (D.C. Cir. 1998), the Court of Appeals for the District of Columbia granted an organization derivative authority to assert the third-party claims of its members. ("The presence of [the chief law enforcement officers] as members gives the Order standing to make these [third-party] claims as well."). The Fraternal Order of Police sued to contest the constitutionality of federal legislation that prohibited supplying firearms to police officers convicted of domestic violence. 152 F.3d at 1000–01. Because a chief law enforcement officer would be liable for supplying a firearm to a subordinate convicted of domestic violence and because the failure to supply a weapon could also violate the subordinate officer's rights, the court of appeals found the chiefs had third-party standing to advance the claims of their officers. Id. at 1002. Since the chiefs were members of the Fraternal Order of Police, the association had standing to advance the chiefs' claims as well as the claims of their subordinates. Similar to this case, none of the members were themselves party to the suit.

The Court of Appeals for the Sixth Circuit also granted an organization derivative authority to enjoin the enforcement of a statute requiring private schools to administer proficiency tests in Ohio Association of Independent Schools v. Goff, 92 F.3d 419, 421–22 (6th Cir. 1996). As parties to the litigation, the association's member schools had standing because failure to comply with the statute would result in the loss of their school charters. Id. at 422. The private schools also had third-party standing to assert the constitutional right of their students' parents to direct their children's education. Because its member schools could be injured by the statute, the Ohio Association of Independent Schools also had standing to assert their claims. Since its member schools had standing to assert the rights of the parents, the court held the Ohio Association of Independent Schools also had standing to sue on behalf of the parents whose children attended its members' schools. Id. ("The member schools ... have standing ... on behalf of parents of students who are threatened with the nonreceipt of diplomas. Consequently, the OAIS itself, as an organization dedicated exclusively to advancing the interests of the member schools, has associational standing to challenge the statutes at issue."). Thus, while some member schools—the intermediate parties—were parties to the dispute, the Sixth Circuit's standing analysis did not rely on that fact. We see a compelling analogy between these cases and the claims before us, and believe the Pennsylvania Psychiatric Society may have standing to assert its members' third-party claims.

* * * It is generally true that third-party standing requires the party who advances the interests of another party to also suffer discrete injury. As noted previously, this prudential requirement sharpens presentation of claims and avoids litigation of general grievances. But when an association, which has not sustained direct injury, obtains standing to pursue the claims of its members, the association may rely on the injuries sustained by its members to satisfy the injury-in-fact requirement. Consequently, once an organization's members establish third-party standing, the prudential concerns are alleviated if the association also has authority to assert its members' claims.

It is a well-recognized anomaly of representational standing that the individuals who have sustained the requisite injury to satisfy the constitutional and prudential standing criteria are not in fact responsible for bringing suit. So long as the association's members have or will suffer sufficient injury to merit standing and their members possess standing to represent the interests of third-parties, then associations can advance the third-party claims of their members without suffering injuries themselves. If on remand the Pennsylvania Psychiatric Society warrants associational standing to represent its members, we conclude it also may have derivative authority to raise the claims of its members' patients.

REMANDED.

Notes and Questions

1. Some states do not recognize the standing of associations to raise claims, or pursue appeals, based on the interests of their members. See W.S. Carnes v. Board of Supervisors, 252 Va. 377, 478 S.E.2d 295 (1996).

2. The federal courts have permitted third-party standing in a wide range of relationships in which the third-parties' interests are sufficiently

aligned with the interests of the rights-holder that standing is appropriate. See e.g., U.S. Department of Labor v. Triplett, 494 U.S. 715, 720–21, 110 S.Ct. 1428, 108 L.Ed.2d 701 (1990) (lawyer-client); Carey v. Population Serv. Int'll, 431 U.S. 678, 682, 97 S.Ct. 2010, 52 L.Ed.2d 675 (1977) (vendor-customer); Singleton v. Wulff, 428 U.S. 106, 96 S.Ct. 2868, 49 L.Ed.2d 826 (1976) (doctor-patient); Pierce v. Society of Sisters, 268 U.S. 510, 536, 45 S.Ct. 571, 69 L.Ed. 1070 (school-students); But see Kowalski v. Tesmer, __ U.S. __, 125 S.Ct. 564, 160 L.Ed.2d 519 (2004) (attorneys with only prospective attorney-client relationship to unknown indigent criminal defendants had no standing to raise latter's rights).

3.   Should a minority and diversity-oriented association be deemed to have standing to challenge the FCC's award of broadcasting licenses to particular groups it believes are insensitive or hostile to its members? As presented in one case, the association declared that it was "committed to furthering social, racial, and economic justice" and that it "seeks to ensure that professional opportunities in broadcasting expand for minorities and that communities have access to diverse broadcasting sources." The association also stated that "several" of its members "live and watch television in the markets that are at issue in this appeal." However, the appellate court noted that the association "submitted nothing more than identical declarations from two of its members, asserting that each ' "would be seriously aggrieved" ' by a grant of the applications because ' "as a consequence . . . members . . . , including myself, would be deprived of . . . program service in the public interest." ' See Rainbow/Push Coalition v. FCC, 330 F.3d 539 (D.C. Cir. 2003).

4.   For direct standing, several courts have taken the position that "the mere fact that an organization redirects some of its resources to litigation and legal counseling in response to actions or inactions of another party is insufficient to impart standing upon the organization." In contrast, an organization could have standing if it had proven a drain on its resources resulting from counteracting the effects of the defendant's actions. Likewise, another court concluded that a housing organization had standing where its staff "stopped everything else" and devoted all attention to the litigation in question and diverted resources to counter the defendant's conduct. See, e.g., Louisiana Acorn Fair Housing v. Leblanc, 211 F.3d 298 (5th Cir. 2000).

3.   STANDING AS A "NEXT FRIEND"

Centuries ago the French legal system recognized a form of representational standing known as the "prochein ami" (the "next friend") in which a family member or other friend of the party who should sue or appeal is allowed to do so on behalf of a person who is not legally able to do so. The doctrine came to England after 1066, and was part of American law at the time of the Nation's independence. It still exists, and is applied by appellate courts. In some states it is routinely used as the rubric for a parent's suit on behalf of a minor child, or a family member's commencement of an action no behalf of an institutionalized relative.

COALITION OF CLERGY v. BUSH

United States Court of Appeals, Ninth Circuit, 2002.
310 F.3d 1153.

WARDLAW, CIRCUIT JUDGE.

A Coalition of clergy, lawyers, and law professors petitioned for a *writ of habeas corpus* on behalf of persons captured in Afghanistan by the Armed Forces of the United States and now held at Guantanamo Naval Base, Cuba, in a secure detention facility known as Camp X–Ray. The Coalition alleged that the detainees have been deprived of their liberty without due process of law, have not been informed of the nature and cause of the accusations against them or afforded the assistance of counsel, and are being held by the United States government in violation of the United States Constitution and the Third Geneva Convention.

The district court dismissed the petition on the grounds that * * * the Coalition lacked next-friend standing to assert claims on behalf of the detainees.

I. BACKGROUND

In an event forever seared upon the soul of America, members of the Al Qaeda terrorist group engaged in a quick series of attacks upon the United States on September 11, 2001, killing thousands of civilians in New York, northern Virginia, and Pennsylvania, with the intent to work even more crippling damage upon the country. As the horror of these events was realized by the American people, the President and Congress united in their commitment of the Armed Forces of the United States to take military action against the Al Qaeda terrorists and those who would harbor them, like the Taliban government of Afghanistan, to prevent any future acts of international terrorism. Authorization for Use of Military Force, Pub. L. No. 107–40, 115 Stat. 224 (Sept. 18, 2001) (authorizing the President "to use all necessary and appropriate force against those nations, organizations, or persons he determines planned, authorized, committed, or aided the terrorist attacks that occurred on September 11, 2001, or harbored such organizations or persons"). American forces were sent to Afghanistan and neighboring countries, and a United States-led alliance attacked the forces of the Taliban government and Al Qaeda.

The United States and its allies successfully removed the Taliban from power and captured, killed, or drove to flight some of the more notorious members of Al Qaeda and the Taliban. Kabul, the capital of Afghanistan, was taken on November 13, 2001, and thousands of Taliban and Al Qaeda combatants were eventually captured or surrendered. Among these captives, the detainees deemed most dangerous by the United States military were transferred to the United States Naval Base at Guantanamo Bay, Cuba.

The detainees are being held at the naval base in a secure facility known as Camp X–Ray. They have been visited by members of the

International Red Cross and diplomats from their home countries. Although the detainees have not been allowed to meet with lawyers, they have had some opportunity to write to friends and family members. * * *

This case stands or falls on whether the Coalition has standing to bring a habeas petition on behalf of the Guantanamo Bay detainees. * * * The Coalition does not assert direct standing, but instead urges us to find next-friend standing under the federal habeas statute or standing under traditional principles of third-party standing. We address these arguments in turn.

A. Next-friend standing under 28 U.S.C. § 2242.

The federal habeas statute provides that the "application for a writ of habeas corpus shall be in writing signed and verified by the person for whose relief it is intended or by someone acting in his behalf." 28 U.S.C. § 2242. Congress added the words "or by someone acting in his behalf" by amendment in 1948. Even before the amendment, however, federal courts had long recognized that under appropriate circumstances, habeas petitions could be brought by third parties, such as family members or agents, on behalf of a prisoner. This species of third-party habeas standing, known as next-friend standing, was examined at length by the Supreme Court in Whitmore v. Arkansas, 495 U.S. 149, 161–64 (1990). In *Whitmore*, the Supreme Court recognized that next-friend standing "has long been an accepted basis for jurisdiction in certain circumstances." The Court explained:

> Most frequently, "next friends" appear in court on behalf of detained prisoners who are unable, usually because of mental incompetence or inaccessibility, to seek relief themselves. As early as the 17th century, the English Habeas Corpus Act of 1679 authorized complaints to be filed by "any one on ... behalf" of detained persons, and in 1704 the House of Lords resolved "That every Englishman, who is imprisoned by any authority whatsoever, has an undoubted right, by his agents, or friends, to apply for, and obtain a Writ of Habeas Corpus, in order to procure his liberty by due course of law." Some early decisions in this country interpreted ambiguous provisions of the federal habeas corpus statute to allow "next friend" standing in connection with petitions for writs of habeas corpus, and Congress eventually codified the doctrine explicitly in 1948.

Whitmore, 495 U.S. at 162–63. * * * The Second Circuit Court of Appeals further elaborated upon the practice and its limitations in 1921:

> It has never been understood that, at common law, authority from a person unlawfully imprisoned or deprived of his liberty was necessary to warrant the issuing of a habeas corpus, to inquire into the cause of his detention.... But the complaint must set forth some reason or explanation satisfactory to the court showing why the detained person does not sign and verify the complaint and who 'the

next friend' is. It was not intended that the writ of habeas corpus should be availed of, as matter of course, by intruders or uninvited meddlers, styling themselves next friends.

United States ex rel. Bryant v. Houston, 273 F. 915, 916 (2d Cir. 1921); see also Rosenberg v. United States, 346 U.S. 273, 291–92 (1953)(denying stranger the right to bring petition on behalf of the Rosenbergs, because there was no authorization); United States ex rel. Toth v. Quarles, 350 U.S. 11, 13 n.3 (1955)(granting next-friend standing to sister on behalf of prisoner in Korea); Gilmore v. Utah, 429 U.S. 1012, 1013–14 (1976) (recognizing, for purposes of stay, next-friend standing of mother on behalf of prisoner); Evans v. Bennett, 440 U.S. 1301 (1979)(Rehnquist, Circuit Justice)(recognizing, for purposes of stay, next-friend standing of mother on behalf of prisoner); Hamilton v. Texas, 485 U.S. 1042, 1042 (1988) (recognizing next-friend standing of mother on behalf of prisoner); Demosthenes v. Baal, 495 U.S. 731, 735 (1990) (denying next-friend standing to parents on behalf of prisoner, when there was no showing of mental incompetence); Vargas v. Lambert, 159 F.3d 1161, 1163 (9th Cir. 1998)(granting next-friend standing to mother on behalf of prisoner); Hamdi v. Rumsfeld, 296 F.3d 278, 281 (4th Cir. 2002)(granting next-friend standing to father on behalf of son).* * *

The Supreme Court surveyed the development of the next-friend doctrine in Whitmore, both at common law and under the federal habeas statute, concluding:

> "Next friend" standing is by no means granted automatically to whomever seeks to pursue an action on behalf of another. Decisions applying the habeas corpus statute have adhered to at least two firmly rooted prerequisites for "next friend" standing. First, a "next friend" must provide an adequate explanation—such as inaccessibility, mental incompetence, or other disability—why the real party in interest cannot appear on his own behalf to prosecute the action. Second, the "next friend" must be truly dedicated to the best interests of the person on whose behalf he seeks to litigate, and it has been further suggested that a "next friend" must have some significant relationship with the real party in interest. The burden is on the "next friend" clearly to establish the propriety of his status and thereby justify the jurisdiction of the court.

Whitmore, 495 U.S. at 163–64 . We have subsequently described the two-pronged Whitmore inquiry as follows:

> In order to establish next-friend standing, the putative next friend must show: (1) that the petitioner is unable to litigate his own cause due to mental incapacity, lack of access to court, or other similar disability; and (2) the next friend has some significant relationship with, and is truly dedicated to the best interests of, the petitioner.

Massie ex rel. Kroll v. Woodford, 244 F.3d 1192, 1194 (9th Cir. 2001).

We first examine whether the Guantanamo Bay detainees are able to litigate their own cause, and then turn to an examination of whether the Coalition has a relationship with any of the detainees sufficient to meet the second prong. * * *

usually seen as a mental capacity question

i. Detainees' inability to litigate own cause.

The first prong of the Whitmore–Massie test, lack of access to the court, has most often been considered a question of mental capacity, usually in the context of an inmate's capacity to bring his own petition. See, e.g., Massie, 244 F.3d 1192; Vargas, 159 F.3d 1161. In Whitmore, the Supreme Court noted:

> One necessary condition for "next friend" standing in federal court is a showing by the proposed "next friend" that the real party in interest is unable to litigate his own cause due to mental incapacity, lack of access to court, or other similar disability. That prerequisite for "next friend" standing is not satisfied where ... his access to court is otherwise unimpeded.

Whitmore, 495 U.S. at 165.

incommunicado argument doesn't work

The Coalition does not urge that the detainees suffer a mental or physical disability precluding their representation of their interests before the court, rather it argues that the first prong of the Whitmore–Massie test is satisfied because the detainees "appear to be held incommunicado," and thus are physically blocked from the courts. This hyperbolic argument fails because it lacks support in the record; in fact, the prisoners are not being held incommunicado.[2]

The record shows that the detainees have been visited by members of the International Red Cross and diplomats from their home countries, and have had limited opportunities to write to friends and family members. Family members have filed habeas petitions on the behalf of some detainees, and diplomats from several countries including Pakistan, Kuwait, Australia, and the United Kingdom have made inquiries into the status of the detainees and sought their release. Rasul v. Bush, 215 F. Supp. 2d 55, 57 (D.D.C. 2002) ("The Court would point out that the notion that these aliens could be held incommunicado from the rest of the world would appear to be inaccurate."); see also Hamdi II, 296 F.3d at 279 (Father filed a petition for a writ of habeas corpus as next friend of his son, who is detained at the Norfolk Naval Station Brig as an alleged enemy combatant captured during ongoing military operations in Afghanistan.). As noted by the District Court for the District of Columbia, "the government recognizes that these aliens fall within the protections of certain provisions of international law and that diplomatic channels remain an ongoing and viable means to address the claims raised by these aliens." Rasul, 215 F. Supp. 2d at 56–57.

international law protections

2. The Coalition requested at oral argument that we remand for an evidentiary hearing on a variety of issues, including the detainees' lack of access to lawyers or courts. We deny this request because the Coalition has not even made a preliminary showing that upon remand it could prove, in light of the record that is before the court, that any individual detainee is being held totally incommunicado. A bald assertion that the detainees are held incommunicado, when the record makes clear the contrary, does not necessitate a hearing; indeed it appears such a hearing would be futile.

Nevertheless, it is evident that the detainees are being held in a secure facility in an isolated area of the world, on a United States Naval Base in a foreign country, to which United States citizens are severely restricted from traveling. The detainees are not able to meet with lawyers, and have been denied access to file petitions in United States courts on their own behalf. As stated by the district court, and conceded by the Government at argument, "from a practical point of view the detainees cannot be said to have unimpeded or free access to court." *Coalition of Clergy*, 189 F. Supp. 2d at 1042. We need not delineate the contours of the access requirement in these circumstances, however, in light of the Coalition's lack of a relationship with the detainees.

lack of access to the court

ii. Significant relationship with and true dedication to the detainees.

Turning to the second prong of Whitmore–Massie, we examine whether the members of the Coalition have some significant relationship with, and are truly dedicated to the best interests of, the detainees. In *Whitmore*, the Supreme Court addressed the limitations on third-party "next friend" standing, and explained that "however friendly" and "sympathetic" a petition may be, and however concerned the petitioner is that "unconstitutional laws [are being] enforced," a petitioner without a significant relationship does not suffer a sufficient grievance for standing purposes. *Whitmore*, 495 U.S. at 166. Otherwise, "however worthy and high minded the motives of 'next friends' may be, they inevitably run the risk of making the actual defendant a pawn to be manipulated on a chessboard larger than his own case." *Lenhard v. Wolff*, 443 U.S. 1306, 1312 (1979)(Rehnquist, Circuit Justice). As the Court explained in *Whitmore*:

A pawn in the chess case

> These limitations on the "next friend" doctrine are driven by the recognition that it was not intended that the writ of habeas corpus should be availed of, as matter of course, by intruders or uninvited meddlers, styling themselves next friends. Indeed, if there were no restriction on "next friend" standing in federal courts, the litigant asserting only a generalized interest in constitutional governance could circumvent the jurisdictional limits of Art. III simply by assuming the mantle of "next friend."

Whitmore, 495 U.S. at 164.

The Coalition argues that the Supreme Court in Whitmore did not impose the requirement of a "significant relationship" between the "next friend" and the detainee, but only noted that the cases it had surveyed suggested as much. In its view, the "significant relationship" requirement is the Ninth Circuit's own erroneous gloss on Whitmore, which need not be followed. All that is necessary, according to the Coalition, is: (1) an adequate explanation for the reason the real party in interest cannot appear on its own behalf; and (2) the true dedication by the next friend to the best interests of the detainee. The "significant relationship" criterion is no more than an additional consideration in determining whether a petitioner is a suitable next friend. See, e.g., *United States v. Ken Int'l. Co.*, 897 F. Supp. 462, 465 (D. Nev.

Coalition's point of view

1995)(stating the two requirements, and then noting: "It is also suggested that a 'next friend' must have some significant relationship with the real party in interest." (citing *Whitmore*, 495 U.S. at 163–64)).

Combining the "significant relationship" requirement, however, with the "dedicated to best interests" consideration, as we did in Massie (and as suggested by Whitmore), meets the concerns the Whitmore Court addressed. The existence of a significant relationship enhances the probability that a petitioner is a suitable next friend, i.e., that a petitioner knows and is dedicated to the prisoner's individual best interests. The more attenuated the relationship between petitioner and prisoner, the less likely a petitioner can know the best interests of the prisoner. The Fourth Circuit adopted the Massie approach in its recent decision in Hamdi v. Rumsfeld, 294 F.3d 598 (4th Cir. 2002) ("Hamdi I"), denying next-friend standing to a public defender and a private citizen who filed habeas petitions on behalf of a military detainee captured as an alleged enemy combatant in Afghanistan. Id. at 604. Construing the language of Whitmore, it noted:

> [The Supreme Court in Whitmore] thought it important to begin by stating that there are "at least two firmly rooted prerequisites for 'next friend' standing," thereby suggesting that there may be more. And after specifying the first two requirements, the Court went out of its way to observe that "it has been further suggested that a 'next friend' must have some significant relationship with the real party in interest." (denying minister and first cousin of prisoner next friend standing) .

Hamdi I, 294 F.3d at 604(quoting Whitmore, 495 U.S. at 163–64). Following *Massie*, "*Whitmore* is thus most faithfully understood as requiring a would-be next friend to have a significant relationship with the real party in interest." Id.

Nevertheless, the contours of the requisite "significant relationship" do not remain static, but must necessarily adapt to the circumstances facing each individual detainee. "Significance" is a relative concept, dependant on the individual prisoner's plight. Not all detainees may have a relative, friend, or even a diplomatic delegation able or willing to act on their behalf. In such an extreme case it is plausible that a person with "some" relationship conveying some modicum of authority or consent, "significant" in comparison to the detainee's other relationships, could serve as the next friend. Moreover, the concept of "true dedication" is a subjective one, difficult of measurement. The existence of some relationship, whether it be from authorized representation to friendship or alliance to familial, serves as an objective basis for discerning the "intruder" or "uninvited meddler" from the true "next friend."

holding

In this case, however, the Coalition has not demonstrated any relationship with the detainees. The record is devoid of any effort to even communicate with the detainees. * * *

iii. The Coalition lacks next-friend standing.

We accept the Coalition's concern for the rights and welfare of the detainees at Camp X–Ray as genuine and sincere. Nevertheless, it has failed to demonstrate any relationship with the detainees, generally or individually. We therefore must conclude that even assuming the detainees are unable to litigate on their own behalf and even under the most relative interpretation of the "significant relationship" requirement the Coalition lacks next-friend standing. * * * At best, the Coalition can only assert "a generalized interest in constitutional governance." *Whitmore*, 495 U.S. at 164. This relationship is insufficient to support next-friend standing.

no next friend standing

B. Third-party standing.

It is a well-established rule that a litigant may assert only his own legal rights and interests and cannot rest a claim to relief on the legal rights or interests of third parties. Singleton v. Wulff, 428 U.S. 106, 113–14 (1976); *Warth*, 422 U.S. at 499. As the prohibition against third-party standing is prudential, rather than constitutional, the Supreme Court has recognized exceptions to this general rule. For example, in Powers v. Ohio, 499 U.S. 400, 410–11 (1991), which upheld a litigant's third-party standing to raise equal protection claims of jurors peremptorily challenged due to race, the Supreme Court recognized three requirements for would-be third-party petitioners.

3rd party standing rule

> We have recognized the right of litigants to bring actions on behalf of third parties, provided three important criteria are satisfied: The litigant must have suffered an "injury in fact," thus giving him or her a "sufficiently concrete interest" in the outcome of the issue in dispute; the litigant must have a close relation to the third party; and there must exist some hindrance to the third party's ability to protect his or her own interests.

3 important criteria

Id.; see also Lujan v. Defenders of Wildlife, 504 U.S. 555, 560–61 (1992); Shaw v. Hahn, 56 F.3d 1128, 1130 n.3 (9th Cir. 1995)(third party must have suffered an injury-in-fact)

Of the three requirements for third-party standing: (1) injury-in-fact; (2) close relationship to the third party; and (3) hindrance to the third party; the Coalition addresses only the last. It contends that a litigant may raise the claims of a third party if there is reason to believe that the individual is unlikely to be able to sue for himself or herself.

coalition only addressed 3rd issue, not 1 and 2

Even if we were to assume satisfaction of the third requirement, a hindrance to the detainees' ability to assert their own claims, we would nevertheless conclude that the Coalition lacks third-party standing because neither it nor its members can demonstrate either the first requirement of an injury-in-fact or the second requirement of a close relationship. As to the first, the Coalition makes no allegation of personal injury to its members, and as to the second, it has alleged no relationship to the detainees. As in Valley Forge Christian College v.

Americans United for Separation of Church and State, Inc., 454 U.S. 464, 485–86 (1982), the members of the Coalition:

> fail to identify any personal injury suffered by them as a consequence of the alleged constitutional error, other than the psychological consequence presumably produced by observation of conduct with which one disagrees. That is not an injury sufficient to confer standing under Art. III, even though the disagreement is phrased in constitutional terms.

Id. Because neither the Coalition nor any of its members has a relationship with the detainees, it cannot assert third-party standing on their behalf. Absent injury-in-fact and any relationship to the detainees, we find no third-party standing.

C. Jurisdiction.

Because we conclude that the Coalition lacks standing, we decline to reach the remaining questions addressed by the district court. * * * We therefore affirm the district court's order as to the lack of standing.

AFFIRMED.

Notes and Questions

1. In a celebrated case in which a non-custodial father (an atheist) sought to appeal in a case against a school district alleging that the system's policy of requiring recitation of the Pledge of Allegiance in his daughter's school violated the First Amendment, the Supreme Court of the United States found that California state law precluded the father from litigating the appeal as "next friend" of the daughter, in light of a custody decree which placed sole responsibility for the child with the mother. The Court found that unlike prior cases of next friend standing, or third-party standing, in this case "the interests of this parent and this child are not parallel and, indeed, are potentially in conflict." Elk Grove Unified School Dist. v. Newdow, 542 U.S. 1, 124 S.Ct. 2301, 159 L.Ed.2d 98 (2004).

SECTION D. INTERVENTION

1. INTERVENTION AND STANDING

Persons with standing to sue, who are not parties, may need to intervene in the action to become parties. By doing so they obtain rights to participate in the proceedings. At the trial level, intervention allows full participation in the motion practice, briefing, presentation of evidence, and post-judgment maneuvering. The later one intervenes the more time and resources will have been expended in preparing the case in its original structure and—in general—the standards for intervention give grounds for denying permission to intervene if the would-be party has waited so long that it causes disadvantage to the pre-existing parties, or messes up a schedule the court has articulated. Late intervention can require that discovery stages be re-done, and can interfere with schedules previously set.

Thus decisions involving intervention to some extent turn upon considerations similar to those ventilated in the standing decisions illustrated earlier in this Chapter. However, there are both procedural and substantive differences that make it profitable to look at intervention cases in addition to basic standing decisions.

MANGUAL v. ROTGER–SABAT

United States Court of Appeals, First Circuit, 2003.
317 F.3d 45.

LYNCH, CIRCUIT JUDGE.

[In a case by a reporter challenging the constitutionality of a criminal libel statute in Puerto Rico that arguably subjected protected speech to criminal prosecution, several other reporters and the Overseas Press Club, a nonprofit association of journalists, sought to intervene, based on allegations that they had been threatened with prosecution for articles critical of government officials. The district court denied intervention.]

The district court, in a summary discussion, found that both Medina's and Caribbean's allegations of injury amount to mere subjective fears and fail to meet the "objectively reasonable" test required to create a case or controversy. We review denial of intervention for abuse of discretion. See Allen Calculators, Inc. v. Nat'l Cash Register Co., 322 U.S. 137, 142 (1944); Daggett v. Comm'n on Governmental Ethics & Election Practices, 172 F.3d 104, 109, 113 (1st Cir. 1999). It is an abuse of discretion for the district court to apply an erroneous standard of law. It is clear that the district court applied several erroneous standards in its legal analysis of Medina's standing and that its conclusion as to the "objective reasonableness" of Medina's fear of prosecution was in error, and so there was an abuse of discretion.

Whether standing is required for intervenors is an as yet unsettled question. The controversy over whether intervention of right under Fed. R. Civ. P. 24(a) requires Article III standing is a well-known one. See Diamond v. Charles, 476 U.S. 54, 68–69 & n.21; *Daggett*, 172 F.3d at 109. The requirement of standing for permissive intervenors has received less attention but is no less unsettled. The traditional rule was that standing was required for permissive intervenors but not for intervenors of right. In part because of the 1990 amendments to the supplemental jurisdiction statute, Judicial Improvements Act of 1990, Pub. L. No. 101–650, Title III, § 310, 104 Stat. 5089, 5113–14 (codified at 28 U.S.C. § 1367 (2000)), the standing requirements for intervenors are now greatly confused. C.A. Wright & M.K. Kane, Law of Federal Courts § 75, at 548 (6th ed. 2002). It is clear that an intervenor, whether permissive or as of right, must have Article III standing in order to continue litigating if the original parties do not do so. Arizonans for Official English v. Arizona, 520 U.S. 43, 65 (1997); *Diamond*, 476 U.S. at 68. However, the circuits are split on the question of whether standing is required to intervene if the original parties are still pursuing the case and thus maintaining a case or controversy, as they are here.[5]

We need not decide this complicated question, because it is clear that Medina has sufficient standing under Article III. Medina is also a journalist working for El Vocero who has been threatened with prosecution under the Puerto Rico criminal libel statute. While the statute of limitations has expired as to that particular threat, he continues to work as a journalist and to risk prosecution under the statute. As such, he is in a position like that of Mangual. Medina has expressed the fear that he may be prosecuted and has articulated his desire to continue publishing, as a journalist, on matters that may draw a libel prosecution. Given the history of threatened and actual prosecution under the statute detailed above, Medina has evidenced enough of a threat to establish standing to intervene in this suit.

Under the circumstances of this case, we see no reason to remand for consideration of Medina's motion to intervene under the correct legal standards. We grant Medina's motion to intervene for several reasons. First, the only objection raised as to intervention was standing, and that has now been resolved in Medina's favor. Second, because we go on to resolve the merits, there is no point in remanding this issue. Third, we have the discretion to permit intervenors at the appellate level, and we choose to do so here. See Ruthardt v. United States, 303 F.3d 375, 386 (1st Cir. 2002). * * *

We hold that the Puerto Rico criminal libel statute incorporates constitutionally invalid standards in the context of statements about public officials or public figures. We hold that Puerto Rico's criminal libel statute, 33 P.R. Laws Ann. §§ 4101–4104, is unconstitutional under the First Amendment as applied to statements regarding public officials or figures. We reverse the denial of Medina's motion to intervene and grant intervention to Medina, reverse the dismissal of the case on jurisdictional grounds, and remand the case with instructions that the district court enter a declaratory judgment and injunctive relief consistent with this opinion. So ordered. Costs are awarded to Mangual and Medina.

Reversed and Remanded.

Notes and Questions

1. It is sometimes argued, particularly when the original parties settle or dismiss their claims, that a party who intervenes without filing a separate pleading (as a plaintiff or defendant) has failed to preserve her right to

5. Some cases have held that intervenors must independently meet Article III standing requirements. See, e.g., EEOC v. Nat'l Children's Ctr., Inc., 331 U.S. App. D.C. 101, 146 F.3d 1042, 1046 (D.C. Cir. 1998); Mausolf v. Babbitt, 85 F.3d 1295, 1300 (8th Cir. 1996). Others have held that intervenors need not show standing if the original parties remain in the case. See, e.g., Ruiz v. Estelle, 161 F.3d 814, 830 (5th Cir. 1998); Chiles v. Thornburgh, 865 F.2d 1197, 1213 (11th Cir. 1989). See generally A.M. Gardner, Comment, An Attempt To Intervene in the Confusion: Standing Requirements for Rule 24 Intervenors , 69 U. Chi. L. Rev. 681, 691–98 (2002) (collecting cases).

continue this case on appeal. Most courts of appeal have concluded, however, that separate pleading is not required where the intervenor and a pre-existing party sought the same result. See Cal. Dept. of Soc. Servs. v. Thompson, 321 F.3d 835 (9th Cir. 2003) citing cases allowing intervenors to proceed without filing separate pleadings where it was clear from the motion to intervene what result intervenors sought, providing sufficient notice of intervenor's position was given. Quoting a leading text, the court said: "If the intervenor is content to stand on the pleading an existing party has filed, it is difficult to see what is accomplished by adding to the papers in the case a new pleading that is identical in its allegations with one that is already in the file."

2. TWO BASES FOR INTERVENTION

There are no rules of appellate procedure on intervention in the federal courts. Many decisions have applied the standards of Federal Rule of Civil Procedure 24, which apply in the trial court, in considering intervention issues on appeal. Pitts v. Thornburgh, 2003 WL 21384601 (D.C. Cir. 2003) ("standards for intervention applicable in the district court also apply in the court of appeals") .

Rule 24(a) allows a party to move for intervention *as a matter of right* if the proceeding will have important, direct impact upon the party. Rule 24(b), on the other hand, allows *permissive* intervention—meaning that the court may choose to exercise its discretion to allow the movant to participate fully in the case because there is some need or advantage served by that step.

Rule 24 provides in part:

Rule 24. Intervention

(a) Intervention of Right. Upon timely application anyone shall be permitted to intervene in an action: (1) when a statute of the United States confers an unconditional right to intervene; or (2) when the applicant claims an interest relating to the property or transaction which is the subject of the action and the applicant is so situated that the disposition of the action may as a practical matter impair or impede the applicant's ability to protect that interest, unless the applicant's interest is adequately represented by existing parties.

(b) Permissive Intervention. Upon timely application anyone may be permitted to intervene in an action: (1) when a statute of the United States confers a conditional right to intervene; or (2) when an applicant's claim or defense and the main action have a question of law or fact in common. When a party to an action relies for ground of claim or defense upon any statute or executive order administered by a federal or state governmental officer or agency or upon any regulation, order, requirement, or agreement issued or made pursuant to the statute or executive order, the officer or agency upon timely application may be permitted to intervene in the action. In exercising its discretion the court shall consider whether the intervention will unduly delay or prejudice the adjudication of the rights of the original parties.

3. APPEAL OF INTERVENTION DECISIONS RENDERED IN THE TRIAL COURT

The doctrine which has arisen holds that if a party claims to be *directly affected* by the lawsuit (and therefore seeks intervention *as a matter of right*) an adverse ruling must be immediately appealed. The penalty for failing to seek an immediate appeal is that a delayed appeal (i.e., an appeal taken when the case is over and final judgment has been entered with respect to the claims of the parties participating in the litigation) *will be dismissed*.

On the other hand, if a party claims only a permissive interest in intervention, that party can wait for the duration of the proceedings and will still be heard on appeal to challenge the decision of the lower court denying intervention. As one might imagine, by that point (after a trial or decision completed without the permissive intervenor being a participant) the appellate courts very rarely conclude that reversible error occurred in denying intervention. It is sometimes said that "[r]eversal of a decision denying permissive intervention is extremely rare, bordering on nonexistent." One federal appellate court called such a reversal "so rare that it is unique." South Dakota v. United States Department of the Interior, 317 F.3d 783 (8th Cir. 2003).

ALTERNATIVE RESEARCH & DEVELOPMENT FOUNDATION v. VENEMAN

United States Court of Appeals, District of Columbia Circuit, 2001.
262 F.3d 406.

Per Curiam.

Alternative Research and Development Foundation filed a petition for rulemaking requesting that the Secretary of Agriculture amend the definition of "animal" in regulations promulgated pursuant to the Animal Welfare Act ("Act") to remove the current exclusion of birds, mice, and rats bred for use in research. Under the Act, the Secretary of Agriculture is authorized to promulgate standards and other requirements to govern the handling, care, and treatment of animals by dealers, research facilities, and exhibitors. 7 U.S.C. § 2143(a)(1). On January 28, 1999, the United States Department of Agriculture ("USDA") published the petition and requested comments. See 64 Fed. Reg. 4356 (1999). While its agency petition was pending, Alternative Research and Development Foundation, as well as In Vitro International, and Kristine Gausz (collectively, "Alternative Research") filed a complaint for declaratory and injunctive relief in the district court, alleging that the USDA's exclusion of birds, rats, and mice from the definition of "animal" in 9 C.F.R. § 1.1 violates the Act. It sought an order enjoining the exclusion and directing USDA to amend the regulation by eliminating the exclusion.

After the district court denied a motion to dismiss filed by USDA, the National Association for Biomedical Research ("NABR"), an association engaged in research using birds, rats, and mice, sought intervention as of right or, alternatively, permissive intervention. Subsequently, Alternative Research and USDA entered into a stipulation of dismissal without prejudice under Federal Rule of Civil Procedure 41(a)(1). The stipulation provides, in pertinent part, that USDA will grant Alternative Research's petition for rulemaking to amend the USDA regulation, and USDA agrees to initiate and complete a rulemaking on the regulation of birds, rats, and mice within a reasonable time. NABR then filed a motion to vacate the stipulation under Rule 60(b)(4). After a hearing, the district court filed the stipulation of dismissal and denied the motions to intervene and to vacate the stipulation under Rule 60(b), concluding that it lacked jurisdiction to decide the motions in light of the stipulated dismissal. Alternatively, the district court denied the motion to intervene as of right on the merits, concluding that NABR's interests would not be impaired by the proposed rulemaking.

NABR appeals from the stipulated dismissal and the order denying intervention and Rule 60(b) relief. Alternative Research moves to dismiss the appeal for lack of jurisdiction. The district court's order denying intervention is appealable, but was not in error; we therefore grant summary affirmance of that ruling. Because intervention was properly denied, NABR is not a party to the action and lacks standing to appeal from the stipulated dismissal and from the order denying relief under Rule 60(b); we therefore grant the motion to dismiss as to those appeals.
* * *

Appealability of denial of intervention as of right. In considering whether it had jurisdiction to review an order of the district court denying intervention to a would-be intervenor, the Supreme Court in Brotherhood of Railroad Trainmen v. Baltimore & Ohio R. Co., 331 U.S. 519, 524 (1947), stated:

> Our jurisdiction to consider an appeal from an order denying intervention ... depends upon the nature of the applicant's right to intervene. If the right is absolute, the order is appealable and we may judge it on its merits.... Our jurisdiction is identified by the necessary incidents of the right to intervene in each particular instance. We must therefore determine the question of our jurisdiction in this case by examining the character of the [would-be intervenor's] right to intervene in the proceeding.

Id. at 524–25.

In *Brotherhood*, and certain subsequent cases, the Supreme Court postponed consideration of whether the denial of intervention as of right was appealable until it decided the appeal on the merits, thus suggesting that the appealability of the denial turned on the merits of the applicant's right to intervene. See Sam Fox Publishing Co. v. United States, 366 U.S. 683, 687–88 (1961) (noting that answer to question whether court has jurisdiction to review order denying intervention as of right also determines merits of appeal from denial); Brotherhood, 331 U.S. at 524–32; see also Sutphen Estates v. United States, 342 U.S. 19, 20–21 (1951). Upon concluding that intervention as of right was properly denied, the Court in *Sam Fox Publishing* and *Sutphen Estates* dismissed the appeals. See *Sam Fox Publishing,* 366 U.S. at 695; *Sutphen Estates,* 342 U.S. at 22–23. More recently, however, the Supreme Court assumed jurisdiction over an appeal from the denial of intervention as of right without first determining the merits of the applicant's right to intervene, and, after concluding that a lower court's denial of intervention was correct, affirmed the decision. Donaldson v. United States, 400 U.S. 517, 530–31 (1971).

The Court's inconsistent treatment is mirrored in the federal courts of appeals. Some decisions make appealability of the denial of intervention automatic once the district court issues its denial; that is, the denial is held to be a final order that is immediately appealable. This approach is followed by a majority of the circuit courts. See Cotter v. Massachusetts Ass'n of Minority Law Enforcement Officers, 219 F.3d 31, 33 (1st Cir. 2000); League of United Latin American Citizens v. Wilson, 131 F.3d 1297, 1302 (9th Cir. 1997); Development Finance Corp. v. Alpha Housing & Health Care, Inc., 54 F.3d 156, 158 (3d Cir. 1995); Shea v. Angulo, 19 F.3d 343, 344–45 (7th Cir. 1994); Corby Recreation, Inc. v. General Electric Co., 581 F.2d 175, 176 n.1 (8th Cir. 1978); Securities and Exchange Comm'n v. Everest Management Corp., 475 F.2d 1236, 1238 n.2 (2d Cir. 1972). Having concluded that this type of order is appealable, these courts review the order denying intervention on the merits and will affirm the district court's ruling if they find no error.

The second approach makes appealability turn on the merits of the motion for intervention as of right, and the denial of intervention is not automatically an appealable, final order. This approach is followed by the Eleventh Circuit. See EEOC v. Eastern Airlines, Inc., 736 F.2d 635, 637 (11th Cir. 1984). Under its self-styled "anomalous rule," the Eleventh Circuit has jurisdiction only to decide whether the district court was correct in denying intervention. Under this rule, if the circuit court concludes that the district court's order was correct, the circuit court's jurisdiction evaporates because the ruling was not a final order, and the circuit court must dismiss the appeal for want of jurisdiction. See id. Conversely, if the circuit court concludes that the district court erred, the circuit court retains jurisdiction and reverses the district court ruling. Either way, the circuit court first decides whether the motion to intervene was properly denied before determining whether the order is appealable. See id. at 641 (concluding that trial court's denial of intervention was correct and that denial was thus not an appealable final order, and dismissing appeal) ; see United States v. Georgia, 19 F.3d 1388, 1393 (11th Cir. 1994) (same).

Our circuit has not been entirely consistent in its approach. * * *

This court now clarifies that the denial of intervention as of right is an appealable, final order regardless of the merits of the claim for intervention as of right. This approach is in accord with * * * Smoke v. Norton, 252 F.3d 468, 470 (D.C. Cir. 2001), this court considered an appeal from a district court order denying a motion to intervene as of right under Rule 24(a). Appellants moved to intervene after the district court granted summary judgment in order to appeal from the underlying judgment, which remanded the case to the agency. The district court denied the motion to intervene as untimely. In reversing the district court's denial, this court stated that the denial of intervention as of right is an appealable final order because it is conclusive with respect to the distinct interest asserted by the movant. See id. (quoting Brotherhood, 331 U.S. at 524). The court treated the denial of intervention as immediately appealable and independent from the underlying judgment, noting that the question whether the underlying judgment is final would not be before the court unless appellants were allowed to intervene and they appealed from that judgment. See id. at 470 n.1. * * *

Furthermore, our jurisdiction to review that denial is not affected by the fact that the district court denied intervention after the stipulated dismissal was entered; the dismissal does not render the appeal moot. United States of America v. Massachusetts School of Law at Andover, Inc., 118 F.3d 776, 780–81 (D.C. Cir. 1997) (where would-be intervenor sought to challenge consent decree, appeal from denial of intervention as of right reviewable even though district court denied intervention after it entered consent judgment). NABR appeals from both the denial of intervention and the denial of its Rule 60(b) motion, which challenged the dismissal. If this court were to conclude that NABR was entitled to intervene in the litigation, NABR would have standing to appeal the district court's denial of the Rule 60(b) motion attacking the stipulated dismissal, and we would review that Rule 60(b) denial. See Purcell v. Bank Atlantic Fin. Corp., 85 F.3d 1508, 1511 n.3 (11th Cir. 1996) (appeal from denial of intervention not mooted by district court's entry of judgment in underlying case); see also League of United Latin American Citizens, 131 F.3d at 1301 n.1 (appeal from denial of intervention not mooted despite district court issuance of memorandum disposing of claims). Because we can potentially grant NABR effective relief, this appeal is not moot. See Purcell, 85 F.3d at 1511 n.3. * * *

Entitlement to intervention as of right. An applicant seeking to intervene as of right must show, among other things, that it is "so situated that the disposition of the action may as a practical matter impair or impede [its] ability to protect [its] interest." Mova Pharmaceutical Corp. v. Shalala, 140 F.3d 1060, 1074 (D.C. Cir. 1998). The relevant inquiry here is whether NABR's concerns about the terms of the stipulated dismissal were sufficient to constitute an interest requiring intervention. See Moten, 543 F.2d at 229, 232–34; see also Natural Resources Defense Council v. Costle, 183 U.S. App. D.C. 11, 561 F.2d 904, 908–11 (D.C. Cir. 1977). NABR asserts that "USDA's collusive stratagem with [Alternative Research] to expand USDA's regulatory jurisdiction without public comment or judicial review" shows that USDA was not adequately representing NABR's interest.

But NABR's rights were not impaired by the initiation of a rulemaking. NABR is a non-profit association whose members are engaged in biomedical research that involves the use of birds, rats, and mice. NABR's position is that the exclusion for birds, rats, and mice should be removed only if regulations can be developed that take into account enforcement needs, current scientific practices, standards already established in other policy statements, and administrative and financial burdens on research facilities. As the district court noted during the hearing on the motion to intervene, NABR will not be precluded from participating in the rulemaking and, if USDA decides to issue a final rule, NABR is not precluded from challenging that rule. Significantly, the stipulated dismissal does no more than what the agency could have done by granting Alternative Research's pending agency petition for rulemaking, and the stipulated dismissal does not bind the agency in its rulemaking. Cf. Massachusetts School of Law at Andover, 118 F.3d at 780–81 (noting that consent decree "with res judicata, collateral estoppel, or stare decisis effect might very well affect MSL's ability to protect its interests," but because the consent decree had no such effect, MSL's interest was not impaired). Accordingly, NABR's concerns about the terms of the stipulated dismissal are insufficient to constitute an interest requiring intervention before the district court under Rule 24(a)(2). * * *

Appeal from stipulated dismissal and denial of Rule 60(b) motion. Finally, because the district court correctly denied intervention, NABR is not a party to the action and lacks standing to appeal from either the stipulation of dismissal or the order denying its Rule 60(b) motion, which challenged the stipulated dismissal. See Fed. R. Civ. P. 60(b) (relief limited to a party); Farmland Dairies v. Commissioner of the New York State Department of Agriculture and Markets, 847 F.2d 1038, 1045 (2d Cir. 1988) (concluding that because court was affirming district court order denying intervention, appellants had no standing to appeal any other order entered by district court, and court dismissed their appeals from those orders).

For the preceding reasons, we conclude this court has jurisdiction to review the denial of intervention as of right and affirm the denial because NABR has not shown that the stipulated dismissal may impair its ability to protect its interest. Because the district court correctly denied intervention, NABR is not a party to the action and does not have standing to appeal from either the stipulated dismissal or the order denying its Rule 60(b) motion; the court dismisses the appeal from those rulings.

Appeal dismissed.

4. TIMELY APPLICATION TO INTERVENE

In considering whether a motion to intervene is timely, several jurisdictions hold that a court must consider five factors:

(1) the point to which the lawsuit has progressed; (2) the purpose for which the intervention is sought; (3) the length of time preceding the application during which the proposed intervener knew or reasonably should have known of the interest in the case; (4) the prejudice to the original parties due to the proposed intervener's failure. after he or she knew or reasonably should have known of his interest in the case, to apply promptly for intervention; and (5) the existence of unusual circumstances militating against or in favor of intervention.

See, e.g., Jordan v. Michigan Conf. of Teamsters Welfare Fund, 207 F.3d 854, 862 (6th Cir. 2000).

PLAIN v. MURPHY FAMILY FARMS

United States Court of Appeals, Tenth Circuit, 2002.
296 F.3d 975.

BALDOCK, CIRCUIT JUDGE.

[In a wrongful death action the adult children of the decedent were denied permission to intervene as beneficiaries of any recovery.]

Those seeking to participate in the underlying resolution of the merits of a lawsuit must make "timely application" to intervene under Fed. R. Civ. P. 24. See Utah Ass'n of Counties v. Clinton, 255 F.3d 1246, 1250 (10th Cir. 2001) (discussing "timeliness" within the meaning of Rule 24). If the district court denies that motion, the proper procedure is to pursue an immediate appeal, and not to file repetitive motions pestering the district court. This is true regardless of how the motions are labeled where the substance of the motions and purported justification for intervention remain unchanged. As we stated in Hutchinson v. Pfeil, 211 F.3d 515, 518 (10th Cir. 2000):

> An order denying intervention is final and subject to immediate review if it prevents the applicant from becoming a party to an action. This is because denial of intervention precludes the proposed intervenor's ability to appeal the later judgment (and at that time to challenge the earlier denial of intervention). Thus, an appeal from the denial of intervention cannot be kept in reserve; it must be taken within thirty days of the entry of the order, or not at all.

The reason for the rule is simple: considering an immediate appeal from a timely pretrial motion to intervene is more efficient and less costly than permitting a proposed intervenor to wait and see if the trial's outcome leaves intervention desirable with its attendant risk of undoing what the trial court has already done. See 15A Charles A. Wright, Arthur R. Miller, & Edward H. Cooper, Federal Practice and Procedure § 3902.1 at 113 (1992).

In this case, the children timely initiated an appeal after the district court denied their pretrial motion to reconsider their first motion to intervene. The children argued then, as they do now, that Plaintiff could not adequately represent their interests and the court should permit counsel of their own choosing to participate in the trial. When Plaintiff moved to dismiss the appeal, however, the children indicated they had no objection to dismissal as the scheduled trial "will render the issues moot." Yet, as evidenced by the children's repetitive motions in the district court and present appeal, the impending trial apparently did not render moot their claim to intervene under Fed. R. Civ. P. 24(a). When the district court refused to stay the trial pending appeal, the proper procedure, as outlined in Fed. R. App. P. 8(a)(2), entailed moving this Court to stay the trial. Such a motion would have provided us with a timely opportunity to review the merits of the children's claim and decide whether a stay was warranted pending final resolution of their appeal.

We do not believe we can review now what we could have reviewed then. The children's current appeal, to the extent its requests a new trial in which they be permitted to participate, seeks "review lost" by their failure to follow proper procedure the first time. See Hutchinson, 211 F.3d at 519 (noting that movant's request to intervene in appeal "is, in effect, an attempt to obtain appellate review lost by her failure to timely appeal the denial of her motion to intervene in district court"); B.H. By Pierce v. Murphy, 984 F.2d 196, 199 (7th Cir. 1993) (rejecting movant's "improper attempt, by filing a virtually identical intervention motion, to circumvent his failure to appeal the first motion's denial within the required time"). Because the children were not parties to the wrongful death suit and because they failed to pursue a timely appeal of the district court's pretrial order denying them the right to intervene, they, as nonparties, may not now attack the judgment by seeking to appeal the district court's denial of their motion for a new trial.

AFFIRMED IN PART; DISMISSED IN PART.

HUTCHINSON v. PFEIL

United States Court of Appeals, Tenth Circuit, 2000.
211 F.3d 515.

Murphy, Circuit Judge.

Plaintiff Thomas R. Hutchinson appeals from the dismissal of his suit under § 43(a) of the Lanham Act, 15 U.S.C. § 1125(a), for lack of standing. He also challenges certain procedural rulings issued in the course of the proceedings. Joining in his notice of appeal are Hope Cobb, whose motion to intervene in district court was denied, and several individuals whom Mr. Hutchinson proposed to add as plaintiffs when he unsuccessfully moved to amend his pleadings. For reasons stated below, we dismiss the appeals of Ms. Cobb and those proposed plaintiffs, deny their joint motion to intervene in the Hutchinson appeal, and affirm all of the rulings challenged by Mr. Hutchinson. * * *

The district court denied Hope Cobb's motion to intervene on February 27, 1998. She did not attempt to appeal that order until she joined Mr. Hutchinson's notice of appeal from the final judgment entered over eight months later.

"An order denying intervention is final and subject to immediate review if it prevents the applicant from becoming a party to an action." Coalition of Ariz./N.M. Counties for Stable Econ. Growth v. Department of the Interior, 100 F.3d 837, 839 (10th Cir. 1996). This is "because denial of intervention precludes the proposed intervenor's ability to appeal the later judgment (and at that time to challenge the earlier denial of intervention)." B.H. ex rel. Pierce v. Murphy, 984 F.2d 196, 199 (7th Cir. 1993). Thus, an appeal from the denial of intervention "cannot be kept in reserve; it must be taken within thirty days of the entry of the order, or not at all." Credit Francais Int'l, S.A. v. Bio–Vita, Ltd., 78 F.3d 698, 703 (1st Cir. 1996); see Hunter v. Department of the Air Force Agency, 846 F.2d 1314, 1316–17 (11th Cir. 1988) (distinguishing a final order denying intervention from appealable interlocutory orders for which immediate review in lieu of appeal from final judgment is optional). Ms. Cobb's appeal is therefore untimely and must be dismissed. See Budinich v. Becton Dickinson & Co., 486 U.S. 196, 203 (1988) ("the taking of an appeal within the prescribed time is mandatory and jurisdictional").

Proposed Plaintiffs' Appeal

After the case had been pending in district court for some time, Mr. Hutchinson filed a motion to amend his pleadings to, among other things, add several new plaintiffs under Fed. R. Civ. P. 21. The proposed plaintiffs did not themselves invoke the power of the court by, for example, moving to intervene under Fed. R. Civ. P. 24. Thus, they are not parties to the action nor have they affirmatively sought and been denied such status.

"A nonparty does not have standing to appeal in the absence of most extraordinary circumstances." Coffey v. Whirlpool Corp., 591 F.2d 618, 619 (10th Cir. 1979) (insurer lacked standing to appeal where district court denied insured's motion to vacate dismissal to permit substitution of insurer as plaintiff). Such circumstances are clearly not present here. Indeed, two distinct considerations undercut the proposed plaintiffs' appellate standing. The first is their indirect, passive relationship to the proceedings conducted in district court. To paraphrase an apt, albeit non-precedential, statement of the Second Circuit, expressly relying on our Coffey decision in a similar case: the plaintiff—not the proposed plaintiffs—moved to amend his complaint, and he—not they—is the proper party to appeal the denial of that motion. See Kahn v. Chase Manhattan Bank, N.A., 1997 WL 734139, at **2 (2d Cir. Nov. 25, 1997) (unpublished). The second consideration relates to the proposed plaintiffs' lack of a substantive interest in the outcome. Because the action was dismissed based on Mr. Hutchinson's lack of standing and thus without any ruling on the merits, the proposed plaintiffs are in the same position as the non-party denied appellate standing in Coffey: "no requirement is imposed upon [the proposed plaintiffs] to do anything" to preserve their claims; the dismissal by the court was without prejudice to their interests. Coffey, 591 F.2d at 619.

APPELLATE INTERVENTION

Ms. Cobb and the proposed plaintiffs also moved to intervene on appeal, in case their joinder in the notice of appeal filed by Mr. Hutchinson was ineffective. We deny the motion for reasons peculiar to each movant. As for Ms. Cobb, the motion is, in effect, an attempt to obtain appellate review lost by her failure to timely appeal the denial of her motion to intervene in district court. Appellate intervention is not a means to escape the consequences of noncompliance with traditional rules of appellate jurisdiction and procedure. See, e.g., United States v. Dorfman, 690 F.2d 1217, 1223 (7th Cir. 1982) (defendants who prematurely appealed suppression order "cannot circumvent the rule against . . . interlocutory appeal" by intervening in third-party appeal); United States v. Ahmad, 499 F.2d 851, 854 (3d Cir. 1974) (party who failed to file notice of appeal "cannot circumvent the requirements for taking an appeal in his own right by a later petition for intervention" in another's appeal).

The proposed plaintiffs lacked standing to obtain direct appellate review and, thus, do not seek intervention to excuse a failure to perfect a proper appeal. Their request, however, is undercut by a different omission. As noted above, they never moved to intervene in the district court. " 'A court of appeals may, but only in an exceptional case for imperative reasons, permit intervention where none was sought in the district court.' " Hall v. Holder, 117 F.3d 1222, 1231 (11th Cir. 1997) (quoting McKenna v. Pan Am. Petroleum Corp. , 303 F.2d 778, 779 (5th Cir. 1962)); see Bates v. Jones, 127 F.3d 870, 873 (9th Cir. 1997); Amalgamated Transit Union Int'l v. Donovan, 771 F.2d 1551, 1552 (D.C. Cir. 1985). Nothing stated in their conclusory motion or inherent in the surrounding circumstances suggests the requisite justification for the proposed plaintiffs' intervention on appeal.

HUTCHINSON'S STANDING TO SUE

On summary judgment, the district court held that Mr. Hutchinson could not satisfy the requirements for standing under the Lanham Act set out by this court in Stanfield v. Osborne Industries, Inc., 52 F.3d 867 (10th Cir. 1995). On de novo review, see Wilson v. Glenwood Intermountain Properties, Inc., 98 F.3d 590, 593 (10th Cir. 1996), we reach the same conclusion. Further, we hold that the standing deficiencies implicate the limitations of Article III of the Constitution. * * *

Mr. Hutchinson is a descendant of nineteenth century American Impressionist artist Theodore Robinson, who painted a work owned by defendants Richard and Mary Joan Pfeil, entitled E.M.J. Betty. Mr. Hutchinson contends that the Pfeils' painting is actually an unfinished version with a forged signature, and that he has an ownership interest in a finished "real" E.M.J. Betty, allegedly stolen after the artist died in 1896. The thrust of Mr. Hutchinson's Lanham Act claim is that by representing their painting as a finished version of the Robinson work in an exhibition catalogue, the Pfeils have "used in commerce [a] false designation of origin, false or misleading description of fact, or false or misleading representation of fact," in violation of 15 U.S.C. § 1125(a)(1). The other defendants are the corporations which produced and printed the catalogue, and the art historians whose professional work was used for the E.M.J. Betty annotation therein. * * *

CONCLUSION

The appeal of intervenor-appellant Hope Cobb is DISMISSED as untimely. The appeal of the proposed plaintiffs-appellants is DISMISSED for lack of appellate standing. With regard to the appeal of plaintiff-appellant Thomas R. Hutchinson, the judgment of the United States District Court for the Northern District of Oklahoma is AFFIRMED in all respects. For reasons explained above, all pending motions are DENIED.

KOOTENAI TRIBE OF IDAHO v. VENEMAN

United States Court of Appeals, Ninth Circuit, 2002.
313 F.3d 1094.

GOULD, CIRCUIT JUDGE.

I

This case involves procedural challenges to a United States Forest Service rule, known commonly as the "Roadless Rule," with a potential environmental impact restricting development in national forest lands representing about two percent of the United States land mass.[1] These challenges in essence urge that the Roadless Rule was promulgated without proper process and that it is invalid. The case also presents constitutional and procedural issues about the ability of the plaintiffs and of the proposed intervenors to be heard.

But we must start closer to the beginning: This appeal arises out of litigation that began on January 8, 2001 when Kootenai Tribe of Idaho and Boise Cascade Corporation, joined by motorized recreation groups, livestock companies, and two Idaho counties[2] filed suit in the United States District Court for the District of Idaho, alleging that the United States Forest Service's Roadless Area Conservation Rule ("Roadless Rule") violated, inter alia, the National Environmental Policy Act ("NEPA"), 42 U.S.C. §§ 4321 et seq., and the Administrative Procedure Act ("APA"), 5 U.S.C. § 553. One day later, the State of Idaho and some state office-holders (collectively "Idaho plaintiffs") filed a separate com-

---

1. The case has generated interest in business, environmental and political communities. We have received amicus briefs from: Washington Legal Foundation and United States Senators Larry E. Craig and Mark Dayton; Nez Perce Tribe; and Montana Attorney General Mark McGrath.

2. The co-plaintiffs joined with the Kootenai Tribe are: the Blue Ribbon Coalition,

Boise County, Idaho, Valley County, Idaho, Idaho State Snowmobile Association, Illinois Association of Snowmobile Clubs, American Council of Snowmobile Associations, Little Cattle Company Limited Partnership, Highland Livestock and Land Company and Boise Cascade Company.

plaint in the District of Idaho and stated similar allegations. Environmental groups intervened. The district court granted plaintiffs' motions for preliminary injunction against the implementation of the Roadless Rule. Although the federal defendants did not appeal the invalidation of the Roadless Rule, an appeal was taken in both cases by intervenors.* * *

A. History of the Roadless Rule

In the 1970s, the United States Forest Service ("Forest Service") began to study and evaluate roadless areas in national forests. The Forest Service developed an "inventory" of roadless areas, each larger than five thousand acres. There are now 58.5 million acres of inventoried roadless areas in the National Forest System.

The Forest Service, in an odd semantic twist,[3] has included in "inventoried roadless areas" some areas with roads. Since 1982, the Forest Service has permitted road construction, industrial logging and other development in the inventoried roadless areas on a local, site-specific basis. See California v. Block, 690 F.2d 753 (9th Cir. 1982). In the past two decades, 2.8 million acres of roadless areas have been developed by the Forest Service.

On October 13, 1999, President William Jefferson Clinton ordered the United States Forest Service to initiate a nationwide plan to protect inventoried and uninventoried roadless areas within our treasured national forests. Within a week of President Clinton's directive, the Forest Service published a Notice of Intent ("NOI") to prepare an Environmental Impact Statement ("EIS") for a nationwide Roadless Rule. The NOI gave sixty days for scoping and public comment. 64 Fed. Reg. 56,306 (Oct. 19, 1999). The Forest Service denied requests to extend the sixty-day scoping period. * * * On January 5, 2001, the Forest Service issued the Final [Roadless] Rule, applicable to the 58.5 million acres. * * * It generally banned road building subject to limited exceptions including: the preservation of "reserved or outstanding rights" or discretionary Forest Service construction necessary for public health and safety. 36 C.F.R. § 294.12(b)(1),(3). Henceforth, this vast national forest acreage, for better or worse, was more committed to pristine wilderness, and less amenable to road development for purposes permitted by the Forest Service.

B. Procedural History

On January 8, 2001, three days after the Final Rule was issued, the Kootenai Tribe, and the private and county plaintiffs joined with it, filed suit alleging that the Roadless Rule was illegal. On January 9, 2001, the Idaho plaintiffs filed suit with similar claims. Both sets of plaintiffs alleged violations of the NEPA and the APA.

---

3. This is perhaps reminiscent of George Orwell's "Newspeak," the name of the artificial language used for official communications in George Orwell's novel Nineteen Eighty–Four, which is now often applied to corrupt English. See Oxford English Dictionary (2d ed. 1989).

On January 20, 2001, newly-inaugurated President George Walker Bush issued an order postponing by sixty days the effective date of all the prior administration's regulations and rules not yet implemented. * * * Before then, on February 20, 2001, the Kootenai Tribe and its co-plaintiffs moved for a preliminary injunction against implementation of the Roadless Rule. * * * Both sets of plaintiffs argued that the Roadless Rule would cause them irreparable harm by preventing their access to the national forests for proper purposes. Plaintiffs argued that such access was necessary to counter wildfires and threats from insects and disease. The plaintiffs based their motion for preliminary injunction upon alleged violations of NEPA, National Forest Management Act ("NFMA") and the APA.

Thereafter, on March 14, 2001, the district court granted the motion of the Idaho Conservation League, joined by other environmental organizations[5] (collectively, "ICL") to intervene as defendants in both cases. The district court also granted the motion of the Forest Service Employees for Environmental Ethics ("FSEEE") to intervene as a defendant in the complaint brought by Kootenai Tribe and its co-plaintiffs.

On April 5, 2001, the district court issued an order in each case, holding that the plaintiffs had a likelihood of success on their motions for a preliminary injunction. However, the district court reserved ruling on plaintiffs' preliminary injunction motions until the administration of President Bush updated the court on its ongoing review of the Roadless Rule. On May 4, 2001, eight days before the Roadless Rule was to go into effect, the Forest Service told the district court that because of "concerns about the process through which the Rule was promulgated," the Forest Service planned to "initiate an additional public process that [would] examine possible modifications to the Rule." Although the Forest Service would let the Roadless Rule go into effect, the Forest Service told the district court that it would also "develop[ ] proposed amendments to the Rule that will seek to maintain the protections embodied in the current rule." In particular, the Forest Service planned to amend the Rule to allow "limited activities to prevent the negative effects of unnaturally severe wildfires, insect infestation and disease."[6]

Thereafter, on May 10, 2001, the district court found that the plaintiffs had shown that there was "a strong likelihood of success on the merits"; that there existed, absent amendments to the Roadless Rule proposed by the federal government under President Bush's administration, a "substantial possibility that the Roadless Rule will result in irreparable harm to the National Forests"; that there was no date certain for amendments nor guarantee that amendments would "cure

---

5. The environmental organizations joined with Idaho Conservation League as co-defendants-intervenors are: Idaho Rivers United, Sierra Club, The Wilderness Society, Oregon Natural Resources Council, Pacific Rivers Council, Natural Resources Defense Council, and the Defenders of Wildlife.

6. As described by the administration of President Bush, the new process would provide accurate mapping data and provide more public comment process for considering amendments to the Rule.

the defects identified by the Court and acknowledged to exist by the Federal Government"; and finally and accordingly, that "the Court finds that Plaintiffs have made the minimal showing of irreparable harm and will order that the injunction issue."

ICL and FSEEE filed their Notices of Appeal on May 11 and May 15, 2001, respectively. The federal defendants did not appeal. [The court found that intervention as a matter of right is not available to private parties in NEPA actions; thus it turned to permissive intervention as a basis for participation of the added parties in the appeal. Eds.]

This appeal presents an unusual procedural setting: The federal defendants, enjoined from "implementing all aspects of the Roadless Area Conservation Rule," have not appealed the injunctions. The interlocutory appeals before us were brought by the environmental groups granted status as defendant-intervenors by the district court. We must determine whether the intervenors may defend the government's alleged violations of NEPA and the APA when the federal defendants have decided not to appeal the district court's preliminary injunction against implementation of the Roadless Rule. Stated another way, if the federal government no longer contests the plaintiffs' positions and the court's ruling, may interested persons as intervenors defend the challenged government processes? * * *

Before we address whether the district court erred in granting intervention under Federal Rule of Civil Procedure 24(b), we must first determine whether intervenors have Article III standing to pursue this appeal in defense of the Roadless Rule without the government as an appellant, leaving intervenors as the only parties on appeal adverse to plaintiffs. In this unusual context, our precedent requires that we find "independent jurisdictional grounds" for the defendant-intervenors' appeal. Beck v. United States Dep't of the Interior, 982 F.2d 1332, 1337–38 (9th Cir. 1992)("A permissive defendant-intervenor must have independent jurisdictional grounds on which to pursue an appeal, absent an appeal by the party on whose side the intervenor intervened. An interest strong enough to permit intervention is not necessarily a sufficient basis to pursue an appeal abandoned by the other parties.").

To establish standing, the defendant-intervenors must first show that they have suffered an injury in fact, " 'an invasion of a legally-protected interest' that is concrete and particularized, and actual or imminent." *Beck*, 982 F.2d at 1340 (quoting Lujan v. Defenders of Wildlife, 504 U.S. 555, 560 (1991)); see also Friends of the Earth, Inc. v. Laidlaw Envtl. Serv., 528 U.S. 167, 180–81 (2000). Considering standing of intervenors, specifically, we have held that "intervenors in environmental litigation satisfy the injury in fact requirement by showing that group members have direct contact with the environmental subject matter threatened by the adverse decision." Idaho Farm Bureau Fed'n v. Babbitt, 58 F.3d 1392, 1398 (9th Cir. 1995). In *Beck,* where intervenors were appealing a decision striking down a regulation protecting Alaskan sea otters, intervenors satisfied the injury in fact requirement by demonstrating that their members were Alaska residents who studied, observed, and enjoyed the otters in Alaska. *Beck*, 982 F.2d at 1340–41.

Here, both sets of intervenors have demonstrated injury in fact. FSEEE's members work in the National Forests containing the roadless areas and regularly use them for a variety of outdoor recreation and nature appreciation, as found by the district court. Similarly, ICL's staff and members hunt, hike, fish and camp in roadless areas. These areas were to be protected by the Roadless Rule but will have less protection from development if the district court's injunction is sustained. This is sufficient to establish an injury in fact. See *Idaho Farm Bureau Fed'n*, 58 F.3d at 1398–99 (finding injury in fact where ICL members' use of endangered species habitat would be impaired by district court ruling overturning species protection). Whatever protections of the involved environmental interests remain in the absence of the Roadless Rule, there can be no doubt that the 58.5 million acres subject to the Roadless Rule, if implemented, would have greater protection if the Roadless Rule stands.

In addition to injury in fact, to establish standing intervenors must show a causal connection between the injury and the conduct complained of and that the injury will likely be redressed by the relief requested. 58 F.3d at 1399. For standing on appeal, intervenors need not show that they independently could have sued the party who prevailed in district court. *Beck*, 982 F.2d at 1338. Intervenors can allege a threat of injury stemming from the order they seek to reverse, an injury which would be redressed if they win on appeal. *Idaho Farm Bureau Fed'n*, 58 F.3d at 1399.

Applying these standards, the intervenors satisfy standing requirements. The injury to both FSEEE and ICL, an increased risk of road development affecting conservation and environmental interests of applicants and their members, is "traceable" to the district court's order granting the injunction. This "injury" would be redressed by a decision of this Court lifting the injunction and allowing the Roadless Rule to have force. We hold that FSEEE and ICL have Article III standing to bring this appeal.

We now analyze permissive intervention under Rule 24(b). A district court's decision to grant or deny permissive intervention under Rule 24(b) is reviewed for an abuse of discretion. See Beckman Indus. Inv. v. Int'l Ins. Co., 966 F.2d 470, 472 (9th Cir. 1992). Under Rule 24(b) the question here is whether the applicants to intervene assert a claim or defense in common with the main action. Here, the intervenors asserted their interests related to the Roadless Rule in moving to intervene, and after intervention was granted asserted defenses of the Roadless Rule directly responsive to the claims for injunction asserted by plaintiffs. Intervenors satisfied the literal requirements of Rule 24(b), and it was within the district court's discretion to decide whether to permit them to participate. It is correct, on the one hand, that the intervenors do not have an independent protectible interest under Wetlands. That decides against intervention under Rule 24(a), but does not control application of Rule 24(b). The intervenors asserted defenses of the Roadless Rule directly responsive to the claim for injunction. Moreover, though intervenors do not have a direct interest in the government rulemaking, they have asserted an interest in the use and enjoyment of roadless lands, and in the conservation of roadless lands, in the national forest lands subject to the Roadless Rule, and they assert "defenses" of the government rulemaking that squarely respond to the challenges made by plaintiffs in the main action.

* * * Rule 24(b)(2) provides that on timely application the court may allow an absentee to intervene "when an applicant's claim or defense and the main action have a question of law or fact in common." The language of the rule makes clear that if the would-be intervenor's claim or defense contains no question of law or fact that is raised also by the main action, intervention under Rule 24(b)(2) must be denied. But, if there is a common question of law or fact, the requirement of the rule has been satisfied and it is then discretionary with the court whether to allow intervention. That appears to be precisely the case here.

Moreover, the court expressly noted that "the magnitude of this case is such that both Applicants' intervention will contribute to the equitable resolution of this case," permitting permissive intervention; thus the court gave a good and substantial reason for exercising its discretion to permit the permissive intervention. In fact, the government declined to defend fully from the outset, suggesting that the government itself saw problems and wanted to amend the Roadless Rule. Under these circumstances it is clear, as the court itself recognized, that the presence of intervenors would assist the court in its orderly procedures leading to the resolution of this case, which impacted large and varied interests. The district court did not abuse its discretion in granting the intervenors permissive intervention under Rule 24(b).

[Reaching the merits of the intervenor's appeal, the court held the initial plaintiffs had standing to bring the challenge to the Rule initially, but that the trial judge erred in considering the need for an injunction.]

Plaintiffs have demonstrated at best a serious question of liability on the merits of their NEPA claim, and plaintiffs cannot prevail at this stage when we assess prospects of irreparable harm to all parties and the balance of hardships that would flow from injunction. Because of its incorrect legal conclusion on prospects of success, the district court proceeded on an incorrect legal premise, applied the wrong standard for injunction, and abused its discretion in issuing a preliminary injunction.

REVERSED AND REMANDED for proceedings consistent with this opinion.

Notes and Questions

1. In an environmental litigation, the Seventh Circuit considered the argument of the Chamber of Commerce that it feared that the parties would settle the proceeding, but the court concluded that "this is a reason to deny

rather than allow intervention. Why should the Chamber receive an entitlement to nix a settlement (if one can be reached) that the Sierra Club, [the power plant operator], and the EPA all favor? Officious intermeddlers ought not be allowed to hijack litigation that the real parties in interest can resolve to mutual benefit." See Sierra Club v. Environmental Protection Agency, 358 F.3d 516 (7th Cir. 2004).

5. POST–JUDGMENT INTERVENTION

Intervention is possible only on "timely application." Fed. R. Civ. P. 24(a), (b). One appellate court commented: "we find it hard to see how a post-judgment motion could be timely." But the court acknowledged that " 'Hard' differs from 'impossible'." In re Navigant Consulting, 275 F.3d 616 (7th Cir. 2001). The Second Circuit has said that post-judgment intervention is particularly disfavored, "because it fosters delay and prejudice to existing parties." Farmland Dairies v. Commissioner of New York State Department of Agriculture & Markets, 847 F.2d 1038, 1044 (2d Cir. 1988).

MASSACHUSETTS v. MICROSOFT CORP.

United States Court of Appeals, District of Columbia Circuit, 2004.
373 F.3d 1199.

GINSBURG, CHIEF JUDGE.

In United States v. Microsoft Corp., 253 F.3d 34 (D.C. Cir. 2001) (Microsoft III), we affirmed in part and reversed in part the judgment of the district court holding Microsoft had violated §§ 1 and 2 of the Sherman Antitrust Act, vacated the associated remedial order, and directed the district court, on the basis of further proceedings, to devise a remedy "tailored to fit the wrong creating the occasion" therefor, id. at 107, 118–19. On remand, the United States and certain of the plaintiff states entered into a settlement agreement with Microsoft. Pursuant to the Antitrust Procedures and Penalties (Tunney) Act, 15 U.S.C. §§ 16(b)–(h), the district court held the parties' proposed consent decree, as amended to allow the court to act sua sponte to enforce the decree, was in "the public interest." Meanwhile, the Commonwealth of Massachusetts and several other plaintiff states refused to settle with Microsoft and instead litigated to judgment a separate remedial decree. The judgment entered by the district court in their case closely parallels the consent decree negotiated by the United States.

Massachusetts alone appeals the district court's entry of that decree. It argues the district court abused its discretion in adopting several provisions Microsoft proposed while rejecting several others Massachusetts and the other litigating states proposed. Massachusetts also challenges a number of the district court's findings of fact. Based upon the record before us in Microsoft III and the record of the remedial proceedings following remand, we affirm the district court's remedial decree in its entirety.

The Computer and Communications Industry Association (CCIA) and the Software and Information Industry Association (SIIA) separately appeal the district court's denial of their motion, following the district court's approval of the consent decree between the United States and Microsoft, to intervene in the case for the purpose of appealing the district court's public-interest determination. * * *

I. BACKGROUND

* * * In May 1998 the United States filed a complaint against Microsoft alleging violations of federal antitrust laws. At the same time, a number of states and the District of Columbia filed a complaint against Microsoft alleging violations of both federal and state antitrust laws. The two complaints, which the district court consolidated, sought various forms of relief, including an injunction against certain of Microsoft's business practices.

After a lengthy bench trial the district court entered findings of fact, and held Microsoft had violated §§ 1 and 2 of the Sherman Act by illegally maintaining its monopoly in the market for "Intel-compatible PC operating systems," by attempting to monopolize the browser market, and by tying its Windows operating system to its Internet Explorer (IE) browser. United States v. Microsoft Corp., 87 F. Supp. 2d 30 (D. D.C. 2000) (Conclusions of Law). The district court also held Microsoft violated the antitrust laws of the several states. Id. at 56. Based upon its findings of fact and conclusions of law, the district court decreed that Microsoft would be split into two separate companies, one selling operating systems and one selling program applications. * * *

The district court denied CCIA's request to intervene in the case, see id. § 16(f)(3), but it did allow CCIA and SIAA to participate in the hearing as amici curiae. In July 2002 the district court concluded both the Government and Microsoft had complied with the requirements of the Tunney Act and held that the matter was ripe for the court to determine whether the decree was in the "public interest."

On November 1, 2002 the district court ruled the Second Revised Proposed Final Judgment would be in the public interest if modified in one respect: The parties would have to provide for the district court to "retain jurisdiction to take action sua sponte in conjunction with the enforcement of the decree." U.S. Consent Decree, at 202. This they did in a Third Revised Proposed Final Judgment, which the district court duly entered. * * *

III. CCIA AND SIIA V. UNITED STATES & MICROSOFT, No. 03–5030

CCIA and SIIA seek to intervene for the purpose of appealing the district court's determination that the consent decree between the Government and Microsoft is in the "public interest," as required by the Tunney Act. They raise * * * a number of issues unique to the settlement proceedings, including the Government's and Microsoft's compliance with the procedural requirements of the Act.

A. Intervention

The district court denied the joint motion of CCIA and SIIA to intervene for purposes of appealing the court's public-interest determination in U.S. Consent Decree. They argue the district court erred in denying intervention because their "claim or defense and the main action have a question of law or fact in common," as required for permissive intervention pursuant to Federal Rule of Civil Procedure 24(b)(2). The district court had also to "consider whether the intervention will unduly delay or prejudice the adjudication of the rights of the original parties." FED. R. CIV. P. 24(b)(2). In denying CCIA's and SIIA's motion, the district court was concerned only with this latter requirement, to which we shall return in a moment. First, we examine whether the would-be intervenors' claim does have a question of law or fact in common with the underlying action.

CCIA and SIIA say they have a "claim or defense" in common with the main action in this case because their members Netscape and Sun Microsystems—"the very firms this Court identified as the victims of Microsoft's anticompetitive conduct"—have brought "antitrust claims that overlap with the Government's case." See Netscape Communications Corp. v. Microsoft Corp., No. 02–00097 (D.D.C., filed Jan. 22, 2002); Sun Microsystems, Inc. v. Microsoft Corp., No. 02–01150 (N.D. Cal., filed March 8, 2002). Unable to deny that point, the Government and Microsoft instead argue CCIA's and SIIA's intervention in this case would not produce the type of efficiency gains that ordinarily make intervention worthwhile when there are common issues because, unlike in MSL, there is no possibility in this case of a "trial on the merits." MSL, 118 F.3d at 782. Of course, there has already been a trial on the merits. Still, if we determine the consent decree is not in the public interest and remand the case for further proceedings on the remedy, then there is a possibility the final court-ordered remedy will provide some additional relief addressed to the issues Netscape and Sun have raised in their private actions.

The Government further contends permissive intervention in this case is inappropriate because Netscape and Sun, having sued Microsoft, may protect their rights apart from this proceeding. The Government cites Roe v. Wade, 410 U.S. 113, 125–27 (1973), in support of its claim that the "pendency of another action in which an applicant can protect its rights ordinarily counsels against permissive intervention." In Roe, however, the Supreme Court denied intervention because the intervenor—a doctor seeking declaratory and injunctive relief in federal court "with respect to the same statutes under which he stands charged in criminal prosecutions simultaneously pending in state court," id. at 126—had made "no allegation of any substantial and immediate threat to any federally protected right that cannot be asserted in his defense against the state prosecutions." Id. Intervention was therefore denied pursuant to the "national policy forbidding federal courts to stay or enjoin pending state court proceedings except under special circumstances." Younger v. Harris, 401 U.S. 37, 41 (1971). No such policy suggests the would-be intervenors in this case should be limited to another forum for airing their grievances. On the contrary, as in MSL, because the private antitrust claims of the associations' members overlap substantially with those here in suit, intervention "might produce efficiency gains." 118 F.3d at 782.

Turning to the second requirement for intervention, recall what we said in MSL:

> Once a common question of fact or law is found, Rule 24(b)(2) says that the district court, in exercising its discretion, "shall consider whether the intervention will unduly delay or prejudice the adjudication of the rights of the original parties." The "delay or prejudice" standard presumably captures all the possible drawbacks of piling on parties; the concomitant issue proliferation and confusion will result in delay as parties and court expend resources trying to overcome the centrifugal forces springing from intervention, and prejudice will take the form not only of the extra cost but also of an increased risk of error.

118 F.3d at 782. Further, "the 'delay or prejudice' standard of Rule 24(b)(2) appears to force consideration of the merits of the would-be intervenor's claims." Id. Hence, the district court in this case noted CCIA's and SIIA's arguments regarding "defects" in the consent decree were "identical to those made in their Tunney Act filings." And having once reviewed those filings in making its public-interest determination and finding them "not to fatally undermine" the proposed consent decree, the court held them insufficient to warrant intervention. Id.

CCIA and SIIA now argue that, if they are allowed to intervene, "There will be no delay caused by [their] appeal because this Court will have to decide the proper remedy for Microsoft's antitrust violations in [Massachusetts'] appeal regardless of what happens here." The Government acknowledges there would be no "undue delay" because the "consent decree is currently in force, as is an identical and unchallenged decree in the litigation between Microsoft and the settling states."

We think it sufficient the consent decree was already in place in the settling states' case when CCIA and SIIA sought intervention in December 2002: Allowing them to appeal from the Tunney Act proceeding will not delay "adjudicating . . . the rights of the original parties," FED. R. CIV. P. 24(b), because the settling states' decree requires Microsoft to conduct itself in the same manner as it must under the decree it entered into with the Government. See New York v. Microsoft Corp., 231 F. Supp. 2d 203, 205–06 (D. D.C. 2002). Nor will the parties be otherwise prejudiced by the intervenors' appeal. CCIA and SIIA had already participated extensively in the proceedings before the district court by submitting public comments in response to the proposed consent decree, see Comments of CCIA (Jan. 28, 2002), 2 J.A. (I) at 455–598; Comments of SIIA (Jan. 28, 2002), 3 J.A. (I) at 990–1057, and appearing as amici in the hearing on the proposed decree, see 3/6/02 pm Tr. at 156–65, 3 J.A. (I) at 1536–45. Because the district court already confronted CCIA's and

SIIA's arguments in rendering its decision, there is no reason to fear "issue proliferation," "confusion," "extra cost," or "an increased risk of error," see MSL, 118 F.3d at 782, if the associations are allowed to appeal the district court's public interest determination. Thus do the unusual procedural and substantive circumstances in this case converge to obviate any undue "delay or prejudice" that might otherwise have attended CCIA's and SIIA's appeal. Accordingly, we reverse the order of the district court denying intervention and permit CCIA and SIIA to intervene for the purpose of appealing the district court's public-interest determination.[19]

B. The Public Interest Finding

Under the Tunney Act, the district court's "public interest" inquiry into the merits of the consent decree is a narrow one: The district court should withhold its approval of the decree "only if any of the terms appear ambiguous, if the enforcement mechanism is inadequate, if third parties will be positively injured, or if the decree otherwise makes a 'mockery of judicial power.'" MSL, 118 F.3d at 783; see also United States v. Microsoft, 56 F.3d 1448, 1462 (D.C. Cir. 1995) (Microsoft I). [The the order approving the consent decree in the public interest was affirmed. Discussion omitted. Eds.]

Notes and Questions

1. In Acree v. Republic of Iraq, 370 F.3d 41 (D.C. Cir. 2004), soldiers who were held as prisoners by Iraq during the Gulf War and their families, filed suit under the terrorism exception to the Foreign Sovereign Immunities Act (FSIA), 28 U.S.C.A. § 1605(a)(7), against defendants, Iraq, its intelligence service, and its president. Judgment was entered in their favor. Two weeks after judgment was entered for the plaintiffs, the U.S. moved to intervene to contest subject matter jurisdiction and argued that provisions of the Emergency Wartime Supplemental Appropriations Act, Pub. L. No. 108–11, § 1503, 117 Stat. 559, 579 (2003), made the terrorism exception inapplicable to Iraq and thus stripped the district court of its jurisdiction. Noting that courts are generally reluctant to permit intervention after a suit has proceeded to final judgment, particularly where the applicant had the opportunity to intervene prior to judgment, the court held that the timeliness of a motion to intervene must be considered in light of all the circumstances of the case, including the purpose for which intervention is

---

19. The Government and Microsoft claim CCIA and SIIA may not intervene because they did not include with their motion to intervene "a pleading setting forth the claim or defense for which intervention is sought." FED. R. CIV. P. 24(c). Neither the Government nor Microsoft explains what type of pleading the would-be intervenors could have filed in a case such as this, where a judgment had already been rendered. In any event, "procedural defects in connection with intervention motions should generally be excused by a court."

McCarthy v. Kleindienst, 239 U.S. App. D.C. 247, 741 F.2d 1406, 1416 (D.C. Cir. 1984). The Government acknowledged as much at oral argument, stating, "this Court and other courts have not been hypertechnical, actually, in making sure that ... potential intervenors do file a pleading." The Government and Microsoft make no claim they had inadequate notice of the intervenors' appeal, and we find no reason to bar intervention based solely upon this technical defect, if defect it be.

sought, the need for intervention as a means of preserving the applicant's rights, and the possibility of prejudice to the existing parties. Weighing the importance of the case to the United States' foreign policy interests and the purposes for which the Government sought to intervene, the D.C. Circuit found that the Government's sole purpose in intervening was to raise "a highly tenable challenge to the District Court's subject matter jurisdiction in a case with undeniable impact on the Government's conduct of foreign policy and to preserve that issue for appellate review." It held that it was an abuse of the trial court's discretion to deny the government's intervention motion as untimely, and found that in light of its clear foreign policy interests, the United States was entitled to intervene as of right pursuant to Rule 24. 370 F.3d at 50.

2.   Bryant v. Yellen, 447 U.S. 352, 100 S.Ct. 2232, 65 L.Ed.2d 184 (1980), is a leading example of a non-party appeal. *Bryant* involved a federal statute governing the allocation of irrigation waters in the West meant to benefit smaller farmers by restricting access to the water to farmers holding no more than 160 acres of land. Id. at 368 n.19. The United States sued a California irrigation agency to force it to comply with the federal statute. Id. at 366. The district court found that the statute did not apply to certain lands in California, owned in parcels larger than 160 acres, that had vested rights to irrigation waters. Id. The government did not appeal this decision. Id. Even though the government declined to appeal, the Supreme Court unanimously recognized the standing of a group of farmworkers to intervene and appeal the decision. Id. at 366–68. The Court reached this conclusion because the intervenors "had a sufficient stake in the outcome of the controversy to afford them standing to appeal." Id. at 368. Other cases often cited as examples of post-judgment appeals by non-parties include United Airlines, Inc. v. Mcdonald, 432 U.S. 385, 395–96, 97 S.Ct. 2464, 53 L.Ed.2d 423 (1977), Hodgson v. United Mine Workers, 473 F.2d 118, 129 (D.C. Cir. 1972), Pellegrino v. Nesbit, 203 F.2d 463, 465 (9th Cir. 1953), United States Casualty Co. v. Taylor, 64 F.2d 521, 526–527 (4th Cir. 1933), and American Brake Shoe & Foundry Co. v. Interborough Rapid Transit Co., 3 F.R.D. 162, 164 (S.D.N.Y. 1942).

3.   In Linda R.S. v. Richard D., 410 U.S. 614, 93 S.Ct. 1146, 35 L.Ed.2d 536 (1973), the Court considered whether a non-party had standing to challenge the government's decision to apply a law in a particular manner. Id. In *Linda R.S.*, the appellant, the mother of an illegitimate child, sued to enjoin the local district attorney from failing to prosecute the father for refusing to pay child support. The district attorney generally prosecuted delinquent fathers of legitimate children but not those of illegitimate children. Id. The Supreme Court found the petitioner lacked standing, albeit in language that helps clarify the standing issues in this case. See id. at 617–19. The Court held that, "appellant has failed to allege a sufficient nexus between her injury and the government action which she attacks to justify judicial intervention." Id. at 617–18. The Court conceded that the lack of child support meant that appellant suffered an injury, but stressed that " 'the party who invokes [judicial] power must be able to show ... that he has sustained or is immediately in danger of sustaining some direct injury as the result of [a statute's] enforcement.' " Id. at 618. The Court noted that the "appellant has made no showing that her failure to secure support

payments results from the nonenforcement" of the child support statute; rather, "if appellant were granted the requested relief, it would result only in the jailing of the child's father. The prospect that prosecution will, at least in the future, result in payment of support can, at best, be termed only speculative." Id. Thus, the Court emphasized that the proposed remedy (arrest) would not redress the injury (lack of child support). Stated differently, the injury (lack of child support) was not traceable to the alleged impropriety (non-prosecution). As the Court concluded, "certainly the 'direct' relationship between the alleged injury and the claim sought to be adjudicated, which previous decisions of this Court suggest is a prerequisite to standing, is absent in this case." Id.

4. The Court decided Linda R.S. thirty years ago, and the Court has since developed the "direct relationship" standing requirement into two more precise sub-requisites; "redressability," and "fairly traceable." See, e.g., Whitmore v. Arkansas, 495 U.S. 149, 155, 110 S.Ct. 1717, 109 L.Ed.2d 135 (1990); Simon v. E. KY. Welfare Rights Org., 426 U.S. 26, 38, 96 S.Ct. 1917, 48 L.Ed.2d 450 (1976). In its first use of the specific phrase "fairly traceable," the Supreme Court explained that standing requires that "the injury is indeed fairly traceable to the defendant's acts or omissions." Village of Arlington Heights v. Metro. Housing Dev. Corp., 429 U.S. 252, 261, 97 S.Ct. 555, 50 L.Ed.2d 450 (1977). The Court has described "redressability" as the causal connection between the injury and the relief sought. See Allen v. Wright, 468 U.S. 737, 752, 104 S.Ct. 3315, 82 L.Ed.2d 556 (1984) (explaining that redressability depends on whether "the prospect of obtaining relief from the injury as a result of a favorable ruling is too speculative").

5. Ultimately, in Valley Forge Christian College v. Americans United for Separation of Church & State, Inc., 454 U.S. 464, 102 S.Ct. 752, 70 L.Ed.2d 700 (1982), the Supreme Court rearticulated its prior standing decisions in a three-part test for standing: someone has standing if he or she (1) suffers and injury in fact that (2) is fairly traceable to the alleged misconduct and (3) redressable by the relief sought. Id. at 472; see also Allen, 468 U.S. at 751 ("A plaintiff must allege personal injury fairly traceable to the defendant's allegedly unlawful conduct and likely to be redressed by the requested relief.").

BAKER v. WADE

United States Court of Appeals, Fifth Circuit, 1985 (en banc).
769 F.2d 289.

REAVLEY, CIRCUIT JUDGE.

Donald F. Baker, a homosexual, sought a declaration that Tex.Pen. Code Ann. § 21.06 is unconstitutional. Section 21.06 proscribes "engag[ing] in deviate sexual intercourse with another individual of the same sex." Id. The district court held that section 21.06 violates the constitutional protections of privacy and equal protection. Baker v. Wade, 553 F.Supp. 1121 (N.D.Tex.1982). Danny E. Hill, the district attorney of Potter County and a member of the defendant class, sought to appeal the district court's judgment. A panel of this court held that Hill did not have the right to intervene and prosecute the appeal. Baker

v. Wade, 743 F.2d 236 (5th Cir. 1984). We granted rehearing en banc and now hold that Hill is a proper appellant and that section 21.06 is constitutional.

1. JURISDICTION

Both Baker and Hill argue that the other is not properly before this court. Hill argues that Baker lacks standing to challenge the statute. Baker maintains that Hill could not appeal the district court judgment. We reject both arguments.

Baker has engaged in, and states that he will continue to engage in, homosexual activities proscribed by section 21.06. The defendant class representatives agreed that violations of section 21.06 have been prosecuted and that they will prosecute future violations where probable cause exists. When a criminal statute is challenged, a plaintiff may demonstrate standing without first exposing himself to arrest. It is enough that there exists a credible threat of prosecution. Babbitt v. United Farm Workers National Union, 442 U.S. 289, 99 S.Ct. 2301, 60 L.Ed.2d 895 (1979).

Coming to our jurisdiction to hear Hill's appeal, as of the date of the entry of the district court's judgment Hill was a member of the class, was enjoined by that judgment, and as district attorney was a proper official under Texas law to represent the state. See Texas Const. art. 5 § 21; State v. Gary, 359 S.W.2d 456, 458 (Texas 1962). As the deadline for giving notice of appeal approached, Hill filed his own notice. Several days later the attorney general of Texas filed a timely notice. It then appeared that the issue of the constitutionality of the Texas statute would be placed before the appellate court. However, several months later the attorney general filed a motion in this court to withdraw his appeal. When Hill learned of this fact, he sought a mandamus in the Supreme Court of Texas to order the attorney general to pursue the appeal, to which the latter responded that Hill had an adequate remedy at law by means of the direct appeal of the federal case, and pointed out to the Texas court: "Petitioner Hill has already filed a timely notice of appeal in the Fifth Circuit of the very decision they seek to have appealed."

Hill promptly filed a motion to intervene and to substitute himself as the class representative, first with the district court and subsequently with this court. A judge of this court granted Hill's motion. Under the peculiar facts of this case the order granting intervention was justified because Hill's position satisfied the requirements of both Fed.R.Civ.P. 23(d)(2) and 24(a)(2). His motion came as soon as he knew that his interests, affected by the judgment, i.e., the declaration of the unconstitutionality of the statute and the injunction against its enforcement, would be pursued. He would be seriously prejudiced were he not allowed to intervene, whereas allowing the appeal to proceed prejudiced no one. As a state official empowered by Texas law to enforce criminal laws, his interest and its impairment by the district court's judgment cannot be questioned. The adequacy of representation of intervenor's interests, and especially those of the class, is ordinarily an issue that would require hearing and determination by the district court. In this case where the district court has rejected binding Supreme Court authority, the circuit court is entitled to conclude as a matter of law that those interests were inadequately represented by those who failed to pursue the appeal and that the state officer seeking to intervene was a proper party to do so.

2. CONSTITUTIONALITY OF SECTION 21.06

The district court held that section 21.06 violated Baker's constitutional right to privacy and to equal protection of the law. Baker v. Wade, 553 F.Supp. 1121, 1141, 1143 (N.D. Tex.1982). Hill assails the district court's holding on the grounds that it fails to give effect to binding precedent and improperly expands constitutional principles. We agree. * * *

Because we hold that section 21.06 is constitutional, the injunction of the district court is vacated and the judgment is REVERSED. * * *

ALVIN B. RUBIN, CIRCUIT JUDGE, with whom GOLDBERG, POLITZ, RANDALL, TATE, JOHNSON, and WILLIAMS, CIRCUIT JUDGES, join, dissenting.

Determined to uphold the constitutionality of a Texas statute whatever obstacles bar the way, the majority opinion tramples every procedural rule it considers. No party to the suit has pursued this appeal, but the majority opinion recognizes an appeal filed by a class member who was not a class representative at the time he filed his appeal, permits a so-called intervention to be filed in the court of appeals by the same class member who sought to intervene only in his own abortive appeal, and decides that the Texas Attorney General together with representatives of a class including all of its prosecutorial officials do not provide adequate representation for the State of Texas in a suit involving the constitutionality of a criminal statute, but that any of the 1085 Texas district, county, and city attorneys is an appropriate party to represent the state and assert its position in the court of appeals. The court's judicial sponsorship of Danny Hill as spokesman for the State of Texas is not only unprecedented but ill-advised. The Texas Attorney General and the class representatives, who have been found wanting in no way save in failing to press the appeal, have decided that the sovereign interests of the state are served by allowing the district court decision to stand. It is neither Hill's province nor ours to question that judgment.

If this en banc decision is precedent, it assuredly rewrites the adjective law. If it is not intended to be precedential, but only a special life-support contrivance, undertaken for the one purpose of salvaging the statute, it denies equal justice both to the litigants before us and to those who, in the future, will be denied equally extreme judicial measures. I, therefore, respectfully dissent from the decision not to dismiss the appeal.

I

Let us first trace the procedural history of this case in somewhat greater detail. The complaint named as defendants Lee Holt, the City Attorney for Dallas, Texas, and Henry Wade, the District Attorney for Dallas County, in their official capacities, and sought a declaratory judgment that the Texas statute is unconstitutional. Later, Baker filed a motion to certify a defendant class of officials responsible for enforcement of the statute.

Before the motion was heard, the Attorney General of Texas was notified of the suit, pursuant to 28 U.S.C. § 2403(b).[1] At the instance of Holt, the district court granted the State of Texas and the Attorney General "leave to intervene for the presentation of evidence and for argument on the question of the constitutionality of § 21.06," and the State of Texas filed what it titled a "Response of the State of Texas" to the complaint. Holt's assistant city attorney then wrote Thomas A. Curtis, the District Attorney of Potter County, Hill's predecessor in office, and thirty-nine other Texas officials, notifying each of the suit and the possibility of certification of a defendant class, and offering each an opportunity to intervene. Curtis did not seek to intervene nor did any other Texas district, county, or city attorney. Only then, and with the consent of the defendants, was the case certified as a defendant class action under Rule 23(b)(2) of the Federal Rules of Civil Procedure. The class was composed of "*all* district, county and city attorneys in the state of Texas responsible for the enforcement of Texas Penal Code Ann. § 21.06," and represented by Holt and Wade. The order named as lead class counsel Holt's assistant city attorney Joe Werner and as associate class counsel Wade's assistant district attorney C.J. Baldree and state assistant attorney general Lonny Zwiener. The class was properly certified as a (b)(2) class because the suit involved only a question generally applicable to the class.

The district court rendered a judgment declaring the statute unconstitutional and enjoining its enforcement on September 30, 1982. Danny Hill was then neither a named defendant nor a class representative, and he had never sought to intervene. Nonetheless, on October 28, Hill filed a notice of appeal. At that time, no named party had sought to appeal. Four days later the Attorney General of the State of Texas filed a notice of appeal on behalf of the State of Texas. Then, before any further proceedings in this court, the Attorney General withdrew his notice of appeal. Hill then unsuccessfully attempted to have the Texas Supreme

---

1. 28 U.S.C. § 2403(b) reads as follows:

In any action, suit, or proceeding in a court of the United States to which a State or any agency, officer, or employee thereof is not a party, wherein the constitutionality of any statute of that State affecting the public interest is drawn in question, the court shall certify such fact to the attorney general of the State, and shall permit the State to intervene for presentation of evi-dence, if evidence is otherwise admissible in the case, and for argument on the question of constitutionality. The State shall, subject to the applicable provisions of law, have all the rights of a party and be subject to all liabilities of a party as to court costs to the extent necessary for a proper presentation of the facts and law relating to the question of constitutionality.

Court mandamus the Attorney General, on March 28, 1983, to force him to pursue his Fifth Circuit appeal.

Hill next filed two motions in the district court on April 12, 1983. One was a motion to intervene and to "substitute" himself as class representative,[2] and the other was a motion to set aside the final judgment and reopen the evidence. These motions were not acted on by the district court until April 3, 1984, a year later. The correctness of that court's decision is not now before us.

While the district court motions were still pending, however, Hill filed a motion in this court to intervene and "substitute" himself as class representative. In that motion, Hill explicitly acknowledged that "[o]n April 12, 1983, appellant filed a Motion to Intervene and Substitute Class Representative in the trial court. The trial court has not ruled on the Motions [sic]." On August 16, 1983, a judge of this court granted "appellant's motion to intervene and substitute class representative." To the extent that evidence, if it may be thus called, was offered in support of the motion, it consisted only of assertions in Hill's brief in support of the motion filed with this court.

Two weeks before oral argument of the case, the trial court denied Hill's motion to intervene and substitute class representative and his motion to set aside the final judgment and reopen the evidence. It found that Hill had not shown that the current class representatives were inadequate or that he could adequately represent the class. It granted Hill leave to refile his motion, however, if he were prepared to make such a showing. From the trial court's denial of a motion to reconsider, that decision has since been appealed but the appeal has not yet been heard.

II

When Hill filed his notice of appeal, he was not a party to the case. He had no right to appeal. The majority does not hold that his appeal was properly lodged, for to do so would recognize that any class member may on his own motion appeal any judgment adversely affecting the class. Instead, it finds that this court has jurisdiction of the appeal because "[u]nder the peculiar facts of this case the order *granting intervention* was justified." Thus, our jurisdiction is created by Hill's motion to intervene in an appeal filed only by Hill himself, the motion coming nine months after the notice of appeal.

This conclusion conveniently overlooks the question whether an intervention does not by its very nature require a subsisting action in which to intervene. An intervenor by definition does not create a suit or an appeal; he intervenes in an action that has already been undertaken. The majority does recognize that a problem is created by its recognition

2. Procedurally, Hill's motion was not a request for substitution under Fed.R.Civ.P. 25, but was a motion to intervene and be named class representative under Fed. R.Civ.P. 23 and 24. See 7A C. Wright & A. Miller, Federal Practice and Procedure § 1951, at 638 (1972).

of a motion to intervene never filed in or acted on by a district court, saying, "The adequacy of representation of intervenor's interests, and especially those of the class, is *ordinarily* an issue that would require hearing and determination by the district court." The majority goes on, however, to assert that, in this case, the question is one of law, a sheer *ipse dixit,* for the three cases cited for this proposition, with the ambiguous reference, "See," provide no support for it whatsoever. Whether the interests of a would-be intervenor have been inadequately represented and whether the interests of a class of which he is a member have also been inadequately represented are factual questions, to be resolved by a trial court, not questions of law.

In *United Airlines, Inc. v. McDonald,*[6] the first of the cases cited in support of this court's admittedly extraordinary recognition of Hill as an intervenor, the Supreme Court considered the timeliness of a motion to intervene filed in the district court for the purpose of appealing that court's earlier denial of class action certification, and no more. The district court had denied the motion[7] to intervene and had earlier denied a motion for class certification. The Supreme Court held that, on the record made in the district court, the motion to intervene for the purpose of appealing the district court's earlier denial of class action certification was timely. The Supreme Court cited a number of lower federal court decisions consistent with its opinion.[8] In every one of these, a motion to intervene was filed in and ruled on by the district court.

Our decision in *Stallworth v. Monsanto Co.,*[10] the next authority cited, gives no greater support. In its first sentence, the opinion states the issue considered and decided: "These consolidated appeals are taken from the district court's denial of two petitions for leave to intervene under Rule 24. * * * "[11] The Seventh Circuit, in *F.W. Woolworth Co. v. Miscellaneous Warehousemen's Union, Local No. 781,*[12] likewise considered only an appeal from the district court's denial of motions to intervene. Indeed, in an opinion that has scarcely had time to reach the advance sheets, a panel of this court held, in *Fuel Oil Supply and Terminaling v. Gulf Oil Corp.,*[13] that whether a party has a right to intervene in a bankruptcy proceeding is a question of fact to be determined by the trial court.[14]

Rules 23(d)(2) and 24(a)(2) of the Federal Rules of Civil Procedure, which are relied upon by the majority, cannot sustain Hill's effort to intervene and create his own appeal in the court of appeals for they both deal, as Rule 1 plainly says, with "the procedure in the United States district courts." The "court" that may make appropriate orders, referred to in Rule 23(d)(2), which applies to class actions, is the district court in

6.   432 U.S. 385, 97 S.Ct. 2464, 53 L.Ed. 2d 423 (1977).

7.   Id. at 390, 97 S.Ct. at 2467, 53 L.Ed. 2d at 429.

8.   See id. at 395 n. 16, 97 S.Ct. at 2470 n. 16, 53 L.Ed.2d at 433 n. 16 * * *.

10.   558 F.2d 257 (5th Cir. 1977).

11.   Id. at 260.

12.   629 F.2d 1204 (7th Cir. 1980).

13.   762 F.2d 1283 (5th Cir. 1985).

14.   Id. at 1287–88.

which the action is filed. The intervention permitted by Rule 24 is intervention in a pending action.

In *Johnson v. Georgia Highway Express, Inc.,*[16] we made it absolutely clear that the determination whether a class member would adequately and fairly represent the class and, thus, whether he should be named class representative is a determination for the trial court:

> Whether [the class member] will adequately represent the class is a question of fact to be 'raised and resolved in the trial court in the usual manner, * * *' * * *. Therefore, the court below, if it doubted appellant's ability to protect the interests of the class, could have had, and on remand still can have an evidentiary hearing on the issue.[17]

A federal court of appeals takes no evidence, creates no record, and decides no factual issues in the first instance. It is a court of review.

A motion filed in a district court by a nonparty who seeks to intervene in order to prosecute an appeal is significantly different from a motion filed in an appellate court by a nonparty who seeks to intervene in an existing appeal, and whether each kind of motion should be granted involves different judicial considerations. When the motion to intervene is filed in a district court, to enable the would-be intervenor to prosecute an appeal, evidence may be taken on such matters as whether the application is timely, whether the applicant's interest is adequately represented by existing parties, the nature and sufficiency of the would-be intervenor's interest, and any other questions pertinent to intervention, as required by Rule 24, or if the action is a class action, Rule 23. An appellate court may then review the district court's action on the basis of the record made in that court. When a motion is filed in an appellate court to intervene in an existing appeal, however, "a court of appeals may, but only in an exceptional case for imperative reasons, permit intervention where none was sought in the district court."[18] Thus we have refused to allow a nonparty to intervene on appeal when he was aware of the action in the district court and of his interest in it but failed to intervene in that court,[19] whereas we have allowed a nonparty who had no notice of the action below to intervene when there was no opposition to his intervention on appeal. Even in these cases, however, an appeal had already been taken by a party to the action, into which the nonparty sought to intervene, and no motions to intervene were pending in the lower courts.

A class member is not precluded from intervening after judgment. To do so, however, he must timely assert his right in the district court. If his application is denied, he may then appeal from the order denying intervention. If no other appeal has been taken, Moore's Federal Practice states, he "may, probably *must,* file a notice of appeal from the judgment

---

16. 417 F.2d 1122 (5th Cir. 1969).

17. Id. at 1124–25 (citation omitted).

18. McKenna v. Pan American Petroleum Corp., 303 F.2d 778, 779 (5th Cir. 1962).

19. Id.

from which he seeks to appeal within the time prescribed by Rule 4(a)." Then, "if the court of appeals reverses the order denying intervention, it will proceed with the merits." On the other hand, "[i]f it affirms denial of intervention, it will dismiss the appeal from the judgment on the merits on ground of want of standing."

Faced with a case similar to the one before this court, the District of Columbia Circuit held the appeal in abeyance and remanded the case to the trial court for its determination of the right to intervene. In this case, district court has considered the motion, decided it, and an appeal from that decision has been taken. The validity of the district court proceedings and the merits of its decision should be considered when that appeal is heard.

III

Hill's membership in the class does not relieve him from meeting the requirements of Rule 24(a) for intervention. Only if Hill meets those requirements may he intervene as a named party to this case.

A class member may intervene without displacing the class representatives. He may, however, choose another, and different, course: he may seek to have the designated class representatives removed for failure adequately to represent the class and seek to have himself designated as class representative. Hill does not dispute that the class representatives adequately represented the class in the trial court. His sole assertion of inadequacy is their failure to appeal. The class representatives' failure to appeal is a factor, but only a factor, in deciding whether their representation is adequate. Hill has never demonstrated that by failing to appeal they have failed "fully and adequately to protect the interests of the class" as a whole, as required by Rule 23(a), as qualified by Rule 23(b)(2), the class action rules, or that as required by Rule 24, the intervention rule, Hill's interest as a state official has not been adequately represented by them.

To determine whether the representatives have adequately represented the interest of the class as a whole, and consequently Hill's interest as a member of that class, we must define that interest. Danny Hill has no personal interest in this case, and indeed no member of the class has any personal interest in it. Hill's only interest, as he admits, stems from his office as District Attorney, and he seeks to appear before us only in that official capacity. No money judgment has been or will be rendered against him, even for costs, as a representative in his official capacity. No judgment has been entered against him in his personal capacity.

That a district attorney is a proper official to represent the state for some purposes cannot be doubted. The issue here, however, is whether the interests of the state and of the class have been adequately and fully represented. In this respect the other class members have an interest identical to Hill's and indeed identical to the State's, for, in their official capacities, they have no interest greater than or different from the

State's interest. None of them has offered to us any indication of dissatisfaction with the action of their representatives.

The real party in interest is the State of Texas, for it is the facial constitutionality of a state statute that is at issue. Whether the Texas Attorney General has power to prosecute for crimes and whether, in the absence of the Attorney General, suit to challenge the constitutionality of a state statute might be brought in federal court against some other official are not at issue here and are indeed irrelevant. Neither the Texas Constitution nor the two cases cited by the majority give a district attorney authority to act for the state in a declaratory judgment action in federal court in which the Attorney General has intervened to protect the state's interest, and they do not dictate to a federal appellate court whether representation of the state's or the class members' interests has been adequately undertaken. When both the State's Attorney General and the class representatives have decided that it is not in the state's interests to appeal, it is not the province of any one of the 1085 district, county, and city attorneys of the State to do so on the priori basis that all others are out of step and that he alone knows the state's true interest.

In deciding who should speak for the state, it is important to consider the result of an adverse judgment against the state on appeal. Not only might the decision of the district court be affirmed but the state might be required to pay the costs of appeal, including the attorney's fees taxable under § 1988. If Hill or any of the multitude of prosecuting attorneys may take it on himself to appeal an adverse ruling, the expense would not fall on Hill or on the other Horatius at the constitutional bridge or on his city or county but on the state.

Whatever Hill's interest in this case may be, it arises solely out of his official capacity as Potter County Attorney, as Hill states in his en banc reply brief. Hill asserts that his official interests have been inadequately represented by the class representatives and the State's Attorney General. The burden of proof, however slight, is on him. He has not borne it.

IV

Soon after the founding of the Republic, the Supreme Court indicated that the power of judicial review should be exercised reluctantly, only because it is essential to the decision of the case before a federal court and because the Constitution and the laws of the United States, as the "Supreme Law of the Land," require it. The justification for federal judicial review of the constitutionality of a federal or state legislative enactment rests upon these principles. As a corollary, the Supreme Court has espoused and this court has followed the prudential principle that a federal court should not and will not reach a constitutional question if it can rest its decision on nonconstitutional grounds. As we stated in *Ramsay v. Bailey,* "[h]owever novel and interesting may be these constitutional claims, it is our duty to decide this case on other grounds if possible." The principle applies with equal force whether decision on the merits would uphold or reject constitutionality. If judicial restraint is a doctrine invoked only to achieve a desired result but to be ignored when following it would not be expedient, it ceases to be a principle and becomes but another rationalization by which judges may achieve their purpose.

Whether the Attorney General, District Attorney Wade, and City Attorney Holt have acted wisely or well in the interests of the State or in the interests of their constituents, are questions to be decided by the Texas electorate and by the institutions of Texas government. It has not been properly shown that they have inadequately represented the interests of the State that they were elected to serve or the interests of the class that they were appointed to represent. From the decision to permit Danny Hill, in his official capacity as District Attorney of Potter County, one of 254 Texas counties, to intervene on appeal and to prosecute this appeal, I respectfully dissent.

Notes and Questions

1. Class actions present some of the most difficult problems in deciding who can appeal, what procedural steps they must take to prosecute an appeal, and when they must take them. In the principal case how do the majority and the minority differ as to what must be done and when? See subsection 6 immediately below.

2. The majority cited United Airlines, Inc. v. McDonald, 432 U.S. 385, 97 S.Ct. 2464, 53 L.Ed.2d 423 (1977) in support of its position, but the minority argued it was not applicable. Which is correct?

3. Another aspect of class actions is whether the named parties can appeal when they have received all of the relief they have claimed in their individual capacities. In Deposit Guaranty Nat'l Bank v. Roper, 445 U.S. 326, 100 S.Ct. 1166, 63 L.Ed.2d 427 (1980), the Supreme Court held that they could appeal the denial of certification of a class, stating as a requirement that the party retain a stake in the appeal to satisfy the requirements of Art. III of the Constitution. In that case the Court found that the named plaintiff's desire to share the costs of litigation with other class members was sufficient.

4. Hill's motion to intervene was granted by a single judge of the Fifth Circuit. What gave the judge the authority to grant the motion? See R. Martineau, Modern Appellate Practice—Federal and State Civil Appeals Ch. 9 (1983). In Amalgamated Transit Union Int. v. Donovan, 771 F.2d 1551, 1552–53 (D.C. Cir. 1985) the court, in refusing to allow intervention after the case had been decided in that court, commented on intervention in the appellate court:

> A court of appeals may allow intervention at the appellate stage where none was sought in the district court "only in an exceptional case for imperative reasons."[3]

---

3. No provision in the Federal Rules of Appellate Procedure provides for interven- tion on appeal, except in proceedings to review agency action. Fed.R.App.P. 15(d).

5. What is the relevance of Federal Rule of Civil Procedure 24 to a motion to intervene in the appellate court?

6. Some state rules expressly authorize a motion to intervene in the appellate court (Wis.Stat.Ann. § 809.13 (West 2003)). In other states, however, the rules do not permit it (Pearman v. Schlaak, 575 S.W.2d 462 (Ky. 1978), noted in 6 No.Ky.L.Rev. 427 (1979)).

7. In one tax case with First Amendment implications, the Ninth Circuit appointed Professor Erwin Chemerinsky to serve as an amicus after oral argument of the appeal. When the taxpayer and the IRS then filed a request for stipulated discontinuance of the appeal, Professor Chemerinsky moved to intervene in the appeal as a party to keep the issue alive for decision by the court. However, the court found that he was not "directly affected" by the question (taxation of a "housing allowance" given to a minister) and could pursue his own claim as in a separate "taxpayer action" if he desired. Hence intervention was denied. See Warren v. Commissioner of Internal Revenue, 302 F.3d 1012 (9th Cir. 2002).

8. Texas Penal Code § 21.06, discussed in the principal case, was eventually held unconstitutional under the Due Process clause in Lawrence v. Texas, 539 U.S. 558, 123 S.Ct. 2472, 156 L.Ed.2d 508 (2003).

6. CLASS ACTION APPEALS: INTERVENORS AND OBJECTORS

CHURCHILL VILLAGE, L.L.C.
v. GENERAL ELECTRIC

United States Court of Appeals, Ninth Circuit, 2004.
361 F.3d 566.

O'SCANNLAIN, CIRCUIT JUDGE.

We must decide various challenges to a class-action settlement of these suits against the manufacturer of consumer dishwashers.

I

Between 1983 and 1989, General Electric ("GE") manufactured and sold approximately three million GE-and Hotpoint-brand dishwashers equipped with a sliding "energy saver" switch. Although some were sold to individual consumers, the dishwashers were considered "low end" products and were primarily marketed to contractors, builders, and owners of commercial or rental properties. The switch, which allows a user to select either a heated drying cycle or drip drying, deteriorates over time and may melt or ignite.

Federal Rules of Civil Procedure Rule 24, relied upon by MARTA, only applies to intervention at the district court level. See Fed.R.Civ.P. 1; International Union, UAW, Local 283 v. Scofield, 382 U.S. 205, 217 n. 10, 86 S.Ct. 373, 381 n. 10, 15 L.Ed.2d 272 (1965). Although the Supreme Court has recognized that "the policies underlying intervention may be applicable in appellate courts," id., courts of appeals have developed their own standards of intervention in order to take account of the unique problems caused by intervention at the appellate stage.

Reports of fires caused by the allegedly defective switch eventually prompted an investigation by the Consumer Product Safety Commission ("CPSC"). Although the investigation found that no consumers had been physically injured, it determined that approximately 50 fires could be attributed to the switch, three of which damaged property other than the dishwasher itself. Under the terms of a formal settlement agreement between GE and the CPSC, GE announced a "recall" of the dishwashers in October 1999. GE advised consumers to stop using the dishwashers immediately, and offered a choice between a $75–125 cash rebate toward the purchase of a GE-brand dishwasher or a $25 cash refund toward the purchase of a non-GE-brand dishwasher, along with a free one-year service agreement with GE. GE also agreed to replace dishwashers still under extended service agreements. The GE–CSPC agreement also permitted GE to reach a separate agreement with owners and operators of commercial and residential properties that could include discounted bulk pricing and instructions to repair the switch by rewiring. Dissatisfied with the rebate program, some consumers turned to the courts.

Following pre-trial motions and discovery, the Churchill plaintiffs reached a settlement agreement with GE. Churchill agreed to file a consolidated amended complaint seeking certification of a class under Fed.R. Civ. P. 23(b)(3). Under the terms of the settlement agreement, GE agreed to provide each class member with either a $20 cash rebate or a one-year service contract.

After Churchill moved the district court for preliminary approval of the proposed settlement, Beckwith—here representing the two sets of plaintiffs pursuing class actions against GE in state court in Illinois and Connecticut—moved to intervene to object. The Beckwith objectors were permitted to present their objections to the proposed settlement in writing and participated in the preliminary approval and fairness hearings. The district court denied the intervention motion and preliminarily approved the proposed settlement.

On January 22, 2002, the district court issued a final order approving the settlement, dismissing with prejudice all claims by members of the settlement class, awarding fees to Churchill's counsel, and denying fees to Florida Counsel. The Beckwith objectors now appeal the district court's approval of the settlement and Florida Counsel appeal the denial of attorneys' fees, claiming that they were responsible for catalyzing Churchill's successful result. Recognizing that Florida Counsel's claim shared a common progenitor with Churchill's settlement, we consolidated these appeals.

II

As a threshold matter, Churchill disputes whether the Beckwith objectors have any right to appeal. Churchill points out that the district court certified the settlement class under Fed. R. Civ. P. 23(b)(3), thereby permitting objecting class members like Beckwith to exclude themselves from the settlement. Because the objectors can opt out,

Churchill contends that they suffer no injury and thus lack standing to appeal.

But the issue is not precisely one of standing. As the Supreme Court has noted, neither Article III nor prudential standing is implicated by the efforts of non-intervening objectors to appeal class-action settlements. See Devlin v. Scardelletti, 536 U.S. 1, 7, 153 L. Ed. 2d 27, 122 S. Ct. 2005 (2002). Instead, the inquiry is best characterized as concerning the definition of a "party" for purposes of appeal. *Id.* And the *Devlin* Court made clear that objectors should be considered parties, holding that "non-named class members . . . who have objected in a timely manner to approval of the settlement at the fairness hearing have the power to bring an appeal without first intervening." Id. at 14.

Churchill urges that we read *Devlin* narrowly. There, the Court relied on the fact that *Devlin* was unable to opt out of the Rule 23(b)(1) class. Here, by contrast, the Beckwith objectors may exclude themselves from the settlement and thus preserve their right to seek relief from GE. Yet this ostensible independence is belied by an essential impracticability. Because each objector's claim is too small to justify individual litigation, a class action is the only feasible means of obtaining relief. By terminating all class actions relating to the dishwasher recall, the settlement will effectively bind the objectors. They therefore occupy precisely the status the *Devlin* Court sought to protect. See id. at 10 ("What is most important to this case is that nonnamed class members are parties to the proceedings in the sense of being bound by the settlement. It is this feature of class action litigation that requires that class members be allowed to appeal the approval of a settlement when they have objected at the fairness hearing.").

We are satisfied that *Devlin* applies here sufficiently to permit the Beckwith objectors to challenge the settlement approved by the district court. Such a reading of Devlin is consistent, moreover, with our long-standing pre-*Devlin* practice of permitting objecting class members to appeal settlements. See Marshall v. Holiday Magic, Inc., 550 F.2d 1173, 1176 (9th Cir. 1977) (allowing class members who had not opted out to appeal settlement); Dosier v. Miami Valley Broad. Corp., 656 F.2d 1295, 1299 (9th Cir. 1981) (noting that unnamed class member who was represented by counsel at settlement conference "could have challenged it by direct appeal"); In re Cement Antitrust Litig., 688 F.2d 1297, 1309 (9th Cir. 1982) ("[A] class member may appeal from an order approving a settlement to which the member objects[.]"); see also 5 Moore's Federal Practice § 23.86[2] (3d ed. 1997) (arguing for a broad reading of *Devlin*).

Because we conclude that Beckwith may appeal the approval of the settlement, we now turn to the merits. * * *

WEINMAN v. FIDELITY CAPITAL APPRECIATION FUND

United States Court of Appeals, Tenth Circuit, 2004.
354 F.3d 1246.

ANDERSON, CIRCUIT JUDGE.

[Plaintiff, trustee for an unsecured creditors' trust, sued over 6,000 recipients of stock distributed in a corporate "spinoff," seeking to recover those shares or their value for the benefit of the trust beneficiaries. A settlement was reached with the named defendants, and steps were taken to give notice to all defendants of the proposed disposition.]

[T]he court ordered the Trustee to submit a report on the deliverability of that notice. The Trustee did so on April 24, 1998. His report indicates that notice of the settlement and hearing was mailed to the 6,423 known members of the class. Of these, approximately 1,455 notices, representing 296,292 shares, were returned as undelivered.

Following the hearing and the Trustee's submission of this report, the district court on July 7, 1999 issued an order and final judgment approving the settlement agreement with the opt-out provision. Pursuant to the court's order, the Trustee gave defendant class members notice of the court's approval both by mail, as before, and by publication. The notice included the deadline—September 15, 1999—by which each class member must either accept the settlement without individual defenses; accept the settlement subject to individual defenses or objections as to the number of shares held; or opt out of the settlement and remain a defendant in the adversary proceeding. Class members who did nothing before the deadline would have individual final judgments entered against them three days after the deadline. Class members who raised individual defenses or objections would not have a final judgment entered against them until their individual issues were judicially resolved. Id. at 843.

According to the Trustee, only some 250 of the more than 6,000 defendants opted out of the settlement—approximately 4–1/2 percent. Additionally, of course, some of the appellants in Integra I, and all of those in this appeal, did not opt out, choosing, instead, to appeal. Individual final judgments have been entered against each of the appellants in this case. Appellant Spengler originally asserted an individual defense but then withdrew it and consented to the entry of final judgment.

DISCUSSION

A. Standing / Right to Appeal

In Integra I we dismissed the appeals for lack of standing. We reasoned first that appellants who had opted out of the settlement lacked standing to contest the settlement on appeal. Integra I, 262 F.3d at 1103. Next, applying our rule in Gottlieb v. Wiles, 11 F.3d 1004 (10th Cir.

1993), we held that unnamed class members who had judgments entered against them but who had failed to file intervention motions in the district court, pursuant to Fed. R. Civ. P. 24(a), lacked standing to appeal. Integra I, 262 F.3d at 1103.

As indicated above, the Supreme Court subsequently ruled in a class action without opt-out rights that an unnamed class member is not required to seek intervention in the district court in order to appeal, although "objection during the fairness hearing" in the district court remains a requirement. Devlin v. Scardelletti, 536 U.S. 1, at 11 (2002). The Court also clarified that the issue relating to whether a class member can appeal from a district court's approval of a class settlement is not one of Article III jurisdiction or of prudential standing, as we characterized it in Integra I. Rather, the issue is "whether [the appellants] should be considered a 'party' for the purposes of appealing the approval of the settlement." Id. at 7. The Court explained that "nonnamed class members . . . may be parties for some purposes and not for others. The label 'party' does not indicate an absolute characteristic, but rather a conclusion about the applicability of various procedural rules that may differ based on context." Id. at 9–10. The Court articulated the issue in terms of "the right to appeal." Id. at 7. Accordingly, we proceed on that characterization.

All of the individuals involved in the five appeals now before us were named as defendants at the outset of the suit, prior to class certification. All but three of them neither filed written objections to the settlement nor moved to intervene; nor did they appear at the fairness hearing. One of the remaining three, Mr. Gioioso, filed a written objection but did not file notice of his intent to appear and object and did not appear at the fairness hearing. As indicated above, two others, Mr. Ulie in his custodial capacity and Mr. Spengler, did file notices of intention to appear and object and did appear at the fairness hearing through counsel, Mr. Bader. As further indicated above, none of the appellants (including Ulie in his capacity as custodian) opted out of the settlement, and all had final judgments entered against them pursuant to the terms of the settlement.

In asserting their right to appeal, the appellants rely on the fact that they were all originally individually named as defendants in this action. They argue that as named defendants having individual judgments entered against them, they have the right to appeal these judgments. In their view, certification of the case as a class action with named class representatives did not diminish their status as named parties. In so arguing, they necessarily contend that our opinion in Integra I was wrong when it classified the originally-named defendants as unnamed members of the class following class certification. See Integra I, 262 F.3d at 1104 n.14. In support, they argue that Devlin not only changed the intervention rules we applied in Integra I, it clarified how we should treat named parties as well. In any event, they argue, Spengler, Ulie and Gioioso have the right to appeal.

At the outset we note that nothing in Devlin overrides the conclusion we reached in Integra I that "despite having been named in the complaint, Appellants nonetheless appear now as unnamed class members, because the district court certified the case as a class action and designated representative defendants. . . ." Id. Accordingly, we reject the argument here, as we did in Integra I, that the appellants have the right to appeal judgments entered against them simply because they were originally named as parties.

Additionally, Devlin reinforces the proposition that an unnamed class member who does not opt out and desires to appeal a class settlement must at least object in the district court. Devlin, 536 U.S. at 11. A motion to intervene pursuant to Rule 24(a) serves the same purpose. Since all but three of the appellants in these appeals neither objected nor sought to intervene in the district court, we hold that they have no right to appeal.

That leaves appellants Gioioso, Ulie and Spengler, who did object, either directly or through counsel, and who did not opt out. As to them, we first address the Trustee's threshold argument that where the option to opt out of a settlement exists, that forecloses any right to appeal the settlement. Contrary to the Trustee's assertions, we did not so hold in Integra I. Rather, our analysis of the intervention requirement necessarily proceeded on the premise that failure to opt out of the settlement was not itself a bar to appeal. While Devlin involved a non-opt out class, the Court's reasoning also suggests that the right of an objecting class member to appeal must be recognized. We now make explicit what we implicitly held in Integra I and hold that a class member who does not opt out of a settlement but objects at the fairness hearing and against whom a final judgment is entered has the right to appeal the district court's approval of the settlement. See Thompson v. Metro. Life Ins., 216 F.R.D. 55, 70 (S.D.N.Y. 2003). This answers the question we left open in Rutter & Wilbanks Corp. v. Shell Oil Co., 314 F.3d 1180, 1185 n.2 (10th Cir. 2002), as to whether Devlin applies to opt-out class settlements.

Under that rule, it would appear that all three objecting class members, Gioioso, Ulie and Spengler, qualify as parties having the right to appeal. But, on further analysis, we cannot reach that conclusion as to Mr. Gioioso because his written objection does not meet the district court's stated requirements for objecting at the fairness hearing. The district court allowed class members to file comments on the settlement agreement in writing without making an appearance at the fairness hearing. However, it specified that in order to preserve a right to contest the approval of the settlement at the fairness hearing, a class member must file a Notice of Intention to Appear and Object. This requirement was included in the Notice of Proposed Class Settlement and Rights of Class Members that was mailed to all known class members. Mr. Gioioso presumably received this Notice since he filed written objections in response. We hold that Mr. Gioioso did not take the procedural steps necessary to have "objected during the fairness hearing" as required by Devlin, 536 U.S. at 11.

Messrs. Ulie as custodian and Spengler, however, have the right to appeal. Both, through counsel, filed the required notice of intent and appeared at the fairness hearing. But there is an overriding and dispositive reason as to Mr. Spengler.

As indicated above, Mr. Spengler was designated by the bankruptcy court as one of the seven class representatives when the court certified this suit as a defendant class action. As an alternative to our holding that objecting unnamed class members have the right to appeal an opt-out settlement, we also hold that an objecting class representative, who has not opted out of the settlement, is a party having the right to appeal. We implied as much in Integra I, 262 F.3d at 1103. Thus, we reject the Trustee's argument that opting out of the settlement was the only permissible avenue for Mr. Spengler to take. In effect, the Trustee's position, unsupported by any direct authority, is that a class action settlement with an opt-out provision can never be appealed, even by a class representative. We disagree. Likewise, we reject the argument that Spengler's consent to a judgment forfeited his right to appeal. A final judgment is a prerequisite to appeal, and was so as to Mr. Spengler. In short, Mr. Spengler is a proper party to appeal, and his appeal is sufficient to bring before us the issues outlined above. * * *

Because Mr. Spengler's appeal is sufficient, and since, as the following discussion shows, we rule for the Trustee on the merits, the other appellants' arguments in support of their right to appeal are, as a practical matter, moot in any event. * * *

AFFIRMED.

Notes and Questions

1. In a securities fraud action brought as a class action by purchasers of $200 million in corporate notes of "Just For Feet," a shoe retailer, several large institutional underwriters were purchasers of 64% of the corporate notes. The underwriters objected to a settlement, and were *excluded* from the definition of the class by the trial court. They attempted to appeal the trial court's approval of the settlement, arguing that the defendant's payments to the class would make defendant "judgment proof"—thereby adversely affecting the underwriters sufficiently to warrant allowing them to appeal. In dismissing the appeal, the Eleventh Circuit reviewed the status of "non-parties" in the sense of non-class members and the right to appeal:

> The Objectors here are not parties. Thus, they could only appeal the denial of their objections to the class settlement if they had intervened in the action. The Objectors argue that the Supreme Court's recent decision in Devlin v. Scardelletti, 536 U.S. 1, 122 S.Ct. 2005, 153 L.Ed.2d 27 (2002), requires a different result. We disagree.

> *Devlin* held that nonnamed members of class actions who have timely objected to a class settlement may appeal the denial of their objections without first moving to intervene. Id. at 14, 122 S. Ct. at 2013. The Supreme Court framed the issue not as a jurisdictional

question,[5] but rather as a matter of determining whether the non-named class member qualified as a "party" for purposes of Fed. R. App. P. 3(c). Id. (citing *Marino*, 484 U.S. at 304, 108 S. Ct. at 587–88). Nonnamed class members who timely object to binding settlements qualify as "parties," the Court held, primarily because they are bound by the judgments they seek to challenge:

> What is most important to this case is that nonnamed class members are parties to the proceedings in the sense of being bound by the settlement.... Particularly in light of the fact that petitioner had no ability to opt out of the settlement, appealing the approval of the settlement is petitioner's only means of protecting himself from being bound by a disposition of his rights he finds unacceptable and that a reviewing court might find legally inadequate.

Id. at 10–11, 122 S. Ct. at 2011; see also id. at 9, 122 S. Ct. at 2010 ("The District Court's approval of the settlement—which binds petitioner as a member of the class—amounted to a 'final decision of [petitioner's] right or claim' sufficient to trigger his right to appeal.").

The Objectors first argue that *Devlin* permits their appeal because they could have or should have been included in the plaintiff class. The argument misses the point of *Devlin*, which was to allow appeals by parties who are actually bound by a judgment, not parties who merely could have been bound by the judgment.[7] Id. at 9, 10–11, 122 S. Ct. 2010, 2011. Parties who are not class members are not bound at all.

Second, the Objectors argue that they are effectively bound by the judgment because it leaves the defendant Officers judgment-proof. That, the Objectors argue, renders their own claims futile. For support, the Objectors cite Karaha Bodas Co. v. Perusahaan Pertambangan Minyak Dan Gas Bumi Negara, 313 F.3d 70 (2nd Cir. 2002), and Plain v. Murphy Family Farms, 296 F.3d 975 (10th Cir. 2002).

Neither case helps the Objectors because each considered very different facts. * * * It is perhaps no accident that in each case the nonnamed party likely met the requirements for intervention as of right under Fed. R. Civ. P. 24(a). The Supreme Court hinted in *Devlin* that those instances may be precisely where the appellate courts should consider allowing nonnamed parties to appeal. See 536 U.S. at 12–13, 122 S. Ct. at 2011–12 (noting that it is "difficult to see the value" of requiring nonnamed objecting class members to intervene because they would easily meet the requirements of Fed. R. Civ. P. 24(a) anyway). No such circumstances exist here. The Objectors do not seek to protect their

---

5. The Court held that the objector's status as a class member satisfied the Article III "case or controversy" requirement and satisfied prudential standing concerns. Id. at 6–7, 122 S. Ct. at 2009.

7. This feature of *Devlin* has led at least one court to believe that it applies only to mandatory class actions. See Ballard v. Advance Am., 349 Ark. 545, 548–49, 79 S.W.3d 835 (2002) ("The petitioner in *Devlin* did not have the ability to opt out of the settle- ment. Here, appellants had the ability to opt out and instead elected to object to the settlement and risk being bound by it, if approved by the court over their objections."). See also In re Gen. Am. Life Ins. Co. Sales Practices Litig., 302 F.3d 799, 800 (8th Cir. 2002) (expressing tentative approval of Ballard in dicta). Because this case does not present that question, we express no opinion on it.

own property, their allotment from an award or settlement, or any other cognizable legal right or interest. They are simply potential plaintiffs who have yet to litigate any claims. Cf. Brennan v. N.Y. City Bd. of Educ., 260 F.3d 123, 129 (2nd Cir. 2001) (stating that to intervene as of right under Fed. R. Civ. P. 24(a)(2), a nonparty must have a "direct," "substantial," and "legally protectable" interest in the action rather than a merely speculative or contingent interest).

Because the Objectors would not qualify as parties even under the most permissive possible reading of Devlin, we decline to determine whether and when *Devlin* may apply outside of the mandatory class action context or to pass judgment on Karaha Bodas and Plain. There is no reason to permit the Objectors to disturb a legal judgment merely because they have outstanding claims they may wish to pursue, and they fear the instant judgment may leave the defendant judgment-proof. We need not determine the precise breadth of *Devlin* to see that the Objectors clearly stretch it too far.

The Objectors are not a party to this action and therefore cannot appeal it under Fed. R. App. P. 3(c). If they had moved to intervene unsuccessfully, we would have entertained an appeal of the denial of intervention. They have not done so. Therefore, we dismiss their appeal.

See AAL High Yield Bond Fund v. Deloitte & Touche LLP, 361 F.3d 1305, 1309–11 (11th Cir. 2004).

2.   Rule 23(f) appeals are discretionary interlocutory appeals permitted from class certification decisions. It has been held that standing is required "may—indeed must—be addressed even under the limits of a Rule 23(f) appeal." Rivera v. Wyeth–Ayerst Labs., 283 F.3d 315, 319 (5th Cir. 2002).

------

7.   THE GOVERNMENT AS INTERVENOR

In federal practice, Rule 24(c) requires a trial court to notify the federal or state government if the constitutionality of a statute is drawn into question in an action where the government or its agencies or employees are not named as parties, thus inviting the government to intervene. Statutes also call for intervention by governmental bodies in certain circumstances. Also, Appellate Rule 29 permits any state, or the United States, to file amicus papers without any requirement for permission of the appellate court.

BRUGGEMAN v. RYAN

United States Court of Appeals, Seventh Circuit, 2003.
318 F.3d 716.

POSNER, CIRCUIT JUDGE.

The United States filed an amicus curiae brief in this appeal on June 24, 2002, and later a brief as an intervenor, pursuant to 28 U.S.C. § 2403(a), which provides that the court "shall permit" the United

States to intervene in a case when the constitutionality of any Act of Congress affecting the public interest is challenged. The requirement that the act affect the public interest is intended to exclude the occasional federal statute that has a purely local or otherwise extremely circumscribed application, see, e.g., Cox v. Schweiker, 684 F.2d 310, 319 (5th Cir. 1982), and that is not the character of the statute at issue here, as will appear. The appellees have moved to strike the second brief on the ground that by filing it the government was trying to circumvent Fed. R. App. P. 29's prohibition against the filing of reply briefs by amici curiae, and that in any event the constitutionality of an Act of Congress is not being challenged and so the government has no right to intervene. We allowed the government to submit both an amicus curiae brief and an intervenor's brief in Doe v. University of Illinois, 200 F.3d 499 (7th Cir. 1999), but we did not discuss the propriety of the dual filing.

The government's amicus brief in this case, which was filed in support of the appellants, was limited to the question whether, consistent with the principle of Ex parte Young, 209 U.S. 123 (1908), suits seeking prospective injunctive relief against state officials in their official capacity may be brought under Title II of the Americans with Disabilities Act. Because an amicus brief must be filed within seven days after the principal brief of the party in support of whom the amicus brief is filed, Fed. R. App. P. 29, the government had no right to intervene at the time it filed its amicus brief unless the constitutionality of a federal statute affecting the public interest was at issue in the appeal. In their response to the appellants' brief, which obviously was filed after the government filed its amicus brief, the appellees argued that the district court had erred in denying their Eleventh Amendment defense to the plaintiffs' claim under section 504 of the Rehabilitation Act. In doing this, the appellees were necessarily challenging the constitutionality of 42 U.S.C. § 2000d–7(a)(1), a provision of the Civil Rights Act of 1964 that states in words that could not be clearer that "a State shall not be immune under the Eleventh Amendment of the Constitution of the United States from suit in Federal court for a violation of section 504 of the Rehabilitation Act."

If the government could not reasonably have been expected to anticipate the constitutional challenge in the appellees' brief, then as a practical matter there was no alternative to the government's filing the two briefs at different times and so the dual filing was proper. See Fordyce v. City of Seattle, 55 F.3d 436, 441–42 (9th Cir. 1995); Mitchell v. Donovan, 290 F. Supp. 642, 645 (D. Minn. 1968), vacated on other grounds, 398 U.S. 427, 26 L. Ed. 2d 378, 90 S. Ct. 1763 (1970) (per curiam). Analysis is complicated, however, by the fact that the government should have anticipated that the appellees would raise the Eleventh Amendment as an alternative ground for upholding the district court's decision, thus inescapably presenting the issue of the constitutionality of the provision of the civil rights act that we just quoted. For the appellees had moved to dismiss the case on Eleventh Amendment grounds in the district court, though apparently no one had mentioned section 2000d–7(a)(1) and the district court had not, as 28 U.S.C. § 2403(a) requires when a federal statute's constitutionality is drawn into question, notified the Justice Department. In these circumstances, we do not think that the Department's failure to intervene before the filing of the appellees' brief should operate as a forfeiture.

The motion to strike is therefore DENIED.

NEWDOW v. U.S. CONGRESS

United States Court of Appeals, Ninth Circuit, 2002.
313 F.3d 495.

FERNANDEZ, CIRCUIT JUDGE.

Once we ruled on the merits of this case, the United States Senate sought to intervene as a party and in that capacity to file a petition for rehearing and a petition for rehearing en banc. We deny the Motion to Intervene, but note our willingness to accept the petition and accompanying brief as an amicus brief, if the Senate consents to the latter use of its filing. Because of the respect that we owe to and have for the Senate, we are constrained to explain the reasons for our denial of intervention.

Initially, of course, we lay aside the usual intervention rule. See Fed. R. Civ. P. 24(a)(2). This case is more in line with Fed. R. Civ. P. 24(a)(1), which allows intervention as of right "when a statute of the United States confers an unconditional right to intervene." There is a special statute that applies to this motion. As relevant here, the statute first provides that the Senate Legal Counsel shall intervene or appear as amicus "when directed to do so by a resolution adopted by the Senate." 2 U.S.C. § 288b(c). There was a resolution here. See Senate Resolution 292, 107th Cong., 2d Sess. (2002), 148 Cong. Rec. S6105–06 (2002). The statute goes on to provide that Counsel shall intervene upon appropriate direction when "the powers and responsibilities of Congress under the Constitution of the United States are placed in issue," but should only do so if there is standing. See 2 U.S.C. § 288e(a). It then states:

> Permission to intervene as a party or to appear as amicus curiae under § 288e of this title shall be of right and may be denied by a court only upon an express finding that such intervention or appearance is untimely and would significantly delay the pending action or that standing to intervene has not been established under section 2 of article III of the Constitution of the United States.

2 U.S.C. § 288l(a).

Because the Senate waited until we had already ruled on the merits of this case on appeal, it would be possible, even accurate, to hold that the attempt to intervene is untimely. However, under the circumstances we are unable to hold that the proposed intervention to seek rehearing or en banc review would "significantly delay" the action. Especially is that true when, as here, some of the current parties to the action have themselves already sought both types of review. We must, therefore, turn our attention to the second exception in § 288l (a)—does the Senate have constitutional standing? To put it more precisely: does the Senate have constitutional standing to intervene in every case where the constitutionality of a United States statute is challenged? Because we determine that the answer to that question is no and because there is nothing about the statute at hand that would distinguish it from other statutes, the Senate does not have standing in this case.

Let it first be said that the issue is not whether the United States has standing to appear in support of the constitutionality of the statute in question. Nobody doubts that it does. See 28 U.S.C. § 2403(a). In fact, in this case it did appear for "the Congress of the United States; the United States of America; and William J. Clinton, President of the United States." The question is whether the Senate, as a separate part of the government, has standing to intervene to support statutes on its own behalf, and not really as a representative of the United States itself. We need not, and do not, decide whether Congress could designate the Senate Legal Counsel, upon a separate resolution of the Senate alone, to appear as the defender of all statutes on behalf of the United States itself. A law of that type might well have its own constitutional problems; it might even trench on the prerogatives of the executive branch of the United States, which has the authority to execute the laws of this country. See U.S. Const. art. II, § 3. At any rate, that has not occurred here. As already stated, a separate statute confers that authority upon the executive branch, and here the Senate seeks to appear to represent itself alone.

As the intervention statute at hand expressly recognizes, the Senate must show that it does have constitutional standing to intervene. That means at the very least that it must show that it has "suffered an 'injury in fact'—an invasion of a legally protected interest which is . . . concrete and particularized." Lujan v. Defenders of Wildlife, 504 U.S. 555, 560 (1992); see also Raines v. Byrd, 521 U.S. 811, 818–20 (1997). That concrete and particularized harm is lacking in this case because no harm beyond frustration of a general desire to see the law enforced as written has been shown here.

In so stating, we are aware that there have been a number of cases wherein Senate intervention has been allowed without any particular remark or detailed consideration. See, e.g., INS v. Chadha, 462 U.S. 919, 930 n.5 (1983); Lear Siegler, Inc., Energy Prod. Div. v. Lehman, 893 F.2d 205, 206 (9th Cir. 1990) (en banc). But those cases are not really apposite because they were of a character that directly (particularly) implicated the authority of Congress within our scheme of government, and the scope and reach of its ability to allocate power among the three branches. Thus, Chadha, 462 U.S. at 956–58, is a case that dealt with individual houses of Congress assuming the authority to review and veto executive decisions regarding the deportation of aliens. It, thus, implicated separation of powers doctrine and the whole scheme of our government. Lear Siegler dealt with whether Congress could allocate to a legislative agent—The Comptroller General—the authority to delay the procurement actions of the executive branch of the government. See

Lear Siegler, Inc., Energy Prod. Div. v. Lehman, 842 F.2d 1102, 1105–06 (9th Cir. 1988) Finally, in In re Benny, 812 F.2d 1133, 1141–42 (9th Cir. 1987), the issue was whether Congress had the authority to prospectively extend the term of office of bankruptcy judges. In other words, in each of these cases the courts were dealing with a statute addressing legislative action regarding allocation of authority within the government, as opposed to action applying that authority to the behavior of the citizenry in general. The issues were the kind that intimately affected Congress's own place within our constitutional scheme.

More closely on point are cases which speak to the standing of legislators to bring actions, where their institutional power as members of the legislature is not being challenged. In Raines, 521 U.S. at 814–16 for example, a number of members of the Senate and House of Representatives sued pursuant to a provision of the Line Item Veto Act which declared that any member of Congress could challenge the Act. See, 2 U.S.C. § 692(a)(1). The Court declared that they had "alleged no injury to themselves as individuals . . . , the institutional injury they allege is wholly abstract and widely dispersed . . . , and their attempt to litigate this dispute at this time and in this form is contrary to historical experience." Id. at 829. The Court did point out that they did not actually represent their separate houses of Congress and those houses actually opposed them, but did not indicate precisely how that affected their standing. Id. The Court distinguished an earlier case wherein state legislators were accorded standing because their votes would have been deprived of all validity if an allegedly improper person were able to vote. See Coleman v. Miller, 307 U.S. 433, 438 (1939). Thus, at least as to individual legislators, there is no standing unless their own institutional position, as opposed to their position as a member of the body politic, is affected.

The District of Columbia Circuit has followed the same approach. In 1977, a congressman sued the director of the Central Intelligence Agency partly on the basis that when that agency misused its budget, his vote as a congressman was impaired. See Harrington v. Bush, 553 F.2d 190, 204 (D.C. Cir. 1977). The court found that he lacked standing, and that a contrary rule would amount to giving him "a roving commission to obtain judicial relief under most circumstances." 553 F.2d at 214. Along the way, the court noted that "his specific rights, interests and prerogatives lie in the power to make laws. As we have noted, this power has not been invaded, diminished, diluted, or injured by the challenged actions in this case." 553 F.2d at 213. A like result was reached when a member of Congress sued to prevent alleged misuse of federal funds by a national commission. See Hansen v. Nat'l Comm'n. on the Observance of Int'l Women's Year, 628 F.2d 533 (9th Cir. 1980). We said: "The injury alleged by appellant is an injury which he suffers along with all other citizens of the United States. He has not presented any facts which show he has sustained or is imminently in danger of sustaining an actual personal injury." Id. at 534. Thus, he had no standing. Id. And, when faced with a claim by congressmen that the military was using its budget to finance combat in other countries, despite laws prohibiting that, the Fourth Circuit had this to say: "Once a bill has become law, however, their interest is indistinguishable from that of any other citizen. They cannot claim dilution of their legislative voting power because the legislation they favored became law." Harrington v. Schlesinger, 528 F.2d 455, 459 (4th Cir. 1975). The court was no more impressed with the claim that their legislative duties would somehow be affected. * * *

These observations also apply to the Senate as a whole, when it seeks to have a roving commission to enter every case involving the constitutionality of statutes it has enacted. In those instances, its own "powers and responsibilities" are not really under attack. Once the Senate has approved a proposed bill, the House of Representatives agrees, and the President has signed the measure, it becomes public law. A public law, after enactment, is not the Senate's any more than it is the law of any other citizen or group of citizens in the United States. It is a law of the United States of America, and the government is already represented in this case by the Attorney General. Of course, every time a statute is not followed or is declared unconstitutional, the votes of legislators are mooted and the power of the legislature is circumscribed in a sense, but that is no more than a facet of the generalized harm that occurs to the government as a whole. By the same token, the President's signing of the legislation is also nullified, judges, who might have felt otherwise, are bound by the decision, and citizens who relied upon or desired to have the law enforced are disappointed.[4] Moreover, if the separate houses of Congress have standing, a challenger of a law would have to contend with fighting the United States itself, and separately defending himself against the Senate and the House of Representatives, each of which would be able to appear as a separate litigating party in the case.[5]

Therefore, the motion of the Senate to intervene is DENIED. However, if the Senate wishes to have us deem its proposed brief to be an amicus brief and to consider it on that basis, we will do that. It should inform us of its desire in that regard within 30 days after the filing of this order.

SECTION E. NECESSARY PARTIES

Every jurisdiction recognizes at the trial court level that in rare cases there is an absent party who is "necessary" to the proceeding. In federal practice, this may arise where a plaintiff does not wish to name

4. All of this is underscored by the Senate's suggestion that it should have standing because it opens its daily sessions with the Pledge of Allegiance. That, of course, is an assertion that could be made by countless other organizations, governmental and otherwise, not to mention thousands of United States citizens.

5. In principle, he might also have to separately contend against the President, whose ability to effectively sign the law in question can be said to have been affected. We see little other than mischief arising from a system of intervention as unregulated as that. Constitutional standing doctrine is the apotropaion for that threatened malady. It must be applied here.

an additional defendant because the added party could destroy diversity of citizenship. In state practice there are often parties who are made mandatory by the statutes creating a cause of action. For example, in "mechanics lien" litigation (where a tradesman or subcontractor sues parties on a construction deal to get paid) statutes often make the property owners and any lenders financing the development "necessary parties" even though the plaintiff might be payable by a construction contractor or from a construction bond.

It may be an unwarranted generalization to assume that any person who was a necessary party at the trial level is a necessary party on appeal, but it is surely most common for the appellant to name the interested parties on the other side in the notice of appeal, and to serve the notice upon them (making them part of the appeal). As we have seen, interested or affected persons who are not technically parties can seek to intervene—both at the trial level, and on appeal. There are some suggestions in case law that where the relief the appellant seeks must come from a particular adverse party, that person should be made part of the appeal. Other, rare, situations may arise where the court on appeal will feel that a particular non-party's interests are so dramatically affected by the appeal that the absent person must be made a party to the appeal. The United States Supreme Court has referred to a duty to "look out" for the interests of non-parties in these unusual cases:

> Third, there is the interest of the outsider whom it would have been desirable to join. Of course, since the outsider is not before the court, he cannot be bound by the judgment rendered. This means, however, only that a judgment is not res judicata as to, or legally enforceable against, a nonparty. It obviously does not mean either (a) that a court may never issue a judgment that, in practice, affects a nonparty or (b) that (to the contrary) a court may always proceed without considering the potential effect on nonparties simply because they are not "bound" in the technical sense. Instead, as Rule 19 (a) expresses it, the court must consider the extent to which the judgment may "as a practical matter impair or impede his ability to protect" his interest in the subject matter. When a case has reached the appeal stage the matter is more complex. The judgment appealed from may not in fact affect the interest of any outsider even though there existed, before trial, a possibility that a judgment affecting his interest would be rendered. *When necessary, however, a court of appeals should, on its own initiative, take steps to protect the absent party, who of course had no opportunity to plead and prove his interest below.*

Provident Tradesmens Bank and Trust Co. v. Patterson, 390 U.S. 102, 110, 88 S.Ct. 733, 19 L.Ed.2d 936 (1968)(emphasis added). In that case the Court cited its own decision Hoe v. Wilson, 9 Wall. 501, 76 U.S. 501, 19 L.Ed. 762 (1869), a case involving the property of a decedent in which the Supreme Court reversed and remanded for the absence of necessary partes—a creditor and other heirs of a decedent—who should have been made parties below but were not. The reversal and remand was ordered on appeal even though the parties and lower court did not raise any "defect" in the naming of parties to the litigation. The Court found the non-participating potential heirs and the decedent's creditor "indispensable parties," because "[n]o relief can be given in the case before us which will not seriously and permanently affect their rights and interests."

WHITE v. CABINET FOR HUMAN RESOURCES

Kentucky Court of Appeals, 1988.
756 S.W.2d 148.

Combs, J.

This is before the Court on motion of the appellee, Cabinet for Human Resources ("CHR") to dismiss this appeal for failure of appellant, Ronald Lee White, to name an indispensable party to this appeal.

White's parental rights with respect to his daughter, Lee Andrea Katherine, were terminated by a September 18, 1987 order of the Circuit Court, from which order White appealed. In his notice of appeal, White named himself as appellant and CHR as appellee. Lee Andrea Katherine was not named as a party. CHR then filed this motion, to which White did not respond.

CHR contends that children are "indispensable" parties to appeals from the termination of parental rights. There is no statute or rule requiring said children to be so named, and this Court has been unable to find any published law regarding this issue. Therefore, this question is one of first impression. In resolving it, this Court must look to general notions as to what makes a party "indispensable."

Civil Rule 19.01, captioned "Persons to be joined if feasible," states:

> A person who is subject to service of process, either personal or constructive, shall be joined as a party in the action if (a) in his absence complete relief cannot be accorded among those already parties, or (b) he claims an interest relating to the subject of the action and is so situated that the disposition of the action in his absence may (i) as a practical matter impair or impede his ability to protect that interest.

Previously, Rule 19.01 turned on whether or not parties were "indispensable." However, the rule was revised in 1969, and now provides a guide from which it may be determined whether or not a party is "necessary" to an action. Within that framework, we examine this question.

Children are required to be parties to termination actions before the circuit court. Additionally, they are entitled to a guardian ad litem who shall represent their specific interests. KRS 625.060, .080. Additionally, CR 17.03 states that actions against unmarried infants shall be defended by a child's guardian or committee, or guardian ad litem, in any event. CR 17.03(3) states "no judgment shall be rendered against an unmarried infant ... until the party's ... guardian ad litem shall have made defense...." Although there is no statutory requirement that these children be likewise named parties to an appeal of said termination action, it would seem to this Court that under the rules previously enumerated, and as a matter of logical extension, said children should be necessary parties to any appeal. The child is, after all, the primary focus of said appeal, and it is no less than the continued health and well-being of child which is at stake. If not named as a party, it appears that the child's ability to protect his interests would be effectively "impaired" or "impeded." CR 19.01. Therefore, this Court finds that children shall be necessary parties to any appeal from an action terminating, or failing to terminate their parents' parental rights.

Failure to name an indispensable party is grounds for dismissal of an appeal. Yocom v. Franklin County Fiscal Court, Ky. App., 545 S.W.2d 296 (1976). Because we hold that children are necessary parties to appeals from termination actions we ORDER that this appeal be, and it is hereby, DISMISSED.

ALL CONCUR.

Notes and Questions

1. If, as the Supreme Court commented in the *Provident Tradesman's Bank* decision, a non-party to the appeal cannot be bound by the ultimate judgment, when could the missing person or entity be adversely affected? Will the absent party's status or rights change depending on the outcome of the appeal?

2. Sometimes there is a potential party to an appeal who either cannot or will not participate. Where the other parties conclude that effective appellate relief will be available without the participation of the absent party, they may elect to stipulate (agree) that the non-participating person or entity is not "necessary"—thus obviating any argument alter on that there is an infirmity with the ultimate judgment. See, e.g., Graves v. United States, 833 F.2d 1012 (6th Cir. 1987) ("By stipulation of the parties, it has been agreed that First Security is not a necessary party to this appeal and will not participate in any way in it").

3. It has sometimes been suggested that an appellate court's jurisdiction is "derivative" such that the absence of a necessary or "indispensable" party in the proceeding below may doom the validity of the appeal. A similar notion suggests that whenever a jurisdiction-affecting defect like the absence of a necessary party is recognized—including at the appellate stage—the court must consider whether it has jurisdiction to proceed in disposing of the appeal. See, e.g., the dissent in Williams v. Kimes, 25 S.W.3d 150, 157 (Mo. 2000): "This Court's jurisdiction is derivative. If the trial court lacks jurisdiction, so does this Court lack jurisdiction on appeal. Whether the bank is characterized as either a necessary party or indispensable party, failure to join the bank in this litigation is so fundamental and jurisdictional as to require its consideration sua sponte whether raised by the parties on appeal or not."

SECTION F. SUCCESSORS AND REPLACEMENT PARTIES

Litigants die, or lose elections. Just as the rules of civil procedure make provision for "substitution" of parties, the appellate system has both rules and doctrine to assure that the real party in interest, including the current representative of any governmental agency, is "substituted in" as the proper party to maintain that portion of the suit. In federal practice, Rule 43 of the appellate Rules deals with these issues:

Rule 43. Substitution of Parties

(a) Death of a Party.

(1) *After Notice of Appeal Is Filed.* If a party dies after a notice of appeal has been filed or while a proceeding is pending in the court of appeals, the decedent's personal representative may be substituted as a party on motion filed with the circuit clerk by the representative or by any party. A party's motion must be served on the representative in accordance with Rule 25. If the decedent has no representative, any party may suggest the death on the record, and the court of appeals may then direct appropriate proceedings.

(2) *Before Notice of Appeal Is Filed—Potential Appellant.* If a party entitled to appeal dies before filing a notice of appeal, the decedent's personal representative—or, if there is no personal representative, the decedent's attorney of record—may file a notice of appeal within the time prescribed by these rules. After the notice of appeal is filed, substitution must be in accordance with Rule 43(a)(1).

(3) *Before Notice of Appeal Is Filed—Potential Appellee.* If a party against whom an appeal may be taken dies after entry of a judgment or order in the district court, but before a notice of appeal is filed, an appellant may proceed as if the death had not occurred. After the notice of appeal is filed, substitution must be in accordance with Rule 43(a)(1).

(b) Substitution for a Reason Other Than Death.

If a party needs to be substituted for any reason other than death, the procedure prescribed in Rule 43(a) applies.

(c) Public Officer: Identification; Substitution.

(1) *Identification of Party.* A public officer who is a party to an appeal or other proceeding in an official capacity may be described as a party by the public officer's official title rather than by name. But the court may require the public officer's name to be added.

(2) *Automatic Substitution of Officeholder.* When a public officer who is a party to an appeal or other proceeding in an official capacity dies, resigns, or otherwise ceases to hold office, the action

does not abate. The public officer's successor is automatically substituted as a party. Proceedings following the substitution are to be in the name of the substituted party, but any misnomer that does not affect the substantial rights of the parties may be disregarded. An order of substitution may be entered at any time, but failure to enter an order does not affect the substitution.

The first three sentences in subdivision (a) of the Rule describe a procedure similar to the rule on substitution in civil actions in federal district court. See Fed. R. Civ. P. 25(a). The appellate Rule then goes on to expressly authorizes an appeal to be taken against one who has died after the entry of judgment. Other portions of subdivision (a) authorize an attorney of record for the deceased to take an appeal on behalf of successors in interest if the deceased has no representative. Under subdivision (c) the substitution of a new office holder is "automatic" and if there is any syncopation in conforming the papers to the new incumbent the "misnomer" will not, according to the rule, affect the merits of the adjudication.

SARMIENTO v. SARMIENTO

United States Court of Appeals, Ninth Circuit, 2004.
100 Fed. Appx. 645.

REINHARDT, THOMAS AND CLIFTON, CIRCUIT JUDGES.

MEMORANDUM

On multiple grounds, Maria Sarmiento appeals the district court's judgment after a bench trial in favor of Gerardo and Rubina Sarmiento. (For clarity, we will refer to these individuals by their first names.) As the parties are familiar with the facts, procedural history, and arguments, we will not repeat them here except as is necessary. We dismiss the appeal for lack of jurisdiction.

I

All federal actions must be prosecuted in the name of the real party in interest. Fed. R. Civ. P. 17(a). An appeal that is not prosecuted in the name of the real party in interest must be dismissed for lack of standing. See Turner v. Cook, 362 F.3d 1219, 1225 (9th Cir. 2004); First State Bank of N. Cal. v. Bank of Am., 618 F.2d 603 (9th Cir. 1980).

In this case, the appellant died while the appeal was pending. Under Fed. R. App. P. 43, a substitution of parties must be accomplished. If substitution is not accomplished within a reasonable time, the appeal must be dismissed. Johnson v. Morgenthau, 160 F.3d 897, 898–99 (2d Cir. 1998); Ward v. Edgeton, 59 F.3d 652, 653–54 (7th Cir. 1995); Crowder v. Housing Auth. of City of Atlanta, 908 F.2d 843, 846 n.1 (11th Cir. 1990); Gamble v. Thomas, 655 F.2d 568, 569 (5th Cir. 1981).

By order of this Court, we granted appellant's counsel considerable time to accomplish the substitution, cautioning that the appeal was subject to dismissal if a substitution of parties could not be accomplished. It has not been accomplished, and we are therefore "unable to proceed without the necessary parties before" us. Maloney v. Spencer, 170 F.2d 231, 233 (9th Cir. 1948). We cannot decide the appeal when there is no party before us who has standing to pursue the appeal. Nor can we exercise hypothetical jurisdiction. Steel Co. v. Citizens for a Better Env't, 523 U.S. 83, 93–101, (1998).

For these reasons, we must dismiss the appeal for lack of jurisdiction.

II

The successors-in-interest to this claim are not prejudiced by this dismissal because it would fail on the merits. [Discussion omitted.]

DISMISSED.

SECTION G.   NON–PARTIES ON APPEAL

1.   IMPACT UPON NON–PARTIES AS A BASIS FOR PARTICIPATION

In Cunningham v. Hamilton County, 527 U.S. 198, 119 S.Ct. 1915, 144 L.Ed.2d 184 (1999), the Supreme Court said, "[A] witness subject to a discovery order, but not held in contempt, generally may not appeal the order." 527 U.S. at 204 n.4

When *parties* get into discovery disputes in the trial court—even disputes about what are perceived to be important, privileged communications—they generally cannot appeal. However, if a party refuses to produce information required by the trial judge, and suffers a criminal contempt citation, an appealable event has occurred. Non-parties, however, are permitted to appeal both civil and criminal contempt citations whenever they are imposed. See generally CFTC v. Armstrong, 269 F.3d 109, 112–13 (2d Cir. 2001)

BURDEN–MEEKS v. WELCH

United States Court of Appeals, Seventh Circuit, 2003.
319 F.3d 897.

Easterbrook, Circuit Judge.

Plaintiffs used to be employees of Country Club Hills, a city in Illinois. They contend in this suit under 42 U.S.C. § 1983 that Mayor Dwight Welch fired them for political reasons, violating the first amendment as it has been understood since Elrod v. Burns, 427 U.S. 347, 49 L. Ed. 2d 547, 96 S. Ct. 2673 (1976). Resolution of that claim has been delayed by a dispute about access to a document prepared for the Intergovernmental Risk Management Agency (IRMA), a body created by modestly sized municipalities in northeastern Illinois to pool their liability risks. The Constitution of Illinois (see Art. VII § 10) permits municipalities to form intergovernmental cooperative agencies, of which IRMA is one.

The document in question was written by IRMA's lawyers after it asked them to investigate whether Country Club Hills is doing enough to curtail litigation exposure. This is a vital question, for insurance creates moral hazard: when someone else pays the tab, the insured will take additional risks and may incur costs deliberately. The other 72 members of IRMA do not want to make it cheap for the Mayor of Country Club Hills to violate the Constitution, knowing that only 1/73 of the consequences will be borne by the local taxpayers. Plaintiffs believe that the report contains information that will help them prevail against the City. IRMA responded to the plaintiffs' subpoena, see Fed. R. Civ. P. 34(c), 45, by invoking the attorney-client privilege. Because plaintiffs' claim arises under federal law, this assertion of privilege also depends on federal law. See Fed. R. Evid. 501.

The district judge added for good measure that the report was not self-critical—it examined the operations of Country Club Hills, not the operations of IRMA itself—and ordered IRMA to give plaintiffs a copy.

Instead of either complying or refusing to do so as a prelude to a citation in contempt of court, the normal way to obtain appellate review of such an order, see United States v. Ryan, 402 U.S. 530, 29 L. Ed. 2d 85, 91 S. Ct. 1580 (1971); Cobbledick v. United States, 309 U.S. 323, 84 L. Ed. 783, 60 S. Ct. 540 (1940), IRMA immediately filed a notice of appeal. Because the district court's order is not a final decision under normal standards, see 28 U.S.C. § 1291, we directed the parties to file supplemental briefs addressing the question whether we have appellate jurisdiction. IRMA analogized the situation to that in Perlman v. United States, 247 U.S. 7, 62 L. Ed. 950, 38 S. Ct. 417 (1918), which held that a party claiming a privilege may appeal immediately when the judge directs a non-party holding the documents to disclose them. The idea behind Perlman is that someone who is neither a party to the suit nor a person aggrieved by the disclosure cannot be expected to put his own neck on the chopping block, standing in contempt of court just to help the privilege holder obtain appellate review. See Church of Scientology v. United States, 506 U.S. 9, 18 n.11, 121 L. Ed. 2d 313, 113 S. Ct. 447 (1992) ("a discovery order directed at a disinterested third party is treated as an immediately appealable final order because the third party presumably lacks a sufficient stake in the proceeding to risk contempt by refusing compliance") (emphasis added). IRMA, however, is not disinterested; it asserts a privilege on its own behalf.

When documents are sought from the entity that claims the privilege, there is every reason to insist that it go through the contempt process, which by raising the stakes helps the court winnow strong claims from delaying tactics that, like other interlocutory appeals, threaten to complicate and prolong litigation unduly. See Powers v. Chicago Transit Authority, 846 F.2d 1139 (7th Cir. 1988). And, independent of how we may evaluate arguments pro and con, there is the holding of Ryan that (subject to the Perlman proviso and another exception limited to the President of the United States, see United States v. Nixon, 418 U.S. 683, 690–92, 41 L. Ed. 2d 1039, 94 S. Ct. 3090 (1974)) non-parties must wait for a contempt citation. Cf. Kerr v. United States District Court, 426 U.S. 394, 48 L. Ed. 2d 725, 96 S. Ct. 2119 (1976) (mandamus not available to escape the rule barring appeal of orders requiring the production of documents said to be privileged). Courts recognize one distinction between appeals by parties and appeals by nonparties: parties must wait until the end of the case or a finding of criminal contempt, while non-parties may appeal from a finding of civil contempt. See Charles A. Wright, Arthur R. Miller & Edward H. Cooper, 15B Federal Practice and Procedure § 3914.23 at 140, 143 & n.44 (2d ed. 1992) (collecting authority). IRMA has not been found in any kind of contempt, however; it has done nothing to demonstrate that it possesses the sort of vital interest that justifies prolongation of a suit by interlocutory review.

Despite all of this, IRMA still holds a trump card: Dellwood Farms holds that non-parties always may appeal immediately when they contest discovery orders. The discussion is brief—just a single sentence—but it is a square holding. We wrote: "When the order is directed against a nonparty, as it is here, [the nonparty] has no appellate remedy at the end of the litigation, so he is entitled to appeal immediately." 128 F.3d at 1125. Dellwood Farms did not discuss the possibility of obtaining review through the contempt process, nor did it mention Ryan, Cobbledick, or similar decisions. Nor did it recognize that other circuits have resolved the same question against appellate jurisdiction. See, e.g., In re Grand Jury Subpoenas, 123 F.3d 695, 698 (1st Cir. 1997) (collecting cases); In re Attorney General of the United States, 596 F.2d 58 (2d Cir. 1979) (holding that even a member of the Cabinet must be cited for contempt of court before a court of appeals will review a discovery order). Instead Dellwood Farms cited three appellate opinions—Ivey v. Harney, 47 F.3d 181, 183 (7th Cir. 1995); Frazier v. Cast, 771 F.2d 259, 262 (7th Cir. 1985); and Boughton v. Cotter Corp., 10 F.3d 746, 749 (10th Cir. 1993)— that suggest the risks of excessive generalization.

Ivey did not entail a discovery dispute; instead a warden was appealing from a writ of habeas corpus ad testificandum, and to the extent the issues were related to discovery it was cousin to Perlman (for the warden, having no interest in the underlying suit, was not about to risk a contempt citation). Frazier likewise did not concern the assertion of privilege by a party resisting discovery; it took up an appeal by a lawyer sanctioned for violating Fed. R. Civ. P. 11. What is more, after we issued *Dellwood Farms* the Supreme Court scuttled Frazier (and decisions like it in other circuits) by holding that an attorney may not appeal immediately from an award of sanctions. See Cunningham v. Hamilton County, 527 U.S. 198, 144 L. Ed. 2d 184, 119 S. Ct. 1915 (1999). *Boughton*, alone of the three opinions cited by *Dellwood Farms*, deals with an interlocutory appeal by someone whose claim of privilege has been rejected by a district judge—but it holds that courts of appeals lack jurisdiction in this situation. The Tenth Circuit collected decisions from many federal appellate courts to the effect that neither the collateral order doctrine nor a related "pragmatic finality doctrine" enables parties to appeal immediately. In passing, *Boughton* remarked that an earlier decision, Covey Oil Co. v. Continental Oil Co., 340 F.2d 993 (10th Cir. 1965), had permitted appeal by a non-party—but it also observed that Covey and similar decisions are of doubtful value in light of *Ryan.*

The most one can say for *Dellwood Farms* is that *Covey Oil* and similar cases in the Tenth Circuit, though questioned in *Boughton*, have not been overruled. That may not have been enough (given *Ryan* and the many decisions in other circuits applying it beyond the grand jury context) to justify our adopting the approach of *Covey Oil,* but it counsels against our overruling *Dellwood Farms*—for, unless the Tenth Circuit also overrules decisions along *Covey Oil*'s lines, a conflict will remain. Indeed, no matter what we (or the Tenth Circuit) do, a conflict will persist—for in recent years some circuits have allowed even parties to appeal immediately from orders rejecting assertions of privilege. Non-parties, which cannot appeal from the final decision following sanctions, other than contempt, under Fed. R. Civ. P. 37, logically have appellate rights at least as extensive as parties do. The most recent of these decisions is United States v. Philip Morris Inc., 314 F.3d 612 (D.C. Cir. Jan. 7, 2003), in which a divided panel held that a party's inability to appeal from an order of civil contempt justifies allowing it to appeal from the discovery order itself. The D.C. Circuit recognized that it was adopting a minority view, and like *Dellwood Farms* it cited neither *Ryan* nor any of the Supreme Court's other cases limiting appeals from discovery orders. Left to our own devices, we would be inclined to agree with Judge Randolph's dissent in *Philip Morris.* But the existence of this decision, and a few like it elsewhere, means that we cannot bring harmony by overruling *Dellwood Farms.* Appellate approaches to this topic are now so disparate that only Congress or the Supreme Court could clear the air. So instead of fussing over jurisdiction, we take circuit law as we found it and resolve the appeal.

The merits are not complex: the district judge was on the mark, for the reasons he gave. * * *

AFFIRMED.

UNITED STATES v. KIRSCHENBAUM

United States Court of Appeals, Seventh Circuit, 1998.
156 F.3d 784.

MANION, CIRCUIT JUDGE.

For those terminally ill, Medicare and Medicaid will pay for hospice care, which treats the patient with pain control and additional medical, social and spiritual assistance for the patient and the family. Defendant Joseph Ari Kirschenbaum owned or controlled a number of entities that delivered hospice services, and over several years he and his business operations received many millions of dollars. But the government has charged him with fraud and money laundering, and, pending trial, has seized about $20 million in assets. * * *

Mr. Kirschenbaum's wife, Julie Kirschenbaum, also brings an interlocutory appeal challenging the district court's jurisdiction to enjoin her, a non-party. To the extent the order purports to enjoin her it is void, but to the extent Mrs. Kirschenbaum now attacks the part of the order directed to Mr. Kirschenbaum rather than to her, we affirm the denial of her motion. * * *

MRS. KIRSCHENBAUM'S APPEAL.

Mrs. Kirschenbaum argued below and argues here that the district court's restraining order, which purports to enjoin her conduct, violates her due process rights because the district court has no personal jurisdiction over her, a nonparty. We must first decide whether Mrs. Kirschenbaum, who did not seek to intervene in the district court and is not a party, can even bring this appeal. Generally, non-parties lack standing to bring appeals. See, e.g., B.H. v. Murphy, 984 F.2d 196, 199 (7th Cir. 1993). But non-parties who are bound by a court's equitable decrees have a right to move to have the order dissolved, United States v. Board of School Commissioners of the City of Indianapolis, 128 F.3d 507, 511 (7th Cir. 1997), and other circuits have held that where a non-party is purportedly bound by an injunction, the non-party may bring an appeal rather than face the possibility of a contempt proceeding. Hilao v. Estate of Marcos (In re Estate of Marcos Human Rights Litigation), 94 F.3d 539, 544 (9th Cir. 1996); In re Piper Funds, Inc., 71 F.3d 298, 301 (8th Cir. 1995) ("A nonparty normally has standing to appeal when it is adversely affected by an injunction."). But see Felzen v. Andreas, 134 F.3d 873, 875 (7th Cir. 1998) (overruling prior cases holding that class members who were not representatives may appeal from judgment without intervening). Because we have held that she had a right to move the district court to modify the restraining order, we conclude that Mrs. Kirschenbaum has standing to bring this appeal from the denial of her motion.

One could argue that the district court's restraining order essentially purports to enjoin the whole world: It provides that "Joseph Ari Kirschenbaum and any of his agents, servants, employees, attorneys (including Thomas Korman), *family members (including Julie Kirschenbaum)*, those persons in active concert or participation with him, and third parties, are prohibited and enjoined...." (Emphasis supplied). A district court may not enjoin non-parties who are neither acting in concert with the enjoined party nor are in the capacity of agents, employees, officers, etc. of the enjoined party. Fed.R.Civ.P. 65(d); Regal Knitwear Co. v. NLRB, 324 U.S. 9, 12, 89 L. Ed. 661, 65 S. Ct. 478 (1945) (court may not grant "injunction so broad as to make punishable the conduct of persons who act independently and whose rights have not been adjudged according to law"); Alemite Manufacturing Corp. v. Staff, 42 F.2d 832 (2d Cir. 1930) (L. Hand, J.) ("no court can make a decree which will bind any one but a party''); Hoover v. Wagner, 47 F.3d 845, 847 (7th Cir. 1995). Of course this does not mean that non-parties are free to knowingly thwart injunctions. Rockwell Graphic Systems, Inc. v. DEV Indus., Inc., 91 F.3d 914, 919 (7th Cir. 1996) (non-parties "may subject themselves to [the injunction]'s proscriptions should they aid or abet the named parties in a concerted attempt to subvert those proscriptions''); Alemite, 42 F.2d at 832 ("a person who knowingly assists a defendant in violating an injunction subjects himself to civil as well as criminal proceedings for contempt''); Regal Knitwear, 324 U.S. at 14 ("In essence it is that defendants may not nullify a decree by carrying out prohibited acts through aiders and abettors, although they were not parties to the original proceeding.''). But even a third-party aider and abettor must have her day in court. "[A] non-party with notice cannot be held in contempt until shown to be in concert or participation. It was error to enter the injunction against the [non-party], without having made this determination in a proceeding to which the [non-party] was a party.'' Zenith Radio Corp. v. Hazeltine Research, Inc., 395 U.S. 100, 112, 23 L. Ed. 2d 129, 89 S. Ct. 1562 (1969).

The government defends the district court's order by arguing that unlike normal injunctions, protective orders under § 853(e)(1), and thus § 982(b)(1) by incorporation, are binding on third-parties. As a matter of statutory interpretation, we cannot accept that argument. * * *

Of course, § 853(e)(1)'s empowering the district court to "take any other action to preserve the availability of property" would certainly allow it to enter orders—restraining orders, injunctions, or otherwise— against persons other than the defendant, but in doing so the court must have jurisdiction over those persons. The district court's attempt to enjoin Mrs. Kirschenbaum and other third-parties over whom the court had no personal jurisdiction is void and so binding on no one. Herrlein, 526 F.2d at 253; cf. United States v. Indoor Cultivation Equipment, 55 F.3d 1311, 1316 (7th Cir. 1995) (addressing challenge under Fed.R.Civ.P. 60(b)(4)). Of course Mrs. Kirschenbaum—like any non-party—could be punished for contempt if, after a hearing and proper findings, it was shown that she aided Mr. Kirschenbaum to violate the injunction. * * *

In Mrs. Kirschenbaum's appeal, No. 98–1592, the order's attempt to enjoin her is void and so we VACATE those parts of the order but we AFFIRM the denial of Mrs. Kirschenbaum's motion to the extent it sought to modify the order relating to Mr. Kirschenbaum.

Recognizing that it has been "lenient" in allowing non-parties to appeal, the Fifth Circuit in SEC v. Forex Asset Management, 242 F.3d 325, 327–30 (5th Cir. 2001) gave an interesting example of the circumstances under which that court has allowed nonparties to appeal:

Michael and Donna Whitbeck * * * learned of a foreign currency investment opportunity with Forex through a radio infomercial given by Kosova, the individual who allegedly controls Forex. Thereafter, the Whitbecks attended a seminar regarding investment opportunities with Forex, and wrote a check to Forex for $100,000. Several months later, after receiving statements reflecting a profitable return on their $100,000 investment, the Whitbecks attended another seminar. After the seminar, the Whitbecks decided to invest additional money, and they took out a loan of $800,000 in order to do so.

* * * After the Whitbecks invested $900,000 with Forex, the Securities and Exchange Commission filed a complaint against Kosova and Forex for allegedly engaging in a scheme to defraud investors. As a consequence of the SEC complaint, the assets of Forex, Kosova and the entities owned and controlled by Kosova were frozen, and a receiver was appointed. The Whitbecks were not named as parties to the suit between the SEC, Forex and Kosova, nor did they move to intervene in accordance with Federal Rule of Civil Procedure 24. * * *

The Receiver appointed to manage the Forex–Kosova assets determined that the Forex program had accumulated approximately $2.5 million of indebtedness, and retained approximately $1,150,000 worth of assets. After analyzing the debts owed and calculating the amount of the remaining assets, the Receiver determined that the assets should be distributed on a pro rata basis in order to treat the creditors equally because none of the creditors had a "secured claim ... or legal preference." According to the plan, each investor "would share in the distribution based upon the percentage of their loss as measured against the losses of all of the unpaid claimants."

Prior to approving the Receiver's distribution plan, the district court sought objections to the plan * * *. After considering the Whitbecks' objections, the district court affirmed the plan because it determined that the "Receiver's Plan provided the most equitable means of addressing all of the victim's harms, ... and the Whitbecks did not present any facts that would elevate their claims above those of the other investors." The court further noted that it was afforded "wide discretion in the supervision of an equity receivership ... and that it could approve a plan as long as it was fair and equitable."

The Whitbecks appeal the district court's order approving the Receiver's distribution plan. Prior to reviewing the merits of the Whitbecks' appeal, there are two threshold issues that require our attention. First, we must determine whether the Whitbecks have standing to bring this appeal. Although the parties have not raised this issue, we may raise it sua sponte. See Lang v. French , 154 F.3d 217, 222 n.28 (5th Cir. 1998) (reaffirming the principle that questions regarding standing may be "raised by an appellate court sua sponte"). Our concern regarding the Whitbecks' standing stems from the fact that the Whitbecks were not named as parties in the

SEC's complaint, nor did they seek to intervene in accordance with Rule 24. As the Supreme Court stated in Marino v. Ortiz, 484 U.S. 301, 304, 108 S.Ct. 586, 587, 98 L.Ed.2d 629 (1988), "the rule that only parties to a lawsuit, or those that properly become parties, may appeal an adverse judgment is well settled."

While there is a general rule that non-parties to a suit do not have standing to appeal, we have previously stated that exceptions exist. For instance, in Castillo v. Cameron County, Tex., 238 F.3d 339 (5th Cir. 2001), where we were asked to determine whether Texas had standing to seek review of a series of injunctions after it was dismissed from the underlying suit, we reaffirmed the principle that " 'if the decree affects a third party's interests, he is often allowed to appeal.' " Id. at 349, citing United States v. Chagra v. San Antonio Light Div. of Hearst Corp., 701 F.2d 354, 358–59 (5th Cir. 1983); see also In re Beef Indus. Antitrust Litig., 589 F.2d 786, 788 (5th Cir. 1979) (stating that "the Fifth Circuit has been lenient in hearing the appeals of non-parties").

Additionally, in Castillo we emphasized that this Circuit applies a three-part test when deciding whether a non-party may appeal. We inquire " 'whether "the non-party actually participated in the proceedings below, the equities weigh in favor of hearing the appeal, and the non-party has a personal stake in the outcome." ' " Id. (citations omitted). Moreover, we favorably cited a case by our sister circuit, Commodity Futures Trading Comm'n v. Topworth Int'l, Ltd., 205 F.3d 1107, 1113 (9th Cir. 1999), in which the court found that a non-party creditor who objected to a proposed receivership distribution plan had standing because he had a legitimate interest in the proceedings, and had participated adequately in the proceedings by timely filing his claim, filing objections, and attending the hearing on the claim. Furthermore, in *Castillo* we reaffirmed the statement that we made in Chagra that "non-party creditors who assert rights in receivership proceedings may appeal orders affecting their legitimate interests." Id., citing *Chagra*, 701 F.2d at 358–59.

To determine whether the Whitbecks' appeal is proper, we apply our three-part test. First, in accordance with the first prong of the test, we find that the Whitbecks participated in the proceedings in the district court to the extent their interests were involved. The Whitbecks' participation is demonstrated by three actions: (1) their filing a notice that they were an interested party; (2) their moving for a turnover of the assets in the FAM Preferred account and replying to the Receiver's response to their turnover request; and (3) their filing an objection to the Receiver's proposed distribution plan.

Second, the equities weigh in favor of hearing the appeal because the distribution order substantially affects the Whitbecks' interests and the district court solicited objections to the distribution order. Moreover, unlike other cases in which standing has been found not to exist, hearing the Whitbecks' appeal will not frustrate another legal principle. See *Searcy v. Philips Elecs. N. Am. Corp.,* 117 F.3d 154, 156 (5th Cir. 1997) (noting that we have more strictly enforced the rule that non-parties may not appeal in the class action context because to do otherwise "could frustrate the Rule 23 mechanism"), citing *Walker v. City of Mesquite,* 858 F.2d 1071, 1074 (5th Cir. 1988) (stating that nonnamed class members should seek to intervene if they desire to appeal a decision regarding the class because to hear an appeal by a nonnamed party who has not intervened "would result in the frustration of the purpose behind class litigation").

Third, we find that the Whitbecks have a personal stake in the outcome of the distribution plan because the method by which the funds are distributed, specifically whether the funds placed in the FAM Preferred account are distributed pro rata or given exclusively to the Whitbecks, will substantially alter the amount allocated to the Whitbecks under the distribution plan.

Accordingly, while the Whitbecks were not parties to the suit nor did they seek to intervene, we find that they have standing to appeal because they meet our three-part test for non-party standing. We caution, however, that this decision does not indicate that parties will be given a free pass to avoid complying with the rules of intervention.[5]

[The appellate court found the decision appealable, and upon consideration of the merits of the Whitbecks' arguments, affirmed the district court's approval of the receiver's plan. Eds.]

Notes and Questions

1. The Ninth Circuit (like some others) permits non-parties to "appeal a district court order where: (1) the appellant participated in the district court proceedings even though not a party, and; (2) the equities of the case weigh in favor of hearing the appeal." *Keith v. Volpe,* 118 F.3d 1386 (9th Cir. 1997). In a case where environmentalists, residents and government officials litigated the question of permitting outdoor advertising billboards along a federally-funded highway being built in Los Angeles, the final consent decree enjoined various agencies from granting any permits to Robert Kudler, identified as "an advertising billboard developer," Kudler participated at the trial court level by responding to an Order to Show Cause, at the district court's request, by filing a Memorandum of Points and Authorities and participating in oral argument. None of the parties appealed the consent decree, but Kudler did. The Court of Appeals allowed the appeal, finding that in this case the equities supporting a nonparty's right to appeal

---

5. We note that granting the parties standing in the present case is at variance with the decisions of the Third and Seventh Circuits. See *S.E.C. v. Black,* 163 F.3d 188, 196 (3d Cir. 1998) (stating that "*Marino* only requires that a court deny an appeal from non-parties who have not obtained or sought intervenor status."); see *S.E.C. v.* *Wozniak,* 33 F.3d 13, 14 (7th Cir. 1994) (stating that a non-party who did not intervene may not appeal). However, this case only emphasizes the circuit split that previously existed based on our analysis of the rule of non-party standing in *Castillo* and our previous cases.

"are especially significant where [a party] has haled the nonparty into the proceeding against his will, and then has attempted to thwart the nonparty's right to appeal by arguing that he lacks standing." 118 F.3d at 1392. In a footnote the court said: "Because Kudler was haled into this action by the district court over his objections, this case is distinguishable from Marino v. Ortiz, 484 U.S. 301, 108 S.Ct. 586, 98 L.Ed.2d 629 (1988) (holding that petitioners did not have standing to appeal from the consent decree because they were not parties to the litigation giving rise to the decree)."

2. Where the losing parties appeal, a purported appeal by a non-party will usually be treated as an attempt to participate as an amicus. See Planned Parenthood of the Columbia/Willamette, Inc. v. American Coalition of Life Activists, 244 F.3d 1007 (9th Cir. 2001)(a case in which a jury awarded more than $100 million in actual and punitive damages against the abortion activists who published threatening and intimidating information against a large number of persons, "including six current members of the Supreme Court, Bill Clinton, Al Gore, Janet Reno, Jack Kevorkian, C. Everett Koop, Mary Tyler Moore, Whoopi Goldberg and, for reasons unknown, Retired Justice Byron White.").

3. A non-party cannot argue that one of the parties is guilty of criminal contempt and thus bootstrap herself into standing to appeal. See Paula Corbin Jones v. William Jefferson Clinton, 206 F.3d 811 (8th Cir. 2000)(non-party witness Dolly Browning filed a motion in the *Paula Jones* litigation seeking to have President Clinton held in criminal contempt; the district judge denied her motion, but sua sponte held the President in civil contempt for "willfully disobeying the court's discovery orders and giving false and misleading deposition testimony." Browning sought to appeal the denial of criminal sanctions, but her appeal was dismissed because, as a non-party, she lacked standing to take an appeal from a rejection of her motion for criminal contempt penalties.).

2. ATTORNEYS AS PARTICIPANTS IN AN APPEAL

The general rule is that "counsel have standing to appeal from orders issued directly against them, but not from orders applicable only to their clients." Uselton v. Commercial Lovelace Motor Freight, Inc., 9 F.3d 849, 854 (10th Cir. 1993). For example, "an attorney lacks separate standing to appeal from a judgment awarding or denying fees to a party, since such concessions are granted to parties, not their attorneys." Pontarelli v. Stone, 978 F.2d 773, 775 (1st Cir. 1992). By contrast, when a monetary sanction is assessed against an attorney personally, only the attorney "possesses standing to appeal from the order," DCPB, Inc. v. City of Lebanon, 957 F.2d 913, 919 (1st Cir. 1992); the client ordinarily has "no pecuniary or ... other sufficient interest in the award to confer standing to appeal," Marshak v. Tonetti, 813 F.2d 13, 21 (1st Cir. 1987). Still other decisions recognize the possibility that "special circumstances" or "an idiosyncratic set of facts" might serve to "deflect the rule's accustomed sweep." *DCPB, Inc.*, 957 F.2d at 919,

Where a party's attorney has been sanctioned and no separate notice of appeal is filed on his behalf, and the notice of appeal filed on behalf of the party does not designate the attorney as an appellant or indicate the attorney's intent to participate in the appeal as a party, the courts of appeal lack jurisdiction to entertain the challenge to the imposition of a sanction against counsel. See, e.g., Fed. R. App. P. 3(c); Agee v. Paramount Communications Inc., 114 F.3d 395, 399–400 (2d Cir. 1997).

In one case where an attorney repeatedly violated the federal rules and a district court's local rules of procedure, and failed to follow directions of the trial judge, the court dismissed the case for lack of diversity jurisdiction, and imposed a formal written admonishment (but not the $9,000 in excess fees that the adversaries alleged were incurred because of the dilatory behavior of the sanctioned attorney). The sanctioned attorney filed a notice of appeal, which read in its entirety:

> PLEASE TAKE NOTICE that plaintiff appeals from the judgment entered January 31, 2001, dismissing the case and effectively denying preliminary injunction, together with all previous orders of Judge William H. Pauley, III, to the United States Court of Appeals for the Second Circuit, pursuant to 28 U.S.C. § 1291.

The notice of appeal was signed by the sanctioned attorney only as "Attorney for plaintiff." There being no indication in this notice that he personally was to be a party to the appeal, and there being no separate notice of appeal filed on behalf of the attorney, the court of appeals concluded: "we have no jurisdiction to entertain [counsel's] challenge to the district court's admonition." Universal Licensing Corp. v. Paola Del Lungo S.P.A., 293 F.3d 579 (2nd Cir. 2002).

CORROON v. REEVE

United States Court of Appeals, Second Circuit, 2001.
258 F.3d 86.

KEARSE, CIRCUIT JUDGE:

This is an appeal, filed in the name of plaintiff Polar International Brokerage Corp. ("Polar"), from an August 7, 2000 Memorandum Order of the United States District Court for the Southern District of New York, Shira A. Scheindlin, Judge, reported at 196 F.R.D. 13 ("August Order"), imposing sanctions on plaintiffs' attorneys pursuant to the Private Securities Litigation Reform Act of 1995, 15 U.S.C. § 78u–4(c)(1) (2000) ("PSLRA"), for violation of Fed. R. Civ. P. 11 in the assertion of a frivolous securities fraud claim, and (b) a September 19, 2000 Memorandum Order of that court, reported at 120 F. Supp. 2d 267 ("September Order"), granting reconsideration and reducing the amount of the sanction imposed on plaintiffs' non-lead counsel and, pro tanto, the total amount of sanctions. The procedures followed in pursuit of this appeal are considerably more problematic than the merits, and we affirm in part and dismiss in part.

The present action was commenced by Polar in 1998 as a class action alleging violations of § 14(e) of the Securities Exchange Act of 1934 (the "1934 Act"), 15 U.S.C. § 78(n)(e), and state law, in connection with a tender offer. Appearing as plaintiffs' lead counsel was Schoengold

& Sporn, P.C. ("Schoengold & Sporn" or the "Schoengold firm"). In late 1999, when a first amended complaint was filed and a claim was added under § 13(e) of the 1934 Act, new plaintiffs were added, one of whom was represented by Berger & Montague, P.C. ("Berger & Montague" or the "Berger firm"), which appeared as non-lead counsel. In an Opinion and Order dated June 27, 2000, reported at 108 F. Supp. 2d 225, familiarity with which is assumed, the district court dismissed the action in its entirety and ordered plaintiffs and their counsel to show cause why sanctions should not be imposed pursuant to Fed. R. Civ. P. 11 for instituting "abusive litigation" within the meaning of the PSLRA, 15 U.S.C. § 78u–4(c)(1).

After hearing from both sides, the court in its August Order imposed sanctions against counsel for asserting the § 14(e) claim but not for asserting the § 13(e) claim, finding that the latter, though meritless, was not frivolous. The court found that the § 14(e) claim "was both legally frivolous and without factual support." August Order, 196 F.R.D. at 16. It also found that lead counsel had made inconsistent representations both to the district court and to the plaintiff class as to the fairness of the challenged tender offer, depending on whether counsel was pressing the merits or urging approval of a proposed settlement. The court stated that "either plaintiffs' counsel violated Rule 11(b)(3) in March 1999 [in advocating settlement] when they repeatedly stated—based upon their examination of documents and consultation with financial experts—that the Tender Offer was fair, or counsel violated Rule 11(b)(3) in October 1999 by filing an amended complaint alleging that the Tender Offer was unfair." August Order, 196 F.R.D. at 18. The court also noted that in the settlement espoused by lead counsel in March 1999, the plaintiff class would have received no money, while counsel would have received $200,000, and the court concluded that

> Lead Counsel was either pursuing meritless litigation in order to force a settlement with respect to attorneys' fees—precisely the behavior the securities laws and Rule 11 abhor—or, equally abhorrent, Lead Counsel was willing to jettison the meritorious claims of its clients in order to obtain attorneys' fees.

In imposing sanctions, the court granted the defendants somewhat less in fees than they had requested, ordering the two firms representing plaintiffs to pay a total of $105,191.43. The court apportioned the award 70 percent, or $73,634, against Schoengold & Sporn, which had been counsel throughout, and 30 percent, or $31,557.43, against Berger & Montague, as a late-comer to the litigation.

Both law firms moved for reconsideration of the August Order on various grounds. In addition, Berger & Montague contended that Schoengold & Sporn had not shared with the Berger firm some of the pertinent substantive documents the Schoengold firm had reviewed or the warning letters the latter had received from defense counsel. In its September Order, the district court concluded that, although it had taken into account the limited duration of the Berger firm's role, it had "not fully appreciated to what extent Berger & Montague [had] acted solely at the direction of Lead Counsel" or that "Berger & Montague was 'not made privy to ... certain matters relevant to the imposition of sanctions.'" September Order, 120 F. Supp. 2d at 269. While remaining of the view that the Berger firm's participation in the litigation warranted some sanction, the court concluded that the amount of the sanction should be reduced from 30 percent of the previously awarded total to 10 percent, or $10,519.14. The court did not reallocate the amount of that reduction to the Schoengold firm but instead simply reduced the total amount of sanctions awarded * * *

The present appeal, timely filed in October 2000, followed. The only notice of appeal, signed by the Schoengold firm, stated as follows:

> Notice is hereby given that Plaintiffs–Appellants, Polar International Brokerage Corp., on its own behalf and on behalf of all similarly situated shareholders of Willis Corroon Group, PLC, hereby appeal to the United States Court of Appeals for the Second Circuit from the Memorandum Orders of Honorable Shira A. Scheindlin, U.S.D.J. of the United States District Court for the Southern District of New York, dated August 7, 2000 ("August 7 Order") imposing sanctions against plaintiffs' counsel for violations of Rule 11 and September 19, 2000 granting reconsideration of the August 7 Order and imposing sanctions. * * *

In February 2001, Berger & Montague moved to intervene in the appeal. Its motion was granted, "limited to the issue raised in Section V.C.3 of appellant's brief," that section having been described in the Berger firm's motion as "Polar International['s] argument that the District Court erroneously reduced Berger & Montague's liability for sanction" (Berger & Montague motion to intervene dated February 14, 2001). Berger & Montague thereafter filed its intervenor brief, which not only defends the district court's reduction but also "joins plaintiffs-appellants' [sic] arguments that no sanctions should be imposed" ("Berger & Montague agrees that sanctions are inappropriate in this case, particularly in light of the affidavits presented to support the allegations of the complaint ... and [because] a majority of claims were found to be nonsanctionable.").

We have several procedural difficulties with the present appeal. To begin with, the notice of appeal is defective. The Federal Rules of Appellate Procedure require, with an exception not pertinent here, that "the notice of appeal must ... specify the party or parties taking the appeal by naming each one in the caption or body of the notice...." Fed. R. App. P. 3(c)(1)(A). In the present case, the notice of appeal specified only the plaintiff Polar as the party taking the appeal. But no sanctions had been imposed against Polar. Hence, as to sanctions, Polar was not entitled to appeal, see, e.g., Deposit Guaranty National Bank v. Roper, 445 U.S. 326, 335, 63 L. Ed. 2d 427, 100 S. Ct. 1166 (1980) (only a party aggrieved by an order may appeal), and the notice of appeal should have been filed in the name of the attorneys challenging the sanctions imposed against them, see generally Agee v. Paramount Communications, Inc., 114 F.3d 395, 400 (2d Cir. 1997) ("Agee") ("placing the bar on notice of the importance of Rule 3(c), the harsh and unfortunate consequences of overlooking it, and the apparent frequency with which these consequences are felt in the context of appeals from sanctions imposed against attorneys").

In Agee, we noted the need for specificity in the notice of appeal as to the identity of the person challenging an order that imposed sanctions against more than one person, and we dismissed for lack of appellate jurisdiction an attorney's challenge to a sanctions award against him where

> [the client was] listed as the sole appellant in the caption of the notice, and the first sentence of the body of that notice refers only to "Plaintiff Agee." Although [attorney] Walshe's name was listed as the appellant's attorney and the notice identifies the August 8, 1995 judgment and order imposing joint and several sanctions against both Agee and Walshe, Walshe's intent to participate as a party rather than as a party's attorney was not clear on the face of the notice.

114 F.3d at 399. We noted that in Garcia v. Wash, 20 F.3d 608 (5th Cir. 1994), the Fifth Circuit had entertained an attorney's challenge to an award of sanctions despite the attorney's not being formally identified as appealing, because the body of the notice of appeal made it clear that the sanction was challenged, and the attorney was the only one sanctioned, see generally Fed. R. App. P. 3(c) Advisory Committee Note (1993) (test for determining the sufficiency of a notice of appeal in this respect is "whether it is objectively clear that a party intended to appeal"). We stated that in Garcia v. Wash, "because the sanctions were imposed solely against the attorney, there was no confusion as to whether the client, the attorney, or both were appealing from the judgment. The same cannot be said in this case involving a joint and several sanction." Agee, 114 F.3d at 399.

In the present case, although no sanctions were imposed against plaintiffs, there exists a confusion similar to that in Agee because sanctions were imposed against two sets of plaintiffs' counsel, and the notice of appeal stated, without differentiation, that the challenge was to sanctions "against plaintiffs' counsel." Nothing in that specification distinguished between the sanction imposed against the Schoengold firm and that imposed against the Berger firm. Moreover, the fact that a plaintiff was specified as the appealing party might have made it seem likely that the sanctions against both of the firms representing the plaintiffs were being challenged. And certainly it was not a reasonable inference that a plaintiff, itself unaffected by the sanctions order, wished to challenge the reduction of the sanction imposed against one of its attorneys. It is thus hardly clear from the body of the notice of appeal that the appeal was not meant to challenge the sanctions against both firms.

Nonetheless, because more than one entity was sanctioned, Berger & Montague surely could not be viewed as an appellant, for it is not "a party whose intent to appeal is otherwise clear from the notice," Fed. R. App. P. 3(c)(4). Berger & Montague not only was not designated as an appellant in the caption or the body of the notice of appeal, it did not even sign the notice of appeal. Had the Berger firm intended to appeal, more than what is in the notice of appeal filed here would have been required.

In fact, however, we were informed at oral argument of this appeal that Berger & Montague had chosen not to appeal the revised award of sanctions against it. This, in turn, brings into question the propriety of so much of the "intervenor" brief filed by the Berger firm as argues that no sanctions at all should have been imposed. Having declined to file an appeal from the August and September Orders, and its appeal deadline having passed, Berger & Montague could not secure the resurrection of its appeal time, which is jurisdictional and strictly enforced, see, e.g., Griggs v. Provident Consumer Discount Co., 459 U.S. 56, 61, 74 L. Ed. 2d 225, 103 S. Ct. 400 (1982) (per curiam); Browder v. Director, Department of Corrections, 434 U.S. 257, 264, 54 L. Ed. 2d 521, 98 S. Ct. 556 (1978), by simply seeking to intervene. Accordingly, when Berger & Montague moved for permission to intervene, we granted its motion only to the extent of allowing it to defend the district court's reduction of its liability for sanctions. Thus, the Berger firm's opposition to the award of any sanctions ("sanctions are inappropriate in this case, particularly in light of the affidavits presented to support the allegations of the complaint ... and [because] a majority of claims were found to be nonsanctionable")), and hence any challenge to the $10,519.14 sanction imposed on Berger & Montague, is not properly before us.

Finally, Schoengold & Sporn, like the Berger firm, was not designated as an appellant in the caption or the body of the notice of appeal. But assuming that the notice of appeal can be objectively read as clearly indicating an intent by the Schoengold firm to appeal in its own right simply because it signed the notice and designated the sanctions orders as the challenged decisions—a proposition of questionable validity under Agee, given that the Schoengold firm was not the only entity sanctioned—we nonetheless conclude that part of the Schoengold & Sporn appeal must be dismissed for lack of standing. To the extent that Schoengold & Sporn attacks the district court's September Order for reducing the sanction imposed against Berger & Montague, the Schoengold firm lacks standing because it is not, in any principled sense, aggrieved by that reduction. The Schoengold firm would have been aggrieved had the district court concomitantly increased the amount of sanction that the Schoengold firm was required to pay; but instead, the total amount of sanctions awarded was reduced, and the amount to be paid by the Schoengold firm remained the same, $73,634. The Schoengold firm's premise that, as a result of the reduction granted the Berger firm, the September Order "held lead-counsel culpable for 90% of sanctions" (Appellant's brief on appeal at 43), is squarely contradicted by the language of that Order, which stated that "Lead Counsel is responsible for 70%, rather than 90%, of the total sanctions previously imposed...." September Order, 120 F. Supp. 2d at 272. The court stated expressly that "the 20% reduction in sanctions assessed against Berger & Montague ... is not allocated to Lead Counsel." Id. Accordingly, we dismiss for lack of standing so much of the appeal by Schoengold & Sporn as argues that the district court erred in "reducing the liability of non-lead counsel".

Assuming that we have jurisdiction over such challenges as Schoengold & Sporn has standing to make, i.e., the alleged errors in the imposition of the $73,634 sanction against the Schoengold firm itself and in the court's refusal to rescind or reduce that amount, we reject its challenges for lack of merit. The district court's decision with respect to the imposition of sanctions pursuant to Rule 11 is reviewable only for abuse of discretion. See, e.g., Cooter & Gell v. Hartmarx Corp., 496 U.S. 384, 405, 110 L. Ed. 2d 359, 110 S. Ct. 2447 (1990); Gurary v. Winehouse, 235 F.3d 792, 798 (2d Cir. 2000), petition for cert. filed (May 29, 2001). We see no abuse of discretion here.

The PSLRA required the court to impose sanctions if it found any violation of Rule 11. See, e.g., Simon DeBartolo Group, L.P. v. Richard E. Jacobs Group. Inc., 186 F.3d 157, 166–67 (2d Cir. 1999). Rule 11 is violated when it is clear under existing precedents that a pleading has no chance of success and there is no reasonable argument to extend, modify, or reverse the law as it stands. See, e.g., Gurary v. Winehouse, 235 F.3d at 798. We see no error of law or clear error of fact in the district court's determination that the § 14(e) claim was without factual support and was legally frivolous, and that its assertion violated Rule 11.

For the foregoing reasons, we affirm so much of the district court's August and September Orders as imposed sanctions of $73,634 against Schoengold & Sporn. In all other respects, the appeal is dismissed for lack of appellate jurisdiction.

Notes and Questions

1.   Some decisions have deemed a notice of appeal naming only the client, but listing only the sanction order as the matter to be challenged on appeal, and signed by the penalized counsel, to be sufficient to permit the attorney to be heard on appeal. See, e.g., Retail Flooring Dealers of America v. Beaulieu of America, LLC, 339 F.3d 1146 (9th Cir. 2003)(over a biting dissent which argues that even in this one circuit there is a split of authority "obscured with a fuliginous cloud" of meaningless explanation for allowing the appeal). What other interpretation is possible if the notice of appeal lists only the sanction order?

2.   "Disqualification orders" are generally held to directly affect the attorney, and thus permit her to seek an appeal. See, e.g., Weeks v. Independent School Dist. No. I–89, 230 F.3d 1201 (10th Cir. 2000) (also holding that even if the underlying case settles, the effect of a reprimand or disqualification order upon counsel's reputation is sufficient to permit an appeal). Ironically, the opposite sort of order—refusing to let an attorney

step aside once a notice of appearance has been filed—has been held not appealable. See United States v. Bertoli, 994 F.2d 1002 (3rd Cir. 1993).

3.   Some courts have noted that sanction orders do not always mention "contempt" even though the predicate for many serious sanctions imposed upon attorneys is the equivalent sense of outrage by the court that its orders have been flouted by counsel. Thus, even where a penalty does not recite that it flows from a finding of contumacious conduct, attorneys will likely be permitted to appeal. See, e.g., Satcorp Int'l Group v. China National Silk Import & Export Corp., 101 F.3d 3 (1996) ($10,000 fine imposed upon counsel, "which [the client] was barred from reimbursing").

4.   Can an attorney for a party to a proceeding appeal from a judgment that adversely affects the attorney's interests because the attorney's fee is dependent upon the success of his client? The general rule is that the attorney cannot appeal. Annotation, 91 A.L.R.2d 618 (1963). This applies even when the attorney's fee is an item of recovery includable in the judgment. The situation is different, however, when the attorney is allowed to file the fee petition in his own name. Boeing Co. v. Van Gemert, 444 U.S. 472, 100 S.Ct. 745, 62 L.Ed.2d 676 (1980). When an attorney is disqualified, a different analysis is made. In Analytica, Inc. v. NPD Research, Inc., 708 F.2d 1263 (7th Cir. 1983), two law firms appealed a district court order disqualifying them from representing a corporate plaintiff. The second firm also appealed the order that directed it to pay $25,000 to the defendant. The Seventh Circuit held that the first law firm did not have standing to appeal because it had not shown that the client wanted to rehire the firm. If it could have shown that the client wanted to keep the firm, the firm would have standing. As to the second firm, because it had standing to appeal the $25,000 assessment the court determined it would have to consider validity of the disqualification in any event.

3.   RIGHTS OF THE MEDIA TO APPELLATE REVIEW

DAVIS v. EAST BATON ROUGE PARISH SCHOOL BOARD

United States Court of Appeals, Fifth Circuit, 1996.
78 F.3d 920.

KING, CIRCUIT JUDGE.

* * * [W]e must now consider whether the news agencies have standing to challenge these orders [precluding disclosure of school desegregation plans]. To establish standing, the news agencies must show an injury in fact that is fairly traceable to the challenged act and that is likely to be redressed by the requested remedy. Valley Forge Christian College v. Americans United For Separation of Church and State, 454 U.S. 464, 472, 70 L. Ed. 2d 700, 102 S. Ct. 752 (1982); Sierra Club v. Cedar Point Oil Co., 73 F.3d 546, 556 (5th Cir. 1996). Several courts have held that news agencies have standing to challenge confidentiality orders in an effort to obtain information or access to judicial proceedings, although they are neither parties to the litigation nor restrained directly by the orders. See, e.g., Pansy v. Borough of Stroudsburg, 23

F.3d 772, 777 (3d Cir. 1994); In re Application of Dow Jones & Co., 842 F.2d 603, 608 (2d Cir. 1988); Journal Publishing Co. v. Mechem, 801 F.2d 1233, 1235 (10th Cir. 1986); Radio & Television News Ass'n v. United States Dist. Court, 781 F.2d 1443, 1445 (9th Cir. 1986); Gurney, 558 F.2d at 1206; CBS, Inc. v. Young, 522 F.2d 234, 238 (6th Cir. 1975).

In this case the only element of standing that is disputable is whether the news agencies have alleged an injury in fact. The district court's March 1st order directs the Board, its attorneys, and several of its employees to refrain from making written or oral comments about any aspects of any drafts of the Board's proposed desegregation plan. The March 8th order directs the Board to meet in private confidential sessions to formulate a proposed desegregation plan, and further orders the Board and its attorneys and employees to keep confidential all of the private sessions and all preliminary versions of the proposed desegregation plan. The combined effect of these orders, as the district court recognized, is to severely impede the news agencies' ability to discover information about the Board's process in formulating a proposed desegregation plan.

The First Amendment provides at least some protection for the news agencies' efforts to gather the news. Branzburg v. Hayes, 408 U.S. 665, 681, 33 L. Ed. 2d 626, 92 S. Ct. 2646 (1972). * * *

In addition, the First Amendment protects the news agencies right to receive protected speech. Virginia State Bd. of Pharmacy v. Virginia Citizens Consumer Counsel, Inc., 425 U.S. 748, 756–57, 48 L. Ed. 2d 346, 96 S. Ct. 1817 (1976) ("Where a speaker exists ... the protection afforded is to the communication, to its source and to its recipients both ... We acknowledge that this Court has referred to a First Amendment right to 'receive information and ideas,' and that freedom of speech 'necessarily protects the right to receive.' "). The Board argues that the First Amendment right to receive speech only comes into existence once a willing speaker has been shown to exist, relying on Virginia State Bd. of Pharmacy, 425 U.S. at 756 ("Freedom of speech presupposes a willing speaker.") The news agencies respond that, even absent a willing speaker, they would have standing by virtue of their independent First Amendment right to gather the news. Indeed, many circuits have found media standing to challenge confidentiality orders without expressly finding the existence of a willing speaker. See, e.g., Dow Jones & Co., 842 F.2d at 607 ("It is hard, in fact, to imagine that there are no willing speakers. Without them there would be no need for a restraining order; it would be superfluous."); CBS, Inc., 522 F.2d at 238 (finding media standing without discussing a willing speaker requirement).

We need not and do not decide whether, in every case, the media must demonstrate the existence of a willing speaker to establish standing to challenge a court's confidentiality order, because, in the present case, we are satisfied that a willing speaker exists. At the district court's February 22nd hearing, the news agencies and the Board stipulated that, prior to the entry of a confidentiality order, the news agencies were able to discover information about desegregation of the school system—i.e., they stipulated that members and employees of the Board were willing speakers on this issue prior to the district court's original confidentiality order. See Dow Jones, 842 F.2d at 607 (discussing the existence of a willing speaker to show that the news agencies had standing to challenge a confidentiality order). The parties also stipulated that the Board's efforts in preparing a desegregation plan were newsworthy and of great public interest in the community. The district court's orders have severely impeded the news agencies' ability to discover newsworthy information from potential speakers.

The following exchange occurred at the February 22nd hearing:

MR. WEISS [attorney for intervenors]: Well, the evidence that we were going to put on, your honor, would have been evidence of the willingness of various representatives of the school board to speak to my clients prior to the entry of the order . . .

Well, we would plan to call Mr. [Bill] Pack, your honor, one of the intervenors, to testify about the effect of the court's order on his ability to gather and report news about this matter . . .

THE COURT: We'll stipulate that if this order is complied with, Mr. Pack will get essentially zero information, and will not be able to report anything.

Do you stipulate to that, Mr. Patin?

MR. PATIN [attorney for Board]: Yes, your honor, we will.

Additionally, the parties stipulated to the following:

MR. WEISS: Let me tell you exactly what Mr. Pack would testify, your honor.

Your honor, first, he would testify that he was given extensive information about the plan prior to the entry of the order, including drafts of the plan, information relating to busing, information relating to student test scores. He would testify that he and Ms. Lightfoot attended workshop sessions called by the superintendent to present and discuss the draft plans, which they disseminated, and the underlying data.

Can we stipulate to that?

MR. PATIN: Your honor, I think my client was a sieve before. We'll stipulate to that.

Thus, the news agencies have alleged an injury in fact that is fairly traceable to the district court's orders and likely to be redressed by the relief requested. The district court's orders impede the news agencies' abilities to gather the news and to receive protected speech, abilities which are arguably protected by the First Amendment. The relief requested—that we vacate the March 1st and March 8th orders—would redress this injury by allowing the news agencies to discover information about the Board's process in formulating a desegregation plan.

We conclude that the news agencies have standing to challenge the district court's March 1st and March 8th confidentiality orders.

––––––––

Notes and Questions

1. In its decision in In Re: Associated Press, 162 F.3d 503 (7th Cir. 1998), the Seventh Circuit summarized its approach in a wide variety of "media" involvement cases:

> In this circuit, we have intimated that the most appropriate procedural mechanism by which to accomplish this task is by permitting those who oppose the suppression of the material to intervene for that limited purpose. See United States v. Andreas, 150 F.3d 766, 767 (7th Cir. 1998) (noting that the newspapers had intervened in the underlying action in order to assert the right of access to materials filed under seal); United States v. Corbitt, 879 F.2d 224, 226–27 (7th Cir. 1989) (explaining that a newspaper publisher moved to intervene in the criminal case to request disclosure of the PSR and testimonial letters on which the district court had relied in sentencing, and that the district court apparently granted the motion to intervene and ultimately granted substantial access to the PSR and the letters); see also United States v. Peters, 754 F.2d 753, 756 (7th Cir. 1985) (noting that the access issue is more appropriately reviewed on direct appeal rather than by mandamus). Other circuits have followed the same practice.

> Several of our cases, although not employing the term "intervention," clearly sanctioned and indeed expressed a preference for proceeding by way of appeal rather than mandamus. In In re Continental Illinois Securities Litigation, 732 F.2d at 1306–07, two reporters informally requested access to a document filed in the litigation and then, upon the district court's instructions, made "formal motions" to that effect. The district court ultimately granted access to the requested materials. In United States v. Edwards, 672 F.2d 1289, 1291 (7th Cir. 1982), a television station and a radio station "informally" requested release of an audio tape that had been played in the criminal trial. The broadcasters sought to copy the tape for broadcast to the public. The court suggested that the broadcasters file "formal" applications requesting the release of the tape. The broadcasters then submitted written applications seeking permission to copy all video and audio tapes that had been or might be admitted into evidence. The court heard oral argument by counsel for the broadcasters, and by counsel for each of the defendants and counsel for the United States. The court then denied the applications in an oral decision from the bench. On appeal, this court held that the issue was not moot and that the district court had not abused its discretion. Similarly, in United States v. Dorfman, 690 F.2d 1230, 1231 (7th Cir. 1982), the court referred to "a motion by newspaper publishers and broadcasters to unseal the sealed exhibits, so that they could be inspected and copied" without addressing how the press procedurally came before the court. The issues on appeal dealt with the

court's appellate jurisdiction under the collateral order doctrine and whether the district court had authority to unseal the exhibits.

2. In Under Seal v. Under Seal, 326 F.3d 479 (4th Cir. 2003) the Fourth Circuit commented on the common use of the writ of mandamus in cases involving denial of media access to court records of various sorts:

> Petitions for mandamus have long been recognized as the appropriate vehicle for challenges to cloture and unsealing orders. Cf. Baltimore Sun Co. v. Goetz, 886 F.2d 60 (4th Cir. 1989) ("Mandamus, not appeal, is the preferred method of review for orders restricting press activity related to criminal proceedings."); In re Washington Post Co., 807 F.2d 383, 388 (4th Cir. 1986) (treating an appeal by a non-party to a district court order sealing documents in a criminal case as a petition for mandamus); Central South Carolina Chapter, Society of Professional Journalists, Sigma Delta Chi v. Martin, 556 F.2d 706 (4th Cir. 1977) (noting that "mandamus is the proper remedy to request the relief prayed for here" where appellant, on an interlocutory appeal, challenges a district court protective order); see also United States v. Gonzales, 150 F.3d 1246 (10th Cir. 1998) (treating an interlocutory appeal from a district court's order to seal the record as a petition for mandamus, in light of the fact that mandamus is the proper vehicle for such review). Mandamus relief, though limited to circumstances where the petitioner's "right to issuance of the writ is clear and indisputable," Kerr v. U.S. Dist. Court, 426 U.S. 394, 403, 96 S.Ct. 2119, 48 L.Ed.2d 725 (1976), 426 U.S. 394, 96 S.Ct. 2119, 48 L.Ed.2d 725, suffices to protect the parties' rights here.

SECTION H. AMICUS CURIAE PARTICIPATION

1. GENERAL STANDARDS

GIAMMALVO v. SUNSHINE MINING COMPANY

Supreme Court of Delaware, 1994.
644 A.2d 407.

HOLLAND, JUSTICE.

The plaintiff-appellant, Salvatore J. Giammalvo ("Giammalvo"), brought this action against Sunshine Mining Company and certain of its directors (collectively "Sunshine Mining"). Giammalvo challenged, inter alia, Sunshine Mining's failure to redeem Cumulative Redeemable Preferred Stock (the "Preferred Stock"). The Court of Chancery held that Sunshine Mining had not breached its contractual obligations to the holders of the Preferred Stock.

The Court of Chancery also certified this matter as a class action, pursuant to Court of Chancery Rule 23(b)(2). Giammalvo was certified as the class representative. Giammalvo appealed from the Court of Chancery's substantive ruling. That appeal is the proceeding which is now before this Court.

Grace Holdings, LP ("Grace") has filed a motion for leave to file a brief in this appeal as a member of the plaintiff class. According to Grace, it has become concerned about whether Giammalvo is able to adequately represent the interests of the class in the proceedings before this Court, in particular, with respect to the mandatory redemption issue. Grace also desires to assist this Court in resolving the other issues presented on appeal.

According to Grace, it does not seek to intervene on appeal, but nevertheless, it desires to file a brief "as a class member." Grace's motion presents the Court with separate and unique concerns to the extent that it implicates a circumvention of conventional procedure. First, motions to intervene on appeal are seldom granted, especially when the movant declined to join in the proceedings at trial. See Ct. Ch. R. 24. See also Maurer v. International Re–Insurance Corp., Del. Supr., 32 Del. Ch. 447, 86 A.2d 360, 362 (1952). Second, permitting an individual class member to intervene at any stage of a class action is somewhat antithetical to the representative nature of such a proceeding. See Ct. Ch. R. 23 and 24. See also Stenson v. Blum, 476 F. Supp. 1331, 1336 (S.D.N.Y. 1979).

Amicus Curiae Status—Discretion of Court

Since Grace has not filed a motion to intervene, this Court has concluded that Grace's present application must be considered in accordance with the standards which apply to a motion to participate as an amicus curiae. Leave to appear as an amicus curiae differs from intervention in its usual sense. First, an intervener becomes a party to the litigation and is bound by the judgment. An amicus curiae does not become a party to the proceedings. Second, an amicus curiae is heard only by leave of the court. Therefore, the privilege to be heard as an amicus curiae, as well as the manner and extent of participation, rests within the discretion of the court.[3]

Amicus Curiae—Historical Role

Translated literally from Latin, amicus curiae means "friend of the court." Courts have considered the desirability of hearing from an amicus curiae for hundreds of years. See The Protector v. Geering, 145 Eng. Rep. 394 (1686). Historically, participation as an amicus curiae has been granted upon a demonstration that such assistance is advisable to protect the court in the consideration of the case, i.e., "for the honor of a court of justice to avoid error." Id.

The history of Anglo–Saxon and American jurisprudence also reflects that the participation of an amicus curiae was generally allowed for the purpose of ensuring a full and complete presentation on questions of either general or public interest which were at issue in the

---

3. For example, Supreme Court Rule 28 provides that an amicus curiae will be permitted to participate in oral argument only in "extraordinary circumstances." Supr. Ct. R. 28.

proceedings before the court. That historical role continues to be the primary function of an amicus curiae. It is now generally recognized that amicus curiae are called upon for the purpose of (1) assisting the court in a case of general public interest by providing adversarial presentations when neither side is represented, e.g., In re Opinion of the Justices, Del. Supr., 575 A.2d 1186 (1990); (2) assisting the court in a case of general public interest, by providing an adversarial presentation when only one point of view is represented, e.g., Red Dog v. State, Del. Supr., 625 A.2d 245 (1993); Matter of Butler, Del. Supr., 609 A.2d 1080 (1992); Appeal of Infotechnology, Inc., Del. Supr., 582 A.2d 215 (1990); Pollock v. Peterson, Del. Ch., 271 A.2d 45, 50 (1970); (3) assisting the court by supplementing the efforts of counsel, even when both sides are represented, in a case of general public interest, e.g., State v. Cohen, Del. Supr., 604 A.2d 846 (1992); Travelers Indem. Co. v. Lake, Del. Supr., 594 A.2d 38 (1991); and (4) drawing the court's attention to broader legal or policy implications that might otherwise escape its consideration in the narrow context of a specific case, e.g., Beattie v. Beattie, Del. Supr., 630 A.2d 1096 (1993) and Gannett Co., Inc. v. State, Del. Supr., 571 A.2d 735 (1989).

Amicus Curiae—Contemporary Role—Supreme Court Rule 28

Over time, however, the traditional role of the amicus curiae has evolved to permit more partisan advocacy. See Krislov, The Amicus Curiae Brief: From Friendship to Advocacy, 72 Yale L.J. 694 (1963). In fact, a recent edition of Black's Law Dictionary also includes the following in its definition of amicus curiae:

> A person with strong interest in or views on the subject matter of an action may petition the court for permission to file a brief, ostensibly on behalf of a party but actually to suggest a rationale consistent with its own views. Such amicus curiae briefs are commonly filed in appeals concerning matters of a broad public interest. . . .

Black's Law Dictionary 75 (5th ed. 1979). See Beattie v. Beattie, Del. Supr., 630 A.2d 1096 (1993).

Supreme Court Rule 28[4] is consistent with both the historical and contemporary roles of amicus curiae. The committee commentary to Supreme Court Rule 28 states that the rule is in substantial compliance with Section 3.33(b)(2) of the ABA Standards Relating to Appellate Courts. That section reads as follows:

> Public Question Cases. In cases involving questions of general public importance, the court may appropriately permit submission of briefs amicus curiae on behalf of those whose circumstances may be affected by the court's decision.

---

4. A brief of an amicus curiae may be filed only by leave of Court granted on motion or stipulation or at the request of the Court. The motion for leave shall identify the interest of the applicant and shall state the reasons why a brief of an amicus curiae is desirable. An amicus curiae shall file a brief within the time allowed by the Court. A motion of an amicus curiae to participate in oral argument will be granted only for extraordinary reasons. Supr. Ct. R. 28.

Standards Relating to Appellate Courts § 3.33(b)(2) (1977). We will examine Grace's application to file a brief from the perspectives of Grace, the parties, and the Court.

GRACE'S PERSPECTIVE—SELF-INTEREST NOT DETERMINATIVE

There is no dispute between the parties about the fact that Grace's rights may be determined by the Court's decision in this case. Thus, Grace's "circumstances may be affected" by this Court's decision. Id. The potential effect of these proceedings upon Grace, however, is not necessarily dispositive of its motion to participate as an amicus curiae.

The opportunity to participate as an amicus curiae, even as it has evolved, is generally afforded to a person who "has no right to appear in a suit, but is allowed to introduce argument, authority or evidence to protect his interests." Ladue v. Goodhead, N.Y. Civ. Ct., 181 Misc. 807, 44 N.Y.S.2d 783, 787 (1943). Grace had the opportunity to intervene as a party in the Court of Chancery. It did not do so. Therefore, it will be granted the privilege of participating as an amicus curiae on appeal only under exceptional circumstances.

The Court concludes that such exceptional circumstances do not exist in this case. First, unlike Elliott, Grace had notice and still did not move to intervene in this proceeding at trial. Second, Grace's interests in this litigation are similar to those of the entire class, which interests are being represented directly on appeal by Giammalvo and indirectly by Elliott.

PARTIES' PERSPECTIVE—GRACE'S ASSISTANCE UNWELCOME

Supreme Court Rule 28 provides for an amicus brief to be filed "upon stipulation." In effect, such stipulations constitute the parties' consent to the motion for participation by an amicus curiae. Although it is not binding upon this Court, the consent of the parties is an important consideration. Stroud v. Milliken Enters., Inc., Del. Supr., 552 A.2d 476 (1989); Riggs v. Riggs, Del. Supr., 539 A.2d 163 (1988). Conversely, the objection of one or more of the actual adversarial parties in interest must also be balanced against the probative value of providing the Court with additional assistance. In this case, the parties have not consented to Grace's application by stipulation. Sunshine Mining objects, Giammalvo states that Grace's assistance is unnecessary, and Elliott takes no position.

JUDICIAL PERSPECTIVE—GRACE'S ASSISTANCE UNNECESSARY

The traditional basis for affording a person an opportunity to participate as an amicus curiae has been a judicial recognition of the need for additional assistance in cases involving questions of general public importance. Usually, courts sought the objective views of "a friend of the court." More recently, courts have permitted assistance by one or more partisan amicus curiae advocates who possess either a unique perspective or expertise regarding an important public issue before the court.

Grace's interest in these proceedings, as set forth in its motion, is not objective, unique, or related to a question of general public importance. Rather, Grace's interest is specific to its status as a class member. To the extent that this case involves any issues of general public importance, Grace has not indicated why those issues will not be adequately addressed by the attorneys for the parties. Consequently, the record does not reflect that this is a case in which the Court would benefit by additional assistance from Grace.

CONCLUSION

It has been noted that a court should be reluctant to exercise its discretion to accept an amicus curiae when it appears that the parties are well represented, the joint consent of the parties to the submission by the amicus curiae is lacking, and the movant's ability to provide the court with some unique supplemental assistance, whether objective or partisan, is not readily apparent. Strasser v. Doorley, 432 F.2d 567, 569 (1st Cir. 1970). The record reflects that this is such a case. Accordingly, Grace's motion is DENIED.

NEONATOLOGY ASSOCIATES, P.A. v. COMMISSIONER

United States Court of Appeals, Third Circuit, 2002.
293 F.3d 128.

ALITO, CIRCUIT JUDGE:

Before me is a motion under Rule 29(b) of the Federal Rules of Appellate Procedure for leave to file a brief as amicus curiae over the opposition of the appellants. The motion has been referred to me as a single judge under our Internal Operating Procedure 10.5.1. Because it appears that the criteria set out in Rule 29(b) are met, i.e., that the amici have a sufficient "interest" in the case and that their brief is "desirable" and discusses matters that are "relevant to the disposition of the case," the motion is granted.

I.

This is an appeal from a decision of the Tax Court. See Neonatology Associates, P.A. v. Commissioner, 115 T.C. 43 (2000). The appeal has been taken by two professional medical corporations (Neonatology Associates, P.A. and Lakewood Radiology, P.A.), physicians who owned the corporations, and spouses who signed joint tax returns. The appellants participated in the Southern California Voluntary Employees' Beneficiary Association ("SC VEBA"), which was promoted by certain insurance brokers. The Commissioner of Internal Revenue determined that the professional corporations had erroneously claimed deductions on their income tax returns for payments made to plans set up under the SC VEBA and that the individual taxpayers had failed to report on their income tax returns income arising from certain related transactions. The appellants filed a petition in the Tax Court challenging the deficiencies and associated penalties. After a trial, the Tax Court sustained the Commissioner's determinations, and this appeal followed.

The motion for leave to file an amicus brief in support of the Commissioner was submitted by five other physicians who also participated in same plan. In the statement of interest in their proposed amicus brief, these five physicians ("the amici") state:

> During pre-trial proceedings in the Tax Court, the Appellants in this case entered into a Settlement Agreement and Release with Commonwealth Life Insurance Company ("Commonwealth") pursuant to which Commonwealth agreed to defend this case at its expense and to pay certain portions of Appellants' tax liabilities in the event of an unfavorable outcome. Appellants (hereafter "the Settling Physicians") then proceeded to trial in what was designated as a "test" case for all of the parties who had challenged the IRS's position. Pursuant to Appellants' settlement with Commonwealth, Commonwealth now controls and is funding the appeal in this litigation.

> Unlike Appellants, amici declined to release their claims and have filed litigation against Commonwealth and its related parties to recover the losses they suffered through their participation in the "VEBA scheme" condemned by the Tax Court in this case. An Amended Complaint in the proposed class action in which amici are plaintiffs, Sankhla v. Commonwealth Life Ins. Co., No. 01–CV–4761 (D.N.J.) (AET), was filed on March 20, 2002 (the "Sankhla Litigation").

> Amici have an interest in the outcome of this case because it has become apparent that Commonwealth, through its control of this appeal, will attempt to induce this Court to address certain non-tax law issues that will impact the rights of amici against Commonwealth and related parties.

Amicus Br. at 1–2. Specifically, the amici are concerned that the appellants have argued that the Employee Retirement Income Security Act ("ERISA") applies to the plan and that our court's discussion of this issue will have a bearing in their litigation on the question whether the plaintiffs' claims against Commonwealth are preempted by ERISA. Amicus Br. at 2. The amici also wish to preserve the factual findings of the Tax Court concerning the roles of various parties in the underlying events because the amici hope to prove that Commonwealth and its agents controlled the Tax Court litigation on behalf of the appellants and that Commonwealth and its agents are therefore bound by those findings.

The appellants argue that the amici do not satisfy the standards for filing a brief as amici. Among other things, the appellants contend that an amicus must be " 'an impartial individual' " and not a person who is "partial to the outcome" or who has "a pecuniary interest in the

outcome.'' Opposition to Motion for Leave to File Amicus Brief (''Opp.'')
at 2–4 (quoting Leigh v. Engle, 535 F. Supp. 418, 420 (N.D. Ill. 1982)).
The appellants also argue that leave to file an amicus brief should not be
granted unless the party to be supported is either unrepresented or
inadequately represented. Opp. at 5–6. In making these arguments, the
appellants cite a small body of judicial opinions that look with disfavor
on motions for leave to file amicus briefs. See, e.g., National Org. for
Women, Inc. v. Scheidler, 223 F.3d 615 (7th Cir. 2000); Ryan v. CFTC,
125 F.3d 1062 (7th Cir. 1997) (single judge opinion); Liberty Lincoln
Mercury, Inc. v. Ford Marketing Corp., 149 F.R.D. 65, 82 (D.N.J. 1993);
Yip v. Pagano, 606 F. Supp. 1566, 1568 (D.N.J. 1985). The appellants
argue that restrictive standards espoused in these opinions represent the
views of ''the judiciary'' and are ''settled law'' ''in this jurisdiction.''
Opp. 3–4.

II.

The standards for filing an amicus brief are set out in Rule 29.
Under Rule 29(a), a private amicus may file if all parties consent or if
the court grants leave. When a party objects to filing by a private amicus
and leave of court is sought, Rule 29(b) provides that the motion for
leave to file must be accompanied by the proposed brief and must state:

(1) the movant's interest; and

(2) the reason why an amicus brief is desirable and why the matters
asserted are relevant to the disposition of the case.

Although the Rule does not say expressly that a motion for leave to file
should be denied if the movant does not meet the requirements of (a) an
adequate interest, (b) desirability, and (c) relevance, this is implicit. With
these requirements in mind, I turn to the restrictive standards that the
appellants urge us to apply.

A.

I begin with the appellants' argument that an amicus must be ''an
impartial individual who suggests the interpretation and status of the
law, gives information concerning it, and whose function is to advise in
order that justice may be done, rather than to advocate a point of view so
that a cause may be won by one party or another.'' Opp. at 3–4. This
description of the role of an amicus was once accurate and still appears
in certain sources, see 3A C.J.S. Amicus Curiae § 2 at 422–23 (1973), but
this description became outdated long ago. See Samuel Krislov, The
Amicus Curiae Brief: From Friendship to Advocacy, 72 Yale L. J. 694,
703 (1962).

Today, as noted, Rule 29 requires that an amicus have an ''interest''
in the case, see Fed. R. App. Proc. 29(b)(1) and (c)(3), and the appellants'
argument that an amicus must be ''impartial'' is difficult to square with
this requirement. An accepted definition of the term ''impartial'' is
''disinterested,'' Black's Law Dictionary 752 (6th ed. 1990), and it is not

easy to envisage an amicus who is "disinterested" but still has an "interest" in the case.

It is particularly difficult to reconcile impartiality and interestedness if the latter requirement is interpreted as a panel of our court did in American College of Obstetricians & Gynecologists v. Thornburgh, 699 F.2d 644 (3d Cir. 1983). In that case, the sharply divided panel denied a motion for leave to file an amicus brief because the proposed amici, a group of law professors, "did not purport to represent any individual or organization with a legally cognizable interest in the subject matter at issue, and [gave] only their concern about the manner in which this court will interpret the law." Id. at 645 (emphasis added). It would be virtually impossible for an amicus to show that it is "an impartial individual . . . whose function is to advise in order that justice may be done" but not a person who is "only . . . concerned about the manner in which [the] court will interpret the law." In any event, whether or not the American College panel was correct in its narrow interpretation of Rule 29's "interest" requirement, the "interest" requirement weighs strongly against the appellants' argument.

B.

The appellants suggest, however, that the very term "amicus curiae" suggests a degree of impartiality. The appellants quote the comment that "the term 'amicus curiae' means friend of the court, not friend of a party." Opp. at 3 (quoting Ryan, 125 F.3d at 1063). The implication of this statement seems to be that a strong advocate cannot truly be the court's friend. But this suggestion is contrary to the fundamental assumption of our adversary system that strong (but fair) advocacy on behalf of opposing views promotes sound decision making. Thus, an amicus who makes a strong but responsible presentation in support of a party can truly serve as the court's friend.

The argument that an amicus cannot be a person who has "a pecuniary interest in the outcome" also flies in the face of current appellate practice. A quick look at Supreme Court opinions discloses that corporations, unions, trade and professional associations, and other parties with "pecuniary" interests appear regularly as amici. (Some of the Supreme Court cases in which the greatest number of amici have filed illustrate this point. See, e.g., Pacific Mut. Life Ins. Co. v. Haslip, 499 U.S. 1, 3, 113 L. Ed. 2d 1, 111 S. Ct. 1032 n.* (1991); Container Corp. of America v. Franchise Tax Bd., 463 U.S. 159, 161, 77 L. Ed. 2d 545, 103 S. Ct. 2933 n.* (1983).) Parties with pecuniary, as well as policy, interests also appear as amici in our court. See, e.g., South Camden Citizens in Action v. New Jersey Dep't of Envtl. Protection, 274 F.3d 771, 773 (3rd Cir. 2001). I thus reject the appellants' argument that an amicus must be an impartial person not motivated by pecuniary concerns.

C.

I also disagree with the appellants' argument that an amicus seeking leave to file must show that the party to be supported is either unrepresented or inadequately represented. Rule 29 does not contain any such provision, and therefore if the requirement is valid it must represent an elaboration on the requirement of "desirability" set out in Rule 29(b)(2). In my view, however, such a requirement is most undesirable. To be sure, an amicus brief may be particularly helpful when the party supported is unrepresented or inadequately represented, but it does not follow that an amicus brief is undesirable under all other circumstances.

Even when a party is very well represented, an amicus may provide important assistance to the court. "Some amicus briefs collect background or factual references that merit judicial notice. Some friends of the court are entities with particular expertise not possessed by any party to the case. Others argue points deemed too far-reaching for emphasis by a party intent on winning a particular case. Still others explain the impact a potential holding might have on an industry or other group." Luther T. Munford, When Does the Curiae Need An Amicus?, 1 J. App. Prac. & Process 279 (1999). Accordingly, denying motions for leave to file an amicus brief whenever the party supported is adequately represented would in some instances deprive the court of valuable assistance. Moreover, requiring a prospective amicus to undertake the distasteful task of showing that the attorney for the party that the amicus wishes to support is incompetent is likely to discourage amici in instances in which the party's brief is less than ideal and an amicus submission would be valuable to the court. See Robert L. Stern, Appellate Practice in the United States 306 (2d ed. 1989) (The lawyer preparing an amicus brief "would normally be unwilling to state, except in most unusual circumstances, that the counsel for the party being supported will do an inadequate job."). The criterion of desirability set out in Rule 29(b)(2) is open-ended, but a broad reading is prudent. The decision whether to grant leave to file must be made at a relatively early stage of the appeal. It is often difficult at that point to tell with any accuracy if a proposed amicus filing will be helpful. Indeed, it is frequently hard to tell whether an amicus brief adds anything useful to the briefs of the parties without thoroughly studying those briefs and other pertinent materials, and it is often not feasible to do this in connection with the motion for leave to file. Furthermore, such a motion may be assigned to a judge or panel of judges who will not decide the merits of the appeal, and therefore the judge or judges who must rule on the motion must attempt to determine, not whether the proposed amicus brief would be helpful to them, but whether it might be helpful to others who may view the case differently. Under these circumstances, it is preferable to err on the side of granting leave. If an amicus brief that turns out to be unhelpful is filed, the merits panel, after studying the case, will often be able to make that determination without much trouble and can then simply disregard the amicus brief. On the other hand, if a good brief is rejected, the merits panel will be deprived of a resource that might have been of assistance.

A restrictive policy with respect to granting leave to file may also create at least the perception of viewpoint discrimination. Unless a court follows a policy of either granting or denying motions for leave to file in virtually all cases, instances of seemingly disparate treatment are predictable. A restrictive policy may also convey an unfortunate message about the openness of the court.

Those favoring the practice of restricting the filing of amicus briefs suggest that such briefs often merely duplicate the arguments of the parties and thus waste the court's time, and I do not doubt that some amicus briefs make little if any contribution. However, a restrictive practice regarding motions for leave to file seems to be an unpromising strategy for lightening a court's work load. For one thing, the time required for skeptical scrutiny of proposed amicus briefs may equal, if not exceed, the time that would have been needed to study the briefs at the merits stage if leave had been granted. In addition, because private amicus briefs are not submitted in the vast majority of court of appeals cases, and because poor quality briefs are usually easy to spot, unhelpful amicus briefs surely do not claim more than a very small part of a court's time. For all these reasons, I think that our court would be well advised to grant motions for leave to file amicus briefs unless it is obvious that the proposed briefs do not meet Rule 29's criteria as broadly interpreted. I believe that this is consistent with the predominant practice in the courts of appeals. See Michael E. Tigar and Jane B. Tigar, Federal Appeals—Jurisdiction and Practice 181 (3d ed. 1999)("Even when the other side refuses to consent to an amicus filing, most courts of appeals freely grant leave to file, provided the brief is timely and well-reasoned."); Robert L. Stern, supra, at 307–08.

III.

Turning to the circumstances of the present case, I believe that the amici have stated an "interest in the case," and it appears that their brief is "relevant" and "desirable" since it alerts the merits panel to possible implications of the appeal. The appellants charge that the amici wish to inject new issues into the case, but it does not appear to me that the amici are attempting to do that. Rather, as I understand their position, they are primarily interested in making sure that our court does not inadvertently stray into issues that need not be decided in this case. Finally, the appellants contend that the proposed amicus brief is full of "spleen" and "invective," Opp. at 10, but no specifics are cited. My reading of the amicus brief did not spot any violations of our LAR 28.1(c), which requires that briefs be phrased in appropriate, professional terms, but if the merits panel views the matter differently, it can of course take appropriate action at that time.

For the reasons noted above, the motion for leave to file the brief as amici curiae over the objection of the appellants is granted.

VOICES FOR CHOICES v. ILLINOIS
BELL TELEPHONE CO.

United States Court of Appeals, Seventh Circuit, 2003.
339 F.3d 542.

POSNER, CIRCUIT JUDGE, in chambers.

I have before me motions for leave to file amicus curiae briefs. Fed. R. App. P. 29. The status of the movants impel me to state publicly my reasons for denying the motions.

[In a case involving whether the Illinois Public Utilities Act provisions regulating telephone companies were preempted by federal statutes, one of the parties filed a brief, which was] long (58 pages) and comprehensive, despite which there are these two motions for leave to file amicus curiae briefs. The first, submitted jointly by Michael J. Madigan, Speaker of the Illinois House of Representatives, and Emil Jones, Jr., President of the Illinois Senate, claims that their proposed amicus curiae brief "presents the opportunity for the Court to consider certain issues from the viewpoint of state officials who play an instrumental role in establishing telecommunications policy for the States." The brief argues that the Federal Telecommunications Act preserves the legislature's plenary authority to set rate-making policy and that the district court failed to consider all the pertinent evidence in the record in concluding that the Illinois statute conflicts with the federal statute. The second brief is submitted by the Communications Workers of America, which represents more than half a million workers in the telecommunications industry, including employees of SBC. The union asserts that the Illinois statute was intended to remedy problems attributable to artificially low lease rates, including employee layoffs and decreased services to customers, that the legislature can adopt standards for rate setting without violating the Federal Telecommunications Act, and that the district court was mistaken to think that rates are to be set only in adjudicative proceedings before the Illinois Commerce Commission.

This court has held that whether to allow the filing of an amicus curiae brief is a matter of "judicial grace." National Organization for Women, Inc. v. Scheidler, 223 F.3d 615, 616 (7th Cir. 2000). The judges of this court will therefore not grant rote permission to file such a brief, and in particular they will deny permission to file an amicus brief that essentially duplicates a party's brief. Id. at 617. The reasons for the policy are several: judges have heavy caseloads and therefore need to minimize extraneous reading; amicus briefs, often solicited by parties, may be used to make an end run around court-imposed limitations on the length of parties' briefs; the time and other resources required for the preparation and study of, and response to, amicus briefs drive up the cost of litigation; and the filing of an amicus brief is often an attempt to inject interest group politics into the federal appeals process. Id. at 616.

All this said, comity might seem to be a compelling reason to allow the filing of an amicus curiae brief by the leaders of a state legislature in an appeal concerning the validity of a statute of their state; and there is no doubt that a union has an interest in the regulatory regime for an employer of its members. It might be argued therefore that I should not trouble myself to determine whether the proposed amicus curiae briefs fill gaps in or otherwise productively supplement the parties' briefs. No doubt many courts would reason so, or would prefer to ignore amicus curiae briefs than to screen them. But in my view the argument from comity bespeaks a misunderstanding of the difference between the legislative and the judicial processes. The legislative process is democratic, and so legislators have an entirely legitimate interest in determining how interest groups and influential constituents view a proposed statute. Statutes pass because there is more political muscle behind than in front of them, not because they are "wise" or "just," though they may be. The judicial process, in contrast, though "political" in a sense when judges are asked to decide cases that conventional legal materials, such as statutory and constitutional texts and binding precedent, leave undetermined, so that some mixture of judges' values, temperament, ideology, experiences, and even emotions is likely to determine the outcome, is not democratic in the sense of basing decision on the voting or campaign-financing power of constituents and interest groups. An appeal should therefore not resemble a congressional hearing.

The fact that powerful public officials or business or labor organizations support or oppose an appeal is a datum that is irrelevant to judicial decision making, except in a few cases, of which this not one, in which the position of a nonparty has legal significance. And even in those cases the position can usually be conveyed by a letter or affidavit more concisely and authoritatively than by a brief.

No matter who a would-be amicus curiae is, therefore, the criterion for deciding whether to permit the filing of an amicus brief should be the same: whether the brief will assist the judges by presenting ideas, arguments, theories, insights, facts, or data that are not to be found in the parties' briefs. The criterion is more likely to be satisfied in a case in which a party is inadequately represented; or in which the would-be amicus has a direct interest in another case that may be materially affected by a decision in this case; or in which the amicus has a unique perspective or specific information that can assist the court beyond what the parties can provide. National Organization for Women, Inc. v. Scheidler, supra, 223 F.3d at 616–17; Ryan v. CFTC, 125 F.3d 1062, 1063 (7th Cir. 1997) (chambers opinion); Georgia v. Ashcroft, 195 F. Supp. 2d 25, 32 (D.D.C. 2002). In my experience in two decades as an appellate judge, however, it is very rare for an amicus curiae brief to do more than repeat in somewhat different language the arguments in the brief of the party whom the amicus is supporting. Those who pay lawyers to prepare such briefs are not getting their money's worth.

While the amicus briefs sought to be filed in this case contain a few additional citations not found in the parties' briefs and slightly more analysis on some points, essentially they cover the same ground the appellants, in whose support they wish to file, do. (The state legislators' brief is a mere seven and a half pages long.) This is not a case in which a party is inadequately represented, or the would-be amici have a direct interest in another case that may be materially affected by a decision in this one, or they are articulating a distinctive perspective or presenting specific information, ideas, arguments, etc. that go beyond what the parties whom the amici are supporting have been able to provide. Essentially, the proposed amicus briefs merely announce the "vote" of the amici on the decision of the appeal. But, as I have been at pains to emphasize in contrasting the legislative and judicial processes, they have no vote.

So saying, I intend no criticism of the movants and in particular no disrespect to Illinois's senior legislative leaders. Nor do I mean to equate states with private persons as would-be participants in litigation in which they are not named as parties at the outset and perhaps do not wish to become parties. A state is entitled to file an amicus curiae brief without leave of court. Fed. R. App. P. 29(a). But Messrs. Madigan and Jones do not purport to be representing the state; nor is their brief signed by the state's attorney general; and they sought leave to file it, which a state need not do. The state could have intervened in the litigation as a matter of right, 28 U.S.C. § 2403(b), but has not done so— maybe the reason it didn't do so is that the state is already a party, because the commissioners of the Illinois Commerce Commission were named as defendants in the case, although the district court granted their motion to be declared nominal parties and to be excused from briefing and pleading requirements and only SBC filed a notice of appeal.

There is something to be said for asking the state to speak in litigation with one voice. And insofar as the district court in the decision that has been appealed placed limitations on what a state legislature may do, not only in this case but presumably in any like case that should arise in the future, it might seem that the leaders of the legislature have a direct interest in other cases, one of the situations in which amicus participation is appropriate. But that argument would imply that any state legislator should have a right to file an amicus curiae brief when the constitutionality of state legislation is challenged—an extreme position that could invite a blizzard of briefs.

The "viewpoint of state officials" to which the Madigan–Jones brief refers does not appear to be any different from that of SBC. Naturally the legislative leaders wish to preserve the prerogatives of state legislatures against federal constitutional challenge, but SBC has the same goal and has briefed the issue more than adequately.

For the reasons explained, the motions for leave to file amicus curiae briefs are DENIED.

Notes and Questions

1. The Seventh Circuit rejected the application of the Illinois Chamber of Commerce to participate in an environmental litigation involving a coal-fired power plant. With respect to potential amicus participation of the

Chamber, the Court found that the Chamber does not have "an interest relating to the property or transaction which is the subject of the action"; its concern is not a legal "interest" (the permit at stake affects only one power plant) "but a political or programmatic one: the Chamber favors more business and less environmental regulation. That does not justify intervention. Indeed, it does not necessarily justify even a filing as amicus curiae. Courts value submissions not to see how the interest groups line up, but to learn about facts and legal perspectives that the litigants have not adequately developed." See Sierra Club v. Environmental Protection Agency, 358 F.3d 516 (7th Cir. 2004).

2. An amicus curiae, by definition, is a friend of the court, not necessarily of the appellant. As one federal appellate court summed up the concern: "An amicus may support the appellant, preferably by providing a broader perspective than the appellant, who may be solely interested in winning its case. But an appellant and an amicus may not split up the issues and expect the court to consider that they have all been raised on appeal. It is the appellant's case, not a joint appeal by the appellant and amicus. Appellant must raise in its opening brief all the issues it wishes the court to address." Amoco Oil Co. v. United States, 234 F.3d 1374 (Fed. Cir. 2000).

3. Amici do not commonly argue the case orally but on occasion, particularly where an amicus is appointed to brief issues on the side of a pro se or incarcerated appellant, the amicus may be permitted to argue the case. See United States v. Hammer, 226 F.3d 229, 231 (3rd Cir. 2000)(federal death penalty appeal; efforts were also made to arrange video hookup allowing the inmate to participate on closed circuit TV).

2. RAISING ARGUMENTS AND BEING HEARD AS AN AMICUS

ELDRED v. ASHCROFT

United States Court of Appeals, District of Columbia Circuit, 2001.
255 F.3d 849.

GINSBURG, CIRCUIT JUDGE:

The plaintiffs-appellants in this case, corporations, associations, and individuals who rely for their vocations and avocations upon works in the public domain, have petitioned for rehearing and filed a suggestion for rehearing en banc. They renew their contentions that the Copyright Term Extension Act of 1998 (CTEA), Pub. L. No. 105–298, 112 Stat. 2827, violates both the First Amendment and the Copyright Clause of the Constitution of the United States.

The plaintiffs-appellants further complain that this court erred in its treatment of the contentions advanced by one of the amici. We are not persuaded. The district court's rejection of the plaintiffs-appellants' constitutional attack followed from its conclusion, in the light of our decision in Schnapper v. Foley, 667 F.2d 102, 112 (1981), that "the introductory language of the copyright clause does not limit [the Congress's] power." Upon appeal, the plaintiffs-appellants did not challenge that determination; rather, they maintained only that the substantive grant of power in the Copyright Clause—authorizing the Congress to grant copyrights for "limited Times"—does not authorize the Congress to extend the terms of copyrights as it did in the CTEA. In sharp contrast, an amicus contended that the CTEA violates the preamble to the Copyright Clause because extending the term of a subsisting copyright does not "promote the Progress of Science and useful Arts."

As we stated in Part III of our opinion, 239 F.3d 372, 378 (2001), the court deems it "particularly inappropriate" in this case to reach the merits of the amicus's position. To elaborate: First, in their brief the plaintiffs-appellants themselves took the position, diametrically opposed to that of the amicus, "that the preamble of the Copyright Clause is not a substantive limit on Congress' legislative power"; when expressly offered the opportunity at oral argument to adopt the position of the amicus, the plaintiffs-appellants did not do so. Therefore, even if we were to read the plaintiffs-appellants' brief broadly as raising the issue whether the Copyright Clause as a whole—including both the preamble and the grant of authority—renders the CTEA unconstitutional, following the lead of the Supreme Court we would still not reach what would then be the supporting argument of the amicus. See New Jersey v. New York, 523 U.S. 751, 781 n.3 (1998) (although arguments of amici and party stem from same article of compact, court "must pass over the arguments of the named amici for the reason that . . . the party to the case has in effect renounced them, or at least any benefit they might provide"); see also Amax Land Co. v. Quarterman, 181 F.3d 1356, 1367 (D.C. Cir. 1999) (remanding where the parties "requested us to remand to the district court for consideration of [legal] issue," whereas "the amicus' preferred that we resolve it" ourselves, which we could readily have done); Narragansett Indian Tribe v. Nat'l Indian Gaming Comm'n, 158 F.3d 1335, 1338 (D.C. Cir. 1998) ("Because we ordinarily do not entertain arguments not raised by parties . . . we consider only the [party's] equal protection challenge" where amicus filed brief "supporting [party's] equal protection claim and reiterating its separation of powers and bill of attainder arguments"); Michel v. Anderson, 14 F.3d 623, 625 (D.C. Cir. 1994) (court ordinarily "would not entertain an amicus 'argument if not presented by a party").

Second, the point advanced by the amicus—that the preamble of the Copyright Clause is a substantive limitation upon the power of the Congress—implicates discrete terms of the Clause that are not otherwise at issue. In that sense it poses an additional constitutional question, subject to the "rule of avoidance"; and there can hardly be a better reason to avoid a constitutional question than that the parties are in agreement. See, e.g., Ashwander v. Tennessee Valley Authority, 297 U.S. 288, 346, 80 L. Ed. 688, 56 S. Ct. 466 (1936) (Brandeis, J., concurring) ("Court will not 'anticipate a question of constitutional law in advance of the necessity of deciding it' ").

Third, because the plaintiffs-appellants did not take the same tack as the amicus, the Government did not on brief address the district court's interpretation of this court's decision in Schnapper. See New Jersey v. New York , 523 U.S. at 781 n.3. Therefore, our usual concern with "avoiding unnecessary or premature constitutional rulings," here as in Harmon v. Thornburgh, 278 U.S. App. D.C. 382, 878 F.2d 484, 494 (D.C. Cir. 1989), "is heightened by the absence of meaningful argument by the parties on this question."

Finally, as explained in Part III of the opinion, id. at 378–80, even if we considered the amicus's position we would not reach a different result in this case: Regardless whether, as the amicus contends, the preamble limits the power of the Congress, the CTEA still passes muster under the "necessary and proper review" applicable to the Congress's "exercise of a power enumerated in Article I." 239 F.3d at 378. The Congress found that extending the duration of copyrights on existing works would, among other things, give copyright holders an incentive to preserve older works, particularly motion pictures in need of restoration. Id. at 379. "Preserving access to works that would otherwise disappear— not enter the public domain but disappear—'promotes Progress' as surely as does stimulating the creation of new works." Id.

We reject the plaintiffs-appellants' challenge under the First Amendment for the reasons stated in the prior opinion. Accordingly, the petition for rehearing is Denied.

ORDER:

Appellants' petition for rehearing en banc and the response thereto have been circulated to the full court. The taking of a vote was requested. Thereafter, a majority of the judges of the court in regular active service did not vote in favor of the petition. Upon consideration of the foregoing, it is DENIED.

SENTELLE, Circuit Judge, dissenting from the denial of rehearing en banc, with whom Circuit Judge TATEL joins:

In my view, the decision in this case is not only incorrect, but is worthy of en banc review on both circuit-specific procedural grounds and fundamental constitutional grounds.

First, procedurally, the Court's opinion in this case effectively eliminates any role for amicus curiae in the practice of this circuit, when it holds that an argument raised by an amicus may not be considered by the Court. See Eldred v. Reno, 239 F.3d 372, 378 (D.C. Cir. 2001). There is no dispute that an amicus curiae may not raise new issues in an appeal. Rather, the role of an amicus is to assist the court in addressing the issues already raised with new arguments and perspectives. In this case, the issue before the Court was, in the panel's words, "whether . . . the Copyright Clause of the Constitution of the United States constrains the Congress from extending for a period of years the duration of copyrights, both those already extant and those yet to come." Eldred, 239 F.3d at 373. The amicus brief submitted on behalf of Eagle Forum addressed this issue more persuasively than did appellants. But amicus did not "expand the scope" of the appeal by "implicating issues" not raised by the appellant. See Resident Council of Allen Parkway Vill. v. HUD, 980 F.2d 1043, 1049 (5th Cir. 1993) ("We are constrained only by the rule that an amicus curiae generally cannot expand the scope of an appeal to implicate issues that have not been presented by the parties to the appeal." (emphases added)). Rather, as the majority noted, amicus adopted a different "argument." Eldred, 239 F.3d at 378. A new "argument" is not a new "issue." This is clear from our circuit's rules. Specifically, an amicus brief "must avoid repetition of facts or legal arguments made in the principal (appellant/petitioner or appellee/respondent) brief and focus on points not made or adequately elaborated upon in the principal brief, although relevant to the issues before this court." Circuit Rule 29. The role of amici is to help in this process, by elaborating upon arguments made by the parties and presenting arguments of their own that bear upon the issues raised by the parties themselves. See White v. Illinois, 502 U.S. 346, 352, 116 L. Ed. 2d 848, 112 S. Ct. 736 (1992) ("We consider as a preliminary matter an argument not considered below but urged by the United States as amicus curiae in support of respondent.").

"When an issue or claim is properly before the court, the court is not limited to the particular legal theories advanced by the parties, but rather retains the independent power to identify and apply the proper construction of governing law." Kamen v. Kemper Fin. Servs., Inc., 500 U.S. 90, 99, 114 L. Ed. 2d 152, 111 S. Ct. 1711 (1991); see also United States Nat'l Bank of Oregon v. Indep. Ins. Agents of Am. Inc., 508 U.S. 439, 446, 124 L. Ed. 2d 402, 113 S. Ct. 2173 (1993) (same). Merely because the parties fail to advance the proper legal theory underlying their claim does not—indeed cannot—prevent a court from arriving at the proper legal disposition. Once the issue is raised, a court has an obligation to determine what the law is which will govern the case at hand. This is so irrespective of whether amici curiae enter an appearance. As it happened, Eagle Forum submitted an amicus curiae brief augmenting appellants' position by making a different argument on the issue before the Court, and at least one member of the panel found it persuasive. Even if the majority did not find amicus's argument compelling, it was properly before the Court.

The majority holds that the "argument" raised by one amicus was "not properly before" this Court because it was effectively renounced by appellants. Eldred, 239 F.3d at 378. This claim is not supported by the record. The relevant amicus brief was submitted some two weeks after appellants' opening brief. Insofar as the oral argument transcript shows anything at all, it illustrates that appellants had not explicitly adopted amicus's arguments in brief but had no problem taking advantage of amicus's argument.[1]

---

1. The relevant portion of the transcript reads as follows:

THE COURT: Have you adopted any point—any arguments that appear in any of these amicus briefs? Or maybe—I don't re-

member—there is more than one, but in any brief other than your own?

[LARRY] LESSIG: Well, in particular, Mr. Jaffe's brief is a brief that makes textu-

The language of New Jersey v. New York, 523 U.S. 767, 781 n.3, 140 L. Ed. 2d 993, 118 S. Ct. 1726 (1998), might be taken to suggest that a court must "pass over ... arguments" raised only by an amicus, but I believe that this is a misreading of the case. In *New Jersey*, the Court noted that only amici took issue with the special master's conclusion affirming the Court's prior holding that "the 'boundary line' between the States established in Article First [of the Interstate Compact]" was the line of sovereignty between the states. Id. at 781. In other words, the amici, and only the amici, sought to overturn Supreme Court precedent. Additionally, insofar as the amici sought to make an exception to the special master's finding with regard to Article First of the compact, it sought to obtain the Court's judgment about a matter about which there was no present controversy. See United States v. Louisiana, 446 U.S. 253, 260–61, 64 L. Ed. 2d 196, 100 S. Ct. 1618 (special master's recommendation not subject to exception by either party accepted by Court due to lack of "present controversy"), reh'g denied, 447 U.S. 930, 65 L. Ed. 2d 1110, 100 S. Ct. 3007 (1980). Thus, even though the Court used the word "argument" to characterize the claims put forward by amici, they were raising issues beyond the purview of the case before the Court.

Contrary to the suggestion of the panel majority, appellants' argument did implicate the "preamble" of the Copyright Clause, just not in the same fashion as amicus. Appellants stipulated to the reading postulated by the district court, as the panel majority notes. Appellants' Opening Brief at 29 n.15. Yet in the very footnote cited by the panel majority, appellants claimed that the remaining portions of the Copyright Clause must be read "in light of the preamble." Id. Contrary to my colleagues' suggestion, this Court was not asked to "anticipate" a question of constitutional law, but to decide a very discreet question— whether the CTEA exceeds the grant of power in the Copyright Clause. Whether appellants asked this Court to recognize that the so-called "preamble" is in fact the enumerated power, or merely to read the rest of the clause "in light of that preamble" should be immaterial. Indeed, the Supreme Court noted long ago that the words of the Copyright Clause should be read "with the words and sentences with which it stands connected." Wheaton v. Peters, 33 U.S. (8 Peters) 591, 661, 8 L. Ed. 1055 (1834); see also Postmaster–General v. Early, 25 U.S. (12 Wheat.) 136, 152, 6 L. Ed. 577 (1827) (it is a "cardinal rule of construction" that "the whole law is to be taken together, and one part expounded by any other which may indicate the meaning annexed ... to ambiguous phrases").

Under the panel's holding, it is now the law of this circuit that amici are precluded both from raising new issues and from raising new arguments. If allowed to stand, this holding will effectively bar future

alist arguments that we believe are quite strong in this way.

    THE COURT: Is there any place in which you have adopted them, in your briefs?

    LESSIG: We formally acknowledge them in our briefs. I don't believe we have, Your Honor, no.

amici from adding anything except possibly rhetorical flourish to arguments already outlined and embraced by the parties. This is particularly the case for those amici who, true to their traditional role as "friends of the court," operate independently to assist the Court in its determinations. If this Court is to adopt such a rule—and I hope we do not—we should do so sitting en banc, not by a divided panel.

3. THE POSSIBILITY OF "AMICUS–PLUS" STATUS

Some courts have attempted to permit a hybrid form of participation sometimes referred to (pejoratively?) as "amicus plus" status. For example, in Maine v. United States Fish & Wildlife Serv., 262 F.3d 13 (1st Cir. 2001) the National Marine Fisheries Service and the U.S. Fish and Wildlife Service issued a final decision designating Atlantic Salmon in an area comprised of seven Maine rivers to be an endangered species protected from capture under the Endangered Species Act. 16 U.S.C. §§ 1531–1544. Several weeks later, the State of Maine and business group plaintiffs sued to have the decision set aside. Several conservation groups, Defenders of Wildlife, Biodiversity Foundation, Conservation Action Project, Forest Ecology Network, and Coastal Waters Project, sought to intervene, also attempting to defend the designation of the Atlantic Salmon as an endangered species. The chief argument of the "Defenders" group was that the federal departments involved had recently been their adversaries in earlier litigation, which the Defenders had brought to force the services to protect the salmon, and this meant the United States did not and could not adequately represent the conservation groups' interests. No party opposed the intervention—but the district court nonetheless denied intervention. Instead, the trial judge said that the court would allow Defenders to participate in the litigation on an amicus-plus status. "As amicus-plus, Defenders have the right to submit briefs (including arguments not presented by the government), a limited right to call and cross-examine witnesses, and a right to receive notice and service of all documents and events as if they were parties in the case. Defenders appealed from the denial of intervention. The plaintiff business interests appeared to defend the district court's order as within its discretion. The State of Maine did not take a position on the appeal.

UNITED STATES v. STATE OF MICHIGAN

United States Court of Appeals, Sixth Circuit, 1991.
940 F.2d 143.

KRUPANSKY, CIRCUIT JUDGE.

The five orders of the United States District Court for the Western District of Michigan [holding the State of Michigan in contempt] presently under appellate review, had their common genesis in the ongoing implementation of a consent decree approved by the court on July 16, 1984 resolving a case * * * pursuant to the Civil Rights of Institutionalized Persons Act (CRIPA), 42 U.S.C. § 1997 et seq. [raising issues of prisoner classification, population limits, and medical care of inmates].

As discussed earlier, the "Knop plaintiffs," inmates in the subject prisons, were denied the right to intervene in this action. However, the district court permitted them to participate in the traditional role of amicus curiae. In July 1984, Michigan and the United States entered into a consent decree and extended the traditional role of amicus curiae to the extent that the defendants were to furnish amicus curiae with reports, plans, pleadings, memoranda, and other documents submitted to the United States and the court pursuant to paragraphs I, J, K, and L of the consent decree. The United States was also to furnish amicus with its responses, if any. The consent decree also permitted the Knop class to respond to any of those materials and to exercise, within the discretion of the trial court, its traditional privileges of participating in any hearing conducted by the court by brief and oral argument.

In July, 1988, after several years of compliance litigation, * * * and over the objections of the United States and Michigan, the district court conferred "litigating amicus curiae" status upon the Knop class. The Knop class subsequently dismissed its pending, parallel civil rights action. This change of status expanded the Knop plaintiffs' role in this action beyond that specified in the consent decree. As ordered by the court, the Knop class as "litigating amicus curiae" was extended full litigating rights of a named party to the action including, but not limited to, the right to file pleadings, conduct discovery, introduce evidence at proceedings, issue and enforce subpoenas, present and enforce the attendance of witnesses, initiate and pursue proceedings in contempt, and file motions to modify and amend the agreement between the United States and Michigan embodied in the July 16, 1984 consent decree and state plan.

There can be little doubt from the record of this appeal that the Knop class, in its role of "litigating amicus curiae" and exercising the authority of a named party/real party in interest, has virtually assumed effective control of the proceedings in derogation of the original parties to this controversy. The creation of this legal mutant characterized as "litigating amicus curiae," as demonstrated by the cascading acrimony among the participants to this litigation, if accorded precedential viability, will implicate and erode the future core stability of American adversary jurisprudence as we know it today. Neither the appellees nor the trial court have advanced, beyond conclusory generalizations and conjecture, a persuasive argument that the trial court's "litigating amicus curiae" order, whatever that term implies, does not seriously impinge the inherent rights of the only real parties in interest to this CRIPA litigation between the United States and Michigan. The district court's order has, by extrajudicial edict, impressed upon the United States and Michigan a third-party legal interloper in the persona of the NPP–ACLU and the ACLUFM acting through their structured willing surrogate, the Knop class, all of whom had been denied real-party-in-interest status and whose efforts to achieve that end had been earlier barred by the trial court. The legal consequence of the district court's order was to achieve, by circumvention, a result that effectively and impermissibly abused all conventional laws and judicial rules of civil practice and procedure for acquiring the status and rights of a named party/real party in interest, including Fed.R.Civ.P. 14 and 17 through 25.

Challenged by the characterization of "litigating amicus curiae," which is not referenced in any legal dictionary, congressional enactment, judicial promulgation, the Federal Criminal Code and Rules, nor the Federal Civil Judicial Procedures and Rules, this court conducted exhaustive research in an effort to search for the identity of this illusive trial court-created mutant. Although a limited number of district courts within the Fifth, Ninth, and Eleventh Circuits and the Ninth Circuit Court of Appeals on a single occasion have applied the characterization of "litigating amicus curiae" to nonparties in interest to a cause of action, the cases afford no assistance in defining or positioning the concept within the evolution of American adversary jurisprudence because, in each instance, the participation of a "litigating amicus curiae" was permitted by agreement of the named parties to the controversy.[13] Accordingly, integral to this appeal as an issue of first impression is the identification of this elusive apparition "litigating amicus curiae."

Historically, "amicus curiae" was defined as one who interposes "in a judicial proceeding to assist the court by giving information, or otherwise, or who conduct[s] an investigation or other proceeding on request or appointment therefor by the court." 4 Am.Jur.2d, Am. Cur. § 1, at 109 (1962). See Leigh v. Engle, 535 F. Supp. 418, 419–20 (N.D. Ill. 1982). Its purpose was to provide impartial information on matters of law about which there was doubt, especially in matters of public interest. Miller–Wohl Co. v. Commissioner of Labor & Indus., State of Montana, 694 F.2d 203, 204 (9th Cir. 1982); 4 Am.Jur.2d, Am.Cur. §§ 1, 2 at 109–10; Leigh, 535 F. Supp. at 420. The orthodox view of amicus curiae was, and is, that of an impartial friend of the court—not an adversary party in interest in the litigation. Miller–Wohl, 694 F.2d at 204. The position of classical amicus in litigation was not to provide a highly partisan account of the facts, but rather to aid the court in resolving doubtful issues of law. New England Patriots Football Club, Inc. v. University of Colorado, 592 F.2d 1196, 1198 n.3 (1st Cir. 1979); Leigh, 535 F. Supp. at 420. Over the years, however, some courts have departed from the orthodoxy of amicus curiae as an impartial friend of the court and have recognized a very limited adversary support of given issues through brief and/or oral argument. Funbus Sys., Inc. v. California Pub. Util. Comm'n, 801 F.2d

13. Appellees have cited the following cases to support their claim that a "litigating amicus" is an entity recognized by the federal court system: Hoptowit v. Ray, 682 F.2d 1237 (9th Cir. 1982); Dove v. Chattanooga Area Regional Transp. Auth., 701 F.2d 50 (6th Cir. 1983), aff'g 539 F. Supp. 36 (E.D. Tenn. 1981); In re Estelle, 516 F.2d 480 (5th Cir. 1975); DeVonish v. Garza, 510 F. Supp. 658 (W.D. Tex. 1981); Pugh v. Locke, 406 F. Supp. 318 (M.D. Ala. 1976); Morales v. Turman, 364 F. Supp. 166 (E.D. Tex. 1973); Wyatt v. Stickney, 344 F. Supp. 373 (M.D. Ala. 1972). These cases do not, however, aid appellee's proposition. In none of the cases was the concept of "litigating amicus curiae" nor the scope of their participation addressed by the court as an issue, nor was the term defined within the context of a "case or controversy" seeking the resolution of the court. The term "litigating amicus curiae" does not appear nor is it alluded to in the Estelle, Wyatt, Pugh, Morales, or Dove opinions.

1120, 1124–25 (9th Cir. 1986); Krislov, The Amicus Curiae Brief: from Friendship to Advocacy, 72 Yale L.J. 694 (1963).

Classical participation as an amicus to brief and argue as a friend of the court was, and continues to be, a privilege within "the sound discretion of the courts," see Northern Sec. Co. v. United States, 191 U.S. 555, 24 S. Ct. 119, 48 L. Ed. 299 (1903); 4 Am. Jur. 2d, Am. Cur. § 4 at 113, depending upon a finding that the proffered information of amicus is timely, useful, or otherwise necessary to the administration of justice. Leigh, 535 F. Supp. at 420. Amicus, however, has never been recognized, elevated to, or accorded the full litigating status of a named party or a real party in interest, Miller–Wohl Co., 694 F.2d at 204, and amicus has been consistently precluded from initiating legal proceedings, filing pleadings, or otherwise participating and assuming control of the controversy in a totally adversarial fashion. Moten v. Bricklayers, Masons and Plasterers Int'l Union of Am., 543 F.2d 224, 227 (D.C. Cir. 1976) (per curiam) (amicus may not appeal judgments); State ex rel. Baxley v. Johnson, 293 Ala. 69, 300 So. 2d 106, 111 (1974) (per curiam) (amicus is not a party and cannot assume the functions of a party nor control litigation); Silverberg v. Industrial Comm'n, 24 Wis. 2d 144, 128 N.W.2d 674, 680 (1964) (amicus brief seeking to challenge validity of testimony in the record stricken because attempt to challenge was not a proper function of amicus); 4 Am. Jur. 2d, Am. Cur. §§ 3, 6 at 111, 114. See City of Winter Haven v. Gillespie, 84 F.2d 285 (5th Cir. 1936). Historically, an amicus could not join issues not joined by the parties in interest, e.g., National Comm'n on Egg Nutrition v. F.T.C., 570 F.2d 157, 160 n.3 (7th Cir. 1977); In re Buffalo, 394 N.Y.S.2d 919, 921 (1977); Phoenix v. Phoenix Civic Auditorium & Convention Center Ass'n, 99 Ariz. 270, 408 P.2d 818, 821 (1965) (amicus cannot create, extend, or enlarge issue), and was not bound by the judgments in actions in which amicus was permitted to brief or argue. Munoz v. County of Imperial, 667 F.2d 811, 816–17 (9th Cir. 1982); TRW, Inc. v. Ellipse Corp., 495 F.2d 314, 318 (7th Cir. 1974); 4 Am. Jur. 2d, Am. Cur. § 3, at 112.

Historically, there has been a bright-line distinction between amicus curiae and named parties/real parties in interest in a case or controversy. Standing to litigate equal to that exercised by named parties/real parties in interest may be acquired or conferred only pursuant to Fed.R.Civ.P. 14 and 17 through 25. See Ex parte Cutting, 94 U.S. 12, 20–21, 24 L. Ed. 69 (1876) (in pre-Civil Rules case, Supreme Court recognized intervention only upon petition for formal intervention, which was granted either expressly or through the actions of the lower court consistent with intervention); Miller–Wohl, 694 F.2d at 204 ("A petition to intervene and its express or tacit grant are prerequisites to this treatment [as an intervenor].") The intent and purpose of the Federal Rules should not be evaded by acts of judicial legerdemain. Amicus curiae may not and, at least traditionally, has never been permitted to rise to the level of a named party/real party in interest nor has an amicus curiae been conferred with the authority of an intervening party of right without complying with the requirements of Fed.R.Civ.P. 24(a), nor accorded permissible intervention without meeting the criteria of Fcd.R.Civ.P. 24(b). Only a named party or an intervening real party in interest is entitled to litigate on the merits, e.g., Miller–Wohl, 694 F.2d at 204; Schneider v. Dumbarton Developers, Inc., 767 F.2d 1007, 1017 (D.C. Cir. 1985); Gilbert v. Johnson, 601 F.2d 761, 768 (5th Cir. 1979) (Rubin, J., concurring); cf. Ross v. Bernhard, 396 U.S. 531, 541 n.15, 90 S. Ct. 733, 740 n.15, 24 L. Ed. 2d 729 (1970), and there is little doubt from the record that the district court, in the instant case, has conferred named party/real party in interest status upon the Knop class under the appellation of "litigating amicus curiae" and has invested the Knop class with equal standing to litigate this CRIPA action on the merits, thus divesting the original parties, the United States and the State of Michigan, of effective control of their litigation. It is reasonable to conclude from the evolution of amicus curiae that the judicial fiat of "litigating amicus curiae" in the instant case transcends the traditional concept of that term within accepted jurisprudence.

Forgetting, for the moment, the lexicology applied by the trial court to its judicial creativity and juxtaposing the broad authority conferred upon the Knop class with the rights equal to those of a named party/real party in interest, it becomes facially apparent that the trial court has, subsequent to the execution of the court-approved consent decree, by judicial legislation, impressed upon the United States as plaintiff and the State of Michigan as defendant in this CRIPA action an intruder with equal litigating rights of a named party/real party in interest, thereby subverting the right of the United States and Michigan to effectively control the future course of the proceedings.

The record of these turbulent proceedings attests to the position, declared in open court, of the NPP–ACLU and the ACLUFM that their interests and the interests of the Knop class were and continue to be adverse to the interests of both the United States and Michigan, the real parties in interest to this litigation. The unnecessary, overly intrusive, and indiscriminate course of litigating conduct demonstrated by the Knop amicus curiae in exercising the court-conferred litigating rights equal to a named party/real party in interest have exacerbated, if not caused, much of the discord, bitter confrontation, and continuing acrimony that has pervaded these proceedings since it moved to secure its domination over the directional course and objectives of these post-judgment proceedings, all of which has noticeably protracted and impeded the orderly implementation of the consent decree and delayed the benefits and results anticipated to be derived therefrom. To condone the fiction of "litigating amicus curiae," in reality an extrajudicial, de facto named party/real party in interest, would extend carte blanche discretion to a trial judge to convert the trial court into a free-wheeling forum of competing special interest groups capable of frustrating and undermining the ability of the named parties/real parties in interest to expeditiously resolve their own dispute and capable of complicating the court's ability to perform its judicial function. The record fails to disclose any result, beyond disrupting the implementation of a court-approved, negotiated consent decree, that the NPP–ACLU, the ACLUFM, and the Knop class cannot achieve as traditional amicus curiae without the necessity of opening this judicial Pandora's box and releasing a prolific source of legal confusion upon the bench, the bar, and the public in this and future cases in controversy.

Accordingly, it is the conclusion of this court that the Knop class is without standing to compel the disclosure of internal medical/mental health/dental care draft peer audits pursuant to the district court's order of April 4, 1990, or to exercise any litigating rights equal to a named party/real party in interest conferred by the district court under the characterization of "litigating amicus curiae" including, as a condition precedent for court consideration, the right to endorse or veto any state-proposed action. The Knop class is, however, not precluded from continued participation in this action in the traditional role of amicus curiae, and may, within the discretion of the court, argue its adversarial position either orally or by written briefs. Michigan shall continue to furnish the Knop class with informational copies of all "reports, plans, pleadings, memoranda, or other documentation" it has agreed to furnish to the court and the United States pursuant to paragraphs I, J, K, and L of the consent decree. Accordingly, the April 4, 1990 order of the district court is REVERSED.

It is ordered that this consolidated appeal is REMANDED to the district court for further proceedings not inconsistent with this decision.

Notes and Questions

1. Based on your current understanding of the various phases, maneuvers, steps and options in appellate practice, if there *were* such a thing as an amicus-plus *on appeal*, what rights or powers would you argue might be conferred on that "participating non-party"? Consider the comments of the Sixth Circuit in Stupak–Thrall v. Glickman, 226 F.3d 467, 467 (6th Cir. 2000):

> Finally, regarding the appellants' third stated purpose, the strength of the appellants' need to participate as parties in this litigation (instead of "only" as amici curiae) is necessarily commensurate with their first two stated purposes. Appellants want to be parties so that they can file motions and appeals, rather than merely amicus briefs—that is, appellants want some say in deciding litigation tactics. Appellants assert that, without these procedural protections, they can neither assure that the litigation will be pursued by the Federal Defendants nor that their positions will be made known to the concerned judicial tribunals. As noted, however, the circumstances of this case are such that the proposed intervenors cannot meaningfully differentiate their concerns from those of the Federal Defendants and, given the fundamental nature of the attack on the authority of the Forest Service, cannot legitimately believe the Federal Defendants might abandon the litigation. In such circumstances, the right to participate as amici curiae is both meaningful and adequate. In sum, the purposes for which appellants seek intervention provide, at most, only lukewarm support for their motion.

SECTION I. LOSING THE RIGHT TO APPEAL

1. THE GENERAL RULE: ACCEPTANCE OF BENEFITS AS WAIVER

"No rule is better settled than that a litigant who accepts the benefits or any substantial part of the benefits of a judgment or decree is thereby estopped from reviewing and escaping from its burdens. He cannot avail himself of its advantages, and then question its disadvantages in a higher court." Albright v. Oyster, 60 F. 644 (8th Cir. 1894). "The general rule is well settled that unless there is a separable controversy, or unless there is some sum to which the appealing party is entitled in any event, he may not accept the benefit of the decree and later appeal." Spencer v. Babylon R. Co., 250 F. 24, 26 (2d Cir. 1918)(L. Hand, J.).

LYON v. FORD MOTOR COMPANY

Supreme Court of North Dakota, 2000.
604 N.W.2d 453.

Neumann, Justice.

Ford Motor Company ("Ford") appealed from a judgment awarding Cary Lyon $10,360.84 in property damages. Because Ford voluntarily satisfied the judgment before appealing, we conclude Ford waived its right to appeal. We therefore dismiss the appeal.

I

On January 30, 1996, Lyon's 1994 Mercury Topaz was destroyed by fire while it was parked unoccupied in a Fargo parking lot. Lyon brought this action against Ford, seeking compensation for property damage. The action was based on theories of negligence, strict liability and breach of warranty. At the December 1998 trial, the court * * * submitted to the jury Lyon's theories of strict liability, negligence, negligent failure to warn and breach of warranty.

The jury returned a verdict in favor of Lyon on his strict liability claim, finding the Mercury Topaz was defective and the defect caused Lyon's damages. The jury also found Ford was not negligent, did not negligently fail to warn Lyon, and although Ford breached an express or implied warranty, that breach did not cause any damages.

Judgment in favor of Lyon for $10,360.84 was entered on February 24, 1999. Lyon requested payment from Ford the following day after receiving notice of entry of judgment. Ford paid Lyon the entire amount of the judgment on March 15, 1999, and Lyon filed a satisfaction of judgment on March 18, 1999. On April 27, 1999, this Court issued its decision in Clarys v. Ford Motor Company, 592 N.W.2d 573 (1999), holding the economic loss doctrine, which bars product liability tort claims when the only damage alleged is to the product itself, applies to consumer purchases. Ford filed its notice of appeal on April 30, 1999, and later received from the trial court an extension to file its notice of appeal under N.D.R.App.P. 4.

Relying on Clarys, Ford argues the trial court erred in denying its motion for judgment as a matter of law because Lyon's product liability tort claim was barred by the economic loss doctrine. Lyon has moved to dismiss Ford's appeal, arguing Ford waived its right to appeal by voluntarily satisfying the judgment.

II

This Court's decisions on the effect of the payment or satisfaction of a judgment on a party's right to appeal have not been consistent.

The most recent, and the longest line of North Dakota cases applies the general rule that a party who voluntarily pays a judgment against him waives the right to appeal from the judgment.[1] See Dakota Northwestern Bank Nat'l Ass'n v. Schollmeyer, 311 N.W.2d 164 (1981); Rolette County v. Pierce County, 80 N.W. 804, 805 (1899). Contrary to the Schollmeyer line of authority, however, other cases in this jurisdiction indicate voluntary payment or satisfaction of a judgment does not waive the right to appeal, if repayment may be enforced or the effect of compliance may be otherwise undone in case of reversal, and unless the payment was intended as a compromise or there was an express agreement to not pursue an appeal. See Workman v. Salzer Lumber Co., 199 N.W. 769, 770 (1924); Fisk v. Fehrs, 155 N.W. 676, 678–79 (1915); State ex rel. Wiles v. Albright, 88 N.W. 729, 731–32 (1901).

Courts in other jurisdictions apply various rules to determine whether payment or satisfaction of a judgment either constitutes a waiver of the right to appeal from the judgment or renders the appeal moot. See, e.g., Annot., Defeated party's payment or satisfaction of, or other compliance with, civil judgment as barring his right to appeal, 39 A.L.R.2d 153 (1955), and cases collected therein; 5 Am.Jur.2d Appellate Review § 623 (1995). Some of the most prevalent rules were summarized by the court in Lytle v. Citizens Bank of Batesville, 630 S.W.2d 546, 547 (Ark. App. 1982):

---

1. This principle is a variation of the similar general rule that one who accepts a substantial benefit of a judgment waives the right to appeal from the judgment. See, e.g., White v. White, 434 N.W.2d 361, 363–64 (N.D. 1989); Geier v. Geier, 332 N.W.2d 261, 264 (N.D. 1983). Even though the acceptance-of-benefits rule of waiver is conceptually related to the voluntary-payment-or-satisfaction-of-judgment rule of waiver, we have sharply limited the acceptance-of-benefits rule to promote a strong policy in favor of reaching the merits, particularly in domestic relations appeals. See, e.g., Wetzel v. Wetzel, 1999 ND 29, P5, 589 N.W.2d 889; Bangen v. Bartelson, 553 N.W.2d 754, 757 (N.D. 1996); Sulsky v. Horob, 357 N.W.2d 243, 245 (N.D. 1984). The limited application of the acceptance-of-benefits rule is justified in divorce cases because it is unreasonable for an appellant to have to choose between economic adversity and the right to appeal. See Spooner v. Spooner, 471 N.W.2d 487, 489–90 (N.D. 1991). Because of the obvious dissimilarity between satisfying a judgment in total and merely accepting some benefit of a multifaceted divorce judgment, and because of the absence of the policy considerations present in divorce cases, we find the acceptance-of-benefits cases unhelpful in resolving the issue in this case.

Some jurisdictions hold that the payment of a judgment under any circumstances bars the payer's right to appeal. However, in the majority of jurisdictions, the effect of the payment of a judgment upon the right of appeal by the payer is determined by whether the payment was voluntary or involuntary. In other words, if the payment was voluntary, then the case is moot, but if the payment was involuntary, the appeal is not precluded. The question which often arises under this rule is what constitutes an involuntary payment of a judgment. For instance, in some jurisdictions the courts have held that a payment is involuntary if it is made under threat of execution or garnishment. There are other jurisdictions, however, which adhere to the rule that a payment is involuntary only if it is made after the issuance of an execution or garnishment. Another variation of this majority rule is a requirement that if, as a matter of right, the payer could have posted a supersedeas bond, he must show that he was unable to post such a bond, or his payment of the judgment is deemed voluntary.

See also Metropolitan Development & Housing Agency v. Hill, 518 S.W.2d 754, 760–66 (Tenn. App. 1974).

A minority of courts have expressed a view similar to the one taken by this Court in Workman, Fisk and Albright, holding unless payment of a final judgment by a judgment debtor is shown to be made with the intent to compromise or settle the matter and to abandon the right to appeal, or the payment in some way makes relief impossible in case of reversal, the payment will not be deemed to either waive the right to appeal or moot the controversy. See, e.g., Dakota County v. Glidden, 113 U.S. 222, 224–25 (1885); Grand River Dam Authority v. Eaton, 803 P.2d 705, 709–10 (Okl. 1990); 11 Wright, Miller & Kane, Federal Practice and Procedure: Civil 2d § 2905, at pp. 525–26 (1995). The courts which follow the minority rule reason allowing the appeal after payment or satisfaction of the judgment simplifies matters by saving the costs of an execution and placing the funds immediately in the hands of the party who, if the appeal fails, will be ultimately entitled to them. Eaton, 803 P.2d at 709. They also reason failing to post a supersedeas bond is immaterial because posting a supersedeas bond is neither a prerequisite to nor a jurisdictional requirement for an appeal.

We reject the minority view, represented in North Dakota by Workman, Fisk and Albright, for both theoretical and practical reasons. The majority of courts view a judgment that is paid and satisfied of record as ceasing to have any existence. See Dorso Trailer Sales v. American Body & Trailer, Inc., 482 N.W.2d 771, 773 (Minn. 1992). Our statutory scheme similarly provides "[a] civil action in a district court is deemed to be pending from the time of its commencement until its final determination upon appeal or until the time for appeal has passed, unless the judgment is sooner satisfied." N.D.C.C. § 28–05–10 (emphasis added). Because a satisfaction of judgment extinguishes the claim, the controversy is deemed ended, leaving the appellate court with nothing to review. See

Becker v. Halliday, 218 Mich. App. 576, 554 N.W.2d 67, 69 (Mich. App. 1996).

The majority rule also promotes the interests of certainty and finality, and the judicial policy of furthering the intentions and legitimate expectations of the parties. See Dooley v. Cal–Cut Pipe & Supply, Inc., 197 Colo. 362, 593 P.2d 360, 362 (Colo. 1979). The rule that a judgment debtor waives the right to appeal is intended to prevent a party who voluntarily pays a judgment from later changing his mind and then seeking the court's aid in recovering payment. See McCallum v. Western Nat'l Mut. Ins. Co., 597 N.W.2d 307, 309 (Minn. App. 1999); Riner v. Briargrove Park Property Owners, Inc., 858 S.W.2d 370 (Tex. 1993). The Supreme Court of Texas reasoned in Highland Church of Christ v. Powell, 640 S.W.2d 235, 236 (Tex. 1982), "[a] party should not be allowed to mislead his opponent into believing that the controversy is over and then contest the payment and seek recovery."

There are existing avenues judgment debtors may pursue to protect themselves from judgment collection efforts during the pendency of an appeal. A supersedeas bond, which may be obtained under the provisions of N.D.R.Civ.P. 62 and N.D.R.App.P. 8, is designed to maintain the status quo and protect the judgment holder against any loss it may sustain as a result of an unsuccessful appeal. See Berg v. Berg, 530 N.W.2d 341, 343 (N.D. 1995). Judgment debtors also have the option of having the judgment released as a lien against their property by depositing sufficient funds with the clerk of the district court in which the judgment is entered. See N.D.C.C. § 28–20–29. Although neither avenue is a jurisdictional prerequisite to an appeal, we see no utility in judicially authorizing yet another avenue for protection from judgment collection efforts during the pendency of an appeal, which would result in little more than a rash of restitution suits for recovery of voluntary payments on later-reversed judgments. We agree with the reasoning of the dissent in Eaton, 803 P.2d at 712:

> The two statutory methods for suspending a judgment pending appeal cast on the judgment debtor the responsibility of securing the principal as well as the interest that will be due at litigation's end. By allowing the obligation's voluntary payment, the court implicitly holds that in the event of reversal the liability for interest will shift to the judgment creditor who will then be bound to make restitution of both the principal and the accrued interest. In my view, the court's pronouncement favors the wrong parties. It accommodates judgment debtors—the parties whose appeal prolongs the litigation's end. It is they who are relieved today from having to pay mid-appeal interest on affirmed judgments—an obligation they would bear if judgment were not paid but secured by either of the two statutory law's authorized methods. Creditors, on the other hand, do not fare as well; they will be stuck with mid-appeal interest when compelled to make restitution following a judgment's reversal. Unlike the court, I would leave undisturbed the legislative allocation of duty to secure mid-appeal interest. It should remain imposed on the appeal-

ing debtor. The party whose appeal postpones the obligation's legal finality should, in the event of affirmance, bear the onus of paying interest accruable during the period between the judgment and mandate dates.

We believe the majority view, represented in North Dakota by the Schollmeyer line of cases, is the better rule and we reaffirm that a party who voluntarily pays a judgment against him waives the right to appeal from the judgment. This view is shared by our sister states. See, e.g., Bartel v. New Haven Tp., 323 N.W.2d 806, 809 (Minn. 1982); Turner v. Mountain Engineering and Const., Inc., 276 Mont. 55, 915 P.2d 799, 804–05 (Mont. 1996); Ray v. Sullivan, 5 Neb. App. 942, 568 N.W.2d 267, 270–72 (Neb. App. 1997); Foster Lumber Co., Inc. v. Glad, 303 N.W.2d 815, 816 (S.D. 1981). This Court's decisions in Workman, Fisk and Albright are overruled to the extent they conflict with the Schollmeyer line of cases and the majority rule.

While a party who voluntarily pays a judgment waives the right to appeal, payment of a judgment under coercion or duress is not a waiver of the right to appeal. See Schollmeyer, 311 N.W.2d at 166. The burden is on the party moving to dismiss the appeal to show the judgment was voluntarily paid and satisfied. See Grady, 57 N.D. at 725, 223 N.W. at 938. Whether a judgment has been voluntarily paid and satisfied depends on the facts and circumstances of the particular case. See Signor, 13 N.D. at 45, 99 N.W. at 71. Where there is no showing other than that the judgment was paid, a presumption arises that the payment was voluntary.

It is undisputed Ford did not pay the judgment because Lyon initiated judgment collection procedures. Lyon did not execute on the judgment. Compare Grady (holding payment of judgment to sheriff armed with an execution is not voluntary so as to work waiver of the right to appeal) . Lyon requested payment from Ford, but made no threats of using legal process to collect the judgment. Although Ford sought to avoid accrued interest on the judgment and the "public relations disaster" which would have ensued if Lyon used legal process to enforce the judgment, these circumstances cannot fairly be interpreted as coercion or duress sufficient to render the payment involuntary. See Poppa Builders, Inc. v. Campbell, 118 Ohio App. 3d 251, 692 N.E.2d 647, 649–50 (Ohio App. 1997). These same allegedly coercive circumstances could be claimed in virtually any case, and Lyon was entitled to request payment because he had a right to payment of the money. See Campbell. Nothing in the record suggests Ford was unable to seek a supersedeas bond or deposit a sufficient amount with the clerk of district court, which would have stayed any enforcement of the judgment. Ford's payment of the judgment itself certainly indicates it had the financial ability to post an adequate appeal bond.

Rather, the record indicates Ford's payment was intended solely as a voluntary satisfaction of the judgment. When it satisfied the judgment, Ford did not indicate to Lyon in any manner it intended to reserve its right to appeal. Indeed, it appears Ford had no intention of appealing when it satisfied the judgment. Ford did not decide to appeal until this Court issued its decision in Clarys more than one month after Ford paid Lyon. The circumstances here are a classic example of what the majority rule was designed to prevent: allowing a party who voluntarily satisfied a judgment to change its mind and seek the court's aid in recovering payment.

Under the circumstances of this case, we conclude Ford voluntarily paid and satisfied the judgment, thereby waiving its right to appeal from the judgment. * * * The appeal is DISMISSED.

2. ARGUMENTS ABOUT "VOLUNTARINESS" OF COMPLIANCE

McCALLUM v. WESTERN NATIONAL MUTUAL INS. CO.

Minnesota Court of Appeals, 1999.
597 N.W.2d 307.

TOUSSAINT, CHIEF JUDGE.

FACTS

After Western National Mutual Insurance Company denied their claim for fire loss at their home, respondents Kim McCallum and Nancy McCallum sued for breach of contract. The jury rendered a verdict in respondents' favor, and judgment awarding respondents $202,699 was entered on December 29, 1998.

This appeal from the December 29, 1998, judgment was filed on February 26, 1999. In their statement of the case, respondents contended that the appeal was moot because appellant paid the judgment and a satisfaction of judgment was filed on or about February 4, 1999. This court questioned jurisdiction. The parties submitted memoranda.

Respondents served a writ of execution on or about January 19, 1999. In its jurisdiction memorandum, appellant states that it was unable to conduct any banking because its bank accounts were frozen after the writ was served. Appellant further states that its bank advised appellant that to release the bank accounts, appellant would have to pay the judgment and file a satisfaction of judgment immediately. On February 1, 1999, appellant forwarded payment to respondents without expressly reserving the right to appeal.

DECISION

Generally, a judgment that is "paid and satisfied of record ceases to have any existence." Dorso Trailer Sales v. American Body & Trailer, Inc., 482 N.W.2d 771, 773 (Minn. 1992) (citation omitted). A "voluntary" payment of damages without reserving the right to appeal results in waiver of appeal rights by satisfaction of the judgment. Bartel v. New Haven Township, 323 N.W.2d 806, 810 (Minn. 1982).

Here, appellant satisfied the judgment without expressly reserving its appeal rights. Because issuance of the writ of execution disrupted appellant's business operations, appellant argues that its payment was not voluntary.

Most jurisdictions hold that payment of a judgment following issuance of execution does not cut off the payor's right to appeal. See E.H. Schopler Annotation, Defeated Party's Payment or Satisfaction of, or Other Compliance With, Civil Judgment as Barring His Right to Appeal, 39 A.L.R.2d 153, 166–68 (1955). As the Texas Supreme Court has explained, the rule that a judgment debtor who voluntarily satisfies a judgment waives the right to appeal is intended to prevent a party who voluntarily pays a judgment from later changing his mind and seeking the court's aid in recovering payment. Riner v. Briargrove Park Property Owners, Inc., 858 S.W.2d 370, 370 (Tex. 1993). But a party does not "voluntarily" pay a judgment if the judgment is satisfied after execution. Id.

In accordance with the majority rule, we hold that appellant's satisfaction of the judgment after issuance of the writ of execution was involuntary and does not operate as a waiver of the right to seek appellate review. By contrast to Bartel, which involved voluntary payment, appellant's payment was not required to expressly reserve its appeal rights.

Respondents contend that appellant could have prevented execution on the judgment for a period of six months by filing a bond with the trial court administrator. See Minn. Stat. § 550.36 (1998) (providing for six-month stay of execution of judgment if judgment debtor files a bond for double the amount of judgment within ten days after entry). It appears that appellant could also have filed an appeal from the December 29, 1998, judgment and obtained a stay of execution by posting an appropriate supersedeas bond. See Minn. R. Civ. App. P. 108.01, subd. 1 (stating that appellant may obtain stay of enforcement by providing supersedeas bond or other security in amount and form which trial court shall order and approve).

A defeated party's compliance with the judgment does not bar an appeal merely because that party failed to obtain a stay of the proceedings or a supersedeas bond. Uyeda v. Brooks, 348 F.2d 633, 635 (6th Cir. 1965); Ronette Communications Corp. v. Lopez, 475 So. 2d 1360, 1361 (Fla. Dist. Ct. App. 1985). The Ronette court held that appellant "did not lose its right to appeal when it paid the judgment after execution to avoid a levy on its property." Ronette, 475 So. 2d at 1360. The court also reasoned that appellant's failure to obtain a stay of execution pending appeal was of "no legal import," because appellant's right to appeal was not conditioned on the posting of a supersedeas bond. Id. at 1361. Similarly, in Minnesota a supersedeas bond is not required to perfect an appeal. All Lease Co. v. Peters, 424 N.W.2d 320, 321 (Minn. App. 1988).

Here, appellant was faced with an emergency situation due to the freezing of its bank accounts as a result of the execution. Appellant's involuntary payment of the judgment did not waive the right to appeal.

Appeal to proceed.

3. EXCEPTIONS TO THE GENERAL RULE

MAY v. STRECKER

Minnesota Court of Appeals, 1990.
453 N.W.2d 549.

HUSPENI, J.

The automobile in which respondent Amy May was a passenger was rear-ended by an automobile driven by respondent Charles Strecker who earlier had been drinking [for four straight hours] at appellant E.J.'s, Inc. bar. The action arising out of this incident was tried to a jury which returned a verdict finding E.J.'s 25% negligent and Charles Strecker 75% negligent. Amy May was awarded $445,227 in damages. E.J.'s motion for judgment notwithstanding the verdict or, in the alternative, a new trial was denied and judgment was entered in accordance with the jury verdict. Insurers for Strecker and E.J.'s tendered their policy limits.

E.J.'s appeals from the denial of a new trial and the entry of judgment; Strecker from the entry of judgment. Amy May moves this court to dismiss the appeal or limit the issues on the grounds that appellants, by tendering part of the judgment, forfeited their right to appeal. We affirm on the merits of all issues appealed. * * *

The insurers of both E.J.'s and Strecker tendered their policy limits directly to Amy May, apparently making the unconditional tender to avoid being liable for continuing interest on the entire judgment. Amy argues that partial payment of the judgment by appellants constituted waiver and seeks to have this appeal dismissed or to bar any challenge to liability. Appellants argue that in any event Amy could have collected these amounts by executing on the trial court judgment, rendering the payment then neither voluntary nor unconditional.

In Bartel v. New Haven Township, 323 N.W.2d 806, 810 (Minn. 1982) the supreme court held that the voluntary payment of a judgment without reserving the right to appeal constitutes a waiver of the appeal rights. In Bartel the township was found 50% negligent and a judgment of $36,438.33 was entered against it. The township paid the judgment, received a partial satisfaction of judgment, and filed the satisfaction with the trial court. Id.

We find this case to be distinguishable from Bartel. There, the township was a party to the action and had direct control over whether payment on the judgment would be tendered. Here, the parties have no control over the insurers who tendered payment. In addition, the parties themselves remain liable for the remainder of the judgment. No satisfaction of judgment was received. It would be unfair in this situation to limit the parties' right to appeal because their insurers sought to limit the insurers' liability. The tender of the policy limits by the insurers is no indication of the parties' acceptance of the judgment. When parties remain personally liable for a portion of the judgment, their rights on appeal should not be affected by their insurers' tender of part of the judgment.

DECISION affirmed.

Notes and Questions

1. In the principal cases the penalty is the same—loss of the right to appeal. Should the same rule be applicable to the defendant who pays a judgment but still wants to appeal and to the plaintiff who accepts payment of the judgment but wants to challenge some portion of it? In the case of the defendant who pays the judgment, how can it be said that the payment is voluntary when enforcement will occur by operation of law unless the defendant takes some action to prevent it? If the judgment is reversed on appeal, the plaintiff will be forced to return the amount of the judgment or undo the action performed. Are there some cases in which this would be impractical or impossible? If so, is this any reason to apply the rule in all cases? Would it be sufficient if the defendant simply filed a document in court saying that he is complying with the judgment only under protest? Is the logic behind the rule that it would be easier for the defendant to obtain a supersedeas bond than pay the judgment? In Illinois it has been held that a person who accepts the benefits of a judgment is precluded from appeal only if the opposing party would be placed at a disadvantage following a reversal, rejecting the flat majority rule. See Del Muro v. Commonwealth Edison Co., 124 Ill.App.3d 473, 79 Ill.Dec. 868, 464 N.E.2d 772 (1984). Is this the better approach?

2. It is possible for the parties to agree that payment of the judgment will not waive the right of the paying party to appeal. See, e.g., La Moureaux v. Totem Ocean Trailer Express, 632 P.2d 539 (Alaska 1981)("The parties also entered into discussions concerning satisfaction of the judgment of the trial court. LaMoureaux's counsel sought to reach an agreement with counsel for Risinger and Sea Star for voluntary payment of the judgment without affecting the pending appeals. These negotiations broke down over LaMoureaux's refusal to guarantee return of any possible overpayment of attorney's fees."). If the parties agree, is the court bound? Does this mean that acceptance of the benefits is not jurisdictional?

3. The "voluntary payment" notion applies in criminal proceedings as well in many jurisdictions. See, e.g., State v. Griffin, 121 Ariz. 540, 592 P.2d 374 (1978)("We hold that appellant's voluntary payment of the fine and restitution must be considered as an acceptance of the sentence and a waiver of the right to appeal from that portion of the judgment").

4. Courts differ on whether the acceptance of a remittitur (a ruling of the trial court that a victorious plaintiff must accept a lowering of the jury's verdict or the judge will grant a new trial) precludes an appeal: Burns v. McGraw–Hill Broad Co., Inc., 659 P.2d 1351 (Colo. 1983) allowed the appeal; while rejecting the appeal was Richards v. Allstate Ins. Co., 693 F.2d 502 (5th Cir. 1982). Which is the better view?

5. There are exceptions to the general rule that payment or acceptance of a judgment award is a waiver of rights to appeal: (1) appellate rights are not waived where the benefit received is an independent and separable part of the judgment being appealed, and (2) where the appellant is entitled to the aspect of the benefit received in any event (i.e., where the appellant seeks even more by appealing). Thus a party who accepts the benefits can still appeal if a reversal on appeal could not affect those benefits. Hilton v. Hilton, 678 S.W.2d 645 (Tex.App.1984). This is a common problem in domestic relations cases. See Comment, Acceptance of Benefits and the Right to Appeal: Divorce, 31 Baylor L.Rev. 81 (1979).

6. A reading of the cases exploring the exceptions plainly discloses that in each the benefit received from a judgment or decree or the part satisfied was not related to and had no effect upon the part from which the appeal was taken. The United States Supreme Court said in one such decision: "There were practically two decrees in this case,—one applicable to the special fund, which, in the bill, the subsequent pleadings, and in the decree, had been kept as a distinct and separate matter. Clearly, his acceptance of a share in the special fund did not operate as a waiver of his appeal from the other part of the decree disposing of the general fund. There is nothing inconsistent in his action." Gilfillan v. McKee, 159 U.S. 303, 311, 16 S.Ct. 6, 40 L.Ed. 161 (1895).

7. Another familiar modality: A judgment is rendered against one defendant in favor of the plaintiff, but in favor of a second defendant and against the plaintiff. The judgment in favor of the plaintiff was satisfied, and plaintiff appealed from the judgment in favor of the other defendant. The court applies the exception to the general rule on the premise that the plaintiff was entitled in any event to collect against the defendant against whom it had succeeded in obtaining a judgment, and furthermore, that the satisfaction of this judgment would not affect the rights either of the plaintiff or the other defendant, irrespective of whether the judgment favorable to such other defendant was affirmed or reversed. See Fifth Avenue Bank of New York v. Hammond Realty Co., 130 F.2d 993 (7th Cir. 1942).

8. Some states have articulated an exception to the "voluntary payment" doctrine for payment of costs awarded in the trial court. Under this view, payment of a cost judgment, which does not "in any way go to the merits of the case," does not defeat the right to appeal in that case. However, if the "costs" are part of a sanction award the voluntary payment rule appears to apply in full force. In one case, the trial court determined that a plaintiff's action was frivolous and, based upon that determination, ordered plaintiff to pay the defendant's "actual costs and attorney's fees in the amount of $36,632." On appeal, the reviewing court held: "Unlike an ordinary judgment for statutory costs to a prevailing plaintiff, an award of actual costs and attorney's fees for bringing a frivolous action is based upon, and goes to, the merits of the case." Thus when the losing plaintiff paid the judgment for actual costs and attorney's fees, it waived its right to appeal from the judgment. Mr. G'S Turtle Mountain Lodge v. Roland Township, 651 N.W.2d 625 (N.D. 2002).

SECTION J.   EFFECT OF APPEAL ON NON–APPEALING PARTIES

HECHT v. CITY OF NEW YORK

Court of Appeals of New York, 1983.
60 N.Y.2d 57, 467 N.Y.S.2d 187, 454 N.E.2d 527.

COOKE, CHIEF JUDGE.

This appeal presents a question respecting the limits of an appellate court's scope of review of a judgment rendered against multiple parties but appealed by only one. Generally, an appellate court cannot grant affirmative relief to a nonappealing party unless it is necessary to do so in order to accord full relief to a party who has appealed. Thus, it was error here for the Appellate Division, 89 A.D.2d 524, 452 N.Y.S.2d 443, to dismiss the action against a joint tort-feasor found liable at trial, but who took no appeal from the judgment.

Plaintiff commenced this negligence action against the City of New York and the Square Depew Garage Corporation for injuries sustained when she fell on a sidewalk located outside a garage operated by defendant corporation. After a jury trial, both defendants were found to be equally liable. Only the City of New York appealed the judgment.

The Appellate Division reversed on the law and dismissed the complaint, holding that there was no actionable defect in the sidewalk. The court added, however, that "[a]lthough only the city prosecuted an appeal, the whole of the judgment is before us * * * and our disposition necessarily effects a dismissal as to the garage defendant as well." This court now modifies the order of the Appellate Division by reinstating the judgment against Square Depew Garage Corporation.

The gravamen of plaintiff's complaint was that defendants failed to maintain the sidewalk in a condition reasonably safe for pedestrians, which failure proximately caused plaintiff's injuries. Plaintiff's proof established that there was a slight gap between two flagstones of the sidewalk. The gap may only be described as trivial. Consequently, it was not error for the Appellate Division to have found no actionable defect in the sidewalk and to have dismissed the complaint against the City of New York.

The other defendant, Square Depew Garage Corporation, however, took no appeal from the judgment. The Appellate Division, therefore, was without power to vacate the judgment against that defendant.

The power of an appellate court to review a judgment is subject to an appeal being timely taken. And an appellate court's scope of review with respect to an appellant, once an appeal has been timely taken, is generally limited to those parts of the judgment that have been appealed and that aggrieve the appealing party. The corollary to this rule is that an appellate court's reversal or modification of a judgment as to an appealing party will not inure to the benefit of a nonappealing coparty unless the judgment was rendered against parties having a united and inseverable interest in the judgment's subject matter, which itself permits no inconsistent application among the parties.

It is, of course, axiomatic that, once an appeal is properly before it, a court may fashion complete relief to the appealing party. On rare occasions, the grant of full relief to the appealing party may necessarily entail granting relief to a nonappealing party (cf. United States Print. & Lithograph Co. v. Powers, 233 N.Y. 143, 135 N.E. 225, supra). At this time, there is no need to detail or enumerate the specific circumstances when such a judgment or order might be appropriate.

Having set forth the rule in general, the court turns to its application here. The appeal by the City of New York to the Appellate Division brought up for its review, with respect to the defendants, only so much of the judgment as imposed liability against the city. As full relief to the city can be achieved without granting relief to Square Depew, it was error to dismiss the complaint as to Square Depew unless the city's interest could be said to be inseparable from that of Square Depew.

When multiple tort-feasors are found to be liable for damages, they may not be said to have an inseverable interest in the judgment, even though the factual basis for each party's liability is identical. Liability is said to be "joint and several", meaning that each party is individually liable to plaintiff for the whole of the damage (see Restatement, Torts 2d, § 875, and Comment [b]). A plaintiff may proceed against any or all defendants. Moreover, a judgment for or against one tort-feasor does not operate as a merger or bar of a claim against other tort-feasors (see Restatement, Judgments 2d, § 49, and Comment [a]). Thus, Square Depew's interest was severable from that of its codefendant. Inasmuch as the judgment here was appealed only by the city, the Appellate Division's reversal was effective only as to that party.

Square Depew argues that the Appellate Division is vested with discretionary power to grant relief to a nonappealing party in the interest of justice, and that the Appellate Division has exercised that discretion in this case. In so arguing, Square Depew relies on CPLR 5522, which provides, in pertinent part, that "[a] court to which an appeal is taken may reverse, affirm, or modify, wholly or in part, any judgment or order before it, as to any party." It has been proposed that the clause "as to any party" vests the Appellate Division with discretionary power to grant relief to a nonappealing party who appears before the court as a respondent. The Appellate Division in the past has claimed this power and applied it on a number of occasions. This court now holds that neither CPLR 5522 nor any other statutory or constitutional authority permits an appellate court to exercise any general discretionary power to grant relief to a nonappealing party.

The common-law concept of a judgment rendered against multiple parties was that, if an error found on appeal required reversal as to one party, the judgment must be reversed as to all. This result obtained even when theories of liability against the defendants differed or when there was error as to only one of the parties (see Sheldon v. Quinlen, 5 Hill 441, 442–443, supra). The rule was derived from the principle "that there can be only one final judgment in an action at law" Draper v. Interborough R.T. Co., 124 App.Div. 357, 359, 108 N.Y.S. 691).

With the advent of statutory provisions permitting appellate courts to reverse, affirm, or modify a judgment, in whole or in part, with respect to any of the parties. Judgments are no longer necessarily viewed as indivisible entireties, reversal of which as to one of the parties necessarily effecting a reversal as to all parties against whom the judgment was rendered. Rather, when multiple parties bring or defend an action or proceeding, and an appeal is taken from an adverse determination below, the appellate court can fashion relief to the various parties within the confines of the governing substantive law. That is the import of CPLR 5522. Moreover, nothing in the legislative history of this provision, its statutory antecedents, or its constitutional counterpart (see N.Y. Const., art. VI, § 5), nor any construction of these provisions by this court indicate that the "as to any party" language vests appellate courts with discretionary power to grant relief to a nonappealing party. The provisions were not meant to expand either the jurisdiction or the scope of review of an appellate court, but were merely intended to enumerate the forms of dispositions an appellate court may order. CPLR 5522, therefore, should be read in harmony with the statutory scheme which limits an appellate court's authority to the grant of relief to those who have appealed, except as discussed above.

Accordingly, the order of the Appellate Division should be modified, with costs to appellant, by reinstating the judgment in favor of plaintiff against Square Depew Garage Corporation and, as so modified, affirmed.

JASEN, JONES, WACHTLER, MEYER and SIMONS, JJ., concur.

Order modified, with costs to appellant, in accordance with the opinion herein and, as so modified, affirmed.

HEGGER v. GREEN

United States Court of Appeals, Second Circuit, 1981.
646 F.2d 22.

MESKILL, CIRCUIT JUDGE.

The plaintiff Hilda Hegger, executrix for the estate of her deceased husband, Fred Hegger, brought this diversity-based medical malpractice action against the defendants Dr. Green and St. Luke's Hospital Center (St. Luke's), claiming that their negligence caused the wrongful death of her husband. The jury found that both defendants had been negligent and that the decedent had been contributorily negligent. In response to special interrogatories, the jury computed the total damages due the plaintiff, deducted a percentage for the decedent's contributory negligence, and apportioned the net damages between the two defendants. St. Luke's appeals, claiming that certain damages were improperly awarded and that, in any event, there was insufficient evidence to support a finding of negligence against it. The plaintiff appeals that portion of the judgment imposing a deduction for the contributory negligence of the decedent. Dr. Green did not appeal. For the reasons stated below, we reverse the judgment against St. Luke's, reverse the deduction for contributory negligence, and modify the remaining judgment to align it with New York precedents governing the recoverability of loss of consortium in wrongful death actions.

* * *

B.   The Plaintiff's Appeal

The plaintiff appeals from the refusal of the court to grant a directed verdict or a judgment n.o.v. in her favor on the issue of the decedent's comparative fault, claiming that there was no evidence of negligence or causation. The jury's deduction of 27 percent from the plaintiff's recovery was based on the supposedly crucial role that the decedent's smoking and stair climbing played in his eventual death. Inasmuch as we have held that those activities were not shown to have proximately caused Hegger's death, the deduction for comparative fault must be set aside.

C.   Disposition of the Case

We are left with the difficult question of how our determination affects the outstanding judgment against Dr. Green. It could be argued that in light of our disposition of the claim against St. Luke's, we cannot be sure that the jury's determination of Dr. Green's liability was based on a proper ground, namely, his failure promptly to operate or to order electronic monitoring, or instead was based upon the doctor's failure to prevent the patient from smoking or climbing stairs. Dr. Green might argue that, to the extent that liability is premised on the latter basis, a new trial is required for him because of our determination that those activities were not shown to have proximately caused Hegger's death. But it is not for us to raise those doubts when Dr. Green has not done so. Ordinarily, a nonappealing party will not benefit from a reversal or modification of a judgment in favor of an appealing party unless the reversal "wipes out all basis for recovery against a non-appealing, as well as against an appealing, defendant * * *," In re Barnett, 124 F.2d 1005, 1009 (2d Cir. 1942); Kicklighter v. Nails by Jannee, Inc., 616 F.2d 734, 742–45 (5th Cir. 1980); Statella v. Robert Chuckrow Construction Co., 28 A.D.2d 669, 670, 281 N.Y.S.2d 215 (1st Dep't 1967); or unless failure to reverse with respect to the nonappealing party will frustrate the execution of the judgment in favor of the successful appellant, In re Barnett, supra, 124 F.2d at 1008–12. See 9 J. Moore, Federal Practice ¶ 204.11[4]-[5] (2d ed. 1980).

It is clear that our holding with respect to the liability of St. Luke's leaves adequate bases upon which the jury could have reasonably found that Dr. Green was negligent. Further, the judgment in favor of St. Luke's does not "wipe out" the basis for the amount of compensatory damages awarded for wrongful death. The compensatory wrongful death damages involved in this case were awarded to provide "fair and just compensation for the pecuniary injuries resulting from the decedent's death to the persons for whose benefit the action is brought." N.Y.E.P.T.L. 5–4.3 (McKinnney 1980). See Franchell v. Sims, 73 A.D.2d 1, 424 N.Y.S.2d 959 (4th Dep't 1980). Unlike Statella v. Robert Chuckrow Construction Co., supra, there is neither a challenge nor a finding that the jury verdicts in this case were "grossly excessive." Finally, the unique situation presented in *Barnett,* supra, bears no similarity to the facts here.

Whether Dr. Green may reap the benefit of our ruling concerning loss of consortium stands in a different light. In this case, the entire basis for an award of loss of consortium has been removed by our holding that the decision of the New York Court of Appeals in *Liff,* supra, applies in this appeal, a holding which effectively "wipes out" the plaintiff's basis of recovery on this point.

CONCLUSION

The judgment holding St. Luke's liable for negligence is reversed. That portion of the judgment holding the decedent liable for contributory negligence is reversed and the judgment modified to eliminate the reduction therefor. Judgment against Dr. Green is modified to eliminate the recovery based on loss of consortium, leaving Dr. Green liable to the plaintiff for $501,984. St. Luke's may recover its costs against plaintiff. No costs between plaintiff and Dr. Green.

MANSFIELD, CIRCUIT JUDGE (concurring in part and dissenting in part):

I concur in the majority's holding that the plaintiff failed to establish (1) negligence on the part of Dr. Green and St. Luke's in failing properly to supervise Hegger's activities in the hospital by preventing him from smoking or climbing stairs and in failing to maintain adequate nursing observation, or (2) that the alleged negligence was the proximate cause of Hegger's death. I also agree that the award of $25,000 for loss of consortium must be reversed in the light of Liff v. Schildkrout, 49 N.Y.2d 622, 427 N.Y.S.2d 746, 404 N.E.2d 1288 (1980), and that the defendants' contributory negligence claim must fail for the reasons stated by the majority. However, I believe that the majority's decision to award against Dr. Green the full amount of the judgment, $501,984 (after deduction of the $25,000 award for loss of consortium) is a denial of substantial justice and an abuse of discretion, amounting to the assumption by this court of the role of trier of the fact and substitution of its views for those of the jury.

In my view the majority's error lies in its assumption that the jury's finding of liability against Dr. Green was based on claims other than those found by us to have been unsustained. If the jury had based its verdict against Dr. Green on the claims that he failed to place Hegger under electronic monitoring and failed to operate promptly, I would have no quarrel with the result reached by my brothers, even though the jury's apportionment of 75% of the award against the hospital and 25% against Dr. Green raises a serious doubt as to whether, if the jury had been precluded from finding the hospital liable, it would have awarded such a substantial amount against Dr. Green.

For present purposes, however, the important point is that the jury based its verdict on impermissible considerations, namely, that Hegger died because of failure on the part of Dr. Green to take more steps to insure that Hegger would not smoke or walk upstairs. By finding the hospital 75% negligent, Dr. Green 25% negligent, and Hegger 27% contributorily negligent, the jury appears in all probability to have rejected plaintiff's claim that Hegger died because of Dr. Green's failure to place him on electronic monitoring and to have based its verdict on the claims based on his smoking and walking upstairs. If the jury had based its award against Dr. Green on claims based on lack of electronic monitoring or delay in operating it would not have decreased its award against Green by 27%, since Hegger could not possibly have been contributorily negligent with respect to these claims. Moreover, as to these claims it could not properly have apportioned liability as between Dr. Green and the hospital, since these claims were not (and could not properly be) asserted against the hospital. Under the circumstances, the proper and equitable course is to reverse the judgment against Dr. Green and remand the case against him for a new trial limited to the claims that he failed to operate promptly and to place Hegger under electronic monitoring.

The majority's decision to increase the verdict against Dr. Green from $125,496 (before deducting 27% for Hegger's contributory negligence) to $501,984 (after deducting the $25,000 improperly awarded for loss of consortium) is not mandated by the authorities relied upon by it. The common law rule, which treated a judgment against joint tortfeasors as an entirety that must be affirmed or reversed as to all parties, Sheldon v. Quinlen, 5 Hill (N.Y.) 441 (1943); Bamberg v. International R. Co., 121 App.Div. 1, 105 N.Y.S. 621 (1907); Annotation, Grant of New Trial, or Reversal of Judgment on Appeal as to One Joint Tort-feasor, 143 A.L.R. 7, 8–9 (1943), including non-appealing defendants, Comment, Judgments Against Joint Tortfeasors—Problems Arising on Appeal by Only One Defendant, 31 Mo.L.Rev. 141, 142 (1962), would mandate reversal of the judgment against Dr. Green. Although that rule has been modified to the extent of permitting an appellate court to affirm as to a defendant properly held liable despite a reversal as to a codefendant, Chiarello Bros. Co. v. Pederson, 242 F. 482, 484 (2d Cir. 1917), see also Dollar S.S. Lines v. Merz, 68 F.2d 594, 595 (9th Cir. 1934), the court may, where it would be in the interest of "substantial justice," reverse a joint judgment in its entirety. For the reasons stated above, a reversal of the judgment against Dr. Green and remand for trial of the validly stated claims against him would clearly be in the interest of substantial justice.

The majority circumvents this eminently equitable course on the ground that Dr. Green did not take a formal appeal. With this holding I must disagree. The fact that a judgment against a non-appealing party will be reversed where the reversal of judgment against a codefendant "wipes out all basis for recovery" against him does not preclude us from entering such a reversal where it would be in the interest of substantial justice. None of the cases cited by the majority would bar such a reversal. Nor have I found any authority holding that, where reversal of a judgment against an appealing defendant would increase or inequitably affect the liability of a non-appealing party, the court may not in its sound discretion reverse the judgment against the latter. On the contrary, the very decisions relied upon by the majority support a reversal here as to Dr. Green. For instance, in In re Barnett, 124 F.2d 1005 (2d Cir. 1942), relied on by Judge Meskill, the court reversed the judgment as to the non-appealing defendant, stating:

> "As previously observed, the other parties adversely affected by the lower court's order did not pray an appeal. Had they done so, it is clear, from our opinion, that we would have held the order erroneous as to them. We are clear that we have the power to order a reversal as to them even though they did not appeal, and that we should do so under the circumstances here disclosed. * * * Hence complete reversal is the only proper way to avoid unnecessary complications and ambiguity." In re Barnett, 124 F.2d 1005, 1008–09 (2d Cir. 1942).

In Kicklighter v. Nails by Jannee, Inc., 616 F.2d 734, 742–45 (5th Cir. 1980), a reversal of a judgment against a third-party defendant was held to inure to the benefit of a non-appealing defendant/third-party plaintiff, permitting all parties to participate in a new trial, on the ground that "an appeal by one defendant [may] operate for the benefit of another defendant," citing In re Barnett, supra and Maryland Casualty Co. v. City of South Norwalk, 54 F.2d 1032 (4th Cir. 1932). In Statella v. Robert Chuckrow Construction Co., 28 A.D.2d 669, 281 N.Y.S.2d 215 (1st Dept.1967), the third case relied upon by the majority, a judgment against multiple tortfeasors was reversed as to a non-appealing defendant, the court stating:

> "Although the defendant Chuckrow did not appeal from the judgment rendered against it in favor of plaintiff, Chuckrow is here on the appeals concerning the determination of its cross complaints and we conclude that the appeals of the codefendants bringing up for review on the merits the question of excessiveness of the verdicts inure also to the benefit of Chuckrow. The verdicts and judgment, insofar as they fix the amounts of recoveries, are in joint form against the several defendants. They occupy the same position and have a common standing with respect to the quantum of plaintiff's recovery. The common-law rule was that verdict or judgment against several tortfeasors might not be reversed as to some and enforced as to others, and that a new trial might not be granted as to some and denied as to others. The judgment was regarded as an entirety which must be affirmed or reversed on appeal as to all or as to none. Today it is quite generally held that a judgment against

multiple tort-feasors may be reversed as to one such defendant without affecting the judgments as to others. In the application of the modern rule, nevertheless, *courts will not enter such a partial reversal where substantial justice requires a reversal as to all defendants, as where it appears there is a right to contribution or indemnity among the codefendants.* Fundamental justice requires, moreover, that judicial discretion be exercised and a new trial ordered as to all defendants unless plaintiff stipulates to reduce the award as to all defendants." Statella v. Robert Chuckrow Construction Co., 28 A.D.2d 669, 670, 281 N.Y.S.2d 215 (1st Dept.1967) (emphasis supplied).

Professor Moore has noted, "the courts of appeals have treated the position of nonparticipants in an appeal on a case to case basis and have not read Rule 3 to limit the *jurisdiction* to reverse or modify a judgment properly brought before it." 9 Moore's Federal Practice Par. 204.11[5], at 4–61 (emphasis in original). I believe this principle should govern here.

Dr. Green's failure to take an appeal is understandable. Both he and the plaintiff were content with the jury's limitation of Dr. Green's liability to 25%. The plaintiff appealed only the 27% deduction based on the jury's finding of contributory negligence. Dr. Green apparently continues to be willing to abide by the 25% verdict even after disallowance of the 27% erroneously deducted by reason of the plaintiff's alleged contributory negligence. He therefore proceeded on the basis that this would be his maximum exposure. The majority, in reversing the judgment against his co-defendant (the hospital), does not merely leave untouched the scope of his liability but increases it by 75%. Under these circumstances, to hold him liable for the full 100%, which was based on impermissible grounds, strikes me as unconscionably harsh. Under the circumstances we should exercise our discretionary power as a matter of fundamental justice to reverse the judgment as to him and remand the validly stated individual claims against him for a new trial, unaffected by the unsustained claims upon which the jury held him liable.

Notes and Questions

1. Is the effect on the non-appealing party in each of the two principal cases the same? Are the two cases inconsistent? If not, on what principled basis can they be reconciled?

2. In Cover v. Cohen, 61 N.Y.2d 261, 473 N.Y.S.2d 378, 461 N.E.2d 864 (1984) the New York Court of Appeals distinguished its decision in *Hecht v. Hecht* and reversed a judgment against a non-appealing car dealer because the judgment against the manufacturer of the car involved in the case was reversed and a new trial ordered. The basis for the distinction was that there was an agreement between the dealer and manufacturer, providing that the manufacturer would indemnify the dealer for any loss arising out of a defect in the car. Upon a new trial if the car manufacturer were found not liable, it would still have to pay the original judgment against the dealer under the indemnity agreement, and this would defeat the purpose of the new trial.

The court reasoned that unless the judgment against the car dealer was also reversed, the purpose of a new trial would be defeated.

3. One federal appeals court concluded that an attempt to renew litigation after failure to pursue a timely appeal in the first litigation "may be dismissed on the ground of claim preclusion (res judicata) even if the decision in the first was transparently erroneous." Gleash v. Yuswak, 308 F.3d 758 (7th Cir. 2002). As another appellate court has noted, "a final judgment is not voided if the precedent upon which it was based is later modified or overruled." United States Philips Corp. v. Sears, Roebuck & Co., 55 F.3d 592 (Fed. Cir. 1995).

4. In the seminal case, Federated Department Stores v. Moitie, 452 U.S. 394, 101 S.Ct. 2424, 69 L.Ed.2d 103 (1981), seven private antitrust actions alleging price fixing were brought against various department stores by plaintiffs seeking to represent classes of retail purchasers. The actions were consolidated in federal district court, but then dismissed for failure to allege an "injury" to the plaintiffs' "business or property" within the meaning of the Clayton Act. Plaintiffs in five of the actions appealed, but Moitie and another group of plaintiffs chose instead to refile their two actions in state court, making similar allegations. After the time for Moitie to appeal the original federal dismissals, but while the five other federal appeals of the dismissals by co-plaintiffs were pending, the United States Supreme Court issued a decision which broadened the understanding of the necessary "injury" in antitrust cases, and the five cases that were appealed got the benefit of the new law. Moitie et al. had their state cases removed to federal court, and these new cases were than dismissed on res judicata grounds (i.e., the prior ruling was a dismissal on the merits that was not appealed, and this final disposition barred a later case on the same theory based on the same transactions). Moitie et al. appealed the res judicata dismissal, but to no avail. The Supreme Court held that res judicata bars relitigation of unappealed adverse judgments, even if the prior judgment may have been wrong or rested on a legal principle subsequently overruled in another case. Justice Rehnquist delivered the opinion of the Court, making several points:

> A final judgment on the merits of an action precludes the parties or their privies from relitigating issues that were or could have been raised in that action. Commissioner v. Sunnen, 333 U.S. 591, 597, 68 S.Ct. 715, 92 L.Ed. 898 (1948); Cromwell v. County of Sac, 94 U.S. 351, 352–353, 24 L.Ed. 195 (1877). Nor are the res judicata consequences of a final, unappealed judgment on the merits altered by the fact that the judgment may have been wrong or rested on a legal principle subsequently overruled in another case. Angel v. Bullington, 330 U.S. 183, 187, 67 S.Ct. 657, 91 L.Ed. 832 (1947); Chicot County Drainage District v. Baxter State Bank, 308 U.S. 371, 60 S.Ct. 317, 84 L.Ed. 329 (1940); Wilson's Executor v. Deen, 121 U.S. 525, 534, 7 S.Ct. 1004, 30 L.Ed. 980 (1887). As this Court explained in Baltimore S.S. Co. v. Phillips, 274 U.S. 316, 325, 47 S.Ct. 600, 71 L.Ed. 1069 (1927), an "erroneous conclusion" reached by the court in the first suit does not deprive the defendants in the second action "of their right to rely upon the plea of res judicata. . . . A judgment merely voidable because based upon an erroneous view of the law is not open to collateral attack, but can be

corrected only by a direct review and not by bringing another action upon the same cause [of action]." We have observed that "[the] indulgence of a contrary view would result in creating elements of uncertainty and confusion and in undermining the conclusive character of judgments, consequences which it was the very purpose of the doctrine of res judicata to avert." Reed v. Allen, 286 U.S. 191, 201, 52 S.Ct. 532, 76 L.Ed. 1054 (1932).

In this case, the Court of Appeals conceded that the "strict application of the doctrine of res judicata" required that Brown II be dismissed. By that, the court presumably meant that the "technical elements" of res judicata had been satisfied, namely, that the decision in Brown I was a final judgment on the merits and involved the same claims and the same parties as Brown II. The court, however, declined to dismiss Brown II because, in its view, it would be unfair to bar respondents from relitigating a claim so "closely interwoven" with that of the successfully appealing parties. We believe that such an unprecedented departure from accepted principles of res judicata is unwarranted. Indeed, the decision below is all but foreclosed by our prior case law.

In *Reed v. Allen* this Court addressed the issue presented here. The case involved a dispute over the rights to property left in a will. A won an interpleader action for rents derived from the property and, while an appeal was pending, brought an ejectment action against the rival claimant B. On the basis of the decree in the interpleader suit A won the ejectment action. B did not appeal this judgment, but prevailed on his earlier appeal from the interpleader decree and was awarded the rents which had been collected. When B sought to bring an ejectment action against A, the latter pleaded res judicata, based on his previous successful ejectment action. This Court held that res judicata was available as a defense and that the property belonged to A:

> "The judgment in the ejectment action was final and not open to assault collaterally, but subject to impeachment only through some form of direct attack. The appellate court was limited to a review of the interpleader decree; and it is hardly necessary to say that jurisdiction to review one judgment gives an appellate court no power to reverse or modify another and independent judgment. If respondent, in addition to appealing from the [interpleader] decree, had appealed from the [ejectment] judgment, the appellate court, having both cases before it, might have afforded a remedy.... But this course respondent neglected to follow." Id., at 198.

This Court's rigorous application of res judicata in *Reed*, to the point of leaving one party in possession and the other party entitled to the rents, makes clear that this Court recognizes no general equitable doctrine, such as that suggested by the Court of Appeals, which countenances an exception to the finality of a party's failure to appeal merely because his rights are "closely interwoven" with those of another party. Indeed, this case presents even more compelling reasons to apply the doctrine of res judicata than did Reed. Respondents here seek to be the windfall beneficiaries of an appellate reversal procured by other independent parties, who have no interest in respondents' case, not a reversal in interrelated cases procured, as in Reed, by the same affected party. Moreover, in contrast to Reed, where it was unclear why no appeal was taken, it is apparent that respondents here made a calculated choice to forgo their appeals. See also Ackermann v. United States, 340 U.S. 193, 198, 71 S.Ct. 209, 95 L.Ed. 207 (1950) (holding that petitioners were not entitled to relief under Federal Rule of Civil Procedure 60(b) when they made a "free, calculated, deliberate [choice]" not to appeal).

The Court of Appeals also rested its opinion in part on what it viewed as "simple justice." But we do not see the grave injustice which would be done by the application of accepted principles of res judicata. "Simple justice" is achieved when a complex body of law developed over a period of years is evenhandedly applied. The doctrine of res judicata serves vital public interests beyond any individual judge's ad hoc determination of the equities in a particular case. There is simply "no principle of law or equity which sanctions the rejection by a federal court of the salutary principle of res judicata." Heiser v. Woodruff, 327 U.S. 726, 733, 66 S.Ct. 853, 90 L.Ed. 970 (1946). The Court of Appeals' reliance on "public policy" is similarly misplaced. This Court has long recognized that "[public] policy dictates that there be an end of litigation; that those who have contested an issue shall be bound by the result of the contest, and that matters once tried shall be considered forever settled as between the parties." Baldwin v. Traveling Men's Assn., 283 U.S. 522, 525, 51 S.Ct. 517, 75 L.Ed. 1244 (1931). We have stressed that "[the] doctrine of res judicata is not a mere matter of practice or procedure inherited from a more technical time than ours. It is a rule of fundamental and substantial justice, 'of public policy and of private peace,' which should be cordially regarded and enforced by the courts...." Hart Steel Co. v. Railroad Supply Co., 244 U.S. 294, 299, 37 S.Ct. 506, 61 L.Ed. 1148 (1917). The language used by this Court half a century ago is even more compelling in view of today's crowded dockets:

> "The predicament in which respondent finds himself is of his own making.... [We] cannot be expected, for his sole relief, to upset the general and well-established doctrine of res judicata, conceived in the light of the maxim that the interest of the state requires that there be an end to litigation—a maxim which comports with common sense as well as public policy. And the mischief which would follow the establishment of precedent for so disregarding this salutary doctrine against prolonging strife would be greater than the benefit which would result from relieving some case of individual hardship." Reed v. Allen, 286 U.S., at 198–199.

3. Reddington v. Beefeaters Tables, Inc., 72 Wis.2d 119, 240 N.W.2d 363 (1976) involved an action by an infant against a restaurant and the driver of an automobile which struck the infant in a driveway next to the restaurant. The trial judge had dismissed the restaurant as a party and the jury found the driver not negligent. The infant appealed the dismissal of the restaurant but did not appeal the judgment in favor of the driver. The supreme court reversed the dismissal of the restaurant and also reversed the judgment in favor of the driver. In explaining its action, the court stated that the judgment was "a nullity, for the action was premised upon a patent error of law [editor's note—presumably the dismissal of the restaurant] that

deprived the plaintiff of their right to try their law suit and deprived [the driver] of any attempt to seek contribution from [the restaurant] or vice versa. * * * In the instant case * * * [the restaurant] was available and was a necessary party to the entire law suit and should not have been dismissed. Under the facts and law, [the restaurant], had it been joined, might well have been assessed some percentage of causal negligence or could have asserted a claim against [the driver]." Is this case consistent with the principal cases? After this case, the Wisconsin statute on appeals was revised to provide expressly that an appellate court can render a judgment only as to a party who is involved in the appeal as an appellant or appellee. Wis.Stat. Ann. § 809.10(4) (West 2003). One of the purposes of the revision was to prevent a court from doing what it did in *Reddington*. R. Martineau & R. Malmgren, Wisconsin Appellate Practice § 604 (1978). Would such a statute prevent what was done in Cover v. Cohen, supra note 2?

Chapter 5

INITIATING AND PERFECTING
AN APPEAL

SECTION A.   THE DECISION TO APPEAL

R. MARTINEAU, MODERN APPELLATE PRACTICE—
FEDERAL AND STATE CIVIL APPEALS

§ 2.1–2.6 (1983).

1.   PRE–LITIGATION APPELLATE CONSIDERATIONS

Most attorneys probably do not think about taking an appeal until they have received an adverse judgment or an adverse ruling on a crucial point in the trial court. Waiting until then is too late. Appeal strategy is far too important to be left until the attorney is faced with an unfavorable decision, for by that time the most effective route to appeal may be inadvertently precluded.

There are both substantive and procedural reasons for making the possibility of appeal part of the litigation strategy from the inception of the law suit. The possibility of appeal may be a factor in deciding in which court to file the action and how to frame the complaint to raise the issues the plaintiff wants to raise. The speed with which appellate review can be had may be just as important as how quickly the trial court can dispose of the case. If the crucial issue in the case will be decided early in the litigation process, the possibility of review of an interlocutory order may be crucial to the plaintiff's case. The quality or predilections of the appellate bench in one jurisdiction may also be a factor, as will the relative expense of taking any appeal. The extent to which oral argument is held may be significant. The scope of review may vary between appellate courts, a factor that could be determinative of the outcome of an appeal.

One of the most important steps for the attorney is to ensure that those issues which he thinks may be significant on appeal are raised in the trial count; to do so he may be required to include them in the complaint. Any potential federal issues must be identified and formally made a part of the case to protect the opportunity to seek review in the United States Supreme Court. Most appellate courts will not consider issues not properly raised in the trial court. It is absolutely necessary, consequently, to determine before filing the complaint those substantive issues that the plaintiff wants to raise and whether including them in the complaint is the best way to do this.

It may also be important from the standpoint of client relations to discuss with the client prior to filing the lawsuit the necessity or desirability of appealing an adverse judgment or ruling. If the client is not interested in appealing no matter what the result in the trial court, the issue of appeal can be ignored in developing a plan for the litigation. If, on the other hand, the client has made up his mind to appeal if not successful in the trial court, building an appeal strategy into the overall litigation plan will make it possible to move quickly once an adverse judgment is rendered. Because the time for appeal begins to run once judgment is entered on the trial court docket, early discussions are particularly important if there is any possibility that the client may not be available to make the decision on appeal, for if he knows what his client desires, the attorney can proceed. If the client is uncertain whether or not he will appeal an adverse decision, the only safe course is to assume that an appeal will be taken and include an appeal as part of the litigation strategy.

2. POST–JUDGMENT APPELLATE CONSIDERATIONS

Whether or not he has held prior discussions with the client about the possibility of an appeal, the attorney should always review the matter after the adverse judgment is received. Various factors may compel a reassessment. The precise form of the adverse judgment, subsequent changes in or clarification of the law, and the individual circumstances of the client may all make a prior decision to appeal or not to appeal no longer appropriate.

The first tactical decision is whether to seek relief in the trial court through a motion for a new trial or other type of post trial motion. It is particularly important to ascertain whether any procedural step in the trial court is a pre-requisite to taking an appeal.

3. OBJECTIVES OF APPEAL

The first consideration in deciding whether to appeal is the objective of the appeal. This objective should be looked at both from the broader standpoint of the ultimate objective of the litigation and from the narrower one of the precise judgment from which the appeal is to be taken. Obviously if the ultimate objective cannot be obtained even if the appeal is successful, then there is no point in taking the appeal. If the issue is likely to be moot when the appeal is decided, or if the judgment cannot be enforced because, for example, the opposing party is judgment proof, dead, or beyond the process of the courts, appeal is futile. The object of the litigation may no longer be in existence or desired. Events may have passed the litigation by, making the issues of the litigation practically if not legally moot. Or the client may have lost all interest in winning the appeal.

The nature of the adverse judgment also cannot be ignored. It must be looked at critically to determine exactly how adverse it is, and whether it can be lived with. The attorney must also determine what type of relief might be awarded in the appellate court. Is the appellate court likely to reverse and award judgment for the appellant, or is it more likely to remand for further proceedings? If the latter, the attorney should consider the possible extent of further proceedings and whether the client's ultimate objective can be obtained through them. If the client is not prepared to pursue the matter through subsequent proceedings in the trial court such as a new trial, or if the subsequent proceedings are not likely to produce the result sought by the client, then there is no point in taking an appeal.

The attorney should consider what function the appeal will ask the appellate court to perform—error correction or law development—and the scope of review of the appellate court. If it seeks error correction, the appeal will probably go no further than the intermediate appellate court. If law development, then the appeal will probably have to be resolved by the supreme court. The cost of the appeal, the likelihood of success, and the length of time to final resolution may each be affected by which function is sought by the appeal.

The chances of prevailing in the appellate court will also be greatly affected by the scope of review of the appellate court over the error asserted. Legal issues are far more likely to be reviewed than factual issues; fact determinations by a judge are more likely to be reviewed than those made by a jury. The scope of review of a matter in the discretion of the trial judge is similarly very small, and appeals attempting to convince the appellate court that the trial judge abused his discretion are seldom successful.

4. COST OF APPEAL

One obvious factor in the decision to appeal is the cost to the appellant. The cost will include filing fees, appeal bond, preparation of the record including the transcript, preparation of the brief and appendix, and the attorney's fees and expenses. A cost-benefit analysis to determine whether the appeal will be cost effective, both in the short run and long run, is essential. If the appeal will cost more than the amount involved in the judgment, there is little point in appealing unless the res judicata or precedential effect of the adverse judgment is such that far more is involved than the amount of the judgment alone. Another cost factor is whether further proceedings in the trial court will be necessary even if the appellant wins in the appellate court. If the client can afford the appeal but not additional trial court proceedings, then an appeal may be a waste of time and money.

If the client strongly desires to appeal but does not have the funds to pay for it, then the attorney must decide whether he has any obligation under the Code of Professional Responsibility to provide his legal services on a reduced or no cost basis. Resolving this question may depend upon whether the case involves only the private interest of the individual litigant or some broader public interest; if the latter, the services of the attorney could be said to be provided pro bono public.

5. DELAY FACTOR

The time it takes for an appeal to move through the appellate process from judgment in the trial court to an enforceable judgment after a successful appeal will also affect the decision to appeal. The attorney must be able to predict not only the likelihood of winning, but the amount of time necessary to obtain and enforce a favorable judgment. If it is not probable that the correct result can be obtained in sufficient time for the client to enjoy the fruits of his victory, then there may be no point in taking the appeal.

It is more likely, of course, that an appeal, if enforcement of the adverse judgment is stayed pending the appeal, will benefit the appellant even if the appellate court affirms the judgment of the trial court. One does not have to be a cynic to believe that many appeals are taken solely or primarily for purposes of delay, particularly when the legal rate of interest is either below the current cost of money or less than the profit the losing party can make from the subject of the litigation while the appeal is pending. In taking an appeal that serves little purpose other than delay, the attorney must consider his obligations under the Code of Professional Responsibility and under the rules of procedure governing the appeal. It may be that the attorney, his client, or both will be found to have taken the appeal solely for purposes of delay and be subjected to a sanction for so doing.

A third possible objective in taking an appeal is to force the successful party in the trial court to agree to a settlement more favorable to the appellant than the original judgment. The winning party will have to make the same analysis as the losing party in deciding how vigorously to try to maintain the original judgment. The appeal, just as the original law suit, may have a settlement value without regard to its substantive merits. It may be to the advantage of the losing party to file an appeal merely to test the willingness of the other side to retain all of the benefits of the judgment it has won.

6. LIKELIHOOD OF APPEAL BY OTHER PARTIES

The decision to appeal must be looked at not only from the standpoint of what can be gained by an appeal, but also from that of what can be lost. If only the appellant appeals, the appellee can seek only to uphold the judgment of the trial court. The appellee has, however, the option of filing a cross appeal that will permit him to challenge any adverse ruling of the trial court that may have had an effect upon the judgment adverse to the appellee. The appellee may decide to take a cross appeal even though he would not have appealed on that issue separately. Because the taking of an appeal by the opposing party may put in jeopardy those portions of the judgment favorable to him, the appellee may be forced to cross appeal to protect himself in the event that the appellant is successful. From an expense standpoint, it is likely to cost little more to take a cross appeal than simply to resist the appellant's appeal.

Filing a cross appeal can, of course, be done solely for purposes of strategy. It may make the appellant think again about the risks of taking an appeal, forcing the appellant either to drop his appeal or be more amenable to a settlement satisfactory to the appellee. Even if the appellant dismisses his appeal, however, the cross appeal remains pending unless dismissed by the cross appellant. It is essential, consequently, to consider the likelihood and the possible negative consequences of a cross appeal when making a decision to appeal.

7. ALTERNATIVES TO APPEAL

In making the decision to appeal, the alternatives to appeal should also be considered. Pursuing post trial motions in the trial court may be a substitute or merely a preliminary step to taking an appeal. Although likely to add to the cost and delay of an eventual appeal, post trial steps may also make an appeal unnecessary. Attempting to work out a settlement is yet another alternative. Settlement and appeal, however, are not mutually exclusive. In fact, the filing of the notice of appeal is more likely to be a strategy in achieving a satisfactory settlement. The opportunities for settlement while an appeal is pending have been substantially increased in view of the settlement programs established by a number of appellate courts.

Notes and Questions

1. On the likelihood of reversal should one appeal, see Eisenberg, Appeal Rates and Outcomes in Tried and Nontried Cases: Further Explorations of Anti–Plaintiff Appellate Outcomes, 1 J. of Legal Studies 659 (2004), noting that based on a massive study of 12 years worth of appeals in the federal courts, appeals are taken in 40% of cases resolved by trial, and only 10% of cases decided without trial. In analyzing those appeals Professor Eisenberg finds that when trial-level defendants are the appellants they obtain reversal in about 10% of the cases, but trial-level plaintiffs who become appellants obtain a reversal of only approximately 4% of adverse trial court judgments. Other studies have probed the question whether certain causes of action are less hospitably reviewed on appeal than others. See, e.g., Clermont & Schwab, How Employment Discrimination Cases Fare in Federal Court, 1 J. Empirical Legal Stud. 429 (2004).

2. Two issues bearing heavily on the decision to take an appeal are preservation of error, which is necessary to provide an opportunity for appellate review (discussed in Chapter 2 of this Casebook), and issues controlling the appealability of the case in various stages of the decision-making process, which are explored in Chapter 3.

3. Bringing an appeal that is ultimately deemed "frivolous" can lead to the imposition of sanctions. The primary objectives of rules governing sanctions for frivolous appeals are:(1) compensation of opposing parties for their time and expense; (2) punishment of the offending party for wasting

the court's time; and (3) deterrence of future frivolous appeals. See generally Martineau, Frivolous Appeals: The Uncertain Federal Response, 1984 Duke L. J. 845. Professor Martineau has suggested that while the core question facing appellate courts in considering imposition of sanctions is whether the appeal has "no legal basis," many factors play into the decision whether to impose sanctions, including a history of misbehavior in the trial court, dilatory conduct in the appeal (such as delay in completing arrangements for the transcript or brief or appendix) and conduct which misleads the appellate court. On key in the application of sanctions is what *scienter* is required for imposition of such a penalty. Writing in 1984 Professor Martineau noted:

> Before a court can decide whether to impose a sanction, it must first decide what evidence it will consider in making that determination. For example, there is a clear distinction between subjective and objective evidence. If subjective evidence is considered, then the court will focus on the personal motives of the appellant or his attorney. Some courts have held that the appellant must have acted in bad faith and brought a meritless appeal in order for an appeal to be considered frivolous. Under this standard the intent of the appellant is the key factor. The bad faith usually consists of deliberately causing delay in order to occasion needless expense for the appellee or of denying the appellee the benefit of the judgment for as long as possible. The sincerity of the appellant can be significant in determining whether an appeal is frivolous.

> Some courts, on the other hand, have applied what appears to be an objective standard. Although no federal court has used the phrase, the California Supreme Court has applied a "reasonably prudent attorney" standard asking whether a reasonably prudent attorney would have brought the appeal in good faith. An examination of the record, briefs, and argument provides the answer to this question, and the actual good faith or sincerity of the appellant is not considered.

> The two standards, subjective and objective, can easily be confused, however, because typically there is no direct evidence of the intent of the appellant in taking the appeal. The court can only infer the bad faith of the appellant from what is reflected in the record, briefs, and oral argument. Thus, whether the court is applying a subjective or objective standard, it will examine the same evidence. In most cases, consequently, there will be little difference in the result regardless of the standard used.

Id. at 854–55. Professor Martineau observed that "the courts of appeals have often confused two distinct issues. The first issue is whether an appeal should be classified as frivolous because of its lack of merit. The second issue is whether, given that an appeal is frivolous on its merits, the conduct of the appellant or the attorney is such that a sanction should be imposed on one or both. Often courts determine that an appeal is frivolous by examining the conduct of the appellant or attorney, rather than by looking at the merits of the appeal. This conduct is then used as the basis for determining the necessity for the sanction and the type to be imposed. This approach causes the courts to vacillate between objective and subjective standards and obscures the extent to which the intent of the appellant or the attorney determines whether an appeal is frivolous." Id. at 870. Nearly 20 years later, the confusion, uncertainty and inconsistency identified by Professor Martineau was still reflected in a "visible disagreement" among the federal courts over whether "bad faith" or a similar subjective mental state was a prerequisite to imposition of sanctions on an attorney or a party. See Note, Keeping the Courts Afloat in a Rising Sea of Litigation: An Objective Approach to Imposing Rule 38 Sanctions for Frivolous Appeals, 100 Mich. L. Rev. 1156 (2002).

4.   Sanctions are assessed at the appellate level for a variety of rule violations and misuses of the appellate process. One encyclopedic survey suggests that attorneys may be sanctioned for numerous reasons which include: (1) filing a deficient brief which fails to conform to court rules; (2) bringing an appeal without any legal or factual basis; (3) bringing an appeal which merely restates arguments rejected and sanctioned by the lower court; (4) failing to research the law and determining that the claim on appeal is without merit; (5) filing an appeal in conflict with overwhelming case authority; (6) failing to provide authority or evidence to establish error in the lower court's decision; (7) appealing an order the attorney knows not to be final; (8) bringing an appeal as part of a vendetta by counsel against the judge or opposing counsel; (9) disregarding the jurisdictional requirements of the court; or (10) aiding a client in bringing an appeal for the purpose of delay or harassment. However, courts generally will determine whether sanctions are warranted on a case-by-case basis. 5 Am. Jur. 2d Appellate Review 949 (1995). What other grounds might warrant sanctions?

5.   Judge Roger Miner has observed that "[i]t is a rare case in which we sanction even those who take frivolous appeals." Miner, Professional Responsibility in Appellate Practice: A View From the Bench, 19 Pace L. Rev. 323, 341 (1999). However, other observers note that the "unpleasant duty" of imposing sanctions is increasingly being undertaken, and that for serious offenses, an award of opposing attorneys fees can result in a sanction of $100,000 or more. See Kravitz, Unpleasant Duties: Imposing Sanctions for Frivolous Appeals, 4 J. App. Prac. & Process 335 (2002). Many lesser forms of sanctions, and a discussion of the reasons for shaping the sanctions and the rules governing them to take cognizance of the broad range of conduct that may spawn consideration of such penalties is explored in Martineau, Frivolous Appeals: The Uncertain Federal Response, 1984 Duke L. J. 845, 848.

6.   In criminal cases, where procedural rules, appellate practice standards and constitutional imperatives collide, counsel's duties in deciding whether to take an appeal are especially complicated. One fascinating aspect of the process is a procedure used in some jurisdictions under the imprimatur of the United States Supreme Court, known as an *Anders* brief. The United States Supreme Court established the procedure in Anders v. California, 386 U.S. 738, 744, 87 S.Ct. 1396, 18 L.Ed.2d 493 (1967), where it approved a mechanism allowing appellate counsel to withdraw from representation in a frivolous or non-meritorious appeal. An *Anders* brief, therefore, is both a motion and brief that is allowed in many states that permit appointed counsel to withdraw from representation in a criminal's first appeal as of right. This brief is submitted after counsel determines that the appeal presents no meritorious or non-frivolous issue that can be raised. The Court held that the request to withdraw was subject to certain constitutional

parameters and would only be considered after the submission of both a brief and a motion to withdraw. The procedure remains controversial, and many jurisdictions struggle to deal with the integration of the aspiration to provide maximum appellate representation for criminal defendants consistent with professional standards. For a survey of current practices, see Comment, The Anders Brief and the Idaho Rule, 39 Idaho L. Rev. 143 (2002).

SECTION B.   THE NOTICE OF APPEAL: BASIC REQUIREMENTS

R. MARTINEAU, MODERN APPELLATE PRACTICE— FEDERAL AND STATE CIVIL APPEALS

§ 6.1 (1983).

The single most important step in the appellate process is the filing of the notice of appeal. Most appellate courts treat timely filing as mandatory and jurisdictional. The failure to file a timely and proper notice of appeal results, consequently, in dismissal of the appeal. In these jurisdictions the filing of a timely notice of appeal is treated the same as the filing of a complaint within the applicable statute of limitations— missing the deadline is usually fatal: the trial court judgment is therefore final.

The steps by which the notice of appeal is prepared and filed must be given the closest attention to avoid the ultimate disservice to the client—the dismissal of the appeal because of a mistake by the appellate attorney.

Thereafter several ministerial steps are required to "perfect" the appeal (paying the filing fees, arranging for the "record" to be processed, and other items), discussed in the final section of this Chapter.

1. FORM AND FUNCTION OF THE NOTICE OF APPEAL

The notice of appeal is typically a one page (indeed, usually one *paragraph*) paper with the caption of the trial court proceeding at the top, which gives the adversaries and the court system notice that a participant in the trial-level proceedings intends to pursue appellate review. The simplicity of this piece of paper is illustrated by Official Form No. 1 annexed to the Federal Rules of Appellate Procedure, which is intended by the drafters of the rules as an example of how simple the notice can be:

Form 1. --Notice of Appeal to a Court of Appeals from a Judgment or Order of a District Court.

UNITED STATES DISTRICT COURT FOR THE ------------------------
     DISTRICT OF   --------------------

                         File number --------------------

A.B., Plaintiff   )
)
     v.   )   **NOTICE OF APPEAL**
)
C.D., Defendant   )

  Notice is hereby given that ------------------------------ (*here name all the parties taking the appeal*) (*plaintiffs*) (*defendants*) in the above case,* hereby appeal(s) to the United States Court of Appeals for the ------------------------Circuit (*from the final judgment*) (*from an order* (*describing it*)) entered in this action on the -------- day of ----------------, 20----.

             (s) -------------------------
             Attorney for --------------
             Address -----------------

* See Rule 3(c) for permissible ways of identifying appellants.

As the sample form illustrates, there are several basic elements that belong in a notice of appeal:

- The caption and docket number of the case at the trial level
- Identification of the party or parties who are appealing
- Specification of the court to which the appeal will be taken
- Designation of the particular order or judgment being appealed
- Signing by an attorney

Every aspect of the notice of appeal process has been goofed up by at least some litigants at some point (wrong party names are listed, some parties are omitted, ambiguous names are used, the wrong court is listed as being appealed to, the notice is filed in the wrong court, it is filed too late, or filed too soon, and myriad other variations of confusion or ineptitude that would make a lawyers' malpractice insurance carrier cringe). Several of the more repetitive kinds of problems have been dealt with in amendments to the rules in recent years, particularly in federal practice. Problems of incarcerated appellants have created the need for special rules. Later sections of this Chapter illustrate the most important aspects in practice. Who would have thought such a simple step could raise so many issues?

Particular problems that have arisen with respect to attorneys attempting to appeal fee or sanction awards involving themselves frequently involve a focus on mistakes in the notice of appeal. These matters are discussed in Chapter 4 of the Casebook, PARTIES.

Notes and Questions

1. When is the notice of appeal *filed* with the clerk of the trial court? Must the notice be stamped "filed"? What is the significance of the *date* stamped on the notice by the clerk? When is a document within the custody and control of the clerk of the trial court?

2. Like the federal rule, most state rules provide that the notice of appeal is to be filed with the clerk of the trial court. Some, however, require the notice to be filed with the clerk of the appellate court or, as in the case of New Hampshire (Supreme Court Rule 26(1) and (2)), with both the trial and appellate court. What are the reasons for preferring the notice filed in the trial court rather than in the appellate court?

3. While some decisions have stated that a court clerk does not have the *authority* to reject a document for filing even if the document on its face does not comply with the rules, many times each year "non-conforming" papers are rejected by the clerks' staff in various courts. What should a clerk do in a case where the papers are in improper form? Often the authority of the clerk on such matters is spelled out in local rules, or "internal operating rules" of the court, which are published. What should the attorney do if the clerk refuses to accept a document?

2. WHEN THE NOTICE OF APPEAL IS DUE

Every jurisdiction has established a specific time limits in which the notice of appeal must be filed for various categories of cases. The most common time limit for civil appeals is 30 days, though jurisdictions vary somewhat on this issue. California, for example, permits 60 days for many appeals to be commenced. Time limits are usually found in the statutes governing appeals, but for federal courts and some state courts, they are found in the appellate rules. Because the time limits are *mandatory and jurisdictional,* they are the most inflexible of the procedural requirements and there is little likelihood that an appellate court will seek to avoid them. Readings in this Chapter explore the rare instances where an extension can plausibly be sought. A late notice of appeal has the same effect as a complaint filed after the statute of limitations has run—it is of no effect and the appeal, like the action, is forever barred.

The standard time limit on filing a notice of appeal applies only if no special time limit is provided. Special time limits for particular categories of cases (particular civil subject matters, appeals from administrative agencies, tax cases, and criminal appeals) can be found in the rules or the statutes, usually in the statutes governing a particular substantive topic. A check of both statutes and rules must always be made to protect against overlooking the applicable time period. In federal practice the criminal appeal period is an incredibly short 10 days. On the other hand, FRAP 4(a) provides a 60–day appeal period for all parties in cases in which the United States or an officer or agency thereof is a party.

Pertinent sections of Federal Rule of Appellate Procedure 4 illustrate the current approach in those courts:

Rule 4. Appeal as of Right—When Taken

(a) Appeal in a Civil Case.

(1) *Time for Filing a Notice of Appeal.*

(A) In a civil case, except as provided in Rules 4(a)(1)(B), 4(a)(4), and 4(c), the notice of appeal required by Rule 3 must be filed with the district clerk within 30 days after the judgment or order appealed from is entered.

(B) When the United States or its officer or agency is a party, the notice of appeal may be filed by any party within 60 days after the judgment or order appealed from is entered.

(C) An appeal from an order granting or denying an application for a writ of error coram nobis is an appeal in a civil case for purposes of Rule 4(a).

* * *

(b) Appeal in a Criminal Case.

(1) *Time for Filing a Notice of Appeal.*

(A) In a criminal case, a defendant's notice of appeal must be filed in the district court within 10 days after the later of:

(i) the entry of either the judgment or the order being appealed; or

(ii) the filing of the government's notice of appeal.

(B) When the government is entitled to appeal, its notice of appeal must be filed in the district court within 30 days after the later of:

(i) the entry of the judgment or order being appealed; or

(ii) the filing of a notice of appeal by any defendant.

Under this rule the key time periods are:

- 30 days after entry of the judgment or order in civil cases (where the United States was *not* a party)

- 60 days *for any party to appeal* if the United States was a party to the civil case.

- 10 days for a convicted defendant in criminal cases.

- 30 days for the government to appeal in a criminal case.

Computing the Date. Rule 26 of the federal rules (conformed in recent years with the comparable provisions of the federal civil procedure rules) illustrates several issues. States vary in the way they handle these topics, but the federal rule is an excellent example of the questions to analyze under comparable state rules. FRAP 26(a) provides:

(a) Computing Time. The following rules apply in computing any period of time specified in these rules or in any local rule, court order, or applicable statute:

(1) Exclude the day of the act, event, or default that begins the period.

(2) Exclude intermediate Saturdays, Sundays, and legal holidays when the period is less than 11 days, unless stated in calendar days.

(3) Include the last day of the period unless it is a Saturday, Sunday, legal holiday, or—if the act to be done is filing a paper in court—a day on which the weather or other conditions make the clerk's office inaccessible.

(4) As used in this rule, "legal holiday" means New Year's Day, Martin Luther King, Jr.'s Birthday, Presidents' Day, Memorial Day, Independence Day, Labor Day, Columbus Day, Veterans' Day, Thanksgiving Day, Christmas Day, and any other day declared a holiday by the President, Congress, or the state in which is located either the district court that rendered the challenged judgment or order, or the circuit clerk's principal office.

Notice that (a)(1) provides that we do not count the triggering day. Looking back at the Rule 4 excerpts above, we see that entry of judgment is the trigger for the notice of appeal time period. For present purposes assume that one can definitively determine the date of "entry" (more on this later in this Chapter).

SECTION C.   CONTENT PROBLEMS WITH THE NOTICE OF APPEAL

1. OVERVIEW

TORRES v. OAKLAND SCAVENGER COMPANY

Supreme Court of the United States, 1988.
487 U.S. 312, 108 S.Ct. 2405, 101 L.Ed.2d 285.

JUSTICE MARSHALL delivered the opinion of the Court.

This case presents the question whether a federal appellate court has jurisdiction over a party who was not specified in the notice of appeal in accordance with Federal Rule of Appellate Procedure 3(c).

Petitioner Jose Torres is one of 16 plaintiffs who intervened in an employment discrimination suit against respondent Oakland Scavenger Co. (hereafter respondent) after receiving notice of the action pursuant to a settlement agreement between respondent and the original plaintiffs. In their complaint, the intervenors purported to proceed not only on their own behalf, but also on behalf of all persons similarly situated. On August 31, 1981, the District Court for the Northern District of California dismissed the complaint pursuant to Federal Rule of Civil Procedure 12(b)(6) for failure to state a claim warranting relief. A class had not been certified at the time of the dismissal.

On September 29, 1981, a notice of appeal was filed in the Court of Appeals for the Ninth Circuit. The Court of Appeals reversed the District

Court's dismissal and remanded the case for further proceedings. *Bonilla v. Oakland Scavenger Co.*, 697 F.2d 1297 (1982). Both the notice of appeal and the order of the Court of Appeals omitted petitioner's name. It is undisputed that the omission in the notice of appeal was due to a clerical error on the part of a secretary employed by petitioner's attorney.

On remand, respondent moved for partial summary judgment on the ground that the prior judgment of dismissal was final as to petitioner by virtue of his failure to appeal. The District Court granted respondent's motion. * * * The Court of Appeals affirmed, judgment order reported at 807 F.2d 178 (1986), holding that "[u]nless a party is named in the notice of appeal, the appellate court does not have jurisdiction over him." * * *

We granted certiorari to resolve a conflict in the Circuits over whether a failure to file a notice of appeal in accordance with the specificity requirement of Federal Rule of Appellate Procedure 3(c) presents a jurisdictional bar to the appeal. We now affirm.

Federal Rule of Appellate Procedure 3(c) provides in pertinent part that a notice of appeal "shall specify the party or parties taking the appeal." The Rule was amended in 1979 to add that an appeal "shall not be dismissed for informality of form or title of the notice of appeal." This caveat does not aid petitioner in the instant case. The failure to name a party in a notice of appeal is more than excusable "informality"; it constitutes a failure of that party to appeal.

More broadly, Rule 2 gives courts of appeals the power, for "good cause shown," to "suspend the requirements or provisions of any of these rules in a particular case on application of a party or on its own motion." Rule 26(b), however, contains certain exceptions to this grant of broad equitable discretion. The exception pertinent to this case forbids a court to "enlarge" the time limits for filing a notice of appeal, which are prescribed in Rule 4. We believe that the mandatory nature of the time limits contained in Rule 4 would be vitiated if courts of appeals were permitted to exercise jurisdiction over parties not named in the notice of appeal. Permitting courts to exercise jurisdiction over unnamed parties after the time for filing a notice of appeal has passed is equivalent to permitting courts to extend the time for filing a notice of appeal. Because the Rules do not grant courts the latter power, we hold that the Rules likewise withhold the former.

We find support for our view in the Advisory Committee Note following Rule 3:

> "Rule 3 and Rule 4 combine to require that a notice of appeal be filed with the clerk of the district court within the time prescribed for taking an appeal. Because the timely filing of a notice of appeal is 'mandatory and jurisdictional,' *United States v. Robinson*, [361 U.S. 220, 224, 80 S.Ct. 282, 285, 4 L.Ed.2d 259 (1960)], compliance with the provisions of those rules is of the utmost importance." 28 U.S.C.App., p. 467.

This admonition by the Advisory Committee makes no distinction among the various requirements of Rule 3 and Rule 4; rather it treats the requirements of the two Rules as a single jurisdictional threshold. The Advisory Committee's caveat that courts should "dispense with literal compliance in cases in which it cannot fairly be exacted," *ibid.*, is not to the contrary. The examples cited by the Committee make clear that it was referring generally to the kinds of cases later addressed by the 1979 amendment to Rule 3(c), which excuses "informality of form or title" in a notice of appeal. Permitting imperfect but substantial compliance with a technical requirement is not the same as waiving the requirement altogether as a jurisdictional threshold. Our conclusion that the Advisory Committee viewed the requirements of Rule 3 as jurisdictional in nature, although not determinative, is "of weight" in our construction of the Rule. Mississippi Publishing Corp. v. Murphree, 326 U.S. 438, 444, 66 S.Ct. 242, 245–246, 90 L.Ed. 185 (1946).

* * * Thus, if a litigant files papers in a fashion that is technically at variance with the letter of a procedural rule, a court may nonetheless find that the litigant has complied with the rule if the litigant's action is the functional equivalent of what the rule requires. See, e.g., Houston v. Lack, 487 U.S. 266, 108 S.Ct. 2379, 101 L.Ed.2d 245 (1988) (delivery of notice of appeal by pro se prisoner to prison authorities for mailing constitutes "filing" within the meaning of Federal Rules of Appellate Procedure 3 and 4). But although a court may construe the Rules liberally in determining whether they have been complied with, it may not waive the jurisdictional requirements of Rules 3 and 4, even for "good cause shown" under Rule 2, if it finds that they have not been met.

Applying these principles to the instant case, we find that petitioner failed to comply with the specificity requirement of Rule 3(c), even liberally construed. Petitioner did not file the functional equivalent of a notice of appeal; he was never named or otherwise designated, however inartfully, in the notice of appeal filed by the 15 other intervenors. Nor did petitioner seek leave to amend the notice of appeal within the time limits set by Rule 4. Thus, the Court of Appeals was correct that it never had jurisdiction over petitioner's appeal.

Petitioner urges that the use of "et al." in the notice of appeal was sufficient to indicate his intention to appeal. We cannot agree. The purpose of the specificity requirement of Rule 3(c) is to provide notice both to the opposition and to the court of the identity of the appellant or appellants. The use of the phrase "et al.," which literally means "and others," utterly fails to provide such notice to either intended recipient. Permitting such vague designation would leave the appellee and the court unable to determine with certitude whether a losing party not named in the notice of appeal should be bound by an adverse judgment or held liable for costs or sanctions. The specificity requirement of Rule 3(c) is met only by some designation that gives fair notice of the specific individual or entity seeking to appeal.

We recognize that construing Rule 3(c) as a jurisdictional prerequisite leads to a harsh result in this case, but we are convinced that the harshness of our construction is "imposed by the legislature and not by the judicial process." Schiavone v. Fortune, 477 U.S. 21, 31, 106 S.Ct. 2379, 2385, 91 L.Ed.2d 18 (1986) (construing Federal Rule of Civil Procedure 15(c) in a similarly implacable fashion). The judgment of the Court of Appeals is affirmed.

Notes and Questions

1. Recall that one pro se party may not file a notice of appeal for another (beyond his or her own spouse).

2. A variety of filings and maneuvers have been reviewed by the courts of appeal under claims that they amount to the equivalent of a proper notice of appeal within the time deadline. These possibilities include:

- a pro se inmate's "informal brief," filed in court of appeals, requesting new trial on all issues triable by a jury. Smith v. Barry, 985 F.2d 180 (4th Cir. 1993).

- a letter from the would-be appellant to the District Court, received within 30 days after the entry of judgment, designating the record on appeal in a fashion which specified the judgment plaintiff was appealing and the court to which she was appealing. Page v. De-Laune, 837 F.2d 233 (5th Cir. 1988).

- Although timely filing of document which is equivalent of notice of appeal will satisfy requirements of Rule 3, requirements of the Rule were not satisfied by filing a "Form for Appearance of Counsel" which failed to indicate whether the party on whose behalf counsel appeared was an appellant or appellee, did not refer to a final order of trial court which was subject of appeal, and was merely a standard form providing information about the attorney planning to appear in the case. Van Wyk El Paso Invest., Inc. v. Dollar Rent-a-Car Systems, 719 F.2d 806 (5th Cir. 1983).

- A litigant's filing of a petition for writ of mandamus with the appellate court has on several occasions been found to be the equivalent of a notice of intent to appeal where the action of the trial judge that is assailed in the mandamus application is a final judgment. See, e.g., SDDS, Inc. v. South Dakota, 97 F.3d 1030 (8th Cir. 1996).

- A "Motion For Reconsideration and to Vacate Judgment or Alternatively Notice of Intent to Appeal," failed to qualify as a notice of appeal because it was seen as asking primarily for reconsideration by the trial judge and only secondarily for an appeal. Washington v. Patlis, 868 F.2d 172 (5th Cir. 1989).

2. NAMING THE PARTIES APPEALING

MEEHAN v. UNITED CONSUMERS CLUB FRANCHISING CORP.

United States Court of Appeals, Eighth Circuit, 2002.
312 F.3d 909.

RILEY, CIRCUIT JUDGE.

[A father and adult son owned a franchise, and filed suit against the franchisor alleging fraud and deceptive practices. The federal district court dismissed the suit with prejudice and an appeal was filed.]

DISCUSSION

A. *Appellant Filing Appeal*

As an initial matter, a question exists about whether both Meehans appealed the district court's order or if only Harry D. Meehan, Jr. appealed. The filings on appeal contain the names of both Meehans and suggest they both appealed; however, the appellees argue only Harry D. Meehan, Jr. appealed. The notice of appeal filed in the district court states:

"Comes now the Complainant and notifies the Court and the defendants that the plaintiff will appeal the Judgment, Order, and Memorandum entered August 17, 2001."

The caption contains only the name Harry D. Meehan, Jr. as "Claimant," without "et al." or any similar designation. The signature line is for the "Attorney for Plaintiff." No other notice of appeal was filed.

Federal Rule of Appellate Procedure 3(c) (4) provides: "An appeal must not be dismissed ... for failure to name a party whose intent to appeal is otherwise clear from the notice." Here, the notice clearly lists only Harry D. Meehan, Jr. and makes no reference to Harry D. Meehan, Sr.'s intent to appeal.

Accordingly, we find Henry D. Meehan, Sr. has not filed an appeal, and we proceed only with the appeal of Harry D. Meehan, Jr. * * *

MAERKI v. WILSON

United States Court of Appeals, Sixth Circuit, 1997.
128 F.3d 1005.

RYAN, CIRCUIT JUDGE.

Kent Maerki and his attorney, Kevin Mirch, appeal from an award of sanctions in favor of the defendants. We will affirm as to Maerki because he has abandoned his appeal, and dismiss as to Mirch for lack of jurisdiction.

I.

In May 1991, Kevin Mirch filed suit against the defendants in district court on behalf of his client, Kent Maerki. The facts giving rise to the complaint, and the specific allegations of the complaint, are not relevant to this appeal. On September 28, 1992, Mirch filed an amended complaint naming both Maerki and the trustee of Maerki's bankruptcy estate, Leroy Bergstrom, as plaintiffs. After the filing of the amended complaint, the parties and the court used the case caption: "Kent Maerki, et al., Plaintiffs, v. Nick Wilson, et. al., Defendants."

On July 2, 1993, the district court dismissed the complaint, with prejudice, for lack of standing and violations of Federal Rules of Civil Procedure 11, 37, and 41(b). In an unpublished decision, this court affirmed the judgment of the district court. Maerki v. Wilson, No. 93–3857, 1995 WL 242004 (6th Cir. Apr. 25, 1995) (unpublished disposition). This court agreed that Maerki and Mirch committed "blatant violations of Rule 11," and that "Maerki ... abused court processes, disregarded court orders, prevented substantive discovery of the factual bases for his claims, and wasted the limited resources of the federal judicial system." Id. at *2–3.

After the district court dismissed the complaint, the defendants moved for an award of sanctions. The district court deferred judgment on the motion, and the defendants renewed their request after this court affirmed the dismissal. On March 19, 1996, the district court entered a lengthy memorandum summarizing the misdeeds of Maerki and Mirch. Pursuant to this memorandum, and also on March 19, 1996, the district court entered a single "Judgment Entry," which stated that "judgment is entered for the defendants against plaintiff's counsel Mr. Kevin Mirch in the sum of $50,000.00 ... and an additional judgment is entered for defendants against the plaintiff Kent Maerki in the sum of $12,141.29."

On April 9, 1996, notice of appeal was filed. The notice used the caption: "Kent Maerki, et. al., Plaintiffs, v. Nick Wilson, et. al., Defendants." The body of the notice stated that "Plaintiffs, Kent Maerki, et al., by and through their attorney of record, Kevin J. Mirch, hereby appeal ... from [the] Judgment entered in this action on March 19, 1996." The March 19 judgment, described above, was attached to the notice.

Pre-argument filings with this court suggested that Mirch was appealing the award of sanctions, but that Maerki was not. The defendants moved to dismiss the appeal, arguing that Maerki had abandoned his appeal and that the notice of appeal was defective as to Mirch. In response, Mirch explained, in part, that the clerk of the court had told him that his April 30, 1996, pre-argument filings "were accepted and filed timely, and that because the sanctions against Mirch were part of the March 19, 1996 order, jurisdiction was proper." On June 13, 1996, a panel of this court entered an order concluding that Maerki could appeal the award of sanctions against him. The court deferred decision as to this court's jurisdiction to review the award of sanctions against Mirch to the panel assigned to hear the case on the merits.

II.

A.

The defendants argue that Maerki has abandoned his appeal and that, accordingly, the judgment against Maerki should be affirmed. We agree.

Despite this court's June 13 order, which made it clear that Maerki could proceed with an appeal from the March 19 judgment, he has not done so. The brief filed with this court under his name addresses only the award of sanctions against Mirch; the brief is, in actuality, Mirch's brief. In his reply brief and at oral argument, Mirch confirmed that no attempt was being made to challenge the sanctions entered against Maerki. Thus, although we have jurisdiction to hear Maerki's appeal, that appeal has been abandoned. Accordingly, we affirm the award of sanctions against Maerki.

B.

Next, the defendants argue that this court does not have jurisdiction to consider Mirch's appeal because Mirch failed to comply with Federal Rule of Appellate Procedure 3(c). Specifically, the defendants argue that the notice of appeal did not specify Mirch as an appellant or otherwise give objectively clear notice of Mirch's intent to appeal. Again we agree with the defendants' argument.

Although resolution of this issue involves a relatively straightforward application of Rule 3(c), we have not found any precise guidance from the published decisions of this court. As the Second Circuit recently noted, "The Rule 3(c) issue has arisen with some frequency in the context of sanctions awards and often is addressed in unpublished opinions." Agee v. Paramount Communications, Inc., 114 F.3d 395, 400 (2d Cir. 1997). * * * In the present case, Mirch relies heavily upon Street v. City of Dearborn Heights, Mich., No. 93–1374, 1994 WL 615672 (6th Cir. Nov. 4, 1994) (unpublished disposition), and the defendants rely exclusively upon published decisions predating critical amendments to Rule 3(c). Because of the lack of published authority, and because we agree that the bar should be reminded "of the importance of Rule 3(c), [and] the harsh and unfortunate consequences of overlooking it," Agee, 114 F.3d at 400, we will take this opportunity to briefly explain, in this published decision, the relatively unremarkable reasons for dismissing Mirch's appeal.

Prior to December 1, 1993, Rule 3(c) provided, in relevant part, that the notice of appeal shall specify the party or parties taking the appeal; [and] shall designate the judgment, order or part thereof appealed from[.] An appeal shall not be dismissed for informality of form or title of the notice of appeal.

Effective December 1, 1993, however, Rule 3(c) was amended to provide that [a] notice of appeal must specify the party or parties taking the appeal by naming each appellant in either the caption or the body of the notice of appeal. An attorney representing more than one party may fulfill this requirement by describing those parties with such terms as "all plaintiffs[.]" * * * A notice of appeal also must designate the judgment, order, or part thereof appealed from, and must name the court to which the appeal is taken. An appeal will not be dismissed for informality of form or title of the notice of appeal, or for failure to name a party whose intent to appeal is otherwise clear from the notice.

Pursuant to the amended rule, then, this court should not dismiss the appeal of a party whose intent to appeal is made "objectively clear" by the notice of appeal. Fed. R. App. P. 3(c) advisory committee's note; Agee, 114 F.3d at 399, Garcia v. Wash, 20 F.3d 608, 610 (5th Cir. 1994). The requirements of Rule 3(c) are jurisdictional in nature, and the court of appeals may not waive or diminish the rule's requirements. Brooks v. Toyotomi Co., 86 F.3d 582, 585 (6th Cir. 1996).

Prior to the 1993 amendments, this court adhered strictly to Rule 3(c)'s requirement that parties intending to appeal be specifically named in the notice of appeal. See, e.g., Minority Employees v. State of Tennessee Dep't of Employment Sec., 901 F.2d 1327 (6th Cir. 1990) (en banc). Although we continue to believe that compliance with the letter of Rule 3(c) is required, what constitutes compliance with the rule has clearly been "liberalized." Thus, we cannot accept the defendants' invitation to simply apply pre-amendment case law. Nevertheless, we agree that the notice of appeal in this case did not give this court jurisdiction to hear Mirch's appeal from the March 19 judgment, because Mirch's intent to appeal was not objectively clear on the face of the notice.

Mirch argues that his intent to appeal was clearly indicated by the notice's reference to the March 19 judgment. In support of this argument, Mirch relies upon *Street*, 39 F.3d 1182. In addition to being nonbinding, *Street* is easily distinguished from the present case. In *Street*, the notice of appeal stated that the plaintiff was appealing the denial of the plaintiff's motion for reconsideration of "the court's order imposing sanctions under Fed. R. Civ. P. 11." Id. at *6. Significantly, "the order appealed from concerned sanctions imposed *only on plaintiff's attorneys and not on plaintiff himself.*" Id. at *5 (emphasis added); see *Hehemann*, 45 F.3d 430.

By way of contrast, the March 19 judgment in this case imposed sanctions on both Maerki and Mirch. Because it is possible that only one party will appeal a judgment entered against multiple parties, and because the notice of appeal in this case clearly indicated Maerki's intent to appeal, it cannot be said that the notice's reference to the March 19 judgment provided objectively clear notice of Mirch's intent to appeal. Accord *Dietrich*, 21 F.3d 427. The court in Agee reached the same conclusion on similar facts; we agree that although [Mirch's] name is listed as [Maerki's] attorney and the notice identifies the [March 19, 1996,] judgment and order imposing * * * sanctions against both [Maerki] and [Mirch], [Mirch's] intent to participate as a party rather than as a party's attorney is not clear on the face of the notice. *Agee,* 114

F.3d at 399. To this end, we believe that the court in *Agee,* id., properly distinguished *Garcia,* 20 F.3d 608, as we have distinguished *Hehemann* and *Street.*

Whether the language, "Plaintiffs, Kent Maerki, et al.," would constitute sufficient notice of Bergstrom's intent to appeal, in the event that he too had been sanctioned by the March 19 judgment, see Fed. R. App. P. 3(c), is not before us and the answer may not be entirely clear. But it is quite clear that this language cannot include Mirch who, unlike Bergstrom, was never himself a plaintiff in this case. Rule 3(c) states that the notice of appeal "must specify the party or parties taking the appeal" and "also must designate the judgment, order, or part thereof appealed from." These are nontaxing, but clearly independent requirements. Although the rule's allowance for "objectively clear" notice may save some failures to specifically identify "the party or parties taking the appeal," it will not do so in this case. * * *

As a final matter, we address the following passage from Mirch's reply brief on appeal:

> Appellees contend that it is improper for Mirch to present his arguments under his client's caption. In doing so, Mirch was following the instruction of a representative of this Court, namely the case manager who called Mirch's office and specifically advised Mirch to proceed in this manner. It is unconscionable to think that this Court would penalize Mirch for following the advice of the Sixth Circuit case manager.

In response to this specific language, we note that Mirch is not being penalized for "presenting his arguments under his client's caption." Rather, he is facing the consequences of his failure to give proper notice of his intent to appeal. It is not the caption in this case, but rather the notice of appeal, that is defective.

To the extent that Mirch intends to argue, as he did in response to the defendants' motion to dismiss the appeal, that he justifiably relied upon a statement by a clerk of the court, to the effect that "jurisdiction was proper," we have two further observations. First, according to Mirch, the alleged statement was made in conjunction with the acceptance of his April 30, 1996, pre-argument filings. By this date, the 30 days permitted for the filing of notice of appeal had already expired. See Fed. R. App. P. 4(a)(1), 26(a). Thus, the alleged statement came too late to create a reliance interest in the validity of the previously filed notice of appeal. More to the point, however, litigants are charged with the responsibility for complying with the Federal Rules of Appellate Procedure. We reject outright any suggestion that the advice of a clerk or case manager affects this court's review of the jurisdictional question presented by this case.

III.

For all of the foregoing reasons, we AFFIRM the judgment of the district court as it relates to Maerki, and DISMISS Mirch's appeal for lack of jurisdiction.

NATHANIEL R. JONES, CIRCUIT JUDGE, dissenting.

I must respectfully dissent from my colleague's opinion. As noted in the majority opinion, the amendments to Rule 3(c) have liberalized its requirements. These amendments have effectively overruled Torres v. Oakland Scavenger Co., 487 U.S. 312 (1988) which strictly construed the requirements of Rule 3(c), and would have mandated the present result. See, e.g., Flaherty v. Gas Research Institute, 31 F.3d 451, 458 (7th Cir. 1994); Garcia v. Wash, 20 F.3d 608, 609 (5th Cir. 1994). Under the amended rule, however, a court is cautioned not to exalt form over substance, as was done here. See Street v. City of Dearborn Heights, Mich., No. 93–1374, 39 F.3d 1182 (6th Cir. Nov. 4, 1994). Although the plaintiff's attorney was not specifically named in the appeal, the appeal clearly referred to the March 19 judgment which imposed sanctions on both Maerki and Mirch. By strictly construing the notice of appeal, the court must dismiss the entire appeal because the claims involving Maerki have been abandoned. There are no reasons of finality or fairness that would require such a result and the court could easily construe the ambiguity in favor of Mirch. Accordingly, I would assert jurisdiction over this appeal and reverse the district court's judgment.

Notes & Questions

1. In a case where a foreign company and its president were held in contempt by the trial judge and appeal was attempted from the contempt citation, the notice of appeal recited that "plaintiff Paramedics Electromedicina Comercial Ltda. hereby appeals [the district court's ruling]," without reference to the individual also held in contempt. The body of the notice mentioned him, once, but only to recite the procedural fact that the district court's order "granted the motion by [GEMS–IT] to hold [Tecnimed] and its President Paulo Werlang in contempt, jointly and severally." The Second Circuit concluded: "Thus the notice of appeal does not make "objectively clear" Werlang's intent to appeal [and his] individual challenge to the contempt order is therefore dismissed." Paramedics Electromedicina Commerckal v. GE Medical Sys. Info Techs., Inc., 369 F.3d 645 (2nd Cir. 2004). See also Agee v. Paramount Communications, Inc., 114 F.3d 395, 399 (2d Cir. 1997) (finding that, although notice of appeal identified order imposing joint and several sanctions against both client and attorney, attorney's intent to participate as a party to the appeal not clear from face of the notice).

2. In a case involving theft of valuable cargo, an insurance company sued several companies responsible for shipping the goods. After the trial court granted summary judgment for the insurer, the following notice of appeal was filed *within* 30 days of the entry of judgment:

> Notice is hereby given that Orient Overseas Container Line (UK), <u>sued herein</u> as Orient Overseas Container (UK) Ltd., OOCL (Europe) Ltd., Orient Overseas Container Line and OOCL (USA), Inc., <u>the above-named Defendant, hereby appeals</u> to the United States Court of Appeals for the Second Circuit from the Opinion and Order issued in this action on November 11, 1999 and the Judgment entered on November 30, 1990. (emphasis added)

Some 45 days after the entry of judgment, an *amended notice of appeal was filed* reading:

> Notice is hereby given that <u>all defendants, to wit</u>: Orient Overseas Container Line (UK), Orient Overseas Container (UK) Ltd., OOCL (Europe) Ltd., Orient Overseas Container Line and OOCL (USA), Inc., <u>hereby appeal</u> to the United States Court of Appeals for the Second Circuit from the Opinion and Order issued in this action on November 11, 1999 and the Judgment entered on November 30, 1990.

The Rules provide that "an appeal must not be dismissed for informality of form * * * or for failure to name a party whose intent to appeal is otherwise clear from the notice." FED. R. APP. P. 3(c) (4). The test for determining whether a Notice of Appeal is adequate "is whether it is objectively clear that a party intended to appeal." FED. R. APP. P. 3(c) advisory committee note (1993 amendment); see also Maerki v. Wilson, 128 F.3d 1005, 1007 (6th Cir. 1997) ("What constitutes compliance with [Rule 3(c)] has clearly been 'liberalized.' "). In this case, the Second Circuit observed that "the initial Notice of Appeal refers in a parenthetical phrase to every defendant." The caption of the Notice also lists each defendant as a party to the case. Such references demonstrate a clear intention by all defendants to appeal the District Court's judgment. Thus the court concluded that it had jurisdiction to hear the appeal of all defendants. Do you agree with this reading, as a matter of grammar, punctuation, or substance? *See* Hartford Fire Ins. Co. v. Orient Overseas Containers Lines, 230 F.3d 549 (2nd Cir. 2000).

3.   In a case where a minor student and her mother sued a school district for failure to properly accommodate disabilities under the Individuals with Disabilities in Education Act, when the defense won at the trial level the mother, "Ms. S," timely filed a pro se notice of appeal, but stated only her own name in the caption, and used the singular term "Petitioner." While the Ninth Circuit generally holds "that a non-attorney parent cannot bring an action on behalf of a minor child without retaining a lawyer," it has also declared that "the infant is always the ward of every court wherein his rights or property are brought into jeopardy, and is entitled to the most jealous care that no injustice be done to him." In this uncounselled disability case appeal, the court adopted the same approach. "For the limited purpose of this jurisdictional notice, Ms. S was constructively proceeding pro se, and her notice of appeal was sufficient under the liberal pleading rules of FED. R. APP. P. 3(c) (2)." Ms. S ex rel. G. v. Vashon Island Sch. Dist., 337 F.3d 1115 (9th Cir. 2003).

4.   Where 25 garment workers sued a union for pressuring their employer to remove work from the factory, a judgment for the defense resulted. The notice of appeal listed only 23 of the 25 workers. When this was noticed, the appellants presented an amended notice of appeal, which the clerk of the court of appeals accepted. The union then moved before a panel of the court to reconsider the deputy clerk's action in correcting the so-called "clerical error" in naming the parties entitled to participate in the appeal. The motions panel of circuit judges found that the omission was a clerical error by counsel in attempting to copy the correct caption from the trial court proceedings. The court also relied on the fact that the workers' opening brief

(filed well after time for a notice of appeal to be lodged) made it clear that all 25 of the workers were appealing. See Simo v. Union of Needletrades, 316 F.3d 974 (9th Cir. 2003). Is it legitimate to consider the brief as a designation of additional appealing parties, if it is filed well after the time for lodging the notice of appeal?

5.   For an interesting survey of problems prior to the present version of the Rule with respect to naming the parties on appeal, see Gegenheimer, Party Names on the Notice of Appeal: Strict Adherence to Federal Appellate Rule 3 After Torres v. Oakland Scavenger Company, 69 Denver U. L. Rev. 725 (1992).

3. IDENTIFYING THE JUDGMENT OR ORDER APPEALED FROM

Rule 3 of the Federal Rules of Appellate Procedure requires the appellant to designate the judgment or order from which an appeal is taken in his notice of appeal. See Fed. R. App. P. 3(c) (1)(B). This rule is jurisdictional and may not be waived by the court. "Although a court may construe the Rules liberally in determining whether they have been complied with, it may not waive the jurisdictional requirements of Rules 3 and 4, even for good cause shown under Rule 2, if it finds that they have not been met." Torres v. Oakland Scavenger Co., 487 U.S. 312, 317, 108 S.Ct. 2405, 101 L.Ed.2d 285 (1988).

Part of the Judgment? The doctrine appears to be that if a party drafts the notice of appeal so as to identify specific "determinations" within the final judgment, only those issues are designated for appeal. Thus in one case the notice of appeal read that the plaintiff "appeals to the United States Court of Appeals for the Sixth Circuit, from an Order granting Defendant's Motion for Summary Judgement, entered in this action on the 1st day of April, 2002." The appellate court concluded: "This notice clearly establishes jurisdiction over the district court's summary judgment ruling. However, the district court denied [plaintiff's] motion for leave to amend in a separate order, albeit an order that was entered on the same day as the order granting summary judgment. Hence, we lack jurisdiction over the district court's denial of the motion for leave to amend." Rushton v. City of Warren, 90 Fed. Appx. 912 (6th Cir. 2004).

Criminal Cases. It appears that in some courts a party must specify whether the appeal challenges a conviction, the sentence, or both. In federal courts this doctrine appears to be explained by the huge fraction of all appeals that involve challenges to sentences, making a tight lid on such challenges to the sentence important. See generally United States v. Avendano–Camacho, 786 F.2d 1392, 1394–95 (9th Cir. 1986).

PARKHILL v. MINNESOTA MUT. LIFE INS. CO.

United States Court of Appeals, Eighth Circuit, 2002.
286 F.3d 1051.

HANSEN, CIRCUIT JUDGE.

[The plaintiff insurance policy holder sought to appeal from rulings of the United States district court granting the defendant insurance company summary judgment on plaintiff's contract and fraud claims related to the insurer's alleged deceptive marketing practices concerning "vanishing premiums" life insurance policies, and the court's denial of class certification of the case on behalf of all policyholders with similar policy forms.]

A district court's decision to deny class certification is normally reviewed for an abuse of discretion. See Prince v. Endell, 78 F.3d 397, 399 (8th Cir. 1996). Minnesota Mutual argues, however, that our review is foreclosed because Parkhill did not indicate in his notice of appeal that he intended to appeal the district court's denial of class certification. We agree and conclude that we lack jurisdiction to review the denial.

Federal Rule of Appellate Procedure 3(c)(1)(B) provides that the notice of appeal must "designate the judgment, order, or part thereof being appealed." When determining whether an appeal from a particular district court action is properly taken, we construe the notice of appeal liberally and permit review where the intent of the appeal is obvious and the adverse party incurs no prejudice. Moore v. Robertson Fire Prot. Dist., 249 F.3d 786, 788 (8th Cir. 2001). Parkhill's notice of appeal indicates only that he appeals from the district court's August 25, 2000, order granting summary judgment in Parkhill (III). No mention is made of the district court's order of a year earlier (Parkhill II) denying class certification. Our court previously has held that an appeal from one order does not "inherently imply" an intent to appeal other orders entered in the action. See Berdella v. Delo, 972 F.2d 204, 208 (8th Cir. 1992). Our court also has held on numerous occasions that a notice which manifests an appeal from a specific district court order or decision precludes an appellant from challenging an order or decision that he or she failed to identify in the notice. See *Moore,* 249 F.3d at 788 (holding that notice indicating appeal was from judgment on date of jury verdict was insufficient to preserve appeal from earlier order granting summary judgment); C & S Acquisitions Corp. v. Northwest Aircraft, Inc., 153 F.3d 622, 625–26 (8th Cir. 1998) (holding that notice indicating the appeal was from summary judgment order was insufficient to confer appellate jurisdiction to reach appellant's challenge to earlier order compelling arbitration); Bosley v. Kearney R–1 Sch. Dist., 140 F.3d 776, 780–81 (8th Cir. 1998) (concluding that notice stating appeal was from entry of judgment as a matter of law was insufficient to confer appellate jurisdiction over earlier summary judgment order). But cf. Greer v. St. Louis Reg'l Med. Ctr., 258 F.3d 843, 846 (8th Cir. 2001) ("Ordinarily, a notice of appeal that specifies the final judgment in a case should be understood to bring up for review all of the previous rulings and orders that led up to and served as a predicate for that final judgment.'').

Parkhill argues that his intent to appeal the denial of class certification was apparent because he filed a motion with the district court to certify the denial for interlocutory appeal. While the intent to appeal may be obvious from the procedural history of a case or from the appeal information form completed by an appellant, see Berdella, 972 F.2d at 208, no such intent is obvious here. Parkhill's appeal information form does not mention the denial of class certification, and the district court's order denying certification did not serve as a predicate to the final disposition of Parkhill's claims; procedurally, the order had no bearing on the merits of his claims. Minnesota Mutual easily could have assumed that Parkhill abandoned his attempt to certify a class when Parkhill failed to include the issue in his notice of appeal and in the appeal information form.

Accordingly, we hold that Parkhill has not complied with Rule 3(c)(1)(B). We therefore lack jurisdiction to review the denial of class certification.

McBRIDE v. CITGO PETROLEUM CORPORATION

United States Court of Appeals, Tenth Circuit, 2002.
281 F.3d 1099.

KELLY, CIRCUIT JUDGE.

[The trial court dismissed the plaintiff employee's Americans with Disabilities Act claim and granted summary judgment in favor of defendant employer on her Family and Medical Leave Act (FMLA) claim. The employee then filed a motion to reconsider, which the district court denied. The employee appealed.]

I. NOTICE OF APPEAL

Ms. McBride's notice of appeal states that she "[does] hereby appeal to the United States District [sic] Court for the Tenth Circuit from the final judgment entered in this action on February [23], 2001." Because the only judgment entered on February 23, 2001 was the grant of summary judgment [on the Family Leave Act claim] and because no mention of the ADA claim was made in any of the other documents filed within thirty days of the February 23rd judgment, CITGO asserts that Ms. McBride failed to perfect an appeal from the dismissal of the ADA claim and is, therefore, barred from raising the issue before this court.

Fed. R. App. P. 3(c) (1)(B) requires the notice of appeal to "designate the judgment, order, or part thereof being appealed." Although the Supreme Court held in Torres v. Oakland Scavenger Co., 487 U.S. 312, 317, 101 L. Ed. 2d 285, 108 S. Ct. 2405 (1988), that Rule 3 is a jurisdictional requirement that cannot be waived, it reaffirmed the principle "that the requirements of the rules of procedure should be liberally construed and that 'mere technicalities' should not stand in the way of consideration of a case on it merits." Torres, 487 U.S. at 316 (citing Foman v. Davis, 371 U.S. 178, 181, 9 L. Ed. 2d 222, 83 S. Ct. 227 (1962)). Thus, if a would-be appellant files papers in a fashion that is technically at variance with the letter of a procedural rule, a court may nonetheless find that the litigant has complied with the rule if his or her action is the functional equivalent of what the rule requires. Torres, 487 U.S. at 317.

Applying this rationale, we have held that a notice of appeal which names the final judgment is sufficient to support review of all earlier orders that merge in the final judgment. Cooper v. American Auto. Ins. Co., 978 F.2d 602, 607–09 (10th Cir. 1992) (notice of appeal that named only the final judgment was sufficient to support review of order entered more than a year earlier granting summary judgment to certain of the defendants); Bowdry v. United Airlines, Inc., 58 F.3d 1483, 1489 n.11 (10th Cir. 1995) (appellant's notice of appeal designated the denial of the motion to reconsider rather than the original order); Cole v. Ruidoso Mun. Sch., 43 F.3d 1373, 1383 n.7 (10th Cir. 1994) (quoting 16 Wright et al., Federal Practice & Procedure § 3949 at 440 (Supp. 1994)) (notice of appeal from final judgment permitted assertion of claims of error in interlocutory orders in the same case). While none of these cases explains which orders can or must "merge" into the final judgment, Professors Wright, Miller and Cooper note that it is a general rule that all earlier interlocutory orders merge into final orders and judgments except when the final order is a dismissal for failure to prosecute. 16A Wright et al., Federal Practice & Procedure § 3949.4 at 72 (3d ed. 1999 & Supp. 2001). Likewise, Professor Moore's treatise states:

> An appeal from a final judgment usually draws into question all prior non final orders and all rulings which produced the judgement. Thus, a failure of the notice of appeal to specifically refer to a preliminary or interlocutory order does not prevent the review of that order on appeal. Having appealed from]the judgment, the appellant is free to attack any nonfinal order or ruling leading up to it.

20 Moore's Federal Practice § 303.21[3][c][iii] (3d ed. 2001) (citing cases).

Because the dismissal of Ms. McBride's ADA claim adjudicated fewer than all the claims and liabilities of all the parties, it was not a final appealable order and would have required certification under Fed. R. Civ. P. 54(b) to be immediately appealable. Bohn v. Park City Group, Inc., 94 F.3d 1457, 1459 (10th Cir. 1996). As an earlier interlocutory order, the order of dismissal merged into the final judgment. The notice of appeal from the February 23, 2001 order and judgment was, therefore, sufficient to support review of the October 16, 2000 order of dismissal of the ADA claim.

GREER v. ST. LOUIS REGIONAL MED. CTR.

United States Court of Appeals, Eighth Circuit, 2001.
258 F.3d 843.

ARNOLD, CIRCUIT JUDGE.

Patrice Greer appeals the District Court's adverse grant of summary judgment in her employment discrimination case against St. Louis Regional Medical Center (Regional), her former employer. Ms. Greer was employed at Regional as a full-time, hourly paid biomedical engineering technician (BET) in the dialysis unit, where she was on call twenty-four hours a day, seven days a week. She was called in to repair equipment on her days off, including days when she was on vacation or sick leave. In her complaint in this action, Ms. Greer alleged that Regional discriminated against her because of her race and gender, in violation of Title VII and 42 U.S.C. § 1981, and treated her differently from white male employees by: (1) requiring her to be on call and calling her in to work when she was sick or on vacation; and (2) subjecting her to less favorable terms with respect to time off and pay for overtime, travel, sickness, and being on call or called back. The plaintiff also alleged she was harassed and constructively discharged in violation of section 1981. * * *

Regional argues first that the appeal is procedurally deficient. Regional filed, and won, three separate motions for summary judgment in the District Court. The first motion, made in June of 1999, concerned claims of harassment and constructive discharge, and argued that plaintiff had failed to exhaust those claims before the Equal Employment Opportunities Commission. The second motion, filed in October of 1999 and granted in November of that year, concerned plaintiff's claims of disparate treatment. The third motion, filed in February of 2000, concerned remaining claims of constructive discharge and racial harassment under 42 U.S.C. § 1981. Final judgment was entered on March 1, 2000. The notice of appeal, filed on March 7, 2000, specified the following as the orders or judgments being appeal: "The final judgment entered in this action on the 18th day of February, 2000; 1st day of March, 2000." We take the reference to "the final judgment entered in this action on the 18th day of February, 2000," to mean the entry of summary judgment on that date in response to Regional's third motion for summary judgment. Thus, the notice of appeal refers expressly only to the final judgment and the third summary-judgment order. It does not mention either of the first two summary-judgment orders.[1]

Fed. R. App. P. 3(c) requires a notice of appeal to "designate the judgment, order, or part thereof appealed from." Fed. R. App. P.

---

1. It may be significant that the notice of appeal was on a form supplied to this pro se litigant by the District Court's Clerk's office. This form contains no space to enter anything as a judgment or order appealed from other than the final judgment disposing of the whole case. The plaintiff wrote in the order of February 18, 2000, in that space, and then underneath that printed line added "1st day of March, 2000," the date of the final judgment.

3(c)(1)(B). Ordinarily, a notice of appeal that specifies the final judgment in a case should be understood to bring up for review all of the previous rulings and orders that led up to and served as a predicate for that final judgment.

Orders granting summary judgment on fewer than all claims are not immediately appealable. Review must await a final judgment disposing of all claims and, normally, attended by the formalities specified in Fed. R. Civ. P. 58. Thus, there is no question that the notice of appeal here is timely. The only question is whether it brings up for review the first two summary-judgment orders. Regional, when reading the notice of appeal, might have thought that the only summary-judgment order contested was the third one, but it does not claim that it took any detrimental action in reliance on such an impression, and plaintiff's brief, when filed, does argue her disparate-treatment theory (the subject of the second summary-judgment order), though it does so inartfully.[2]

We do not think that the rules specifying the contents of notices of appeal should be interpreted strictissimi juris, especially in dealing with pro se litigants, where the appellee shows no prejudice. In addition, the judgment entered on March 1 recites, as its basis, the fact that "summary judgment has been ordered against the plaintiff on all counts of her complaint." It is fair to interpret this language as incorporating the three summary-judgment orders previously entered. Accordingly, we hold that the entire case is properly before us for review on this appeal. "It is important that the right to appeal not be lost by mistakes of mere form." Advisory Committee Note to 1979 Amendments to Fed. R. App. P. 3(c).

LUSARDI v. XEROX CORP.

United States Court of Appeals, Third Circuit, 1992.
975 F.2d 964.

POLLAK, DISTRICT JUDGE.

* * * This age discrimination case, filed in the District Court for the District of New Jersey more than nine years ago, is, from a procedural perspective, a cautionary tale. It has been assigned to three different district court judges and has twice been addressed here. As this case comes to this court for the third time, some irony attaches to efforts to breathe new life into age discrimination claims that are so old. [The court then discussed the facts and procedural history, in which a class of 25,000 former Xerox Corporation workers was certified by Judge Stern in 1984, then de-certified by Judge Lechner in 1988. Then in 1991 the claims were dismissed by Judge Politan as moot after a settlement of numerous claims.]

At oral argument, appellants presented their two preferred outcomes to this appeal: reversal of Judge Politan's ruling that the class

---

2. The brief asserts that "Ms. Greer was placed on a 24 hour call status and given a pager to be called back to work," Brief for Appellant 1, and that "two white males were not subjected to 24 hour call status...." Id. at 2.

action claims were moot or reversal of Judge Lechner's 1988 decertification order. Because of alleged defects in the notice of appeal, we must decide, as an initial matter, whether we have jurisdiction to review Judge Lechner's order.

In his August 13th letter opinion, Judge Politan informed the named plaintiffs that, although he was dismissing their motion to certify as moot, they could appeal Judge Lechner's 1988 decertification order. Apparently disregarding this invitation, appellants filed a notice of appeal which reads as follows:

> Please take notice that the plaintiffs ... as well as the proposed plaintiffs-intervenors ... hereby appeal to the United States Courts of Appeals for the Third Circuit from an opinion and order dated September 30, 1991 of District Judge Nicholas H. Politan denying a motion of the named plaintiffs filed pursuant to Rule 59(e) of the Federal Rules of Procedure seeking to alter or amend an August 13, 1991 opinion and order constituting a final judgment dismissing all class action claims asserted by the named plaintiffs and denying a supplemental motion of the proposed plaintiffs-intervenors for leave of court to file a complaint in intervention.

App. at 2088–89. The notice of appeal does not mention the June 1988 decertification order.

Because of an ambiguously worded question in appellants' Civil Information Statement, Xerox realized that appellants might actually be challenging the Lechner order and moved to dismiss that portion of the appeal as untimely filed. In response to Xerox's partial motion to dismiss, appellants stressed that "it is the denial by Judge Politan of the plaintiff's motion for recertification ... that is the subject of the instant appeal." Appellants' Brief in Opp. to Motion to Dismiss at 5. Similarly, appellants' initial brief makes clear that they were "appealing from the August 15, 1991 final judgment rendered by Judge Politan [i.e. the August 13th letter opinion docketed on August 15, 1991] *rather than the October 21, 1988 decertification order of Judge Lechner* ...". Appellants' Brief in Sup. at 27 (emphasis added). Only in later submissions did appellants express an oblique intention to challenge Judge Lechner's conclusions to the extent that they were "discussed and adopted" by Judge Politan in his opinions. Appellants' Reply Brief and Response to Cross Appeal at 20. Still, appellants maintained that they were appealing Judge Politan's orders. See id. at 16–7 ("[we] clearly identified as the basis for ... appeal the August 13, 1991 opinion and order of Judge Politan ... [and] the district court's September 30, 1991 opinion and order denying the plaintiff's Rule 59(e) reconsideration motion ...") Therefore, appellants never purported to be appealing Judge Lechner's second decertification order.

Federal Rule of Appellate Procedure 3(c) states that "the notice of appeal shall ... designate the judgment, order or part thereof appealed from." Xerox argues that this rule precludes us from reviewing Judge Lechner's order due to appellants' failure to specify this order in their notice of appeal and their repeated representations that they were not appealing that order. We agree.

In trying to avoid the swath of Rule 3(c), appellants rely upon our liberal construction of notices of appeal. See Drinkwater v. Union Carbide Corp., 904 F.2d 853, 858 (3d Cir. 1990). Specifically, they argue that the simple description of Judge Politan's August 13th opinion as "constituting a final judgment dismissing all class action claims" effectively drew into question all prior non-final orders. Appellant's Reply Brief at 16. In support of this proposition, they rely on the suggested form for a notice of appeal set out in the Appendix of Forms to the Federal Rules of Appellate Procedure, which allows an appeal simply from "the final judgment," identifying it only by date. However, appellants did not appeal generally from "the final judgment" on the class claims. Rather, appellants stated that they were appealing from an opinion and order of Judge Politan which declined to amend an earlier opinion and order of Judge Politan. Having referred specifically to those two district court orders, appellants had the responsibility to designate any separate orders that they sought review of:

> When an appeal is taken from a specified judgment only or from a part of a specified judgment, the court of appeals acquires thereby no jurisdiction to review other judgments or portions thereof not so specified or otherwise fairly to be inferred from the notice as intended to be presented for review on the appeal.

Elfman Motors, Inc. v. Chrysler Corp., 567 F.2d 1252, 1254 (3d Cir. 1977).

Recently, we translated the standard into a three-pronged test, under which it is proper to exercise appellate jurisdiction over unspecified prior orders only if there is a connection between the specified and unspecified order, the intention to appeal the unspecified order is apparent and the opposing party is not prejudiced and has a full opportunity to brief the issues. Williams v. Guzzardi, 875 F.2d 46, 49 (3d Cir. 1989). None of these factors is present here.

Where a connection between the unspecified and specified orders has been found, the link has been clear and direct. See, e.g., Matute v. Procoast Nav. Ltd., 928 F.2d 627, 629 (3d Cir. 1991), cert. denied, 116 L. Ed. 2d 270, 112 S.Ct. 329 (1991) (appealing from order denying motion for reconsideration gives notice of intent to appeal underlying order of dismissal); *Drinkwater*, 904 F.2d at 858 (reviewing unspecified summary judgment order only insofar as it included a claim that was "inextricably meshed" with claim in the specified summary judgment order); *Williams*, 875 F.2d at 50 (denial of directed verdict "underlies" the specified final judgment notwithstanding the verdict); United States v. Certain Land in the City of Paterson, N.J., 322 F.2d 866, 869 (3d Cir. 1963) (order denying motion to amend prior order includes the prior order); see also Foman v. Davis, 371 U.S. 178, 181 (1962) (denial of motion to vacate judgment and amend complaint and denial of prior judgment dismissing complaint). In each of these cases, the specified order either was predicated upon the unspecified order or raised intertwined issues that could not be decided without assessment of the unspecified order.[14]

In this case, Judge Politan's order denying class certification only depends on Judge Lechner's earlier order if we accept one of appellants' theories, cast in the alternative, that (1) Judge Politan "discussed and adopted" Judge Lechner's decertification order, Appellants' Reply Brief at 20, or (2) "had [Judge Politan] conducted the de novo class certification hearing contemplated by the MOU, the district court would have adopted Judge Lechner's conclusions." Appellants' Brief in Sup. at 27. Judge Politan never reached the merits of class certification, much less adopted Judge Lechner's conclusions on that issue. Judge Politan's August 13th letter opinion reads, "Since I find that there no longer exists a live case or controversy within the meaning of Article III of the Constitution, *I will not rule on the merits of the motion to recertify the class.*" App. at 2042 (emphasis added). Moreover, any counterfactual speculation about what conclusions Judge Politan might have reached had he conducted a de novo hearing is insufficient to constitute genuine interdependence. Finally, Judge Politan's jurisdictional determination was only in the most remote sense based on the earlier decertification ruling. Judge Politan might not have dismissed the class action as moot had Judge Lechner not previously decertified the class; however, one could with equal force contend that Judge Lechner would not have dismissed the claims but for Judge Stern's denial of Rule 23 certification back in 1983, but it would strain credulity to argue that the 1983 order, too, was incorporated in appellants' notice of appeal.

Second, the intention to appeal Judge Lechner's order was hardly "apparent". Aside from an explicit recital that they were not appealing the 1988 order, appellants' general presentation indicated that they did not intend this court to review the validity of Judge Lechner's decertification order. Appellate review of class certification determinations is normally limited to whether the district court abused its discretion in denying the motion, see Weiss v. York Hosp., 745 F.2d 786, 807 n.33 (3d Cir. 1984); Bogus v. American Speech & Hearing Ass'n., 582 F.2d 277, 289 (3d. Cir. 1978); however, appellants have made no serious attempt to recreate the record that was actually before Judge Lechner when he decertified the class. Nor did their original brief discuss the abuse of discretion standard of review with respect to Judge Lechner's ruling. Indeed, while Judge Politan's letter opinions were attached as exhibits to appellant's initial brief, appellants did not include excerpts from the transcript of proceedings before Judge Lechner or Judge Lechner's 1988 decertification order until more than two months later, in their Supple-

---

14. We have occasionally exercised appellate jurisdiction over a third class of cases—where (1) appellant designated a summary judgment order dismissing remaining counts of the complaint, yet not an earlier order dismissing other counts; (2) the parties nonetheless fully briefed and argued all of the issues; and (3) the earlier order could not be appealed until final judgment. See Murray v. Commercial Union Ins. Co., 782 F.2d 432, 434–35 (3d Cir. 1986); Gooding v. Warner–Lambert Co., 744 F.2d 354, 357 n.4 (3d Cir. 1984). In this case, only the last condition is met.

mental Appendix. Moreover, appellants repeatedly urged this court to mandate certification of four subclasses, relief that was never formally requested from Judge Lechner.

Xerox in its submissions on this appeal has not undertaken to defend Judge Lechner's order. Given the clarity of appellants' representation that they were not appealing Judge Lechner's order and appellants' failure to provide this court with a record sufficient to make a judgment on Judge Lechner's decertification order, there was no evident reason to brief that issue. Therefore, prejudice to appellee is likely to result if review is granted of an order that was not designated in the notice of appeal, and we hold that Rule 3(c) of the appellate rules bars us from reviewing Judge Lechner's order.

Accordingly, the only issues properly before us are whether the district court erred in concluding that it lacked subject matter jurisdiction over the motion for class certification, and whether the district court abused its discretion in denying the motion for leave to file a complaint in intervention on behalf of four members of the putative class.

Notes and Questions

1. As the principal cases indicate, a notice of appeal designating the final judgment itself is generally said to "bring up" to the appellate court all prior orders intertwined with final judgment. See R. Martineau, Modern Appellate Practice—Federal and State Civil Appeals, § 6.4 (1983). Thus an attorney may elect to list specific pre-judgment rulings as specifically subject to the appeal, to avoid any doubt about those events being appealed, but individualized references to orders or decisions will not be a substitute for the necessary practice of naming the final judgment in the notice of appeal as well. Several courts of appeal have held that where party designates in notice of appeal particular orders only (and not the final judgment), the appellate court is without jurisdiction to hear challenges to other rulings or orders not specified in the notice of appeal. See, e.g., Trust Co. v. N.N.P. Inc., 104 F.3d 1478 (5th Cir. 1997).

2. Consider a case in which the trial judge made two summary judgment rulings. Later the court entered a "Final Judgment." A party moved for reconsideration and new issues were raised during the briefing on that post-judgment motion. Ultimately, the trial court denied relief and reinstated the judgment. The notice of appeal specifically designated the summary judgment rulings, and did not list the decision on the motion for reconsideration as being appealed. The appellate court held that because the appellant's notice of appeal referenced only the district court's summary judgment rulings, the court did not have jurisdiction to consider issues raised in a motion for reconsideration not referenced in the notice of appeal. See United States v. Universal Mgmt. Servs. Inc., 191 F.3d 750, 756 (6th Cir. 1999).

3. In another case, the trial court dismissed a foreign affiliate of the U.S. defendant as a party defendant. Months later, the court granted summary judgment for the remaining defendant, and the plaintiff appealed. Reading the briefs, the appellate court noted that the plaintiff argued that

the district court erred when it dismissed the foreign company from the action for lack of personal jurisdiction. The court ruled, however: "We do not reach the merits of Whetstone's argument because we do not have jurisdiction to decide the issue. In its Notice of Appeal, Whetstone gave notice that it was appealing only the district court's summary judgment decision. It did not give notice of its intention to appeal the district court's earlier decision to dismiss Kraft UK for lack of personal jurisdiction, and no notice of appeal was sent to any representative of Kraft UK. Where an appellant notices the appeal of a specified judgment only, this court has no jurisdiction to review other judgments or issues which are not expressly referred to and which are not impliedly intended for appeal." Whetstone Candy Co. v. Kraft Foods, Inc., 351 F.3d 1067 (11th Cir. 2003).

4.   Some appellate courts have stated that they will "exercise jurisdiction over orders not designated in the notice if there is a connection between the specified and unspecified order, the intention to appeal the unspecified order is apparent and the opposing party is not prejudiced and has a full opportunity to brief the issues." See, e.g., Williams v. Guzzardi, 875 F.2d 46, 49 (3d Cir. 1989). Recent unpublished applications of this doctrine in the Third Circuit allow the appellate court to reach the merits in the following situation: The trial court grants summary judgment ending the case. The loser seeks reconsideration, which is denied without discussion. The notice of appeal cites only the reconsideration decision, but it is apparent that the underlying summary disposition is the gravamen of the appeal.

5.   In a case where the validity and application of two different patents was adjudicated in the trial court, but the notice of appeal sought review only as to one, plaintiff was not granted permission to "amend" its notice of appeal to include a designation of the decision relating to other patent, with relation back to date of filing. The Federal Circuit held that the original notice was not technically defective, and that amendment of a notice of appeal is permitted only to cure misdescription or technical deficiency. The court concluded that there is no doctrine that permits appellant to "amend" a notice so that time for appealing is extended beyond prescribed period. Durango Assoc. v. Reflange, Inc., 912 F.2d 1423 (Fed. Cir. 1990).

6.   Despite the "jurisdictional" and hence "fatal" nature of violations of Rule 3 under *Torres,* some courts of appeal nevertheless from time to time opine that "a party's failure to designate the proper order it intends to appeal is 'not necessarily fatal'." Martin v. FERC, 199 F.3d 1370, 1372 (D.C. Cir. 2000). The D.C. Circuit explains that "a party may demonstrate its intention to appeal from one order despite referring only to a different order in its petition for review if the petitioner's intent can be fairly inferred from the petition or documents filed more or less contemporaneously with it." Independent Petroleum Ass'n of America v. Babbitt, 235 F.3d 588 (D.C. Cir. 2001). A related consideration sometimes articulated is that without a showing of "prejudice" by the appellee, "technical errors in the notice of appeal are considered harmless." Id. (noting that an appellee did suffer any prejudice where it fully briefed the merits of the ruling the appellant failed to specify, and where the content of its papers demonstrated that it understood the true nature of the appeal).

7. In a case where a mother and her daughter, proceeding without counsel, sued an insurance company and the daughter's former legal guardians for allegedly depriving plaintiffs of proceeds from a settlement of a personal injury claim, the defendants moved for dismissal of the action for venue and other defects. The plaintiffs failed to respond to the motion, were threatened with dismissal, failed to respond again, then sought an extensions of time. The trial court denied a further extension of time to respond, and dismissed the suit. The plaintiffs designated only the denial of their motion for enlargement of time in their notice of appeal. The Seventh Circuit commented that even "a technically imperfect notice satisfies the rule if no genuine doubt exists about who is appealing, from what judgment, and to which appellate court." On the other hand, after Torres v. Oakland Scavenger Co., 487 U.S. 312, 108 S.Ct. 2405, 101 L.Ed.2d 285 (1988), that circuit had held that an appellant who identified specific issues in his notice of appeal would be limited to those matters on appeal, Brandt v. Schal Ass'n, Inc., 854 F.2d 948, 954 (7th Cir. 1988), and that designating an interlocutory order that serves as the sole basis for the final judgment is sufficient to call up the final judgment but excludes other decisions in the case, Chaka v. Lane, 894 F.2d 923, 924–25 (7th Cir. 1990). Surveying its post-Torres oeuvre on this subject the Court gave this summary:

> But we have allowed appeal of matters not specifically identified in the notice of appeal if the intention of the appellant is clear. See, e.g., Badger Pharmacal, Inc. v. Colgate–Palmolive Co., 1 F.3d 621, 625 (7th Cir. 1993) ; United States v. Michelle's Lounge, 39 F.3d 684, 692 (7th Cir. 1994)(claimants designating "any adversary hearing" effectively appealed specific order even thought it was not identified in notice of appeal); Librizzi v. Children's Mem. Med. Ctr, 134 F.3d 1302, 1306 (7th Cir. 1998) (notice of appeal identifying final judgment rather than order denying reconsideration of final judgment was effective to challenge later order); see also Foman v. Davis, 371 U.S. 178, 181–82, 83 S.Ct. 227, 9 L.Ed.2d 222 (1962) (designation of order denying motion to amend judgment effectively appealed judgment itself). The reason why an appellant is required to clearly state his intention on appeal is "to ensure that the filing provides sufficient notice to other parties and the courts." Smith v. Barry, 502 U.S. 244, 248, 112 S.Ct. 678, 116 L.Ed.2d 678 (1992) (holding that inmate's brief in response to briefing order could have qualified as functional equivalent of notice of appeal). A faulty notice of appeal will still be effective, then, if the intention of the appellant is clear and the notice "did not mislead or prejudice" the appellee. Foman, 371 U.S. at 181.

In the instant case, the Seventh Circuit noted that the district court had denied the mother and daughter's pro se motion for enlargement of time simultaneously with its ruling dismissing the suit. The plaintiffs' notice of appeal stated that they, "being entitled to an extension of time to file their response to the Defendant's Motion to Dismiss of which was denied by this court on April 9, 2001 [, appeal] said order to the United States Court of Appeals." The appellate court concluded that although this notice did not point specifically to the dismissal, an appellant's failure to directly identify the order intended for appeal was not fatal. Citing Barrow v. Falck, 977 F.2d 1100, 1102 (7th Cir. 1992) ("Defendants had only to draw the court's attention to the final judgment of March 19. Although this notice of appeal pointed to the order of October 1, such a gaffe is not fatal."), the court of appeals noted that the defendants discerned the plaintiffs' intent "and were in no way misled." See Farmer v. Levenson, 79 Fed. Appx. 918 (7th Cir. 2003)(the court proceeded to hear the merits of the appeal).

8.   What about rulings entered after a notice of appeal is initially filed? In a case where a Georgia golf cart manufacturer sued a Canadian golf cart distributor, and won, the defendants promptly filed a notice of appeal. Thereafter, the victorious plaintiff applied to the trial court for an award of attorneys fees. In a post-judgment motion, the president of the Canadian distributor also asked for reconsideration of the ruling that he was personally liable as a guarantor of the amounts due from the distributorship. The trial court granted attorney's fees to the Georgia plaintiff, and denied the Canadian defendant's motion on his personal guarantee. On appeal, the defendants/appellants briefed all of the issues on the merits, including the award of attorneys fees to plaintiff and the validity of the personal guarantee by the Canadian corporate officer individually. The Eleventh Circuit was able to avoid ruling upon the latter two issues, however. It held:

> Finally, CCQ and Murphy challenge rulings awarding attorney fees to Club Car and rejecting Murphy's claims that the personal guaranty contract was unenforceable. Both issues arose in rulings on motions for judgment as a matter of law entered after the initial judgment was entered and the initial notice of appeal was filed. In light of this, CCQ and Murphy were required to amend their notice of appeal to designate the rulings and amended judgment affected by those rulings. Fed. R. App. P. 4(a)(4)(B)(ii). They amended their notice, but failed to designate the rulings and judgment they now challenge.
>
> Fed. R. App. P. 3(c) requires a notice of appeal to "designate the judgment, order or part thereof appealed from." We have jurisdiction to review only those judgments or orders specified-expressly or impliedly-in the notice of appeal. Pitney Bowes, Inc. v. Mestre, 701 F.2d 1365, 1374–75 (11th Cir. 1983). Where a notice of appeal specifies a particular judgment or ruling, we infer that others are not part of the appeal. Id. The failure to designate the post-trial rulings on attorney fees and the personal guaranty precludes CCQ and Murphy from challenging them in this appeal.

Club Car Inc. v. Club Car (Quebec) Imp., Inc., 362 F.3d 775 (11th Cir. 2004). The court distinguished the situation before it from the general principle that rulings made *prior* to the final judgment, are deemed "merged" in the judgment and hence fair game for argument on appeal when the judgment itself is named in the notice of appeal ("The appeal from a final judgment draws in question all prior non-final orders and rulings which produced the judgment"). Does the entry of the final judgment provide a clear line of demarcation after which separate rulings will need to be specifically designated for appeal in order to assure that they are subject to review?

9.   Many courts apply a test similar to that in the Ninth Circuit, which says that when "a party seeks to argue the merits of an order that does not appear on the face of the notice of appeal, we generally consider two factors:

(1) whether "the intent to appeal a specific judgment can be fairly inferred" and (2) whether "the appellee [was] prejudiced by the mistake." See Lolli v. County of Orange, 351 F.3d 410 (9th Cir. 2003). In such a court, if the appellant files an opening brief arguing points that do not seem to be within the scope of the order identified in the notice of appeal as the target of the appeal, has the appellant satisfied the first prong of the test already by virtue of spelling out the arguments in the brief? If the appellee includes opposing argument in its brief, has the appellee satisfied the second prong itself (since appellee would be availing itself of an opportunity to be heard fully on these topics)? Would it be safe to omit those arguments from the brief in opposition? Is there any alternative?

10. A notice of appeal in the federal system is *not* required to specify the *issues* which the appellant intends to pursue. See, e.g., Draper v. Coombs, 792 F.2d 915 (9th Cir. 1986). Thus the prevailing system differs from the "assignment of error" approach still used in some American courts, in which the appellant must give specific notice of the claimed mistakes in the judgment being appealed.

11. Some federal circuits use appellate "information forms" which must be completed in connection with filing and processing the appeal. It has been held in some circuits that the court of appeals, in determining the scope of appeal, can rely on both the notice of appeal and the appeal information form. Burgess v. Suzuki Motor Co., 71 F.3d 304 (8th Cir. 1995). Does this provide a means of expanding an inadequate notice of appeal? Would it make a difference whether the information form was filed within the time allowed for filing the initial notice of appeal? See Clay v. Fort Wayne Community Sch., 76 F.3d 873 (7th Cir. 1996)(refusing to consider topics raised in the brief as an expansion of the notice of appeal where the briefs were filed after the 30 days originally available to file a notice of appeal and designate the orders appealed from).

12. If the issue is "jurisdictional" the appellate court may (or must) reach it—whether or not it is specified in the notice of appeal. For example, in a case where a landowner sued a town over its refusal to allow the landowner to place a mobile home on a residential lot, the town was not precluded under Fed. R. App. P. 3(c) from raising on appeal *the issue of ripeness* even though the town's notice of appeal did not refer to the orders of the district court that addressed this issue, because ripeness affected justiciability of the landowner's claims, and an appellate court is always required to address that issue if it applies. Lauderbaugh v. Hopewell Twp., 319 F.3d 568 (3rd Cir. 2003).

13. Most notices of appeal track the example form, and identify the order being appealed by its date. An unambiguous designation of the order by topic or title has sometimes sufficed in the absence of a date in the notice. See, e.g., United States v. Garcia, 65 F.3d 17 (4th Cir. 1995). Notices of appeal that give the wrong date for the judgment being appealed have been effective, at least where there is only one judgment and other factors make it clear what the appellant intends to appeal.

4. NAMING THE COURT TO WHICH APPEAL IS TAKEN

GRAVES v. GENERAL INSURANCE CORPORATION

United States Court of Appeals, Tenth Circuit, 1967.
381 F.2d 517.

WILBUR K. MILLER, SENIOR CIRCUIT JUDGE:

In this suit filed by Glen Graves on a fire insurance policy, the United States District Court for the District of New Mexico on July 15, 1966, awarded summary judgment to the defendant insurance company. Graves' counsel, on July 20, 1966, mailed to the clerk of the District Court at Albuquerque a notice of appeal from that action. The Clerk received the notice on July 21, but did not mark it "Filed" because it seemed to him to be defective.

The notice was correctly captioned, showing the name of the District Court and the style of this case as it appeared on the docket; but in the text of the notice it was erroneously recited that the appeal was being taken to the Supreme Court of the State of New Mexico instead of the United States Court of Appeals for the Tenth Circuit. Because of this error, the Clerk of the District Court did not file the notice of appeal, but returned it to Graves' counsel, calling his attention to the misnomer of the appellate court.

Graves' counsel prepared a corrected notice of appeal but, due to fortuitous circumstances, it was not received by the Clerk of the District Court until after the expiration of the period of 30 days from the entry of summary judgment.

After the District Court had announced its intention to deny his motion to file the tardily tendered corrected notice of appeal on the ground of excusable neglect, Graves filed on October 13, 1966 a written motion that the Clerk be directed to docket his appeal on the notice of appeal received by him on July 21, 1966. The motion included the following grounds:

> "That on July 20, 1966, Plaintiff mailed to the Clerk of this Court a Notice of Appeal wherein Plaintiff erroneously stated that he was appealing the Order of this Court granting Summary Judgment in favor of the Defendant to the Supreme Court of the State of New Mexico; that a true and correct copy of said Notice of Appeal is attached hereto and made a part hereof.

> "That said Notice of Appeal was received by the Clerk of this Court on July 21, 1966, and that the Clerk failed and refused to file the same and returned it to Plaintiff's attorneys; that the Notice of Appeal was adequate under the law and rules of the United States Courts and should have been filed in this cause by the Clerk."

On the same day—October 13—the District Court denied the motion just described, and this appeal followed.

Of course, the Clerk of the District Court was trying to be helpful when he returned to Graves' counsel the first notice of appeal and pointed out the obvious inadvertence in naming the court to which the appeal was taken. But it is not the function of the clerk of a district court to pass on the sufficiency of a notice of appeal which is tendered to him for filing. The sufficiency of such a notice may be challenged in the Court of Appeals by the appellee's motion to dismiss; or the appellate court itself, with or without motion, may dismiss for lack of jurisdiction, if it considers the notice of appeal fatally defective. Trivette v. New York Life Insurance Company, 270 F.2d 198 (6th Cir. 1959).

We hold that the Clerk of the District Court should have filed the notice of appeal which he received July 21; but that his failure to mark it "Filed" is immaterial, since it is the time when the clerk of a district court receives actual custody of the notice which establishes the jurisdiction of the appellate court. The Fifth Circuit said, in Ward v. Atlantic Coast Line Railroad Company, 5 Cir., 265 F.2d 75, 81 (1959):

> " * * * It is the time when the clerk receives actual custody of the notice which determines whether this court has jurisdiction over the appeal, and under circumstances such as are present in this case, the notice may be received in the clerk's custody and control even though it has not yet been manually handled and marked 'filed' by the clerk or his deputy."

It was there held that the notice of appeal was seasonably filed because the clerk's office had actual custody of it within the 30–day period, even though it was not marked "Filed" until after that period had expired.

Accordingly, we hold that the District Court erred in denying the appellant's motion of October 13, which asked that the Clerk of the District Court be directed to file the notice of appeal lodged with him July 21.

The next question is whether the notice of appeal was fatally defective because it recited that the appeal was being taken to the Supreme Court of New Mexico, instead of the United States Court of Appeals for the Tenth Circuit. Of course, because of the posture of the case, the appellee has not had an opportunity to test the sufficiency of the notice of appeal by filing in this court a motion to dismiss the appeal. We shall therefore, on our own motion, examine the jurisdictional question and consider whether the misnomer of the court to which the appeal was being taken made the notice of appeal fatally defective.

Rule 73(b) does indeed provide that a notice of appeal from a district court to the court of appeals "shall name the court to which the appeal is taken." Rule 1 provides, however, that the rules "shall be construed to secure the just, speedy, and inexpensive determination of every action." And it has been expressly held that Rule 73 should be liberally construed. Thus, in Gunther v. E.I. du Pont de Nemours & Company, 4 Cir., 255 F.2d 710, 717 (1958), the Fourth Circuit said:

"The courts of appeal [*sic*] should be liberal in passing on the sufficiency of a notice of appeal taken under Rule 73. It is provided in Rule 73(b) that the notice shall specify the parties taking the appeal, the judgment or the part thereof appealed from, and the name of the court to which the appeal is taken. The purpose of the notice is to acquaint the appellee and the appellate court with the fact that an appeal has been taken from a specific judgment in a particular case. When it appears that adequate information is given by the notice, the appeal should not be dismissed for mistakes which do not mislead or prejudice the appellee. * * * "

The Third Circuit had occasion to discuss this subject in Donovan v. Esso Shipping Company, 3 Cir., 259 F.2d 65, 68 (1958). It said:

"The filing of a simple notice of appeal was intended to take the place of more complicated procedures to obtain review, and the notice should not be used as a technical trap for the unwary draftsman. A defective notice of appeal should not warrant dismissal for want of jurisdiction where the intention to appeal from a specific judgment may be reasonably inferred from the text of the notice and where the defect has not materially misled the appellee. * * * "

In like manner, we think a defective notice of appeal should not warrant dismissal for want of jurisdiction where the intention to appeal to a certain court of appeals may be reasonably inferred from the notice, and where the defect has not materially misled the appellee.

Here, the notice of appeal's caption correctly showed the style of the case as one which had lately been decided by the United States District Court for the District of New Mexico. The United States Court of Appeals for the Tenth Circuit is the only court to which an appeal could have been taken. In these circumstances the notice's recital that the appeal was being taken to the Supreme Court of the State of New Mexico was an obvious inadvertence which could not possibly have prejudiced or misled the appellee. We hold that the notice of appeal of July 21 was sufficient to give this court jurisdiction.

The order appealed from will be reversed, the first notice of appeal will be treated as having been properly filed on July 21, 1966, and, due to the circumstances, the 40–day period for docketing the appeal fixed by Rule 73(g) will begin to run on the date of this opinion.

It is so ordered.

Notes & Questions

1. While the principal case was decided under earlier rules, it has been held under the current style of rules that—while the notice of appeal must explicitly name court to which appeal is taken when there is more than one potential appellate forum—where only one avenue of appeal exists, Federal Rule of Appellate Procedure 3(c)(1)(C) is satisfied even if notice of appeal does not name the appellate court. Dillon v. United States, 184 F.3d 556 (6th Cir. 1999). In the federal system, when would there be alternative appellate forums available?

2.   A notice of appeal indicating that appeal will be to a different federal circuit from that in which the district court is located (a move not open to a party) has been deemed effective to give notice of appeal to the one and only circuit to which an appeal may be taken in the federal system. United States v. MUSA, 946 F.2d 1297 (7th Cir. 1991). Likewise, a notice of appeal was not fatally defective because it mistakenly stated that appeal from an order of district court was being taken to U.S. Supreme Court instead of court of appeals: the intention to appeal to the court of appeals could be inferred from notice, and the flaky entry did not materially mislead the appellee. See Anderson v. District of Columbia, 72 F.3d 166 (D.C. Cir. 1995).

3.   According to the principal case, when is the notice of appeal filed with the clerk of the trial court? Must the notice be stamped "filed"? What is the significance of the date stamped on the notice by the clerk? When is a document within the custody and control of the clerk of the trial court?

4.   Like the federal rule, most state rules provide that the notice of appeal is to be filed with the clerk of the trial court. Some, however, require the notice to be filed with the clerk of the appellate court or, as in the case of New Hampshire (Supreme Court Rule 26(1) and (2)), with both the trial and appellate court. What are the reasons for preferring the notice filed in the trial court rather than in the appellate court?

5.   A number of states have not adopted the provision of Fed.R.App.P. 4(a)(1) that permits a notice of appeal mistakenly filed in the appellate court to be treated as valid. What are the reasons for treating as valid a notice of appeal filed in the wrong court? What are the reasons for rejecting this approach? What if the notice is filed in the wrong trial court? The wrong appellate court? In federal court rather than state court or vice versa? Can all of these questions be answered by analyzing the reasons for requiring a notice of appeal to be filed formally rather than just serve the notice on the opposing party?

6.   The court in the principal case stated that a court clerk does not have the authority to reject a document for filing even if the document on its face does not comply with the rules. What should a clerk do in such a case? What should the attorney do if the clerk refuses to accept a document?

7.   In the principal case the appeal could have been properly taken only to the Tenth Circuit. What if the appeal could have been taken to one of several courts? The court in In Re Wisner's Guardianship, 148 Ohio St. 31, 72 N.E.2d 751 (1947) said the possibility that the appeal could have been taken to more than one court did not make any difference because the statute specifying the content of the notice of appeal did not require the name of the court to which the appeal was taken to be included in the notice. Most modern rules, however, do include this requirement. Should this change the result?

8.   Consolidation of cases under Fed.R.Civ.P. 42(a) and its state counterparts can create, at times, confusion as to the number of notices of appeal that must be filed. If cases are consolidated into a single case and only one judgment is entered, then only one notice of appeal need be filed. Harcon Barge Co., Inc. v. D & G Boat Rentals, Inc., 746 F.2d 278 (5th Cir. 1984). If, however, actions are merely consolidated for trial but separate judgments are entered, then a separate notice of appeal must be filed in each case.

Kittery Electric Light Co. v. Assessors of Town of Kittery, 219 A.2d 744 (Me.1966). What is the basis for distinction? Is it valid?

SECTION D. SIGNING THE NOTICE OF APPEAL

The notice of appeal is supposed to be signed by counsel, or in person by a pro se litigant. In a case appealed all the way to the United States Supreme Court on this issue, a prisoner's action against state officials relating the conditions of his confinement was dismissed in the trial court. He filed a timely notice of appeal but forgot to sign it. The Sixth Circuit dismissed the appeal for lack of a handwritten signature on the original appeal notice of appeal. The Supreme Court agreed that the governing Federal Rules of Appellate Procedure and Fed. R. Civ. P. 11(a) direct that the notice of appeal, like other papers filed in district court, are to be signed by counsel or, if the party was unrepresented, by the party himself. But the Court reversed the dismissal order, holding that if the notice was timely filed and adequate in other respects, jurisdiction vested in the appellate court, where the case could have proceeded so long as petitioner promptly supplied the signature once the omission was called to his attention. Thus, the appellate court should have accepted a corrected notice of appeal as a means of perfecting the prisoner's appeal. Becker v. Montgomery, 532 U.S. 757, 121 S.Ct. 1801, 149 L.Ed.2d 983 (2001) (set forth in part below).

Note also that under Rule 3(c)(2) of the federal appellate rules, a pro se notice of appeal is considered filed on behalf of the signer and the signer's spouse, a term that was added after some unfortunate snafues in a large number of uncounselled immigration appeals. However, this provision does not reach beyond spouses. Thus in a case where several Hispanic landowners sued the government for taking their land in the Manhattan Engineering District of Los Alamos New Mexico without adequate compensation, after the government succeeded in having the case dismissed on a Rule 12(b)(6) motion in the trial court, there was a "falling out between counsel and some or all of the plaintiffs." Ms. Sylvia Molina filed and signed a notice of appeal purporting to launch an appeal on behalf of herself and "all named individual plaintiffs." However, the 10th Circuit held tersely: a "notice of appeal must be signed by the appellant's counsel or, if the appellant is proceeding pro se, by the appellant." (citing 10th Cir. R. 3.1 and Fed. R. App. P. 3 (c)(2)), The Court continued: "A non-lawyer may not represent another individual on appeal and cannot file a notice of appeal on another's behalf," and concluded that Ms. Molina may appeal the district court's order only as it applies to herself and the estate of [her deceased husband]. Pajarito Plateau Homesteaders, Inc. v. United States, 346 F.3d 983 (10th Cir. 2003).

BECKER v. MONTGOMERY

Supreme Court of the United States, 2001.
532 U.S. 757, 121 S.Ct. 1801, 149 L.Ed.2d 983.

JUSTICE GINSBERG delivered the opinion of the Court.

Petitioner Dale G. Becker, an Ohio prisoner, instituted a *pro se* civil rights action in a Federal District Court, contesting conditions of his confinement. Upon dismissal of his complaint for failure to state a claim for relief, Becker sought to appeal. Using a Government-printed form, Becker timely filed a notice of appeal that contained all of the requested information. On the line tagged "(Counsel for Appellant)," Becker typed, but did not hand sign, his own name. For want of a handwritten signature on the notice as originally filed, the Court of Appeals dismissed Becker's appeal. The appellate court deemed the defect "jurisdictional," and therefore not curable outside the time allowed to file the notice.

We granted review to address this question: "When a party files a timely notice of appeal in district court, does the failure to sign the notice of appeal require the court of appeals to dismiss the appeal?" 531 U.S. 1110, 121 S.Ct. 853, 148 L.Ed.2d 768 (2001). Our answer is no. For want of a signature on a timely notice, the appeal is not automatically lost. The governing Federal Rules direct that the notice of appeal, like other papers filed in district court, shall be signed by counsel or, if the party is unrepresented, by the party himself. But if the notice is timely filed and adequate in other respects, jurisdiction will vest in the court of appeals, where the case may proceed so long as the appellant promptly supplies the signature once the omission is called to his attention.

This case originated from a civil rights complaint under 42 U.S.C. § 1983 filed *pro se* by Ohio prison inmate Dale G. Becker in the United States District Court for the Southern District of Ohio. Becker challenged the conditions of his incarceration at the Chillicothe Correctional Institution, specifically, his exposure to second-hand cigarette smoke. The District Court dismissed Becker's complaint for failure to exhaust prison administrative remedies and failure to state a claim upon which relief could be granted.

Within the 30 days allowed for appeal from a district court's judgment, see 28 U.S.C. § 2107(a); Fed. Rule App. Proc. 4(a)(1), Becker, still *pro se,* filed a notice of appeal. Using a notice of appeal form printed by the Government Printing Office, Becker filled in the blanks, specifying himself as sole appellant, designating the judgment from which he appealed, and naming the court to which he appealed. See Fed. Rule App. Proc. 3(c)(1). He typed his own name in the space above "(Counsel for Appellant)," and also typed, in the spaces provided on the form, his address and the date of the notice. The form Becker completed contained no statement or other indication of a signature requirement and Becker did not hand sign the notice.

The District Court docketed the notice, sent a copy to the Court of Appeals, and subsequently granted Becker leave to proceed *in forma pauperis* on appeal. Becker received a letter from the Sixth Circuit Clerk's Office telling him that his appeal had been docketed and setting a briefing schedule. The letter stated: "The court is aware that you are not an attorney and it will *not* hold you to the same standards it requires of them in stating your case." App. 14.

Becker filed his brief more than two weeks in advance of the scheduled deadline. He signed it both on the cover and on the last page. Some six months later, on its own motion, the Sixth Circuit dismissed the appeal in a spare order relying on that court's prior, published decision in Mattingly v. Farmers State Bank, 153 F.3d 336 (1998) (*per curiam*). In Becker's case, the Court of Appeals said, summarily:

> "This court lacks jurisdiction over this appeal. The notice of appeal is defective because it was not signed by the pro se appellant or by a qualified attorney." App. 16–17.

No court officer had earlier called Becker's attention to the need for a signature, and the dismissal order, issued long after the 30–day time to appeal expired, accorded Becker no opportunity to cure the defect.

Becker filed a timely but unsuccessful motion for reconsideration, to which he appended a new, signed notice of appeal. Thereafter, he petitioned for this Court's review. The Attorney General of Ohio, in response, urged us "to summarily reverse the judgment below," Brief in Response to Pet. for Cert. 1, stating:

> "We cannot honestly claim any uncertain[t]y about petitioner Becker's intention to pursue an appeal once he filed his timely, though unsigned, notice of appeal in the district court. We never objected to the lack of a signature on his notice of appeal, and fully expected the court of appeals to address his appellate arguments on the merits." *Id.* at 5.

We granted certiorari to assure the uniform interpretation of the governing Federal Rules, and now address the question whether Becker's failure to sign his timely filed notice of appeal requires the Court of Appeals to dismiss his appeal.

In Mattingly v. Farmers State Bank, 153 F.3d 336 (1998) (*per curiam*), the Sixth Circuit determined that a notice of appeal must be signed, and that a signature's omission cannot be cured by giving the appellant an opportunity to sign after the time to appeal has expired. For this determination, that court relied on the complementary operation of two Federal Rules: Federal Rule of Appellate Procedure (Appellate Rule) 4(a)(1), which provides that "the notice of appeal required by Rule 3 [to commence an appeal] must be filed with the district clerk within 30 days after the judgment or order appealed from is entered"; and Federal Rule of Civil Procedure (Civil Rule) 11(a), which provides that "[e]very ... paper [filed in a district court] shall be signed." We agree with the Sixth Circuit that the governing Federal Rules call for a signature on notices of appeal. We disagree, however, with that court's dispositive ruling that the signature requirement cannot be met after the appeal period expires.

Civil Rule 11(a), the source of the signature requirement, comes into play on appeal this way. An appeal can be initiated, Appellate Rule 3(a)(1) instructs, "only by filing a notice of appeal with the district clerk within the time allowed by [Appellate] Rule 4." Whenever the Appellate Rules provide for a filing in the district court, Appellate Rule 1(a)(2) directs, "the procedure must comply with the practice of the district court." The district court practice relevant here is Civil Rule 11(a).

Rule 11(a)'s first sentence states the signature requirement:

"Every pleading, written motion, and other paper shall be signed by at least one attorney of record in the attorney's individual name, or, if the party is not represented by an attorney, shall be signed by the party."

Notices of appeal unquestionably qualify as "other paper[s]," so they "shall be signed."

Becker maintains that typing one's name satisfies the signature requirement and that his original notice of appeal, containing his name typed above "(Counsel of Record)," met Civil Rule 11(a)'s instruction. We do not doubt that the signature requirement can be adjusted to keep pace with technological advances. A 1996 amendment to Civil Rule 5 provides in this regard:

"A court may by local rule permit papers to be filed, signed, or verified by electronic means that are consistent with technical standards, if any, that the Judicial Conference of the United States establishes. A paper filed by electronic means in compliance with a local rule constitutes a written paper for the purpose of applying these rules." Fed. Rule Civ. Proc. 5(e).

See, e.g., Rule 5.1 (ND Ohio 2000) (permitting "papers filed, signed, or verified by electronic means"). The local rules on electronic filing provide some assurance, as does a handwritten signature, that the submission is authentic. See, *e.g.,* United States District Court for the Northern District of Ohio, Electronic Filing Policies and Procedures Manual 4 (April 2, 2001) (available at http://www.ohnd.uscourts.gov/Electronic_Filing/user.pdf) (allowing only registered attorneys assigned identification names and passwords to file papers electronically). Without any rule change so ordering, however, we are not disposed to extend the meaning of the word "signed," as that word appears in Civil Rule 11(a), to permit typed names. As Rule 11(a) is now framed, we read the requirement of a signature to indicate, as a signature requirement commonly does, and as it did in John Hancock's day, a name handwritten (or a mark handplaced).

As plainly as Civil Rule 11(a) requires a signature on filed papers, however, so the rule goes on to provide in its final sentence that "omission of the signature" may be "corrected promptly after being called to the attention of the attorney or party." "Correction can be made," the Rules Advisory Committee noted, "by signing the paper on file or by submitting a duplicate that contains the signature." Advisory Committee's Notes on Fed. Rule Civ. Proc. 11, 28 U.S.C.App., p. 666.

Amicus urges that only the first sentence of Civil Rule 11(a), containing the signature requirement—not Rule 11(a)'s final sentence, providing for correction of a signature omission—applies to appeal notices. Appellate Rule 1(a)(2)'s direction to "comply with the practice of the district court" ceases to hold sway, *amicus* maintains, once the notice of appeal is transmitted from the district court, in which it is filed, to the court of appeals, in which the case will proceed. Brief of *Amicus Curiae* in Support of the Judgment Below 15–18, and nn. 18–20.

Civil Rule 11(a), in our view, cannot be sliced as *amicus* proposes. The rule was formulated and should be applied as a cohesive whole. So understood, the signature requirement and the cure for an initial failure to meet the requirement go hand in hand. The remedy for a signature omission, in other words, is part and parcel of the requirement itself. Becker proffered a correction of the defect in his notice in the manner Rule 11(a) permits—he attempted to submit a duplicate containing his signature, see *supra,* at 1804—and therefore should not have suffered dismissal of his appeal for nonobservance of that rule.

The Sixth Circuit in *Mattingly* correctly observed that we have described Appellate Rules 3 and 4 as "jurisdictional in nature." 153 F.3d, at 337 (citing Torres v. Oakland Scavenger Co., 487 U.S. 312, 315, 108 S.Ct. 2405, 101 L.Ed.2d 285 (1988), and Smith v. Barry, 502 U.S. 244, 248, 112 S.Ct. 678, 116 L.Ed.2d 678 (1992)). We do not today hold otherwise. We rule simply and only that Becker's lapse was curable as Civil Rule 11(a) prescribes; his initial omission was not a "jurisdictional" impediment to pursuit of his appeal.

Appellate Rules 3 and 4, we clarify, are indeed linked jurisdictional provisions. Rule 3(a)(1) directs that a notice of appeal be filed "within the time allowed by Rule 4," *i.e.,* ordinarily, within 30 days after the judgment appealed from is entered, see *supra,* at 1805, and n. 2. Rule 3(c)(1) details what the notice of appeal must contain: The notice, within Rule 4's timeframe, must (1) specify the party or parties taking the appeal; (2) designate the judgment from which the appeal is taken; and (3) name the court to which the appeal is taken. Notably, a signature requirement is not among Rule 3(c)(1)'s specifications, for Civil Rule 11(a) alone calls for and controls that requirement and renders it nonjurisdictional.

Amicus ultimately urges that even if there is no jurisdictional notice of appeal signature requirement for parties represented by attorneys, *pro se* parties, like Becker, must sign within Rule 4's time line to avoid automatic dismissal. See Tr. of Oral Arg. 34–36. Appellate Rule 3(c)(2) is the foundation for this argument. That provision reads: "A pro se notice of appeal is considered filed on behalf of the signer and the signer's spouse and minor children (if they are parties), unless the notice clearly indicates otherwise."

We do not agree that Rule 3(c)(2)'s prescription, added in 1993 to a then unsubdivided Rule 3(c), see Advisory Committee's Notes on Fed. Rule App. Proc. 3, 28 U.S.C.App., p. 590, places *pro se* litigants in a singularly exacting time bind. The provision, as we read it, does not dislodge the signature requirement from its Civil Rule 11(a) moorings and make of it an Appellate Rule 3 jurisdictional specification. The current Rule 3(c)(2), like other changes made in 1993, the Advisory Committee Notes explain, was designed "to prevent the loss of a right to appeal through inadvertent omission of a party's name" when "it is objectively clear that [the] party intended to appeal." Advisory Committee's Notes on Fed. Rule App. Proc. 3, 28 U.S.C.App., p. 590. Seen in this light, the Rule is entirely ameliorative; it assumes and assures that the *pro se* litigant's spouse and minor children, if they were parties below, will remain parties on appeal, "unless the notice clearly indicates a contrary intent." *Ibid.*

If we had any doubt that Appellate Rule 3(c)(2) was meant only to facilitate, not to impede, access to an appeal, we would find corroboration in a related ameliorative rule, Appellate Rule 3(c)(4), which provides: "An appeal must not be dismissed for informality of form or title of the notice of appeal, or for failure to name a party whose intent to appeal is otherwise clear from the notice." Cf. this Court's Rule 14.5 ("If the Clerk determines that a petition submitted timely and in good faith is in a form that does not comply with this Rule [governing the content of petitions for certiorari] or with Rule 33 or Rule 34 [governing document preparation], the Clerk will return it with a letter indicating the deficiency. A corrected petition received no more than 60 days after the date of the Clerk's letter will be deemed timely.").

In Torres v. Oakland Scavenger Co., 487 U.S. 312, 108 S.Ct. 2405, 101 L.Ed.2d 285 (1988), it is true, we held, that a notice of appeal that omitted the name of a particular appellant, through a clerical error, was ineffective to take an appeal for that party. *Id.,* at 318, 108 S.Ct. 2405 (construing Rule 3(c) prior to the ameliorative changes made in 1993. Becker's notice, however, did not suffer from any failure to "specify the party or parties taking the appeal." Fed. Rule App. Proc. 3(c)(1)(A). Other opinions of this Court are in full harmony with the view that imperfections in noticing an appeal should not be fatal where no genuine doubt exists about who is appealing, from what judgment, to which appellate court. See Smith v. Barry, 502 U.S. 244, 245, 248–249, 112 S.Ct. 678, 116 L.Ed.2d 678 (1992) (holding that "a document intended to serve as an appellate brief [filed within the time specified by Appellate Rule 4 and containing the information required by Appellate Rule 3] may qualify as the notice of appeal"); Foman v. Davis, 371 U.S. 178, 181, 83 S.Ct. 227, 9 L.Ed.2d 222 (1962) (holding that an appeal was improperly dismissed when the record as a whole—including a timely but incomplete notice of appeal and a premature but complete notice—revealed the orders petitioner sought to appeal). * * *

In sum, the Federal Rules require a notice of appeal to be signed. That requirement derives from Civil Rule 11(a), and so does the remedy for a signature's omission on the notice originally filed. On the facts here presented, the Sixth Circuit should have accepted Becker's corrected notice as perfecting his appeal. We therefore reverse the judgment dismissing Becker's appeal and remand the case for further proceedings consistent with this opinion. It is so ordered.

Notes and Questions

1. No rule of the Federal Rules of Appellate Procedure deals with the requirement that documents filed in the appellate process be signed.

2. In the principal case, Dale Becker proceeded pro se, but can the decision be read as a rule limited to pro se cases? The Court's rationale centers on Federal Rule of Civil Procedure 11, which the Court finds to be the font of the requirement for signing pleadings, including specifically the notice of appeal. When the Court rejects the notion that the provisions of Rule 11 apply only to counseled appeals, is it holding in effect that the signing requirement applies at a minimum in cases where counsel represents the appellant? Is the case for allowing pro se litigants the same "cure" option for supplying a signature after the fact that is open attorneys a convincing one?

SECTION E. FILING AND SERVICE OF THE NOTICE OF APPEAL

1. FILING THE NOTICE OF APPEAL—IN THE TRIAL COURT

The notice of appeal in American courts is normally required to be filed in the trial court. That is the court that has entered a final judgment, and the court that may be involved in authorizing and superintending efforts to enforce the judgment. It is the court that has physical custody of the docket sheet, the judgment papers, and all of the preceding pleadings, motions, briefs, and exhibits.

Numerous cases have occurred over the years in which a litigant has erroneously filed the notice of appeal with the appellate court, rather than the trial court as required under the rules. The rules have been amended to deal with this recurring problem, and Rule 4 now states:

> **(d) Mistaken Filing in the Court of Appeals.** If a notice of appeal in either a civil or a criminal case is mistakenly filed in the court of appeals, the clerk of that court must note on the notice the date when it was received and send it to the district clerk. The notice is then considered filed in the district court on the date so noted.

Only a few states have adopted provisions modelled upon Fed.R.App.P. 4(a)(1), permitting a notice of appeal mistakenly filed in the appellate court to be treated as valid. What are the reasons for treating as valid a notice of appeal filed in the wrong court? What are the reasons for rejecting this approach? What if the notice is filed in the wrong trial court? The wrong appellate court? In federal court rather than state court or vice versa? Can all of these questions be answered by analyzing the reasons for requiring a notice of appeal to be filed formally rather than just serve the notice on the opposing party? Oregon v. Champion International Corp., 680 F.2d 1300 (9th Cir. 1982) held that filing in a state trial court rather than the federal district court was not excusable neglect or good cause for the purpose of extending the time for filing the notice of appeal.

2. PRISONER FILING: THE WARDEN'S MAILBOX RULE

In Houston v. Lack, 487 U.S. 266, 108 S.Ct. 2379, 101 L.Ed.2d 245 (1988) the Supreme Court found that the situation of prisoners seeking to appeal without the aid of counsel is unique:

"Such prisoners cannot take the steps other litigants can take to monitor the processing of their notices of appeal and to ensure that the court clerk receives and stamps their notices of appeal before the 30–day deadline. Unlike other litigants, pro se prisoners cannot personally travel to the courthouse to see that the notice is stamped 'filed' or to establish the date on which the court received the notice. Other litigants may choose to entrust their appeals to the vagaries of the mail and the clerk's process for stamping incoming papers, but only the pro se prisoner is forced to do so by his situation. And if other litigants do choose to use the mail, they can at least place the notice directly into the hands of the United States Postal Service (or a private express carrier); and they can follow its progress by calling the court to determine whether the notice has been received and stamped, knowing that if the mail goes awry they can personally deliver notice at the last moment or that their monitoring will provide them with evidence to demonstrate either excusable neglect or that the notice was not stamped on the date the court received it. Pro se prisoners cannot take any of these precautions; nor, by definition, do they have lawyers who can take these precautions for them. Worse, the pro se prisoner has no choice but to entrust the forwarding of his notice of appeal to prison authorities whom he cannot control or supervise and who may have every incentive to delay. No matter how far in advance the pro se prisoner delivers his notice to the prison authorities, he can never be sure that it will ultimately get stamped 'filed' on time. And if there is a delay the prisoner suspects is attributable to the prison authorities, he is unlikely to have any means of proving it, for his confinement prevents him from monitoring the process sufficiently to distinguish delay on the part of prison authorities from slow mail service or the court clerk's failure to stamp the notice on the date received. Unskilled in law, unaided by counsel, and unable to leave the prison, his control over the processing of his notice necessarily ceases as soon as he hands it over to the only public officials to whom he has access—the prison authorities—and the only information he will likely have is the date he delivered the notice to those prison authorities and the date ultimately stamped on his notice.''

The Court concluded that Federal Rules of Appellate Procedure 3(a) and 4 should be construed such that delivery to prison authorities is deemed the moment of filing. Rule 25(a) of the Federal Rules of Appellate Procedure has subsequently been promulgated to codify the prison mail box rule. It provides:

> Papers filed by an inmate confined in an institution are timely filed if deposited in the institution's internal mail system on or before the last day for filing. Timely filing of papers by an inmate confined in an institution may be shown by a notarized statement or declaration (in compliance with 28 U.S.C. § 1746) setting forth the date of deposit and stating that first-class postage has been prepaid.

3. SERVING THE NOTICE ON ALL PARTIES

Court rules vary in American jurisdictions, but in the federal system and several states, the notice of appeal is served upon the parties to the trial court proceeding *by the clerk of court*. Even though the appellant has just filed the notice of appeal, the clerk serves a copy on that party too. In criminal cases, the notice is served on the defendant individually—as well as counsel. FRAP 3(d) provides:

(d) Serving the Notice of Appeal.

(1) The district clerk must serve notice of the filing of a notice of appeal by mailing a copy to each party's counsel of record—excluding the appellant's—or, if a party is proceeding pro se, to the party's last known address. When a defendant in a criminal case appeals, the clerk must also serve a copy of the notice of appeal on the defendant, either by personal service or by mail addressed to the defendant. The clerk must promptly send a copy of the notice of appeal and of the docket entries—and any later docket entries—to the clerk of the court of appeals named in the notice. The district clerk must note, on each copy, the date when the notice of appeal was filed.

(2) If an inmate confined in an institution files a notice of appeal in the manner provided by Rule 4(c), the district clerk must also note the date when the clerk docketed the notice.

(3) The district clerk's failure to serve notice does not affect the validity of the appeal. The clerk must note on the docket the names of the parties to whom the clerk mails copies, with the date of mailing. Service is sufficient despite the death of a party or the party's counsel.

Double Service. It might bear noting that, in general, every paper one files at the trial level is also served by counsel on the counsel of record for all other parties (and on pro se parties). In the federal system,

Rule 5 requires that *"every written notice* ... and similar paper shall be served upon each of the parties."* Thus, most commonly, even though the Clerk will be serving the notice on opposing parties that a notice of appeal has been filed, when a party files a notice of appeal a copy is served (typically by mail) on all other parties. The adversaries of the appellant thus receive the notice from the appellant, and then from the clerk of the trial court.

Sending Notice to the Court of Appeals. In the federal system, as Federal Rule of Appellate Procedure 3(d)(1) indicates, the clerk of the trial court is required to "promptly send a copy of the notice of appeal and of the docket entries—and any later docket entries—to the clerk of the court of appeals named in the notice." Because the untimely lodging of a notice of appeal will likely be fatal (it deprives the appellate court of jurisdiction to hear the appeal) the Rule quoted above requires that the district court clerk note, on each copy of the notice of appeal, the date on which the notice of appeal was filed.

RHYNER v. SAUK COUNTY

Court of Appeals of Wisconsin, 1984.
118 Wis.2d 324, 348 N.W.2d 588.

PER CURIAM.

The trial court entered judgments dismissing the complaint against Sauk County and other defendants. Plaintiff has appealed. Sauk County moves to dismiss the appeal on grounds that * * * Sauk County was not timely served with the notice of appeal. Because we conclude that Sauk County was not timely served with the notice of appeal and did not waive its rights by participating in the appeal, we dismiss the appeal as to Sauk County. * * *

August 10, 1983, the trial court entered an order for judgment and a judgment dismissing the complaint against Sauk County. August 11, 1983, the court entered an order for judgment and judgment dismissing the complaint against Village of Lake Delton and Jeffrey Woodruff. September 12, 1983, plaintiff filed his notice of appeal, but did not serve Sauk County or its attorney until December 5, 1983. * * *

Sauk County moves to dismiss on the ground that it had no notice that an appeal was pending against it until after the appellant's brief and appendix were served on November 25, 1983. Attorney Mercer states that he wrote a letter to plaintiff's attorney on that date inquiring whether the appeal also applied to Sauk County. December 5, 1983, Attorney Mercer received a letter from plaintiff's attorney containing a copy of the notice of appeal and apologizing for the late service. December 7, 1983, Sauk County filed its motion to dismiss in this court.

Plaintiff argues there is no requirement in the Rules of Appellate Procedure to serve opposing counsel with the notice of appeal. There is no express service requirement in Rule 809.10. Rule 809.80(2), however, requires service as provided in secs. 801.14(1), (2) and (4), Stats., of any paper required to be filed under the Rules in a trial or appellate court. State v. Rhone, 94 Wis.2d 682, 685, 288 N.W.2d 862, 864 (1980). A notice of appeal is a paper required to be filed under the Rules. Sections 801.14(1) and (2) require service of all papers on opposing counsel. Section 801.14(4) provides that filing constitutes certification that the paper filed has been served on all parties required to be served. The Rules therefore require service upon all opposing parties before filing. *Rhone,* supra, 94 Wis.2d at 687, 288 N.W.2d at 864–65.

Rule 809.10(1)(b) provides that the filing of a timely notice of appeal is necessary to give the court jurisdiction over the appeal. The *Rhone* court held, however, that service of a petition for review on the opposing parties is not necessary to confer jurisdiction on the Wisconsin Supreme Court under Rule 809.61. *Rhone,* supra, 94 Wis.2d at 687, 288 N.W.2d at 864–65. By analogy, we conclude that service of the notice of appeal on opposing parties is not necessary to confer jurisdiction on this court.

Plaintiff contends that Attorney Mercer had notice of the appeal on September 22, 1983, when the clerk of the trial court issued notice that the record was assembled and ready for inspection. The appeal record does not show that Attorney Mercer received notice at that time. Moreover, because Attorney Mercer's name was not on the notice of appeal, he did not receive notices from this court that an appeal was pending or that the record had been filed. It is undisputed that he was not served with the notice of appeal until December 5, 1983, which was after he was served with the appellant's brief and after he inquired whether the plaintiff intended the appeal to apply to Sauk County.

Although a party may move to dismiss an appeal under Rule 809.83(2) for late service of the notice of appeal, this court may extend the time for service of the notice of appeal under Rule 809.82(2). *Rhone,* supra, 94 Wis.2d at 687–88, 288 N.W.2d at 865. We are without guidance under the new Rules of Appellate Procedure when considering a motion to dismiss for late service of the notice of appeal. Martineau and Malmgren in *Wisconsin Appellate Practice,* sec. 601, recommend that the cases arising under the old law on waiver by participation in the appeal be followed. Id. at pp. 37–39. Under those cases, the signing of a stipulation or the filing of a brief on the merits during the pendency of an appeal constituted a waiver of defects on appeal. Retaining an appellant's brief prior to filing a motion to dismiss was not considered waiver. We conclude those cases are applicable to determine whether the appeal should be dismissed as to Sauk County.

We conclude there was no waiver by participation in the appeal by Sauk County. Sauk County promptly moved to dismiss upon learning that the appeal was intended to apply to it and did not participate in the appeal.

We conclude that the motion to dismiss the appeal as to Sauk County should be granted. The appeal continues as to Village of Lake Delton and Jeffrey Woodruff.

Appeal dismissed as to Sauk County.

Notes and Questions

1. Court rules differ regarding who should serve the notice of appeal—the appellant or the clerk of court. Which is preferable?

2. What should be the effect of failure to serve the notice of appeal? Should it be the same as failure to notify the parties of the entry of judgment? Should the party not served have to show prejudice before dismissal of the appeal as to it? For a case refusing to dismiss a cross appeal because no prejudice was shown from the failure of the cross appellant to serve the cross appellee for almost two months after it was filed, see Rowen v. Lemars Mutual Ins. Co., 347 N.W.2d 630 (Iowa 1984).

3. Would the result in the principal case have been different had Sauk County been the only appellee? Should it have been?

4. Problems that arise when *no notice* of a judgment is provided to the losing party are discussed in later portions of the present Chapter of this Casebook.

SECTION F. TIMING PROBLEMS WITH NOTICES OF APPEAL

1. WHEN THE JUDGMENT IS ENTERED

WILLIAM CHERRY TRUST v. HOFMANN

Court of Appeals of Ohio, 1985.
22 Ohio App.3d 100, 489 N.E.2d 832.

HANDWORK, JUDGE.

This matter is before the court, sua sponte. The case sub judice is a civil appeal purportedly from a judgment of the Toledo Municipal Court. For the following reasons, we conclude that the "judgment" sought to be appealed is not one that is final and appealable.

On July 24, 1984, the municipal court ruled on matters relating to an earlier default judgment which had been entered against defendants-appellees and which, at some later point, had been vacated. The July 24th ruling appears to have been directed to motions to correct and clarify the record as to what it was the trial court had intended to do in granting and then vacating the previous default judgment. On August 17, 1984, appellant filed a motion for reconsideration, asking the court to reconsider its ruling of July 24th and requesting a hearing on the matter. Subsequently, on August 21, 1984, appellant filed its notice of appeal from the July 24th "clarification" order. Despite its lack of jurisdiction after the notice of appeal was filed, the trial court, on August 30th, granted the requested hearing, which was held on September 26, 1984. On October 19, 1984, the trial court "reaffirmed" its July 24th ruling.

The July 24th order, the order from which this appeal has been taken, is handwritten in ink on a 15 x 10 inch case file-envelope. It appears as follows:

"7/24/84. In ruling on its Pltf's motion #84–631 the court finds, that although Defts' motion #83–682 filed on 6–2–83 makes reference only to George Hofmann DBA Hofmann Furniture Store, the court in its entry of 6–8–83 nevertheless states in part as follows: 'Defts' motion #83–682 to vacate default judgment entered on 4–26–83 is found well-taken & granted and it is hereby ordered that said default judgment is vacated & set aside.'

"The default judgment entry of 4–26–83 granted a default judgment against all defendants including Frank Riege and therefore the vacation of that default judgment on 6–8–83 applied to all defendants.

"The court also transferred the entire case, including all the parties, to the court of common pleas for determination of all matters against all parties.

"/s/ Judge Robt. W. Penn"

Two deficiencies exist in this "entry," though only one of them prevents it from being a final appealable judgment or order for purposes of appellate jurisdiction.

I

The first problem lies in the *form* of the "judgment." Aside from various other entries on the same file-envelope, all of which are written in ink but with an occasional typewritten note, no *separate* document (a "judgment entry") has been *separately* filed as such. It is, therefore, difficult to say that there is an identifiable "judgment" or "order." Arguably, the handwritten notations here are not even the kind of "half-sheet" entry commonly used, but frequently criticized. See Hall v. K.V.V. Enterprises (1984), 15 Ohio App.3d 137, 140, 473 N.E.2d 833 (Whiteside, J., dissenting).

Whether cryptically scribbled notations on a case file-envelope suffice, in form, as a proper "judgment/journal entry" for purposes of final appealability is at least open to serious doubt. Civ.R. 54(A) does little more than define "judgment" as including "a decree and any order from which an appeal lies." The language of Civ.R. 58, however, implies the formal "preparation" of a written journal or judgment entry by trial courts. Civ.R. 58 mandates, in pertinent part:

"[U]pon a general verdict of a jury, or upon a decision announced, the court *shall promptly cause the judgment to be prepared and, the court having signed it, the clerk shall thereupon enter it. A judgment is effective only when filed with the clerk* for journalization. * * * "(Emphasis added)

In this regard, too, M.C.Sup.R. 7 states:

"The *judgment entry* specified in Civil Rule 58 and in Criminal Rule 32[B] shall be journalized within thirty days of the judgment. If such entry is not prepared and presented for journalization by counsel, *it shall be prepared by the court and filed with the clerk for journalization.*" (Emphasis added.)

Many cases suggest that Civ.R. 58 requires the drafting of a separate document, complete in itself, which incorporates the order, decree or determination of the court. They further suggest that this document must be filed separately from other material with the clerk of the trial court who is responsible for its journalization. The underlying premise here is that a judge speaks as the court only through journalized judgment entries.

Mere "notations" on case jackets are insufficient to rise to the dignity and finality of properly drafted judgment entries filed with the clerk for journalization. Civ.R. 58; A document not labeled "judgment" or "judgment entry," nor unequivocally intended to be a judgment, does not constitute a "judgment" in the formal sense. This is often true where no separate document is ever filed by the court.

In Peters v. Arbaugh (1976), 50 Ohio App.2d 30, 361 N.E.2d 531 [4 O.O.3d 17], the court stated, in the syllabus:

> "*Before a document filed by a judge in a civil action can qualify under Civ.R. 58 as a judgment from which an appeal can be taken, it must contain a sufficiently definitive formal statement showing an intent to effect a termination of the case.*" (Emphasis added.)

Indeed, a "judgment is final, effective and imbued with a permanent character *when filed* with the clerk [of the trial court] pursuant to Civ.R. 58." (Emphasis added.) Cale Products, Inc. v. Orrville Bronze & Alum. Co. (1982), 8 Ohio App.3d 375, 457 N.E.2d 854. But there is more to a "judgment" than merely its form as a separate document. As the court noted in Peters v. Arbaugh, supra, the document's language must reasonably indicate an intent to effect "a termination of the case." Although these sentiments regarding the form and character of a formal judgment might appear self-evident, confusion has manifested itself in the ambivalent distinction between a court's "decision" and its "judgment."

The question is not only "when is a judgment a judgment?"—but also: "what constitutes a judgment?" The question, in each case, is essentially *sui generis*. However, insofar as this distinction between "decisions" and "judgments" is concerned, the current wisdom appears to hold that while Civ.R. 58 does *not* require a court's "judgment" to be incorporated on a written document *separate from* its "decision," *the better practice* is clearly for a trial court to file a separate document with the clerk, preferably one identifiable as a "judgment entry," which the clerk may then date and "enter" on the record. Millies v. Millies, supra, 47 Ohio St.2d at 44, 350 N.E.2d 675 ("[T]he case before us concerns an equivocal order not readily identifiable as a judgment entry, but rather one arguably intended by the trial judge as an announcement of his decision." Id.); see, also, Civ.R. 58. However, the Ohio Supreme Court has yet to hold, clearly and authoritatively, that Civ.R. 58 requires that a trial court's "judgment" be prepared and filed with the clerk as a separate document.

Yet, regardless of whether "decisions" and "judgments" should be filed and entered separately, it is clear under the current interpretation of Civ.R. 58 that in order to be "effective" a court's judgment, whatever its form may be, must be *filed* with the trial court clerk for journalization. See Civ.R. 58; see, also, App.R. 4(A) (civil cases) and App.R. 4(B) (criminal cases). (We note that the following language is contained in both appellate rules: "A judgment or order is entered * * * *when it is filed* with the clerk of the trial court for journalization." [Emphasis added.])

This interpretation of what Civ.R. 58 requires goes far toward bringing into the twentieth century the judicial practice and procedure for entering formal judgments. This it does, not only "for the sake of a 'more intelligible record,' "see L.T.M. Builders v. Jefferson, supra, 61 Ohio St.2d at 96, 399 N.E.2d 1210, but also to augment the more rudimentary appellate concern of determining when a particular judgment is entered, "effective," and therefore final and appealable in civil cases under App.R. 4(A). See Peters v. Arbaugh, supra, 50 Ohio App.2d at 32–33, 361 N.E.2d 531 ("Upon the entry of such a document on the court's record, the judgment becomes effective and the time in which a notice of appeal must be filed begins to run.").

Accordingly, handwritten "notations" by a municipal judge on a case file-envelope or case jacket do not rise to the dignity and finality of a "judgment" from which an appeal will lie, *in the absence of evidence that it has been filed with the clerk of the trial court.* Columbus v. McCreary, supra (first and second paragraphs of the syllabus); cf. Lima v. Elliott, supra. For the same reason, the thirty-day time limit within which to file the notice of appeal does not begin to run unless and until that which the municipal court has ordered or decreed in its judgment is *filed* with the clerk of the trial court. And this brings us to the second problem with this appeal.

II

App.R. 4(A), which applies to civil cases, *requires* that a "notice of appeal * * * be filed with the clerk of the trial court *within thirty days of the date of the entry of the judgment or order appealed from.*" (Emphasis added.) This rule also states: "A judgment or order is *entered* * * * *when it is filed with the clerk of the trial court for journalization.*" (Emphasis added.) The same requirements apply in criminal cases. See App.R. 4(B); Crim.R. 32(B). Furthermore, R.C. 1901.31, which establishes the office of municipal court clerk and which mandates certain duties for the clerk, provides, in pertinent part:

> "(E) [The clerk] shall file and safely keep all journals, records, books, and papers belonging or appertaining to the court, record its proceedings, perform all other duties that the judges of the court

may prescribe, and keep a book showing all receipts and disbursements, which book shall be open for public inspection at all times.

"The clerk shall prepare and maintain a general index, a docket, and other records that the court, by rule, requires, of all which shall be the public records of the court. * * * *Under proper dates, he shall note the filing of the complaint, issuing of summons or other process, returns, and any subsequent pleadings. He shall also enter all reports, verdicts, orders, judgments, and proceedings of the court, clearly specifying the relief granted or orders made in each action.*" (Emphasis added.)

This section, standing alone, strongly implies that the municipal court clerk is required, as part of his duties, to record the date various documents are filed in his office, including orders and judgments. As noted earlier, M.C.Sup.R. 7 requires compliance, in civil cases, with Civ.R. 58 and in criminal cases, with Crim.R. 32(B) regarding the preparation, entry and journalization of judgments. In particular, M.C.Sup.R. 7 requires that such judgments be "*filed with the clerk* for journalization." (Emphasis added.) Id.

Since M.C.Sup.R. 7 refers to Civ.R. 58, and since R.C. 1901.21(A) (regarding procedure in municipal courts) provides a "gap-filler" rule which incorporates the practice and procedure in the courts of common pleas, Civ.R. 58's mandate regarding the filing and entry of judgments controls such procedure in municipal courts. That rule requires that a municipal court's order or judgment be reduced to writing promptly (called "preparing the judgment") and, once signed by the trial judge, the rule also requires that the document be filed with the clerk for journalization (i.e., that it be "entered"). Civ.R. 58; see, also, App.R. 4(A). Any judgment or order not filed with the trial court clerk is not a "final appealable judgment or order." App.R. 4(A); Such filing is usually evidenced by "file-stamping" the date of filing on the face of the document itself.

Of course, the practice of file-stamping judgment entries is not necessarily the only or the exclusive method that may be used to comply with Civ.R. 58, so long as there is some indication on the document *that* it was filed with the trial court clerk and, most importantly, *when*. But, whatever the particular method used, the practice of endorsing the date of filing on the judgment entry (or, for example, on notice of appeal) has been held to be "evidence that it was filed on that date," which is all that an appellate court needs to determine the timeliness of the appeal for jurisdictional purposes.

Here, by contrast, even assuming that the trial court had prepared and filed a separate, formal judgment entry on July 24th, there is no indication on the face of the document *that* it was filed with the clerk—or, if it was so filed, *when*. Hence, the "order" at issue here lacks final appealability for this reason, and the thirty-day time limit for appeal has not commenced to run.

Based upon the grounds heretofore explained in this opinion, the appeal *sub judice* is premature, and this court is without jurisdiction to entertain it. Accordingly, the instant appeal is hereby dismissed. This case is remanded to the Toledo Municipal Court for further proceedings not inconsistent with this opinion. It is so ordered.

Appeal dismissed.

Connors, P.J., and Resnick, J., concur.

Notes and Questions

1. Entry of judgment in federal practice is governed by Fed.R.Civ.P. 58 and 79(a).

Rule 79. Books and Records Kept by the Clerk and Entries Therein

(a) Civil Docket. The clerk shall keep a book known as "civil docket" of such form and style as may be prescribed by the Director of the Administrative Office of the United States Courts with the approval of the Judicial Conference of the United States, and shall enter therein each civil action to which these rules are made applicable. Actions shall be assigned consecutive file numbers. The file number of each action shall be noted on the folio of the docket whereon the first entry of the action is made. All papers filed with the clerk, all process issued and returns made thereon, all appearances, orders, verdicts, and judgments shall be entered chronologically in the civil docket on the folio assigned to the action and shall be marked with its file number. These entries shall be brief but shall show the nature of each paper filed or writ issued and the substance of each order or judgment of the court and of the returns showing execution of process. The entry of an order or judgment shall show the date the entry is made. When in an action trial by jury has been properly demanded or ordered the clerk shall enter the word "jury" on the folio assigned to that action.

* * *

Rule 54. Judgments; Costs

(a) Definition; Form. "Judgment" as used in these rules includes a decree and any order from which an appeal lies. A judgment shall not contain a recital of pleadings, the report of a master, or the record of prior proceedings.

* * *

Rule 58. Entry of Judgment

(a) Separate Document.

(1) Every judgment and amended judgment must be set forth on a separate document, but a separate document is not required for an order disposing of a motion:

     (A) for judgment under Rule 50(b);

     (B) to amend or make additional findings of fact under Rule 52(b);

     (C) for attorney fees under Rule 54;

(D) for a new trial, or to alter or amend the judgment, under Rule 59; or

(E) for relief under Rule 60.

(2) Subject to Rule 54(b):

(A) unless the court orders otherwise, the clerk must, without awaiting the court's direction, promptly prepare, sign, and enter the judgment when:

(i) the jury returns a general verdict,

(ii) the court awards only costs or a sum certain, or

(iii) the court denies all relief;

(B) the court must promptly approve the form of the judgment, which the clerk must promptly enter, when:

(i) the jury returns a special verdict or a general verdict accompanied by interrogatories, or

(ii) the court grants other relief not described in Rule 58(a)(2).

(b) Time of Entry. Judgment is entered for purposes of these rules:

(1) if Rule 58(a)(1) does not require a separate document, when it is entered in the civil docket under Rule 79(a), and

(2) if Rule 58(a)(1) requires a separate document, when it is entered in the civil docket under Rule 79(a) and when the earlier of these events occurs:

(A) when it is set forth on a separate document, or

(B) when 150 days have run from entry in the civil docket under Rule 79(a).

Notes of Advisory Committee on 2002 amendments. Rule 58 has provided that a judgment is effective only when set forth on a separate document and entered as provided in Rule 79(a). This simple separate document requirement has been ignored in many cases. The result of failure to enter judgment on a separate document is that the time for making motions under Rules 50, 52, 54(d)(2)(B), 59, and some motions under Rule 60, never begins to run. The time to appeal under Appellate Rule 4(a) also does not begin to run. There have been few visible problems with respect to Rule 50, 52, 54(d)(2)(B), 59, or 60 motions, but there have been many and horridly confused problems under Appellate Rule 4(a). These amendments are designed to work in conjunction with Appellate Rule 4(a) to ensure that appeal time does not linger on indefinitely, and to maintain the integration of the time periods set for Rules 50, 52, 54(d)(2)(B), 59, and 60 with Appellate Rule 4(a).

Rule 58(a) preserves the core of the present separate document requirement, both for the initial judgment and for any amended judgment. No attempt is made to sort through the confusion that some courts have found in addressing the elements of a separate document. It is easy to prepare a separate document that recites the terms of the judgment without offering additional explanation or citation of authority. Forms 31 and 32 provide examples.

Rule 58 is amended, however, to address a problem that arises under Appellate Rule 4(a). Some courts treat such orders as those that deny a motion for new trial as a "judgment," so that appeal time does not start to run until the order is entered on a separate document. Without attempting to address the question whether such orders are appealable, and thus judgments as defined by Rule 54(a), the amendment provides that entry on a separate document is not required for an order disposing of the motions listed in Appellate Rule 4(a). The enumeration of motions drawn from the Appellate Rule 4(a) list is generalized by omitting details that are important for appeal time purposes but that would unnecessarily complicate the separate document requirement. As one example, it is not required that any of the enumerated motions be timely. Many of the enumerated motions are frequently made before judgment is entered. The exemption of the order disposing of the motion does not excuse the obligation to set forth the judgment itself on a separate document. And if disposition of the motion results in an amended judgment, the amended judgment must be set forth on a separate document.

Rule 58(b) discards the attempt to define the time when a judgment becomes "effective." Taken in conjunction with the Rule 54(a) definition of a judgment to include "any order from which an appeal lies," the former Rule 58 definition of effectiveness could cause strange difficulties in implementing pretrial orders that are appealable under interlocutory appeal provisions or under expansive theories of finality. Rule 58(b) replaces the definition of effectiveness with a new provision that defines the time when judgment is entered. If judgment is promptly set forth on a separate document, as should be done when required by Rule 58(a)(1), the new provision will not change the effect of Rule 58. But in the cases in which court and clerk fail to comply with this simple requirement, the motion time periods set by Rules 50, 52, 54, 59, and 60 begin to run after expiration of 150 days from entry of the judgment in the civil docket as required by Rule 79(a).

A companion amendment of Appellate Rule 4(a)(7) integrates these changes with the time to appeal.

The new all-purpose definition of the entry of judgment must be applied with common sense to other questions that may turn on the time when judgment is entered. If the 150–day provision in Rule 58(b)(2)(B)—designed to integrate the time for post-judgment motions with appeal time—serves no purpose, or would defeat the purpose of another rule, it should be disregarded. In theory, for example, the separate document requirement continues to apply to an interlocutory order that is appealable as a final decision under collateral-order doctrine. Appealability under collateral-order doctrine should not be complicated by failure to enter the order as a judgment on a separate document—there is little reason to force trial judges to speculate about the potential appealability of every order, and there is no means to ensure that the trial judge will always reach the same conclusion as the court of appeals.

Appeal time should start to run when the collateral order is entered without regard to creation of a separate document and without awaiting expiration of the 150 days provided by Rule 58(b)(2). Drastic surgery on Rules 54(a) and 58 would be required to address this and related issues, however, and it is better to leave this conundrum to the pragmatic disregard that seems its present fate. The present amendments do not seem to make matters worse, apart from one false appearance. If a pretrial order is set forth on a separate document that meets the requirements of Rule 58(b), the time to move for reconsideration seems to begin to run, perhaps years before final judgment. And even if there is no separate document, the time to move for reconsideration seems to begin 150 days after entry in the civil docket. This apparent problem is resolved by Rule 54(b), which expressly permits revision of all orders not made final under Rule 54(b) "at any time before the entry of judgment adjudicating all the claims and the rights and liabilities of all the parties."

New Rule 58(d) replaces the provision that attorneys shall not submit forms of judgment except on direction of the court. This provision was added to Rule 58 to avoid the delays that were frequently encountered by the former practice of directing the attorneys for the prevailing party to prepare a form of judgment, and also to avoid the occasionally inept drafting that resulted from attorney-prepared judgments. See 11 Wright, Miller & Kane, Federal Practice & Procedure: Civil 2d, § 2786. The express direction in Rule 58(a)(2) for prompt action by the clerk, and by the court if court action is required, addresses this concern. The new provision allowing any party to move for entry of judgment on a separate document will protect all needs for prompt commencement of the periods for motions, appeals, and execution or other enforcement.

Would the result in the principal case be the same under today's federal rules?

2. The quotation in footnote 4 of the opinion in the principal case suggests four possibilities for beginning the running of the appeal time period. Have Ohio and federal rules selected the best possibility? In some jurisdictions, the running of the appellate time begins when service of notice of entry of judgment occurs (e.g., Cal.Civ.Pro.Code § 664.5). "Service" means the date counsel mails the paper to other attorneys in the case. What problems can this create?

2. JUDGMENTS "WITH PREJUDICE" OR WITH LEAVE TO REPLEAD

DUBICZ v. COMMONWEALTH EDISON COMPANY

United States Court of Appeals, Seventh Circuit, 2004.
377 F.3d 787.

MANION, CIRCUIT JUDGE.

The appellants, current or retired employees of Commonwealth Edison Company ("ComEd"), appeal from a decision of the District

Court for the Northern District of Illinois to deny their motion for leave to file a second amended complaint. Also at issue, however, is the jurisdiction of that court to consider the motion. For the reasons set forth below, we conclude that the district court had jurisdiction to consider the motion, but that under the unique circumstances of this case, it was an abuse of discretion to deny the appellants leave to file a second amended complaint.

I.

This case began as a pro se action by certain current or retired employees of ComEd. In a complaint filed with the District Court for the Northern District of Illinois, the initial plaintiffs (the "Cook Plaintiffs") alleged that ComEd discriminated against them on account of their age in relation to ComEd's pension plan (the "Plan").

The Cook Plaintiffs subsequently retained counsel and filed a first amended complaint. This complaint had six counts. In Count I, the Cook Plaintiffs alleged age discrimination and misrepresentation in relation to the Plan. In Counts II, III, and IV, individual plaintiffs raised allegations of age discrimination. In Count V the Cook Plaintiffs alleged that ComEd made material misrepresentations with respect to the Plan in violation of the Employee Retirement Income Security Act of 1974, 29 U.S.C. §§ 1001, et seq. ("ERISA"). In Count VI, the Cook Plaintiffs alleged breach of contract resulting from material misrepresentations by ComEd with regard to the Plan.

ComEd moved to dismiss the complaint in its entirety for failure to state a claim and, with respect to Count V, for failure to plead a claim of fraud with particularity. On September 25, 2002, the district court issued a memorandum opinion explicitly dismissing Counts II, III, and IV with prejudice and Counts I, V, and VI without prejudice. Accompanying the decision was form AO4050 (the "Judgment Form"). That form, titled "Judgment In A Civil Case," signed by the clerk of the court and dated the same day as the memorandum opinion, stated that "Counts I, V, and VI of Plaintiffs' first amended complaint are dismissed without prejudice." The Judgment Form, however, also included what purported to be an entry of final judgment: "All matters in controversy having been resolved, final judgment is hereby entered in favor of the defendant and against the plaintiffs."

Eight months after the dismissal of the first amended complaint, the Cook Plaintiffs, now joined by a second group of plaintiffs (together with the Cook Plaintiffs, the "Appellants"), filed a motion for leave to file a second amended complaint pursuant to Rule 15(a) of the Federal Rules of Civil Procedure. On July 3, 2003, the district court denied the motion and also converted its earlier dismissal of Counts I, V, VI without prejudice to dismissals with prejudice. The district court found that the passage of eight months was an undue delay and that the eight-month delay was also prejudicial to ComEd. In a memorandum opinion accompanying its decision, the court found that "eight months is beyond the pale in light of what was required of [the Appellants]." The district court attributed the delay in filing the motion for leave to an effort by Appellants' trial counsel to add new plaintiffs: "Instead of taking what should have been weeks, Plaintiffs' counsel spent eight months busily hunting up new clients." The district court also agreed with ComEd that ComEd was prejudiced because during the eight-month delay, "memories faded and documents were lost." This appeal followed.

II.

The Appellants argue that the district court abused its discretion in denying their motion for leave to amend. Before we reach that issue, however, we must consider whether the district court had the jurisdiction to consider the motion for leave to file the second amended complaint. ComEd argued before the district court, and repeats its arguments here, that the entry by the district court of the Judgment Form accompanying the district court's September 25, 2002 decision made that decision a final judgment and thus the district court did not have jurisdiction eight months later to consider the Rule 15(a) motion. The district court rejected ComEd's jurisdictional argument and stated that "we dismissed the claims at issue without prejudice and fully intended that the Plaintiffs be given the opportunity to amend their complaint."

When there has been an entry of final judgment, a complaining party may amend a complaint pursuant to Rule 15(a) only after that party has successfully altered or amended the judgment pursuant to Rule 59(e) or the judgment has been vacated pursuant to Rule 60(b). See Sparrow v. Heller, 116 F.3d 204, 205 (7th Cir. 1997). The Appellants did not move to set aside or alter this judgment. Therefore, if the district court's September 25, 2002 order and the accompanying Judgment Form represented a final judgment, the district court should not have considered, and had no juris-diction to consider, the Appellants' Rule 15(a) motion. Paganis v. Blonstein, 3 F.3d 1067, 1073 (7th Cir. 1993) (holding that, absent a Rule 59(e) or 60(b) motion, a district court lacks the jurisdiction to review a Rule 15(a) motion where final judgment has been entered).

Interwoven with the district court's jurisdiction to hear the Appellants' motion for leave to file the second amended complaint is this court's jurisdiction. With some exceptions not applicable here, this court's jurisdiction is limited to the review of final decisions. 28 U.S.C. § 1291. A party seeking to appeal a final decision of a district court must file a notice of appeal with that court "within 30 days after the judgment or order appealed from is entered." Fed. R. App. P. 4(a)(1)(A). The Appellants did not, of course, file a notice of appeal within 30 days after the district court's September 25, 2002 decision. Thus, if that decision were a final decision, any appeal would be untimely and this court would not have jurisdiction. Budinich v. Becton Dickinson & Co., 486 U.S. 196, 203, 100 L. Ed. 2d 178, 108 S. Ct. 1717 (1988) (holding that the filing of a timely notice of appeal is mandatory and jurisdictional).

Despite the language in the district court's order of judgment, the district court's dismissal of the complaint was not a final judgment. With a limited exception, a dismissal without prejudice "does not qualify as an appealable final judgment because the plaintiff is free to re-file the case." Larkin v. Galloway, 266 F.3d 718, 721 (7th Cir. 2001); see also Furnace v. Bd. of Trustees of Southern Ill. Univ., 218 F.3d 666, 669 (7th Cir. 2000); Principal Mut. Life Ins. Co. v. Cincinnati TV 64 Ltd. Partnership, 845 F.2d 674, 676 (7th Cir. 1988) ("An order dismissing a complaint is not final because a plaintiff may file an amended complaint, resurrecting the lawsuit."). The exception to this rule arises "when it is clear from the record that the district court 'found that the action could not be saved by any amendment of the complaint which the plaintiff could reasonably be expected to make.' " Furnace, 218 F.3d at 670.

The September 25, 2002 dismissal of three of the Cook Plaintiffs' claims was without prejudice. This is made clear both in the district court's opinion and, more importantly, in the Judgment Form. The Judgment Form states that three of the counts "are dismissed without prejudice." A review of the record does not suggest that amendments to the complaint would be futile. To the contrary, the district court's opinion accompanying the Judgment Form makes it clear that the first amended complaint was capable of being amended. For example, with respect to Counts V and VI, the district court concluded that the counts should be dismissed because the Cook Plaintiffs had not met the requirements of particularity for an averment of fraud required by Federal Rule of Civil Procedure 9(b). Specifically, the district court found that "there are many dates, documents, and names that need to be included in the complaint in order to meet the Rule 9(b) requirements." Requiring a party to provide more specific dates, names and certain documents suggests that the party need only provide more detail, and the record does not show that adding such detail would have been impossible.

The problem arises, of course, because immediately after the Judgment Form states that certain of the counts are dismissed without prejudice, the Judgment Form also states that the final judgment is entered in favor of ComEd. Thus, the Judgment Form appears to be inconsistent—it tells the Appellants that their claim is dismissed without prejudice (meaning the Appellants could amend their complaint) but then goes on to state that all matters at issue have been resolved and that a final judgment had been reached. The district court's labeling of its decision as final (apparently inadvertently) should not, however, be conclusive. A district court's decision is a final judgment only when the decision meets the requirements for being a final judgment. The September 25, 2002 decision was not final, regardless of the label attached to it. See Dodge v. Cotter Corp., 328 F.3d 1212, 1221 (10th Cir.2003) (labeling a decision as a final judgment is not controlling). The district court dismissed three counts of the complaint without prejudice and, as discussed above, there is no indication from the record at that stage that attempts to amend the complaint would have been futile. There was no final judgment.

Potentially at odds with this conclusion, however, is the decision of this court in Hoskins v. Poelstra, 320 F.3d 761 (7th Cir. 2003). In that case, the district court dismissed a complaint without prejudice but also entered a judgment against the plaintiff "dismissing the 'case' without any suggestion that Hoskins was entitled to plead again." *Id. at 763.* Hoskins immediately appealed the district court's decision and this court held that the decision was immediately appealable. This court noted that "the district judge sent inconsistent signals." *Id.* Further, this court noted that, "when the district court's resolution looks both ways, the only safe route is to treat it as final: the alternative lays a trap for unwary (or even wary) litigants, who may forego appeal in reliance on the 'without prejudice' language only to learn later, and to their sorrow, that the original order was appealable and the time for appellate review has lapsed." *Id. at 764.*

In *Hoskins*, therefore, this court permitted a litigant to take an immediate appeal from a district court's decision dismissing a complaint without prejudice because the district court's form of judgment stated that the case (rather than only the complaint) was dismissed. At first glance, it appears, therefore, that this court should hold likewise—that the September 25, 2002 decision because it "looked both ways" was immediately appealable, and that because the Appellants failed to appeal in a timely fashion, this court has no jurisdiction to hear the appeal. Likewise, because the Appellants failed to reopen the judgment or have it vacated, the district court did not have jurisdiction to hear the Rule 15(a) motion.

Hoskins is not, however, wholly incompatible with our approach. First, it is not clear from that opinion what exactly the Rule 58 judgment form (as opposed to the actual decision of the district court) stated. The opinion says only that there was no suggestion Hoskins was entitled to plead again. In this case, however, there was such a suggestion; in fact, the Judgment Form quite clearly suggests that the Appellants were entitled to plead again. The Judgment Form stated that certain of the counts were dismissed with-out prejudice. Second, it is also not clear to what extent Hoskins should apply in the reverse—in other words, should this court refuse to hear an appeal (and should the district court be stripped of jurisdiction to consider a *Rule 15(a)* motion) because the district court inadvertently labeled its decision a final judgment but also in the same form stated that certain of the counts were dismissed without prejudice? As discussed above, a district court's label cannot convert an otherwise non-final judgment into a final judgment, and a litigant, relying on the explicit language of the district court's Judgment Form bolstered by its written opinion, should not bear the price for the district court's inadvertence. We therefore hold that the district court properly considered the Appellants' Rule 15(a) motion.

That is not to say the Appellants chose the wisest course. The Appellants would have been better served had their trial counsel, upon receiving the Judgment Form, taken steps to confirm the status of the case (for instance, by requesting clarification from the district court). We see no reason why trial counsel could not have done so and doing so would have likely cleared up the discrepancy well before it reached this court. We turn next to the actual decision of the district court on that motion [and hold that] the district court abused its discretion in denying the Appellants' motion for leave to amend. * * *

CASEY v. ALBERTSON'S INC.

United States Court of Appeals, Ninth Circuit, 2004.
362 F.3d 1254.

SILVERMAN, CIRCUIT JUDGE:

We hold today that when the parties treat a fully dispositive summary judgment order as if it were a final judgment, the requirement in Federal Rule of Civil Procedure 58 that the judgment "be set forth on a separate document" can be waived. Bankers Trust Co. v. Mallis, 435 U.S. 381, 382, 55 L. Ed. 2d 357, 98 S. Ct. 1117 (1978).

I. FACTS

Appellant Shannon Casey filed this lawsuit against Albertson's, her employer, alleging sexual harassment and discrimination based on marital status in violation of California's Fair Employment and Housing Act. She alleged that Pete King, the manager of the Albertson's where she worked, sexually harassed her and then transferred her to another store when she returned to work following her pregnancy. Casey alleges that her transfer to another store was illegal because there was another employee, Pepper Smith, who was less senior than Casey who should have been transferred instead. She claims that her transfer "was in response to Casey's rebuffing King's sexual advances and King learning that Casey had not divorced her husband as King wanted her to do and that she had become pregnant."

Casey failed to respond to Albertson's requests for admissions. As a result, under Federal Rule of Civil Procedure 36(a), she was deemed to have admitted that, among other things, (1) King did not discriminate against her on the basis of gender; (2) King did not discriminate against her on the basis of her marital status; (3) King did not discriminate against her on the basis of her pregnancy; and (4) King did not make the decision to transfer her. Casey's attorney also failed to attend a hearing on Albertson's motion for summary judgment.

The district court granted Albertson's summary judgment on all claims on August 28, 2001. Summary judgment was granted in the form of a civil minute order. Although the judge's seven page civil minute order disposed of all of Casey's claims and concluded with "IT IS SO ORDERED," no separate judgment was entered.

On August 28, 2002, exactly one year from the entry of summary judgment, Casey moved for relief from judgment under Federal Rule of Civil Procedure 60(b), arguing that the judgment should be set aside because of excusable neglect, new evidence, and fraud, misrepresentation, or misconduct. The gist of her motion was that by means of an inexpensive Internet investigation service, of which she had only recently become aware, Casey was able to locate Pepper Smith, who could confirm that Smith had less seniority than Casey but was not transferred to another store. The court noted that the one year filing limit for relief from judgment under Rule 60(b)(1), (2), & (3) "is an outer limit," and that "plaintiff delayed filing this motion until the last possible day." The court also ruled that the delay in locating Pepper Smith was unjustified. On November 26, 2002, the court denied Casey's motion, ruling that Casey had not demonstrated excusable neglect, newly discovered evidence, or fraud, misrepresentation, or misconduct, pursuant to Rule 60(b)(1), (2), & (3), respectively. Casey filed her notice of appeal from that ruling on December 19, 2002.

At some point after the district court denied her Rule 60(b) motion and the notice of appeal had been filed, Casey noticed that the district court had failed to enter a final judgment on a document separate from its summary judgment ruling. On July 22, 2003, eight months after the district court denied her Rule 60(b) motion, Casey lodged with the district court a proposed form of judgment. On August 8, 2003, the district court entered a minute order acknowledging that "although summary judgment was granted in favor of Defendant Albertson's, Inc. on August 28, 2001, thereby terminating the case, a final judgment on a separate document was not entered." However, the court held that it no longer had jurisdiction over the case because a notice of appeal had been filed. It continued: "However, if either Plaintiff or Defendant Albertson's Inc. believes that a separate document is necessary ... and that this court does have jurisdiction to enter a judgment ... , either party may file a brief ... to that effect...." After briefing by both sides, the district court ruled that, pursuant to Bankers Trust Co. v. Mallis, 435 U.S. 381, 55 L. Ed. 2d 357, 98 S. Ct. 1117 (1978), the litigants had waived strict compliance with the separate judgment requirement by proceeding as if a separate judgment had been entered.

II. Jurisdiction and Standard of Review

We have jurisdiction pursuant to 28 U.S.C. § 1291. Motions for relief from judgment pursuant to Rule 60(b) are addressed to the sound discretion of the district court and will not be reversed absent an abuse of discretion. SEC v. Coldicutt, 258 F.3d 939, 941 (9th Cir. 2001). A district court abuses its discretion if it does not apply the correct law or if it rests its decision on a clearly erroneous finding of material fact. Bateman v. United States Postal Serv., 231 F.3d 1220, 1223 (9th Cir. 2000).

III. Discussion

Casey spends the bulk of her time on appeal rearguing the merits of the district court's grant of summary judgment. However, her notice of appeal expressly states she is appealing only the denial of her Rule 60(b) motion. Normally, the merits of a case are not before the panel in reviewing a Rule 60(b) motion. See Wages v. I.R.S., 915 F.2d 1230, 1234 (9th Cir. 1990) ("an appeal from a denial of Rule 60(b) relief does not bring up the underlying judgment for review") (internal quotation marks omitted). There are thus two issues before the court: First, does the fact that the district court did not enter a judgment separate from its summary judgment minute order somehow allow the district court or this court to revisit the merits of the summary judgment ruling; and, second, did the district court abuse its discretion in denying Casey's Rule 60(b) motion?

A. *The Separate Judgment Rule*

Federal Rule of Civil Procedure 58(a)(1) provides that "every judgment . . . must be set forth on a separate document." It further states that "unless the court orders otherwise, the clerk must, without awaiting the court's direction, promptly prepare, sign, and enter the judgment when . . . the court denies all relief." Fed. R. Civ. P. 58(a)(2)(A)(iii); but see Fed. R. App. P. 4(a)(7)(B) ("A failure to set forth a judgment or order on a separate document when required by Federal Rule of Civil Procedure 58(a)(1) does not affect the validity of an appeal from that judgment or order."). "Only when both" rules Rule 58 and Rule 79(a)—which tells the parties how the clerk must enter documents on the civil docket— "are satisfied is there an 'entry of judgment'" that tells the parties they may appeal. Radio TV Espanola S.A. v. New World Entertainment, Ltd., 183 F.3d 922, 930 (9th Cir. 1999). "The separate document requirement . . . exists so that the parties will know exactly when the judgment has been entered and they must begin preparing post-verdict motions or an appeal." Carter v. Beverly Hills Sav. & Loan Ass'n, 884 F.2d 1186, 1194 (9th Cir. 1989)(Kozinski, J., dissenting).

"Although a final judgment requires a 'separate document,' neither the Supreme Court nor this court views satisfaction of Rule 58 as a prerequisite to appeal." Kirkland v. Legion Ins. Co., 343 F.3d 1135, 1140 (9th Cir. 2003). "A ruling is final for purposes of § 1291 if it (1) is a full adjudication of the issues, and (2) clearly evidences the judge's intention that it be the court's final act in the matter." National Distrib. Agency v. Nationwide Mut. Ins. Co., 117 F.3d 432, 433 (9th Cir. 1997).

The Supreme Court's decision in Bankers Trust, while not on all fours with this case, leads us to the conclusion that the district court's failure to file a separate judgment does not affect any of the issues in this appeal. In Bankers Trust, "the issue posed is whether a decision of a district court can be a 'final decision' for purposes of § 1291 if not set forth on a document separate from the opinion." 435 U.S. at 383. There, the district court failed to enter a judgment as a separate document, but the district court's "opinion and order" contained the language "complaint dismissed in its entirety. So ORDERED." Id. at 382 & n.1. The Court concluded that "it could not have been intended that the separate document requirement of Rule 58 be such a categorical imperative that the parties are not free to waive it." Id. at 384.

If, by error, a separate judgment is not filed before a party appeals, nothing but delay would flow from requiring the court of appeals to dismiss the appeal. Upon dismissal, the district court would simply file and enter the separate judgment, from which a timely appeal would then be taken. Wheels would spin for no practical purpose.

. . . The need for certainty as to the timeliness of the appeal [i.e., the purpose of Rule 58] . . . should not prevent the parties from waiving the separate-judgment requirement where one has accidentally not been entered.

. . . Here, the District Court clearly evidenced its intent that the opinion and order from which an appeal is taken would represent the final decision in the case. A judgment of dismissal was recorded in the clerk's docket. And petitioner did not object to the taking of the appeal in the absence of a separate judgment. Under these circumstances, the parties should be deemed to have waived the separate document requirement of Rule 58, and the Court of Appeals properly assumed appellate jurisdiction under § 1291.

Id. at 385–86, 387–88; see also Kirkland, 343 F.3d at 1139–40 (holding that a district court settlement order that effectively ended the litigation on the merits was a final, appealable order despite the absence of entry of a separate judgment, and a party that had attempted to enforce the agreement waived the right to question this issue); Pac. Employers Ins. Co. v. Domino's Pizza, Inc., 144 F.3d 1270, 1278 (9th Cir. 1998) ("under Rule 58, a district court is not even required to file two separate documents"); Beaudry Motor Co. v. Abko Props., Inc., 780 F.2d 751, 754–55 (9th Cir. 1986) (holding that a civil minute order that is prepared at the direction of the district judge, noted in the docket, file stamped, and ended with the language "IT IS SO ORDERED" "clearly put plaintiff's counsel on notice that an order had been entered against his client" and satisfied Rule 58 despite the lack of entry of a formal, separate document).

Here, Casey unequivocally indicated her belief that the August 28, 2001 summary judgment minute order served as a judgment by filing a Rule 60(b) motion. In Bankers Trust, the filing of an appeal and the parties proceeding before an appellate court as if a separate judgment had been entered was indicative of acknowledgment by the parties that a final judgment had been entered. The same is true in this case. Casey filed a Rule 60 motion, indicating an unambiguous belief that a judgment had been entered. Judge Matz's order explicitly granted summary judgment for Albertson's on all the claims and indicated that the matter was concluded. Thus, as Bankers Trust can be said to stand for the proposition that a party's actions indicating its belief that a final judgment was entered can be sufficient to waive any Rule 58 objections, Casey exhibited such a belief by filing a Rule 60 motion and subsequently waived any Rule 58 objection to the district court's failure to file a separate judgment.

It is true that there are cases stating that "a mechanical application of Rule 58" is required. See, e.g., Long v. Coast Resorts, Inc., 267 F.3d 918, 922 (9th Cir. 2001). However, in those cases, Rule 58 is used to salvage the appealability of a case where it may have been unclear in the district court which document was the final judgment. See Long, 267 F.3d at 922 (applying the "mechanical" Rule 58 separate document requirement to salvage the validity of an appeal where it was not clear which district court entry was the final order for appeal purposes); Radio TV, 183 F.3d at 929–32; Carter, 884 F.2d at 1189–91; Paddack v. Morris, 783 F.2d 844, 846 (9th Cir. 1986). We have found no cases that apply Rule 58 as Casey would urge, as a sword to reopen a case in which the parties and the judge all have indicated that they treat a district court entry as a final, separate judgment.

In these circumstances, the district court's failure to enter a separate judgment apart from its August 28, 2001 minute order does not create a loophole through which we can reach past Casey's Rule 60(b) motion to get to the merits of the district court's summary judgment ruling. However, the Rule 60(b) motion is properly before us, and we turn to it now. * * *

LOCAL UNION NO. 1992 OF THE INTERNATIONAL BROTHERHOOD OF ELECTRICAL WORKERS v. THE OKONITE COMPANY

United States Court of Appeals, Third Circuit, 2004.
358 F.3d 278.

CHERTOFF, CIRCUIT JUDGE.

Rule 58 of the Federal Rules of Civil Procedure mandates that district courts set forth a judgment on a separate document, apart from any accompanying opinion. The precise definition of that requirement is important because the docketing of a judgment in correct form triggers the beginning of the time period within which an appeal must be filed. Misapprehension of Rule 58 can be jurisdictionally fatal to an appeal.

The disposition of this appeal turns on precisely that jurisdictional issue. Appellant, The Okonite Company ("Okonite"), argues that Appellate Rule 4(a)'s thirty-day period to file an appeal never began to run because the District Court failed to comply with Rule 58's "separate document requirement." For the reasons set forth below, we disagree with Okonite's interpretation of Rule 58 . We find that Okonite has not timely appealed the District Court's original rulings. Accordingly, we have no jurisdiction to entertain an appeal of those rulings. The only ruling properly before us is Okonite's timely appeal from the District Court's more recent judgment awarding plaintiff attorneys' fees. We will vacate that judgment and remand for further proceedings.

I.

In 1997, plaintiff Local 1992 of the International Brotherhood of Electrical Workers ("Local 1992") brought suit against Okonite under the Worker Adjustment Retraining and Notification Act ("WARN Act"), 29 U.S.C. §§ 2101–09, claiming that Okonite failed to provide the sixty-day notice of a plant closing that the statute requires. [The parties filed] cross-motions for summary judgment. The District Court denied them, and the case went to trial. After a jury returned a verdict in its favor, Local 1992 filed post-trial motions for attorneys' fees, costs, and prejudgment interest. Okonite opposed Local 1992's motions and cross-moved for judgment as a matter of law (under Federal Rule of Civil Procedure 50(b)) or, alternatively, a new trial (under Federal Rule of Civil Procedure 59).

The District Court issued an opinion, dated May 7, 2002, in which it (1) denied Okonite's Rule 50 and 59 motions for judgment as a matter of law or a new trial; (2) denied Local 1992's motion for prejudgment interest; (3) granted in part and denied in part Local 1992's motion for attorneys' fees and costs; and (4) referred Local 1992's application for attorneys' fees and costs to a Magistrate Judge to determine the total amount of fees and costs that was reasonable. The comprehensive opinion was accompanied by a separately-captioned "order," dated May 7, 2002. The Clerk of the Court separately entered the opinion and order on the docket on May 8, 2002.

After the referral by the District Court, the Magistrate Judge issued a Report and Recommendation on September 24, 2002. She recommended that the District Court (a) award Local 1992 $51,340 in attorneys' fees for the period since July 9, 1998; and (b) deny, without prejudice, Local 1992's request for costs for failing to comply with Local Civil Rule 54.1(a). Local 1992 objected to the Magistrate Judge's Report and Recommendation on the grounds that the Magistrate Judge wrongly excluded the time Local 1992's attorneys spent working on Okonite's appeal from the initial decision granting Local 1992 summary judgment.

In papers filed on October 11, 2002, Okonite opposed Local 1992's objection. In addition, also on October 11, 2002, Okonite filed a motion requesting that the District Court enter what Okonite termed three separate final judgments, pursuant to Federal Rule of Civil Procedure 58, for (1) the denial of Okonite's Rule 50 and 59 motions, (2) the denial of Local 1992's motion for prejudgment interest, and (3) the partial denial and partial grant of Local 1992's motion for attorneys' fees and costs. Okonite also urged the District Court to exercise its discretion under Rule 58 and order that Local 1992's motion for attorneys' fees "have the same effect under Rule 4(a)(4) of the Federal Rules of Appellate Procedure as a timely motion under Rule 59." Fed. R. Civ. P. 58.

On November 27, 2002—while the parties' motions were pending before the District Court and 203 days after the District Court's May 8 order—Okonite filed a notice of appeal from several of the District Court's orders from before, during, and after the trial. Okonite's principal argument in that appeal is that the District Court erred by denying its Rule 50 motion for judgment as a matter of law.

Local 1992 filed a motion with this Court, arguing that we should dismiss Okonite's appeal as untimely. Local 1992 also protectively cross-appealed the District Court's denial of prejudgment interest, but acknowledged that its appeal is also untimely if we dismiss Okonite's appeal.

Meanwhile, in a January 30, 2003 opinion, the District Court rejected the Magistrate Judge's recommendation to exclude the 186.3 hours Local 1992's attorneys spent working on the appeal from the initial summary judgment decision, and the Court accepted the Magistrate Judge's recommended $200 hourly attorneys' fees rate. The District Court further denied Okonite's motion for separate judgments under Rule 58 and declined to order that Local 1992's motion for attorneys' fees be treated like a *Rule 59* motion for purposes of extending when the time to file a notice of appeal would begin to run. Okonite timely filed a notice of appeal from the January 30, 2003 decision on February 24, 2003.

To summarize, we have before us Okonite's November 27, 2002 appeal, Local 1992's motion to dismiss the November 27, 2002 appeal, Local 1992's cross-appeal, and Okonite's February 24, 2003 appeal. Both parties agree that Okonite's appeal from the District Court's final attorneys' fees determination (decided in the January 30, 2003 decision) is properly before us, and we address it below. The primary question we must decide, however, is the timeliness of Okonite's November 27, 2002 appeal, which Okonite filed more than six months after the District Court's May 8 opinion and order. That issue underlies both Local 1992's motion to dismiss Okonite's November 27, 2002 appeal and Okonite's appeal from the District Court's January 30, 2003 order denying Okonite's motions for separate judgments and for an order extending the time for appeal.

II.

Federal Rule of Appellate Procedure 4(a) requires that a notice of appeal "be filed with the district clerk within thirty days after the judgment or order appealed from is entered." Fed. R. App. P. 4(a)(1)(A). With regard to an appeal from a jury verdict, the thirty days does not begin to run—i.e., "entry of judgment" has not occurred—until the judgment is set forth in a separate document pursuant to Federal Rule of Civil Procedure 58 and the clerk of the court enters the judgment into the civil docket pursuant to Federal Rule of Civil Procedure 79(a). * * *

The separate document requirement was added to Rule 58 in 1963. The Advisory Committee's notes to the 1963 Amendment explain:

> Hitherto some difficulty has arisen, chiefly where the court has written an opinion or memorandum containing some apparently directive or dispositive words, e.g., 'the plaintiff's motion [for summary judgment] is granted[.]' . . . . Where the opinion or memorandum has not contained all the elements of a judgment, or where the judge has later signed a formal judgment, it has become a matter of

doubt whether the purported entry of judgment was effective, starting the time running for post-verdict motions and for the purpose of appeal.

The amended rule eliminates these uncertainties by requiring that there be a judgment set out on a separate document—distinct from any opinion or memorandum—which provides the bases for the entry of judgment.

Fed. R. Civ. P. 58 advisory committee's notes. In other words, the separate document requirement was "intended to avoid the inequities that were inherent when a party appealed from a document or docket entry that appeared to be a final judgment of the district court only to have the appellate court announce later that an earlier document or entry had been the judgment and dismiss the appeal as untimely." Bankers Trust Co. v. Mallis, 435 U.S. 381, 385, 55 L. Ed. 2d 357, 98 S. Ct. 1117 (1978) (per curiam). As a result, Rule 58's separate document provision "must be mechanically applied in order to avoid new uncertainties as to the date on which a judgment is entered." United States v. Indrelunas, 411 U.S. 216, 222, 36 L. Ed. 2d 202, 93 S. Ct. 1562 (1973).

In order to satisfy the separate document requirement, a judgment must, generally speaking, " 'be a self-contained document, saying who has won and what relief has been awarded, but omitting the reasons for this disposition, which should appear in the court's opinion.' " James Wm. Moore et al., Moore's Federal Practice P 58.05[4][a] (3d ed. 2003) (quoting Otis v. City of Chicago , 29 F.3d 1159, 1163 (7th Cir. 1994)).[11] Here, the District Court accompanied its eighteen-page May 8, 2002 opinion with a two-page document, denominated an "Order," that read as follows:

> For the reasons expressed in the accompanying written opinion,
>
> IT IS on this 7th day of May 2002,
>
> ORDERED that Defendant's motion for judgment as a matter of law or, alternatively, a new trial is denied, and it is further
>
> ORDERED that Plaintiff's motion for prejudgment interest is denied, and it is further
>
> ORDERED that Plaintiff's motion for attorney's fees and costs is granted in part and denied in part. To the extent the Plaintiff moves for a recalculation of fees for the period between October 16, 1996 and July 8, 1998, the motion is denied. However, to the extent

---

11. We have not had the occasion to consider what suffices to satisfy Rule 58 's separate document requirement since our decision in Gregson & Assocs. Architects v. Gov't of the Virgin Islands, 675 F.2d 589 (3d Cir. 1982) (per curiam). There,

the judgment of the district court was set forth within a four-page document including a memorandum opinion by the court. The district court's order of February 26

carried the heading "MEMORANDUM OPINION AND JUDGMENT." On the last of the four pages of the document there appeared a separate heading, "JUDGMENT," under which the judgment of the court was stated.

Id. at 591. We concluded that the District Court had failed to comply with Rule 58's separate document requirement, but we did not explain precisely why. Id. at 591 n.1.

that Plaintiff moves for an award of attorney's fees and costs for services performed since July 9, 1998, the motion is granted. Accordingly, the Court refers the Plaintiff's application to Magistrate Judge Arleo for a report and recommendation as to a reasonable award of fees and costs in this case.

This order satisfies the separate document requirement. First, the order is self-contained and separate from the opinion. It has a separate caption; the opinion and order are not consecutively paginated (the opinion contains page numbers along the bottom of each page, while the order does not); the District Judge separately signed the last page of both the opinion and the order; the first page of both the opinion and order are separately file-stamped; and the Clerk of the Court docketed the opinion and order separately on May 8, 2002. See generally United States v. Johnson, 254 F.3d 279, 285–86 (D.C. Cir. 2001).

Second, the order sets forth the relief granted. It succinctly states that the District Court denied Okonite's post-trial motions for judgment as a matter of law and a new trial, denied Local 1992's motion for prejudgment interest, and granted in part (for the period prior to July 8, 1998) and denied in part (for the period after July 8, 1998) Local 1992's motion for attorneys' fees. Of course, a district court's recitation of the relief granted will vary depending on the circumstances of the particular judgment. A judgment granting a plaintiff summary judgment, for example, may have to contain any damages or injunctive relief awarded. Cf. Massey Ferguson Div. of Varity Corp. v. Gurley, 51 F.3d 102, 104–05 (7th Cir. 1995). Where a court denies a post-trial motion for judgment as a matter of law or a new trial, however, simply stating that the motion is denied suffices.

Third, the order omits the District Court's reasons for disposing of the parties' motions as it did. Some courts of appeals have found that including a bit of analysis does not run afoul of the separate judgment requirement. See, e.g., Kidd v. District of Columbia, 340 U.S. App. D.C. 362, 206 F.3d 35, 39 (D.C. Cir. 2000). We express no opinion as to the propriety of that approach, however, because we see nothing in the order that can fairly be characterized as reasoning.

The order's denomination as an "order," rather than a "judgment," does not mean that it fails to satisfy the separate document requirement. We acknowledge that the Second Circuit has held that Rule 58 is not satisfied by a separate document denominated "order," rather than "judgment." See Kanematsu–Gosho Ltd. v. M/T Messiniaki Aigli, 805 F.2d 47, 48–49 (2d Cir. 1986) (per curiam). But we agree with the more comprehensive analysis of the D.C. Circuit in United States v. Johnson, 254 F.3d at 209 n.7. See also Mirpuri v. ACT Mfg., Inc., 212 F.3d 624, 628 (1st Cir. 2000); 11 Charles A. Wright & Arthur R. Miller, Federal Practice and Procedure § 2785, at 22 (2d ed. 1995). Federal Rule of Civil Procedure 54(a), by its literal terms, defines "judgment" as including "a decree and any order from which an appeal lies." Fed. R. Civ. P. 54(a) (emphasis added). And Federal Rule of Appellate Procedure 4(a) provides that an appeal must be filed within thirty days "after the judgment or order appealed from is entered." Fed. R. App. P. 4(a)(1)(A) (emphasis added). Finally, Federal Rule of Appellate Procedure 4(a)(7) provides that "judgment or order" is entered for purposes of Appellate Rule 4(a) when it is entered in compliance with Rule 58 and Rule 79(a). Fed. R. App. P. 4(a)(7) (emphasis added). In light of these specific references to judgments or orders as subjects of appeal, we believe that a separate document denominated an "order" may comply with Rule 58.

Okonite argues, as it did before the District Court, that Rule 58 required the District Court to enter three separate judgments for (a) its denial of Okonite's Rule 50 and 59 motions; (b) its denial of Local 1992's motion for prejudgment interest; and (c) its partial denial and partial grant of Local 1992's attorneys' fees motion. This argument is frivolous. Rule 58 " 'require[s] that there be a judgment set out an a separate document—distinct from any opinion or memorandum—which provides the basis for the entry of judgment.' " Kidd, 206 F.3d at 38 (quoting Fed. R. Civ. P. 58 advisory committee's notes). Nowhere does it mandate— either expressly or implicitly—that the resolution of each issue or motion have a separate judgment.

Okonite also argues that the District Court failed to comply with Rule 58 because neither it nor Local 1992 thought the May 8 order was final and appealable. In other words, Okonite contends that the parties' subjective state of mind controls whether the District Court complied with Rule 58 . Local 1992 disputes Okonite's characterization of how it interpreted the May 8 order, but whether Local 1992 believed the May 8 order was final and appealable is immaterial because Okonite's contention is meritless as a matter of law. The parties' intent is only relevant when a district court has failed to comply with the separate document requirement. In that case, a court of appeals can infer (from the parties proceeding on the assumption that the court's order is final) that the parties waived the requirement. See Bankers Trust Co. v. Mallis, 435 U.S. at 387–88; Spain v. Gallegos, 26 F.3d 439, 445 n.9 (3d Cir. 1994).

Finally, Okonite argues that the May 8 order does not satisfy Rule 58's separate document requirement because it included a "detailed discussion" of Local 1992's motion for attorneys' fees. We find, however, that including a referral of the attorneys' fees issue to the Magistrate Judge did not negate the clear notice that the separate document requirement is intended to create. See Haynes, 158 F.3d at 1329 ("The sole purpose of Rule 58 's separate document requirement was to clarify when the time for an appeal begins to run.").

As the Supreme Court explained in Budinich v. Becton Dickinson & Co., the pendency of a motion for attorneys' fees does not preclude entry of a final judgment. 486 U.S. at 199, 202 (1988) ("An unresolved issue of attorney's fees for the litigation in question does not prevent judgment on the merits from being final."). As a result, it is often the case than an order embodying a final judgment leaves open the assessment of attorneys' fees. Indeed, Rule 58 contemplates that "entry of the judgment shall not be delayed, nor the time for appeal extended, in order to tax costs or award fees." Fed. R. Civ. P. 58. Because Rule 58 expressly allows a court to defer the determination of attorneys' fees, the succinct statement in a judgment that an attorneys' fees motion is deferred for future resolution is perforce consistent with Rule 58 . Okonite's failure to appeal in this case cannot be excused under the pretense that the District Court violated Rule 58. * * *

We will dismiss the parties' appeals from all of the District Court's decisions in this case except for the District Court's determination of reasonable attorneys' fees. We will vacate the District Court's determination of attorneys' fees and remand for further proceedings in accordance with this opinion.

CREAGHE v. ALBEMARLE CORPORATION

United States Court of Appeals, Fifth Circuit, 2004.
98 Fed. Appx. 972.

PER CURIAM.

Appellant St. George Creaghe was employed by Appellee Albemarle Corporation and its predecessor-in-interest for nearly thirty years before being dismissed in 1996. Creaghe, who was 72 at the time of his dismissal, alleged that his firing was motivated by his age and filed suit in district court, raising claims of discrimination under the Age Discrimination in Employment Act ("ADEA"). The district court concluded that Creaghe failed to make out a prima facie case of discrimination and granted summary judgment in favor of Albemarle Corporation. Creaghe now appeals, urging that he produced evidence that his discharge was motivated by discriminatory animus and that the non-discriminatory reasons offered by Albemarle are pretextual. For the following reasons, we AFFIRM the district court's decision.

I

Before addressing Creaghe's ADEA claims, we must first assess whether we have jurisdiction over this appeal. Creaghe filed his notice of appeal on September 29, 2003. Albemarle contends that this notice was untimely because the district court's February 28, 2001, "Ruling on Motion for Summary Judgment" was a final judgment that dismissed Creaghe's suit. In response, Creaghe argues that the time for filing his appeal did not commence until the court issued its "Judgment" on September 22, 2003. He insists that the February 2001 order was not a final judgment because it did not comply with the requirements of Rule 58 of the Federal Rules of Civil Procedure and because it did not, by its terms, dismiss the case.

Rule 58 requires that every judgment be (1) set forth on a separate document and (2) entered on the district court's civil docket sheet. "The sole purpose of Rule 58 's separate-document requirement was to clarify when the time for an appeal begins to run."[2] Thus, it must be "mechanically applied in order to avoid new uncertainties as to the date on which a judgment is entered."[3] However, the separate document requirement "should be read, where reasonably possible, to protect the right to appeal."[4] "It must be remembered that the rule is designed to simplify and make certain the matter of appealability. It is not designed as a trap for the inexperienced.... "[5] Thus, "the rule should be interpreted to prevent loss of the right of appeal, not to facilitate loss."[6]

Contrary to Creaghe's assertions, the district court's February 2001 order appears to satisfy Rule 58's separate document requirements. To be "separate," a judgment must be apart from any document detailing either the court's factual findings or the legal basis of the court's ruling; it may not be part of a memorandum or opinion.[7] The order in this case fully complies with this directive: it contained no discussion of the reasoning behind the court's decision, did not mention the facts of the case, did not discuss the parties' contentions, and cited no legal authority. Indeed, it contained only four sentences, the final and most prominent of which clearly stated that "IT IS ORDERED that the Motion for Summary Judgment filed on behalf of defendant Albemarle Corporation is hereby GRANTED, and this action will be dismissed." To be sure, the order did include some other basic information—specifically, a brief introductory statement identifying the matter before the court and a sentence defining the court's jurisdiction. However, the inclusion of this bare information alone does not transform the order into a memorandum or opinion.[8] Nor does the fact that the order was called a "Ruling" rather than a "Judgment" affect its status under Rule 58.[9]

2. Ludgood v. Apex Marine Corp. Ship Management, 311 F.3d 364, 368 (5th Cir. 2002) (citing Bankers Trust Co. v. Mallis, 435 U.S. 381, 55 L. Ed. 2d 357, 98 S. Ct. 1117 (1978)).

3. United States v. Indrelunas, 411 U.S. 216, 222, 36 L. Ed. 2d 202, 93 S. Ct. 1562 (1973).

4. Seiscom Delta, Inc. v. Two Westlake Park, 857 F.2d 279, 282 (5th Cir. 1988).

5. Seiscom, 857 F.2d at 283 (internal citations omitted).

6. Id.

7. See, e.g., Whitaker v. City of Houston, Tex., 963 F.2d 831, 833 (5th Cir. 1992) ("Until set forth on a separate document in compliance with Rule 58 , a statement tacked on at the end of an opinion is not a judgment."); see also Notes of Advisory Committee on Rules, 1963 Amendment to FED. R. CIV. P. 58 ("The amended rule eliminates these uncertainties by requiring that there be a judgment set out on a separate document—distinct from any opinion or memorandum—which provides the basis for the entry of judgment.").

8. See, e.g., Nunez–Soto v. Alvarado, 956 F.2d 1 (1st Cir. 1992) (holding that an order was a "separate document" despite the inclusion of a single explanatory sentence); Hamilton v. Nakai, 453 F.2d 152 (9th Cir. 1971) (holding that an order, designated as such, was a "separate document" even though it included a one-sentence explanation); cf. Taylor v. Sterrett, 527 F.2d 856 (5th Cir. 1976) (holding that an order which included the court's opinions, findings, and conclusions was not a "separate document"); Hughes v. Halifax County Sch. Bd., 823 F.2d 832 (4th Cir. 1987) (finding that an order which included procedural history, arguments presented, and reasons for disposition was not a separate document).

9. Meadowbriar Home for Children, Inc. v. Gunn, 81 F.3d 521, 528 (5th Cir. 1996) ("The Supreme Court has held that no form of words and no peculiar formal act is necessary to evince the rendition of a judgment" (citations and internal quotations omitted)).

Nonetheless, there are weighty considerations discouraging us from concluding that Creaghe's appeal was untimely. The February Ruling, most notably, clearly stated that the action "will" be dismissed; it did not, by its express terms, *dismiss* the suit. The order thus contemplated that a separate final judgment would later issue, and Creaghe was justified in relying on the court's clear representation.[10] Moreover, the district court itself stated that it "never intended it's [sic] Ruling of February 28, 2001 to be a final decision. The document is not, nor was it ever intended to be, a judgment."[11]

Although the question is fairly close, we agree in light of the ambiguous language in the district court's February 2001 Ruling and our generous approach to Rule 58 issues—that the time for filing the notice of appeal did not commence until September 22, 2003, the date on which the court issued its Judgment. We interpret Rule 58's requirements to prevent the loss of an appeal whenever reasonable. Even if the February 2001 Ruling might have been sufficient to satisfy Rule 58's requirements, "we are reluctant to hold that because such an order has been entered, the parties may not appeal from a later separate order which clearly meets the requirements of Rule 58 ."[12] Accordingly, we acknowledge our jurisdiction and proceed to consider the merits of Creaghe's appeal.

II

The district court concluded that Creaghe failed to establish a prima facie case of discrimination under the ADEA and granted Albemarle's motion for summary judgment. We [affirm.]

Notes and Questions

Amended Judgments: Each year a number of "final" judgments are revised: Spelling is corrected, math is fixed, provisions for interest or recovery of attorneys fees are added. The revised judgment is signed and docketed.

[The] mere fact that a judgment previously entered has been reentered or revised in an immaterial way does not toll the time within which review must be sought. Only when the lower court changes matters of substance, or resolves a genuine ambiguity, in a judgment previously rendered should the period within which an appeal must be taken or a

---

10. We have stated in the past that "the mere fact that a court reenters a judgment or revises a judgment in an immaterial way does not affect the time within which litigants must pursue an appeal." Offshore Prod. Contractors Ins. Co. v. Republic Underwriters, 910 F.2d 224, 229 (5th Cir. 1990). Given the wording of the February order, the later September Judgment cannot fairly be considered a simple "reentry" of judgment.

11. Creaghe v. Albemarle Corp., No. 97–cv–803 (M. D. La. Feb. 10, 2003) (order granting Creaghe an extension of time to file a notice of appeal).

12. Kline v. HHS, 927 F.2d 522, 523 (10th Cir. 1991).

petition for certiorari filed begin to run anew. The test is a practical one. The question is whether the lower court, in its second order, has disturbed or revised legal rights and obligations which, by its prior judgment, had been plainly and properly settled with finality.

Federal Trade Commission v. Minneapolis-honeywell Regulator Co., 344 U.S. 206, 73 S.Ct. 245, 97 L.Ed. 245 (1952).

3. EXTENSION OF TIME TO APPEAL

There are very limited circumstances in which any form of relief from the mandatory and jurisdictional filing deadline. This section explores, first, cases where a party gets no notice of the entry of a judgment, and hence misses the normal deadline for filing an appeal. Later cases raise issues with respect to parties who *got notice* but nonetheless failed to lodge a timely appeal, and who seek relief from the appellate court under the "excusable neglect or good cause" provision of Rule 4(a)(5).

AVOLIO v. COUNTY OF SUFFOLK

United States Court of Appeals, Second Circuit, 1994.
29 F.3d 50.

PRATT, CIRCUIT JUDGE:

This appeal requires us to interpret and apply, apparently for the first time in this circuit, a 1991 amendment to rule 4(a) of the Federal Rules of Appellate Procedure. The amendment extends until 180 days after entry of judgment the time within which a district court may permit late filing of a notice of appeal.

Plaintiffs' § 1983 action against Suffolk County, New York, the Suffolk County Police Department, Suffolk County Detectives Joseph Avella and Angelo Carrion, and Detective Sergeant Donald Risener was dismissed, partly as a matter of law during trial, and partly by a jury verdict. On February 4, 1993, the clerk entered judgment against the plaintiffs and, as required by Fed.R.Civ.P. 77(d), mailed notice of entry of the judgment to all parties.

In his affirmation supporting plaintiffs' motion for an extension of time to appeal, counsel for plaintiffs indicated that his office had never received a copy of the judgment. His affirmation implies that he first learned the judgment had been entered when on or soon after March 18, 1993, his client told him that he had contacted the court and was advised that a judgment had been signed on January 19, 1993. Counsel confirmed that information by telephone in a conversation with a deputy clerk and immediately obtained a copy of the judgment. Counsel further asserted that he could "conceive of no prejudice to any of the defending parties to this action" resulting from an extension of time to appeal.

On March 26, 1993, plaintiffs' attorney moved "pursuant to Rule 4(a)(6) of the Federal Rules of Appellate Procedure to reopen the time for plaintiffs to file a Notice of Appeal". Counsel for defendant Risener, by letter dated April 8, 1993, "vigorously oppose[d]" the motion "[i]n view of the complete lack of merit in Plaintiff's [sic] case". The other defendants raised no opposition. By memorandum and order dated June 9, 1993, the district court denied the motion. Despite the facts that the clerk's office had mailed copies of the judgment to all parties and that none of the copies was returned, the court assumed for purposes of the motion that plaintiffs' attorney never received a copy of the judgment. Thus, the court turned to rule 4(a)(6), as amended in 1991. That rule reads as follows:*

> The district court, if it finds (a) that a party entitled to notice of the entry of a judgment or order did not receive such notice from the clerk or any party within 21 days of its entry and (b) that no party would be prejudiced, may, upon motion filed within 180 days of entry of the judgment or order or within 7 days of receipt of such notice, whichever is earlier, reopen the time for appeal for a period of 14 days from the date of entry of the order reopening the time for appeal.

The district court construed the word "may" as allowing it discretion to determine whether under the circumstances an extension should be granted, and it found that the circumstances "do not warrant such an extension". To guide its discretion the district court turned to the law as it existed before the 1991 amendment. Under that law, during a period of 30 days after the time to file a notice of appeal has expired, the district court could grant an extension only upon a showing of excusable neglect. In the second circuit, the clerk's failure to mail a notice of judgment did not constitute excusable neglect. *Bortugno v. Metro–North Commuter Railroad*, 905 F.2d 674, 676 (2d Cir. 1990) (per curiam) (reversing district court's grant of extension). As pointed out by the district court, a party was obligated to find out when the judgment was entered, and counsel's failure to investigate when he did not receive notice of a judgment from the clerk, constitutes "unexcusable neglect and does not warrant an extension of time in which to file a notice of appeal."

In short, the district court interpreted the word "may" in the 1991 amendment to have incorporated into Fed.R.App.P. 4(a)(6) the same standard of excusable neglect that had guided our earlier rulings on motions for extensions of time to appeal.

We do not think the district court's decision correctly reflects either the purpose or effect of rule 4 as now amended. As pointed out in the notes of the advisory committee that accompanied the 1991 amendment,

> The amendment provides a limited opportunity for relief in circumstances where the notice of entry of a judgment or order, required to be mailed by the clerk of the district court pursuant to Rule 77(d) of the Federal Rules of Civil Procedure, is either not received by a

---

* [Revisions in the wording of this rule since the date of this opinion have not altered its substance. Eds.]

party or is received so late as to impair the opportunity to file a timely notice of appeal.

This provision establishes an outer time limit of 180 days for a party who fails to receive timely notice of entry of a judgment to seek additional time to appeal.

In a civil case not involving the United States, a notice of appeal must be filed within 30 days after the date of entry of the judgment or order appealed from, Fed.R.App.P. 4(a)(1), unless the time is extended under one of the other subdivisions of rule 4(a). Under subdivision (5), the district court may extend the time upon a motion filed not later than 30 days after expiration of the original period, provided there is "a showing of excusable neglect or good cause". Plaintiffs could not qualify for this kind of extension because the mere failure to discover that the judgment had been entered, even when the clerk had failed to mail a notice of judgment as directed by Fed.R.Civ.P. 77(d), does not constitute excusable neglect. *Bortugno*, 905 F.2d at 676.

Subdivision (6) of rule 4(a), however, was added in 1991 to address precisely the type of problem presented by this case. It authorizes an extension of time when the appellant did not receive notice of the entry of the judgment or order within 21 days of its entry.

To qualify under subdivision (6), the movant must establish: (1) that he was entitled to notice of the entry of the judgment; (2) that he did not receive such notice from the clerk or any party within 21 days of its entry; (3) that no party would be prejudiced by the extension; and (4) that he moved within 180 days of entry of the judgment or within 7 days of his receipt of such notice, whichever is earlier.

Plaintiffs in this case claimed to have met these requirements. As to the first, there is no dispute that plaintiffs were entitled to notice of the entry of the judgment against them. As to the second—whether plaintiffs received such notice—there appears to be no problem, although the district court may wish to inquire further on the remand that we are ordering. Counsel's affirmation in support of the motion for an extension of time, as well as the district court's decision, both speak in terms of receipt of a copy of the judgment; the rule contemplates receipt of notice of the entry of the judgment. Whether the difference is significant or not in this case, we leave to the district court to determine.

In other respects, although the record lacks clarity, non-receipt of the notice seems to have been established. The moving papers reflect that while plaintiffs' counsel was out of the state for an 8–day period in March, one of the plaintiffs contacted the court and was advised that the judgment had been signed on January 19, 1993. Since plaintiffs were then represented by counsel, the notice of entry had to be received by counsel, not the party. See Fed.R.Civ.P. 5(b) ("[W]henever * * * service is required or permitted to be made upon a party represented by an attorney the service shall be made upon the attorney."). Furthermore, the notice must be received "from the clerk or any party". Finally, the notice contemplated by this rule is written notice; an oral communication simply is not sufficient to trigger the relevant time periods. In short, it appears at least until March 18, no notice was received by plaintiffs within the meaning of subdivision (6).

As to the third requirement—prejudice—the district court did not reach the question. Plaintiffs' counsel argued that no prejudice would follow in the circumstances here, and none of the defendants urged the district court to find prejudice. Nevertheless, a finding on this point by the district court will be required before the extension may be granted.

As to the fourth requirement—timeliness—counsel's affirmation asserts that after he returned to New York on March 18, 1993, he obtained a copy of the judgment from the clerk. Presumably at that point he did receive from the clerk the required written notice that the judgment had been entered. His motion under subdivision (6), filed on March 26, 1993, was well within 180 days of the entry of judgment. It was also within the required seven days, since the intervening Saturday and Sunday are excluded from the calculation. Fed.R.Civ.P. 6(a). Plaintiffs' motion was therefore timely.

The district court did not reach some of these issues, because it interpreted the word "may" as granting to the district court discretion in deciding whether or not to grant the motion. To guide its exercise of discretion, the district court then incorporated into subdivision (6) the standard of "excusable neglect" that applies to applications for extensions of time under subdivision (5). This was error. The purpose of subdivision (6) was to relieve parties of the rigors of subdivision (5) when the failure to timely appeal was caused by not having received notice of the entry of judgment.

Were we to accept the district court's interpretation, we would subvert the central purpose of subdivision (6). As noted by the civil rules advisory committee in recommending a companion amendment to Fed. R.Civ.P. 77(d), "The purpose of the revisions is to permit district courts to ease strict sanctions now imposed on appellants whose notices of appeal are filed late because of their failure to receive notice of entry of a judgment." Advisory Committee Note to 1991 amendment of Fed. R.Civ.P. 77(d).

To balance the potentially substantial extension of the time to appeal, subdivision (6) in effect encourages the prevailing party to send its own notice of entry of judgment to the losing party. See David D. Siegel, Changes in Federal Rules of Civil Procedure, 142 F.R.D. 359, 378 (1992). As noted by the Advisory Committee, "Winning parties are encouraged to send their own notice in order to lessen the chance that a judge will accept a claim of non-receipt in the face of evidence that notices were sent by both the clerk and the winning party." Advisory Committee Note to Fed.R.App.P. 4(a)(6).

In sum, if a party does not receive notice of entry from the clerk or another party within 21 days of entry of the judgment, he may seek an extension of time under subdivision (6) at any time up to 180 days after entry of the judgment, provided he moves within 7 days of receipt of notice of entry; and he may succeed if he can establish that no party would be prejudiced by the delay. We need not determine to what extent discretion may lie in the district court under this rule; we do determine, however, that a denial of relief may not be based on a concept of inexcusable neglect for not having learned of the entry of judgment. That concept has no place in the application of subdivision (6).

We therefore vacate the order of the district court and remand for further proceedings with respect to plaintiffs' motion consistent with this opinion.

Notes and Questions

1. In Marcangelo v. Boardwalk Regency, 47 F.3d 88 (3d Cir. 1995), a party was represented by "local" counsel and out-of-state, principal counsel. Delivery of notice to the local attorney was deemed effective, and thus an application for extension under the rule discussed in the principal case was denied.

2. The time limits provided by Fed.R.App.P. 4(a)(6) and 28 U.S.C. § 2107 are "mandatory and jurisdictional." Consequently, the courts are required to dismiss untimely appeals sua sponte. Browder v. Director, Dep't of Corrections, 434 U.S. 257, 264, 98 S.Ct. 556, 54 L.Ed.2d 521 (1978). The parties may not confer jurisdiction on the appellate court by consent. Therefore, even in the absence of opposition by the appellees in Marcangelo, the motion could not have been granted. Accord Riggs v. Riggs, 539 A.2d 163 (Del. 1988).

3. Consider the alternative systems used by various states to deal with the issue of a losing party that does not get notice of the judgment in time to lodge an appeal. One pattern is to place primary reliance on the service of *notice* of the judgment on the clerk of court. For example, in Ohio if the clerk of court fails to serve notice of a judgment on a party within three days of its entry, the running of the time for appeal is tolled until service is made. Ohio Appellate Rule 4(A). Several states follow this model, including Colorado [Colo. R. Civ. P. 58(A)]; Kansas [Kan. Stat. Ann. § 60–258]; and North Carolina [N.C. R. Civ. P. 58]. Is there no outer limit on the time for such applications?

Other states make it clear that there is no notice requirement at all if the judgment is rendered in open court. Rhode Island's version of R. Civ. P. 77 (d) has such a provision.

Massachusetts allows, under its Rule 4 of the Rules of Appellate Procedure, for the extension of time to file a notice of appeal upon a finding of "excusable neglect."

In Tennessee, parties must request to receive notice of the judgment. Under Tenn. R. Civ. P. 58.03(1), if so requested, the clerk will provide notice to all the parties in the case.

Wisconsin provides that if notice is not served on a party within 21 days of the entry of a judgment, the time period to file an appeal is increased from 45 to 90 days. Wis. R. Civ. P. 808.04. Under that rule, notice may be served by any party upon the other.

Montana [Mont. R. Civ. P. 77(d)], North Dakota [N.D. R. Civ. P. 77 (d)] and Utah [Utah R. Civ. P. 58A (d)] require the prevailing party to *serve* notice on the adverse party as a triggering event in the appellate process.

However, in Texas [Tex. R. App. P. 5(b)(4)] and South Carolina [S.C. R. Civ. P. 74] the initiation of the time for appeal is contingent upon the parties' *receipt* of the notice of entry. Texas also places an outer limit on the amount of time an appeal can remain open due to lack of notice of entry of a final order.

Finally, Virginia Code § 8.01–428(C) provides:

> **C. Failure to notify party or counsel of final order.**—If counsel, or a party not represented by counsel, who is not in default in a circuit court is not notified by any means of the entry of a final order and the circuit court is satisfied that such lack of notice (i) did not result from a failure to exercise due diligence on the part of that party and (ii) denied that party an opportunity to file an appeal therefrom, the circuit court may, within sixty days of the entry of such order, grant the party leave to appeal. The computation of time for noting and perfecting an appeal shall run from the entry of such order, and such order shall have no other effect.

How would one demonstrate exercise of "due diligence" under this section? Is 60 days after entry of the judgment a sufficient period of time for seeking an "extension" of the time for appeal?

4. THE EXCUSABLE NEGLECT STANDARD UNDER APPELLATE RULE 4(a)(5)

PINCAY v. ANDREWS

United States Court of Appeals, Ninth Circuit, 2004 (en banc).
389 F.3d 853.

SCHROEDER, CHIEF JUDGE.

This appeal represents a lawyer's nightmare. A sophisticated law firm, with what it thought was a sophisticated system to determine and calendar filing deadlines, missed a critical one: the 30–day time period in which to file a notice of appeal under Federal Rule of Appellate Procedure 4(a)(1)(A). The rule, however, provides for a grace period of 30 days within which a lawyer in such a fix may ask the district court for an extension of time, and the court, in the exercise of its discretion, may grant the extension if it determines that the neglect of the attorney was "excusable."[1] Here an experienced trial judge found excusable neglect, and the appellee asks us to overturn that ruling.

The underlying dispute began in 1989 when Laffit Pincay, Jr. and Christopher McCarron (Pincay) sued Vincent S. Andrews, Robert L.

---

1. The rule provides in relevant part: "The district court may extend the time to file a notice of appeal if: (i) a party so moves no later than 30 days after the time pre- scribed by this Rule 4(a) expires; and (ii) ... that party shows excusable neglect or good cause." Fed. R. App. P. 4(a)(5)(A).

Andrews, and Vincent Andrews Management Corp. (Andrews) for financial injuries stemming from alleged violations of the Racketeer Influenced and Corrupt Organizations Act (RICO) and California law. In 1992, a jury returned verdicts in Pincay's favor on both the RICO and the California counts. Pincay was ordered to elect a remedy, and he chose to pursue the RICO judgment. This judgment was reversed on appeal on the ground that the RICO claim was barred by the federal statute of limitations. Pincay v. Andrews, 238 F.3d 1106, 1110 (9th Cir. 2001). On remand, Pincay elected to pursue the remedy on his California law claim. Judgment was entered in his favor on July 3, 2002.

Andrews's notice of appeal was due 30 days later, but a paralegal charged with calendaring filing deadlines misread the rule and advised Andrews's attorney that the notice was not due for 60 days, the time allowed when the government is a party to the case. See Fed. R. App. P. 4(a)(1)(B). Andrews's counsel learned about the error when Pincay relied upon the judgment as being final in related bankruptcy proceedings, and Andrews promptly tendered a notice of appeal together with a request for an extension within the 30–day grace period. By that time the matter had been in litigation for more than 15 years. Everyone involved should have been well aware that the government was not a party to the case, and any lawyer or paralegal should have been able to read the rule correctly. The misreading of the rule was a critical error that, had the district court viewed the situation differently, would have ended the litigation then and there with an irreparably adverse result for Andrews. The district court, however, found the neglect excusable and granted the motion for an extension of time to file the notice of appeal.

Pincay appealed to this court, and a majority of the three-judge panel concluded that Andrews's attorney had improperly delegated the function of calendaring to a paralegal, and held that the attorney's reliance on a paralegal was inexcusable as a matter of law. Pincay v. Andrews, 351 F.3d 947, 951–52 (9th Cir. 2003). It ordered the appeal dismissed. The dissent would have applied a more flexible and deferential standard and affirmed the district court. Id. at 952–56 (Kleinfeld, J., dissenting).

A majority of the active non-recused judges of the court voted to rehear the case en banc to consider whether the creation of a per se rule against delegation to paralegals, or indeed any per se rule involving missed filing deadlines, is consistent with the United States Supreme Court's leading authority on the modern concept of excusable neglect, Pioneer Investment Services Co. v. Brunswick Associated Ltd. Partnership, 507 U.S. 380, 123 L. Ed. 2d 74, 113 S. Ct. 1489 (1993). We now hold that per se rules are not consistent with Pioneer, and we uphold the exercise of the district court's discretion to permit the filing of the notice of appeal in this case.

The Pioneer decision arose in the bankruptcy context and involved the "bar date" for the filing of claims. The Court in Pioneer established a four-part balancing test for determining whether there had been "excusable neglect" within the meaning of Federal Rule of Bankruptcy Procedure 9006(b)(1). The Court also reviewed various contexts in which the phrase appeared in the federal rules of procedure and made it clear the same test applies in all those contexts. The Pioneer factors include: (1) the danger of prejudice to the non-moving party, (2) the length of delay and its potential impact on judicial proceedings, (3) the reason for the delay, including whether it was within the reasonable control of the movant, and (4) whether the moving party's conduct was in good faith. 507 U.S. at 395.

In this case, the district court analyzed each of the Pioneer factors and correctly found: (1) there was no prejudice, (2) the length of delay was small, (3) the reason for the delay was carelessness, and (4) there was no evidence of bad faith. It then concluded that even though the reason for the delay was the carelessness of Andrews's counsel, that fact did not render the neglect inexcusable. The district court relied on this court's decision in Marx v. Loral Corp., 87 F.3d 1049 (9th Cir. 1996), in which we affirmed an order granting an extension of time in a case that involved an attorney's calendaring error.

Because the panel majority decided the case in part on the issue of delegation of calendaring to a paralegal, we consider that issue first. This issue was not presented to the district court, and it was raised sua sponte by the three-judge panel.

In the modern world of legal practice, the delegation of repetitive legal tasks to paralegals has become a necessary fixture. Such delegation has become an integral part of the struggle to keep down the costs of legal representation. Moreover, the delegation of such tasks to specialized, well-educated non-lawyers may well ensure greater accuracy in meeting deadlines than a practice of having each lawyer in a large firm calculate each filing deadline anew. The task of keeping track of necessary deadlines will involve some delegation. The responsibility for the error falls on the attorney regardless of whether the error was made by an attorney or a paralegal. See Model Rules of Prof'l Conduct R. 5.5 cmt. 2 (2002) ("This Rule does not prohibit a lawyer from employing the services of paraprofessionals and delegating functions to them, so long as the lawyer supervises the delegated work and retains responsibility for their work."). We hold that delegation of the task of ascertaining the deadline was not per se inexcusable neglect.

The larger question in this case is whether the misreading of the clear rule could appropriately have been considered excusable. Resolution of that question requires some effort to try to distill any principles that have evolved in the 10 years since Pioneer. In Pioneer itself, the Court adopted a broader and more flexible test for excusable neglect. A narrower test existed in many circuits before Pioneer that limited excusable neglect to situations that were beyond the control of the movant for an extension as, for example, the messenger being hit by a truck on the way to the court clerk's filing desk. See Pioneer, 507 U.S. at 387–88 & n.3.

The district court followed our decision in Marx, where we acknowledged that Pioneer had worked a change in our circuit's law as to what constitutes excusable neglect. 87 F.3d at 1053–54. As we explained in Marx, our "strict standard," which required both a showing of extraordinary circumstances that prevented timely filing and injustice resulting from denying an extension, id. at 1053, gave way to an equitable determination that involves consideration of the four Pioneer factors. Id. at 1054. We therefore affirmed the district court's grant of an extension of time to file a notice of appeal in Marx because the district court correctly considered the Pioneer factors. We found that the district court did not abuse its discretion, and we said: "The district court's analysis of the Pioneer Inv. factors in this case, although considerably lenient to the plaintiffs, was not a clear error of judgment." Id.

Our court, in other cases, has also described Pioneer's flexible approach, saying, for example, "we will ordinarily examine all of the circumstances involved rather than holding that any single circumstance in isolation compels a particular result regardless of the other factors." Briones v. Riviera Hotel & Casino, 116 F.3d 379, 382 n.2 (9th Cir. 1997); see also Bateman v. United States Postal Serv., 231 F.3d 1220, 1224 (9th Cir. 2000).

We seemed to take a more narrow approach in Kyle v. Campbell Soup Co., 28 F.3d 928 (9th Cir. 1994). In that case our court reversed the district court's finding of excusable neglect. We emphasized the fact that the attorney had made a mistake in interpreting rules that were not ambiguous and we focused on the particular facts of Pioneer, including a "dramatic ambiguity" in the notice of the filing deadline at issue. Id. at 931.

Our circuit's confusion is not isolated. The authorities interpreting Pioneer in a number of circuits are in some disarray. In fact, the confusion begins with Pioneer itself, and various subsequent circuit opinions have cited similar portions of Pioneer to support their respective but differing conclusions. The key passage in Pioneer, having a little something for everyone, is as follows:

> Although inadvertence, ignorance of the rules, or mistakes construing the rules do not usually constitute "excusable" neglect, it is clear that "excusable neglect" under [Bankruptcy] Rule 6(b) is a somewhat "elastic concept" and is not limited strictly to omissions caused by circumstances beyond the control of the movant.

507 U.S. at 392 (internal footnotes omitted).

The experience of the Seventh and Fifth Circuits is instructive. The Seventh Circuit in Prizevoits v. Indiana Bell Telephone Co., 76 F.3d 132 (7th Cir. 1996), dismissed an appeal for lack of jurisdiction because the notice was not filed within the 30 days required by the Rule. In that case the attorney had missed the deadline for filing a motion under Federal Rule of Civil Procedure 59(e) to alter or amend the judgment and filed a motion to extend the time. The district court denied this motion because no extension is allowed under Rule 59. The time for filing a notice of appeal expired, however, while the motion was pending before the district court, and so the attorney moved for an extension under Rule 4. The district court granted the extension of time to appeal, but the Seventh Circuit reversed. Id. at 133. The Prizevoits majority cited Pioneer for the proposition that "excusable neglect" is not limited to situations where the failure to timely file 'is due to circumstances beyond the control of the filer,' " id. at 134 (quoting Pioneer, 507 U.S. at 391), but limited the reach of Pioneer to such things as "plausible misinterpretations of ambiguous rules." Id. The majority then concluded: "Here the rule is crystal clear, the error egregious, the excuses so thin as to leave the lapse not only unexcused but inexplicable. If there was 'excusable' neglect here, we have difficulty imagining a case of inexcusable neglect." Id.

Judge Eschbach's dissent also relied on Pioneer and criticized the majority's choice "not to address the impact of Pioneer on our past decisions." 76 F.3d at 136. The dissent said: "In Pioneer, the Court held that attorney negligence may, in certain circumstances, constitute 'excusable neglect,' considerably liberalizing its meaning and prescribing a new analytical test." Id.

In the Fifth Circuit, a majority relied on Prizevoits in Midwest Employers Cas. Co. v. Williams, 161 F.3d 877 (5th Cir. 1998), over a strong dissent by Judge Garza. Judge Garza cited authority, seemingly contrary to the majority, from both the Fifth and Seventh Circuits, interpreting the equitable factors of Pioneer. Id. at 882–84, 885. He cited United States v. Evbuomwan, 36 F.3d 89 (5th Cir. 1994) (unpublished opinion) (reported at 36 F.3d 89 (table case)), "where the court found that the district court did not abuse its discretion in finding that a good faith misinterpretation of plain rules was excusable neglect. He also cited Lackey v. Atlantic Richfield Co., 990 F.2d 202, 205 (5th Cir. 1993), where the court found that the district court did not abuse its discretion in finding excusable neglect because the attorney's obvious error was mitigated by the lack of prejudice to the nonmovant and the shortness of the delay. Finally, he cited United States v. Brown, 133 F.3d 993 (7th Cir. 1998), where the Seventh Circuit affirmed the district court's finding that an attorney's confusing of state rules with federal rules amounted to excusable neglect. Id. at 996. The Seventh Circuit said: "Pioneer made clear that the standard is a balancing test, meaning that a delay might be excused even where the reasons for the delay are not particularly compelling." Id. at 997.

The Eleventh Circuit seems to have set forth a more categorical test. In Advanced Estimating System, Inc. v. Riney, 130 F.3d 996 (11th Cir. 1997), the court stated: "The ancient legal maxim continues to apply: ignorance of fact may excuse; ignorance of law does not excuse. Accordingly, [Appellant's] counsel's misunderstanding of the law cannot constitute excusable neglect." Id. at 999 (citations omitted). That decision seemed to move the Eleventh Circuit back toward the approach it had taken before Pioneer, and which Pioneer rejected, i.e., excusable neglect is limited to matters beyond the control of the attorney. See In re

Analytical Systems, 933 F.2d 939, 942 (11th Cir. 1991) (reciting the Eleventh Circuit's pre-Pioneer standard for establishing excusable neglect); Pioneer, 507 U.S. at 387 n.3 (citing In re Analytical Sys. as an example of a court that had taken a narrow view of excusable neglect). In Pioneer, the Supreme Court rejected "a bright-line rule of the sort embraced by some Courts of Appeals, erecting a rigid barrier against late filings attributable in any degree to the movant's negligence" as "irreconcilable with our cases." 507 U.S. at 395 n.14.

Despite this confusion, there appears to be general agreement on at least one principle: the standard of review. We review for abuse of discretion a district court's decision to grant or deny a motion for an extension of time to file a notice of appeal. Marx, 87 F.3d at 1054; see also Pioneer, 507 U.S. at 398 ("To be sure, were there any evidence of prejudice to petitioner or to judicial administration in this case, or any indication at all of bad faith, we could not say that the Bankruptcy Court abused its discretion in declining to find the neglect to be 'excusable.' "); Kyle, 28 F.3d at 930; Silivanch v. Celebrity Cruises, Inc., 333 F.3d 355, 362 (2d Cir. 2003); Midwest Employers Cas. Co., 161 F.3d at 879; Advanced Estimating Sys., 130 F.3d at 997. We must therefore affirm unless we are left with the definite and firm conviction that the lower court committed a clear error of judgment in the conclusion it reached after weighing the relevant factors. Marx, 87 F.3d at 1054.

In this case the mistake itself, the misreading of the Rule, was egregious, and the lawyer undoubtedly should have checked the Rule itself before relying on the paralegal's reading. Both the paralegal and the lawyer were negligent. That, however, represents the beginning of our inquiry as to whether the negligence is excusable, not the end of it. The real question is whether there was enough in the context of this case to bring a determination of excusable neglect within the district court's discretion.

We therefore turn to examining the Pioneer factors as they apply here. The parties seem to agree that three of the factors militate in favor of excusability, and they focus their arguments on the remaining factor: the reason for the delay. Appellee Andrews characterizes the reason for the delay as the failure of a "carefully designed" calendaring system operated by experienced paralegals that heretofore had worked flawlessly. Appellant Pincay, on the other hand, stresses the degree of carelessness in the failure to read the applicable Rule.

We recognize that a lawyer's failure to read an applicable rule is one of the least compelling excuses that can be offered; yet the nature of the contextual analysis and the balancing of the factors adopted in Pioneer counsel against the creation of any rigid rule. Rather, the decision whether to grant or deny an extension of time to file a notice of appeal should be entrusted to the discretion of the district court because the district court is in a better position than we are to evaluate factors such as whether the lawyer had otherwise been diligent, the propensity of the other side to capitalize on petty mistakes, the quality of representation of the lawyers (in this litigation over its 15-year history), and the likelihood of injustice if the appeal was not allowed. Had the district court declined to permit the filing of the notice, we would be hard pressed to find any rationale requiring us to reverse.

Pioneer itself instructs courts to determine the issue of excusable neglect within the context of the particular case, a context with which the trial court is most familiar. Any rationale suggesting that misinterpretation of an unambiguous rule can never be excusable neglect is, in our view, contrary to that instruction. "The right way, under Pioneer, to decide cases involving ignorance of federal rules is with an 'elastic concept' equitable in nature, not with a per se rule." Pincay v. Andrews, 351 F.3d 947, 953 (9th Cir. 2003) (Kleinfeld, J., dissenting).

We are also mindful that Rule 4 itself provides for leniency in limited circumstances. It could have been written more rigidly, allowing for no window of opportunity once the deadline was missed. Many states' rules provide for an extension of the time for filing a notice of appeal under few, if any, circumstances. See, e.g., Ariz. R. Civ. App. P. 9 (providing for an extension of time to file a notice of appeal only if a party did not receive notice of the entry of judgment and no party would be prejudiced); Matter of Appeal in Pima County Juvenile Action No. S–933, 135 Ariz. 278, 660 P.2d 1205, 1207 (Ariz. 1982) ("Excusable neglect affords no basis for relief from the dismissal of an untimely appeal."); Cal. R. Ct. 3 (listing circumstances in which the time to appeal is extended and not including an extension for excusable neglect); In re Hanley's Estate, 23 Cal. 2d 120, 142 P.2d 423, 424–25 (Cal. 1943) ("In the absence of statutory authorization, neither the trial nor appellate courts may extend or shorten the time for appeal even to relieve against mistake, inadvertence, accident, or misfortune.") (internal citations omitted). The federal rule is a more flexible one that permits a narrow 30-day window for requesting an extension, and the trial court has wide discretion as to whether to excuse the lapse.

We understand several of our sister circuits have tried to fashion a rule making a mistake of law per se inexcusable under Rule 4. See, e.g., Silivanch, 333 F.3d at 368–69, which in turn quotes a series of pre-Pioneer cases including In re Cosmopolitan Aviation Corp., 763 F.2d 507, 515 (2d Cir. 1985)) (" 'the excusable neglect standard can never be met by a showing of inability or refusal to read and comprehend the plain language of the federal rules.' "); Advanced Estimating Sys., 130 F.3d at 998 ("An attorney's misunderstanding of the plain language of a rule cannot constitute excusable neglect.")). Prizevoits , 76 F.3d at 133 ("An unaccountable lapse is not excusable neglect."); We agree that a lawyer's mistake of law in reading a rule of procedure is not a compelling excuse. At the same time, however, a lawyer's mistake of fact, for example, in thinking the government was a party to a case and that the 60-day rule applied for that reason, would be no more compelling.

We are persuaded that, under Pioneer, the correct approach is to avoid any per se rule. Pioneer cautioned against "erecting a rigid barrier against late filings attributable in any degree to the movant's negligence." 507 U.S. at 395 n.14. There should similarly be no rigid legal rule against late filings attributable to any particular type of negligence. Instead, we leave the weighing of Pioneer's equitable factors to the discretion of the district court in every case.

We hold that the district court did not abuse its discretion in this case. Therefore, the district court's order granting the defendant's motion for an extension of time to file the notice of appeal is AF-FIRMED. The merits of the appeal are before the three judge panel in appeal number 02–56491. The panel should proceed to decide that appeal.

BERSON, CIRCUIT JUDGE, CONCURRING:

Although I join the majority opinion in full, I write separately to briefly emphasize the two points that I believe dispositive of this case and that explain why I cannot agree with an otherwise persuasive dissent.

First, in his dissent, Judge Kozinski concludes that "most of the work" is done by Pioneer's third factor—the reason for the delay. But Pioneer portends a balancing test, and does not ascribe determinative significance to any single factor. In other words, whether neglect is "excusable" is the conclusion one reaches after considering the pertinent factors, not an independent element with moral content. Pioneer thus indicates that a district court may find neglect "excusable" if it is caught quickly, hurts no one, and is a real mistake, rather than one feigned for some tactical reason—even if no decent lawyer would have made that error. There is no linguistic flaw in terming such errors "excusable," meaning nothing more than "appropriate to excuse."

Second, even if I agreed with the dissent that the defendants had to show "something" in satisfaction of Pioneer's third prong, I would hold that there is "something" here. The dissent's position is seemingly that, for neglect to be excusable, the reason for the error must be one that an appellate court views as understandable or sympathetic—a "good" reason in some respect. Such an assessment is necessarily subjective. The examples Judge Kozinski gives indicate that courts have recognized personal difficulties, client communication problems, and confusing rules as "good" reasons—as "something"—that weigh positively in the Pioneer balance, while viewing misreading clear rules as not a "good" reason—not "something."

If this were an essential inquiry, I would hold that the district court did not abuse its discretion in holding that even the complete misfiring of a generally well-conceived calendaring system is "something"—as compared, for example, to letting court orders pile up on desks, with no effort to read them or calculate appeal deadlines (a not-so-hypothetical hypothetical, as we have had such cases). Here, the lawyer did within the appeal deadline period make an effort, although an exceedingly poor one, to ascertain the appeal deadline; he did not ignore the issue entirely.

The existence of some effort to meet appeal deadlines is not simply evidence of good faith. The good faith consideration goes to the absence of tactical or strategic motives, not to the degree of negligence. Here, as Judge Kozinski recognizes, given the lack of prejudice or delay and the absence of any evidence of ulterior motives, "defendants need not have offered a terribly good countervailing reason to make their neglect excusable." In my view, a district court does not abuse its discretion by regarding the existence of a system designed to prevent the error from happening—even a system that is overly reliant on non-lawyers and that entirely misfired in this instance (probably as a result of over-reliance on non-lawyers)—as "something" weakly positive in the reason category.

I therefore join the opinion of the court in its entirety.

KOZINSKI, CIRCUIT JUDGE, with whom Judges RYMER and McKEOWN join, dissenting:

We must never forget that it is "excusable neglect" we are expounding. Before Pioneer Investment Services Co. v. Brunswick Associates Ltd. Partnership, 507 U.S. 380, 123 L. Ed. 2d 74, 113 S. Ct. 1489 (1993), four circuits had forgotten; they interpreted this phrase as "requiring a showing that the delay was caused by circumstances beyond the movant's control." Id. at 387 n.3. But how could circumstances beyond one's control be neglect? A jurisprudence that refused to excuse anything one could fairly call "neglect" was inconsistent with the clear text of rules that, by their terms, provide exceptions for "excusable neglect." Pioneer corrected the error and gave us a four-part test for recognizing when admitted neglect—inadvertence, miscalculation, negligence, carelessness—can nonetheless be excused.

But if excusable neglect must be neglect, it must also be excusable. Pioneer's four-part test isn't just a black box into which we throw (1) prejudice to the adverse party, (2) the length of the delay, (3) the reason for the delay, and (4) the good faith of the movant, and accept whatever comes out. When all the weighing and balancing is done, we must have something we can say with a straight face is excusable. Factors one, two and four will almost always cut one way: Delays are seldom long, so prejudice is typically minimal. Bad-faith delay is rare, given that we're only dealing with "neglect," not deliberate flouting of the rules, see Pioneer, 507 U.S. at 387–88—though flouting does happen on occasion. See Laurino v. Syringa Gen. Hosp., 279 F.3d 750, 758 (9th Cir. 2002) (Kozinski, J., dissenting). Most of the work, then, is done by factor three, the most important one, see, e.g., Lowry v. McDonnell Douglas Corp., 211 F.3d 457, 463 (8th Cir. 2000), which may balance out any findings under the other factors: The greater the delay, the prejudice to the adverse party and the movant's bad faith, the better a reason the movant must show for having missed the deadline.[1] In this case, the

---

1. We know from the Supreme Court's opinion in Pioneer that not all excuses are created equal. Respondents in Pioneer offered two excuses for failing to file a timely proof of claim: (1) "Respondents' counsel ... was experiencing upheaval in his law practice at the time of the bar date," 507 U.S. at 398; and (2) the notice of the bar

district court found there was no prejudice to Pincay, the delay was short and there was no bad faith. Thus, defendants need not have offered a terribly good countervailing reason to make their neglect excusable.

But they needed to show something. Was this a class action that bristled with client "consultation difficulties"? See Marx v. Loral Corp., 87 F.3d 1049, 1053–54 (9th Cir. 1996). Was the client distracted by a divorce and job change, and had he lost his lawyer to boot? See Laurino, 279 F.3d at 753. Was the rule confusing or notice of the deadline unusual? See Pioneer, 507 U.S. at 398. No, no and no. The action was not complicated; the lawyer worked at a large, sophisticated law firm; and the rule is as clear as legal rules get:

> In a civil case, except as provided in Rules 4(a)(1)(B), 4(a)(4), and 4(c), the notice of appeal required by Rule 3 must be filed with the district clerk within 30 days after the judgment or order appealed from is entered.

Fed. R. App. P. 4(a)(1)(A). As the text indicates, the rule only has three exceptions. The first is that the notice of appeal may be filed in 60 days instead of 30 if "the United States . . . is a party." Fed. R. App. P. 4(a)(1)(B). It isn't. The second exception only applies if certain motions are filed. Fed. R. App. P. 4(a)(4). None were. The third exception applies to inmates, which defendant is not. Fed. R. App. P. 4(c). Thus, the number of days to file a notice of appeal was 30—no ifs, ands or buts about it. There surely are complicated rules in the law, but this isn't one of them. The majority agrees: "Any lawyer or paralegal should have been able to read the rule correctly."

Rather than present a reason for the neglect, defendants call the error " 'inexplicable,' " Appellees' Br. at 32 (quoting Appellants' Br. at 10), and "aberrational." Id. But "inexplicable" and "aberrational" are not synonyms for excusable. In such circumstances, I have trouble seeing how the balance can tilt in favor of excusability.

Defendants do point to one exonerating circumstance, though it is not so much a "reason" for the delay as a proof of their good faith, which we assume anyway: their lawyer's "carefully designed and staffed," "reliable and successful[]" calendaring system. Appellees' Br. at 7–8; see also id. at 10 (describing counsel's additional efforts to avoid error). But this doesn't help them: Extreme good faith has no exonerating power of its own; bad faith can sink an excusable neglect claim, and good faith is nothing but the absence of this negative. In any event, the calendaring system here did not fail. The wrong date was calendared with meticulous efficiency and accuracy. But the lawyer did fail by

date contained a "dramatic ambiguity," id. (quoting Brunswick Assocs. Ltd. P'ship v. Pioneer Inv. Servs. Co. (In re Pioneer Inv. Servs. Co.), 943 F.2d 673, 678 (6th Cir. 1991)) (internal quotation marks omitted). The Court dismissed the first excuse as carrying "little weight," id., but found the second one compelling. This passage in Pioneer, where the Court performed precisely the kind of review we are doing today, precludes the majority's argument that any excuse, or no excuse, can be sufficient to support a finding of excusable neglect.

abdicating his basic duty—to determine the applicable appeal deadline based on a clear-as-day rule.

At bottom, what the sophisticated-calendaring-system excuse comes down to is that the lawyer didn't bother to read the rule; instead, he relied on what a calendaring clerk told him. While delegation may be a necessity in modern law practice, it can't be a lever for ratcheting down the standard for professional competence. If it's inexcusable for a competent lawyer to misread the rule, it can't become excusable because the lawyer turned the task over to a non-lawyer. Errors made by clerks performing lawyerly functions are probably less excusable than those made by the lawyer himself; they certainly can't be more so.

The majority may be right that any competent lawyer or clerk should have been able to read the rule correctly, but that is quite different from saying that a lawyer and a non-lawyer would be equally likely to misread the rule. Studying and practicing law develops certain skills and habits of mind that, one hopes, make lawyers more careful than non-lawyers about reading rules. When a lawyer turns this function over to a non-lawyer, it increases the likelihood an error will be made. Had the lawyer in this case read the rule himself, rather than relying on what a clerk told him, he doubtless would have gotten it right. Indeed, the 30–day rule for appeals in federal court is so well known among federal practitioners that, had the lawyer but thought about the rule, rather than relying entirely on the calendaring clerk's representation, he would surely have realized that the 60–day period is wrong. Instead, the lawyer delegated the calendaring issue to the calendaring "system," which is made up entirely of non-lawyers. If turning large chunks of law practice over to para-professionals can itself be an excuse for misreading rules, then we'll probably see more such delegation and misreading. It is the cold logic of the marketplace that conduct that is rewarded will be repeated.[2]

The Supreme Court told us in Pioneer that "inadvertence, ignorance of the rules, or mistakes construing the rules do not usually constitute 'excusable' neglect." 507 U.S. at 392. Pioneer forecloses any per se rule against "mistakes construing the rules." Still, the word "usually" suggests that we should not apply the balancing test so that virtually no type of mistake is off limits for excusable negligence. Yet this is precisely what the majority has done here, because if this mistake is excusable, I can't imagine a mistake that isn't. See Prizevoits v. Ind. Bell Tel. Co., 76 F.3d 132, 134 (7th Cir. 1996) ("If there was 'excusable' neglect here, we have difficulty imagining a case of inexcusable neglect."). No circuit has taken a position as charitable to lawyer errors as we do today; the

2. Judge Berzon suggests that "even the complete misfiring of a generally well-conceived calendaring system" is a better excuse than, say, "letting court orders pile up on desks, with no effort to read them or calculate appeal deadlines." But it's not clear why Judge Berzon believes the lawyer who procrastinates his professional duties is acting inexcusably while the lawyer who foists them off onto a non-lawyer is not. Procrastination and delegation are different ways of shirking professional obligations. They both occasionally result in missed deadlines, for more or less the same reason: The lawyer paid insufficient attention to his cases.

majority is at odds with decisions in at least six other circuits. See Silivanch v. Celebrity Cruises, Inc., 333 F.3d 355, 369–70 (2d Cir. 2003); Midwest Employers Cas. Co. v. Williams, 161 F.3d 877, 879 (5th Cir. 1998); Prizevoits, 76 F.3d at 134; Lowry, 211 F.3d at 464; United States v. Torres, 372 F.3d 1159, 1163–64 (10th Cir. 2004); Advanced Estimating Sys., Inc. v. Riney, 130 F.3d 996, 998–99 (11th Cir. 1997).

Identifying classes of cases where Pioneer balancing cannot excuse neglect is not, as the majority suggests, adopting a per se rule. It is merely providing the sort of guidance that we are entitled and required to give district courts. This is, in fact, what the Supreme Court did in Pioneer: It re-weighed the factors assessed by the bankruptcy court and found an abuse of discretion. If a finding that neglect is not excusable can be an abuse of discretion (as the Supreme Court held in Pioneer), it surely makes no sense to hold that a finding of excusable neglect can never be an abuse of discretion (as the majority holds today). See id. at 15911 ("We leave the weighing of Pioneer's equitable factors to the discretion of the district court in every case."). To do so abdicates our responsibility of appellate review and, if taken literally, results in as many rules as there are district judges.[4]

I would hold that the error here—whether made by the lawyer, the calendaring clerk or the candlestick-maker—is inexcusable and dismiss the appeal as untimely.

Note

In Silivanch v. Celebrity Cruises, Inc., 333 F.3d 355 (2nd Cir. 2003), discussed in the principal case, numerous victims of an outbreak of Legionnaires' Disease on board a cruise ship sued several defendants. A jury awarded certain of the plaintiffs damages in excess of $4 million against the manufacturer of a filter which allegedly failed to remove bacteria in the ship's spa. On January 28, 2002, the clerk of court formally entered the presiding judge's "Second Supplemental Judgments" ordering post-judgment interest for plaintiffs and making other directions which finally resolved some of the cases. Counsel for the plaintiffs mentioned this judgment in a letter to this defendant's attorneys ten days later. Three weeks after the Second Supplemental Judgments had been entered, counsel for several parties participated in a pre-argument telephone conference with Second Circuit staff counsel regarding a separate appeal filed in other cases arising from the same cruise. During the conference, staff counsel sought to set a briefing schedule that would take into account the timing of the filter manufacturer's expected appeals, and asked the lawyers when they would know whether they were pursuing such other appeals. In that multi-party telephone conversation, one of the attorneys for another party referred to March 4, 2002 as the "control date" for the appeals of the cases resolved in January. While Fed. R. App. P. 4(a)(1)(A) requires parties to file notices of appeal "within 30 days after the judgment or order appealed from is

---

4. Imagine what will happen the next time we get a case on materially indistinguishable facts, except that the district court found the delay inexcusable. Will it be just to tell the litigant that his case is lost because he happened to draw the wrong district judge?

entered," the filter manufacturer filed a notice of appeal on March 1, 2002, which was 32 days after the supplemental judgments were docketed. Soon thereafter, realizing that the appeal was filed too late, the filter manufacturer filed a motion in the district court requesting an extension of time to file a notice of appeal pursuant to Fed. R. App. P. 4(a)(5), asserting that it had filed its notice of appeal late because its counsel had been misled by the statement of another attorney during the conference call that the deadline was March 4. The district court granted the motion, concluding that late filing in reliance on the other attorney's statement constituted "excusable neglect" under Fed. R. App. P. 4(a)(5)(A)(ii). The Second Circuit's consideration of Pioneer Investment Services Co. v. Brunswick Associates Limited Partnership, 507 U.S. 380, 113 S.Ct. 1489, 123 L.Ed.2d 74 (1993), discussed in the principal case, led it to observe that "the equities will rarely if ever favor a party who fails to follow the clear dictates of a court rule" and that where "the rule is entirely clear, we continue to expect that a party claiming excusable neglect will, in the ordinary course, lose under the Pioneer test." The Court observed that in most cases "the court's sympathy will lie with the applicant: the hardship of being denied an appeal is great ... , while the hardship to the prospective appellee is usually small." Further, "[t]he prejudice to [the filter company] of denying its motion [for an extension] would be significant, since it would be denied the opportunity to appeal a multimillion dollar verdict." The Court further said, however:

> We operate in an environment, however, in which substantial rights may be, and often are, forfeited if they are not asserted within time limits established by law. Judges, of course, make mistakes. We, like the district court, have considerable sympathy for those who, through mistakes—counsel's inadvertence or their own—lose substantial rights in that way.[8] And there is, indeed, an institutionalized but limited flexibility at the margin with respect to rights lost because they have been slept on. But the legal system would groan under the weight of a regimen of uncertainty in which time limitations were not rigorously enforced—where every missed deadline was the occasion for the embarkation on extensive trial and appellate litigation to determine the equities of enforcing the bar.

After a review of numerous decisions, the Second Circuit found itself "compelled, on these facts, to conclude that the district court abused its discretion when it decided that [the filter company's] counsel's determination of the wrong date by which [it] had to file a notice of appeal in sole reliance on a remark by counsel for another party during a scheduling conference for another appeal constituted excusable neglect." For these reasons, the plaintiffs' motion to dismiss the appeal was granted.

---

8. Judge Learned Hand said of statutes of limitations:

They are often engines of injustice; their justification lies in furnishing an easy and certain method of solving problems which are often intrinsically insoluble, or soluble only with so much uncertainty and after so

much trouble that in the long run the game is not worth the candle. Perhaps they are not justifiable at all.... But where they do exist one must be prepared for hard cases, and it is no answer that this is one.

Helvering v. Schine Chain Theaters, Inc., 121 F.2d 948, 950 (2d Cir. 1941).

GRAPHIC COMMUNICATIONS INT'L UNION v. QUEBECOR PRNTG. PROVIDENCE, INC.

United States Court of Appeals, First Circuit, 2001.
270 F.3d 1.

LIPEZ, CIRCUIT JUDGE.

On December 16, 1998, Quebecor Printing Providence, Inc. and Quebecor Printing (USA) Corp. (collectively, "Quebecor") announced the permanent closure of their gravure printing plant in Providence, Rhode Island, effective that same day. Graphic Communications International Union, Local 12–N and Graphic Communications International Union, Local 239–M ("the Unions") filed a lawsuit in the United States District Court for the District of Rhode Island, claiming that Quebecor had violated the Worker Adjustment and Retraining Notification Act ("WARN Act"), 29 U.S.C. § 2102(a), which requires that employers provide 60 days notice of a plant closing. On July 21, 2000, the district court entered judgment pursuant to a memorandum and order granting Quebecor's motion for summary judgment and denying the Unions' cross-motion for summary judgment. The Unions filed a notice of appeal with the district court on August 22, 2000, one day after the 30–day period for filing the notice of appeal had expired. The Unions then moved for an extension of time to file the notice of appeal due to excusable neglect, and the district court denied their motion. The Unions appeal both the denial of that motion and the district court's disposition of the cross-motions for summary judgment. Because the district court acted within its discretion in rejecting the Unions' motion for an extension of time to file the notice of appeal, we affirm that decision, and do not reach the merits of the Unions' WARN Act claim.

I.

The district court decided the summary judgment motions in favor of Quebecor on the merits of the Unions' WARN Act claims in a memorandum and order issued on July 20, 2000, and the clerk entered judgment the next day. Pursuant to Fed. R. App. P. 4(a)(1)(A), the Unions had until August 21, 2000 to file the notice of appeal.

On Thursday, August 17, Peter J. Leff, the Unions' Washington counsel, sent a notice of appeal and a check for the cost via Express Mail to Marc Gursky, the Unions' Providence counsel. Leff telephoned Gursky, either on August 17 or the day before, to alert him to expect the package. Although it was guaranteed to arrive at its destination the morning of Friday, August 18, the Postal Service did not attempt to deliver the package to Gursky's firm until 7:00 a.m. on Saturday, August 19, when no one was there to sign for it. A second delivery attempt was made at 2:14 p.m. on Monday, August 21, and was successful.

The apparent reason for the Postal Services' failure to deliver the package on Friday, August 18 was an incorrect address on the package. In March of 2000, Gursky's firm had relocated within Providence. In preparing the Express Mail package, however, Leff's office copied the old address off a letter Gursky's firm had written before the move.

When the package did arrive at 2:14 p.m. on Monday, August 21, there was still time (until the end of the day) to file the notice of appeal. A secretary at Gursky's firm, Cheryl Dichiara, received the package, and placed it on her desk with the intention of giving it to Gursky when he returned to the office. Dichiara, who was preparing an arbitration brief for another client that was due the next day, lost track of the package under other documents on her desk, and did not give it to Gursky until August 22.[1] The Unions filed the notice of appeal that same day, and informed Quebecor of the error and of their intention to file a motion for extension of time to file the notice of appeal on the ground of excusable neglect, pursuant to Fed. R. App. P. 4(a)(5) (the motion was filed on August 24). At a hearing before the district court the next month, Gursky indicated that, as of August 21, the deadline for filing the notice of appeal, he believed the period for filing the notice of appeal was 60 days, rather than 30.

II.

Under the Federal Rules of Appellate Procedure, with exceptions not relevant here, the notice of appeal "must be filed with the district clerk within 30 days after the judgment or order appealed from is entered." Fed. R. App. P. 4(a)(1)(A). "The district court may extend the time to file a notice of appeal if: (i) a party so moves no later than 30 days after the time prescribed by this Rule ... expires; and (ii) that party shows excusable neglect or good cause." Fed. R. App. P. 4(a)(5)(A). The Unions argue that while the late filing was not due to forces beyond their control, any neglect on their part was excusable, and that the district court should therefore have granted an extension.

Our review of the district court's interpretation of Fed. R. App. P.4(a)(5) is de novo, "but otherwise [we] defer to its denial of the requested extension in the absence of an abuse of discretion." Pontarelli v. Stone, 930 F.2d 104, 109 (1st Cir. 1991).

Before the Supreme Court's decision in Pioneer Investment Services Co. v. Brunswick Associates Limited Partnership, 507 U.S. 380, 123 L. Ed. 2d 74, 113 S. Ct. 1489 (1993), the rule in this circuit was that "neglect is excusable within the meaning of FRAP 4(a)(5) only in unique or extraordinary circumstances." Pontarelli, 930 F.2d at 111 (finding no excusable neglect where notice of appeal failed to specify each party

---

1. It is unclear whether Gursky returned to the office on the afternoon of August 21. He offered the following account to the district court:

   THE COURT: What happened on Monday the 21st? Apparently, this package arrived, and you weren't there?

   MR. GURSKY: That's right.

   THE COURT: Which is understandable.

   MR. GURSKY: I don't know what happened on Monday the 21st because I

wasn't there. I only know what happened on Tuesday which would have been-

   THE COURT: Did you go back to the office on the 21st?

   MR. GURSKY: Judge, I don't know. I'm sure I must have been back at the office at some point on the 21st.

Leff indicated to the district court that he "believed" Gursky's secretary had said in the declaration that he had returned to the office that afternoon, but the declaration contains no such statement.

taking appeal, as required under Fed. R. App. P. (3)(c)); see also Rivera v. Puerto Rico Tel. Co., 921 F.2d 393, 396 (1st Cir. 1990) (attorney's failure to list all plaintiffs on notice of appeal "does not constitute excusable neglect for purposes of Rule 4(a)(5) except in unusual or extraordinary circumstances"); Airline Pilots in the Service of Executive Airlines, Inc. v. Executive Airlines, Inc., 569 F.2d 1174, 1175 (1st Cir. 1978) ("A mistake made by an attorney or his staff [secretary wrote down incorrect deadline for notice of appeal] is not, except in unusual or extraordinary circumstances ... excusable neglect.... "); Spound v. Mohasco Indus., Inc., 534 F.2d 404, 411 (1st Cir. 1976) ("Excusable neglect calls for circumstances that are unique or extraordinary."). We did find excusable neglect in In Re San Juan Dupont Plaza Hotel Fire Litigation, 888 F.2d 940, 941–42 (1st Cir. 1989), but there the circumstances were extraordinary: the failure to name each plaintiff on a notice of appeal stating that "all plaintiffs, through the Plaintiffs'Steering Committee hereby appeal," was deemed excusable on the grounds of "the extraordinary size [over 2,000] of the plaintiff group," the representative status of the Plaintiffs' Steering Committee, and the reasonableness of the plaintiffs' filing (which, we suggested, may in fact have complied with Rule (3)(c)). Id. at 942.

In *Pioneer* the Supreme Court endorsed a more generous reading of the phrase "excusable neglect." The Court interpreted the "excusable neglect" provision in Rule 9006(b)(1) of the Federal Rules of Bankruptcy Procedure, which "empowers a bankruptcy court to permit a late filing if the movant's failure to comply with an earlier deadline 'was the result of excusable neglect.'" 507 U.S. at 382. Rejecting what it termed a "narrow view of 'excusable neglect,'" under which the failure to meet a deadline had to be "caused by circumstances beyond the movant's control," the Court advanced "a more flexible analysis." Id. at 387. The Court observed that the ordinary meaning of the word "neglect" encompasses not just unavoidable omissions, but also negligent ones, and concluded that "Congress plainly contemplated that the courts would be permitted, where appropriate, to accept late filings caused by inadvertence, mistake, or carelessness, as well as by intervening circumstances beyond the party's control." Id. at 388.

The Court then identified factors to be weighed in evaluating a claim of excusable neglect:

> we conclude that the determination is at bottom an equitable one, taking account of all relevant circumstances surrounding the party's omission. These include ... the danger of prejudice to the [nonmoving party], the length of the delay and its potential impact on judicial proceedings, the reason for the delay, including whether it was within the reasonable control of the movant, and whether the movant acted in good faith.

507 U.S. at 395. Although the excusable neglect provision interpreted in *Pioneer* was located in the Bankruptcy Rules, the Court cited a disagreement among the circuits on the meaning of "excusable neglect" in Fed.

R. App. P. 4(a)(5) as a reason for granting certiorari. 507 U.S. at 387 & n.3. In Virella–Nieves v. Briggs & Stratton Corp., 53 F.3d 451 (1st Cir. 1995), we concluded that *"Pioneer"*'s exposition of excusable neglect, though made in the context of late bankruptcy filings, applies equally to Fed. R. App. P. 4(a)(5)." Id. at 454 n.3; see also Pratt v. Philbrook, 109 F.3d 18,19 (1st Cir. 1997) (*"Pioneer* must be understood to provide guidance outside the bankruptcy context.").

We have recognized that *Pioneer* marked a shift in the understanding of excusable neglect. In *Pratt,* we vacated the district court's denial of the plaintiff's motion to reopen a case under Fed R. Civ. P. 60(b)(1), and remanded for reconsideration under the "latitudinarian standards" for excusable neglect announced in *Pioneer.* 109 F.3d at 19. We noted that the Supreme Court had "adopted a forgiving attitude toward instances of 'excusable neglect,' a term *Pioneer* suggests will be given a broad reading." Id. at 22. In Hospital Del Maestro v. National Labor Relations Board, 263 F.3d 173, 174 (1st Cir. 2001) (per curiam), we observed that excusable neglect after *Pioneer* is "a somewhat elastic concept" Other circuits have come to the same conclusion. See Robb v. Norfolk & W. Ry. Co., 122 F.3d 354, 359 (7th Cir. 1997) ("Pioneer broadened the definition of 'excusable neglect.' "); United States v. Thompson, 82 F.3d 700, 702 (6th Cir. 1996) (Pioneer establishes "a more liberal definition of what constitutes excusable neglect when an individual seeks a motion for an extension of time in the district court under Fed. R. App. P. 4"); Fink v. Union Cent. Life Ins. Co., 65 F.3d 722, 724 (8th Cir. 1995) (*Pioneer* "established a more flexible analysis of the excusable neglect standard"); United States v. Hooper, 9 F.3d 257, 258 (2nd Cir. 1993) (*Pioneer* advances "a more lenient interpretation" of excusable neglect).

Although the *Pioneer* standard is more forgiving than the standard in our prior case law, there still must be a satisfactory explanation for the late filing. We have observed that " 'the four *Pioneer* factors do not carry equal weight; the excuse given for the late filing must have the greatest import. While prejudice, length of delay, and good faith might have more relevance in a closer case, the reason-for-delay factor will always be critical to the inquiry....' " Hosp. Del Maestro, 263 F.3d at 175 (quoting Lowry v. McDonnell Douglas Corp., 211 F.3d 457, 463 (8th Cir. 2000)). This focus comports with the *Pioneer* Court's recognition that "inadvertence, ignorance of the rules, or mistakes construing the rules do not usually constitute 'excusable' neglect." 507 U.S. at 392.

Even in the wake of *Pioneer,* therefore, when a party's or counsel's misunderstanding of clear law or misreading of an unambiguous judicial decree is the reason for the delay in filing the notice of appeal, we have continued to uphold findings of "no excusable neglect" where the court cited the absence of unique or extraordinary circumstances. In Mirpuri v. ACT Manufacturing, Inc., 212 F.3d 624, 631 (1st Cir. 2000), counsel misread a clear statement in the district court's memorandum decision dismissing plaintiff's complaint "with finality," id. at 627, as leaving open the possibility of subsequent amendment, see id. at 630. We indicated that the memorandum decision had "explained in the most transparent of terms the court's intention to act with 'finality in this case,'" and concluded that "[a] misunderstanding that occurs because a party (or his counsel) elects to read the clear, unambiguous terms of a judicial decree through rose-colored glasses cannot constitute excusable neglect." Id. at 631. We held that "because the plaintiffs' failure to file a timely notice of appeal was not excused by any extraordinary circumstances, the district court did not abuse its discretion in denying their motion for an extension of time."[3] Id.

Most recently, in *Hospital Del Maestro*, we affirmed the denial of an excusable neglect claim where appellant had filed exceptions to the decision of an administrative law judge with the National Labor Relations Board one day late. 263 F.3d at 175. Appellant had misunderstood the Board's rule requiring that mailings be postmarked before, not on, the due date. Id. at 174. We held that "we have no basis for finding [appellant's] neglect 'excusable' when there is no proffered reason that would justify, or even plausibly explain, its misreading of the rules," the meaning of which we described as "plain" and "unambiguous." Id. at 175. We concluded: the favorable juxtaposition of the other Pioneer factors does not, therefore, excuse [appellant's] oversight. Id.

Viewed together, *Mirpuri* and *Hospital Del Maestro* illustrate that a trial judge has wide discretion in dealing with a litigant whose predicament results from blatant ignorance of clear or easily ascertainable rules, and, if the trial judge decides that such neglect is not excusable in the particular case, we will not meddle unless we are persuaded that some exceptional justification exists. See *Mirpuri*, 212 F.3d at 631; *Hospital Del Maestro*, 263 F.3d at 175.

Other circuits have been even harder on excusable neglect claims involving ignorance of the rules. In Advanced Estimating System, Inc. v. Riney, 130 F.3d 996, 997 (11th Cir. 1997), the Eleventh Circuit held that "as a matter of law, the lawyer's failure to understand clear law cannot constitute excusable neglect." The court explained that "nothing in Pioneer indicates otherwise, and we believe that the law in this area

---

3. In Gochis v. Allstate Insurance Co., 16 F.3d 12, 14 (1st Cir. 1994), the appellants offered as an excuse for an untimely notice of appeal their (allegedly) "plausible misconstruction" of the requirement of Fed. R. App. P. 3(c) that a notice of appeal name each of the parties taking the appeal. The original notice of appeal had listed "William Gochis, et. al."as appellants, rather than naming each of the 79 parties taking the appeal. See id. at 13. We concluded that this misconstruction of the rule was not plausible, but rather "was due to nothing more than counsel's ignorance of the law." Id. at 15. We held that the district court had abused its discretion in excusing the appellants' neglect: "in order to show excusable neglect, appellant must demonstrate unique or extraordinary circum-

stances." Id. at 14. This statement seems to require a showing of unique or extraordinary circumstances to establish excusable neglect when there has been a misunderstanding of clear law. That was the pre-Pioneer view, and it indicates that Gochis, although decided ten months after Pioneer, should be regarded as part of our pre-Pioneer precedent. Such a conclusion becomes virtually irresistible when one considers that (a) insofar as we can tell, neither side cited Pioneer to the Gochis panel; (b) the opinion in Gochis makes no reference to Pioneer; and (c) the panel decided Gochis before Virella–Nieves, in which we held for the first time that Pioneer's exposition of excusable neglect applied outside the bankruptcy context to Fed. R. App. P. 4(a)(5). 53 F.3d at 454 n.3.

remains as it was before Pioneer." Id. at 998; see also Midwest Employers Cas. Co. v. Williams, 161 F.3d 877, 880 (5th Cir. 1998) (noting that it would be a "rare case indeed" in which "misinterpretations of the federal rules could constitute excusable neglect"); Prizevoits v. Ind. Bell Tel. Co., 76 F.3d 132, 133 (7th Cir. 1996) (notwithstanding *Pioneer*, "the excusable neglect standard can never be met by a showing of inability or refusal to read and comprehend the plain language of the federal rules." (internal quotation marks omitted)); Weinstock v. Cleary, Gottlieb, Steen & Hamilton, 16 F.3d 501, 503 (2nd Cir. 1994) (same). These cases confirm that our post-*Pioneer* precedents do not conflict with *Pioneer* in refusing lightly to excuse an untimely notice of appeal caused by ignorance of the rules.

III.

The district court found that one of the salient reasons for the untimely notice of appeal was local counsel's ignorance of the Federal Rules of Appellate Procedure. That finding was based on an exchange between the court and local counsel that began with the court asking counsel if he had known, on August 21, that the notice of appeal was due that day:

> MR. GURSKY: Well, by the math, obviously, when you add 60 days to the-
>
> THE COURT: How many days?
>
> MR. GURSKY: Well, at this point, it's more than 60 because you-
>
> THE COURT: Thirty.
>
> MR. GURSKY: Okay. Thirty. . . .

This factual finding[4] informed the court's application of the four *Pioneer* factors to its excusable neglect determination. See 507 U.S. at 395. The district court observed that there would be "little danger of prejudice" to Quebecor if the court granted the motion for extra time; that "the length of the delay was minimal (one day), and ... would not have a serious impact on judicial proceedings"; and that there was no evidence the Unions had acted in bad faith. Nevertheless, it held that the "reason for the delay" was insufficient to justify an extension of time:

---

4. The Unions reject the district court's conclusion that Gursky was mistaken about the period of time in which a notice of appeal could be filed, arguing that his actions, in their totality, suggest that he knew the deadline was 30 days. The Unions assert that once he realized on August 22 that the notice of appeal had not been filed on time,

> Mr. Gursky immediately called lead counsel, Peter Leff, in Washington, D.C. to inform him of the mishap and seek counsel on remedying the situation. . . . Additionally, on August 22, 2000, Mr. Gursky filed the Notice of Appeal with

the district court. . . . Obviously, if Mr. Gursky believed that the Appellants had 60 days to file the Notice of Appeal, he would not have taken such action on August 22nd.

The inference the Unions would have us draw, that Gursky's actions on August 22 indicate that he knew the deadline had passed, is tenuous. It could be that Gursky believed the deadline was 60 days, and only discovered that it was 30 when he opened the package from Leff, which presumably indicated the date the notice of appeal was due. In any event, the court's factual finding is not clearly erroneous.

While the delay here was brief and Defendants have suffered no prejudice, the fact remains that counsel's failure to comply with a rule that is "mandatory and jurisdictional" was the result of ignorance of the law and inattention to detail. Gochis, 16 F.3d at 15 (citing [United States] v. Robinson, 361 U.S. 220, 229, 4 L. Ed. 2d 259, 80 S. Ct. 282 (1960)). There were no "unique or extraordinary circumstances" at play here. 16 F.3d at 14. This Court therefore concludes that Plaintiffs' motion must be denied. To find this neglect to be "excusable" would only serve to condone and encourage carelessness and inattention in practice before the federal courts, and render the filing deadline set in Fed. R. App. P. 4(a)(1) a nullity. For these reasons, Plaintiffs' Motion for Extension of Time to File Notice of Appeal is DENIED.

The Unions argue that the district court erred in its application of the *Pioneer* standard when it rested its finding that their neglect was not excusable on the absence of "unique or extraordinary circumstances." We read the district court's decision differently. Having found that the reason for the delay was, in addition to "inattention to detail," counsel's ignorance of a simple procedural rule, the court cited the absence of "unique or extraordinary circumstances" not as a talisman, but as a check on its conclusion that this degree of carelessness and inattention warranted no relief. In taking this approach, the court acted within its discretion and in conformity with our post-*Pioneer* precedents in declining to excuse the Unions' neglect. *See Mirpuri*, 212 F.3d at 631.

Denial of the Motion for Extension of Time to File Notice of Appeal is Affirmed.

Notes and Questions

1. When and under what circumstances should an extension of time be granted to allow the late filing of a notice of appeal? This is a continuing problem for both trial and appellate courts. As the foregoing cases suggest, litigants and attorneys will make almost any argument to avoid the dismissal of an appeal. The problems applying Rule 4(a)(5) have been compounded by a 1979 amendment that allowed an extension for "good cause" as well as "excusable neglect." What does this amendment add?

2. A thorough survey of the issues with respect to excusable neglect and "ignorance of the law" may be found in May, Pioneer's Paradox: Appellate Rule 4(a)(5) and the Rule Against Excusing Ignorance of the Law, 48 Drake L. Rev. 677 (2000).

5. THE EFFECT OF POST–TRIAL MOTIONS IN THE LOWER COURT ON THE APPEAL DEADLINE

Several issues have arisen from scenarios in which a party makes a post-verdict or post-judgment motion in the trial court, seeking reconsideration, a new trial, or vacation/modification of the judgment from the trial judge. The federal rules have been amended several times in this regard, and most states have refined their rules in recent years. There remain some pitfalls, especially in the designation of what order a party is appealing when the party has (1) lost the underlying judgment, and (2) thereafter lost the motion for reconsideration or relief from that judgment. These matters are explored in this Section.

JACKSON v. CROSBY

United States Court of Appeals, Eleventh Circuit, 2004.
375 F.3d 1291.

Tjoflat, Circuit Judge:

I.

On December 15, 2003, the district court entered a final judgment in this case denying petitioner habeas corpus relief from his conviction and sentence for capital murder. On January 5, 2004, petitioner filed a motion to alter or amend judgment pursuant to Federal Rule of Civil Procedure 59(e). The motion was untimely because petitioner failed to file it within ten days of the entry of final judgment as Rule 59(e) requires. On January 29, 2004, the district court entered a written order stating that the motion was "DENIED."[2] On February 27, 2004, petitioner filed a notice of appeal in the district court; the notice stated that he was appealing the final judgment of December 15, 2003 and the order of January 29, 2004.

On April 7, 2004, this panel dismissed petitioner's appeal of the December 15, 2003 judgment in an order containing the following language:

Appellant's motion to alter or amend, made pursuant to Fed. R. Civ. P. 59(e) was not filed within ten business days of and did not toll the appeal period for the December 15, 2003, judgment. Fed. R. App. P. 4(a)(4)(A); Fed. R. Civ. P. 6(a), 58, 60(b). Therefore the appeal is DISMISSED as to that order.[3]

On April 20, 2004, petitioner moved this court to reconsider its April 7 order dismissing his appeal of the December 15, 2003 judgment. In his motion, petitioner conceded that the Rule 59(e) motion he filed in the district court on January 5, 2004 might be untimely. If untimely, he asks that we treat the motion as timely under the "unique circumstances" doctrine. He cites Willis v. Newsome, 747 F.2d 605 (11th Cir. 1984), in which we granted relief under that doctrine, and states that the unique

---

2. The order consisted of one sentence. The sentence contained no reason for the ruling.

3. Our April 7 order stated that petitioner's notice of appeal was:

timely to appeal the district court's January 29, 2004, order denying the Rule 59(e) motion, construed as a motion under Fed. R. Civ. P. 60(b), for relief and the appeal MAY PROCEED from that

order. Rice v. Ford Motor Co., 88 F.3d 914 918–19 (11th Cir. 1996); Cavaliere v. Allstate Ins. Co., 996 F.2d 1111, 1115 (11th Cir. 1993). The appeal shall be limited to a determination of whether the district court abused its discretion in denying the motion for relief and to set aside the judgment, and shall not extend to the validity of the underlying order per se.

circumstances surrounding the filing of petitioner's Rule 59(e) motion "fall squarely within the situation compelling relief in Willis."

The "unique circumstances" petitioner relies on are set out in the affidavit of one of the attorneys who filed his Rule 59(e) motion, David R. Gemmer. In his affidavit, Gemmer states that "[o]ne of my tasks [in filing the Rule 59(e) motion] was to determine the deadline for filing the motion." To this end, he reviewed the Federal Rules of Civil Procedure and the district court's local rules. He

> understood from that review that the Motion had to be timely filed within ten days from the date of entry of the order in question. However, [he] also was aware of Fed. R. Civ. P. 6 and Local Rule 4.20, which provided for three additional days to file when there had been service of a notice or paper by mail.[5] While the [December 15,

---

5. In referring to Rule 6, Gemmer was apparently focusing on the provisions of part (e) of the rule, which states:

Whenever a party has the right or is required to do some act or take some proceedings within a prescribed period after the service of a notice or other paper upon the party and the notice or paper is served upon the party under Rule 5(b)(2)(B), (C), or (D), 3 days shall be added to the prescribed period.

Rule 5 governs "Serving and Filing Pleadings and Other Papers." Part (a), speaks, in pertinent part, to "Service: When Required."

> Except as otherwise provided in these rules, every order required by its terms to be served, every pleading subsequent to the original complaint unless the court otherwise orders because of numerous defendants, every paper relating to discovery required to be served upon a party unless the court otherwise orders, every written motion other than one which may be heard ex parte, and *every written notice*, appearance, demand, offer of judgment, designation of record on appeal, *and similar paper* shall be served upon each of the parties. No service need be made on parties in default for failure to appear except that pleadings asserting new or additional claims for relief against them shall be served upon them in the manner provided for service of summons in Rule 4.

(emphasis added). Subparts (b)(2)(B), (C), and (D), respectively, authorize service [under part (a)], by mail, by leaving a copy with the clerk of the court "if the person served has no known address," and by "other means, including electronic means."

The district court's order denying petitioner habeas corpus relief did not require

"by its terms" that it be "served" on the parties. The final judgment entered pursuant to that order on December 15, 2003 was "set forth on a separate document," as required by Federal Rule of Civil Procedure 58. The clerk thereafter served copies of the order and final judgment on the parties as required by Rule 77(d). It is important to note that the clerk's failure to notify a party of the issuance of an order or the entry of final judgment "does not affect the time to appeal or relieve or authorize the court to relieve a party for failure to appeal within the time allowed, except as permitted in Rule 4(a) of the Federal Rules of Appellate Procedure." Fed. R. Civ. P. 77(d). By the same token, the fact that the clerk serves the parties by mail with notice of the entry of judgment does not extend the time for filing a notice of appeal by three days pursuant to Rule 6(e).

For purposes of Rule 59(b) and (e)'s ten-day limitations periods, we focus on when the judgment is entered, not when it is served. Fed. R. Civ. P. 59(b), (e) (stating that such motions "shall be filed no later than 10 days *after entry of the judgment*" (emphasis added)). Rule 58 governs entry of judgment. Part (a)(1) requires, "Every judgment and amended judgment must be set forth on a separate document...." Part (a)(1) then lists exceptions to the separate document requirement that are not applicable here. Part (b) states, in pertinent part:

Judgment is entered for purposes of these rules: ...

(2) if Rule 58(a)(1) requires a separate document, when it is entered in the civil docket under Rule 79(a) and when the earlier of these events occurs:

(A) when it is set forth on a separate document, or

2003 judgment] had been mailed to [his office, he] was not sure whether the local rule applied to the Motion. [He] either had no knowledge or had no recollection of Cavaliere v. Allstate Insurance Co., 996 F.2d 1111 (11th Cir. 1993)."

After reviewing the above rules, Gemmer telephoned "the office of the Clerk in the Federal District Court . . . several days before December 31, 2003."[6] During his conversation with the woman who answered the telephone, he mentioned Local Rule 4.20 and asked whether Local Rule 4.20 "applied. She affirmatively told [him] that Local Rule 4.20 applied to [his] situation." Responding to his statement that he was having "problems with counting the holidays," she said that "December 25 and 26th were official court holidays, the extra day being established by the President in a special order." He then "counted off the days accounting for the holidays and Rule 4.20 and determined that Monday, January 5, 2004, would be the deadline for filing the [m]otion." "Had the clerk expressed any doubt . . . about the application of Rule 4.20, [he] would have conducted additional research, but her answer was clear, emphatic, and unreserved, as was her affirmation that, accounting for holidays, weekends, and Rule 4.20, January 5, 2004 was [his] deadline." Nonetheless, "[b]oth the clerk and [Gemmer] acknowledged that the clerk's representations were not binding."

Gemmer goes on to state that his

> confidence that the motion had passed muster as timely was increased when the state and the court addressed the Application for Certificate of Appealability substantively [i.e., for the purpose of identifying claims that satisfied the criterion of 28 U.S.C.

(B) when 150 days have run from the entry in the civil docket under Rule 79(a).

In this case, Rule 58(a)(1) required a separate document for the December 15, 2003 judgment. The judgment satisfied both prongs of Rule 58(a)(2) on December 15, 2003, when it was both entered on the docket and set forth in a separate document. December 15 was therefore the date the judgment was entered under Rule 58, and the date from which the Rule 59(e) limitations period ran. Because Rule 6(e) only applies when a party "has the right or is required *to do some act or take some proceedings within a prescribed period after the service*" (emphasis added), while Rule 59(b) and (e) require action to be taken within "10 days *after entry of the judgment*," (emphasis added) Rule 6(e) can never extend the time for filing a Rule 59(b) or (e) motion.

Local Rule 4.20 provides:

(a) Pursuant to Fed.R.Civ.P. 6(a) and (e), whenever a period of time prescribed or allowed by the Federal Rules of Civil Procedure or the Rules of the District Court of the United States for the Middle District of Florida, or by any applicable statute is less than eleven (11) days and there has been service of a notice or other paper upon a party by mail, then the period of time which that party has to act shall be computed as follows: (1) By first calculating the original prescribed period pursuant to Fed.R.Civ.P. 6(a); and (2) By then adding three (3) days to the original prescribed period pursuant to Fed. R.Civ.P. 6(e). The three (3) days shall be calculated beginning with the day following the last day of the original prescribed period, and shall be counted consecutively regardless of whether any day of this three (3) day period is a Saturday, Sunday, or legal holiday as defined in Fed. R.Civ.P. 6(a). The third day shall be treated as the last day of the period unless it is a Saturday, Sunday, or legal holiday in which event the period runs until the end of the next day which is not a Saturday, Sunday, or legal holiday.

M.D. Fla. Local R. 4.20.

6. Gemmer "did not obtain or recall the name of the clerk [he] spoke with."

§ 2253(c)(3)], rather than dismissively as based on a void notice of appeal. This buttressed [his] belief that the denial of the Motion to Alter or Amend was based on the merits.

In the body of his motion for reconsideration, petitioner urges that, in determining whether the unique circumstances doctrine applies, we should take into account, in addition to what Gemmer says in his affidavit, the following factors. First, the State, in responding to his Rule 59(e) motion, did not contend that it was untimely. "Had it done so in a timely fashion . . . , [petitioner] could have filed the Notice of Appeal in a timely fashion." Second,

> [h]ad the trial judge denied the Motion for untimeliness January 27, 2004, [petitioner] would have had more than two weeks to seek relief for excusable neglect under Fed. R. App. P. 4(a)(5). Instead, the lack of any objection or notice of the issue in this case lulled counsel into proceeding on the schedule based on the assumption the Rule 59(e) motion was timely.

II.

A notice of appeal challenging the final judgment in a civil action must be filed no later than thirty days after the judgment is entered on the district court's docket. Fed. R. App. P. 4(a)(1)(A). A timely Rule 59(e) motion to alter or amend the judgment automatically tolls this thirty-day period, so that it begins to run from the date of the order denying the motion. Fed. R. App. P. 4(a)(4)(A).[8] The motion to alter or amend the judgment is timely if filed "no later than 10 days after entry of judgment." Fed. R. Civ. P. 59(e); see Advanced Estimating Sys., Inc. v. Riney, 77 F.3d 1322, 1323 (11th Cir. 1996) ("Untimely motions under Rule[] 59 . . . will not toll the time for filing an appeal.").

Because the time period for filing a motion to alter or amend the judgment is less than eleven days, intermediate Saturdays, Sundays, and legal holidays are not included in the computation. Fed. R. Civ. P. 6(a). Legal holidays include, inter alia, Christmas Day, New Year's Day, and "any other day appointed as a holiday by the President or the Congress of the United States. . . ." Id.

In this case, the judgment was entered on Monday, December 15, 2003. To toll the time for filing an appeal, petitioner's motion to alter or amend the judgment had to have been filed by Tuesday, December 30, which was ten days later, not counting two weekends and Christmas Day. The motion was actually filed on January 5, 2004.[9] The motion was

---

8. Federal Rule of Appellate Procedure 4(a)(4)(A) also tolls the time for filing a notice of appeal when the appellant moves the district court for the entry of judgment under Rule 50(b), to amend or make additional factual findings under Rule 52(b), for attorney's fees under Rule 54, for a new trial under Rule 59, or for relief under Rule 60 "if the motion is filed no later than 10 days after the judgment is entered." When one of these motions is filed, the time for filing an appeal challenging the final judgment runs "from the entry of the order disposing of the last such remaining motion." Fed. R. App. P. 4(a)(4)(A).

9. According to petitioner, the motion was timely if one takes into account three days under Local Rule 4.20 and December

therefore untimely and did not toll the time for filing a notice of appeal from the December 15 judgment. Accordingly, the notice of appeal was due, as prescribed by Federal Rule of Appellate Procedure 4(a)(4)(A), on January 14, 2004, which was thirty days after the entry of the December 15 judgment. The notice of appeal petitioner filed on February 27, 2004 was therefore untimely.

According to his affidavit, Gemmer believed that "Fed. R. Civ. P[.] 6 and Local Rule 4.20 ... provided for three additional days to file when there had been service of a notice or paper by mail." He had received the December 15, 2003 judgment by mail; nevertheless, he was "not sure whether the local rule applied to [his Rule 59(e)] Motion."

The Rule 6 provision Gemmer was referring to is part (e), which we quote in the margin. Gemmer was unfamiliar with our decision in Cavaliere v. Allstate Ins. Co., 996 F.2d 1111 (11th Cir. 1993). Had he read it, he would have discovered that the appellant there, Cavaliere, made the same argument about Rule 6(e) that he and his co-counsel advance here. Cavaliere argued that because the final judgment was "served" by the clerk of the court by mail,[10] Rule 6(e) provided him with three extra days to file his Rule 50(b) motion for new trial. We rejected Cavaliere's argument. We held that Rule 6(b), which bars the district court from "extend[ing] the time for taking any action under Rules 50(b) ... and [59](e)," renders Rule 6(e) ineffective with respect to the time for filing Rule 59 motions. Given this holding, is petitioner's argument that Local Rule 4.20 provided him with three extra days for filing his Rule 59(e) motion valid? The answer has to be no.

The district court promulgated Local Rule 4.20 under the authority provided by 28 U.S.C. § 2071(a), which states:

> The Supreme Court and all courts established by Act of Congress may from time to time prescribe rules for the conduct of their business. Such rules shall be consistent with Acts of Congress and rules of practice and procedure prescribed under [28 U.S.C. § 2072].

(emphasis added.). Federal Rule of Civil Procedure 6 (and each of its subparts) was prescribed under § 2072. Rule 83 states in part (a) that

26 as a "day appointed as a holiday by the President." See Fed. R. Civ. P. 6(a). In his affidavit, Gemmer states that the clerk's office employee with whom he spoke over the telephone told him that the President had appointed December 26 a holiday. The record does not indicate whether December 26 was in fact such a holiday, and we decline to take judicial notice of the matter on our own initiative. Whether December 26 was a declared holiday is of no moment, however. Petitioner fails to convince us that Local Rule 4.20 provided him three extra days to file his Rule 59(e) motion. In short, even if December 26 was a holiday ordered by the President, petitioner had to file his motion no later than Wednesday, December 31, 2003.

10. The panel's opinion in Cavaliere does not indicate whether Cavaliere contended that he received the final judgment by mail. According to the opinion, his argument was "as follows: Under Rule 77(d), the court clerk was required to serve the judgment on Cavaliere by mail; Cavaliere had the 'right' to file his motion for a new trial 'within a prescribed period'; therefore, Cavaliere was entitled to three extra days." 996 F.2d at 1113. The fact that Rule 77(d) requires the clerk to notify the parties of the entry of final judgment does not extend the time for filing a notice of appeal and, thus, the time for filing a Rule 59 motion.

"[a] local rule shall be consistent with—but not duplicative of—Acts of Congress and rules adopted under 28 U.S.C. § 2072...." Local Rule 4.20, to the extent it is inconsistent with Rule 6(e), is therefore invalid. Local Rule 4.20's allowance of three extra days for filing Rule 59 motions is inconsistent with Rule 6(b)'s ban on extending the rule's ten-day limitations period and is therefore a nullity. In sum, petitioner's Rule 59(e) motion was untimely.

III.

Petitioner asks that we treat his motion as timely under the "unique circumstances" doctrine. The unique circumstances doctrine excuses a litigant's failure to abide by the jurisdictional time limitations established by the rules, such as the ten-day limitations period prescribed by Rule 59, when the failure is caused by the litigant's reasonable reliance on a specific assurance by a judicial officer. Hollins v. Dep't of Corr., 191 F.3d 1324, 1327 (11th Cir. 1999). In determining whether the doctrine should be invoked, we focus on "the reasonableness of the appellant's reliance on the action of the district court." Pinion v. Dow Chem., U.S.A., 928 F.2d 1522, 1532 (11th Cir. 1991). "[A]ny judicial action prior to the expiration of the relevant time period for appeal that could have lulled the appellant into inactivity may permit our application of the doctrine." Hollins, 191 F.3d at 1327 (citing Pinion, 928 F.2d at 1529) (marks and citations omitted).

The unique circumstances petitioner cites are set out in Gemmer's affidavit and the body of petitioner's motion for reconsideration. Reduced to their essentials, they are: (1) that Gemmer obtained the assistance of someone in the clerk's office to calculate the number of days he had in which to file petitioner's Rule 59(e) motion; specifically, the holidays that were to be counted and whether, under Rule 6(e) and Local Rule 4.20, he had three extra days, in addition to the ten days provided by the rule, to file the motion; (2) that the State did not object to the motion as untimely; and (3) that the district court, in denying the motion, did not do so on the ground that it was untimely filed.

The facts petitioner relies upon to satisfy the unique circumstances inquiry mirror those relied upon by appellant Dow Chemical in Pinion. If anything, Dow Chemical presented a stronger case for the application of the doctrine than petitioner has. In Pinion, the district court, giving effect to the jury's verdict, entered a $2,450,000 judgment against Dow Chemical. 928 F.2d at 1524. Two days later, Dow Chemical presented the court with a consent order (signed by counsel for Dow Chemical and the plaintiffs) purporting to give Dow Chemical a thirty-day extension to file post-trial motions. Id. The court signed that consent order and another consent order several weeks later. Id. Within the time provided by the second extension, Dow Chemical filed a motion for judgment notwithstanding the verdict pursuant to Rule 50(b) of the Federal Rules of Civil Procedure and, alternatively, a motion for new trial pursuant to Rule 59. Id. The court denied both motions, and Dow Chemical appealed. Id.

Dow Chemical filed its notice of appeal ninety-six days after the entry of final judgment, long after the thirty-day appeal period Rule 4(a) of the Federal Rules of Appellate Procedure provides.[11] Although the plaintiffs did not question our jurisdiction to entertain the appeal, we did so own our own initiative. Id.

After concluding that Dow Chemical's post-trial motions were untimely and thus did not toll the time for taking an appeal under Rule 4(a), we launched into the unique circumstances inquiry, assessing the "reasonableness of [Dow Chemical's] reliance on the action of the district court." Id. at 1532. Specifically, "[w]as it reasonable for Dow to rely upon the district court's improper extension of the time for filing post-trial motions, in spite of the explicit language of Rule 6(b) prohibiting the district court from granting such an extension?" Id. Our answer was clear: "When the problem is framed in this manner, we must answer 'No.' " Id. "[T]he more apparent it becomes that the party's filing error stems as much from the party's own negligence in simply not reading or inquiring about the Rules, as it does from actual reliance on some action by the district court, the circumstances become far less 'unique.' " Id. at 1533.

In Pinion, counsel admitted that they " 'inadvertently overlooked the Rule 6(b) prohibition.' " Id. In the case at hand, petitioner's counsel was similarly neglectful, overlooking Rule(6)(b)'s prohibition and our decision in Cavaliere. In Pinion, we cited the Third Circuit's comments in a case presenting a similar scenario:

> The unique circumstances doctrine has never been extended to an attorney's miscalculation of the applicable time limits, and we see no reason to do so here even if the trial judge also shared that incorrect assumption.

Id. (quoting Kraus v. Conrail, 899 F.2d 1360, 1365–66 (3d Cir. 1990)). We also cited a Tenth Circuit case for the proposition that an attorney cannot reasonably rely on an improper enlargement of the time to file a notice of appeal "in light of his 'duty to familiarize himself with the appellate rules.' " See id. (quoting Certain Underwriters at Lloyds of London v. Evans, 896 F.2d 1255, 1257–58 (10th Cir. 1990)). In rejecting the argument that counsel were justified in relying on the district court's unlawful ruling, the Certain Underwriters court said: counsel either "knew or should have known" that the district court had exceeded the maximum allowable extension under App. Rule 4(a)(5). 896 F.2d at 1258. So, too, in Pinion: counsel were not entitled to rely on the district court entry of an order extending the ten-day period for filing post-trial motions under Rules 50(b) and 59. To this effect we cited a Seventh Circuit observation in "United States v. Hill, 826 F.2d 507, 508 (7th Cir. 1987) ('The Supreme Court has not held or even hinted that a defendant's own neglect, or that of his lawyer, extends a jurisdictional time limit.')." Pinion, 928 F.2d at 1533.

---

11. The notice of appeal was so late that any extension Federal Rule of Appellate Procedure 4(a)(5) may have provided was unavailable.

Pinion makes clear that it was unreasonable for petitioner's counsel to rely on the State's failure to oppose petitioner's Rule 59(e) motion as time-barred or to read the district court's denial of the motion as a ruling on its merits. And, if counsel in Pinion could not rely on the district court's extension orders, certainly counsel in this case could not rely on an unknown clerk's office employee's statement that Local Rule 4.20 gave counsel three extra days to file petitioner's motion, especially after the employee told counsel, in Gemmer's words, that her "representations were not binding."[12]

Precedent requires that we deny petitioner's motion for reconsideration. It is, accordingly,

DENIED.

BLACK, CIRCUIT JUDGE, specially concurring:

Because this is a capital case, I find the result reached today very troubling. Ultimately, however, the facts in this case do not permit us to apply the "unique circumstances" doctrine.

There was no reliance upon a representation or order from the district court. See Butler v. Coral Volkswagen, Inc., 804 F.2d 612, 613 (11th Cir. 1986) (discussing petitioner's reliance on the district court's extension of the time in which a new trial motion could be amended); Inglese v. Warden, U.S. Penitentiary, 687 F.2d 362, 362–63 (11th Cir. 1982) (discussing petitioner's reliance on the district court's order extending the time in which a Rule 59(e) motion could be filed). Nor was there reliance on assurances received from the clerk's office pertaining to the administrative functions of the clerk's office, about which attorney familiarity could not be presumed. See Hollins v. Department of Corrections, 191 F.3d 1324, 1326 (11th Cir. 1999) (observing that the district court's [Internet accessible computer docket reporting] system failed to show the district court's entry of a final order); Willis v. Newsome, 747 F.2d 605, 606 (11th Cir. 1984) (noting that the clerk's office gave assurances regarding "local custom" and practice for stamping notices of appeal).

Here, Petitioner's counsel called and asked the clerk for legal advice—specifically, how to interpret the procedural rules regarding the time for filing a Rule 59(e) motion. Petitioner thus did not rely on either representations made by the district court or assurances from the clerk's office pertaining to an administrative function.

The "unique circumstances" doctrine does not permit us to reassign the lawyer's obligation to read the relevant rules and case law. In other

---

12. Petitioner argues that Willis v. Newsome, 747 F.2d 605 (11th Cir. 1984), in which we provided relief under the unique circumstances doctrine, dictates our decision. We disagree. The circumstances in that case and the circumstances here cannot reasonably be considered analogous. There, "the district court's filing clerk" told appellant's attorney that appellant's notice of appeal would be stamped filed on the date he placed the notice in the United States mails. Id. at 606. In essence, what the filing clerk told counsel was that the post office was a repository of the clerk's office, a representation that counsel could neither affirm nor refute by consulting the Federal Rules of Procedure or the case law.

words, it is not the responsibility of the clerk's office to inform the lawyer of the law. See Rezzonico v. H & R Block, Inc., 182 F.3d 144, 152 (2d Cir. 1999) (finding no unique circumstances where appellants relied on representations from the clerk's office involving legal matters). As we have previously noted, even in a case as grave as this, an equitable remedy such as the "unique circumstances" doctrine does "not exist merely to rehabilitate attorney oversight or inadvertence." Pinion v. Dow Chemical, U.S.A., 928 F.2d 1522, 1534 (11th Cir. 1991). Therefore, I must very reluctantly join in the opinion.

CARNES, CIRCUIT JUDGE, specially concurring:

Like Judge Black, I'm not fond of the result in this case but recognize that the law and the facts with which we are presented require it.

This would-be appellant has an experienced attorney who serves as Assistant Capital Collateral Regional Counsel–Middle Region of Florida. Experienced as this counsel is, he screwed up. If one credits his affidavit, which given the present posture of the case we must, he unjustifiably sought and relied upon the advice of an unidentified person in the local clerk's office when he could and should have found the answer to his legal question himself. Not only that, but his affidavit discloses that both the person in the clerk's office and counsel acknowledged during their telephone conversation "that the clerk's representations were not binding."

In these circumstances, reliance upon that advice was unreasonable to say the least, and more to the point, it is outside our unique circumstances doctrine. See Pinion v. Dow Chem. U.S.A., 928 F.2d 1522 (11th Cir. 1991); Willis v. Newsome, 747 F.2d 605, 606 (11th Cir. 1984). If counsel had sufficiently researched the matter about which he had a question, as he should have, he would have turned up our decision in Cavaliere v. Allstate Ins. Co., 996 F.2d 1111 (11th Cir. 1993), and Fed.R.Civ.P. 83(a)(1). Instead, he put at risk his client's right to appeal the judgment against him in return for the prospect of gaining a few days extra time for filing a Rule 59(e) motion.

If this were a case involving two corporations, we would apply the established rules, which require that we dismiss the appeal, and would do that with little or no discussion. What has brought forth more in response to the motion for reconsideration in this case is the fact that the party whose appeal is being dismissed is on death row, and the judgment he is seeking to appeal is one denying him federal habeas relief. That makes us as judges want to hear and decide the appeal instead of dismiss it for lack of jurisdiction because of an untimely notice of appeal. However, the rules relating to timeliness of filing and appellate court jurisdiction apply without respect to the identity of the parties or the nature of the case. We do not have one set of rules for petitioners and their attorneys in capital cases and another set for everyone else.

As judges we are obligated to follow the law, regardless of whether we personally like the result of doing so. We have done that.

Notes and Questions

1. A post-judgment motion that tolls the time to appeal must itself be timely to have that effect. The taking of the motion under consideration by the trial court does not reasonably mislead litigants that the motion was timely. Center for Nuclear Responsibility v. United States Nuclear Reg. Com'n, 781 F.2d 935 (D.C. Cir. 1986).

2. In United Computer Systems v. AT & T Corporation, 298 F.3d 756 (9th Cir. 2002) the court reviewed a complex suit by a software concern against a communications company, in which several rulings were made by the trial court:

> April 3: the doctrine of res judicata barred all claims against defendants AT & T, Lucent Technologies and NCR Corporation.

> April 4: all claims were dismissed against Jan Stredicke, an employee of the American Arbitration Association, on substantive grounds (not res judicata grounds).

> April 14: the action would not be remanded to state court, as plaintiff had hoped.

On April 14th plaintiff filed a motion for relief under Rule 60(b) because of a recently released Ninth Circuit decision on res judicata that suggested a different outcome in the present case. That motion was not decided until May 25th.

On May 1st plaintiff filed a notice of appeal designating the res judicata and remand rulings, but not the dismissal of Ms. Stredicke as a defendant.

AT & T then moved for sanctions against plaintiff's counsel, which were granted on June 28th.

On July 14 plaintiff filed an amended notice of appeal, now referencing the April 4 order (Stredicke's dismissal), the May 25 order (denial of the Rule 60(b) motion) and the June 28 order (sanctions).

> As a threshold matter, both UCS's appeal of the Stredicke dismissal and the denial of the Rule 60(b) motion are untimely. The judgment against Stredicke was entered by the district court on April 4. Under Fed. R. App. P. 4(a)(1)(A), UCS had thirty days, until May 4, to file its notice of appeal. The Federal Rules of Appellate Procedure state that a "notice of appeal must ... (B) designate the judgment, order, or part thereof being appealed." Fed. R. App. P. 3(c)(1). In this case, the original notice of appeal (specifying only the April 3 and April 14 judgments) was filed before the district court made its ruling on the Rule 60(b) motion. Since that ruling was entered on May 25, the appeal of the April 3 and the April 14 judgments became effective on that date. See Fed. R. App. P. 4(a)(4)(B)(i) ("If a party files a notice of appeal after the court announces or enters a judgment—but before it disposes of any motion listed in Rule 4(a)(4)(A)—the notice becomes effective to appeal a judgment or order, in whole or in part, when the order

disposing of the last such remaining motion is entered.''). Even if we assume that the filing deadline for the Stredicke dismissal was thirty days after the court entered the denial of the Rule 60(b) motion (entered on May 25), *which is a plausible but not necessarily correct reading of Fed. R. App. P. 4(a)(4)(A)*, the latest possible date for filing a timely appeal would have been June 25. In this case, however, UCS did not file its amended notice of appeal until July 14.

In summary, this court has jurisdiction only over the April 3rd judgment dismissing the corporate defendants, the April 14th judgment denying the motion to remand to state court and the June 28th judgment imposing sanctions on UCS.

Is it clear why the order dismissing Ms. Stredicke is not before the court of appeals? Secondly, what is the strength of the plaintiff's argument (described by the court as "plausible but not necessarily correct") that the time to file an appeal from the Stredicke dismissal runs from the ruling on the Rule 60(b) motion? If the Rule 60(b) motion relates only to possible reconsideration of the res judicata ruling as to other defendants, why should the pendency of that motion extend time to appeal a dismissal not subject to the reconsideration motion, involving a different defendant and different legal theory? If the pendency of the Rule 60(b) motion is NOT sufficient to extend the time to appeal another disposition not subject to such a motion, does this mean that multiple notices of appeal are required?

3.   Should it ever be permissible for a trial court to vacate and then reenter a judgment solely to give a party a second opportunity to appeal? Was Fed.R.Civ.P. 60 intended for this purpose? What does this do to the time limits on taking appeals and the limited authority of a trial court to grant an extension for taking an appeal?

4.   In considering whether to grant more time for appeal, prejudice to the opposing party is supposed to be one of the factors to be taken into consideration. How can the opposing party be anything but prejudiced when the court allows an appeal that would otherwise be dismissed?

5.   Case law generally warns that it is unreasonable to rely on legal advice from clerks of court, and that jurisdictional requirements are not obviated by reliance on such advice. See Strock v. Vanhorn, 919 F.Supp. 172 (E.D. Pa. 1996). A court clerk's advice on proper procedure, such as serving various papers on an appeal, is also no defense to an error—it has been held that reliance on the clerk's advice is not "good cause" under the rules. Gabriel v. United States, 30 F.3d 75 (7th Cir. 1994). The appellate courts have applied this stringent doctrine to misleading advice by both district court and appellate court clerks' office Personnel. Spinetti v. Atlantic Richfield Company, 552 F.2d 927 (Temp. Emerg. Ct. Ap. 1976) ("attorneys may not escape from their procedural errors by claiming reliance on a court clerk's advice").

MEDRANO v. CITY OF LOS ANGELES

United States Court of Appeals, Ninth Circuit, 1982.
973 F.2d 1499 (9th Cir. 1992).

WIGGINS, CIRCUIT JUDGE.

The widow, parents, and siblings of Ruben Medrano seek damages from Los Angeles Police Department officers and the City of Los Angeles under 42 U.S.C. section 1983 for the shooting of Medrano. The Medranos appeal from directed verdicts and a jury verdict against their section 1983 claims. This court has jurisdiction over the appeal pursuant to 28 U.S.C. section 1291.

BACKGROUND

On March 21, 1988, Ruben P. Medrano left a suicide note, locked himself in his bathroom with a loaded .357 magnum revolver, injected himself with a lethal dosage of heroin, and threatened to kill anyone who tried to enter the bathroom to prevent his suicide. After his wife of three weeks, Linda Medrano, and his sister, Lucia Medrano, were unable to persuade Ruben Medrano to come out of the bathroom, they called 911 for emergency assistance. Paramedics and Los Angeles Police Department officers responded to the call. The police officers removed all of the family members from the area and initiated communication with Medrano. Medrano informed the police that he wanted to commit suicide and that he would kill anyone who came through the bathroom door to interfere.

During the communications with Medrano, the Medrano family members were allowed to speak with Ruben Medrano to persuade him to come out of the bathroom. The police took measures to prevent these family members from being shot in case Ruben Medrano opened fire. After Ruben became agitated and demanded that the family members leave, the police determined that they should be removed from the immediate area. The police continued to communicate with Ruben Medrano until he no longer responded and they could hear him snoring in the bathroom. Aware that Ruben Medrano could die of a heroin overdose if he was not removed from the bathroom, the police decided that Officer Mowry, a qualified crisis negotiator, should attempt to negotiate Ruben Medrano out of the bathroom if he was awake or to enter the bathroom to take custody of Medrano if he was still sleeping.

After listening at the bathroom door, the police formed the opinion that Ruben Medrano was in a drug induced state of unconsciousness and decided to enter the bathroom. Officer Mowry forced the door open and entered the bathroom. Lying on the floor, Ruben Medrano woke up and fired one shot into the wall behind him. Officer Mowry grabbed the gun in Ruben Medrano's hand and struggled with Medrano for possession of the gun. Officer Romero then entered the bathroom and fired two shots into Ruben Medrano's chest. After Ruben Medrano continued struggling for possession of the gun, Officer Romero fired a final shot into Ruben Medrano's head. Medrano died at the scene.

However, the exact circumstances surrounding the fatal shooting of Ruben Medrano are disputed. When the police entered the bathroom, the Medranos heard three consecutive shots and then a delayed shot at the end. The Medranos believe that Ruben Medrano never fired his .357 magnum. According to the Medranos, the police shot Medrano three times and then staged a shot from Medrano's .357 magnum after he was already dead.

Ruben Medrano's wife, parents, and siblings brought suit against many of the police officers involved in this incident and against the City of Los Angeles. Seeking damages under 42 U.S.C. section 1983, the Medranos alleged that the police violated Ruben Medrano's constitutional rights by using excessive force and that the police conspired to cover up the actual events that occurred when the police entered the bathroom. The Medranos also brought several state law claims in this action, but the district court refused to exercise pendent jurisdiction over these claims and dismissed them. The district court directed a verdict in favor of the City of Los Angeles. In addition, the district court either dismissed or directed verdicts in favor of all the individual defendants except for Officers Mowry and Romero, the two police officers who struggled with and shot Ruben Medrano. The jury returned a verdict in favor of these two officers. The Medranos appeal the directed verdicts against them, the dismissal of Chief Gates from the lawsuit, and numerous rulings that the court made during the trial.

DISCUSSION

I. *The Notice of Appeal*

The appellees argue that our review should be limited to the denial of the Medranos' new trial motion because the notice of appeal mentions only the district court's order denying the motion for a new trial and says nothing about the earlier judgment. The appellees rely on Rule 3(c) of the Federal Rules of Appellate Procedure: "The notice of appeal ... shall designate the judgment, order or part thereof appealed from...." Fed. R. App. P. 3(c). This argument, however, ignores the Supreme Court's holding in Foman v. Davis, 371 U.S. 178 (1962). Like the Medranos in the case at bar, the appellant in Foman had filed an appeal from the judgment that was premature because of a pending motion to alter or amend the judgment under Fed. R. Civ. P. 59. Id. at 180. Like the Medranos, the appellant in *Foman* filed a second notice of appeal after the district court denied the Rule 59 motion. Id.

Also like the present case, the appellee in *Foman* argued that the second appeal was limited to the district court's denial of the Rule 59 motion because the notice of appeal failed to specify that the appeal was being taken from the judgment as well as from the order denying the Rule 59 motion. The Supreme Court squarely rejected this analysis:

The defect in the second notice of appeal did not mislead or prejudice the respondent. With both notices of appeal before it (even granting the asserted ineffectiveness of the first), the Court of Appeals should have treated the appeal from the denial of the motions as an effective, although inept, attempt to appeal from the judgment sought to be vacated. Taking the two notices and the appeal papers together, petitioner's intention to seek review of both the [judgment] and the denial of the motions was manifest. Not only did both parties brief and argue the merits of the earlier judgment on appeal, but petitioner's statement of points ... similarly demonstrated the intent to challenge the [judgment].

It is too late in the day and entirely contrary to the spirit of the Federal Rules of Civil Procedure for decisions on the merits to be avoided on the basis of such mere technicalities.

Id. at 181.

The appellees are unable to distinguish the present case from *Foman*. Contrary to the appellees' assertions, when a prior notice of appeal from a judgment is premature, Fed. R. App. P. 3(c) allows a later notice of appeal from the denial of a Rule 59 motion to serve as a notice of appeal from the underlying judgment. Id.; In re Nicholson, 779 F.2d 514, 515–16 (9th Cir. 1985); see also Torres v. Oakland Scavenger Co., 487 U.S. 312, 316–17 (1988) (explaining *Foman*). *Foman* clearly governs this issue, and we therefore treat the Medranos' notice of appeal as an appeal from the earlier judgment of the court.

Notes and Questions

As noted in the following section, current provisions or Federal Rules of Appellate Procedure 3 and 4 deal specifically with "premature" notices of appeal. Under current rules, how would the principal case be decided? If the facts were that there was no notice of appeal prior to disposition of the Rule 59 motion, would either the FRAP or the doctrine of the principal case save the appeal? Why?

6. FILING THE NOTICE OF APPEAL TOO EARLY

FIRSTIER MORTGAGE COMPANY v. INVESTORS MORTGAGE INSURANCE COMPANY

Supreme Court of the United States, 1991.
498 U.S. 269, 111 S.Ct. 648, 112 L.Ed.2d 743.

JUSTICE MARSHALL delivered the opinion of the Court.

Federal Rule of Appellate Procedure 4(a)(2) provides that a "notice of appeal filed after the announcement of a decision or order but before the entry of the judgment or order shall be treated as filed after such entry and on the day thereof." In this case, petitioner filed its notice of appeal after the District Court announced from the bench that it intended to grant summary judgment for respondent, but before entry of judgment and before the parties had, at the court's request, submitted proposed findings of fact and conclusions of law. The question presented is whether the bench ruling is a "decision" under Rule 4(a)(2). We hold that it is.

Respondent, Investors Mortgage Insurance Co. (IMI), issued eight insurance policies to petitioner, FirsTier Mortgage Co. (FirsTier). The parties intended these policies to insure FirsTier for the risk of borrower default on eight real estate loans that FirsTier had made. After the eight borrowers defaulted, FirsTier submitted claims on the policies, which IMI refused to pay. Invoking the District Court's diversity jurisdiction under 28 U.S.C. § 1332, FirsTier filed suit, seeking damages for IMI's alleged breach of contract and breach of its duty of good faith and fair dealing.

On January 26, 1989, the District Court held a hearing on IMI's motion for summary judgment. After hearing argument from counsel, the District Court announced from the bench that it was granting IMI's motion. The judge stated that FirsTier's eight policies had been secured from IMI through fraud or bad faith and therefore were void:

> "I find that the policies should be and are cancelled as void for want of [sic] fraud, bad faith. The Court has heard no evidence in the matter of this hearing to change its mind from holding that the policies are void.

> "Of course in a case of this kind, the losing party has a right to appeal. If the Court happens to be wrong, I don't think I am, but if the Court happens to be wrong, it could be righted by the Circuit.

> "The Court does find that [IMI] relied on the package [of information furnished by FirsTier] in each of these loans and the package was not honest. In fact it was dishonest. The dishonesty should and does void the policy." App. 27.

The District Court then requested that IMI submit proposed findings of fact and conclusions of law to support the ruling, adding that FirsTier would thereafter be permitted to submit any objections it might have to IMI's proposed findings:

> "The Court will then look at what you submit as your suggestion and it is your suggestion only. The Court then will modify, add to it, delete and write its own findings of fact and conclusions of law and judgment in each of these eight policies that we have talked about.

. . . . .

> "And if [FirsTier] cares to do so, within five days you may file with the Court your objection or suggestion wherein you find that the suggestions of [IMI] are in error, if you care to do so." Ibid.

Finally, the District Court clarified that its ruling extinguished both FirsTier's claim for breach of contract and FirsTier's claim for breach of the duty of good faith and fair dealing. Id., at 28.

FirsTier filed its notice of appeal on February 8, 1989, identifying the January 26 bench ruling as the decision from which it was appealing. On March 3, 1989, the District Court issued its findings of fact and conclusions of law in support of its ruling that IMI was entitled to summary judgment. In a separate document, also dated March 3, 1989, the District Court entered judgment. See Fed.Rule Civ.Proc. 58 (requiring that "[e]very judgment shall be set forth on a separate document").

After notifying the parties that it was considering dismissing FirsTier's appeal for lack of jurisdiction, the Court of Appeals requested that the parties brief two issues: first, whether the February 8 notice of appeal was filed prematurely; and, second, whether the January 26 bench ruling was a final decision appealable under 28 U.S.C. § 1291. See App. to Pet. for Cert. B–2. The Court of Appeals dismissed the appeal on the ground that the January 26 decision was not final under § 1291. The court did not address whether FirsTier's notice of appeal could be effective as a notice of appeal from the March 3 final judgment despite the fact that it identified the January 26 ruling as the ruling appealed from. See id., at A–2. We granted certiorari, 494 U.S. 1003, 110 S.Ct. 1295, 108 L.Ed.2d 472 (1990), and now reverse.

The issue before us is whether FirsTier's February 8 notice of appeal is fatally premature. Federal Rule of Appellate Procedure 4(a)(1) requires an appellant to file its notice of appeal "within 30 days after the date of entry of the judgment or order appealed from." See also 28 U.S.C. § 2107. In this case, FirsTier filed its notice of appeal close to a month before entry of judgment. However, under Federal Rule of Appellate Procedure 4(a)(2) a notice of appeal "filed after the announcement of a decision or order but before the entry of the judgment or order shall be treated as filed after such entry and on the day thereof."[1] Added to the Federal Rules in 1979, Rule 4(a)(2) was intended to codify a general practice in the courts of appeals of deeming certain premature notices of appeal effective. See Advisory Committee's Note on Fed.Rule App.Proc. 4(a)(2), 28 U.S.C.App., p. 516. The Rule recognizes that, unlike a tardy notice of appeal, certain premature notices do not prejudice the appellee and that the technical defect of prematurity therefore should not be allowed to extinguish an otherwise proper appeal. See In re Grand Jury Impaneled Jan. 21, 1975, 541 F.2d 373, 377 (CA3 1976) (cited with approval in Advisory Committee's Note on Fed.Rule App.Proc. 4(a)(2), supra, at 516); Hodge v. Hodge, 507 F.2d 87, 89 (CA3 1975) (same).

---

1. Rule 4(a)(2) applies "[e]xcept as provided in (a)(4) of this Rule." Rule 4(a)(4) states, in pertinent part:

"If a timely motion under the Federal Rules of Civil Procedure is filed in the district court by any party: (i) for judgment under Rule 50(b); (ii) under Rule 52(b) to amend or make additional findings of fact, whether or not an alteration of the judgment would be required if the motion is granted; (iii) under Rule 59 to alter or amend the judgment; or (iv) un-der Rule 59 for a new trial, the time for appeal for all parties shall run from the entry of the order denying a new trial or granting or denying any other such motion. A notice of appeal filed before the disposition of any of the above motions shall have no effect. A new notice of appeal must be filed within the prescribed time measured from the entry of the order disposing of the motion as provided above."

IMI maintains that the relation forward provision of Rule 4(a)(2) rescues a premature notice of appeal only if such notice is filed after the announcement of a decision that is "final" within the meaning of 28 U.S.C. § 1291. IMI further contends that the January 26 bench ruling did not constitute a final decision. For a ruling to be final, it must "en[d] the litigation on the merits," Catlin v. United States, 324 U.S. 229, 233, 65 S.Ct. 631, 633–34, 89 L.Ed. 911 (1945) (citation omitted), and the judge must "clearly declar[e] his intention in this respect," United States v. F. & M. Schaefer Brewing Co., 356 U.S. 227, 232, 78 S.Ct. 674, 678, 2 L.Ed.2d 721 (1958). IMI contends that the judge did not clearly intend to terminate the litigation on the merits. Although the judge stated from the bench his legal conclusions about the case, he also stated his intention to set forth his rationale in a more detailed and disciplined fashion at a later date. Moreover, the judge did not explicitly exclude the possibility that he might change his mind in the interim.

We find it unnecessary to resolve this question whether the bench ruling was final. For we believe the Court of Appeals erred in its threshold determination that a notice of appeal filed from a bench ruling can only be effective if the bench ruling is itself a final decision. Rather, we conclude that Rule 4(a)(2) permits a notice of appeal filed from certain nonfinal decisions to serve as an effective notice from a subsequently entered final judgment.[4]

To support its contention that Rule 4(a)(2) cannot permit a premature notice of appeal from a nonfinal decision, IMI relies on Federal Rule of Appellate Procedure 1(b). Rule 1(b) provides that the appellate rules "shall not be construed to extend or limit the jurisdiction of the courts of appeals as established by law." According to IMI, construing Rule 4(a)(2) to cure premature notices of appeal from nonfinal decisions would contravene Rule 1(b) by enlarging appellate jurisdiction beyond that conferred by 28 U.S.C. § 1291, the relevant jurisdictional statute.

IMI misinterprets Rule 4(a)(2). Under Rule 4(a)(2), a premature notice of appeal does not ripen until judgment is entered. Once judgment is entered, the Rule treats the premature notice of appeal "as filed after such entry." Thus, even if a bench ruling in a given case were not "final" within the meaning of § 1291, Rule 4(a)(2) would not render that ruling appealable in contravention of § 1291. Rather, it permits a premature notice of appeal from that bench ruling to relate forward to judgment and serve as an effective notice of appeal from the final judgment.

Applying this principle to the case at hand, we conclude that the District Court's January 26 bench ruling was a "decision" for purposes

---

4. Rule 4(a)(2) refers to "a notice of appeal filed after the *announcement of a decision or order but before the entry of the judgment or order*" (emphasis added). Thus, under the Rule, a premature notice of appeal relates forward to the date of entry of a final "judgment" only when the ruling designated in the notice is a "decision" for purposes of the Rule. We define "decision" with this situation in mind. We offer no view on the meaning of the term "order" in Rule 4(a)(2) or on the operation of the Rule when the jurisdiction of the court of appeals is founded on a statute other than § 1291.

of Rule 4(a)(2). Even assuming that the January 26 bench ruling was not final because the District Court could have changed its mind prior to entry of judgment, the fact remains that the bench ruling did announce a decision purporting to dispose of all of FirsTier's claims. Had the judge set forth the judgment immediately following the bench ruling, and had the clerk entered the judgment on the docket, see Fed.Rules Civ.Proc. 58 and 79(a), there is no question that the bench ruling would have been "final" under § 1291. Under such circumstances, FirsTier's belief in the finality of the January 26 bench ruling was reasonable, and its premature February 8 notice therefore should be treated as an effective notice of appeal from the judgment entered on March 3.[7]

In reaching our conclusion, we observe that this case presents precisely the situation contemplated by Rule 4(a)(2)'s drafters. FirsTier's confusion as to the status of the litigation at the time it filed its notice of appeal was understandable. By its February 8 notice of appeal, FirsTier clearly sought, albeit inartfully, to appeal from the judgment that in fact was entered on March 3. No unfairness to IMI results from allowing the appeal to go forward.

Because the District Court rendered a final judgment on March 3, and because, by virtue of Rule 4(a)(2), FirsTier's February 8 notice of appeal constituted a timely notice of appeal from that judgment, the Court of Appeals erred in dismissing FirsTier's appeal. Accordingly, the judgment of the Court of Appeals is reversed, and the case is remanded for further proceedings consistent with this opinion.

SECTION G.   CROSS–APPEALS

A contentious aspect of modern appellate practice involves cross-appeals. As this edition of the casebook goes to press, the Advisory Committee on the Appellate Rules has publicly declared that there is a "vacuum" of directions under the rules in federal practice, which have generally *failed* to address cross-appeals. Since cross-appeals are not uncommon, the situation has "frustrated judges, attorneys, and parties who have sought guidance in the rules." The absence of definitive resolution of common issues ranges from bedrock questions like deciding who is the "appellant" in cross-appeal situations, to management of the briefing process. As is noted in Chapter 8, briefing size limitations are a key restriction on appellate practice today, and some observers have suggested that sometimes attorneys file a cross-appeal simply to expand the number of available lines and characters for briefing (most circuits have allowed four briefs in cross-appeal situations).

Many lawyers file unnecessary cross-appeals either out of carelessness or, worse, an effort to obtain a self-help increase in the allowable type volume. Many lawyers do not realize that they do not

---

7. Because FirsTier did not file any of the motions enumerated under Federal Rule of Appellate Procedure 4(a)(4), see n. 1, supra, Rule 4(a)(4) does not render its premature notice of appeal ineffective.

need to file a cross-appeal to defend a judgment on a ground not relied on by the district court. Or they do realize it, but file a cross-appeal anyway, in order to get additional brief space.

See Advisory Committee Report, May, 2004, Notes to Proposed Rule 28.1 (quoting formal written comments submitted by Judge Frank Easterbrook of the Seventh Circuit). Efforts by the rules drafters are underway to bring order from chaos, and to unify the quite dramatically approaches of various circuits in local rules governing the cross-appeal process.

In most if not all circuits, each appeal, including a cross-appeal, is assigned a separate docket number and thus is technically a distinct appellate "case," even though the separate cases are typically consolidated. Thus the key is that these are related cases involving cross-appeals from the same judgment or order. Until uniform national rules on cross-appeals are prescribed, there are differing page limits, briefing schedules and other provisions relating to cross-appeals in the federal court system.

More importantly, the cross-appeal process raises fundamental questions about the relief available on appeal to each party, and the grounds on which the trial-level disposition may be attacked or defended. Much more is at stake than who gets to file the first brief, or how many lines of argument text can be included in the appellate briefs. At times, failure to cross-appeal limits the ability to obtain certain aspects of relief, or the ability to have certain arguments heard by the appellate court.

1. THE PROCEDURE FOR CROSS–APPEALING

Standard Notice of Appeal Format. There is no rule of procedure in the federal court system directly and separately addressing cross-appeals. Thus, when an attorney concludes that a cross-appeal is appropriate, the general guidance of Rules 3 and 4 will control the procedure. The cross-appeal is begun with a notice of appeal, or notice of cross-appeal (no preference regarding the labelling is stated in the rules), which should have the same content as required in the original notice of appeal by the first appellant.

Time to Serve Notice for a Cross–Appeal. The timing for commencement of a cross-appeal is specified in federal practice by Rule 4(a)(3), helpfully entitled "Multiple Appeals." That subdivision of the basic time-to-appeal provision for federal practice states that the would-be cross-appellant has the same 30 days from the entry of judgment as is allowed to all parties (or 60 if the United States government is a party). However, if another party has appealed, a cross-appeal is permitted within 14 days after that initial notice of appeal is *filed*. Thus, a party who has not elected to appeal may learn that on the 29th day after entry of judgment, an adversary filed a notice of appeal. The party has 14 days from the date the notice of appeal was filed by the adversary in which to notice (by filing) a cross-appeal. Rule 4(a)(3) reads:

(3) *Multiple Appeals.* If one party timely files a notice of appeal, any other party may file a notice of appeal within 14 days after the date when the first notice was filed, or within the time otherwise prescribed by this Rule 4(a), whichever period ends later.

Under the structure of this rule 14–day window for filing is not always applicable. The rule provides an extension of the 30–day period for filing a notice of appeal after entry of the judgment only in those situations where the appellant files a notice of appeal during the last 14 days of the basic 30–day appeal time period. Thus, under the federal rule a 14–day period is commenced from the date the initial notice was filed. As Professor Martineau has noted, the full 14–day period is not tacked on to the last day for filing an initial notice of appeal unless the initial notice is filed on the last day. It should also be noted that, regardless of what time period is applicable, the time period commences upon the filing of the initial notice, not from the date the notice is received by the party. The fact that up to an additional 14 days may be allowed *does not mean* that the absolute maximum amount of time for filing notice of a cross-appeal is 44 or 74 days from entry of the judgment being appealed. R. Martineau, Modern Appellate Practice—Federal and State Civil Appeals, § 6.18.

The notice of cross-appeal is filed in the district court, even though an appeal is in some sense pending once the original appellant files the first notice of appeal. See Martin v. Alamo Community College Dist., 353 F.3d 409 (5th Cir. 2003).

Other Federal Procedures. Until uniform national rules are promulgated, the procedure after a cross-appeal is filed will be controlled largely by local rules of the federal circuits. Often a briefing schedule order is issued directing the parties on exactly what to file, and when. Many appellate courts have "information sheets" that must be completed shortly after an appeal is noticed, and the existence of related appeals will be entered on such forms.

State Practice. In many of states the content of the notice of cross-appeal is the same as is used for the initial notice. While several states follow the federal rule, others limit or increase the content requirements. Some states require that the notice identify the court from which the appeal is taken as well as the court to which the appeal is taken. Others may require an "assignment of errors" to be assailed on appeal. A few states require that the portions of the transcript to be ordered be included in the notice. Apart from knowing whether a cross-appeal must be filed, knowing the time in which a notice must be filed is crucial for the appellate attorney. Some states follow federal timetables, while others specify a differing number of "extra" days available to the appellee for the lodging of a cross-appeal after an initial notice of appeal by the appellant.

JOHNSON v. TEAMSTERS LOCAL 559

United States Court of Appeals, First Circuit, 1996.
102 F.3d 21.

CAMPBELL, SENIOR CIRCUIT JUDGE.

In the principal appeal now before us, Teamsters Local 559 and Robert Dubian appeal from state law tort judgments against them arising out of a workplace conflict. They argue, inter alia, that there is insufficient evidence to support the judgments under the Norris–LaGuardia Act's "clear proof" requirement. * * * .

C.   GILMARTIN'S LIABILITY

In their cross-appeal, the Johnsons contend that the district court erred when it overturned the jury's judgment in their favor on their claims against Gilmartin for intentional infliction of emotional distress and loss of consortium. This cross-appeal was, however, filed too late to give this court jurisdiction over the Johnsons' appeal. As "timely filing of a notice of appeal is 'mandatory and jurisdictional' ", Acevedo–Villalobos v. Hernandez, 22 F.3d 384, 387 (1st Cir. 1994), we dismiss the Johnsons' cross-appeal for lack of appellate jurisdiction.

There has been a split in authority among the circuits as to whether the late filing of a notice of a cross-appeal has the same dire jurisdictional consequences as does the late filing of an appeal. Some of the circuits have held that courts should use a "rule of practice" approach allowing more flexibility in administering the 14–day requirement applicable to cross-appeals. See Young Radiator Co. v. Celotex Corp., 881 F.2d 1408, 1415–17 (7th Cir. 1989) (citing cases on both sides); United States v. Lumbermens Mutual Casualty Co., Inc., 917 F.2d 654, 662 (1st Cir. 1990) (recognizing the split but not adopting a rule).

In *Young Radiator*, while noting the earlier circuit split, the Seventh Circuit inferred from the Supreme Court's recent decision in Torres v. Oakland Scavenger Co., 487 U.S. 312 (1988), that the timely filing of a cross-appeal should henceforth be treated as mandatory and jurisdictional. Although *Torres* dealt only with whether the failure to name a party presented a jurisdictional bar to appeal, the Young Radiator court believed that the Supreme Court's broad language in that case, about the mandatory nature of the timing rules in Federal Rules of Appellate Procedure 3 and 4, indicated that the time limit for cross-appeals in Rule 4(a)(3) was also jurisdictional.

The two circuits employing the "rule of practice" approach to have reconsidered this issue after Torres have either expressly held that Torres rendered the cross-appeal time limit jurisdictional or have stated as much in dicta. See EF Operating Corp. v. American Bldgs., 993 F.2d 1046, 1049 n.1 (3d Cir. 1993) (holding that the cross-appeal time limit is jurisdictional); Stockstill v. Petty Ray Geophysical, 888 F.2d 1493, 1496–97 (5th Cir. 1989) (stating in dicta that it is "doubtful" whether cases adopting the rule of practice approach remain good law after Torres). We agree, post-*Torres*, that the cross-appeal time limit in Federal Rule of Appellate Procedure 4(a)(3) is mandatory and jurisdictional.[4] See also Fed. R. App. P. 26(b) ("The court may not enlarge the time for filing a notice of appeal, a petition for allowance, or a petition for permission to appeal.")

A notice of appeal must be filed with the clerk of the district court within 30 days after the date of entry of the judgment or order appealed from. Fed. R. App. P. 4(a)(1). A cross-appeal must be filed within 14 days after the date when the first notice of appeal was filed or within the time otherwise prescribed by Appellate Rule 4(a). Fed. R. App. P. 4(a)(3). Under the provisions of Appellate Rule 4(a)(4), the timely filing of certain types of motions, such as motions under Federal Rules of Civil Procedure 50(b) or 59, will extend the time for appeal for all parties, causing the time limits to run from the date of the entry of the order disposing of the last such motion outstanding.

The district court entered its judgment on May 24, 1995. But on June 8, 1995, the defendants timely served a motion under Rules 50(b) and 59, thereby extending the time available for filing an appeal. The district court entered its orders deciding this motion on September 28, 1995. The defendants timely filed their notice of appeal within 30 days, on October 25, 1995. But the Johnsons did not file their cross-appeal until November 13, 1995, 19 days after the defendants filed their notice of appeal. Their filing was five days too late. * * *

We dismiss the Johnsons' cross-appeal for lack of appellate jurisdiction.

Note

In Endicott Johnson Corporation v. Liberty Mutual Insurance Co., 116 F.3d 53 (2d Cir. 1997) the court held that where an *appellant*'s notice of appeal was untimely, and was to be stricken, the *appellee*'s notice of cross-appeal must be stricken as well (presumably, the cross-appeal was not lodged within 30 days of the judgment, and thus required the 14–day grace period of Rule 4(a)(1) to be deemed timely).

2. THE DECISION WHETHER TO CROSS–APPEAL

One of the most difficult problems facing the attorney for the appellee is whether to file a cross-appeal. The decision depends upon what types of issues the appellee wishes to raise in the appellate court.

---

4. Although the core holding in *Torres* has been superseded by the 1993 amendments to the Federal Rules of Appellate Procedure, see Fed. R. App. P. 3(c) ("An appeal will not be dismissed ... for failure to name a party whose intent to appeal is otherwise clear from the notice."); Garcia v. Wash, 20 F.3d 608 at 608–09 (5th Cir. 1994) (per curiam), the advisory committee notes to that amendment state that the amendment was intended to put an end to the satellite litigation over whether an ambiguous reference to a party was sufficient to identify an appellant under *Torres*. Fed. R. App. P. 3(c) advisory committee's note. The amendment does not indicate any intent to change the mandatory nature of the time limits in Rules 3 and 4. Nor has there been any corresponding amendment to Rule 26(b), which prohibits courts from enlarging the time for filing a notice of appeal and upon which the *Torres* court in part relied.

The Basic Rule and its Converse. The general rule for cross-appeals is that an appellee seeking only to affirm judgment below need not file a cross appeal. The rule that cross-appeals are necessary only when an appellee seeks to change the judgment of the lower court, not when he wishes to advance in support of the judgment arguments rejected or not considered by that court, finds its primary justification in the notion that a person who is satisfied with the action of a court should not have to appeal from it, no matter what his adversary does. Thus, the rule in federal courts and many state courts is that an appellee need not appeal or cross-appeal in order to urge in support of a decree any matter appearing in the record, although his argument may involve an attack upon the reasoning of the lower court or an insistence on matters overlooked or ignored by it. A prevailing party need not cross-appeal to defend a judgment on any ground properly raised below, as long as it seeks to preserve rather than to change the judgment. Importantly, even if the trial judge rejected some of the appellee's arguments, these contentions may be used on appeal to defend the outcome on appeal. The appellee, it is sometimes said, can argue that the trial court came out at the right place, but for the wrong reasons.

The converse of the rule is that when an appellee seeks to overturn a ruling adverse to it on an independent claim, then a cross appeal must be filed. The cross appeal must be filed regardless of whether the appellee seeks to increase the award or the scope of relief or obtain certain remedies rejected by the lower court. This requirement applies to defenses as well as to affirmative claims for relief. Thus an appellee who fails to file a cross-appeal "may not attack the decree with a view either to enlarging his own rights thereunder or of lessening the rights of his adversary, whether what he seeks is to correct an error or to supplement the decree with respect to a matter not dealt with below." United States v. American Ry. Express Co., 265 U.S. 425, 435, 44 S.Ct. 560, 68 L.Ed. 1087 (1924); see Francis v. Clark Equip. Co., 993 F.2d 545, 552 (6th Cir. 1993) (stating that "the filing of a notice of cross-appeal is jurisdictional where an appellee wishes to attack part of a final judgment in order to enlarge his rights or to reduce those of his adversary").

Accordingly, in the absence of a cross-appeal, the court of appeals need not consider any argument urged by the prevailing party whose acceptance would result in a modification of the judgment as entered below. When an appellee seeks to have findings of a trial court revised, a cross appeal is required if such revision carries with it as an incident a revision of the judgment. Although the rule seems clear on the surface, the law surrounding what exactly constitutes a modification of the judgment requiring a cross-appeal is confusing. See generally 15A C. Wright, A. Miller & E. Cooper, Federal Practice & Procedure § 3904, at 206–09 (2d ed. 1992) (discussing the uncertain modern value of the cross-appeal requirement and general lack of reasoning for its application a number of prominent cases).

State Variations. State rules—indeed, state doctrinal expositions—are not extensive on the topic of cross-appeals. Most states appear to follow the federal rule that a notice of cross-appeal is necessary only when the appellee seeks to alter in some way his rights under the judgment. A few states, however, hold that an appellee who has not cross-appealed cannot defend his judgment by attacking findings adverse to him which he contends would, if correctly decided, have furnished additional grounds to support his judgment. See Littlefield v. Littlefield, 292 A.2d 204 (Me. 1972). By such a rule, the courts seek to provide as much notice of what is being reviewed as is possible to opposing parties. Although this is a worthwhile objective, it is doubtful that the notice required by these states will meet the objective: in most states the appellant's notice does not notify the other parties of the specific issues to be raised. The appellee can still only speculate as to what findings or grounds the appellant will attack. Thus, the appellee may not know for certain whether it will be necessary to attack certain other findings of the lower court until the appellant's brief is received. It is the appellant's brief that alerts the appellee to what arguments he must make and it is the appellee's brief which alerts the appellant as to whether a reply brief will be required. Thus, the minority rule does not achieve its objective.

A unique approach to the problem is to eliminate completely the need for a cross appeal, which was done in Tennessee. Under this approach all questions are before the court as long as the initial notice of appeal is timely filed. The reason for eliminating the requirement of a cross-appeal is that the notice of appeal is not designed to inform the other parties of the issues to be presented or the arguments to be made. See Advisory Commentary to Tennessee R. App. P. 13. While elimination of the need for a notice of cross-appeal would avoid any possible confusion, it is probably more often helpful than harmful for notice to be provided at least in accordance with the general rule applied in the federal courts and a majority of states.

Separate Claims. Cross-appeals are necessary to present arguments relating to a different claim than that covered by the initial appeal. Though this principle appears simple, the attorney must be aware of those situations in which various claims merge into a judgment with only one provision. For example, claims for interest, costs and attorney's fees are separate from the principal, and the disposition of these claims could result in a judgment for a single amount, but require an appeal and a cross-appeal. When a plaintiff claims damages and attorneys fees, the judgment may award damages which the appellant thinks inadequate and attorneys fees to which the appellee objects. If the appellant appeals from the judgment to attack the amount of the damages, the appellee cannot challenge the award of attorneys fees unless he files a cross appeal.

Venue Challenges. In Peoria & P. U. R. Co. v. United States, 263 U.S. 528, 44 S.Ct. 194, 68 L.Ed. 427 (1924) the Supreme Court held that the defense of improper venue was waived if not raised by cross-appeal in a case in which the plaintiff's claim was dismissed on the merits. This requirement makes sense in light of the fact that the consequences of a dismissal for improper venue differ from those flowing from a dismissal on the merits.

LANGNES v. GREEN

Supreme Court of the United States, 1931.
282 U.S. 531, 51 S.Ct. 243, 75 L.Ed. 520.

MR. JUSTICE SUTHERLAND delivered the opinion of the Court.

[The Supreme Court reviewed a case in which a trial court's judgment was attacked in the court of appeals on two grounds. The court of appeals rejected the appellant's first theory, but accepted the second. Having won, the original appellant did not cross-petition for a writ of certiorari when the party who lost in the court of appeals sought a hearing in the Supreme Court. The Supreme Court reversed the judgment based on the theory the court of appeals had rejected.]

[W]e deem it unnecessary to consider the second contention further, since the conclusion to which we have come rests upon the first contention, in respect of which, for reasons presently to be stated, we are of opinion both courts below were in error.

The preliminary objection is urged by petitioner that, since the decision below upon this point was against respondent and he has not applied for certiorari, the point is not open here for consideration; but the objection is without merit, as a brief review of the decisions of this court will disclose. * * *

The question then arises: What is the scope of inquiry in this court when the case is brought up by certiorari from the Circuit Court of Appeals? It has been decided that upon writ of error from an intermediate appellate tribunal we are not limited to a consideration of the points raised by the plaintiff, but "must enter the judgment which should have been rendered by the court below on the record then before it." Baker v. Warner, 231 U.S. 588, 593, 34 S.Ct. 175, 177, 58 L.Ed. 384. And in Delk v. St. Louis & San Francisco R. R., 220 U.S. 580, 588, 31 S.Ct. 617, 55 L.Ed. 590, following Lutcher & Moore Lumber Co. v. Knight, 217 U.S. 257, 267, 30 S.Ct. 505, 54 L.Ed. 757, it was held that on certiorari, likewise, the entire record is before this court with power to review the action of the Court of Appeals and direct such disposition of the case as that court might have done upon the writ of error sued out for the review of the Circuit [now District] Court. In Watts, Watts & Co. v. Unione Austriaca, etc., 248 U.S. 9, 21, 39 S.Ct. 1, 2, 63 L.Ed. 100, 3 A.L.R. 323, it was said that: "This court, in the exercise of its appellate jurisdiction, has power not only to correct error in the judgment entered below, but to make such disposition of the case as justice may at this time require"; and "the rule is the more insistent, because in admiralty cases are tried de novo on appeal." See, also, Dorchy v. Kansas, 264 U.S. 286, 289, 44 S.Ct. 323, 68 L.Ed. 686.

The authorities relied upon by petitioner are not to the contrary. They contain no challenge to the rule laid down in the decisions cited immediately above, but proceed upon the theory that the court is not bound to consider objections to the decree urged by respondent, in the absence of cross-petition for certiorari. In Warner Co. v. Pier Co., 278 U.S. 85, 91, 49 S.Ct. 45, 46, 73 L.Ed. 195, where the authorities are collected, it is said:

> "Objections to the decree below were offered by counsel for respondents in their briefs and arguments here. But no application for certiorari was made in their behalf and we confine our consideration to errors assigned by the petitioner."

In Hubbard v. Tod, 171 U.S. 474, 494, 19 S.Ct. 14, 21, 43 L.Ed. 246, the court disposed of the matter by saying:

> "And, as respondents did not apply for certiorari, we shall confine our consideration of the case to the examination of errors assigned by petitioner."

In Federal Trade Comm. v. Pac. Paper Ass'n, 273 U.S. 52, 47 S.Ct. 255, 71 L.Ed. 534, respondents, without presenting a cross-petition for certiorari, sought a reversal of a distinct portion of the decree. This court, in declining to consider the matter, said (page 66 of 273 U.S., 47 S.Ct. 255, 259):

> "A party who has not sought review by appeal or writ of error will not be heard in an appellate court to question the correctness of the decree of the lower court. This is so well settled that citation is not necessary. The respondents are not entitled as of right to have that part of the decree reviewed. And, assuming power, we are not moved by any persuasive consideration to examine the parts of the Commission's order to which respondents object."

These decisions simply announce a rule of practice which generally has been followed; but none of them deny the power of the court to review objections urged by respondent, although he has not applied for certiorari, if the court deems there is good reason to do so. In the present case, however, it is not necessary to consider this rule of practice because the respondent offers no objection to the decree of the Court of Appeals. In that court he attacked the decree of the District Court upon the two grounds above stated, and the Circuit Court of Appeals sustained the attack but upon one of such grounds only. Respondent here defends that decree upon the ground upon which it was based, and, in addition, continues to urge the rejected ground, not to overthrow the decree, but to sustain it. His right to do so is beyond successful challenge, quite apart from the fact that this is a proceeding in admiralty, and is here from an intermediate appellate court. United States v. American Ry. Exp. Co., 265 U.S. 425, at page 435, 44 S.Ct. 560, 564, 68 L.Ed. 1087, where it is said:

> "It is true that a party who does not appeal from a final decree of the trial court cannot be heard in opposition thereto when the case is brought here by the appeal of the adverse party. In other words, the appellee may not attack the decree with a view either to

enlarging his own rights thereunder or of lessening the rights of his adversary, whether what he seeks is to correct an error or to supplement the decree with respect to a matter not dealt with below. But it is likewise settled that the appellee may, without taking a cross-appeal, urge in support of a decree any matter appearing in the record, although his argument may involve an attack upon the reasoning of the lower court or an insistence upon matter overlooked or ignored by it. By the claims now in question, the American does not attack, in any respect, the decree entered below. It merely asserts additional grounds why the decree should be affirmed.''

And, obviously, the right or duty of this court to consider these additional grounds will neither be affected by their rejection in the court below nor be made to depend upon the effect finally given to them here. * * *

The decrees of both courts below must be reversed and the cause remanded to the District Court for further proceedings in conformity with this opinion.

Reversed.

Notes and Questions

1. The principal case addresses the general rule followed by the federal courts and most states. Some deviations from the rule are noted and discussed in Stern, When to Cross–Appeal or Cross–Petition—Certainty or Confusion?, 87 Harvard L.Rev. 763 (1974).

2. Some states, however, do not follow the federal rule. In Littlefield v. Littlefield, 292 A.2d 204 (Me.1972) the court held that an appellee cannot defend the judgment by attacking adverse findings. This variation is discussed in Note, Cross–Appeals in Maine: Pitfalls for the Winning Litigant, 25 Me.L.Rev. 105 (1973).

3. It has been observed that a cross-appeal is required "when the logical result of acceptance of a respondent's additional argument would be to change more of the judgment than is brought into issue by the initial appeal." Stern, When to Cross–Appeal or Cross–Petition—Certainty or Confusion?, 87 Harv. L. Rev. 763, 767 (1974). Consider NLRB. v. International Van Lines, 409 U.S. 48, 93 S.Ct. 74, 34 L.Ed.2d 201 (1972), where an employer discharged picketing employees. The Board held that this was an unfair labor practice and ordered that the employees be reinstated with back pay. The reinstatement portion of the Board's order was set aside by the court of appeals and the Supreme Court reversed. Before the Supreme Court, the employer argued that the employees' picketing was not a protected activity. Since the Board's decision to reinstate the employees was based on the fact that it is an unfair labor practice to discharge an employee who is participating in a protected activity, a finding by the Supreme Court that the picketing was not protected would, as a practical matter, result in affirmance of the appellate court. The Court would not hear the protected activity argument,' however, on the ground that the logical result of the argument would go farther than was necessary to resolve the issue raised on appeal.

The need for a cross-appeal in such an instance has been sharply criticized and rightfully so because the parties are interested in the argument's logical conclusion only in so far as it results in affirmance or reversal of the order.

4. The principal case above was an admiralty case, and some of the comments it makes are dicta. It may be argued that Trans World Airlines v. Thurston, 469 U.S. 111, 105 S.Ct. 613, 83 L.Ed.2d 523 (1985), suggests that *Langnes* is no longer good law. There the court of appeals held that TWA was liable in damages to the plaintiffs-respondents for violation of the Age Discrimination in Employment Act; and it also held that the Air Line Pilots Association (ALPA) had violated the ADEA, but that the plaintiffs could not recover damages from the ALPA because the ADEA did not permit monetary recovery from unions. TWA petitioned for certiorari, but the plaintiffs-respondents did not cross-petition. The Supreme Court held it "was without jurisdiction" to consider the correctness of the court of appeals' ruling as to the ALPA's lack of liability for damages, which plaintiffs-respondents (as well as TWA) urged it to reverse. Id., 105 S. Ct. at 620 n.14. The Court stated:

> In its petition for a writ of certiorari, TWA raised the issue of a union's liability for damages under the ADEA. Although we granted the petition in full, we now conclude that the Court is without jurisdiction to consider this question. TWA was not the proper party to present this question. The airline cannot assert the right of others to recover damages against the Union. Both the individual respondents and the EEOC argue that the issue of union liability is properly before the Court. But the respondents failed to file a cross-petition raising this question. A prevailing party may advance any ground in support of a judgment in his favor. An argument that would modify the judgment, however, cannot be presented unless a cross-petition has been filed. In this case, the judgment of the Court of Appeals would be modified by the arguments advanced by the EEOC and the individual plaintiffs, as they are contending that the Union should be liable to them for monetary damages.

MASSACHUSETTS MUTUAL LIFE INSURANCE CO. v. LUDWIG

Supreme Court of the United States, 1976.
426 U.S. 479, 96 S.Ct. 2158, 48 L.Ed.2d 784.

Per Curiam.

This is a diversity case. Petitioner (the insurer) issued a life insurance policy in Michigan to Dean E. Cane providing for double indemnity if Cane's "death was the result of an injury sustained while the insured was a passenger in or upon a public conveyance then being operated by a common carrier to transport passengers for hire ..." Cane was killed in Illinois by a freight train while crossing a railroad track in order to board a commuter train which had not yet arrived at the station. The insurer paid Cane's estate ordinary benefits, but denied liability under the double indemnity provision of the policy.

The administrator of Cane's estate (respondent) sued the insurer in the District Court for the Northern District of Illinois to recover benefits under the double indemnity provision. The District Court held that under Illinois conflict-of-laws rules, the law of the situs of the contract (Michigan) applied, and that under Michigan law the insurer was liable only for ordinary benefits. The administrator appealed. The insurer argued in the Court of Appeals for the Seventh Circuit that the District Court's application and interpretation of Michigan law was correct, and alternatively that Illinois conflict-of-laws rules required application of Illinois—not Michigan—substantive law in this case, and that under Illinois substantive law its liability was also only for ordinary benefits. The Court of Appeals reversed, 524 F. 2d 376 (1975), but without reaching the question of which State's substantive law would be applicable under the Illinois conflicts rule. The court held that the insurer was precluded from arguing on appeal the applicability of Illinois substantive law, because it had not cross-appealed from the District Court's ruling that Michigan law applied. Id., at 379 n. 1.

The Court of Appeals' decision on this issue is plainly at odds with the "inveterate and certain" rule, Morley Co. v. Maryland Cas. Co., 300 U.S. 185, 191 (1937), of United States v. American Ry. Exp. Co., 265 U.S. 425, 435 (1924), where a unanimous Court said:

> "It is true that a party who does not appeal from a final decree of the trial court cannot be heard in opposition thereto when the case is brought here by the appeal of the adverse party. In other words, the appellee may not attack the decree with a view either to enlarging his own rights thereunder or of lessening the rights of his adversary, whether what he seeks is to correct an error or to supplement the decree with respect to a matter not dealt with below. But it is likewise settled that the appellee may, without taking a cross-appeal, urge in support of a decree any matter appearing in the record, although his argument may involve an attack upon the reasoning of the lower court or an insistence upon matter overlooked or ignored by it." * * *

The argument of the insurer before the Court of Appeals that Illinois, not Michigan, substantive law applied was no more than "an attack upon the reasoning of the lower court," and as such required no cross-appeal.

Because the Court of Appeals did "not reach the issue nor express any opinion on the effect of the tort claim conflicts of law doctrine" of Illinois, 524 F. 2d, at 379 n. 1, we think it "appropriate to remand the case rather than deal with the merits of that question in this Court." Dandridge v. Williams, 397 U.S. 471, 476 n. 6 (1970). Accordingly, the petition for writ of certiorari is granted, the judgment of the Court of Appeals is vacated, and the case is remanded for further proceedings in conformity with this opinion.

So ordered.

Mr. Justice Stevens took no part in the consideration or decision of this case.

MARTS v. HINES

United States Court of Appeals, Fifth Circuit, 1997 (en banc).
117 F.3d 1504.

POLITZ, CHIEF JUDGE.

We have taken this case en banc to resolve relevant conflicting circuit precedents, to continue our development of procedures to address and dispose appropriately of a continually burgeoning prisoner pro se docket, both at the trial and appellate levels, and to note an appropriate awareness of the intervening Prison Litigation Reform Act of 1995.

The facts concerning the appeal by Sidney Marts of his 42 U.S.C. § 1983 complaint against an assistant district attorney for Orleans Parish, Louisiana, a public defender, and a private attorney representing a codefendant in a state court criminal action, are set forth in the panel opinion. Marts' complaint implicated the integrity of the state court criminal proceeding, thus requiring the district court to make a threshold determination whether his action was not frivolous and justified the retention of federal jurisdiction. The trial court dismissed without prejudice the claim for money damages against the private counsel and public defender because they were not state actors, and that against the prosecutor on the basis of absolute immunity. Finding no factual basis for the conspiracy charge it was dismissed as frivolous, also without prejudice. The panel modified the dismissals to be with prejudice, except for the conspiracy claim, and affirmed the trial court. We determined that because of conflicting circuit precedents it was necessary to revisit this issue en banc.

ANALYSIS

Once again we consider the application of limited judicial resources to an ever increasing number of prisoner pro se filings. Our task, simply stated, is to implement procedures which will aid in the separation of the wheat from the chaff in such filings as early in the judicial process as is possible, in an effort to ensure that judicial resources will not be wasted and that the meritorious claims may receive the timely attention and disposition warranted.

The rule that the in limine dismissals of actions by the district court generally are to be with prejudice particularly fits dismissals under the former 28 U.S.C. § 1915(d), now a part of 28 U.S.C. § 1915(e)(2). Dismissals under the in forma pauperis statute are in a class of their own, acting not as dismissals on the merits but, rather, as denials of in forma pauperis status. Typically, but not exclusively, such dismissals may serve as res judicata for subsequent in forma pauperis filings, but they effect no prejudice to the subsequent filing of a fee-paid complaint making the same allegations. Exceptions included complaints containing claims which, on their face, were subject to an obvious meritorious defense, or instances in which the plaintiff was given an opportunity to expound on the factual allegations by a Watson questionnaire or a Spears hearing and could not assert a claim with an arguable factual basis, or claims without an arguable basis in law.

On en banc reconsideration, considering the distinct features of such in forma pauperis proceedings, we now hold that dismissals as frivolous or malicious should be deemed to be dismissals with prejudice unless the district court specifically dismisses without prejudice. When the trial court dismisses without prejudice it is expected that the court will assign reasons so that our appellate review of the trial court's exercise of discretion may be performed properly. Unexplained dismissals without prejudice will necessitate a remand.

We reserve for another day and an appropriate appeal the question of the full application of this rule to the expanded bases for denial of in forma pauperis status specified in the Prison Litigation Reform Act.

In reaching today's decision we have determined and now hold that in cases involving dismissals as frivolous or malicious under the in forma pauperis statute, in which the defendant has not been served and was, therefore, not before the trial court and is not before the appellate court, the appellate court, notwithstanding, has the authority to change a district court judgment dismissing the claims without prejudice to one dismissing with prejudice, even though there is no cross-appeal by the obviously non-present "appellee." This limited exception is the product of our effort to make effective the prudential rule announced herein.

Consistent with today's holding we must now vacate and remand this action to the district court for entry of an order of dismissal with prejudice except as relates to the conspiracy claim and for such further proceedings as may be deemed appropriate.

VACATED and REMANDED.

GARWOOD, CIRCUIT JUDGE, with whom, KING, HIGGINBOTHAM, SMITH, DUHE, GARZA, BENAVIDES and DENNIS CIRCUIT JUDGES, join, dissenting.

I respectfully dissent from this Court's sua sponte action, taken where only the plaintiff has appealed, changing the district court's judgment of dismissal without prejudice to one of dismissal with prejudice. I likewise dissent from the majority's conclusory announcement that in all pre-service dismissals without prejudice if in forma pauperis suite where the plaintiff alone appeals, this Court will determine whether the dismissal could properly have been with, rather than without, prejudice and will modify the judgment accordingly.

The Court provides no explanation, justification, or authority for this action, and does not even tip its hat to the Federal Rules or the relevant jurisprudence. Its decision hence appears to be more an exercise of will than of judgment.

Some sixty years ago, just before the Federal Rules went into effect, the Supreme Court had occasion to review a decision of the Eighth Circuit which had modified in a manner favorable to the appellee a judgment of the district court, despite the absence of any cross-appeal.

The Supreme Court reversed the Eighth Circuit in a unanimous opinion by Justice Cardozo. Morley Construction Co. v. Maryland Casualty Co., 300 U.S. 185 (1937). The opinion begins by stating the question before the Supreme Court: "The *power* of an appellate court to modify a decree in equity *for the benefit of an appellee in the absence of a cross-appeal* is here to be admeasured." Id. at 326 (emphasis added). The Court went on to hold that the appellate court had no such power, stating:

> "Without a cross-appeal, an appellee may 'urge in support of a decree any matter appearing in the record, although his argument may involve an attack upon the reasoning of the lower court or an insistence upon matter overlooked or ignored by it.' United States v. American Railway Express Co., 265 U.S. 425, 435 [1924]. What he may not do in the absence of a cross-appeal is to 'attack the decree with a view either to enlarging his own rights thereunder or of lessening the rights of his adversary, whether what he seeks is to correct an error or to supplement the decree with respect to a matter not dealt with below.' Ibid. The rule is inveterate and certain." Id. at 327–28.[2]

The Supreme Court did not suggest that the Eighth Circuit had abused its discretion or that the circumstances were not sufficiently exceptional to justify its action, but rather held that the Eighth Circuit simply did not have the "power" to do what it did "in the absence of a cross-appeal."

Yet this Court now, in violation of the "inveterate and certain" rule of Morley, does just what the Supreme Court held the Eighth Circuit lacked the power to do.[3]

2. * * *The Supreme Court has likewise continued to apply the Morley principles in refusing to consider a contention of a respondent who did not cross-petition where if the contention were sustained the judgment of the court of appeals would be modified in a manner adverse to the petitioner. See, e.g., Mills v. Electric Auto–Lite Company, 396 U.S. 375, 90 S. Ct. 616, 620 n.4, 24 L. Ed. 2d 593 (1970) (citing Morley). See also Trans World Airlines v. Thurston, 469 U.S. 111, 105 S. Ct. 613, 620 n.14, 83 L. Ed. 2d 523 (1985); Federal Energy Admin. v. Algonquin SNG, Inc., 426 U.S. 548, 96 S. Ct. 2295, 2303 n.11, 49 L. Ed. 2d 49 (1976) (citing Mills); United States v. ITT Continental Baking Co., 420 U.S. 223, 95 S. Ct. 926, 929 n.2, 43 L. Ed. 2d 148 (1975) (citing Morley). Most recently, in Northwest Airlines, Inc. v. County of Kent, 510 U.S. 355, 114 S. Ct. 855, 862, 127 L. Ed. 2d 183 (1994), the Court wrote: "A cross-petition is required, however, when the respondent seeks to alter the judgment below."

3. It is well-settled that where the plaintiff alone appeals a dismissal without prejudice, the appellate court may not change the judgment to one of dismissal with prejudice, as this enlarges the rights of the defendant-appellee under the judgment, for which a cross-appeal is required. See, e.g., Transcapital Financial v. Office of Thrift Supervision, 310 U.S. App. D.C. 134, 44 F.3d 1023, 1026 (D.C. Cir. 1995); Tredway v. Farley, 35 F.3d 288, 296 (7th Cir. 1994); New Castle County v. Hartford Acc. & Indem. Co., 933 F.2d 1162, 1206 (3d Cir. 1991); Benson v. Armontrout, 767 F.2d 454, 455 (8th Cir. 1985). We similarly so held in Arvie v. Broussard, 42 F.3d 249 (5th Cir. 1994). In Arvie, we declined to follow earlier decisions in Graves v. Hampton, 1 F.3d 315, 319 (5th Cir. 1993), and Ali v. Higgs, 892 F.2d 438 (5th Cir. 1990), in which this Court had changed dismissal without prejudice to with prejudice without even commenting on the absence of a cross-appeal, much less making any attempt to justify such unusual action. Cf. Pennhurst State School v. Halderman, 465 U.S. 89, 104 S. Ct. 900, 918, 79 L. Ed. 2d 67 (1984) (decisions assuming jurisdiction sub silentio are not binding precedent on that issue).

I.

Over the years, decisions of the courts of appeals have divided on whether the *Morley* rule requiring a cross-appeal in order to modify the judgment to enlarge the appellee's rights thereunder, or diminish those of the appellant, is a rule governing the power or jurisdiction of the appellate court or is rather a rule of practice as to which exceptions may be made on a case by case basis in highly unusual and compelling circumstances. * * * Likewise in this Court there are decisions viewing the question as one of power or jurisdiction, and others which treat it as a rule of practice or as at least subject to exception in particularly unusual circumstances. * * * On the other hand, there are a few decisions of this Court which have treated the cross-appeal requirement as a rule of practice subject to exceptions in rare particular cases. * * *

The last three times we have expressly addressed the "rule of practice" argument we have declined to either adopt or reject it, but have denied relief to the appellee due to the failure to cross-appeal. * * *

The Committee Note to Rule 3 made at the time the Federal Rules of Appellate Procedure were adopted states:

> "Rule 3 and Rule 4 combine to require that a notice of appeal be filed with the clerk of the district court within the time prescribed for taking an appeal. Because the timely filing of a notice of appeal is 'mandatory and jurisdictional,' United States v. Robinson, 361 U.S. 220, 224, 4 L. Ed. 2d 259, 80 S. Ct. 282 (1960), compliance with the provisions of those rules is of the utmost importance." 9 Moore's Federal Practice (2d ed.) § 203.01[2].

Since then, the Supreme Court has time and again reiterated that the filing of a timely notice of appeal is "mandatory and jurisdictional." See, e.g., Torres v. Oakland Scavenger Co., 487 U.S. 312 (1988) ("... a court of appeals ... may not waive the jurisdictional requirements of Rules 3 and 4, even for 'good cause shown' under Rule 2"); Budinich v. Becton Dickinson And Co., 486 U.S. 196 (1988) ("the taking of an appeal within the prescribed time is mandatory and jurisdictional"); Griggs v. Provident Consumer Discount Co., 459 U.S. 56 (1982) ("It is well settled that the requirement of a timely notice of appeal is mandatory and jurisdictional" [internal quotations marks omitted]); Browder v. Director, 434 U.S. 257 (1978) (" 'mandatory and jurisdictional,' " citing Robinson).* * *

As the Supreme Court observed in *Torres* respecting the above quoted Committee Note to Rule 3: "This admonition by the Advisory Committee makes no distinction among the various requirements of Rule 3 and Rule 4; rather it treats the requirements of the two Rules as a single jurisdictional threshold." Torres at 2408. * * *

The notion that the requirement of a cross-appeal in order to modify the judgment in a manner favorable to the appellee is merely a "rule of practice" which the appellate court may disregard at its discretion is founded on essentially three propositions. I consider these seriatim.

First, reliance is placed on Langnes v. Green, 282 U.S. 531 (1931), which does indeed contain "rule of practice" language. Id. at 245–246. However, *Langnes* cannot sustain the weight thus sought to be placed on it. In the first place, *Langnes* predates *Morley,* and *Morley* expressly speaks to the "power" of the appellate court. The Supreme Court has never retreated from *Morley.* If *Langnes* and *Morley* conflict, the latter clearly controls. Second, the "rule of practice" language in *Langnes* is dicta. * * *

The next argument in favor of the "rule of practice" approach is founded on Fed. R. App. P. 2 (allowing courts of appeals to suspend the rules in particular cases) and Fed. R. Civ. P. 1 (rules "shall be construed and administered to secure the just, speedy and inexpensive determination of every action"). See, e.g., Robicheaux v. Radcliff Materials, Inc., 697 F.2d at 628 (declining to exercise "any power we might have under Fed. R. App. P. 2 to suspend the requirement for a timely cross-appeal, Fed. R. App. P. 4(a)(3)"). Of course, as previously noted, Fed. R. App. P. 2 is expressly made subject to Fed. R. App. P. 26(b), which provides that a court of appeals "may not enlarge the time for filing a notice of appeal." As to Fed. R. Civ. P. 1, the Rules of Civil Procedure have long been inapplicable to giving notice of appeal, and when they were applicable former Rule 6(b) prohibited notice of appeal time enlargements not provided for in former Rule 73(a). See note 8, supra, and accompanying text. In related contexts, the Supreme Court has consistently rejected these or similar arguments.

The final and most frequently invoked justification for the "rule of practice" approach to cross-appeals is that the initial appellant's notice of appeal gives the court of appeals jurisdiction over the whole case, so notice of appeal by any other party is not a necessary precondition to exercise appellate power or jurisdiction to modify the judgment in a manner adverse to the appellant. However, as pointed out above, this approach ignores the reason for the 1966 addition of the extra fourteen days for cross-appeal by clause (3) of former Rule 73(a) and is likewise inconsistent with the treatment in former Rule 73(a), and now in Fed. R. App. P. 4(a), of the "cross appeal" time limits in the very same way as the initial appeal time limits, except for the extra fourteen days allowed for the "cross-appeal." Nor does this approach account for the provision in the second paragraph of former Rule 73(a), now in Fed. R. App. P. 3(a), that "failure of an appellant to take any steps *other than* the timely filing of a notice of appeal does not affect the validity of the appeal" (emphasis added). This provision was plainly as applicable to appeals under clause (3) of the first sentence of former Rule 73(a) as to appeals under the other provisions of that sentence, just as it is now as applicable to Fed. R. App. P. 4(a)(3) as to Fed. R. App. P. 4(a)(1). Further, the rule of practice approach cannot reasonably account for the provisions of Fed. R. App. P. 26(b)—formerly contained in Fed. R. Civ. P. 6(b)—prohibiting enlargement of the fourteen-day period specified in Fed. R. App. P. 4(a)(3) (and previously in former Rule 73(a)) or the fact that the flexibility authorized to the courts of appeal by Fed. R. App. P. 2 is expressly made subject to this restriction.

Finally, the theory that the initial appeal fulfills all jurisdictional prerequisites so as to empower the appellate court to dispose of all aspects of the entire case appears to be necessarily inconsistent with *Torres*. The Seventh and Third Circuits have expressly so recognized. See Young Radiator, 881 F.2d at 1416; E.F. Operating Corp., 993 F.2d at 1029 & n.1. We, too, have twice recognized the strength of the Young Radiator analysis of Torres in this connection, although not ultimately resolving the matter. See Crist at 1289; Stockstill at 1296–97. In *Torres*, notice of appeal was timely filed naming as appellants fifteen of the sixteen plaintiffs, but the name of the sixteenth plaintiff, Jose Torres, was inadvertently left off the notice of appeal. The Supreme Court held that because Torres' name was left off the notice of appeal, the court of appeals never acquired jurisdiction on appeal over the case as to Torres. Obviously, had the notice of appeal of the other plaintiffs—which was indisputably timely and adequate—sufficed to bring up the whole case or the entire judgment, then this would not have been so. *Torres* thus necessarily rejects the notion that a valid notice of appeal by one party suffices to vest the court of appeals with jurisdiction over the entire judgment of the district court, even as to parties not giving notice of appeal. As the *Young Radiator* Court stated:

> "... it could have been argued in Torres that the notice of appeal naming fifteen of the sixteen plaintiffs invoked the jurisdiction of the court over the whole case, so that a separate appeal by the sixteenth plaintiff would not be jurisdictionally required. Yet the Court's holding made clear that the requirements of Rules 3 and 4 must be satisfied as to each party, and precludes the argument in this case that Celotex's noncompliance with Rule 4(a)(3) can be waived." Id., 881 F.2d at 1416.

The theory that an initial appeal by one party brings up the entire judgment so as to render appeals by other parties irrelevant for purposes of the jurisdiction or power of the court of appeals is likewise rejected, at least implicitly, by Osterneck v. Ernst & Whinney, 489 U.S. 169 (1989).[15]

15. There, the plaintiffs Osterneck, stockholders in a corporation which merged into Barwick Industries, sued defendants Barwick Industries, its officers, E.T. Barwick, Keller, and Talley, and its accountants, Ernest & Whinney (E & W), claiming that the merger was induced by fraud. On January 30, 1985, judgment was entered on the jury verdict awarding the Osternecks damages against Barwick Industries, Keller, and Talley, but exonerating E.T. Barwick and E & W. Within ten days, the Osternecks filed a motion for prejudgment interest. While this motion was pending, on March 1, 1985, the Osternecks filed a notice of appeal naming all defendants, and on the same day Talley and Keller filed notices of appeal. On July 9, 1985, the district court entered an amended judgment, granting the Osternecks some but not all the prejudgment interest they had requested (but otherwise not changing the January 30 judgment). Within thirty days thereafter, Keller and Talley filed notices of appeal, as did the Osternecks on July 31. The Osternecks' July 31 notice of appeal named all the defendants except E & W. Before the court of appeals the Osternecks claimed that the judgment erroneously exonerated E & W and E.T. Barwick, and also that the award of prejudgment interest was inadequate; Keller and Talley argued, inter alia, that the Osternecks' claims against them were

In summary, the language and history of Fed. R. App. P. 3, 4(a), and 26 (b), and the Supreme Court's decisions in *Morley* and *Torres,* compel the conclusion that a court of appeals, despite a timely and proper appeal from a district court judgment by one party, lacks power or jurisdiction to modify that judgment so as to make it either more favorable to another party who has not timely appealed it or less favorable to the only party who has appealed it. The majority errs in its implicit holding to the contrary.

II.

Finally, even if we were dealing with a rule of practice which the Court might waive in a particular case, cf. Fed. R. App. P. 2, I would still dissent from the majority's modification of the judgment, which only the plaintiff has appealed, from one of dismissal without prejudice to one of dismissal with prejudice, and from its apparent announcement of a new rule of practice that in all pre-service dismissals without prejudice of in forma pauperis suits where only the plaintiff appeals this Court will sua sponte determine whether the dismissal of any claim could properly have been with, rather than without, prejudice, and will modify the judgment accordingly.

Courts that have espoused the rule of practice approach have almost always emphasized that waiver or excuse of the failure to file a protective or cross-appeal was available only in most narrowly defined circumstances. Those circumstances we listed in Anthony, 693 F.2d at 497–98, and there refused to go beyond them, as we similarly so refused in Robicheaux, Stockstill, and Crist. Other courts that have assumed arguendo that a rule of practice "waiver" might theoretically be available

barred by limitations and that the evidence was insufficient. The court of appeals held it had jurisdiction over the July 1985 appeals of Keller and Talley, but found that the issues raised by those defendants were without substantive merit. Osterneck v. E.T. Barwick Industries, Inc., 825 F.2d 1521 (11th Cir. 1987). The court likewise concluded that it had jurisdiction over the Osternecks' July 31, 1985, notice of appeal, but that this notice of appeal did not suffice to bring forward the Osternecks' claims against E & W, as E & W was not named therein. Id. at 1528–1529. See, also, e.g., Capital Parks v. Southeastern Advertising, 30 F.3d 627, 630 (5th Cir. 1994); Pope v. MCI, 937 F.2d 258, 266 (5th Cir. 1991). The court of appeals further held that the Osternecks' March 1, 1985, notice of appeal (and that of Keller and Talley filed the same day) was rendered ineffective by the then provisions of Fed. R. App. P. 4(a)(4) because it was filed while the motion for prejudgment interest, which the court concluded was a Rule 59(e) motion, was pending. Osterneck, 825 F.2d at 1525–1529. The Osternecks petitioned for certiorari com-

plaining of the dismissal of their appeal as to E & W. The Supreme Court granted the writ and affirmed. It noted that "the Court of Appeals dismissed petitioners' appeal as to Ernest & Whinney for lack of jurisdiction." Osterneck, 108 S. Ct. at 989. It agreed with the court of appeals that the Osternecks' motion for prejudgment interest was a Rule 59(e) motion, and since it was pending when the March 1 notice of appeal was filed that notice of appeal was nugatory under the then provisions of Fed. R. App. P. 4(a)(4). Id. at 990–992. The Court declined to make any equitable exception to this ruling. Id. at 992–93. The Osternecks did not contend in the Supreme Court that their July 31, 1985, notice of appeal was effective as to E & W. Id. at 990 n.1. Of course, had the July 1985 notices of appeal by Keller and Talley—which were properly before the court of appeals— brought the whole July 9, 1985, judgment into the court of appeals for jurisdictional purposes, then the court of appeals would have had jurisdiction over the Osternecks' complaints of that judgment's denial to them of recovery against E & W.

in some cases have refused to invoke it in similar circumstances. See, e.g., Lumbermens Mut. Cas. Co., 917 F.2d at 662–663. Where "rule of practice" waiver of failure to appeal has been invoked it has almost always been in highly unusual cases involving three or more parties where the rights of the parties are interdependent and on the appeal by one party the appellate court changes the judgment in a way that adversely affects the rights of one nonappealing party as against another or eliminates the basis of the judgment against a nonappealing party. Thus, 15A Wright, Miller & Cooper, Federal Practice and Procedure, (2d ed.) § 3904 at 219, states "the cases that have excused separate appeal requirements virtually all involved circumstances in which appeals were taken by one or more defendants or third party defendants, but not by others. The decision on appeal was inconsistent with the judgment against those who did not appeal." See also 9 Moore's Federal Practice (2d ed.) ¶ 204.11[5] ("In some cases, however, the rights of the parties are tied together so closely that the court of appeals can render no judgment that would be just without affecting the rights of the parties who did not file a notice of appeal.").

No cases have been found granting a "rule of practice" waiver of the failure to file a cross-appeal or protective appeal in a situation, such as the present, where absent such a waiver the only result would have been a simple affirmance of the judgment below. The waiver is granted only where on the appeal timely taken the appellate court properly grants relief to the appellant and accordingly changes the judgment below in some respect; because of that appellate change, nonappealing parties are sometimes, in certain narrow and extreme cases, allowed to request other or further changes in the judgment below under the "rule of practice" theory notwithstanding their failure to appeal, because the appellate change in the judgment affects their rights against some other nonappealing party or eliminates the basis of the judgment against them. The Court's decision in the instant case represents a sharp break with this rationale, and in effect simply creates a wholly new rule of practice.

Moreover, our departure from the "inveterate and certain" rule of *Morley* gains us next to nothing in judicial efficiency. Any gain in judicial efficiency presupposes both that if we had merely affirmed the dismissal without prejudice the appellant would in fact have timely filed another suit on the same claim against the same defendant, and that because we have changed the dismissal so that it is with prejudice, he will not actually do so. This is a lot of assuming. But, to promote the efficiency of this Court—and I believe the district courts generally can pretty well take care of their own efficiency concerns—we must also further assume that when the district court disposes of the second suit, which will again doubtless be by dismissal, the plaintiff will again appeal to us, but would not have done so had we on the first appeal changed the district court's original dismissal to be with prejudice. Nor are these hypothetical efficiency gains without costs (apart from the systemic costs of casually departing from established legal rules), for we must now not only determine whether the dismissal without prejudice violated the appellant's rights, but we must also sua sponte determine the sometimes rather close question of whether the dismissal should instead have been made with prejudice. In this case, for example, we hold that the dismissal should have been with prejudice as to three of the claims, but was properly without prejudice as to the fourth.

III.

The plaintiff alone has appealed the judgment dismissing all his claims without prejudice. Instead of entering the obviously merited simple affirmance, we have undertaken to change the judgment to one of dismissal with prejudice as to three of the four claims. That change exceeds our power and jurisdiction. Even were we to follow the theory that the failure to take a protective or cross-appeal may in certain rare instances be waived by a court of appeals, this simple case—where absent the waiver there would be only a plain vanilla affirmance—is totally beyond the universe of cases in which that approach has been followed and is wholly unsupported by their rationale.

From one point of view, this is certainly a "nothing" case. But as a court of appeals it is vitally important that we understand and observe the rules which govern our jurisdiction, power, and proceedings. We should not so casually depart from such inveterate and certain rules.

Notes & Questions

1. In Anthony v. Petroleum Helicopters, 693 F.2d 495, 497–98 (5th Cir. 1982), PHI, owner of a helicopter which crashed, was sued by an injured passenger, who also sued the manufacturer, MBB, the distributor, Boeing, and Texaco; PHI brought claims for contribution and for loss of the helicopter against MBB and Boeing; and MBB and Boeing sought contribution against Texaco. The trial court granted summary judgment exonerating MBB, Boeing, and Texaco from all liability. The surviving passenger appealed the judgment exonerating MBB, Boeing, and Texaco, but then settled. PHI appealed the judgment but only insofar as it exonerated MBB and Boeing. The Fifth Circuit reversed, holding that summary judgment for MBB and Boeing was improper, as there were genuine issues of fact. The appellate court refused to consider the request of appellees MBB and Boeing, who had not cross-appealed, to also set aside the summary judgment in favor of Texaco, stating "[since] neither party [MBB and Boeing] filed a protective appeal against Texaco pursuant to Fed. R. App. P. 4(a)(3), we dismiss the appeal with respect to Texaco." Id. at 498. The court also observed that "MBB and Boeing do not fall within any of the exceptional circumstances in which the appellate courts have exercised their discretionary powers." Id.

2. The Seventh Circuit has written: "Although appellate courts have 'discretionary power to retain all parties in the lawsuit [on] remand ... to insure an equitable resolution at trial,' Bryant v. Technical Research Co., 654 F.2d 1337, 1342 (9th Cir. 1981), this discretion has been exercised only in narrowly defined situations: when the reversal 'wipes out all basis for recovery against the nonappealing, as well as against the appealing defendant,' Daniels v. Gilbreath, 668 F.2d 477 (10th Cir. 1982); Kicklighter v.

Nails by Jannee, Inc., 616 F.2d 734, 742–45 (5th Cir. 1980); when the failure to reverse with respect to the nonappealing party will frustrate the execution of the judgment in favor of the successful appellant, In re Barnett, 124 F.2d 1005, 1008–12 (2d Cir. 1942); or when the appealed decision could reasonably be read as not being adverse to the nonappealing party. Bryant, 654 F.2d at 1342–43." Young Radiator Co. v. Celotex Corp., 881 F.2d 1408 (7th Cir. 1989).

3.   So far as the "rule of practice" approach is followed by the Supreme Court on certiorari, it seems only to limit the rights of a respondent who has not cross-petitioned to seek to sustain the judgment of the court of appeals on a different basis than that relied on by the court of appeals. See, e.g., United States v. ITT Continental Baking Co., 420 U.S. 223, 95 S.Ct. 926, 929 n.2, 43 L.Ed.2d 148 (1975):

> Respondent recognizes that, not having cross-petitioned, it cannot attack the judgment insofar as it sustained the findings of violations and imposed penalties for such violations. United States v. American Railway Express Co., 265 U.S. 425, 435, 44 S.Ct. 560, 563, 68 L.Ed. 1087 (1924). Cf. Morley Construction Co. v. Maryland Casualty Co., 300 U.S. 185, 57 S.Ct. 325, 81 L.Ed. 593 (1937). Respondent argues that it may nevertheless seek to sustain the Court of Appeals' limitation on the penalties on the theory that no penalty should have been awarded at all. Ordinarily, however, as a matter of practice and control of our docket, if not of our power, we do not entertain a challenge to a decision on the merits where the only petition for certiorari presents solely a question as to the remedy granted for a liability found to exist, even if the respondent is willing to accept whatever judgment has already been entered against him.

This contrasts with the absolute duty of the court of appeals to rule on issues properly presented by appellee and preserved below which would result in affirmance of the district court's judgment, albeit on a different ground and even though no cross-appeal has been taken. Massachusetts Mutual Life Ins. Co. v. Ludwig, 426 U.S. 479, 96 S.Ct. 2158, 2159, 48 L.Ed.2d 784 (1976)(set forth earlier in this Section of the Casebook).

4.   It follows from the general principles discussed in this Chapter that a party may need to file a protective notice of cross appeal in some instances. Suppose your client won some and lost some in the trial court, and on balance is not unhappy with the outcome. On the 31st day after the judgment, the adversary appeals. There is a good argument under the basic timing rules that the appellant's case should be dismissed on appeal for the jurisdictional defect of being untimely. However, what if there could be some basis for allowing the late appeal? Given that the opponent has appealed, and for the time being that appeal is pending, one may need to file a "protective" notice of cross appeal, essentially to preserve the option to raise the adverse rulings below in the event that the opponent is allowed to pursue the late appeal on the points won in the trial court.

5.   In some instances a party may lodge a "conditional" cross-appeal. As the Federal Circuit has said in patent cases: "[A] party who prevails on noninfringement has no right to file a 'conditional' cross-appeal to introduce new argument or challenge a claim construction, but may simply assert

alternative grounds in the record for affirming the judgment." Phillips v. AWH Corp., 363 F.3d 1207, 1216 (Fed. Cir. 2004). However that same court has cautioned: "It is only necessary and appropriate to file a cross-appeal when a party seeks to enlarge its own rights under the judgment or to lessen the rights of its adversary under the judgment." Bailey v. Dart Container Corp. Of Mich., 292 F.3d 1360, 1362 (Fed. Cir. 2002). Thus, a cross-appeal is proper only when acceptance of the argument advanced "would result in a reversal or modification of the judgment rather than an affirmance." Id.

6. The nature of a conditional cross-appeal is to say to the appellate court, *in the event* that you are disposed to reverse the lower court on the grounds assigned by that court, please consider these other arguments which were preserved in the trial court, and while the trial judge did not decide the case on this basis, they uphold the validity of the outcome below. In a protective cross-appeal, a party who is generally pleased with the judgment and would have otherwise declined to appeal, will cross-appeal to insure that any errors against his interests are reviewed so that if the main appeal results in modification of the judgment his grievances will be determined as well. Hartman v. Duffey, 19 F.3d 1459, 1465 (D.C. Cir. 1994). A protective cross-appeal differs from a cross-appeal because the protective cross-appel-lant is not necessarily "dissatisfied with the judgment." Id. Appellate courts generally allow protective cross-appeals but do not consider them unless it is appropriate to do so after disposition of the appeal. Id. at 1465–66.

7. "Cross-appeals for the sole purpose of making an argument in support of the judgment are worse than unnecessary. They disrupt the briefing schedule, increasing from three to four the number of briefs, and they make the case less readily understandable to the judges. The arguments will be distributed over more papers, which also tend to be longer. Unless a party requests the alteration of the judgment in its favor, it should not file a notice of appeal. Jordan v. Duff & Phelps, Inc., 815 F.2d 429, 439 (7th Cir. 1987). These comments are doubly appropriate when parties overlay their dispute with a further quarrel regarding the propriety of a cross-appeal." Boehringer Ingelheim Vetmedica, Inc. v. Schering-Plough Corporation, 320 F.3d 1339 (Fed. Cir. 2003).

8. If the district court enters a judgment that denies all relief to a plaintiff, and the plaintiff appeals from that judgment, a defendant-appellee seeking to uphold the judgment need not cross-appeal and may urge affir-mance on any ground appearing in the record (appellate court may affirm on any ground supported by the record, even if not relied upon by the district court). If the court of appeals agrees with the plaintiff-appellant and alters the judgment in some way, it provides relief that was not provided by the district court, and thereby "enlarges" the rights of the plaintiff-appellant and "lessens" the rights of the defendant-appellee. But if the court of appeals agrees with the defendant-appellee and sustains the judgment, it only affirms what the district court did. Even if it affirms on the alternative ground, its decision leaves the parties where the district court left them. In that event, the court of appeals does not "enlarge" the rights of the defendant-appellee or "lessen" the rights of the plaintiff-appellant. Rivero v. City and County of San Francisco, 316 F.3d 857 (9th Cir. 2002).

9. Imagine a case where the plaintiff brings numerous § 1983 theories against government and non-state actors, but some theories are abandoned by the plaintiff and others are dismissed at the trial level. Plaintiff is allowed to go to trial and recovers a judgment solely on the theory of malicious prosecution. On appeal by the defendants, plaintiff does not cross appeal. The appellate court invalidates the concept of suing under § 1983 for malicious prosecution, but remands the case for new trial on all of the plaintiff's other theories. Is this outcome a mistake under cross-appeal principles? Does an appellate judgment *invalidating* a judgment stand on the same footing for granting the appellee relief he has not asked for as a situation where the appellee (who has not filed a cross-appeal) seeks to uphold the trial court's judgment on a ground other than that relied upon by the trial court itself? See Castellano v. Fragozo, 352 F.3d 939 (5th Cir. 2003)(en banc decision in which the majority provides the plaintiff with such relief, over the dissent of some of the judges on that court that "the majority mistakenly stretches this rule far beyond its intended scope. [O]ur court is not affirming a judgment; instead, we are vacating a judgment premised on a jury's verdict based on a malicious prosecution, not a due process, claim. [T]he exception to the cross-appeal rule only applies where the appellee urges affirmation on the basis of a claim rejected by the district court; Castellano did not do so. He was quite satisfied with, and clung tenaciously to, his judgment based on malicious prosecution.") Which side has the stronger argument here in cases where the judgment is being reversed on appeal? Is it appropriate to give the appellee a second chance below by authorizing retrial on issues that were not appealed in the first instance?

10. In the event that the appellant's appeal is unsuccessful, protective or conditional cross-appeals are normally dismissed, denied as moot, or simply not addressed. As one appellate court said: "Upon review, we conclude that we need not address the defendants' protective cross-appeal because the plaintiffs' appeal has been dismissed. The defendants' protective cross-appeal was dependent upon the plaintiffs' appeal such that the dismissal of the plaintiffs' appeal warrants dismissal of the defendants' cross-appeal. See Abrams v. Lightolier Inc., 50 F.3d 1204, 1211, 1213 (3d Cir. 1995); Moore v. Subaru of Am., 891 F.2d 1445,1453 (10th Cir. 1989); see also Avery Prods. Corp. v. Morgan Adhesives Co., 496 F.2d 254, 258 (6th Cir. 1974). Indeed, Conwood agrees with this result, as footnote six of its appellate brief states that 'because this Court has dismissed Anderson's and Hollingsworth's direct appeal, Conwood wishes to abandon its cross-appeal.'" Anderson v. Roberson, 90 Fed. Appx. 886 (6th Cir. 2004).

11. Consider Rangolan v. County of Nassau, 370 F.3d 239 (2d Cir. 2004) in which a an inmate was severely beaten by another detainee, and recovered a judgment for $820,000 against the County and its Sheriff's Department. The United States Marshal's Service sought $4,792 for transporting the victim to and from court appearances in the action, and protecting him, either from the plaintiffs or from the defendants. The trial court awarded recovery of the costs from the defendants. On appeal, in the face of arguments that costs were not recoverable from the County, the government asked the court of appeals to declare that these costs were recoverable from the plaintiffs. Judge Kearse wrote:

[T]he government, while it does not lack standing, has done nothing to preserve its right to assert in this Court a right to reimbursement from the Rangolans. The district court expressly rejected the contention that the Marshals Service expenses should be taxed against the Rangolans. If the government wished to have that determination reversed, it was incumbent on the government to file a cross-appeal, at least conditionally challenging that ruling in the event that this Court overturned the taxation of costs in favor of USMS against the County. See, e.g., Morley Construction Co. v. Maryland Casualty Co., 300 U.S. 185, 191, 57 S.Ct. 325, 81 L.Ed. 593 (1937) (an appellee generally "may not . . . in the absence of a cross-appeal . . . attack the [district court's] decree with a view either to enlarging his own rights thereunder or of lessening the rights of his adversary, whether what he seeks is to correct an error or to supplement the decree with respect to a matter not dealt with below" (internal quotation marks omitted)); see also Kaplan v. Rand, 192 F.3d 60, 67 (2d Cir. 1999) (a "nonparty may appeal when the nonparty has an interest that is affected by the trial court's judgment" (internal quotation marks omitted)). Although "the requirement of a cross-appeal is a rule of practice which is not jurisdictional and in appropriate circumstances may be disregarded," Finkielstain v. Seidel, 857 F.2d 893, 895 (2d Cir. 1988), "exercise of the power [to disregard the failure to cross-appeal] has been rare, . . . requiring a showing of exceptional circumstances," 15A C. Wright, A. Miller & E. Cooper, Federal Practice and Procedure § 3904, at 228 (2d ed. 1992). No such circumstances have been suggested here. This appeal was reinstated by the County's filing of a new notice of appeal in April 2003. The government not only did not file a notice of cross-appeal, it did not even file a brief in opposition to the County's appeal until expressly requested by this Court to do so in 2004.

12.   An exception to this general rule permits the prevailing party to cross-appeal from a summary judgment in its favor if a collateral adverse ruling can serve as the basis for collateral estoppel in subsequent litigation. Ruvalcaba v. City of Los Angeles, 167 F.3d 514, 520 (9th Cir. 1999). However, only findings necessary to the judgment could conceivably have collateral estoppel effect in other cases, and hence incidental or immaterial recitals by the trial court will not sustain a cross-appeal. See Pension Trust Fund for Operating Engineers v. Federal Insurance Co., 307 F.3d 944 (9th Cir. 2002).

13.   While ordinarily an appellee need not file a cross-appeal in order to rely upon any matter appearing in the record in support of the judgment below, see Blum v. Bacon, 457 U.S. 132, 137 n.5, 102 S.Ct. 2355, 72 L.Ed.2d 728 (1982), this rule has a somewhat uncertain application when a habeas petitioner seeks affirmance on the basis of a constitutional claim after the enactment of the Antiterrorism and Effective Death Penalty Act. Prudence has led some courts to treat a cross-appeal as an application for a "certificate of appealability" so as to comply with current rules. See, e.g., Szuchon v. Lehman, 273 F.3d 299 (3rd Cir. 2001).

14.   Consider the issue of sanctions. In one case where a police officer wrote a letter to the local paper supporting his embattled chief, and was later fired after the chief was replaced, the officer sued the locality and the

Fraternal Order of Police on numerous state and federal theories for conspiracy to injure him. The defendants won the case on summary judgment, but the trial judge refused the police union's request that the court slap the plaintiff with attorney's fee sanctions for bringing unnecessary litigation. The plaintiff officer appealed but the FOP did not file a cross-appeal. In response to the union's arguments in appellate papers that the trial judge abused his discretion in failing to award fees for truly baseless litigation, the appellate court said:

> Because the FOP failed to file a cross-appeal, we do not consider its request for this Court to decide whether Mr. Montgomery should have been awarded attorneys' fees. It is well-recognized that an appellee who has failed to file a cross-appeal cannot "attack the decree with a view either to enlarging his own rights thereunder or of lessening the rights of his adversary." Burgo v. Gen. Dynamics Corp., 122 F.3d 140, 145 (2d Cir. 1997) (quoting Morley Constr. Co. v. Maryland Cas. Co., 300 U.S. 185, 191, 57 S.Ct. 325, 81 L.Ed. 593 (1937) (Cardozo, J.)); see Int'l Ore & Fertilizer Corp. v. SGS Control Servs., Inc., 38 F.3d 1279, 1286 (2d Cir. 1994) ("Although an appellee who has not cross-appealed may urge alternative grounds for affirmance [of the judgment], it may not seek to enlarge its rights under the judgment by enlarging the amount of damages or scope of equitable relief.").

Montgomery v. City of Ardmore, 365 F.3d 926 (10th Cir. 2004).

15.   The federal government not infrequently takes a cross-appeal in a criminal case to challenge the "downward departure" of a trial judge from the sentencing guidelines. See, e.g., United States v. Lang, 364 F.3d 1210 (10th Cir. 2004). Is this practice a form of "conditional cross-appeal"? Will the government's cross-appeal be reached on the merits if the defendants successfully challenge their convictions? In other instances, such as when the trial court dismisses some counts of an indictment, and the defendant is convicted on others, when the defendant appeals the conviction the government's cross-appeal is not really "conditional" is it? Why not? See United States v. Carucci, 364 F.3d 339 (1st Cir. 2004).

16.   Consider this puzzle: where criminal defendants were awarded a new trial *by the trial judge*, and the government appealed, the defendants attempted to cross-appeal the district court's failure to grant their motions for outright acquittal on three counts of the indictment. The appellate court ducked: "Because the district court did not rule on these motions, we dismiss the cross-appeal for lack of jurisdiction." See United States v. Viayra, 365 F.3d 790 (9th Cir. 2004). Was this not an effort by the defendants to "improve" their position under the trial court's disposition? Assuming that the defendants had fully developed their arguments for outright dismissal of the charges, and received only a new trial, why should they not be allowed to raise their grounds on appeal?

17.   Courts generally express concern about exercising pendent appellate jurisdiction, a "disfavored" exercise of federal judicial power, where the the issues involved in a cross-appeal are not "inextricably

intertwined" with the appealable order. Swint v. Chambers County Comm'n, 514 U.S. 35, 51, 115 S.Ct. 1203, 131 L.Ed.2d 60 (1995); see also Armijo v. Wagon Mound Public Schs., 159 F.3d 1253, 1265 (10th Cir. 1998) (refusing to exercise pendent appellate jurisdiction to consider cross-appeal in case in which proper interlocutory appeal on qualified immunity is before the court); Erickson v. Holloway, 77 F.3d 1078, 1081 (8th Cir. 1996) (same); Woods v. Smith, 60 F.3d 1161, 1167 (5th Cir. 1995) (same). Issues of qualified immunity frequently raise this issue. In one case, the court said:

> Our jurisdiction over Plaintiffs' cross-appeal, however, is less certain. Plaintiffs cross-appeal the district court's partial grant of qualified immunity to Officer Hall. The jurisdictional exception for qualified immunity cases—allowing interlocutory appeals from the denial of qualified immunity—does not encompass Plaintiffs' cross-appeal. So, we have jurisdiction of Plaintiffs' cross-appeal only if it properly falls within our pendent appellate jurisdiction.
>
> Under the pendent appellate jurisdiction doctrine, we "may address [otherwise] nonappealable orders if they are 'inextricably intertwined' with an appealable decision or if 'review of the former decision [is] necessary to ensure meaningful review of the latter.' " Summit Med. Assoc., P.C. v. Pryor, 180 F.3d 1326, 1335 (11th Cir. 1999); see also Swint v. Chambers County Com'n, 514 U.S. 35, 50–51, 115 S.Ct. 1203, 1212, 131 L.Ed.2d 60 (1995); Tamiami Partners, Ltd. v. Miccosukee Tribe of Indians of Fla., 177 F.3d 1212, 1221–22 (11th Cir. 1999).
>
> As we have explained, we independently have jurisdiction of Officer Hall's appeal. Because the issues raised by Plaintiffs' cross-appeal are sufficiently related to and intertwined with Officer Hall's appeal, we conclude that Plaintiffs' cross-appeal of the partial grant of qualified immunity to Officer Hall falls within our pendent appellate jurisdiction. See Lopez–Lukis, 102 F.3d at 1167 n. 10 (finding issues sufficiently related to permit exercise of pendent appellate jurisdiction); cf. Tamiami Partners, 177 F.3d at 1221–22 (concluding issues not sufficiently related to permit exercise of pendent appellate jurisdiction). For the sake of judicial economy, we choose to exercise this pendent appellate jurisdiction over Plaintiffs' cross-appeal of the partial grant of qualified immunity to Officer Hall.

Hudson v. Hall, 231 F.3d 1289 (11th Cir. 2000)(§ 1983 action arising out of a traffic stop; the court noted that the totality of circumstances test applied to the officer's appeal, making decision of plaintiff's issues particularly appropriate).

18. Cross-appeals that are not briefed are deemed to have been abandoned. See, e.g., Johnson v. Wyandotte County, 371 F.3d 723 (10th Cir. 2004).

SECTION H.   PERFECTING THE APPEAL

Following the filing of the notice of appeal, the appellant and court personnel must take several other steps necessary to "perfect" the appeal. These include the payment of any necessary filing and docketing fees, the sending of certain information to the appellate court such as copies of the notice of appeal and the trial court docket entries, ordering the transcript, sending the record to the appellate court, and the filing of a bond for costs. The requirements as to the record, including provisions for generation of a printed transcript, are explored in Chapter 7. For a discussion of the other requirements, see R. Martineau, Modern Appellate Practice—Federal and State Civil Appeals §§ 6.10–6.12 (1983).

1. OVERVIEW OF THE STEPS IN COMPLETING THE APPEAL

After a timely notice of appeal has been lodged, and leading up to the expected oral argument, there are several additional required steps, often referred to as "perfecting" the appeal. While federal circuits and state courts differ in how draconian a view to take of the failure to promptly complete these steps, there is no doubt that they are important and, in a given case, failure to complete any of these steps can lose the appeal. Starting with the notice, there are seven major steps or phases in completing the appeal, some with subparts. Here is an overview:

STEP ONE: Timely Filing the Required Notice in the District Court

As noted in preceding sections of this Chapter, appeals from the district court as a matter of right are taken by filing a notice of appeal with the clerk of the district court within the time prescribed. This is the key first step in "perfecting" the appeal.

STEP TWO: Pay the Required Filing and Docketing Fees

Unless a party is given permission to proceed *in forma pauperis* (a process recognized in the federal courts by statute and by statute or rule in many—but not all—states, under which a person demonstrates indigence and is given permission to proceed without paying the fees required of solvent litigants) it is necessary to pay a "filing fee" to the trial court clerk's office for filing the notice of appeal as a trial court document, and a separate fee increment as a "docketing fee" in the Court of Appeals. In the federal system, the trial-level clerk collects both fees. As this edition of the Casebook goes to press, federal clerks' offices collect a $5 filing fee for the notice of appeal, and a $250 docketing charge for lodging the appeal in the appellate court. See 28 U.S.C. § 1913 for the governing statutory provisions in federal cases. State fees are usually less than those for filing a federal appeal, and are adjusted frequently by state legislatures and rules promulgation bodies in the various states.

STEP THREE: Arrange Any Needed Bonds

Bond for Costs on Appeal in Civil Cases. A bond for costs on appeal may be required by the district court with the notice of appeal in civil cases. This potential requirement is not regularly required. It is discussed in the last section of the present Chapter of this Casebook.

Supersedeas Bonds. As noted in Chapter 6, if the appellant desires relief from the effects of the trial court judgment, a different form of bond, known as a *supersedeas bond* must be obtained.

While a bond for costs is only occasionally required, and is a small undertaking, a supersedeas bond is required to hold off the effect of the trial court's judgment, and the size of a supersedeas bond can be very substantial. This topic is explored in Chapter 6 of the Casebook.

STEP FOUR: Arranging for the Record to be Produced

Civil, criminal and Tax Court cases. The record on appeal consists of the original papers and exhibits, filed with the district court or Tax Court, the transcript of proceedings, if any, and a certified copy of the docket entries prepared by the clerk of the court. The topic is discussed in detail in Chapter 7 and only a short description of the process is presented here to complete an overview.

Within 10 days after filing of a notice of appeal, the appellant is to order from the reporter a transcript of such part of the proceedings not already on file as is thought proper to include. Notwithstanding the requirement that the appellant order a transcript within 10 days after the filing of the notice of appeal, parties are urged to order the necessary parts of the transcript immediately after the filing of the notice of appeal. If the appellant does not include the entire transcript, appellant must file and serve on the appellee a description of what appellant intends to include in the transcript and a statement of the issues he intends to present on the appeal, so that the appellee may designate additional parts to be included. Rules provide that only those parts of the transcript should be ordered which relate to the issues to be raised on appeal.

Upon receipt of the order for a transcript the reporter must acknowledge at the foot of the order the fact that it has been received and the date on which he expects to have the transcript completed. A copy of the order, so endorsed, must be forwarded to the Clerk of the Court of Appeals by the reporter.

Where, as is sometimes the case, a complete transcript is obtained during the trial for the judge's use and is filed with the clerk, no further designation is made; but the parties are free to print in the appendix only so much of the transcript as seems pertinent to the appeal.

If no transcript is available, under F.R.App.P. 10(c) the appellant may prepare a statement of the evidence or proceedings from the best available means, including his recollection, and serve it on the appellee, who may serve objections or proposed amendments within 10 days. The district court then settles and approves the statement and objections or amendments, and the result is included in the record on appeal.

The parties may prepare and sign a statement of the case in lieu of the record on appeal. The statement should contain how the issues on appeal arose and were decided in the district court including the essential and relevant facts averred and proved or sought to be proved. This statement should be submitted to the district court for approval, and then certified as the record on appeal.

Disputes about the correctness or composition of the record should be decided in the trial court, although the Court of Appeals has power, either on motion or of its own accord, to require that the record be corrected or amplified.

Administrative agencies. The record on review consists of the order sought to be reviewed or enforced, the findings or report on which it is based, and the pleadings, evidence, and proceedings before the agency. The record may be corrected or supplemented by stipulation or by order of the Court of Appeals.

STEP FIVE: Filing Docketing Forms & Statements in the Appellate Court

United States Courts of Appeal require filing of various forms in conjunction with the commencement of an appeal.

Appearance. In many circuits, whenever any matter is docketed in the Court of Appeals, an "entry of appearance" form bearing only the docket number will be sent by the clerk to all counsel (or the parties, if not represented by counsel) of record in the court or agency whence the matter emanated. Only counsel for parties participating in the appeal should complete and return the appearance form. The title of the case, the name and address of counsel (or the party), and the name, address, and telephone number of the firm.

Docketing statement. Some circuits (e.g., the Tenth) have required a "docketing statement" in addition to any filing forms prescribed by the Administrative Office of the United States Courts. A docketing statement may require such information as:

- The statutory authority believed to confer jurisdiction on this court to hear the appeal. In multi-party or multi-issue cases, particular attention should be paid to Fed.R.Civ.P. 54(b);

- A concise statement of the nature of the proceeding, e.g., this appeal is from a final order of the district court or this petition is for review of an order of an administrative agency;

- The date of the judgment or order sought to be reviewed; the date of any order respecting a motion pursuant to Fed.R.Civ.P. 50(b), 52(b), or 59, and the date the notice of appeal or petition for review or enforcement was filed;

- A concise statement of the case containing facts material to a consideration of the questions presented;

- The questions presented by the appeal, expressed in terms and circumstances of the case but without unnecessary detail. One local appellate rule states: "The questions should be brief and not repetitious. General conclusory statements such as 'the judgment of the trial court is not supported by the law or facts' are unacceptable";

- A statement setting forth the reasons why in the party's opinion, oral argument should be heard;

- A reference to all related or prior appeals. If the reference is to a prior appeal, the appropriate citation should be given.

Where used, docketing statements are primarily helpful in determining which of the court's calendar tracks will be used in scheduling an appeal. Additionally, docketing statements enhance the court's ability to monitor pending appeals and to identify at the initial stages those cases which involve: complex and/or multiple issues requiring more detailed consideration; less substantial issues requiring less detailed consideration; or jurisdictional defects (e.g., non-appealable orders, untimely notices of appeal). The docketing statement is not a brief. It should not contain argument or procedural motions.

Corporate Disclosure Statement. Rule 26.1 of the F.R.App.P. requires filing as part of the briefing of a statement identifying corporations, parents, subsidiaries and affiliates of named parties, to facilitate recognition of judicial conflicts of interest. By local rule, some circuits require such statements to be filed in advance of the briefing.

STEP SIX: Transmitting the Record (and any exhibits to be included)

Civil, Criminal and Tax Court cases. The record on appeal is to be transmitted to the Court of Appeals from the district court or the Tax Court as soon as required transcripts have been lodged there, and if transcripts are not required as soon as practicable after designation. The appeal is docketed in the Court of Appeals upon receipt of the notice of appeal and of a certified copy of the docket sheet of the district court. [Fed.R.App.P. 3(d).] Unless the required docketing fee is paid to the clerk of the District Court or Tax Court when the appeal is filed, it must be paid within ten days or the appeal is subject to dismissal. Notice of docketing of the appeal is sent to all parties. The appeal is docketed under the same title as in the district court with the appropriate parties designated as appellant or appellee. The title may be changed, however, to delete any party no longer involved in the matter at the appellate level. All further actions regarding progression of the appeal are controlled by the court of appeals from the time of docketing in the court of appeals.

The record is transmitted to the court of appeals when the transcript is complete. It is expected that the transcript will be completed and the record transmitted within 30 days of the date of the final order for parts of the transcript. If the transcript cannot be completed within the 30 day period contemplated by F.R.App.P. 11, the reporter must request an extension from the clerk of the court of appeals. Any extension granted by the clerk must be entered on the docket and the parties are notified. When the reporter files the transcript with the clerk of the district court he must notify the clerk of the court of appeals that he has done so. The clerk of the district court must then transmit the entire record forthwith to the clerk of the court of appeals.

The parties may agree, or on motion the district court may order, that the record be temporarily retained in the district court for use in preparing appellant's appendices and briefs. The district court may also on its own motion direct retention of the record for its use in ongoing proceedings. In such cases the clerk of the district court transmits a certificate of readiness indicating that the record is complete for purposes of the appeal. When the record is retained the Clerk of the district court will ordinarily transmit the record at the time the appellee's brief is served and filed, subject to agreement by the parties to earlier transmission. The appellant is responsible for notifying the clerk of the district court that appellee's brief has been served. The parties may also agree that parts of the record be retained indefinitely in the trial court unless the Court of Appeals or any party requests their transmittal. if such a stipulation is filed, the parts of the record designated therein need not be sent to the Court of Appeals absent request by the Court or of a party to do so.

Failure of the appellant to cause the record to be timely transmitted or to pay the docket fee (unless he is exempt) is ground for dismissal of the appeal.

Exhibits are generally not required to be transmitted as part of the record. If exhibits are a necessary part of the record, the attorney or party having possession of the designated exhibits must file such exhibits with the clerk of the district court so that they can be transmitted to the clerk of the Court of Appeals along with the rest of the record. Unusually large, heavy, or bulky exhibits are generally excluded from this transmission requirement. It is the responsibility of each party to produce the designated exhibits at the argument and to make them available to the court if so requested.

Administrative agencies. Within 40 days of the filing of the petition for review or application for enforcement (unless the statute authorizing review fixes a different time), the administrative agency transmits the record to the Court of Appeals.

The agency may file the entire record or only such parts as the parties agree to by stipulation filed with the agency; or it may file a certified list and description of all the papers comprising the record before it, or of such parts as the parties agree upon by stipulation. If the actual record (or portion thereof designated by stipulation filed with the agency) has not been filed with this Court by the date on which appellee's brief is filed, the Court will order the agency to forthwith prepare and forward the record. The date on which the first of a stipulation, certified list or the actual record is filed in the Court of Appeals is considered the date on which the record is filed. If the entire record is not filed, the agency retains the record or segments of it, but any party or the Court of Appeals may require further materials to be transmitted. All portions of the record retained by the agency are still a part of the record on review for all purposes.

STEP SEVEN: Serving and Filing Briefs

Service of briefs is discussed in Chapter 8 of this Casebook. Suffice it to say here that it is necessary to timely complete and file the brief in order to have "perfected" the appeal. The following periods apply absent contrary local procedures:

Within 40 days after the record is filed, the appellant or petitioner must serve and file his brief, unless the Court otherwise orders.

Within 30 days after service of the appellant's brief, the appellee or respondent must serve and file his answering brief.

Within 14 days after service of the appellee's brief, appellant or petitioner may serve a reply brief, but it must be served at least 3 days before argument. To dispose of the Court's business a case may be reached prior to the filing of a reply brief, in which case application must be made to the Court for leave to file a reply.

The court may shorten the periods prescribed above for serving and filing briefs, either by rule for all cases or classes of cases, or by order for specific cases.

As might be imagined, the federal courts of appeal do not look with favor upon applications for extensions of time for the filing of briefs and appendices. In order to keep the docket reasonably current, such applications generally are denied. And applications for extensions of time for the filing of briefs and appendices in criminal cases are not granted except in the most extraordinary circumstances.

STEP EIGHT: Preparing and Serving Appendix (if used in this Appellate Court)

Nature of the Appendix. As is explored in Chapter 8 of this Casebook, the appendix is in effect "the vitals" of the record. It is those parts of the record which the parties desire each judge to have before him as he studies the briefs. While the entire original record or designated portions thereof will most likely have been transmitted to the clerk of the Court of Appeals, it would be cumbersome for all the judges to refer to that record. On the other hand, to require the entire record to be reproduced for each of the judges would be burdensome to the parties and would present each judge with more than may be necessary to a just disposition of the case, especially since many points raised in the trial may not be pertinent to the issues raised on appeal. The appendix enables the parties to reduce the record to manageable size.

In some circuits, the requirement for an appendix has been severely limited by local rules reflecting streamlined processes. Some categories of cases may be exempted from the requirement to create an appendix (e.g., appeals from denials of Social Security benefits or habeas corpus petitions), or an appendix may be required only if the trial record exceeds a set number of pages (e.g., 300 pages).

The appellant has the duty to prepare and file the appendix, but the parties are encouraged to agree on the contents. The parties and the court may rely on any material in the record, even if it is not included in the appendix, although excessive reference to the original record should not be necessary if the appendix is properly prepared.

Purpose. An appendix to the briefs should contain only those parts of the record which the parties believe are essential for each judge to have before him when he studies the briefs. Ten copies of the appendix are required. However, the appendix is not the record, and the judges are not restricted to examining the material the parties put in the appendix. Portions of the transcript contained in the appendix shall be suitably indexed.

Usual method of preparation. If the parties do not agree on the contents of the appendix, the appellant must serve on the appellee a designation of the parts of the record he intends to include in the appendix, and a statement of the issues be intends to present for review. This designation and statement must be served not later than 10 days after the record is filed. The appellee has 10 days after receiving the designation to cross-designate anything he thinks is necessary and should be included which the appellant has omitted, and the appellant must include it in the appendix but he may require appellee to advance the necessary cost. The appellant must file the appendix with his brief unless the court allows it to be deferred. 10 copies are filed with the clerk, and 1 copy served on counsel for each party separately represented. Thus fewer copies of the appendix than of the brief are served and filed.

Deferred preparation of the appendix. Fed.R.App.P. 30(c), provides that the preparation of the appendix by the appellant may be deferred until after the briefs have been filed, and the appendix may be filed 21 days after the service of the brief of appellee. If the preparation and filing of the appendix is thus deferred, the provisions of subdivision (b) of Rule 30 apply. References in the briefs to the record may be to the pages of the parts of the record involved, in which event the original paging of each part of the record shall be indicated in the appendix by placing in brackets the number of each page at the place in the appendix where that page begins. The index to the appendix should show both the record page and appendix page. Or if a party desires to refer in the brief directly to pages of the appendix, the party may serve and file a copy of his brief within the time required by Fed.R.App.P. 31(a), with appropriate references to the pages of the parts of the record involved. Only one copy of this preliminary brief should be filed in court. Within 14 days after the appendix is filed, the parties then serve and file the required number of copies of the brief in the form prescribed by Rule 32(a), containing references to the pages of the appendix in place of or in addition to the initial references to the pages of the parts of the record involved. No other changes may be made in the brief as initially served and filed, except that typographical errors may be corrected.

Contents of appendix. In each case the appendix must contain the relevant docket entries in the proceedings below; relevant portions of the pleadings, charge, findings, or opinion; the judgment, order, or decision in question; and any other parts of the record (usually the transcript and exhibits) to which the parties wish to direct the court's attention. The appendix is required to have the date of filing or of entry of each pleading, judgment, decree, order, decision, or other document set out at the beginning; and each document contained in the appendix must conform to the original as to content, dates, and signatures. Inclusions in the appendix are arranged chronologically but the exhibits may be separately bound.

When an appendix is filed, it should contain the findings or opinion and other parts of the record, such as portions of the pleadings or charge, which are essential to a determination of the issues on appeal. If the parties jointly agree on what the appendix should contain, so much the better.

At the beginning of any appendix should be a table of contents describing each item included therein (e.g., relevant docket entries, pleadings, judgment) and listing the appendix page on which each of these items can be found. The table of contents is followed by the relevant items in chronological order. If the appendix contains portions of the transcript of proceedings, the table of contents should include an index of those portions.

Method of citing record. Local rules often control the format of record references. Typically, a part of the record reproduced in an appendix may be cited by making reference to page numbers within the appendix (e.g., App. 247; II App. 749). When no appendix is filed, citations must be to the original pages of the record (e.g., R.O.A. at 27; TR. at 59).

2.   THE BOND FOR "COSTS" ON THE APPEAL

Recovery of Costs. In the federal courts and those of many states, there is a possibility for the party who wins an appeal to recover the "costs" of appealing. This is a small exception to "the American Rule" about recovery of one's litigation expenses, which is generally that each party bears its own attorneys' fees and expenses, and the winner does not have the option to collect those fees from the loser, absent some contractual provision or statute that expressly changes the groundrules by clearly creating a right to recover specific expenses. By rule of court in the federal system, a victorious part can recover costs at the trial court level (usually limited to filing fees and transcription fees). See F.R.Civ.P. 68. The appellate rule in the federal system is Rule 39, which provides that—unless the substantive law is to the contrary, or the court orders otherwise—"costs are taxed" against the parties (but not the United States government) as follows:

  (1) if an appeal is dismissed, costs are taxed against the appellant, unless the parties agree otherwise;

  (2) if a judgment is affirmed, costs are taxed against the appellant;

  (3) if a judgment is reversed, costs are taxed against the appellee;

(4) if a judgment is affirmed in part, reversed in part, modified, or vacated, costs are taxed only as the court orders.

Taxable costs normally relate to the costs of producing the appellate papers, and Rule 39 goes on to make specific provisions to keep copying costs under control by requiring local courts of appeal to specify the copying charges standard in various communities. The rule sets up procedures for the prevailing party on the appeal to file the "bill of costs" claiming the recoverable charges, and it allows for an objection procedure.

Interestingly, the party entitled to recover costs files the bill of costs with the appellate court's clerk, for inclusion in the "mandate" issued by the appellate court. Costs on appeal are actually taxable (hence collected) in the district court, however. And on occasion the district court clerk must complete the finalization of the recoverable costs after the appellate court's mandate has been issued.

Current Rule 39 of the Federal Rules of Appellate procedure lists these costs incurred during the appeal as recoverable:

(1) the preparation and transmission of the record;

(2) the reporter's transcript, if needed to determine the appeal;

(3) premiums paid for a supersedeas bond or other bond to preserve rights pending appeal; and

(4) the fee for filing the notice of appeal.

Putting aside item (3) temporarily, one may accurately surmise that in most appeals costs are not huge sums. Transcription of a four-day trial record may cost $4,000 in per–page typing fees, and copying of the record, printing of the briefs and filing fees may be a few hundred to a few thousand dollars. Some federal courts of appeals have held, however, that in statutory causes of action where the legislation allows recovery of attorneys' fees "as a part of costs" it is appropriate for the appeal bond to reflect an estimate of the attorneys' fees the non-appealing party will incur as a result of appeal. See Adsani v. Miller, 139 F.3d 67, 74 (2nd Cir. 1998) (Copyright cause of action); Montgomery & Assocs. v. CFTC, 816 F.2d 783, 784 (D.C. Cir. 1987)(similar statutory provision). Where, however, the right to recover fees is more general (not defined as a recovery "as costs") the prevailing party will need to pursue recovery of those fees without using the bond mechanism. See, e.g., O'Keefe v. Mercedes–Benz USA, 2003 WL 1826501 (E.D. Pa. 2003) (plaintiff in a product liability class action sought "a cost based appeal bond totaling $268,467." The requested bond covered copying, printing, and reproduction costs in a complex case—and projected attorney's fees on appeal. Since there was no statute prescribing that fees be recovered "as part of costs," the bond was set at only $13,467).

Bond for Costs. In the federal system and similar state appellate regimes, the appealing party may be required to post a bond for the potentially recoverable costs to be incurred on appeal. Rule 7 of the F.R.App. P. provides:

Rule 7. Bond for Costs on Appeal in a Civil Case

In a civil case, the district court may require an appellant to file a bond or provide other security in any form and amount necessary to ensure payment of costs on appeal. Rule 8(b) applies to a surety on a bond given under this rule.

For many years the federal system automatically fixed this bond at $250. That provision is no longer in force, but such bonds are often still for relatively small amounts. One reason is that the appellant normally undertakes the bulk of the preparation expense (and, for example, may be the party that pays the principal transcription costs) so the function of the bond under Rule 7 is to insure the appellee of recovery of fees which it must incur as a result of the appellant's decision to appeal. In many systems, the clerk of court fixes the amount of the bond for costs, subject to supervision or revision by the trial judge.

Note

Failure of an appellant to file the bond for costs will not always be fatal to an appeal, but case law clearly states that it can be grounds for dismissal of the appeal. Compare Perry v. Pogemiller, 16 F.3d 138 (7th Cir. 1993) (failure to file bond for costs on appeal may warrant dismissal) with Carr v. Grace, 516 F.2d 502 (5th Cir. 1975)(court should be loathe to dismiss a putatively meritorious appeal for failure timely to file a bond for costs).

Chapter 6

RELIEF PENDING APPEAL

R. MARTINEAU, MODERN APPELLATE PRACTICE—
FEDERAL AND STATE CIVIL APPEALS

§ 7.1 (1983).

Almost as important as the fundamental question whether to take an appeal are issues relating to the need to seek some type of stay, injunction or other relief pending appeal. In many cases, if relief is not obtained the appeal will be moot, perhaps because the property in dispute will be destroyed or consumed, or because the losing party is not financially secure.

In every case with a dollar judgment there is the question whether the losing party will have the money to pay the amount awarded to the prevailing party if execution is put off for 18 months or two years by an appeal. In other cases the losing party may wish to enjoy the object of the judgment as long as possible or at least to deny the benefit of it to the winning party. Whatever the reason, when an attorney and the client discuss the possibility of appeal, they should also decide whether to seek relief while the appeal is pending, and if so, the type of relief to request. A variety of possibilities exist in civil practice. (Example Rules of Court are set forth in this Section of the Chapter, and case law is explored in ensuing Sections). In criminal cases, the modern rules also acknowledge the possibility of post-judgment relief on behalf of a convicted defendant, though the instances of such relief are far fewer (See Section D at the end of this Chapter).

Overlaying these questions is a general doctrine in American law that a case generally has only one locus: it is either "in" the trial court, or it is before the appellate tribunal. In the period immediately after a trial court judgment, however, both the trial and the appellate court may take actions concerning status of the judgment or order while an appeal is processed. Thus in considering procedural provisions for the various options that need exploration immediately after a judgment and pending an appeal, the civil and criminal trial level rules are juxtaposed with the similar provisions in the higher ranking appellate court. Which court can or will act becomes interesting.

SECTION A.   STAY OF THE TRIAL COURT JUDGMENT—GENERAL PRINCIPLES

Intuitively, one might think that taking an appeal would hold off the effectiveness of the trial court's disposition of a case until the higher court has ruled on whether the judgment is valid—and one might imagine that once an appeal is filed the trial court's judgment would be suspended until all possibilities for further appeal are exhausted. In practice it's not quite that simple.

Historically, English and American practice has vacillated over the effect of the writ of error as supersedeas and whether security was required either to obtain the writ of error in the first instance or for it to have a supersedeas effect. Similar confusion existed as to an appeal. For a description of these developments, see R. Pound, Appellate Procedure in Civil Cases 148–152 (1941) and R. Martineau, Modern Appellate Practice—Federal and State Civil Appeals § 7.2 (1983). Should the appeal itself be effective to interdict the judgment? In a few jurisdictions it still is. See Pa.R.App.P. 1731 (money judgments are stayed by the filing of a notice of appeal, without any further step).

Today in the federal courts, and those of most states, if no "stay" is obtained to preclude further steps, *even though an appeal is formally filed and validly pending* the party holding a judgment can arrange for property to be seized, and normal execution of judgment procedures will be available, such as attachment, selling off property at public auction, and garnishment of the debtor's wages.

The Rules do create an initial 10–day zone of protection for the losing party in money and property cases, known as the automatic stay, and other options spelled out in the rules of civil and appellate procedure require a focus on the nature of the outcome which a party seeks to appeal. However, not all judgments are subject to the automatic stay of enforcement, and after the first 10 days more steps are required even in cases where the automatic stay applies initially.

1.   THE AUTOMATIC STAY: THE FIRST 10 DAYS AFTER MONEY OR PROPERTY JUDGMENTS

Under Rule 62(a) of the F.R.Civ.P. there is an initial 10–day period in which "no execution shall issue upon a judgment involving monetary recovery or property rights nor shall proceedings be taken for its enforcement." This provision precludes a party from taking steps to enforce a judgment until the "the expiration of 10 days after its entry." This portion of civil Rule 62 provides:

(a) Automatic Stay; Exceptions—Injunctions, Receiverships, and Patent Accountings. Except as stated herein, no execution shall issue upon a judgment nor shall proceedings be taken for its enforcement until the expiration of 10 days after its entry. Unless otherwise ordered by the court, an interlocutory or final judgment in an action for an injunction or in a receivership action, or a judgment or order directing an accounting in an action for infringement of letters patent, shall not be stayed during the period after its entry and until an appeal is taken or during the pendency of an appeal. The provisions of subdivision (c) of this rule govern the suspending, modifying, restoring, or granting of an injunction during the pendency of an appeal.

Saturdays, Sundays and Legal Holidays. Two interesting points should be noted: (1) because this is a procedural rule setting a period of only 10 days, it is governed by Rule 6(a) of the F.R.Civ.P., which says that in calculating periods of less than 11 days, Saturdays, Sundays and legal holidays are *not counted*. This generous provision is not applicable to longer periods such as the 30–day period for filing a notice of appeal in a civil case, in which all intervening days, including weekends and holidays, *count*. (2) If the last day of the automatic stay period falls on a legal holiday or a weekend, the stay will continue in effect through the first day thereafter that is not a holiday or weekend day.

Injunctions and Other Exceptions: Rule 62(a), quoted above, does *not* automatically stay the effect of judgments involving the issuance of an injunction, appointment of a receiver to take over a troubled business, or directions for an accounting in patent suits. Thus, absent a specific court order, such rulings are not automatically stayed after entry, and are not stayed either during the period when filing a notice of appeal is permitted, or even during the pendency of an appeal. Rule 62(c) makes specific provisions for suspending, modifying, restoring, or granting of an injunction during the pendency of an appeal. It provides in part:

> **(c) Injunction Pending Appeal.** When an appeal is taken from an interlocutory or final judgment granting, dissolving, or denying an injunction, the court in its discretion may suspend, modify, restore, or grant an injunction during the pendency of the appeal upon such terms as to bond or otherwise as it considers proper for the security of the rights of the adverse party.

Appellate Rule 8 provides options in those instances where the trial court denies relief pending the appeal with respect to injunctive relief.

2. GENERAL CONSIDERATIONS FOR STAYS PENDING APPEAL

The fact that the rules prevent the trial-level winning party from acting upon a money or property judgment for 10 days sets the stage for several possible maneuvers. The party that lost the case can do a number of things during the first 10 days following entry of judgment, and it is important to understand the effect—if any—that these steps have on the judgment itself. Perhaps the most important point is this: *Simply filing a notice of appeal* (even if the papers are prepared, served and filed within the first 10 days after judgment) does *not* preclude enforcement of the judgment once the 10 day automatic stay expires.

Parties who lose trial-level decisions can also sometimes file a post-trial motion with the trial court, such as a motion under Rule 59 or 60 seeking a new trial, modification or relief from the judgment. The effect of such motions (discussed in Chapter 3 of the Casebook) is generally to put off the time for appeal. However, neither of those rules specifically contains any explicit provision addressing the possibility of the victorious party seeking enforcement of the trial court's disposition while such post-trial motions are under consideration. Rule 62(b) of the civil rules provides no automatic relief, either. Rather, it puts the onus on the party who lost the judgment to make an application to the trial court for relief from the effects of the judgment while the post-trial motion is under consideration. The Rule provides:

> **(b) Stay on Motion for New Trial or for Judgment.** In its discretion and on such conditions for the security of the adverse party as are proper, the court may stay the execution of or any proceedings to enforce a judgment pending the disposition of a motion for a new trial or to alter or amend a judgment made pursuant to Rule 59, or of a motion for relief from a judgment or order made pursuant to Rule 60, or of a motion for judgment in accordance with a motion for a directed verdict made pursuant to Rule 50, or of a motion for amendment to the findings or for additional findings made pursuant to Rule 52(b).

Under this provision, parties moving for reconsideration of a judgment entered by the trial court often include in their motion papers a request for relief from the judgment until the motion attacking the judgment is decided. Note that Rule 62(b) strongly implies that the trial court should condition any deferral of the effectiveness of the judgment by requiring the posting of a security bond, or some other express directions (such as prescribing how a particular asset will be treated pending resolution of the pending motions). Such "security" is intended to prevent a party that has lost a judgment from taking steps while procedural motions are pending to dispose of its assets or make the ultimate effectuation of the judgment more difficult for the winning party.

Another thing the losing party can do during the initial days after entry of judgment in the trial court is to seek relief that will provide protection for the entire duration of an appeal. Rule 8 of the F.R.App. P. specifies the procedure which governs in civil cases where a party seeks a stay of the judgment or order of a district court pending an appeal. It also addresses the mechanisms for approving a supersedeas bond, and for seeking an order granting, suspending, modifying, or restoring an injunction.

Try Below First. Appellate Rule 8 allows a party to seek various forms of relief from the appellate court during a pending appeal *once efforts to obtain relief from the trial court have been exhausted.* See F.R.App.P. 8(a). A litigant seeking relief from the appellate court must be able to represent that the trial court has denied relief, or that it is not practical to obtain the needed relief from the trial court.

One factor mentioned in a number of decisions is whether the trial court's disposition is made under newly enacted law, or applies principles where there is very little guidance. "A stay is frequently issued where the trial court is charting new and unexplored ground and the court determines that a novel interpretation of the law may succumb to appellate review." Stop H–3 Ass'n v. Volpe, 353 F.Supp. 14 (D. Haw. 1972).

3. SIMPLE MONEY OR PROPERTY JUDGMENTS

In fact there are two very favorable rules protecting defendants hit with money or property judgments. The first we have already seen: an automatic 10–day stay against enforcement of the judgment. The second favorable rule is that the party who lost the case has a *right* to preclude enforcement of the judgment upon the filing of a *supersedeas bond*. See Section B, below.

SECTION B.   THE SUPERSEDEAS BOND

A defendant who has lost a money judgment is normally will file a bond as a condition of pursuing an appeal. Generally referred to as a *supersedeas* bond, this obligation is intended to assure the holder of the judgment that if the appeal is unsuccessful, payment of the judgment will be assured by "going against the bond." In Hovey v. McDonald, 109 U.S. 150, 159, 3 S.Ct. 136, 27 L.Ed. 888 (1883) the Supreme Court gave the following definition:

> A *supersedeas,* properly so called, is a suspension of the power of the court below to issue an execution on the judgment or decree appealed from; or, if a writ of execution has issued, it is a prohibition emanating from the court of appeal against the execution of the writ. It operates from the time of the completion of those acts which are requisite to call it into existence. If, before those acts are performed, an execution has been lawfully issued, a writ of *supersedeas* directed to the officer holding it will be necessary; but if the writ of execution has been not only lawfully issued, but actually executed, there is no remedy until the appellate proceedings are ended, when, if the judgment or decree be reversed, a writ of restitution will be awarded.

In most courts only a "summary proceeding" is required to collect on such a bond. After winning an appeal where a bond was in place, a plaintiff whose judgment was upheld can make a motion for payment from the bond, and let the bonding company worry about collecting any sum from the judgment-debtor defendant. Since the courts maintain a list of solvent bonding companies, the judgment creditor who has had to wait during an appeal before collecting is assured of a solvent source of payment once the judgment is upheld.

By its terms, FRAP 8(a) places initial responsibility for determining the propriety and amount of a supersedeas bond with district court, and

FRCP 62(d) permits the trial court to set the supersedeas bond even after the notice of appeal is filed, so that, although filing of a notice of appeal generally divests the trial court of its jurisdiction over any matters dealing with merits of the appeal, the trial judge retains jurisdiction over any issues relating to enforcement of judgment or the supersedeas bond.

The pertinent portion of Rule 62 provides:

> **(d) Stay Upon Appeal.** When an appeal is taken the appellant by giving a supersedeas bond may obtain a stay subject to the exceptions contained in subdivision (a) of this rule. The bond may be given at or after the time of filing the notice of appeal or of procuring the order allowing the appeal, as the case may be. The stay is effective when the supersedeas bond is approved by the court.

Several important principles are packed into that paragraph of Rule 62. One is that the filing of a supersedeas bond does not interrupt the applicability of an injunction. If a party wants to be relieved from injunctive provisions during the post-judgment and appeal period, a separate application for an order granting relief (a motion) will need to be pursued. Second, the bond can be filed with or after the notice of appeal (*i.e.*, no technical trap invalidating a bond that somehow is not lodged contemporaneously with the notice of appeal). Thus, while the judgment is not stayed if there is a delay while the defendant scurries around to find a bonding company willing to underwrite the bond, a subsequent filing of proof that there is a proper surety bond in place will be valid. Third, the trial court must approve the bond (Note that in many courts the Clerk of Court is authorized to accept bonds so long as the surety is on the approved list of bond supplying companies).

1. THE LOSING PARTY'S ELECTION TO FILE THE BOND AND OBTAIN A STAY

One common scenario is the defendant found liable for a money judgment who thinks that there is a basis for appeal, and wants to defer paying the judgment until appellate review is exhausted. A leading treatise summarizes advice to a party contemplating appeal after entry of a money judgment where no post-judgment motion for reconsideration or new trial seems likely to prove fruitful:

> If the party elects to appeal immediately, he should file his notice of appeal within the ten-day period and immediately present to the district court the supersedeas bond required by Civil Rule 62(d). Filing the motion or appealing during the automatic stay period prevents the prevailing party from acting on the judgment to the detriment of the appellant.

Moore's Federal Practice—Civil § 308.20 (2004).

The appellant is assured of a stay because it applies as a matter of law when the bond is approved. Rule 62(d) provides that "by giving a supersedeas bond" the appellant will obtain a stay. Under this provision, the stay is effective as a matter of law "when the supersedeas bond is approved by the court."

Timing. A would-be appellant who will benefit from a stay should act promptly. If it is not clear that post-trial motions will be pending, the notice of appeal should be filed within the initial 10 days after judgment. If post-trial motions (in the federal system, motions under Rules 59 and 60 among others) Rule 62(b) provides that the trial court may grant a stay "pending the disposition" of such motions, which appears to mean that a stay may be entered while the motions are pending.

A stay may be sought after the 10–day automatic period of non-enforcement ends, but the losing party runs the risk in that situation that an aggressive judgment creditor will take immediate steps to seize or encumber the losing party's assets. A stay obtained after some steps have been taken to enforce the judgment will be valid, but generally does not retroactively "undo" the effects of the initial enforcement steps that have taken place (such as an attachment).

Note

If the aggrieved party has no appeal "as a matter of right"—i.e., must seek permission to appeal some interlocutory disposition—merely proffering a supersedeas bond will not force the trial court to stay the disposition below. In a colorful antitrust case (there are such things) in which a large number of college athletic coaches sued the National Collegiate Athletic Association (NCAA), the trial court ordered the NCAA to pay daily contempt fines for as long as it refused to pay various fees and costs the court had awarded to the coaches. The NCAA argued on appeal that the coercive sanctions were improper because upon filing of a supersedeas bond it was entitled to a stay of the daily fines imposed by the trial court. The Tenth Circuit ruled this argument out of bounds:

> The NCAA's argument is based on its belief that it had a right to appeal and hence a right to a stay if it was able to file a sufficient supersedeas bond. It argues that Fed. R. Civ. P. 62(d) provides district courts with only a ministerial duty in approving bonds.

> The NCAA's argument fails primarily because it had no right to appeal the interim attorneys' fee awards. It could ask this appellate court to take its appeal. But whether we would do so depended upon both an exercise of our discretion and a determination that our decision on the related injunction appeal necessarily resolved the appeal the NCAA sought to take. When there is no appeal of right there is no duty on the district court to grant a stay upon the filing of a supersedeas bond.

> The NCAA can find no solace in Fed. R. Civ. P. 62. As applied to the injunction order that was appealable of right, Rule 62(c) gives discretion to the district court whether to issue a stay during the pendency of the appeal. If discretion is given to the district court when the order is appealable of right, it would be incongruous to read Rule 62(d) to require a stay upon presentation of a supersedeas bond when the appeal

must piggy-back on the injunction appeal, and depends on an exercise of discretion by the appellate court.

The NCAA's proper course of action, if it sought to avoid or delay paying the interim fee awards, would be to follow the dictates of Fed. R. App. P. 8. It first should have sought a stay in the district court before April 29, and when the district court refused, then applied, as it did belatedly, in this court.

Law v. National Collegiate Athletic Association, 134 F.3d 1025, 1030–31 (10th Cir. 1998).

2. APPROVAL OF THE AMOUNT OF THE BOND BY THE COURT

Rule 62 does not prescribe a formula for determining the amount of a supersedeas bond. In most cases the amount of the supersedeas bond is tied to the amount of the judgment. Sometimes the bond is in the exact amount of the judgment. However, many state and federal courts follow a formula calling for the bond to cover the judgment amount plus interest for the expected appeal period, costs, and an increment for any other damages that delay in enforcement of the judgment is calculated to cause. Cases in this Chapter refer to former Rule 73(d) of the Federal Rules of Civil Procedure as to the items covered by the bond. That rule was repealed when the Federal Rules of Appellate Procedure were adopted in 1968, and no similar statement was included in the new rules. Notwithstanding, federal courts still sometimes refer to former Rule 73(d) as a matter of practice or include similar provisions in their local rules prescribing the amount of a bond.

In some reported cases, a lower bond has been approved when accompanied by an agreed-order or an injunction restricting the use or location of certain assets while the appeal is pending, thus helping to assure that the judgment creditor will not have difficulty enforcing the judgment if it is upheld on appeal. See, e.g., Olympia Equipment Leasing Co. v. Western Union Tel. Co., 786 F.2d 794, 796 (7th Cir. 1986). The United States District Court for the District of Massachusetts has a local rule, Rule 62.2, setting forth a common formula:

MASSACHUSETTS LOCAL RULE
62.2—SUPERSEDEAS BOND

A supersedeas bond staying execution of a money judgment shall be in the amount of the judgment plus ten (10%) percent of the amount to cover interest and any award of damages for delay plus Five Hundred and no/100 ($500.00) Dollars to cover costs, unless the court directs otherwise.

In general, therefore, if the appellant wishes to post a supersedeas bond in the "standard" amount recognized in that jurisdiction (applying prevailing interest and cost increments to the actual amount of the judgment in the pending case) such an application is likely to be approved ministerially in most American courts. Once accepted, the bond will normally have the automatic effect of staying enforcement of the judgment. If, however, the appellant wishes to obtain a stay with a lesser form of surety, it is most common for the applicant to file a motion asking the trial court to fix the amount of the security required for the stay.

Some state courts have defined the amount of a proper supersedeas bond by listing the categories of factors it is required to cover, in a fashion not unlike former federal Rule 73. For example, Washington Rules of Appellate Procedure, which in Rule 8.1(c) provides:

> *(1) Money judgment.* The supersedeas amount shall be the amount of the judgment, plus interest likely to accrue during the pendency of the appeal and attorney fees, costs, and expenses likely to be awarded on appeal.

> *(2) Decision affecting property.* The supersedeas amount shall be the amount of any money judgment, plus interest likely to accrue during the pendency of the appeal and attorney fees, costs, and expenses likely to be awarded on appeal entered by the trial court plus the amount of the loss which the prevailing party in the trial court would incur as a result of the party's inability to enforce the judgment during review. Ordinarily, the amount of loss will be equal to the reasonable value of the use of the property during review. A party claiming that the reasonable value of the use of the property is inadequate to secure the loss which the party may suffer as a result of the party's inability to enforce the judgment shall have the burden of proving that the amount of loss would be more than the reasonable value of the use of the property during review. If the property at issue has value, the property itself may fully or partially secure any loss and the court may determine that no additional security need be filed or may reduce the supersedeas amount accordingly.

> *(3) Stay of portion of judgment.* If a party seeks to stay enforcement of only part of the judgment, the supersedeas amount shall be fixed at such sum as the trial court determines is appropriate to secure that portion of the judgment. * * *

Bonds Can be Expensive. A supersedeas bond is purchased by the appellant from one of the approved surety companies. A premium is charged in the form of a percentage of the gross amount of the bond. Typically, the appellant must pledge assets to secure the bond, so that if the appeal fails, and the appellee collects on the bond, the surety company will seek to execute on the collateral securing the bond. As cases below indicate, in small cases where the parties have little money, and in multi-million dollar cases involving major corporations or wealthy individuals, the bond premium—and the collateralization with assets—can be a significant problem. In many cases the bonding companies want complete (yes, 100%) collateralization, so it may be necessary to encumber assets equaling the entire judgment amount in order to have a bond that the court will accept.

ALEXANDER v. CHESAPEAKE, POTOMAC & TIDEWATER BOOKS

United States District Court, Eastern District of Virginia, 1999.
190 F.R.D. 190.

ELLIS, DISTRICT JUDGE.

MEMORANDUM OPINION

The post-judgment issue presented in this copyright, contract, and tortious interference case is whether a judgment debtor may obtain a stay of the judgment pending appeal without posting a full supersedeas bond. * * *

The first question is whether a district court has discretion to stay a judgment pending appeal without first requiring a bond that secures the full amount of the judgment. Analysis of this question properly begins with Rule 62(d), Fed. R. Civ. P., which provides, in pertinent part, that "when an appeal is taken the appellant by giving a supersedeas bond may obtain a stay." The plain meaning of the language is unmistakable: A judgment debtor wishing to appeal a judgment is entitled to a stay of the judgment if the debtor provides a supersedeas bond. Even assuming, then, that the term "supersedeas bond" as used in the Rule means a bond that fully secures the entire judgment,[1] Rule 62(d), by its terms, says no more than that an appellant may obtain a stay as a matter of right by posting such a bond.

Significantly, Rule 62(d) does not address, and hence does not preclude, issuance of a stay on the basis of some lesser bond, or indeed, no bond. It follows, logically, that this Rule leaves unimpaired a district court's inherent, discretionary power to stay judgments pending appeal on terms other than a full supersedeas bond. Indeed, every circuit that has addressed the issue has reached precisely this result. * * * In

---

1. As Black's reflects, the typical use of the term "supersedeas bond" connotes "[a] bond required of one who petitions to set aside a judgment or execution and from which the other party may be made whole if the action is unsuccessful." Black's Law Dictionary 1438 (6th ed. 1990). But Black's also notes that the term "supersedeas" is simply "the name of a writ containing a command to stay the proceedings at law" and "is often used synonymously with a 'stay of proceedings,' and is employed to designate the effect of an act or proceeding which of itself suspends the enforcement of a judgment." Id. at 1437–38. Thus, a supersedeas bond is arguably any bond that, by order of a district court, stays enforcement of a money judgment, even if the bond secures only a portion of the money judgment. Notwithstanding this potential ambiguity in the phrase "supersedeas bond," it seems clear that the supersedeas bond contemplated in Rule 62(d) is a full security bond, one that secures the entire amount of the judgment, and any deviation from such a bond requires a district court's approval. See Federal Prescription Serv., 636 F.2d at 760 ("[A] full supersedeas bond should be the requirement in normal circumstances. . . ."); Poplar Grove Planting & Refining Co., Inc., v. Bache Halsey Stuart, Inc., 600 F.2d 1189, 1191 (5th Cir. 1979) (holding that a party who wishes to stay judgment on less than a full security supersedeas bond must "objectively demonstrate the reasons for such a departure").

summary, then, the answer to the first question presented is that a district court's inherent discretionary power to stay judgments pending appeal on the basis of less than a full supersedeas bond, or no bond, is not addressed or affected by Rule 62(d), which establishes only the narrow proposition that a full supersedeas bond entitles an appellant to the issuance of a stay pending disposition of the appeal.

Left to be resolved is a second question, namely, what principle guides a district court's exercise of discretion to issue a stay of the judgment on less than a full bond securing the entire judgment.

The Fifth Circuit's statement of the governing principle is lucidly succinct: In determining whether to issue a stay pending appeal on the basis of less than a full bond, a district court should act to "preserve the status quo while protecting the non-appealing party's rights pending appeal." Poplar Grove, 600 F.2d at 1190–91. In the typical case, of course, this principle is best served by requiring a full supersedeas bond as a condition to the issuance of a stay of judgment pending appeal. But, the Fifth Circuit also noted that in light of the purpose of a bond on appeal, a full bond may not be necessary in either of two polar circumstances: (i) when the judgment debtor can currently easily meet the judgment and demonstrates that it will maintain the same level of solvency during appeal, and (ii) when "the judgment debtor's present financial condition is such that the posting of a full bond would impose an undue financial burden." Id. at 1191. In the former case, the court may "substitute some form of guaranty of judgment responsibility for the usual supersedeas bond." Id. In the latter case, "the court . . . is free to exercise a discretion to fashion some other arrangement for substitute security through an appropriate restraint on the judgment debtor's financial dealings, which would furnish equal protection to the judgment creditor." Id. In these circumstances, fashioning an alternative to a full supersedeas bond in the latter case can be "a very difficult task," as the district court must find some way "to make the judgment creditor as well off during the appeal as it would be if it could execute at once, but no better off." Olympia Equip. Leasing Co., 786 F.2d at 800 (Easterbrook, J., concurring).

Therefore, where, as here, the judgment debtor has not the means to secure a full supersedeas bond, a stay may issue if the judgment debtors * * * provide security such that plaintiffs will be in nearly the same position at the conclusion of the appeal of this case as they are currently. Such a bond or security may well be significantly less valuable than the amount of the damages award. See Olympia Equip. Leasing, 786 F.2d at 800 (Easterbrook, J. concurring) ("When the judgment debtor lacks the assets or credit necessary to pay at once and in full, this means that the judge should give the creditor less than complete security.").

In other words, any security or bond offered by defendants in this case should simply reflect and preserve defendants' current ability to satisfy the judgment. At present, the record reflects that both defendants are arguably insolvent, and that their combined assets could not satisfy half the judgment, even putting aside their current liabilities. Yet, defendants did set aside $16,175.50 for payment to plaintiffs in this case, which is all defendants appear able to pay in satisfaction of the current judgment. Thus, to put plaintiffs in the same position as they are now at the conclusion of appeal, defendants must secure that amount for plaintiffs' benefit.

Accordingly, defendants may either post a bond in the amount set aside, or, if the parties agree, place the sum into an escrow account, to be released to plaintiffs if they prevail on appeal. Accordingly, stay of judgment has been conditioned on the happening of one of these.

TRANS WORLD AIRLINES, INC. v. HUGHES

United States District Court, Southern District of New York, 1970.
314 F.Supp. 94.

METZNER, DISTRICT JUDGE.

Defendants move for a stay of execution, pending appeal, of the judgment entered in favor of the plaintiff without posting the usual supersedeas bond. Practically speaking, defendant Hughes Tool Company (hereinafter called Toolco) is the party involved in this motion.

F.R.C.P. 62(d) provides that "When an appeal is taken the appellant by giving a supersedeas bond may obtain a stay subject to the exceptions contained in subdivision (a) of this rule." Rule 33 of the General Rules of this court provides that such bond shall be in the amount of the judgment plus 11% and an additional $250 to cover costs. Plaintiff in this antitrust action was awarded single damages of $45,870,478.65, which after trebling and adding costs and a reasonable attorney's fee amounts to $145,448,141.07. The bond would have to be in the amount of $161,447,686.59.

[T]he General Rules of this court provides that every bond or undertaking must either:

(1)be secured by the deposit of cash or government bonds in the amount of the bond, undertaking or stipulation, or be secured by (2) the undertaking or guaranty of a corporate surety holding a certificate of authority from the Secretary of the Treasury . . . . .

It is Toolco's contention that either of the alternatives contained in [this] Rule * * * "could not be effected without imposing an added penalty on [Toolco] by requiring it to engage in disruptive and time-consuming liquidation of assets or a costly and time-consuming financing program." It proposes that it either not be required to post any bond or undertaking, or that whenever the net worth of Toolco goes below three times the judgment the stay pending appeal shall be lifted.

Although the final judgment in this matter was not entered until April 14, 1970, the report of the special master recommending damages in the amount of $137,611,435.95 was confirmed by this court on December 23, 1969. Defendants apparently did nothing from that time until May 5, 1970 (the date of the order to show cause bringing on this motion) to arrange for the posting of the required bond except to make inquiry of surety companies. Appended to the order to show cause are two letters from surety companies indicating that a bond of this size could be arranged only if secured with a deposit of collateral in the form of cash or government bonds or documents of similar liquidity in the full amount of the bond. The inability of surety companies to undertake such an obligation is fully understood and appreciated by the court.

Because of the unprecedented size of the judgment against what is in essence a single defendant, the court signed the order to show cause in an attempt to see if some satisfactory arrangement could be worked out whereby the interests of the successful plaintiff could be reconciled with the understandable, practical problems facing Toolco. Hearings were held on May 11, May 20 and June 3 which were unproductive in bringing the parties close to a solution of the problem.

At the outset the brief submitted by Toolco took the position that the law was clear to the effect that the court has the power "in extraordinary circumstances such as those presented by this case, to grant a stay of execution without requiring the filing of a supersedeas bond in the ordinary form or the posting of any security." It argued that its net worth was in excess of $500,000,000 and that this was ample assurance that the plaintiff would be able, in the event of affirmance, to obtain satisfaction of its judgment without the posting of any security at the present time. In addition, it offered that a lien could be created on specific property having a value in excess of $45,000,000, the amount of the compensatory portion of the judgment. The plaintiff took the position that Rule 33, requiring a bond in the amount of 111% of the judgment, indicates that any lower figure is most unlikely to be sufficient security for the payment of a judgment.

With the adoption of the Federal Rules of Appellate Procedure, effective July 1, 1968, Rule 73(d) of the Federal Rules of Civil Procedure, which referred to supersedeas bonds on appeals to the Court of Appeals, was repealed. It had provided, among other things, that:

> "the amount of the bond shall be fixed at such sum as will cover the whole amount of the judgment remaining unsatisfied, costs on appeal, interest, and damages for delay, unless the court, after notice and hearing and for good cause shown, fixes a different amount."

These words had been inserted in the original rule in 1938 to cover situations where money judgments of enormous sums had been entered and defendants were unable to give a supersedeas bond to stay the execution of a judgment. The language allowed the court, in a case of hardship of that kind, to issue a stay of execution so that, in effect, the defendant's right of appeal would not be destroyed. The language was not transferred to any other section of the rules by the amendment of 1968, and consequently the court is faced with F.R.C.P. 62(d) and our local district Rule 33. Despite the repeal of Rule 73(d), I am of the opinion that the court has the inherent power in extraordinary circumstances to provide for the form and amount of security for a stay pending appeal, based on the conditions it finds to exist in a particular case.

At the first hearing on May 11, the parties adhered to their diametrically opposed positions. The plaintiff pointed out that there was no assurance that Toolco's present net worth would continue to exist. It further took the position that during the period from December to May Toolco, with its asserted net worth, could have arranged for a loan to be used as an undertaking. Plaintiff suggested that Howard Hughes, the sole owner of the stock of Toolco, should guarantee the payment of the judgment and place his stock with the court as collateral for such guaranty.

If consideration was to be given to Toolco's proposal, plaintiff asserted that it should receive the same treatment as would be afforded any lending institution approached for a loan by Toolco. This would include certified, detailed financial statements, regular certificates by responsible officers of defendants as to the maintenance of net worth and limitations on transactions between Toolco and its 100% stockholder. However, plaintiff adhered to its view that Toolco should arrange for financing in order to secure the judgment in full.

The hearing was adjourned to May 20 with a direction to the defendants to conduct negotiations with lending institutions. Counsel were admonished to have continuing discussions so that on the adjourned date the plaintiff would not be faced with a new proposal for the first time. * * *

The hearing proceeded on May 20, in which counsel for Toolco outlined the discussions had with the banks. * * * The hearing was adjourned to June 3 with a direction to Toolco to furnish the plaintiff with the audited financial statements of its operations for the year 1969 and a list of its assets worth $10,000,000 or more. This was done for the purpose of giving the plaintiff an opportunity to know what was being offered and to be in a position to evaluate whether it would be sufficient to secure its judgment.

Aside from charges and counter-charges of bad faith, a large portion of the hearing on June 3 was devoted to a statement by defense counsel as to the huge capital demands being made on Toolco by its subsidiaries and affiliates. The sum total of all this was that there could be nothing available for the plaintiff by way of cash security. Business was to continue as usual with Toolco being the sole arbiter of what it wanted to do. Cash could be converted to fixed assets which would not affect the net worth of the company as reflected on a balance sheet. However, it could certainly affect what I would call the quality of that net worth insofar as the collection of the judgment is concerned. We read every day about the liquidity squeeze.

The figures which were furnished the plaintiff indicate that in the three-month period ending March 31, 1970 the quick current assets have been reduced by a third. In addition, the court received a letter from

Toolco's counsel dated May 22, 1970 stating that the court should not be surprised to read an announcement in the press, either late that day or the next day, that Toolco had acquired the Dunes Hotel for a cash consideration of $35,000,000 and that there was a contemplated transaction in which Toolco would be called upon to lay out another $11,000,000 within the next six or eight months. There are additional examples of cash commitments in the financial notes to which I need not specifically refer.

Part of business as usual must include some recognition of the rights of this plaintiff that has acquired a judgment against Toolco for violation of the antitrust laws of the United States. Toolco requests plaintiff to forgo both immediate collection of its judgment and full security for that judgment pending appeal. It must be prepared to assume some financial burden to achieve "business as usual." At the same time, I fully appreciate that under present conditions a supersedeas bond in the amount contemplated by [the local] Rule * * * is not practicable under the circumstances. I have come to the conclusion that Toolco can arrange to post security in the form required * * * in the amount of $75,000,000. This shall be done on or before June 22, 1970. The balance of $86,447,686.59 shall be secured along the lines suggested by the defendants as to the maintenance of Toolco's net worth at three times the amount of such balance. The details of this arrangement shall be worked out between counsel. Each knows what the other has proposed. The court cannot be expected, on the papers before it, to come up with a satisfactory resolution embodying such detailed and intricate financial considerations. It should not be required to devote the time necessary to preside over such a conference between counsel. Obviously, there has to be flexibility on both sides for this endeavor to be successful.

Counsel are directed to meet in continuous session and appear before the court on June 16 in Room 1106 at 10:30 A.M. with a proposal in such form that any needed resolution of disputes can easily be disposed of.

So ordered.

Notes and Questions

1. What is the source of a court's authority to set a bond amount different from that established by the local rules? Could a court issue a stay without requiring any bond? Should it be able to do so? In a case involving a money judgment only, could the trial court refuse to set the amount of a bond so as to deny relief pending appeal? According to American Mfg. Mut. Ins. Co. v. American Broadcasting-Paramount Theaters, Inc., 87 S.Ct. 1, 17 L.Ed.2d 37 (1966) (not published in U.S. Reports) the answer is no.

2. What do the foregoing cases suggest about the importance of relief pending appeal, both to the appellant and the appellee? For a discussion of some of the tactical aspects of relief pending appeal, see Towers, Stay of Execution Pending Appeal, 22 Trial 57 (March, 1986). Professor Towers suggests that whenever possible the attorney for a plaintiff who has won a money judgment should *resist* efforts of the defendant to obtain a stay,

because the defendant will retain the use of the money pending the appeal (the value of which may or may not exceed the post-judgment interest plaintiff will eventually collect when the judgment is ultimately paid) and because a defendant who benefits from a stay has more leverage to negotiate a settlement on appeal—particularly if the plaintiff is in financial straits and desperately needs some proceeds from the litigation. If defendant has an ethical basis to undertake the appeal in the first place, could it ever be improper for the defendant to seek the advantages of a stay of enforcement of the judgment pending resolution of the appeal?

———

3. SELECTION OF AN ACCEPTABLE SURETY

Many state and federal courts maintain lists of persons and companies approved to provide surety bonds. In some jurisdictions these approved bond suppliers are set forth in statutes or rules. The federal court for the District of Massachusetts follows its supersedeas bond rule with a lengthy rule concerning approved sureties, part of which reads:

MASSACHUSETTS LOCAL RULE 67.1 SURETIES

(a) Members of the Bar and Court Officers. No judge, clerk, marshal, member of the bar or other officer or employee of the court may be surety or guarantor of any bond or undertaking in any proceeding in this court.

(b) Form of Bond. Surety bonds shall be signed and acknowledged by the party and his surety or sureties. They shall refer to the statute, rule, or court order under which given, state the conditions of the obligation, and contain a provision expressly subjecting them to all applicable federal statutes and rules.

(c) Security. Except as otherwise provided by law or by order of the court, a bond or similar undertaking must be secured by:

(1) The deposit of cash or obligations of the United States in the amount of the bond (note Rule 67.4 with regard to the court's cash policy); or

(2) The guaranty of a company or corporation holding a certificate of authority from the Secretary of the Treasury pursuant to 6 U.S.C. § 8; or

(3) The guaranty of two (2) individual residents of this district each of whom owns unencumbered real or personal property within the district worth the amount of the bond, in excess of legal obligations and exemptions.

(d) Deposits of cash or obligations of the United States shall be accompanied by a written statement, duly acknowledged, that the signer is owner thereof, that the same is subject to the conditions of the bond, and that the clerk may collect or sell the obligations and apply the proceeds, or the cash deposited, in case of default as provided in the bond. Upon satisfaction of the conditions of the bond, the monies or obligations shall be returned to the owner on the order of a magistrate or district judge.

Many clerks offices have "master lists" of bonding companies and others who are accepted sources of surety bonds for appeal (and other) purposes.

4. SEEKING A STAY WITHOUT THE FILING OF A SUPERSEDEAS BOND

By far the most common procedure is for the party held liable for a money or property judgment to file a bond covering the value of the judgment. However, there is discretion in the applicable rules for the court to adjust the requirement for a bond. One federal appellate court has commented that "an inflexible requirement of a bond would be inappropriate in two sorts of case: where the defendant's ability to pay the judgment is so plain that the cost of the bond would be a waste of money; and—the opposite case, one of increasing importance in an age of titanic damage judgments—where the requirement would put the defendant's other creditors in undue jeopardy." Olympia Equipment Leasing Co. v. Western Union Telegraph Co., 786 F.2d 794, 796 (7th Cir. 1986)(finding that the defendant, while maintaining assets of over $2 billion, was "financially distressed and illiquid" making the posting of a $36 million bond difficult and possibly an unnecessary threat to the company's other creditors—the court approved the district judge's actions in allowing an appeal without a traditional supersedeas bond, relying instead on a pledge of accounts receivable and other nontraditional security measures). See also Poplar Grove Planting & Refining Co. v. Bache Halsey Stuart, Inc., 600 F.2d 1189, 1191 (5th Cir. 1979).

DILLON v. CITY OF CHICAGO

United States Court of Appeals, Seventh Circuit, 1989.
866 F.2d 902.

COFFEY, CIRCUIT JUDGE.

Plaintiff-appellee Joseph Dillon won a sizable jury verdict in his employment discrimination case against the defendant-appellant City of Chicago ("the City"), and also was awarded attorneys' fees and costs as the prevailing party. The City has filed two motions asking this court to stay the execution of both the judgment and the attorneys' fees. Because the district court erred in refusing to waive the requirement of bond or to otherwise stay the execution of the judgment and award of fees and costs, we reverse.

* * * Rule 62(d) of the Federal Rules of Civil Procedure allows an appellant to obtain an automatic stay of execution of judgment pending appeal by posting a bond. In the alternative, the appellant may move

that the district court employ its discretion to waive the bond requirement. When determining whether to waive the posting of bond, the
district court may look to several criteria enumerated by this court: (1)
the complexity of the collection process; (2) the amount of time required
to obtain a judgment after it is affirmed on appeal; (3) the degree of
confidence that the district court has in the availability of funds to pay
the judgment; (4) whether the defendant's ability to pay the judgment is
so plain that the cost of a bond would be a waste of money; and (5)
whether the defendant is in such a precarious financial situation that the
requirement to post a bond would place other creditors of the defendant
in an insecure position.

Applying these principles to the present case leads to the conclusion
that the City should not be required to post bond, or other alternate
security, to obtain a stay of the execution of the judgment or payment of
fees and costs. * * *

The City presents a strong case in favor of staying the execution of
the judgment, as well as attorneys' fees and costs, without requiring a
bond. The City submitted affidavits to the district court, which the
plaintiff did not dispute, outlining the mode of payment of employment
discrimination judgments against the Chicago Police Department. The
entire process of payment of the judgment and fees and costs should take
less than thirty days, and is guaranteed to be paid from the Corporate
Payroll Fund of the City of Chicago. In 1988, $484 million were appropri-
ated for this Fund, which would appear to be more than adequate to
guarantee payment of the $115,359.59 backpay award and the
$51,882.53 attorneys' fees and costs award. As the affidavit of the City
Comptroller states, "Appropriations are made into the Chicago Police
Department's Corporate Payroll Fund annually by the City Council in an
amount designed to provide adequate funds for payment of such
awards." Appellant's Motion to Stay without Security, Appendix C,
Affidavit of Ronald D. Picur, Comptroller of the City of Chicago. Further,
unlike the City's desultory record in payment of sizable tort judgments,
the City has a history of more than adequate provision for payment of
employment discrimination judgments, paid out of the budget of the
relevant departmental unit. * * * This case emulates the procedure
recommended in [a prior decision] in providing a previously appropriated
fund, out of which judgments may be paid.

The City has demonstrated the existence of previously appropriated
funds, available for the purpose of paying judgments without substantial
delay or other difficulty. The plaintiff makes a general attack on the
sufficiency of these funds, but has failed to demonstrate a single instance
in which a claim of this type has gone unpaid. The City, on the other
hand, presented clear evidence to the contrary in the district court. On
the facts of this case then, the district court's orders with regard to the
stay of execution of the judgment and payment of fees and costs pending
appeal were unreasonable and so are reversed.

Accordingly, IT IS ORDERED that the execution of judgment and payment of fees and costs are stayed without bond pending appeal.

Notes and Questions

1. In another case, a discharged lawbook salesman sued the largest lawbook publisher in the world for firing him when he was out sick, in violation of the Family Medical and Leave Act, 29 U.S.C. § 2611 et seq. After a jury trial, plaintiff was awarded a verdict of $119,000 along with $11,449 in interest, $85,657 in attorney's fees, plus $8,962 in costs. When the defendant appealed, the trial court granted its motion for a stay of execution of the judgment without the filing of a supersedeas bond. On appeal, the Sixth Circuit concluded that in case where there was a mere $225,000 judgment against one of the largest and most financially healthy companies in the world, it was well within the trial court's discretion to allow a stay without going through the motions of requiring the filing of a bond:

> [Plaintiff] Arban now argues that for West to obtain a stay of execution of the judgment, West must give a supersede as bond pursuant to Fed. R. Civ. P. 62(d). This court reviews a district court's denial of a supersedeas bond for an abuse of discretion. * * * However, the Rule in no way necessarily implies that filing a bond is the only way to obtain a stay. It speaks only to stays granted as a matter of right, it does not speak to stays granted by the court in accordance with its discretion. Arban claims that West must make "at least a showing that it has adequate resources to satisfy the bond." West has done so here. At the hearing on West's motion for stay without bond * * * counsel for West stated that "the revenues of the group of which West is a part is approximately 2.5 billion dollars." The Seventh Circuit has noted that "an inflexible requirement of a bond would be inappropriate * * * where the defendant's ability to pay the judgment is so plain that the cost of the bond would be a waste of money." Olympia Equip. Leasing Co. v. Western Union Tel. Co., 786 F.2d 794, 796 (7th Cir. 1986). In light of the vast disparity between the amount of the judgment in this case and the annual revenue of the group of which West is a part, the district court's decision to grant a stay without a bond was not an abuse of discretion.

Arban v. West Publishing Corp., 345 F.3d 390, 408–09 (6th Cir. 2003). Accord: Federal Prescription Serv. v. American Pharmaceutical Ass'n, 636 F.2d 755, 761 (D.C. Cir. 1980) (it was not an abuse of discretion for the trial court to decline to require a bond where the net worth of judgment debtor was unequivocally shown on the record to be 47 times amount of judgment, and it was clear that judgment debtor would remain in the community and be available for enforcement of the judgment).

2. Does *inability* to pay the judgment logically justify a reduced bond? Consider Miami International Realty Co. v Paynter, 807 F.2d 871 (10th Cir. 1986), in which a lawyer was found liable for legal malpractice, and sought to appeal but could not afford to post a supersedeas bond in the full amount of the judgment. The defendant attorney filed an affidavit that he had

insufficient assets to post the full bond amount and that execution of judgment would cause irreparable harm and place him in insolvency (which would injure his other creditors and his clients). Plaintiff was allowed the opportunity to produce evidence that the defendant lawyer had other, hidden assets, but failed to offer such proof. The court concluded that evidence of *financial inability* justified granting a stay on a lesser bond.

3. **The Most Favored Appellant.** Considering the showings the City of Chicago had to make in the preceding case, compare Rule 62(e), which provides that the federal government simply does not need file a bond, and that upon the filing of any appeal the enforcement of any judgment against the United States of America, or any of its officers or agencies, is stayed:

> **(e) Stay in Favor of the United States or Agency Thereof**. When an appeal is taken by the United States or an officer or agency thereof or by direction of any department of the Government of the United States and the operation or enforcement of the judgment is stayed, no bond, obligation, or other security shall be required from the appellant.

5. STAYS OF NON–MONETARY JUDGMENTS

J. PEREZ & CIA., INC. v. UNITED STATES

United States Court of Appeals, First Circuit, 1984.
747 F.2d 813.

BREYER, CIRCUIT JUDGE.

The appellant, J. Perez & Cia., Inc. ("Perez"), is a grocery business that participated in the federal food stamp program. The Department of Agriculture found that the business repeatedly violated program rules. And, it decided to suspend Perez from the program for two months. Perez sought judicial review of the Department's decision; the federal district court found the decision lawful; and Perez decided to appeal. Perez and the Department agreed to a stay of the suspension pending appeal. Perez posted a $12,500 "supersedeas bond," stipulating that the bond was "in consideration of the Government's acquiescence" to the stay. This court affirmed the district court on the merits in an unpublished opinion. Perez & Cia., Inc. v. United States, No. 821356 (1st Cir. Dec. 29, 1982). But, by that time the Department had terminated the relevant food stamp program. Since there no longer existed a program to suspend Perez from, the Department asked for the $12,500 secured by the bond. The district court ordered Perez to forfeit the bond money. 578 F.Supp. 1318. And Perez now appeals from that "forfeiture" decision.

The parties here argue in part about the district court's power to authorize a bond to secure nonmonetary relief. The bond was posted under Fed.R.Civ.P. 62. The district court apparently believed the bond fell within the scope of subsection (d), which states that when

> an appeal is taken the appellant by giving a supersedeas bond may obtain a stay . . . .

This particular subsection, however, is likely aimed at money judgments, the value of which can be calculated and secured with relative ease. See

Donovan v. Fall River Foundry Co., 696 F.2d 524, 526 (7th Cir. 1982). A case in which a party seeks review of an agency's suspension order, in which the court can either permit the order to take effect or forbid the agency from enforcing it, is more naturally viewed as a case involving an order to do, or not to do, something (that is, involving something like an injunction) rather than a case involving a money judgment. Cf. Donovan v. Fall River Foundry Co. supra (order to submit to government health inspection). Thus, the applicable subsection is more likely to be (c), which provides

> When an appeal is taken from a ... judgment granting, dissolving, or denying an injunction, the court in its discretion may suspend, modify, restore, or grant an injunction during the pendency of the appeal upon such terms as to bond or otherwise as it considers proper for the security of the rights of the adverse party.

We need not decide definitely, however, which subsection applies, for the district court possesses adequate power under Rule 62 to require a bond that will "protect an enforceable judgment" in favor of its winner, Redding & Co. v. Russwine Construction Corp., 417 F.2d 721, 727 (D.C. Cir. 1969), and protect the winner from any subsequent harm suffered through appellate delay, whether or not the judgment is monetary in nature. The issue here is not one of the court's power to act; it is one of interpreting the court's action. What were the conditions of the stay that the court originally ordered? To be more specific, what were the bond forfeiture conditions? And, since the district court simply ratified the agreement of the parties, the issue is what terms of forfeiture the parties intended. See Aviation Credit Corporation v. Conner Air Lines, Inc., 307 F.2d 685, 688 (5th Cir. 1962) (extent of liability under supersedeas bond to be determined in accordance with real or presumed intention of parties).

Appellant argues that the only purpose of the bond was to compensate the Department for the actual harm it suffered through appeal. In fact, appellant argued to the district court that the bond was in reality one for appellate costs under Fed.R.App.P. 7 (Bond for Costs on Appeal in Civil Cases). It says that the harm suffered by not being able to suspend appellant has no monetary equivalent; since the program has ended, suspension is now beside the point. And, the district court agreed that the Department "has not suffered monetary setback."

On the other hand, the delay, by preventing punishment where warranted, interferes at least in a general way, with the "deterrence" objective of the Department's law enforcement programs. The district court specifically found that the parties intended the $12,500 to represent the abstract value of the suspension judgment to the Department and to be forfeited should the program terminate before the appeal was decided. There is evidence in support of that conclusion.

For one thing, the parties' joint stipulation for a stay used the term "supersedeas bond." The term "supersedeas bond" traditionally describes a bond designed to secure the value of the judgment, not a bond that simply secures costs on appeal. Former Fed.R.Civ.P. 73(d), for example, described a supersedeas bond as one

> conditioned for the satisfaction of the judgment in full together with costs, interest, and damages for delay ... as the appellate court may adjudge and award.

For another thing, the parties knew before the appeal that termination of the food stamp program was likely. Further, the Department filed an affidavit stating in some detail how the $12,500 figure was arrived at, namely, by calculating the sort of monetary penalty that the Department believed equivalent to the two-month suspension. Although the affidavit does not state that appellant was aware of this calculation, appellant does not deny awareness. Instead, it argues that the "parol evidence rule" bars the affidavit (a fallacious argument, since the affidavit is being used to explain the written agreement, not to contradict it.) Finally, appellant did not seek a hearing or seek to adduce any additional evidence designed to show that it did not understand that the full $12,500 was to be forfeited.

Although this evidence supporting the district court's finding is not overwhelmingly strong, we believe it an adequate basis for a lower court, familiar with the controversy, to conclude that the parties intended the forfeiture that was enforced to be a condition of the stay that the court allowed. The judgment of the district court is therefore

Affirmed.

Notes and Questions

If plaintiff, for example, is denied a particular form of liability jury instruction requested, and loses the case, the plaintiff may appeal. In that situation there is no need for plaintiff as the appellant to file a supersedeas bond—there is no award to enforce. If, however, a plaintiff wins a partial victory and seeks to appeal trial court rulings that may have wrongfully limited the recovery, what is the effect on the enforcement of the initial judgment? On this general issue, see Trustmark Insurance Co. v. Gallucci, 193 F.3d 558, 558–59 (1st Cir. 1999) (the prevailing party's appeal would not automatically suspend enforcement of the trial court's disposition unless the theory of the appeal is inconsistent with enforcement of the judgment while the appeal is pending).

6. COMPLEX CASES: MULTIPLE CLAIMS AND MULTIPLE PARTIES

Under F.R.Civ. P. 54(b) the trial court enter a final judgment against fewer than all of the parties or on fewer than all the claims. For example, in the middle of a long case, the trial court could enter summary judgment with respect to the claims against one defendant, while allowing the remaining claims against other defendants to go forward for further litigation. Rule 62(h) contains a provision dealing with such possibilities, and it specifies that if such partial final judgments are entered the court has power to stay enforcement of such rulings. Further, the trial court may direct any necessary steps or protections to assure that the party in whose favor the partial final judgment has been entered obtains the benefit of the judgment.

7. STAYS UNDER STATE ENFORCEMENT LAWS

Each state has a complex web of laws regarding the enforcement of judgments. There are detailed procedures, as well as numerous "exemptions" and other rules, governing the process by which a judgment is satisfied. By contrast, the federal rules contain almost no provisions on this topic: Instead, most federal judgments are enforced in accordance with the state procedures of the jurisdiction where the federal court is located. In accord with this "borrowing" approach to enforcement of judgments in the federal courts generally, Rule 62(f) calls for adherence to any stay procedures under applicable state law concerning enforcement of judgments:

> **(f) Stay According to State Law.** In any state in which a judgment is a lien upon the property of the judgment debtor and in which the judgment debtor is entitled to a stay of execution, a judgment debtor is entitled, in the district court held therein, to such stay as would be accorded the judgment debtor had the action been maintained in the courts of that state.

Despite the broad language of this section of the Rule, courts have noted that it is not self-executing. Thus, even if a stay would be automatic in state court a party must file a motion in the federal court asserting entitlement to the benefits of the state rules. Whitehead v. Food Max of Miss., Inc., 277 F.3d 791 (5th Cir. 2002).

8. LATE POSTING OF A BOND: EFFECT ON PRIOR EN-FORCEMENT ACTIVITIES

In Sheldon v. Munford, 128 F.R.D. 663 (N.D. Ind. 1989) plaintiffs in a franchise lawsuit won a verdict in the amount of $300,000 and judgment was entered on May 24th. When they attempted to collect the judgment the defendant requested a stay of the enforcement of the judgment pending appeal. Pursuant to Federal Rule of Civil Procedure 62(d), the court granted the stay on July 13 conditioned upon the posting of a supersedeas bond in the amount of $325,000 by August 1. When defendant failed to post the required bond, the plaintiffs continued with the collection process. On October 10th the defendant finally filed a supersedeas bond in the amount of $325,000 with the Insurance Company of North America as surety. The plaintiffs did not file any objections to that bond, and it was approved by the court. In the meantime, however, plaintiffs had obtained a "Writ of Execution" on the judgment from the United States District Court in another state, where defendant was attempting to complete a real estate transaction. The Writ of Execution is a cloud on the property's title. The court held that it had jurisdiction even with an appeal pending "to regulate the collection proceedings" because of the power it had to adjust the supersedeas bond and to assure that the bond provided the protection to which the plaintiffs were entitled. The court concluded:

> Finally, the Sheldons suggest that Munford's failure to post the bond in a timely fashion required them to expend time and effort to secure the judicial liens. The Sheldons argue that it would be inequitable to vacate those liens at this time. However, this argument ignores the purpose of a supersedeas bond. As previously stated, the purpose of the bond is to guarantee that the plaintiffs will be able to collect their judgment if the verdict is affirmed on appeal. Regardless of when the bond is posted, Rule 62(d) provides that the bond is the only security which the plaintiffs are entitled to pending appeal. Since there has been no showing that the Sheldons will not be able to collect on the bond, they may not continue to disrupt Munford's legitimate business activities with judicial liens.

9. RECOVERY OF THE BOND PREMIUM (IF THE APPELLANT WINS THE APPEAL)

If an appellant incurs a premium expense in purchasing a supersedeas bond, and then wins the appeal, the bond premium can be recouped in the taxation of "costs" that is normally permitted after an appeal is concluded. See F.R.App.P. 39(e).

Notes and Questions

1. Why does Federal Rule of Civil Procedure 62 provide for an automatic delay of 10 days in the execution of a judgment?

2. Is there a difference between obtaining a stay of a judgment for money or property and any other type of judgment? Why?

3. Is obtaining a stay secured by a bond the only way to preserve the status quo pending appeal?

4. What is the *res judicata* effect of a judgment that has been appealed but that has not been stayed? While the current Restatement of Judgments clearly provides that for such claim preclusion to apply there must be "a final judgment on the merits," Restatement (Second) of Judgments §§ 17, 24 (1982), a pending appeal does not interrupt the judgment. Id. at § 13 cmt. f. Thus, according to Hunt v. Liberty Lobby, Inc., 707 F.2d 1493 (D.C. Cir. 1983) the res judicata effect is the same as if no appeal had been taken. See also See Huron Holding Co. v. Lincoln Mine Operating Co., 312 U.S. 183, 189, 61 S.Ct. 513, 85 L.Ed. 725 (1941) (holding that availability or even the pendency of an appeal does not affect finality of federal judgment). The same applies to registering the judgment in another jurisdiction. Kaplan v. Hirsh, 696 F.2d 1046 (4th Cir. 1982).

5. What is the effect of a bond filed by a party other than the appellant? According to Young v. Kilroy Oil Co., 673 S.W.2d 236 (Tex. App.1984) and Fogelson v. Fogelson, 39 Conn.Sup. 63, 467 A.2d 1272 (1983) it has no effect. Should it make a difference who files the bond?

SECTION C. RULINGS INVOLVING INJUNCTIVE FORMS OF RELIEF

No Built–In Stay After Injunction Rulings. As noted in the preceding sections, under Rule 62(a) of the civil rules the automatic stay of enforcement principle is not applicable to injunction rulings. If the trial judge enters an order that particular conduct be done or that a party refrain from acting, that ruling is immediately effective unless a phase-in provision is set forth in the ruling itself. Under present federal court rules a trial court's injunction ruling is immediately enforceable (no 10–day stay) and it remains in force even if an appeal is properly commenced by the losing party.

Supersedeas is Not a General Answer. The rules do not provide for the filing of a supersedeas bond to stop the effect of an injunctive decree. In part this is no doubt due to the fact that injunctive relief is normally awarded when fixing the amount of dollar relief would be difficult. If precise calculation of damages has already been shown to be impractical, it would be odd to allow posting of a dollar bond to supersede the injunction. Thus, in general, there is no automatic right to interrupt or defer the operation of injunctive relief by filing a bond.

Crafting a Special Purpose Modification of Injunctive Relief. Arguments for stays of injunctive relief commonly center around the issue of preserving the "status quo" to allow an effective appellate ruling. Of course, sometimes it is difficult to identify the state of affairs that needs to be preserved. In a complicated commercial transaction, such as a takeover bid to acquire controlling shares in another enterprise and effectuate a merger, finding a stage of the proceedings at which to call a halt pending appellate review may be difficult, even if both parties and the trial court are in agreement that appellate guidance would be helpful. See, e.g., Simon Property Group v. Taubman Centers, Inc., 262 F. Supp. 2d 794 (E.D. Mich. 2003) where an injunction was issued against the target party's lobbying efforts to oppose an ongoing takeover bid. In that context, is an ongoing "process" of tendering for shares the status quo, and can it continue to completion while an injunction against interference is appealed by the restrained party?

As a general matter, as the Second Circuit has observed, a stay of a preliminary injunction pending appeal will almost always be logically inconsistent with the prior finding the trial court will have just made in granting the injunction that there will be irreparable harm that is imminent. Nonetheless, district court has authority to grant a brief stay of even from the operation of a preliminary injunction in appropriate cases in order to permit a court of appeals the opportunity to consider an application for a stay pending appeal under expedited motion practice procedures. See Rodriguez v. DeBuono, 175 F.3d 227 (2d Cir. 1999)(injunction requiring daily "safety monitoring" for a statewide class of mentally disabled persons as part of Medicaid personal home care services was stayed pending appeal).

In Hilton v. Braunskill, 481 U.S. 770, 107 S.Ct. 2113, 95 L.Ed.2d 724 (1987) the United States Supreme Court summarized the applicable law:

> Different Rules of Procedure govern the power of district courts and courts of appeals to stay an order pending appeal. See Fed. Rule Civ. Proc. 62(c); Fed. Rule App. Proc. 8(a). Under both Rules, however, the factors regulating the issuance of a stay are generally the same: (1) whether the stay applicant has made a strong showing that he is likely to succeed on the merits; (2) whether the applicant will be irreparably injured absent a stay; (3) whether issuance of the stay will substantially injure the other parties interested in the proceeding; and (4) where the public interest lies. See, e. g., Virginia Petroleum Jobbers Assn. v. FPC, 259 F.2d 921, 925 (D.C. Cir. 1958).

Applying these principles in concrete factual situations is challenging. The Supreme Court concluded that these factors "contemplate individualized judgment in each case, [and] the formula cannot be reduced to a set of rigid rules."

WASHINGTON MET. AREA TRANSIT COM'N v. HOLIDAY TOURS, INC.

United States Court of Appeals, District of Columbia Circuit, 1977.
559 F.2d 841.

LEVENTHAL, CIRCUIT JUDGE.

The District Court granted the Washington Metropolitan Area Transit Commission a permanent injunction restraining Holiday Tours from operating a motor coach sightseeing service without a certificate of public convenience and necessity. Then, on motion of Holiday Tours, the District Court stayed its injunction pending appeal. We deny the Commission's motion to vacate the District Court's stay, and in doing so find it necessary to refine the discussion in Virginia Petroleum Jobbers Association v. FPC, 259 F.2d 921 (D.C. Cir. 1958).

On the merits, this appeal turns on the proper interpretation of Holiday Tours, Inc. v. Washington Metropolitan Area Transit Commission, 372 F.2d 401 (1967), in which we affirmed the Commission's ruling that Holiday Tours was not entitled to a certificate of public convenience and necessity under the "grandfather clause" of the pertinent statute. In our concluding paragraph of that opinion, we stated (at 402):

> Finally, we note that the Commission concedes that appellant may continue to operate in the future a sightseeing business by limousine, as well as with buses and drivers supplied by licensed bus operators. * * *

This language is central to the current dispute because Holiday Tours, which was primarily a limousine tour service when our earlier opinion was rendered, has recently transformed itself into primarily a bus tour service. Holiday Tours contends that this conversion is authorized by the quoted language so long as the buses are rented from licensed operators rather than owned by Holiday Tours itself. The Commission, however, argues that the language is merely the court's observation that no certificate is required if Holiday Tours occasionally rents buses to accommodate additional customers as an *adjunct* to its primary business of providing limousine tours. The Commission emphatically rejects an interpretation which sanctions Holiday Tours' conversion from a limousine to a bus tour service.

The District Court adopted the Commission's interpretation but stayed the permanent injunction pending appeal. Although the District Court did not make detailed findings, it recited that all four of the *Virginia Petroleum Jobbers* factors favored a stay.

These factors are by now familiar to both the bench and bar in this Circuit.

> (1) Has the petitioner made a strong showing that it is likely to prevail on the merits of its appeal? Without such a substantial indication of probable success, there would be no justification for the court's intrusion into the ordinary processes of administration and judicial review. (2) Has the petitioner shown that without such relief, it will be irreparably injured? . . . (3) Would the issuance of a stay substantially harm other parties interested in the proceedings? . . . (4) Where lies the public interest? . . .

Virginia Petroleum Jobbers Ass'n, 259 F.2d at 925.

Despite the Commission's protestations to the contrary, the final three factors enumerated above clearly favored the District Court's grant of a stay. The harm to Holiday Tours in the absence of a stay would be its destruction in its current form as a provider of bus tours. In contrast to this irreparable harm, there is little indication that a stay pending appeal will result in substantial harm to either appellee Commission or to other tour bus operators. As to harm to the public interest, this is not a case where the Commission has ruled that the service performed by appellant is contrary to the public interest. Indeed for all that the record discloses, appellant might obtain a certificate, perhaps not precisely for the operation it prefers, if it made application. The interest of the Commission and of the riding public is largely the same as that of the general public in having legal questions decided on the merits, as correctly and expeditiously as possible. But the question is whether there is a further interest, that precludes maintaining the status quo while the merits are being decided on appeal.

In this context, Holiday Tours was undoubtedly not entitled to a stay on a showing "that it is likely to prevail on the merits of its appeal." Implicit in the Commission's argument against the stay is the view, commonly shared by litigants interpreting *Virginia Petroleum Jobbers*, that a stay is never appropriate unless the movant can show that success on appeal is "probable." Adherents of this view maintain that a lesser showing, of, say, a chance of prevailing that is only fifty percent or less is insufficient even though the "balance of equities," as determined by a consideration of the other three factors, clearly favors a stay.

Although this approach adopts a linguistically permissible interpretation of *Virginia Petroleum Jobbers,* it is mandated only if one assumes that the Court was using language in an exceedingly precise, technical sense. In light of the unnecessarily harsh results sometimes engendered by this approach, we decline to entertain this assumption. Instead, we hold that under *Virginia Petroleum Jobbers* a court, when confronted with a case in which the other three factors strongly favor interim relief may exercise its discretion to grant a stay if the movant has made a substantial case on the merits. The court is not required to find that ultimate success by the movant is a mathematical probability, and indeed, as in this case, may grant a stay even though its own approach may be contrary to movant's view of the merits. The necessary "level" or "degree" of possibility of success will vary according to the court's assessment of the other factors.

This approach is reflected in the *Virginia Petroleum Jobbers*, 259 F.2d at 925, where the court wrote:

> But injury held insufficient to justify a stay in one case may well be sufficient to justify it in another, where the applicant has demonstrated a higher probability of success on the merits.

The view that a 50% plus probability is required by that opinion, although frequently encountered, is thus contrary to both the language and spirit of that opinion.

Our holding is generally in accord with the movement in other courts away from a standard incorporating a wooden "probability" requirement and toward an analysis under which the necessary showing on the merits is governed by the balance of equities as revealed through an examination of the other three factors. In a leading case, Judge Frank, speaking for the Second Circuit, stated:

> To justify a temporary injunction it is not necessary that the plaintiff's right to a final decision, after a trial, be absolutely certain, wholly without doubt; if the other elements are present (i.e., the balance of hardships tips decidedly toward plaintiff), it will ordinarily be enough that the plaintiff has raised questions going to the merits so serious, substantial, difficult and doubtful, as to make them a fair ground for litigation and thus for more deliberative investigation.

Hamilton Watch Co. v. Benrus Watch Co., 206 F.2d 738, 740 (2d Cir. 1953). More recently, the same court declared:

> One moving for a preliminary injunction assumes the burden of demonstrating either a combination of probable success and the possibility of irreparable injury or that serious questions are raised and the balance of hardships tips sharply in his favor.

Charlie's Girls, Inc. v. Revlon, Inc., 483 F.2d 953, 954 (2d Cir. 1973) (per curiam). To the same effect, see also Costandi v. AAMCO Automatic Transmissions, Inc., 456 F.2d 941 (9th Cir. 1972).

We believe that this approach is entirely consistent with the purpose of granting interim injunctive relief, whether by preliminary injunction or by stay pending appeal. Generally, such relief is preventative, or protective; it seeks to maintain the status quo pending a final determination of the merits of the suit. An order maintaining the status quo is appropriate when a serious legal question is presented, when little if any harm will befall other interested persons or the public and when denial of the order would inflict irreparable injury on the movant. There is substantial equity, and need for judicial protection, whether or not movant has shown a mathematical probability of success.

Another weakness of adherence to a strict "probability" requirement is that it leads to an exaggeratedly refined analysis of the merits at an early stage in the litigation. If, to use Judge Frank's phrase, there exists "a fair ground for litigation and thus for more deliberative investigation," a court should not be required at an early stage to draw the fine line between a mathematical probability and a substantial possibility of success. The endeavor may be necessary in some circumstances when interim relief would cause substantial harm to another party or person, or when the balance of equities may come to require a more careful heft of the merits. However, it is not required in all cases.

The doctrine thus stated is congruent with Rules 8 and 18 of the Federal Rules of Appellate Procedure, which state that motions for stay "must ordinarily be made in the first instance" to the district court or agency which issued the challenged order. Prior recourse to the initial decision maker would hardly be required as a general matter if it could properly grant interim relief only on a prediction that it has rendered an erroneous decision. What is fairly contemplated is that tribunals may properly stay their own orders when they have ruled on an admittedly difficult legal question and when the equities of the case suggest that the status quo should be maintained.

Applying this standard to the instant motion, we cannot say that the District Court abused its discretion in staying its permanent injunction. Although a more searching inquiry into the merits might compel the tentative conclusion that Holiday Tours is less likely than not to prevail on the merits, we have satisfied ourselves that the case is a difficult one warranting plenary review. In light of the balance of equities in this case, that suffices to sustain the stay.

The Commission's motion to vacate the District Court's order staying its permanent injunction is denied.

So ordered.

Notes and Questions

What are the criteria established in the principal case for determining whether a stay pending appeal should be granted? Are the criteria cumulative or alternative? Is it realistic to ask the losing party to persuade the trial judge who has ruled against it that it is likely to prevail on appeal? Are these criteria applicable only to the stay of an injunction or to other types of orders and judgments as well?

GRUTTER v. BOLLINGER

United States District Court, Eastern District of Michigan, 2001.
137 F. Supp. 2d 874.

BERNARD A. FRIEDMAN, DISTRICT JUDGE.

This matter is presently before the court on defendants' motion to stay injunction. Plaintiffs have filed a response in opposition. For the following reasons, the motion is denied.

In an opinion and order dated March 27, 2001, the court found that the University of Michigan Law School has violated the Equal Protection Clause and Title VI of the Civil Rights Act of 1964 by using race as a factor in considering applications for admission. Accordingly, the court ordered that the law school "is hereby enjoined from using applicants' race as a factor in its admissions decisions." Defendants have indicated that they intend to appeal the court's decision. In the instant motion, defendants ask that the court stay the injunction pending appeal. The intervenors concur in the motion; plaintiffs oppose it.

LEGAL STANDARDS

* * * In deciding such a motion, the court considers the following factors:

> (1) whether the stay applicant has made a strong showing that he is likely to succeed on the merits; (2) whether the applicant will be irreparably injured absent a stay; (3) whether issuance of the stay will substantially injure the other parties interested in the proceeding; and (4) where the public interest lies.

Hilton v. Braunskill, 481 U.S. 770, 776 (1987). The Sixth Circuit has provided considerable guidance as to how these factors should be weighed:

> These factors are not prerequisites that must be met, but are interrelated considerations that must be balanced together.

> Although the factors to be considered are the same for both a preliminary injunction and a stay pending appeal, the balancing process is not identical due to the different procedural posture in which each judicial determination arises. Upon a motion for a preliminary injunction, the court must make a decision based upon "incomplete factual findings and legal research." Even so, that decision is generally accorded a great deal of deference on appellate review....

> Conversely, a motion for a stay pending appeal is generally made after the district court has considered fully the merits of the

underlying action and issued judgment, usually following completion of discovery. As a result, a movant seeking a stay pending review on the merits of a district court's judgment will have greater difficulty in demonstrating a likelihood of success on the merits. In essence, a party seeking a stay must ordinarily demonstrate to a reviewing court that there is a likelihood of reversal. Presumably, there is a reduced probability of error, at least with respect to a court's findings of fact, because the district court had the benefit of a complete record that can be reviewed by this court when considering the motion for a stay.

To justify the granting of a stay, however, a movant need not always establish a high probability of success on the merits. The probability of success that must be demonstrated is inversely proportional to the amount of irreparable injury plaintiffs will suffer absent the stay. Simply stated, more of one excuses less of the other. This relationship, however, is not without its limits; the movant is always required to demonstrate more than the mere "possibility" of success on the merits. For example, even if a movant demonstrates irreparable harm that decidedly outweighs any potential harm to the defendant if a stay is granted, he is still required to show, at a minimum, "serious questions going to the merits."

In evaluating the harm that will occur depending upon whether or not the stay is granted, we generally look to three factors: (1) the substantiality of the injury alleged; (2) the likelihood of its occurrence; and (3) the adequacy of the proof provided.... In addition, the harm alleged must be both certain and immediate, rather than speculative or theoretical....

Of course, in order for a reviewing court to adequately consider these four factors, the movant must address each factor, regardless of its relative strength, providing specific facts and affidavits supporting assertions that these factors exist.

Michigan Coalition of Radioactive Material Users, Inc. v. Griepentrog, 945 F.2d 150, 153–54 (6th Cir. 1991). "Because the burden of meeting this standard is a heavy one, more commonly stay requests will not meet this standard and will be denied." 11 C. Wright & A. Miller, Federal Practice and Procedure § 2904, pp. 503–505 (1995).

APPLICATION

Defendants first argue that "there is a reasonable possibility that Defendants' position will ultimately prevail." Defendants' Mem. of Law in Support of Motion to Stay Injunction, p. 4. "Reasonable possibility" is not the standard. Rather, as noted above, defendants must make a "strong showing" that they are likely to succeed on the merits; they must, at a minimum, demonstrate the existence of "serious questions going to the merits."

Defendants have failed to demonstrate the existence of "serious questions going to the merits." While the status of Justice Powell's endorsement of the diversity rationale is debatable, the court is convinced that in Part IV–D of his opinion in Regents of the Univ. of Cal. v. Bakke, 438 U.S. 265 (1978), Justice Powell was speaking only for himself, not for a majority of the Supreme Court. A majority of the Court has never recognized racial diversity in university admissions as a compelling state interest. And as this court noted in its March 27, 2001, opinion, post-Bakke Supreme Court decisions cast further doubt on the constitutionality of any use of race that is not strictly remedial. * * *

The cases cited by defendants are not to the contrary. Oliver v. Kalamazoo Bd. of Educ., 706 F.2d 757 (6th Cir. 1983), was a school desegregation case in which the district court imposed a racial hiring quota for teachers as part of the remedy for the intentional racial segregation of students. The court of appeals reversed on the grounds that the quota was arbitrary and because the school district was acting in good faith to remedy the effects of past discrimination. See id. at 762–63. In dictum, the court stated that hiring quotas as not per se improper, but "generally, the wiser approach is a more flexible affirmative action program rather than a hiring quota. Cf. University of California v. Bakke, 438 U.S. 265 (1978) (affirmative action admission programs of educational institutions may take race into account, but racial quotas are prohibited)." 706 F.2d at 763. Nothing in Oliver supports defendants' argument that diversity in university admissions has ever been recognized as a compelling state interest, or that the Sixth Circuit has held that Bakke stands for such a proposition. * * *

Nor are defendants assisted by Hopwood v. State of Texas, 236 F.3d 256, 276 (5th Cir. 2000), in which the Fifth Circuit reversed the district court's order enjoining the University of Texas School of Law "from taking into consideration racial preferences in the selection of those individuals to be admitted as students." The first reason for the reversal was that the district court failed to make findings of fact and conclusions of law, as required by Fed. R. Civ. P. 52(a), something which cannot be said of this court's injunction. The second reason for the reversal was that the injunction "forbids the University from using racial preferences for any reason, despite Bakke's holding that racial preferences are constitutionally permissible in some circumstances." Id. at 276–77. This court's injunction should not be understood as prohibiting "any and all use of racial preferences," id. at 277, but only the uses presented and argued by the defendants and the intervenors in this case—namely, in order to assemble a racially diverse class or to remedy the effects of societal discrimination. No other justifications were offered by the parties to this lawsuit, none others were considered by this court, and none others are enjoined by this court's order.

Even if a higher court rules that assembling a racially diverse class can be a compelling state interest, defendants cannot overcome the overwhelming evidence, and this court's findings based on that evidence, that their use of race is not narrowly tailored to the achievement of that interest. At pages 49–54 of its opinion, the court listed five reasons why the law school's admissions policy is not narrowly tailored. In their motion to stay, defendants do not even mention narrow tailoring or suggest why the court's analysis of this prong of the strict scrutiny test is likely to be reversed on appeal. As the Sixth Circuit has observed, defendants' task is more difficult than it would be if they were seeking a stay of a preliminary injunction, as the injunction in question was issued after an exhaustive consideration of the merits. See Griepentrog, 945 F.2d at 153.

Defendants next argue that they will be irreparably harmed unless the injunction is stayed. Defendants claim that the admissions process for the current season will be disrupted, that they will be prevented from admitting a racially diverse class, and that their First Amendment rights to academic freedom and the pursuit of educational goals will be infringed.

Defendants' arguments do not satisfactorily establish a certain and immediate threat of irreparable harm. Taking the arguments in reverse order, defendants' First Amendment rights to select the student body and to pursue educational goals are not seriously infringed by an injunction prohibiting the unconstitutional consideration of race in making admissions decisions. In any event, the equal protection rights of all applicants to be considered for admission without regard to their race clearly outweighs the First Amendment rights claimed by the law school.

Defendants' second argument is that the injunction will "thwart[] the Law School's ability to enroll a meaningful number of underrepresented minority students, which is critical to its educational mission." Defendants' Mem. of Law in Support of Motion to Stay Injunction, p. 9. This goes to the heart of the case and is in effect an argument for reconsideration of the merits. The court heard extensive testimony during a 15–day bench trial as to the reasons why defendants believe they must consider race in order to admit a critical mass of underrepresented minority students. However, for the reasons explained at length in its March 27, 2001, opinion, the court has concluded that the attainment of a racially diverse class is not a sufficiently compelling interest to justify race-based admissions decisions. The court has found that defendants' use of race is indistinguishable from a quota system, and there is no doubt that racial quotas in this context and for this purpose are unconstitutional. Defendants are not irreparably harmed by an injunction that requires them to comply with the Constitution.

Nor is the court convinced that the law school "will have to halt its entire admissions process immediately" unless a stay is granted. Defendants' Mem. of Law in Support of Motion to Stay Injunction, p. 7. Defendants claim that they cannot predict how many offers they must make under a race-blind system in order to enroll the desired number of students; that they will need "several weeks" to analyze the new situation statistically; and that the best candidates will enroll elsewhere during the delay.[1]

---

1. Defendants indicate they have made 826 offers of admission to date, and that 70 of these are for students who will begin studying in the summer of 2001. Therefore,

These arguments, which are supported by an affidavit of the acting dean of admissions, are unpersuasive. The court's injunction is simply and easily complied with: race is not to be used as a factor to achieve a racially diverse class or to remedy societal discrimination. Defendants testified at trial that they review every application individually. They should continue to do so, but without considering the race of the applicants. Defendants indicate the immediate urgency is that "approximately 100 additional offers need to be extended in the next 10 days in order to fill [the summer] section." Defendants' Mem. of Law in Support of Motion to Stay Injunction, p. 8. With their extensive experience in reviewing law school applications, defendants should have no difficulty identifying 100 excellent candidates within this time frame without considering race. Nor should the law school be unduly hindered in finishing the admissions process for the class entering in the fall of 2001. Defendants indicate they have already made over 750 offers of admission and that approximately 300–450 more offers must be made in order to round out the entering class. The court sees no insurmountable obstacle in completing the admissions process while obeying the injunction.

The final two factors—the interests of other parties and the public interest—also weigh against granting a stay. Because this is a class action, the plaintiffs are not merely one individual but all non-minority applicants whose applications are reviewed less favorably than those of minority applicants. Clearly, the members of the plaintiff class with pending applications have a strong interest in keeping the injunction in place. There is also a strong public interest in ensuring that public institutions comply with the Constitution.

For these reasons, the court concludes that defendants have failed to demonstrate their entitlement to a stay of the injunction. Defendants have not shown they are likely to succeed on the merits on appeal; defendants have not demonstrated that they will be irreparably harmed if the injunction is not stayed; and the interest of the other parties and of the public would be harmed by a stay. Accordingly,

IT IS ORDERED that defendants' motion to stay injunction is denied.[2]

Notes

1. The outcome in the principal case was reversed on appeal. See Grutter v. Bollinger, 539 U.S. 306, 123 S.Ct. 2325, 156 L.Ed.2d 304 (2003),

approximately 756 offers of admission have been made for the class entering in the fall of 2001. Defendants further indicate that they generally must make a total of between 1,050 and 1,200 offers of admission in order to enroll a fall class of 350. Therefore, it appears that between 294 and 444 offers must still be made. The court's injunction does not require the law school to rescind any offers it has already extended.

2. Defendants' alternative request for a 10–day "administrative stay" is also denied.

Defendants seek this alternative relief "to permit Defendants an opportunity to file their notice of appeal and seek a stay from the Court of Appeals." Defendants are free at any time to apply to the court of appeals for a stay of this court's injunction. See Fed. R. Civ. P. 62(g). Indeed, defendants state in their brief that they intended to file a notice of appeal on April 2, 2001, and to seek a stay from the court of appeals if this court did not grant one by that date. Thus, it does not appear that any purpose would be served by a 10–day stay.

holding that the University of Michigan Law School's narrowly tailored use of race in admissions decisions to further a compelling interest in obtaining the educational benefits that flow from a diverse student body is not prohibited by the Equal Protection Clause, Title VI, or § 1981.

2. Where "the public interest" served by the trial court's initial disposition is strong, even a temporary stay of that order may be denied. See, e.g., Friends of the Wild Swan, Inc. v. United States EPA, 130 F. Supp 2d 1207 (D. Mo. 2000) (a stay of the trial court's order setting a timetable for compliance with federal water quality standards in Montana was denied, despite arguments by the state government that compliance with the order during an appeal would bring highway construction and other necessary projects to a complete halt). On the other hand, where a stay of relief will not present "life or death dangers" the trial court has discretion to stay even rulings that serve constitutional purposes, pending appellate review.

GLASSROTH v. MOORE

United States District Court, Middle District of Alabama, 2002.
242 F. Supp. 2d 1068.

Myron H. Thompson, United States District Judge.

Order

On November 18, 2002, this court held that defendant Roy S. Moore, Chief Justice of the Alabama Supreme Court, violated the Establishment Clause of the First Amendment to the United States Constitution by placing a Ten Commandments monument in the rotunda of the Alabama State Judicial Building. Chief Justice Moore was given thirty days to remove the monument voluntarily, and he failed to do so. On December 19, 2002, the court issued a permanent injunction requiring the Chief Justice to remove the monument by January 3, 2003. On that same day, the Chief Justice filed a notice of appeal from that injunction. Currently before the court is the Chief Justice's motion asking that the court stay the injunction, pursuant to Fed. R. Civ. P. 62(c), while the case is pending on appeal. The motion will be granted.

Four factors inform a trial court's decision whether to stay an injunction: (1) the applicant's likelihood of prevailing on the merits of the appeal; (2) whether the applicant will suffer irreparable damage absent a stay; (3) the harm that the other parties will suffer if a stay is granted; and (4) where the public interest lies. Hilton v. Braunskill, 481 U.S. 770, 776 (1987); United States v. Bogle, 855 F.2d 707, 708 (11th Cir. 1988). These factors, however, should not be applied as "a set of rigid rules," *Hilton*, 481 U.S. at 777; rather these "traditional stay factors contemplate individualized judgments in each case." Id. For example, when the "balance of the equities [identified in factors 2, 3, and 4] weighs heavily in favor of granting the stay," only a "substantial case on the merits" is necessary to satisfy the first factor. Garcia–Mir v. Meese, 781 F.2d 1450, 1453 (11th Cir. 1986).

The Monument

For the reasons given in the November 18 opinion, the court does not believe that the Chief Justice has presented even a substantial case on the merits. Additionally, the Chief Justice cannot show he will suffer irreparable harm unless the injunction is stayed, because the monument can be easily returned if this court's decision is reversed. Nevertheless, the court is convinced that a stay is warranted based on the other two factors of the stay inquiry.

It is almost certain that the Eleventh Circuit Court of Appeals would grant a temporary or short stay, at the very least, in order to have adequate time to consider whether a longer stay pending appeal should be granted. To review this court's denial or grant of a stay, the appellate court would need beyond the January 3 deadline to review the record to determine, among other things, whether this court's decision that the Chief Justice does not have a substantial case for appeal is correct. Indeed, if this court were sitting as an appellate court unfamiliar with the record, the undersigned (as a member of that court) would counsel granting a temporary stay for this reason. Therefore, aside from the issue of the merits of this case, there is no realistic likelihood that the monument will be removed by January 3; this court and the parties are looking at a date beyond the January 3 deadline before the Eleventh Circuit can even determine whether a stay pending appeal is warranted. Moreover, if an expedited review on the merits is feasible, there is also a strong likelihood that the appellate court would delay reaching the merits on the stay issue and would simply address them on the final appeal.

To be sure, the plaintiffs will suffer continuing irreparable harm pending the appeal. See Elrod v. Burns, 427 U.S. 347, 373 (1976) ("The loss of First Amendment freedoms, for even minimal periods of time, unquestionably constitutes irreparable injury"). But this case does not present a circumstance where the magnitude of the harm requires the appellate court to shoot from the hip, such as a life-or-death situation or a situation where to delay a decision on relief pending appeal would leave a party without relief at all.

The court, therefore, finds that the plaintiffs', as well as the public's, main goal of the vindication of the First Amendment through the expeditious and orderly removal of the monument would be better furthered by expeditious appellate review of the case on its merits. The plaintiffs did not seek a preliminary injunction in this court; instead, the parties and this court devoted their time and resources to expedited preparation and consideration of the merits of the case. This case was, therefore, litigated in a little over a year, including the development of a complete record, the holding of a week-long trial, and the issuance of a judgment. Moreover, the appellate record is now almost complete. There is no reason why the Eleventh Circuit, if it were to choose, could not similarly expedite its review. Toward this end, the parties should devote their immediate time and resources to an expedited appellate review of the case on the merits rather than whether a stay should be granted.

Finally, it should be repeated that the court does not discount the harm to the plaintiffs in allowing the monument to remain pending appeal of this case, nor does the court discount the public interest in having the unconstitutional actions by the Chief Justice remedied forthwith. Therefore, the court emphasizes that, upon receipt of an appellate mandate affirming this court's decision and injunction, the court will immediately lift the stay and enter another injunction, along the lines of the December 19 injunction, requiring the removal of the Ten Commandments monument within fifteen days.

According, it is ORDERED that the motion for a stay of the injunction pending appeal, filed by defendant Roy S. Moore on December 19, 2002 is granted.

GOTANDA, THE EMERGING STANDARDS FOR ISSUING APPELLATE STAYS

45 Baylor L. Rev. 809, 819–823 (1993).*

Surprisingly, no uniform standards exist in the federal appellate courts for granting stays. Courts have not only disagreed over what the relevant factors are for granting such equitable relief, but also the procedure that should be used to weigh the various factors in rendering their rulings. These disparities have resulted in forum shopping and inconsistent decisions, and they have made it impossible to accurately predict a court's ruling on a motion for stay. * * *

In general, four procedures have been used to weigh the above factors in deciding whether to grant the stay: (1) the sequential test; (2) two-alternative test; (3) balancing-of-the-factors test; and (4) the two-tier sliding scale test. * * *

A. The Sequential Test. The most difficult of four tests under which to obtain a stay is the sequential test. Under that approach, the movant is required to establish in sequence each of the four factors. Movant therefore must show:

> (1) a substantial likelihood that movant will prevail on the merits, (2) a substantial threat that movant will suffer irreparable injury if the stay is not granted, (3) that the threatened injury to movant outweighs the threatened harm the stay may do to the other parties, and (4) that granting the stay will not disserve the public interest.

If the movant is unable to carry the burden of persuasion on any one of the factors, the stay will be denied. By requiring the movant establish all

* Copyright © 1993, Baylor Law Review. Reprinted by permission. All rights reserved.

four factors in order to obtain a stay, this test does not contemplate a lesser showing on one factor to be compensated by a stronger showing on one or more of the other factors.

B. The Two–Alternative Test. The two-alternative test appears to be the most lenient of the various procedures for weighing the four stay factors. Under this test, a stay will be granted "only upon clear showing of either (1) probable success on the merits and possible irreparable injury, or (2) sufficiently serious questions going to the merits to make them a fair ground for litigation and a balance of hardships tipping decidedly toward the party requesting the preliminary relief." This test thus appears to allow a movant to prevail without proof of probable irreparable injury if probable success could be shown.

C. The Balancing-of-the-Factors Test. In contrast to the strict standard imposed by the sequence approach, the balance-of-the-factors test allows the court flexibility in determining whether to grant or deny the stay by permitting a lesser showing on one factor to be compensated by a strong showing on one or more of the other factors. Under the balancing test, no single factor is determinative since all four factors are "balanced" to determine whether a stay is warranted in a particular case. Thus, the movant is not required to demonstrate a more than fifty percent chance of prevailing on the merits since that requirement will vary with the balance of the other factors. For example, a stay may be granted where the likelihood of success on the merits is low if the balance of harms and the public interest tips decidedly in the movant's favor. Conversely, a stay may be granted where there is "a high probability of success and some injury."

D. The Two–Tier Sliding Scale Test. The Seventh Circuit has formulated a two-tier sliding scale test that basically incorporates features from the above tests. Under the Seventh Circuit's approach, the movant, as a threshold matter, "must demonstrate (1) some likelihood of succeeding on the merits, and (2) that it has 'no adequate remedy at law' and will suffer "irreparable harm" if . . . relief is denied." If the movant cannot satisfy both of these inquiries, the stay would be denied and no further inquiry would be necessary. If the movant is able to clear these initial hurdles, however, the court would then take into consideration the remaining factors (i.e., the harm to the non-moving party and the public interest) and weigh all four factors using a sliding scale approach to decide whether to grant or deny the stay, seeking at all times to minimize the costs of being mistaken.

Under the sliding scale approach, the more likely that the movant "will succeed on the merits, the less the balance of irreparable harms need weigh towards its side." Conversely, "the less likely it is that the movant will succeed, the more the balance need weigh toward its side." Thus, where both the overall balance of harms and the court's assessment of the merits favors the movant, the court would grant the stay. If, however, the overall balance of harms and the court's assessment of the merits favors the non-moving party, the court would deny the stay.

Where the balance of harms are in equipoise or near equipoise, the court would decide in favor of the party that appears more likely to prevail on the merits. Also, if each party has an equal chance of prevailing on the merits, the court would rule in favor of the party that will suffer the most irreparable injury.

In situations where the merits favor one party and the balance of harms favors the other, the court would evaluate the degree of irreparable injury with the prospects of prevailing on the merits. Thus, a stay may be granted with a high probability of success and some injury, or vice versa.

Seventh Circuit Judge Posner has sought to clarify the relationship under the sliding scale approach through the use of a mathematical formula: $P \times Hd > (1-P) \times Hg$. Under this formula, a stay will be granted only if "the harm to the movant if the stay is denied, multiplied by the probability that the denial would be an error i.e., that the movant will ultimately prevail, exceeds the harm to the other parties if the stay is granted, multiplied by the probability that granting the stay would be an error." Judge Posner further explained that "the left-hand side of the formula is simply the probability of an erroneous denial weighted by the cost of denial to the movant, and the right-hand side simply the probability of an erroneous grant weighted by the cost of the grant to the other parties." Essentially, the formula is designed to minimize the costs of being mistaken.

Analysis of the Various Procedures. A uniform procedure for weighing the various stay factors is needed. As noted, however, there has been much debate over what should be the uniform procedure. Any procedure should strive to satisfy the following goals. First, the test for granting a stay should allow a court flexibility to exercise its equitable discretion. As the Supreme Court has noted, the formula for granting a stay "cannot be reduced to a set of rigid rules." Rather, it should allow for "individualized judgments in each case." Second, the test should be easy to apply and promote judicial efficiency. In many cases, the decision whether to issue a stay often is made under severe time constraints and without a hearing. Furthermore, given the nature of the requested relief, the court is usually presented with complex legal issues in hastily drafted pleadings. A clear and easy to apply uniform test would facilitate, rather than hinder, the decision making process. Third, the test should maintain the burden imposed upon the movant to show that he or she is entitled to relief. It seems appropriate to place a heavy burden upon the party seeking a stay because that party's arguments have already received full consideration by the trial court or agency. Fourth, and most importantly, the test should achieve the purpose of preserving the court's power to render a meaningful decision on the merits. To realize that objective, courts should not focus on preserving the status quo, but on minimizing the harm that would result from an erroneous decision.
* * *

SECTION D.   POWERS OF THE TRIAL COURT AFTER THE APPEAL IS LAUNCHED

Trial Court Power to Adjust Injunctive Relief After Judgment. The *trial courts* in the federal system and those of many states do have the power to make rulings with respect to the injunctive relief—even after the judgment setting forth the disposition is final. Thus under federal civil Rule 62(c) it is expressly provided that a district court has the power to suspend, modify, restore, or grant an injunction during the pendency of an appeal from an interlocutory or final judgment granting, dissolving, or denying an injunction. The court has discretion to require the posting of a bond or some other form of security to protect the rights of any other party which may be adversely affected by the ruling.

Notice that the federal rule contemplates that a trial court can adjust or otherwise deal with an existing injunctive decree *while* the case in on appeal, a rare counter-example to the general principle that the trial court loses all jurisdiction over the case once an appeal is properly commenced. See, e.g., Natural Resources Defense Council v. Southwest Marine Inc., 242 F.3d 1163, 1166 (9th Cir. 2001) (recognizing this exception). In *Southwest Marine* the Ninth Circuit expressed the view that the trial judge's power in this regard should be confined to instances where the supplemental ruling serves to preserve the status quo to allow the appellate court to rule effectively. And in one of the numerous "Napster" appellate rulings involving unauthorized copying and distribution of musical works over the Internet, that same Circuit held that a trial court's modification of a preliminary injunction—while that ruling was on appeal—exceeded the bounds of the trial judge's powers, since such a ruling could purport to adjudicate substantial rights directly involved in appeal, and interfere with appellate review of the case. See A & M Records, Inc. v. Napster, Inc., 284 F.3d 1091, 1099 (9th Cir. 2002).

FARMHAND, INC. v. ANEL ENGINEERING INDUSTRIES

United States Court of Appeals, Fifth Circuit. 1982.
693 F.2d 1140.

Politz, Circuit Judge.

This patent dispute, one of the final patent cases to be considered by this court, involves device for transporting large, compacted haystacks and cotton modules. Returning special verdicts, the jury found the patent to be valid and infringed, and determined the factual basis for damages. The district court entered judgment assessing damages and enjoining defendant Anel. Anel appealed (our docket number 811157), posting a supersedeas bond for the money damages. After this appeal was noticed, plaintiffs charged Anel with violations of the injunction. The district judge refused to adjudge Anel guilty of contempt. Plaintiffs appealed this decision (our docket number 811384), and the two appeals were consolidated. Finding no error in either case, we affirm the district court. * * *

Motion for Contempt

When the district court issued its permanent injunction, Anel had fifteen infringing machines. Anel subsequently purchased Craven Welding Company, thereby acquiring the license to sell chain-type movers which Craven had purchased from Farmhand. After Anel attempted to sell and in fact sold some of its machines, Farmhand and Reynolds sought a contempt citation. The motion was denied by the district judge.

Generally, when an appeal is noticed the district court is divested of jurisdiction; the matter is transferred immediately to the appellate court. The rule, however, is not absolute. The district court maintains jurisdiction as to matters not involved in the appeal, such as the merits of an action when appeal from a preliminary injunction is taken, see Ex parte National Enameling & Stamping Co., 201 U.S. 156 (1906), or in aid of the appeal, as by making clerical corrections. See 16 C. Wright, A. Miller, E. Cooper & E. Gressman, Federal Practice and Procedure § 3949, at 359 (1977). The district court maintains jurisdiction for other matters, such as ordering stays or modifying injunctive relief. The Ninth Circuit in Hoffman v. Beer Drivers & Salesmen's Local, 536 F.2d 1268, 1276 (9th Cir. 1976), upheld the district court's "continuing duty to maintain a status quo" in recognizing the jurisdiction of the trial court to issue further contempt orders while an appeal from the first contempt order was pending.

We have recognized the continuing jurisdiction of the district court in support of its judgment, as long as that judgment has not been superseded. In Brown v. Braddick, 595 F.2d 961 (5th Cir. 1979), a patent interference action, the district court held contempt hearings on violations of its discovery orders. Jurisdiction was sustained:

> Since Braddick failed to ask the district court for a stay pending appeal and to post supersedeas bond as required by F.R.C.P. 62(d), the district court retained power to enforce its order by civil contempt proceedings. * * *

Anel did not seek a stay of the injunction nor post a supersedeas bond relative thereto. The district court, accordingly, maintained jurisdiction to supervise its injunction—to execute its unsuperseded judgment—and properly entertained the motion for contempt. See Sirloin Room, Inc. v. American Employers Insurance Co., 360 F.2d 160 (5th Cir. 1966) (order to enforce unsuperseded money judgment may be entered by district court even after appeal noticed); International Paper Co. v. Whitson, 595 F.2d 559 (10th Cir. 1979) (same). * * *

The judgment of the district court is, in all respects, AFFIRMED.

UNITED STATES OF AMERICA v. POWER ENGINEERING COMPANY

United States District Court, District of Colorado, 1998.
10 F. Supp. 2d 1165.

BABCOCK, J.

Plaintiff, United States of America ("the United States"), acting on behalf of the Environmental Protection Agency, moves for the issuance of an order requiring defendants, Power Engineering Company * * * to obtain financial assurances in the form of a surety bond that satisfies state regulations adopted by the Colorado Department of Public Health and Environment. * * * For the reasons set forth below, I grant the United States' motion.

I. PROCEDURAL HISTORY

The United States commenced this action on August 1, 1997, alleging eight claims: (1) treatment of hazardous waste without a permit or interim status; (2) disposal of hazardous waste without a permit or interim status; (3) shipment of hazardous waste to an un-permitted facility; (4) improper container management; (5) storage of hazardous waste without a permit or interim status; (6) failure to provide employee training; (7) failure to have a hazardous waste contingency plan; and (8) illegal operations (failure to have a groundwater monitoring program, failure to have a closure plan, failure to minimize releases of hazardous waste, and failure to obtain and provide financial assurances for closure and post-closure). * * *

I issued a Memorandum Opinion and Order ("the June 10 order") granting the United States' motion for preliminary injunction. The June 10 order directs defendants to provide financial assurances in the amount of $3,500,000 or show cause why they have not provided such financial assurances within thirty days. * * *

A status conference was held on August 6, 1998 to address defendants' compliance with the June 10 order. At the commencement of the hearing, I raised the issue of whether defendants' Notice of Appeal, filed July 22, 1998, divested this court of jurisdiction to enforce the June 10 order. * * *

Generally, a party's filing of a notice of appeal divests the district court of jurisdiction. Stewart v. Donges, 915 F.2d 572, 574–576 (10th Cir. 1990). "The filing of a notice of appeal, whether from a true final judgment or from a decision within the collateral order exception, 'is an event of jurisdictional significance—it confers jurisdiction on the court of appeals and divests the district court of its control over those aspects of the case involved in the appeal." Id. at 575 (quoting Griggs v. Provident Consumer Discount Co., 459 U.S. 56, 58 (1982)). The principle of jurisdictional transfer is not, however, absolute. No transfer occurs if the appeal is taken from a non-appealable order, Riggs v. Scrivner, Inc., 927

F.2d 1146, 1148 (10th Cir. 1991), or if the district court certifies that the appeal is frivolous, forfeited, or dilatory.

Further, appeals from interlocutory orders granting or denying injunctive relief present special considerations. Interlocutory, appellate review of a preliminary injunction order pursuant to 28 U.S.C. § 1292 (a)(1) will not divest the district court of its jurisdiction to act on the merits of the case pending appeal. State of Colorado v. Idarado Mining Co., 916 F.2d 1486, 1490 (10th Cir. 1990); Wright, Miller & Kane, Federal Practice and Procedure: Civil 2d § 3921.2. * * *

Although the language of Rule 62(c) appears to afford district courts extensive authority to grant injunctive relief pending appeal, courts addressing the issue have construed the rule more narrowly. Several circuits have held that the district court may not alter the injunction once an appeal has been filed except to maintain the status quo of the parties pending the appeal. See, e.g., Coastal Corp. v. Texas Eastern Corp., 869 F.2d 817, 820 (5th Cir. 1989); Ideal Toy Corp. v. Sayco Doll Corp., 302 F.2d 623, 625 (2d Cir. 1962). This narrow interpretation of Rule 62(c) derives from Sayco Doll, which involved a motion to vacate an injunction based on new evidence brought before the district court while the validity of the injunction was on appeal to the Second Circuit, which held:

Once the appeal is taken, ... jurisdiction passes to the appellate court. Thereafter the appellant is not usually entitled as of right to present new evidence or argument to the trial court, which in the exercise of a sound discretion will exercise jurisdiction only to preserve the status quo as of the time of appeal. Appellant's proper procedure is then to request leave of the court of appeals to proceed in the lower court. He need not even dismiss his appeal, for we have always been ready to suspend proceedings while new matter was introduced below. But absent permission of the appellate court to reopen, sound judicial administration demands that unless the judge is satisfied that this order was erroneous he shall use his power under Rule 62(c) only to preserve the status of the case as it sits before the court of appeals.

Sayco Doll, 302 F.2d at 625.

More recently, in Coastal Corp. v. Texas Eastern Corporation, the district court granted the plaintiffs' motion for a preliminary injunction, prohibiting the defendants from filing lawsuits challenging a tender offer in other jurisdictions. After the defendants appealed the preliminary injunction order, the trial court dissolved the injunction based on newly discovered evidence. The Fifth Circuit reversed, concluding that Rule 62(c) did not allow the district court to dissolve the injunction and eliminate the appeal Coastal, 869 F.2d at 820. According to the Fifth Circuit, "the powers of the district court over an injunction pending appeal should be limited to maintaining the status quo and ought not to extend to the point that the district court can divest the court of appeals from jurisdiction while the issue is before us on appeal." Id.

Two circuits have concluded that, in some circumstances, the district court may alter the status quo by modifying an injunction during the pendency of an appeal. See Board of Educ. of St. Louis v. State of Missouri, 936 F.2d 993, 996 (8th Cir. 1991) (district court's ongoing supervision of integration of vocational educational programs requires it to retain the broadest discretion possible); Ortho Pharmaceutical Corp. v. Amgen, Inc., 887 F.2d 460, 464 (3d Cir. 1989) (district court may alter status quo pursuant to Rule 62(c) if alteration "preserves the integrity" of the appeal). See also Basicomputer Corp. v. Scott, 973 F.2d 507, 513 (6th Cir. 1992) (declining to rule on issue). In Ortho, the plaintiff sought a modification of an injunction while an appeal was pending. The Third Circuit, like the Second and Fifth Circuits, held that Rule 62(c), though purporting to convey extensive authority to the district courts, did not permit a district court unlimited authority to modify a preliminary injunction. The Third Circuit, however, adopted a less narrow construction, holding that Rule 62(c) authorized the district court to take any of the listed actions as long as such action "preserved the integrity of the proceedings in the court of appeals." Ortho, 887 F.2d at 464. Since the modification requested by the plaintiff would impose additional requirements on the defendant, the district court concluded that the motion to modify transgressed the "status quo" limitation. On appeal, the Third Circuit implicitly agreed that the modification would alter the status quo, but concluded that the modification would preserve the integrity of the appeal by protecting the rights of the plaintiff, which rights were jeopardized in a manner not anticipated by the original injunction. Thus, the Third Circuit concluded that the modification was within the authority provided by Rule 62(c) even though it altered the status quo.

The Tenth Circuit came closest to addressing this issue in Chief Freight Lines Co. v. Local Union No. 886, 514 F.2d 572 (10th Cir. 1975), in which an employer commenced an action in district court to enjoin a union from striking. On February 27, 1974, the district court judge announced orally in open court that he would enter an order granting the preliminary injunction; the union filed a notice of appeal on March 29, 1974. Id. at 578. On April 9 and 10, 1974, the district court heard further evidence and oral argument. The district court judge then entered detailed written findings and conclusions together with an injunctive order on April 10, 1974. Id. The union filed a second notice of appeal on April 17, 1994. Id. The Tenth Circuit concluded that the district court judge "intended to, and did on February 27, merely announce orally his conclusion to grant the preliminary injunction, but that he did not enter the preliminary injunction until April 10." Id. Thus, the Tenth Circuit deemed the written injunctive order of April 10 as the order from which an appeal was taken. Chief Freight Lines, however, does not mention Rule 62(c) or Sayco Doll. While one commentator suggests that Chief Freight Lines implies the Tenth Circuit would follow the majority rule, see, e.g., Wright, Miller & Kane, Federal Practice and Procedure: Civil 2d § 3921.2 n. 28, I am not convinced that Chief Freight Lines provides guidance for the particular issue presented here. Thus, I conclude that the issue is one of first impression in this circuit.

The two predominant formulas are articulated by Coastal and Ortho. Coastal requires maintenance of the status quo as of the time of appeal, and Ortho speaks of preserving the integrity of the appeal. The difference is subtle. Ortho recognizes, and Coastal fails to recognize, that the status quo itself may cause one of the parties irreparable injury and thereby threaten the appeal. Ortho Pharmaceutical, 882 F.2d 806 at 814. Under such circumstances, it may be necessary to alter the status quo to prevent the injury and preserve the appeal. Id. The two formulas, however, have much more in common than in conflict. Regardless of the precise formula used, it is clear that any injunctive action taken pursuant to Rule 62(c) "must be designed to aid the appeal and, accordingly, may not materially alter the status of the case on appeal." A. Ides, The Authority of a Federal District Court to Proceed After a Notice of Appeal Has Been Filed, 143 F.R.D. 307, 321–322 (1992). Where, as here, modification of the injunction would not materially alter the status of the case on appeal, either paradigm allows the district court to modify the injunction pursuant to Rule 62(c). Thus, I need not decide between the subtly different formulas.

As noted above, the June 10 order requires defendants to "provide financial assurance in the amount of $3,500,000 pursuant to 6 COLO. CODE REGS. 1007–3 § 266 and all applicable subparts." Defendants could have complied with the June 10 order by providing any type of financial assurance allowed by § 266, including a bond, trust, insurance, or any combination thereof. In light of defendants' insufficient trust proposal, however, the United States now moves for issuance of an order requiring defendants to provide a specific form of financial assurance allowed by § 266, a "Surety Bond Guaranteeing Payment into a Closure and/or Post Closure Trust Fund." See 6 COLO. CODE REGS. 1007–3 § 266.14(f). The United States' motion can be characterized as either a motion to enforce the June 10 order or as a request for modification of the order. As noted above, the United States does not raise the issue of contempt. Nor does the United States seek to re-litigate any of the issues presented at the injunction hearing.

If construed as a motion to enforce the June 10 order, this court has continuing jurisdiction to address the United States' motion. See Tyler v. City of Manhattan, 118 F.3d 1400, 1402 n. 1 (10th Cir. 1997) (district court necessarily retained jurisdiction over parties until they complied with the terms of injunctive order even though injunctive order appealed). If construed as a motion to modify the June 10 order, jurisdiction also exists. The requested modification, if granted, does not materially alter the status of the appeal. Nor would granting the modification deprive or otherwise affect the jurisdiction of the Tenth Circuit over the appeal.

As no risk of interference exists, I conclude that this court has jurisdiction to entertain the United States' motion to enforce or modify the injunction. I also conclude that this court retains jurisdiction to proceed with the action on the merits. See State of Colorado v. Idarado Mining Co., 916 F.2d at 1490. Lastly, I conclude that the June 10 order, as an interlocutory order granting mandatory injunctive relief, is not automatically stayed by defendant's notice of appeal. Fed.R.Civ.P. 62(a); Wright, Miller & Kane, Federal Practice and Procedure: Civil 2d § 2904. Thus, the June 10 order remains in effect. Contrary to the United States' assertion, the order need not be "restored." Accordingly, I address the merits of the United States' motion. [Discussion on the merits is omitted. Eds.]

Notes and Questions

1.   The concept that trial court retains some jurisdiction after an appeal has been taken appears to be inconsistent with the traditional notion that each case is a single judicial unit and only one court can have jurisdiction over it at any given time. See generally Sears, Roebuck & Co. v. Mackey, 351 U.S. 427, 431–32, 76 S.Ct. 895, 100 L.Ed. 1297 (1956) discussed supra Chapter 3. Can the contrary approach of the cases immediately above case be explained on a theoretical basis, a practical basis, or both?

2.   If the trial court has the primary responsibility for determining the terms and conditions of a bond, why should it not have the power to revise its own action? Under the present rules, when is it appropriate to bypass the trial court and seek relief directly in the appellate court?

3.   Does the judicial unit theory also explain why in some states relief pending appeal must be sought in the trial court before the notice of appeal is filed but after in the appellate court?

4.   Questions concerning the continuing jurisdiction of the trial court can arise in various ways. (a) Authority to Amend Judgment: Ivor B. Clark Co. v. Hogan & Talcott, 411 F.2d 788 (2d Cir. 1969) involved an appeal from a judgment requiring the payment of rentals. The trial court, asked to set the amount of a supersedeas bond, amended the judgment in order to fix the amount of rental required to be paid. In holding that the trial court had the authority to amend the judgment, the Second Circuit reasoned that the lower court could not have fixed the amount of the supersedeas bond without first having the amount of the rentals established, and that the failure to include the rental amount in the judgment was simply an oversight. (b) Authority to Grant Temporary Injunction. In General Motors Corp. v. Miller Buick, Inc., 56 Md.App. 374, 467 A.2d 1064 (1983), the trial court issued a temporary injunction during the pendency of the proceeding. The appellate court held that the temporary injunction was dissolved when the final judgment was entered. If the trial court wishes to preserve the *status quo* pending an appeal, it must issue a new injunction to be effective during the pendency of the appeal.

5.   In Powell v. Turner, 16 Ohio App.3d 404, 476 N.E.2d 368 (1984) the court held that after the notice of appeal was filed the trial court could not act except in aid of the appeal. It thus was without jurisdiction over motions for a new trial, judgment n.o.v., or remittitur but could rule on a motion for stay of execution pending appeal. Is this consistent with the principal case?

6. One court of appeals has recognized one form of simultaneous jurisdiction between the appellate court and the district court. In Jason's Foods, Inc. v. Peter Eckrich & Sons, Inc., 768 F.2d 189 (7th Cir. 1985) the court of appeals remanded a case to the district court to hear evidence on the principal place of business of the defendant, a matter that could affect diversity jurisdiction. The Seventh Circuit held it could make a limited remand to make a ruling that could terminate the appeal, but retained nominal jurisdiction over the appeal. Isn't it more accurate to say the trial court did not reacquire jurisdiction but was merely serving as a master for the court of appeals so it could rule on the question of jurisdiction?

7. Note also that where interlocutory appeal is permitted for a ruling on part of the case, for example by virtue of the issuance of a preliminary injunction, it is sometimes permissible for the trial court to continue supervision of other aspects of the case (e.g., discovery on the merits). In a few cases, the trial court has been permitted to rule on the availability of a permanent injunction while the preliminary injunction ruling is on appeal. See Railway Labor Executives' Ass'n v. Galveston, 898 F.2d 481 (5th Cir. 1990).

8. For a very thoughtful discussion of the need for modification of an injunction to allow parties to operate successfully while an appeal is pending, see Chandler v. James, 998 F.Supp. 1255, 1270–71 (M.D. Ala. 1997), in which a large school system was enjoined on Establishment Clause grounds from permitting a wide range of religious activity. While an appeal was pending, the trial court modified a portion of the injunction to clarify obligations pending an appellate review, and attempted to explain the remainder of the injunction so that thousands of students and teachers would have as much guidance as possible during the time the appellate court considered the case.

SECTION E. RELIEF FROM THE APPELLATE COURT DURING AN APPEAL

Powers of the Appellate Court. It should be apparent from the foregoing readings that the appellate court may also entertain applications by way of motions by the parties for rulings with respect to injunctions—or other aspects of the litigation—while the appeal is pending. Rule 62(g) confirms aspects of this power:

> **(g) Power of Appellate Court not Limited.** The provisions in this rule do not limit any power of an appellate court or of a judge or justice thereof to stay proceedings during the pendency of an appeal or to suspend, modify, restore, or grant an injunction during the pendency of an appeal or to make any order appropriate to preserve the status quo or the effectiveness of the judgment subsequently to be entered.

The text of this rule continues the theme noted above that a central mission of rulings while the case is on appeal is to preserve the case in a posture allowing the court of appeals to effectively decide the issues and implement its decision.

To make sure that the appellate court is not inundated with applications for relief, Rule 8(a) of the appellate rules underscores the fact that applications for the three basic forms of relief discussed in this Chapter of the Casebook (approving a bond, obtaining a stay of the judgment, and altering the injunctive relief) should all be made in the first instance in front of the trial judge:

(1) Initial Motion in the District Court. A party must ordinarily move first in the district court for the following relief:

(A) a stay of the judgment or order of a district court pending appeal;

(B) approval of a supersedeas bond; or

(C) an order suspending, modifying, restoring, or granting an injunction while an appeal is pending.

The procedural provisions of this rule emphasize the exhaustion of district court remedies requirement, and give a flavor of the exceptional nature of the application:

(2) Motion in the Court of Appeals; Conditions on Relief. A motion for the relief mentioned in Rule 8(a)(1) may be made to the court of appeals or to one of its judges.

(A) The motion must:

(i) show that moving first in the district court would be impracticable; or

(ii) state that, a motion having been made, the district court denied the motion or failed to afford the relief requested and state any reasons given by the district court for its action.

(B) The motion must also include:

(i) the reasons for granting the relief requested and the facts relied on;

(ii) originals or copies of affidavits or other sworn statements supporting facts subject to dispute; and

(iii) relevant parts of the record.

(C) The moving party must give reasonable notice of the motion to all parties.

(D) A motion under this Rule 8(a)(2) must be filed with the circuit clerk and normally will be considered by a panel of the court. But in an exceptional case in which time requirements make that procedure impracticable, the motion may be made to and considered by a single judge.

Any form of relief may be sought from the appellate court by motion, relating to the relations of the parties, the enforcement of the trial court's judgment, or the conduct of the appeal. Most appellate courts have local rules providing powers to the Clerk of Court to grant minor scheduling relief, and for a panel of judges—or, sometimes, an individual member of the appellate court—to grant substantive relief of various kinds. These matters are also addressed in Rule 27 of the Federal Rules of Appellate Procedure at some length.

Stay Applications Seek Emergency Relief. In many courts, applications for stays are lumped together with other applications for emergency relief when it comes to procedural requirements and internal processing practices of the court. It bears noting that counsel asking for this sort of relief must "make the case" that such relief is warranted. The showings required include not only the exhaustion of efforts to obtain help from the trial court, but also some evidentiary material to document that an exigency exists. As one federal court of appeals summarizes the guidance for attorneys in these situations:

> Application for a stay or any other appropriate emergency relief must first be made to the district court or agency whose order is being appealed, or the motion filed in this Court must explain why such relief was not sought. If the district court or agency denies the relief requested, an application may then be made to this Court. A motion for a stay must describe any prior applications for relief and their outcome.

> If the facts are in dispute, evidentiary material supporting the request for a stay should be furnished. Relevant portions of the record must be included with the motion. At a minimum, these include a copy of the judgment or order involved, and any explanation, written or oral, that accompanied the ruling. The motion also should contain, in a prominent place, a specific statement of the time exigencies involved.

> Because many motions for stay are filed on an emergency basis, Circuit Rules 8, 18, and 27(f), which prescribe the procedures for seeking emergency relief, should be reviewed carefully. In particular, counsel or a party must identify the motion as an "Emergency Motion," and file it at least 7 calendar days before the date on which court action is necessary, or explain why the motion could not have been filed sooner. Where counsel or a party gives only a vague or general explanation as to why it was not filed at least 7 calendar days before the date of the requested court action, the Court may conclude that expedited consideration of the motion is unwarranted.

SECTION F. STAYS AND SIMILAR RELIEF IN CRIMINAL CASES AFTER CONVICTION

Criminal Rule 38 governs post-trial applications in criminal cases analogous to the stay concepts discussed in this chapter. Practitioners specializing in criminal practice will occasionally have need for use of the procedures of that rule.

For present purposes it may be sufficient to note that there are provisions in Rule 38 of the Criminal Rules for such relief as a stay of the sentence of imprisonment, a stay of a sentence to pay a fine or costs, a stay of a sentence of probation, and a stay of civil or employment disabilities that arise under federal statutes by reason of a conviction or sentence. However, under the federal Bail Reform Act and case law such relief is rarely available to convicted defendants. State law is similarly negative.

In general, a convicted defendant will be incarcerated unless there is a finding by clear and convincing evidence that the accused is not likely to flee or pose a danger to others. There are celebrated examples where convicted felons have been released on bail pending appeal (See Chambers v. Mississippi, 410 U.S. 284, 93 S.Ct. 1038, 35 L.Ed.2d 297 (1973)(convicted murderer of police officer released during pendency of his appeal to the United States Supreme Court) but these are exceedingly rare rulings, and will not be further pursued in this Casebook.

Chapter 7

THE RECORD ON APPEAL

FEDERAL RULES OF APPELLATE PROCEDURE

RULE 10. THE RECORD ON APPEAL

(a) Composition of the Record on Appeal. The following items constitute the record on appeal:

(1) the original papers and exhibits filed in the district court;

(2) the transcript of proceedings, if any; and

(3) a certified copy of the docket entries prepared by the district clerk.

(b) The Transcript of Proceedings.

(1) Appellant's Duty to Order. Within 10 days after filing the notice of appeal or entry of an order disposing of the last timely remaining motion of a type specified in Rule 4(a)(4)(A), whichever is later, the appellant must do either of the following:

(A) order from the reporter a transcript of such parts of the proceedings not already on file as the appellant considers necessary, subject to a local rule of the court of appeals and with the following qualifications:

(i) the order must be in writing;

(ii) if the cost of the transcript is to be paid by the United States under the Criminal Justice Act, the order must so state; and

(iii) the appellant must, within the same period, file a copy of the order with the district clerk; or

(B) file a certificate stating that no transcript will be ordered.

(2) Unsupported Finding or Conclusion. If the appellant intends to urge on appeal that a finding or conclusion is unsupported by the evidence or is contrary to the evidence, the appellant must include in the record a transcript of all evidence relevant to that finding or conclusion.

(3) Partial Transcript. Unless the entire transcript is ordered:

(A) the appellant must—within the 10 days provided in Rule 10(b)(1)—file a statement of the issues that the appellant intends to present on the appeal and must serve on the appellee a copy of both the order or certificate and the statement;

(B) if the appellee considers it necessary to have a transcript of other parts of the proceedings, the appellee must, within 10 days after the service of the order or certificate and the statement of the issues, file and serve on the appellant a designation of additional parts to be ordered; and

(C) unless within 10 days after service of that designation the appellant has ordered all such parts, and has so notified the appellee, the appellee may within the following 10 days either order the parts or move in the district court for an order requiring the appellant to do so.

(4) Payment. At the time of ordering, a party must make satisfactory arrangements with the reporter for paying the cost of the transcript.

(c) Statement of the Evidence When the Proceedings Were Not Recorded or When a Transcript Is Unavailable. If the transcript of a hearing or trial is unavailable, the appellant may prepare a statement of the evidence or proceedings from the best available means, including the appellant's recollection. The statement must be served on the appellee, who may serve objections or proposed amendments within 10 days after being served. The statement and any objections or proposed amendments must then be submitted to the district court for settlement and approval. As settled and approved, the statement must be included by the district clerk in the record on appeal.

(d) Agreed Statement as the Record on Appeal. In place of the record on appeal as defined in Rule 10(a), the parties may prepare, sign, and submit to the district court a statement of the case showing how the issues presented by the appeal arose and were decided in the district court. The statement must set forth only those facts averred and proved or sought to be proved that are essential to the court's resolution of the issues. If the statement is truthful, it—together with any additions that the district court may consider necessary to a full presentation of the issues on appeal—must be approved by the district court and must then be certified to the court of appeals as the record on appeal. The district clerk must then send it to the circuit clerk within the time provided by Rule 11. A copy of the agreed statement may be filed in place of the appendix required by Rule 30.

(e) Correction or Modification of the Record.

(1) If any difference arises about whether the record truly discloses what occurred in the district court, the difference must be submitted to and settled by that court and the record conformed accordingly.

(2) If anything material to either party is omitted from or misstated in the record by error or accident, the omission or misstatement may be corrected and a supplemental record may be certified and forwarded:

(A) on stipulation of the parties;

(B) by the district court before or after the record has been forwarded; or

(C) by the court of appeals.

(3) All other questions as to the form and content of the record must be presented to the court of appeals.

RULE 11. TRANSMISSION OF THE RECORD

(a) Appellant's Duty. An appellant filing a notice of appeal must comply with Rule 10(b) and must do whatever else is necessary to enable the clerk to assemble and forward the record. If there are multiple appeals from a judgment or order, the clerk must forward a single record.

(b) Duties of Reporter and District Clerk.

(1) Reporter's Duty to Prepare and File a Transcript. The reporter must prepare and file a transcript as follows:

(A) Upon receiving an order for a transcript, the reporter must enter at the foot of the order the date of its receipt and the expected completion date and send a copy, so endorsed, to the circuit clerk.

(B) If the transcript cannot be completed within 30 days of the reporter's receipt of the order, the reporter may request the circuit clerk to grant additional time to complete it. The clerk must note on the docket the action taken and notify the parties.

(C) When a transcript is complete, the reporter must file it with the district clerk and notify the circuit clerk of the filing.

(D) If the reporter fails to file the transcript on time, the circuit clerk must notify the district judge and do whatever else the court of appeals directs.

(2) District Clerk's Duty to Forward. When the record is complete, the district clerk must number the documents constituting the record and send them promptly to the circuit clerk together with a list of the documents correspondingly numbered and reasonably identified. Unless directed to do so by a party or the circuit clerk, the district clerk will not send to the court of appeals documents of unusual bulk or weight, physical exhibits other than documents, or other parts of the record designated for omission by local rule of the court of appeals. If the exhibits are unusually bulky or heavy, a party must arrange with the clerks in advance for their transportation and receipt.

(c) Retaining the Record Temporarily in the District Court for Use in Preparing the Appeal. The parties may stipulate, or the district court on motion may order, that the district clerk retain the record temporarily for the parties to use in preparing the papers on appeal. In that event the district clerk must certify to the circuit clerk that the record on appeal is complete. Upon receipt of the appellee's brief, or earlier if the court orders or the parties agree, the appellant must request the district clerk to forward the record.

(d) [Abrogated]

(e) Retaining the Record by Court Order.

(1) The court of appeals may, by order or local rule, provide that a certified copy of the docket entries be forwarded instead of the entire record. But a party may at any time during the appeal request that designated parts of the record be forwarded.

(2) The district court may order the record or some part of it retained if the court needs it while the appeal is pending, subject, however, to call by the court of appeals.

(3) If part or all of the record is ordered retained, the district clerk must send to the court of appeals a copy of the order and the docket entries together with the parts of the original record allowed by the district court and copies of any parts of the record designated by the parties.

(f) Retaining Parts of the Record in the District Court by Stipulation of the Parties. The parties may agree by written stipulation filed in the district court that designated parts of the record be retained in the district court subject to call by the court of appeals or request by a party. The parts of the record so designated remain a part of the record on appeal.

(g) Record for a Preliminary Motion in the Court of Appeals. If, before the record is forwarded, a party makes any of the following motions in the court of appeals:

- for dismissal;
- for release;
- for a stay pending appeal;
- for additional security on the bond on appeal or on a supersedeas bond; or
- for any other intermediate order—

the district clerk must send the court of appeals any parts of the record designated by any party.

SECTION A. THE PURPOSE OF THE RECORD ON APPEAL

NOTE, FORM OF APPELLATE RECORDS IN IOWA

48 Iowa L. Rev. 77, 81–82 (1962).*

THE PURPOSE AND NATURE OF THE APPELLATE RECORD

A. EFFECTIVE COMMUNICATION OF THE RELEVANT FACTS

The purpose of the appellate record is to communicate efficiently to the reviewing court the relevant facts adduced at the trial necessary for rendering a fair and accurate appellate decision. These relevant facts are found from the proceedings below in the transcript, pleadings, motions, judgments, orders and exhibits. The degree of detail in presentation for review should depend on the extent original fact issues will be tried. In federal cases tried without a jury or with an advisory jury, the federal appellate court has to examine facts to determine whether the lower court was clearly erroneous. The Iowa court differs since in some cases fact issues will be triable de novo from information found in the record. Therefore, in some Iowa appeals all the original papers may be relevant for fair review of facts. Nonetheless, a detailed fact background is unnecessary where an appeal is taken on a strictly legal issue not dealing with sufficiency or weight of evidence. Thus, the degree of detail of the relevant facts necessary for review will vary according to the degree and scope of review given by the appellate court.

The record or factual presentation must communicate the facts to the reviewing body. An excessively long record will force a judge to rush over the material and perhaps miss important facts; a cryptic record will omit information necessary for the judge to decide the case; a fragmentary record will likewise be ineffective because lack of continuity makes it difficult to see the fact picture as a whole. A narrative record runs the danger of distorting the original courtroom testimony thereby becoming an unworthy communication to the reviewing judge. A non-adversary record will sometimes mislead appellate judges into believing crucial fact issues are no longer disputed. The ideal appellate presentation avoids these pitfalls, for the primary purpose of a good appellate record is to accurately *and* effectively communicate the relevant facts necessary to decide the issues before the court.

B. OTHER INTERESTS

The test of a good appellate record has been defined in terms of good jurisprudence. While the described record should be the ideal, there are involved special interests of the attorneys, clients, and judges which often affect the shape of the appellate record.

* Copyright © 1962, University of Iowa (Iowa Law Review). Reprinted by permission. All rights reserved.

A *court's* special interest is in the ease of handling the record to enable an efficient disposition of the case. Although the narrative form of testimony eases the reading of facts by the court, it conflicts with good jurisprudence in that it tends to communicate less accurately the lower court proceedings.

The *attorney's* special interest is reducing the time and effort needed to prepare a record. Yet this motive conflicts with good jurisprudence if it forces the court to read an inadequately prepared factual presentation.

The *litigant's* special interest is minimizing the cost of making the record. Printing expenses and legal and secretarial time and labor increase the cost to the litigant of making the appellate paper. However, there is the danger of a cheap record encouraging "cheap" justice. "The rule requiring abstracting * * * is for the benefit of both court and litigant, designed not only to minimize labor and costs but to ensure a better understanding by the court of the real merits of the case."

These special interests deserve consideration when not in conflict with the primary purpose of the record—to insure a fair and accurate appellate decision. Practically speaking, they surely have considerable influence on the form of the appellate record.

Notes and Questions

1. What does the Note mean when it states that the degree of detail necessary in the record depends on the extent original facts will be tried and that in some cases in Iowa fact issues are triable *de novo* in the Iowa Supreme Court? When does an appellate court try facts *de novo?* See Chapter 2, section A 1, supra.

2. Is the Note correct in stating that a detailed fact background is unnecessary when an appeal is taken on a strictly legal issue? Is a case ever decided on a legal issue as to which facts are not important? See the discussion of the importance of facts in an appeal, see Chapter 8, section D, infra.

SECTION B. CONTENT OF RECORD

1. BASIC COMPONENTS

In federal practice Rule 10(a) of the FRAP specifies the basic elements composing the record on appeal. It provides that the record will contain:

(1) the original papers and exhibits filed in the district court;

(2) the transcript of proceedings, if any; and

(3) a certified copy of the docket entries prepared by the district clerk.

I.B.M. CORP. v. EDELSTEIN

United States Court of Appeals, Second Circuit, 1975.
526 F.2d 37.

PER CURIAM.

International Business Machines ("IBM") petitions this Court for extraordinary relief in the form of a writ of mandamus, pursuant to 28 U.S.C. § 1651 and Fed.R.App.P. 21. The petition focuses on certain rulings and practices adopted by Chief Judge Edelstein of the Southern District of New York in the conduct of a lawsuit currently being tried before him, United States v. International Business Machines Corp., 69 Civ. 200, Civ. No. 72–344.

More specifically, IBM seeks relief from the acts of the trial judge in * * * refusing to file IBM's papers with the Clerk of the Court as required by Fed.R.Civ.P. 5(e); * * * Before responding to these requests, we first give consideration to our jurisdiction and such limitations as there may be on the exercise of our discretionary power relating to the petition.

This is not an ordinary case, and this will not be an ordinary trial. The complaint was filed on January 17, 1969. In substance, it charged IBM with violations of Section 2 of the Sherman Act (15 U.S.C. § 2). The trial commenced on May 19, 1975 and the Government estimates that it will "last well over a year". It expects to call "more than one hundred witnesses", and to "offer several thousand exhibits" (Gov't.'s Br. 1 and 2). IBM will undoubtedly have a comparable number of witnesses and exhibits. So much for the magnitude of the trial which, having commenced in May 1975 and recessed for the summer, has now resumed.

The Government asks that we "discourage in the strongest possible language the filing of petitions for extraordinary relief raising issues as insubstantial as those raised in this case". (Gov't. Br. 5). We decline to do so because we do not regard the issues as "insubstantial". We recognize that mandamus is not a substitute for an appeal, and that every disputed ruling during a trial should not be made the subject of a mandamus petition. However, the relief sought here is more fundamental. The errors complained of are not errors involving improper exercise of discretion; see Stans and Mitchell v. Gagliardi, 485 F.2d 1290 (2d Cir. 1973); rather they concern actions which, petitioner has charged, are entirely outside the permissible bounds of the trial court's discretion, and which exceed the trial court's jurisdiction. Such actions are properly reviewable by writ of mandamus. See Parr v. United States, 351 U.S. 513, 520, 76 S.Ct. 912, 917, 100 L.Ed. 1377 (1956). Moreover, appellate review will be defeated if the writ does not issue, for petitioner's claims are not of the kind that will be merged into any final judgment and thus capable of correction on appeal. This, too, is a proper ground for the issuance of a writ of mandamus. Parr v. United States, supra.

The asserted errors are wholly collateral to the resolution of the legal issues involved. They deal only with the manner of developing such issues. Restrictions which may impede the development, presentation and determination of facts should be avoided wherever possible—particularly at the comparative outset of such a trial as here. * * *

NON-FILING OF PAPERS SUBMITTED BY PETITIONER

In his Trial Order No. 3 of September 23, 1975, the trial judge formalized a procedure instituted by him in mid–1974 whereby all papers connected with *U.S. v. IBM* were to be sent to the Court's chambers instead of being filed with the Clerk.

Petitioner has submitted a lengthy appendix consisting of papers which Judge Edelstein has refused to forward to the Clerk for filing, primarily on grounds of untimely submission or faulty proof of service. Petitioner contends that the Court's refusal to file some of these papers is based upon an erroneous interpretation of the Southern District's Local General Rule 9 and Rule 6(a) of the Federal Rules. While the correctness of Judge Edelstein's construction of those rules will not be reviewed on this mandamus petition, we must consider whether the manner in which the judge gave effect to his construction of the Rules was within the ambit of his proper authority.

Had the trial judge chosen simply to deny Petitioner's motions, IBM could complain of no usurpation of power. The judge's refusal to file IBM's papers, however, does raise such issue, because the Petitioner is thereby prevented from making a record for purposes of appeal. It need hardly be stated that the trial record is composed of the proceedings in the District Court including all papers, exhibits, and affidavits on file with the Court. It is not the type of paper submitted but rather the fact of filing which determines whether a particular item will be included in the record. Todd v. Nello L. Teer Co., 308 F.2d 397, 399 (5th Cir. 1962) (letter addressed to court properly regarded on appeal as part of trial record where it had been previously filed with the trial court).

Filing at the trial court level with a view to "making a record" is crucial because, absent extraordinary circumstances, federal appellate courts will not consider rulings or evidence which are not part of the trial record. This is true whether the record is merely ambiguous or is affirmatively deficient with respect to any papers or orders of any kind.

Moreover, it is of no avail to an appellant that the trial court itself may have prevented him from including a particular item in the trial record; the appellate court will not speculate about the proceedings below, but will rely only upon the record actually made. Little v. Green, 428 F.2d 1061, 1070 (5th Cir. 1970) (Court of Appeals refused to consider question on appeal on grounds that it did not appear in trial record, where counsel claimed that trial judge prevented him from interposing an objection during trial).

Under the Federal rules, both Rule 10(a) and its forerunner former Rule 75(a) the parties on appeal have the right to submit to the appellate court, for its consideration, those parts of the trial record which they choose to challenge or defend on review. The policy that it is the appealing parties, and not the trial court, who control the issues to be presented on appeal has been embodied in federal practice since the Federal Rules were adopted in 1938. This Circuit formally adopted that policy in 1942, when Judges Swan and Augustus Hand joined in Judge Clark's opinion in Treasure Imports v. Henry Amdur & Sons, 127 F.2d 3 (2d Cir. 1942):

> The record is in a somewhat confused state, owing in part to an order of the district court that several of the matters designated by defendants for inclusion in the record should not be so included or transmitted to us. * * * [T]he Federal Rules do not permit the district court to prevent parties from including in the record any part of the occurrences below which they wish thus included. 127 F.2d at 4.

On the basis of this policy, district courts have refrained from exercising any degree of control over the contents of the trial record, even where parties have petitioned the trial court to exclude certain items from the record.

Since Petitioner has no other means of presenting its arguments to the appellate court—whether as appellant or appellee—save by making the necessary record at the trial level, Judge Edelstein's refusal to file petitioner's motions has constituted an impermissible interference with petitioner's right to make the record it chooses for purposes of appeal.

It is true that filing papers directly with the judge is permitted (to a limited extent) under Fed.R.Civ.P. 5(e):

> The filing of pleadings and other papers with the court as required by these rules shall be made by filing them with the clerk of the court, except that the judge may permit the papers to be filed with him, in which event he shall note thereon the filing date *and forthwith transmit them to the office of the clerk.* (Emphasis supplied)

Filing directly with the Court may be necessary for the protection of the parties where, for example, the delay occasioned by first filing with the clerk will cause irreparable harm. [Citations omitted.] It is not, however, a procedure to be invoked by the Court for the purpose of selectively determining what papers should properly constitute the trial record of the controversy before it. Rule 5(e), it should be emphasized, speaks only of the granting of permission to file papers with the Court; it does not speak of any judicial discretion to refuse thereafter to file papers with the Clerk. Moreover, we specifically note the rule's language that the Court "*may permit* the papers to be filed" with it (emphasis supplied); the use of "may permit" instead of "may order" suggests to us that such filing is proper only when the Court's discretion has been invoked by one of the parties for good cause, and that the rule was not intended to be invoked by the Court *sua sponte.*

We therefore conclude that all papers previously submitted to Judge Edelstein's chambers should have been considered filed within the meaning of Federal Rule 5(d) and 5(e), and transmitted to the Clerk's office, as contemplated by Rule 5(e).

[Petition for writ of mandamus granted.]

2. "OFF THE RECORD" EPISODES IN THE TRIAL COURT

BADAMI v. FLOOD

United States Court of Appeals, Eighth Circuit, 2000.
214 F.3d 994.

FLOYD R. GIBSON, CIRCUIT JUDGE.

Plaintiffs Philomena T. Badami, Stephen J. Badami, Michael James Badami, Thomas Joseph Badami, Kimberly Ann Badami, John Paul Badami, Patrick Raymond Badami, Daniel Vincent Badami, David Christopher Badami, and Matthew Lawrence Badami (hereinafter "the Badamis") brought suit under the Fair Housing Act, 42 U.S.C. §§ 3601–3631 (1994), claiming the defendants discriminated against them, based on the size of their family, in their search for a rental home. After a two-day trial, a jury awarded the Badamis $1,100 in compensatory damages. Terry W. Flood, Robert C. Conn, Flood & Conn Enterprises, Jay Ann Flood, and Terry W. Flood Real Estate Company, (hereinafter "the defendants") do not appeal this verdict. The Badamis, however, appeal several rulings of the district court. We affirm in part, reverse in part, and remand. * * *

EVIDENTIARY EXCLUSIONS

The Badamis * * * contend that the district court erred in excluding certain evidence of actual damages. Mrs. Badami submitted to this Court an affidavit asserting that the district court excluded evidence of damages incurred by her family. Mrs. Badami alleges that the court excluded damages such as alternative housing costs, lost wages, and mental anguish and humiliation damages. Mrs. Badami avers that the conference during which the court excluded the evidence was off the record and urges us to consider her affidavit as a record of the court's ruling. The defendants have moved to strike the affidavit, and we hereby grant that motion.

Federal Rule of Evidence 103(a) provides that "error may not be predicated upon a ruling which ... excludes evidence unless ... the substance of the evidence was made known to the court by offer or was apparent from the context within which questions were asked." In order to challenge a trial court's exclusion of evidence, the issue must be preserved for appeal by making an offer of proof on the record. See Dupre v. Fru–Con Engineering Inc., 112 F.3d 329, 336 (8th Cir. 1997); Holst v. Countryside Enterprise, Inc. 14 F.3d 1319, 1323 (8th Cir. 1994). Mrs. Badami failed to make an offer of proof to the district court regarding the evidence allegedly excluded by the court.

Further, Mrs. Badami failed to follow the proper appellate procedure in her attempt to have this Court consider the excluded evidence. The Federal Rules of Appellate Procedure provide the course of action Mrs. Badami should have taken. Mrs. Badami's affidavit is not entirely improper, as FRAP 10(c) does allow an appellant to prepare a statement recounting unrecorded proceedings before the district court. However, Rule 10(c) requires that the statement "be submitted to the district court for settlement and approval." Mrs. Badami failed to provide the district court with an opportunity to review, correct or approve the affidavit she submitted to this Court.

Alternatively, Mrs. Badami could have moved, pursuant to FRAP 10(e), to modify the record. Rule 10(e) provides that, when differences arise as to whether the record on appeal truly discloses what occurred in the district court, "the difference shall be submitted to and settled by [the district court]." Again, Mrs. Badami failed to provide the district court with an opportunity to correct any errors in the record. On appeal Mrs. Badami requests that, as she tried the case pro se, we forgive her procedural error. While we are mindful of the difficulties faced by pro se litigants, we must decline. Absent a record of the proffered evidence and the trial court's reasons for excluding it, meaningful appellate review is virtually impossible.

Even if this issue had been preserved on appeal, we have carefully reviewed the district court's rulings that are contained in the record and find no abuse of discretion. See United States v. Looking, 156 F.3d 803, 811 (8th Cir. 1998) (stating standard of review of district court's exclusion of evidence). We find the Badamis' other contentions on appeal to be without merit.

Accordingly, the district court's order denying the submission of punitive damages is reversed and the case is remanded for trial on the issue of punitive damages. The defendants' motion to strike the affidavit of Mrs. Badami is granted. In all other respects the trial court's decision is affirmed.

Notes and Questions

Nonverbal communication will not appear in the record in the absence of some affirmative action by the trial attorney. See Note, Let the Record Show: Modifying Appellate Review Procedures for Errors of Prejudical Nonverbal Communication by Trial Judges, 95 Colum. L. Rev. 1273 (1995).

SECTION C.   ARRANGING FOR COMPLETE OR PARTIAL TRANSCRIPTION

1.   BASIC REQUIREMENT OF DESIGNATION

POZO v. ESSER

United States Court of Appeals, Seventh Circuit, 2004.
90 Fed. Appx. 968.

PER CURIAM.

Wisconsin inmate Rodosvaldo Pozo filed this pro se suit under 42 U.S.C. § 1983 against officials in the Wisconsin Department of Corrections, alleging that they violated his rights under the Eighth Amendment by using excessive force and by being deliberately indifferent to his serious medical needs. Pozo also alleged that the officials' actions were in retaliation for complaining about prison conditions. The parties proceeded to trial, and a jury found in favor of the defendants. Pozo appeals, but because he has failed to provide us with trial transcripts, we must dismiss his appeal. See Fed. R. App. P. 10(b)(2).

Pozo's allegations stem from an April 2001 incident in which the defendants transferred him from one prison cell to another. During the transfer, Pozo contends, he was assaulted by the defendants, causing injuries to his head and back. Pozo submits that those injuries were not treated until five or six days later. Further, Pozo claims, he was then placed in a cold cell without clothing or bedding for three days. Pozo argues that the defendants' actions were malicious and intended to cause him harm and that as a result of the incident he suffers from post-traumatic stress disorder, nightmares, phobias, and difficulty sleeping and concentrating.

On appeal Pozo challenges the district court's evidentiary and procedural rulings at trial as well as the jury's verdict. First, Pozo contests the district court's admission of a videotape of the April 2001 cell transfer; he believes that the defendants altered the videotape by erasing the portion showing them using excessive force. Next, Pozo submits that the district court erred at trial by refusing to give him copies of two prison policies concerning the transfer of inmates. Pozo also argues that the district court erred in refusing to permit several of Pozo's witnesses to testify at the trial. Further, Pozo challenges the jury's conclusion that the defendants were not deliberately indifferent to his medical needs. Finally, Pozo contends that the trial was unfair both because the district court did not appoint counsel to represent him and because the court made negative comments about him that biased the jury toward the defendants.

Pozo, however, has not included a trial transcript in the record, so we cannot meaningfully review any of his arguments or verify any of his claims. See LaFollette v. Savage, 63 F.3d 540, 544 (7th Cir. 1995).

Federal Rule of Appellate Procedure 10(b)(2) provides that "if the appellant intends to urge on appeal that a finding or conclusion is unsupported by the evidence or is contrary to the evidence, the appellant must include in the record a transcript of all evidence relevant to that finding or conclusion." Fed. R. App. P. 10(b)(2); see Learning Curve Toys, Inc. v. Playwood Toys, Inc., 342 F.3d 714, 731 n.10 (7th Cir. 2003). Without the transcript, "we are unable to evaluate the evidence submitted in this case." Hotaling v. Chubb Sovereign Life Ins. Co., 241 F.3d 572, 581 (7th Cir. 2001) (citation omitted). Since all of Pozo's arguments require us to evaluate the evidence presented at trial, all of his arguments are forfeited and we may dismiss his appeal. LaFollette, 63 F.3d at 544 ("dismissal is the appropriate course if the absence of a complete record precludes meaningful appellate review"). We note that Pozo's pro se status does not prohibit dismissal. See Woods v. Thieret, 5 F.3d 244, 245–46 (7th Cir. 1993) (dismissing appeal of pro se plaintiff for failure to provide transcript).

Although we have the authority under Federal Rule of Appellate Procedure 10(e) to order Pozo to supplement the record to include the trial transcript, we decline to exercise that authority because Pozo has "had ample opportunity to correct the problem but [has] failed to do so." *LaFollette*, 63 F.3d at 545. Pozo twice requested a copy of the trial transcript from the district court, noting that he needed the transcript to prepare his appeal. The district court denied both motions, concluding that because the transcript was not necessary for his appeal, Pozo would have to prepay to receive it. But he never paid to have the transcript prepared. Afterwards in this court Pozo four times renewed his motion to receive a free transcript; each motion was denied. In denying one of his motions, we notified Pozo that he was not entitled to receive free transcripts because he was not proceeding in forma pauperis on appeal. See 28 U.S.C. § 753(f). Since Pozo still did not order and arrange to purchase the transcript, we see no purpose in affording him yet another chance to do so.

The defendants request that Pozo be sanctioned for filing a frivolous appeal, but they have not submitted the "separately filed motion" necessary for us to consider their request. See Fed. R. App. P. 38 (requiring "notice" and a "reasonable opportunity to respond" before sanctions can be imposed); LINC Fin. Corp. v. Onwuteaka, 129 F.3d 917, 924–25 (7th Cir. 1997).

DISMISSED.

Note

In Loren v. Sasser, 309 F.3d 1296 (11th Cir. 2002) the Circuit court canvassed several other courts' approaches to applying the strictures of Federal Rule of Appellate Procedure 10(b)(2) to pro se litigants. It noted that where a district court denies in forma pauperis status, an appellant may apply to the appellate court for such status, which would provide funding for the transcript. Absent a transcript, the trial court will be affirmed because the appellant fails to provide all the evidence that the trial court had before it when making various contested evidentiary rulings. The Eleventh Circuit concluded that pro se appellants, like appellants represented by counsel, must provide trial transcripts in the appellate record to enable this court to review challenges to sufficiency of the evidence.

2. RELYING UPON ALL OR PART OF THE TRANSCRIBABLE MATERIAL

CONWAY v. FORD MOTOR CO.

Court of Appeals of Ohio, 1976.
48 Ohio App.2d 233, 356 N.E.2d 762.

KRENZLER, JUDGE.

The plaintiff appellee, hereinafter referred to as the appellee filed a claim for workmen's compensation benefits with the administrator of the Bureau of Workmen's Compensation in which he alleged that he injured his back in a work related accident on February 18, 1973 at the Ford Motor Company. On July 18, 1973 the deputy administrator of the Bureau of Workmen's Compensation disallowed the claim. On appeal the decision of the deputy administrator was upheld by the Cleveland Regional Board of Review of the Bureau of Workmen's Compensation and by the Industrial Commission of Ohio.

Pursuant to R.C. 4123.519, the appellee appealed to the Court of Common Pleas. After a trial de novo, the jury found that the appellee was entitled to participate in the Workmen's Compensation Fund and final judgment to this effect was entered on March 26, 1975.

The appellants, the Ford Motor Company, the Bureau of Workmen's Compensation and the Industrial Commission of Ohio, appeal this decision and assign as error:

"1. The trial court erred in overruling, in part, employer's motion for a directed verdict at the completion of claimant's case and there is insufficient evidence supporting the jury verdict for the reason claimant failed to prove by expert medical testimony that he, in fact, suffered a substantial aggravation of a preexisting condition which was the direct and proximate result of an alleged accident occurring on February 18, 1973.

"A. Claimant has failed to establish by credible and competent expert medical testimony that claimant suffered an aggravation of a preexisting condition.

"B. Claimant has failed to establish by credible and competent expert medical testimony that claimant suffered a substantial aggravation of a preexisting condition."

"It is noted that the praecipe accompanying the notice of appeal in this case specifically requested the clerk of courts to "Please file with the Court of Appeals of Cuyahoga County, Ohio, Eighth Appellate District, the transcript of the docket and journal entries together with the original and other miscellaneous papers which are found

in the court file in this case. Please do not prepare a trial transcript.
* * * "

In this case the appellee maintains that he suffered injury to his lower back when, in the course of his employment, he attempted to retrieve a falling conveyor chain on February 18, 1973. The appellants maintain that the appellee's back was injured before February 18, 1973 and that the accident on that date did not aggravate his back problems.

Before addressing the assignment of error stated above, it is necessary to first resolve a procedural problem concerning the record. In the present case, the record on appeal consists of the original papers and a certified copy of the docket and journal entries prepared by the clerk of the trial court. We do not have before us a verbatim transcript of proceedings as provided for in Appellate Rule 9(B), a narrative statement as provided for in Appellate Rule 9(C), or an agreed statement as provided for in Appellate Rule 9(D). Among the original papers is a deposition of Dr. Earl Brightman, a prospective witness called on behalf of the appellee.

It is well established that an appellant has the burden of demonstrating from the record the errors he complains of. The record on appeal consists of the original papers and exhibits thereto filed in the trial court, the transcript of proceedings, if any, including exhibits, and a certified copy of the docket and journal entries prepared by the clerk of the trial court. Appellate Rule 9(A). If a party can demonstrate the error complained of by the use of the original papers and exhibits thereto or by the docket and journal entries, it is not necessary for him to provide an appellate court with a transcript of proceedings, a narrative statement, or an agreed statement as provided for in Appellate Rules 9(B), 9(C) and 9(D). However, if an appellant intends to urge on appeal that a finding or conclusion is unsupported by the evidence, is contrary to the weight of the evidence, that there was error in the trial court's charge to the jury, or some other similar issue, it is necessary for him to provide the court with either a complete or partial verbatim transcript of the testimony, as required by Appellate Rule 9(B), or a narrative statement, as provided for in Appellate Rule 9(C), or an agreed statement as provided for in Appellate Rule 9(D).

If a verbatim transcript of proceedings is to be used in an appeal, the appellant has the responsibility of initially ordering either a complete or partial transcript of the proceedings from the court reporter. The reporter shall certify such transcript as correct and state whether it is a complete or partial transcript. Appellate Rule 9(B). If a narrative or an agreed statement is to be used, the appellant has the responsibility of preparing these statements and submitting them to the appellee. Such statements must also be submitted to the trial court for settlement and approval, and then be included by the clerk of courts, as approved, in the record on appeal. Appellate Rules 9(C) and 9(D).

We must now determine the status of a witness's deposition when it is filed with the clerk of courts. The mere filing of a deposition of a witness with the clerk of courts pursuant to Civil Rules 30(F) and 32(A) does not automatically make such deposition a part of the transcript of proceedings. The transcript of proceedings is a verbatim transcription of the trial proceedings, including the testimony and exhibits, which is prepared and certified by the court reporter pursuant to Appellate Rule 9(B). When a deposition is read verbatim at a trial in lieu of the personal appearance and testimony of a witness, and one of the parties desires to use this testimony on appeal, that party can request the court reporter to prepare a verbatim transcript of testimony. The reporter will certify it as correct and state whether it is a complete or partial transcript. Appellate Rule 9(B).

Additionally, it is recognized that a party may want to minimize his costs of appeal by not paying for the preparation of the above verbatim transcript of proceedings. Therefore, in a case where a deposition of a witness is read at the trial and the appellant wants to minimize his costs, he can request the court reporter to certify the deposition itself as a partial verbatim transcript of proceedings pursuant to Appellate Rule 9(B), or he can attempt to comply with Appellate Rule 9(D) by seeking to use the deposition as an agreed statement. In this case he must seek approval of the other party and then submit the statement to the trial court for settlement and approval. An approved agreed statement will then be included by the clerk of courts in the record on appeal.

In this case, because the appellants are relying on the testimony of Dr. Brightman to sustain their burden in regard to their assignment of error, it is necessary to have Dr. Brightman's testimony as a part of the transcript of proceedings. There is nothing in the record before this court to show whether Dr. Brightman was a witness at the trial either in person or by the reading of his deposition. Therefore, the testimony of Dr. Brightman is not before this court in this appeal, and we cannot say that the assignment of error is well taken. We affirm the judgment of the trial court.

Judgment affirmed.

Notes and Questions

1. Is there a difference between the trial court record and the record on appeal? Why should it be so important that the trial record indicate that an issue was raised in the trial court?

2. Federal Rule of Appellate Procedure 10(a) provides that all papers and exhibits filed in the trial court along with the transcript of testimony and a copy of the docket entries constitute the record on appeal; Rule 11 permits the parties to stipulate that specific items need not be forwarded to the court of appeals. This is the rule in many jurisdictions. Other jurisdictions, however, list specific items that are to be included in the record and permit the parties to stipulate to agree to include other items. E.g., Wis.Stat. Ann. § 809.15 (West 1994), Mo.R.Civ.P. 81.12. Does one type of rule put a heavier burden on the attorneys for the parties than the other?

3. An appellant is generally held to have no obligation to order a complete transcript, if portions of the record are not pertinent to the appeal. On occasion, this doctrine has had the effect of denying opposing parties the opportunity to advance arguments that would be based solely on omitted portions of the record. It remains the responsibility of other parties, therefore, to assess whether the appellant has ordered a complete transcript and, if not, what other portions of the record need to be transcribed to permit ventilation of the expected issues. See United States on Behalf of Cal's A/C and Electric v. Famous Construction Corp., 220 F.3d 326 (5th Cir. 2000) (the appellant "satisfied in toto the requirements of rule 10(b)(3)(A). It served [the adversaries] with its transcript order and with its notice of appeal, which adequately articulated a statement of the issues that the appellant intends to present on the appeal. The appellate rules do not require ... that an appellant specifically warn appellees that it is not ordering a complete transcript").

4. The rule that the appellate court will not consider anything outside the record applies to documents (United States v. Gilmore, 698 F.2d 1095 (10th Cir. 1983)), testimony (Cormier v. Walker, 473 A.2d 871 (Me. 1984)), and oral arguments made to the trial court (Spillios v. Green, 137 Ariz. 443, 671 P.2d 421 (App.1983)). On occasions, however, a court will deviate from the general rule. For example, in Whedon v. Whedon, 68 N.C.App. 191, 314 S.E.2d 794 (1984) the court held that the absence of a record of the qualifications of an expert witness did not prevent a challenge to the testimony of the witness. The court reasoned that if the record indicates that such a finding could have been made, it will be assumed that the judge found him to be an expert. Similarly, in Plawecki v. Angelo Tomasso, Inc., 1 Conn.App. 48, 467 A.2d 944 (1983) the court reviewed the issue of the admissibility of a written statement even though it had not been marked as an exhibit for identification as is generally required. The court reasoned that the fact that the trial court examined the statement and found it inconsistent with the testimony of the person who gave the statement, and that the offering party did not argue it was not inconsistent, was an adequate substitute for the record. Some admission by the opposing party may also suffice such as conceding that an issue had been raised orally (Bickerstaff v. Denny's Restaurant, Inc., 142 Ariz. 27, 688 P.2d 673 (App.1984)) or a stipulation as to essential facts made in a memorandum of law included in the record (Lakeland Property Owners Ass'n v. Larson, 121 Ill.App.3d 805, 77 Ill.Dec. 68, 459 N.E.2d 1164 (1984)). More unusual was the case of Orthmann v. Apple River Campground, Inc., 757 F.2d 909 (7th Cir. 1985) in which the court considered documents included in an appendix to the brief, some of which had been created after the lower court's dismissal of the complaint and some of which were generated by discovery in another lawsuit. The court acknowledged that the documents were not part of the record. It reasoned that because the appeal was from dismissal of the complaint for failure to state a claim upon which relief could be granted, plaintiff on appeal could attempt to show dismissal was improper by offering even an unsubstantiated version of the events. This being the case, it could go farther and offer proof of the allegations. Is this a sound analysis?

5. The *"Daubert* hearings" prevalent in federal practice under Daubert v. Merrell Dow Pharmaceuticals, Inc., 509 U.S. 579, 113 S.Ct. 2786, 125

L.Ed.2d 469 (1993) consider issues relating to the scope and admissibility of expert opinion. The appellate review of such rulings requires that the record of the separate hearing on these issues be presented to the appellate court. See Learning Curve Toys, Inc. v. Abraham, 342 F.3d 714 (7th Cir. 2003) (review "forfeited" by failure to include the transcripts). The Court said:

> We recognize that, as an alternative to forfeiture, we have the authority under Rule 10(e) of the Federal Rules of Appellate Procedure to order PlayWood to supplement the record to include the *Daubert* hearing. See Fed. R. App. P. 10(e). However, we decline to exercise that authority in this case because PlayWood "has had ample opportunity to correct the problem but has failed to do so." LaFollette, 63 F.3d at 545. Learning Curve pointed out in its answer brief that the *Daubert* hearing was not made part of the record on appeal. See Appellees' Br. at 41 ("PlayWood would have this Court undertake a de novo review and reverse the trial court's ruling on the admissibility of expert testimony, rendered after a *Daubert* hearing, without any reference to the evidence introduced at that hearing! Indeed, PlayWood has not included the hearing transcript in the record before the Court."). Despite notice of Learning Curve's objection to the incomplete record, PlayWood made no attempt to supplement the record or to explain why a transcript of the hearing was not necessary to permit meaningful appellate review.

6.   Where a spotty record is prepared, the appellate court may choose to limit review to those issues on which the appellant has discharged the burden to present a record from which a proper decision can be made. See, e.g., Crompton Mfg. Co. v. Plant Fab Inc., 91 Fed. Appx. 335 (5th Cir. 2004)(appellant provided only the transcript of a pretrial conference and a notice of appeal).

7.   Where additional material takes the form of docket records in other court proceedings, the appellate court will sometimes take judicial notice of indisputable facts (such as the fact that a case with certain named parties was filed or pending). See United States v. Verlinsky, 459 F.2d 1085, 1089 (5th Cir. 1972) (taking judicial notice of "the records of the district court and the court of appeals here involved"); Paul v. Dade County, 419 F.2d 10, 12 (5th Cir. 1969) (taking judicial notice of a prior state case, even though it "was not made part of the record on . . . appeal").

3.   DEPOSITION TRANSCRIPTS

CHURCH v. PERALES

Tennessee Court of Appeals, 2000.
39 S.W.3d 149.

WILLIAM C. KOCH, JR., JUDGE.

This appeal involves a dispute between an elderly patient and her physicians regarding their treatment of a severe post-operative infection caused by a bowel perforation that occurred during gynecological surgery. The patient filed suit in the Circuit Court for Davidson County against five physicians and a hospital alleging medical battery and malpractice. The trial court granted a summary judgment to the physicians and the hospital and dismissed the patient's case. * * *

Before we address the substance of Ms. Church's medical battery and lack of informed consent claims, we must turn our attention to a flaw in the appellate record that materially affects the scope of our review. The parties' briefs contain numerous references to Ms. Church's deposition testimony. While the record indicates that Ms. Church's lawyer may have filed Ms. Church's deposition in the trial court as part of her response to Dr. Perales's summary judgment motion, the deposition was never made part of the record on appeal.[6] This is a material omission because the record contains no other direct evidence of Ms. Church's version of her pre-operative conversations with Dr. Perales.

When this court noted the absence of Ms. Church's deposition during oral argument, Dr. Perales's lawyer endeavored to assume responsibility for the oversight. However, Ms. Church was responsible for ensuring that all parts of the trial court record germane to the issues she intended to raise on appeal were included in the appellate record. See Tenn. R. App. P. 24(a), (e); State v. Banes, 874 S.W.2d 73, 82 (Tenn. Crim. App. 1993). There was ample opportunity to discover that Ms. Church's deposition was not in the record because the appellate record had been on file with this court and available to the parties for six months prior to oral argument, and Ms. Church's lawyer actually had the record in her possession for two weeks prior to oral argument.

Once the fact that Ms. Church's deposition was not included in the record was brought to her attention, Ms. Church's lawyer could have supplemented the record pursuant to Tenn. R. App. P. 24(e). She did not do so, and as a result, the record contains no testimony by Ms. Church regarding her pre-operative conversations with Dr. Perales. We cannot take judicial knowledge of her testimony, even if parts of it are cited in the briefs, because it is outside the record. See Richmond v. Richmond, 690 S.W.2d 534, 535 (Tenn. Ct. App. 1985).

Thus, in accordance with Tenn. R. App. P. 36(a), Ms. Church must bear the consequences of absence of her deposition from the record. * * *

[W]e affirm the summary judgment dismissing Ms. Church's medical battery and informed consent claims against Dr. Perales * * *.

Notes and Questions

1. Some 30 years before the principal case, an appellate court facing a very similar failure to include deposition transcripts in the appellate record held: "Such a failure is not automatically 'fatal' to an appeal because, under Rule 10(a), all of the original papers and exhibits filed in the district court are a part of the record on appeal whether or not brought before this court." Thus following oral argument, and pursuant to Rule 10(e), that court

---

6. Only four depositions were included in the appellate record filed with this court. These included the depositions of Drs. Perales, Dunbar, and Ross, as well as the deposition of Dr. Gary J. Wolf, a Lewisburg surgeon, who was Ms. Church's expert witness.

directed plaintiff to file a supplemental transcript containing the missing depositions. See Chapman v. Rudd Paint and Varnish Company, 409 F.2d 635 (9th Cir. 1969). Do you think the inexorable crush of increased case filings in recent decades makes it less likely that, today, spontaneous use of the supplementation process will be undertaken to cure such errors?

2. In federal practice, are such gaps in the record matters most directly addressed as correction of the record under Fed.R.App.P. 10(e) or transmission of the record under Fed.R.App.P. 11? Do Rules 10 and 11 cover all of the possibilities when a part of the record in the trial court is not forwarded to the appellate court. Is the statement that the appellate court can always call up any missing part of the record accurate? On changes in the record under Rule 10(e) see Annotation, 60 A.L.R.Fed. 183 (1982).

3. As noted under section B, supra, some jurisdictions do not follow the principle that the entire record in the trial court constitutes the record on appeal. Would those jurisdictions follow the rule stated in the principal case that the appellate court is always free to call up from the trial court any part of the trial record that was through error or oversight not forwarded to the appellate court? If not, how could the additional item be included in the record? A motion filed in the trial court? In the appellate court?

4. If an event occurs after the notice of appeal has been filed that may affect the outcome of the appeal such as making the matter moot, how can the event be brought to the attention of the appellate court? The court in Strand Century, Inc. v. Dallas, 68 Or.App. 705, 683 P.2d 561 (1984) approved the procedure of filing an affidavit in the appellate court. Would it be preferable to remand the case to the trial court to take evidence on the question? Is Federal Rule of Appellate Procedure 10(e) applicable to this situation? In Birdsey v. Grand Blanc Community Schools, 130 Mich.App. 718, 344 N.W.2d 342 (1983), however, the court refused to consider a claim that a case was moot because the appellant had graduated because the fact of graduation was not a matter of record. Does this make sense?

SECTION D. UNAVAILABILITY OF THE NORMAL TRANSCRIPT

1. A RANGE OF POSSIBLE PROBLEMS

PALMER v. ESPEY HUSTON & ASSOCIATES

Court of Appeals of Texas, 2002.
84 S.W.3d 345.

OPINION BY JUSTICE RODRIGUEZ.

Appellants, G.J. Palmer, Jr., individually and as managing partner on behalf of Queen Isabella Development Joint Venture and Queen Isabella Development Joint Venture and 1629 Service Corp., appeal from directed verdicts granting take nothing judgments in favor of appellees, Max Burkhart, MBA Architecture Group (MBA), Michael J. Blum, Valcon, Inc., and Espey Huston & Associates, Inc. By six points of error, appellants complain that (1) the record is neither complete nor proper for this appeal, and (2) the trial court erred in granting appellees' motions for directed verdict, and in excluding evidence. We affirm.

I. BACKGROUND

This case involves the development of a marina in the Laguna Madre at Port Isabel, Texas. Queen Isabella Development Joint Venture (QID) hired MBA, an architectural, engineering and planning firm, to assist with the development of the marina. MBA worked on the planning and design phase of the project, including the design of a breakwater to create an artificial harbor by forming a barrier between waters outside the harbor and the interior of the marina.

MBA hired Espey Huston, an engineering firm, to (1) assist in handling permit applications with the Army Corps of Engineers; (2) conduct a bathymetric study; (3) conduct a wave-attenuation or "wave-climate" study; and (4) later, perform a written analysis of four different types of generic breakwaters, and how they typically would react to the wave-climate/attenuation study. Espey Huston's final report was completed in February 1985.

Because MBA did not provide in-house structural engineering services, it sub-contracted this work to Donald Dragutsky, a licensed civil engineer. Prior to the completion of the breakwater design, MBA withdrew from the project. Thereafter, Dragutsky contracted with appellants, and modified the design prepared by Espey Huston. Dragutsky's design was a variation on a timber-wall breakwater depicted in Espey Huston's February 1985 report. Bellingham Marine constructed the breakwater. After construction was complete, a series of storms with prevailing northerly winds generated waves which overtopped or went under the breakwater and caused damage to the docks and boats inside the marina.

In 1988, appellants sued appellees for breach of contract, negligence, breach of warranty, strict liability, and violations of the Texas Deceptive Trade Practices and Consumer Protection Act (DTPA). Nine years later, in October 1997, the case went to trial. After appellants' case-in-chief, the trial court found "there [was] no evidence of probative force to support a recovery for Plaintiffs or to submit the case to a jury," and granted all appellees' motions for directed verdict.

II. THE APPELLATE RECORD

By their first point of error, appellants contend the appellate record is not complete or proper. They complain of (1) unrecorded bench conferences, (2) inaccuracies and missing testimony and arguments in the trial transcript, (3) lost or misplaced original exhibits, and (4) an improperly certified statement of facts.[7]

A. Unrecorded Bench Conferences

Appellants complain of four unrecorded bench conferences. First, they contend the court reporter failed to record a bench conference that

---

7. Appellants dispute the accuracy of the reporter's record, not the clerk's record.

occurred during appellants' examination of Burkhart. Espey Huston objected to a question asked of Burkhart because it called for an opinion. An unrecorded bench conference followed. After the bench conference, appellants asked Burkhart the same question and he responded. Again, Espey Huston objected, this time on the basis that the response was non-responsive, hearsay, an opinion, and was not based on personal knowledge. The court sustained the objection and struck the response. Appellants did not challenge the ruling and no bench conference, recorded or unrecorded, followed.

The second unrecorded bench conference occurred after appellants offered their fourth exhibit into evidence. Immediately following the unrecorded bench conference, outside the presence of the jury, the trial court and counsel had a lengthy discussion on exchanging exhibits, not interrupting the trial with objections regarding exhibits, and witnesses rendering expert testimony. This exchange was recorded and appears in the transcript of the trial proceeding.

The third unrecorded bench conference occurred during appellants' direct examination of Dragutsky, presented by way of deposition testimony. During the course of the testimony, after the trial court sustained appellee's objection that the testimony called for an opinion, appellants requested a bench conference. Following the bench conference, appellants continued presenting the deposition testimony of Dragutsky.

The last unrecorded bench conference occurred during appellants' case-in-chief; after they had offered excerpts of the deposition testimony of Paul Jensen, the vice-president of Espey Huston, passed the witness, and discussed exhibits entered. Appellant Palmer's trial counsel asked to approach the bench on another issue. After the bench conference, counsel called Palmer as the next witness.

A court reporter is required to make a full record of the proceedings unless excused by agreement of the parties. Tex. R. App. P. 13.1(a). No such agreement is apparent on the record. We recently held, in a criminal proceeding, the reporter's duty to record proceedings, including bench conferences that occur after the trial commences, is mandatory pursuant to appellate rule 13.1, and, thus, noncompliance is error. See Tanguma v. State, 47 S.W.3d 663, 667 (Tex. App.-Corpus Christi 2001, pet. ref'd); but see Polasek v. State, 16 S.W.3d 82, 88–89 (Tex. App.-Houston [1st Dist.] 2000, pet. ref'd) (rule 13.1(a) conflicts with section 52.046(a) of Texas Government Code, and is void). Likewise, in this civil case, we conclude the court reporter's failure to record and transcribe the identified bench conferences that occurred after the trial commenced, without agreement of the parties, constitutes error. See Tex. R. App. P. 13.1(a). However, a failure to record bench conferences does not automatically result in reversal.

We may not reverse unless the error complained of probably caused the rendition of an improper judgment or prevented an appellant from properly presenting the case to the appellate court. Tex. R. App. P. 44.1; cf. *Tanguma*, 47 S.W.3d at 667 (pursuant to appellate rule 44.2, this

Court analyzed whether error was reversible constitutional error or reversible non-constitutional error affecting substantial rights). Appellants asserted no consequences from the failure of the court reporter to record the four bench conferences. They do not claim the error probably caused rendition of improper judgments. See Tex. R. App. P. 44.1(a)(1). Neither have they set out how the failure of the court reporter to record the four bench conferences prevented appellants from properly presenting their case to this Court. See id. at 44.1(a)(2). Furthermore, based on our review of the record, we cannot ascertain support for these arguments, had they been made. Accordingly, while we conclude the court reporter's failure to completely record the bench conferences at trial was error, such failure is not reversible. See id. at 44.1(a). We must, therefore, disregard the error. See id.

B.   Inaccurate/Lost Record

Appellants next argue the statement of facts is replete with inaccuracies which call the entire statement of facts into question. Appellants refer us to inaccuracies in eight lines of transcription in the five-volume reporter's record. Although the referenced portions of the record contain some unintelligible words or phrases, when reviewed in context, the meaning is understandable. Thus, we cannot conclude the entire statement of facts is called into question on this basis.

Appellants also generally refer us to other inaccuracies in the reporter's record, inaccuracies they contend are impossible to set out "without enormously exceeding the page limits of [their] brief." However, a party asserting error on appeal bears the burden of showing that the record supports the contention raised, and of specifying the place or places in the record where matters upon which they rely or of which they complain are shown. Tex. R. App. P. 38.1(h); Happy Harbor Methodist Home, Inc. v. Cowins, 903 S.W.2d 884, 886 (Tex. App.—Houston [1st Dist.] 1995, no writ). "We will not do the job of the advocate." Happy Harbor, 903 S.W.2d at 886. Appellants have not carried their burden on this contention.

Finally, to the extent appellants are complaining that the above referenced portions of the record were lost or destroyed, we apply a similar analysis. An appellant is entitled to a new trial when a reporter's record is lost or destroyed if (1) appellant timely requested the record; (2) a significant portion of the court reporter's notes has been lost or destroyed; (3) the lost portion is necessary to the appeal, and the parties cannot agree on a complete reporter's record. Tex. R. App. P. 34.6(f). We have reviewed the complained-of portions of the record, and have concluded the nature of the testimony or argument is apparent from the record. We cannot conclude that a significant portion of the reporter's notes has been lost or destroyed. See id. at 34.6(f)(2). Furthermore, appellant has not established how the lost portions, if any, are necessary to the appeal. See id. at 34.6(f)(3).

C. Lost or Destroyed Exhibits

Appellants next assert "it appears that the original exhibits presented to the court at the underlying proceedings were lost and/or misplaced
by the court." Appellants do not complain that the exhibits were, in fact,
lost or misplaced, and App are, thus, unavailable for our review, as is
contemplated by appellate rule 34.6(f). See Tex. R. App. P. 34.6(f). They
argue only that markings on the exhibits are missing, markings that
indicated how the evidence was to be limited for our review.

While there are no markings on the copies of the exhibits filed in
this appeal, we conclude, nonetheless, appellants have provided record
cites, or could have done so, limiting their evidence for our review.
Moreover, appellants must show this Court that the missing markings
on the exhibits in the appellate record are necessary for the resolution of
their issues on appeal. See id. at 34.6(f). They have not done so. Neither
have they provided authority to support their argument, or offered
record cites to specific exhibits about which they complain. See Tex. R.
App. P. 38.1(h). Furthermore, to the extent appellants are complaining
that the exhibits do not contain notations indicating which exhibits, or
portions thereof, were admitted in the presence of the jury and which
were admitted only for the bill of exception, the reporter's record affords
that information.

D. Certification of Record

Finally, appellants contend the statement of facts is improperly
certified by the three court reporters involved in its completion. Appellants complain the court reporter's certification is not identical to the
form set out in the appendix of the Texas Rules of Appellate Procedure.
See Tex. R. App. P. Appendix, Order Directing the Form of the Appellate
Record in Civil Cases, § B(1)(q). However, by order of the Texas Supreme Court, section B(1)(q) provides only that the certificate contain
certain information in substantially the form outlined in the appendix.
Id.

The court reporter certified the five volumes of the reporter's record
with the following:

> I, RONALD DUNAGAN, Certified Shorthand Reporter in and for
> the State of Texas, with the assistance of Elizabeth Jimenez, hereby
> certify to the following:
>
> That the testimony given in the above-mentioned matter is a
> true and accurate record of the proceedings.
>
> I further certify that this transcription of the record of the
> proceedings truly and correctly reflects the exhibits, if any, offered
> by the respective parties.

Although not verbatim, the court reporter's certificate in this case is
in substantial compliance with the suggested language found in the
appendix of the appellate rules, that the "foregoing contains a true and
correct transcription of all portions of evidence and other proceedings

. . . all of which occurred in open court or in chambers and were reported by me." Id.

Appellants also argue the record is not properly certified because court reporter Catalina Reyes informed this Court the record could not be completed. However, at a show cause hearing to determine why the original court reporter, Elizabeth Jimenez, should not be held in contempt for failure to file the reporter's record, Reyes offered her opinion that Jimenez should be able to provide assistance for those portions that were not transcribed. In our July 13, 2000, order, we directed the trial court to hold a hearing to determine whether the record could be completed with Jimenez's assistance, and "to take all steps necessary in order to secure a complete reporter's record." In compliance with the July 13 order, the trial court appointed Dunagan to complete the record, with assistance from Jimenez. On August 10, 2000, a complete and certified reporter's record was filed with the clerk of this Court.

Appellants' first point of error is overruled [and] judgment of the trial court is affirmed.

Note

In some courts, jury instructions are not transcribed. Instead, copies of the tendered instructions—marked to indicate which were given and which were refused by the trial court—are made a part of the record in the manner of exhibits. However, as one might expect, judges sometimes experience slips of the tongue (or improvisation) in reading from pages upon pages of printed text. For a glimpse into a fascinating effort by an appellate court to "reconstruct" which instructions were actually given, by looking at drafts submitted, handwritten notations by the trial judge, recollections of the parties involved, including use of the law clerk's affidavit and the trial judge's "laptop computer notes," see United States v. Zichettello, 208 F.3d 72 (2nd Cir. 2000).

2. COPING WITH LOSS OR ALL OR PART OF THE TESTIMONY

TANSOR v. CHECKER TAXI COMPANY

Supreme Court of Illinois, 1963.
27 Ill.2d 250, 188 N.E.2d 659.

SCHAEFER, JUSTICE.

This court granted leave to Jo D. Tansor, the plaintiff, to file her original petition in this court for a writ of *mandamus* directed to the respondent, Hon. Elmer N. Holmgren, a judge of the superior court of Cook County. We also allowed her petition for leave to appeal from an order of the Appellate Court for the First District, which denied her motion for leave to file in that court a similar petition for a writ of *mandamus* directed against the same respondent. The two cases were consolidated in this court. Both concern the plaintiff's efforts to obtain a report of proceedings at a trial conducted before the respondent as trial judge, in furtherance of her appeal from an adverse judgment.

From the record before the Appellate Court and the plaintiff's original petition in this court, it appears that the plaintiff prosecuted a claim for personal injuries against the Checker Taxi Company, the defendant. Upon a trial before the respondent judge, the jury returned a verdict in the plaintiff's favor in the sum of $4,500. On the motion of the defendant, the respondent entered judgment for the defendant notwithstanding this verdict, and conditionally granted the defendant's motion for a new trial in the event of reversal, in accordance with section 68.1 of the Civil Practice Act. (Ill.Rev.Stat.1961, chap. 110, par. 68.1.) The plaintiff filed her notice of appeal to the Appellate Court and undertook to procure the record on appeal.

No officially appointed court reporter, as authorized by statute (Ill. Rev.Stat.1961, chap. 37, pars. 163a, 163b,) attended the trial. The stenographers who reported the proceedings were employed by a private court reporting firm hired by the defendant. In an effort to obtain a copy of the stenographic report to complete her record on appeal, the plaintiff presented a motion in the trial court for an order directing the defendant or the court reporter to supply a transcript. The motion was accompanied by a tender of the reporter's full fee for attendance, reporting, and transcribing, and by an offer to prove, through the testimony of the reporter himself, that the testimony had already been transcribed and was available subject to the directions of the defendant. The reporter declined to supply the transcript, however, without the authorization of the defendant, and the respondent denied the motion to compel production.

Plaintiff's attorney thereupon prepared a report of proceedings, in the form of a "condensed statement." (Ill.Rev.Stat.1961, chap. 110, par. 101.36.) Since no stenographic transcript was available to him, he based this account upon his trial notes and his own recollection of the proceedings. The statement so prepared was submitted to the respondent as a report of proceedings for his certificate of correctness as required by Rule 36 of this court. (Ill.Rev.Stat.1961, chap. 110, par. 101.36.) The defendant objected, and the respondent refused to certify the submitted report.

The plaintiff thereupon filed a motion in the Appellate Court where her appeal was pending, seeking leave to file a petition for a writ of *mandamus* directing the respondent to certify the report of proceedings. The respondent opposed this motion, and supported his opposition with a statement that the tendered report was inaccurate in certain respects. The defendant's attorney also opposed the motion with an affidavit that recited, so far as is pertinent, that the tendered report "is substantially incorrect and substantially incomplete. It does not contain the full substance of testimony as to how the accident occurred. Nor does it correctly reflect the trial court's rulings during the trial." By an order entered without opinion, the Appellate Court denied leave to file the petition for a writ of *mandamus*. The plaintiff then sought relief in this court.

The report of proceedings under the present practice serves the function of the former bill of exceptions. (Ill.Rev.Stat.1961, chap. 110, par. 74(2).) It affords the means for putting before the reviewing court matters not included in the formal common-law record. (See Miller v. Anderson, 269 Ill. 608, 109 N.E. 1048.) Here the plaintiff seeks review of a judgment entered notwithstanding the verdict. The sufficiency of the evidence introduced is determinative of this issue, and the evidence can be placed before a reviewing court only through a report of proceedings. Unless a report can be supplied, certified by the trial judge in accordance with our Rule, the plaintiff will be denied adequate appellate review.

Under the Rules, the burden of procuring the report of proceedings rests upon the appellant. (Rule 36(1)(c), Ill.Rev.Stat.1961, chap. 110, par. 101.36(1)(c).) In modern practice, this burden is ordinarily met simply by ordering a transcript of the stenographic record from the court reporter. In this case the respondent had ready means at hand to verify the tendered report and to single out errors. It is not denied that the defendant had been supplied with a complete transcript of the testimony. Since the stenographer's fee was tendered, the defendant's attorney might have been called upon to furnish that transcript, or the respondent might have called upon the stenographer himself, either to read from his notes or to supply a transcript. See People ex rel. Hall v. Holdom, 193 Ill. 319, 322, 61 N.E. 1014.

In Beebe v. State ex rel. Starr Piano Co., 106 Ohio St. 75, 139 N.E. 156 (1922), the stenographer who reported the trial had been hired, as here, by the prevailing party. The loser, preparing an appeal, tendered the reporter's fee for a transcript but, as here, the tender was refused upon the direction of the attorney for the prevailing party. The appellant then prepared a narrative statement, from consultation with witnesses and trial counsel, setting out in substance the evidence introduced. The trial judge refused to certify this statement on the ground that it was incorrect and untrue, and declined to compel the stenographer to read from his notes to facilitate correction. The Supreme Court of Ohio directed the issuance of a writ of *mandamus* to compel the respondent to correct and to sign the submitted report. The holding of the case is officially summarized in the syllabi prepared by the court as follows:

"2. It is the duty of the trial judge to allow and sign a bill of exceptions when duly presented, if the same be correct; it is likewise his duty to correct errors therein, and upon refusal to do so a writ of mandamus may issue.

"3. If the trial judge from memory or from memoranda in his possession cannot make such correction, it is his duty to refresh his memory from available information, including that which may be obtained from the stenographer who has shorthand notes of the testimony and other proceedings of the trial, even though such stenographer was not an official reporter appointed by the court, but was employed therein by the party prevailing in the suit. * * * " 106 Ohio St. 75–76, 139 N.E. at 156.

That the stenographer was hired and paid by the defendant poses no obstacle to this course. Full disclosure of information at the appellate stage does not threaten the adversary system, invade the lawyer's work product, or probe his trial strategy. The transcript of the testimony given in open court is not the product of the advocate's effort and diligence, but of the power of the State to compel witnesses to testify in the interest of justice. No claim of privilege can justify withholding of a report made by a stenographer under the auspices and with the facilities of the court. We so held in McGill v. Illinois Power Co., 18 Ill.2d 242, 163 N.E.2d 454, where the plaintiff had taken the depositions of certain witnesses in the prosecution of a workmen's compensation claim. In a subsequent proceeding on a common-law claim against a different defendant, the plaintiff refused to produce transcripts of these depositions or to permit the stenographer to supply copies upon the defendant's tender of the fee for copying or transcribing them. We there said: "The documents with which we are concerned are depositions taken pursuant to law. They are the product of the power of the State to compel the testimony of witnesses rather than of the ingenuity or resourcefulness of any lawyer. The State makes available its compulsory process to compel witnesses to attend and give testimony on a pretrial deposition in order to assist in the ascertainment of the truth. To sanction something akin to a property right in the transcript of testimony so taken would frustrate that purpose." 18 Ill.2d at 246, 163 N.E.2d at 457.

Both the respondent and the Appellate Court appear to have approached this case under the influence of Western Store and Office Fixture Co. v. A.L. Randall Co., 223 Ill.App. 225, decided in 1921. There a somewhat similar problem had arisen in the municipal court of Chicago and in the course of its opinion the Appellate Court stated, "The stenographer was an employee of the party who hired him and was bound by the terms of that hiring and, as to transcribing his notes and furnishing a typewritten copy, was not amenable to orders of the trial judge." No reason was advanced by the Appellate Court in support of the curious barrier thus erected around the court reporter, as contrasted with all other persons, who, as shown by the decisions of this court and other courts, can be compelled to testify fully as to what occurred at a trial at which they were present.

But we need not consider the intrinsic merits or demerits of the Appellate Court's opinion. Any notion that a court reporter or a litigant may have a proprietary interest in a transcript of the evidence introduced in a judicial proceeding can not survive the statute which provides for official court reporters. That statute authorizes each judge of the circuit and superior courts to appoint an official shorthand reporter, and provides that the salaries of the reporters so appointed shall be paid for by the State. (Ill.Rev.Stat.1961, chap. 37, pars. 163a, 163b.) The fee to be paid to the reporter for preparing a transcript of his shorthand notes is fixed by the statute, which states that "The fees for making transcripts shall be paid in the first instance by the party in whose behalf such transcript is ordered and shall be taxed in the suit." (Ill.Rev.Stat.1961, chap. 37, par. 163b.) Under this statute neither party can claim a proprietary interest in the official reporter's notes or transcript. And certainly the absence of an official reporter can not, in the face of the governing statute, give to either party a proprietary interest in a court reporter's transcript that would not exist if the statute was complied with.

This court has already denied the motion of the respondent and the defendant to dismiss the petition for *mandamus* on the ground that the time for filing the report of proceedings had expired. Allowance of that motion would have effectively precluded the plaintiff's efforts to review the judgment against her. The order of the Appellate Court denying the plaintiff's petition for *mandamus* is reversed. This court's writ of *mandamus* is awarded commanding the respondent as judge of the superior court of Cook County to direct the defendant's attorney to furnish the transcript, or to direct the court reporter to transcribe his notes and deliver the transcript to the plaintiff. The respondent is also directed to certify the report of proceedings for filing in the Appellate Court for the First District. The Appellate Court will then fix the time within which the abstracts and briefs of the parties may be filed.

No. 37104. Order reversed; No. 37158. Writ awarded, with directions.

Notes and Questions

1. Is the decision in the principal case dependent upon the Illinois statutes cited in the opinion, or does the case stand for general principles of broader application? Does the court answer the question of who owns the transcript of testimony? Under the decision, if a transcript is filed in the court records of a case is anyone entitled to make a copy of it the same as any other court record without paying the court reporter the fee for a transcript? Is this question answered by 28 U.S.C. § 753, the federal statute governing federal court reporting and transcripts of court proceedings?

2. For a discussion of the problems caused by the manner in which court reporters are paid for their services, see R. Leflar, Internal Operating Procedures of Appellate Courts 19–20 (1976).

COMMERCIAL CREDIT EQUIP. CORP.
v. L & A CONTRACTING CO.

United States Court of Appeals, Fifth Circuit, 1977.
549 F.2d 979.

GODBOLD, CIRCUIT JUDGE.

This is an appeal by L & A Contracting Company (L & A) from a jury verdict of $25,000 in favor of Commercial Credit Equipment Corporation (CCEC). We affirm. Only one issue on appeal, the failure of the court reporter to record the closing arguments of the attorneys, warrants full discussion here.

L & A financed the purchase of an airplane through CCEC under an agreement known as a finance lease. Under the terms of this arrangement CCEC owned the plane and leased it to L & A for a monthly sum. After this lease had been in effect for almost a year and a half, L & A, under the terms of the lease, wished to have the aircraft sold and end its obligation to CCEC. The plane was sold and, through an error, CCEC undercalculated its interest in the plane by $27,000 and subsequently overpaid L & A $27,000 from the proceeds of the sale. This suit was brought to recover the overpayment.

The court reporter failed to transcribe the closing arguments of the attorneys. L & A contends that this is reversible error because it precludes review of whether there was a critical error committed in the closing argument of the attorney for CCEC. We disagree.

The Court Reporters Act, 28 U.S.C. § 753(b), requires that all open court proceedings in civil cases be recorded unless otherwise agreed by the parties. While the requirements of this Act are mandatory and not permissive, a violation is not reversible error per se.

This court has set up three hurdles in interpreting the Court Reporters Act, and L & A must clear two of them in order to gain a reversal. The first is that there must be a contention that error was committed in the omitted portion of the record. Id. L & A has made this contention with enough specificity to meet this threshold burden. Next, L & A must show that in its present form the record is insufficient to permit review of the claim of error. Id. L & A has failed to meet this requirement. The record as now constituted is enough to allow us to pass on the error alleged. Here all counsel for both sides filed post-trial affidavits concerning the contents of the omitted closing arguments, and, at a hearing on L & A's motion for new trial, the court reporter and attorneys for both sides testified about the nonrecorded portion of the record. This testimony and these affidavits tell approximately the same story and contain no major contradictions. The affidavits and testimony concerning the omitted closing argument make the record complete enough for us to pass upon L & A's claim of error contained in the closing argument of CCEC's attorney.

The final hurdle L & A must clear if it is to obtain a reversal is that it must show that a portion of the closing argument of CCEC's attorney was so prejudicial as to require us to vacate the jury verdict and order a new trial. L & A has not made this showing. L & A complains that after the trial court had agreed to give a jury instruction saying that L & A had relied on CCEC's representation as to the amount of CCEC's interest in the airplane, CCEC's attorney questioned whether L & A in fact had relied. CCEC's attorney states that he was questioning whether L & A's reliance was justified and in good faith. L & A objected to this portion of CCEC's closing argument at the time it was made and the objection was overruled. L & A also raised this point in a motion for mistrial after the closing arguments. The motion was denied.

Generally, an attorney is to be given a good deal of leeway in his argument to the jury, and a trial judge has wide discretion in regulating the scope of the argument. This discretion was not abused in this case.

CCEC's attorney's questioning of the nature of L & A's reliance was taken from the evidence and reasonable inferences which could be drawn from the evidence and thus was allowable. Whether L & A's reliance was justified and in good faith and to what extent L & A had changed its position based on the reliance were fair issues to raise to the jury. From reading the record, the affidavits and testimony on the closing arguments and the jury instructions we hold that the trial court was within the bounds of its discretion in allowing the argument.

L & A's other contentions are without merit.

AFFIRMED.

Notes and Questions

1. Why did the court not adopt the rule that if an alleged error was not recorded through no fault of the appellant, reversal would be automatic? Does the rule the court adopted place an impossible burden on the attorneys?

2. Failure of the court reporter to include a crucial objection in the transcript was handled somewhat differently than in the principal case in Reichert v. Ingersoll, 18 Ohio St.3d 220, 480 N.E.2d 802 (1985). In that case the Ohio Supreme Court held that court of appeals improperly refused to permit the record to be supplemented, taking the view that the omission was made in good faith, not part of a continuing course of conduct for purposes of delay, there would be no prejudice to the appellee, and denial would frustrate the policy of deciding cases on the merits. Is this decision surprising in light of the fact that the appellant did not discover the absence of the objection from the record until it was pointed out in the appellate court's opinion refusing to consider the alleged error?

3. If the appellant does not order a transcript of testimony, it cannot rely on findings of fact made by the trial judge referring to testimony at trial. Abood v. Block, 752 F.2d 548 (11th Cir. 1985).

4. Does Federal Rule of Appellate Procedure 10(e) cover the situation that arose in the principal case? If so, why wasn't the rule cited by the court of appeals? Was the procedure followed consistent with Rule 10(e)? Were there other persons who should have been asked to testify on the unreported argument?

3. CONSTRUCTING A SUBSTITUTE FOR A TRANSCRIPT OF THE RECORD

HAWLEY v. CITY OF CLEVELAND

United States Court of Appeals, Sixth Circuit, 1994.
24 F.3d 814.

BOYCE F. MARTIN, JR., CIRCUIT JUDGE.

Pursuant to an ordinance passed by the Cleveland City Council, the Catholic Diocese of Cleveland operates a chapel, in a space the diocese leases from the City of Cleveland, in the terminal building of Cleveland

Hopkins International Airport. Claiming that the lease agreement and its authorizing ordinance violate the Establishment Clause of the First Amendment, three Cleveland taxpayers and an advocacy organization brought suit under 42 U.S.C. § 1983 against the city, the city's Director of Port Control, the diocese, and diocese Bishop Anthony M. Pilla. Plaintiffs now appeal the district court's judgment in favor of defendants. For the following reasons, we affirm the judgment of the district court. * * *

Before turning to the substantive analysis of whether the chapel violates the Establishment Clause, we must first address the procedural ramifications of the death of the trial's court reporter, and plaintiffs' subsequent failure to avail themselves of Federal Rule of Appellate Procedure 10(c). Because of the inability of other court reporters to decipher the trial reporter's notes, no transcript of the proceedings in this case is available. Moreover, plaintiffs have chosen not to supplement the record on appeal pursuant to Rule 10(c), but rather to rely solely on the small portion of the transcript that the reporter was able to complete (less than one day's worth of a six-day trial), coupled with trial exhibits and depositions that were filed with the district court in advance of trial. Plaintiffs claim that they have chosen not to comply with Rule 10(c) because "the inevitable disputes with opposing counsel over what was said at trial would only prolong this appeal even further." Plaintiffs' Brief at 2. In response, defendants argue that plaintiffs' failure to provide a record of the evidence adduced at trial essentially precludes this Court from granting the relief sought by plaintiffs.

Two sections of Rule 10 are applicable to this dispute. First, Rule 10(b)(2) provides, in pertinent part:

> If the appellant intends to urge on appeal that a finding or conclusion is unsupported by the evidence or is contrary to the evidence, the appellant shall include in the record a transcript of all evidence relevant to such finding or conclusion.

Second, Rule 10(c) provides:

> If no report of the evidence or proceedings at a hearing or trial was made, or if a transcript is unavailable, the appellant may prepare a statement of the evidence or proceedings from the best available means, including the appellant's recollection. The statement shall be served on the appellee, who may serve objections or proposed amendments thereto within 10 days after service. Thereupon the statement and any objections of proposed amendments shall be submitted to the district court for settlement and approval and as settled and approved shall be included by the clerk of the district court in the record on appeal.

Although the preliminary language of Rule 10(c) is not mandatory ("appellant may prepare a statement"), Rule 10(c) supplies the only possible means of meeting the Rule 10(b)(2) requirement in cases where transcripts of the proceedings are unavailable. Read as a whole, therefore, Rule 10 provides that an appellant need not invoke Rule 10(c) in every case where a transcript is unavailable, but must do so if the transcript is unavailable and the appellant "intends to urge on appeal that a finding or conclusion is unsupported by the evidence or is contrary to the evidence." FED.R.APP.P. 10(b)(2).

Although not explicitly adopting the above reading of Rule 10 in a case such as the instant matter, this Court has drawn the same conclusion in similar contexts. In Herndon v. City of Massillon, 638 F.2d 963 (6th Cir. 1981), for example, the appellant challenged jury instructions that had not been transcribed by the court reporter. Without availing himself of Rule 10(c), the appellant argued that the absence of a record so insulated any error in the instructions from review that he should be entitled to a new trial. Id. at 965. In rejecting this contention, this Court cited with approval its earlier holding that plaintiffs' failure to avail themselves of "the procedure designed to reconstruct unrecorded proceedings [leaves] them with no objection based on the missing record." Id.[2] This Court has also held that the sufficiency of the evidence to support a verdict cannot be challenged on appeal in the absence of either a transcript or a statement of the evidence in narrative form. King v. Carmichael, 268 F.2d 305, 306 (6th Cir. 1959).

Other circuits have reached a similar conclusion in cases in which appellants have failed to invoke Rule 10(c). In United States v. Mills, 597 F.2d 693, 698 (9th Cir. 1979), for example, a defendant sought to submit an affidavit of counsel, which purportedly described an unreported pretrial conference in chambers, in support of his claim on appeal that the district court improperly enhanced his sentence as a result of his decision to stand trial. The Ninth Circuit refused to consider the affidavit on the ground that the defendant had not followed the provisions of Rule 10(c) for augmenting "the record on appeal concerning proceedings which were not reported." Id. As the Fifth Circuit has succinctly observed, "[w]here an appellant fails to provide an adequate appellate record on an issue finally decided by a prior court, that failure makes his road to victory difficult at best." In re Evangeline Refining Co., 890 F.2d 1312, 1322 (5th Cir. 1989).

In light of the foregoing, plaintiffs cannot justify their failure to invoke Rule 10(c) merely by asserting that to do so would have led to disputes with opposing counsel and a further delay of the appeal. Plaintiffs' presentation of a significant number of exhibits and depositions is no substitute for a statement of the proceedings that, pursuant to Rule 10(c), has been scrutinized and critiqued by defendants, and, perhaps most importantly, approved by the district court. Because the record on appeal in this case does not allow for an objective evaluation of the actual evidence presented at trial, we adopt the district court's findings of fact in their entirety.

---

2. In affirming a conviction despite the trial court's failure to record side-bar conferences, this Court noted in a more recent case that the appellant could have, but failed to, avail himself of Rule 10(c). See United States v. Ellzey, 874 F.2d 324, 331 (6th Cir. 1989).

Notes and Questions

1. In a classic case, Clawans v. White, 112 F.2d 189 (D.C. Cir. 1940), Justice Rutledge, sitting as Circuit Justice, reviewed an appeal in which one party disagreed with the "narrative" summary approved by the trial court, which was prepared to describe portions of the proceedings for which a court reporter had not been present. The court wrote:

> The case therefore must be treated as one in which appellant assigns as error the honest refusal of the trial court to accept her version of what transpired at the trial. Such a refusal is neither an accidental error nor judicial fraud. Although the trial court may be mistaken and the consequences may be serious for the appellant, we have no power to take corrective action in such circumstances. The situation is one in which the law must give credence either to the appellant or to the trial court. It is settled that the court's version, in such circumstances, must be accepted as correct.

The appeal was dismissed for failure of the appellant to perfect the appeal with a record sufficient to sustain her claims of error. Under today's Federal Rule of Appellate Procedure 10(c) and (e) can a party who disagrees with the trial judge as to the facts developed at trial do anything to challenge the trial judge's statement of evidence or proceedings?

2. According to one state's view of a similar problem, Associated Estates Corp. v. Fellows, 11 Ohio App.3d 112, 463 N.E.2d 417 (1983), the court cannot resolve disputes about the record in the course of the appeal, and mandamus is the only remedy. Does this make sense in view of the appellate court's general power over a case pending in the court?

SECTION E.   "EXPANDING" THE RECORD

1. THE GENERAL RULE: MATERIALS ACTUALLY CONSID-ERED BELOW

The record on appeal is generally limited to material considered—or at least offered—in the trial court. A party must offer all of the testimony and exhibits it wishes to rely upon for a given issue in the trial court proceedings.

LOWRY v. BARNHART

United States Court of Appeals, Ninth Circuit, 2003.
329 F.3d 1019.

ALEX KOZINSKI, CIRCUIT JUDGE.

* * * Save in unusual circumstances, we consider only the district court record on appeal. See Barilla v. Ervin, 886 F.2d 1514, 1521 n.7 (9th Cir. 1989). Federal Rule of Appellate Procedure 10(a) explains which materials constitute the record. Fed. R. App. P. 10(a). And Circuit Rule 30–1 provides that the appellant (and, if necessary, the appellee) shall prepare "excerpts" of that record. See 9th Cir. R. 30–1.1(a). The rather obvious implication is that the "excerpts of record" are just that: "excerpts" of the "record."

This limitation is fundamental. As a court of appeals, we lack the means to authenticate documents submitted to us, so we must be able to assume that documents designated part of the record actually are part of the record. To be sure, the fact that a document is filed in the district court doesn't resolve all questions of authenticity, but it does ensure that both opposing counsel and the district court are aware of it at a time when disputes over authenticity can be properly resolved. Litigants who disregard this process impair our ability to perform our appellate function.

There are exceptions to the general rule. We may correct inadvertent omissions from the record, see Fed. R. App. P. 10(e)(2)(C); cf. United States v. Garcia, 997 F.2d 1273, 1278 (9th Cir. 1993), take judicial notice, see Fed. R. Evid. 201(f); EEOC v. Ratliff, 906 F.2d 1314, 1318 n.6 (9th Cir. 1990), and exercise inherent authority to supplement the record in extraordinary cases,see Dickerson v. Alabama, 667 F.2d 1364, 1366–68 & n.5 (11th Cir. 1982). Consideration of new facts may even be mandatory, for example, when developments render a controversy moot and thus divest us of jurisdiction. See Arizonans for Official English v. Arizona, 520 U.S. 43, 68 n.23, 137 L. Ed. 2d 170, 117 S. Ct. 1055 (1997) ("It is the duty of counsel to bring to the federal [appellate] tribunal's attention, 'without delay,' facts that may raise a question of mootness."). One constant runs through all these exceptions, however: Only the court may supplement the record. "[It is a] basic tenet of appellate jurisprudence . . . that parties may not unilaterally supplement the record on appeal with evidence not reviewed by the court below." Tonry v. Sec. Experts, Inc., 20 F.3d 967, 974 (9th Cir. 1994). Litigants should proceed by motion or formal request so that the court and opposing counsel are properly apprised of the status of the documents in question.

Sadly, this is not the first time a party has graced us with so-called "excerpts of record" that have never before seen the light of courtroom day. It is, however, a particularly serious violation. Lowry's strongest argument was that the Administration had not complied with its own procedures for handling bias claims by completing review of his complaint. He relied heavily on this argument in his opening brief to our court. Two weeks after he filed his brief, the agency conveniently plugged this hole in the record by generating a letter that undercut Lowry's claim. It then filed it as an excerpt of record and relied on it in its own brief. It's certainly conceivable that this one-page letter was the natural terminus of a three-and-a-half year review process, but its timing creates at least some appearance of a connection between appellees' need for the evidence and its sudden materialization.

Appellees' unilateral supplementation of the record was also unfair to Lowry. Because the agency generated the letter after Lowry filed his opening brief, he argued the case on a record different from the one the agency relied on. The appellate process is for addressing the legal issues a case presents, not for generating new evidence to parry an opponent's arguments.

We ordered the parties to brief whether appellees should be sanctioned. Appellees essentially concede the impropriety of their conduct and move to strike the excerpt. They nonetheless ask that we refrain from imposing sanctions, explaining that "it was not their intent to act inappropriately" and that, although the letter "may not have met the legal standard for supplementing the record," it was nonetheless not "irrelevant, because it was responsive to an assertion made by Mr. Lowry" that "they knew ... was no longer true at the time they filed their Appellees' Brief."

We are not satisfied by this response. The issue is not whether the letter "met the legal standard for supplementing the record." That might be a question open to reasonable dispute. Appellees never moved to supplement the record. They merely designated the letter an excerpt of record and referred to it as such in their brief.

Lowry asks for two sanctions. First, he seeks to supplement the record with his own materials in response. Because we will shortly grant appellees' motion to strike, this request will soon be moot. As an alternative sanction, he asks us to "strike the defendant-appellees' appearance in this case, reverse the District Court's decision, and remand the case for entry of judgment in plaintiff's favor * * * including an order requiring the SSA to finalize and publish the final judicial bias procedures promised 10 years ago." While not wanting in ambition, this proposed sanction is, we believe, excessive.

Nonetheless, merely striking appellees' supplemental excerpts seems insufficient to deter abuse. If the only penalty for including forbidden material in the excerpts of record is removal of that material, it's hard to see why anyone would think twice before violating the rule. Circuit rules authorize monetary sanctions, see 9th Cir. R. 30–2(d), and we believe this is the appropriate remedy in this case. Lowry responded to the government's improper excerpts by addressing them in his reply brief, filing a motion to supplement the record and preparing a supplemental brief at our direction. As the government notes, however, Lowry's motion to supplement improperly cites an unpublished memorandum disposition of our court and therefore violates Circuit Rule 36–3. See Hart v. Massanari, 266 F.3d 1155(9th Cir. 2001). Lowry shall therefore recover his reasonable attorney's fees for his reply brief and supplemental brief, but not for his motion to supplement.

The case is referred to the Appellate Commissioner, who is authorized to enter a judgment in the appropriate amount. Appellees' motion to strike the supplemental excerpts of record is GRANTED.

AFFIRMED.

2. MOTIONS IN THE TRIAL COURT TO ENLARGE THE REC-ORD

TENEBAUM v. CALDERA

United States District Court, Eastern District of Michigan, 2001.
135 F. Supp. 2d 803.

ROBERT H. CLELAND, DISTRICT JUDGE.

ORDER DENYING "MOTION FOR ENLARGEMENT OF THE RECORD"

Now pending before the court is Plaintiff David Tenenbaum's "Motion for Enlargement of the Record," filed on January 10, 2001. A response and reply memorandum were filed on February 2, 2001, and February 15, 2001, respectively. Having reviewed the parties' submissions, the court will deny Plaintiff's motion.

I. BACKGROUND

On January 19, 2000, Plaintiff filed a Title VII action claiming religious discrimination arising out of his employment with the United States Army. On March 31, 2000, Defendant Louis Caldera filed a motion to dismiss, arguing that the claim was time-barred because Plaintiff had failed to contact an Equal Employment Opportunity counselor in a timely manner. The matter was fully briefed by the parties and subsequently addressed at oral argument on October 18, 2000. At the conclusion of the hearing, this court issued a bench opinion dismissing the case. An order and judgment were issued the following day.

Subsequent to the October 19, 2000 order, Plaintiff filed a notice of appeal to the United States Court of Appeals for the Sixth Circuit. Currently before the court is Plaintiff's motion to expand the record on appeal by adding documents that were obtained during discovery but not submitted to the court on the motion to dismiss.

II. DISCUSSION

Federal Rule of Appellate Procedure 10 provides as follows:

If anything material to either party is omitted from or misstated in the record by error or accident, the omission or misstatement may be corrected and a supplemental record may be certified and forwarded:

  (A) on stipulation of the parties;

  (B) by the district court before or after the record has been forwarded; or

  (C) by the court of appeals.

Fed. R. App. P. 10(e)(2). Cases interpreting application of this rule have held that its purpose is "to allow the district court to correct omissions from or misstatements in the record for appeal, not to introduce new evidence in the court of appeals." S & E Shipping Corp. v. Chesapeake & Ohio Ry. Co., 678 F.2d 636, 641 (6th Cir. 1982). Thus, the rule allows "modification of the record transmitted to the court of appeals so that it accurately reflects what happened in the district court," but does not permit adding material that was never before the district court in the first place. Id. at 641 n.9 (citing United States ex rel. Mulvaney v. Rush, 487 F.2d 684, 687 n.5 (3d Cir. 1973)). Accord United States v. Barrow, 118 F.3d 482, 487–88 (6th Cir. 1997) ("We have not allowed the rule to be used to add new evidence that substantially alters the record after notice of appeal has been filed; rather we have allowed enough modification to ensure the accuracy of the record."); United States v. Kennedy, 225 F.3d 1187, 1190 (10th Cir. 2000) ("Federal Rule of Appellate Procedure 10(e) authorizes the modification of the record only to the extent it is necessary to 'truly disclose[ ] what occurred in the district court.' "). These cases comport with the firmly established rule that "the only proper function of the court of appeals is to review the decision below on the basis of the record that was before the district court." Fassett v. Delta Kappa Epsilon, 807 F.2d 1150, 1165 (3d Cir. 1986). Relying upon these cases, and on Plaintiff's failure to cite any authority to the contrary,[1] the court concludes that Rule 10(e) does not authorize supplementing the record in this matter.

Seeking to avoid the consequences of his failure to satisfy the requirements of Rule10(e), Plaintiff argues that the record on appeal may be supplemented pursuant to Local Rule 26.2(e) instead. Rule 26.2(e) provides that "if discovery material not previously filed with the Clerk is needed for an appeal in a case, the party maintaining custody of the discovery material shall file it with the Clerk either on stipulation of the parties or on order of the Court." E.D. Mich. LR 26.2(e). The court questions the authority of the Local Rules to permit what plainly is forbidden under the case law interpreting Federal Rule of Appellate Procedure 10. Rather, it seems more accurate that Local Rule 26.2(e) merely states the process by which the record may be supplemented if authorized under Rule 10. See Chrysler Int'l Corp. v. Cherokee Exp. Co., 134 F.3d 370 (6th Cir. Jan. 27, 1998) ("If the local rule attempts to broaden and expand upon the limits of Fed. R. App. P. 10(e), it cannot accomplish this end."). Accordingly, the court concludes that Local Rule 26.2 cannot be used to circumvent the limitations of Federal Rule of Appellate Procedure 10.

The cases cited by Plaintiff are not to the contrary. In Brown v. Crowe, 963 F.2d 895 (6th Cir. 1992), the Sixth Circuit recognized that "a

---

1. The court notes that a minority of courts have discussed the existence of an "inherent equitable power to supplement the record on appeal to include information not presented to the district court," but only in unique cases that, in the interest of justice, require special consideration. See Chrysler Int'l Corp. v. Cherokee Exp. Co., 134 F.3d 370 (6th Cir. 1998) (quoting In re Capital Cities/ABC, Inc.'s Application for Access, 913 F.2d 89, 97 (3d Cir. 1990)). To this court's knowledge, however, the Sixth Circuit has never adopted such a view. Moreover, Plaintiff has not even relied upon this line of authority, let alone demonstrated why this lawsuit warrants special consideration.

federal appellate court is always empowered to resolved any issue not considered below 'where the proper resolution is beyond any doubt or where injustice ... might result.' " Id. at 898. This holding, however, is inapplicable to the facts presently before the court because Plaintiff is not seeking to introduce new issues on appeal. Whether the appellate court would agree to hear issues not addressed in the trial court is a distinct issue from whether this court may expand the record where there is no showing that justice so requires. The other cases cited by Plaintiff in support of his motion similarly do not contradict the court's holding, but merely supplement it by holding that cumulative or irrelevant material may not be added to the record. See Nugent v. Wise, No. 83–1205, 723 F.2d 910 (6th Cir. Nov. 2, 1983); Wolf v. Buckeye Incubator Co., 296 F. 680, 682 (6th Cir. 1924).

III. Conclusion

Federal Rule of Appellate Procedure 10(e)(2) prohibits adding evidence not considered by the trial court to the record of appeal. Plaintiff has failed to cite any circumstances which even raise the issue of whether an equitable exception to the Rule should apply. Similarly, Local Rule 26.2 is an inappropriate vehicle for circumventing Rule 10. Accordingly,

IT IS ORDERED that Plaintiff's "Motion for Expansion of the Record" is DENIED.

3. SUPPLEMENTATION OF THE RECORD ON APPEAL

INLAND BULK TRANSFER CO.
v. CUMMINS ENGINE CO.

United States Court of Appeal, Sixth Circuit, 2003.
332 F.3d 1007.

KAREN NELSON MOORE, JUDGE.

The principal controversy on appeal is whether the contract between Inland Bulk and Cummins included the associated provision requiring arbitration. Cummins argues that the parties agreed upon Revision A and that the arbitration provision became part of that contract, and argues alternatively that Revision B would also have incorporated an arbitration provision. Inland Bulk asserts that the parties agreed upon Revision B and that the arbitration provision was not incorporated into that document, and alternatively, that Revision A did not contain an arbitration provision. For the reasons explained infra, we conclude that the contract included an arbitration provision, regardless of whether the parties agreed upon Revision A or Revision B. * * *

THE MOTION TO SUPPLEMENT THE RECORD

Before addressing the merits of this appeal, we must resolve Inland Bulk's motion to supplement the record, which was filed on March 29, 2002. Inland Bulk seeks to supplement the record with four documents that allegedly show that the parties agreed upon Revision B as their contract. None of these documents was considered by the district court at the time of its ruling. The first is an internal invoice of Cummins's, dated December 10, 1998, which states that Revision B is the proper contract between the parties. The second is a change order request from Cummins, dated September 2, 1998, also listing Revision B as the operative contract. The third piece of evidence is a copy of Revision B with the original price, $558,270, crossed out and a new price $545,190, written in.[4] Inland Bulk does not state where this copy of Revision B came from, and the document has no date on it other than the date that Revision B was sent to Inland Bulk.

The fourth and final piece of evidence is a handwritten copy of the district judge's notes from a status conference. This status conference, which took place on April 24, 2002, addressed Inland Bulk's motion in the district court to supplement the record on appeal.[5] In rejecting Inland Bulk's motion to supplement the record, the district judge suggested that his decision on the arbitration-related issues was predicated on his belief that Revision B was the operative version of the contract.

Inland Bulk argues that we should allow the record to be supplemented with this new evidence either under Federal Rule of Appellate Procedure 10(e), the inherent powers of this court, or the rule that district courts retain jurisdiction to handle matters "in aid of the appeal." Upon reflection, we deny Inland Bulk's motion to supplement the record.

1. *Supplementation under the Federal Rules of Appellate Procedure*

Inland Bulk contends that Federal Rule of Appellate Procedure 10(e) allows the admission of these pieces of evidence. Normally, the record on appeal consists of "the original papers and exhibits filed in the district court," "the transcript of proceedings, if any" and "a certified copy of the docket entries prepared by the district clerk." Fed. R. App. P. 10(a).

---

4. This piece of evidence also tends to support Inland Bulk's assertion that Revision B was the true contract in the following way: The purchase order form sent by Inland Bulk listed the price as $545,190, which was the price of Revision A, but not Revision B, which listed the price as $558,270. Standing alone, the purchase order form therefore suggests that Revision A was the true contract between the parties. With this piece of evidence, Inland Bulk seeks to explain away the price listed on the purchase order form, by suggesting that although Revision B's price was changed to match the price of Revision A, it was Revision B (not Revision A) that the parties were agreeing upon.

5. Inland Bulk apparently filed contemporaneous and identical motions to supplement the record in this court and in the

district court below. Under Federal Rule of Appellate Procedure 10, the district court can correct or modify the record on appeal under Fed. R. App. P. 10(e)(2)(B), just as this court can under Fed. R. App. P. 10(e)(2)(C). Both motions were attempts by Inland Bulk to have the record supplemented with the first three documents: the internal invoice, the change order form, and the copy of Revision B with the price altered by hand.

After the district court denied Inland Bulk's motion to supplement the record with these three documents, Inland Bulk then filed on May 24, 2002, in this court, an amended motion to supplement the record. It was in this motion that Inland Bulk sought to supplement the record with the fourth document—the district judge's handwritten notes from the status conference.

However, "if anything material to either party is omitted from or misstated in the record by error or accident," the rule allows "the omission or misstatement [to] be corrected and a supplemental record [to] be certified and forwarded." Fed. R. App. P. 10(e)(2). Rule 10(e) allows correction of the record either by agreement of the parties, by order of the district court, or by order of the court of appeals. Fed. R. App. P. 10(e)(2). However, as is clear from the rule's wording, "the purpose of the rule is to allow the [] court to correct omissions from or misstatements in the record for appeal, not to introduce new evidence in the court of appeals." S & E Shipping Corp. v. Chesapeake & O. Ry. Co., 678 F.2d 636, 641 (6th Cir. 1982). "In general, the appellate court should have before it the record and facts considered by the District Court." United States v. Barrow, 118 F.3d 482, 487 (6th Cir. 1997); cf. Sovereign News Co. v. United States, 690 F.2d 569, 571 (6th Cir. 1982) ("A party may not by-pass the fact-finding process of the lower court and introduce new facts in brief on appeal."), cert. denied, 464 U.S. 814, 78 L. Ed. 2d 83, 104 S. Ct. 69 (1983).

Rule 10(e) does not justify supplementation of the record in this case. Inland Bulk's motion to supplement the record is not aimed towards correcting some misstatement or omission in the district court's record. Inland Bulk has not even suggested that the record inaccurately reports the proceedings in the district court. Instead, Inland Bulk is simply attempting to add new material that was never considered by the district court. This is not permitted under the rule.

2. Supplementation Under the Equitable Power of this Court

Inland Bulk next claims that we should permit the record to be supplemented under the equitable power of this court. Several circuits have held that they have an inherent equitable authority to supplement the record on appeal under circumstances where Fed. R. App. P. 10 would not apply. See United States v. Kennedy, 225 F.3d 1187, 1192 (10th Cir. 2000); Ross v. Kemp, 785 F.2d 1467, 1474 n.12 (11th Cir. 1986); Turk v. United States, 429 F.2d 1327, 1329 (8th Cir. 1970). Commentators have noticed this inherent equitable power as well, although they point out that the practice is only justified in rare instances. See Charles Alan Wright et al., Federal Practice & Procedure § 3956.4, at 349–51 (3d ed. 1999 & Supp. 2003) ("In special circumstances, however, a court of appeals may permit supplementation of the record to add material not presented to the district court."); 20 Moore's Federal Practice § 310.10[5][f], at 310–19 (3d ed. 2000) ("In extraordinary situations, the circuit court may consider material not presented to the district court when it believes the interests of justice are at stake."). While other circuits have embraced the notion that the record can be supplemented under an appellate court's equitable authority, we as of yet have not. See Chrysler Int'l Corp. v. Cherokee Exp. Co., 134 F.3d 370 (6th Cir. 1998); see also Hadix v. Johnson, 144 F.3d 925, 945 (6th Cir.

1998) (noting that " 'because of their very potency,' the inherent powers of the courts 'must be exercised with restraint and discretion' ").

We will not allow Inland Bulk to supplement the record pursuant to any inherent equitable power this court may have. Even assuming such a power exists, we do not find any special circumstances present that would justify its exercise here. Most of the new evidence Inland Bulk seeks to add to the record could have been presented to the district court below, and none of it establishes beyond doubt the proper disposition of this case. See CSX Transp., Inc. v. City of Garden City, 235 F.3d 1325, 1330 (11th Cir. 2000) ("A primary factor which we consider in deciding a motion to supplement the record is whether acceptance of the proffered material into the record would establish beyond any doubt the proper resolution of the pending issues."). Lastly, we need not consider this new information because the point Inland Bulk is trying to establish with this material—that Revision B (rather than Revision A) is the operative contract between the parties—is ultimately not material to our legal analysis * * *.

3. *Supplementation Under the "In Aid of the Appeal" Exception*

Finally, Inland Bulk makes the claim that there is a particular justification for supplementation of the record with the district judge's handwritten notes because they were created in aid of the appeal. It is established that "the filing of a notice of appeal divests the district court of jurisdiction and transfers jurisdiction to the court of appeals," but that the "district court retains jurisdiction to proceed with matters that are in aid of the appeal." Cochran v. Birkel, 651 F.2d 1219, 1221 (6th Cir. 1981). Several appellate courts have allowed district courts to use this exception to memorialize oral opinions soon after a decision was rendered; that action has been considered one "in aid of the appeal." See In Re Grand Jury Proceedings Under Seal, 947 F.2d 1188, 1190 (4th Cir. 1991) (considering a district court's written opinion that memorialized its oral ruling made one day earlier, even though the written opinion was subsequent to the appellant's filing of the notice of appeal); Blaine v. Whirlpool Corp., 891 F.2d 203, 204 (8th Cir. 1989) (considering a district court's written opinion filed one week after the appellants filed their notice of appeal from the district court's oral ruling); see generally Charles Alan Wright et al., Federal Practice & Procedure § 3949.1, at 51 (3d ed. 1999). However, appellate courts have generally prevented trial courts from developing supplemental findings after the notice of appeal has been filed. See Pro Sales, Inc. v. Texaco, U.S.A., 792 F.2d 1394, 1396 n.1 (9th Cir. 1986) (noting that the losing party had already filed its notice of appeal, and therefore the district court "had no power to amend its opinion [with a supplemental explanation] at the time it attempted to do so"); see also Ced's Inc. v. U.S. EPA, 745 F.2d 1092, 1095 (7th Cir. 1984) (coming to the same conclusion and stating that "the parties to an appeal are entitled to have a stable set of conclusions of law on which they can rely in preparing their briefs") "The distinction, although sometimes blurred, is between actions that merely aid the appellate process and actions that alter the case on appeal." Allan Ides, The Authority of a Federal District Court to Proceed After a Notice of Appeal Has Been Filed, 143 F.R.D. 307, 323 (1992).

We hold that the "in aid of the appeal" exception is inapposite in this case. First, there is no indication that the district judge's comments were actually created to aid the appeal. The district judge's comments were not directed to this court for our consideration. Instead, they were off-hand, handwritten comments, never published or formalized. They were apparently made in a status conference that occurred roughly a year and a half after the notice of appeal was filed, at which the district court considered a motion to supplement the record with certain documents. There is no evidence that these comments were meant to aid our analysis. Second, we note that Inland Bulk is not prejudiced by our refusal to consider the purported legal conclusions or reasoning of the district judge created a year and a half after his ruling because in any event we give no deference to such material on de novo review.

For all these reasons, Inland Bulk's motion to supplement the record must be denied.

Notes and Questions

1. In Ross v. Kemp, 785 F.2d 1467 (11th Cir. 1986), the Eleventh Circuit recognized its "inherent equitable authority" to supplement the record on appeal to include material not before the district court. The *Ross* court set forth the following non-exclusive list of factors it would consider when deciding to supplement the record on appeal: 1) whether "acceptance of the proffered material into the record would establish beyond any doubt the proper resolution of the pending issue;" 2) whether remand for the district court to consider the additional material would be contrary to the interests of justice and a waste of judicial resources; and 3) whether supplementation is warranted in light of the "unique powers that federal appellate judges have in the context of habeas corpus actions." The *Ross* court determined the movant had not established the first factor, and had not established the threshold issue of whether his failure to present the information before the district court was the result of excusable neglect. However, the Ross court concluded based on the facts of that case, the interests of justice demanded remand to the district court to determine whether to allow Mr. Ross to supplement the record and if so, to determine whether an evidentiary hearing was warranted.

2. In United States v. Kennedy, 225 F.3d 1187 (10th Cir. 2000), the appellate court in the 10th Circuit noted the reasoning of *Ross* but found that use of an an inherent equitable power to supplement the record on appeal was not appropriate because the spectre of gullible attorneys relying on misleading instructions from state officials (the arguable situation in *Ross*) was not present.

3. Proceedings before Bankruptcy Judges and United States Magistrate Judges, particularly in non-urban districts, may present problems due to the lack of regular, official court reporters attending such proceedings. For a fascinating discussion of problems arising in such cases, particularly the

partial availability of "official" reporters, see Bitler v. A.O. Smith Corp., 252 F. Supp. 2d 1123 (D. Colo. 2003) (an 11–day trial, half of which was reported accurately by the official reporter, and half of which was "covered" by an unofficial reporter using tape recording. The audiotape transcript contained "hundreds of instances in which the proceedings were inaudible to the transcriber. Indeed, on the very first page of audiotaped transcript, the transcriber notes that "there appear to be no microphones turned on except the Judge's and the speakers are barely audible.").

SECTION F.   THE PROBLEMS OF DELAY AND TECHNOLOGY

R. MARTINEAU, MODERN APPELLATE PRACTICE— FEDERAL AND STATE CIVIL APPEALS

§ 8.7 (1983).

In courts of general jurisdiction in both federal and state judicial systems a court reporter usually makes a verbatim record of all proceedings in open court and sometimes of those in the judge's chambers. This verbatim record may be required by statute or rule or may be at the option of the parties or the court. There is seldom any difficulty in having the court reporter, who is usually paid by the government, to make the verbatim record of the proceedings.

The major problem is in converting the reporter's stenographic notes into a typewritten transcript for use by the parties and the appellate court. One authority has stated that "slow preparation of trial transcripts has been a major cause of delayed appellate decision[s]." Speeding up preparation of the transcript has been a major focus of virtually every effort to expedite the appellate process.

Some jurisdictions have eliminated much of the delay in a few simple measures, two of which involve the attorneys in the appeal. Appellate rules may require the appellant's attorney to order and to make arrangements to pay for the transcript within a short time after the notice of appeal is filed and for notice of these steps to be given to the appellate court. Second, the rules may provide that the attorneys for both sides order only those portions of the transcript necessary for prosecuting the appeal. To be effective in preventing delay and unnecessary costs, appellate rules must provide for effective sanctions against attorneys who do not comply with these rules. Delay in transcript preparation can be eliminated or sharply reduced only if the appellate court is willing to take control of the preparation and to impose sanctions on those who cause the delay. Federal Rules of Appellate Procedure 10 and 11 were designed to expedite the process and put the burden on the court reporter to prepare the transcript in a timely fashion. Many of the circuits have adopted case management plans which include ordering of the transcript as an essential element.

ST. PAUL FIRE AND MARINE INS. CO. v. ARKLA CHEM. CORP.

United States Court of Appeals, Eighth Circuit, 1970.
431 F.2d 959.

PER CURIAM.

This is a civil proceeding involving both a direct appeal and cross-appeal from the judgment of the district court. The matter comes before us on a motion for an extension of time in which to file the appellants' appendix and brief; the motion is accompanied by a letter from the district court reporter that she will not be able to complete the transcript for "several months." We deny leave for such an extension.

There is no showing that the appellant has attempted to invoke Rules 10(c) or (d) of the Federal Rules of Appellate Procedure. * * * Under the circumstances as outlined by appellant, we view the "transcript * * * unavailable."

Rule 10(d) reads as follows:

"*Agreed Statement as the Record on Appeal.* In lieu of the record on appeal as defined in subdivision (a) of this rule, the parties may prepare and sign a statement of the case showing how the issues presented by the appeal arose and were decided in the district court and setting forth only so many of the facts averred and proved or sought to be proved as are essential to a decision of the issues presented. If the statement conforms to the truth, it, together with such additions as the court may consider necessary fully to present the issues raised by the appeal, shall be approved by the district court and shall then be certified to the court of appeals as the record on appeal and transmitted thereto by the clerk of the district court within the time provided by Rule 11. Copies of the agreed statement may be filed as the appendix required by Rule 30."

Rule 10(e) supplements the above procedure[.]

* * *

All of these rules may be utilized to prepare an abbreviated appendix in compliance with Rule 30. We further call attention to the parties to the use of a deferred appendix under Rule 30(c).

The above rules are designed to alleviate congestion and delay in the courts. They should be utilized whenever possible. Although Rule 10 is derived from the former Federal Rules * * * we observe the abbreviated procedure has seldom been invoked. In rare instances a complete transcript, with all questions and answers and the testimony of all witnesses transcribed, may be deemed essential by the parties to certain appeals. Our experience in the majority of cases indicates otherwise. For example, we recently reviewed a record where only three pages from a 1500 page transcript were relevant to the question on appeal. Full utilization of the abbreviated, stipulated record under Rule 10 not only will avoid unnecessary delays and court congestion, but its practical application will save litigants thousands of dollars in high printing costs. Furthermore, a true focus on the relevant issues and testimony can better achieve an efficient, as well as a fair, administration of justice.

Motion denied.

Notes and Questions

1.   To the same effect as the principal case is Cecil Grain, Inc. v. Gillen Oil Co., 22 Ohio Misc.2d 14, 489 N.E.2d 838 (1982).

2.   Why should the appellant be blamed if the court reporter, who is an employee of the court and not of the parties, is unable to prepare a transcript? Are the alternatives of an agreed statement of facts or a statement prepared by one party and subject to amendment or modification by the trial court adequate substitutes for a transcript of testimony?

3.   There has been a substantial amount of effort in recent decades to develop means of recording testimony other than by a court reporter using shorthand or a stenotype machine. Recent efforts have concentrated on computer assisted transcripts in which the transcript is produced by a voice generated computer. For a description of early developments in this area see Clifford & Delaplain, Computer–Aided Transcription: Not for Every Court, 5 State Court J. 27 (Summer, 1981). More recent improvements have created the prospect of allowing hearing impaired persons to serve as jurors, or witnesses, by use of immediate computer-assisted transcription technologies. Note, The Digital Divide and Courtroom Technology: Can David Keep Up With Goliath? 54 Fed. Comm. L.J. 567 (May, 2002). See generally Hewitt & Levy, Computer-aided Transcription: Current Technology and Court Applications (1994). Surprisingly, in one state where "most court reporters in the state use computer-aided transcription (CAT) to prepare appellate transcripts, the filing of civil records is [nonetheless still] slow." Symposium: Managing Caseflow in State Intermediate Appellate Courts: What Mechanisms, Practices, and Procedures Can Work to Reduce Delay? 35 Ind. L. Rev. 467 (2002) (discussing the Indiana experience).

4.   Criminal cases are beyond the scope of this Casebook. Suffice it to say that delays, errors and "untranscribable" records in criminal cases present special constitutional and criminal procedure issues, and no small amount of headaches for appellate courts with large criminal dockets. Compare United States v. Locust, 95 Fed. Appx. 507 (4th Cir. 2004) (absence of a transcript of the opening and closing arguments and the district court's jury instructions); United States v. Johnson, 231 F.3d 43 (D.C. Cir. (2000)(the court reporting company lost the entire transcript of a sentencing proceeding in a felony case). See generally United States v. Tucker, 964 F.2d 952 (9th Cir. 1992), where two year delay in transcribing the testimony of defendant's felony trial only ended when the appellate court entered the following order:

> If Ms. Daily [as court reporter] fails to file the transcript, or fails to submit proof of service to this court or the United States Marshal, the United States Marshal shall proceed immediately to arrest and confine Ms. Daily with her notes and transcribing equipment until she has completed the transcript for February 3, 1987, including the transcrip-

tion of all jury instructions and all closing arguments. Should incarceration be necessary, the Marshal is directed to assist Ms. Daily in obtaining the necessary notes and equipment. Ms. Daily shall be released upon providing the transcript to the Marshal. Should Ms. Daily fail to comply with this order, the district court is requested to issue promptly a bench warrant for Ms. Daily's arrest.

Chapter 8

THE BRIEF AND APPENDIX

SECTION A. THE IMPORTANCE
OF THE BRIEF

R. MARTINEAU, MODERN APPELLATE PRACTICE—
FEDERAL AND STATE CIVIL APPEALS

§§ 11.1–.2 (1983).

Understanding the role of the briefs filed by the parties is essential for an appellate attorney. The traditional English practice was exclusively oral once the record was filed in the appellate court. The arguments made on behalf of the parties were oral; the decision was announced at the conclusion of the oral argument with each judge stating his reasons for joining or not joining in the decision. Briefs, to the extent that there were any, were mere summaries or outlines of the oral argument and were not of major consequence. In this country as well, until recently, the emphasis was on the attorneys' oral presentations. Stories about arguments that lasted several days before the United States Supreme Court by leading attorneys such as Daniel Webster are common. Gradually, as courts became busier they began to impose limitations on the length of oral argument. At first each side was allowed several hours, then one hour, then 30 minutes or even less. As the length of oral argument was reduced, attorneys and courts began to rely more heavily on the written briefs. As appellate courts began to hear oral arguments in several cases each day, it became impossible for judges to decide and to give opinions on each case upon the conclusion of the oral arguments. Written briefs then became necessary for the judges to use when they prepared written opinions.

Although the length was reduced in most courts, the practice of oral argument in every case was maintained. In recent years, however, even the practice has been largely eliminated. Now only a few appellate courts provide for oral argument as a matter of course in every case. In those cases in which oral argument is not allowed, the importance of the brief is evident because the brief is the only means available for presenting arguments to the appellate court. Because the attorney may not know whether the court will order oral argument when he prepares the brief, he must therefore write on the assumption that there will be no oral argument.

Changes in the internal operating procedures of appellate courts also emphasize the importance of the brief. Prior to the 1940's it was common for judges not to read the briefs prior to oral argument and the initial decision conference. Now in almost every court the briefs are read and studied before oral argument and some courts have a conference on cases prior to oral argument.

What has happened is that the roles of the brief and oral argument have been reversed. The brief is the central feature of modern appellate practice. This dramatic change, although discussed in a number of recent articles by judges on busy appellate courts, has not been recognized by many attorneys. This lack of understanding results primarily from the fact that few attorneys specialize in appellate practice, and even those who do may not be conscious of the cumulative effect of changes in appellate rules and the internal operating procedures of appellate courts. Judge Aldisert of the Third Circuit has expressed the relative importance of the brief and oral argument in the following terms: "The appellate brief is far more important than oral argument. To judge their relative importance, consider this: oral argument in a federal appellate court may take fifteen minutes, with most of the time devoted to answering questions from the bench; analyzing a brief consumes hours, if not days, for the judge and his staff." The appellate attorney must understand that *the brief affords the principal and perhaps the only opportunity he will have to present arguments on behalf of his client to the appellate court.* Otherwise, he does not understand the nature of modern appellate practice and his brief is likely to be ineffective or not as effective as it might be. In either event, his client may be harmed.

SECTION B. THE FORMAL REQUIREMENTS

FEDERAL RULES OF APPELLATE PROCEDURE

Rule 28. Briefs

(a) Appellant's Brief. The appellant's brief must contain, under appropriate headings and in the order indicated:

(1) a corporate disclosure statement if required by Rule 26.1;

(2) a table of contents, with page references,

(3) a table of authorities–cases (alphabetically arranged), statutes, and other authorities–with references to the pages of the brief where they are cited,

(4) a jurisdictional statement, including:

(A) the basis for the district court's or agency's subject-matter jurisdiction, with citations to applicable statutory provisions and stating relevant facts establishing jurisdiction;

(B) the basis for the court of appeals' jurisdiction, with citations to applicable statutory provisions and stating relevant facts establishing jurisdiction;

(C) the filing dates establishing the timeliness of the appeal or petition for review; and

(D) an assertion that the appeal is from a final order or judgment that disposes of all parties' claims, or information establishing the court of appeals' jurisdiction on some other basis;

(5) a statement of the issues presented for review;

(6) a statement of the case briefly indicating the nature of the case, the course of proceedings, and the disposition below;

(7) a statement of facts relevant to the issues submitted for review with appropriate references to the record (see Rule 28(e));

(8) a summary of the argument, which must contain a succinct, clear, and accurate statement of the arguments made in the body of the brief, and which must not merely repeat the argument headings;

(9) the argument, which must contain:

(A) appellant's contentions and the reasons for them, with citations to the authorities and parts of the record on which the appellant relies; and

(B) for each issue, a concise statement of the applicable standard of review (which may appear in the discussion of the issue or under a separate heading placed before the discussion of the issues);

(10) a short conclusion stating the precise relief sought; and

(11) the certificate of compliance, if required by Rule 32(a)(7).

(b) Appellee's Brief. The appellee's brief must conform to the requirements of Rule 28(a)(1)-(9) and (11), except that none of the following need appear unless the appellee is dissatisfied with the appellant's statement:

(1) the jurisdictional statement;

(2) the statement of the issues;

(3) the statement of the case;

(4) the statement of the facts; and

(5) the statement of the standard of review.

(c) Reply Brief. The appellant may file a brief in reply to the appellee's brief. An appellee who has cross-appealed may file a brief in reply to the appellant's response to the issues presented by the cross-appeal. Unless the court permits, no further briefs may be filed. A reply brief must contain a table of contents, with page references, and a table of authorities–cases (alphabetically arranged), statutes, and other authorities–with references to the pages of the reply brief where they are cited.

(d) References to Parties. In briefs and at oral argument, counsel should minimize use of the terms "appellant" and "appellee." To make briefs clear, counsel should use the parties' actual names or the designations used in the lower court or agency proceeding, or such descriptive terms as "the employee," "the injured person," "the taxpayer," "the ship," "the stevedore."

(e) References to the Record. References to the parts of the record contained in the appendix filed with the appellant's brief must be to the pages of the appendix. If the appendix is prepared after the briefs are filed, a party referring to the record must follow one of the methods detailed in Rule 30(c). If the original record is used under Rule 30(f) and is not consecutively paginated, or if the brief refers to an unreproduced part of the record, any reference must be to the page of the original document. For example:

- Answer p. 7;
- Motion for Judgment p. 2;
- Transcript p. 231;

Only clear abbreviations may be used. A party referring to evidence whose admissibility is in controversy must cite the pages of the appendix or of the transcript at which the evidence was identified, offered, and received or rejected.

(f) Reproduction of Statutes, Rules, Regulations, etc. If the court's determination of the issues presented requires the study of statutes, rules, regulations, etc., the relevant parts must be set out in the brief or in an addendum at the end, or may be supplied to the court in pamphlet form.

(g) [Reserved]

(h) Briefs in a Case Involving Cross–Appeal. If a cross-appeal is filed, the party who files a notice of appeal first is the appellant for the purposes of this rule and Rules 30, 31, and 34. If notices are filed on the same day, the plaintiff in the proceeding below is the appellant. These designations may be modified by agreement of the parties or by court order. With respect to appellee's cross-appeal and response to appellant's brief, appellee's brief must conform to the requirements of Rule 28(a)(1)-(11). But an appellee who is satisfied with appellant's statement need not include a statement of the case or of the facts.

(i) Briefs in a Case Involving Multiple Appellants or Appellees. In a case involving more than one appellant or appellee, including consolidated cases, any number of appellants or appellees may join. In a brief, and any party may adopt by reference a part of another's brief. Parties may also join in reply briefs.

(j) Citation of Supplemental Authorities. If pertinent and significant authorities come to a party's attention after the party's brief has been filed–or after oral argument but before decision–a party may promptly advise the circuit clerk by letter, with a copy to all other parties, setting forth the citations. The letter must state the reasons for the supplemental citations, referring either to the page of the brief or to a point argued orally. The body of the letter must not exceed 350 words. Any response must be made promptly and must be similarly limited.

Rule 31. Serving and Filing Briefs

(a) Time to Serve and File a Brief.

(1) The appellant must serve and file a brief within 40 days after the record is filed. The appellee must serve and file a brief within 30 days after the appellant's brief is served. The appellant may serve and file a reply brief within 14 days after service of the appellee's brief but a reply brief must be field at least 3 days before argument, unless the court, for good cause, allows a later filing.

(2) A court of appeals that routinely considers cases on the merits promptly after the briefs are filed may shorten the time to serve and file briefs, either by local rule or by order in a particular case.

(b) Number of Copies. Twenty-five copies of each brief shall be filed with the clerk and 2 copies must be served on each unrepresented party and on counsel for each separately represented party. An unrepresented party proceeding in forma pauperis must file 4 legible copies with the clerk, and one copy must be served on each unrepresented party and on counsel for each separately represented party. The court may by local rule or by order in a particular case require the filing or service of a different number.

(c) Consequence of Failure to File. If an appellant fails to file a brief within the time provided by this rule, or within an extended time, an appellee may move for dismissal of the appeal. An appellee who fails to file a brief will not be heard at oral argument unless the court grants permission.

Rule 32. Form of Briefs, Appendices, and Other Papers

(a) Form of a Brief

(1) Reproduction

(A) A brief may be reproduced by any process that yields a clear black image on light paper. The paper must be opaque and unglazed. Only one side of the paper may be used.

(B) Text must be reproduced with a clarity that equals or exceeds the output of a laser printer.

(C) Photographs, illustrations, and tables may be reproduced by any method that results in a good copy of the original; a glossy finish is acceptable if the original is glossy.

(2) Cover. Except for filings by unrepresented parties, the cover of the appellant's brief must be blue; the appellee's, red; an intervenor's or amicus curiae's, green; any reply brief, gray; and any supplemental brief, tan. The front cover of a brief must contain:

(A) the number of the case centered at the top;

(B) the name of the court;

(C) the title of the case (see Rule 12(a));

(D) the nature of the proceeding (e.g., Appeal, Petition for Review) and the name of the court, agency, or board below;

(E) the title of the brief, identifying the party or parties for whom the brief is filed; and

(F) the name, office address, and telephone number of counsel representing the party for whom the brief is filed.

(3) Binding. The brief must be bound in any manner that is secure, does not obscure the text, and permits the brief to lie reasonably flat when open.

(4) Paper Size, Line Spacing, and Margins. The brief must be on 8 ½ by 11 inch paper. The text must be double-spaced, but quotations more than two lines long may be indented and single-spaced. Headings and footnotes may be single-spaced. Margins must be at least one inch on all four sides. Page numbers may be placed in the margins, but no text may appear there.

(5) Typeface. Either a proportionally spaced or a monospaced face may be used.

(A) A proportionally spaced face must include serifs, but sans-serif type may be used in headings and captions. A proportionally spaced face must be 14–pont or larger.

(B) A monospaced face may not contain more than 10 ½ characters per inch.

(6) Type Styles. A brief must be set in plain, roman style, although italics or boldface may be used for emphasis. Case names must be italicized or underlined.

(7) Length.

(A) Page limitation. A principal brief may not exceed 30 pages, or a reply brief 15 pages, unless it complies with Rule 32(a)(7)(B) and (C).

(B) Type-volume limitation.

(i) A principal brief is acceptable if:

● it contains no more than 14,000 words; or

● it uses a monospaced face and contains nor more than 1,300 lines of text.

(ii) A reply brief is acceptable if it contains no more than half of the type volume specified in Rule 32(a)(7)(B)(i).

(iii) Headings, footnotes, and quotations count toward the word and line limitations. The corporate disclosure statement, table of contents, table of citations, statement with respect to oral argument, any addendum containing statutes, rules or regulations, and any certificates of counsel do not count toward the limitation.

(C) Certificate of compliance.

(i) A brief submitted under Rule 32(a)(7((B) must include a certificate by the attorney, or an unrepresented party, that the brief complies with the type-volume limitation. The person preparing the certificate may rely on the word or line count of the word-processing system used to prepare the brief. The certificate must state either:

● the number of words in the brief; or

● the number of lines of monospaced type in the brief.

(ii) Form 6 in the Appendix of Forms is a suggested form of a certificate of compliance. Use of Form 6 must be regarded as sufficient to meet the requirements of Rule 32(a)(7)(C)(i).

(b) Form of an Appendix. An appendix must comply with Rule 32(a)(1), (2), (3), and (4), with the following exceptions:

(1) The cover of a separately bound appendix must be white.

(2) An appendix may include a legible photocopy of any document found in the record or of a printed judicial or agency decision.

(3) When necessary to facilitate inclusion of odd-sized documents such as technical drawings, an appendix may be a size other than 8 ½ by 11 inches, and need not lie reasonably flat when opened.

(c) Form of Other Papers.

(1) Motion. The form of a motion is governed by Rule 27(d).

(2) Other Papers. Any other paper, including a petition for panel rehearing and a petition for hearing or rehearing en banc, and any response to such a petition, must be reproduced in the manner prescribed by Rule 32(a), with the following exceptions:

(A) A cover is not necessary if the caption and signature page of the paper together contain the information required by Rule 32(a)(2). If a cover is used, it must be white.

(B) Rule 32(a)(7) does not apply.

(d) Signature. Every brief, motion, or other paper filed with the court must be signed by the party filing the paper or, if the party is represented, by one of the party's attorneys.

(e) Local Variation. Every court of appeals must accept documents that comply with the form requirements of the rule. By local rule or order in a particular case a court of appeals may accept documents that do not meet all of the form requirements of this rule.

Note on Rules of Procedure

The rules set forth above establish the general requirements for briefs filed in the federal courts of appeals. The Federal Rules of Appellate Procedure also permit each circuit to establish additional requirements or to change those in the Federal Rules of Appellate Procedure. The rules of each circuit must be checked, consequently, before the precise requirements for a particular brief can be established.

Similarly in some states with intermediate appellate courts there are generally applicable rules of appellate procedure; these may or may not be changed or supplemented by individual appellate court rules.

The United States Supreme Court also has a separate set of rules that govern the briefs filed with that court. The Federal Rules of Appellate Procedure do not apply to the Supreme Court. In the states, however, usually the general appellate rules are applicable to briefs filed in both the state intermediate appellate court and the state supreme court, unless specific exceptions are made.

SECTION C. EFFECT OF NON–COMPLIANCE WITH RULES

STATE EX REL. QUEEN CITY CHAPTER SIGMA DELTA CHI v. McGINNIS

Supreme Court of Ohio, 1984.
10 Ohio St.3d 54, 461 N.E.2d 307.

This original action in mandamus was brought by relators, Queen City Chapter of the Society of Professional Journalists, Sigma Delta Chi, a non-profit voluntary association of working journalists, and three of its members who are journalists and residents of Hamilton County. They sought the issuance of a writ to compel respondents, the Safety Director for the city of Cincinnati and the Sheriff for Hamilton County, to disclose the names of law enforcement officers who were involved in a shooting incidental to a robbery in Cincinnati, Ohio.

Respondents have claimed exemption from disclosure under R.C. 149.43(A)(2)(d) for the reason that they believe release of the officers' names would endanger the officers' lives and safety.

This matter has been before the court twice on motions. On December 10, 1982 relators filed a motion for summary judgment. Depositions and affidavits were filed in support of and in opposition to this motion through January 1983. On June 1, 1983, the court denied relators' motion for summary judgment and ordered relators to file their brief by June 16, 1983.

No brief was filed by relators at that time. On June 23, 1983 respondent Bret McGinnis filed a motion to dismiss. On July 1, 1983, relators filed a second motion for summary judgment, incorporating the arguments and evidence in support of the first motion for summary judgment. No new arguments or facts were submitted.

On October 28, 1983, an additional affidavit was filed. A "Brief in Support of Relators' Complaint" was also filed on that date, which was a *one-page* document stating, in its entirety, "[r]elators here adopt by reference their memorandum previously filed in support of their first motion for summary judgment."

By entry of November 23, 1983, the court ordered relators' second motion for summary judgment stricken, *sua sponte,* and overruled respondent's motion to dismiss. That entry also ordered relators to file their brief on or before December 8, 1983.

On December 7, 1983, relators filed their second brief in support of complaint. The brief is a verbatim copy of relators' first motion for summary judgment with a new introduction and cover page. It does not set forth propositions of law denominated as such, and contains no table of contents, table of authorities or appendix.

*   *   *

PER CURIAM.

Pursuant to Section 10, Rule VIII of the Supreme Court Rules of Practice, briefs filed by plaintiffs in original actions must comply with the requirements of Sections (1), (3), (4) and (6) of Rule V and with Rule VI of the Supreme Court Rules of Practice governing the form of briefs on the merits in appeal cases. Section 1 of Rule V requires that merit briefs contain a table of contents, a table of authorities, arguments headed by propositions of law and an appendix.

Relators' brief does not comply with any of these requirements. Moreover, by this "brief," relators have, in essence, submitted the same motion to the court for consideration for the third time. Relators' failure to file a brief in compliance with the Rules of Practice after being ordered to do so twice is inexcusable. As we stated in Drake v. Bucher (1966), 5 Ohio St.2d 37, 39–40, 213 N.E.2d 182:

> "[T]here is no excuse for the failure of any member of the bar to understand or to comply with the rules of this court. They are promulgated so that causes coming before the court will be presented in a clear and logical manner, and any litigant availing himself of the jurisdiction of the court is subjected thereto. Not to be minimized is the necessity of compliance as an accommodation to the correct dispatch of the court's business. * * *

> "In order to promote justice, the court exercises a certain liberality in enforcing a strict attention to its rules, especially as to mere technical infractions. But a substantial disregard of the whole body of these rules cannot be tolerated." See, also, Vorisek v. North Randall (1980), 64 Ohio St.2d 62, 65, 413 N.E.2d 793.

Here, relators apparently concluded that their first motion for summary judgment, shielded by skilled draftsmanship, could not be challenged and that if they persisted, this court would agree. There is no rational framework for this conclusion.

Accordingly, this cause is dismissed *sua sponte* for the reason that relators' have failed to minimally comply with the Rules of Practice of this court.

Cause dismissed.

HOLMES, J., dissents.

HOLMES, JUSTICE, dissenting.

In my view, the relators have, in essence, complied with the rules of this court. Disregarding the technical infractions, the law to be asserted was sufficiently set forth within the memoranda surrounding relators' motions for summary judgment.

Therefore, I would decide the case on its merits in order to resolve this important issue.

Notes and Questions

1. Appellate rules govern both the content and the form of the briefs and appendix as well as when and how they must be served and filed. Violations of the rules can thus relate to content, form, filing, or service of the briefs, and can be committed by either the appellant or the appellee. In considering whether to impose a sanction for failure to comply with one or more rules, the court will consider several factors: (1) the purpose of the rule; (2) the harm caused by the violation; (3) by whom the harm is suffered; (4) the nature of the sanction; and (5) the person upon whom the burden of the sanction falls. The principal opposing considerations are reflected in the principal case: on the one hand, what purpose do procedural rules serve if the court does not insist upon compliance with them; on the other hand, should the court refuse to hear the merits of a case simply because the attorney has failed to comply with a procedural rule?

One of the best statements of the reasons for insisting upon compliance with rules, even if it means the merits will not be addressed was made by the federal court of appeals for the District of Columbia in United States v. Seigel, 168 F.2d 143 (D.C. Cir. 1948). The court, in dismissing an appeal by federal government, which had not become a party in the proceeding, stated:

"[r]ules of procedure such as the one here pertinent are not mere naked technicalities. As we recently had occasion to observe, reasonable adherence to clear, reasonable and known rules of procedure is essential to the administration of justice. Justice cannot be administered in chaos. Moreover, the administration of justice involves not only meticulous disposition of the conflicts in one particular case but the expeditious disposition of hundreds of cases. If the courts must stop to inquire where substantial justice on the merits lies every time a litigant refuses or fails to abide the reasonable and known rules of procedure, there will be no administration of justice. Litigants must be required to cooperate in the efficient disposition of their cases.

"We are told that in substance no injustice would result from ignoring the rules in this case. That may be, but it cannot justify the departure. Just as soon as the rules of procedure are ignored in order to do substantial justice on the merits in a particular case, there are no rules.

What is done in one case must be done in all. Of course, the prevention of manifest injustice may present another problem."

Are the reasons given by the court persuasive? If the appeal is dismissed for an action or non-action by the attorney, is a malpractice action an adequate remedy? See generally, Annotation, Sanctions, In Federal Circuit Courts of Appeals, for Failure to Comply with Rules Relating to Contents of Briefs and Appendices, 55 A.L.R.Fed. 521 (1981).

2.   When the violation is a late filing of the brief by the appellant, some courts will accept the brief rather than dismiss the appeal on the ground that the opposing side has shown no prejudice from the delay. Such a case was Perry v. Perry, 7 Ohio App.3d 318, 455 N.E.2d 689 (1982). The court, however, did assess all appeal costs against the appellant without regard to the outcome of the case. Is a monetary sanction an appropriate penalty? Is liability for costs only a sanction if the appellant wins? Is there a sanction if the appellant loses?

3.   What should the court do when the appellee fails to file a brief? In State Bd. of Health v. Lakeland Disposal Service, Inc., 461 N.E.2d 1145 (Ind.App.1984), the court said that the appellant had to show only *prima facie* reversible error to prevail. Another approach was taken in Dymek v. Nyquist, 128 Ill.App.3d 859, 83 Ill.Dec. 52, 469 N.E.2d 659 (1984), in which the appellate court reviewed the trial court's judgment on the merits because it was of the opinion that a judgment should not be reversed solely because of the failure of the appellee to file a brief. Does the procedure for permitting a default judgment in the trial court provide a model for what the appellate court should do? Court rules often provide that if the appellee does not file a brief, then the appellee loses the right to be heard at oral argument. E.g., Fed.R.App.P. 31(c). Does this make sense? Does it not create as many problems for the court as for the appellee? Why would an appellee not file a brief?

SECTION D.   STANDARD OF REVIEW

1.   IMPORTANCE OF STANDARD OF REVIEW

R. MARTINEAU, FUNDAMENTALS OF MODERN APPELLATE ADVOCACY

§ 7.21   (1985).

A question basic to the appellate process but often overlooked by appellate attorneys is the standard of review used by the appellate court in deciding whether the trial court has committed reversible error. The attorney must be aware of the applicable standard because it tells the attorney how much deference the appellate court must give to the actions of the trial court that the appellant seeks to challenge. Ultimately, it affects the probability that the appellate court will either affirm or reverse the trial court.

From the attorney's standpoint, the issue should have a substantial effect on the decision to appeal. If the standard of review is very restrictive on the appellate court, the chances of success on appeal are reduced, and thus an appellant may consider it not worthwhile to appeal. If, on the other hand, the appellate court is free to substitute its judgment for that of the trial court on the disputed issue, then it may be much easier for the appellant to prevail, and thus encourage the prosecution of the appeal.

The standard of review will also be important in the preparation of the briefs and the oral argument. The types of arguments made and their focus will obviously vary depending upon the standard of review. The appellant will have to show that not only is there a factual or legal basis for his argument, but under the applicable standard of review he is entitled to prevail. The argument will have to be developed with the standard of review in mind. In the case of the appellant, it must be designed to overcome the standard or, in the case of the appellee, to show that the standard has not been met. The appellant, in choosing the issues to be raised on appeal, should attempt to choose those issues that have the lower threshold because the appellate court will have greater freedom to reverse the trial court.

Knowledge of the standard of review is also be necessary simply to comply with the formal requirements of the brief. Federal Rule of Appellate Procedure 28(a)(9)(B) expressly requires that the argument section of the appellant's brief contain "for each issue, a concise statement of the applicable standard of review."

2. FINDINGS OF FACT

ANDERSON v. BESSEMER CITY

Supreme Court of the United States, 1985.
470 U.S. 564, 105 S.Ct. 1504, 84 L.Ed.2d 518.

JUSTICE WHITE delivered the opinion of the Court.

In Pullman–Standard v. Swint, 456 U.S. 273, 102 S.Ct. 1781, 72 L.Ed.2d 66 (1982), we held that a District Court's finding of discriminatory intent in an action brought under Title VII of the Civil Rights Act of 1964, 78 Stat. 253, as amended, 42 U.S.C. § 2000e et seq., is a factual finding that may be overturned on appeal only if it is clearly erroneous. In this case, the Court of Appeals for the Fourth Circuit concluded that there was clear error in a District Court's finding of discrimination and reversed. Because our reading of the record convinces us that the Court of Appeals misapprehended and misapplied the clearly-erroneous standard, we reverse.

Early in 1975, officials of respondent City of Bessemer City, North Carolina, set about to hire a new Recreation Director for the city. Although the duties that went with the position were not precisely delineated, the new Recreation Director was to be responsible for managing all of the city's recreational facilities and for developing recreational programs—athletic and otherwise—to serve the needs of the city's residents. A five-member committee selected by the Mayor was responsible for choosing the Recreation Director. Of the five members, four were men; the one woman on the committee, Mrs. Auddie Boone, served as the chairperson.

Eight persons applied for the position of Recreation Director. Petitioner, at the time a 39–year-old schoolteacher with college degrees in social studies and education, was the only woman among the eight. The selection committee reviewed the resumes submitted by the applicants and briefly interviewed each of the jobseekers. Following the interviews, the committee offered the position to Mr. Donald Kincaid, a 24–year-old who had recently graduated from college with a degree in physical education. All four men on the committee voted to offer the job to Mr. Kincaid; Mrs. Boone voted for petitioner.

Believing that the committee had passed over her in favor of a less qualified candidate solely because she was a woman, petitioner filed discrimination charges with the Charlotte District Office of the Equal Employment Opportunity Commission. In July 1980 (five years after petitioner filed the charges), the EEOC's District Director found that there was reasonable cause to believe that petitioner's charges were true and invited the parties to attempt a resolution of petitioner's grievance through conciliation proceedings. The EEOC's efforts proved unsuccessful, and in due course, petitioner received a right-to-sue letter.

Petitioner then filed this Title VII action in the United States District Court for the Western District of North Carolina. After a 2–day trial during which the court heard testimony from petitioner, Mr. Kincaid, and the five members of the selection committee, the court issued a brief memorandum of decision setting forth its finding that petitioner was entitled to judgment because she had been denied the position of Recreation Director on account of her sex. In addition to laying out the rationale for this finding, the memorandum requested that petitioner's counsel submit proposed findings of fact and conclusions of law expanding upon those set forth in the memorandum. Petitioner's counsel complied with this request by submitting a lengthy set of proposed findings (App. 11a–34a); the court then requested and received a response setting forth in detail respondent's objections to the proposed findings (id., at 36a–47a)—objections that were, in turn, answered by petitioner's counsel in a somewhat less lengthy reply (id., at 48a–54a). After receiving these submissions, the court issued its own findings of fact and conclusions of law. 557 F.Supp. 412, 413–419 (1983).

* * *

On the basis of its findings that petitioner was the most qualified candidate, that the committee had been biased against hiring a woman, and that the committee's explanations for its choice of Mr. Kincaid were pretextual, the court concluded that petitioner had met her burden of establishing that she had been denied the position of Recreation Director because of her sex. Petitioner having conceded that ordering the city to hire her would be an inappropriate remedy under the circumstances, the court awarded petitioner backpay in the amount of $30,397.00 and attorney's fees of $16,971.59.

The Fourth Circuit reversed the District Court's finding of discrimination. 717 F.2d 149 (1983). In the view of the Court of Appeals, three of the District Court's crucial findings were clearly erroneous: the finding that petitioner was the most qualified candidate, the finding that petitioner had been asked questions that other applicants were spared, and the finding that the male committee members were biased against hiring a woman. Having rejected these findings, the Court of Appeals concluded that the District Court had erred in finding that petitioner had been discriminated against on account of her sex.

* * *

Because a finding of intentional discrimination is a finding of fact, the standard governing appellate review of a district court's finding of discrimination is that set forth in Federal Rule of Civil Procedure 52(a): "Findings of fact shall not be set aside unless clearly erroneous, and due regard shall be given to the opportunity of the trial court to judge of the credibility of the witnesses." The question before us, then, is whether the Court of Appeals erred in holding the District Court's finding of discrimination to be clearly erroneous.

Although the meaning of the phrase "clearly erroneous" is not immediately apparent, certain general principles governing the exercise of the appellate court's power to overturn findings of a district court may be derived from our cases. The foremost of these principles, as the Fourth Circuit itself recognized, is that "a finding is 'clearly erroneous' when although there is evidence to support it, the reviewing court on the entire evidence is left with the definite and firm conviction that a mistake has been committed." United States v. United States Gypsum Co., 333 U.S. 364, 395, 68 S.Ct. 525, 542, 92 L.Ed. 746 (1948). This standard plainly does not entitle a reviewing court to reverse the finding of the trier of fact simply because it is convinced that it would have decided the case differently. The reviewing court oversteps the bounds of its duty under Rule 52 if it undertakes to duplicate the role of the lower court. "In applying the clearly erroneous standard to the findings of a district court sitting without a jury, appellate courts must constantly have in mind that their function is not to decide factual issues de novo." Zenith Radio Corp. v. Hazeltine Research, Inc., 395 U.S. 100, 123, 89 S.Ct. 1562, 1576, 23 L.Ed.2d 129 (1969). If the district court's account of the evidence is plausible in light of the record viewed in its entirety, the court of appeals may not reverse it even though convinced that had it been sitting as the trier of fact, it would have weighed the evidence differently. Where there are two permissible views of the evidence, the factfinder's choice between them cannot be clearly erroneous.

* * *

This is so even when the district court's findings do not rest on credibility determinations, but are based instead on physical or documentary evidence or inferences from other facts. To be sure, various Court of Appeals have on occasion asserted the theory that an appellate court may exercise *de novo* review over findings not based on credibility determinations. [Citations omitted.] This theory has an impressive genealogy, having first been articulated in an opinion written by Judge Frank and subscribed to by Judge Augustus Hand, see Orvis v. Higgins, supra, but it is impossible to trace the theory's lineage back to the text of Rule 52, which states straightforwardly that "findings of fact shall not be set aside unless clearly erroneous." That the Rule goes on to emphasize the special deference to be paid credibility determinations does not alter its clear command: Rule 52 "does not make exceptions or purport to exclude certain categories of factual findings from the obligation of a court of appeals to accept a district court's findings unless clearly erroneous." Pullman–Standard v. Swint, 456 U.S., at 287, 102 S.Ct., at 1789.

The rationale for deference to the original finder of fact is not limited to the superiority of the trial judge's position to make determinations of credibility. The trial judge's major role is the determination of fact, and with experience in fulfilling that role comes expertise. Duplication of the trial judge's efforts in the court of appeals would very likely contribute only negligibly to the accuracy of fact determination at a huge cost in diversion of judicial resources. In addition, the parties to a case on appeal have already been forced to concentrate their energies and resources on persuading the trial judge that their account of the facts is the correct one; requiring them to persuade three more judges at the appellate level is requiring too much. As the Court has stated in a different context, the trial on the merits should be "the 'main event' * * * rather than a 'tryout on the road.'" Wainwright v. Sykes, 433 U.S. 72, 90, 97 S.Ct. 2497, 2508, 53 L.Ed.2d 594 (1977). For these reasons, review of factual findings under the clearly-erroneous standard—with its deference to the trier of fact—is the rule, not the exception.

When findings are based on determinations regarding the credibility of witnesses, Rule 52 demands even greater deference to the trial court's findings; for only the trial judge can be aware of the variations in demeanor and tone of voice that bear so heavily on the listener's understanding of and belief in what is said. [Citations omitted.] This is not to suggest that the trial judge may insulate his findings from review by denominating them credibility determinations, for factors other than demeanor and inflection go into the decision whether or not to believe a witness. Documents or objective evidence may contradict the witness' story; or the story itself may be so internally inconsistent or implausible on its face that a reasonable factfinder would not credit it. Where such factors are present, the court of appeals may well find clear error even in a finding purportedly based on a credibility determination. [Citations omitted.] But when a trial judge's finding is based on his decision to credit the testimony of one of two or more witnesses, each of whom has told a coherent and facially plausible story that is not contradicted by extrinsic evidence, that finding, if not internally inconsistent, can virtually never be clear error. [Citations omitted.]

IV

Application of the foregoing principles to the facts of the case lays bare the errors committed by the Fourth Circuit in its employment of the clearly-erroneous standard. In detecting clear error in the District Court's finding that petitioner was better qualified than Mr. Kincaid, the Fourth Circuit improperly conducted what amounted to a *de novo* weighing of the evidence in the record. The District Court's finding was based on essentially undisputed evidence regarding the respective backgrounds of petitioner and Mr. Kincaid and the duties that went with the position of Recreation Director. The District Court, after considering the evidence, concluded that the position of Recreation Director in Bessemer City carried with it broad responsibilities for creating and managing a recreation program involving not only athletics, but also other activities for citizens of all ages and interests. The court determined that petitioner's more varied educational and employment backgrounds and her extensive involvement in a variety of civic activities left her better qualified to implement such a rounded program than Mr. Kincaid, whose background was more narrowly focused on athletics.

The Fourth Circuit, reading the same record, concluded that the basic duty of the Recreation Director was to implement an athletic program, and that the essential qualification for a successful applicant would be either education or experience specifically related to athletics. Accordingly, it seemed evident to the Court of Appeals that Mr. Kincaid was in fact better qualified than petitioner.

Based on our own reading of the record, we cannot say that either interpretation of the facts is illogical or implausible. Each has support in inferences that may be drawn from the facts in the record; and if either interpretation had been drawn by a district court on the record before us, we would not be inclined to find it clearly erroneous. The question we must answer, however, is not whether the Fourth Circuit's interpretation of the facts was clearly erroneous, but whether the District Court's finding was clearly erroneous. [Citations omitted.] The District Court determined that petitioner was better qualified, and, as we have stated above, such a finding is entitled to deference notwithstanding that it is not based on credibility determinations. When the record is examined in light of the appropriately deferential standard, it is apparent that it contains nothing that mandates a finding that the District Court's conclusion was clearly erroneous.

Somewhat different concerns are raised by the Fourth Circuit's treatment of the District Court's finding that petitioner, alone among the applicants for the position of Recreation Director, was asked questions regarding her spouse's feelings about her application for the position. Here the error of the Court of Appeals was its failure to give due regard to the ability of the District Court to interpret and discern the credibility of oral testimony. The Court of Appeals rested its rejection of the District Court's finding of differential treatment on its own interpretation of testimony by Mrs. Boone—the very witness whose testimony, in the view of the District Court, supported the finding. In the eyes of the Fourth Circuit, Mrs. Boone's testimony that she had made a "comment" to Mr. Kincaid about the feelings of his wife (a comment judged "facetious" by the District Court) conclusively established that Mr. Kincaid, and perhaps other male applicants as well, had been questioned about the feelings of his spouse.

Mrs. Boone's testimony on this point, which is set forth in the margin, is certainly not free from ambiguity. But Mrs. Boone several times stated that other candidates had not been questioned about the reaction of their wives—at least, "not in the same context" as had petitioner. And even after recalling and calling to the attention of the court that she had made a comment on the subject to Mr. Kincaid, Mrs. Boone denied that she had "asked" Mr. Kincaid about his wife's reaction. Mrs. Boone's testimony on these matters is not inconsistent with the theory that her remark was not a serious inquiry into whether Mr. Kincaid's wife approved of his applying for the position. Whether the judge's interpretation is actually correct is impossible to tell from the paper record, but it is easy to imagine that the tone of voice in which the witness related her comment, coupled with her immediate denial that she had questioned Mr. Kincaid on the subject, might have conclusively established that the remark was a facetious one. We therefore cannot agree that the judge's conclusion that the remark was facetious was clearly erroneous.

Once the trial court's characterization of Mrs. Boone's remark is accepted, it is apparent that the finding that the male candidates were not seriously questioned about the feelings of their wives cannot be deemed clearly erroneous. The trial judge was faced with the testimony of three witnesses, one of whom (Mrs. Boone) stated that none of the other candidates had been so questioned, one of whom (a male committee member) testified that Mr. Kincaid had been asked such a question "in a way," and one of whom (another committeeman) testified that all the candidates had been subjected to similar questioning. None of these accounts is implausible on its face, and none is contradicted by any reliable extrinsic evidence. Under these circumstances, the trial court's decision to credit Mrs. Boone was not clearly erroneous.

The Fourth Circuit's refusal to accept the District Court's finding that the committee members were biased against hiring a woman was based to a large extent on its rejection of the finding that petitioner had been subjected to questioning that the other applicants were spared. Given that that finding was not clearly erroneous, the finding of bias cannot be termed erroneous: it finds support not only in the treatment of petitioner in her interview, but also in the testimony of one committee member that he believed it would have been difficult for a woman to perform the job and in the evidence that another member solicited applications for the position only from men.[4]

4. The Fourth Circuit's suggestion that any inference of bias was dispelled by the fact that each of the male committee members was married to a woman who had

Our determination that the findings of the District Court regarding petitioner's qualifications, the conduct of her interview, and the bias of the male committee members were not clearly erroneous leads us to conclude that the court's finding that petitioner was discriminated against on account of her sex was also not clearly erroneous. The District Court's findings regarding petitioner's superior qualifications and the bias of the selection committee are sufficient to support the inference that petitioner was denied the position of Recreation Director on account of her sex. Accordingly, we hold that the Fourth Circuit erred in denying petitioner relief under Title VII.

In so holding, we do not assert that our knowledge of what happened 10 years ago in Bessemer City is superior to that of the Court of Appeals; nor do we claim to have greater insight than the Court of Appeals into the state of mind of the men on the selection committee who rejected petitioner for the position of Recreation Director. Even the trial judge, who has heard the witnesses directly and who is more closely in touch than the appeals court with the milieu out of which the controversy before him arises, cannot always be confident that he "knows" what happened. Often, he can only determine whether the plaintiff has succeeded in presenting an account of the facts that is more likely to be true than not. Our task—and the task of appellate tribunals generally—is more limited still: we must determine whether the trial judge's conclusions are clearly erroneous. On the record before us, we cannot say that they are. Accordingly, the judgment of the Court of Appeals is

Reversed.

JUSTICE POWELL, concurring.

I do not dissent from the judgment that the Court of Appeals misapplied Rule 52(a) in this case. I write separately, however, because I am concerned that one may read the Court's opinion as implying criticism of the Court of Appeals for the very fact that it engaged in a comprehensive review of the entire record of this case. Such a reading may encourage overburdened Court of Appeals simply to apply Rule 52(a) in a conclusory fashion, rather than to undertake the type of burdensome review that may be appropriate in some cases.

In this case, the Court of Appeals made no arbitrary judgment that the action of the District Court was clearly erroneous. On the contrary, the court meticulously reviewed the entire record and reached the conclusion that the District Court was in error. One easily could agree with the Court of Appeals that the District Court committed a mistake in its finding of sex discrimination, based, as it was, on fragmentary statements made years before in informal exchanges between members

worked at some point in the marriage is insufficient to establish that the finding of bias was clearly erroneous. Although we decline to hold that a man's attitude toward his wife's employment is irrelevant to the question whether he may be found to have a bias against working women, any relevance the factor may have in a particular case is a matter for the district court to weigh in its consideration of bias, not the court of appeals.

of the selection committee and the applicants for the position to be filled. On the record before us, however, the factual issue fairly could be decided for either party. Therefore, as the Court holds, the District Court's decision was not clearly erroneous within the meaning of Rule 52(a).

JUSTICE BLACKMUN, concurring in the judgment.

* * *

Notes and Questions

1. How does the Court in the principal case characterize the "clearly erroneous" standard of review? Does it help in understanding the proper role of the court of appeals in reviewing a finding of fact?

2. As discussed in the principal case, some appellate courts have exercised greater review of findings of facts based on documentary evidence or undisputed facts. Note, Rule 52(a): Appellate Review of Findings of Fact Based on Documentary or Undisputed Evidence, 49 Virginia L.Rev. 506 (1963). Federal Rule of Civil Procedure 52(a) was amended in 1985 to state expressly that both oral and documentary evidence are subject to the clearly erroneous rule. Does the principal case indicate that the standard of review for findings of fact based on credibility of witnesses is the same or different as for documentary evidence or undisputed facts?

3. The principal case involves findings of fact made by a judge. When the findings of fact are made by a jury, what should the standard of review be? R. Martineau, Fundamentals of Modern Appellate Advocacy § 7.23 (1985):

> Because of the constitutionally protected right to a jury trial in both federal and state courts, the standard of review by appellate courts over facts found by a jury is extremely narrow. The standard is usually stated in terms of a requirement that the jury finding must be upheld if there is sufficient evidence to support the verdict. Sufficiency of the evidence is defined to mean that there are in the record probative facts from which the ultimate fact found by the jury could reasonably be inferred. The appellate court may not substitute its judgment for that of the jury. This standard of review applies, however, only if a motion for directed verdict or for a motion for judgment n.o.v. has been filed. If one or both of these motions is not filed, then the review is even more limited. The review then is restricted to ascertaining whether there is *any* evidence in the record to support the jury finding. If there is, then the verdict must be upheld.

4. What is the difference between a fact and an ultimate fact? The Supreme Court in Pullman–Standard v. Swint, 456 U.S. 273, 282, 289, 102 S.Ct. 1781, 1789, 1790, 72 L.Ed.2d 66, 78, 80 (1982) discussed the distinction between basic facts and ultimate facts in two footnotes as follows:

> **16.** There is some indication in the opinions of the Court of Appeals for the Fifth Circuit (see n. 14) that the circuit rule with respect to "ultimate facts" is only another way of stating a standard of review with respect to mixed questions of law and fact—the ultimate "fact" is

the statutory, legally determinative consideration (here, intentional discrimination) which is or is not satisfied by subsidiary facts admitted or found by the trier of fact. As indicated in the text, however, the question of intentional discrimination under § 703(h) is a pure question of fact. Furthermore, the Court of Appeals' opinion in this case appears to address the issue as a question of fact unmixed with legal considerations.

At the same time, this Court has on occasion itself indicated that findings on "ultimate facts" are independently reviewable. In Baumgartner v. United States, 322 U.S. 665, 64 S.Ct. 1240, 88 L.Ed. 1525 (1944), the issue was whether or not the findings of the two lower courts satisfied the clear and convincing standard of proof necessary to sustain a denaturalization decree. The Court held that the conclusion of the two lower courts that the exacting standard of proof had been satisfied was not an unreviewable finding of fact but one that a reviewing court could independently assess. The Court referred to the finding as one of "ultimate" fact, which in that case involved an appraisal of the strength of the entire body of evidence. The Court said that the significance of the clear and convincing proof standard "would be lost" if the ascertainment by the lower courts whether that exacting standard of proof had been satisfied on the whole record were to be deemed a "fact" of the same order as all other "facts not open to review here". 322 U.S., at 671, 64 S.Ct., at 1243.

The Fifth Circuit's rule on appellate consideration of "ultimate facts" has its roots in this discussion in *Baumgartner*. In Galena Oaks Corp. v. Scofield, 218 F.2d 217 (CA5 1954), in which the question was whether the gain derived from the sale of a number of houses was to be treated as capital gain or ordinary income, the Court of Appeals relied directly on *Baumgartner* in holding that this was an issue of "ultimate fact" that an appellate court may review free of the clearly erroneous rule. Causey v. Ford Motor Co., 516 F.2d 416 (CA5 1975), relying on Galena Oaks Corp. v. Scofield, supra, said that "although discrimination *vel non* is essentially a question of fact, it is, at the same time, the ultimate issue for resolution in this case" and as such, was deemed to be independently reviewable. The passage from East v. Romine, Inc., 518 F.2d 332, 339 (CA5 1975), which was repeated in the case before us now, supra, at 1788, rested on the opinion in *Causey v. Ford Motor Co.*

Whatever *Baumgartner* may have meant by its discussion of "ultimate facts", it surely did not mean that whenever the result in a case turns on a factual finding, an appellate court need not remain within the constraints of Rule 52. *Baumgartner's* discussion of "ultimate facts" referred not to pure findings of fact—as we find discriminatory intent to be in this context—but to findings that "clearly impl[y] the application of standards of law." 322 U.S., at 671, 64 S.Ct., at 1243.

19. We need not, therefore, address the much-mooted issue of the applicability of the Rule 52(a) standard to mixed questions of law and fact—i.e., questions in which the historical facts are admitted or established, the rule of law is undisputed, and the issue is whether the facts satisfy the statutory standard, or to put it another way, whether the rule of law as applied to the established facts is or is not violated. There is substantial authority in the circuits on both sides of this question. [Citations omitted.] There is also support in decisions of this Court for the proposition that conclusions on mixed questions of law and fact are independently reviewable by an appellate court, [Citations omitted.]

Does the above suggest that the Supreme Court was abolishing the distinction between basic fact and ultimate fact, acknowledging the difference but merely saying that the question of intent in that case was a basic fact rather than an ultimate fact, or simply not ruling on the issue because it was not necessary to decide the case?

5. Appellate review of trial court disposition of motions for summary judgment or directed verdicts are especially troublesome. For two cases in which the Supreme Court found the court of appeals had applied the wrong standard of review, see Anderson v. Liberty Lobby, Inc., 477 U.S. 242, 106 S.Ct. 2505, 91 L.Ed.2d 202 (1986) and Celotex Corporation v. Catrett, 477 U.S. 317, 106 S.Ct. 2548, 91 L.Ed.2d 265 (1986).

3. ABUSE OF DISCRETION

KERN v. TXO PRODUCTION CORP.

United States Court of Appeals, Eighth Circuit, 1984.
738 F.2d 968.

Arnold, Circuit Judge.

TXO Production Corporation appeals from the District Court's order dismissing without prejudice Frances Kern's action against it. TXO claims that the dismissal, which came after the trial had begun, should have been with prejudice, or, in the alternative, should at least have been conditioned on the payment by plaintiff of its costs and lawyers' fees. We cannot agree that it was an abuse of discretion to dismiss the complaint without prejudice, but we do hold that conditions should have been attached to protect TXO. We therefore affirm in part, reverse in part, and remand with instructions.

I

The plaintiff owns the surface of five acres of land in Logan County, Arkansas. TXO holds an oil-and-gas lease granted by the owner of the mineral interest. Plaintiff brought this action for damages, claiming that a gas well drilled on her property by TXO had reduced the value of her surface ownership more than reasonably necessary in the exercise of a mineral lessee's rights. Suit was filed in the Circuit Court of Logan County, Arkansas, Northern District, for $15,000.00 in damages, later increased by amendment to $25,000.00. TXO removed the case to the District Court on the basis of diversity of citizenship.

After some discovery had taken place, the District Court set the case for trial. Plaintiff then moved to dismiss her complaint without prejudice under Fed.R.Civ.P. 41(a)(2). The District Court informed counsel by letter that it would grant the motion, but "only upon the express condition that, if the case is refiled in any court, the defendant will be awarded all costs of this action, including all attorney's fees incurred in preparing this case for trial." Designated Record (D.R.) 19. Plaintiff, evidently believing this condition too burdensome, withdrew her motion to dismiss, and the case went to trial before a jury about two weeks later.

After plaintiff had presented four out of the five witnesses she intended to call, the court and counsel conferred out of the presence of the jury. The intended testimony of the fifth witness, a real-estate expert, was fully discussed. The court informally indicated the view that plaintiff would be unable to make out a submissible fact question for the jury: "at the close of your [the plaintiff's] case, the court will more than likely direct a verdict in favor of the defendant." Tr. 137. After a 15–minute recess to allow plaintiff's lawyer to consult with his client, the plaintiff renewed her motion for dismissal without prejudice. This time the motion was granted, and no conditions as to costs and expenses were imposed. The court said (Tr. 143):

> The court sees Ms. Kern, sees TXO. Under the circumstances, I think that if I'm going to err, I want to err in favor of giving Ms. Kern another chance because TXO will survive. I'm just certain of that.

TXO objected to this action, and it now appeals.

II

Under Fed.R.Civ.P. 41(a)(1) a plaintiff may voluntarily dismiss her complaint, without prejudice to the filing of a new action based on the same claim, as a matter of right, provided only that the dismissal must occur before the defendant has either answered or moved for summary judgment. Otherwise,

> an action shall not be dismissed at the plaintiff's instance save upon order of the court and upon such terms and conditions as the court deems proper.

Fed.R.Civ.P. 41(a)(2).

Motions to dismiss without prejudice are addressed to the sound discretion of the district courts. But "the discretion vested in the court is a judicial and not an arbitrary one * * *." International Shoe Co. v. Cool, 154 F.2d 778, 780 (8th Cir.) *cert. denied,* 329 U.S. 726, 67 S.Ct. 76, 91 L.Ed. 678 (1946). That is, when we say that a decision is discretionary, or that a district court has discretion to grant or deny a motion, we do not mean that the district court may do whatever pleases it. The phrase means instead that the court has a range of choice, and that its decision will not be disturbed as long as it stays within that range and is not influenced by any mistake of law. An abuse of discretion, on the other hand, can occur in three principal ways: when a relevant factor that should have been given significant weight is not considered; when an irrelevant or improper factor is considered and given significant weight; and when all proper factors, and no improper ones, are considered, but the court, in weighing those factors, commits a clear error of judgment. And in every case we as an appellate court must be mindful that the district courts are closer to the facts and the parties, and that not everything that is important about a lawsuit comes through on the printed page.

At common law, dismissals without prejudice were, in general, freely allowed at any time before the case was ready for decision. That is still the rule in the Arkansas state courts. Ark.R.Civ.P. 41. But in the federal courts, after answer, such dismissals should be granted only "if no other party will be prejudiced." 9 Wright & Miller, *Federal Practice & Procedure—Civil* § 2362 (1971). By "prejudice" in this context is meant something other than the necessity that defendant might face of defending another action. That kind of disadvantage can be taken care of by a condition that plaintiff pay to defendant its costs and expenses incurred in the first action. One sort of prejudice that cannot be cured by the attachment of conditions is the loss by defendant of success in the first case. If defendant has already won its case, reimbursement of fees and expenses cannot make it whole from the injury of being sued again, perhaps this time to lose.

A series of cases in this Court has applied this principle. The most recent example is Williams v. Ford Motor Credit Co., 627 F.2d 158 (8th Cir. 1980). The jury verdict had gone for plaintiff. Defendant moved for judgment notwithstanding the verdict. Plaintiff opposed the motion, but asked the court, if it decided the verdict could not stand, to grant her a voluntary nonsuit, so that she could sue again in a state court. The motion for nonsuit was granted. We reversed. "Under the circumstances we feel the court abused its discretion in granting the motion to dismiss without prejudice at such a late time in the proceedings." Id. at 160. We noted, among other things, that the dismissal might prejudice the defendant with respect to a third-party claim it had asserted in the first action.

TXO urges that *Williams* is controlling. It must be admitted that the differences between the case and this one are not great. Certainly if the District Court had refused the plaintiff's motion for voluntary dismissal, or insisted that the dismissal, if suffered, would be with prejudice, it would not have abused its discretion. It is true here, as it was in *Williams,* 627 F.2d at 159–60, that

> Plaintiff's motion fails to disclose the reason for seeking the dismissal without prejudice. Plaintiff did not indicate that new evidence might be shown [on a second trial]. Even if there were such evidence, there is no indication that plaintiff could not have presented it during [the first] trial.

That the denial of the motion would not have been reversible as an abuse of discretion, however, does not mean that granting it was such an abuse. The very concept of discretion presupposes a zone of choice within which the trial courts may go either way.

We think the differences between this case on the one hand, and *Williams* and its precursors on the other, are great enough, though perhaps not by much, to justify a decision not to interfere with the choice made by the District Court. The trial here was not so far along as in *Williams* and the other cases cited. The plaintiff had not yet rested, and defendant had not yet moved for directed verdict. Although it was likely that that motion, when made, would have been granted, we cannot say that it was certain. The final witness's testimony might have differed somewhat from the parties' expectations. The District Court might have decided, as trial courts often do, to let the case proceed despite its initial view as to the insufficiency of plaintiff's case. Furthermore, by granting the nonsuit without prejudice the District Court allowed the plaintiff the opportunity to seek a state-court ruling on a state-law issue. The District Court's action here was immediately preceded by a thorough discussion of Arkansas law on surface damages. The court and plaintiff's counsel differed on the meaning of certain opinions of the Supreme Court of Arkansas. We have no reason to suppose that the District Court's view was not wholly reasonable, but its decision would still have been only a forecast, an educated guess about what the Arkansas state courts would do. The state courts, by contrast, can give an authoritative answer. This factor cuts in favor of the decision to allow plaintiff to try again.

In short, we cannot bring ourselves to say that it was an abuse of discretion to allow the dismissal without prejudice, and to that extent the judgment will be affirmed.

III

We turn now to defendant's alternative contention that it was an abuse of discretion not to impose a condition with respect to costs and attorneys' fees. In New York, C. & St. L.R.R. v. Vardaman, 181 F.2d 769, 771 (8th Cir. 1950), we said:

> Our view is that payment to the defendant of the expenses and a reasonable attorney fee may properly be a condition for dismissal without prejudice under Rule 41(a) but that omission of such condition is not necessarily an arbitrary act.

In *Vardaman* the trial court had required payment of costs but not fees. We affirmed on the ground that much of the defendant's fee request was attributable to services rendered in other cases, and that during the argument on the motion to dismiss without prejudice no specific request for fees had been made. We added the comment that, whatever the state of the record in the particular case, "it would not have necessarily been an abuse of discretion to omit payment of expenses and attorney fees as a requirement for the dismissal." Id. at 772.

In *Vardaman,* though, the case had not gone to trial. The time and effort invested by the parties, and the stage to which the case had progressed, are among the most important factors to be considered in deciding whether to allow a dismissal without prejudice, and, if so, on what conditions. A closer case is Home Owners' Loan Corp. v. Huffman,

134 F.2d 314 (8th Cir. 1943). There, plaintiff had gained a verdict. We reversed and remanded for a new trial. Prior to the commencement of the new trial, plaintiff was granted a nonsuit without prejudice and without payment of costs. We approved the dismissal without prejudice but held that "the court abused its discretion in permitting dismissal without prejudice unless conditioned on payment of costs." Id. at 319. "The rule has long prevailed in both law and equity that a plaintiff may dismiss the case without prejudice only by payment of the costs * * *." Id. at 317. The question of lawyers' fees is not covered by our opinion.

This case is in some ways between *Vardaman* and *Huffman*. The trial had begun but was not over. In all the circumstances presented here, we think it was an abuse of discretion not to compensate defendant in some fashion both for costs proper and for attorneys' fees. Such a condition will almost always be appropriate in cases where dismissal is allowed after the trial has begun. In addition, with all deference to the District Court, we believe it considered an improper factor in making its ruling. The only reason the court gave for dismissing without prejudice and without condition was that "TXO will survive." The fact that a party is a corporation, or is thought to be rich, or both, is and must be irrelevant in courts of justice. The courts' duty is to "administer justice without respect to persons, and do equal right to the poor and to the rich * * *." 28 U.S.C. § 453.

The District Court's refusal to impose conditions must be reversed. On remand, it should determine the amount of defendant's costs, including the premium for the removal bond, and fees reasonably incurred up through the order of dismissal. Plaintiff need not be required to pay any amount now. But she should be required to make a payment to defendant as a condition of maintaining a second action, if she decides to file one and does so within the relevant period of limitations. If the second suit is filed in a federal court, payment of the sum found to be appropriate will be a condition precedent to any action's taking place in the suit subsequent to the filing of the complaint. If, as seems likely, the second suit is filed in a state court, with the demand for damages reduced below the jurisdictional amount, so as to defeat removal, this method of collection will not work. But the District Court should enter an order now stating that if plaintiff refiles in a state court it will forthwith enter judgment against her, which may be executed as provided by law, for the amount of costs and fees that it has fixed.

We leave to the District Court the ascertainment of this amount. It may not be appropriate to include all of the lawyers' fees reasonably incurred by TXO. Some of its lawyers' work may not have to be repeated in a second action. We assume, for example, that any discovery taken in the first action should be freely usable in the second, whether the refiling is in a state or a federal court. Plaintiff should be required to pay only for those lawyers' services that will have to be repeated if the case is refiled. See McLaughlin v. Cheshire, 676 F.2d 855 (D.C.Cir. 1982).

Defendant also asks us to condition the dismissal on a requirement that plaintiff refile, if at all, only in a federal court. We decline to do so. The state courts, unlike us, are courts of general jurisdiction. It would be unwise for us (assuming our power to do so) to forbid a citizen to resort to the courts of her own state. "[O]ne court is as good as another." Young v. Southern Pac. Co., 25 F.2d 630, 632 (2d Cir. 1928) (L. Hand, J., concurring). We have no reason to think the state courts will not do justice. See Lawson v. Moore, 29 F.Supp. 175 (W.D.Va. 1939), where a similar condition was refused. Indeed, in this case, as we have remarked, the state courts can give a more accurate, or at least a more authoritative, answer to the questions of Arkansas law that will govern this case. And defendant gets some advantage, too: its maximum exposure will be reduced from $25,000.00 to $10,000.00.

IV

The order of the District Court, to the extent that it allowed dismissal of the complaint without prejudice, is affirmed. The decision not to impose conditions is reversed, and the cause remanded for further proceedings consistent with this opinion.

It is so ordered.

Notes and Questions

1. There are numerous matters left to the discretion of the trial judge. For example, in the West Key Number System, key numbers 811 through 830 under Federal Courts are dedicated to the different type of legal matters that by statute, rule, or court decision are within the discretion of the trial judge.

2. It has been suggested that discretionary decisions fall within three main categories: (1) absolute discretion, such as the discretion of the judge under Federal Rule of Civil Procedure 49(a) to request a special verdict; (2) limited discretion, where standards for the exercise of discretion under a rule have been expressly set forth in the rule itself or by judicial decision, such as under Rule 24(b) regulating intervention; (3) limited discretion, where the limitations have been prescribed and developed exclusively by the courts, such as want to stay an action pending completion of a state court proceeding. Project, Civil Appellate Jurisdiction: An Interlocutory Restatement, 47 Law and Contemporary Problems 13, 62–63 (1984).

3. In the principal case, the court states that discretion means that the trial court has a range of choices and its action will not be disturbed if it falls within that range of choices. How can the range of choices be identified? The court also says that the trial judge can be reversed for a "clear error of judgment." Does the opinion give any guidance as to how a clear error of judgment can be identified? If not, does the standard mean anything more than when the appellate court thinks not only that the trial judge made a mistake, but a bad mistake, or that the appellate court not only disagrees with the trial judge but strongly disagrees? Is anything more definite possible or desirable? See generally, Rosenberg, Appellate Review of Trial Court Discretion, 79 F.R.D. 173 (1979).

4. QUESTIONS OF LAW

Project, Civil Appellate Jurisdiction: An Interlocutory Restatement, 47 Law and Contemporary Problems 13, 52 (1984).*

> Rule 52(a) of the Federal Rules of Civil Procedure delineates the scope of review which appellate courts are to apply to findings of fact. The Rules provide no standard of review for conclusions of law. Given this silence and the long-established principles of law and equity, it is clear that the appellate court may freely review the trial courts' conclusions of law. Therefore, although Rule 52 requires the trial court to separately state its conclusions of law or legal premise, the appellate court is not bound by that view of the law or application of a legal standard.
>
> Rule 44.1 of the Federal Rules of Civil Procedure explicitly states that the trial judge's determination regarding the law of a foreign country "shall be treated as a ruling on a question of law." Similarly, a determination of state law is generally freely reviewable as a question of law, though appellate courts give great weight to a lower court's conclusion in consideration of the district judge's experience in the law of that state.

Notes and Questions

1. Why should an appellate court have greater discretion to review questions of law than findings of fact? Should this rule affect the types of issues an appellant should raise on appeal?

2. On questions of state law, shouldn't the conclusions of the district judge be given greater weight than on questions of federal law?

3. Review of rulings on summary judgment and motions for directed verdicts are treated as questions of law and not as questions of fact. Roberts v. Browning, 610 F.2d 528, 536–37 (8th Cir. 1979); Keiser v. Coliseum Properties, 614 F.2d 406, 410 (5th Cir. 1980). What would be the rationale for this rule? Is it valid?

4. The standards of review on treated comprehensively in S. Childress & M. Davis, Federal Standards of Review (2d ed. 1992). For an excellent treatment of the subject for the brief writer see R. Aldisert, Winning on Appeal 56–72 (2d ed. 2003).

SECTION E. EFFECTIVE BRIEF WRITING

1. HOW TO TEACH AND TO LEARN BRIEF WRITING SKILLS

One of the most common complaints of appellate judges and their law clerks is the inadequacy of most briefs filed in appellate courts. Yet almost every law student is required to write at least one appellate brief

---

* Copyright © 1984 Law and Contemporary Problems.

prior to graduation and many make participation in moot court programs the non-classroom staple of their law school experience. Further, almost every appellate judge and many appellate attorneys feel constrained at one time or another to write an article or give a speech to lawyers on the basic principles of brief writing. The problem is that neither the law school activity nor the efforts of the judges and practitioners appear to have any positive effect on the quality of briefs.

There are several possible explanations for the ineffectiveness of brief writing training in law school. It could be either that this skill simply cannot be taught in law school or that the law schools are not doing it properly. The Committee on Appellate Skills Training of the A.B.A. Appellate Judges Conference in its report "Appellate Litigation Skills Training: The Role of the Law Schools" (published in 54 U. of Cin. L.Rev. 129 (1985)) concluded that brief writing skills not only can be taught, but should be taught. It further concluded that the current efforts in law schools are misdirected because they are designed to teach only legal analysis skills, not brief writing skills, and are taught by persons who themselves have no experience or training in brief writing, usually either third year law students or research and writing instructors their first year out of law school. The major defect in law school brief writing programs as identified by the Committee is that they do not train students to work with an actual record, the skill that most distinguishes appellate brief writing from all other forms of legal writing. All cases involve the application of law to facts. The central function of the appellate litigator is to select from the record the key issues to be presented to the appellate court and to identify in the record the facts that the appellate court must know in order to decide those issues.

This is a skill that can be mastered only after many years of practice. The law student can, however, be exposed to the fundamentals of the skill in a law school course and, under the supervision of an experienced instructor, develop a base that can be further sharpened in practice, much in the same way that a trial practice course provides a base for becoming a competent trial lawyer.

There are several ways to approach learning brief writing skills in a basic course in appellate practice and procedure. One approach is for the instructor to obtain actual records from an appellate court, to assign students to represent one side or the other, and to have them write briefs. Another approach is to assign students to an actual case pending in an appellate court and to have them write a critique of the work of the lawyers in the case, including their briefs written in the case, using the record in the case as the focal point for the critique. The author has used the latter format for a number of years and believes that it is the best way for the students to utilize the knowledge they have gained in the course and to be introduced to the real world of appellate practice. In the author's view, students can learn more quickly by just observing and critiquing what lawyers have done in a real case. Ideally, upon completion of the basic course that includes a written critique of the briefs filed in an actual appeal, the students should take a follow up course in brief writing and oral argument in which they will receive advanced training in these skills, using an actual record and under the supervision of a skilled instructor. For a further development of these ideas, see Martineau, Appellate Litigation: Its Place in the Law School Curriculum, 35 J. Legal Ed. 71 (1989).

The following materials include some of the classic articles on brief writing. They provide the basic guidelines for writing an effective brief. What is said in these articles has been repeated in hundreds of other articles over the years. The only thing that is difficult to understand is why so few lawyers seem to have learned them.

2. WRITING THE EFFECTIVE BRIEF

TATE, THE ART OF BRIEF WRITING: WHAT A JUDGE WANTS TO READ

4 Litigation 11–15, 56–57 (Winter, 1978).*

An appellate advocate wants his brief and argument to contribute to the success of his client's cause. My primary theme, however, is how the appellate brief can help the court, not the client. A court only uses briefs that help it make decisions. If counsel regards the appellate brief as more than a perfunctory, functionless tool, he therefore must prepare it primarily for the court. The judges may then rely on it as they prepare the decision. Win or lose, this always benefits the client, because *his* counsel has contributed to the decision-making.

To help the judge, the brief need not be eloquent or even persuasive about the client's cause. It is sufficient that it furnish ready access to the record, the authorities, and the reasoning by which the lawyer's client is to prevail. If the client is to lose, the brief and oral argument should at least enable the judges to understand the authorities and reasoning that support the client's position. (Perhaps 50 percent of the briefs filed with our courts are so one-sided or superficial as to be essentially discarded after an initial skimming. From the point of view of both client and court, it is as if no brief at all had been filed.)

Before suggesting in more detail how briefs may perform this function most effectively, I should perhaps consider the appellate judge for whom the briefs are prepared.

As counsel writes the brief, he should visualize the judge, what he thinks he is trying to do in deciding the case, and how he will use the brief. He should keep in mind what the judge's approach may be to the problem, what will interest him, and what he may disregard as irrelevant or useless. The brief is not written to be fed into an impersonal, computerized justice machine, but to be read and studied and weighed by fellow human beings.

* Copyright © 1978 American Bar Association. Reprinted with permission. All rights reserved.

The present-day appellate judge performs in a milieu of ever-increasing appellate volume. In less than a decade, the law explosion has tripled the number of cases many appellate courts must decide each year. In my own court, for instance, each of the seven judges must participate in deciding nearly 2,000 appeals or supervisory writs during the year.

Yet the appellate judge today is essentially the same sort of man as his predecessor of two (or ten) decades ago. He shares the same central perception of his function and duty: in each case that comes before him, he accepts as his personal responsibility the duty of seeing that individual justice is done, within the framework of the law.

The result that seems "just" for the present case must be a principled one that will afford just results in similar conflicts of interest. The brief, then, is addressed to a human judge, not an abstract legal technician. This judge has an initial human concern that the litigants receive common-sense justice, but he also realizes that the discipline of legal doctrine governs his determination of the cause.

High Volume

In writing for this judge, counsel must also keep in mind that the volume of cases exposes him to several hundred appeals a year. Consequently, he knows much law and has seen many approaches to appellate advocacy. He quickly recognizes sham and superfluous arguments. Each appeal in his burgeoning caseload competes for his interest and limited time. Considering all this, the appellate advocate will do well to concentrate on the strengths of his case, as concisely and lucidly as possible, if he wants to attract the judge's interest in and reliance upon his own brief.

In this era of high volume, the brief serves a function that is increasingly important: to obtain oral argument or, at least, an articulated opinion deciding the appeal.

Perhaps 80 percent of appeals present issues clearly destined to appellate rejection. They may involve the contested but correct application of settled law, or an attack upon a factual finding of the trier not clearly erroneous. They may even involve frivolous contentions or ones the appellate court has consistently rejected in the past. Since an articulated and published opinion will add nothing to the law or the parties' understanding of why the appeal resulted in an affirmance, some appellate courts have devised summary proceedings to eliminate full-scale consideration of such appeals and to provide for their disposition without opinion or oral argument. This helps to preserve more time to hear, study, and prepare opinions in appeals involving more substantial or uncertain issues.

In the summary instances, the appellant's brief is the primary basis upon which the screening is made. To assure a hearing beyond the brief, let alone to prevail, the appellant must strongly demonstrate the possibility of individual unfairness or of a truly arguable question of law, or its application, in need of articulated resolution. The appellee's brief, of course, should demonstrate the lack of merit to these contentions, if indeed there is none.

Although my suggestions primarily concern preparing a brief to help the court in deciding a case by an articulated opinion, after oral argument, the same considerations apply even more strongly where the appeal may be decided without oral argument or by summary affirmance or reversal.

I should not overemphasize the skills of advocacy in determining the result in the bulk of litigation. Although appellate advocates frequently disagree, most appellate judges feel that they might ultimately have blundered upon the correct result without the assistance of counsel. Litigation should be decided on the basis of the law and the facts, not on the technical skills of counsel. Most appeals are decided by the pleadings and evidence in the trial court and the law in the books, and not on the basis of appellate advocacy. This of course is as it should be.

On the whole, the effective appellate advocate's contribution will be to sharpen and hasten the decisional process, while assuring full consideration of his client's position. Also, by his choice of issues and authorities, counsel may add important dimensions and perspectives to the rationale and future usefulness of the decision.

Generally speaking, the form and organization of a brief should serve two purposes: First, it should be so complete within itself that in writing the opinion the judge need not refer to extrinsic sources, except to confirm the accuracy of the presentation. Second, the brief should allow the court to understand it and obtain access to the record or authorities cited without spending any unnecessary effort.

Court rules about the form of the brief typically provide for (1) a "preliminary statement," which states in one or two sentences the general nature of the action and the procedural history of the case; (2) a "statement of the issues"—a succinct listing of the questions presented for decision; (3) a "statement of facts," a concise narrative summary of the material facts in the context of which the litigation arises; (4) the "argument"—points of law or fact, discussed under appropriate point headings, with analysis of the legal problems on argument of law, and with presentation of the accurately cited evidence on argument of fact; and (5) the "conclusion"—a succinct summarized reiteration of why the judgment should be reversed or affirmed, sometimes including a suggested decree. Whether the rule of court so provides or not, this format presents for ready comprehension by the judge the essential issues of law in their factual context.

The "preliminary statement" and the "conclusion" are self-explanatory. Before I note what I find helpful to the client's cause and to the court in a brief's statement of the issues, statement of the facts, and argument, I have some general observations applicable to the brief as a whole.

Be Concise, Lucid

Recognizing the mass of reading and research competing for the judge's time and attention, appellate counsel should revise to be concise and lucid. From the mass of materials available, he should repeatedly select and discard—*select* essential issues, facts, and authorities; *discard* and winnow others ruthlessly, along with excess words and repetitious argument.

Counsel's worry, of course, is that what he winnows as superfluous might, if left, somehow catch the court's eye. Hence, he errs unwisely on the side of inclusion. Unless there is particular reason to believe otherwise, however, a safe rule is to assume that appellate judges will have the same good sense as counsel in concluding that the winnowable issue or fact is indeed non-contributory. Part of the craft of counselling is the ability to balance the *possible* contribution of the issue or fact against the undoubted loss of impact and persuasion of a brief that wastes the court's time on side trails that lead nowhere.

Need I add that accuracy and candor should guide counsel's selection of the issues and statements of factual argument and of the arguable import of the authority relied upon? Inaccuracy in statement or misleading argument will obviously destroy the court's confidence in the brief.

For readability and easy comprehension, the brief should be coherently organized, with appropriate headings and subheadings to facilitate ready reference to topics of special interest. Short sentences and relatively short paragraphs allow immediate understanding. Italics should be sparingly used, exclamation points practically never, and capitalized boldface type not at all; rather, the emphasis should result from the content and arrangement of the thoughts. From reading several thousand briefs a year, a judge has learned that what is shouted and exclaimed could usually be whispered, if it needs mouthing at all.

Counsel should accurately note page numbers for facts in the record and have someone proofread for accuracy of doctrinal and decisional citations, including page numbers of quotations; case citations must be Shepardized to assure their current viability. Inaccurate citations will waste the court's time and subconsciously undermine confidence in the reliability of counsel's argument as well.

Judge's Companion

The brief is a companion of the judge from before the oral argument until after the rehearing is denied, and it will be referred to or reread as often as necessary. The judge to whom the decision is assigned will continually consult the effective appellate brief—issue by issue and fact by fact—in his research and as he drafts the proposed opinion. Primarily on the basis of the briefs, each other judge of the panel will decide to sign the proposed opinion or instead to dissent, concur, or suggest changes in it.

Even before the opinion is assigned and circulated, the participating judges all use primarily the briefs to prepare for oral argument and to reach a tentative conclusion for the opinion-assignment conference immediately following argument. After the opinion is issued, they again consult the briefs in deciding whether to grant a rehearing. At all stages, each participating judge relies largely upon the briefs when deciding whether to engage in independent research of the record or the law.

At the outset, the statement of the issues acquaints the court with the essence of the case. It should provide a concise statement of the controlling questions for decision. The statement of the issues is not the same as a statement of counsel's contentions; it is rather an attempt to state fairly to the court the crux of the case in terms of the precise legal issue to be decided and of the ultimate facts that gave rise to this issue. Ideally, the question should be stated so that the opponent must accept it. When the opposing parties frame an issue differently, the party who misstates what the court concludes to be the real issue loses much credibility.

The questions should be stated in the briefest and most general terms, without names, amounts, or details. The conciseness of what is expected is indicated by some court rules that provide that this statement should not ordinarily exceed fifteen printed lines and never more than a page. Of course, the statement of a central issue includes every subsidiary issue fairly comprised within it, which then may be developed more fully in subheadings of the argument proper.

In my experience, counsel often overlook the importance of the statement of the central issues and sometimes prepare it as an afterthought after having written the argument. The judge's initial reaction to the seriousness and merit of the appeal is often based upon this indication of what issues counsel considers to be vital to his case; in the light of this statement, and of the statement of facts, the judge tends unconsciously to screen the appeal as substantial or not, even though this impression may yield to later study. When the questions at issue are effectively stated, the judge is able to decide and to read and understand more quickly the argument that follows in the brief.

The questions should be one or few in number. Rare is the appeal with a great number of reversible errors; when a great number of questions are presented as serious issues, the judge's expectation that most or all of them are insubstantial is rarely disappointed. It has sometimes seemed to me that a great number of insubstantial issues raised might have been abandoned, and the argument section more tightly concentrated on the arguable issues, if counsel had attempted to articulate concisely the precise questions he wished the court to decide *before* writing his brief. I have never been able to understand the motives of counsel who raise a great number of issues they must realize the court will decide adversely to them: the few arguable issues raised by them tend to be regarded as non-meritorious by association. It is like shooting with a blunderbuss crammed with eggshell, which will annoy and distract without affecting the outcome.

Selecting and characterizing the issues may determine the course of the appeal. Llewellyn once described an unsuccessful appeal, stated in terms of the duty of an "agent," and suggested that a contrary result would have been reached if the issue had been instead characterized as the duty owed by a "broker." In my own experience, an appeal—stated and briefed in terms of a subrogation issue—was nearly lost, until our court, after much study, discovered that the issue was one of indemnity. The issues stated should be selected not only in view of the facts and the state of the law, but also in the light of what will appeal to the particular reviewing court.

The most helpful statement of an issue is in terms of its facts, not as an abstract question of law. The statement should show the precise point of substantive law and its applicability to the facts at hand. Thus, "Was plaintiff guilty of contributory negligence?" does vaguely indicate the general issue; but how much more helpful to the court's concentration and understanding of the issue is: "Plaintiff's car struck the rear of a vehicle operated by the defendant, who had made an emergency stop without signalling. Where plaintiff admits that he could not have stopped his car within an assured clear distance ahead, is he chargeable with contributory negligence so as to bar his recovery?"

Don't Argue too Much

An overly argumentative statement of the issues turns me off. Self-evident, overtly self-serving, or overgeneralized statements are not helpful and may be misleading (and thus prejudicial to the court's appreciation of counsel's sincerity). Thus, the issue in a tax case, if stated as, "Whether a man is taxable on income which his son receives?", is not indicative of the true issue: "Whether the owner of coupon bonds should include in his gross income the amount of coupons which he detached and gave to his son several months before maturity?" I should note that, if fairly stated, a formulation of the issue is not out of order when it subtly suggests the response desired by the litigant; as, for instance, in the tax collector's reformulation of the above issue to suggest the taxpayer's evasion of tax on income from property still owned by him: "The taxpayer owned coupon bonds. Several months prior to maturity of the interest coupons he detached them and gave them to his son, retaining the bonds themselves. Is he relieved of income tax with respect to such interest coupons?"

The statement of the facts is regarded by many advocates and judges as the most important part of the brief. In the first place, regardless of how much the judge knows about the legal issues beforehand, he does not know the facts until he reads this statement. Second, law and legal principles are designed to produce fair and socially useful results when applied to *facts*. This fundamental aim of law lurks always in the mind of the judge. If the application of the given legal principle produces a result deemed unfair by the judge, he will wish to study carefully whether indeed the given principle was truly intended to apply to the particular facts before him.

This initial statement of facts should not be confused with any argument about the facts to be advanced in the subsequent section of the brief. By this initial statement, counsel attempts to state accurately and with reasonable fairness the material facts, without failing to disclose those which are contested. The attempt is to summarize, without too much unnecessary detail, only those facts that are most cogent and persuasive, without omitting unfavorable circumstances, so that the court may understand the basic factual background of the legal issues. Accurate reference to the transcript or appendix should be provided to allow the court immediately to verify counsel's facts as stated. Counsel's selection, arrangement, and emphasis of these facts, if without sacrifice of accuracy, may readily suggest to the court how the legal issues presented should be decided.

WHAT THEY SAID

John W. Davis and Frederick B. Wiener are numbered among America's greatest appellate advocates. Davis said:

> [I]t cannot be too often emphasized that in an appellate court the statement of the facts is not merely a part of the argument, it is more often than not the argument itself. * * * The court wants above all things to learn what are the facts which give rise to the call upon its energies; for in many, probably in most, cases when the facts are clear there is no great trouble about the law. Davis, The Argument of an Appeal, 28 A.B.A.J. 895, 896 (1940).

Wiener has said:

> The real importance of facts is that courts want to do substantial justice and that they are sensitive to the "equities." Consequently the objective of the advocate must be so to write his statement that the court will want to decide the case his way after reading just that portion of the brief. Wiener, Essentials of an Effective Appellate Brief, 17 Geo.Wash.L.Rev. 143, 145 (1949). See also, to the same effect, K. Llewellyn, The Common Law Tradition: Deciding Appeals 238 (1960).

Judicial writers agree on the importance of the statement of facts, among them Justice Robert H. Jackson:

> It may sound paradoxical, but most contentions of law are won or lost on the facts. The facts often incline a judge to one side or the other. Jackson, Advocacy Before the Supreme Court, 37 A.B.A.J. 801, 803 (1951).

Chief Judge Irving R. Kaufman of the Federal Second Circuit has said:

> Let the narrative of facts tell a compelling story. The facts are, almost without exception, the heart of the case on appeal. * * * The

facts generate the force that impels the judge's will in your direction. "Appellate Advocacy in the Federal Courts," Address before Association of the Bar of the City of New York (April 21, 1977).

THE ARGUMENT

In the "argument" section of the brief, counsel is a partisan advocate urging the court to adopt his analysis of the legal authorities and his view of the facts. Here, the points of law will be treated consecutively. Succinct headings and subheadings should indicate to the court the thrust of the argument on each point (e.g., "Appellant had notice of the defect and therefore is not a holder in due course"), following which counsel will analyze and argue the legal and factual data in support of each heading. If there are numerous points, a final summary may provide for the court a ready synthesizing review of the arguments covered that point toward counsel's position.

From the court's point of view, the principle of "select and discard" should here apply also. Only truly arguable points should be selected and relied upon; unessential or diversionary points rarely affect the result, and normally they should be discarded.

Generally, a point that goes to the very heart of the case should be argued first. An experienced judge will usually select the strongest issue for study first. But the judge initially may not know what is counsel's strongest issue, unless counsel, based on his knowledge of the facts and his legal research, so directs the court.

When the judge has decided on affirmance or reversal, he usually addresses the appellant's strongest premise first in drafting the opinion. If the judge accepts the premise and decides to reverse, often he need not research or address other points relied upon by the appellant. As a psychological matter, appellant's counsel should force the court early to face head-on his strongest argument; otherwise, the judicial impression of its forcefulness may be lessened, if its study is not reached until after the judge has half-decided on affirmance, having rejected counsel's previous arguments.

In many instances, of course, counsel cannot argue his strongest point first because of reasons of logical priority. He must then set forth his arguments in a logical step-by-step progression, relying upon placement, emphasis, and the "Statement of the Issues" to indicate the greater importance of a particular point. Also, the appellee's order of argument is normally directed by sequential response to the points raised by the appellant; if, however, the appellant has minimized some overriding argument in favor of affirmance, the appellee should likewise emphasize early the forcefulness of his strongest argument. An appellee may safely ignore an illogical sequence of insubstantial arguments, although he should explain why he does so, and he should explain at some point why the appellant's arguments lack merit, rather than ignore them.

The type of argument must of course vary with the type of case and the type of issue. However, counsel should prepare it, as he selected its points and the issues of his appeal, with some knowledge of the tribunal to which the brief is submitted. For example, a Louisiana intermediate court decides many workmen's compensation cases each year; detailed jurisprudential and statutory argument may unnecessarily burden a brief to that court, whereas it might enlighten the Supreme Court of Louisiana, which in this legal area only occasionally issues full-scale opinions. Similarly, there is no point in urging that a court overrule a prior decision if you know that court never overrules decisions. The same court may not be as reluctant to "distinguish" the same prior decision, with identical practical consequences. Some courts, or some panels of a court, are more oriented to technical issues of law or to innovative arguments than are others.

Use Few Citations

About citations: a lawyer should include as few as practical, mainly those of the leading or more recent cases. Also, where possible, citation should be made to decisions of the court that hears the appeal; the judges are more likely to be familiar with them and accept them without additional verifying research. If counsel intends to rely heavily on a particular decision, it is well for him to make the effort to summarize its facts, and to show that the cited case is applicable to the *facts* of the present case. Quotations from the case, if used at all, should be restricted to the relevant sentences. Opposing authorities should be distinguished, not ignored, lest the court feel that counsel cannot answer them.

Blind citation of precedent without functional analysis is of minimal assistance. As Justice Rutledge observed:

> What judges want to know is why this case, or line of cases, should apply to these facts rather than that other line on which the opponent relies with equal certitude, if not certainty. Too often the *why* is left out. Rutledge, The Appellate Brief, 28 A.B.A.J. 251, 253 (1942).

Further, to me, it is always useful and often persuasive to find counsel's position supported by an authoritative treatise or illuminated by law review commentaries and ALR annotations.

Arguments over facts are rarely persuasive if founded solely upon long excerpts of questions and answers from the transcript. The most useful and persuasive technique, if accurately done, is a concise summary of the factual evidence on the issue, including that opposed to counsel's position, with accurate reference to the pages in the transcript that verify these statements. Key phrases or statements, rather than entire dialogues, may usefully be quoted to give flavor and force, if not done out of context. The strongest factual arguments emphasize the commonsense fairness of the client's position, or call into play the undoubted application of settled law; but it is important that, in so arguing, counsel does not distort or ignore contrary facts, however much he evades their forcefulness by explaining their context or supposed lack of weight.

For appropriate cases, such as where the court is essentially concerned with weighing policy values in the selection or creation of a rule with future consequences, I personally would like to see more nondecisional authority. Social statistics of which we may take judicial notice, for instance, sometimes afford data by which to evaluate practical implications of a proposed interpretation. Thus, in deciding whether a personal-injury lawyer violated ethical canons by his occasional advance of small loans to his impoverished client when the latter was beset by financial emergencies, we found to be of some aid the Bureau of Census reports concerning the population's poverty level. Louisiana State Bar Association v. Edwins, 329 So.2d 437, 447 (La.1976). In criminal cases the standard of fairness, or a better interpretation of our own procedural law, may often be formulated with the aid of studies and recommendations founded on both scholarship and practical experience, such as the American Bar Association Standards for Criminal Justice, the American Law Institute Model Code of Pre–Arraignment Procedure, or the National Conference of Commissioners on Uniform State Laws' Model Code of Criminal Procedure.

I have already mentioned the importance of headings and subheadings to clarity and immediate understanding. I should add that charts or tables may inform the judge at a glance of what he could similarly understand only with minutes of reading and of puzzling out words and figures. Complex machines or locales, such as unusual intersections, may likewise be quickly demonstrated or understood by a diagram, where it might take hours for counsel to write (and minutes for the court to read with understanding) words purporting to convey the same information.

Some Other Writings

Before concluding, I should note several publications that treat with much greater detail, with practical illustrations of effective and ineffective technique, effective appellate briefing: G. Rossman, ed., Advocacy and the King's English (1960); E.D. Re, Brief Writing and Oral Argument (4th ed., 1977); and F.B. Wiener, Effective Appellate Advocacy (1950). See also Wiener, Essentials of an Effective Appellate Brief, 17 Geo.Wash.L.Rev. 143 (1949).

In summary, the truly effective appellate brief, from the point of view of the court, is one quite similar to a superior law clerk's memorandum. It contains discussion and analysis and summary of all factual considerations and legal rationales necessary for the decision. Once the contents are verified, through the ready means furnished by accurate citation to the record and published material, the judge ideally should be able to dictate his opinion from the brief, including liberal paraphrasing or plagiarizing of its concise and accurate wording. In serving through his brief as a valued research assistant to the court, counsel has certainly aided the administration of appellate justice, whether his client wins or loses.

I have emphasized my concept of the appellate brief as chiefly a vehicle to enable the judge to understand quickly the issues and facts, disputed or not, of the appeal, and for him most readily to grasp the argument of counsel, in its strengths and weaknesses. I do not, however, imply that the brief's usefulness is negatived by its advocacy. By selection, emphasis, and articulation, counsel properly attempts to persuade the court of the correctness of his client's position, although (if he wishes his brief to be useful to and used by the court) he must do so accurately and with candor about the factual and legal data applicable to the issues of the case. The more clear, concise, complete, and coherent is the brief furnished for the court's use, the more certainly will the brief afford the court access not only to the legal materials furnished by it for decision, but also to counsel's persuasiveness in his brief's contention that the law and the facts demand that his client prevail.

Notes and Questions

1. Judge Tate states that the most effective appellate brief is one that is quite similar to a good memorandum prepared by the judge's law clerk. Does this mean that the brief should be impartial and not advocate the position of the client?

2. Another excellent article written by a federal court of appeals judge is Bright, Appellate Briefwriting: Some "Golden" Rules, 17 Creighton L.Rev. 1069 (1984). For an article written by two former law clerks to court of appeals judges on effective practice in one circuit, see Gerhardt & Martineau, Jr., Reflections on Appellate Practice in the Sixth Circuit, 16 U. Tol. L. Rev. 625 (1985).

R. MARTINEAU, FUNDAMENTALS OF MODERN APPELLATE ADVOCACY

120–31 (1985).

§ 7.14. Who should write the brief

The first question to be confronted when there is a possibility that a brief may have to be filed in an appellate court is who should prepare the brief. This question should be considered as soon as possible so that the person who is supposed to prepare the brief can become familiar with the case before he starts work on it. It is most important that the decision be made before the time for filing the brief begins to run. Typically, a party has only 30 days in which to prepare a brief. This is not very much time for researching, writing, typing, rewriting, checking citations, printing, checking galleys and page proofs, and filing and serving. None of that precious time should be wasted on deciding who is to write.

The choice is usually between the attorney who has tried the case and an attorney who is skilled in appellate practice. In making this decision, the competing factors are knowledge of the facts and issues in the individual case and knowledge and experience in appellate practice. Unfortunately, the two seldom go hand in hand. Too often the attorney who is handling the case is skilled neither as a trial attorney nor as an appellate attorney. Although the deficiencies in the skills of trial attorneys have been commented upon extensively and steps have been taken to correct the situation, a similar concern has not been expressed for the skills of appellate attorneys. In large part this is because the trial is the most dramatic part of the entire judicial process, and proceedings in the appellate court, particularly the written briefs, are thought to be dull and dry.

Until recently few attorneys were exposed to trial skills courses in law school, but almost every attorney participated in law school appellate moot court competitions. To the extent an attorney believes that an appellate brief involves primarily legal research, he assumes he has been adequately prepared to write an appellate brief by his legal education. The result is that almost every attorney thinks that he can handle an appeal without difficulty, even if he has never done so previously. Most attorneys are unlikely to have had much appellate experience, because the ratio between the number of cases disposed of in the trial courts and the number of appeals taken is such that few attorneys except for those who serve in the appellate divisions of public prosecutor offices or legal aid agencies are likely to have written many appellate briefs. In a particular geographical area there are usually one or more attorneys who are skilled appellate advocates and consideration should be given to employing one of them to handle the appeal or at least to assist in preparation of the brief.

A far too common practice among busy trial attorneys is to leave the task of brief writing to either the newest attorney in the office or to a law student working as a law clerk in the attorney's office. This practice is probably premised on the theory that law students are as well or better equipped than trial attorneys to do the research and writing necessary in the preparation of a brief.

Nothing could be more inimical to the preparation of an effective appellate brief than this attitude. As will be seen in the remainder of this chapter, effective handling of an appeal requires as much knowledge of the facts of a case and as many specialized skills as those necessary to try a case effectively. Ideally, the attorney who should write the brief is the one who best combines these two attributes. Realistically, this ideal is seldom achieved. The balance that must be struck will vary from case to case. All that can be said is that the person who decides who will write the brief should be aware of the importance of the decision and of the factors to be weighed in making it. The decision should not be made by default, but should be carefully thought out and made only after all the competing factors have been considered.

While choosing between the trial attorney and an appellate specialist to write the brief is not a problem in most appellate moot court competitions or other appellate advocacy programs, these programs have another practice which create a special problem. Usually, in these programs students work in teams of two and the brief writing is divided between them either on the basis of issue or sections of the brief. A good brief must be a single, unified document with all of its parts woven together so that they all lead to a decision in favor of the client of the author of the brief. The likelihood is not high that two law students who may not know each other well or at all at the beginning of the brief writing can in a short period of time develop a working relationship that will enable them to write a truly effective brief. While there is nothing wrong with having more than one person work on a brief, only one person should ultimately be responsible for the final product, including the selection of the issues to be raised, the arguments to be made, the statement of facts, and the final editing. This should dictate that if a multi-member team is utilized, one person should be designated as the lead writer with final responsibility for making the brief read as though it came from the pen of a single person.

§ 7.15. Overriding principle of simplicity

The law student and the appellate attorney must develop an overall approach to or philosophy of brief writing. The author's experience as a law clerk to an appellate judge, an appellate attorney, appellate court administrator, and observer of the appellate process has convinced him that the one principle that should dominate the preparation of the appellate brief is simplicity—simplicity in both substance and style.

Simplicity in substance means that the number and kind of issues presented to the court should be as few and as uncomplicated as the attorney can make them. Simplicity in style means that the principles of good writing style demanding brevity and short, simple declarative sentences should be closely followed.

Simplicity in substance and style have long been characteristics of a good brief. Articles on effective brief writing have always urged that the brief contain no extraneous matter, that the issues be kept to a minimum, and that good grammar and a forceful style be used. The importance of this advice is now, however, far greater than ever before. In an earlier era when both judges and attorneys could operate at a more relaxed pace, the submission of a high quality brief was the mark of a true professional but not necessarily crucial to the outcome of the case. Today, the sheer volume of the cases that an appellate court must decide and the limited time that can be devoted to an individual case mean that the effect of the brief is far greater than ever before. A brief that adheres to the principle of simplicity in substance and style is no longer just a luxury to be enjoyed by those who can afford the best appellate advocate, but an absolute necessity for any litigant if he is to have his side of the case receive the full attention of the appellate court. The simple fact is that today judges must read so many briefs and decide so many cases that, unless the principal points of a brief can be absorbed very quickly and on first reading, the brief is likely to have little effect upon the decision. If the essential point the appellate attorney is trying to make is buried among a whole range of issues or in language that is convoluted, obscure, or oratorical in nature, there is a good chance it may be overlooked. Even if discovered, its full impact may be lost because of its lack of clarity. Few things exasperate a judge more than not being able to ascertain the point the attorney is making or to have to struggle to find out why the point is relevant.

A widely known principle of the real estate business is that there are three main factors that affect the value of property; (1) location; (2) location; and (3) location. The same approach can be taken to effective brief writing—the three most important attributes of an effective brief are (1) simplicity; (2) simplicity; and (3) simplicity. If the law student or appellate attorney keeps that principle in mind, he will most likely write a brief that will be of service to his real or hypothetical client, the appellate judges, and his professional reputation.

The principle of simplicity is just as difficult if not more so to follow and apply in appellate moot court competitions or in appellate advocacy programs as it is in actual practice. The law student is usually dealing in an area of law in which he or she has little expertise and has not had the benefit of dealing with the case in the trial court. Similarly, the law student has had little or no persuasive writing experience. It is to teach the skill of making things simple—both in substance and style—that moot court competitions and other appellate advocacy programs should exist. It is for this reason that only persons who are skilled in brief writing should teach or supervise the programs and competitions. Most intramural appellate moot court competitions are, unfortunately, supervised by instructors in their first year out of law school or third-year law students. Few if any of these instructors have ever written a real appellate brief or ever been in an appellate courtroom. At most, they have had law review or moot court experience under the direction of persons with no more qualifications than they have. Appellate skills training, particularly brief writing and oral argument, require instructors with the same level of training and experience demanded for trial practice or any other professional skill. This is another area in which major changes are required in the manner in which appellate advocacy is taught in the law school.

§ 7.16. Compliance with appellate rules

The requirements for appellate briefs have been reviewed in §§ 7.4–7.10, supra. Most appellate rules are themselves sufficiently clear—or consultation with the appellate court clerk's office will make them so—that compliance with them is relatively easy. Nevertheless, it is surprising how often appellate briefs do not comply with the rules or customs of the appellate court. Although the failure to comply with a technical rule usually has no major adverse effect, each minor deviation may have a more subtle, negative impact. If the cover of the brief is the wrong color it may be mislaid by the judge and not looked at when the judge wants to check something. If the statement of facts does not contain the appendix or record reference supporting a particular fact, the judge may not find it in the record and thus may not accept the fact as stated in the brief. If the portions of the brief are not in the correct order, the judge may overlook a significant issue or argument.

Even without any specific harm, the judge may infer from failure to comply with the rules that the attorney is not careful in what he does, so that his statements on the law or the facts are suspect.

As an advocate, the appellate attorney's principal task is one of persuasion. To be effective, the appellate attorney must, among other things, create in the appellate judges a feeling of confidence in himself or herself. One of the easiest ways to help build that confidence is by demonstrating that the appellate attorney both knows the rules and abides by them. This same principle is, of course, just as applicable in appellate moot court competitions and appellate advocacy programs as in appellate practice.

§ 7.17. Guidelines, generally

In addition to the overriding principles of simplicity and compliance with the rules, the appellate attorney should keep in mind general principles of persuasion as he prepares the brief. These guidelines, unlike the specific ones relating to each section of the brief and discussed in § 7.18, infra, are applicable not only to the brief but in most instances to oral argument as well. Numerous authors have set down similar guidelines. Whether denominated as rules, maxims, essentials, or commandments, these guidelines are similar in content. The similarity should not be surprising because in the art of persuasion there is little new to be learned, given the constancy of human nature.

The appellate brief is merely one form of persuasion. It has its own special features because it operates in a special environment. What is set forth here is, consequently, not some new approach to appellate advocacy, but merely a restatement of points made previously by many others. These guidelines are derived primarily from articles written by appellate judges rather than by appellate lawyers. As John W. Davis has stated, if you want to know how to catch a fish, the best one to ask is the fish, not the fisherman.

§ 7.18. Understand roles of appellate judge and appellate attorney

Before the appellate attorney can understand his own role in the appellate process, he must first understand the role of the appellate judge. The judge is the focus of the appellate process. It is he who must be persuaded. It is he who makes the decision that determines whether the appellate attorney's client will win or lose.

The first thing to understand is that in every case the appellate judge has two primary concerns. His task is to render a decision that will simultaneously do individual justice between the parties in the case and be consistent with the demands of the law. The appellate judge wants to "do justice" but at the same time he knows that the decision in the case will serve as precedent for other cases. He is bound not only by the facts and the issues in the record before him, but also by the laws of the jurisdiction in which he sits as contained in constitutional and statutory provisions and the prior opinions of his and superior courts. The judge thus must be convinced that the result the appellate attorney is seeking not only does justice between the parties but is also either consistent with prior law or establishes a rule that will have a similar result in other cases. The type of function the appellate court is being asked to perform—error correction or law development, as discussed in Chapter 1, supra—is relevant here.

The role of the appellate attorney is determined by the role of the appellate judge. The attorney must show the appellate judge both why justice demands that the court rule in his client's favor and how a decision in his client's favor is consistent, or at least not inconsistent, with the law as it is or should be. The attorney must show the appellate court how it can fit a favorable ruling for his client into the general pattern of cases raising similar issues and must show that such a decision would be valid precedent in future cases.

The function of the brief in this process is to serve as the vehicle through which the attorney communicates to the judge how the facts and the law can be woven together for a favorable result. The traditional view of the appellate attorney as an advocate has included the notion that the brief must be a highly partisan document in which both the facts and the law are painted in black and white terms and which suggests that only a fool or a blackguard could see any merit in the opposing party's case. Writings by the most perceptive appellate judges suggest that this approach to the brief is no longer correct, if it ever was. Judge Albert Tate, Jr., now of the U.S. Court of Appeals for the Fifth Circuit and formerly of the Louisiana Supreme Court, has expressed a substantially different concept of the brief. He points out that a properly written brief can be an invaluable tool for the judge. If the judge has concluded that he can rely upon a brief, it will be used and referred to constantly by the judge. Judge Tate refers to such a brief as the judge's companion. Obviously, a brief used in this way has enormous influence on the ultimate decision and greatly enhances the chances of success.

How can this objective be accomplished? It is not by being the ultimate partisan, claiming everything and conceding nothing. It is, rather, by making sure that the judge understands the issues and what are the significant facts and legal authorities. The brief should be viewed not so much as a partisan effort but as a contribution to the appellate process. Judge Tate has gone so far as to state that "the truly effective appellate brief, from the point of view of the court, is one quite similar to a superior law clerk's memorandum. . . . Once the contents are verified, . . . the judge ideally should be able to dictate his opinion from the brief, including liberal paraphrasing or plagiarizing of its concise and accurate wording. . . . The more clear, concise, complete, and coherent is the brief furnished for the court's use, the more certainly will the brief afford the court access not only to the legal materials furnished by it for decision, but also to counsel's persuasiveness in his briefs contentions that the law and the facts demand that his client prevail.''

It may seem peculiar in an appellate advocacy course or appellate moot court competition to urge law students to use restraint in their advocacy on behalf of their hypothetical client. The students in other courses are being imbued with the philosophy that they must do everything legally and morally possible to advance the cause of their clients, and the moot court competition is usually the first opportunity to demonstrate just how zealous they can be on behalf of a client. What the students must learn right at the beginning, however, is that the most effective advocacy is almost never the advocacy that goes beyond the fair statement, the reasoned plea, the attempt to be fair. Excessive zeal is almost always counterproductive, especially in an appellate court. If law students fail to learn this in their initial efforts at advocacy in moot court competitions, it will be learned later at the expense of their clients.

§ 7.19. Develop confidence in appellate attorney and brief

The objective in preparing the brief is to develop a document that the appellate judge can use and rely on in the same manner as he would upon a law clerk's memorandum. This objective can be achieved only if the judge has absolute confidence in the accuracy of every statement in the brief. The appellate attorney thus must prepare the brief with meticulous care to ensure that statements of fact and law are accurate, that statements requiring documentation or citation have it, and that the documentation and citation are accurate and correct. Over-statements, excessive partisanship, inaccurate statements, statements that cannot be supported, hyperbole, attacks on the integrity of the trial judge or opposing counselor their clients, arguments that on their face are unsound, a scatter gun approach to allegations of error, misrepresentations, sloppiness, and the like, individually or in combination, will undermine the confidence an appellate judge has in the attorney and the brief he has filed. The judge will conclude that the attorney and his brief are unreliable. This type of brief will be read once and put aside, not to be consulted again. Such a brief may well do more harm than no brief at all.

A recurring issue of legal ethics is whether adverse precedent should be brought to the attention of the court. The Code of Professional Responsibility dictates that only binding precedent in the appellate court's jurisdiction must be brought to its attention. Effective brief writing principles dictate that any precedent, binding or not, that the appellate court may find relevant should be brought to its attention. If it is not, the appellate judge will necessarily conclude that the appellate attorney either has not been thorough in his research or is attempting to hide an adverse opinion. In either event, the judge will decide that he cannot rely on the brief and will look elsewhere for the basis for his decision. Failure to deal with an adverse authority also means loss of the opportunity to show why the authority should not be followed or does not require a decision against the appellate attorney's client, an opportunity that should never be ignored.

In appellate moot court competitions, the brief will not, of course, be used in the same manner as in an actual appellate case. The role of the judge in an actual appellate case is to decide the case and to write an opinion giving the reasons for the decision based on the facts in the case and the applicable law. The judge will have as much time as he wants to study the briefs, examine the record, and to research the law. He will be aided by law clerks, and his work will be subject to the scrutiny of two other judges. When filed it will be reviewed by the attorneys in the case and if published will be open to critical analysis by the bench and bar generally, including legal scholars and law reviews. All of these pressures will force the judge to perform the judicial task as well as possible. The judge will, consequently, rely on a brief only if he is certain he can safely do so. On the other hand, the judge in a moot court competition reads the briefs only to prepare for oral argument while other persons grade the brief against moot court standards. No one is concerned with deciding a case or writing an opinion nor, of course, in using the briefs in connection with either. This does not mean, however, that the moot court brief should be any different in form or style than an actual appellate brief. The whole purpose of the moot court exercise is, or should be, to develop the brief writing skills the law student will use in practice. The moot court brief should, consequently, adhere to the same standards for simplicity and developing confidence in the writer of the brief as an actual appellate brief. A well designed moot court competition will include checks on the accuracy of statements made in the briefs as to both the facts and the law to test this aspect of brief writing. In an appellate advocacy course where the briefs are written for the instructor rather than a moot court competition, the instructor will be more familiar than the students with the facts and law of the subject matter of the brief and any statement or non-statement that would diminish the confidence of a judge in the brief will be readily apparent to the instructor and should be reflected in the grading of the brief.

§ 7.20. Brevity

Brevity in brief writing is one of those ideals observed more in the breach than in the observance. Everyone agrees in theory that brevity in brief writing is a virtue. The reality is, most appellate attorneys either cannot write in a succinct style or, if they can, think that the particular appeals they are working on are exceptions to the general rule. As a defense to overly long briefs, most appellate courts have imposed page limitations on briefs. Even so, many appellate attorneys use the full number of pages when fewer will suffice, or ask for an allowance of additional pages when the permitted number should be adequate. The excessive length of many briefs is a reflection of the lack of importance that many appellate attorneys place on the brief. It is a generally accepted principle that it takes longer to write something short than something long. It is safe to say that the amount of time devoted to a brief usually has a reverse relation-ship to its length. Excessive length suggests to the appellate judge that the attorney did not think the appeal important enough to warrant the additional time required to revise the brief and make it as concise as possible.

The effect of volume on the appellate process has now made brevity in brief writing not just a desirable goal but an absolute requirement. Appellate judges in most jurisdictions simply have too many briefs to read to tolerate a brief that is anything but brief. If the brief is too long it will not be read carefully, and if it is not read carefully the points made in it may not be appreciated by the appellate court.

Brevity in brief writing is not a goal that has a high priority in most appellate moot court competitions, given their structure. In view of the heightened importance of brevity in modern appellate practice, this aspect of brief writing should become one of the highest priorities and this should be reflected in the bases for the grading of briefs.

3.   SPECIFIC SECTIONS OF THE BRIEF

a.   Summary of argument

R. ALDISERT, WINNING ON APPEAL
183–86 (2d ed. 2003).*

§ 13.1   Overview

In 1994, the Federal Rules of Appellate Procedure were amended to make mandatory where theretofore had been only a suggestion. The new amendment at Rule 28(a)(8) now provides that briefs of the appellant and appellee must contain:

> a summary of the argument, which must contain a succinct, clear, and accurate statement of the arguments made in the body of the brief, and which must not merely repeat the argument headings.

In earlier editions I referred to old Rule 28(a)(5) and commented: "Although this language is permissive, the good brief writer will consider it mandatory." I cannot overemphasize that every appellate brief should contain a summary of the argument even if your specific state rules may not require it. In many ways, the summary of the argument is the most import part of the brief.

To understand my strident recommendation, you must recall the manner in which appellate judges study briefs. They generally read the appellants' statement of issues first. If the trial court has written an opinion, they then read the court's treatment of those issues. The next step, which is crucial, is to turn to the appellant's summary of the argument—if there is one—and then to the appellee's summary. This provides the "flavor" of the case.

The summary is critical because it gives the reader a concise preview of the argument. The summary should be crafted so as to allow the judge

* Copyright © 2003, National Institute for Trial Advocacy. Reprinted by permission. All rights reserved. Further reproduction is prohibited.

to construct a practical outline of a memorandum. Alas, this often does not occur, because the brief writer either has not prepared a summary or has slapped one together without the thought necessary to create a statement that is both comprehensive and concise.

Preparing an effective summary may be the brief writer's most challenging and most important task. Former Mississippi Supreme Court Justice James L. Robertson remarks:

> I think the most important part of the brief is the Summary of the Argument. I invariably read it first. It is almost like the opening statement in a trial. From clear and plausible argument summary, I often get an inclination to affirm or reverse that rises almost to the dignity of a (psychologically) rebuttable presumption.

> I do not mean to denigrate the importance of a fully developed and technically sound argument. But I read the subsequent argument in a "show me" frame of mind, testing whether it confirms my impression from the summary of the argument.

Loyola School Dean David W. Burcham, one of my former clerks who went on to clerk for Justice Byron White, and to practice law with a large Los Angeles firm before donning academic robes, offers these comments: "A brief writer should understand that the summary or argument will likely create the first, and perhaps last, impression of the Court toward the legal merits of the client's case. It should be the structural centerpiece of the entire brief.

§ 13.2 The Critical Opening Paragraph

Readers of appellate briefs tend to be very busy. As a result, they have highly selective reading habits. They need and expect to know what a given case is about, and the opening of the summary of argument should tell them immediately. Detective mysteries and narratives with O. Henry-style surprise endings have their place—in fiction. But apply these techniques to brief writing and you risk losing your audience. In reading a summary, judges are impatient. They want to know up front what the case is about. They do not want to wait until the end. With the number of appeals constantly increasing, it is important that the brief writer give an early signal to the reader. That signal is the opening or orientation of the summary of the argument.

The introduction of your summary—the *exordium* in the schema of the rhetoricians—must let the reader know, in few sentences, the scope, theme, content, and outcome of the brief. It sets the stage for the discussion to follow. It dispatches your argument to the reader at once in succinct, concise, and minimal terms. It describes the equitable heart of the appeal.

The critical portion of your summary is the orientation sentence or sentences that announce the theme of your argument. To craft the theme or focus on your argument takes skill and concentration. It is the *first* thing you write and the *last* thing you rewrite. It is the dominant argument of maximum potency that must be compatible with ruling case

law or consistent with known policy considerations of the judicial tribunal before which you appear. The theme should be all-inclusive and
subsume the various points to be discussed in the brief. It should be
aphoristic, in a sense of being a short, pithy, pointed sentence containing
some important legal precept, one that Cardozo, in a related context,
described as "a brief and almost sententious statement at the outset of
the problem to be attacked." If you are proceeding on alternative
theories, you necessarily will have multiple themes.

Justice William A. Bablitch of the Wisconsin Supreme Court reminded us that, as a basic principle of good writing, "a reader should not be
forced to confront details before the writer has provided a framework for
understanding." Thus, the introductory paragraph must alert the reader
to the upcoming issues, their importance and any conclusions to be
drawn. You may have the opportunity to write an effective introductory
paragraph in other parts of your brief, depending on the court's rules,
but it is essential that you prepare one as the introduction to your
argument summary and repeat it in your first point of the argument.
Justice Bablitch aptly observes:

> It is not easy to write a good introductory paragraph. It takes great
> effort, but it is time well spent. A properly written introduction
> makes the rest of the brief-writing task comparatively easy. If you
> are unable to write a cogent, succinct, encompassing introduction,
> you probably do not have a solid grasp of the subject matter.

> The fundamental question is, "What does the reader need to know
> to decide the final resolution?" If the introduction offers context
> before detail, then the reader is able to discern the important from
> the unimportant.

Appellate lawyers are professional writers. Whether they write well
or poorly, they write for a very discriminating audience, an audience of
professional readers of legal text. By force of circumstance, everything
the brief writer does must be expressed in words, preferably with a high
degree of clarity and precision. Other writers may have the assistance of
elegant typography and graphic illustration. The appellate lawyer is
armed only with the pen.

Judges crave an immediate sense of overview. At the beginning of a
brief, they are not interested in hearing all the details of the case. They
want to know what kind of case this is and what issues the brief
addresses. Only then are they prepared to digest, in Cardozo's words, "a
fuller statement of the facts, rigidly pared down, however, in almost
every case, to those that are truly essential as opposed to those that are
decorative and adventitious. If these are presented with due proportion
and selection, our conclusion ought to follow so naturally and inevitably
as almost to prove itself.

If you have trouble expressing the theme of the brief in the introductory pages of your summary of argument, look to West Publishing
Company's headnote writers for guidance. These people are highly
professional; they are trained to describe an issue as comprehensively as

possible, with minimal wordage. If you still have trouble, look to the *exordium* or introductory paragraph of judicial opinions written by those judges who spend much care in fashioning the opening. A sampling of some excellent opening sentences from United States Supreme Court justices in volume 484 of the United States Reports in 1987 discloses how one can combine tight writing with excellent orientation.

b. Tables of contents and authorities

R. MARTINEAU, FUNDAMENTALS OF MODERN APPELLATE ADVOCACY
140–55 (1985).

Rule 28 of the Federal Rules of Appellate Procedure and most other appellate rules require a table of contents and a table of authorities at the beginning of the brief. Most appellate attorneys refer to this section as a table of contents only, thereby misstating the principal purpose of this portion of the brief.

The table of contents is, of course, the simplest of all, indicating the page at which each of the five sections of the brief begins. This table is of marginal use to the appellate judge because the brief is short and the order in which the sections appear is fixed by appellate rule. The table of contents is important for only two reasons—the rule requires it and the judge expects it. It is highly unlikely that a sanction will be imposed upon the appellate attorney or his client for failing to include a table of contents. The failure to observe the rule, however, may create the appearance of not knowing or not caring about the requirements, thereby weakening the court's confidence in the appellate attorney and his brief. The same point can be made about the accuracy of the table of contents. The table of contents can also serve as a check to ensure that the sections of the brief are in the order called for by the applicable rule.

The table of authorities is, however, far more likely to be used by the appellate judge and thus far more important. There are three subdivisions in a table of authorities—cases, statutes, and other authorities. Cases are arranged alphabetically. While no order is specified for the statutes and other authorities, an alphabetical arrangement should also be used. Any other order will simply create confusion.

The appellate judge may use the table of authorities for various purposes. He may wish to compare the comments in one party's brief or a case or statute with those in the other party's brief. Or believing that a particular case or statute is relevant to the pending appeal, he might look in the table of authorities to locate in the brief the discussion on the case or statute. He may also use the table of authorities during the opinion writing stage of the appellate process to cite or quote what the brief says about a case, or one of the authorities used in the brief. He may also use the table simply for purposes of locating the authority in the law library or writing out the correct citation form. A complete and accurate table of authorities will encourage the judge to make constant use of the brief. The objective, as stated by Judge Tate of the Fifth Circuit, is to have the brief become the companion of the judge, for the more the judge uses the brief, the more likely he is to be influenced by what is said in it.

The table of contents and table of authorities can be prepared only after the rest of the brief is completed. It should be prepared by a law clerk, paralegal, or competent secretary. Given the premium on accuracy, however, it is essential for the appellate attorney to review carefully both tables to ensure that they are in proper form and, above all, accurate.

c. Statement of issues presented for review; when to prepare

All portions of the brief—the statement of the case, the statement of facts, the argument and the conclusion—should be prepared in light of and in support of the issues that the appellate attorney wishes the appellate court to consider. It follows, therefore, that the first portion of the brief that should be prepared is the statement of issues. The statement of the case and the statement of facts must in particular provide the information necessary for the appellate court to be able to review the issues presented in the brief. It is important, consequently, that the appellate attorney have not only a general idea of the issues he wishes to raise in the appellate court but that he have them precisely formulated before preparing any other portion of the brief.

Another approach to brief writing suggests that the statement of issues should not be prepared until after the statement of the case, the statement of facts, and the argument have been written. Under this approach, it is the remainder of the brief that determines the precise statement of the issues. The author does not agree with this order of preparation. Before any portion of the brief is drafted, the brief writer must be completely familiar with the record and generally familiar with the relevant law. This familiarity should enable the brief writer to ascertain those issues he wishes to raise and to prepare an initial draft of them. These draft issues can then give focus to the preparation of the other sections of the brief. As these other sections are written, it may develop that some modifications should be made in the statement of an issue to reflect a more accurate reading of the record or assessment of the state of the law. The writing of the brief should begin, however, with a draft of the statement of the issues.

d. Number of issues

One of the universally accepted principles of effective brief writing is to keep the number of issues raised to a minimum. This is another principle that is violated as often as it is observed. Most appellate attorneys appear to lack the confidence necessary to focus their briefs on one or two main issues and forget the rest. This is, understandably, even more true for law students. They apparently take the position that because they do not know which issue of many may be found to involve reversible error and are afraid of making the wrong choice, they will discuss all of the potential issues, hoping that lightning may strike at least one of them. Another justification for including many issues rather than focusing on one or two is that the appellate court may conclude that while no one error of the trial court justifies a reversal, the cumulative effect of many small errors may do so.

Neither of these approaches has real merit. The result of either is to convince the appellate court that the appellate attorney has no real confidence in any of the issues he is raising and merely hopes he will be lucky. The principle of limitation of issues has always been valid and is especially so today. The appellate judge simply does not have the time that is required to spend on each case if he is presented with a whole range of issues and asked to discover one of them that may justify a reversal. Because the appellate judge relies upon the attorneys to identify critical issues, the only effect of a brief that raises multiple issues is to make the appellate judge impatient with the attorney and to make it less likely that the judge will find anything of merit in the brief.

How many issues are too many? Ideally, the brief should raise only one issue. If this is simply not possible, an absolute maximum should be three issues, presented in descending order of importance. To raise more than three issues reduces the effectiveness of each. A brief which contains more than three issues is not an exercise in appellate advocacy, but merely a throwing of the dice in the hope that something in the brief might find a receptive mind on the appellate court. That is not advocacy; it is, rather, a confession that the attorney does not know how to be an advocate.

e. Framing of issues

Although those who write on appellate practice are unanimously in favor of limiting the number of issues in a brief, there is far less agreement on how the issues should be framed. Authorities do agree that the issues should not be framed too generally or too narrowly, but that advice is of little help in practice.

One aspect of the appellate process to keep in mind in preparing the statement of issues is the dual interest of the appellate judge—his desire to do justice in the individual case and at the same time to follow or establish principles of law that are applicable generally and not just to the instant case. This dual interest suggests that the issues should be framed so that they incorporate both the individual aspects of the particular case and the general aspects that make the issue one of broader application.

This principle can be illustrated by example. Assume that the main issue in an automobile accident case is the admissibility of evidence relating to the defendant's driving behavior before the accident. A common formulation of the question would be: "Did the trial court err in admitting [or not admitting] evidence relating to the defendant's prior driving behavior?" This formulation is poor for several reasons. The introductory words "Did the trial court err" are unnecessary—the issue in an appeal is always whether there was an error by the trial court. The phrase "evidence relating to the defendant's driving behavior" is too broad because it does not identify those factors that will determine the admissibility of the evidence—the type of driving behavior and when and where it occurred. Thus if the driver was driving at a high rate of speed three blocks from the scene of the accident and two minutes before it occurred, the question should be: "Is testimony that a person involved in an automobile accident was driving in excess of the speed limit two minutes prior to the accident three blocks away from where it occurred admissible?" Because this formulation presents the issue in a general form but also includes the particulars, the appellate judge knows what the parties are fighting about and what he should be looking for as he reads each section of the brief. Other details could be added to the statement of the issue if they are in the record such as the extent to which the speed was excessive (3 or 30 miles per hour), the similarity between the location of the accident and that of the observed speeding (highway or residential street), the type of witness (policeman or 12–year-old child) which may affect the admissibility. Details such as the name of the witness, the name of the street, the type of car, and the like should be included only if they may affect the decision of the appellate court.

It is sometimes suggested that the appellate attorney should frame the issue so that it will suggest the desired answer. It is very doubtful that any attempt to color the statement of the issue can be successful and it is far more likely to do harm. If at all possible the appellate court wants the parties to agree on what the issue is so that the focus of the parties and the court can be on what the answer to the question should be, not on what the question is. The best formulation of the issue by a party is one that is so fair and so accurate that both the opposing parties and the appellate court have no alternative but to accept it. The worst thing that can happen is for the court to accept the other party's statement of the issue or to make up its own. If either occurs it means that the brief of the party whose formulation of the issue is rejected is addressed to an issue different from the one being considered by the appellate court. In such a circumstance, the value of the brief is greatly reduced if not eliminated.

The importance of the framing of the issues cannot be overemphasized. How the judges perceive the issues in the case will to a large extent determine how the case will be resolved. Selecting the principal issue in the case and framing it properly deter-mines which facts are important as well as which statutes, rules, and cases are controlling. It is with the selection and the framing of the issues that the art of advocacy becomes of crucial significance. It is, consequently, the skill that requires substantial attention by both the instructor and the student. Substantial time should be spent in any appellate advocacy program in the drafting and redrafting of issues. Examples can be found in briefs filed in any appellate court or in any appellate opinion. Most helpful would be to have the entire class participate in the drafting of an issue as part of an in-class exercise. This should then be followed by assigning another issue to each member of the class to draft and submit separately with the instructor then demonstrating in class the proper formulation of the issue.

In developing the statement of the issues, it is important to remember the relationship between the statement and the argument. The issue should be framed in such a way that the heading of the companion portion of the argument is simply the answer to the question posed in the statement of the issue. This will be discussed in § 7.38 infra.

f. Statement of case

The next portion of the brief is designated as the statement of the case. Many jurisdictions separate the statement of the case from the statement of facts, but FRAP 28(a)(3) and some states include both under the statement of the case heading. The two will be treated separately here because of their basically different nature and purpose.

The statement of the case includes "the nature of the case, the course of proceedings, and its disposition in the court below." FRAP 28(c)(3). All that is required is an outline of the procedural history of the case in the trial court so that the appellate judge can tell at a glance how the case got before him. The statement of the case is nothing more than the principal events in the case as reflected in the docket entries put in narrative form.

The two problems presented to the appellate attorney in preparing the statement of the case is how much detail to include and in what order to set forth the information. A correct but unhelpful description of the amount of detail to include is "enough but not too much." The best approach for the brief writer is to try to put himself in the place of the appellate judge and include in the statement the information about the procedural history of the case that he would want to know if he had to decide the issues presented by the statement of issues. With one major exception, the best presentation is chronological: that is, the information should be arranged in the order in which it developed as reflected in the docket entries. There is however, one critical exception to this principle: the first sentence of the statement of the case should state what the appellate judge is most interested in—what is being appealed. Thus the first sentence should recite that this is an appeal, the judgment or order appealed from, the date it was entered, the court in which it was entered, and the relief granted by the judgment. Thus an appeal by a defendant of a judgment against him would read: .'This is an appeal from a judgment entered July 1, 1983, by the United States District Court for the Northern District of Illinois (Eastern Division) for $100,000 against the defendant—appellant Jones Corporation." An appeal of a judgment against a plaintiff would read: "This is an appeal from a judgment entered July 1, 1983, by the United States District Court for the District of Maryland dismissing a complaint by the plaintiff—appellant Thomas Smith seeking damages and a permanent injunction." Reference to the opposing party need be included only if there is more than one.

This type of statement gives the appellate judge the heart of the appeal and the frame of reference for everything else in the brief in its most basic form. It also forces the appellate attorney to focus on the essential nature of the appeal and what the dispute between the appellant and appellee is all about. In the absence of unusual circumstances, all of the information should be contained in a single sentence.

The remainder of the statement should contain the chronological narrative. It should begin with the complaint, giving the date of the filing, the names of the parties and their status in the trial court, the nature of the complaint, and the relief sought. Ordinarily this is too much information for one sentence. It should not give the basic facts out of which the dispute arose, that is the function of the statement of facts. An example would be: "This case began with the filing on August 15, 1979, of a complaint by the plaintiff—appellant Steven Smith against Jones Corporation, the defendant—appellee. The complaint alleged that Smith was injured as a result of his use of an electric toaster manufactured by Jones Corporation. It alleged that the toaster was defectively designed and claimed $500,000 in damages."

How much detail to include about what transpired between the filing of the complaint and the entry of the judgment appealed from will depend upon the issues raised upon appeal. If there is an issue concerning discovery, then the procedural details as to discovery and the dispute over it should be given including the type of discovery sought, the objection to it, and the ruling of the trial court. If the issue relates to the admissibility of evidence at the trial, then all that it is necessary to say about discovery is that it was conducted. The statement would then indicate when the trial began and give details as to how the dispute arose at the trial.

A difficult problem is whether to include the date of any event referred to. Dates should be included, of course, if the time when something happened is significant to the appeal, such as whether a motion was timely. Dates are also helpful in putting major events into a chronological context, even though the dates are not significant to the appeal. Three dates that should always be given are the date the complaint was filed, the date of the judgment, and the date the notice of appeal was filed.

The length of the statement of the case will vary depending upon the complexity of the case. It should, as with the entire brief, be no longer than necessary to give the appellate judge what he needs to know to understand the remainder of the brief.

The statement of the case should ordinarily end with a recital of the filing of the notice of appeal, including the date on which it was filed. Events which occurred after the filing of the notice of appeal should be included only if they are relevant to the appeal, for example, a dispute over the record or the intervention of a new party.

If the appellate attorney was also the trial attorney, he will usually be so familiar with the case that he may unconsciously assume that everyone else including the appellate judges are just as knowledgeable as he is about the case. He must force himself to remember that the appellate judge will know only as much of the case as is set forth in the briefs. The information is, of course, available in the docket entries, but the attorney's objective should always be to present enough information so that the judge can read the brief without having to turn to the appendix, the record, or the brief of the other party to obtain some procedural fact about the case.

The statement of the case more than any other section of the brief should be as fair and as objective as possible. Ideally the statements of the case by the parties should be identical. Neither the appellant nor the appellee should try to obtain any advantage out of its statement of the case. The appellate judge will resent an effort to color the statement of the case to favor one party or the other and any such attempt will simply back-fire.

g. Statement of facts, generally

Another point on which authorities on brief writing are unanimous is that although every portion of the brief is important, the statement of facts is the heart of the brief upon which all of the other parts depend and to which they are related. If no part of the brief can be downgraded by describing it as less important than any other part, then the statement of facts is *primus inter pares*. No matter how good all the other parts are, a brief cannot be effective unless the statement of facts provides "the appellate court with a sufficient factual basis upon which to decide the appeal in favor of the party upon whose behalf the brief is filed.

The statement of facts acquires its importance from the influence of the facts upon the appellate judges. It has been pointed out previously that in each case the appellate judge wants to do justice between the parties in a manner consistent with the applicable legal principles. Where substantial justice lies depends upon the judge's perception of the facts of the case. The source of the judge's perception of the facts is, of course, the statement of facts contained in the briefs of the parties. The statement of facts that will have the most influence upon the judge is the statement most clearly written, best supported by references to the record, and which sets forth the facts in the most logical and understandable way. A statement of facts written in the traditional legal style of convoluted sentences, excessive verbiage, hyperbole, and without adequate references to the record will leave the appellate judge without a clear understanding of what actually occurred and thus make it difficult for him to decide the case in favor of the party submitting the brief.

One of the basic elements of understanding the law as developed in the opinions of appellate courts is that abstract rules of law do not exist independent of the facts of a case. This has special significance in the argument section of the brief as will be discussed in § 7.38, infra, but it has particular importance to the statement of facts because it is here that the facts to be used in the argument are established. If they are not set forth in the statement of facts, it is highly unlikely they will be considered. The entire basis for the decision must be laid out in the statement of facts so that the judges can perform their basic judicial function of applying the law as developed in the factual context of prior cases to the factual context of the case pending before it. While the foregoing is necessarily of a general nature, the following are some specific guides to the appellate attorney in preparing the statement of facts.

Know facts

Before the appellate attorney can prepare an effective statement of facts it is essential that he familiarize himself with the facts as shown by the record including the transcript. He must know what is in the record because insofar as the appellate court is concerned only those facts in the record are facts. This is particularly important for the appellate attorney who was also the trial attorney. He will know an enormous amount about the case from his investigation of the case, much of which, for one reason or another, will not be reflected in the record. This information cannot, of course, be considered by the appellate court and thus cannot be included in the statement of facts. Because his recollection of what the documents show and what the testimony was will not always be accurate, the attorney must read the record carefully before preparing the statement of facts. Needless to say, the appellate attorney who was not the trial attorney must read the record.

The more familiar he is with the record, the better able the appellate attorney is to put all of the facts into a narrative that can be read and understood by a person unfamiliar with the case. It is far more important that the attorney be familiar with the facts of his case than that he be a leading authority on the relevant legal principles. Appellate judges feel quite confident determining for themselves what a prior case stands for. What they look to the attorney for in a particular case is a complete knowledge of the facts to aid them in understanding those facts in the case that make other cases more or less relevant.

FRAP 28(a)(3) and most appellate rules require that the statement of facts be supported by references to the record or the appendix. Compliance with this requirement is most important. Nothing frustrates the appellate judge more than to find an important fact in the statement unsupported by a reference to the record. The judge must himself then look for the support in the record. If he finds it, he will be annoyed with the appellate attorney for making the judge do the attorney's work. If he does not find the support, the judge's faith in the credibility of the attorney and in his statement of facts will be substantially if not irreparably harmed.

Be accurate and candid in telling facts

One of the principal objectives of the brief is to develop the appellate judge's confidence in the brief and its author. This confidence can be developed only if the appellate judge, upon investigation, determines that the statements are accurate and that the brief writer has not misstated the facts or the law or ignored a fact or case that may be adverse to the position of the party on whose behalf the brief is filed. There is no section of the brief in which accuracy and candor are more important then the statement of facts. It, unlike the argument portion of the brief, does not purport to be partisan in nature, but is rather a summary of what is contained in the record. The judge will, of course, check the record references in the statement of facts to test their accuracy. It is almost inevitable that the judge will discover any inaccuracy or failure to state a significant but unhelpful fact. Even if the judge does not make the discovery on his own, the appellate attorney can be certain that the opposing brief will make the most of the adverse fact. It is, consequently, virtually assured that any inaccuracy or lack of candor will be discovered. The consequences of discovery will be far worse that revealing the fact and attempting to minimize its effect. The ideal statement of facts is one, like the ideal statement of an issue, that both the appellee and the court can accept without change.

Tell facts in compelling narrative

An accurate and candid statement of facts need not be dull. Too many briefs contain statements of fact that are boring in the extreme, and unnecessarily so. Every case or appeal involves human drama. If a dispute is important enough to the parties to cause them not only to engage in litigation but to appeal the judgment of the trial court, it is almost inevitable that the facts as developed at the trial will provide interesting reading even to a casual reader and most certainly to the judges who must decide the appeal. The raw material is there. It is up to the appellate attorney to turn the cold record into a warm, human story.

The worst format is a seriatim recitation of each witness's testimony: "Witness A testified that ... , Witness B testified that ... , and Witness C testified that. ..." Not only is such a recitation dull but it makes it almost impossible to obtain a clear picture of what happened. Witnesses do not testify in such a logical and comprehensive manner, and thus summarizing their testimony in the order given will not contribute as fully as possible to an understanding of the facts.

The best structure for the narrative is usually chronological as the facts actually developed, not in the order testified to at the trial. Taking a fact testified to by the first witness, and combining it with a statement of a rebuttal witness may give the most accurate picture of a particular event. The attorney should imagine how the appellate court will set forth the facts in its opinion and use that as a model. The highest tribute that can be paid to a statement of facts in a brief is for the appellate court to adopt verbatim the statement of facts in the brief of one of the parties as its statement of facts.

If, as will often happen, there is a conflict in the testimony between two or more witnesses, then that conflict should be set forth clearly. The statement of facts is not, however, the place to argue which of the conflicting version of the facts should be accepted-the place for this is in the argument.

Too often attorneys interrupt the flow of the narrative by including unnecessary detail, such as insignificant dates. If the type of car driven, the width of a road, the place where people met, or the date on which something occurred is important, be sure to say so. Otherwise, leave it out.

Finally, and above all else, do not attempt to color the facts or to argue the case in the statement of facts. Set forth the salient facts accurately, succinctly, in an interesting manner, and in a way that puts the client of the brief writer in the most favorable light, and then move on to the argument.

h. Argument

All of the prior sections of the brief lead up to the argument. It is here that the appellate attorney has the opportunity to persuade the appellate court that as between the parties before the court, justice demands that his client win, and that a decision in his client's favor is consistent with the applicable law.

Perhaps the greatest weakness in most appellate briefs is the writer's failure to use the facts of his case in the argument section to demonstrate the basic justice of his client's cause and to demonstrate similarities to facts in cases that establish favorable precedents and distinguish them from facts in unfavorable precedents. Many appellate attorneys mention facts only in the statement of facts and discuss the "law" as abstract principles in the argument. This separation reveals a basic misunderstanding of the role of facts in the decision of a case, and the role of the argument portion of the brief in relating the law to the facts of the case.

Facts are central to both the statement of facts and the argument. The difference between the two is not that one deals with facts and the other with law, but in the use of facts in each section. In the statement of facts, as already pointed out, the facts are used to give the appellate court an accurate and complete picture of the incident that gave rise to the lawsuit. Editorializing on the facts is completely out of place. Just the opposite is true in the argument. The entire focus of this section of the brief is to stress, to downplay, to comment, to point out, to highlight, to explain away, to identify with, to disassociate from, to distinguish, to find controlling—in short, to argue. It is here that all of the compulsion to be an unabashed advocate, repressed in the other sections of the brief, should come into full flower. The object of the argument is to show why the case should be decided in favor of the attorney's client and how this can be done in a manner consistent with law.

The above describes the basic approach to be followed in writing an effective argument. Some generally accepted precepts that will make the argument as readable and persuasive as possible are:

(a) Follow the same order as the statement of issues.

(b) Use one section of the argument for each issue.

(c) Give the answer in each section heading to the issue discussed in that section.

(d) Present your strongest point first.

(e) Use only the most pertinent citations.

(f) Do not use footnotes.

(g) Do not ignore adverse facts or contrary authority.

(h) Rely upon decisions of the court in which the appeal is pending as the most persuasive.

(i) Quote from the record or an opinion sparingly but accurately.

(j) Underestimate the judges' knowledge of the facts.

(k) Overestimate the judges' knowledge of general principles and particularly the court's own decisions.

(*l*) Do not use hyperbole or exaggeration.

(m) Be accurate.

(n) Be brief.

i. Conclusion

Most appellate rules call for a conclusion to the brief. Although a conclusion seems unnecessary, the experience of appellate courts dictates its inclusion. The purpose of the conclusion is to state exactly what action the party wants the appellate court to take. The type of action requested will depend upon the nature of the judgment appealed from and the party submitting the brief. It may be a request that the appellate court reverse, affirm, reverse and remand, vacate, take action as to all or only part of the judgment, decrease or increase the judgment, and so on. The variety in the type of relief sought is almost endless. The important thing is that it tell the precise relief sought. The appellate attorney should never assume that the appellate court knows what relief is sought. Not only does he chance annoying the court by forcing it to guess, but he runs the risk that the court will guess incorrectly.

The conclusion should not be long, never more than a short paragraph. Several sentences usually suffice.

Note

To learn how one judge uses briefs, see F. Coffin, On Appeal 107–25 (1994).

4. EFFECTIVE BRIEF WRITING AND PROFESSIONAL RESPONSIBILITY

DAY v. NORTHERN INDIANA PUBLIC SERVICE CORP.

United States Court of Appeals, Seventh Circuit, 1999.
164 F.3d 382.

EASTERBROOK, CIRCUIT JUDGE.

Wonda Day found herself behind the eight ball in this employment-discrimination suit when her lawyer ignored the district court's rule requiring all statements of fact in support of or opposing motions for summary judgment to be supported by citations to the record. Day's lawyer submitted a narrative statement of facts that contained only a single citation, to the whole of one deposition. The district judge deemed this insufficient, observing that the function of the rule is to provide pinpoint citations so that the judge can find the facts readily; citing a whole deposition frustrates that function. As a result the judge treated the employer's factual position as uncontested, as judges properly may do in order to enforce their rules about summary-judgment practice. * * *

In order to get anywhere on this appeal Day had to persuade us that the district court abused its discretion by disregarding her version of the facts. That objective, hard to achieve given deferential appellate review, was put out of reach when her lawyer repeated in this court the very performance that led the district court to disregard her affidavit. Circuit Rule 28(c) provides: "The statement of the facts required by Fed. R.App.P. 28(a)(7) shall be a fair summary without argument or comment. No fact shall be stated in this part of the brief unless it is supported by a reference to the page or pages of the record or the appendix where that fact appears." (We quote Circuit Rule 28(c) as amended on December 1, 1998, to update its reference to the national rule; no substantive change has been made in Circuit Rule 28(c) for more than a generation.) Day's lawyer violated both sentences of Circuit Rule 28(c), the first because the statement of facts is argumentative (it treats Day's position as established, even though the district court found it to be unsupported), and the second because it does not support the propositions with citations. Day's statement of facts is 8 1/2 pages long; the first six pages are unadorned by a single record reference. Eventually the brief cites one deposition, NIPSCO's statement of uncontested facts, and Day's affidavit. Just as in the district court, counsel expected the court to peruse the record without the help of pinpoint citations. It takes a brave, or foolhardy, lawyer to repeat in the court of appeals the very strategy that cost his client the case in the district court!

NIPSCO filed a motion asking us to strike Day's brief, but that step is inappropriate. Striking the brief would lead either to dismissal for want of prosecution (if we then denied Day's request to file a corrected but untimely brief) or to a whole new round of briefs (if Day replaced the defective brief and NIPSCO responded). Neither approach matches the transgression. Dismissal for want of prosecution would foreclose any possibility that the original brief, deficient as it was, might persuade us that the district court erred. A second round of briefs would multiply the costs of resolving the case and condone a violation of the court's rules. Sometimes we permit repair work when lawyers have good reasons (the category of "excusable neglect"), but that's hardly an apt description of the omission here, given what happened in the district court. * * *

NIPSCO's motion to strike included a request for sanctions under Fed.R.App.P. 38. Counsel had an opportunity to reply, and the motion is now granted. The sanction is a public reprimand and a fine of $500, payable to NIPSCO. The monetary sanction is small because NIPSCO offers us no reason to think that the expense it incurred in responding to the appeal was enhanced by counsel's neglect; to the contrary, noncompliance with the rule likely enabled NIPSCO to reduce its attorneys' fees by making the appeal less formidable (and creating the possibility of summary affirmance). A public reprimand is in order because this deficient performance by counsel Michael J. Foley follows hard on the heels of another. In Filippo v. Northern Indiana Public Service Corp., 141 F.3d 744 (7th Cir. 1998), attorney Foley filed a brief that violated Fed.R.App.P. 28(a)(6) (as it stood before December 1, 1998) by reducing to a skeleton the argument on the merits. Foley contended that the district court misunderstood the facts, but as we pointed out he "fail[ed] to elaborate on how the court erred." 141 F.3d at 751. Because the brief was "not entirely devoid of citation or factual reference" (ibid.) we bent over backward to avoid a forfeiture, while informing Foley that the brief "must stand as the irreducible minimum" (ibid.). Our opinion in Filippo, issued on April 10, 1998, counseled Foley never to repeat the performance. Only a few weeks later, on May 21, 1998, Foley filed the appellate brief in Day's case. In response to the motion for sanctions Foley observed that we counseled him in Filippo to comply with Fed.R.App.P. 28(a)(6), while this case involves noncompliance with Circuit Rule 28(c). This "response" shows that Foley didn't get the point. A lawyer need not be counseled one subsection at a time until the rules have been exhausted—and anyway the failure on this appeal is the same as Foley's failure in the district court. In Filippo attorney Foley filed a brief that was so deficient that only by the grace of the court did the judges consider the merits. Foley learned nothing from either Filippo or the district court's conclusion that his factual presentation on behalf of Day was deficient.

Attorney Michael J. Foley is reprimanded for persistent noncompliance with the rules of appellate procedure and fined $500. The judgment of the district court is affirmed.

Notes and Questions

1.   Are a reprimand and a $500 fine an adequate penalty for a persistent failure to follow the rules relating to the preparation of briefs?

2. Would it not be more effective simply for the court to find that the brief does not support the party's position and then rule against the party, as was done in State *ex rel.* Queen City Chapter Sigma Delta Chi v. McGinnis, *supra*? If so, does this unfairly punish the client for the sins of the attorney?

SECTION F. THE APPENDIX

FEDERAL RULE OF APPELLATE PROCEDURE 30

APPENDIX TO THE BRIEFS

(a) Appellant's Responsibility

(1) Contents of the Appendix. The appellant must prepare and file an appendix to the briefs containing:

(A) the relevant docket entries in the proceeding below;

(B) the relevant portions of the pleadings, charge, findings, or opinion;

(C) the judgment, order, or decision in question; and

(D) other parts of the record to which the parties wish to direct the court's attention.

(2) Excluded Material. Memoranda of law in the district court should not be included in the appendix unless they have independent relevance. Parts of the record may be relied on by the court or the parties even though not included in the appendix.

(3) Time to File; Number of Copies. Unless filing is deferred under Rule 30(c), the appellant must file 10 copies of the appendix with the brief and must serve one copy on counsel for each party separately represented. An unrepresented party proceeding in forma pauperis must file 4 legible copies with the clerk, and one copy must be served on counsel for each separately represented party. The court may by local rule or by order in a particular case require the filing or service of a different number.

(b) All Parties' Responsibilities.

(1) Determining the Contents of the Appendix. The parties are encouraged to agree on the contents of the appendix. In the absence of an agreement, the appellant must, within 10 days after the record is filed, serve on the appellee a designation of the parts of the record the appellant intends to include in the appendix and a statement of the issues the appellant intends to present for review. The appellee may, within 10 days after receiving the designation, serve on the appellant a designation of additional parts to which it wishes to direct the court's attention. The appellant must include the designated parts in the appendix. The parties must not engage in unnecessary designation of parts of the record, because the entire record is available to the court. This paragraph applies also to a cross-appellant and a cross-appellee.

(2) Costs of Appendix. Unless the parties agree otherwise, the appellant must pay the cost of the appendix. If the appellant considers parts of the record designated by the appellee to be unnecessary, the appellant may advise the appellee, who must then advance the cost of including those parts. The cost of the appendix is a taxable cost. But if any party causes unnecessary parts of the record to be included in the appendix, the court may impose the cost of those parts on that party. Each circuit must, by local rule, provide for sanctions against attorneys who unreasonably and vexatiously increase litigation costs by including unnecessary material in the appendix.

(c) Deferred Appendix.

(1) Deferral Until After Briefs Arc Filed. The court may provide by rule for classes of cases or by order in a particular case that preparation of the appendix may be deferred until after the briefs have been filed and that the appendix may be filed 21 days after the appellee's brief is served. Even though the filing of the appendix may be deferred, Rule 30(b) applies; except that a party must designate the parts of the record it wants included in the appendix when it serves its brief, and need not include a statement of the issues presented.

(2) References to the Record.

(A) If the deferred appendix is used, the parties may cite in their briefs the pertinent pages of the record. When the appendix is prepared, the record pages cited in the briefs must be indicated by inserting record page numbers, in brackets, at places in the appendix where those pages of the record appear.

(B) A party who wants to refer directly to pages of the appendix may serve and file copies of the brief within the time required by Rule 31(a), containing appropriate references to pertinent pages of the record. In that event, within 14 days after the appendix is filed, the party must serve and file copies of the brief, containing references to the pages of the appendix in place of or in addition to the references to the pertinent pages of the record. Except for the correction of typographical errors, no other changes may be made to the brief.

(d) Format of the Appendix. The appendix must begin with a table of contents identifying the page at which each part begins. The relevant docket entries must follow the table of contents. Other parts of the record must follow chronologically. When pages from the transcript of proceedings are placed in the appendix, the transcript page numbers must be shown in brackets immediately before the included pages. Omissions in the text of papers or of the transcript must be indicated by asterisks. Immaterial formal matters (captions, subscriptions, acknowledgments, etc.) should be omitted.

(e) Reproduction of Exhibits. Exhibits designated for inclusion in the appendix may be reproduced in a separate volume, or volumes, suitably indexed. Four copies must be filed with the appendix, and one copy must be served on counsel for each separately represented party. If a transcript of a proceeding before an administrative agency, board, commission, or officer was used in a district-court action and has been designated for inclusion in the appendix, the transcript must be placed in the appendix as an exhibit.

(f) Appeal on the Original Record Without an Appendix. The court may, either by rule for all cases or classes of cases or by order in a particular case, dispense with the appendix and permit an appeal to proceed on the original record with any copies of the record, or relevant parts, that the court may order the parties to file.

MINER, COMMON DISORDERS OF THE APPENDIX AND THEIR TREATMENT
3 J. App. Prac. & Process 39 (2001).*

"Appendix" is a Latin word meaning appendage or addition. To the medical profession, it is "a general term used in anatomical nomenclature to designate a supplementary, accessory, or dependent part attached to a main structure." The term often is used specifically to designate the vermiform appendix of the colon. Inflammation of the vermiform appendix may require surgical intervention. For the legal profession, appendix is defined as "[s]upplementary materials added to [an] appellate brief." Like its anatomical counterpart, the appendix to a brief receives little attention until the onset of an acute disorder. Such a disorder may give rise to judicial intervention. Careful attention to the preparation of a proper appendix will avoid this consequence.

A disordered appendix evidences a breach of a lawyer's professional duty of competence in appellate practice. It is just as important for a member of the appellate bar to be knowledgeable about the rules and techniques pertaining to appendices as it is to be knowledgeable about the rules and techniques pertaining to briefs and oral arguments. The three elements of appellate advocacy—preparation of the brief, compilation of the appendix, and presentation of oral argument—are co-equal in importance. Indeed, it is excellence in all three elements of a case on appeal that is the hallmark of successful appellate advocacy. My purpose here is to discuss the function of an appendix, to review the rules that govern its preparation, to identify some deficiencies and disorders commonly associated with it, to examine the consequences of an improper appendix, and in doing so, to focus attention on the importance of this neglected element of appellate practice.

I. THE FUNCTION OF AN APPENDIX

Before an appellate court can consider an appeal, a record of the proceedings in the trial court generally must be filed with the appellate

* Judge Roger J. Minor, copyright © 2001 Journal of Appellate Practice and Process, University of Arkansas School of Law. Reprinted by permission. All rights reserved.

court. In federal appellate practice, the record on appeal consists of the original exhibits and papers filed in the district court, all transcripts of proceedings, and a certified copy of the district court clerk's docket entries. The documents constituting the record must be numbered and forwarded to the circuit clerk by the district clerk along "with a list of the documents correspondingly numbered and reasonably identified." By stipulation or court order, some or all of the documents, especially the exhibits, may be retained by the attorneys or by the district court clerk. However, the retained documents must remain available to the appellate court if needed. The purpose of an appendix is to facilitate appellate review by placing before the appellate court only those portions of the record that are pertinent to the specific issues raised in the briefs submitted by the parties. This abbreviated record serves to focus the attention of the judges on the arguments of counsel in much the same way as the briefs. By efficient preparation of the appendix, the attorneys show the judges what parts of the proceedings that transpired in the trial court are important to their points on appeal. A proper appendix is especially important where the entire record is not in the custody of the circuit court clerk.

II. The Contents of an Appendix

The Federal Rules of Appellate Procedure impose upon the appellant the obligation to prepare and file an appendix to the briefs. The contents of the appendix are itemized as follows:

(A) the relevant docket entries in the proceeding below;

(B) the relevant portions of the pleadings, charge, findings, or opinion;

(C) the judgment, order, or decision in question; and

(D) other parts of the record to which the parties wish to direct the court's attention.

This provision of the rules is simple enough, and it obviously provides for a great deal of discretion on the part of the attorneys who are to prepare the appendix. Unfortunately, that discretion is often abused, to the great detriment of the attorney who attempts to make a point in his brief or in his oral argument that finds no support in the appendix. Such an omission causes the judge to scurry back to the full record to look for the material omitted from the appendix. Sometimes, the judge discovers the material quickly and sometimes not. In neither case is the judge satisfied with the conduct of counsel.

On a number of occasions, I have found such basic items as pleadings and intermediate orders missing from the appendix. I have found appendices in which summary judgment motion papers, or some of them, were missing. I have seen materials that apparently were randomly inserted in the appendix as well as items that were unidentified. In one case presented for review, I found the partial transcripts of two trials in the appendix but no indication where one began and the other left off.

On occasion, I have been constrained to track down an indictment or other charging instrument that has been omitted from the appendix in a criminal appeal.

Solving the problem of missing materials is time-consuming, as well as annoying. In the circuit in which I serve, the original record remains with the clerk of the district court, and it is transmitted to a judge of the court of appeals only on request through our own circuit court clerk. The delay does not sit well with the judge assigned to draft the opinion or with the other judges on the panel, for that matter. And what item is most often included that should not be included? It is the Memorandum of Law that is filed in the district court, and that the rules specifically exclude from inclusion in the appendix.

Many federal courts of appeals have established rules requiring additional materials to be included in an appendix. Our local rule in the Second Circuit Court of Appeals requires that the Notice of Appeal be included. The Notice of Appeal is an important item in any appeal. The Notice of Appeal needs to specify whether part or all of the judgment is being appealed from and must also specify the parties taking the appeal. Without a proper and timely Notice of Appeal, the appellate court has no jurisdiction. We are very particular about verifying our jurisdiction, and it is not unusual for us to find a lack of jurisdiction that counsel has failed (purposely or not) to bring to our attention. So, what is often missing from the appendix in our court? The Notice of Appeal, of course.

Reported cases detailing the difficulties posed by underinclusive appendices abound. In a case before my court, United States v. Urena, the issue presented was whether the attorneys representing the defendants should be permitted to withdraw from representation of their clients pursuant to Anders v. California. The panel, in preliminarily denying permission to withdraw, noted that both attorneys had "not even included the sentencing transcripts in the appendices" and that one of the attorneys had "not included his client's plea agreement." These materials were obviously necessary for the determination of the application. In United States v. Tom, the court noted the omission of the relevant docket entries as well as the indictment. In a Fourth Circuit case, United States v. Banks, the appendix was characterized as "skimpy" and "wholly inadequate to permit the evidentiary assessment required by the critical sufficiency issues raised by appellants."

In United States v. Friedman, the court, faced with the issue of whether the prosecutor's summation warranted reversal of conviction, "fault[ed] both sides for neglecting to include in the joint appendix the pages of the trial transcript containing the summations." The following plea for an understanding of the importance of a joint appendix preceded a detailed review of the rules governing the preparation and filing of appendices:

> We take this opportunity to remind the bar of the vital function of the joint appendix in the consideration of appeals heard by this Court. Most of the judges of this Court maintain their permanent

chambers outside of New York City. For them, the single copy of the trial transcript filed with the Clerk's office at Foley Square is not readily available for inspection before or after their attendance in New York City to hear argument. The bar has come to expect that the judges of this Court will attend argument fully informed about the appeal. The joint appendix, available to all members of the panel at their resident chambers, provides the basis for thorough pre-argument preparation and for further study of the issues as an opinion is being written and considered by the panel.

Rule 30(e) of the Federal Rules of Appellate Procedure, entitled "Reproduction of Exhibits," provides that "[e]xhibits designated for inclusion in the appendix may be reproduced in a volume, or volumes, suitably indexed." Our local rules require that the index for such a separate volume "shall include a description of the exhibit sufficient to inform the court of its nature; designation merely by exhibit number or letter is not a suitable index." This direction is simple enough, and it should be followed even in the absence of a local rule. Yet, we continue to receive separate volumes containing multiple exhibits designated only by letter or number. Compliance with local rules is essential, and no competent appellate attorney will ignore them.

There are some circuits that require specific excerpts of the record in lieu of the appendix prescribed by the Federal Rules, and the contents of these excerpts vary widely. In the Second Circuit, the appendix is dispensed with altogether as to appeals in forma pauperis under the Social Security Act and those taken pursuant to the Criminal Justice Act. In those types of cases, appeals are heard on the original record, and the court must be provided with

> five clearly legible copies of the reporter's transcript or of so much thereof as the appellant desires the court to read (or in the case of social security decisions, of the administrative records), and both parties in their briefs shall direct the court's attention to the portions of the transcript or administrative record deemed relevant to each point.

It is always a good idea to consult the local rules for dispensing with the appendix and other matters relating to appropriate presentation of the record.

The foregoing rule of course deals with transcripts in cases where an appendix is not required. It is also germane in cases where the appendix is required, for it points out the necessity of coordinating the brief and the portion of the record included in the appendix. It is, after all, the brief's appendix that must contain the "parts of the record to which the parties wish to direct the court's attention." Actually, the appendix and the brief must work together to "direct the court's attention." Indeed, the brief must include citations to the appropriate pages in the appendix when referring "to the parts of the record contained in the appendix." Specific provision is made for reference to evidence whose admissibility is in question. In such cases the pages of the appendix (or transcript) must be cited.

An underinclusive appendix is probably worse than an overinclusive appendix, provided of course that the latter is properly formatted. As previously noted, references in briefs to materials not included in the appendix cause no end of problems, the principal one being a waste of time. Often, the omitted materials have a critical bearing upon the issues with which the appellate judges are concerned. Counsel blithely go forward with their written and oral arguments without a clue that the appendix is barren of the material to which they refer. Here is an example: In an argument of a case before a panel of which I was a member, counsel discussed whether certain evidence should have been admitted under the residual exception to the hearsay rule. Under that rule, hearsay not otherwise admissible may be received in evidence, in the interest of justice, if it meets certain criteria and if the particulars of the evidence were made known to the opposing party in advance of trial. The problem was that the letter relied upon to provide the requisite notice in advance of trial was missing from the appendix.

An overinclusive appendix also is unacceptable and can bring forth the wrath of an appellate court. Some courts are so concerned about the problems caused by overinclusion that they have adopted specific rules designed to foreclose it. For example, the Fourth Circuit rules specifically allow for the imposition of "sanctions against attorneys who unreasonably and vexatiously . . . inclu[de] unnecessary material in the appendix." Such sanctions may be imposed by the court sua sponte or upon motion of any party. The Fourth Circuit rule makes it clear that the only parts of the record to be included are those that are "vital to the understanding of the basic issues on appeal." Familiarity and compliance with local rules governing the preparation of the appendix will help to avoid the offense of overinclusion. Indeed, familiarity and compliance with local rules will avoid many other disorders of the appendix as well. No competent appellate attorney will undertake the preparation of an appendix without a review of all the court rules governing contents and form of the appendix. My own experience with overinclusive briefs makes me wish that the Second Circuit had a rule similar to the Fourth Circuit rule regarding the inclusion of unnecessary material. There are, however, other ways to deal with that problem.

The court may invoke the procedures allowing the imposition of disciplinary sanctions upon appellate counsel who fail to comply with the rules governing appellate practice. The court may also use the statutory provision for the assessment of excess costs, expenses and fees upon any counsel who "multiplies the proceedings in any case unreasonably and vexatiously" to correct the problem.

The responsibility for the preparation of the appendix lies with the appellant, at least in the first instance. The appellant must compile the appendix and make sure to comply with the contents requirement. However, "[t]he parties are encouraged to agree on the contents of the appendix," to the end that all necessary portions of the record are before the court. There would seem to be no reason for any disagreement as to what an appendix should contain. Since some "Rambo" litigators (wrongfully) perceive that it is their duty to disagree about everything, the Federal Rules establish a procedure for determining the contents of an appendix in the absence of the preferred agreement of counsel.

First, the appellant is to serve on the appellee, within ten days of the filing of the record, "a designation of the parts of the record the appellant intends to include in the appendix and a statement of the issues the appellant intends to present for review." The appellee is given ten days after receipt to "serve on the appellant the designation of additional parts [of the record] to which it wishes to direct the court's attention." Although the appellant has no choice but to include the additional parts, the Federal Rules caution the parties not to engage in "unnecessary designation."

Despite the provisions regarding designation, we often see two separate appendices filed in the case—one by appellant and one by appellee. Aside from there being no such thing as a separate appendix for each party provided by the rules, the judges become cross when they have to skip from one appendix to another. They may as well have reference to the original record, for two appendices certainly do not accomplish the purpose of facilitating appellate review. More than thirty years ago, a panel of the court on which I serve condemned the filing of a separate appendix by each party. Noting the requirement for the filing of a single appendix, the court stated:

> The parties chose instead to file an appellants' appendix and an appellee's appendix. Thus, in order to consider a given witness' testimony in this highly technical case, it was necessary for us to jump from one appendix to the other. The rule requiring a single appendix was adopted to facilitate our task of judicial review.

The facilitation of judicial review seems far from the minds of many appellate attorneys as they go about the work of assembling appendices. The rules do provide for the situation where an appellant, who is responsible for the cost of the appendix in the first instance, considers unnecessary the additional record parts designated by the appellee. In that situation, the appellant is authorized to notify the appellee, who then must advance the costs of including the additional parts.

The court's power to allocate the cost of an appendix serves as a brake on the inclusion of unnecessary materials. While the cost of the appendix is taxable to the loser, the court may impose the costs of unnecessary parts of the record included in the appendix upon the party who causes the inclusion of those parts. The real sword of Damocles that discourages the inclusion of unnecessary material is the provision requiring circuits to promulgate rules for "sanctions against attorneys who unreasonably and vexatiously increase litigation costs by including unnecessary material in the appendix."

III. THE FORMAT AND APPEARANCE OF AN APPENDIX

The format of the appendix is dictated by the applicable rules of appellate procedure, including local rules in the various circuits. In federal practice, "[t]he appendix must begin with a table of contents identifying the page at which each part begins." The relevant docket entries come next, followed by the other parts of the record in chronological order. When an appendix includes any pages from the transcript of proceedings, the brief writer should provide the transcript page numbers, in brackets, immediately before the included pages. Omissions in the transcript or in other included papers are to be noted by asterisks. The appendix should omit formal matters immaterial to the case on appeal, including such items as acknowledgments and captions. The items to be omitted are specified in the vain hope that the appendix will be no larger than necessary to assist the judges in resolving the issues presented on appeal. The hope is a vain one because almost every appendix is cluttered with unnecessary and immaterial formal matters that should be omitted.

Counsel should pay close attention to all the rules governing the physical appearance of the appendix. The Federal Rules of Appellate Procedure refer to the rules governing the appearance of briefs for such matters as reproduction, binding, paper size, line spacing and margins except that "[t]he cover of a separately bound appendix must be white." Interim local rules recently adopted by the Second Circuit Court of Appeals require "[s]equentially numbered pages beginning with A–1," "[a] detailed index referring to the sequential page numbers" and one-inch-high type for the docket number printed on the appendix cover. These rules already have been honored in the breach. The Federal Rules allow the inclusion of "legible photocop[ies]" of any documents or decisions and an appendix of a size other than 8–1/2 by 11 inches "to facilitate inclusion of odd-sized document such as technical drawings." The interim local rules allow printing on both sides of an appendix page, the employment of tabs in addition to sequential page numbering to identify documents, and the use of the minuscript form of transcripts. Minuscript allows the printing of as many as four pages of transcript on one page of the appendix. This method greatly reduces the size of the print in the interest of a more compact appendix. For me, it is too hard on the eyes, and fortunately, I have not been subjected to it very frequently.

A frequently encountered problem is the appendix that is so poorly bound that it falls apart. An appendix whose pages become scattered all over the judge's desk as the binding falls apart loses its efficacy. And while the rules require that there be a single appendix, there is nothing that says the appendix cannot be in two volumes. Sometimes there are so many papers that three or more volumes of a joint appendix are required. No matter how many pages there are per volume, a careful lawyer sees that each volume presented to the court is bound properly. In an unpublished opinion dealing with an Age Discrimination in Employment claim, the Fourth Circuit described the appendix submitted as "a mess—too many pages were put in a volume so that the volumes fell apart." In addition, the court found the page numbers "unreadable," and the appendix index "useless," and noted that the appendix contained more than 1,000 pages but "failed to contain the complaint and other crucial portions of the record." The court summed up its view in that case as follows: "In short, the joint appendix was a disaster that utterly failed to comply with the letter or spirit of Fed. R. App. P. 30." All too often are appellate judges confronted with unhelpful appendices that can only be characterized as unmitigated disasters!

Aside from disastrous matters, I insert here a point of personal annoyance. Often, the lower court opinion included in the appendix is a photocopy of the opinion received by counsel from the court. When counsel marks up that opinion by underlinings and comments in the margin, the result is very distracting when counsel's copy is included in the record. I am not the only appellate judge to comment upon this distraction. In Allen v. Seidman, the court noted its displeasure with the appendix copy of the lower court's opinion in which a lawyer for the Department of Justice "had scribbled critical marginalia, such as the word 'WRONG' beside several findings of [the Judge] with which she took particular issue." Characterizing this conduct, which it had observed in other cases, as "indecorous and unprofessional," the court expressed the hope that it would not recur. In the same vein, my preference is that the photocopy of a published opinion, if available (and clean, of course) should be included in the appendix rather than the typewritten opinion received from the lower court.

IV.   The Supplemental Appendix

Although it should be avoided if at all possible, it sometimes becomes necessary to file a supplemental appendix. If the procedure for designation of the record is followed, there should be no need for it. However, as is often the case, the failure of counsel to cooperate in the preparation of an appendix often calls for a supplemental appendix to be filed by an attorney who asks for the inclusion of designated material but is refused. Leave should always be sought before a supplemental appendix is filed.

In one case a motion to strike a supplemental appendix (apparently filed without permission) was denied "because the materials in defendants' supplemental appendix merely correct and clarify factual misstatements in plaintiffs' appellate brief." The court's rationale for allowing the supplemental index was grounded in Rule 10(e) of the Federal Rules of Appellate Practice, which actually has reference to the record on appeal rather than the appendix. It allows the appellate court to direct a "supplemental record" in the event that "anything material to either party is omitted from or misstated in the record."

A supplemental appendix should not be confused with the duplicate appendix problem previously described. As noted, the use of a separate appendix by each party has been roundly condemned. In one case a panel of my court was confronted with a situation where "[s]ix counsel submitted appendices in addition to the appendices submitted by the United States and by the public defender for the District of Connecticut, who represented an eighth defendant." This was excessive duplication and obviously caused considerable confusion. The panel warned the bar "that henceforth costs of reproducing appendices in multi-defendant appeals will not be reimbursed to the extent that the same document or the same pages of transcript are reproduced by more than one lawyer." In my view, duplicative appendices should call for sanctions greater than the mere denial of the costs of reproduction of the duplicative material. The problem of course can be entirely avoided by the preparation of a single joint appendix in accordance with the requirements of the Federal Rules.

V. PENALTIES FOR THE IMPROPER APPENDIX

Courts have not hesitated to impose substantial sanctions as a penalty for improper preparation of an appendix. Costs on appeal have been imposed upon a prevailing party that failed to include a copy of the trial court's opinion and omitted thirteen pages of the appendix, "demonstrating extreme carelessness." The cost of preparing a supplemental appendix has been imposed upon a party whose appendix "did not contain all the materials required by court rule and was not properly paginated." An assessment of a sum of money toward the payment of appellees' attorneys' fees was awarded in the case where appellant refused to accommodate a request by appellees to include designated parts of the trial record. In that case, the attorney was directed not to charge any part of the sanctions against his client. Financial sanctions equal to the defendant's attorneys' fees were imposed against plaintiff's counsel in a case where counsel finally "submitted a joint appendix 11 months after he was given extensive and explicit instructions on how to prepare and file a joint appendix."

Where the appellant at first failed to include parts of the record designated by the appellee but later filed a corrected appendix when ordered to do so by the court, attorneys' fees incurred in the preparation of a successful motion to strike the appendix as originally filed were allowed as sanctions. In a case where the court found the first three volumes of appendices "poorly indexed, not in chronological order, and not consecutively paginated," the court invited and granted a motion to allow the filing of a two-volume supplemental appendix. The supplementary materials did not contain all the documents desired but did contain "unindexed documents of uncertain relevance." The court noted that "appellants did not seek leave to repaginate and rearrange the first three volumes of their appendices ... [and did not] revise their record references to the documents cited in their briefs." This all resulted in a chilling conclusion for appellants. The court stated as follows: "[I]n the instant case, wherever material uncertainties result from an incomplete or indecipherable record and impede or affect our decision, we resolve such uncertainties against appellants."

The most severe sanction of all is described in a case decided by the Third Circuit Court of Appeals in 1980. In Kushner v. Winterthur Swiss Insurance Co., the court described its frustration thus:

> Because appellants here failed to provide the court with a list of docket entries or a notice of appeal, much valuable time had to be expended by three judges and personnel of the Clerk's office repairing an incomplete brief and appendix, when this time would have been better spent in considering the merits of cases that are presented to us in proper form.

The court then announced its decision in the following words:

> We now decide not to expend any more valuable judicial time performing the work of errant counsel, a practice that worked a tremendous disservice to the bulk of the litigants who appear before us represented by diligent counsel who do observe our rules. We are deciding this case deliberately, with an awareness of the institutional and precedential value of our decision. We dismiss this appeal for failure to file an appendix that conforms to our rules.

VI. CONCLUSION

It is to be hoped that the foregoing will provide some guidance to the bar as its members go about preparing that essential part of a case on appeal—the appendix. Although dismissal as a sanction for an improper appendix is a rare event, it remains as the most severe of the sanctions available. The preparation of a proper appendix is not a difficult task and can avoid the imposition of any sanctions at all. One needs only to follow the rules governing preparation and to see the appendix as an essential part of appellate advocacy.

A well-written brief coordinated with a properly prepared appendix is a joy for an appellate judge to behold. It will earn many points for the client and for the attorney who prepares it on his behalf. A disordered appendix, on the other hand, may have to be removed, with all the unfortunate consequences that may result. Removing (or striking) such an appendix in its entirety is a sanction that will leave the references in the brief without meaning. In such a case, a new joint appendix and new briefs would be required by leave of the court. The case would be delayed, and expenses would proliferate, all chargeable to the offending attorneys, who would then have to explain all to their clients. The attorneys would be subject to severe disciplinary sanctions, but the innocent clients would not suffer the extreme prejudice of dismissal or the resolution of the issues against them. After fifteen years on the appellate bench, and with appendices getting worse all the time, that is my view of an appropriate sanction.

Notes and Questions

1. Is the separate appendix necessary, desirable, or simply an unnecessary expense? If the client can afford it, should the separate appendix be prepared?

2. Does it make sense to prepare the appendix after the briefs have been prepared, as is permitted by Federal Rule of Appellate Procedure 30(c)?

3. One of the principal reasons behind the drive to eliminate the appendix was the fact that its cost made taking an appeal prohibitive for many persons. Willcox, Karlen & Roemer, Justice Lost—By What Appellate Papers Cost, 33 N.Y.U.L.Rev. 934 (1958).

4. Abstracting the record is a practice that was quite common at one time but is used in only a few places today. The attorney for the appellant condenses all the material that would otherwise be included in an appendix into an abstract, including the transcript of testimony. According to Justice Smith of the Arkansas Supreme Court the practice "creates more problems for the court and for the appellate bar than all the court's other rules put together." The reason for this, he states, is that the practice "requires a lawyer, in the midst of his advocacy, to lay aside his role as a partisan and prepare an *impartial* condensation of the record." [Emphasis in original.] Smith, Arkansas Appellate Practice: Abstracting the Record, 31 Ark.L.Rev. 359, 360 (1977). Notwithstanding, Justice Smith further commented that he did not oppose the practice because none of the members of the Arkansas Supreme Court could think of a better alternative. Does the fact that almost all other courts have abandoned the system in favor of the appendix, the original record, or some combination, suggest that there are adequate alternatives?

5. Have computerizing court records and fax and photocopy machines eliminated the problem of relying on the original record?

6. Are the problems different with a court in which all of the members have their offices in the same city than with a court where the judge's office is in separate locations?

DREWETT v. AETNA CASUALTY & SURETY COMPANY

United States Court of Appeals, Fifth Circuit, 1976.
539 F.2d 496.

LEWIS R. MORGAN, CIRCUIT JUDGE.

Plaintiff Glen Drewett sued defendant National Flood Insurers Association in federal district court to recover on a flood insurance policy issued under the provisions of the National Flood Insurance Act of 1968, as amended, codified at 42 U.S.C. s 4001 et seq. After a bench trial the district court denied recovery, and Drewett appeals. For the reasons stated herein, we affirm.

This court also must dispose of appellant Drewett's motion to tax to the appellee the cost of allegedly unnecessary portions of the appendix on appeal ordered by appellee. For the reasons stated herein, we grant this motion. * * *

Appellant filed a 31 page Appendix with his brief to this court, containing reproductions of the docket entries in the district court; his complaint and appellee's answer; appellee's motion for summary judgment, appellant's response in opposition, and the district court's partial grant of the motion; both parties' trial memoranda; the written opinion of the district court holding for appellee on the merits; the judgment; and the contract of insurance. The Appendix cost $76.30 to print.

Appellee designated, as additional portions of the record to be reproduced as a Supplemental Appendix, literally everything else in the record below. This Supplemental Appendix is 212 pages long. Among other things, it contains a reproduction of the entire trial transcript; a copy of the insurance contract, which was already reproduced in the original Appendix; copies of 24 photographs of appellant's camp house; two separate reproductions of the same diagram of the floor plan of the camp house; two separate copies of the same statement of Glen Drewett dated August 8, 1973; copies of miscellaneous correspondence among the parties and the district court relating to such matters as the filing of pleadings, bonds, interrogatories, and motions; copies of the parties' motions and memoranda of law to the trial court on a variety of issues at all stages of the proceedings; copies of interrogatories, answers, and affidavits; a copy of the pre-trial order; copies of the notice of appeal and receipt for appeal bond; and more. This Supplemental Appendix cost $533.68 to print.

Appellant alleges that appellee's designation of the entire record for reproduction in the Supplemental Appendix was not necessary to enable us to decide the issue on appeal, and he moves that the cost of printing the Supplemental Appendix be charged to appellee. Fed.R.App.P. 30(a) and (b) describe the portions of the record which are to be reproduced in the appendix and the methods by which the parties are to determine the contents of the appendix; and (b) authorizes the court of appeals to impose the cost of unnecessary portions of the appendix on the party designating them. * * *

(b) Contents of Appendix: Counsel should bear in mind the Court's desire to minimize the cost of reproducing the appendix, consistent with the obligation and responsibility of the parties to reproduce therein those parts of the record which are essential to the Court's consideration and determination of the issues raised by the appeal. Any parts of the record which are inadvertently omitted from the reproduced appendix may be referred to by appropriate references to the original record. . . .

We think that appellee here clearly has disregarded the dictates of Fed.R.App.P. 30 and Local Rule 13(b). For instance, because the issue on appeal is one of law and involves no dispute as to the salient facts, it was wholly unnecessary to order reproduction of the entire trial transcript and all the exhibits in the Supplemental Appendix. Similarly, reproduction in the Supplemental Appendix of all the memoranda of law submitted to the trial court by both parties on all issues not one of which memoranda is referred to in appellee's brief was unnecessary. The same is true of the correspondence among the parties and the district court, the interrogatories, answers, and affidavits, the pre-trial order, and the notice of appeal and receipt for appeal bond none of which is cited in appellee's brief. There is, of course, no excuse for printing the same matter in the Supplemental Appendix twice or for duplicating in the Supplemental Appendix material already in the Appendix.

Appellee's "Opposition to Plaintiff–Appellant's Motion to have Appellee Pay Cost of Unnecessary Portion of Appendix Requested" states in conclusory fashion that inclusion of "all testimony, evidence and the entire record ... is essential to the just disposition of this matter and reference thereto is made in the brief of defendant-appellee ..." The fact of the matter, however, is that appellee's brief refers to only minute portions of the record that is reproduced in the Supplemental Appendix, and the portions therein referred to have no bearing on the issue of law on appeal. Compare Brief for Appellee at 5–8 with text and note at note 6 supra.

Although we have no desire or intent to discourage litigants from reproducing all the relevant portions of the record in their appendices to this court, we cannot condone the extravagance practiced by appellee here. Because of the evident carelessness and disregard for Fed.R.App.P. 30 and Local Rule 13(b) with which appellee's Supplemental Appendix was assembled, appellant's motion to tax the costs of the Supplemental Appendix against appellee is granted.

Notes and Questions

1. Does the Drewett case mean that the general rule for including items in the appendix is "not too much but not too little"?

2. If so, is this rule too vague to offer much guidance?

3. Is the practical answer that in most cases content of the appendix not a problem?

Chapter 9

ORAL ARGUMENT

FEDERAL RULE OF APPELLATE PROCEDURE 34

Oral Argument

(a) In General.

(1) Party's Statement. Any party may file, or a court may require by local rule, a statement explaining why oral argument should, or need not, be permitted.

(2) Standards. Oral argument must be allowed in every case unless a panel of three judges who have examined the briefs and record unanimously agrees that oral argument is unnecessary for any of the following reasons:

    (A) the appeal is frivolous;

    (B) the dispositive issue or issues have been authoritatively decided; or

    (C) the facts and legal arguments are adequately presented in the briefs and record, and the decisional process would not be significantly aided by oral argument.

(b) Notice of Argument; Postponement. The clerk must advise all parties whether oral argument will be scheduled, and, if so, the date, time, and place for it, and the time allowed for each side. A motion to postpone the argument or to allow longer argument must be filed reasonably in advance of the hearing date.

(c) Order and Contents of Argument. The appellant opens and concludes the argument. Counsel must not read at length from briefs, records, or authorities.

(d) Cross–Appeals and Separate Appeals. If there is a cross-appeal, Rule 28(h) determines which party is the appellant and which is the appellee for purposes of oral argument. Unless the court directs otherwise, a cross-appeal or separate appeal must be argued when the initial appeal is argued. Separate parties should avoid duplicative argument.

(e) Nonappearance of a Party. If the appellee fails to appear for argument, the court must hear appellant's argument. If the appellant fails to appear for argument, the court may hear the appellee's argument. If neither party appears, the case will be decided on the briefs, unless the court orders otherwise.

(f) Submission on Briefs. The parties may agree to submit a case for decision on the briefs, but the court may direct that the case be argued.

(g) Use of Physical Exhibits at Argument; Removal. Counsel intending to use physical exhibits other than documents at the argument must arrange to place them in the courtroom on the day of the argument before the court convenes. After the argument, counsel must remove the exhibits from the courtroom, unless the court directs otherwise. The clerk may destroy or dispose of the exhibits if counsel does not reclaim them within a reasonable time after the clerk gives notice to remove them.

SECTION A. THE ROLE OF ORAL ARGUMENT IN THE APPELLATE PROCESS

R. MARTINEAU, FUNDAMENTALS OF MODERN APPELLATE ADVOCACY

§ 8.1 (1985).

In [earlier sections of this treatise,] the changes in the nature and role of the brief in the appellate process were reviewed. These changes necessarily reflect changes in the nature and role of oral argument. The brief and the oral argument are the appellate attorney's only means for communicating with the appellate court. As the role of the brief has been expanded, that of oral argument has been diminished.

Oral argument has held center stage for most of the history of appellate review, in part for historical reasons. Appellate review developed in England primarily as an oral process, because of the preferences of those involved and the cost and difficulty of printing. Oral arguments often lasted for several days. That tradition was carried over to this country. However, as printing became quicker and less expensive and the courts and judges wanted more time for reflection and writing opinions prior to handing down decisions, they began to limit the time allotted for oral argument in each case. Restrictions on oral argument caused attorneys to turn to the brief as a means of expressing their views to the appellate courts. The courts also encouraged the change.

The shift in emphasis from oral argument to brief was gradual. Well into the 1950's oral argument remained the major influence on the ultimate decisions of the appellate courts. In almost all appellate courts oral argument was heard in most cases, and many judges came to oral argument "cold," that is, without having read the briefs beforehand and thus knew nothing about the case. Because some courts made tentative decisions on cases immediately after oral argument, it was inevitable that the oral argument would have a far greater influence upon their decisions than did the briefs.

Sustaining the continued importance of oral argument was the fact that the oral argument was the only part of the appellate process easily available to other attorneys and the press. Briefs were filed without public notice or fanfare. The oral argument was, however, a public confrontation between the opposing attorneys. It was an event that could be observed and reported even by persons not knowledgeable about legal matters. It could capture the attention not only of the news media and the public but of the participants and other attorneys. It also provided the perfect model for a moot court in the law schools. Appellate moot court became a requirement in almost every law school curriculum, so every attorney came out of law school thinking that the ability to make a dramatic oral argument was one of the hallmarks of a great attorney.

Beginning in the mid 1950's, however, increasing case loads began to influence how a court dealt with each case. Oral arguments became shorter. Oral argument was no longer automatic in every case. Judges, with the help of the staff, prepared for oral argument by reading the briefs beforehand. Oral argument was no longer a time for attorneys to introduce the judges to the case with ample time for demonstrating the oratorical arts. Rather, in the limited number of cases in which it was allowed, oral argument gave an opportunity for the judges to clear up questions that had occurred to them in reading the briefs, for the appellant's attorney to emphasize his principal argument, and for the appellee's attorney to make his most telling point in opposition. Appellate attorneys must now rely primarily upon their briefs to define the issues, present their version of the facts, and develop their legal arguments. Oral argument is no longer the central focus of the appellate process but rather just one step in the process through which the appellate court performs its function of error correction or law development.

This is not to say that oral argument is no longer important. But it is important in a much different way than it once was. In earlier times oral argument was the principal difference between winning and losing the appeal, a head-to-head confrontation at the conclusion of which one side prevailed over the other. Today judges take advantage of oral argument to explore with the attorneys particular difficult legal or factual points in the case; failure to satisfy the judges on that point may result in an adverse decision. Persuasion remains the principal objective of oral argument, but not the kind of persuasion in which an appellate attorney by the force of his personality and the eloquence of his argument convinces a court with little or no prior knowledge about a case to decide it in his client's favor. The modern appellate attorney should view the oral argument as an opportunity to sit in on a conference of the judges to discuss the case with them, to point out the essential elements of each side of the case, and most importantly to answer any questions the judges may have.

Given the changes in the appellate process oral argument is not as decisive as it once was. If the court, however, chooses only some cases for oral argument, the appellate attorney whose case is selected can be certain that the court is bothered by the case and the outcome is not certain. By ordering oral argument when it has discretion not to order it, the court is sending a clear signal to the attorneys that the judges are open to being influenced by oral argument. With that kind of invitation, the appellate attorney who does not treat oral argument as potentially decisive is ignoring what the court is telling him.

Another of the major ways in which appellate moot court competitions fail to reflect the realities of modern appellate practice is in the relative importance of the brief and the oral argument. In the moot court competitions, the oral argument still remains the climax of the competition, the feature that distinguishes the competitions from all other law school activities and probably the principal cause for their dramatic increase in popularity. In large part, the same factors that made oral argument the central focus of appellate practice for so long lie behind its continuing to occupy that role in moot court competitions. It is at the oral argument that the attorney meets an opponent face to face; it is the last step in the process just before a decision is made; it is where the attorney can demonstrate his or her skills in a public forum before an audience; it is where the attorney not only faces directly the symbols of the judicial process but becomes a live participant in that process; it is where the attorney deals directly with people and not just paper, pen, and books. Moot court competitions even have one attraction that usually does not occur in actual appellate practices—there is an instant decision and, for half of the participants, instant gratification.

The structure of a moot court competition is also very similar to that of oral argument in the appellate courts of 25 to 50 years ago. There is oral argument in every case; the oral argument in every case is the same length; the judges are not likely to have made substantial preparation for the argument; the arguments are designed more to permit the attorneys to tell the judges about the case rather than having the judges ask questions based on their prior study of the briefs and the record; and the attorney can prevail by the sheer force of personality, skill in technique, and powers of oral persuasion.

The problem is, of course, that modern appellate practice has changed so much in the past 25 years that none of these elements of the oral argument continues to exist in most appellate courts—but moot court competitions continue to include all of them. The result is that the oral argument portion of moot court competitions is training in skills that are no longer relevant. The only purpose now served by moot court oral arguments is experience in public speaking. This type of training is helpful, but not nearly as helpful as participating in an oral argument that approximates as closely as possible an oral argument in a real appellate court.

SECTION B. THE NECESSITY
FOR ORAL ARGUMENT

1. ARGUMENTS FAVORING ORAL ARGUMENT

MARTINEAU, THE VALUE OF APPELLATE
ORAL ARGUMENT: A CHALLENGE TO
THE CONVENTIONAL WISDOM

72 Iowa L. Rev. 1, 11–20 (1986).*

I. INTRODUCTION

The last several decades have witnessed a host of substantive and procedural developments that have had a dramatic impact on the legal process. The system of appellate review has not been immune from these developments; in fact, many of the changes have had more of an effect at the appellate level than at the trial level. The expansion of substantive rights through legislative and judicial action, the growth of the administrative and bureaucratic state, the effort to make both trial and appellate courts more accessible, and the growth in the number of lawyers have dramatically increased the appellate court caseload. This 'crisis of volume,' in turn, has generated reform measures that address the structure, personnel, and processes of appellate courts, with any type of response in one area affecting the others. The most common structural change has been the creation of one or more intermediate appellate courts, with a right of appeal only to the first appellate level; further review is discretionary in the supreme court. The most immediate and typical response to the increased appellate caseload has been an addition of appellate judgeships at the intermediate level or at the supreme court level in jurisdictions without an intermediate appellate court.

While structural and personnel changes have required legislative or voter approval, procedural changes have been initiated by state and federal appellate courts. Whether it has been simplifying the notice of appeal form or supervising the preparation of the testimony transcript, the appellate courts have made strenuous efforts to increase the number of appeals terminated and reduce the amount of time between judgment in the trial court and judgment in the appellate court. Efficiency and expediting have become bywords of the appellate process.

Many, if not most, of these developments have been recognized as either helpful to a meaningful appellate review or at least not a hindrance to that process. In several areas, however, there is substantial debate over whether particular reforms have done more harm than good to a sound appellate process. The principal areas of concern have been limitations on oral argument, the growth of court staffs, and limitations on the writing and publication of opinions.

[handwritten margin note: more harm than good to appellate process]

* Copyright © 1986, University of Iowa (Iowa Law Review). Reprinted by permission. All rights reserved.

Of all of these controversial developments, the one that has probably caused more concern among both appellate judges and appellate lawyers is the extent to which many appellate courts have eliminated or severely restricted oral argument. To most observers of and participants in the appellate process, these restrictions on oral argument are highly regrettable, forced upon the courts by an overwhelming caseload, and adopted only with great reluctance. Very few, on the other hand, argue that the relative importance of oral argument has been greatly overestimated and that the appellate brief is and should be the principal focus of the appellate process.

caseload is the cause of limited oral arg.

* * *

III.   THE ARGUMENTS FOR ORAL ARGUMENT

In analyzing the importance of oral argument to the appellate process, the most appropriate methodology is to examine the reasons given by those who believe that oral argument is an essential element of effective appellate review in virtually every case. These represent four distinct interests: the appellate courts as an institution, the appellate judges, counsel, and the litigants. The reasons given on behalf of each interest will be examined separately.

A.   *Institutional Purposes*

A principal justification for oral argument is stated in terms of the appellate court's importance as an institution of government in democratic society. The premise underlying this approach is that the governmental processes should, to the extent possible, be conducted in public, to assure the public and the participants in the process that decisions are based on publicly acknowledged considerations and interests. The underlying principle is discussed today in terms of public accountability and visibility. For the judicial system, accountability is crucial, since it depends on public confidence and acceptance of the results of its processes. Otherwise, the system could not function. This imperative lies behind the often-stated principle that it is essential not only that justice be done but that it appear to be done.

Accepting all of the foregoing as true does not mean, however, that oral argument must be heard on every aspect of every case, or on the merits of every case, or even on a substantial majority of cases. The starting point of the analysis should be an <u>awareness</u> that, in order for the judicial process to satisfy the demands for accountability, it has never been a requirement that all proceedings be conducted in public or that the participants have the right to make oral presentations. Instead, the essentials for accountability are: (1) interested parties must be able to present their views to the decisionmaker; (2) the factors that serve as the basis for the decision—the record—must be available to the public; (3) the decision must be publicly announced and become part of the record; and (4) the process must appear fair to the parties and the public. If the judicial process has these ingredients, the participants in the process cannot legitimately complain that they are unable to present their views or that they are unaware of the bases for the decision.

demands of accountability

Moreover, the public cannot complain that there is no public accountability because they have full access to the parties' presentations, the record, the decision, and the reasons given to support the decision.

Orality and visibility, however, have never been absolute requirements for every step in the appellate process. The confidentiality of the court's conference room, draft opinions, and communications among judges and their staffs is virtually unquestioned. Many decisions on motions, both substantive and procedural, and on whether to have oral arguments, written or published opinions, or rehearings are made on written submissions to the court without oral arguments, even though many of these decisions may be 'outcome determinative.' The question then becomes when will orality be required. That question should be the focus of debate, rather than the question of how to preserve oral argument in every case.

To say that oral argument is not required in all cases does not mean that it should not be held in a substantial number of cases, even some in which the judges may have concluded that briefs are adequate to decide the case properly. There are some cases which, by virtue of the importance of the issues involved, or the public interest in those issues, demand the full panoply of the traditional appellate process, including oral argument and a full, signed published opinion. If these cases and those in which the judges think oral argument would be helpful are not sufficient to legitimate the appellate process, then the judges should assign additional cases for oral argument to satisfy those institutional interests. With a large caseload, the need for oral argument to satisfy these interests becomes particularly important when the court utilizes different features of the appellate process such as dispositions on motion, an enlarged central staff, disposition without opinion, and unpublished opinions. When oral argument is held for reasons other than to assist judges in deciding cases, this fact should be acknowledged by judges, counsel, and litigants.

B.   The Judge's Purposes

Many proponents of oral argument cite its usefulness to the appellate judge as one of the principal reasons for having it in virtually every case. The core justification, stated in various ways by different commentators, is that oral argument can assist judges in understanding issues, facts, and arguments of the parties, thereby helping judges decide cases appropriately. According to this theory, assistance comes in several ways, depending on the nature of the case or the quality of the briefs. For example, there may be matters that are unclear or omitted from the briefs that can be clarified only by questioning opposing counsel, particularly in cases with complicated facts or novel legal issues. Moreover, some ideas are better transmitted orally than by written means.

Other justifications for oral argument are based on the nature or practices of the individual judge. It is contended that some judges, for example, assimilate ideas more effectively through oral rather than written communication.

Another justification concerns the judge not so much from the standpoint of the individual case, but from that of the judge's role in the judicial process. Oral argument helps judges avoid becoming too isolated, and serves to remind them that they are not the only participants in the judicial process, and that their decisions directly affect individual lives. Moreover, it is important for judges to have direct personal contact with the litigant's attorney. Without this contact, a judgeship would be reduced merely to processing paper and thus, fewer well-qualified persons may be attracted to the bench.

An analysis of these justifications supports the use of oral argument in the appellate process. These justifications do not support, however, the necessity of oral argument in every case or even in a large majority of cases. At best they suggest why there should be oral argument in some cases.

In examining the first justification—that oral argument facilitates the judge's understanding of the issues, facts, and arguments—it is clear that the usefulness of oral argument in a particular case depends on the quality of the briefs, and the extent to which the judges and their staffs study the briefs and the record, and use means other than oral argument to clarify ambiguities. To suggest that most cases involve issues and facts so complicated and briefs so poorly written that oral argument is virtually indispensable ignores a basic fact about most appellate cases: they are not exceedingly complicated. By reading the briefs and the relevant portions of the record, judges are usually provided a sufficient basis to decide a case.

On the other hand, if briefs are so bad that even after careful scrutiny confusion still remains over the facts, issues, or contentions of the parties, it is doubtful whether a fifteen-or twenty-minute oral argument will do much to clarify matters, particularly when there is no advance notice as to the matters on which the judges seek clarification. Attorneys who cannot write an adequate brief are not likely to be better at oral argument; thus, oral argument may be a wasted effort. The idea that an attorney can respond better orally to an unanticipated question, under the pressures of a personal appearance in a public courtroom, relying exclusively on memory, than in a written brief over which the attorney has had thirty or more days to prepare, with full access to the record, and to the texts of relevant cases, simply defies the realities of the situation.

This is not to suggest that oral argument will never be helpful. Among other things, exploring the limitations of precedent and the implications of a decision, as well as the public's interest in the decision, may all justify oral argument in a particular case. Such exploration, however, does not justify a general policy in favor of oral argument, particularly in the usual case that involves only error correction issues.

The two remaining justifications for oral argument—one relating to the nature of the case and the other to judges' abilities—are closely related and yet are opposite sides of the same coin. The first justification is that some ideas or arguments are better communicated by oral rather than written means, while the second justification is that some judges assimilate ideas more effectively when they are transmitted orally. What validity there may be to either of these arguments, when comparing oral versus written communication generally, is without merit when applied to oral argument as it is conducted in most appellate courts.

Oral arguments are fifteen or twenty minutes in length per side. During that period attorneys hope to summarize one or two of their best points set forth in the brief and to answer questions from the judges. Some attorneys have a sufficient command of the record and the relevant law, and are competent enough at public speaking, to make effective oral argument succinctly and coherently and to respond competently to questions from the judges. Most attorneys, however, do not make good use of oral argument, whether for lack of skill, insufficient knowledge of the purposes of oral argument, or inadequate preparation for the particular argument. It simply flies in the face of common sense that the transitory, spontaneous, and soon forgotten oral statement can communicate an idea better than a carefully prepared brief that can be studied as long as necessary.

Communicating emotion is one aspect of advocacy that is unquestionably done more effectively in oral form. This emotive quality is achieved by making what is essentially a jury argument to the appellate court, emphasizing the equities of the case. Judges, however, do not respond well to this kind of argument; although they are concerned with doing justice, they are more concerned with rendering justice on a principled basis, not on an emotional basis induced, in part, by counsel's rhetoric. Consequently, the ability to communicate emotion should not justify preference for oral argument over the written brief. Furthermore, the idea that some judges assimilate ideas better from oral presentations than from written documents ignores the limitations of oral argument and the generally accepted principles on the amount that can be absorbed orally at one time.

Notwithstanding these inherent weaknesses of oral argument, it must be acknowledged that oral argument does allow judges to explore their ideas of the case with counsel. In recognizing this fact, however, the question must be asked whether oral argument is the most effective means for judges to test their ideas. This function is usually served by the judge meeting with the staff and other judges on the panel. Often they are just as conversant as counsel on the strengths and weaknesses of the judges' ideas, particularly as they may be affected by the record or other cases. Furthermore, a short oral argument is hardly the most appropriate time to obtain a thoughtful response from counsel about a novel idea. Attorneys will be far more likely to give a reasoned response if given an opportunity to reflect on the idea, review the record, and do additional research. If put in this position at oral argument, the wise advocate will ask for permission to submit a short memorandum on the idea, avoiding a spur of the moment response.

There is no doubt that participation in oral argument on occasion can be important to the appellate judge for all of the reasons suggested by its supporters. Likewise, this fact supports oral argument in some, but not in all cases, and not even in some predetermined percentage of cases. It proves only that it is important for an appellate court to hear oral argument in some cases. The key question is in which cases.

C. *For Litigants and Counsel*

In addition to justifying oral argument as an institutional necessity and aid for the appellate judge, many assert that oral argument is also advantageous for litigants and their counsel. Much of the support for this argument is virtually identical to that given in the institutional and appellate judge context.

1. *Influence on Result*

First and foremost among the reasons why counsel and their clients wish to have oral argument is that it may determine the result of the case. Since it is the last opportunity to win the case, most attorneys, and presumably their clients, want to preserve oral argument in as many cases as possible. Statements by a number of judges on the percentage of cases in which oral argument is decisive or changes the judge's view about the proper result can be cited.

2. *Highlighting Issues*

Oral argument gives counsel both the opportunity to concentrate on the principal issue of the case from their own perspective as well as from that of the judges. This rationale properly assumes that the briefs will raise several issues of which only one or two will be dispositive. Moreover, oral argument allows counsel to focus the judge's attention on these crucial issues. Furthermore, should the judges and counsel differ in identifying the key issue, this difference may be addressed during oral argument; in this way, counsel at least has an opportunity to focus on the pertinent issue in stating the client's position.

3. *Responding to Questions*

Just as it is important for judges to question counsel in a particular case, it is equally important that counsel have an opportunity to respond, in hopes of resolving any doubts the judge may have about the parties' positions. At this stage of the appellate process, the issues have been narrowed and the case is ready for disposition. By asking questions, the judges identify the weak spots of the case as presented by counsel's brief. Satisfactory responses to these questions, may result in a victory for the responding counsel's client. Thus, oral argument becomes crucial to the outcome of the appeal.

4. *Participation in the Process*

From the attorney's and the litigant's perspectives, oral argument can be justified as a way of engaging them more in the appellate process.

This involvement reinforces their confidence in the result of the process, and strengthens their respect for the courts and the adversary system. This justification is essentially the same as the public accountability and visibility justification given in section III A, in which the institutional interests of the court were considered.

In analyzing the reasons why counsel and litigants desire oral argument, several questions about the effect oral argument has on the result of the appeal process must be considered: (1) how reliable are the estimates of the percentage of cases in which oral argument is decisive; (2) if oral argument is decisive in a relatively small percentage of cases, can those cases be identified before making a decision on whether to have oral argument; and (3) are there less expensive, more expedient alternatives to oral argument in some cases. These questions will be discussed more fully in section VI. At this point, analysis will be limited to the viewpoint of counsel and the litigant. In most cases, it is clear that they will prefer to incur the time and expense of oral argument for one last opportunity to win the case. Having spent a great deal time and money of both at the trial level as well as in the briefing stage on appeal, they will find that the additional cost in time and money is only marginal. The more fundamental question is, however, the extent to which the desires of the attorney or the client should be determinative of whether oral argument is held. There are those whose principal oral argument thesis is that either party should have it on request, and that at most the appellate court should be able only to suggest the waiver of oral argument but never to order that it be forgone.

At the heart of this question is the issue of whether the procedures of appellate review are to be directed primarily at permitting the litigants to control the appellate process for their own advantage, or whether they are to be controlled by the court to enable it to perform its functions in the manner that the court considers most effective and efficient, balancing the interests of all of the litigants who bring or will bring cases to the court. If the developments in the appellate process over the past two decades show anything, they demonstrate that appellate courts have, as a matter of necessity, taken control over each step in the appellate process to enable them to cope with the deluge of appeals, while still attempting to develop the law and do justice between the parties.

No one has disputed most of the steps taken by the courts in this direction, such as dramatic shortening of the time in which a notice of appeal can be filed or the transcript of testimony can be ordered, mandating settlement conferences, allowing motions for summary disposition, imposing page limitations on briefs, dismissing appeals for failure to comply with the appellate rules, shortening the time allowed for oral argument, and generally assuming control of the pace of the appellate process and insisting that the rules, and particularly the time limits, be complied with by litigants before the court. What is perhaps most incongruous is that some who are most insistent upon the court not being able to eliminate oral argument in any case in which counsel wishes to have it propose that briefs be done away with, forcing counsel and litigants to rely exclusively on oral argument. Why the appellate court should be able to eliminate the written brief, but not oral argument is not explained.

The remarkable efforts of appellate courts to deal with the crisis of volume have demonstrated one point most clearly—no aspect of appellate procedure is sacrosanct. Every part of it, major or minor, can and must be examined from the standpoint of its assistance to the appellate court in performing its functions of error correction and law development, fairly and quickly. The guiding principle should be that an appellate court is required to devote only as much time as necessary for the court to consider the submissions of the parties, to decide which result is correct, and to provide a statement of reasons for its decisions, as well as to serve the institutional interests of the court and the judges. To insist upon more is to require the court to devote time to one case that it could devote to the next case, thereby delaying consideration of all pending and subsequently filed appeals.

guiding principal

The second and third reasons why counsel and the litigant might wish to have oral argument—to highlight issues and respond to questions—are identical to those reasons given for why the judges would want to have oral argument and are discussed in section III B. Similarly, the last reason, participation in the process, is essentially the same as the institutional purpose of the court discussed in section III A.

Notes and Questions

1. According to table 1.8 from the 2003 report of the Administrative Office of the United States Courts, the following table shows for each year the percentage of cases decided after oral argument:

Year	Percent
1988	51%
1989	48%
1990	45%
1991	44%
1992	44%
1993	40%
1994	41%
1995	40%
1996	39%
1997	40%
1998	39%
1999	37%
2000	35%
2001	32%
2002	33%
2003	33%

In state supreme courts the statistics from a 1973 survey are as follows:

The use of oral arguments as part of the initial decision-making process varies from state to state. Of the forty-three states responding to this section of the questionnaire, twenty-five reported that 90 per cent or more of their cases are accompanied by oral argument of counsel. Only six of the responding states hear oral argument in fewer than 50 per cent of cases. Kentucky hears oral argument in only 2 per cent of cases, followed by Oklahoma with only 10 to 20 per cent. In Indiana, all civil cases are accompanied by oral arguments but criminal cases rarely are. In Utah, 66 per cent of the civil cases but only 10 per cent of the criminal cases are presented orally.

McConkie, Decision–Making in State Supreme Courts, 59 Judicature 337, 338 (1976). No later state court statistics are available but it is reasonable to assume that as the number of appeals to state appellate courts have increased, the percentage of appeals argued orally has declined.

2. Why are there such variances in the percentage of cases in which oral argument is heard? What other information would be necessary to answer this question? Is it a reasonable explanation that in some courts the judges believe more strongly in the value of oral argument than in others?

3. What are the principal arguments in favor of oral argument? Against it?

4. Is there a difference between admitting the value of oral argument in some cases and requiring it in all cases?

5. Should a party be able to insist upon oral argument even though the court thinks it is unnecessary? In P. Carrington, D. Meador, and M. Rosenberg, Justice on Appeal 16–24 (1976) the authors suggest that at most a court should be able to suggest to counsel that the opportunity for oral argument may be waived, but that if the attorney for either side wants oral argument, it will be held. Is this a practical approach to the problem? Does this raise the question of for whose benefit oral argument is held—the judges, the litigants, the attorneys, or the court as an institution? Does it raise a question as to who should have control over how the court spends its time in deciding appeals.

6. The English system relies almost exclusively on oral argument rather than briefs as the means for communication between the attorneys and the judges. R. Martineau, Appellate Justice in England and the United States: A Comparative Analysis 101–03 (1990). It has been suggested that this approach should be used in this country to help appellate courts handle their workload. Meador, Toward Orality and Visibility in the Appellate Process, 42 Maryland L.Rev. 732, 739 (1983). For a criticism of this proposal, see Martineau, The Value of Appellate Oral Argument: A Challenge to the Conventional Wisdom, 72 Iowa L.Rev. 1, 25–28 (1986). What advantages are there to this system? What disadvantages?

SECTION C. EFFECTIVE ORAL ARGUMENT

Introductory Note

Unless a lawyer has been a law clerk for an appellate judge, the lawyer is essentially in the dark about how a judge prepares for oral argument. The following description by Judge Ruggero Aldisert of his preparation is one of the few detailed descriptions written by a judge. While other judges' preparations may not be identical, they will have many of the same characteristics. A wise lawyer will prepare for oral argument by keeping in mind how the judges will prepare for it. For descriptions of other judges preparations see F. Coffin, On Appeal 120–25 (1994) and Panel Discussion, What Appellate Advocates Seek from Appellate Judges and What Appellate Judges Seek from Appellate Advocates, 31 N.M. L. Rev. 255 (2001).

R. ALDISERT, WINNING ON APPEAL

305–307 (2d ed. 2003).*

Preparing for Oral Argument

§ 22.1 How Judges Prepare

Judges follow different chambers practices. Our work habits differ. Our experiences differ. I came to the federal appellate bench after an active career as a trial lawyer and state trial judge. I served as an adjunct law professor for twenty-three years. I like to study, do research, and write. My chambers practice is a mix of the pragmatic and the scholastic. Let me describe what takes place in my chambers prior to oral argument.

1. We receive the briefs and appendices a minimum of four weeks (usually six or seven weeks) in advance of the calendar week.

2. I am the first in chambers to read the briefs and the appendices. Depending on the circuit, there are at least six to eight cases each day on the week's calendar. This is how I read the briefs:

(a) Read the statement of issues in the appellant's brief.

(b) Read the district court's opinion with special emphasis on the facts and that portion of the opinion dealing with the issues raised on appeal.

(c) Read appellant's summary of argument.

(d) Read appellee's summary of argument.

(e) Read appellant's brief cover to cover.

(f) Read appellee's brief cover to cover.

(g) Skim, not read, reply brief to see if any point is legitimate.

* Copyright © 2003, National Institute for Trial Advocacy. Reprinted by permission. All rights reserved. Further reproduction is prohibited.

(h) If appellant raises a point with which I am not familiar, I do not proceed to next point. Instead, I immediately read the appellee's brief on this point.

(i) I reach a tentative decision.

3. I dictate a bench memorandum in each case analyzing the issues. If I am not familiar with controlling cases, I go to the Reporters and often have the full text of cases photocopied and attached to my memo together with excerpts from the record. I then make three decisions: (1) whether I desire oral argument; (2) whether my clerks should do further work on the case; and (3) reach a very tentative decision as to disposition.

4. After dictating the memo, I then prepare a document entitled "Synopsis." I synthesize the *major* contentions in the brief. By typing it myself rather than dictating, I am able to summarize the contentions, and ascertain, wherever possible, the single theme on which the appeal will stand or fall.

Important enough for oral argument

5. If the case is important enough for oral argument, I require my law clerks to prepare a detailed, formal bench memorandum, separate and apart from the one I already prepared. I instruct that their analysis and recommended disposition be their own product and they not be influenced by my original analysis. The clerks examine the relevant cases cited, do original research, and prepare a quality memorandum. Their memos are written in a formal style so that if the presiding judge assigns the case to me for an opinion, I can use excerpts from their memo for use in the first draft of the opinion. While preparing their bench memos, the clerks often confer with me.

6. Where another judge on the panel requests argument in additional cases, those too are assigned to the clerks for the "full court press."

7. I carefully study the bench memoranda prepared by the law clerks, either approving them or ordering more research and analysis.

develops questions

8. In the week prior to argument, my clerks and I devote at least a day to what I call "Case Conference." The day before Case Conference I reread all bench memos and will list on a "pink sheet" any questions I might have. My clerks (and sometimes interns) and I then sit around a conference table and discuss every case on the calendar—emphasizing those that will be argued but also those in which the clerks have not written a memo. My "position papers" at the conference are at least two bench memoranda: mine and the law clerks. During the course of discussion, I may order additional materials to be affixed to the memoranda, such as excerpts from the briefs, parts of the record and photocopies of cases. Often, I will have a clerk prepare a concise account of our conference summarizing our

discussions and indicating what questions I may ask counsel. This is listed on a document entitle "Case Conference Notes." The law clerk who had worked on the cases leads this discussion, and I lead the discussion on the cases to be submitted without argument.

9. The law clerks then prepare a thick, spiral-bound "Bench Memorandum" that includes a table of contents, my bench memo, the clerk's memo, my "pink sheet" and Case Conference Notes, all opinions of the trial court or administrative agency, and full text copies of *all* relevant cases. This is the document that I have before me on the bench during oral argument. I also require that all briefs and appendices be on the bench as well.

doc. created & used on the bench

We then travel to the city where the court will be sitting. On the morning of the argument, before I ascend the bench, my clerks and I meet again for about forty-five minutes to discuss the day's calendar.

Even with all this preparation, I recognize that a sort of chambers inbreeding takes place. I require oral argument in all cases except the "slam dunks" to discover whether my clerks and I have missed something in reading the briefs. I await the emphasis counsel will put on the case in their presentations, and I always listen closely to my colleagues' questions. These furnish clues as to their interests or concerns. Unlike other judges, I do not take notes during argument. My clerks do this. Instead, I concentrate completely on what every counsel says.

R. MARTINEAU, FUNDAMENTALS OF MODERN APPELLATE ADVOCACY

§§ 8.2–8.13 (1985).

§ 8.2. When to seek oral argument

The percentage of cases being heard orally is declining each year in response to the pressures of caseload. When appellate courts first began selecting only some cases for oral argument, they usually did so without any clearly defined criteria and without asking the attorneys in the case whether they thought oral argument was necessary. Now after substantial experience with selecting cases for oral argument, it is possible for these courts to establish criteria for making the decision, to announce the criteria to the attorneys in advance, and to ask the attorneys for their views on the necessity for oral argument in a particular case prior to making the decision. FRAP 34(a) and Wisconsin Appellate Rule 809.22 provide examples of the criteria. The negative criteria are essentially divided into two main categories: (1) the appeal is without merit either on the law or the facts; or (2) the briefs are adequate to present the issues and oral argument would be of marginal benefit. The first goes to the merits of the case, the second to the quality of the briefs.

It may be appropriate for an appellate attorney to suggest that oral argument is not necessary in a particular appeal in which he is involved. When oral argument was the central focus of the appellate process, the advice that it should never be waived was understandable, but there are many circumstances under which that advice is no longer appropriate. A busy appellate court seeking advice from the attorneys on whether to have oral argument will not appreciate being told in every case by every attorney that oral argument is essential. The court will not conclude that an attorney considers his case without merit if he does not ask for oral argument. It will, rather, look at the reasons given for the position taken.

From the viewpoint of the appellant, it is obvious that the appellant's attorney can never concede that his appeal is without merit. If the facts or the law or both are heavily against his position, then he must argue that there are nuances that can best be explored at oral argument. If his argument is novel or requires the overturning of prior law, the attorney can argue that the intricacies of the argument necessitate an oral explanation and the opportunity to explain the impact of adopting the attorney's argument on other cases. It is perfectly appropriate, however, for the appellant's attorney to waive oral argument on the basis that the briefs adequately set out the arguments on both sides. The attorney for the appellant may legitimately take the position that even though the briefs are adequate, the issues are such that the court should have the opportunity to question the attorney in open court, but only if he truly believes that to be the case.

The appellee's attorney can, of course, argue that the appeal is without merit and thus oral argument is a waste of time. He should not fear, however, conceding that the appellant raises difficult issues that require additional development in oral argument. Oral argument may be particularly important if the brief of the appellant makes a strong argument and the appellee wants an opportunity to refute.

Attorneys for the appellant and the appellee, in short, should always give the court their candid views on the value of oral argument. The one exception to this ground rule is that the appellant's attorney should never concede that the appeal is frivolous. The appellate court will not criticize the attorney who requests oral argument rather than infer that his case is without merit. In moot court competitions, oral arguments are held as a matter of course, although perhaps they should not be.

§ 8.3. Protocol of oral argument

The clerk of the appellate court will always notify the attorneys of the day oral argument will be heard, and usually the order in which the cases set for that day will be heard. If the day or the order is not suitable, the attorney may request a change by motion or by letter. Federal Appellate Rule 34(b) and some state rules require a motion. It is always wise to consult with other parties to see if they have any objection before filing the motion. Such a change should never be requested for merely personal reasons. The better alternative for the attorney who has something planned which will be difficult to reschedule is to notify the clerk of the potential conflict before the schedule is made up and request that the appeal be scheduled to avoid the conflict. It is

[margin handwritten note: give candid views on oral arg. →]

always easier for the court to take an attorney's preferences into account in making up the schedule than to change the schedule after it is once published.

If the appellate attorney is new to the appellate court before which he is to argue, he should visit the court when it is in session. He should observe whether there is more than one courtroom, their locations, the arrangement of counsel tables and lectern, how the cases are called, how the court controls the length of oral argument (lights or other signals), whether a clock can be seen from the lectern, where he can place his notes and other materials he plans to use during oral argument, whether a sound system is used, the acoustics, and anything else that may affect his argument. The more familiar an appellate attorney is with the surroundings and details of the appellate court before which he is appearing, the more comfortable and relaxed he will be when making his oral argument. A minor *faux pas* will probably not upset the court, but may be enough to disrupt the attorney's concentration on his argument.

If the appellate attorney wants to do something unusual during oral argument such as giving the court a letter calling a recently decided case to its attention, distributing copies of an exhibit, showing a movie, using visual aids, or the like he must check with the clerk of the court first to make the necessary arrangements and obtain the approval of the court. He should also notify the attorneys for the other parties. The beginning of oral argument is not the time to surprise the court or the opposing party. Anything that is to be distributed to the court should normally be given to the clerk for him to distribute.

The appellate attorney should always check in with the clerk's office on the morning of oral argument well before the beginning of the court session, no matter where his case is scheduled on the docket for the day. The court may change the order of cases for some reason, placing the attorney's case first to be argued. Nothing irritates an appellate court more than to wait for an attorney to show up even though the attorney would have been on time if the schedule had remained as announced.

The judges, of course, sit on a bench facing the attorneys, with the presiding judge in the center, and the other judges on either side of him in order of seniority alternating from his right to his left. Despite obvious value to the attorney, appellate courts seldom place name plates in front of the judges. In a court in which all of the judges sit on every case, it is easy to know who the judges are and where they will sit. In many intermediate appellate courts, however, the panels rotate on varying bases and thus the attorney may not know before whom he will argue until he sees the judges on the bench, although usually it is possible to learn who the judges are from the clerk's office prior to the day of argument, or at least on the day of argument. Whatever the situation, the appellate attorney should have before him a sheet of paper showing the names and seating arrangement of the judges so that the attorney can know which judge is asking him a question and can use that judge's name at the beginning of his response.

The appellant will always lead off the oral argument. He usually has an opportunity for a rebuttal but he must reserve time for this purpose out of the total allotted time. The shorter the total time available, of course, the less that can be saved for rebuttal.

§ 8.4. Effective oral argument, generally

Justice Robert Jackson before he was appointed to the Supreme Court served as Solicitor General of the United States and in that capacity participated in many oral arguments. Looking back on his experience he concluded that for each case he made three oral arguments. "First came the one that I had planned—as I thought, logical, coherent, complete. Second was the one I actually presented—interrupted, incoherent, disjointed, disappointing. The third was the utterly devastating argument that I thought of after going to bed that night." Justice Jackson's experience is common to most veteran appellate attorneys. The validity of his description is even greater today in an era of very short oral arguments before a busy but well prepared panel of judges.

To be effective in this situation means to be able to provide the court with the answers to the questions that it has about the case. As it has evolved, oral argument is now an exchange between the judges and the attorneys for the parties. An effective oral argument is one in which the attorney participates in such a way as to eliminate any doubts that the judges may have about the validity of the points made in his brief, the justice of his client's cause, or the effect of a decision in his client's favor upon the state of the law and future cases.

§ 8.5. Preparation

A complete mastery of the record is prerequisite to preparing an effective brief and equally as important in preparing for the oral argument. The only difference is that oral argument requires a far more complete knowledge of the record because of the difference in the circumstances under which the appellate attorney will be asked to demonstrate that knowledge. The appellate attorney writes the brief while sitting in his own office with the record before him. He can spend as much time as necessary checking the record to find a statement of a witness or a sentence in a document. At oral argument, while he may have a copy of the record with him, he cannot leisurely search out the exact language with which to respond to a question. If he does not have the fact at his fingertips, he is forced to say he will provide the answer in a letter to be submitted later. A delayed letter is a poor substitute for an immediate response. In addition, the attorney must have a thorough command not only of his own brief but also that of his opponent because he may well be asked about a statement or argument in either and must be able to respond intelligently and immediately.

The attorney must, of course, also have a thorough knowledge of the case law and other authorities relied upon. He must know the facts of the pertinent cases and be able to argue factual similarities and differences. This ability presupposes complete mastery of the facts of the case being argued. Despite the fact that cases get decided on the basis of the law and the facts, lack of familiarity with the record is the most glaring weakness in most oral arguments. Notwithstanding all of the articles and books about effective appellate advocacy stressing the importance of the facts in the ultimate disposition of an appeal, many if not most appellate attorneys fail even to demonstrate that they have ever heard of the advice. Whether the result inadequate preparation time, misdirected moot court programs in law schools, or laziness, most appellate attorneys are simply not sufficiently grounded in the facts of their own cases to respond adequately to questions from the bench about the facts and their relationship to the facts of cases relied upon as precedent.

Many appellate attorneys appear to think that preparation for oral argument means writing out a complete statement and memorizing as much of it as possible. This is the worst type of preparation possible because he is preparing an oral argument that will not be given and will detract from the spontaneity that makes an oral argument interesting. This is not to say that no preparation for what will be said is necessary, only that writing out a formal statement is a waste of time. The appellate attorney should prepare an outline or some other listing of the principal points he wishes to make so that his remarks are in logical sequence and he will not overlook any of the critical points. He should attempt to anticipate the questions he may be asked by the judges and be prepared to answer them.

If brevity is the single most important quality of an effective brief, flexibility is the most important element of preparation for oral argument. The appellate attorney must be prepared to give a full presentation because the court may ask few or no questions, although this situation is unlikely. He must also be prepared to spend much if not all of his time, responding to questions. Typically, the attorney's presentation is interspersed with questions and dialogues with the judges, but the possibility of no questions or of many questions cannot be disregarded. All the attorney can do is be prepared to deal with any of the three types, and to make an effective argument no matter what develops.

These same principles are true for appellate moot court competitions. The problem is, however, that most moot court competitions do not include a realistic record as discussed supra in Chapter 6. The type of preparation for oral argument essential in modern appellate practice is, consequently, not the type of preparation engaged in by law students for oral arguments in moot court competitions. They spend their time making one practice argument after another, usually with a prepared text devoted primarily to discussing the cases cited in their brief. In so doing, they are not learning the skills necessary for an effective oral argument in a real appellate court. It is the facts that determine the result of real cases and they are what an appellate court is concerned with during an oral argument. Only when appellate moot court competitions are structured to include a realistic record can the preparation of a moot court argument begin to stimulate preparation for an oral argument in an appellate court.

§ 8.6. Applicability of principles of public speaking, generally

An oral argument in an appellate court is a special type of public speaking, but it is nonetheless public speaking, and most of the principles of effective public speaking are applicable to it.

These principles are reviewed here in substantial detail because many law students and appellate attorneys have not been exposed to them previously or, if they have, may not remember them or may not understand their relevance to oral argument in an appellate court.

§ 8.7. Written preparation

In preparing for oral argument, the law student or appellate attorney is first faced with the question of the desired form of delivery. The options are: (1) to read from a manuscript, (2) memorize a manuscript, (3) speak without written preparation, or (4) use notes to provide organization and aid memory but speak without a written text. Of these four types, authorities on public speaking are unanimous that the first three types have major defects. Both the read and memorized texts bore the listener, lack sincerity, reduce audience rapport, and most importantly, inhibit the flexibility essential to an effective oral argument. The practice of some lawyers reading their briefs during oral argument has even prompted some appellate rules to specify that brief reading is prohibited.

At the other end of the spectrum is the impromptu delivery where the speaker makes no advance preparation of what to say. This type of delivery is suitable only when the speaker need only respond to questions and has no responsibility to take the initiative. Notwithstanding the fact that oral argument in a modern appellate practice has become primarily a forum for the judges to ask questions of the attorneys, as noted supra at § 8.1, the extent to which judges ask questions varies from court to court, judge to judge, and case to case. The appellate attorney must always be prepared to speak on his own without the aid of questions, and it would be very difficult to make a logical argument without having worked out carefully in advance the points to be covered.

Public speaking authorities are also agreed that the most effective type of delivery is the one that has everything worked out in advance except the precise words to be used in the speech. This type of speech, which is termed extemporaneous, is precise in its organization and thought content, but flexible in word choice. It combines the best features of all of the other forms of delivery but does not suffer any of their drawbacks. It permits good audience contact and a feeling of sincerity and spontaneity while at the same time allowing the speech to have a logical organization and smooth progression. Rather than preparing a manuscript, all that is necessary is to prepare notes on the key words and phrases of the speech and the authorities cited, and to arrange them in the proper order. These notes can be typed or printed on cards or sheets of paper so that they can glanced at briefly during the course of the speech, but not used so much as to interfere with good eye contact with the audience. For oral argument, this type of delivery is ideal because it gives the flexibility so essential to an effective oral argument. The attorney is prepared to speak until a question is asked, to respond to the question immediately, and to resume with the notes when the question has been answered to the judge's satisfaction. Any other type of delivery is certain to create problems and not be as effective as the extemporaneous.

§ 8.8. Audience contact

It is essential in public speaking for the speaker to acquire and maintain contact with the audience. This is achieved in part by the speaker exercising careful control over his or her body, movements, and voice. Particularly important is eye contact. The speaker must look at individual faces of the audience. If the speaker looks over the heads of the audience or at notes, this essential contact is lost. One of the many drawbacks of reading a prepared text is that it makes good eye contact difficult. Eye contact is important not only because it helps keep the attention of the audience, but it conveys the attitudes of sincerity and sureness—two important attributes of any speaker but especially the courtroom advocate. When speaking to a multi-judge appellate court, eye contact should be divided between the judges.

The speaker must also control his or her body so as not to make movements that distract the audience. The effect of the body on the message communicated by a speaker has recently come to be known as "body language." Under this theory, we communicate as much with our bodies as with our voices. There is no doubt that this theory is as applicable to public speaking as it is to private conversation. Body control is achieved by standing evenly on both feet, avoiding rocking, swaying, shifting back and forth from one foot to the other, or leaning on the table or lectern.

A major problem for most speakers is what to do with their hands. Some speakers, in an artificial attempt at casualness, put their hands in their pockets. This creates an impression of indifference or even disrespect for the audience. Other speakers use their hands for gestures in an effort to add emphasis. Gestures can be effective, but only if used very sparingly, and only if they appear natural. If used too often or if awkward or nervous, they only distract from the content of the speech and interfere with the contact between the speaker and the audience. The best thing to do with hands is to keep them loosely on the lectern, ready to adjust the notes or to make gestures, but not gripping the lectern so tightly that it appears as a means of support.

§ 8.9. Voice control

Equally as important as eye contact and body control is control of the speaker's voice. It is, of course, crucial that the speaker be heard, so the speaker must use the volume necessary for the audience to hear without strain. Usually this calls for a volume somewhat above a conversational level, but this will vary depending upon the acoustics of the room and whether there is a sound amplifier system. The only standard is one of comfortable listening for the audience. If possible, the speaker should test the acoustics and sound system first so that the volume level most appropriate can be anticipated. The speaker who cannot do this should be sensitive to the problem at the beginning of the speech and make any adjustments which are thought to be necessary. The worst thing is for the audience to have to indicate in some way that the speaker's volume is either too low or too high.

Voice pitch can also affect the attention given by the audience to the speaker. A monotone pitch is boring to listen to, and conveys a lack of interest or sincerity. Some speakers also have a pattern to their pitch, with it rising and falling at regular intervals. This also is distracting to the audience. Both the monotone and pattern tone can be avoided by giving emphasis to certain words, phrases, or sentences. Emphasis is a change in volume and pitch to give added meaning to the words being used. Often, it is as important as the words themselves.

Additionally, the speaker must be concerned with the pace of his delivery. Too slow a rate will permit the attention of the audience to wander, while too fast a rate will make it difficult for the audience to absorb the content of the speech. The proper rate of delivery is probably somewhat faster than ordinary conversation, but not too much. The rate also can be slowed down as a means of emphasis.

§ 8.10. Questions from audience

Questions from the audience should not be viewed as an interruption to the speech but as an important part of the presentation. Questions are used by the audience to clarify their understanding of the speaker's position and to obtain additional information. Responses to them thus should not be just a repetition of what has already been said, but should provide additional information or different emphasis. Questions are important because they identify the difficulties the audience is having in accepting the speaker's position and enable the speaker to address directly those problems.

A speaker should always anticipate questions and be prepared to answer them. This can best be done by thinking through the objections likely to be raised by the opposing view and mentally preparing responses to them. The matter of questions is, of course, particularly important in oral argument before an appellate court, as noted in § 8.1, supra. The opportunity for the judges to ask questions is the principal purpose of oral argument in modern appellate practice.

§ 8.11. Limiting number of points raised

In a speech of 20–30 minutes, authorities suggest that an audience will retain only a small part of a speech. It is recommended that the speaker attempt to make only two or three points. An audience is also most likely to remember what is said at the beginning of the speech and at the end; interest is likely to lag in the middle. With these factors in mind, it is recommended that the main points be repeated several times for emphasis during the course of the speech. It is also helpful to identify the principal points with phrases that highlight their importance such as "this case turns upon" or "the heart of the dispute between the parties is." This emphasis should also be made by changes in the voice pitch and volume and gestures as noted in §§ 8.8–8.9, supra.

Limiting the number of points raised has special significance in appellate practice. In § 7.31, supra, the necessity of keeping the number of issues raised on appeal and addressed in the brief to a minimum was discussed. This principle has even greater application to oral argument given the minimum amount of time available for oral argument, often only 15 or 20 minutes per side. When this time is even further reduced by questions from the bench it is obvious that oral argument can be used to urge only the strongest and most basic points in support of the attorney's case. If anything more is attempted, the oral argument will have little or no effect or may even be counterproductive.

§ 8.12. Know the audience

A speaker, in order to have the greatest effect on the audience, should try to become familiar with the makeup of the audience. No matter what general type the audience falls into, it is necessary to understand that the audience is plural and thus will hear the ideas conveyed by the speaker differently and will make judgments about the speaker and his cause depending upon the outlook and frame of reference of the individual listener. The speaker must thus view the speech from the perspective of the audience. The speaker should ask himself, "What am I asking of the audience, and what do they need to know to do it." The answer to this question will depend on the cultural, economic, and political background of the audience. The more the speaker knows about these aspects of his or her audience, the more likely the speaker will be able to frame an argument to appeal to that audience.

The speaker also must show respect for the audience. The speaker must neither speak down to it, or be obsequious. Respect for the audience also means not being overzealous in attacking opposing ideas or persons, particularly not on a personal basis.

As with all of the preceding points, the principle of knowing the audience is relevant to oral argument. Judges are as different from one another as any other individuals. Fortunately, it is usually possible to review opinions of the judges prior to the argument, as well as their judicial, legal, and social philosophies. Above all, it is important to remember the two basic interests of the judge: to do justice between the parties, but in accordance with the law.

The appellate attorney must also be clear what he is asking the court to do. In one sense this is dictated by the request for relief stated in the conclusion of the brief and the standard of review. The whole point of the brief and the oral argument is to give the court the "why" it should rule in favor of the attorney's client and the wherewithal to do it.

§ 8.13. Special rules of oral argument

No matter how primed the appellate judges are to ask questions, almost invariably the appellant's attorney will have the opportunity to give an opening statement. He should first identify himself and his client, then tell the court as succinctly as possible just what the case is about. The description of the case should not be as structured as the first sentence of the statement of the case in the brief. In fact, it is seldom desirable to recite that this is an appeal from the X court. Stating the central issue in the appeal is far more effective. How the issue is stated varies. Although it is certainly proper to say "This appeal presents the issue of the authority of the Director of the Department of [name of department] to [do whatever he did]," it may be more effective to say "The appellant was ordered by the Director of [name of department] to [name of the act]. He is here to argue that the order was beyond the Director's statutory authority." How the issue is formulated will vary from attorney to attorney and from case to case. The important thing is to frame the opening so that it catches the attention of the judges and focuses on what the attorney considers the main point.

After opening, the appellant's attorney is responsible for presenting those facts about the case which put the argument in context. FRAP 34(c) requires the appellant in his opening argument to give a fair statement of the case, including the facts. However, this requirement is less important than it once was because almost all appellate judges familiarize themselves with the facts before oral argument and it is usually most unwise to devote any substantial portion of a short 15 or 20 minute oral argument to a recital of the facts. Nevertheless, the appellant's attorney should be sure to relate those facts he thinks crucial to the outcome of the case because the facts control the outcome.

The attorney for the appellee can be somewhat more flexible in his opening statement. He need not tell the court what the case is about unless he disagrees with the opposing attorney's description of the case. He should not give a formal statement of facts, but he should correct any misstatements of fact by the appellant. He may also want to add facts omitted by the appellant.

The body of the argument is devoted to discussing the relationship between the facts and the law, implications to be drawn from the facts, and the most relevant statutes and cases. The traditional advice has been to limit oral argument to only one or two issues, each supported by the one or two most relevant cases. This advice has risen to the level of an imperative in the abbreviated oral argument of today. Fifteen or twenty minutes is simply not sufficient time to do more.

Another item of traditional advice that has been reinforced by changes in the appellate process is that questions from the judges indicate interest and should be welcomed and answered as thoroughly as possible. Resentment of questions from the bench because they interrupt the flow of a prepared oral argument has always reflected a failure to understand the role of an appellate judge in oral argument. Today the principal object of oral argument is to give the judges the opportunity to ask questions. An appellate attorney who resents questions misunderstands the purpose of oral argument and is thus unlikely to make an effective presentation.

Every question asked must almost always be answered when it is asked. It is seldom wise to put off a judge with the comment that the question will be answered later. The judge may infer from this failure to answer immediately that the attorney cannot answer the question, or worse, that the attorney fears that a candid answer will be damaging. There is also the possibility that through an oversight the attorney may neglect to answer the question. In short, the possible results of delaying an answer may harm the effectiveness of the oral argument.

For various reasons many appellate attorneys divide their oral argument between two or more attorneys. This is almost always harmful, particularly in modern practice. An oral argument of 30 minutes or less cannot be divided into neat packages, one per attorney. Such a division will almost inevitably result in less effective or even no answers to questions from the judges. The exchange between the judges and the attorneys is clearly hampered if the attorney arguing must tell the judge asking the question to wait until his partner argues because the latter is responsible for that portion of the case. Some courts have even included in their rules a prohibition against split arguments.

The common practice in most moot court competitions of having two person teams on each side with the members of the team sharing the oral argument is highly undesirable. It is exactly contrary to a basic principle of effective advocacy. The appellate attorney must always resist the temptation to interrupt the argument of the opposing attorney who misstates a fact or answers a question with misinformation or claims lack of information. Unless otherwise directed by a judge, the attorney should never interrupt the other side, but should wait until the other side is finished to provide the correct information. The appellee's attorney, who does not have a right of rebuttal, must request permission of the court to correct a statement made by the appellant in his rebuttal.

Almost all appellate courts have some means of keeping track of the time used by each side, usually warning lights that signal when the time is elapsed. The appellate attorney must not presume upon the good will of the court or the other side by going beyond the allotted time. Some presiding judges are more generous than others in allowing the attorney to finish his remarks, but unless invited by the presiding judge to continue, the attorney should end his argument as soon as he sees the signal that his allotted time is up.

An appellant's attorney should never tell an appellate court that he does not intend to make an oral argument but is available to answer questions. If the court has ordered argument or has not suggested it be waived, the attorney should assume the court wants to hear an oral argument. He does not have to use the full time, but he should make his main points. It may well be appropriate, however, for the appellee's attorney, after hearing the appellant's argument, to decide that further argument is unnecessary and to advise the court that he will make no argument but will answer any questions the judges may have. The appellee should waive oral argument in this manner only when it appears that the appellant has made no impression and that the court's mind is already made up. Waiver would not, of course, be appropriate in a moot court competition.

The oral argument should end in the same manner as the brief— with a short statement of the relief that the party seeks. Not only is such a statement a simple way to end the argument, but it reminds the appellate court why the party is before the court. If the party's time has expired, however, it is better to leave out the final statement than to go over the time.

R. ALDISERT, WINNING ON APPEAL

355–71 (2d ed. 2003).*

Delivering the Argument

§ 24.1 Appearance and Demeanor

When your case is called, you approach the lectern and identify yourself: "I am attorney So and So representing the appellant Such and Such." This is not only necessary for the moment of the argument but if the case is being recorded, in reviewing the tape or a transcript of it, the judges will know exactly who is speaking.

My advice is to dress conservatively. Men should wear a dark business suit and a conservative tie. For women, the basic black dress is always appropriate, as is a traditionally tailored, dark-colored suit. Judges are more tolerant today—much more tolerant than they were when I came to the bar in 1947—but it would not hurt to remember the words of King Lear: "Through tattered clothes small vices do appear." No court will stop a lawyer from arguing if he or she shows up in technicolor splendor; yet keep in mind that the judges appear in black robes in the appellate courtroom—the most formal of settings. How you dress may be of little moment to most judges, but if your appearance offends one judge who is a stickler for proper appearance, then you are starting off on the wrong foot in your responsibility to persuade.

Keep your voice well modulated. Your appearance before an appellate court is not an appearance before a jury. If the lectern is fairly close to the bench, it is well to keep your voice on the same level and in the same tone that you would use in a conversation at a dinner table with one sitting across from you. I recognize that acoustics in many courtrooms will not permit this and you may have to project your voice. In many courtrooms, the bench is somewhat elevated and is set at some distance from the lectern. In this situation, you should pitch your voice accordingly. Some microphones are placed on the podium for amplifica-

* Copyright © 2003, National Institute for Trial Advocacy. Reprinted by permission. All rights reserved. Further reproduction is prohibited.

tion purposes. Others are there for recording purposes only. Find out in advance what the situation is.

You should attempt to make your presentation as if you and the judges are sitting around a conference table. When the present courtrooms in the third circuit were designed, we deliberately arranged the design so that the attorney and the judges were almost on eye level. This was to encourage the private conversational give-and-take between counsel and the court.

Should the client be present at oral argument? I do not think so. Clients have a tendency to make the sort of suggestions that are least admired by judges. Many times I have had the experiences described by Justice H. Jackson:

> When I hear counsel launch into personal attacks on the opposition or praise of a client, I instinctively look about to see if I can identify the client in the room—and often succeed. Some counsel have become conspicuous for the gallery that listens to their argument, and when it is finished, ostentatiously departs. The case that is argued to please a client, impress a following in the audience, or attract notice from the press, will not often make a favorable impression on the bench. An argument is not a spectacle.

Although I have emphasized the conversational nature of your oral presentation, it is extremely important that you speak loud enough for the judges to hear you. Many lawyers are understandably quite nervous and have difficulty speaking. This is unfortunate. All is lost in oral argument unless the judge understand you; and we cannot understand you unless we hear you. Justice Jackson also adds:

> If your voice is low, it burdens the hearing, and parts of what you say may be missed. On the other hand, no judge likes to be shouted at as if he were an ox. I know of nothing you can do except to bear the difficulty in mind, watch the bench, and adapt your delivery to avoid causing apparent strain.

§ 24.2 Nervous? Yes, We Know

Judges know that appearing before a panel of the court is a formidable experience. There is an accompanying nervousness, and this is to be expected. The stress level is always high as the lawyer stands, ready to sell the case. Alan L. Dworsky put it very well:

> Experienced lawyers feel that way too. In fact, polls show that most people are more afraid of public speaking than dying. To me this only proves that most people who are polled don't think much about the questions. My point is you're human. Don't interpret your nervousness as personal flaw. Be gentle with yourself. Nervousness is a normal human experience in an exciting and scary challenge. It shows that you care about your performance and your case. When you stop being nervous, start worrying. You've either stopped caring or stopped breathing.

There is, however, one antidote to this; and I guarantee that it will work every time. If you walk into that courtroom better prepared on the subject than anyone else in the room, you have nothing to be nervous about. It is *your* case. You have lived with it. You have written the brief after researching and becoming familiar with every case touching the subject matter. You know more about the subject matter than any judge on the bench. Judges are generalists, not specialists in any idiosyncratic part of the law. It is you who is the specialist. You are there to help the judges by sharing your knowledge.

Notice that I used the phrase "know more about the *subject matter*." I did not say "know more about *your case*." You must have a broad comprehension of the entire branch of the law of which your case is but a part. You will have a ready answer for any hypothetical thrown at you, and *you*, not the judges, are now the master in this little domain. In the words of Franklin D. Roosevelt, "You have nothing to fear but fear itself."

Assume that you are still nervous. Not to worry. Ultimately, judges are interested in what you say; not how you say it. We are not out there judging a debate or a law school moot competition. We have asked for oral argument because we need a little more substantive help from the lawyers, not an Oscar-worthy performance.

Do not mumble. Always speak clearly so that you may be understood. Oklahoma Supreme Court Justice Yvonne Kauger adds:

> Don't whine.... Nervous tension seems to raise voices by octaves. Take a deep breath and lower your register. It should go without saying—but don't chew gum! As incredible as this sounds, it has happened.

§ 24.3 Ten Golden Rules of Oral Argument

	John W. Davis, Esq.		Judge Myron H. Bright
1.	Change places (in your imagination of course) with the court.	1.	Know your customer, the court.
2.	State first the nature of the case and briefly its prior history.	2.	A.B.P.—always be prepared.
3.	State the facts. (Follow the three Cs: chronology, candor and clarity.)	3.	Go for the jugular.
4.	State next the applicable rules of law on which you rely.	4.	Questions, questions, good and bad. Answer directly, then return to your main theme.
5.	Always go for the jugular vein.	5.	Be flexible and innovative.
6.	Rejoice when the court asks questions.	6.	One lawyer is better than two.
7.	Read sparingly and only from necessity.	7.	Look up, speak up.
8.	Avoid personalities.	8.	Don't snatch defeat from the jaws of victory

John W. Davis, Esq.	Judge Myron H. Bright
9. Know your record from cover to cover.	9. Believe in your case and be natural.
10. Sit down.	10. Above all, don't kid yourself. Oral argument is important; indeed, it may be crucial.

§ 24.4 Payoff Time: The Actual Delivery

§ 24.4.1 Overview

We all have our own personality, our own way of speaking, our own way of convincing. We say things in a certain manner, communicate in individual styles of tone, modulation, and gesture. We are comfortable as we do this, and we are usually effective.

In oral argument be as natural and comfortable as possible. Be yourself. Do not try to cast yourself in the image of another, because you run the risk of appearing artificial and insincere; you fail to project the appearance of confidence and credibility. When this happens, you lack persuasion. If you have prepared enough, you can afford to be yourself.

To launch your argument you might wish to commit to memory a few opening sentences, but do not start out by reading. To read your argument is to antagonize the court. Never, never do it. Do not even think about it. Have an outline or notes, but your notes must be a safety net, not a crutch. Look at your notes when you are making a short quote from the record or a case. Referring to your notes at this time adds the appearance of reliability to your quoting. If you have prepared sufficiently, or have rehearsed adequately, you should know exactly what to say.

Your oral argument should never exceed three points. You do not have the time to develop more. After identifying yourself, it is imperative to inform the court what issues you intend to discuss. You will then explain that your are relying on the brief for the others. At this point, you may be interrupted by one of the judges who wishes to hear argument on another issue. You should be sufficiently prepared to accommodate the court.

Former Wisconsin Supreme Court Chief Justice Nathan S. Heffernan advises counsel: "At the outset, tell the judges what you are going to tell them, tell them, and if it appears necessary, tell them what you told them."

§ 24.4.2 When to Say What

You always lead off with your best point—your strongest one. Your strongest point is *the argument that objectively considered, and based on precedent, and stated policy concerns of the court, is most likely to persuade the court to your point of view.*

[handwritten margin note: lead w/ strongest point]

It is what John W. Davis characterized as the "cardinal point around which lesser points revolve like planets around the sun." This determination must be made dispassionately. No matter how great the cause you hope to advance, no matter how deep the passions run, your presentation must be at all stages cool, calculating, and logical. I have had some of the nationally famous civil rights lawyers appear before me over the years, great advocates whose out-of-court interviews and televised sound bites resounded in flamboyant, purple prose. But in courtroom the role-playing and posturing were gone. They were very professional and, in general, extremely effective advocates in the finest tradition.

After setting out your first point, you then move to your second strongest argument, and if there is more, then to the final one. The presentation should be in the form of an inverted pyramid, with the best material presented first and the lesser following after in order of diminishing importance. This is how reporters are taught to write a newspaper article—to permit the editor to cut it off at the end and still leave a complete and important story.

Ideally, your second and third points should be self-sufficient and independent of the court's acceptance of the first argument. If the first point is rejected by the court, be prepared to shift ground immediately. I have heard too many arguments in which the advocate elected to slug it out with the judges on the first point. The advocate persisted, even though the effort was a manifest failure, and even though counsel was losing valuable time by not moving on to a point that might have gotten a more sympathetic hearing.

§ 24.4.2 [*sic*]Do Not Hide Facts and Cases That Hurt

You are the appellant. There are facts in the record and a case or two that may hurt you. Your opponent is sitting at the counsel table waiting to slam you with them as soon as you sit down. Or even worse, the judges are about to trump your opponent and launch an attack of their own. It is time to take the wind out of your adversary's sails. Mention these facts up front and tell us why they do not hurt you. Explain why the adverse case really is not a death knell. This will defuse any potential attack.

If you do this well, some of the fire and brimstone is taken out of the appellee's main argument. What is more, you have earned the respect of the court because this has heightened your credibility. This does not mean that you should pitch your entire argument as a rebuttal to the appellee's case. Rather, you, not your opponent, must control the direction of your argument.

If this is not done, you will surely get a question from one of the judges: "Help us out. In a few minutes, your friend is going to talk about these facts or this case, may we have your views on this now." Address these points before the court has an opportunity to ask. Where the case is fact-driven, as in a sufficiency of the evidence case, too often the appellant gives us a reprise of a jury speech, arguing evidence that has been rejected by the jury. Avoid this temptation and provide the court, up front, a worse-case scenario of facts against you. This will engender respect every time.

§ 24.4.3   How to Say It

Spicing your argument with a quote from one of the literary masters can be effective if used properly. A familiar quotation can eloquently sum up your position or vividly illustrate the equities that favor your client. Do not repeat it if it appears already in your brief. Do use it if the quote fits perfectly, is memorable, and you are confident that it is well known to the judges. Make certain that it does not provide fodder to your adversary and thus boomerang on you.

Keep your main points simple and hard-hitting. Limit discussion of citations and precedents. It is better to leave detailed discussion of cases to the briefs. Concentrate instead on the logic and force of your position. Keep always in mind the focus of your argument and do not get sidetracked, even by a single judge. Stay with the theme that represents your best hope of winning. Do not waste your severely rationed time on unnecessary elaboration.

Tell the court what you want and why. Explain how the rule you want the court to adopt will work, and show how it is consistent with what these judges have said before. Explain that there is impressive, respectable authority for it and that it fairly accommodates relevant values and interests.

This is but a modern version of the *confirmatio*; your argument confirms the acceptability of the proposition you are urging before the court. It proves the case. At the same time you must set forth what the ancients called the *confutatio*, a refutation of the proposition urged by your adversary. Quickly, forcefully, and effectively show why that position should not be accepted, why it is not supported by good reason or authority and why it will not work.

Know your record cold. Be prepared to answer questions and *all* its relevant parts. Remember, different judges may focus on different aspects of the prior proceeding. One judge may question you about an event or finding, because that judge has already studied the record and is seeking only to question the factual predicate of your position. This is simply a quiz. Another judge may ask about a portion of the record to substantiate that judge's support of your proposition. As we will develop later in this chapter, not all questions asked by judges are zingers. Many are designed to help you. Many are designed as part of an open internal advocacy of positions on the bench.

The corollary of knowing the record is sticking to it. Unless asked by a judge, never go outside the record in oral argument.

As soon as you perceive that the judges understand your point, move to the other issues. When you perceive that they understand these arguments, *sit down*. I cannot emphasize too much the necessity to quit while you are ahead.

A certain atmosphere or mood characterizes an argument in every case. Experienced lawyer-observers can sense this as they watch other lawyers' performances. Even law clerks, fresh out of law school but thoroughly acquainted with the case, can sense this. There comes a time when the man or woman at the lectern reaches the maximum possible advantage of the oral presentation. That is the moment to quit talking and sit down. Do not think that talking for a few more minutes cannot hurt. It *will* hurt. It can dispel the positive, confident atmosphere created by your presentation. A somewhat cynical old adage teaches: "'Tis better to remain silent and be thought a fool, than to open your mouth and remove all doubts."

There is a level of theater in appellate courtroom rhetoric, with recognized highs and lows. To abandon a high point that has been successfully reached and then proceed to fill the air with meaningless padding and verbal filler is to transform your sizzle into drizzle. But even more dangerous, the anticlimactic speech used to fill the air between the close of your real argument and the expiration of your allotted time may call attention to a weaker point in your position. One of the judges may pick up on this, start probing and wind up destroying the court's prior willingness to accept your argument. I have seen this happen many, many times. Judges carry impressions—weak or strong, good or bad—from the close of oral argument to the decision conference that immediately follows the day's calendar.

§ 24.4.4 A Special Delivery

The Opening. Walk to the lectern. Wait to be recognized by the presiding judge. Then open by saying:

> If it please the court. My name is John J. Jones and I represent the appellant, Santa Barbara Olive Company. We ask to reserve X minutes for rebuttal. We request this court to reverse the judgment of the trial court for the reasons set forth in our brief. Today, I will address two points in support of our position. We will rely on our brief for the other arguments. I request two minutes for rebuttal time. [Pause for reaction from the presiding judge.] We believe that the judgment should be reversed for the following reasons.

Your outline. Have an outline of your argument, together with supporting papers, at the lectern. Remember: your outline is a safety net, not a crutch.

Maintain eye contact. You look directly at the judges at all times. It is eyeball-to-eyeball time.

Be courteous and respectful. But do not be timorous or overawed. Maintain a position of respectful equality. Do not be disturbed or pushed around simply because a judge disagrees with your position. Stand your ground firmly but with courtesy and dignity.

Be prepared to modify your planned presentation. You may have to modify your argument for several reasons. The judges may agree immediately with one point. If you sense this, move quickly to another point. A series of questions may have taken much time from your planned presentation on one point; when you move to the next point, deliver it in truncated fashion, otherwise time may run out. If you are the appellee, and the questions put to the appellant demonstrate that the judges understand your position on one point, alter your planned argument.

Your closing. Do not let the presentation peter out simply because time has been called. Save time for a concise, punchy summary.

Sit Down. Exactly that.

§ 24.4.5 Watch Your Time

Place your watch on the lectern and keep track of your time. In some courts, a series of lights are placed on the podium. The green light signals the start of your argument; the amber comes on when you have two minutes remaining and the red light signifies that you should stop. When the red light comes on, immediately close your argument in thirty seconds or so; do no antagonize the judges by prolonging the discussion when your time has expired.

Save at lease one minute for a summary of your argument. Watch your rebuttal time. If you are the appellant, arrange in advance how much time you are reserving for rebuttal. In some courts you may ask the presiding judge at the beginning of the argument. In other courts, you make arrangements with the clerk in which case you advise the court what you have done.

Do not intrude on your rebuttal time by prolonging your argument in chief. The time will be subtracted from you. Do not expect to use rebuttal simply as a chance to include arguments that should have been made in the case in chief. There are presiding judges, and I was one of them, who were very strict about what could be said in rebuttal. It is not spillover time from your case in chief. The appellee always has the right to respond, so you may not save for rebuttal material what should have been started earlier.

When the red light goes on or you are told that your time is up, and you are in the middle of a sentence or a thought or a response to a question, it is good practice to ask the presiding judge for a brief moment to conclude. Then wrap it up in fifteen to twenty seconds.

§ 24.4.6 Be Flexible

In the modern appellate argument, you must be able to think on your feet. Watch how the wind is blowing from the bench. When the judges ask persistent questions that seem to indicate that they do not agree with your position, and their questions are really not designed to elicit further information, it is time to shift gears. You may wish to provide a transition by saying, "If the court please, we have stated our position and I believe that your honors understand our argument. Permit me now to address the second point."

Be careful about making concessions. If in the preparation of your argument you believe that it may be appropriate to make concessions, then do it. Do not make careless concessions at oral argument on the spur of the moment. They may come back to haunt you.

When two of the judges engage in private conversation during your presentation, do not stop. Address your argument to other judge or judges. In any event, never stop talking. The judge or judges who are paying attention to you will resent that you have interrupted your delivery to them.

It is a normal reaction to more vigorously try to persuade in the face of a bench that is not buying your argument. If the point in controversy is the major premise on which your second and third argument depend, you must hang tough. If, however, the point under attack is independent of other points in your argument, as soon as you get the storm signals from the bench, it is time to move on to another argument.

* * *

§ 24.6   How to Answer Questions

§ 24.6.1   In General

Oral argument is no longer the formal, uninterrupted presentation characteristic of appellate proceedings of yesteryear. Wisconsin Supreme Court Chief Justice Shirley Abrahamson reports: "At one time oral argument in the Wisconsin Supreme Court was so quiet that you could hear the justices' arteries clogging."

In most appellate courts today, however, oral presentations consist primarily of a dialogue between the judges and the advocate. Answering questions from the judges is a vial part of modern advocacy. Answering them properly is critical to the modern art of persuasion. Certain general suggestions are in order.

To answer a question intelligently, you must first *listen* to the question. Judges recognize that some lawyers may be a little nervous, and understandably so. But judges also recognize that lawyers, just like you and I in private conversation, sometimes have a tendency to "hear" only a part of the question asked. In appellate advocacy, it is important to listen to the entire question and to answer the entire question, not only a discrete part of it.

In listening to the question, be certain that you *understand* it before attempting to answer. This is especially true in federal appellate courts, where the judges deal with specialized subject matter and have a tendency to speak in shorthand expressions. Less experienced lawyers may not be familiar with the jargon used. For example, the court may inquire, "Counsel, do the authorities you rely on come up in the context of a *Teague* matter?" What the court is really asking goes to the distinction between a direct appeal in a criminal case and an appeal on collateral review. If you do not understand the question, say so. You will not necessarily lose any points.

Answer the question directly. Do not evade. If the question calls for "yes or no" answer, respond with a yes or a no. Then elaborate. You do not have time to beat around the bush, and you do not want to give the impression that you are stonewalling. Do not postpone the answer by saying, "I have not got to that point in my argument yet." The judge will respond, "Yes, you have."

This problem often arises where more than one lawyer is representing a single party. The practice of divided representation is appropriate to avoid conflicts of interest, but it is otherwise disfavored. To be sure, we understand that clients want their own lawyers to argue. We also understand the converse: Lawyers who have lived through the trial and have prepared a brief want a chance to get in at least five minutes of argument (and have their names in the Reporter showing that they argued the case). But, if cases of severely rationed time, judges want to get to the heart of what interests them and do not like to hear, "If the court please, my colleague is handling that part of the argument."

Your responses should be clear and concise. Judges know the time limitations you are under, and ordinarily the questions put are not designed for a lengthy response. One or two sentences usually will suffice.

Yet there are questions that demand a longer response and will take up substantial amounts of your limited time. In this situation, be cheerful, or at lest pretend that you are. Do not create the impression that the mere putting of the question annoys you. In my many years on the bench I have received enough responses of this type; they come under the category, "How to Wean Friends on the Bench."

A number of years ago, a constitutional law professor appeared before us, and he had brought along his entire class to witness his dazzling performance as the appellant's lawyer. Early in his presentation, I interrupted and asked him to address the question of our court's jurisdiction in the appeal. He sloughed me off with a scowl, saying that there was no such issue in the case. A little while later I tried again and he responded with some annoyance, "I've already answered that question." When I was rebuffed the third time, the presiding judge, William H. Hastie, unloaded on him, "Counsellor, answer the question and answer it right now. For your information, the question of jurisdictions has been in this case ever since the moment Judge Aldisert raised it ten minutes ago." The professor glared, and then stumbled, and stumbled some more. The opinion was assigned to me, and we dismissed the appeal for lack of jurisdiction.

When the questions put by the court are relevant—and most of the time they are, especially when more than one judge pursues a particular line of inquiry—it is a clear signal that this is the direction in which the judges are moving. Throw away your planned argument and proceed in the direction of the questions. This probably is the issue the judges will talk about in conference.

It may be that one of the judges goes off on a tangent that is completely irrelevant. We will discuss later how to handle questions from the judge who, by persistent irrelevant questions, appears to have gone off on an intellectual frolic of his or her own. If you are fully prepared on the subject matter of the case, you will know what questions are totally off base.

What do you do when you are asked a point-blank question about a case that you do not know, notwithstanding thorough preparation? My answer: Do not bluff. Be frank with the court, "If Your Honor will refresh my recollection of the holding, I would appreciate it." If the explanation does not ring my bells, my suggestion is that you say, "Your Honor, I'm sorry I must have overlooked that case. May I please have the opportunity of filing a supplemental brief discussing it within forty-eight hours?" It would be the most hard-hearted judge who would refuse such a request. Counsel should not overlook the opportunity of seeking to file a post-argument supplemental brief where a judge's question plowed novel ground. But to be effective, promise to have the supplement filed in a matter of days, not weeks.

Be careful about making concessions in response to questions. When you go through the questions checklist contained in § 21.7 in preparation for oral argument, you may decide that you are willing to concede some points. This decision can serve two important goals. First, you may wish to clear away the underbrush of questionable points that may possibly detract from the jugular point. It is better to prune than to be subjected to time-consuming interrogation on minor points. Second, it is one thing to plan a concession after calm and careful reflection in the environment of your office; it is quite another thing to concede hastily in open court while under pressure from the bench.

To concede or not to concede a point at oral argument depends upon the extent of your advance preparation. You should know what will hurt or help you. Without sufficient preparation, you may be faced with a dilemma. On this one hand you do not want to concede something that may come back to haunt you, but on the other hand you do not want the judges to conclude that you are stonewalling.

§ 24.6.2   Questions: User–Friendly and Otherwise

Many lawyers are instinctively suspicious of questions from the bench, and they answer so cautiously that they sound evasive. When this happens, I am inclined to say, "Look here, all the questions put to you are not designed to trap you. Please listen to the question before attempting to answer." Too many lawyers operate under the impression that bench questions are all cross-examination. Actually, there are several discrete categories.

The most important question is where a judge sweeps away all the clutter and zeroes in on the basic issue in the case. It is the question that sums up the case in the single sentence. If you have prepared thoroughly, you should expect this, notwithstanding the structure of your brief or your game plan at argument. When this question comes thundering down, you can run but you cannot hide. It will reappear in the opening sentence or paragraph of the opinion: "The major question for decision in this appeal is whether . . ." Be ready for it.

Many questions are designed to clarify something in the record. I vote for oral argument often because I need help from counsel in getting to this information. Often the problem is caused in federal courts by an incomplete appendix accompanying the brief. This is especially true in the courts where the judges require only an Excerpt of Record instead of the full appendix. Thus the question will proceed, "Counsel, on page so-and-so of the brief you refer to such-and-such evidence in the record. Will you please tell us where we can locate it?" Often when this factual predicate is established, it will serve as the springboard to other questions.

Many questions relate to the standard of review. Often, counsel will argue the evidence presented at trial instead of the facts as found by the fact-finder. This provokes the questions: "What did the fact-finder find? If the jury found it, can we touch it in view of the Seventh Amendment? If found by the judge, is it clearly erroneous? If found by the agency, was there substantial evidence in the record as a whole to support it?

Often we get ambiguous standards of review in the briefs. Oral argument provides the opportunity to focus on the correct standard. In many cases, the standard of review determines the outcome of the appeal.

Then there are what I call the quiz questions, which are utilized by individual judges for at least three objectives: Socratic or debating purposes, for internal judicial advocacy, and to communicate outright hostility to the lawyer's position. Judges used the Socratic Method to test the validity of the logic employed and to determine by means of hypotheticals where a proposed rule will take the court. Lawyers must expect that the logic of the argument will be put to the test. They must be prepared to defend their reasoning, both in form and content.

Be prepared for the hypothetical. Do not antagonize the court by saying, "Well, those facts are not before the court here. That is a different case." The judges know that. Counsel must understand that there is a limit to every principle, as immutable in the law as the principle may be; that there comes a pont when the extension of the legitimate principle brings it into conflict with another, equally legitimate, and the court must decide where along the line the axe must fall. Accordingly, counsel should not try to move the application of a principle too far or too fast.

In a multijudge appellate court, judges do not usually discuss cases in advance. In the United States courts of appeals and state appellate courts, judges often do not live in the same city. They meet for the first time at oral argument, and often questions are put to counsel by a judge solely to test the jural waters. When this occurs, the lawyer is merely a conduit. He or she is simply the medium by which the questioning judge may disclose to the other judges some inclination on the case.

* * *

Chapter 10

INTERNAL OPERATING PROCEDURES

SECTION A. IMPORTANCE FOR APPELLATE ATTORNEY

R. MARTINEAU, MODERN APPELLATE PRACTICE— FEDERAL AND STATE CIVIL APPEALS

§ 13.1 (1983).

Once an appeal is docketed in the appellate court, the pace at which it moves through the court and the manner in which it is handled are dictated by the court's case management policies and internal operating procedures. Both of these terms—case management policies and internal operating procedures—have only recently been applied to appellate courts. Formerly appellate courts functioned and cases moved through the appellate process in accordance with unwritten practices and procedures that had seemed always to exist, and about which no one ever thought. Persons connected with the parties or officials of the trial or appellate court usually acted independently of each other and without regard to what anyone else was doing. Things were done either because the adversary system carried over from the trial court to the appellate court or because they had always been done that way. It was a process or system only in the sense that it happened, not that it was designed to function in a particular way to achieve an ultimate objective.

Beginning in the late 1930's under the leadership of such persons as Roscoe Pound, Arther Vanderbilt, Edson Sunderland, and John Parker, lawyers, judges, and professors began to examine what courts did, why they did it, and how the entire process could be improved to aid in disposing of appeals fairly, expeditiously, and inexpensively, doing justice between the parties, and developing the law. Judicial administration and court management became new disciplines.

These developments occurred first and primarily at the trial court level because of those courts greater visibility. Judges at the appellate level thought case management unnecessary, assuming that the competing interests of the parties would ensure that each appeal would be

884

decided expeditiously enough to suit the parties. The internal operating procedures of the appellate courts were thought to be the province solely of the appellate judges; the secrecy surrounding the court's decision and opinion until announced publicly was expanded from the substance of the decision and the content of the opinion to the procedures whereby they were developed and formalized. Those procedures were something only the appellate judges knew about, and they seldom talked.

There has been a dramatic change, however, in the past 20 years. The pressures of caseload and the increase in the number of appellate courts and judges have compelled the courts to take firm control of the pace at which cases move through the appellate process and to examine their own procedures to ensure that each case receives the attention it deserves but nothing more. As oral argument was reduced or eliminated, as appeals were decided without any opinion or published opinion, and professional appellate court staffs developed, it became clear that case management and internal operating procedures had a direct effect upon the parties, their attorneys, and the outcome of appeals. Appellate courts realized that they could not change appellate rules, case management policies, or their own internal procedures without considering the effect upon the parties and their attorneys. They thus began to publicize their case management policies and internal procedures and to consult with the bar before making changes.

The increased publicity given by appellate courts to their case management policies and internal operating procedures is a clear signal to appellate attorneys that familiarity with these policies and procedures can enable the attorney to use them for the benefit of his client and avoid their having an adverse impact on the interests of his client. An appellate attorney should, consequently, obtain a copy not only of the rules of the appellate court before which he contemplates taking an appeal, but also of its case management policies and internal operating procedures so that he can adjust his efforts to the court's requirements. Descriptive statements may be obtained from the court itself or from an article or book describing practice in that court.

SECTION B. TIME LIMITATIONS AND CONTROL OF THE APPELLATE PROCESS

MARTINEAU, THE APPELLATE PROCESS IN CIVIL CASES: A PROPOSED MODEL

63 Marquette L.Rev. 163, 200–201 (1979).

It has been recognized for some time that in order for trial courts to function effectively, they must control the flow of cases through the court. This control is referred to as case management. It was discovered that the adversary system was not a sufficient guarantee for the expeditious disposition of cases and that the court must assume responsibility for imposing time limitations on each successive step in the litigation process, monitoring compliance with the limitations and imposing sanctions for failure to comply with the limitations. Recent studies have shown that of all the possible variables in the litigation process, the only one which had any substantial impact upon pace of the litigation process is the extent to which judges are willing to exercise control over it.

Appellate rules have traditionally set time limits on each step of the appellate process. Except for the time limit on filing the notice of appeal, however, compliance with these rules has not been enforced either by the appellate court on its own initiative or on motion of the opposing party. There was, consequently, little or no relationship between the time limits as set forth in the rules and the actual median time spans between the steps in the appellate process. As appellate courts began to develop statistics which demonstrated this fact, they realized that only through the adoption of a case management system could the entire appellate process be speeded up and actual median time spans begin to approximate the time limits as set forth in the rules. The success of those courts that have implemented case management systems clearly proves the desirability of each appellate court adopting a similar plan.

Appellate courts cannot, of course, simply set and enforce time limits against the litigants. They must simultaneously adopt and enforce time limits on their internal procedures. This means that standards have to be set for the processing of all petitions and motions, the scheduling of cases for oral argument or briefs only, the circulation of opinions after submission and the opinion conference. These internal time limits cannot, of course, be enforced by any formal sanctions, but the peer pressure resulting from monthly statistics showing the status of all pending cases and of the cases of each judge along with encouragement by the chief judge should in all but extreme cases be sufficient.

Notes and Questions

1. In an adversary system who should control the pace of litigation, the parties or the courts? If the parties are willing to delay, why should this concern the court? Does society have an interest independent of the parties in having cases disposed of expeditiously? Who should protect this interest— the courts? the attorneys? Do attorneys have a professional responsibility to ensure that cases are not delayed even though the delay may be for the benefit of the client or the attorney? See Model Rule of Professional Conduct 3.2 (2002); Federal Rules of Civil Procedure 11 and 16.

2. For opposing viewpoints of the propriety of judges taking an active role in expediting cases at the trial level, compare Resnik, Managerial Judges and Court Delay: The Unproven Assumptions, 23 Judges' J. 8 (Winter, 1984) with Flanders, Blind Umpires—A Response to Professor Resnik, 35 Hastings L.J. 505 (1984). There has been little question about the necessity for courts to have control over the appellate process. Section 3.50 of the A.B.A. Standards Relating to Appellate Courts provides: "[a]n Appellate Court should supervise and control the preparation and presentation of all appeals coming before it." The commentary to the section states: "[d]elay in appel-

late litigation is rarely the result of a single cause * * *. The first and most important is that appellate courts generally have exercised inadequate supervision of the movement of cases coming before them." For a good summary of developments, see Cameron, Improvement of Appellate Justice, in A.B.A. Judicial Administration Division, The Improvement of the Administration of Justice 203 (6th ed.1981) and Summary, Reducing Appellate Delay, 9 State Court J. 27 (Fall, 1985). At least one judge has argued against efficiency for the sake of efficiency. See Bazelon, New Gods for Old: "Efficient" Courts in a Democratic Society, 46 N.Y.U. L.Rev. 653 (1971).

SECTION C.   PREHEARING OR SUMMARY DISPOSITION

MARTINEAU, THE APPELLATE PROCESS IN CIVIL CASES: A PROPOSED MODEL

63 Marquette L.Rev. 163, 201, 203–04 (1979).

Not all appeals taken to an appellate court are disposed of on the merits in consecutive order after the briefs have been filed. Many appeals are disposed of at an earlier stage or, even if the briefs have been filed, not in the order in which cases are normally taken. Appeals can be disposed of by voluntary abandonment by the appellant, as a result of a settlement, by virtue of a procedural ruling by the appellate court on a motion, or on the merits, either on a motion by a party or on the court's own motion.

* * *

Although appellate rules do not usually provide for a motion to dismiss or a motion for summary disposition, some appellate courts receive them and act on them. A motion to dismiss is for the purpose of raising procedural questions such as appealability, timeliness, adequacy of the record or compliance with the appellate rules. A motion for summary disposition will seek affirmance or reversal on the merits and can be filed either before or after the briefs are filed. Such motions are useful in that they permit a case to be disposed of without the full treatment given to appeals taken under submission in the ordinary course. To the extent that this procedure can shorten the time for disposition of appeals with a reduced expenditure of judges' time the procedure is valuable. If the only thing accomplished is double consideration of most appeals, both the time for disposition of appeals and the efficient utilization of judicial time will be adversely affected. The rules should provide for such motions so that attorneys know they can be filed, but the appellate court should stress that the motions are appropriate only in appeals which have little merit to them on one side or the other.

The appellate court may also become aware of an appeal that should be affirmed or reversed summarily. In such an event, the court should dispose of the case immediately to avoid further delay and expense for the litigants and to leave more time for appeals that have merit. Again the appellate rules should provide for this type of disposition so that the parties and their attorneys are aware that it can occur.

Notes and Questions

1. When should a motion for summary disposition be filed—before or after the briefs are filed? Does the answer depend on whether the motion is based on procedural grounds or on the merits? Who should be able to file— the appellant, the appellee, or both? Would it ever be appropriate for the appellant to file a motion for summary disposition? Should a panel other than the panel assigned to hear the case on the merits be assigned the motions?

2. Would it ever be appropriate for a court to dispose of an appeal summarily on its own motion?

3. A number of appellate courts have divided cases into classes and apply different procedures to each class. This is called "differentiated case management" or "tracking." The most common differentiation is between those cases in which oral argument is heard and those in which it is not. These issues are discussed in Chapter 9, supra. Other classifications are cases decided: (a) with oral argument but without the filing of briefs or with only limited briefs (A.B.A. Action Commission to Reduce Court Costs and Delay, Attacking Litigation Costs and Delay 25–43 (1984)); (b) with abbreviated briefing schedules and abbreviated oral argument; (c) with neither briefs nor oral argument (Douglas, Innovative Appellate Court Processing: New Hampshire's Experience with Summary Affirmance, 69 Judicature 147 (1985)); (d) without a written opinion. See generally J. Martin & E. Prescott, Appellate Court Delay: Structural Responses to the Problems of Volume and Delay 6–16 (1981). In examining any of these procedures, two questions must always be asked: (1) what are the essentials of the appellate process and (2) do the procedures adopted retain these essentials?

SECTION D. ALTERNATIVE DISPUTE RESOLUTION

EXAMINING THE WORK OF STATE COURTS

National Center for State Courts 2003 p. 70.*

Alternative dispute resolution (ADR) consists of dispute resolution processes outside of (or adjacent to) the traditional court case structure. Processes as diverse as mediation, arbitration, early neutral evaluation (ENE), summary jury trials, settlement conferences, parenting classes for divorcing couples, and group or family conferencing are all considered types of ADR.

The focus of many appellate court ADR programs is to encourage or require counsel for the parties to discuss settlement at a conference

* Copyright © 2000, National Center for State Courts. Reprinted by permission. All rights reserved.

facilitated by a non-judicial court employee or other third-party neutral. Although these attorney-neutrals have different titles depending on the court, their role is primarily that of a mediator. The conferences are usually held before the filing of appellate briefs and, in nearly all cases, before oral argument. Some appellate programs are geared exclusively toward settlement, while other programs also address case management and procedural issues.

Local court rules or procedures identify the criteria each court uses to determine whether a case is eligible for the program and whether a conference should be scheduled.

In twenty-one states, appellate courts are addressing increasing caseloads by offering alternative dispute resolution before and during the appeal

Case types that are often referred to mediation include general civil (tort, contract, and real property rights), domestic relations, and workers' compensation cases.

R. MARTINEAU, MODERN APPELLATE PRACTICE— FEDERAL AND STATE CIVIL APPEALS

§ 13.3 (1983).

Settlement is a traditional means of disposing of appeals, but until recently had to be reached by the parties themselves without any aid or encouragement from the appellate court, unlike the situation in the trial court where the judge often plays a significant role in the settlement process. More recently, following the lead of the United States Court of Appeals for the Second Circuit, a number of federal and state appellate courts have experimented with having an active or retired member of the court or a court official meet with the parties shortly after the filing of the notice of appeal. The purpose of the conference is to ascertain whether there are any possibilities of settlement and, if so, to provide a favorable setting to aid the parties in coming to an agreement. If no settlement is possible, an attempt can be made to narrow the issues on appeal, thereby reducing the amount of the transcript that need be prepared. So far there is no conclusive evidence that this procedure results in more dispositions of more cases more quickly with less judicial effort than the traditional hands-off approach. Consequently, more testing and experimentation is necessary. A stated theory of the settlement conference is that it provides an opportunity and a setting in which the parties can work out a settlement by themselves, and that the court officer plays no role in encouraging settlement or suggesting terms. The reality is that the officer often plays an active role in the settlement process. Any exception to the contrary is unrealistic. If he did not participate actively, there would be no need for his presence; the same purpose could be accomplished by appellate rules mandating that the parties meet for settlement discussions.

Whether the court officer should be a judge is debatable, but in at least one court the settlement officer is an active member of the appellate court. This is a questionable practice for several reasons. First, it reduces the number of judges available to hear appeals which are not settled without any clear evidence that an active judge can settle more cases than a retired judge or a nonjudge. Further, and of more importance, any comments during the conference by the judge on the state of the law or on the possible outcome of the appeal may be perceived as representing the views of the court. This perception may destroy one of the essential features of a court mandated settlement conference—that the parties believe that their discussions are confidential and that no member of the court will be aware of the content of those discussions. Participation by an active member of the court may diminish that essential confidence.

Another key feature of the settlement conference system is that the conference be held as early in the appellate process as possible, preferably before there has been any substantial preparation of the transcript or the briefs. Once the parties have a major financial investment in the appeal, the chances of settlement will be reduced. Absent special circumstances, the settlement conference should not, however, be a reason to delay the other steps in the appellate process. Otherwise, the settlement process becomes nothing more than a delaying tactic. Nothing will promote early settlement better than firm deadlines, for they promote an understanding that failure to reach settlement within the allotted time will result in substantial expense to the client, which can otherwise be avoided.

Although appellate rules do not usually provide for motion to dismiss or for summary affirmance or reversal, some appellate courts receive and act on such motions. A motion to dismiss may be based upon procedural questions such as appealability, timeliness, adequacy of the record, or compliance with the appellate rules. A motion for summary affirmance or reversal seeks disposition on the merits and can be filed either before or after the briefs are filed. Either type of motion is useful in that it permits an appeal to be disposed of without the full treatment given to appeals taken under submission in the ordinary course. To the extent that the motion shortens the time for disposition of the appeal and reduces the time the judges must spend, the procedure is valuable. If the only thing accomplished is that the appeal must be considered twice, then the motion has postponed ultimate disposition and adversely affected the court's use of its own time. The rules should provide for such motions so that attorneys know they can be filed, but the appellate court should stress that the motions are appropriate only in appeals with little merit on one side or the other.

Even without a motion the appellate court may become aware that an appeal should be affirmed or reversed summarily. In such an event, the court should dispose of the case immediately to avoid further delay and expense for the litigants and to leave more time for meritorious appeals. Again, the appellate rules should provide for this type of disposition so that the parties and their attorneys are aware that it can occur.

NEWMAN AND FRIEDMAN, APPELLATE MEDIATION IN PENNSYLVANIA: LOOKING BACK AT THE HISTORY AND FORWARD TO THE FUTURE

5 J. App. Prac. & Process 409 (2003).*

I. INTRODUCTION

In recent years, appellate courts have increasingly integrated alternative dispute resolution methods into their procedures in an effort to reduce ever-expanding caseloads. The Pennsylvania Commonwealth Court, for example, adopted an appellate mediation program in September of 1999 and reports that it has been successful. This Article includes a summary of the foundations of appellate mediation that traces its primary development in the federal courts of appeal, a discussion of the extension of appellate mediation programs to state appellate courts, and an examination of the specifics of the Commonwealth Court's program. In its final section, the Article concludes that the Commonwealth Court's report of its program's success is well-founded and advocates for extension of that program.

II. FOUNDATIONS OF APPELLATE MEDIATION

A. *The Second Circuit*

In 1974, Chief Judge Irving R. Kaufman of the Second Circuit instituted the first appellate alternative dispute resolution (ADR) program, hoping to expand upon the successes of ADR in reducing the caseload of courts of original jurisdiction. Chief Judge Kaufman created the Civil Appeals Management Plan (CAMP), which had four main goals: (1) to preserve judicial resources, most notably time, by encouraging dispute resolution without judicial involvement; (2) for cases not subject to ADR, to reduce the time from the filing of an appeal to its disposition; (3) for cases that ADR will not be able to resolve, to help clarify the ultimate issues in the case; and (4) to quickly consider basic procedural motions without expending judicial resources. Originally, the CAMP program employed one separate full-time Staff Attorney (also called staff counsel), who searched through the Second Circuit's appellate docket for the cases that appeared to be most conducive to settlement. The Staff Attorney also conducted the settlement conference and served as program administrator.

The CAMP program was the first response to Federal Rule of Appellate Procedure 33, adopted in 1967, which now provides as follows:

* Sandra Schultz Newman and Scott E. Friedman, copyright © 2003 Journal of Appellate Practice and Process, University of Arkansas School of Law. Reprinted by permission. All rights reserved.

The court may direct the attorneys—and, when appropriate, the parties—to participate in one or more conferences to address any matter that may aid in disposing of the proceedings, including simplifying the issues and discussing settlement. A judge or other person designated by the court may preside over the conference, which may be conducted in person or by telephone. Before a settlement conference, the attorneys must consult with their clients and obtain as much authority as feasible to settle the case. The court may, as a result of the conference, enter an order controlling the course of the proceedings or implementing any settlement agreement.

Pursuant to CAMP, as originally designed, the Staff Attorney would peruse all new appeals for cases that would most benefit from a settlement conference. For those cases that the Staff Attorney determined to be candidates for a successful conference, the Staff Attorney would issue a scheduling order, which would delineate the date of argument, the date of the CAMP conference, and the due date for filing briefs and the record. The Staff Attorney, counsel for the parties, and in some situations, the parties themselves, would participate in any number of conferences, each lasting from one to several hours. However, the parties always maintained their right to proceed with an appeal if they were unable to resolve the dispute at the conferences.

The CAMP program remains the cornerstone of ADR in the federal appellate courts. The Second Circuit currently employs three Staff Attorneys, each of whom conducts approximately three conferences each day. Whereas the Staff Attorney once culled the docket for potential CAMP participants, the court now requires all appellants in civil matters, with the exception of pro se and habeas corpus cases, to submit a pre-argument statement within ten days of filing an appeal. In the vast majority of cases, the parties will appear before a Staff Attorney for a mandatory conference within three weeks of the date on which the appeal is docketed. If, after the mandatory conference, the Staff Attorney believes that the case will not settle, the court will schedule oral argument. Otherwise, the Staff Attorney will schedule another conference; this process will continue until (1) the parties settle; (2) the Staff Attorney determines that additional conferences will not have any benefit; or (3) the case is otherwise dismissed. By 1985, settlement conferences reduced the number of cases argued before the Second Circuit by almost twenty percent. By 1995, half of all appeals to the Second Circuit were resolved prior to argument.

B. The Sixth Circuit

The judges on the other federal circuits were so impressed by the success of CAMP that they began to institute similar programs in the early and mid–1980s. The first to follow the Second Circuit was the Sixth, which modified the CAMP program to address geographic differences between the Second and Sixth Circuits. Whereas the Second Circuit is small in area and has a large caseload, the Sixth Circuit covers a much larger swath of the country but addresses far fewer cases. Accordingly, the Sixth Circuit conducts most conferences by telephone and focuses more on encouraging settlement than on case-management issues. Additionally, while the Second Circuit attempts to evaluate the parties' arguments, often by issuing a non-binding advisory opinion, the Sixth Circuit favors an interest-based or facilitative approach, in which the Staff Attorney will discuss the parties' interests with each of them separately.

The geographic spread of the Sixth Circuit and its mediation program's resultant reliance on telephone conferences posits another interesting question: Are telephone or videoconferences as effective as live mediation? Telephone or video conferences allow persons in different places to effectively be at the same place at the same time without having to make the expenditure in time and money to meet at some potentially far-away location; however, a common perception is that participants in live conferences are more inclined to settle. While this article does not address these issues, they are interesting to consider nonetheless. The authors look forward with interest to the results of others' scholarly investigation of this topic.

C. The Third Circuit

The Third Circuit, based in Philadelphia, instituted an appellate mediation program in 1995 that is very similar to the Sixth Circuit's program. Virtually all civil matters, other than cases involving prisoners or pro se litigants, are eligible for appellate mediation. The Program Director selects from the list of eligible cases those that involve non-frivolous issues that are capable of extra-judicial resolution. From May through October of 1995, parties filed 422 cases eligible for appellate mediation; from this group, the Program Director selected 107. This rate of scheduling roughly twenty-five percent of eligible cases for mediation has remained relatively consistent throughout the life of the program. Cases can also be referred to mediation by the parties or by the court itself immediately prior to or after oral argument.

Approximately two weeks after the parties are notified that their case has been selected for appellate mediation, confidential position papers, not in excess of ten pages, are due to the mediator. These papers must articulate counsel's views concerning the possibility of settlement, summarize prior settlement discussions (if any), and identify other ancillary issues that must be resolved in order to effectuate any type of settlement; these confidential statements are never made available to the court or to opposing counsel. The Program Director conducts approximately half of all mediation conferences and the senior circuit judges mediate the remainder. No more than twenty percent of all initial conferences are conducted by telephone; unless distance or other factors preclude them, in-person conferences are preferred. While the briefing schedule and other appellate deadlines theoretically remain in effect while a case is being mediated, in reality, the clerk of court usually does not set a briefing schedule until the matter is no longer in mediation.

However, in instances where pending mediation will affect the briefing schedule or other appellate deadlines, the mediator will usually recommend staying all court-related proceedings until mediation is concluded. Cases for which mediation does not result in an ultimate settlement return to a full briefing schedule, usually within sixty days of the original reference to mediation.

D. The Ninth Circuit

Like the Sixth Circuit, the Ninth Circuit does not engage in case management. The Ninth Circuit takes the facilitative approach one step further, however, by attempting to focus the parties more on the real-world implications of a case, deemphasizing the legal aspects. Facing many times more cases than the Sixth Circuit, the Ninth Circuit's Staff Attorneys are far more selective in determining which cases to schedule for appellate mediation. The Staff Attorneys utilize a two-step process to select cases, and "[b]y hand-picking the cases they handle and devoting their full attention to settlement, the Ninth Circuit's mediators have been able to accrue an impressive seventy-three percent settlement rate."

E. The D.C. Circuit

The D.C. Circuit instituted a unique program that relies on local attorneys who volunteer to mediate disputes. The court approves experienced attorneys to participate as volunteer mediators and then trains them in mediation skills in an intensive program. While using members of the local bar in mediation has always been a staple of trial court programs, the D.C. Circuit remains the only appellate court to exploit this resource. To ensure that these attorneys are protected from suits filed by unhappy parties to a mediation, the D.C. Circuit has provided, by rule of court, that voluntary mediators enjoy quasi-judicial immunity while mediating, as (1) "the functions of the official in question are comparable to those of a judge"; (2) "the nature of the controversy is intense enough that future harassment or intimidation by litigants is a realistic prospect"; and (3) "the system contains safeguards which are adequate to justify dispensing with private damage suits to control unconstitutional conduct."

The D.C. Circuit program is also distinctive in its selectivity and its well-developed criteria for admission. The program director selects approximately sixty cases each year for mediation, based on (1) the nature of the underlying dispute; (2) the relationship of the issues on appeal to the underlying dispute; (3) the availability of incentives to reach settlement or limit the issues on appeal; (4) the susceptibility of the issues to mediation; (5) the possibility of effectuating a resolution; (6) the number of parties; and (7) the number of related pending cases. Because the court only attempts to mediate sixty cases in a given year, its goal is to "offer a service to parties whose needs may be better served by creative settlement than by judicial resolution," not to control the docket. The D.C. Circuit does not go as far to facilitate settlement as does the Ninth

Circuit. As a result, the court's program has accrued a less-impressive thirty percent settlement rate, although it considers more time-consuming and multi-issue cases, especially suits against agencies of the federal and D.C. local governments, which are the sorts of cases from which other appellate mediation programs shy away.

F.　Early State Programs

Numerous state courts have followed suit, instituting appellate mediation programs to handle burgeoning caseloads. California's Third District Court of Appeals, an intermediate appellate court sitting in Sacramento, was the first state appellate court to enter the ADR realm, instituting a program almost identical to the Second Circuit's CAMP, with a group of retired judges serving as voluntary mediators. The program succeeded, routinely settling thirty to forty percent of its cases, but the court abandoned the initiative in 1993 due to budget cuts. Unfortunately, most state court appellate mediation programs created in the 1970s and early 1980s did not fare as well as the California program, in many cases fizzling out after one or two years. These programs failed in large part because they were developed as projects that were strongly supported by only one judge on the relevant court, did not employ enough persons qualified to mediate the disputes, and suffered from debilitating financial constraints.

The Missouri Court of Appeals for the Eastern District, an intermediate appellate court based in St. Louis, boasts one of the oldest continuously operating state court appellate mediation programs, founded in 1976. One of the sitting judges on that court serves as Settlement Judge; the assignment rotates among the fourteen judges on an annual basis. With jurists serving as mediators, this program tends to be more evaluative than facilitative, similar to that of the Second Circuit. It is unclear if the jurists are required to recuse themselves if they happen to be assigned to a panel hearing a case that they considered while serving as mediator.

The court established the settlement conference procedure pursuant to a local court rule, which provides that

> [a]fter the notice of appeal has been filed, the court may schedule a conference for the purpose of exploring the possibility of settlement. The court may stay the requirements for ordering the record on appeal, filing the record, or briefs in order to facilitate the settlement process.

The Settlement Judge screens cases on the appellate docket to determine those cases in which the best interests of the parties would be to settle. The program utilizes sitting judges as mediators because "their assessment of the merits of the case will hold more weight among the parties." Additionally, clients are not permitted to attend the conferences, because their presence would hamper the ability of the lawyers to discuss the strengths and weaknesses of their positions openly, and that of the

Settlement Judge to give a fair and accurate assessment of the case to the attorneys.

The Missouri program has achieved significant and sustained success, settling approximately forty percent of the cases referred to it for disposition. The court as a whole considers approximately 1,500 cases each year, 300 to 400 of which are scheduled for mandatory settlement conferences. While this is not a statewide program, this single Missouri court has illuminated the path for appellate courts in other states to effectively implement some form of ADR.

III.   The Second Wave

Within the past decade many states have either re-instituted or created new appellate mediation programs. As of 2002, thirty-one states had ADR programs at some appellate level; six of these programs were at the highest court of that state.

A.   *The Massachusetts Appeals Court*

In the summer of 1992, Chief Justice Liacos of the Supreme Judicial Court of Massachusetts spearheaded a push to bring mediation to the Massachusetts Appeals Court, an intermediate appellate court. He applied for and received a Massachusetts Bar Foundation grant to establish the program as an experiment. The money funded the creation of a staff position to manage the operations of the program and the program budget for two years; the Appeals Court selected a retired federal trial judge, a dean of one of the in-state law schools, and an experienced private lawyer to conduct mediation conferences. During its first six months of operation, the program accepted approximately ten cases per month; in April of 1993, the court appointed eleven additional attorneys to conduct conferences and the caseload of the program expanded concomitantly. From July of 1993 through July of 1994, the group of arbiters conducted conferences in about 170 cases.

The program considers civil cases except those involving, for example, (1) litigants who are proceeding pro se; (2) adoption and other care-of-minors issues; and (3) civil commitment petitions. The Justices of the Supreme Judicial Court decided to make entry into the program mandatory; in other words, the attorneys for parties in cases selected for appellate mediation had to participate in one settlement conference, but the decision about whether to participate in additional conferences or to proceed with the appeal is made independently by the parties and their attorneys. The attorneys of record in cases that might be required to participate in the conference program were contacted within two weeks of docketing the appeal in the Appeals Court and were asked to complete a Conference Statement, which gave the Conference Program staff a quick view of the case and allowed them to determine whether the case was suitable for the program. The Program has retained these features.

By July of 1994, the funds provided by the Massachusetts Bar Foundation had been exhausted, but after reviewing the experiment, the

Justices of the Supreme Judicial Court concluded that the program was a resounding success and, accordingly, institutionalized it within the court system. In its first official year, the Massachusetts Appeals Court Conference Program provided approximately three hundred conferences, almost forty percent of which reached full settlement without further recourse in the courts. The Boston Bar Journal reported that

[t]his settlement rate is more than triple the settlement rate for civil appeals in the two years before the program began, and more than seventy-five percent higher than the combined rate of settlements and dismissals for lack of prosecution in the same period.

In more than a third of the cases that did not reach full settlement through the program, the parties nevertheless benefitted palpably from presenting their positions to a conference leader—either simplification or clarification of issues on appeal. In 2000, of the approximately 980 civil cases filed in the Massachusetts Court of Appeals, 359 were selected for settlement conferences, with forty-four percent of those cases reaching full settlement.

B.   The New Mexico Court of Appeals

In September of 1998, the New Mexico Court of Appeals, an intermediate appellate court, instituted a pilot mediation program for much the same reasons that the Massachusetts Court of Appeals and the myriad other state and federal appellate courts had employed appellate mediation—chiefly, to reduce burgeoning caseloads. Similar to the Massachusetts Appeals Court, the New Mexico Court of Appeals decided not to use a sitting judge as a mediator. The program creators considered using volunteers to run the mediation conferences. They noted the benefits of utilizing volunteers—"prestige for the program, no cost for conferences, bar involvement, geographic diversity, and specialized knowledge"—but ultimately determined that the inherent problems— "limitations on availability, lack of quality control, difficult recruitment/exclusion issues, experience spread thin, need to provide training, administrative burden, and immunity concerns"—of such an approach would vitiate the intended benefit of the program. In the end, the program creators settled on a single staff appellate mediator, and chose as the first mediator a lawyer who had worked with the program creators, served as a staff attorney for the New Mexico Court of Appeals for almost a decade, and had functioned as a mediator in numerous New Mexico courts of original jurisdiction.

All pending civil cases except those involving a prisoner, a pro se litigant, a driver's license revocation, a petition for extraordinary relief, or those arising from either the Mental Health and Development Code or the Children's Code, are potential targets of the mediation program. The majority of cases scheduled for mediation conferences are selected by the mediation program staff at random from all eligible appeals. In some instances, however, the panel of judges assigned to hear the appeal will transfer cases to the program either before or after briefing, and counsel for either party can request a mediation conference, which request the program staff usually grants. The court determined that random selection would be the best method of picking cases in part because the program creators' review of myriad other appellate mediation programs taught them that it is nearly impossible to predict the cases in which mediation conferences will ultimately be successful. Participation in a mediation conference is mandatory if the case is selected.

Typically, the program staff will contact the litigants in cases chosen for mediation before the commencement of briefing to cut down on the costs to the parties. However, the appellate schedule remains in effect. At the beginning of a conference, the mediator will attempt to resolve any outstanding procedural issues before discussing the substantive elements of the conflict. Once the preliminary matters are addressed,

> [t]he legal issues may be directly discussed. However, the purpose is not to decide or reach a conclusion about the merits of the appeal, but rather to facilitate an understanding of the issues and an evaluation of the risks and opportunities for each side.

If the parties are unable to come to a settlement agreement after one or several conferences, the mediator can make suggestions to the parties, which the parties are free to reject if they so choose.

From the program's inception in September of 1998 until June of 2000, 308 cases were scheduled for settlement conferences, of which eighty-eight settled—a twenty-nine percent settlement rate. Approximately 500 civil appeals are filed each year in the court, meaning that almost one-third of all civil cases are scheduled for appellate mediation. A report prepared for the New Mexico Administrative Office of the Courts and the Court of Appeals of New Mexico pursuant to a grant from the State Justice Institute concluded in March of 2001 that the New Mexico program had achieved an excellent rate of settlement. Robert Hanson, the author of Appellate Review and Mediation in New Mexico, asked attorneys who had participated in settlement conferences between September 15, 1998, and September 30, 2000, to complete surveys rating their experiences, whether the mediation conferences ultimately proved successful. Sixty-one percent of all attorneys who completed the surveys reported that the mediator improved communication between the sides and sixty-seven percent agreed that the mediator helped to identify options. Interestingly, more than half of the attorneys whose cases did not settle indicated that the mediator helped to clarify some issues, and almost half reported that he also helped them resolve some issues.

Hanson found that the cost of running the program for one year, leading to settlement of an average of forty-four cases, amounted to approximately $97,000.00. Hanson equated the forty-four cases settled each year with the average workload of a New Mexico Court of Appeals judge and determined that the $97,000.00 spent on mediation conferences was an efficient use of that money. Furthermore, the study found that the time spent from docketing of an appeal until a case reaches settlement is 266 days, far fewer than the 450 days it takes for the court to rule on an average appeal.

C. Supreme Court of Nevada

One of the most successful and prolific appellate mediation programs resides in the Supreme Court of Nevada, the only appellate court in that state. In March of 1997, the Supreme Court of Nevada turned to appellate mediation to, according to one of the settlement judges, "deal with the exponential growth in appeals over the past several years." To effectuate an appellate mediation program, the Justices of the Nevada Supreme Court adopted Nevada Rule of Appellate Procedure 16, which permits a settlement conference for any civil appeal. As soon as the Clerk of the Court notifies the parties that a settlement conference will be scheduled, all appellate requirements, such as the filing of transcripts and briefs, are stayed. Instead, the litigants must file a settlement statement, not to exceed five pages, which sets forth

> (1) the relevant facts; (2) the issues on appeal; (3) the argument supporting the party's position on appeal; (4) the weakest points of the party's position on appeal; (5) the settlement proposal that the party believes would be fair or would be willing to make in order to conclude the matter; and (6) all matters which, in counsel's professional opinion, may assist the settlement judge in conducting the settlement conference.

The Clerk assigns one of approximately ninety mediators to cases on a rotating basis, while also considering the type of case.

Unlike those used in the appellate mediation programs in Massachusetts and New Mexico, Nevada Supreme Court mediation conferences do not follow any pre-determined structure; the mediators are permitted great discretion in setting the agenda and sequence of presentation. Ten days after the conference, the mediator files a report with the Supreme Court detailing the course of the negotiations (but not disclosing matters discussed at the conference) and also disclosing the result, if any. The rules only require that all parties participate in good faith:

> The failure of a party, or the party's counsel, to participate in good faith in the settlement conference process is grounds for sanctions against the party, the party's counsel, or both. The filing of a frivolous appeal is also grounds for sanctions. Sanctions include, but are not limited to, payment of attorney's fees and costs of the opposing party, dismissal of the appeal, or reversal of the judgment below.

The Court takes the requirement that all parties act in good faith very seriously; the Court has shown its willingness to impose sanctions in several cases in which the parties did not genuinely attempt to settle.

Between institution of the program in 1997 and the end of 2001, the settlement judges attempted mediation in approximately 2,500 cases; almost 1,400 of these cases have reached settlement, representing an effective settlement rate of fifty-six percent. This is an impressive rate of settlement, but not necessarily surprising given that the Court allocates a much larger percentage of its financial resources and human capital to the appellate mediation program than do programs in other states. The program is also very prolific. In 2001, for example, parties filed 713 civil appeals, 546 of which (or approximately eighty percent) were assigned to the settlement program.

While most other courts spend no more than $100,000 per year on appellate mediation, Nevada budgets approximately $350,000 each year for this program. Additionally, with ninety mediators at the disposal of the Court, Nevada's program administrator can choose one who is familiar with the issues at hand and will consequently be able to more fairly adjudge the relative positions of the parties, making the process more user-friendly.

IV. THE PENNSYLVANIA EXPERIENCE: THE COMMONWEALTH COURT

Recognizing the numerous and varied benefits of appellate mediation generally, and the marked successes that appellate mediation programs had reaped in other states during the 1990s, the Commonwealth Court of Pennsylvania established an appellate mediation program effective January 1, 2000. Cases eligible for mediation are: (1) counseled appeals of orders of the courts of common pleas; (2) counseled appeals of administrative agency decisions; (3) counseled actions filed in the original jurisdiction of the Commonwealth Court. These cases "may be referred at the discretion of the Court to the Court's Mediation Program to facilitate settlement and otherwise to assist in the expeditious resolution of matters before the Court."

The President Judge of the Commonwealth Court selects one of the Senior Judges of that court to serve as the coordinator of the Mediation Program; the coordinator screens eligible cases to determine whether any are suitable for inclusion. The parties can also request inclusion and, for cases not selected, the judges may direct the parties to enter the program.

Within ten days of filing an appeal or a petition for review, the party challenging the lower tribunal's decision or seeking relief must file a Statement of Issues with the normal appellate docketing statement. According to the Internal Operating Procedures of the Commonwealth Court,

> [t]he Statement of Issues shall be no more than two pages in length and shall set forth a brief summary of the issues and a summary of the case necessary for an understanding of the nature of the appeal, petition for review or complaint.

Once the coordinator selects a case for participation in the program, the court clerk notifies counsel for the parties, who then have ten days to provide the mediation judge with a Mediation Statement. The Mediation Statement cannot be longer than five pages, and must set forth the key facts and issues, whether the parties have attempted to settle out of court, and the disposition of any motions filed in the court.

As in the New Mexico program, but unlike that of the Nevada Supreme Court, scheduled proceedings before the Commonwealth Court are not stayed unless the mediation judge so directs the court in order to accommodate additional mediation sessions. The mediator has the discretion to mandate the attendance of the parties at the mediation conference. However, according to the 2000 Annual Report of the Commonwealth Court, the mediation judge does not ask the parties to attend, but does request that they be available by telephone. Additionally, each party must send counsel with authority to settle.

If, after the original mediation conference, the parties have not agreed on a settlement but the mediation judge believes that additional sessions will lead to settlement, the mediation judge can order additional conferences. Failure to comply with the procedures set out in the I.O.P. can lead to sanctions. If the mediation conferences do not end in settlement, neither the mediation judge nor the parties can disclose the substance of the negotiations to the court. According to the court rule,

> [n]o information obtained during settlement discussions shall be construed as an admission against interest, and counsel shall not use any information obtained during settlement discussions as the basis for any motion or application.

All confidential documents other than those related to the Court's briefing or argument scheduling that have been submitted to the mediation judge are destroyed immediately upon the termination of mediation proceedings.

In 2000, the first year of the program, 286 cases were referred to appellate mediation, representing approximately eight percent of all appeals filed in the Commonwealth Court. Of those 286 cases, 263 proceeded to at least one mediation conference and 123, or approximately 47%, settled extrajudicially. In 2001, approximately 4,100 new appeals were filed, 331 of which were referred to mediation. Of the 309 cases actually mediated in 2001, 141 settled, resulting in a settlement rate of approximately forty-five percent. The number of cases that the program settled over the first two years is equivalent to the workload of a three-judge panel over that same time period, which the program administrator considers a success.

V. The Pennsylvania Experience: Extending The Commonwealth Court's Program

The Commonwealth Court's appellate mediation program is a proven success in its first two-and-one-half years of existence. The program was instituted to eliminate the expense and time of taking an appeal, with the added benefit that a settlement, by definition, is a result with which all parties are satisfied. It has reaped those benefits in at least the forty-seven percent of mediated cases in which the mediation judge is able to broker a settlement.

The Commonwealth Court's program, however, was not the first foray into the realm of appellate mediation in Pennsylvania. In the early 1980s, operating on a limited-term grant from the National Center of State Courts, President Judge Emeritus William F. Cercone and Judge J. Sydney Hoffman created a settlement conference program in the Superior Court in an attempt to reduce backlogs in that court—the average appeal at that time took almost three years from docketing to decision. The program was a marked success and, along with the creation of new judgeships on the court, helped to drastically reduce the backlog. The program continued for at least several months after the grant expired, but as a result of the decrease in time it took for the court to dispose of cases, as well as the expiration of the National Center for State Courts funding, the program was disbanded.

While the Superior Court has maintained an excellent record in disposing of cases in relatively short stead and the Commonwealth Court appellate mediation program has proved successful, now is not a time for our courts to rest on their laurels. The experiences of appellate courts in other states indicate that appellate mediation programs can reach greater percentages of litigants with no decrease in success rates. We should devote additional funds to expand the Commonwealth Court's program and engage in further research to determine if reinstitution of an appellate mediation program in the Superior Court would prove beneficial. The more we are able to encourage parties to settle amicably, the more efficient our system of justice becomes and the more time we have to devote to those cases that remain before us. Appellate mediation benefits not only the courts, but also the parties, who are able to save time and money by mediating their disputes.

Notes and Questions

1. For an early study of the CAMP procedure in the Second Circuit, see Goldman, The Appellate Settlement Conference: An Effective Procedural Reform?, 2 St. Ct. J. 3 (Winter 1978). Based on an experimental study of appellate cases that were subject to the procedure, and those that were not, as well as other evidence (such as a survey of judges), the author concluded that the benefits of CAMP were not significant. Many policymakers, however, were more enthusiastic, as demonstrated by the Newman & Friedman article. The Second Circuit is, however, the only court to have conducted the type of empirical study described by Professor Goldman. For a more positive evaluation of CAMP, see Kaufman, Must Every Appeal Run the Gamut?—The Civil Appeals Management Plan, 95 Yale L.J. 755 (1986).

2. One of the major questions about a settlement conference procedure is whether it should be conducted by an active member of the appellate court. What would be the advantage of using an active judge? The disadvantages? What other types of persons could conduct them? The Minnesota Supreme Court changed the purpose of its prehearing conference from assisting settlements to weighing the merits of the cases and determining the extent of additional appellate review. See Scott & Moskal, The Prehearing Conference—Perhaps Your Only Opportunity to Present Oral Argument to the Minnesota Supreme Court, 7 William Mitchell L.Rev. 283 (1981). For

a more general discussion of how settlement conferences work, see R. Martineau, Modern Appellate Practice—Federal and State Civil Appeals §§ 10.7–.9 (1983).

SECTION E. DISPOSITION AFTER SUBMISSION ON BRIEFS OR ORAL ARGUMENT

R. LEFLAR, INTERNAL OPERATING PROCEDURES OF APPELLATE COURTS
30, 36–42, 53–54 (1976).

PREARGUMENT MEMORANDA

Another aid to intelligent preargument understanding of issues is the preparation and distribution to each judge of memoranda summarizing each case and its problems, with relevant citations of authority. These memoranda could be prepared by the judges themselves under some preassignment system—preferably not by the judge who later writes the opinion for the court. They could be prepared by a law clerk of the assigned judge, or by staff attorneys in a court with a central research staff. Though a judge may be tempted not to read the brief if he knows that he will receive good memoranda before the case is submitted, failure to read it would be a betrayal of his judicial obligation, an improper delegation of his duty to participate independently in the collegial process of decision in each case on which he sits. In New Jersey, for instance, each judge prepares his own preargument memorandum on each case. There can be no substitute for personal study and preparation.

PREARGUMENT CONFERENCES

In a number of courts, preargument conferences are standard procedure. They may take different forms and serve a variety of purposes. In some states, as in California and New Jersey, a short conference is held before oral argument in order to facilitate the hearing of argument by the court—the idea being to identify issues that need clarification and to plan for questions to elicit the information needed by the judges. A careful planning for the judges' part in the presentation can shorten the oral argument and make it more useful at the same time. This type of preargument conference, however informal, can be worthwhile only if the judges have prior familiarity with the cases. If they do, the conference can substantially speed up the decisional process.

* * *

THE DECISION CONFERENCE

It is important that the decision conference be held as soon as possible after oral argument, assuming that briefs have been read and that appropriate memoranda have been prepared before argument. Thus, all the judges deciding the case have it fresh in mind. Each sitting judge will then, presumably, have his own memorandum or notes on the case. The best time to hold the conference would be in the afternoon, after arguments have been heard in the morning. If there is no free time then, it should be held at the earliest time available thereafter. If a court hears argument for several days continuously, it is preferable that the conference not wait until all the arguments are finished, but that successive daily conferences be held on the cases argued, or at least that conferences be held before a great number of cases accumulate.

The reason is evident: judicial reactions are more complete, facts and argument are clearer in the minds of all the members of the panel soon after the briefs have been read and the oral argument has been heard. As time passes, cases and analyses become blurred and confused; they must be reviewed before intelligent discussion can take place. The review takes additional time and may not bring back as clear an understanding of the case as was present when the original study and argument were fresh in the minds of the judges. Time is saved and analysis is better when consideration is prompt.

For judges who are by nature dilatory, prompt preparation of opinions may be aided by a rule such as that in the United States Court of Appeals for the Fourth Circuit under which assigned cases are monitored, judges warned after a fixed time, and cases reassigned if not duly written. A few courts prescribe some official publication of the fact if any judge falls more than a stated length of time behind on cases assigned to him. Even the California constitutional provision under which judges are not to be paid their salaries if their work does not maintain a designated currency confers certain undeniable, though indirect, benefits upon some appellate judges.

ONE-JUDGE OPINIONS

It seems odd that in a few states a judge is expected to write an opinion for his court without any decision conference and therefore without knowing beforehand the views of the other judges on what the significant issues are, what reasons should be relied upon in dealing with the issues, or how the case should be decided. Worse yet, after a substantial lapse of time—perhaps weeks—during which he was preparing his unguided opinion, the other judges may have become vague about facts and principles they considered important when the case was submitted; they may be more disposed to forgo views that might have proved to be controlling if developed earlier. The one-man opinion, the very opposite of what should be produced by a multijudge court, must too frequently be the natural result.

Even when all the judges on the court intelligently concur in an opinion prepared without a conference, it is unlikely that the writer will have written the opinion in the same way he would have written it had he known the views of his colleagues in advance. He cannot express views of which he is unaware; he may have included unnecessary incidental argument that he erroneously felt might be persuasive. Even more important, his view of the case might have been altered by a thoughtful exchange of opinions around the conference table, thus saving the time and effort expended in unsound writing.

Of course, a vote taken around the conference table shortly after submission may not always stand up against further research and thought. In some cases it will not. In a few cases the vote may be postponed pending further study. If, as he works on the case, the judge assigned to write the opinion finds that new analysis is required, he must report to the court for further conference; but even that necessity is made easier by a prior knowledge of the views of the other judges. If the case has to be reassigned because the first judge assigned turns out to be in the minority, less time and energy are wasted by reassigning it as soon as possible. Only if the assigned writer knows, at least tentatively, how the other judges feel about the case, can he sensibly present to them new ideas that might put him into a minority position.

CONDUCT OF CONFERENCES

No general rule can be stated about how conferences should be conducted beyond the obvious requirement that they should be conducted in an orderly fashion. If for any reason one judge has made a special study of a particular case, there will be some value in having that judge lead off in the discussion of the case. The order in which the judges speak can be determined by seniority, either directly or inversely, though there would be some virtue in varying the order, perhaps from month to month, and letting the successive orderings be set by lot. One thing is certain: no judge should cast his vote on a case until all the judges have spoken and the discussion has ended. The vote of each judge should be based on the entire analysis, and each judge should hold himself free to make up or change his mind after he has heard all of it.

One other point deserves emphasis. Every case that is decided on appeal ought to be brought up in conference of the judges who decide it. This includes cases submitted without oral argument as well as those that are argued; it also includes those which, by some method of prior screening, have been classified as susceptible to only one conclusion or even as frivolous. If by reason of the classification the court refuses to hear the appeal, no further consideration is called for. But if the case is actually being decided on appeal, the decision should be made by the whole panel or the whole court, in accordance with the rules, and not by a single writing judge. If the case is truly an easy one, the court need not spend much time on it. Nevertheless, it is obligated to spend some time on it.

ASSIGNMENT OF CASES

There has been as much variety in methods of assigning cases for preparation of opinions as in any aspect of appellate operating procedures.

In the federal courts, including the United States Supreme Court, and in a minority of the states, assignment is made by the presiding judge after the decision conference. If the court is divided, the assignment is of course made to one of the majority. Presumably, assignments are designed to keep the workload of all the judges fairly even, with difficult cases and easy ones being divided equally and with fewer cases being assigned to judges who are ill or for any reason are unable to keep up with their work. Expertise or experience in particular fields of law are often taken into account in making assignments in spite of the popular feeling that ordinary appellate courts should be made up of generalists, not specialists, and the fear that recurring assignments of specialized cases to a judge with expertise in the area will result in one-man opinions and noncollegial decisions. Probably the fact that goes furthest to justify satisfaction with this system is that the assignment comes after the judges in the decision conference have voted on the case. Then the assigned judge knows how the case stands, and the other judges know that he has heard their views on it.

Assignment by Rotation

In contrast is the system formerly followed in Alabama, under which cases were assigned before submission by automatic rotation to numbered positions on the court. If, for instance, the judge numbered "5" were ill, or if that position were vacant due to retirement or death, every ninth case would in rotation still be assigned to that position, and stacked up to await opinions to be written without benefit of conference by whoever next occupied position 5. Judges who were slow with their work never caught up; others stayed even with the submissions. The amazing thing is that it was not until recently that the Alabama Supreme Court was able to discard that system.

A large number of state courts employ rotation systems less mechanical and more practical than the old Alabama system. Their outstanding feature is that at some time before it is submitted, each case is automatically assigned to a particular judge. There may be a single rotation for all the cases ready for submission or separate rotations for various categories of cases. Separate rotations could make the process sufficiently complex that counsel would have no chance to time their cases so as to throw them to preferred judges. A judge is expected to make special preparation before argument on his cases. He is usually expected not only to study the briefs but to check the record as well. Because he is better prepared than the other judges to ask questions of counsel, counsel might be able to guess which judge has his case and concentrate his argument on that judge, who would lead off in discussion of the case in conference. Each preassigned judge would normally spend much more time on the case assigned to him than on the cases of the other judges. In an ordinary case that had not attracted the special interest of the other judges, the preassigned judge would exert more influence than any of the others in determining how the case should be dealt with. This does not mean that a one-judge decision or a one-man opinion would inevitably ensue. That would not happen if the case were an important or interesting one that attracted the attention of all the judges, or even of several of them. In ordinary cases, however, the advance rotation system tends toward one-judge emphasis to a degree that is not present if the entire study-and-decision process precedes the assignment.

THE "CHECK JUDGE"

A partial deterrent to one-judge emphasis has been developed in a few courts that use a presubmission rotation for assignment of cases. It involves a "check judge" or "second judge," also preassigned by independent rotation to each case, whose duty it is to study the case in advance with, presumably, the same thoroughness as does the assigned judge. This system, apparently first developed in Mississippi, was later followed with small variations in Arkansas, Louisiana, Wisconsin, and possibly other states. It has the obvious virtue of largely eliminating the danger of one-man decisions; at the same time, it suggests the possibility of two-judge conference emphasis when the ideal would be a system of equal participation in the decision conference by all members of the court. Any court that is for any reason firmly committed to assignment of cases by presubmission rotation would do well to supplement the system with a check-judge arrangement.

An assignment system recently devised in Tennessee appears to achieve many of the advantages and avoid many of the disadvantages of the older systems. All the judges of the Tennessee Supreme Court read the briefs in advance of oral argument and come to the postargument decision conference acquainted with all the cases that have been submitted. Tentative decisions are then reached on all submitted cases. At the end of the decision conference, during which no judge's prior assignment gave him any superior status in the discussion, all cases then decided are assigned by lot. Neither the presiding judge's predilections nor any deference to expertise enters into the assignment. As under other random systems, it is of course possible that cases will have to be exchanged if, for example, a drawee is in the minority, but that does not affect the virtues of the system.

ASSIGNMENT TO PANELS

A preliminary assignment problem exists in courts that sit in two or more panels. This is the situation in all of the federal courts of appeals, in intermediate appellate courts such as the California Courts of Appeal, and in any court that sits in divisions. The problem is which cases are to be assigned to which panel. Here again a sort of expertise could develop, with criminal appeals assigned to one panel, personal injury cases to another, and so on. Most jurists would disapprove of what would thus in practical effect be specialized subcourts. The general feeling is that appellate judges and appellate courts should be generalists, taking cases across the board unless a real need for expertise in a particular legal area induces the court-creating authority in the jurisdiction to set up separate courts. Even in that event, specialized separate courts are more appropriate at the trial than at the appellate level, where all areas of the law need to be coordinated. When a court sits in panels, there is good reason for using some random method of allocating cases to the panels, always subject to the condition that related cases and cases presenting similar issues may best be heard together.

The same reasoning that argues against specialized panels supports the practice of rearranging the membership of panels in such a way that, as in the federal courts of appeals, each judge will over a year or so be assigned to sit with every other judge on the court an approximately equal number of times. The goal is to work together as much as possible and thus participate equally in the court's total decisional and precedent-creating process even though individual cases are decided by panels.

* * *

ADOPTING OPINIONS

After a full-scale opinion has been written by the assigned judge, with such assistance as was appropriate from his law clerk and other members of his staff, what is the procedure for making it the opinion of the court?

The former practice in some jurisdictions was that all opinions written or rewritten after a previous decision or opinion conference were read aloud to the members of the court in a later opinion conference. Many judges had difficulty staying awake through hours of continuous reading; others reacted sporadically to what they heard; nearly all knew that it was impossible to evaluate the parts of any given opinion with reference to its whole. It is surprising that in some courts this practice was continued until quite recently; the only explanation is unquestioning acceptance of a tradition that dated back to the time when it was not easy to reproduce copies of opinions.

CIRCULATION OF OPINIONS

At present, the accepted procedure is that copies of the written opinions are made and distributed simultaneously to all other members of the court or panel, whose prompt attention to them is supposed to take precedence over all other work. Giving such priority to the opinions of colleagues may be required by court rule, or it may be a matter of custom and courtesy. The most efficient practice is for each judge to tell the opinion writer at once whether he thinks changes should be made. Although oral suggestions may be valuable, written suggestions have the advantage of being clearer. The opinion writer may accept some or all of the suggestions, or he may reject them. If he subsequently makes substantial changes in the opinion, he will want to recirculate the rewritten version. Later at the opinion conference, the whole opinion need not be read aloud. Only those parts that produced differences among the judges need to be discussed. If it is then approved by the majority of the court, the opinion can become final, with time allowed for the preparation of dissents or concurrences if insisted on. At this stage it is still possible to agree on a further rewriting that will produce a more nearly unanimous agreement of the court. If it must be rewritten, the opinion should be recirculated and reconsidered at a later conference.

Some courts have used variations of the above procedure. In a few courts, especially those whose judges live in different cities and do not have offices near each other, suggestions may await the opinion conference. This is inefficient. It takes the time of the whole court to do what two judges alone could have accomplished less formally. It comes at a time when it interferes with putting the opinion in final form, which is the purpose of the conference. If unable to meet in person before the conference, the two judges could have communicated by telephone. Another variation in procedure was, and in a few courts still is, the circulation of a single copy of each opinion to one judge at a time, with each one noting agreement or proposing changes, then passing it on to the next. This could take weeks, even months. The consensus today is that simultaneous circulation is proper, that speedier approval or disapproval of opinions by the whole court is desirable, and that unnecessary delay in the handing down of decisions is bad.

HALL, OPINION ASSIGNMENT PROCEDURES AND CONFERENCE PRACTICES IN STATE SUPREME COURTS

73 Judicature 209 (December 1989–January 1990).*

Despite their importance as policymakers, much about state supreme courts remains unknown. Up-to-date information on such details as their internal operating procedures, as provided in this study, will help facilitate understanding.

State supreme courts are becoming increasingly interesting to political scientists as the importance of these institutions as policymakers is recognized. Despite the significant advances made in the study of state supreme courts, however, much remains unknown. One of the serious problems in researching these institutions is the lack of easily attainable data. Few centralized sources of information are available and much of the published data are not current. This article attempts to contribute to the study of judicial institutions by providing up-to-date information about a number of the internal operating procedures of state supreme courts. Such data permit comparisons of these institutions and facilitate the testing of hypotheses about the effects of various institutional rules on judicial decisionmaking.

THE SURVEY

In 1976, Stanford McConkie published information about a number of the internal operating procedures of state supreme courts in Judica-

* Melinda Gann Hall, copyright © 1989. Reprinted by permission. All rights reserved.

ture. McConkie obtained these interesting and significant data from questionnaires mailed to chief justices in 1973, with follow-up telephone calls to complete the survey. These data have been used extensively in research on state supreme courts and constitute an important contribution to the study of judicial politics.

However, 16 years have passed since the gathering of McConkie's data. In order to evaluate whether this information is still accurate, a telephone survey was conducted in the fall of 1988 and spring of 1989. Calls were placed to the offices of the chief justices of the 50 state supreme courts and questions were asked about the types of rules and protocol both formal and informal, governing the operation of each institution.

In particular, information was sought from each court about the method of opinion assignment, as well as the order among justices for discussing cases and casting votes in conference. In a majority of the states, the chief justice or a sitting justice was interviewed about the various types of decision rules utilized within his or her court. In other instances, when the purpose of the call was explained to the secretary of the chief justice, an appropriate person was designated, usually by the chief justice, to provide the information. Most typically, the person interviewed in this situation was the administrative assistant to the chief justice or the clerk of court. In all cases where the clerk's office conducts case assignments, the clerk of court or a deputy clerk was also interviewed. In a small minority of states, the chief justice asked that the questions be submitted in writing. As a result of the telephone calls and letters, a complete description of the internal operating rules currently used in each state supreme court was obtained. These data are reported in Table 1.

Table 1

Internal operating procedures of state supreme court

State	Size of Court	Method of opinion assignment	Order of discussion	Order of voting
Alabama	9	Rotation, by clerk's office	Reporting justice, then open	Reverse seniority
Alaska	5	Rotation, by clerk's office	Reporting justice, then reverse seniority	Reporting justice, then reverse seniority
Arizona	5	Chief justice	No formal order	No formal order
Arkansas	7	Rotation, by clerk's office	Reporting justice, justice, back-up justice, then reverse seniority from back-up justice re-	No formal order (Same as discussion)

State	Size of Court	Method of opinion assignment	Order of discussion	Order of voting
			turning to seniority after most junior	
California	7	Chief justice	Seniority, chief justice last	Seniority, chief justice
Colorado	7	Chief justice if the majority, else senior majority justice	Reverse seniority	Reverse seniority
Connecticut	7	Chief justice	Most junior justice, then open	Most junior justice, then open
Delaware	5	Chief justice	Reverse seniority	Reverse seniority
Florida	7	Rotation, by clerk's office	Reporting justice, then seniority chief justice, last	Reporting justice, then seniority chief justice, last
Georgia	5	Rotation, by clerk's office	Reporting justice then open	No formal order
Hawaii	5	Chief justice	No formal order	No formal order
Idaho	5	Random draw, by clerk's office	Reporting justice, then reverse seniority	Reporting justice, then reverse seniority
Illinois	7	Rotation, by chief justice	Reporting justice, then open	Reporting justice, then open
Indiana	5	Consensus of the majority	Reverse seniority	Reverse seniority
Iowa	9	Rotation, by chief justice	Reporting justice, then open	Reporting justice, then open
Kansas	7	Chief justice	Reporting justice, then open	Reporting justice, then open
Kentucky	7	Chief justice	No formal order	No formal order
Louisiana	7	Random draw, by central staff	Reporting justice, then open	Reporting justice, then open
Maine	7	Rotation, by chief justice	Reporting justice, then reverse seniority	Reporting justice, then reverse seniority
Maryland	7	Chief justice, if in the majority, else senior majority justice else senior	Reverse seniority	Reverse seniority
Massachusetts	7	Chief justice	Seniority, chief justice last	Seniority, chief justice last

State	Size of Court	Method of opinion assignment	Order of discussion	Order of voting
Michigan	7	Random draw, after oral argument	Rotation	Rotation
Minnesota	7	Rotation, by commissioner's office	Reporting justice, then seniority chief justice last	Reporting justice, then seniority chief justice last
Mississippi	9	Random draw, by clerk's office	Reporting justice, then alternating seniority and reverse seniority	Reporting justice, then alternating seniority and reverse seniority
Missouri	7	Rotation, by chief justice after oral argument	Reverse seniority	Reverse seniority
Montana	7	Rotation, by chief justice	Reporting justice, then open	Reporting justice, then open
Nebraska	7	Rotation, by clerk's office	Reporting justice, then open	Seniority
Nevada	5	Rotation, by clerk's office	Reporting justice, then around table	Reporting justice, then around table
New Hampshire	5	Random draw, after oral argument	No formal order	No formal order
New Jersey	7	Chief justice if in the majority else senior majority justice	Rotation	Seniority
New Mexico	5	Rotation, by clerk's office	Reporting justice, then open	Reporting justice, then open
New York	7	Random draw, after oral argument	Reporting justice, then reverse seniority	Reporting justice, then reverse seniority
North Carolina	7	Rotation, by chief justice, after oral argument	Reverse seniority	Reverse seniority
North Dakota	5	Rotation by clerk's office	Reverse seniority	No formal order
Ohio	7	Random draw, after oral argument	Seniority	Reverse
Oklahoma	9	Rotation, by chief justice	Reporting justice, then reverse seniority	Reporting justice, then reverse seniority
Oregon	7	Chief justice	Rotation	Rotation
Pennsylvania	7	Chief justice	Seniority	Seniority
Rhode Island	5	Rotation, by chief justice	Reverse	Reverse

State	Size of Court	Method of opinion assignment	Order of discussion	Order of voting
South Carolina	5	Rotation, by clerk's office	Reporting justice, then seniority	Reporting justice, then seniority
South Dakota	5	Random draw, by clerk's office	Reporting justice, then seniority	Reporting justice, then seniority
Tennessee	5	Random draw, after oral argument	No formal order	No formal order
Texas	9	Rotation and random draw	Reporting justice, then around table	Reporting justice, then around table
Utah	5	Rotation, by clerk's office	No formal order	No formal order
Vermont	5	Rotation, by chief justice	Reverse seniority, reporting justice last	Reverse seniority, reporting justice last
Virginia	7	Random draw, by clerk's office	Reporting justice, then around table from assignee	Reporting justice, then around table from assignee
Washington	9	Random draw, by clerk's office	Reporting justice, then around table	Reporting justice, then around table
West Virginia	5	Rotation, by chief justice	Reporting justice, then reverse seniority	Reverse seniority
Wisconsin	7	Random draw, after oral argument	Seniority	Seniority
Wyoming	5	Chief justice	Rotation	Rotation

Immediately apparent to those familiar with the McConkie data are the differences between the information obtained in the more recent survey and the data published in 1976. All data missing from the McConkie survey have been replaced. In addition, there are reported differences between the earlier data and this survey in virtually every American state. More precisely, in 46 states there are deviations in at least one category of information from the results reported in 1976. While there are a number of possible explanations for these discrepancies, it is clear that the McConkie data no longer portray an accurate portrait of the operational practices of state supreme courts.

METHODS OF OPINION ASSIGNMENT

The process of assigning a particular justice to write the majority opinion, or the opinion of the court, is a critical one. Whether such decisions will be subject to the discretion of particular justices or whether opinion assignments will be performed in a purely random fashion has significant ramifications for the operating environment of the institution.

An internal rule which empowers designated justices, usually the chief justice or senior majority justice for each case, to determine who writes for the court allows the justices, if they so desire, to develop various degrees of specialization. With the cooperation of the assigning justices, members can volunteer for cases in their areas of interest and serve as experts for the court.

A system of discretionary opinion assignments also creates strategic opportunities for the assigning justices. The ability to reward members of the court with desirable opinion assignments or to punish colleagues with a barrage of uninteresting or unimportant cases can be used to discourage the expression of disagreement with the assigning justices, leading to greater consensus within the institution and greater power for those with assignment responsibilities. A second advantage for any justice with opinion assignment power is the ability to increase the chances of holding together tenuous majorities of which he or she is a member by assigning opinions to the most marginal members of the coalitions.

An opinion assignment procedure which is random in nature has important consequences as well. Distributing case assignments among the members of a court by the luck of the draw rather than on the basis of individual discretion disperses power among the members of a court rather than concentrating power in the hands of particular court members. Within this structure, which lacks a system of effective rewards and sanctions in the opinion assignment process, a court can actually be expected to have a higher level of dissent than a court that designates certain members as assigners. Random assignments also insure that each justice will write on a wide variety of legal questions and mitigate against the development of policy specialists within the court.

As Table 1 reveals, the overwhelming preference among state supreme courts for assigning majority opinions is to allocate cases in a random or rotating manner. Thirty-five states (70 per cent) provide for an opinion assignment procedure in which no justice on the court has discretionary assignment authority. Conversely, only 15 states (30 per cent) utilize a process which allows such decisions to be made completely at the discretion of the chief justice or senior-most justice in the majority or by the consensus of the justices in the majority for each case.

Although opinion assignment procedures can be described broadly as either discretionary or nondiscretionary, more specifically there are five types of opinion allocation processes currently being utilized in the states: (1) a random or rotating system of opinion assignment which takes place before oral argument or consideration of cases on the merits; (2) a random or rotating system of opinion assignment in which opinions are assigned among the members of the court after oral argument, if held, and after the court specifically addresses the issues of the cases; (3) a procedure which always grants the power of assignment to the chief justice, to be exercised at his or her discretion; (4) an opinion assignment technique which grants the power of assignment to the chief justice when in the tentative majority on the merits of each case or to the senior-most justice in the majority when the chief justice is in the minority; and (5) an opinion distribution plan in which opinions are assigned in conference by the consensus of the justices in the majority for each case. Within the first four methods, there are tremendous variations in specific implementation.

Random assignment prior to conference consideration. Twenty-seven states utilize random or rotating systems of assignment in which cases are allocated among the justices of a court prior to consideration of case merits. Of these 27, 18 utilize a system whereby the actual assignment is performed by the clerk of court or the central staff, while nine states follow the practice of having the random distribution of opinions supervised by the chief justice in conference.

In the states in which the responsibility for allocating opinions rests with the clerk's office, most typically the clerk creates a roster of the justices, who are usually listed in order of seniority, and then assigns cases from a chronological list or by docket number to the justice next on the list from the previous assignment. Some states, however, sort cases into various categories and then make assignments from each of the categories. For instance, Arkansas identifies each case as either a death penalty, oral argument, criminal or civil case, with the categories prioritized. The clerk then distributes cases among the justices to provide each justice with approximately the same number of each type of case.

Rather than assigning cases on a rotational basis, the clerks of court or central staff in Idaho, Louisiana, Mississippi, South Dakota, Virginia and Washington distribute cases randomly among the justices by drawing docket numbers from a hat or other similar lottery-type procedure. The random drawing is performed in the clerk's office or the offices of the central staff, with the clerk, law clerks, secretaries or even the justices themselves participating in the process.

As previously mentioned, rather than having the clerk's office or central staff randomly allocate opinions among the justices prior to oral argument or consideration of case merits, nine states (Illinois, Iowa, Maine, Montana, Oklahoma, Rhode Island, Texas, Vermont, West Virginia) permit the chief justice to oversee the distribution of opinions in conference. Either on a rotational basis or through a blind draw, opinions are assigned in conference without the direct participation of the clerk or other court personnel.

The Texas Supreme Court and Rhode Island Supreme Court are excellent examples of the different methods used by the states to distribute opinions randomly in conference prior to oral argument or a tentative vote. In Texas, each week the clerk of court places three case titles on index cards, indicating the cases in which oral argument will be heard during the week. The clerk gives these three cards to the chief justice, who then insures that the three justices who are next in rotation draw for the cases listed on the index cards. In Rhode Island, however, each case from a list of cases pending review is distributed in conference by seating, which is in order of seniority. The justices simply go down the list and around the table, with each person in turn taking the next available case.

When cases are assigned to the justices of a court prior to oral argument or discussion of each case, there is always the possibility that, upon addressing the merits of the case, the person to whom the opinion was originally assigned will find himself or herself in the minority rather than the majority. As a result, states which make random assignments prior to review on the merits have developed processes for reassigning cases in the event the original justice charged with writing the court's opinion is not in the majority.

A variety of reassignment practices have emerged in the 27 states which allocate cases prior to the consideration of case merits. These practices largely are informal in nature and rely upon the collegial nature of the institutions. In most states, when the original assignment justice fails to win the support of the majority, such norms as volunteering, trading cases, having the first dissenter take the opinion or simply reaching a consensus on the reassignment without a formal rule, are utilized to redirect the opinion to someone in the majority. In some states, the chief justice is given the power of reassignment, with complete discretion to give the case to any member of the majority. In Arkansas, a back-up justice is assigned with the original writer who will take over the responsibility for the majority opinion if the original assignment justice fails to capture the support of the majority. Finally, in Nebraska, an assignment judge who ends up on the losing side has two options: either write a per curiam opinion for the court majority and then write a dissent or, if the justice has strong feelings against writing for the majority, send the case back to the clerk's office for reassignment in a random manner.

Random assignment after consideration of case merits. While 27 states assign opinions to justices in a random or rotating manner before oral argument or consideration of the merits of the cases, eight states (Michigan, Missouri, New Hampshire, New York, North Carolina, Ohio, Tennessee, Wisconsin) distribute opinions randomly after oral argument, if held, and after tentative votes are taken on the disposition of the cases. In a majority of these states, once preliminary votes are cast and a tentative majority is identified for each case, opinions are rotated or drawn only by members of the winning coalition. This practice eliminates the problem of having justices who were assigned majority opinions actually end up in the minority. However, in a few states, the rotation or drawing takes place among all members of the court. In this type of procedure, if the justice drawing the opinion or first in rotation is not in the majority, the case is simply returned for redrawing or given to the justice next in rotation.

Assignment at the discretion of the chief justice. As Table 1 indicates, in 10 state supreme courts, the chief justice has complete discretion to make opinion assignments, whether or not the chief justice is a member of the winning coalition. These assignments are made after oral argument, if held, and after a tentative vote on the merits of the case has been taken, except in Kansas, where assignments are made prior to oral argument but nonetheless at the discretion of the chief justice.

Several informal norms and guidelines for making these decisions were reported. Virtually all of the states emphasized the importance of equalizing the workload among the justices, a norm generally recognized within appellate courts. While a few states indicated a preference for distributing cases according to the interests and specializations of the justices, most do not foster the development of expertise in given areas, although the option is available with this type of assignment process. Surprisingly, no chief justice spontaneously expressed the belief that the chief should write on the most important cases, a practice expected somewhat in the U.S. Supreme Court. However, several chief justices gave some limited acknowledgment to the practice when specifically asked.

Assignment by the chief justice only when a majority member. Only Arizona, Colorado, Maryland and New Jersey follow the practice of the U.S. Supreme Court for distributing opinions among the justices. In these four states, the chief justice designates the writer of the majority opinion for those cases in which the chief justice is a member of the winning coalition. However, when the chief justices' votes place them outside the majority, the power of assignment reverts to the senior justice in the majority for each case. As mentioned earlier, this type of procedure maximizes the influence of the chief justice and more senior justices and leads to greater consensus within the court.

Assignment by the consensus of the majority coalition. The Indiana Supreme Court has a unique and interesting method for assigning opinions. There, opinions are distributed by the consensus of the justices in the majority for each case, either by volunteering or nominating writers. The chief justice does not have any particular power to direct or control the assignments other than as a member of the majority.

Table 2 summarizes the above patterns of opinion assignment. Clearly the states are quite diverse in their approach to this important process, although the preference for randomizing opinion allocation is pronounced.

Table 2

Opinion assignment procedures in state supreme court

Random assignment prior to conference consideration   27
    -by the clerk of court or central staff (18)
    -by the chief justice in conference (9)

Assignment at the discretion of the chief justice	10
Random assignment after consideration of the case merits	8
Assignment by the chief justice when a majority member, else assignment by the senior majority justice	4
Assignment by consensus of the majority coalition	1
	50

Procedures Governing Participation

The order in which the justices of a court discuss cases and cast votes in conference can affect significantly the internal decision dynamics of the institution. By rotating or randomizing the sequence in which justices are allowed to raise issues or express preferences, the effects of dominant personalities or more senior members controlling the agenda or always being in a preferred position to influence the other justices are minimized. In other words, rules which randomize the order for conference participation provide no particular individual or group an edge over the other members and diffuse leadership and power within the group.

Conversely, conference procedures which grant either the most senior or most junior members the opportunity always to speak or vote first create important advantages. In these situations, the senior-most members potentially can maximize their influence over more junior colleagues, while the least senior members are more easily socialized into the role appropriate for the institution. Indeed, recent research demonstrates that the members of a court are less likely to express disagreement when discussion takes place in order of seniority and when opinions are assigned at the discretion of the chief justice.

Although every state supreme court has specific procedures governing the assignment of opinions, only 44 states reported having rules, either written or by custom, which designate a particular sequence among the justices for discussing cases. Only 43 states have rules specifying an order for voting on cases. The remaining states have no guidelines for participation in conference. More importantly, however, even in the face of existing procedures, the overwhelming majority of states indicated that the rules, regardless of whether they were in writing, were not rigidly adhered to by the justices. Informality and collegiality appear to govern the conferences of most state supreme courts rather than formality or attention to procedure. Despite the informality, however, an interesting variety of methods for conducting conferences are followed in all 50 states.

Conference discussion rules. Because of the tendency for state supreme courts to assign opinions to justices before oral argument or the consideration of the particular issues involved in the cases, typically the reporting, or assignment, justice begins the discussion. Twenty-five states provide that the reporting justice speak first on those cases specifically assigned to him or her. After the reporting justice has made opening remarks, the remaining justices speak.

As Table 1 demonstrates, the sequence for the other justices to become involved in the discussion varies significantly by state. Nine states open the discussion to any member wishing to participate, without any type of sequence, after the reporting justice has relinquished the floor. Six states provide that the discussion follow in order of reverse seniority after the presentation by the reporting justice, while four states specify an order of seniority. Nevada, Texas, Virginia and Washington simply have the discussion proceed around the table in order of seating from the reporting justice. Arkansas is the only state to specify an order that moves from the reporting justice to the back-up justice, and then to the remaining justices in reverse seniority from the back-up justice. Finally, Mississippi provides for an interesting rotation of justices according to seniority and reverse seniority.

Of the states which do not initiate discussions of each case with comments from a reporting justice, nine states require that remarks begin with the most junior member and then proceed in order of reverse seniority. Five states provide that the most senior member speak first, followed by the remaining justices in order of seniority.

Michigan, New Jersey, Oregon and Wyoming rotate the position of first speaker, with three of these states permitting the chief justice to name the person who will begin the discussion of each case. In Michigan, the role of discussion leader rotates counterclockwise from the chief justice, with the discussion proceeding counterclockwise from the discussion leader. The chief justice in New Jersey chooses a justice to launch the discussion and after that justice has spoken, the remaining justices proceed in order of seniority from the speaker, moving from the most senior to the least junior. In Oregon, although there are no formal written rules, the chief justice has elected to implement a rotational system whereby the chief justice designates who will begin the discussion of each case based on a schedule for randomizing the first speaker position. After the first speaker surrenders the floor, discussion proceeds around the table to the left or right of the discussion leader, at the direction of the chief justice. In Wyoming, the chief justice also assigns each case a discussion leader, a responsibility which is rotated among the justices. Interestingly, the person the chief justice designates as discussion leader is not necessarily the justice who will be assigned the opinion for that case.

Only Connecticut begins discussion with the junior-most justice and then opens the floor to any member, rather than continuing according to inverse seniority. Finally, six states do not have any preordained sequence among the justices for contributing comments about the cases.

Table 3 summarizes the rules for conference discussion currently followed in state supreme courts. The variation among the states in this process is most pronounced, with the dominate preference fairly evenly divided between an order of reverse seniority and open discussion.

Table 3

Order of discussion among justices in conference in state supreme courts

Reporting justice first	25
-then open discussion (9)	
-then reverse seniority (6)	
-then seniority (4)	
-then around table from the assignee (4)	
-then back-up justice and reverse seniority from the back-up justice (1)	
-then alternating seniority and reverse seniority (1)	
Reverse seniority	9
Open discussion with no specified order	6
Seniority	5
Rotation	4
Most junior justice, then open	1
	50

Conference voting rules. Of the states having rules, however flexible in application, which establish a sequence among the members of a court for participating in conference, most maintain the same order for discussing cases and casting votes. Five states (Alabama, Nebraska, New Jersey, North Dakota and Ohio), however, alter somewhat the order of participation among the justices from the discussion stage to the voting stage.

At the discussion stage, Alabama and Nebraska begin with the reporting justice and then open the floor to any other members in no particular sequence. However, the justices in Alabama vote in order of reverse seniority, while the justices in Nebraska cast votes in order of seniority. New Jersey permits the chief justice to choose the discussion leader, who is followed in sequence by the other justices in increasing seniority from the speaker; voting, however, takes place in order of seniority. Members of the North Dakota Supreme Court discuss cases according to reverse seniority but follow no particular order for voting. Finally, the justices in Ohio discuss cases in order of seniority but vote in reverse seniority. Table 4 summarizes the various voting rules in conferences in state courts of last resort.

Table 4

Order of voting among justices in conference in state supreme courts

Reporting justice first	21
-then open (6)	
-then reverse seniority (5)	
-then seniority (4)	
-then around table from the assignee (4)	
-then back-up justice and reverse seniority from the back-up justice (1)	
-then alternating seniority and reverse seniority (1)	
Reverse seniority	11
Open, no specified order	8
Seniority	6
Rotation	3
Most junior justice, then open	1
	50

CONCLUSION

One of the most interesting characteristics of the opinion assignment procedures and conference practices in state supreme courts today is their continued diversity. As McConkie noted in 1976, each institution has adopted rules uniquely suited to the professional norms and expectations of the justices who historically have composed the institution and which promote and maintain the type of internal environment desired. Also noteworthy is the fact that the rules used in the U.S. Supreme Court have not been adopted by the states. On the contrary, the states appear to prefer a more informal and flexible operating environment in which norms of professionalism and collegiality structure behavior.

More study is needed of the internal operating procedures of state supreme courts. Why courts have adopted particular practices and why courts choose to change their rules are issues of tremendous importance.

The consequences of specific internal practices also deserve further examination. The environment created by a particular rule system may be a crucial determinant of judicial behavior. Already there is evidence that the method of opinion assignment and voting order influence one important form of judicial behavior, the expression of dissent.

The variations in rules and procedures among state supreme courts provide an outstanding opportunity for researchers to estimate the impact of other types of institutional arrangements on judicial decision-making. Continued research is needed to determine how important each institutional characteristic is to appellate court politics and policies. Given the data becoming available because of the increased attention to state supreme courts, investigations of these intriguing relationships can proceed.

Notes and Questions

1.   What are the different types of conferences a court can hold on an individual case? Is each type of conference essential to a sound decision making process? Is any type of conference essential? Could a telephone conference or circulation of memoranda substitute for conferences? Are there other values that flow from conferences other than as part of the decision making process?

2.   Are the same type and number of conferences necessary for a case submitted on the briefs as for one in which oral argument is heard? Does the answer to this question depend on the effect of oral argument on the number of cases an appellate court can dispose of in any given period of time?

3.   Note the differences in decision making procedures identified in the Hall article. Would any of these differences have a possible significant effect on the outcome of a case? Should it?

4.   When and how often a court holds decisional conference also varies substantially. According to Smith, The Appellate Decisional Conference, 28 Ark. L. Rev. 425, 434–35 (1975):

> In at least 32 of the 37 conferencing courts of last resort the decision-making conference is held immediately after oral arguments. Michigan seems to be alone in having its conference before the oral argument. That practice is also followed in the intermediate California courts, where the judges believe that by reaching a tentative decision in advance they are better able to control the oral argument and to put the right questions to the attorneys.
>
> There is much to be said in favor of holding short conferences frequently rather than long ones infrequently. In Kansas, for example, the court sits to hear oral arguments eight times a year. Each conference begins on the following Wednesday and usually lasts for from ten to fourteen days. Under such a schedule it is inevitable that some of the cases will have gotten cold in the judge's mind when he begins to write his opinion. He must then, at least to some extent, reread the briefs, re-examine the record, reassemble the facts, and resurvey the authorities. In short, much of his work is done twice. In Arkansas we pretty well avoid that lost motion by holding a conference every Monday and usually writing a first draft of our opinions within the next forty-eight hours.

Is Justice Smith correct in favoring frequent short conferences over infrequent long ones? Should it make a difference whether all of the judges live in the same city or reside throughout the territorial jurisdiction of the court? Should all of the judges of an appellate court reside in the city where the court has its principal office? Are there any advantages to having a judge reside in different cities? Appellate courts also differ as to whether they sit only in one city or hold hearings in various cities. What are the advantages and disadvantages of each system? For a discussion of both issues as they relate to one court, see R. Leflar, R. Martineau, & M. Solomon, Pennsylvania's Appellate Courts 12–13 (1978) (published as a report of the American Judicature Society).

SECTION F. PROFESSIONAL STAFF AND SCREENING

P. CARRINGTON, D. MEADOR, M. ROSENBERG, JUSTICE ON APPEAL

44–55 (1976).

PROFESSIONAL STAFF

In response to the pressure of workload, many high volume courts have made increasing use of supporting professional personnel. The emerging practice is to be distinguished from the more familiar use of the personal law clerk assigned to the individual judge. That innovation, itself a development of recent decades, was motivated more by the desire for professional quality than by the need for efficiency.[1] The personal law clerk customarily performs any service that he is directed by his judge to perform, most frequently to assist in legal research.[2] Many appellate judges now have two, or even more, personal law clerks. The new development is the creation of a staff of similarly qualified professionals who serve the court as a whole, and who have no personal relationship with individual judges.[3] Typically, this central staff is headed by a mature lawyer with administrative experience who is responsible to the court for hiring and supervising.[4]

A. THE PERSONAL LAW CLERK: COSTS AND BENEFITS

Because the personal law clerk is a familiar institution, it has been tempting to increase the efficiency and productivity of high volume court by increasing the number of such clerks. They are usually recent law school graduates and cost less per capita than judges. Experience indicates, however, that there is a fairly low point of diminishing return in judicial productivity resulting from the creation of such clerkships. There is also reason to believe that the non-economic costs of proliferation are substantial. Increased personal clerkships threaten several imperatives.

Probably the most substantial threat is the risk to the working conditions of judges. A judge with a large staff is less a professional craftsman, and more an administrator. He must devote more of his time to hiring his staff, to the supervision of their work, and to the handling of their personal problems. His work inevitably becomes less the product of his own mind and more the product of a team. This concern is

---

1. Baier, The Law Clerks: Profile of an Institution, 26 Vand.L.Rev. 1125 (1973).

2. Wright, Observations of an Appellate Judge: The Use of Law Clerks, 26 Vand. L.Rev. 1179 (1973).

3. See generally D. Meador, Appellate Courts: Staff and Process in the Crisis of Volume (1974).

4. For a more detailed description of the most fully developed central staff, see Lesinski & Stockmeyer, Prehearing Research and Screening in the Michigan Court of Appeals: One Court's Method for Increasing Judicial Productivity, 26 Vand. L.Rev. 1211 (1973).

magnified exponentially by increasing clerkships; whereas the first clerk is a companion and a source of intellectual stimulation, the third or fourth is more of a distraction and a burden than a help to the performance by the judge of his own work. While this is not true for every judge, some being more attuned to the demands of office management, it will be true for most. And, over time, the judicial office will be made less attractive to persons who should be attracted to it, if the judgeship is systematically transformed into a flywheel for the satellite clerks who do the bulk of the work.

This transformation of the relationship between the judge and the clerk poses a collateral risk that is worth noting. At the present time, appellate judge clerkships are in great demand among the most talented law school graduates. It is unlikely that a clerkship will remain so popular if the relationship is depersonalized by continued increases in the number of clerks.

A second imperative that may be jeopardized by continued enlargement of the judges' personal staffs, is the imperative of collegiality. Numerous clerks serve to insulate the judges from one another. The larger the judge's personal retinue becomes, the greater is the tendency for the judge to confer with his staff rather than with his judicial colleagues. He may become less receptive to peer argument in conference. This kind of relationship between peers, which seems to be a probable outcome of the proliferation of personal clerks, can be seen in the working of several federal administrative agencies.

A third risk, which is implicit in the two previously stated, is the risk to the imperative of personal responsibility. Increasing the number of clerks strains the supervisory ability and energy of the judge. At some point, which will vary greatly among individual judges, the judge cannot know what his subordinates are doing and will become dependent on them to do some or all of his thinking for him.

In light of these risks, the advantages of increasing the number of personal law clerks must appear to be substantial if the increase is to be justified. In fact, it is not clear that there is a significant increase in judicial productivity to be gained by enlarging the personal staffs of the judges. In Michigan, it was determined that the second personal law clerk contributed more to the length than to the number of decisions rendered by the judges. While this experience is not universal, it should not be surprising if it is common. Unless there is to be an improper delegation of decision-making responsibility, there is little that the individual judge's third and fourth clerk can do which will make the basic work of deciding cases faster or less demanding of effort by the judge himself. For these reasons, we oppose increases beyond two, in the number of law clerks regularly assigned to individual judges in high volume courts.

B. Central Staff

The use of central staff carries some of the same risks associated with excessive dependence on personal law clerks. If it is used in the wrong way, such a staff can become a sprawling bureaucracy which could dominate the court, and thus threaten the imperatives of identifiability, personal responsibility, collegiality, and inspiring working conditions. In fact, these risks seem greater in regard to the use of central staff, if central staff were to be used in precisely the same way that the more familiar personal law clerks are used, as a source of help in thinking. A central staff which acquired all the functions of the personal law clerks and provided the same service to all judges in every case would be quite likely to dominate the institution. The most powerful office in the court could come to be that of the staff director.

But this need not be. As the previous chapter's discussion of efficiency suggested, there are a number of steps which can be taken to abbreviate and accelerate the process which do not require the full attention of all the judges. It is these functions which can be assisted efficiently by the central staff. The crucial step in the effective utilization of central staff is to alter the traditional appellate procedure which operates in all cases the same in favor of a differentiated procedure which measures the court's efforts to fit the needs of the particular case. It is in the operation of a differentiated procedure that the central staff can be used to substantial advantage.

The benefit to be secured has been proven by experience in several states. The Illinois Appellate Court experienced an increase in efficiency of almost 50% which was achieved largely by means of the use of a central staff functioning in a differentiated process. Smaller, but similar gains were observed in the New Jersey Appellate Division. These data were secured by means of a study conducted under the auspices of the National Center for State Courts. The same study revealed that the use of central staff was not an effective means to secure efficiency in courts in which the differentiated process was not used; such was the experience in Nebraska and Virginia.

The adverse risks of the use of central staff are also less where the central staff functions are primarily associated with the routing procedures that are necessary to the differentiated process. Nevertheless, there is just reason for caution in the enlargement of the central staff. The staff functions are not, and cannot be, so clearly defined that there will be no danger of undue dependence, if there are a small number of judges served by a large central staff in a high volume situation. Prudence dictates that the central staff should not be permitted to become so large that it will be possible for it to compete for judicial functions. As a sound rule of thumb, we propose that no central staff be enlarged to include more professionals than there are judges to be served by the staff. To place this rule in relation to one previously suggested, we propose as a rule that not less than one professional of four serving in a high volume court should be a full-fledged judge; such a judge may be appropriately assisted by as many as two personal law clerks and the equivalent of one additional clerk serving in the central staff. To surround a judgeship in such a court with more supporting personnel would create risks we regard as excessive to the imperatives of appellate justice.

As long as this rule is observed, there need be little concern about staff usurpation or the "bureaucratization" of the judiciary.

If this precaution is taken, there is then no need to distinguish sharply between the functions of personal law clerks and the functions of central staff. After identifying a limited number of cases in which a centralized staff service would be both efficient and feasible within its capacity, the limited central staff can perform some of the traditional law clerk functions of preparing research memoranda and draft opinions. The energies of the personal law clerks can then be reserved for the more difficult cases in which centralized treatment is unsuitable.

C. The Routing Preview

If appeals are to be classified for different kinds of procedural treatment, a procedure for classification is needed. Such a procedure is often described as screening. This term is used in so many senses that it has lost meaning. We avoid it, and describe the process of initial classification as a "routing preview." The decision to be made at a routing preview is the extent of central staff participation in the handling of the appeal, but this in turn involves predictions about the degree of judicial attention the case is likely to merit.

The routing preview could be placed in the hands of one or more judges. One judge could examine each appeal as the briefs are filed and make the tentative decision as to whether it should be sent to the staff, or by what process it should be considered and decided. This would have the advantage of involving the judges directly in every stage of the process. But it does entail a cost in judicial energy which does not seem worth the advantage in light of the very tentative character of the decision which is made at this point. Indeed, there may be some risk that judicial participation will make the tentative decisions more difficult to alter if they prove to be improvident, because at least one judge will have some involvement of ego in the preliminary decision.

Accordingly, we favor the more common practice in courts having central staffs, which is to make the routing preview the responsibility of the staff director. Experience demonstrates that an able staff director, operating with adequate guidelines or rules of court, can predict with a high degree of accuracy the appeals which the judges themselves would classify as appropriate for staff assistance. The step of sending the case through the staff director in this way is not a method of determining the merits or even unalterably fixing the procedural course of the appeal. If the staff director makes a mistake and sends to the staff a case the judges themselves would not have sent to the staff, the result is simply that the judges have a staff memorandum and draft opinion they would not have had if they had done the routing preview. There is no harm done. The judges may still deal with the case as they see fit as far as oral argument and conference are concerned; and they can write a full opinion if they think that appropriate. If the staff director makes a mistake and sends directly to the judges a case they would have routed to staff, they retain the capability of dispatching the case to the staff.

The routing preview should be performed entirely by the staff director, not shared with other staff attorneys. The staff director is the member of the staff selected by the judges themselves by reason of their confidence in his ability and judgment. Normally the director is a more experienced lawyer than the other staff attorneys. A single individual reviewing all appeals can provide a higher assurance of consistency in application of routing criteria than is likely to result from a division of the function among multiple individuals. He acquires a facility for appraising cases that expedites the routing decision. Experience has shown that even with a high volume of cases, a staff director alone can conduct this kind of preliminary routing. For example, in the New Jersey Appellate Division the staff director has reviewed in this fashion over 1,600 appeals annually. On the average, the process required less than one half hour a day of the director's time. The volume could be increased substantially without more than one person having to handle the routing preview.

In doing the routing preview the staff director should examine the opposing briefs and glance at the record. Typically the task will take from five to ten minutes for each case. Even less time will be required in some cases: for example, it may be instantly obvious that the issues are too substantial and that the case is inappropriate for staff treatment. Proficiency in this work usually comes fairly quickly with experience and with proficiency comes speed. If not, it is a signal of trouble. If the staff director in a high volume court routinely spends much more than ten minutes per case, something is wrong. And if the director is not moving the cases coming through his office within ten days, something is wrong. In either case, the routing preview is in danger of becoming a bottleneck. It must be overhauled.

In conformity with the suggested measures of efficiency described in the previous chapter, the staff director should assign to a staff member for central staff work all cases which seem to be likely candidates for disposition by memorandum decisions. These, it will be recalled, include the following situations:

    (1) The issues involve no more than the application of well-settled rules of law to a recurring fact situation.

    (2) The issue is whether the evidence is sufficient, and it clearly is.

    (3) Disposition of the appeal is clearly controlled by a prior holding and no reason appears for questioning or qualifying the holding.

    (4) The decision reviewed is accompanied by a full opinion which is essentially correct.

The hopeless or unanswerable appeal will be included within one of these categories.

D. THE STAFF ATTORNEY'S MEMORANDUM

1. Work of the Staff Attorney. Like the director, the staff attorney should remain current in his work. If the director cannot assign a case to a staff attorney with a backlog of three or fewer cases, he should not assign it at all, but should send it on to the judges without central staff work. In this way, the staff can be prevented from becoming a bottleneck.

Moreover, the staff attorney should be responsible for the use of his own time. If the staff director assigns him a case which proves to be too difficult, he should return it. An appropriate test is whether the staff attorney can complete his work on the case within two and one half working days. If more time is required, the case is not an appropriate one for central staff handling.

2. Contents of the Memorandum. In the few days which the staff attorney is to spend with a case, he can be expected to achieve a solid grasp of a simple case. He will study the briefs and read the entire record. He will examine the pertinent legal authorities and perform enough independent library research to be satisfied that no controlling authority is overlooked. If the briefs are weak, the library research will be more time-consuming. He should then prepare a memorandum which contains: (1) a description of the procedural history and posture of the case; (2) a statement of the issues; (3) a summary of the facts necessary for decision of the issues, with appropriate references to the record; (4) a summary of the opposing arguments; (5) his own analysis of the law and the facts; (6) his own recommendation of a disposition; (7) a draft of a memorandum decision; (8) a recommendation as to whether the court should invite waiver of oral argument if it has been requested, or order it *sua sponte* if it has not been requested; and (9) a suggestion of issues to be discussed at oral argument, if such an argument is recommended. While memoranda will differ in length, brevity is a primary virtue. A typical staff memorandum is set forth in Appendix A.

The staff attorney's memorandum should be read by the staff director before transmittal to the judges. He will perform whatever steps are necessary to assure reasonable quality control on the work of his staff. In particular, he should apply his broader experience to the questions of the oral argument and the form of the proposed disposition.

3. Uses of the Memorandum. Guided by such a memorandum, the judges can make much shorter work of those cases which were properly assigned to the staff attorney. It will remain necessary for them to examine the brief of the party who will be disfavored by the proposed decision, and to check the record to assure that factual analysis is well-founded. A judge still in doubt will have more reading to do. It will also be necessary for the judges to confer, however briefly, about the recommended disposition. And it may be necessary to hear oral argument.

One proposal for safeguarding the adversary interests and the integrity of the judicial process is that in every staff-processed case the staff memorandum and staff-drafted opinion be sent to counsel. Counsel would then be afforded an opportunity to respond to the staff work, either in writing or by oral argument. Staff errors or misconceptions would thereby be subject to corrections by counsel. The process would be made more visible, thus dispelling apprehension about undue staff influence. The points of contention could be sharpened, thus insuring that the judges' minds are directed to the real issues. The practice has long proved beneficial to the working of administrative tribunals. Against these apparent advantages, however, must be set possible difficulties that would be generated by this practice. Delay is one; time must be allowed counsel to study the staff papers and to respond. New points of dispute are likely to be introduced; the staff work might become a target of argument instead of the issues in the case. There is also a judicial reluctance to disclose internal documents that supposedly are solely for the judges' use in deciding cases.[11] Whether the judges should review the staff work before it is sent to counsel is a troublesome question that would need to be resolved. If the judges do consider the papers first, another step is introduced into the process, thereby adding to the work burden. Yet if the staff work goes to counsel without any judicial review, time and attention may be drawn off to matters that will ultimately be of little concern to the judges.

In view of these potential difficulties and the lack of any experience with the practice of disclosure of staff work, we are reluctant at this point to endorse the idea unqualifiedly.[12] It would be useful, however, for some appellate court with a central staff to try the practice experimentally.

4. Staff Role on Oral Argument. If an oral argument has been requested, and the staff recommends sending counsel an invitation to waive, the court must take action on this recommendation before the waiver letter can be sent. In light of the relative inconsequence of the decision to send the letter, it is one that can be made without a conference of the judges. If a majority of the judges report their agreement to the recommendation, the staff director or clerk's office could be empowered to send the letter. If no oral argument has been requested, the staff should nevertheless suggest that oral argument be conducted on order of the court if there are issues worthy of discussion which have not been adequately treated in the briefs. Like the recommendation for invited waiver, this action should require no conference by the judges; and, indeed, the request of a single judge should suffice to cause oral argument to be ordered. For those who share our attraction to orality, there is a possibility of fuller use of staff to provide for appellate proceedings that are largely oral. A model for such a system was described in the previous chapter. Such a process is best suited to criminal proceedings which tend to be simpler and more demanding of expedition. We will consider that system in connection with other

11. The central staff attorney should be sharply distinguished from the personal law clerk in regard to the need for privacy. The latter is a relationship of personal confidence which requires privacy, the former is not.

12. It is arguable that disclosure of central staff reports is constitutionally required. Cf. Mazza v. Cavicchia, 15 N.J. 498, 105 A.2d 545 (1954) (per Vanderbilt, C.J.). And see B. Schwartz, Administrative Law 396–399 (1975).

proposals for the improvement of the criminal appellate process, which is the subject of the next chapter.

5. Proposed Decision. Even with the stated precautions, some readers will be concerned about the risks which inhere in allowing the staff attorney to propose a decision. There is the obvious danger that the judge, especially if very busy, will be tempted to become a rubber stamp if he is not forced to do his own work. In large measure, we have assumed this much risk in allowing the judge to have a personal law clerk. There is also a danger that the staff attorney is pre-empting the function of counsel; this risk could be placed under control by the assurance that the memorandum will be visible, and subject to comment by counsel. If the staff attorney were not permitted to take a position at all, the value of his work would be much more limited. And, anyway, the effort to disguise conclusions often fails. Nevertheless, sensitivity to these concerns does indicate that the staff attorney should be constrained in style. He should, in writing his memorandum, let the parties' briefs do the persuading and should not seek to sell his viewpoint.

6. Frequency of Use. In what percentage of the court's cases should such staff work be performed? Perhaps as many as fifty percent of the appeals in a high volume court of first review may meet the test for staff assignment stated in the previous section of this chapter. Prudence dictates that the proportion should not in any event exceed one half, lest this "fast track" approach come to be the norm. Appropriate regard for the imperatives dictates that the fuller procedure be preserved in at least half of the court's proceedings. Moreover, the staff work is simply not cost-justified in more difficult cases in which the judges will, and should, read and brood longer. On the other hand, the proportion of cases handled by the staff should be sufficient to assure the economies of scale. For this reason, we favor the use of a staff large enough to perform this service in about half of the court's cases, if that many meet the test and provided that this does not require a staff larger than permitted by the rule earlier stated of not more than one staff attorney for each judgeship. At a minimum, if a staff is to be used at all, it should be large enough to work on at least a fourth to a third of the cases.

R. HANSON, C. FLANGO & R. HANSEN, THE WORK OF APPELLATE COURT LEGAL STAFF

National Center For State Courts 2000, pages 1–5*

Every appellate court employs a legal staff to assist the justices. Staff members may include clerks of court, central staff attorneys, short-term in-chambers law clerks, and possibly career in-chambers law clerks. The literature is replete with conflicting views on whether the justices rely too much on legal staff, but there is very little information on what tasks the staff actually performs. . . .

* Copyright © 2000, National Center for State Courts. Reprinted by permission. All rights reserved.

The National Center for State Courts (The National Center) with the support of the State Justice Institute (SJI), examined the work of the nation's state appellate court legal staff, to help fill a void in the literature. What are the basic work areas of legal staff? Are different types of legal staff devoted to particular areas? Does the work domain of legal staff depend on the type of court or some other specific characteristic? . . .

The research came to three major conclusions:

The work of state appellate court legal staff can be divided into nine distinct work areas. Each area consists of a particular combination of tasks. The nine areas are:

- assisting justices in opinion preparation

- handling cases at key procedural events (case management)

- training staff and court management

- prehearing assistance

- researching substantive motions and applications for writs

- attending decisional conferences

- conducting settlement conferences

- managing settlement conferences

- preparing memoranda on discretionary petitions

Each of the work areas tends to be the domain of a particular type of legal staff person. Short-term law clerks tend to be the primary staff in providing assistance to justices in the preparation of opinions; however, central staff attorneys are also involved and even clerks of court assist individual justices on specific cases. Clerks of court are the key players in case management and in court management assistance, although some career law clerks play some role in court management. Central staff attorneys have a more diverse portfolio, working on more areas than their colleagues. Their responsibilities include: assistance in opinion preparation, prehearing assistance, researching motions and writs, attending decisional conferences, conducting and managing settlement conferences and preparing memoranda on discretionary petitions. Interestingly, the work of legal staff in U.S. courts of Appeal parallels the work patterns of their counterparts in state appellate court systems.

There is a uniformity in the relative amount of time spent by each type of legal staff in intermediate appellate courts, courts of last resort without an intermediate appellate court, and courts of last resort with an intermediate appellate court in some of the work areas, such as case management and preparing memoranda on motions and writs. However the type of court affects the amount of time spent in several of the work areas.

* * *

R. HANSON, C. FLANGO & R. HANSEN, THE WORK OF APPELLATE SUPPORT STAFF IN FEDERAL COURTS

National Center For State Courts (2000), 59–66*

STRUCTURE OF U.S. COURTS OF APPEALS

There are thirteen U.S. courts of appeals under the purview of the Judicial Conference of the United States. These thirteen consist of twelve regional courts of appeals including those for the eleven numbered circuits and the U.S. Court of Appeals for the District of Columbia. The thirteenth court is the U.S. Court of Appeals for the Federal Circuit which is a national court that was created to centralize the review of certain kinds of appeals from the U.S. district courts and the board of contract appeals. Of the regional courts of appeals, the First Circuit is the smallest with six judges, and the Ninth Circuit has the largest number of judges (27). The First through the Eleventh Circuits each include at least three states. The D.C. Circuit is the reviewing court for the U.S. Courts of Appeals for the District of Columbia and decides a large proportion of appeals from administrative agencies. In addition to the thirteen courts under the Judicial Conference of the U.S., this project surveyed two other federal appellate courts: the U.S. Court of Appeals for the Armed Forces and the U.S. Court of Appeals for Veterans Claims, which are courts of limited jurisdiction that handle specialized cases.

Federal courts increasingly use support staff to help manage court operations or to handle other duties that were previously handled only by judges. Appellate support staff in the federal courts of appeals includes, but is not limited to, a circuit executive, a court clerk, central staff attorneys, elbow clerks, pro se law clerks, and, in nearly all courts, circuit mediators.

At mid-century, each court of appeals judge had single in-chambers law clerk. Today, judges in these courts generally hire three or four law clerks, depending on the number of secretaries (two to one, respectively) they choose to have. Chief judges may hire four or five clerks, and senior judges may have from one to three, depending on the size of the caseload they elect to maintain. Some federal judges have begun hiring career, or permanent law clerks to fill an opening in their chambers, which will reduce their need for temporary staff.

BACKGROUND ON THE FEDERAL PART OF THE STUDY

To determine how each of the federal courts of appeal (or federal appeals courts) use their legal staff, a set of surveys similar to those sent to the state courts was sent to a head staff attorney in each court for

* Copyright © 2000, National Center for State Courts. Reprinted by permission. All rights reserved.

distribution to the clerk of the court, a circuit executive, a circuit mediator, a central staff attorney, a short-term in-chambers law clerk, and a career law clerk where applicable. The survey listed 40 tasks similar to those that were used in the state court inquiry. The response rate from the federal appeals courts was 75 percent. All but one federal appeals court participated in the study, but some circuits did not return a complete set of surveys.

SURVEY FINDINGS: DUTIES OF FEDERAL APPELLATE SUPPORT STAFF

Circuit Executive. The tasks of a circuit executive are assigned by statute and by the circuit council and are exercised under the supervision of the chief circuit judge. The Circuit executive is usually responsible for a range of standard non-judicial administrative tasks, especially oversight of the personnel system and the budget for the court of appeals. Some of these tasks involve serving as a liaison to state courts, bar groups, the media, and the public. The circuit executive also collects statistical data on the flow and management of cases within the circuit and prepares reports for the circuit and the Administrative Office of the U.S. Courts. All federal appeals courts have circuit executives except for the U.S. Court of Appeals for the Armed Forces and the U.S. Court of Appeals for Veterans Claims.

Circuit Mediator. Mediators, also termed conference attorneys, spend most of their time on appellate settlement conferences, including reviewing the settlement conference statements, managing the logistics of the settlement conferences, acting as a host for the settlement conferences, and other related work. All of the courts of appeals have provisions for civil settlement conferences, but the Federal Circuit does not use a circuit mediator. The Court of Appeals for the Armed Forces, the Court of Appeals for the Federal Circuit, and the Court of Appeals for Veterans Claims do not have circuit mediators, and the other courts have even more circuit mediators.

Clerk of Court. Each circuit court has a clerk who is appointed by and serves at the pleasure of the court. The clerk of court may be a lawyer, but a law degree is not a requisite for appointment. The clerk of court appoints necessary deputies and clerical assistants with the approval of the court and manages a variety of complex, non-judicial functions delegated by the court. The Administrative Office establishes the number of authorized employees and their salary schedules.

This study identified two major work areas for federal clerks of court. These are 1) handling cases procedurally and 2) overall court management. In the First, Second, Sixth, Eighth, Tenth, and Federal Circuits, the clerks of court spend almost half of their work time on the procedural handling of cases with these six courts spending from 86 percent to 43 percent of their time on this activity. In contrast, in the Third, Fifth, and Ninth Circuits, and the Court of Appeals for Veterans Claims, the clerks of court spend most of their time on court management with their times for this activity ranging from 81 to 45 percent.

The graph below shows the time distribution for federal clerks of court in handling cases procedurally and court management. These are the same two major work areas found in the state courts for clerks of court.

Figure 4.1
U.S. Courts of Appeals: Clerks of Court

	Handling Cases Procedurally	Court Management
First Circuit	53%	23%
Second Circuit	86%	14%
Third circuit	41%	59%
Fourth Circuit	31%	55%
Fifth Circuit	37%	45%
Sixth Circuit	50%	25%
Eighth Circuit	43%	20%
Ninth Circuit	40%	50%
Tenth Circuit	64%	14%
Armed Forces	70%	30%
Veterans Claims	18%	61%
Federal Circuit	50%	30%

Central Staff Attorneys. In 1951, the Court of Appeals for Veterans Claims began to use central staff attorneys, with most of the regional federal courts of appeal following suit in the mid seventies. Because of its geographic size and number of judges, the Ninth Circuit has a somewhat larger staff. The administrative manager of the office is usually called the director of the staff attorneys' office or the senior staff attorney.

Central staff attorneys were originally employed to help the courts process cases filed by unrepresented prisoners, but in most courts their duties now extend to other types of cases. In almost all courts, central staff attorneys perform a screening function, reviewing appeals as they become ready for the court's attention and routing them into an oral argument track or a non-argument track. In addition to preliminarily determining whether a case will be decided with or without argument, staff attorneys generally review the briefs and records and prepare memoranda to assist the judges; in some courts they also recommend dispositions and draft proposed opinions, usually in the non-argued cases.

In most courts of appeals, central staff attorneys review all or most of the appeals before judicial review. In some courts, staff attorneys are involved primarily in civil cases; in a few circuits, they handle only procedural motions. Central staff attorneys may also be involved in appellate settlement conferences. The Sixth Circuit reported wide case diversity with its central staff attorneys working in criminal, social security, black lung, immigration, bankruptcy, death penalty, civil, and habeas corpus.

In the federal court surveys, as in the state surveys, central staff attorneys show the greatest variation in tasks among appellate legal staff. The procedural handling of appeals and prehearing assistance are the two areas that have the highest percentage of reported work time.

Figure 4.2 shows the wide variety of tasks performed by central staff attorneys in the federal appeals courts. The four major areas that the survey indicated are: 1) prehearing assistance, 2) handling cases procedurally, 3) researching substantive motions and writs, and 4) opinion preparation.

Figure 4.2
U.S. Courts of Appeals: Central Staff Attorneys

	Opinion Preparation	Prehearing Assistance	Handling Cases Procedurally	Researching Substantive Motions & Writs
First Circuit	18%	6%	4%	45%
Second Circuit	7	12	3	15
Third Circuit	37	27	36	0
Fifth Circuit	5	5	18	60
Sixth Circuit	1	6	81	0
Seventh Circuit	18	6	32	20
Eighth Circuit	38	3	40	3
Ninth Circuit	11	15	12	10
Tenth Circuit	43	2	5	3
Armed Forces	5	0	0	0
Veterans Claims	9	19	34	7
Federal Circuit	0	21	0	55

Depending on an individual court's practices, these tasks are defined more specifically below:

PREHEARING ASSISTANCE

Preliminary Jurisdictional Analysis. Central legal staff or attorneys employed by the clerk's office flag apparent jurisdictional flaws for the judge or a panel of judges who will dispose of the cases or claims lacking jurisdiction.

Screening Cases for Oral Argument Calendar. Central staff attorneys familiar with the court's practices and preferences may review cases for routing to argument or nonargument disposition.

Issue Coding and Appeal Classification. In some circuits, central staff attorneys screening cases for argument or nonargument disposition also classify appeals according to the nature and complexity of the issues presented. This work facilitates equitable distribution of the court's workload among its panels. Issue coding is also sometimes used to route cases presenting the same issues to the same panel and to route cases that present the same issue as one already being decided in another case to the same panel. The coding also facilitates staff review of opinions for consistency before they are used.

HANDLING CASES PROCEDURALLY

Some federal appellate courts also use central staff attorneys to prepare materials for cases not slated for oral argument. Staff attorney responsibilities vary from court to court. In some instances, staff attorneys are asked to review the record research the law, prepare a memorandum on the case, and draft a recommended disposition and order. In other instances, central staff attorneys participate in a panel's decisional conference on the case.

Researching Substantive Motions and Writs. In some courts, the power to decide procedural motions has been delegated to the clerk's office or to central staff attorneys. Typically, these motions concern what paper will be filed in an appeal, and when it will be filed. For example, staff may decide motions for extensions of time, unopposed motions to file amicus curiae brief; and motions related to the length and nature of appendices.

Opinion Preparation. The amount of time central staff dedicate to this task varies by federal appellate court. It includes contributing to opinion preparation, preparing memoranda on opinions of other judges, consulting with individual judges, shepardizing and preparing footnotes, editing opinions, and proofing mandates.

In-Chambers Law Clerks. Judges differ in how they use their law clerks, but most law clerks research the law and prepare bench memoranda for cases in which oral argument will be heard. Most also have some involvement in producing written opinions—some producing the first draft, others working with a first draft written by the judge.

Usually clerks attend oral argument and discuss cases with the judge. After oral argument, if the judge is assigned to write the opinion, the clerk will usually be asked to write a first draft, which the judge will revise and edit. In some chambers, however, it is the judge who provides the first draft, and the clerk is asked to comment, edit, and provide additional research. If the judge is not writing the opinion, often the clerk is expected to read the proposed opinion from another judges' chambers once it is circulated. The amount of advice a clerk is asked to render on these opinions varies with the judge.

Both short-term in-chambers and long-term in-chambers clerks spend most of their time on opinion preparation. Prehearing assistance is the second most frequently performed task by elbow clerks. Survey respondents noted that there are no career clerks in the Second or Federal Circuits. The adjacent graphs show how clerks in the reporting circuits distribute their time between opinion preparation and prehearing assistance.

Figure 4.3
U.S. Court of Appeals: Career and Short–Term In–Chambers Legal Staff

	Opinion Preparation	Prehearing Assistance
Career		
First Circuit	65%	25%
Second Circuit	38%	40%
Fifth Circuit	57%	33%
Sixth Circuit	15%	66%
Eighth Circuit	59%	25%
Ninth Circuit	32%	47%
Tenth Circuit	45%	50%
Armed Forces	29%	15%
Veterans Claims	25%	6%
Short-Term		
First Circuit	85%	5%
Second Circuit	38%	40%
Fifth Circuit	50%	26%
Sixth Circuit	51%	39%
Eighth Circuit	45%	39%
Ninth Circuit	32%	47%
Tenth Circuit	46%	50%
Armed Forces	28%	3%
Veterans Claims	74%	9%
Federal Circuit	40%	53%

SUMMARY

The most important finding is that the work of legal staff in federal appeals courts closely parallels the work of legal staff in state appellate courts. Clerks of court are involved primarily in administrative tasks. The two areas of handling cases procedurally and court management make up most of clerks of courts' work time as it does in the state courts.

Short-term and career in-chambers law clerks are used primarily for opinion preparation and then for prehearing assistance, just as they are in state courts. Finally, as in the state courts, the central staff attorneys who work for each court show the most variation in the time spent on different tasks. Opinion preparation, handling cases procedurally, prehearing assistance, and researching substantive motions and writs are the tasks on which they spend most of their time, but each court uses their central staff attorneys differently and shows a different percentage of time for each task.

SECTION G. TECHNOLOGY

TALMADGE, NEW TECHNOLOGIES AND APPELLATE PRACTICE

2 J. App. Prac. & Process 363 (2000).*

Many appellate courts are doing their work at the dawn of the twenty-first century in a fashion not entirely dissimilar to the way they were doing their work at the dawn of the twentieth. Appellate courts process paper files physically transmitted to them by the trial courts. Appellate judges and their staffs read paper briefs. Upon the publication of a written opinion, the paper record is placed in physical storage. Too often, because of resistance from attorneys, staff, and the judges themselves, and because resources are unavailable to move to an electronic environment, appellate courts have not utilized new technology that can facilitate the business of those courts.

By necessity, appellate courts currently use some forms of new technology. Few appellate courts or their staffs could survive without modern word processing or electronic legal research services. But as trial courts change how they do their work, and as attorneys employ new technology to make the practice of law more productive, the appellate courts, too, must use more new technology in their decisionmaking. Appellate judges may be surprised to discover their ability to resolve cases will be enhanced as new technology is brought to bear. In many instances, appellate courts can abandon the unnecessary use of paper, including the storage of vast volumes of paper records, in favor of digitized submissions and records. The most significant reform resulting from the use of new technology in appellate practice will be a more accessible record for judges and law clerks, and briefs that give judges and clerks fingertip access to cases and record citations. This will improve the ability of appellate courts to process materials and decide cases.

In five particular respects, new technology can improve the operation of the appellate courts: (1) electronic filing and argument of appellate cases; (2) digital maintenance of the record; (3) briefs; (4) dissemination of opinions; and (5) record storage. I will discuss each in turn.

I. ELECTRONIC FILLING AND ARGUMENT OF CASES

Many appellate courts already allow electronic filing of documents. Through electronic filing courts may accept pleadings by facsimile transmission, as attachments to e-mail, or as direct file transfers. All of these formats require attention to the particular court rules for electronic submission of documents. Many courts, including those of the federal system and Washington State, confer substantial local discretion on courts to allow electronic filing.

Many attorneys still do not utilize electronic filing of documents because of concerns about the reliability of transmission. The comfort

* Philip A. Talmadge, copyright © 2003 Journal of Appellate Practice and Process, University of Arkansas School of Law. Reprinted by permission. All rights reserved.

level of attorneys might be enhanced if, for example, filing fees are adjusted to provide financial incentives for electronic filing and courts send out official confirmation of receipt. E-filing must offer tangible rewards to practicing attorneys if it is to succeed.

In addition to e-filing, appellate courts could allow argument of motions in electronic form. Today, many appellate courts serving large areas frequently allow telephonic argument of motions. The technology to support interactive video communications—or even argument in a chat room or asynchronous e-mail format—is readily available and should be considered for argument of appellate motions, and perhaps even for final arguments on the merits.

II. APPELLATE RECORDS

In most appeals, copies of the clerk's papers (pleadings in a case) and the trial transcript are physically reproduced at the trial court and mailed to the intermediate appellate court. If further appellate review is sought, the record is again transmitted to the next level of appellate court. This process requires the expenditure of considerable time and effort on the part of support staff in both trial and appellate courts, not to mention substantial reproduction and mailing costs. Further, after the record is used by the appellate court, considerable costs are incurred in the storage of these records.

The implications of paper records for the judges' work on cases are also profound. No two appellate judges can work on the same case file simultaneously unless the court has reproduced the whole record for each judge, an expensive proposition. Moreover, for a voluminous record, the judge and his or her staff do not have the luxury of keyword searches through the record. Judicial personnel must rely on laborious treks through the record, relieved only by the sketchy indices prepared by trial court staffs and court reporters.

Ironically, more and more court reporters use computer technology to create transcripts. The steno machines of most court reporters are nothing less than small computers and many reporters can provide the court and counsel with real time transcripts. But often reporters must reduce an electronic record to paper for appellate courts. Transcripts can and should be processed electronically.

Many courts now use new forms of record keeping. In the Chelan County Superior Court and several other Washington State counties, all pleadings received are scanned and electronically maintained. Washington courts have also experimented with scanned records in appellate cases. The obvious benefit of an electronic record is that an appellate court judge and his or her staff can access the record through keyword searches. A court does not have to rely on the rudimentary index most court reporters provide for trial and deposition transcripts, or the all too cursory index to the clerk's papers that trial court clerks prepare.

The benefit of electronic processing of an appellate case was recently demonstrated in Washington. In Aluminum Company of America v.

Aetna Casualty & Surety Company, the parties agreed to provide the Washington Supreme Court an electronic record in the case in the form of CD–ROM disks produced and formatted with operating software by a commercial enterprise. This agreement was born of near necessity. The clerk's papers consisted of over 57,000 pages, and the report of proceedings (the trial transcript) was over 12,000 pages in length.

The CD–ROMs containing the briefs, clerk's papers, trial exhibits, appendices, and transcripts in the Alcoa case were all located on a central server so that any justice or law clerk could access any part of the record from their own computer terminals. Considering that the paper record in this case was stored in approximately fifty banker's boxes, the availability of the record via computer made access immeasurably more convenient.

While scanned records are a distinct improvement over paper records, it is something of an interim technology, reinforcing business practices built on paper. Scanning may actually impede transition of court systems to true electronic case processing, unless courts are cautious in choosing the technology so that the transition to direct electronic data interchange is built into the system. Some form of electronic record will inevitably be adopted by appellate courts. A CD–ROM record might be a means of ensuring an electronic record without a vast investment and major planning with local trial courts. Alternatively, remote access to trial court record keeping could be used, requiring significant trial court-appellate planning and coordination of effort. In this model, lawyers submit pleadings to the trial courts in digital form and the trial courts are the repositories of the records in digital form. Appellate courts across a state would be able to access the records directly from the trial court's storage system. No reproduction or mailing costs would be entailed in such a system. However, it is also true that adoption of this approach is hindered by the lack of bandwidth, or equal access to sufficient bandwidth, for the telecommunications portion of the necessary infrastructure.

As this day of the electronic appellate court is rapidly approaching, judges and court administrators must address several troubling issues associated with using the electronic medium. Security is an enormous concern. Protection against hackers is vital to the integrity of the court. No court can tolerate tampering with an electronically-maintained record. In particular, the possibility of introducing counterfeit documents into an electronic record would be very troublesome. The sealing of documents raises another important issue. How an appellate court handles public access to the electronic record and limits public access to sealed documents will be an important consideration of any electronic record system. These problems, though significant, can be overcome.

III. BRIEFS

The old system of paper briefs is simply archaic. Lawyers should submit briefs in electronic form to appellate courts. The technology exists, and it should be used.

In the Alcoa case, all the briefs were submitted to the Washington Supreme Court on CD–ROMs. A justice and his or her staff could hyperlink immediately to the record or to the key portion of the case cited by the parties straight from the text of the party's brief. Additionally, footnotes in the briefs are hyperlinked. Clicking once on a hyperlinked footnote superscript brings one to the footnote itself, which typically contains a reference to the record, also a hyperlink. Clicking once on that reference, a clerk's paper page number, for instance, brings one instantly to that actual document. Compare clicking a mouse button twice with getting up from one's chair, walking to the place in our Temple of Justice where the record is stored, rummaging through fifty boxes to find the one with document you are looking for, and then, perhaps, making a copy of the document to take back to your office for perusal.

While this scanned record clearly was more convenient than traditional paper-based approaches to case processing, such a system has its costs. This quantity of detailed material is not always easy to read in an electronic setting, as not all of us find scrolling through information on a computer terminal to be entirely enjoyable, nor as efficient. Moreover, there are limitations to the utility of records in an electronic format. Absent electronic books and software, such records are not entirely portable. Attention to user needs is a critical issue for such records, if their use is to become widespread.

While the Alcoa case involved a very large record, attorneys can submit briefs in electronic form along with paper briefs in the average appellate case. This would help the appellate court and its staff. However, each judge must have a ready means of reading the brief in electronic format, and that judge and judicial staff must become comfortable reading briefs electronically in the routine appellate case. Moreover, as of this writing, most appellate court rules are silent as to whether briefs may be submitted electronically; this silence does not suggest the courts would welcome briefs in electronic format.

IV.   Dissemination of Opinions

The traditional method for dissemination of appellate opinions is by means of a printed volume. With the explosion of information on the Internet, the print medium is no longer the best way of disseminating appellate opinions for public use. The Washington appellate court opinions are available in the traditional printed volume format. Paper opinions by Washington appellate courts are posted physically in those courts and given to the Associated Press. But few other printed copies are distributed. The Washington courts also publish opinions on their home page on the Internet. As soon as an opinion is issued by the Washington Supreme Court or Court of Appeals, it is posted on the Internet and remains on the Washington court system's home page for a period of ninety days. This is an effective means of giving public access to court opinions, particularly for the Washington Supreme Court. The court broadcasts all of its oral arguments on Television Washington (TVW), Washington's version of C–SPAN.

Dissemination of opinions on the home page, however, raises the question of published versus unpublished opinions. Washington Court of Appeals opinions may be unpublished. It is difficult to make a distinction between a published and unpublished opinion disseminated over the Internet. New terminology will be required. Plainly all of the opinions disseminated through the Internet are "published," but the real issue is whether or not they have precedential value. Appellate courts should eschew the "published/unpublished" terminology in favor of "precedential/non-precedential" opinions.

A final problem with respect to dissemination of opinions is the citation of cases. The traditional method of citation to cases by printed volume and page number must certainly give way as more and more of the opinions are electronically published. I advocate the addition of an electronic case citation to the traditional state and regional reporter citations for cases.

V. RECORD STORAGE

An increasingly difficult problem for appellate courts is the storage of case files. Courts must bear the cost of storage themselves or pay another public or private entity to store their records. The maintenance of vast volumes of paper records over a long period of time becomes a significant space and cost factor for appellate courts, particularly in criminal cases where collateral attacks on judgments are a reality and records must be retained for prolonged periods.

Trial court record keeping in digital format would do much to limit the cost of storage for appellate courts. And the elimination of paper briefs in favor of briefs submitted in an electronic format would dramatically reduce the volume of records stored by the average appellate court. This effort could effect a significant cost savings for an appellate court, although court managers must also carefully balance these cost savings against the added cost of periodic copying of records into new media as the technology for record storage evolves over time.

VI. CONCLUSION

New technology will make the processing of appellate cases in the twenty-first century more efficient for appellate court judges and staffs. The transition of appellate courts from paper to electronic systems will require a change in attitude on the part of lawyers, judges, and judicial staffs. Several important steps suggest themselves in order to encourage the development of new technology for the deciding of appellate cases.

First, lawyers, judges, and judicial staffs must together explore ways of increasing competence and comfort with new technology for case processing. Continuing legal education and judicial education seminars, perhaps jointly conducted, on the use of new technology in appellate cases would be a very useful way of encouraging lawyers, judges, and judicial staffs to process appellate cases electronically. Moreover, courts must address the question of pro se court access in this context because many pro se litigants may not have ready access to the needed technology for electronic case handling. Electronic case processing will only be as successful as the system users permit it to be.

Second, appellate courts must be certain their information systems have the capacity to handle the kind of electronic case processing recommended here. In particular, a court must be certain its digital infrastructure is ready to access a higher volume of cases processed in electronic form. Careful attention to this issue by court information technology staffs is critical.

Third, courts should assess their internal and external policies regarding court records. Internally, appellate courts must decide how best to maintain electronic records storage in a secure environment and when to begin, if at all, the process of putting older stored records in electronic format. Externally, the information revolution will make public records, like all information, more easily available to anyone, anywhere. Court policies on security and information disclosure deserve serious discussion.

Fourth, courts must evaluate their own rules of procedure to ensure that new technologies may readily be accommodated. In particular, court rules for electronic filing of all forms of pleadings should be examined to encourage electronic records and briefs. Moreover, filing fees should be set to offer financial incentives for electronic filing of appellate pleadings.

Finally, the rules for costs on appeal should be amended to allow prevailing parties in appellate litigation who submit their case in electronic format to recover the full costs of such submissions. In particular, attorneys who agree to provide the court an electronic record and submit briefs in electronic format should be able to recover the costs of so doing.

In an era when the public demands more government efficiency in the handling of public issues, courts are not immune. The employment of new technology for the handling of appellate cases can bring greater efficiency to appellate court operations. Moreover, in improving review by judges and judicial staffs of the record and briefs in a case, this new technology advances the administration of justice.

As opposed to being reluctant participants in new technology, dragged kicking and screaming into the twenty-first century, courts and judges should instead be technological leaders. Appellate courts must be friendly to new technology that can only enhance the process by which appellate cases are decided, thereby improving public access to, and confidence in, the appellate courts.

Notes and Questions

1. The implications of voluminous appeals for the practitioner are discussed in Vitiello, The Appellate Lawyer's Role in the Caseload Crisis, 58 Miss. L.J. 437 (1988).

2. Several appellate courts have adopted expedited procedures for certain kinds of cases. For a critical examination of the expedited procedures used in several jurisdictions, including the District of Columbia, Indiana, Kentucky, Massachusetts, New Hampshire, New York, Ohio, Vermont and West Virginia, *see* Symposium, Expedited Appeals in Selected State Courts, 4 J. App. Prac. & Process 191 (2002). Why is a knowledge of an appellate court's internal operating procedures important in expediting an appeal?

3. It is helpful to know how an appellate court assigns the writing of opinions prior to oral argument because preassignment frequently results in the assigned jurist asking most of the questions during oral argument.

Chapter 11

OPINIONS AND MANDATES

SECTION A. THE FUNCTIONS
OF A WRITTEN OPINION

LEFLAR, SOME OBSERVATIONS CONCERNING
JUDICIAL OPINIONS

61 Col. L.Rev. 810–13, 816–19 (1961).*

One function that is recognized both by detached students of the judicial process and by opinion writers themselves is that the necessity for preparing a formal opinion assures some measure of thoughtful review of the facts in a case and of the law's bearing upon them. Snap judgments and lazy preferences for armchair theorizing as against library research and time-consuming cerebral effort are somewhat minimized. The checking of holdings in cases cited, the setting down of reasons in a context of comparison with competing reasons, the answering of arguments seriously urged, the announcement of a conclusion that purportedly follows from the analysis set out in the opinion, are antidotes to casualness and carelessness in decision. They compel thought. It is even necessary that the thought have some of the quality of rigorousness in it. This does not assure that any particular opinion will be a good one, but it does increase the likelihood that it will be fairly good. That is a genuine function of judicial opinions, everyone will agree.

In a legal system built on stare decisis, the law-announcing function of opinions as precedents is constantly though about. It is the function most emphasized among law students, law teachers and members of the bar, particularly as they study opinions in an attempt to ascertain "what the law is" on one point or another. Quite a bit has been written about the opinion writing process as an aspect of the law's function in guiding society's future, and it appears that the literature on the topic is about ready to multiply. Much of what we call Jurisprudence bears on this function of the common law judicial opinion. When judicial opinions

* Copyright © 1961 by the Directors of the Columbia Law Review Association, Inc. All rights reserved. Reprinted by permission.

originate the legal rules, principles, standards, and policies that comprise the main body of a society's law, effectiveness in the presentation and initial implementation of these norms is, on the face of things, one of the main objectives that opinion writers ought to have.

The functions of law itself, or at least of the formulation and publication of law, are functions of the opinion writing process. The achievement of predictability in law, so that expectations based on knowledge of the law may be justified and justified expectations be realized, is a function that opinions should serve. It is a function of law to grow; growth enables law to satisfy a changing society's new needs instead of restricting and strangling them, and a common law judge's opinions must yield this growth. It is also a part of law's function to maintain the society's historic and traditional continuity with its past, and it is the writer of appellate opinions who in our system is principally responsible for maintaining this continuity. Logical symmetry in the whole body of law is a virtue, and in a system under which law derives from opinions it is well that the virtue be at least latent in them. Ethical decency, perhaps even ethical superiority, is generally agreed to be a proper end of law, and should therefore be aimed at by opinions that make law.

The most immediate function of an opinion is to explain to parties and their counsel what is being done with their case. The law-making aspect of the common law appellate judicial process does not outweigh the dispute-deciding aspect of it, even though the latter is sometimes overshadowed. Actually, the theory is that the dispute-deciding part is the court's main job, and that the law-making part is a consequence of the decision of the dispute because that is the way we think law should develop. At least this is the traditional way in which our common law has developed. The dispute must be decided and the adversary procedure is supposed to assure us that there is inquiry into all facets of the problem. Whether this breadth of inquiry is achieved or not, the case is decided, reasons are given for the decision, and the parties or their counsel read the reasons. Ordinarily they will be more interested in the reasons than will anybody else at that time, though their interest may decrease as their concern moves on to other problems, whereas the interest of others may increase with time if the decision has potentialities for future influence.

* * *

One of the major functions of any system of law is to assure its own acceptance in the society it governs, and this is part of the job of each judicial opinion. Law that is rejected by the people it undertakes to control, or that is received by them with doubts and misgivings, is not good law, and may not even be accepted as law at all. To a great extent the validity of law for a people depends on their confidence in it.

Law made by legislators is in a measure explained to the people by the legislative debates and reports that precede its enactment. These are directed as much to the electorate generally as to fellow-legislators.

Further explanations may come in later campaigns for reelection. For judge-made law the only comparable explanation is the judicial opinion. It is the appellate judges' and courts' major communication, almost their sole communication, with society. It is their interpretation of themselves to practicing lawyers, to trial judges, to law teachers, to laymen. * * * Pride of authorship is by no means an unmitigated evil. When it builds a protective fence around poor writing and preserves it at the law's expense it is vicious. When it preserves minor defects that without it would have been easily eliminated, it is unfortunate. When it induces a judge to forego the advantages of group criticism it is all bad. But this pride can drive a man to hard work and with meticulous effort. The poorest opinions are apt to be written by judges who take no pride in them, who regard the preparation of them as mere chores. Pride in work well done is a proper incident of good craftsmanship in any field of work, including law. An opinion in which the author takes no pride is not likely to be much good. I will even say that one proper function of good judicial opinions is to give a sense of satisfaction, of work well done, to their authors. A feeling of the value and importance of one's work is as legitimate in the appellate judiciary as in any other craft, and it is part of the judge's job to merit and create in himself and in his fellows a proper sense of pride in the judicial writing that he does.

* * *

A substantive flaw in opinion writing that frequently gives rise to misunderstanding is over-reliance on logic. Some opinions are written as though the cited precedents and the formally accepted rules, theories and doctrines inevitably require the exact result that is announced. This may create the impression that a result that can not be tortured into the conceptual mold prescribed by logic is "wrong." Yet the same court may start a seemingly similar case from a different premise and with equal inevitability by pure logic arrive at a different result. The careless reader may still think that the logic is all-important. The judge is at fault in his writing, obviously, for pretending that the logic is more important than it is. But the reader is at fault too; he ought to be able to do a better job of analysis, at least after he has read both opinions. He probably knew all the time that logic is only a tool, not an end in itself, and he should not have been misled by the opinion's implication that logic alone was the basis for its conclusions. He probably knew all the time that "judges make law," but he was forgetting *how* they do it.

It is hard on the reader to tell him that what was said in the decision conference may be different from what is said in the opinion, and that the opinion must be read in the light of that understanding; nevertheless, that is largely the situation. The reasons for the decision relied on in the conference may have been neither fully developed nor expressed in terms of formal legal principles or rules, but they were real reasons. The judge to whom the case is assigned is then in effect told to make it look good. That is an overstatement, because he is expected to be honest in what he writes, and is expected to set forth the case accurately.

But he *is* expected to make the court's decision, or the majority's position, look good. And logic is an excellent tool, like a brush in an artist's hand, for doing this job. Comparatively few judicial opinions, with the possible exception of those of the United States Supreme Court, undertake to go fully into all the reasons underlying the decision at the conference table stage. There is no dishonesty in this; it is only that these "real" conference table reasons do not read like law, that they often are practical social and economic reasons rather than technical legal reasons, and that many opinion writers think their opinions ought to read like pure law undiluted by the facts of sociology and life. Some state court judges, and most United States Supreme Court justices, realize that these "real" reasons are as much part of the law as are the legal rules and concepts that tie them together, and these judges try to put the whole combination of reasons into their opinions. When judges writing opinions narrowly omit such relevant factors, the lawyer reader has to read between the lines and fill them in. It may be difficult to do this, if a judge who really had nothing to hide has nevertheless done a neat job of concealing his court's true reasons for the decision. But competent lawyers can and regularly do so.

On the other hand, some misimpressions are created by the reader or critic who takes a sentence or paragraph from an opinion, sometimes out of context, and analyzes it as a Shakespeare scholar would, or as though it were a verse from Holy Writ, discovering hidden meanings, innuendoes, and subtleties never intended. This sometimes amounts almost to an attempt to psychoanalyze the judge who wrote the few words. This happens not only in lawyers' briefs but in law review casenotes and even in full-length articles by law teachers and legal scholars. The opinion-writer may do a little to avoid this by unifying his whole piece so that it is harder to take parts out of context. Generally, however, the fault is the commentator's; he ought to know enough about the nature of judicial opinions to realize that they are not designed to undergo that sort of exegesis. It is unlikely that all the members of a court will agree with every sentence in an opinion, despite its being a unanimous one. Other judges, and sometimes the author of the opinion, may not recognize its full import.[6] If they do recognize the import they still may not want to hurt his feelings by insisting on a change that is not immediately urgent. It may just be too much trouble to get the opinion rewritten. The case may have been poorly briefed, and a crowded calendar may leave too little time for new research and study. When a case comes out of conference assigned to a particular judge for writing, after majority or even unanimous vote, it is an incomplete thing; much is

6. When I became a member of the Arkansas Supreme Court, draft opinions were not regularly circulated among the judges, but were read aloud by the writing judge at an opinion conference. Disagreements and corrections were supposed to be noted then. Complete alertness for three hours of such reading was humanly impossible. Listening judges could do little more than give agreement to blobs of words, toward the end of the reading time. Fortunately the court soon changed its practice to circulation of draft opinions in advance, but there still are American courts in which uncirculated opinions are read aloud at opinion conferences.

left to the judge who has the writing assignment, and there is a tendency in some courts to let each judge do his job his own way.

Moreover, an opinion may represent a compromise. An unwanted paragraph may have been inserted to secure one judge's agreement, another important paragraph may have been deleted so that another judge would not dissent, two theories may be stated as alternative justifications to obtain a majority of votes. No opinion, however much rewritten, can represent the separate thinking of all the members of a court, and the more it is rewritten the less likely it is to represent the actual thinking of the one whose name is on it. Lawyers and law teachers know all this, but they sometimes forget.

No one would contend that every consideration that influences a judge toward agreement with a result announced ought invariably to be included in the opinion. Some motivations are negligible, some never become explicit, and some may better be left unmentioned. The urge to do justice in the particular case does not demand detailed explanation, when doing justice does not disrupt existing principle and theory. Lines of hoped-for growth need not be spelled out fully when the first seed is planted; often beginnings must be tentative, and one who plants a tentative seed flies in the face of fate if he then announces the full-grown tree that he hopes will ultimately emerge,[7] though he must say enough to indicate to others that a plant is growing so they will be encouraged to help tend it. Candor is a virtue, in judicial opinions as elsewhere, and we need much more of it. But to "tell all," with complete and unmitigated candor, is not always a virtue in judicial opinions or elsewhere. Restraint may be a virtue too, for reasons sometimes of decency and sometimes of wise planning. The problem of when to be candid, when silent, and how candid to be, is one that antedates the invention of pen and ink.

In terms of the writing of judicial opinions, it is a problem of what best achieves the useful functions that the opinion should be designed to serve. The creation of false impressions of what judges do when they decide cases will seldom do this. No writer can completely avoid misunderstanding in his readers, but he need not deliberately promote it. An opinion that tries to hide the true reasons for a decision, or that pretends that the reasons are different from what they really are, is not likely to perform its proper functions very well. Almost as bad are opinions that disregard the possibility of misunderstanding, ignore it as though it made no difference. Few opinions are written with wanton and deliberate disregard of what readers may think or understand, but failure to give affirmative thought to probable reactions can defeat an opinion's function just as fully. Effective communication with readers is something that has to be worked at; it seldom just happens.

7. This cautionary thought need not apply to professors whose law review articles propose new lines of growth in law. The exercise of imagination is part of their function. But judges who largely lay the foundations for new developments in the law know that they had better do so cautiously, without anticipating the ultimate result before a decision demands it.

Conscious thought directed anew as each opinion is drafted to the questions "To whom is this bit of writing addressed?" and "What ideas should it convey *to that reader*?" will go far toward enabling the opinion to achieve its functions. Since different opinions may properly have different functions, this conscious thought compels identification of the functions contemplated for the particular opinion. It makes the writing job a more specific and exact one, and makes the legal job a clearer one too. Judges, like everyone else, are aided mightily in doing their jobs well by being first clearly aware of exactly what each job is.

The purposes served by judicial opinions may properly be identified with the functions of appellate courts in our legal system. These could be thought of as the functions of a magic priesthood, and some remnant of this thought undoubtedly remains with us. Our sane intelligence rejects the thought, but it persists. Judicial opinions are the voices of our courts, and they serve the purposes that the courts serve. Stated most broadly, those are the purposes of government itself, though not all the purposes of government. Opinions are the public voice of appellate courts, and so represent the judiciary to the public, but they are not voices merely. They are what courts do, not just what they say. They are the substance of judicial action, not just news releases about what courts have done, though they have that function too.

ADVISORY COUNCIL ON APPELLATE JUSTICE, STANDARDS FOR PUBLICATION OF JUDICIAL OPINIONS

2–3 (1973).

One purpose of a judicial opinion is to permit the parties and their attorneys to see that the judges have considered their positions and arguments and to see the reasoning on which the court reached its conclusion. Thus, a written opinion may be required for reasons having nothing to do with whether an opinion should be published.

Still another basis for requiring a written statement of reasons in connection with the disposition of cases relates to the process of deciding cases. Most people find that their thinking is disciplined by the process of written expression. The reduction of ideas to paper, the organization of ideas on paper, significantly affects ultimate decisions; fuzzy thinking is exposed and in the collegial setting of an appellate court, errors are corrected. This likewise does not have anything to do with whether or not the reasons that support a decision are published or are filed and given only to the parties and their lawyers.

A wholly different purpose of judicial opinions is to provide the stuff of the law: to permit an understanding of legal doctrine, and to accommodate legal doctrine to changing conditions. Statutes and Constitutions must be interpreted and the common law developed. The reasoning of the court in significant cases must therefore be made widely available to judges, lawyers and the public. In such cases the law can be better developed if judges writing opinions have adequate time and energy thoroughly to research and reflect upon the difficult cases which will result in published opinions.

The judge's opinion also serves as a teaching device. Many people in society have special obligations to know what actions conform to law. Opinions of judges help not only the litigants; they help other citizens and public officials in similar situations to know how to act within the bounds of the law; and they also instruct lawyers besides those at bar in counseling their clients. Therefore, certain opinions should be publicly disseminated as rapidly as possible: for example, opinions involving alteration or modification of a rule of law, a critique of existing law or a resolution of a conflict of authority.

It is clear also that the judicial time and effort essential for the development of an opinion to be published for posterity and widely distributed is necessarily greater than that sufficient to enable the judge to provide a statement so that the parties can understand the reasons for the decision.

LASKY, OBSERVING APPELLATE OPINION FROM BELOW THE BENCH
49 California L.Rev. 831, 838 (1961).*

Where a judge need write no opinion, his judgment may be faulty. Forced to reason his way step by step and set down these steps in black and white, he is compelled to put salt on the tail of his reasoning to keep it from fluttering away. * * * Holmes said that the difficulty is with the writing rather than the thinking. I am sure he meant that for the conscientious man the writing tests the thinking.

Notes and Questions

1. How many functions does a written judicial opinion serve? How does Leflar make this analysis? Is one function more important than any of the others?

2. Can opinions in different cases serve different functions? Consider this question in relation to the issue of publication of opinions discussed in Section D, infra.

SECTION B. THE NECESSITY FOR A WRITTEN OPINION

McCLAIN, THE EVOLUTION OF THE JUDICIAL OPINION
36 American L.Rev. 801, 819–21, 823–24 (1902).

The judicial opinion is not essential in the decision of a case so far as the parties themselves are concerned. An official judgment, which suc-

* © 1961 by California Law Review. Reprinted by permission.

cinctly states the relief awarded, is all that is necessary in a case so far as that controversy is concerned, and no one now imagines for a moment that such judgments need be promulgated as matters of public interest. When they are entered on the records of the courts, all has been done that is necessary. Moreover, while it is generally assumed to be a satisfaction to the parties and their attorneys to which they are fairly entitled, to know the reasons on which the result reached is based, there is no public necessity for the announcement of these results as far as the case itself is concerned. * * * The desire of a judge deciding a case to vindicate the result which he reaches so that he shall not be chargeable with incompetence or partiality, is commendable; but where it is not customary to make any such explanation, the administration of justice is quite as effectual without as with it. Moreover, we have not yet reached, and probably in the near future cannot expect to reach, the general perfection of impartial judgment by which the unsuccessful litigant and his lawyer can be made to see the absolute justice and correctness of an adverse decision. Let us then abandon in the appellate courts, as we have already abandoned in the trial courts, the effort to satisfy the parties immediately concerned in the case that justice has been done, and that all the ingeniously devised points of counsel have been duly and fairly considered, and turn our attention more definitely to the discharge of the proper function of a court in giving expression to the reasons on which its decision is found. That function is discharged by preserving in permanent form the conclusions of the court on the controlling point or points in a case, which on the one hand involve a somewhat new or instructive application of legal principles to a controversy which is capable of decision by the announcement of something in the nature of a rule or principle. If, when the ultimate facts are determined by the court, it appears that there is no reasonable doubt as to the principles of law applicable to the controversy and indicating its solution, then reiteration of the principles which are applied is useless. Undoubtedly it is true that it is easier in writing an opinion to select the facts of a cause with reference to which previous decisions have established the law, and then cite the unquestioned authorities on which the same conclusion is reached, than it is to individualize the case from others and discuss the possible new propositions or applications of legal principles of it, and yet it is only opinions in which some new question or new phase of an old question arises which are of any value, and it is only those cases which can be individualized that are worth discussing in an opinion which is to be preserved as a precedent. On the other hand, if the facts involved are merely evidential facts, and the only thing which the court can say about them in the end is that they bring the case within an already established rule, then plainly an opinion is useless.

* * *

To summarize, the reduction would be brought about by writing a memorandum only in one-half the cases and putting it in such form that the case could not possibly be cited in support of any proposition whatever. Then in cases where opinions should be written, the length of the opinion could be greatly reduced by considering only the points of some practical importance, and as to which an opinion is worth while, and finally, the discussions of the points which are worth while could be made much shorter by the statement only of ultimate facts, instead of elaborating the reasons and facts which the judge considers and rejects in reaching those which he finds satisfactory and for which he is willing to vouch.

P. CARRINGTON, D. MEADOR, M. ROSENBERG, JUSTICE ON APPEAL

31–35 (1976).

E.   OPINIONS

1.   **Indispensability of Statements of Reasons.** The integrity of the process requires that courts state reasons for their decisions. Conclusions easily reached without setting down the reasons sometimes undergo revision when the decider sets out to justify the decision. Furthermore, litigants and the public are reassured when they can see that the determination emerged at the end of a reasoning process that is explicitly stated, rather than as an imperious ukase without a nod to law or a need to justify. Especially in a case in which there is no oral argument, the opinion is an essential demonstration that the court has in fact considered the case. In many circumstances, appellate courts have required administrative agencies to write opinions. It is paradoxical for appellate courts to claim the power now to do without them.[8]

On the other hand, it is advantageous that beleaguered courts not expend undue energy and time on opinion writing. It is clearly established that this is the most time-consuming and expensive phase of the traditional American process. Some judges are prone to write more than is necessary and to polish and refine the literary style at considerable cost in time and with insignificant gain for the judicial function. Refined editing is particularly likely when the opinion is destined to be preserved in print between hard covers under the author's name.

The pressures of heavy workloads have led some appellate courts to overreact by curtailing too sharply the explanation that accompanies the decision. Some have adopted the practice of issuing curt or perfunctory rulings that say nothing more than "Judgment affirmed." These and other cryptic styles of judgment orders tend to give an impression of an imperious judiciary that acts without the need to justify its judgments. They should not be used. But this does not mean that lengthy opinions must be employed in every case. A reasonable accommodation is possible.

2.   **The Memorandum Decision.** A short form of opinion can, in many cases, serve both of the interests involved: It can give reasons sufficient to explain the decision, while at the same time avoiding the

---

8. We are not overlooking the advice said to have been given by Lord Mansfield to the businessman appointed judge that he should only give judgments, which would probably be right, and no reasons, which would almost certainly be wrong.

expenditure of undue energy or time in trying to lay out a full exposition of the facts and the analysis in deathless legal prose for posterity—and pride. Thus we recommend much more use of the short form.

We have labelled this short form of opinion a "memorandum decision." Some courts call them "per curiam" opinions. Other labels such as "memorandum opinions" or even "judgment orders" are also used. The name, of course, is of little importance so long as the style and content of this type of opinion is understood, in contrast to the traditional, more elaborate style which we are calling a "full opinion." The essential characteristics of the memorandum decision are that it is not signed by a single author; it is addressed to the parties, not to the public at large; and it is as short as possible, consistent with the imperatives.

The principles we recommend as governing the use of opinions are as follows:

(1) Every decision of an appeal should be accompanied by a statement of reasons, however brief, except a decision that does no more than affirm a sentence in a criminal case. Not every decision on appeal requires the same sort of statement of reasons.

(2) A full opinion will be appropriate when any one of the following circumstances is present:

(a) In deciding the appeal the court enunciates a new rule of law or modifies an existing rule.

(b) In deciding the appeal the court resolves a conflict or apparent conflict of authority between its own panels or between subordinate courts.

(c) The court is not unanimous in the disposition.

(d) The decision is of substantial public interest.

(3) A memorandum decision will otherwise be employed, especially in cases in which:

(a) The issues involve no more than the application of well settled rules of law to a recurring fact situation.

(b) The issue asserted is whether the evidence is sufficient, and it clearly is. This issue may arise upon review of a jury verdict, a trial judge's finding of fact, or an administrative agency's finding.

(c) Disposition of the appeal is clearly controlled by a prior holding of the deciding court or of a higher court, and no reason appears for questioning or qualifying that holding.

(d) The decision on appeal is accompanied by an opinion of the court or the agency being reviewed, that opinion identifies and discusses all the issues presented, and the appellate court approves of the conclusions and reasons in the opinion.

Memorandum decisions can vary in style and in length. In Appendix B seven memorandum decisions are reprinted in their entirety. These illustrate the variations in this opinion form and show different situations in which the form can be employed. Whatever the length, it is essential that the memorandum decision convey at least three elements: (1) the identity of the case that the judges were deciding; (2) the ultimate result or disposition; (3) the reasons for the result. In addition, it is often desirable that the issues—or the appellant's contentions—be explicitly stated. The illustrations in Appendix B all contain the three essential elements, but not all fully reveal the issues.

An opinion that contains these elements, even though it be less than a page in length, adds assurances that the judges did in fact bring their minds together on the same matter, and it tells the parties what the judges considered and why they decided as they did. Less than this raises doubts about collegiality and the degree of attention that the judges gave the case.

The full opinion, by contrast, would typically set forth the facts and the procedural history at greater length, and it would spell out the reasoning as well as give the reasons. This latter point is a key difference between the opinion forms. A memorandum decision gives only the reasons; it does not lay bare the reasoning. The full opinion presents both.

F. COFFIN, THE WAYS OF A JUDGE

57–58 (1980).*

THE CONSTRAINT OF WRITING

A remarkably effective device for detecting fissures in accuracy and logic is the reduction to writing of the results of one's thought processes. The custom of American courts of embodying decision in a written opinion setting forth facts, law, logic, and policy is not the least of their strengths. Somehow, a decision mulled over in one's head or talked about in conference looks different when dressed up in written words and sent out into the sunlight. Sometimes the passage of time or a new way of looking at the issue makes us realize that an opinion will simply not do, and back we go to the drawing board. Or we may be in the very middle of an opinion, struggling to reflect the reasoning all judges have agreed on, only to realize that it simply "won't write." The act of writing tells us what was wrong with the act of thinking.

One can canvass other kinds of deciders who come to mind and find few who accompany their routine decisions with written explanations. If explanations there are, they are likely to be incomplete, informal, oral, and perhaps meant to be forgotten. Or, if in writing, there is little guarantee that they reveal the real reason for decision. A legislature may vote down a tax increase, invoking impressive economic data; one may suspect that the prospect of an impending election had more to do with

* © Copyright 1980 by Frank M. Coffin.
Reprinted by permission of Houghton Mifflin Company.

the result. A chief executive may announce a policy decision and marshal sophisticated reasons in support; in reality he may have been reacting to interest groups or congressional pressures.

What makes the "in writing" tradition a demanding one for appellate courts is that judges do not write on a clean slate. Prior decisions in other cases of different degrees of similarity demand to be reconciled with, or distinguished from, the present one. If results differ, the court must explain why. While conscientious and competent judges may disagree, the rigors of dealing honestly with facts, of recognizing and respectably treating precedent, and of reasoning logically, reduce the occasions for differences and narrow the gulf of such as remain.

Notes and Questions

1. In considering whether a written opinion is necessary, it must be remembered that this issue is different from that of whether every opinion should be published, although the two are closely related. The latter question is discussed in Section D, infra.

2. In *Justice on Appeal*, the authors argue that a statement of reasons is necessary in every case. Can a decision without an opinion ever be justified? Must the statement be a written statement? The English tradition, that still continues, involves oral opinions that are taken down by a court reporter and published either officially or unofficially. Some American courts, including the Second and Sixth Circuits, have adopted this technique as part of an effort to retain oral argument in every case. This approach has been urged as a solution to the crisis of volume (A.B.A. Action Commission to Reduce Court Costs and Delay, Attacking Litigation Costs and Delay 25–43 (1984) and Meador, Toward Orality and Visibility in the Appellate Process, 42 Md. L.Rev. 732 (1983)). It is also criticized as placing a higher value on what should be at best a duplicative means of persuasion (oral argument in addition to a written brief) over the one procedure that distinguishes the appellate process from all other means of dispute resolution (the written opinion) (Martineau, The Value of Appellate Oral Argument: A Challenge to the Conventional Wisdom, 72 Iowa L.Rev. 1 (1986) and Martineau, Practice in the Sixth Circuit: Oral Argument and Decisions from the Bench, 16 U. Tol. L.Rev. 655 (1985)). What arguments favor oral argument over a written opinion? What arguments favor a written opinion over oral argument? What values are emphasized by each of the two positions? Which values should prevail? Does the answer to this question depend upon whether the issue is viewed from the standpoint of the litigants, the attorneys, the judges, or the court as an institution?

SECTION C. MEASURING THE QUALITY OF A JUDICIAL OPINION

LEFLAR, QUALITY IN JUDICIAL OPINIONS
3 Pace L.Rev. 579, 580–83 (1983).

It has been said that appellate judges are, by the very nature of their work, professional writers. Yet few of them have gained acclaim, even among members of the bar, for their performance of that part of the judicial task. There has been a considerable volume of writing about opinion writing, and most of it has been critical.

Dean Wigmore's comments are among those most quoted. Writing early in the century, in the first edition of his great treatise on the law of evidence, he listed six major shortcomings in the bulk of the many thousands of opinions he had read. Five of the shortcomings had to do with content and form. First was the failure to exhibit knowledge of and reliance upon broad legal principles as distinguished from narrow rules. Others were disregard of controlling precedents, overemphasis on techniques and technicalities, undue bondage to the servitude of precedent, and overconsideration of every point of law raised in the briefs. The sixth, probably not in point here though now a common basis for criticism, was the one-man opinion. Mercifully, he did not dwell upon the too-frequent clumsiness of legalistic style and even grammar that more ordinary critics have often observed.

One rather obvious consideration that has bearing on how an opinion should be written is: for whom is the opinion written, for what readership? Not all opinions are destined for posterity. The first readership quite definitely consists of the writer's fellow judges. Their preferences and special concerns, or at least those of a majority of them, have to be satisfied, else the opinion must be revised as a dissent. Apart from that, it is evident that some opinions will be of real interest primarily, or even only, to the immediate parties and their counsel. Such opinions can be written simply, without much effort expended on achievement of literary quality. A clear statement is enough. If the case is one that has excited wide public interest, the opinion should be so written that the interested public can understand it, even when they read about it in the newspapers. That requires that it be so written that newspaper reporters can understand it. The public is the employer for whom the judge is working.

If the decision is one that will, or may, have precedential significance, and especially if it involves genuine policy considerations, it is being written not only for the parties, fellow judges, and the reading public, but for the bar, for law students, and for future judges. It may even be written for members of the legislature; they sometimes attempt to straighten out mixed-up and obsolete areas of the law—both wisely and unwisely. At any rate, it is these most important opinions that commentators are concerned about, and it is to the writing of them that much critical advice is principally directed.

Of prime importance is a common-sense requirement that the *real* reasons for the decision be set forth in such opinions. Often, neither formal logic nor interpretations of prior precedent constitute real reasons either for moving the law in new directions or for refusing to move it. The real reasons are apt to be socioeconomic or even political. They underlie all law and all legal rules, whether laid down in England in 1607 to meet the needs of that time and place, in New England to fit conditions there in post-Civil War days, or in New York in 1983 to fit whatever are thought to be the demands of the current society. Citation of 1607 or 1870 precedents, or even those of 1970, too often does not adequately explain 1983 decisions. Along with his formal analysis of precedents and restatement of applicable law, the good opinion writer must both understand what the real socioeconomic or political reasons actually are and be able to explain them clearly and honestly.

Clear and honest explanations call for more than good intentions on the writer's part, for more even than sound learning and moral integrity. Those judicial qualities, we can hope, may be assumed. Effective exposition also calls for good expository writing.

Careful organization of the materials to be presented is the first prerequisite to effective exposition. Standards for organization of judicial opinions are not materially different from those for other writing of the same general character. No one standard can be applied to all cases. But most opinions are sufficiently similar in content and purpose that some generalization is possible. Judge Frederick G. Hamley, then Chief Justice of the Supreme Court of the State of Washington and later on the United States Court of Appeals for the Ninth Circuit, in 1956 prepared for the Appellate Judges Seminars an organizational outline that has come to be accepted by hundreds of judges for most opinions. It divides an opinion into five major parts.

The first part is usually short. It states the nature of the action and how it reached the appellate court. The next, also short, sets out the question or questions to be decided. Then comes a statement of the facts—not all the facts in the record, but only essential facts. If there be more than one question in the case, so that issues have to be discussed one at a time, incidental facts that are relevant to one issue only are not set out until that issue is discussed. The fourth part is an analysis of the issue or issues one at a time in an order based on their interrelationship. This is referred to as "the meat of the opinion." The facts relevant to each issue must be tied into the discussion of it, but facts already stated need not be repeated except as emphasis is required. Some kind of a conclusion is called for on each issue that is deemed worthy of discussion, though one possible conclusion may be that the issue should be laid aside as irrelevant. Finally, there is the disposition of the case. If the judgment below is simply affirmed, or reversed and dismissed, that is all there is to say. For other dispositions, however, more detailed directions such as the scope of a new trial, corrected instructions, allocation of costs, and the like, are necessary and should be fully anticipated. These five elements, in varying lengths but in this order, are appropriate to the great majority of all appellate judicial opinions.

Opinion writers have received a plenitude of advice to the effect that they should use good English. Most judges do not need the advice except when they are hurried or get careless. Law clerks and fellow judges usually catch common errors before they come out in print. Yet dangling participles, mixed metaphors, strange punctuations, misspelt words, and dozens of other mistakes do get into the reports. It is interesting that so-called "typographical errors" rarely appear in the reports of opinions written by real masters of the language.

HOPKINS, NOTES ON STYLE IN JUDICIAL OPINIONS
8 Trial Judges J. 49–51 (1969).*

1.   Judges write opinions for an audience. The audience varies as the case varies.

2.   The opinion, as an expression of judgment, is an essay in persuasion. The value of the opinion is measured by its ability to induce the audience to accept the judgment.

3.   The nature of the audience is defined by the case. When the issue is essentially factual, the audience usually consists of the parties and their attorneys. When the issue is essentially legal, the audience usually consists of the parties, their attorneys, and the bench and bar. When the issue has public implications, the audience includes the legislature, public officials, the news media, and the community.

4.   The focus of the opinion will be as narrow or broad as the nature of the audience. The style responds to the focus of the opinion—that is, the style is adapted to the audience.

5.   The style of an opinion has two aspects—the organization of the discussion, and the composition of the language.

6.   The organization of the discussion means first, the approach of the author to the issue, and second, the method employed to make the discussion clear and concise.

7.   The approach should always be measured, temperate, and objective. Rhetoric is best suited for the advocate; an opinion expresses a decision above the individual passions in the case.

8.   The method of the discussion is not bound by any one rule. An opinion considering several issues may be divided into branches. Footnotes are useful when they inform the reader as to relevant citations and material not crucial to the decision or contain quotations at length of statutory provisions and pivotal testimony. Footnotes breed irritation when their number and proximity interrupt the flow of the discussion.

9.   The operative facts should be stated in depth preceding the discussion in the opinion concerning their effect and the operative law. This is not an absolute: sometimes disparate issues arise from unrelated facts, and divisions of the discussion as to both fact and law pertinent to each issue assist understanding.

10.   One cardinal rule: do not omit the facts which are stressed by the unsuccessful party or a doctrine which may be at war with the ultimate disposition. Otherwise the standing of the case both as to persuasiveness and as a precedent is impaired.

* © 1969 American Bar Association. Reprinted with permission.

11. The language of an opinion implies grammatical construction, sentence and paragraph structure, and choice of words.

12. The nature of the appeal and the relationship of the parties should appear in the opening paragraph of the opinion.

13. Simple declaratory sentences are the easiest to read. Modifying clauses, if not carefully composed, entangle the thought and deflect understanding.

14. Strong words move to persuasion. They are not many-syllabled but induce the sense of action. E.g., say "shows" rather than "provides evidence", or "distrusted" rather than "did not have confidence in."

15. Too many adjectives and adverbs weaken the movement of the sense. Nouns and verbs usually are enough.

16. Use the active voice. A person acts, sometimes a thing or a force acts. The passive voice indicates an anonymous actor, a vague thing, and an unknown force.

17. An affirmative statement is preferable to a negative one. The reader may doubt the scope of the negative.

18. A cliché cannot always be avoided—it is shorthand to evoke a response. But it should be restricted to the necessities. A cluster robs the opinion of the sudden insight which imparts persuasion.

19. Metaphors illuminate, yet may also be delusive. Be sure that they truly fit the pattern illustrated, and are not so remote in their bearing that the reader loses his way in underbrush.

20. Emphasis does not require reiteration. Once a point is expressed well, saying it a second time denotes a concealed doubt of the author.

21. Dictating an opinion invites amendment and re-writing to shorten and strengthen its structure. Time does not always allow a handwritten draft, but it usually is more effective than a dictated draft. Remember that even a handwritten draft shows flaws when it reaches the eye in plain type.

22. Humor has a dubious place in an opinion. It is not an universal commodity and the decision of the rights of the parties is a serious matter. Irony may be an effective tool of expression, when sparingly used, but sarcasm directed toward the parties is seldom in good taste.

23. All rules of organization and language have exceptions. The objectives always in mind are clarity, conciseness and movement. If the rules must be violated to accommodate the objectives, violate the rules.

24. Do not quote at length from citations. One or two sentences, suitably culled, promote the movement; more impedes it.

25. One or two citations to support a general rule are sufficient. If more are needed or comment is relevant, put them in a footnote.

26. At some point in the opinion appears its fulcrum. That is where the author ends his discussion of the operative facts and law and begins

his explanation of the decision. The value of the opinion largely hinges on this section. Make sure that it expresses the intent of the decision fully and clearly.

27. The statement of the relief granted should be sharply defined. Otherwise the preparation of the judgment (or order) to be entered becomes difficult and subject to mistake.

28. Distinguish between opinions which end a case and opinions which decide preliminary questions. The latter may entail instruction to the parties as to future procedure and therefore may be more discursive. Only in the rare case of a new statute or a question of public importance should an opinion ending a case expand beyond the limits of the question presented for decision, and then only to instruct as to future behavior which appears inevitable.

29. Put the decision on a major ground. Recall that the opinion loses worth as a precedent if the decision rests on alternative grounds. Sometimes this cannot be helped: the grounds are equally significant and each is necessary to the proper disposition of the case. But generally the opinion should determine the issue on only one major ground.

30. Be sure that a precedent distinguished is truly distinguishable. The reasoning of the opinion is suspect if the distinction fails.

31. An opinion construing a statute gains little by reliance on a rule of construction. For each rule favoring a certain construction another rule can be cited favoring a different construction. Give effect to what you believe to be the spirit and intent of the statute, even though you legislate.

32. Brevity is the soul of wisdom. Yet, do not be so brief as to be cryptic. The audience may not always appreciate the author's desire to shorten the opinion to the irreducible minimum.

33. Everything said here has its exceptions. Be certain that the exception is justified.

Notes and Questions

1. What are the hallmarks of a good opinion? Will they vary depending upon whether the opinion will be published? Practical suggestions on writing opinions are contained in Douglas, How to Write a Concise Opinion, 22 Judges' J. 4 (Spring 1983).

2. Should anyone other than the judge be interested in the quality of an opinion? Should the result in a case be delayed so that a better quality opinion can be prepared? Will the answer to this question depend upon which player in the appellate process is being asked?

3. What role should other members of the appellate court play in the preparation of an opinion? The procedure described by Leflar in footnote 6 of the Columbia Law Review article included in Section A, supra, was common at one time. Today the judges take far more collegial responsibility for an opinion. See R. Martineau, Modern Appellate Practice—Federal and State Civil Appeals § 13.5 (1983) and R. Leflar, Internal Operating Procedures of

Appellate Courts 53–54 (1976). For an inside look at how one judge approaches the opinion writing task and how he works with law clerks and judges in crafting an opinion, see F. Coffin, On Appeal, 171–229 (1994)

SECTION D. PUBLICATION AND CITATION OF OPINIONS

MARTINEAU, RESTRICTIONS ON PUBLICATION AND CITATION OF JUDICIAL OPINIONS: A REASSESSMENT

28 U. Mich. J.L. Reform 119 (1994).*

In response to the "crisis of volume," state and federal appellate courts have been restricting the opinions they write to those opinions which will: (1) establish a new rule of law or expand, alter, or modify an existing rule; (2) involve a legal issue of continuing public interest; (3) criticize existing law; or (4) resolve a conflict of authority. All other opinions are limited to brief statements of the reasons for the decision, go unpublished, and generally carry a prohibition against their being cited as precedent. Recently, critics have alleged a number of faults with this practice, including the supposed loss of judicial accountability, the difficulties of appellate review, the problems of predicting precedential value, the inequalities of parties' access to unpublished opinions, and the illusory nature of the claims of judicial and litigant economy. In this Article, Professor Martineau demonstrates that these criticisms are based on false premises and ignore the realities of legal research and the appellate decision making process. Professor Martineau writes that limited publication and citation rules are an essential way to respond to increasing caseloads, so long as: (1) they are crafted and administered to ensure that the criteria for publication are maintained with several checks on judges' discretion not to publish and (2) the prohibitions against citing unpublished opinions be enforced strictly through good example, sanctions, and structural mechanisms intended to make the opinions available less readily to people other than the immediate parties.

INTRODUCTION

The phrase "crisis of volume" is a trite but nonetheless accurate description of the principal cause of the problems confronting the appellate justice system in the United States. Responses to the crisis have ranged from new structures, such as establishing intermediate appellate courts, to new equipment, such as providing judges and law clerks with word processors and computer terminals. The appellate courts themselves also have made major changes in how they function. Some of the most common and most controversial changes concern judicial opinions.

* Copyright © 1994, University of Michigan Journal of Law Reform. Reprinted by permission. All rights reserved.

In some cases judges do not write an opinion. If they do write one, then they make it shorter than a full opinion and designate it as "not for publication." An unpublished opinion usually carries a prohibition against its being cited as precedent.

Although a few commentators have criticized the restrictions on publication and citation from the beginning, in the past decade commentators have been nearly unanimous in calling for their repeal, arguing that they are both fundamentally flawed in concept and unworkable in practice.

The purpose of this Article is to analyze the validity of publication and citation restrictions in light of the criticisms of them and the increased numbers of unpublished opinions included in computer databases. Part I reviews the reasons given originally for the adoption of the restrictions: the time and expense involved in preparing, publishing, and researching full opinions. Part II summarizes and critiques the principal criticisms of the restrictions: the supposed loss of judicial accountability, the difficulties of appellate review, the problems of predicting precedential value, inequalities of access to unpublished opinions, and the illusory claims of judicial and litigant economy. This Article demonstrates that the criticisms are based on false premises and ignore the realities of legal research and the appellate decision making process. It argues that eliminating the restrictions would create problems far worse than those attributed to their existence. Finally, Part III identifies problems that exist with the restrictions, examines their causes, and proposes remedies that will enhance rather than weaken their effectiveness. This Article concludes that although there are several weaknesses in the administration of rules restricting citation and publication of judicial opinions, the rules should not be eliminated. Rather, several changes should be made to provide for improved administration of the rules.

I. THE DEVELOPMENT OF RESTRICTIONS ON THE PUBLICATION AND CITATION OF OPINIONS

A. *Early Commentary*

Although restrictions on the publication and citation of judicial opinions did not become widespread until the last two decades, calls for a reduction in the number of opinions added to the body of common-law precedent are nothing new. Faced with roughly thirty volumes of reported decisions in 1777, England's Lord Coke warned judges not to report all decisions. Similar concerns about the growing wealth of case law appeared on this side of the Atlantic Ocean as early as 1915. It was not until the early 1970s, however, that judges, scholars, and attorneys in the United States embarked on a serious effort to reduce the growing body of reported case law facing the bar and the bench.

Initial discussion of curtailing publication stemmed from a concern for maintaining a manageable body of law in light of the growing number of cases heard by appellate courts. The Judicial Conference of

964   OPINIONS AND MANDATES   Ch. 11

the United States first took note of the problem in 1964, recommending that federal courts authorize "the publication of only those opinions which are of general precedential value."

B. The 1973 Advisory Council for Appellate Justice Report

Little happened until 1973, when the Advisory Council for Appellate Justice issued a report urging appellate courts to adopt publication rules to reduce the number of published appellate opinions. In proposing limited publication, the Advisory Council report identifies several principal concerns. Limited publication could "help redress the balance between what must be produced and assimilated and the resources available for production and assimilation." In contrast, the continuation of unlimited publication threatened to "crush[ ] [the common law of the United States] by its own weight if the rate of publication [was] not abated."

1. Benefits of Limited Publication—The report identifies the benefits to be gained from limited publication: saving the judge and the appellate court bench the time spent preparing a polished, published opinion; saving the lawyer the time spent researching opinions; reducing the logistical burden and expense of maintaining a law library; reducing the burden on publishing companies to supply the increasing number of opinions at affordable rates; and reducing the burden on the entire system of creating new devices to point the bar and the bench to the opinions constituting precedent.

2. Purposes of Judicial Opinions—After distinguishing as two separate inquiries whether an opinion should be written and whether an opinion should be published, the report lists three purposes for judicial opinions. First, an opinion permits the parties and their attorneys to see that the judges have considered their arguments and have provided a reasoned justification for the decision. Second, the process of writing an opinion can force judges to clarify their thinking. "[T]hinking is disciplined by the process of written expression," because "[t]he reduction of ideas to paper" allows for the exposure and correction of error. Third, certain judicial opinions "provide the stuff of the law." They facilitate the "understanding of legal doctrine" and its applicability to current conditions by providing a look at the court's reasoning, and they teach people in society what actions conform to the law. They help not only the litigants, but also other citizens, public officials, and lawyers, and thus should be disseminated widely.

Not all opinions, however, serve this third purpose. Only those that do clarify or expand the law, as opposed to those that only settle disputes, deserve publication. A written opinion not designed for publication would require less refinement, polish, and time spent by the writing judge, yet could still serve the first two purposes of an opinion.

3. Proposals—The report recommends that the courts adopt rules under which courts would: (1) continue to write an opinion in every case; (2) establish standards for publication and procedures to determine

whether an opinion should be published; and (3) prohibit citation of unpublished opinions. The report proposes several criteria for the rules. First, to ensure consistency within a judicial system, the highest court of each jurisdiction should promulgate rules governing publication and citation rather than let each court design its own plan. Second, "to avoid wasted effort," a tentative decision regarding publication should be made at the earliest possible point, such as at a conference on the case either before it is assigned or at the time of assignment. An early decision maximizes the time saved by the judge, but the decision must be only tentative so that publication would not be precluded were the opinion writing process to demonstrate that publication would be prudent. Third, an opinion should be published only if a majority of the judges participating in the decision agrees that the opinion meets the publication standards set forth in the rules. Further, a concurring opinion should be published only if it accompanies a published majority opinion. In contrast, a dissenting opinion should be published only if the dissenter or dissenters find that it meets the standards for publication on its own merits, regardless of the status of the majority opinion. When an entire opinion does not warrant publication, the court should publish those portions of it that do meet the standards.

The report proposes that an opinion be published if it does any one of the following: (1) "lays down a new rule of law, or alters or modifies an existing rule"; (2) "involves a legal issue of continuing public interest," as opposed to "general public interest . . . of a fleeting nature"; (3) "criticizes existing law," especially when it calls for change by a higher court or the legislature; or (4) resolves a conflict of authority and "rationaliz[es] apparent divergencies in the way an existing rule has been applied."

The report further recommends that unpublished opinions not be cited as precedent by a court or in material presented to a court. Allowing the citation of unpublished opinions would give lawyers or others having special knowledge of those opinions an unfair advantage to use or withhold that knowledge. It also would thwart the intended goal of judicial economy because citation would require the bar and bench to examine unpublished opinions. Allowing citation by litigants also would encourage judges to craft their unpublished opinions more carefully, thus increasing the time judges spend preparing them.

C. Responses to the Advisory Council's Report

Every federal court of appeals and a majority of state appellate courts responded to the Advisory Council report by adopting rules that restrict publication and citation of unpublished opinions. Although the rules differ in procedure and degree of specificity, they typically have several common characteristics that follow the report's recommendations. First, most of the adopted rules provide that a majority of the deciding panel make a tentative publication decision as early in the decision making process as possible. Second, in general, if there is a dissenting opinion, both it and the majority opinion are published. Third, most rules outline specific criteria on which judges should rely in making the publication decision: principally whether the opinion makes new law, criticizes existing law, or involves a matter of great public interest. Finally, most rules forbid citation to unpublished opinions except for the limited purposes of establishing res judicata, collateral estoppel, or law of the case.

II. THE PRINCIPAL CRITICISMS AND A CRITIQUE OF EACH

Just as there are features common to most restrictions on publication and citation, a consensus exists on the criticisms of them. Set out below are the five principal criticisms, each followed by a critique.

A. *Judicial Accountability*

1. The Criticism—First and foremost, critics argue that restrictions on publication and citation deal a crushing blow to judicial accountability and thus foster judicial irresponsibility. Courts, critics maintain, are more apt to issue arbitrary rulings "if their past [decisions] cannot be cited to them to guide and restrict their future action." Courts can use unpublished opinions to address "troublesome cases presenting issues the court does not wish to address in public" or to decide a case contrary to existing precedent without also changing the path and direction of the current law. One commentator links limited publication and citation rules with the success of tyranny. Tyranny flourishes when the law is unwritten, because then the law is known to few and is unreviewable by the masses. Written law, on the other hand, allows for a check of the government and gives the citizens a method to review the government's application of the law. For these reasons, this commentator argues that publication of opinions, not a limited publication system, better maintains an ordered system of civil liberties.

2. The Critique—Are the critics correct in arguing that an appellate court is more likely to be irresponsible by ignoring binding precedent, hiding controversial rulings, or acting arbitrarily because some of its opinions are not published and cannot be cited to it? Theoretically these practices may be achievable, but practically, several reasons make this assertion untenable. First is the desire of almost every judge to do the right thing. Second are the constraints imposed upon the appellate court by the appellate process itself. In most instances, an appellate decision is a collegial one reached by three judges, at least two of whom must agree on the result. If one disagrees and writes a dissenting opinion, then both the majority and dissenting opinions qualify for publication under most adopted rules. In addition, other members of the same court usually keep abreast of the decisions of panels on which they do not sit, so one panel is unlikely to do something irresponsible without other members of the court knowing about it. Further, the decision ordinarily is subject to additional review, either by the entire court through an en banc procedure, or by a higher court, or both. One of the most effective ways for a litigant to obtain further review is to show that the present decision is inconsistent with prior decisions. This can be

done best if the appellate court provides a written statement of reasons supporting its decision, and thus a statement should be prepared in every case. The present system, under which many cases are decided by order without a written statement of reasons, has a much greater potential for judicial irresponsibility.

Also supporting the Proposition that restrictions on publication do not result in increased judicial irresponsibility are empirical studies which examine the operation of the restrictions in appellate courts and the experience with trial courts. Only two in-depth studies, one in California and the other in Wisconsin, have attempted to determine empirically whether appellate courts actually make controversial or potentially unpopular decisions and then hide them by either not writing an opinion or by writing an opinion but designating it as not for publication, hiding behind limited publication and citation rules. Both studies came to the same conclusion: the courts used the rules in good faith and seldom used them to render improper decisions.

Even more significantly, the federal and state trial court systems both operate without a mandatory opinion writing and publication requirement. Judges rarely write opinions in cases disposed of at trial, and only a small fraction of those opinions are published, and then only at the initiative of the trial judge. Nobody has suggested, however, that the lack of published trial court opinions encourages irresponsible behavior by trial judges.

Not quite as relevant, but nonetheless significant, is the English experience. While only a very small percentage of the opinions of the English Court of Appeal—England's intermediate appellate court—are published because most are delivered orally from the bench, and only published opinions can be cited, it has never been argued that their limited publication rule has resulted in judicial irresponsibility.

If an appellate court writes a statement of reasons which goes unpublished, the decision is not necessarily secret and hidden from public attention. The losing party still may use the written statement of reasons to appeal to a higher court or to complain to the legislature, the news media, or interest groups; the party, or more likely its attorney, even may write a law review article about it. If the case is of public interest, the news media will publicize the decision. A case involving a controversial crime or issue such as obscenity, abortion rights, gay rights, sex or race discrimination, or an election dispute will receive attention regardless of whether the opinion is published. In any event, the limited publication rules usually do call for the publication of an opinion in these types of cases.

For those who wish to study a court's decisions in a particular area, whether concerning the substantive law, procedure, the parties involved, or on any other basis, the researcher may review and critique the court's own records, the briefs submitted, the trial court record, and the court's statement of reasons. Researchers regularly do this with the United States Supreme Court's denial of certiorari petitions, which rarely are accompanied by opinions except in dissent, as well as with appellate court actions on which no opinion is written, such as disposition of interlocutory appeals. Neither the California nor the Wisconsin study suggested that the lack of published opinions supporting these decisions has led to judicial irresponsibility.

Perhaps the weakest part of the judicial accountability criticism is that it demonstrates a lack of understanding about the relationship between the real reasons for a judicial decision and the reasons given in the opinion supporting that decision. As I have explained in a recent article, there is no necessary relationship between the two. The written statement of reasons merely seeks to legitimize the court's decision by making it appear consistent with prior opinions and the facts as shown by the record. If a court is intent upon acting irresponsibly, it can do so with a published opinion just as well as without one. The leeways of precedent and the fuzziness of the record almost always enable a court to make any decision appear reasonable. Consequently, the protection against irresponsibility comes not from the published opinion, but from the other constraints upon the appellate process, particularly the parties' ability to examine and dispute the required written statement of reasons.

Fear of judicial irresponsibility is a legitimate concern. American appellate systems, however, have many built-in protections to prevent against this irresponsibility without mandatory publication of opinions. Accordingly, this fear of irresponsibility does not justify mandatory publication.

B. Review by a Higher Court

1. The Criticism—Critics contend that review by a higher level is hampered by limited access to all opinions. They argue that the law announced in published cases and the results reached in unpublished decisions may differ. The potential for perceptions of judicial impropriety also increases, because litigants may conclude that the opinion was not published because the court lacked sufficient reasons to support a coherent rationale. Further, judges can use unpublished opinions to hide embarrassing information about litigants, to send messages to government agencies on how the agencies should act in the future without disapproving of past actions, or to save lawyers from embarrassment by not revealing that an attorney's improper or negligent conduct was the basis for the decision—none of which furthers a responsible judiciary. Judges even can use unpublished opinions to rely on the rationale of a past unpublished opinion, without disclosing the source of its reasoning. "If '[s]unlight is said to be the best of disinfectants,' then limited publication may permit sores to fester."

2. The Critique—The criticism that restrictions on publication and citation interfere with review by a higher court, like the criticism that they encourage judicial irresponsibility, ignores the constraints upon judges inherent in the appellate process and misunderstands the appellate process itself. If an intermediate appellate court does in fact decide a

case with an unpublished statement of reasons contrary to the published case law, the losing party is in a perfect position to seek review in a higher court by pointing out the discrepancy. Even if the losing party cannot cite unpublished decisions of cases not following the published case law, that party's appeal is not weakened. It is the inconsistency of the lower court's unpublished opinion with prior published opinions that is important. As long as the litigant can cite published cases that contradict the lower court's decision in his case, the fact that there are also other cases in which the court did not follow binding precedent is irrelevant to the party's chances for obtaining appellate review.

In any event, the statements of reasons in those unpublished, inconsistent cases are unlikely to be of much help because they will seldom, if ever, show a conscious disregard of the published case law. At most, unpublished opinions will show lack of awareness of the accepted published law, but that unawareness is best attributed not to the deciding courts' schemes but to the failure of counsel to bring it to the courts' attention. If appellate judges really are intent upon deciding a case contrary to binding precedent, they are more likely to do so by reading the precedent so narrowly or construing the facts in such a way as to make the precedent inapplicable to the present case. If the assumption is that judges are dishonest, it does not follow that they are foolish enough not to cover their tracks.

C. Predicting Precedential Value

1. The Criticism—The third common criticism of restricted publication and citation rules attacks the very foundation on which the restrictions are based. Though standards have been adopted to aid judges in determining whether to publish, critics often question the ability of judges to decide conclusively what is or is not of precedential value. In the first place, the rules' attempt to limit the scope of the term "precedent" at all is a doubtful endeavor. In the common law system, all decisions are precedent, regardless of whether they are published. To deny that they are precedent is to deny that they exist, an impossibility. An unpublished, uncitable decision cannot fit with the definition of stare decisis and the purpose of the common law, regardless of its compliance with a set of standardized guidelines to determine its precedential value. This is because "all decisions make law, or at least contribute to the process, for each shows [prospective litigants] how courts actually resolve disputes."

Additionally, it is debatable whether judges actually can predict precedential value, especially when that prediction is made early in the decision making process. "An early decision not to publish entails significant costs, ... for value inheres in the actual writing of the opinion." An early decision not to publish may affect not only the form in which the final decision is rendered, but also the actual reasoning or result. If that occurs, the judicial process may suffer. Furthermore, what is determined to be nonprecedential now may be of value to future litigants. Limited publication and citation rules require judges to determine in advance the rule of law that will emerge from a case, and then to determine the effect of their decisions on the development of the law. Because our common law system emphasizes the importance of facts in each case, judges hardly can hope to predict the facts of future disputes. They cannot know today what will be crucial to litigants of tomorrow, even when they follow the standards designed to aid them in this determination. There is no such thing as the "mere application of a rule, for every case constitutes a needed reaffirmation and/or extension, at least temporarily, of the rule."

Some commentators even have argued that the rules' precedential criteria are flawed. Numerous studies have demonstrated that opinions that were precedential have not been published.

Moreover, the fact that an opinion raises no new issue of law does not necessarily diminish the decision's importance. Rather, "the frequency with which issues arise is some measure of their importance." It is not always the new question that requires attention, but sometimes the old one. Change results in our system of law not only because a "new" issue of law arises, but also because an old issue recurs repeatedly. A well established rule might need to be changed. Limiting the precedent available in a certain area hurts those litigants who wish to use that precedent to establish change. The accumulation of decisions in an area allows litigants to assess the stability of a doctrine with greater confidence and helps them "flesh out a precedent ... [to] make it more understandable." "[T]he sweep of a group of cases makes it easier to understand the principles involved."

2. The Critique—The criticism that restricted publication and citation rules fly in the face of stare decisis and thus are inconsistent with the fundamental principle of the common-law system ignores the historical development and present operation of the system of reporting opinions in England, where our common-law system and the principles of precedent and stare decisis developed. The English opinion-reporting system has never published and does not today publish every opinion of English appellate courts, even though the total number of opinions issued each year in the English Court of Appeal and House of Lords is little more than 1000. In fact, these courts always have published only a very small percentage of their opinions, limited to those for which a barrister prepares a summary of the opinion. This system was a necessary product of the practice of English courts to render most opinions orally rather than in writing. It was not until 1951 that transcripts of the oral opinions were produced and placed in England's Supreme Court library in the Royal Courts of Justice. Today this library is the only place in which the actual opinions can be found, other than on computer databases. An official transcript will not be cited in the courts, however, because it does not meet the two requisites for citation: the transcript is not a summary prepared by a barrister and it is not published somewhere, whether in a report or a newspaper. There is no official report, only reports published under the auspices of a committee comprised of the bar (barristers), the Law Society (solicitors), and private publishers.

Moreover, the texts of the opinions included in the computer databases cannot be cited. The American rules limiting publication and citation are, in fact, far closer to the English system than the policies of unlimited publication and citation advocated by the critics of the American rules.

The criticism based on the unpredictability of a case's precedential value also is misplaced, although for a different reason. Essentially this criticism is premised on an extreme version of legal realism holding that all precedent is fact based and that because the facts of every case are different, every case is a unique precedent and thus should be published. This argument not only overstates legal realism, but if carried to its logical conclusion would destroy the underlying principle of stare decisis, that similar cases should be decided similarly. If all cases are different because their facts are different, there can be no precedent. The doctrine of stare decisis assumes that some opinions do make law that is valid beyond the narrow facts of the individual case. Limited publication and citation rules reflect this assumption and seek to publish only those opinions that can fairly be said to make law. There is no reason why in most cases the judges faced with deciding a case cannot determine early whether their decision will make law worthy of writing an opinion. As to citation rules, to prove that an area of law requires change, litigants need not necessarily cite recent published opinions, but only trial and appellate court decisions which the proponents of change assert reflect an outmoded legal principle.

D. *Equality of Access*

1. The Criticism—Critics of restricted publication and citation also raise the issue of unfairness. They argue that although the citation restrictions were designed to prevent certain litigants from gaining an advantage over those with less access to unpublished opinions, that advantage still exists. The restrictions reduce, "but do not eliminate[, the] effective use of unpublished opinions." Experienced litigants can use "arguments, exact language, and hypotheticals" of an unpublished opinion without ever revealing to the bench or the other side the source of this material. If the question is really fairness, critics argue, the proper solution is not to prohibit citation, but to require litigants to acknowledge the source of their reasoning and conclusions so that the other side stands on an equal footing before the bench.

2. The Critique—The supposed benefits of having access to unpublished opinions that may not be cited are marginal at best. For the benefits to be substantial, the unpublished arguments, language, or hypotheticals must be so appealing that the court will be more likely to adopt the position of the party advancing the borrowed argument than that of his opponent. There is little merit in this contention. Far more persuasive would be to cite the court itself as the source of the argument, language, or hypothetical because a court is always most concerned with its own precedent. Without citation, the unpublished material has no more persuasive force than if its proponent were its creator.

Essentially the only difference is between the court thinking that the court agrees with the party rather than the court agreeing with its own unattributed prior reasoning. In either event, the court will arrive at the same result.

To the extent that some persons gain an advantage from being able to afford access to unpublished opinions while others cannot, unlimited citation is not the only alternative. Others are to publish all opinions or to prevent access to unpublished opinions. The former would, of course, eliminate all of the advantages of limited publication. The latter is discussed in the next section.

E.   Judicial and Litigant Economy

1.   The Criticism—Finally, advocates of unlimited publication and citation attack the concept of restricted publication and citation at its base. They question whether or not the restrictions actually bring about the judicial and litigant economy predicted by their supporters. Empirical assessments have examined the federal circuits' caseloads, publication standards, time lapses between oral argument and opinion, and total productivity. Unfortunately, all of these have been relatively inconclusive. The critics argue that these data do not demonstrate conclusively that restricted publication rules increase judicial productivity.

Critics also contend that the reports of the staggering number of opinions are exaggerated. Some argue that there is no indication that the "present trend" of opinion proliferation will continue. Further, they argue that even if the current boom should continue, technologies such as microfiche, microfilm, computer databases, and CD–ROM storage could alleviate space and storage dilemmas at a reasonable cost. One critic argues that with the advent of LEXIS and Westlaw, the justification for restricting publication loses strength. She contends that with the availability of the computer data banks, there should be no reason for limited publication. She further predicts that the competition between electronic database services soon will lead to on-line access to all opinions, resulting in a system of universal publication.

The critics also dispute the argument that nonpublication saves time. Were cases published more frequently, judges would have more available precedent to work with, and the work required to decide cases would in fact decrease. "[M]erely cumulative opinions [should not] threaten the cohesiveness of the common law." Instead, "they should, if anything, make research and discernment of principle easier, since there will be more cases elaborating a principle, and some of those cases will be more recent as well."

Proposals for change have not been lacking either in number or in variety. Some commentators have argued for a complete repeal of publication and citation restrictions. Others have proposed compromise along a middle ground. One proposal is to permit citation of unpublished opinions as persuasive but not binding authority. This would put unpublished opinions on at least an equal footing with other nonprecedential matters currently citable to the court such as sociological data, treatises, and law review articles. A court then could follow the unpublished opinion if the court found the reasoning persuasive enough when applied to the facts of the case at hand. Under this scheme, the proper use of unpublished opinions is not set out by a bright line rule, but "depends on the wisdom and integrity of judges." Other commentators believe that a solution exists in partial publication, which permits the publication and citation of a portion of an opinion, leaving unpublished the portions that do not satisfy the criteria for publication. Partial publication would reduce the length of published opinions, yet permit the publication of portions of more opinions, thus increasing access and judicial accountability. "A partial publication rule would result in fewer published pages with more precedentially useful 'meat' on each page than the present 'all or nothing' rule." Most advocates of restricted publication and citation, meanwhile, have stood firm or proposed slight changes that they believe would make the rules work more effectively.

2. The Critique—Those who argue that writing a short memorandum for use solely by the parties involves just as much time as writing a full opinion for publication simply do not understand the appellate opinion writing process. The only empirical study of how appellate judges spend their time shows that they devote approximately one half of their time to writing opinions, more than they spend on any other duties. Clearly, the ability of a court to cope with its caseload is determined in large part by how much time a judge must devote to a particular opinion. If that opinion is intended solely for the parties to the appeal and their attorneys, the judge can write in an almost shorthand fashion, with little space or time devoted to a recital of the procedural history or the facts. The statement of reasons can and should be limited to addressing the one or two main issues raised by the appellant and why, with a citation to only one or two cases, the appellant's argument is rejected. Only when the trial judge ignored obvious controlling authority should a reversal be by unpublished opinion. The judge need devote little time writing the unpublished statement of reasons, because they often can be written by a law clerk or staff attorney.

In contrast is the time and care that goes into a published opinion that makes new law, criticizes or rejects existing law, explains the court's decision in a highly controversial case, or applies existing law to facts substantially different from prior cases. This opinion becomes the object of study by the bar, judges, and scholars, who will dissect, analyze, and apply or distinguish the language of an opinion with the care given to few written works apart from the Bible and the works of Shakespeare. Judicial opinions, like the Bible, become the bases on which people arrange their lives and conduct their affairs. As time permits, these opinions should be written with the greatest of care and precision in language. Therefore, a brief statement of reasons by the court is appropriate only when the court is performing its limited "review-for-correctness function." The statement of reasons should inform the parties that their contentions have been considered, and provide a rational basis for the court's conclusion. A full opinion, on the other hand, is appropriate when the court performs its law development function. An opinion developing law demands far greater care and time than the review-for-correctness statement of reasons. Because review-for-correctness statements of reasons generally go unpublished, since judges rarely find error, the judges and their staffs can and do devote much less time to them. The savings in judicial time are, consequently, real and substantial. Were they not, appellate courts could not have had the dramatic increases in cases disposed of on the merits per judge that have occurred in the past thirty years.

The argument that the number of opinions is not increasing and that legal research would not be more difficult if all opinions were published also has little validity. The number of appeals decided on the merits by the federal courts of appeal rose from 3552 in 1964, when the U.S. Judicial Conference first called for limited publication, to 23,597 in 1992, almost a sixfold increase. Just between 1985 and 1992, the number of appeals terminated on the merits by these courts increased from 16,369 to 23,597, an increase of over fifty percent in just seven years. The number increases each year, with no end in sight. In 1964, virtually all opinions were published because there were no limited publication rules. In 1992, only 29.7% of the opinions were published, but the total published was 6980, still over twice as many as in 1964. Notwithstanding the three-fourths reduction in the percentage of opinions published by the courts of appeals, the growth in the number of pages published was so great that in October 1993, West Publishing Company (West) issued the first volume of the Federal Reporter, Third Series (F.3d) after completing 999 volumes of the Federal Reporter, Second Series (F.2d). Each of the more recent volumes of F.2d contains approximately 1500 pages, compared to 1000 when F.2d was first published in 1925. It took fifty years to issue the first 500 volumes of F.2d, but only eighteen years, 1975 to 1993, for the last 499. The number of opinions sent to West for publication each year by both state and federal courts increased from 27,336 in 1964 to 66,500 in 1992, even with the large number of unpublished opinions and dispositions issued without opinion. Significantly, the 1964 total of 27,336 opinions was approximately 200 less than in 1929, and only about 8000 more than in 1895.

The effect of limited publication rules can be seen by comparing the number of opinions published by West in its various reporters and the number included in its computer-based Westlaw system. In addition to the 66,500 opinions received for publication, approximately 33,500 additional opinions are included in Westlaw. Essentially, 100,000 opinions are being added to the database each year. And these do not include all of the opinions being written, because some courts, including several federal courts of appeals, do not send their opinions to Westlaw or LEXIS. If every opinion of every court were included, the total would probably exceed 150,000 per year. Those who argue that opinion proliferation is not a problem are ignoring or are unaware of the facts.

Another argument is that the inclusion of both published and unpublished opinions in the commercial computer based systems of LEXIS and Westlaw eliminates the rationale behind the limited publication and citation rules. This argument identifies the right culprit, but the wrong problem and the wrong solution. There is no doubt that computer based systems have to a large degree destroyed the effectiveness of rules restricting publication. Judges know their "unpublished" opinions will be read by a far larger audience than merely the parties to the appeal. Thus, they may feel compelled to write for the larger audience, thereby negating one of the principal benefits of unpublished opinions: reduced writing time. Even more importantly, those who engage in legal research—judges, attorneys, and scholars—must now search all opinions in the database, whether designated for publication or not, to ensure that they have not missed anything that might be useful. Research in the databases is not, however, free or even cheap, whether considering the cost of the researcher's time or the cost of access to the databases.

Whether done in books or computer databases, legal research takes time, and time is money. The more opinions available to research, the more time the research takes, and the greater the cost. The only solution to the computer database problem is not to abandon limited publication, but to keep out of the databases statements of reasons not designated for publication.

III.   PROBLEMS AND SOLUTIONS

As demonstrated in Part II, the problems with restricted publication and citation do not justify eliminating or even weakening the restrictions. That is not to say, however, that the restrictions are not without problems. These problems stem from three primary causes: (1) the lack of a fail-safe system to ensure that all precedential opinions are published; (2) the failure to enforce strictly the rules restricting citation; and (3) the inclusion in computer databases of statements of reasons designated "not for publication."

As to the first, there is no question that some opinions that make law are still designated "not for publication." Whatever the reason—and there is no basis for suspecting that the decision is based on improper grounds—the rules should provide means to correct the error. One means should be preventive, avoiding the problem before it occurs. This can be done by establishing an internal review system within each court. An advisory publication panel of judges, staff attorneys, or both, would review each statement of reasons tentatively designated as "not for publication" to determine whether the statement meets any of the criteria for publication. Were the publication panel to conclude that it does, the authoring judge would be required to expand the statement to make it suitable for publication, primarily by adding facts sufficient to make the opinion understandable to those who are not parties to the appeal.

Another means should be remedial, correcting the problem after it occurs. The court's rules should provide that subsequent to issuance of the unpublished statement of reasons, any person, including the parties, who becomes aware of the statement, and who believes that the statement meets one of the criteria for publication, could petition the court or publication panel to order the statement published. If the original deciding panel or the advisory publication panel agreed, the statement could be published as an opinion, again after the addition of a statement of facts necessary to make the opinion understandable to outsiders. Because there is no fixed time in which nonparties will discover the statement of reasons or determine its significance, the rules should allow for an unlimited time to submit a petition for publication. This double system of checks on the initial publication decision should ensure the publication of virtually all opinions of precedential value.

The second and third problems, the lack of strict enforcement and the availability of unpublished opinions from computer databases, are related closely and the correction of one should eliminate the other. The best way to make restricted publication and citation rules work effectively is to enforce strictly the rules against both attorneys and the courts, primarily the latter. If a court relies on an unpublished opinion, even once, that court not only invites, but almost demands, that other judges on that court, lower courts, and attorneys practicing in the court's jurisdiction research the court's unpublished as well as its published opinions. If lightning strikes once, the prudent judge or attorney must assume that it can and will strike again. The inevitable result is that the computer based research systems will include every opinion a court issues, unpublished and published. On the other hand, once the legal community learned that citing unpublished opinions to the court brings no advantage, and perhaps even brings disadvantage, the need to research them should cease and thus the research companies would lose the economic incentive to include unpublished opinions in their computer databases.

Although strict adherence to the no-citation rule would be the principal means to eliminate the unofficial publication of unpublished opinions, the courts could take additional steps to discourage the unofficial publication of the statements of reasons designated as "not for publication." One simple step would be to refrain from sending the statements to persons other than parties. Although a statement of reasons placed in the pleading file of a case is no doubt a public document and subject to being copied, at the very least the court could refuse to send copies to nonparties, including Westlaw and LEXIS, and insist that anyone who wants a copy come to the court clerk's office to copy it, the same as for any other document on file with the court. Many courts, including four United States courts of appeals, now follow this practice, with the result that their unpublished opinions are not included in the computer databases. If every court followed the same practice, the problem of published "unpublished" opinions would be eliminated.

Another simple step, one perhaps even more useful, would be for the court not to place the unpublished statement of reasons in the case's pleading file or in its electronic counterpart, but to incorporate it in the letter from the clerk to the parties notifying the parties of the court's decision in the case. The letter would go on to state: "The Court has directed me to advise you that its reasons for its decision were...." Because this letter would be placed in the correspondence file rather than the pleading file, it would not be part of the formal record in the case. This letter would be subject to inspection by others, but would not look like an opinion or be easily incorporated into a computer database.

Notes and Questions

1.   What are the arguments in favor of publication? Non-publication?

2.   Can the question of publication be separated from that of citation? Can a non-publication rule be effective if there is no ban on citation? How can a non-citation rule be enforced in a court other than in the one that adopts the rule?

3.   Is there an effective response to the argument that in a common law system what a court has done is always precedent, and to deny the ability of lawyers and courts to acknowledge a particular precedent is attempting to deny the existence of a fact? Is the objection to non-publication that a court may attempt to cover up what it is doing valid?

4.   A procedure designed to be a safety valve for a non-publication—non-citation rule is one that allows a person desiring to cite an unpublished opinion to petition the court that issued it to publish it. Seventh Circuit Rule 35(d)(3) and Wis.Stat.Ann. § 809.23(4) (West 2004) so provide. For a criticism of this type of procedure, see Walther, The Noncitation Rule and the Concept of Stare Decisis, 61 Marq.L.Rev. 581 (1978). The Wisconsin State Bar appointed a committee to study the Wisconsin non-publication non-citation rule. The committee concluded that the rule worked well and did not require a change. 57 Wisconsin Bar Bull. 40 (August, 1984).

5.   Does the principal case prove or disprove any of the contentions raised by those on opposite sides of the issue? If you were asked to advise a court on how to deal with the problem what would you advise? Would it make a difference whether you were speaking as a disinterested observer, practicing attorney, or court staff member?

6.   Who should decide whether an opinion should be published? Most court rules provide that either the author of the opinion or a majority of the panel adopting the opinion. In Wisconsin, a committee of the entire court of appeals makes the decision. This was done to avoid conflicting precedents between different panels of the court. Wisconsin Stat.Ann. § 809.23(2) (West 2004). In Ohio, the official reporter of decisions makes the decision. For a criticism of the Ohio rule, see Richman & Reynolds, The Supreme Court Rules for the Reporting of Opinions: A Critique, 46 Ohio St.L.J. 313 (1985). Why is this issue important? The rule in some circuits is that a decision by one panel binds all subsequent panels until overturned by the court sitting en banc or the Supreme Court. Dickinson v. Petroleum Conversion Corp., 338 U.S. 507, 70 S.Ct. 322, 94 L.Ed. 299 (1950), describes how this policy

works in one circuit. Should one panel of a court be bound by a prior decision of another panel? If not, then it becomes less important to have some control over what opinions a panel publishes.

7. For a listing of the rules limiting publication and citation, see Serfiss & Cranford Federal and State Court Rules Governing Publication and Citation of Opinions, 3 J. App. Prac. & Process, 251, 253–85 (2001). A critical analysis of the publication practices of the federal courts of appeals is contained in Reynolds & Richman, An Evaluation of Limited Publication in the United States Courts of Appeals: The Price of Reform, 48 U. Chi. L.Rev. 573 (1981).

8. In 2003 the Federal Advisory Committee on Appellate Rules recommended to the Standing Committee on Rules of Practice and Procedure a proposed rule that would require all federal circuit courts to accept citations to unpublished or non-precedential opinions. The committee gave two reasons for its proposal—the conflict between the circuits on allowing the citations, and because it considered the restrictions bad policy. The Standing Committee refused to accept the proposal and sent it back to the Advisory Committee for further study. In making its proposal the Advisory Committee stated that 80% of all opinions of the federal courts of appeals are not published. Does this fact support or weaken the proposal? Does it make sense to increase the research burden on attorneys fivefold?

HART v. MASSANARI

United States Court of Appeals, Ninth Circuit, 2001.
266 F.3d 1155.

KOZINSKI, CIRCUIT JUDGE.

Appellant's opening brief cites *Rice v. Chater,* No. 95–35604, 1996 WL 583605 (9th Cir. Oct.9, 1996). *Rice* is an unpublished disposition, not reported in the Federal Reporter except as a one-line entry in a long table of cases. *See* Decisions Without Published Opinions, 98 F.3d 1345, 1346 tbl. (9th Cir. 1996). The full text of the disposition can be obtained from our clerk's office, and is available on Westlaw® and LEXIS®. However, it is marked with the following notice: "This disposition is not appropriate for publication and may not be cited to or by the courts of this circuit except as provided by 9th Cir.R. 36–3." Our local rules are to the same effect: "Unpublished dispositions and orders of this Court are not binding precedent . . . [and generally] may not be cited to or by the courts of this circuit. . . ." 9th Cir. R. 36–3.

We ordered counsel to show cause as to why he should not be disciplined for violating Ninth Circuit Rule 36–3. Counsel responds by arguing that Rule 36–3 may be unconstitutional. He relies on the Eighth Circuit's opinion in Anastasoff v. United States, 223 F.3d 898, *vacated as moot on reh'g en banc,* 235 F.3d 1054 (8th Cir.2000). *Anastasoff,* while vacated, continues to have persuasive force. *See, e.g.,* Williams v. Dallas Area Rapid Transit, 256 F.3d 260 (5th Cir.2001) (Smith, J., dissenting from denial of reh'g en banc). It may seduce members of our bar into violating our Rule 36–3 under the mistaken impression that it is unconstitutional. We write to lay these speculations to rest.

I

A. *Anastasoff* held that Eighth Circuit Rule 28A(i), which provides that unpublished dispositions are not precedential—and hence not binding on future panels of that court[2]—violates Article III of the Constitution. *See* 223 F.3d at 899. According to *Anastasoff,* exercise of the "judicial Power" precludes federal courts from making rulings that are not binding in future cases. Or, to put it differently, federal judges are not merely required to follow the law, they are also required to *make* law in every case. To do otherwise, *Anastasoff* argues, would invite judicial tyranny by freeing courts from the doctrine of precedent: " 'A more alarming doctrine could not be promulgated by any American court, than that it was at liberty to disregard all former rules and decisions, and to decide for itself, without reference to the settled course of antecedent principles.' " *Id.* at 904 (quoting Joseph Story, *Commentaries on the Constitution of the United States* § 377 (1833)).[3]

We believe that *Anastasoff* overstates the case. Rules that empower courts of appeals to issue nonprecedential decisions do not cut those courts free from all legal rules and precedents; if they did, we might find cause for alarm. But such rules have a much more limited effect: They allow panels of the courts of appeals to determine whether future panels, as well as judges of the inferior courts of the circuit, will be bound by particular rulings. This is hardly the same as turning our back on all precedents, or on the concept of precedent altogether. Rather, it is an effort to deal with precedent in the context of a modern legal system, which has evolved considerably since the early days of common law, and even since the time the Constitution was adopted.

2. Our rule operates somewhat differently from that of the Eighth Circuit, though it is in essential respects the same. While Eighth Circuit Rule 28A(i) says that "[u]npublished decisions are not precedent," we say that unpublished dispositions are "not binding precedent." Our rule, unlike that of the Eighth Circuit, prohibits citation of an unpublished disposition to any of the courts of our circuit. The Eighth Circuit's rule allows citation in some circumstances, but provides that the authority is persuasive rather than binding. *See* 8th Cir. R. 28A(i) ("Parties may . . . cite an unpublished opinion of this court if the opinion has persuasive value on a material issue and no published opinion of this or another court would serve as well."). The difference is not material to the rationale of *Anastasoff* because both rules free later panels of the court, as well as lower courts within the circuit, to disregard earlier rulings that are designated as nonprecedential.

For a comprehensive table of nonpublication and noncitation rules across all circuits and states, see Melissa M. Serfass & Jessie L. Cranford, Federal and State Court Rules Governing Publication and Citation of Opinions, 3 J.App. Prac. & Process 251, 253–85 tbl. 1 (2001).

3. In the passage cited by *Anastasoff,* Justice Story argued only that the judicial decisions of the Supreme Court were "conclusive and binding," and that inferior courts were not free to disregard the "decisions of the highest tribunal." He said nothing to suggest that the principle of binding authority constrained the "judicial Power," as *Anastasoff* does; rather, he recognized that the decisions of the Supreme Court were binding upon the states because they were the "supreme law of the land." Story, *supra,* § § 376–78.

The only constitutional provision on which *Anastasoff* relies is that portion of Article III that vests the "judicial Power" of the United States in the federal courts. U.S. Const. art. III, § 1, cl. 1. *Anastasoff* may be the first case in the history of the Republic to hold that the phrase "judicial Power" encompasses a specific command that limits the power of the federal courts. There are, of course, other provisions of Article III that have received judicial enforcement, such as the requirement that the courts rule only in "Cases" or "Controversies," *see, e.g.,* Lujan v. Defenders of Wildlife, 504 U.S. 555, 559, 112 S.Ct. 2130, 119 L.Ed.2d 351 (1992), and that the pay of federal judges not be diminished during their good behavior. *See, e.g.,* United States v. Hatter, 532 U.S. 557,————, 121 S.Ct. 1782, 1790–91, 149 L.Ed.2d 820 (2001). The judicial power clause, by contrast, has never before been thought to encompass a constitutional limitation on how courts conduct their business.

There are many practices that are common or even universal in the federal courts. Some are set by statute, such as the courts' basic organization. *See, e.g.,* 28 U.S.C. § 43 (creating a court of appeals for each circuit); 28 U.S.C. § 127 (dividing Virginia into two judicial districts); 28 U.S.C. § 2101 (setting time for direct appeals to the Supreme Court and for applications to the Supreme Court for writs of certiorari). *See generally* David McGowan, Judicial Writing and the Ethics of the Judicial Office, 14 Geo. J. Legal Ethics 509, 509–10 (2001). Others are the result of tradition, some dating from the days of the common law, others of more recent origin. Among them are the practices of issuing written opinions that speak for the court rather than for individual judges, adherence to the adversarial (rather than inquisitorial) model of developing cases, limits on the exercise of equitable relief, hearing appeals with panels of three or more judges and countless others that are so much a part of the way we do business that few would think to question them. While well established, it is unclear that any of these practices have a constitutional foundation; indeed, Hart (no relation so far as we know), in his famous Dialogue, concluded that Congress could abolish the inferior federal courts altogether. *See* Henry M. Hart, Jr., The Power of Congress to Limit the Jurisdiction of Federal Courts: An Exercise in Dialectic, 66 Harv. L.Rev. 1362, 1363–64 (1953). While the greater power does not always include the lesser, the Dialogue does suggest that much of what the federal courts do could be modified or eliminated without offending the Constitution.

Anastasoff focused on one aspect of the way federal courts do business—the way they issue opinions—and held that they are subject to a constitutional limitation derived from the Framers' conception of what it means to exercise the judicial power. Given that no other aspect of the way courts exercise their power has ever been held subject to this limitation, we question whether the "judicial Power" clause contains any limitation at all, separate from the specific limitations of Article III and other parts of the Constitution. The more plausible view is that when the federal courts rule on cases or controversies assigned to them by

Congress, comply with due process, accord trial by jury where commanded by the Seventh Amendment and generally comply with the specific
constitutional commands applicable to judicial proceedings, they have
ipso facto exercised the judicial power of the United States. In other
words, the term "judicial Power" in Article III is more likely descriptive
than prescriptive.

If we nevertheless were to accept *Anastasoff*'s premise that the
phrase "judicial Power" contains limitations separate from those contained elsewhere in the Constitution, we should exercise considerable
caution in recognizing those limitations, lest we freeze the law into the
mold cast in the eighteenth century. The law has changed in many
respects since the time of the Framing, some superficial, others quite
fundamental. For example, as Professor William Nelson has convincingly
demonstrated, colonial juries "usually possessed the power to find both
law and fact in the cases in which they sat," and were not bound to
follow the instructions given to them by judges. *See* William E. Nelson,
Marbury v. Madison: The Origins and Legacy of Judicial Review 16–17
(2000). Today, of course, we would consider it unfair—probably unconstitutional—to allow juries to make up the law as they go along.

Another example: At the time of the Framing, and for some time
thereafter, the practice that prevailed both in the United States and
England was for judges of appellate courts to express separate opinions,
rather than speak with a single (or at least majority) voice. The practice
changed around the turn of the nineteenth century, under the leadership
of Chief Justice Marshall. *See* George L. Haskins & Herbert A. Johnson,
Foundations of Power: John Marshall, 1801–15, in 2 The Oliver Wendell
Holmes Devise: History of the Supreme Court of the United States 382–
89 (Paul A. Freund ed., 1981).

And yet another example: At the time of the Framing, and for some
time thereafter, it was considered entirely appropriate for a judge to
participate in the appeal of his own decision; indeed, before the creation
of the Circuit Courts of Appeals, appeals from district court decisions
were often taken to a panel consisting of a Supreme Court Justice riding
circuit, and the district judge from whom the decision was taken. Act of
March 2, 1793, ch. 22, § 1, 1 Stat. 333; *see also* Charles Alan Wright,
Arthur R. Miller & Edward H. Cooper, Federal Practice and Procedure
§ 3504 (2d ed.1984). Today, of course, it is widely recognized that a
judge may not hear the appeal from his own decision. There are
doubtless many more such examples.

One danger of giving constitutional status to practices that existed
at common law, but have changed over time, is that it tends to freeze
certain aspects of the law into place, even as other aspects change
significantly. This is a particularly dangerous practice when the constitutional rule in question is not explicitly written into the Constitution, but
rather is discovered for the first time in a vague, two-centuries-old
provision. The risk that this will allow judges to pick and choose those
ancient practices they find salutary as a matter of policy, and give them

constitutional status, is manifest. *Compare* Richard S. Arnold, Unpublished Opinions: A Comment, 1 J.App. Prac. & Process 219 (1999) (suggesting that all opinions be published and given precedential value), *with Anastasoff*, 223 F.3d 898 (holding that the Eighth Circuit's rule barring citation to unpublished opinions violates Article III). Thus, in order to follow the path forged by *Anastasoff*, we would have to be convinced that the practice in question was one the Framers considered so integral and well-understood that they did not have to bother stating it, even though they spelled out many other limitations in considerable detail. Specifically, to adopt *Anastasoff*'s position, we would have to be satisfied that the Framers had a very rigid conception of precedent, namely that all judicial decisions necessarily served as binding authority on later courts.

This is, in fact, a much more rigid view of precedent than we hold today. As we explain below, most decisions of the federal courts are not viewed as binding precedent. No trial court decisions are; almost four-fifths of the merits decisions of courts of appeals are not. To be sure, *Anastasoff* challenges the latter practice. We find it significant, however, that the practice has been in place for a long time, yet no case prior to *Anastasoff* has challenged its constitutional legitimacy. The overwhelming consensus in the legal community has been that having appellate courts issue nonprecedential decisions is not inconsistent with the exercise of the judicial power.

To accept *Anastasoff*'s argument, we would have to conclude that the generation of the Framers had a much stronger view of precedent than we do. In fact, as we explain below, our concept of precedent today is far stricter than that which prevailed at the time of the Framing. The Constitution does not contain an express prohibition against issuing nonprecedential opinions because the Framers would have seen nothing wrong with the practice.

B. Modern federal courts are the successors of the English courts that developed the common law, but they are in many ways quite different, including how they understand the concept of precedent. Common law judges did not make law as we understand that concept; rather, they "found" the law with the help of earlier cases that had considered similar matters. An opinion was evidence of what the law is, but it was not an independent source of law. *See* Theodore F.T. Plucknett, A Concise History of the Common Law 343–44 (5th ed.1956). The law was seen as something that had an existence independent of what judges said: "a miraculous something made by nobody ... and merely declared from time to time by the judges." 2 John Austin, Lectures on Jurisprudence or The Philosophy of Positive Law 655 (4th ed. 1873) (emphasis omitted). Opinions were merely judges' efforts to ascertain the law, much like scientific experiments were efforts to ascertain natural laws. If an eighteenth-century judge believed that a prior case was wrongly decided, he could say that the prior judge had erred in his attempt to discern the law. *See Bole v. Horton*, 124 Eng. Rep. 1113, 1124

(C.P.1673). Neither judges nor lawyers understood precedent to be binding in *Anastasoff*'s strict sense. * * *

III

While we agree with *Anastasoff* that the principle of precedent was well established in the common law courts by the time Article III of the Constitution was written, we do not agree that it was known and applied in the strict sense in which we apply binding authority today. It may be true, as *Anastasoff* notes, that "judges and lawyers of the day recognized the authority of unpublished decisions even when they were established only by memory or by a lawyer's unpublished memorandum," 223 F.3d at 903, but precedents brought to the attention of the court in that fashion obviously could not serve as the kind of rigid constraint that binding authority provides today. Unlike our practice today, a single case was not sufficient to establish a particular rule of law, and case reporters often filtered out cases that they considered wrong, or inconsistent with their view of how the law *should* develop. The concept of binding case precedent, though it was known at common law, ... was used exceedingly sparingly. For the most part, common law courts felt free to depart from precedent where they considered the earlier-adopted rule to be no longer workable or appropriate.

Case precedent at common law thus resembled much more what we call persuasive authority than the binding authority which is the backbone of much of the federal judicial system today. The concept of binding precedent could only develop once two conditions were met: The development of a hierarchical system of appellate courts with clear lines of authority, and a case reporting system that enabled later courts to know precisely what was said in earlier opinions. As we have seen, these developments did not come about—either here or in England—until the nineteenth century, long after Article III of the Constitution was written.

The question raised by *Anastasoff* is whether one particular aspect of the binding authority principle—the decision of which rulings of an appellate court are binding—is a matter of judicial policy or constitutional imperative. We believe *Anastasoff* erred in holding that, as a constitutional matter, courts of appeals may not decide which of their opinions will be deemed binding on themselves and the courts below them. For the reasons explained, the principle of strict binding authority is itself not constitutional, but rather a matter of judicial policy. Were it otherwise, it would cast doubt on the federal court practice of limiting the binding effect of appellate decisions to the courts of a particular circuit. Circuit boundaries—and the very system of circuit courts—are a matter of judicial administration, not constitutional law. If, as *Anastasoff* suggests, the Constitution dictates that every "declaration of law ... must be applied in subsequent cases to similarly situated parties," 223 F.3d at 900, then the Second Circuit would have no authority to disagree with a ruling of the Eighth Circuit that is directly on point, and the first circuit to rule on a legal issue would then bind not only itself and the courts within its own circuit, but all inferior federal courts.

Another consequence of *Anastasoff*'s reasoning would be to cast doubt on the authority of courts of appeals to adopt a body of circuit law on a wholesale basis, as did the Eleventh Circuit in *Bonner,* and the Federal Circuit in *South Corp.* Circuits could, of course, adopt individual cases from other circuits as binding in a case raising a particular legal issue. *See, e.g.,* Charles v. Lundgren & Assocs., P.C., 119 F.3d 739, 742 (9th Cir.) ("Because we have the benefit of the Seventh Circuit's cogent analysis, we will not replow plowed ground. Instead, we adopt the reasoning of the Seventh Circuit....") *cert. denied,* 522 U.S. 1028, 118 S.Ct. 627, 139 L.Ed.2d 607 (1997). But adopting a whole body of law, encompassing countless rules on matters wholly unrelated to the issues raised in a particular case, is a very different matter. If binding authority were a constitutional imperative, it could only be created through individual case adjudication, not by a decision unconstrained by the facts before the court or its prior caselaw.

Nor is it clear, under the reasoning of *Anastasoff,* how courts could limit the binding effect of their rulings to appellate decisions. Under *Anastasoff*'s reasoning, district court opinions should bind district courts, at least in the same district, or even nationwide. After all, the Constitution vests the same "judicial Power" in all federal courts, so *Anastasoff*'s conclusion that judicial decisions must have precedential effect would apply equally to the thousands of unpublished decisions of the district courts.

No doubt the most serious implication of *Anastasoff*'s constitutional rule is that it would preclude appellate courts from developing a coherent and internally consistent body of caselaw to serve as binding authority for themselves and the courts below them. Writing an opinion is not simply a matter of laying out the facts and announcing a rule of decision. Precedential opinions are meant to govern not merely the cases for which they are written, but future cases as well.

In writing an opinion, the court must be careful to recite all facts that are relevant to its ruling, while omitting facts that it considers irrelevant. Omitting relevant facts will make the ruling unintelligible to those not already familiar with the case; including inconsequential facts can provide a spurious basis for distinguishing the case in the future. The rule of decision cannot simply be announced, it must be selected after due consideration of the relevant legal and policy considerations. Where more than one rule could be followed—which is often the case— the court must explain why it is selecting one and rejecting the others. Moreover, the rule must be phrased with precision and with due regard to how it will be applied in future cases. A judge drafting a precedential opinion must not only consider the facts of the immediate case, but must also envision the countless permutations of facts that might arise in the universe of future cases. Modern opinions generally call for the most precise drafting and re-drafting to ensure that the rule announced sweeps neither too broadly nor too narrowly, and that it does not collide with other binding precedent that bears on the issue. *See* Fred A. Bernstein, How to Write it Right, Cal. Lawyer, at 42 (June 2000). Writing a precedential opinion, thus, involves much more than deciding who wins and who loses in a particular case. It is a solemn judicial act that sets the course of the law for hundreds or thousands of litigants and potential litigants. When properly done, it is an exacting and extremely time-consuming task.

It goes without saying that few, if any, appellate courts have the resources to write precedential opinions in every case that comes before them. The Supreme Court certainly does not. Rather, it uses its discretionary review authority to limit its merits docket to a handful of opinions per justice, from the approximately 9000 cases that seek review every Term. While federal courts of appeals generally lack discretionary review authority, they use their authority to decide cases by unpublished—and nonprecedential—dispositions to achieve the same end: They select a manageable number of cases in which to publish precedential opinions, and leave the rest to be decided by unpublished dispositions or judgment orders. In our circuit, published dispositions make up approximately 16 percent of decided cases; in other circuits, the percentage ranges from 10 to 44, the national average being 20 percent. Administrative Office of the United States Courts, *Judicial Business of the United States Courts* 44 tbl. S–3 (2000).

That a case is decided without a precedential opinion does not mean it is not fully considered, or that the disposition does not reflect a reasoned analysis of the issues presented. What it does mean is that the disposition is not written in a way that will be fully intelligible to those unfamiliar with the case, and the rule of law is not announced in a way that makes it suitable for governing future cases. As the Federal Judicial Center recognized, "the judicial time and effort essential for the development of an opinion to be published for posterity and widely distributed is necessarily greater than that sufficient to enable the judge to provide a statement so that the parties can understand the reasons for the decision." Federal Judicial Center, Standards for Publication of Judicial Opinions 3 (1973). An unpublished disposition is, more or less, a letter from the court to parties familiar with the facts, announcing the result and the essential rationale of the court's decision. Deciding a large portion of our cases in this fashion frees us to spend the requisite time drafting precedential opinions in the remaining cases.

Should courts allow parties to cite to these dispositions, however, much of the time gained would likely vanish. Without comprehensive factual accounts and precisely crafted holdings to guide them, zealous counsel would be tempted to seize upon superficial similarities between their clients' cases and unpublished dispositions. Faced with the prospect of parties citing these dispositions as precedent, conscientious judges would have to pay much closer attention to the way they word their unpublished rulings. Language adequate to inform the parties how their case has been decided might well be inadequate if applied to future cases arising from different facts. And, although three judges might agree on the outcome of the case before them, they might not agree on the precise reasoning or the rule to be applied to future cases. Unpublished concurrences and dissents would become much more common, as individual judges would feel obligated to clarify their differences with the majority, even when those differences had no bearing on the case before them. In short, judges would have to start treating unpublished dispositions—those they write, those written by other judges on their panels, and those written by judges on other panels—as mini-opinions.[36] This new responsibility would cut severely into the time judges need to fulfill their paramount duties: producing well-reasoned published opinions and keeping the law of the circuit consistent through the en banc process. The quality of published opinions would sink as judges were forced to devote less and less time to each opinion.

Increasing the number of opinions by a factor of five, as *Anastasoff* suggests, doesn't seem to us a sensible idea, even if we had the resources to do so. Adding endlessly to the body of precedent—especially binding precedent—can lead to confusion and unnecessary conflict. Judges have a responsibility to keep the body of law "cohesive and understandable, and not muddy[ ] the water with a needless torrent of published opinions." Martin, note 36 *supra,* at 192. Cases decided by nonprecedential disposition generally involve facts that are materially indistinguishable from those of prior published opinions. Writing a second, third or tenth opinion in the same area of the law, based on materially indistinguishable facts will, at best, clutter up the law books and databases with redundant and thus unhelpful authority. Yet once they are designated as precedent, they will have to be read and analyzed by lawyers researching the issue, materially increasing the costs to the client for absolutely no legitimate reason. Worse still, publishing redundant opinions will multiply significantly the number of inadvertent and unnecessary conflicts, because different opinion writers may use slightly different language to express the same idea. As lawyers well know, even small differences in language can have significantly different implications when read in light of future fact patterns, so differences in phrasing that seem trivial when written can later take on a substantive significance.

The risk that this may happen vastly increases if judges are required to write many more precedential opinions than they do now, leaving much less time to devote to each. Because conflicts—even inadvertent ones—can only be resolved by the exceedingly time-consuming and inefficient process of en banc review, *see* Atonio v. Wards Cove Packing Co., 810 F.2d 1477, 1478–79 (9th Cir. 1987) (en banc) (conflict in panel opinions must be resolved by en banc court), *cert. denied,* 485 U.S. 989, 108 S.Ct. 1293, 99 L.Ed.2d 503 (1988), an increase in intracircuit conflicts would leave much less time for us to devote to normal panel

36. *See* Boyce F. Martin, Jr., In Defense of Unpublished Opinions, 60 Ohio St. L.J. 177, 196 ("[I]t will not save us any time if [unpublished opinions] are being cited back to us. We will have to prepare unpublished opinions as we do published opinions—if they were creating precedent.").

opinions. Maintaining a coherent, consistent and intelligible body of caselaw is not served by writing more opinions; it is served by taking the time to make the precedential opinions we do write as lucid and consistent as humanly possible.

IV

Unlike the *Anastasoff* court, we are unable to find within Article III of the Constitution a requirement that all case dispositions and orders issued by appellate courts be binding authority. On the contrary, we believe that an inherent aspect of our function as Article III judges is managing precedent to develop a coherent body of circuit law to govern litigation in our court and the other courts of this circuit. We agree with *Anastasoff* that we—and all courts—must follow the law. But we do not think that this means we must also make binding law every time we issue a merits decision. The common law has long recognized that certain types of cases do not deserve to be authorities, and that one important aspect of the judicial function is separating the cases that should be precedent from those that should not.[40] Without clearer guidance than that offered in *Anastasoff,* we see no constitutional basis for abdicating this important aspect of our judicial responsibility.

Contrary to counsel's contention, then, we conclude that Rule 36–3 is constitutional. We also find that counsel violated the rule. Nevertheless, we are aware that *Anastasoff* may have cast doubt on our rule's constitutional validity. Our rules are obviously not meant to punish attorneys who, in good faith, seek to test a rule's constitutionality. We therefore conclude that the violation was not willful and exercise our discretion not to impose sanctions.

The order to show cause is DISCHARGED.

Notes and Questions

1.   The opinion of the Eighth Circuit in Anastasoff v. United States, 223 F.3d 898 (8th Cir. 2000) added a constitutional dimension to the no publication-no citation debate. The Court held that its rule prohibiting the citation of its unpublished opinions went beyond the grant of judicial power to federal courts in Art. III of the Constitution. As the opinion of the Ninth Circuit in the Hart case, supra, shows, that court disagreed. For an excellent debate on the merits of the two cases, see Capalli, The Common Law's Case Against Non–Precedential Opinions, 76 S. Cal. L. Rev. 755 (2003) (supporting Anastasoff) and Laretto, Precedent, Judicial Power, and the Constitutionality of "No–Citation" Rules in the Federal Courts of Appeals, 54 Stan. L. Rev. 1037 (2002) (supporting Hart).

---

40.   This is hardly a novel view:

[C]ertain types of cases do not deserve to be authorities. One type, already alluded to, is that in which there is no discoverable *ratio decidendi*. Others are cases turning purely on fact, those involving the exercise of discretion, and those which judges themselves do not think worthy of being precedents.

[R.W.M. Dias, Jurisprudence 55 (2d ed. 1964)] (footnotes omitted) (citing *R. v. Stokesley* (Yorkshire) Justices, Ex parte Bartram [1956] 1 All E.R. 563 at 565).

2. Isn't the fact that under the English system only a small percentage of opinions of appellate courts has ever been published and only published opinions could be cited a complete answer to those who argue that the citation of previous opinions whether published or not? For a more complete description of the English system see R. Martineau, Appellate Justice in England and the United States: A Comparative Analysis, 104–08, 112–19, 133–39 (1990).

SECTION E. JUDGMENT AND MANDATE

FEDERAL RULE OF APPELLATE PROCEDURE 41

Issuance of Mandate; Stay of Mandate

(a)Date of Issuance. The mandate of the court shall issue 21 days after the entry of judgment unless the time is shortened or enlarged by order. A certified copy of the judgment and a copy of the opinion of the court, if any, and any direction as to costs shall constitute the mandate, unless the court directs that a formal mandate issue. The timely filing of a petition for rehearing will stay the mandate until disposition of the petition unless otherwise ordered by the court. If the petition is denied, the mandate shall issue 7 days after entry of the order denying the petition unless the time is shortened or enlarged by order.

CALVERT, APPELLATE COURT JUDGMENTS OR STRANGE THINGS HAPPEN ON THE WAY TO JUDGMENT

6 Tex.Tech. L.Rev. 915–925 (1975).

Drafting of judgments in cases reaching appellate courts by appeal should be a simple clerical task. The task will not be simple, however, unless certain fundamental concepts are fully understood and kept in mind; and clerks of the courts who are not lawyers and by and large are untrained in the technical aspects of judgment drafting need the help of judges who are aware of the concepts and are alert to their observance.

* * *

THE BASIC CONCEPTS

The concepts essential to proper judgment drafting center around certain words of art used in our rules of civil procedure, *viz,* decision, opinion, judgment, and cause or case.

A sound approach to proper judgment drafting by a court of appeals or the supreme court must recognize the necessity of keeping clear lines of demarcation between the distinct functions of an appellate court, which are; (1) *to decide* issues and causes; (2) *to write opinions* which reflect the reasons for the court's decisions, (3) *to render judgments* which must act upon lower court judgments; and (4) *to dispose of causes.*

An increasing number of appellate court opinions and judgments indicate an unfamiliarity with, or indifference toward, these basic concepts and an erroneous application of them. Although most errors in judgment drafting go unnoticed or unchallenged, the distinctive place each of the concepts has in the appellate court adjudicatory process is no better, nor more graphically, illustrated than in the recent case of *Merchandise Mart, Inc. v. Marcus*. This case is singled out for analysis not to discredit or to criticize the courts which decided or reviewed it, but merely because it illustrates more than one of the common errors committed by appellate courts in the drafting of judgments and supporting opinions.

Merchandise Mart sued Marcus for rentals alleged to be payable under a lease contract for a term of 9 years and 5 months beginning May 1, 1964, and providing for monthly rentals of 468.66 dollars. Marcus had vacated the premises at the end of 5 months and defended the suit on the ground of fraud in the inducement of the contract. The jury answered in favor of Marcus in response to such special issues on fraud as were submitted. On the basis of these answers, the trial court rendered judgment that Merchandise Mart take nothing. The court of civil appeals decided and held that the jury's answers to the submitted issues did not establish the defense of fraud. At the end of its opinion, the court stated: "The judgment of the trial court is reversed and judgment is here rendered for appellant [Merchandise Mart]."

The court made a preliminary finding in its judgment as entered in its minutes as follows:

> [I]t is the opinion of the court that there was error in the judgment as entered by the trial court and that the same should be *reversed and rendered*.

As entered in the minutes, the decretal part of the court's judgment reads:

> It is therefore ORDERED, ADJUDGED and DECREED by the Court that the judgment of the trial court in favor of Herman Marcus be, and the same is hereby, reversed and judgment is rendered for the appellant, Merchandise Mart, Inc., in accordance with the opinion of this Court * * *.

When Merchandise Mart was unable to execute its judgment because of failure of the court of civil appeals to state the amount for which judgment was rendered, it sought, but was unable to obtain, relief from the trial court and the court of civil appeals. In an opinion on Motion to Amend Mandate, which it dismissed, the court of civil appeals referred to the fact that it had earlier *"reversed and rendered this cause* for appellant." Merchandise Mart then filed in the supreme court a "Motion to Clarify Judgment." The supreme court dismissed the motion and issued a per curiam opinion.

In its per curiam opinion the supreme court reviewed the history of the litigation and, with reference to the original appeal from the trial court's judgment, stated: "On appeal the court of civil appeals *reversed* *and rendered judgment for Merchandise Mart * * *.''* The court continued:

> The judgment entered by the court of civil appeals in this case determines the issue of liability but not the amount of recovery. Since the judgment does not dispose of all necessary issues, it is an interlocutory judgment and the cause is still pending before the court of civil appeals.

It is suggested with utmost respect that the supreme court reached a correct result for a technically wrong reason. In the first place, the issue of liability was not determined by the *judgment* of the court of civil appeals as stated by the court; it was decided or determined by the court of civil appeals in its *opinion* as a reason or basis for its *judgment of reversal* of the trial court's judgment. In the second place, the supreme court's statement that the court of civil appeals "rendered judgment for Merchandise Mart" is also erroneous. The court of civil appeals said it did, but it did not. Moreover, the decision or determination of issues in a case, even all necessary issues, does not satisfy the requirement for rendition of a final judgment.

* * * The *sine qua non* of a final judgment is the pronouncement by a court of the sentence of the law upon the matters and issues in a cause. The court stated in *Kuehn v. Kuehn* that to be a final judgment, "[I]t is not sufficient that the court make a ruling which would logically lead to a final disposition of it [the case], but the consequences of the ruling to the parties must also be declared." And the supreme court has said that a judgment "not expressly disposing of the case is not a final judgment." On that reasoning, the supreme court held long ago that failure of a judgment for money to state the amount of the recovery, as in *Merchandise Mart,* is not a final judgment. A simple example will further serve to demonstrate the verity of the court's declarations.

A sues B in trespass to try title to recover title to, and possession of, land which he claims as owner of the record title under a regular chain of title. B defends on grounds that (1) the deed to A was never delivered, and (2) he owns title by adverse possession under the 10–year statute of limitation. By counterclaim B seeks to recover title and possession of the premises. The jury finds on conflicting evidence that A's deed was delivered, but that B has had the requisite adverse possession to satisfy the 10–year statute. On motion, the trial court disregards the jury's answer to the limitation issue on the ground that it is not supported by probative evidence and renders judgment that A recover title and possession of the land. On appeal B contends only that the answer of the jury to the limitation issue is supported by probative evidence and argues that for that reason the trial court's judgment should be reversed, and judgment should be rendered awarding title and possession of the land to him. The appellate court decides the no-evidence issue in B's favor, holding expressly that the jury's answer to the limitation issue has ample support in the evidence, and on the basis of the holdings the court reverses the trial court's judgment, but does not award title to, and possession of, the premises to B. The judgment obviously is not a final one even though the appellate court has decided the only issue before it and the only issue necessary to the entry of judgment awarding title and possession to B.

* * *

CAUSES

When an appeal from a trial court judgment to a court of civil appeals is perfected, the entire *cause,* and not just the trial court's judgment, is removed from the trial court to the appellate court. Likewise, the granting of writ of error by the supreme court removes a cause to that court from a court of civil appeals. It follows that a judgment of an appellate court which does not dispose of *the cause* is technically incomplete and not final. To dispose of a pending cause, an appellate court must render a final judgment by which it must either dismiss the cause, affirm the judgment or judgments below, modify and affirm the judgment or judgments below, reverse the judgment or judgments below and award such relief as the trial court should have awarded, reverse the judgment or judgments of the court or courts below and remand the cause to the trial court or to the court of civil appeals for further proceedings, or sever the cause into parts when authorized by the rules and affirm the judgment in one severed part and reverse in the other and either award relief to the opposite party or remand for further proceedings.

DECISIONS

The word "decision" is used to describe different actions of an appellate court. It may refer to the action of a court in resolving one or more of the issues in a case; or it may refer to action outlining the type of judgment which a court expects to render; or it may refer to a judgment which a court has rendered. The word "decision" found in statutes and rules is sometimes held to mean "judgment;" but the word "judgment" is a more all-inclusive term.

OPINIONS

The "opinion" of an appellate court is not at all the legal equivalent of its decision or judgment. The supreme court, in a commissioner's opinion, has said that "there is a wide and well-recognized legal difference between the 'opinion' and the 'decision' of a court." A court of civil appeals' rule, titled "Decision and Opinion," directs the courts to "decide" issues and to "announce their conclusions" in writing. When one of these courts reverses a judgment and remands a cause, it is required "to state its reasons for the judgment," and if one of the courts "hands down an opinion" in connection with a judgment overruling a motion for rehearing, a further motion is in order. The supreme court is directed to render "opinions" in answering certified questions. A supreme court rule requires that the court's "judgments or decrees" be announced in open court, but leaves strictly to the court's discretion whether "the opinion of the court will be reduced to writing." Not only do these rules make a clear distinction between "opinions" on the one hand, and "decisions" or "judgments" on the other, they also clearly imply that an opinion is in addition to, and cannot serve the purpose of, a decision or a judgment in a cause. Moreover, it is the judgment and not the opinion of a court which brings the rule of res judicata into play.

JUDGMENTS

It is in the drafting of judgments that appellate courts and their clerks are not as careful as they should be in the selection and use of accurate and proper terminology. The central ingredient to good appellate court judgment drafting in appealed cases is the conscious knowledge at all times that, except in cases in which appeals are dismissed, or writ of error is denied, appellate court judgments must always operate upon lower court judgments.

* * *

There is a custom with appellate judges, not required by the Texas Rules of Civil Procedure, to close an opinion in a case with a statement of the nature of the judgment being rendered. A correct statement in the opinion of the substantive provisions of the judgment being rendered and announced in open court will be of tremendous help to the clerk in correctly recording the judgment in the court's minutes, and, after all, it is the minute record of the judgment which controls in case of conflict. An equally important reason for using the utmost care in preparing the statement of the nature of the judgment to be included in the opinion is that, at least until the court's mandate comes down, it is the only written evidence of the judgment actually rendered that counsel or the litigants ever see.

CHIPS AND WHETSTONES: BITS AND PIECES

Perhaps the message of care in appellate court judgment drafting will be more forcibly and graphically demonstrated by looking with a critical eye at frequently used and faulty judgment expressions found in appellate court opinions.

1. "The trial court (or the court of civil appeals) is affirmed (or reversed)."

Comment: Neither of the courts is ever before a higher court for approval or disapproval, affirmance or reversal. Their judgments are, but the courts are not.

2. "This case (or cause) is affirmed (or reversed)."

Comment: The judgment in a cause may be affirmed or reversed, but the cause definitely is not. When a judgment is reversed, the cause may be remanded, but it remains the same.

3. "The opinion of the court of civil appeals is affirmed (or reversed)."

Comment: There is no authority in the rules or statutes for the supreme court to affirm or reverse an opinion of a court of civil appeals. The supreme court may expressly approve or disapprove an opinion or a specific part of an opinion of a court of civil appeals, or the court may approve an opinion in a given case by refusal of writ of error, but in neither instance does the court affirm or reverse an opinion.

4. "The judgment of the trial court is reversed and rendered."

Comment: An appellate court has no power or jurisdiction to render a trial court's judgment. Only the trial court can render its judgments. An appellate court can, and often does, render a judgment which the trial court should have rendered.

5. "The judgment of the trial court (or the court of civil appeals) is reversed and remanded."

Comment: This type of judgment leaves the cause pending in, and undisposed of by, the deciding court. How can a lower court possibly proceed to re-try or re-hear a cause which is still pending in a higher court?

6. "The judgment for the plaintiff is reversed and judgment is here rendered for the defendant."

Comment: The appellate court judgment in this situation will be favorable to the defendant, but the judgment should be one denying relief to the plaintiff and not one granting relief to the defendant.

7. "The judgment that the plaintiff take nothing is reversed and judgment is here rendered for the plaintiff."

Comment: This judgment, like that in *Merchandise Mart,* is obviously incomplete and not final.

8. "The judgment of the trial court is reversed in the interest of justice and the cause is remanded to the trial court for a new trial."

Comment: The rules do not authorize reversal of a trial court judgment in the interest of justice. Once a court finds reversible error, it may remand in the interest of justice rather than render judgment for the opposite party.

CONCLUSION

Pride should be the hallmark of the appellate judge who puts his work product in books of judicial history, and it is unthinkable that failure of a judge to observe the most elementary principles of judgment drafting can be charged to deliberate disregard of those principles. Carelessness cannot be defended on the theory that "everyone knows what the court meant." If *Merchandise Mart* teaches nothing else, it teaches that, when an incorrectly drafted judgment is called into question, the defense of "everyone knows what the court meant" will not work. Moreover, if the court's intention is so easy to discover, its intention should be equally easy for the court to express correctly and clearly.

A correct draft of a judgment to be included in an opinion which has been written with care should be the final challenge to the writing judge. Sometimes, as in situations requiring modification or severance, the drafting process may seem difficult, but observance of the four basic concepts itemized in the forepart of this article will simplify the task. In that event, perhaps this writing will have been helpful to my brethren of the bench.

Notes and Questions

1. What is the mandate? What is the relationship between the judgment of the appellate court and its mandate?

2. Who prepares the judgment and the mandate? The judge who wrote the opinion? The clerk of the appellate court? The attorney for the winning party in the appellate court? Why should the attorney be concerned with the exact language of the mandate? See R. Martineau, Modern Appellate Practice—Federal and State Civil Appeals § 17.1 (1983).

BRIGGS v. PENNSYLVANIA RAILROAD CO.

Supreme Court of the United States, 1948.
334 U.S. 304, 68 S.Ct. 1039, 92 L.Ed. 1403.

MR. JUSTICE JACKSON delivered the opinion of the Court.

This case first presents the question whether a plaintiff recovering under the Federal Employers' Liability Act, 45 U.S.C. § 51, is entitled to have interest on the verdict for the interval between its return and the entry of judgment, where the Circuit Court of Appeals' mandate which authorized the judgment contains no direction to add interest and is never amended to do so.

The jury returned a verdict of $42,500. The District Court then granted a motion, as to which decision had been reserved during the trial, to dismiss the complaint for lack of jurisdiction, and the judgment entered was therefore one of dismissal. However, the Circuit Court of Appeals reversed, 153 F.2d 841, and directed that judgment be entered on the verdict for plaintiff. When the District Court entered judgment, it added to the verdict interest from the date thereof to the date of judgment. The mandate of the Circuit Court of Appeals had made no provision for interest. No motion to recall and amend the mandate had been made and the term at which it was handed down had expired. Motion to resettle so as to exclude the interest was denied by the District Court. The Circuit Court of Appeals has modified the judgment to exclude the interest in question and to conform to its mandate, 164 F.2d 21, and the case is here on certiorari, 333 U.S. 836.

In its earliest days this Court consistently held that an inferior court has no power or authority to deviate from the mandate issued by an appellate court. [Citations omitted.] The rule of these cases has been uniformly followed in later days; [Citations omitted.] Chief Justice Marshall applied the rule to interdict allowance of interest not provided for in the mandate, [Citations omitted.] Mr. Justice Story explained and affirmed the doctrine. [Citations omitted.] We do not see how it can be questioned at this time. It is clear that the interest was in excess of the terms of the mandate and hence was wrongly included in the District Court's judgment and rightly stricken out by the Circuit Court of Appeals. The latter court's mandate made no provision for such interest and the trial court had no power to enter judgment for an amount different than directed. If any enlargement of that amount were possible, it could be done only by amendment of the mandate. But no move to do this was made during the term at which it went down. While power to act on its mandate after the term expires survives to protect the integrity of the court's own processes, [Citations omitted.] it has not been held to survive for the convenience of litigants. [Citations omitted.]

The plaintiff has at no time moved to amend the mandate which is the basis of the judgment. That it made no provision for interest was apparent on its face. Plaintiff accepted its advantages and brings her case to this Court, not on the proposition that amendment of the mandate has been improperly refused, but on the ground that the mandate should be disregarded. Such a position cannot be sustained. Hence the question whether interest might, on proper application, have been allowed, is not reached. [Citations omitted.]

Affirmed.

MR. JUSTICE RUTLEDGE, with whom MR. JUSTICE BLACK, MR. JUSTICE DOUGLAS and MR. JUSTICE MURPHY join, dissenting.

We granted certiorari to resolve a conflict between the decision of the Circuit Court of Appeals, 164 F.2d 21, and one rendered by the like court for the Fifth Circuit in Louisiana & Arkansas R. Co. v. Pratt, 142 F.2d 847.

In each case the jury returned a verdict for the plaintiff, but the trial court nevertheless gave judgment for the defendant as a matter of law; upon appeal that judgment was reversed; and the cause was remanded with directions to enter judgment on the verdict. In both cases the appellate courts' mandates were silent concerning interest, but the trial courts included in the judgments interest from the date of the verdict, not merely from the time when judgment was entered following receipt of the appellate courts' mandates. In the *Pratt* case this action of the trial court was sustained as conforming to the mandate; in this case the trial court's like action was reversed as being in excess of and, to that extent, contrary to the mandate.

The two cases thus present squarely conflicting decisions on two questions: (1) whether the appellate court's mandate includes the interest provided by 28 U.S.C. § 811, although the mandate makes no explicit mention of interest; (2) whether, if so, the interest allowed by the section properly runs from the date of the verdict or only from the time of entering judgment after receipt of the appellate court's mandate. Both questions are necessarily involved on petitioner's presentation and should now be decided.

This Court, however, declines to answer the second question, because it determines the first in respondent's favor, accepting, erroneously I think, the decision of the Circuit Court of Appeals in this phase of the case. That court construed its mandate as not including interest. This was on the basis that the mandate was silent concerning interest, mentioning expressly only the principal sum awarded by the verdict. In such a case the court said, "the District Court is without power to enter judgment for a different sum." Hence, it was held, the mandate was violated when interest was added to that sum. 164 F.2d at 23. And even upon the assumption that the mandate might have been amended to include interest by timely application for that purpose, this could not be done after expiration of the term at which the judgment was rendered, as petitioner sought to have done. Ibid.

It is this treatment of the court's mandate, now accepted by this Court and forming the basis for its disposition of the case without reaching the question certiorari was granted to review, from which I dissent. It confuses settled lines of distinction between different statutes and of decisions relating to them. I think these were correctly drawn and ought to be maintained. If that were done, we would be forced to reach and decide the question now avoided concerning the effect of § 811.

Ordinarily it is for the court issuing a mandate to determine its scope and effect, and other courts are bound by its determination. But this is not always so. If it were true, for example, that the silence of a mandate or a judgment regarding interest invariably precluded its recovery, the Court's decision and that of the Circuit Court of Appeals would be correct. But an explicit provision for interest is not always necessary to its inclusion, whether in a judgment or a mandate. In some instances interest attaches as a matter of law, even though the mandate or judgment is wholly silent regarding it. In others explicit mention is necessary to its inclusion. Blair v. Durham, 139 F.2d 260, and authorities cited.

Where the claim for interest rests upon statute, whether the one or the other effect results depends upon the terms and effect of the particular statute on which the claim is founded. Because not all statutes are alike in this respect, the terms and intent of each must be examined, when put in question, to ascertain whether the interest allowed attaches to the judgment or the mandate by operation of law or only upon explicit judicial direction. Usually this is resolved by determining whether the interest allowed is to be given in the court's discretion or as a matter of right.

* * * The extent to which the section gives interest is, of course, a distinct question, depending in this case on whether the section contemplates that the interest shall begin to run at one date or another.

Since the Court does not decide that question, I reserve decision upon it. But I dissent from the refusal to decide it now. The question is of considerable importance for the proper and uniform administration of the statute; it is not entirely without difficulty; and the uncertainty as well as the conflict of decision should be ended.

Notes and Questions

1. The authority of the appellate court over its mandate after it has been issued usually arises in one of two situations: (1) the authority of the appellate court to amend its own mandate and (2) the authority of the appellate court to compel the trial court to comply with the mandate.

In the principal case, it is stated that the appellate court lost authority to amend its mandate after the term in which it was issued expired. The legal concept of a term of a court is no longer of legal significance. The Fifth Circuit has stated that although it retains jurisdiction over its mandates to prevent injustice, there is no procedure established in the Federal Rules of Appellate Procedure to recall the mandate. The court stated that either a motion in the court of appeals or in the district court seeking a clarification of the interest question would be appropriate. Home Life Insurance Co. v. Equitable Equipment Co., Inc., 694 F.2d 402 (5th Cir. 1982). In Reeves v. International Tel. & Tel. Corp., 705 F.2d 750 (5th Cir. 1983), however, the court affirmed a district court refusal to award post judgment interest after an original appeal. The district court's action was on the ground that the mandate in that appeal did not include interest. The Fifth Circuit treated the appeal from the refusal as a request to modify the mandate to allow interest, which it did. Are the two cases consistent? Based on these two cases, what is the proper procedure to follow to seek an amendment to a mandate, either for interest or any other purpose? Some state rules specify the procedure to follow. E.g., Cal.R.App.P. 25(d), Colo.R.App.P. 41.1. A useful discussion is found in Note, Recall of Appellate Mandates in Federal Civil Litigation, 64 Cornell L.Rev. 704 (1979).

2. Some courts take the position that after the mandate issues, the appellate court no longer has jurisdiction over the case. Jones v. Board of Fire and Police Comm'rs., 127 Ill.App.3d 793, 82 Ill.Dec. 859, 469 N.E.2d 393 (1984). Under this view, is there any procedural remedy to make the trial court comply with the mandate?

JORDAN v. JORDAN

Supreme Court of Arizona, 1982.
132 Ariz. 38, 643 P.2d 1008.

Feldman, Justice.

This marriage dissolution action presents the novel question of whether a trial court may deviate from the mandate of an appellate court because of an intervening change in controlling law and, on remand, decide the case contrary to the instructions contained in that mandate. The court of appeals held that the trial court was without jurisdiction so to do and reversed. Jordan v. Jordan, 132 Ariz. 51, 643 P.2d 1021 (App.1981). We granted appellee wife's petition for review.

The parties were married in 1959 and lived in Oklahoma before moving to Arizona. In 1972, they bought a residence in Tucson, taking title as joint tenants with right of survivorship. At that time, Arizona law provided that courts had no jurisdiction to apportion joint tenancy property in dissolution proceedings. Becchelli v. Becchelli, 109 Ariz. 229, 508 P.2d 59 (1973). In 1973, after *Becchelli*, the legislature amended A.R.S. § 25–318 to provide that on dissolution of marriage the court had jurisdiction to include joint tenancy property in an equitable division of marital property. In 1975, the wife filed a petition for dissolution in Pima County Superior Court.

In the initial dissolution hearing, the trial court assumed jurisdiction over the joint tenancy property and awarded it to the wife. To offset the award of the residence to the wife, the trial court awarded certain community property to the husband. The trial court also made an award of spousal maintenance to the wife. The husband appealed, challenging the division of property and the award of spousal maintenance.

In an unpublished memorandum decision rendered in 1979, the court of appeals, per Richmond, Judge, held that the 1973 amendment to A.R.S. § 25–318 operated only prospectively and, therefore, joint tenancy property acquired before the effective date of the amendment was not subject to equitable division. The court stated:

> Because the joint tenancy residence cannot be awarded to appellee [wife] as her sole and separate property, the matter must be remanded. Inasmuch as appellant [husband] was awarded certain community assets to offset the award of the residence, the division of other property must be reconsidered (footnotes omitted).

The husband moved for rehearing; it was denied, and he petitioned for review. We denied this petition on December 4, 1979. The mandate then issued from the court of appeals to the trial court. The court of appeals reversed the portion of the trial court's decree which pertained to the division of property and the case was remanded for further proceedings. In all other respects the decree was affirmed.

Between the date of the court of appeals' mandate and the trial court's reconsideration of the property division, in what, we assume, would have been obedience to that mandate, the statute was amended again. The 1980 amendment gave the statute prospective and retrospective operation, thereby conferring jurisdiction on the trial court to make an equitable division of joint tenancy property even though the property had been acquired before 1973, the date of the first amendment to the statute.

Thus, when the trial court sat to obey the dictates of the mandate from the court of appeals, the legislature had given it jurisdiction to do that which the court of appeals had held it could not do—include the joint tenancy home in the equitable division of the marital property.

Accordingly, the trial court ordered that "in light of the change in the statute the original decree of dissolution which had been entered on August 21, 1978, * * * 'is hereby confirmed and validated.'" Thus, for the second time, the trial court awarded the joint tenancy residence to the wife with an offset of community property to the husband. The husband again appealed. By opinion filed December 17, 1981, the court of appeals, 132 Ariz. 51, 643 P.2d 1021, held that the trial court still lacked jurisdiction to make an equitable apportionment of the joint tenancy property. The holding was based entirely on the theory that by applying the 1980 amendment to the statute the trial court had ignored the mandate of the first appeal. Stating that "[a] remand sends a matter back to the body from which it came where further action will be limited by the terms of the mandate," the court of appeals ruled that when there is a "specific remand with specific directions" the lower court is without jurisdiction to enter a judgment which varies from the one it has been ordered to enter. Although we approve this statement as a general rule, we do not agree with its application to this unusual situation and, therefore, vacate the opinion of the court of appeals and affirm the trial court.

At the outset, we acknowledge that the trial court's ruling on remand conflicted with the mandate rendered after the first appeal. We acknowledge also numerous Arizona cases holding that on remand the lower tribunal has no choice but to enter a judgment which complies exactly with that which the higher court has ordered. [Citations omitted.] "To hold otherwise would be to strip judicial proceedings of their dignity and respect, while creating a circular process that would provide no end to litigation * * *." Tovrea v. Superior Court, 101 Ariz. at 297, 419 P.2d at 81. Nevertheless, none of these cases involves a situation where there has been a change in controlling law between the date of the mandate and the date of the trial court's reconsideration of the case.

The cases cited above present situations in which the trial court allegedly had attempted to substitute its view in lieu of the instructions contained in the mandate from the higher court. Each of the cases correctly holds that the trial court could not act in violation of the mandate. However, the general rule that the lower tribunal must follow the mandate of the higher court is part of the doctrine of the "law of the case." [Citations omitted.] Courts have not given this doctrine the same conclusive effect as the doctrine of *res judicata*. Compare Stuart v. Winslow Elementary School District No. 1, 100 Ariz. 375, 414 P.2d 976 (1966) (an erroneous judgment is conclusive between the parties) with Employers Mutual Liability Insurance Co. v. Industrial Commission, 115 Ariz. 439, 565 P.2d 1300 (App.1977) (law of the case inapplicable if different evidence is provided at the second hearing).

Thus, the general rule that the mandate must be followed has always had its exceptions. In Arizona, application of the general principle has been conditioned upon the proviso that the facts and issues on the subsequent proceedings after remand must be substantially the same as those on which the first decision rested. [Citations omitted.] The applicability of the "law of the case" doctrine has been limited to instances where the evidence on the second proceeding is substantially the same as that of the first. [Citations omitted.]

If on the new hearing the *facts* are not shown to be different, then the conclusion is that the [Industrial] Commission must follow the law already applied [by the appellate court] to substantially identical facts. * * * Correspondingly, if different evidence is presented in the hearings *de novo,* then the factual matters should be evaluated against this new evidence and the law of the case might well not be applicable since *its application is conditioned upon substantial identicality of facts, issues and evidence.*

Employers Mutual Liability Insurance Co. v. Industrial Commission, 115 Ariz. at 442, 565 P.2d at 1303 (emphasis supplied).

If the trial court has power to apply different law when the facts have changed, we must, then, consider whether the trial court can apply different law when the law changes between the date of the mandate and the date of the new hearing held in obedience to that mandate. Before discussing this question, it is necessary to deal with the use of the word "jurisdiction" in the numerous Arizona cases already cited and which, in different situations, state that a trial court is "without jurisdiction" to stray from the mandate of the higher court. Arizona authority indicates that the use of the word "jurisdiction" in the law of the case rule is incorrect. In State v. Maxwell, 19 Ariz.App. 431, 508 P.2d 96 (1973), Division One of the Court of Appeals considered whether a criminal defendant was entitled to a trial court hearing on the question of whether, at the time of his guilty plea, he had been given the rights to which he was entitled under the rule of Boykin v. Alabama, 395 U.S. 238, 89 S.Ct. 1709, 23 L.Ed.2d 274 (1969). On defendant's first appeal, Division Two of the Court of Appeals had held that Maxwell could not seek appellate review of his guilty plea on alleged *Boykin* defects without first petitioning the trial court to set aside the plea. [Citations omitted.] This ruling became final. Thereafter, the trial court held a hearing and denied defendant's motion to withdraw his guilty plea. Defendant filed a second appeal from this denial. On the second appeal, no record of the trial court proceedings could be obtained because the court reporter had left the jurisdiction, taking his notes with him. Defendant contended on the second appeal that since it was the law of the case that the determination of his *Boykin* rights must initially be made in the trial court and since the transcript of the trial court proceedings was unavailable for review, the case must be sent back to the trial court for another *Boykin* hearing. The second appeal was decided by Division One of the Court of Appeals. Between the date on which the first appeal became final and the decision of the second appeal, we held in a different case, State v. Sullivan, 107 Ariz. 98, 482 P.2d 861 (1971), that an appellate court could determine the *Boykin* issue without first requiring defendant to petition the trial court to set aside the plea. Maxwell claimed that Division One of the Court of Appeals was bound by the decision of Division Two in the first appeal, because that decision had become final and was "the law of the case." Division One disagreed, holding that:

"the law of the case doctrine is a *procedural rule which is generally followed, not because the court is without power to reconsider a former determination,* but because the orderly processes of judicial procedure require an end to litigation. In the absence of exceptional circumstances of hardship and injustice the need for attributing finality to considered judicial determinations compels the adherence to the previous decision. But the rule should never be made the instrument of injustice. Thus, where the controlling rules of law have been altered or clarified in the interval between the first and second appeal and adherence to the previous decision would result in defeating a just cause, it has been held that the court will not hesitate to reconsider its prior determination." State v. Maxwell, 19 Ariz.App. at 435, 508 P.2d at 100 (quoting Gore v. Bingaman, 20 Cal.2d 118, 122–23, 124 P.2d 17, 20 (1942)) (emphasis supplied).

Thus, Arizona has already recognized that notwithstanding the use of the word "jurisdiction" in the law of the case doctrine, an appellate court is not always required to follow the law as mandated in a previous opinion or order in the same case.

An analogous issue is discussed in Lennig v. New York Life Insurance Co., 130 F.2d 580 (3d Cir. 1942). *Lennig* was a diversity case which the Third Circuit Court of Appeals had remanded to the trial court with a mandate requiring action in accordance with the law announced in the body of the decision. Pennsylvania law controlled the substantive rights of the parties. On remand, the trial court decided it was not bound by the mandate because of a subsequent, inconsistent pronouncement on a point of state law in a different case decided by the Pennsylvania Supreme Court. On the second appeal, the Third Circuit stated as follows:

> If, as the learned trial judge apprehended, the later decision in [a state case] interpreted the law of Pennsylvania differently than we had perceived it to be in our earlier opinion [in this case], then the court below was quite right in applying to the retrial of this case the rule if and as made plain subsequently by binding state court decision * * * [w]here a federal court of appeals in a given case has ascertained and applied what it apprehends to be the pertinent state law, such ascertainment of the local law is binding upon the trial court at the retrial of the case unless it is clearly made to appear by subsequent statute, no more than declaratory, or by binding state court decision that the law of the state was other than what the federal appellate court had understood it to be.

Id. at 581.

Similar conclusions have been reached when a court of last resort is forced to decide whether its own final decision which has become "the law of the case" is binding upon it on a second appeal when in the interim the appellate court has found contrary controlling statutory law which had previously escaped its attention. [Citations omitted.]

Of course, we are well aware that the issue here is not whether an appellate court is bound to follow the mandate of its previous final decision under the "law of the case" doctrine, nor even whether one appellate court is bound to follow the final decision of another appellate court in the same case. The issue here is whether a lower tribunal is bound by the mandate of a higher court, even when there has been a change in controlling law. The leading case on this issue is Banco Nacional de Cuba v. Farr, 383 F.2d 166 (2d Cir. 1967), *cert. denied*, 390 U.S. 956, 88 S.Ct. 1038, 20 L.Ed.2d 1151 (1968). In a previous appeal of the same case, Banco Nacional de Cuba v. Sabbatino, 376 U.S. 398, 84 S.Ct. 923, 11 L.Ed.2d 804 (1964), the United States Supreme Court had reversed the Second Circuit Court of Appeals, 307 F.2d 845, and had ruled that the "act of state" doctrine applied to the case and prevented the trial court from examining the validity of an expropriation by the Cuban government. The Supreme Court remanded the case to the district court to decide other litigable issues of fact in proceedings consistent with its opinion and mandate. Before the district court issued a final judgment on the remanded issues, Congress enacted the Hickenlooper Amendment to the Foreign Assistance Act of 1964, 22 U.S.C. § 2370(e). The amended statute provided that "no court in the United States shall decline on the ground of the federal act of state doctrine * * * [to determine expropriation cases on the merits] giving effect to the principles of international law * * * [where the case involved an asserted confiscation by a foreign country in violation of the principles of international law]." Id. The effect of this amendment was to render inapplicable the "act of state" doctrine which the Supreme Court had relied upon to reverse the case. On the second appeal, the Second Circuit was faced with the question of whether the trial court was bound by the mandate of the Supreme Court following the first appeal, or whether it had jurisdiction to disregard the mandate and decide the case under the newly amended statute. The Second Circuit held that the statute governed over the previous mandate. Judge Waterman wrote:

> We have learned of no case involving the effect on the rights of litigants of a federal statute, inconsistent with a Supreme Court mandate, which became law after the Supreme Court had remanded a case to the trial court but before the trial court had acted upon the merits after the remand. None has been called to our attention by the parties and we have found none by independent research. We must therefore determine whether the mandate rule should cover this novel situation; it is our view that it should not be extended to do so.

> The Supreme Court mandate rule is nothing more than one specific application of a general doctrine appellate courts apply to their orders to lower courts, a doctrine commonly referred to as the law of the case, * * *. Other courts in applying the law of the case rule have held that a lower court is not bound to follow the mandate of an appellate court if the mandate is, in the interim, affected by an authority superior to the court issuing the mandate, such as by a higher appellate court, either state or federal * * * or by an *en banc* decision of the same court * * *. This principle has also been applied when the mandate of the court is affected by intervening

statutory enactment * * *. The same principle should apply here; any limiting language in the Supreme Court mandate should not preclude judicial application of the [Hickenlooper] Amendment in this case for the rule of law expressed by the mandate has been affected by a subsequently enacted federal statute.

Banco Nacional de Cuba v. Farr, 383 F.2d at 178 (citations omitted). [Citations omitted.]

The authorities discussed above compel our conclusion that the "law of the case" doctrine is inapplicable where the policy of the law has been changed, by legislative enactment or decision of a higher court, while the case is still pending resolution. In reaching our decision, we do not depart from our long-held rule that after decision on appeal and remand the lower court is bound to follow the law set forth in the appellate court's opinion and to carry out the directions contained in the mandate, whether the lower court agrees or disagrees, approves or disapproves of the opinion and the mandate. We hold, however, that this general rule is subject to the exception that the lower court may deviate from the mandate and apply different law from that specified by the appellate court where, while the case is still pending, and in the interim between the rendition and implementation of the mandate, there has been a change in controlling law. Such being the case here, the decision of the court of appeals is vacated and the decree of the trial court is reinstated.

Notes and Questions

1. What is the status of the rule of the law of the case? Why should it have any less status than the principle of *res judicata?* Does this not invite the trial court to ignore the mandate of the appellate court?

2. Another approach when there is a change in the law subsequent to the issuance of the mandate of the appellate court is to request that court to amend its mandate to reflect the change. This procedure was permitted in Judkins v. Beech Aircraft Corp., 745 F.2d 1330 (11th Cir. 1984). Is this preferable to the procedure followed in the principal case?

3. The principal case is discussed in Comment, Appellate Decisions 1981–82, 24 Ariz. L.Rev. 993 (1982).

4. If a matter is not within the scope of the mandate, what is the authority of the trial court on remand to act on other issues? See Sprague v. Ticonic Nat. Bank, 307 U.S. 161, 59 S.Ct. 777, 83 L.Ed. 1184 (1939) (permitting trial court to consider other issues).

CHAPTER 12

SUPERVISORY JURISDICTION

EXTRAORDINARY WRITS

R. MARTINEAU, MODERN APPELLATE PRACTICE— FEDERAL AND STATE CIVIL APPEALS

§ 19.1 (1983).

One of the traditional means for appellate review of an action of a lower court as an alternative to an appeal or writ of error has been through an extraordinary or supervisory writ (hereafter referred to as extraordinary writ). The availability of the extraordinary writs in an appellate court for review of a lower court action must be examined in the context of the final judgment rule. The overriding principle of appealability is that a judgment or order must be final to be appealable. The goal underlying this rule is judicial economy. Competing with this goal, however, is the litigant's need for effective review of intermediate rulings which may prejudice his rights in the case. In an attempt to satisfy the litigant's need with as little judicial disruption as possible, exceptions to the final judgment rule have arisen. The extraordinary writs were not, however, designed as an exception to the rule, but rather as ways for the appellate court to ensure that the appellate courts did not go beyond their jurisdictional authority and that they assumed jurisdiction when required to do so. For example, the writ of mandamus traditionally was used to confine an inferior court to exercising only its prescribed jurisdiction or to compel it to act when required to do so. The writ of prohibition was used to prevent a lower court from acting when it had no jurisdiction. However, as with the final judgment rule, exceptions to the extraordinary writs have arisen. Writs have been used as a supplement to appeal and to supervise the intermediate rulings of the lower courts.

PFANDER, JURISDICTION–STRIPPING AND THE SUPREME COURT'S POWER TO SUPERVISE INFERIOR TRIBUNALS

78 Tex. L. Rev. 1433, 1442–51 (2000).*

"SUPREME COURTS" AND THE RISE OF SUPERVISORY POWERS

A. *King's Bench Supervision of Inferior Tribunals Through Prerogative Writs*

1. The Development of Prerogative Writs.—The supervisory role of King's Bench developed in England during the troubled years of the seventeenth century with the demise of Star Chamber and other forms of conciliar jurisdiction, King's Bench acceded to the summary forms of process that we now associate with the prerogative writs of mandamus, habeas corpus, prohibition, certiorari, and quo warranto. These writs, which made up the heart of the supervisory powers of King's Bench, received an important boost in the battles with James II that culminated in the Glorious Revolution. In the end, of course, James II abdicated and cleared the way for the accession of William and Mary and the beginning of constitutional monarchy. But just as his predecessor's attempts to place royal prisoners beyond the reach of habeas corpus had led to an important strengthening of the availability of that writ in the Habeas Corpus Act of 1679, James II's attempt to set up a separate tribunal, known as the Court of Commissioners for Ecclesiastical Purposes, rekindled a struggle with Parliament and the common law courts that eventually led to the prohibition of such courts in the English Bill of Rights.

By the time of Blackstone's Commentaries, some seventy-five years after the Revolution of 1688, the supervisory writs of King's Bench had taken on a definite shape. The writ of mandamus issued by King's Bench directed inferior courts and administrative officials to take action clearly required of them by law. Habeas corpus ad subjiciendum, the "Great Writ" of freedom, directed the jailer to bring the "body" of an inmate before the court for an adjudication of the legality of further confinement. Prohibition directed a lower court to refrain from exercising authority over a matter beyond its jurisdiction. Certiorari effected the removal of a judicial record or cause (often an indictment) from a lower court for trial or other disposition in King's Bench. Quo warranto tested the title of an individual to royal office and supplied the means of ousting those who held office unlawfully.

These writs shared many characteristics by the time they were first lumped together as "prerogative" writs by Lord Mansfield in 1759. First, the writs were closely associated with the exercise of royal authority and with King's Bench, having long been used by the Crown in the adminis-

*James E. Pfander, copyright © 1994 by permission. All rights reserved. University of Texas Law Review. Reprinted

tration of the state. Second, the prerogative writs were issued by the court after reviewing the sufficiency of the petition and supporting affidavits; in contrast to these "extraordinary" writs, most common law writs issued as a matter of course without any required showing of cause. Third, the prerogative writs were seen as the "suppletory means of substantial justice"—the remedial mode to which the subject turned whenever remedies at law were unavailable. Fourth, the writs were adjudicated by way of summary proceedings, and were enforceable through contempt sanctions.

Although different from them in certain key aspects, the writ of scire facias bore some resemblance to the prerogative writs in its provision for the individual suitor to assert claims in the name of the King and seek relief from government wrongdoing. Scire facias initiated a proceeding to cancel the King's letters patent, a legal document that passed one of the official seals of state and ordinarily provided conclusive evidence of the lawfulness of the ownership interest (in land, office, or "patented" invention) that it described. Corrective scire facias process was required any time letters patent were issued in error....

B. Supervisory Use of the Prerogative Writs in American State Courts

Americans quite consciously borrowed the model of King's Bench in contending that their supreme courts enjoyed supervisory authority to monitor inferior tribunals. In Massachusetts, shortly after the new state constitution took effect in 1780, the legislature empowered the Supreme Judicial Court to hear writs of error and other proceedings in the ordinary course and to issue writs of prohibition and mandamus to "all courts of inferior judiciary powers." A similar linkage appeared in New York, where the supreme court had asserted broad supervisory powers by the early eighteenth century. By 1804, the Supreme Court of Pennsylvania had drawn the following express link between its status as a "supreme" tribunal and its authority to issue the prerogative writs of habeas corpus, certiorari, mandamus, and prohibition to courts of inferior jurisdiction:

> It is a position beyond contradiction, that the king's bench, in England, (and this court is clothed with the same common law authority,) has jurisdiction.... that wherever new jurisdictions are erected ... they are subject to the inspection of the king's bench by writ of error, certiorari and mandamus.... The necessity of a superintending power to restrain and correct partialities and irregularities which may be committed by inferior officers, is so obvious and indispensable, that the court ought by no means to deny themselves a jurisdiction of such salutary influence.

Similar developments occurred in other states and generally corresponded to the growing recognition of the importance of the doctrine of separation of powers and the need to secure the judicial role against legislative dominance. Indeed, as Leonard Goodman has noted in summarizing the incorporation of the prerogative writs into the supervisory power of the American supreme or superior courts, "some degree of separation of powers was a necessary ingredient in the assertion of supervisory jurisdiction by colonial courts." Needless to say, the Constitution itself rests upon notions of separated powers that appear quite congenial to the assertion of a vigorous supervisory function.

ALL WRITS ACT

"The All Writs Act, provides: 'The Supreme Court and all courts established by Act of Congress may issue all writs necessary or appropriate in aid of their respective jurisdictions and agreeable to the usages and principles of law.' This statute, based upon language that has been a part of American law since the Judiciary Act of 1789, authorizes United States courts of appeals to review and control the exercise of power by federal district courts without the necessity of a final judgment."[1]

"The principal extraordinary writs are mandamus, prohibition, habeas corpus, and certiorari. The writ of certiorari under § 1651(a), generally described as the 'common law' writ, is not the same, jurisdictionally, as the writ of certiorari provided for in 28 U.S.C. §§ 1254 and 1257, which govern the bulk of the cases coming to the Supreme Court in the ordinary course of appellate review."[2]

FEDERAL RULE OF APPELLATE PROCEDURE 21 WRITS OF MANDAMUS AND PROHIBITION, AND OTHER EXTRAORDINARY WRITS

(a) **MANDAMUS OR PROHIBITION TO A COURT: PETITION, FILING, SERVICE, AND DOCKETING.**

(1) A party petitioning for a writ of mandamus or prohibition directed to a court shall file a petition with the circuit clerk with proof of service on all parties to the proceeding in the trial court. The party shall also provide a copy to the trial court judge. All parties to the proceeding in the trial court other than the petitioner are respondents for all purposes.

(2) (A) The petition shall be titled *in re [name of petitioner]*.

    (B) The petition shall state:

        (i) the relief sought;

        (ii) the issues presented;

        (iii) the facts necessary to understand the issues presented by the petition; and

        (iv) the reasons why the writ should issue.

    (C) The petition shall include copies of any order or opinion or parts of the record that may be essential to understand the matters set forth in the petition.

---

1. M. Tigar, Federal Appeals: Jurisdiction and Practice 135–36 (2d ed. 1987).

2. R. Stern, E. Gressman, S. Shapiro, & K. Geller, Supreme Court Practice 580 (8th ed. 2002).

(3) When the clerk receives the prescribed docket fee, the clerk shall docket the petition and submit it to the court.

(b) **DENIAL; ORDER DIRECTING ANSWER; BRIEFS; PRECEDENCE.**

(1) The court may deny the petition without an answer. Otherwise, it shall order the respondent, if any, to answer within a fixed time.

(2) The clerk shall serve the order to respond on all persons directed to respond.

(3) Two or more respondents may answer jointly.

(4) The court of appeals may invite or order the trial court judge to respond or may invite an amicus curiae to do so. The trial court judge may request permission to respond but may not respond unless invited or ordered to do so by the court of appeals.

(5) If briefing or oral argument is required, the clerk shall advise the parties, and when appropriate, the trial court judge or amicus curiae.

(6) the proceeding shall be given preference over ordinary civil cases.

(7) The circuit clerk shall send a copy of the final disposition to the trial court judge.

(c) **OTHER EXTRAORDINARY WRITS.** Application for an extraordinary writ other than one of those provided for in subdivisions (a) and (b) of this rule shall be made by filing a petition with the circuit clerk with proof of service on the respondents. Proceedings on such application shall conform, so far as is practicable, to the procedure prescribed in subdivisions (a) and (b) of this rule.

(d) **FORM OF PAPERS; NUMBER OF COPIES.** All papers may be typewritten. An original and three copies shall be filed unless the court requires the filing of a different number by local rule or by order in a particular case.

WISOTSKY, EXTRAORDINARY WRITS: "APPEAL" BY OTHER MEANS

26 American Journal of Trial Advocacy 577 (2003).*

INTRODUCTION

In the course of litigation, civil or criminal, counsel may be confronted with a pretrial order that materially impairs the client's case or the lawyer's ability to continue to represent the client. One of the first questions the attorney should ask is whether appellate relief may be available. If the order in question is not an appealable interlocutory

* Steven Wisotsky, copyright © 2003, American Journal of Trial Advocacy, Sam-   ford University. Reprinted by permission. All rights reserved.

order, if it does not qualify for appeal under the collateral order doctrine, and if it is not one that the trial judge will certify as presenting "a controlling question of law" the resolution of which would "materially advance" termination of the case, counsel may yet find a remedy in the extraordinary writs. This Article presents an overview of the ways in which trial lawyers may, in effect, "appeal" to the court of appeals by means of the extraordinary writs.

I. The Functions of Extraordinary Writs

The extraordinary writs play a statistically small but occasionally vital part of appellate practice. Technically, an extraordinary writ is not appellate review of a trial court order; rather, it is an original proceeding filed directly in the appellate court. Nevertheless, an extraordinary writ can in some situations accomplish the functional equivalent of appellate review by providing a remedy for an adverse trial court order. Most commonly, the order sought to be reviewed by writ is entered during the pretrial phase of litigation, although trial and post-trial orders have sometimes also been challenged. The writs utilized for these purposes are mandamus and prohibition, and are the only writs specifically listed in Federal Rules of Appellate Procedure 21.

Extraordinary writs may also lie to review final judgments (e.g., a writ of certiorari to certify and send up the record on appeal, a writ of habeas corpus to secure the liberty of a petitioner in custody, or a writ of error coram nobis for collateral attack on a criminal conviction by a petitioner who is not in custody). The primary focus of this Article is on the use of writs by a trial lawyer to obtain the equivalent of an interlocutory appeal. In this usage, the writs may be viewed as an exception to the final judgment rule. For that reason, it is essential for appellate counsel to consider whether appeal from a collateral order under 28 U.S.C. § 1291 or appeal from an interlocutory order under 28 U.S.C. § 1292(b) are viable alternatives. The interrelationship between and among mandamus (or prohibition), collateral orders, and interlocutory appeals is explored in Part VI.

II. Jurisdiction for Extraordinary Writs

The jurisdiction of federal courts of appeals to issue extraordinary writs arises from the All Writs Act: "The Supreme Court and all courts established by Act of Congress may issue all writs necessary or appropriate in aid of their respective jurisdictions and agreeable to the usages and principles of law."

The "aid of" jurisdiction language indicates that the power to issue writs is remedial in nature and not ipso facto a basis of jurisdiction. Rather, the writs may be issued to implement a court's independently-based jurisdiction, whether or not it has been invoked or perfected. Thus, the court of appeals has writ jurisdiction over trial court orders before final judgment because it would have jurisdiction "at some (later) stage of the ... proceedings"—that is, upon appeal from final judgment.

In short, the writs may issue in aid of present or future jurisdiction or, in the case of a completed appeal, to enforce its mandate.

In most cases, the challenge to counsel seeking a writ is not jurisdictional but practical and prudential-the need to persuade the court that it ought to exercise its jurisdiction to grant the particular relief sought. The granting of an extraordinary writ is a matter of discretion, and appellate courts have been warned by the Supreme Court to avoid disrupting the trial court's authority over an ongoing trial except when there has been a " 'usurpation of judicial power' or clear abuse of discretion." Thus, writs are to be issued sparingly. Indeed, the Supreme Court, alluding to Gilbert & Sullivan, has issued this guideline: "What never? Well, hardly ever!"

The rationale for this parsimonious approach overlaps the final judgment rule and the corresponding policy against interlocutory appeals to avoid piecemeal litigation. "All our jurisprudence is strongly colored by the notion that appellate review should be postponed, except in certain narrowly defined circumstances, until after final judgment has been rendered by the trial court." Accordingly, the extraordinary writs "may not be used to thwart the congressional policy against piecemeal appeals. Mandamus . . . does not 'run the gauntlet of reversible errors.' " Nevertheless, the case law has established situations where the case for relief by way of extraordinary writ is deemed strong. These are reviewed in Part IV.

III.   NATURE OF THE REMEDY: MANDAMUS AND PROHIBITION

At common law, mandamus would lie to compel performance of a ministerial or nondiscretionary duty, and prohibition would lie to prevent a judge or other official from acting in excess of his jurisdiction. Modern usage has expanded beyond those parameters. Yet, as the Supreme Court noted, mandamus and prohibition are similar to injunctions insofar as they compel or restrain performance of a specified act or course of conduct. Compared to injunctions, the writs are narrower in scope; they lie only against public officials, typically the trial judge or an administrative agency.

A petition is often presented in the alternative because it is usually possible to phrase an order either in the affirmative or in the negative. For example, a petition alleging that the trial court lacks jurisdiction and should not proceed may be framed either as one for prohibition, preventing the trial judge from proceeding further, or for mandamus, compelling the trial judge to grant a motion for dismissal.

IV.   STANDARDS FOR ISSUANCE

Supreme Court jurisprudence respecting the issuance of extraordinary writs has been inconsistent. No single test prevails, and only generalities provide guidance. "The preemptory common-law writs are among the most potent weapons in the judicial arsenal. . . . '(T)hey are reserved for really extraordinary causes.' " Here again is a parallel to the standards for issuing an injunction insofar as petitioner must make a showing of exceptional need. He must "have no other adequate means to attain the relief he desires, and ... satisfy 'the burden of showing that (his) right to issuance of the writ is "clear and indisputable." ' " Few things in law are "clear and indisputable." Beyond that, one of the recognized uses of the writ is "to settle new and important problems" on "issues of first impression." Still, the point is made: petitioner's claim to relief must be a compelling one that requires an immediate remedy—an exceptional situation.

To implement this broad policy directive, the circuit courts of appeals have developed similar, but not identical, multi-prong tests. For example, the Sixth Circuit looks to four criteria: (1) petitioner "has no other adequate" remedy, including interlocutory appeal or appeal from the final judgment; (2) "the district court's order is clearly erroneous as a matter of law"; (3) the order reflects a persistent or systemic problem in the district courts; or (4) "the district court's order raises new" or unresolved and important "issues of law." Not all the criteria must coexist to justify relief by way of an extraordinary writ; indeed, factors 2 and 4 are facially inconsistent. Further, factors 3 and 4 would not apply at all (nor would factor 1) to the fairly routine exercise of mandamus in cases where a trial judge has refused to recuse himself upon a proper challenge to his impartiality.

In comparison, the Ninth Circuit has a five-part set of guidelines for determining whether to grant mandamus relief:

(1) The party seeking the writ has no other adequate means, such as a direct appeal, to attain the relief he or she desires. (2) The petitioner will be damaged or prejudiced in a way not correctable on appeal.... (3) The district court's order is clearly erroneous as a matter of law. (4) The district court's order is an oft-repeated error, or manifests a persistent disregard of the federal rules. (5) The district court's order raises new and important problems, or issues of law of first impression.

As with the Sixth Circuit "test," at least two of the criteria, numbers (4) and (5), are in conflict, as an oft-repeated error could not constitute a new legal problem. It might also be argued that numbers (3) and (5) are similarly in tension, as a new legal issue could not be clearly erroneous as a matter of law. Furthermore, factors (1) and (2) seem to be duplicative and in any event would not apply to the erroneous refusal of a judge, challenged for (the appearance of) partiality, to grant a recusal motion; that would certainly be correctable on appeal from final judgment.

The Ninth Circuit later acknowledged, in United States v. Harper, that it had listed "conflicting indicators" and that they were meant only as "a useful starting point ... regarding the propriety of mandamus relief." This indirectly admits that writ jurisprudence is a muddle. The muddle is caused by the formalistic pretense that writ usage is governed by hard legal standards when, in reality, writ usage is governed by soft situational discretion. For that reason, the various "tests" or "criteria" articulated by the several circuits do not square with one another, sound more like shibboleths than rules (e.g., "usurpation of power"), and do not produce consistent, coherent adjudication, so far as we can tell-most petitions are decided without any reported opinion. Writ jurisprudence is a legal realist's paradise.

The simple truth of the matter is that the decision whether or not to issue an extraordinary writ cannot be cabined by any black letter rule, even if (or especially if) expressed as a multi-factor analysis. Rather, equity and discretion necessarily play a very large role. The decision to grant or deny relief must be highly fact-specific and contextual, akin to the decision whether or not to issue a temporary restraining order or preliminary injunction. In that domain, the equitable considerations of urgency or irreparability of harm predominate. Thus, counsel and client must evaluate a potential writ filing against a normative standard based on the justice of the cause-that is, whether the writ should issue, not whether it must issue.

V.   Common Uses of the Writs

"(T)here is enough flexibility in the (Supreme) Court's teaching that courts of appeals can justify hearing a very broad range of issues on mandamus." Indeed, the range is so broad as to encompass one-time-only review of new and important legal issues that might create trouble for a district court judge (a review that might be called advisory in nature) and recurring problems that fall into recognizable categories (a review that might be called supervisory in nature).

A.   *Review of Denial of Motion to Disqualify Trial Judge*

Federal law provides for disqualification of judges for bias or prejudice for or against a party. The Code also mandates disqualification on a variety of grounds including conflicts of interest or financial stake in the outcome of the case. The failure of a trial judge to grant a legally sufficient motion for disqualification under section 144 would be grounds for appeal after final judgment, and at least two circuits require that path to be followed. But rather than force a party to go through the effort and expense of a trial before a judge whose impartiality "might reasonably be questioned" under section 455, a pretrial petition for writ of mandamus to compel a trial judge to recuse himself will be entertained. "Interlocutory review of disqualification issues on petitions for mandamus is both necessary and appropriate to ensure that judges do not adjudicate cases that they have no statutory power to hear, and virtually every circuit has so held." Diplomacy sometimes prevails: more than one opinion has formally denied the writ, with the court of appeals suggesting that the trial judge will have the good judgment to either voluntarily remove himself or to modify objectionable orders.

Finally, it is not only the erroneous denial of a recusal motion that is reviewable; the erroneous grant of such a motion under section 455 may also be reviewed by mandamus where there is an actual injury not correctable on appeal. Thus, in a nationwide class action case where the trial judge recused himself after several years of pretrial litigation, the court of appeals held that mandamus would lie pursuant to the court's "supervisory mandamus authority" because the recusal order would "significantly impair the progress of this litigation" by requiring the parties to educate a new judge on the issues involved in the complex multi-district litigation consisting of twenty-one consolidated antitrust lawsuits.

B. *Review of Orders on Motions to Disqualify Opposing Counsel*

An older, now obsolete, body of case law treats orders granting or denying motions to disqualify opposing counsel under the collateral order doctrine of Cohen v. Beneficial Industrial Loan Corp. But the Supreme Court put an end to such interlocutory review by appeal in a series of cases. The Court first held that an order refusing to disqualify counsel in a civil case was not immediately appealable under the collateral order doctrine. It then held that an order granting disqualification in a criminal case was likewise not immediately appealable as a collateral order. Finally, it held that an order disqualifying counsel in a civil case was not immediately appealable under the collateral order doctrine, even if the disqualification was coupled with a monetary sanction imposed upon the trial lawyer.

Despite these holdings, the Court stated in dictum in Firestone Tire & Rubber Co. v. Risjord that such orders on motions to disqualify counsel might be remediable in "exceptional circumstances" by writ of mandamus. Similarly, Justice Kennedy's concurring opinion in Cunningham v. Hamilton County stated that mandamus may be justified to avoid "an exceptional hardship itself likely to cause an injustice."

Thus, even if there are exceptional circumstances, orders on motions to disqualify opposing counsel remain unreviewable by collateral appeal, although mandamus may lie. Judge Posner elaborated upon this differentiation, quoting Professor Moore: " '(W)ith respect to the demands of justice made by individual cases, it seems clear that discretionary review by mandamus is to be preferred to enlarging by judicial interpretation the categories of interlocutory orders that are appealable as of right.' "

1. *Civil Cases*

Infrequently, courts of appeals have reviewed orders disqualifying counsel by mandamus. The few cases to do so have been civil cases, although, formally speaking, the standards for issuance of an extraordinary writ are the same whether the case is civil or criminal.

The Seventh Circuit issued writs of mandamus at least twice in the 1990s to reinstate disqualified lawyers even after the Supreme Court decided Richardson–Merrell, Inc. v. Koller. For example, in In re Sandahl, the court of appeals held that, "(t)o avoid the collapse of mandamus into appeal, we hold that a litigant who seeks mandamus to set aside an order of disqualification must show that the order is patently erroneous." In a later case denying the writ for lack of "irreparable injury" to the plaintiff class, the Seventh Circuit distinguished the earlier two cases as ones involving "obvious blunders by the district courts, blunders that imposed pointless costs on litigants." Regarding costs, it is apparent that a late-in-the-day motion, after considerable pretrial litigation has occurred, is more disruptive and expensive. It requires the party suffering the disqualification to replace one firm with a new one whose attorneys will have to educate themselves about the case at the client's expense. Such a case presents a more compelling set of equities for relief from the court of appeals by issuance of an extraordinary writ.

2. *Criminal Cases*

As stated above, there is no formal or doctrinal difference in the standard required for relief by mandamus in a criminal case. Nonetheless, the different context is important. Recalling that relief by extraordinary writ is the functional equivalent of interlocutory appeal, it is important to reiterate that the final judgment rule "takes on added weight in criminal cases." Correspondingly, the prohibition against interlocutory appeals "is at its strongest in the field of criminal law." Part of the reason is that the Government has a much more limited right to appeal than does the defendant, and the Government cannot appeal at all from an acquittal because of double jeopardy rules.

When the Government moves to disqualify defense counsel based on a conflict of interest, the paradoxical effect of the defendant's Sixth Amendment right to the counsel of his choice is to make it harder to obtain relief from an erroneous disqualification. The criminal trial is not merely a dispute between private litigants; it also involves the public interest in seeing that justice is done. Thus, the prosecution itself has a duty to avoid a trial that may be "tainted" by conflicted representation. Further, the prosecution interest is heightened by the possibility that a convicted defendant will seek appellate or post-conviction relief based upon that very conflict of interest, even in cases where the defendant has waived that right in open court. "An actual or potential conflict cannot be waived if, in the circumstances of the case, the conflict is of such a serious nature that no rational defendant would knowingly and intelligently desire that attorney's representation."

For this reason, the Supreme Court has held that a trial judge has "substantial latitude" to reject a defendant's waiver of conflict of interest, whether actual or potential, and to order defense counsel disqualified. Such orders are reviewed on direct appeal only for abuse of discretion, so mandamus will rarely lie to overturn a disqualification order unless, perhaps, it is flagrantly wrong or unfair.

C. *Discovery Disputes—Orders Compelling Disclosure*

Ordinarily, a judge's orders on pretrial discovery are not reviewable until after final judgment because of their interlocutory nature. This applies equally to orders compelling discovery and orders granting protection from discovery. However, if the pretrial discovery order involves potentially irreparable injury resulting from compelled disclosure of privileged information or trade secrets, the writ should be issued. The rationale is that the harm resulting from improperly compelled disclosure cannot be undone even if the objecting party wins a new trial or outright reversal on appeal. The damage done is collateral to the issue of merits liability; the party who is improperly compelled to disclose suffers competitive injury or invasion of privacy.

In re BankAmerica Corp. Securities Litigation is a good example of a writ issued to protect against the potential for unwarranted disclosure. In that case, a securities class action lawsuit arose out of the merger of Nationsbank and BankAmerica. During pretrial discovery, the plaintiffs moved to compel production of eleven documents as to which defendants asserted the attorney-client privilege. The district court ordered the documents produced under the crime-fraud exception. The bank petitioned the court of appeals for a "writ of mandamus and (also) moved for an emergency stay of the district court's order." The court of appeals granted the stay pending disposition of the petition and issued the writ of mandamus.

The appellate court explained that, "(t)hough mandamus is an extraordinary remedy, we will issue the writ when the district court has committed a clear error of law or abuse of discretion in ordering the disclosure of privileged materials." The appellate court also emphasized the importance of the attorney client privilege to the administration of justice and the irreparable nature of the injury: "(A)n appeal after disclosure of the privileged communication is an inadequate remedy."

D. Discovery Disputes–Orders Denying Disclosure

This is a much rarer use of the writ, but a few cases have issued an extraordinary writ to compel a trial judge to order that disclosure be made. For example, mandamus has been ordered to require the trial judge to compel disclosure of discovery materials for use in related litigation.

E. Orders Restraining Media Coverage

Where the trial judge attempts to prevent prejudicial pretrial publicity by restraining disclosure of information about the proceedings to news media, the affected news organizations may seek relief by appeal under the collateral order doctrine in some circuits. In other circuits, review of a pretrial gag order is by writ of mandamus, whether the gag order is challenged by a participant in the proceeding or by a news organization covering it. Whether review is by appeal or by writ, the news organization has standing to intervene as a nonparty who has suffered legally cognizable injury as a result of the court's order. Several cases hold that news organizations can obtain access to case materials in civil or criminal cases by writ of mandamus.

F. Preventing a Trial Judge From Exceeding His "Jurisdiction"

Creative uses of the extraordinary writs have been approved in a variety of circumstances where petitioning counsel asserts that the trial judge has acted in excess of his lawful jurisdiction. For example, where the district judge had entered an order granting an untimely motion for a new trial, the Seventh Circuit Court of Appeals issued a writ of mandamus directing the trial judge to reinstate the jury verdict. This would seem to conflate a legal error with a lack of jurisdiction to rule. After all, the court had subject matter jurisdiction over the case and personal jurisdiction over the parties. As a practical matter, however, the district court's error in granting an untimely Rule 59 motion was clear and reversal was a foregone conclusion. Rather than compelling the petitioner to go through the greater time and expense of taking an appeal from final judgment after a retrial, it was more expeditious to grant relief by issuing the extraordinary writ.

Analogous cases of jurisdiction-stretching under state law can be seen in the issuance of writs of prohibition to stop a trial from proceeding in violation of the speedy trial rule or after expiration of the statute of limitations. In substance, the same relief is obtained in federal court by means of appeal under the collateral order doctrine where the trial judge erroneously refuses to grant a motion to dismiss based on double jeopardy grounds.

VI. Writs Compared to Collateral Order
Appeal and Interlocutory Appeal

There may be functional overlap in seeking review of nonfinal orders under section 1292(b) or under the collateral order doctrine and the extraordinary writs. For example, the concurrence in Cunningham v. Hamilton County suggests that mandamus may fill the need for review in situations (disqualification of trial counsel) where the collateral order doctrine would not. Judge Posner made essentially the same point in In re Sandahl. Until 1998, courts sometimes allowed mandamus review of class action certification orders before Rule 23(f) was amended to permit direct appeals in the discretion of the court of appeals. Appellate review may occasionally be obtained if the district judge certifies "a controlling question of law" under 28 U.S.C. 1292(b). Thus, appellate review of nonfinal orders may potentially be obtained in several different ways. Therefore, when appellate counsel sets out to obtain appellate review of a nonfinal order, he must consider all possible and plausible alternatives. Sometimes, the prudent course of action will be to proceed on two tracks at once. The procedure for doing so is addressed in Part VII.C.

VII. Practice and Procedure

Practice and procedure for writs of mandamus and prohibition are controlled by Federal Rule of Appellate Procedure 21 and supplemented by local rules of court. In general, the procedure is streamlined and much less onerous than the requirements for an appeal from a final judgment.

A. *Petitioner*

The petition must be filed with the clerk of the circuit court, unlike an appeal where the notice of appeal is filed in the district court. Of course, copies must be served on all parties, who become respondents. Although the trial judge's action or inaction is the focus of the petition, he or she is not named as a party and does not participate as one. Rather, the party or parties who benefit from the district court's order under challenge are the real parties in interest. Petitioner is required, however, to serve a copy of the petition upon the district judge.

Because it is an original proceeding in the court of appeals, the rules of appellate procedure do not specify any time limit on the filing of a petition for an extraordinary writ. Nonetheless, in most cases it would be prudent to observe the thirty-day time limit for ordinary civil appeals; filing after a longer lapse of time may suggest that there is a lack of urgency to the petition. On the other hand, if the petition challenges the district judge's impartiality, that is not a matter that is cured or mitigated by the passage of time.

Rule 21(a)(2)(B) specifies that the petition must state (a) the relief sought, (b) the issues presented, (c) the facts necessary to understand the issue presented by the petition, and (d) the reasons why the writ should issue. Petitioner's burden is to establish that the order under review was not only wrong but of such a magnitude as to justify the intervention of the court of appeals by means of a writ of mandamus or prohibition. In this regard, the petition should emphasize the severity of the immediate harm and the lack of an effective remedy by appeal from final judgment.

An appendix should accompany the petition sought to be reviewed consisting of the order and any parts of the record "that may be essential to understand" the petition. If the petition is filed by a non-governmental corporate entity, Federal Rule of Appellate Procedure 26.1 also requires the contemporaneous filing of a corporate disclosure statement. Once filed, a petition takes precedence on the court's docket over ordinary civil cases.

B. *Respondent*

In many cases, the respondent will not be required to take any action at all because the petition will be denied summarily. If the court perceives some substance to the petition, it will usually require an answer before ruling. Traditionally, a respondent was required to show cause why the writ should not be granted. Rule 21(b) speaks simply of an answer, but in substance the same showing is required (i.e., reasons why the petition should be denied). Respondent's burden in this regard is less than petitioner's; respondent need not even show that the challenged order is correct, only that it is not so patently injurious as to justify relief by extraordinary writ. As a practical matter, however, it will usually be prudent to argue, first, that the order was correct and, second, that the stringent prerequisites for issuance of an extraordinary writ are lacking (e.g., the petitioner will have an adequate remedy by appeal from final judgment). The trial judge is not permitted to respond unless the court so orders. With or without his participation, a copy of the ruling on the writ must be provided to the trial judge.

C. *Petitioning in the Alternative*

As shown above, some orders may be reviewable by interlocutory appeal under section 1292(b) or as a collateral order under section 1291 as well as by extraordinary writ. In such a case, petitioning counsel ought to seek relief in the alternative. However, if the order is potentially reviewable by appeal, then it will be prudent to file a notice of appeal in the district court in addition to the petition for extraordinary writ in the circuit court. In such a case, appellate counsel should cross-reference the two proceedings in each set of documents. For example, the petition for writ of mandamus should forthrightly acknowledge that the party is also seeking relief by interlocutory appeal or collateral order appeal, supplying the appropriate docket numbers, because both methods of review appear to apply; counsel should state that he acts in good faith out of an abundance of caution to protect the rights of the party he represents and to avoid inadvertently defaulting on the appropriate remedy. The appellate court will appreciate the candor. Indeed, a court of appeals may itself guide appellate counsel who has chosen the incorrect remedy, as where the court of appeals treated a notice of appeal as an application for mandamus. On the other hand, it is not wise to rely on such generosity, and the lawyer who chooses the wrong remedy may be stuck with his error. It is better to keep all options open.

CONCLUSION: EVALUATING THE CLIENT'S NEEDS AND
DECIDING WHETHER TO FILE FOR A WRIT

As with all decisions to initiate legal action, the prospective petitioner must make an informed cost-benefit analysis. Factors to be considered include the likelihood of success, the importance of the relief sought to the future conduct of the case, and the costs to be incurred in litigating the writ.

Notes and Questions

1.   For another historical view of the extraordinary or prerogative writs see J. High, A Treatise on Extraordinary Legal Remedies (1874) and Jenks, The Prerogative Writs in English Law, 32 Yale L.J. 523 (1923).

2.   The procedure for filing a petition for a writ in a federal court of appeals is set forth in Federal Rule of Appellate Procedure 21. For a description of practice under this rule as well as in several states see R. Martineau, Modern Appellate Practice—Federal and State Civil Appeals § 19.8 (1983).

3.   A writ of mandamus is an order directing a public official to perform a duty exacted by law. An order prohibiting certain judicial action is termed a *writ of prohibition*—the obverse of mandamus—but there is no practical distinction in procedures dealing with them in appellate tribunals. In re Atlantic Pipe Corp., 304 F.3d 135, 138 n.1 (1st Cir. 2002). Mandamus can be "supervisory," "ordinarily appropriate [only] in those rare cases in which

the issuance (or nonissuance) of an order presents a question anent the limits of judicial power, poses some special risk of irreparable harm to the [petitioner], and is palpably erroneous." *See Glotzer v. Martha Stewart*, 374 F.3d 184 (2d Cir. 2004) (issuing writ of mandamus to vacate an order compelling compliance with a subpoena). Compare Cole v. United States District Court for the District of Idaho, 366 F.3d 813 (9th Cir. 2004) (declining to issue a writ of mandamus to correct a clear error because the petitioner did not pursue an available alternative remedy). Mandamus also can be "advisory," employed without a showing of irreparable harm "where a previously unaddressed question regarding the limits of judicial power anent a systemically important issue (one that is capable of significant repetition before other, effective review may be had) is presented." *Id.* at 139 and 140, n.8.

4. The Fifth Circuit accepts mandamus petitions to correct a denial of a 28 U.S.C. § 1404(a) motion to transfer venue "if the district court failed to correctly construe and apply the relevant statute, or to consider the relevant factors incident to ruling upon the motion, or otherwise abused its discretion in deciding the motion." *See, e.g.,* In re Volkswagen AG, 371 F.3d 201 (5th Cir. 2004). Are there policy reasons justifying carving out specific motions or procedures for greater access to mandamus review? Would you include denial of transfer motions among those warranting special rights of access to appellate review? Why?

5. If a court has before it both an appeal and a petition for mandamus, and the order is properly reviewable by way of appeal, the court must review the order through appeal rather than mandamus. *See* In re Kozeny, 236 F.3d 615, 618 (10th Cir. 2000).

6. Federal courts have no jurisdiction to issue a writ of mandamus to a state judge or a state court. Olson v. Hart, 965 F.2d 940, 942 (10th Cir. 1992).

ALLIED CHEMICAL CORP. v. DAIFLON, INC.

Supreme Court of the United States, 1980.
449 U.S. 33, 101 S.Ct. 188, 66 L.Ed.2d 193.

PER CURIAM.

Respondent, Daiflon, Inc., is a small importer of refrigerant gas that brought an antitrust suit against all domestic manufacturers of the gas. Petitioner E. I. du Pont de Nemours & Co. was accused of monopolizing the industry in violation of § 2 of the Sherman Act, 15 U.S.C. § 2. All petitioners were accused of conspiring to drive respondent out of business in violation of § 1 of the Sherman Act, 15 U.S.C. § 1.

After a 4–week trial, the jury returned a verdict for the respondent and awarded $2.5 million in damages. In a subsequent oral order, the trial court denied petitioners' motion for a judgment notwithstanding the verdict, but granted a motion for new trial. The trial court acknowledged in its oral order that it had erred during trial in certain of its evidentiary rulings and that the evidence did not support the amount of the jury award.

Respondent then filed a petition for a writ of mandamus with the Court of Appeals for the Tenth Circuit, 612 F.2d 1249, requesting that it instruct the trial court to reinstate the jury verdict. The Court of Appeals, without a transcript of the trial proceedings before it, issued a writ of mandamus directing the trial court to restore the jury verdict as to liability but permitting the trial court to proceed with a new trial on damages. Daiflon, Inc. v. Bohanon, 612 F.2d 1249. Petitioners seek review of this action of the Court of Appeals by their petition for certiorari with this Court.

An order granting a new trial is interlocutory in nature and therefore not immediately appealable. The question presented by this petition is therefore whether a litigant may obtain a review of an order concededly not appealable by way of mandamus. If such review were permissible then the additional question would be presented as to whether the facts in this particular case warrant the issuance of the writ.

It is not disputed that the remedy of mandamus is a drastic one, to be invoked only in extraordinary situations. On direct appeal from a *final* decision, a court of appeals has broad authority to "modify, vacate, set aside or reverse" an order of a district court, and it may direct such further action on remand "as may be just under the circumstances." 28 U.S.C. § 2106. By contrast, under the All Writs Act, 28 U.S.C. § 1651(a), courts of appeals may issue a writ of mandamus only when "necessary or appropriate in aid of their respective jurisdictions." Although a simple showing of error may suffice to obtain a reversal on direct appeal, to issue a writ of mandamus under such circumstances "would undermine the settled limitations upon the power of an appellate court to review interlocutory orders." Will v. United States, [389 U.S. 90, 98 n.6, 88 S.Ct. 269, 19 L.Ed.2d 305 (1967)].

This Court has recognized that the writ of mandamus "has traditionally been used in the federal courts only 'to confine an inferior court to a lawful exercise of its prescribed jurisdiction or to compel it to exercise its authority when it is its duty to do so.' " Will v. United States, supra, 389 U.S., at 95, 88 S.Ct., at 273, quoting Roche v. Evaporated Milk Assn., 319 U.S. 21, 26, 63 S.Ct. 938, 941, 87 L.Ed. 1185 (1943). Only exceptional circumstances, amounting to a judicial usurpation of power, will justify the invocation of this extraordinary remedy.

The reasons for this Court's chary authorization of mandamus as an extraordinary remedy have often been explained. Its use has the unfortunate consequence of making a district court judge a litigant, and it indisputably contributes to piecemeal appellate litigation. It has been Congress' determination since the Judiciary Act of 1789 that as a general rule appellate review should be postponed until after final judgment has been rendered by the trial court. A judicial readiness to issue the writ of mandamus in anything less than an extraordinary situation would "run the real risk of defeating the very policies sought to be furthered by that judgment of Congress." In order to insure that the writ will issue only in extraordinary circumstances this Court has required that a party seeking issuance have no other adequate means to attain the relief he desires, and that he satisfy the "burden of showing that [his] right to issuance of the writ is 'clear and indisputable.'" In short, our cases have answered the question as to the availability of mandamus in situations such as this with the refrain: "What never? Well, *hardly* ever!"

A trial court's ordering of a new trial rarely, if ever, will justify the issuance of a writ of mandamus. On the contrary, such an order is not an uncommon feature of any trial which goes to verdict. A litigant is free to seek review of the propriety of such an order on direct appeal after a final judgment has been entered. Consequently, it cannot be said that the litigant "has no other adequate means to seek the relief he desires." The authority to grant a new trial, moreover, is confided almost entirely to the exercise of discretion on the part of the trial court. Where a matter is committed to discretion, it cannot be said that a litigant's right to a particular result is "clear and indisputable." Will v. Calvert Fire Ins. Co., 437 U.S. 655, 666, 98 S.Ct. 2552, 2559, 57 L.Ed.2d 504 (1978) (plurality opinion).

To overturn an order granting a new trial by way of mandamus indisputably undermines the policy against piecemeal appellate review. Under the rationale employed by the Court of Appeals, any discretionary order, regardless of its interlocutory nature, may be subject to immediate judicial review. Such a rationale obviously encroaches on the conflicting policy against piecemeal review, and would leave that policy at the mercy of any court of appeals which chose to disregard it.[3]

The petition for a writ of certiorari is therefore granted, and the order of the Court of Appeals granting the writ of mandamus is

Reversed.

JUSTICE STEWART and JUSTICE STEVENS took no part in the consideration or decision of this case.

JUSTICE BLACKMUN, with whom JUSTICE WHITE joins, dissenting.

I have no quarrel with the general principles enunciated by the Court in its *per curiam* opinion. Of course, only exceptional circumstances justify the extraordinary remedy of mandamus. I sense, however, from the rather voluminous material that is before us (as contrasted with the average petition for certiorari), and from the Court of Appeals'

3. Even if it be appropriate in certain circumstances to use mandamus to review a discretionary order by a trial court, the new-trial order entered in this case would not appear to be a likely candidate. A trial judge is not required to enter supporting findings of facts and conclusions of law when granting a new-trial motion. See Fed. Rule Civ.Proc. 52(a). It cannot be contended with any certainty that the trial court in this case, when entering its oral order granting a new trial, intended to set forth each and every reason for its order. The trial court did note, however, that it had made errors in the admission of certain documentary evidence and that it felt the petitioners had not received a fair trial. Given that the Court of Appeals did not have a complete transcript of the proceedings before it, and that there could be other unarticulated bases for the new-trial order, it would seem all but impossible for the Court of Appeals to hold as a matter of law that the trial court clearly abused its discretion in entering the new-trial order.

careful review of the law and the decided cases concerning the use of the mandamus power, that this is an unusual case and that there well may be more here than appears at first glance. I therefore would not decide, peremptorily and summarily, what circumstances, if any, justify a federal appellate court's issuance of a writ of mandamus to overturn a trial court's order granting a new trial.* Instead, I would grant the petition for certiorari and give the case plenary consideration so that we may examine carefully the factors and considerations that prompted the Court of Appeals to issue the writ. I feel that the case deserves at least that much.

Notes and Questions

1. Federal appellate courts' use of writs of mandamus or prohibition to review orders or actions by district court not appealable under the final judgment rule or the exceptions to it [see Chapter 3, supra] has long been a matter of controversy. Several Supreme Court decisions, particularly La Buy v. Howes Leather Co., 352 U.S. 249, 77 S.Ct. 309, 1 L.Ed.2d 290 (1957) and Schlagenhauf v. Holder, 379 U.S. 104, 85 S.Ct. 234, 13 L.Ed.2d 152 (1964) led federal courts of appeals to use the writs as a general substitute for interlocutory appeal. See Note, Mandamus as a Means of Federal Interlocutory Review, 38 Ohio St.L.J. 301 (1977). Supreme Court decisions have been more restrictive. Will v. United States, 389 U.S. 90, 88 S.Ct. 269, 19 L.Ed.2d 305 (1967); Will v. Calvert Fire Ins. Co., 437 U.S. 655, 98 S.Ct. 2552, 57 L.Ed.2d 504 (1978); and Allied Chemical Corp. v. Daiflon, Inc., supra. For an excellent review of these cases that argues for a more extensive use of the writ, see Berger, The Mandamus Power of the United States Courts of Appeals: A Complex and Confused Means of Appellate Control, 31 Buffalo L.Rev. 37 (1982).

2. When interlocutory appeal becomes more available the demand for a supervisory writ as a substitute will be reduced. Has the Supreme Court, by its renewed insistence upon adherence to the final judgment rule and its restricting the availability of mandamus as an alternative, put an undue burden on litigants?

IN RE DALTON

United States Court of Appeals, Tenth Circuit, 1984.
733 F.2d 710.

WILLIAM E. DOYLE, CIRCUIT JUDGE.

Involved herein is an effort by Petitioner/Appellant Eugene Dalton to persuade this court to review two bankruptcy orders which were issued by the United States District Court for the District of Colorado (hereinafter, Colorado District Court). The first of these was issued March 8, 1983. It withdrew reference of the pending bankruptcy proceedings from the United States Bankruptcy Court for the District of

---

* To the extent that the Court's decision in this case is based upon the inadequacy of the record before the Court of Appeals, the proper remedy is to remand for further proceedings based upon a complete record.

Colorado (hereinafter, Colorado Bankruptcy Court). The second order, issued September 22, 1983, granted the motion of Respondents/Appellees United States of America and the Receiver (hereinafter the government) to transfer venue of the Dalton bankruptcy proceedings from the Colorado District Court to the United States District Court for the District of Arizona (hereinafter, Arizona District Court).

* * *

The basic issues in the case are whether this court lacks appellate jurisdiction to review the Colorado District Court's withdrawal of reference and transfer of venue orders, and if such jurisdiction is lacking, whether an extraordinary writ should issue.

[The court reviewed the applicable law and concluded that the orders were not reviewable under the *Cohen* exception to the final judgement rule.]

* * * Thus, if this court has jurisdiction to review the two orders which have been specified here of the Colorado District Court that jurisdiction lies exclusively in the issuance of an extraordinary writ. The appropriateness of the issuance of such writ in these facts must be now considered.

IV.   APPROPRIATENESS OF AN EXTRAORDINARY WRIT

A.   SUMMARY STATEMENT OF CONTENTIONS

We must now ask whether Dalton has succeeded in showing that his right to issuance of a writ of mandamus is clear and undisputable. Dalton contends that there is an alternative to appellate review of the withdrawal of reference and transfer of venue orders. He contends that review is available under the All Writs Act, 28 U.S.C. § 1651(a) and its implementing rule, Rule 21 of the Federal Rules of Appellate Procedure. Dalton principally argues that the Colorado District Court's order of transfer was entered without a hearing and is, therefore, appropriate for mandamus since it was violative of due process.

Dalton also offers another argument for review of the interlocutory orders, although he presents the argument in the context of appealability rather than review by mandamus. He asserts that the instant case is distinguishable from decisions holding transfer orders interlocutory and nonappealable, because here in addition to the transfer order two other appeals are currently pending and undecided: the Colorado Bankruptcy Court's withdrawal of reference order; and the Colorado Bankruptcy Court's Section 543 turnover order. These pending appeals will be extinguished when the case is transferred. Dalton contends that a party's appellate routes cannot be so easily destroyed and this court's appellate jurisdiction avoided by simply changing venue. Such an argument deriving jurisdiction to review an interlocutory order based on a concern to protect or preserve the reviewing court's jurisdiction is more properly an argument for an extraordinary writ and not for appellate jurisdiction. Because courts of appeal have long recognized that they may issue an appropriate writ in aid and preservation of both their then-existing and prospective jurisdiction over district courts, Dalton's argument for "protective review" will be considered in determining the appropriateness of mandamus.

B. APPLICABLE STANDARDS

It is well established and oft repeated that "mandamus is an extraordinary writ, and the requirements for its issuance are strict." United States v. Winner, 641 F.2d 825, 830–31 (10th Cir. 1981), quoting State Farm Mutual Auto Insurance v. Scholes, 601 F.2d 1151, 1154 (10th Cir. 1979). Courts have consistently held that while "a simple showing of error may suffice to obtain a reversal on direct appeal, to issue a writ of mandamus under such circumstances [for simple error] 'would undermine the settled limitations upon the power of an appellate court to review interlocutory orders.'" Allied Chemical Corp. v. Daiflon, Inc., 449 U.S. 33, 35, 101 S.Ct. 188, 190, 66 L.Ed.2d 193 (1980) (per curiam), *quoting* Will v. United States, 389 U.S. 90, 96, 88 S.Ct. 269, 274, 19 L.Ed.2d 305 (1967). Suffice it to add that issuance of writs of mandamus in aid of appellate jurisdiction has been limited strictly. It is limited to those exceptional cases where the inferior court acted wholly without jurisdiction or so clearly abused its discretion as to constitute usurpation of power. Moreover, in order to justify the invocation of this extraordinary remedy, the petitioning party has the burden of showing that its right to issuance of the writ is "clear and undisputable". *Winner,* supra, at 831; quoting Bankers Life & Casualty Company v. Holland, 346 U.S. 379, 74 S.Ct. 145, 98 L.Ed. 106 (1953).

C. STANDARDS APPLIED

We have stated previously that this court has long recognized mandamus to be an appropriate remedy to test the validity of a transfer order. Whether the standards for issuance of the writ are satisfied in this case must be determined.

Five specific guidelines have been formulated by courts of appeal for determining the propriety of mandamus relief in particular cases.

First, the party seeking the writ has no other adequate means to secure the relief desired. *Second,* the petitioning party will be damaged or prejudiced in a way not correctable on appeal. *Third,* the district court's order constitutes an abuse of discretion. The Ninth Circuit Court of Appeals has phrased this third guideline as whether the district court's order is "clearly erroneous as a matter of law." "Clearly erroneous" and "abuse of discretion" are often used interchangeably by courts, including the Ninth Circuit Court of Appeals. However, to avoid any confusion, we have phrased this third guideline in terms of abuse of discretion. *Fourth,* the district court's order represents an often repeated error and manifests a persistent disregard of federal rules. *Fifth,* the district court's order raises new and important problems or issues of law of the first impression. While these guidelines are not entirely conclusive, they are eminently reasonable and certainly provide a manageable framework for our determination.

The possibility of an appeal from the final judgment in the transferee circuit, even with the difficult burden of demonstrating prejudice there, will preclude relief by writ. The remedy of a future appeal from a final judgment in the transferee court is inadequate and therefore justifies mandamus only when the appeal is totally unavailable or when it cannot correct extraordinary hardship because of the particular circumstances. No such extraordinary hardship is alleged in this case. Dalton merely alleges that review now is necessary to preserve the two previously mentioned pending appeals.

Thus, the argument is for protective review. We must hold that it is insufficient to satisfy the first two guidelines mentioned above as standards to be considered for issuing an extraordinary writ. It is to be noted that the appeal in the Colorado District Court from the Colorado Bankruptcy Court's Section 543 turnover order was instituted by the government; its pendency cannot be used by Dalton to support the request for mandamus. Indeed, the government's appeal may properly be deemed withdrawn as a result of the government's motion for transfer of venue. Dalton may not now assert the protection of this court's appellate jurisdiction over an allegedly pending appeal which was withdrawn by the government as a basis for mandamus. So Dalton's contention in this respect is not persuasive.

Extinguishment of the pending appeal of the Colorado District Court's order withdrawing reference from the bankruptcy court is also inadequate to justify mandamus. Dalton concedes that "to be realistic the venue order must not be divorced from the withdrawal since together they effected a single scheme." Brief of Debtor/Petitioner, at 16. Because as already stated the extinguishment of the appeal to this court from the district court's transfer order is not sufficient to justify mandamus, the extinguishment of the appeal from the withdrawal of reference order, too, necessarily fails to justify mandamus.

This court has held that determining whether to transfer venue of an action lies within the formal discretion of the district court and its determination should not be rejected unless the court of appeals determines that there is a clear abuse of discretion. All of the relevant factors were considered and weighed by the district court on the motion for change of venue. We are not called on to engage in a balancing of completing factors which bear upon convenience and the interests of justice. It is not our function to substitute our judgment for that of the judge most familiar with the problem. The district court considered the applicable law in its transfer order and clearly set forth the reasons for granting the venue change. Dalton has failed to show that the district court abused its discretion. Accordingly, he failed to satisfy the third guideline for issuing a writ.

The fourth and fifth guidelines are intertwined somewhat and are subject to being considered together. The allegation is that mandamus is appropriate because the Colorado District Court violated Dalton's federal due process rights by transferring venue without convening a hearing. He cites the court's hospitality for considering petitions for mandamus in those cases where challenged transfer orders were entered without hearings. Even though this argument is not clearly articulated, Dalton is evidently contending that mandamus should issue under these circumstances because the allegation of denial of due process raises issues and problems of peculiar public importance involving disregard of federal rights. Superficially this contention appears to satisfy the fourth and fifth guidelines for the issuance of mandamus; however, Dalton misreads the decisions he cites in support of his argument.

The assertion is that several courts have held that mandamus is particularly appropriate to review orders issued without a hearing. A close reading of the cited decisions reveals that none of the courts of appeal has held that a district court's failure to hold a hearing on a motion to transfer venue constitutes an abuse of discretion reviewable by mandamus. The contrary is true; the decisions evidence the appellate courts' explicit refusal to hold that a hearing is necessarily required on every transfer motion. Rather, the decisions stand for the proposition that "the failure to provide notice and an opportunity to be heard to the party opposing transfer [constitutes] a violation of due process and [can] be remedied by granting a writ of mandamus to secure vacation of the transfer order."

From a review of the record it is plain that Dalton had extended to him a fair opportunity to be heard concerning his opposition to transfer. The government's motions for withdrawal of reference and transfer of venue were properly filed with notice to Dalton, and Dalton properly responded by filing substantial reply memoranda in opposition to the government's motions. Over seven months elapsed from the government's filing of its motion to withdraw reference to the Colorado District Court's transfer of venue to the Arizona District Court. The interim period involved an exchange of motions and memoranda between the parties and the court. There is no evidence that during that period Dalton requested oral argument or a hearing on any of the motions. Therefore, it is plain once again that Dalton's due process rights were not violated or even threatened by the issuance of the venue transfer order. Consequently, the fourth and fifth guidelines for issuance of a writ are not satisfied.

V. Conclusion

It is clear that the circumstances of the instant case are not so extraordinary as to warrant review by mandamus. Dalton is not irrevocably and prejudicially precluded from securing relief by other means. The district court's order does not constitute an abuse of discretion, nor does it manifest a disregard for federal rights and it does not raise important questions of first impression. Indications are that Dalton is searching for a court that has not had extensive exposure to his problems, and at the same time is seeking to avoid facing up to the ultimate decision. Finally, we are convinced that this court lacks appellate jurisdiction to review the district court's withdrawal of reference and transfer of venue orders, because neither order is a final order of the district court nor does either order satisfy the collateral order exception established in *Cohen,* supra.

Hence, the appeal must be dismissed. We conclude that Dalton has also failed to satisfy the requisite bases for an extraordinary writ, and the petition for an extraordinary writ must, therefore, be denied.

It is so ordered.

Notes and Questions

1. Does the *Dalton* case suggest an answer to Note 2 following the *Allied Chemical* case *supra?*

2. If the standards set forth in *Dalton* were applied to the facts in *Allied Chemical,* would it be decided the same way?

3. The relationship between the availability of interlocutory review and the need for supervisory writ is demonstrated by the experience in California and New York. In California, interlocutory review is not generally available so the use of mandamus is widespread. In New York, however, the situation is the opposite. R. Martineau, Modern Appellate Practice—Federal and State Civil Appeals §§ 19.4–19.5 (1983).

4. State courts have problems similar to federal courts in attempting to restrict the use of extraordinary writs. The failure of the Missouri Supreme Court to abide by its own limitations is detailed in Note, Prohibition in Missouri: Prodigal Writ or Ad Hoc Remedy?, 53 U.Missouri–Kansas City L.Rev. 311 (1985).

5. In many states, the supreme court is given express authority in the constitution to issue the prerogative or extraordinary writs. For example, Article IV § 11(6) authorizes the Delaware Supreme Court to issue "writs of prohibition, quo warranto, certiorari, and mandamus." Some supreme courts use this as the basis for taking original jurisdiction to hear cases of great public importance. See, for example, In re Exercise of Original Jurisdiction, 201 Wis. 123, 229 N.W. 643 (1930) and Petition of Heil, 230 Wis. 428, 284 N.W. 42 (1938). This type of case is one that could have been filed in a court of general jurisdiction, but because of the statewide importance of the issues involved and the need for a prompt decision, the lower courts were bypassed and the complaint was filed directly in the supreme court. For a discussion of the use of their power in Ohio, see Herbert, Obtaining Certification in the Supreme Court of Ohio: Cases of Public or Great General Interest, 18 Western Reserve L.Rev. 32 (1966).

INHERENT SUPERVISORY POWER
UNITED STATES v. HORN

United States Court of Appeals, First Circuit, 1994.
29 F.3d 754.

SELYA, CIRCUIT JUDGE.

We decide today a question of first impression: Do principles of sovereign immunity bar a federal district court, exercising its supervisory power, from assessing attorneys' fees and costs against the federal government in a criminal case? We answer this question affirmatively and, therefore, annul the district court's fee-shifting orders.

1. FACTUAL BACKGROUND

This appeal arises out of unpardonable misconduct committed by a federal prosecutor who should have known better. The factual background of the criminal case in which the misconduct occurred—a multi-defendant prosecution for, *inter alia,* conspiracy to defraud a federally insured financial institution—is memorialized in a recent opinion of this court. *See* United States v. Lacroix, 28 F.3d 223, 225–226 (1st Cir. 1994). The facts pertaining to the misconduct are recounted in the opinion below. *See* United States v. Horn, 811 F.Supp. 739, 741–44, 748–51 (D.N.H.1992). For purposes of deciding the abstract question of law that confronts us today, we largely omit the former set of facts, and limn the latter in less than exegetic detail.

The court referred the lead prosecutor to the disciplinary committees of her two bar associations, and, in the portion of its order that sparked the current controversy, the court directed the government to pay the fees and costs incurred by the defendants in litigating the misconduct issue. See id. Although the court's original order was inexplicit concerning the source of its authority to assess fees and costs, the court, in denying the government's motion to reconsider, explained that it grounded this sanction in the judiciary's supervisory power. See id. at 753–54.

Zsofka, Lee, and Lacroix stood trial early in 1993. They were each convicted on at least one count, and were sentenced in July. On August 18, 1993, the district court quantified its earlier order, assessing a grand total of $46,477.80 in fees and costs. The other sanctions have been carried out and the defense no longer presses the claim that the district court should have dismissed the indictment. Hence, all that remains of the case is the government's appeal from the assessment of fees.

The government contests the award chiefly on the ground that it is prohibited by principles of sovereign immunity. Extracted from its complicated factual predicate, drained of rancor, and separated from other, essentially extraneous disputes, this appeal requires us to serve as the dispatcher at a crossing where two powerful engines—the judiciary's supervisory power and the government's sovereign immunity—are on a collision course.

II. Doctrinal Background

In ascertaining what happens when doctrines clash, derivation frequently becomes important. Thus, we turn to this task.

A. Supervisory Power.

Supervisory power, sometimes known as inherent power, encompasses those powers which, though "not specifically required by the Constitution or the Congress," United States v. Hasting, 461 U.S. 499, 505, 103 S.Ct. 1974, 1978, 76 L.Ed.2d 96 (1983), are nonetheless "necessary to the exercise of all others," Roadway Express, Inc. v. Piper, 447 U.S. 752, 764, 100 S.Ct. 2455, 2463, 65 L.Ed.2d 488 (1980) (quoting United States v. Hudson, 11 U.S. (7 Cranch) 32, 34, 3 L.Ed. 259 (1812)). *See generally* United States v. Santana, 6 F.3d 1, 9–10 (1st Cir. 1993).

Although the doctrine's ancestry can be traced to the early days of the Republic, *see, e.g., Hudson,* 11 U.S. at 34; *see also* Ex parte Robinson, 86 U.S. (19 Wall.) 505, 510, 22 L.Ed. 205 (1873) (observing that the "moment the courts of the United States were called into existence ... they became possessed of [inherent] power"), a full-scale genealogical dig would serve no useful purpose. It suffices to say that the doctrine emerged in modern form roughly a half-century ago, *see* McNabb v. United States, 318 U.S. 332, 341, 63 S.Ct. 608, 613, 87 L.Ed. 819 (1943), and it has since developed most robustly in the area of criminal procedure, *see* Sara Sun Beale, Reconsidering Supervisory Power in Criminal Cases, 84 Colum.L.Rev. 1433, 1435–64 (1984). While supervisory power is sometimes understood to derive from the Constitution, either as incidental to the Article III grant of judicial power, *see id.* at 1464–83, or as implicit in the separation of powers, *see* Eash v. Riggins Trucking, Inc., 757 F.2d 557, 562 (3d Cir. 1985), the Court has made it clear that, at least as a general proposition, Congress may limit the power of lower federal courts by rule or statute, *see* Chambers v. NASCO, Inc., 501 U.S. 32, 47, 111 S.Ct. 2123, 2134, 115 L.Ed.2d 27 (1991).

In what is not necessarily an exhaustive listing, the Court has recognized three purposes to which the supervisory power may be dedicated: "to implement a remedy for violation of recognized rights, to preserve judicial integrity ... and ... as a remedy designed to deter illegal conduct." *Hasting,* 461 U.S. at 505, 103 S.Ct. at 1978 (internal citations omitted). Invoking this third theme, we have warned that we will consider unleashing the supervisory power in criminal cases "[w]hen confronted with extreme misconduct and prejudice," in order "to secure enforcement of 'better prosecutorial practice and reprimand of those who fail to observe it.' "United States v. Osorio, 929 F.2d 753, 763 (1st Cir. 1991) (quoting United States v. Pacheco–Ortiz, 889 F.2d 301, 310–11 (1st Cir. 1989)).

The supervisory power has definite limits. *See Hasting,* 461 U.S. at 505, 103 S.Ct. at 1978. For one thing, the supervisory power doctrine is interstitial in the sense that it applies only when there is no effective alternative provided by rule, statute, or constitutional clause. *See Chambers,* 501 U.S. at 50–51, 111 S.Ct. at 2135–36. For another thing, even when inherent powers legitimately can be invoked, they must be exercised with restraint and circumspection, both "because [they] are shielded from direct democratic controls," *Roadway Express,* 447 U.S. at 764, 100 S.Ct. at 2463, and "[b]ecause of their very potency," *Chambers,* 501 U.S. at 44, 111 S.Ct. at 2132.

In particular, it is inappropriate for courts to attempt to use the supervisory power to justify an extreme remedy when, short of such heroic measures, the means are at hand to construct a satisfactory anodyne more narrowly tailored to the objective. *See Hasting,* 461 U.S. at 506, 103 S.Ct. at 1979 (overturning use of supervisory power to deter prosecutorial misconduct through reversal of conviction). It is equally inappropriate for a court to gear up the supervisory power in an effort to circumvent a limitation firmly established under conventional doctrine. *See* Bank of Nova Scotia v. United States, 487 U.S. 250, 254–55, 108 S.Ct. 2369, 2373–74, 101 L.Ed.2d 228 (1988) (overturning use of supervisory power to evade the harmless error inquiry); United States v. Payner, 447 U.S. 727, 735–36, 100 S.Ct. 2439, 2446–47, 65 L.Ed.2d 468 (1980) (overturning use of supervisory power to craft a new exclusionary rule designed to reach situations in which the constitutional exclusionary rule is not triggered). Illustrating the same point, this court has ruled it inappropriate to use the supervisory power to redress misconduct that did not result in harm, *see Santana,* 6 F.3d at 11 (citing cases), or that resulted in harm to someone other than the complaining defendants, *see id.*

It has been squarely held that a court's array of supervisory powers includes the power to assess attorneys' fees against either parties or their attorneys in befitting situations. *See Roadway Express,* 447 U.S. at 764–67, 100 S.Ct. at 2463–65; In re Cordova Gonzalez, 726 F.2d 16, 20 (1st Cir. 1984). The Court recently reaffirmed this rule, *see Chambers,* 501 U.S. at 49, 111 S.Ct. at 2135, and clarified its contours. While a court may invoke its supervisory power to assess fees only when the fees are intended as a sanction responding to a display of bad faith, the bad faith may occur in connection with "a full range of litigation abuses." *Id.* at 46, 111 S.Ct. at 2134. Moreover, even though a particular abuse is covered by a specific statute or rule, a court still may invoke its supervisory power to address the abuse if the existing remedial provision is inadequate to the task. *Id.* at 50–51, 111 S.Ct. at 2135–36.

B. *Sovereign Immunity*

The principle of sovereign immunity, in its primary form, dictates that the United States may not be sued except with its consent. This tenet was first stated, *ipse dixit,* by Chief Justice Marshall in Cohens v. Virginia, 19 U.S. (6 Wheat.) 264, 411–12, 5 L.Ed. 257 (1821) (dictum). It has been reaffirmed as recently as this past term. *See* FDIC v. Meyer, 510 U.S. 471,——, 114 S.Ct. 996, 1000, 127 L.Ed.2d 308 (1994); *see also* Gonsalves v. IRS, 975 F.2d 13, 16 (1st Cir. 1992) (per curiam).

The secondary principle that monetary penalties cannot be collected from the federal government absent its consent was first articulated, in the narrow context of an assessment for costs, in United States v. Hooe, 7 U.S. (3 Cranch) 73, 90–91, 2 L.Ed. 370 (1805). However, the *Hooe* Court made no explicit reference to sovereign immunity, and it was not until four decades later that the two principles formally converged, *see* United States v. McLemore, 45 U.S. (4 How.) 286, 287–88, 11 L.Ed. 977 (1846). They have been taken in tandem ever since in cases involving costs. *See, e.g.,* United States v. Bodcaw, 440 U.S. 202, 203–04 n. 3, 99 S.Ct. 1066, 1067 n. 3, 59 L.Ed.2d 257 (1979) (per curiam); Fairmont Creamery Co. v. Minnesota, 275 U.S. 70, 73–74, 48 S.Ct. 97, 98–99, 72 L.Ed. 168 (1927); United States v. Chemical Found., Inc., 272 U.S. 1, 20, 47 S.Ct. 1, 8, 71 L.Ed. 131 (1926); Shewan v. United States, 267 U.S. 86, 87, 45 S.Ct. 238, 238–39, 69 L.Ed. 527 (1925).

V.   CONCLUSION

Having satisfied ourselves that appellate jurisdiction inheres, we now recapitulate. We agree with the lower court that the government committed egregious acts of prosecutorial misconduct. We do not believe, however, that the court had the right to ignore sovereign immunity in responding to that misconduct. The court's supervisory power, although potent, cannot intrude, unaided, into the sovereign's protected preserves.

We need go no further. Because principles of sovereign immunity bar a federal court from invoking its supervisory power to compel the federal government to pay attorneys' fees and costs as a sanction for prosecutorial misconduct in a criminal case, we reverse the orders of the district court insofar as they purport to shift such fees and costs. All parties shall bear their own costs in this court.

Reversed. No costs.

FRAZIER v. HEEBE

Supreme Court of the United States, 1987.
482 U.S. 641, 107 S.Ct. 2607, 96 L.Ed.2d 557.

JUSTICE BRENNAN delivered the opinion of the Court.

The question for decision is whether a United States District Court may require that applicants for general admission to its bar either reside or maintain an office in the State where that court sits.

Petitioner David Frazier is an attorney having both his residence and his law office in Pascagoula, Mississippi. An experienced litigator, he is a member of the Mississippi and Louisiana State Bars, and also of the Bars of the United States Courts of Appeals for the Fifth and Eleventh Circuits and the United States District Court for the Southern District of

Mississippi. In April 1982, Frazier applied for admission to the Bar of the United States District Court for the Eastern District of Louisiana. His application was denied because he neither lived nor had an office in Louisiana, as required by the court's local Rule 21.2. In addition, Frazier was ineligible for admission under the court's local Rule 21.3.1, which requires continuous and uninterrupted Louisiana residence or maintenance of a Louisiana law office for continuing eligibility in that bar.

Frazier challenged these District Court Rules by petitioning for a writ of prohibition from the Court of Appeals for the Fifth Circuit. The petition alleged that the restrictions in Rules 21.2 and 21.3.1 were unconstitutional, on their face and as applied to him. The Court of Appeals did not rule on the petition, but remanded the case to the District Court for the Eastern District for appropriate proceedings and entry of an appealable judgment. All the judges of the Eastern District recused themselves. The matter was assigned to Judge Edwin Hunter, a Senior Judge of the Western District of Louisiana. The District Court held a 1–day bench trial in which two District Court Judges, two Magistrates, and the Clerk of the Eastern District testified in support of the challenged Rules.

Frazier challenged the District Court Rules on several constitutional grounds, primarily under the equal protection requirement of the Due Process Clause of the Fifth Amendment. Applying the standard of intermediate scrutiny, the District Court upheld Rule 21.2 as constitutional. 594 F.Supp. 1173, 1179 (1984).

The District Court found that the Rule serves the important Government objective of the efficient administration of justice. It relied on testimony by court officials that proximity to the New Orleans courthouse is important when emergencies arise during proceedings, and that participation by nonresident attorneys complicates the scheduling of routine court matters. The court also found that the office requirement is not unduly restrictive and that it increases the availability of an attorney to the court. Finally, it stated the failure to require in-state attorneys to open a local office was reasonable, since such attorneys "must of necessity open an office," and, even absent an office, an in-state attorney is likely to be available. Without further explanation, the court declared that the in-state attorney's admission to the bar "does not raise the same concern for the efficient administration of justice that admission of nonresident attorneys does." After reviewing petitioner's other claims, the District Court denied Frazier's petition for extraordinary relief and dismissed his suit.

The Court of Appeals affirmed over a dissent. 788 F.2d 1049 (1986). The court found that the discrimination at issue did not warrant heightened scrutiny, and held that the exclusion was rationally related to the District Court's goal of promoting lawyer competence and availability for hearings. It characterized the testimony before the District Court as "of one voice: lawyers admitted pro hac vice, who neither reside nor maintain an office in Louisiana, fail to comply with the local rules and impede the efficient administration of justice more than members of the bar of the Eastern District." The court also noted that out-of-state attorneys were not unduly disadvantaged by this restriction, since they could affiliate with Louisiana counsel and appear pro hac vice. Finally, the court denied petitioner's alternative request to invalidate these Rules through use of the Court of Appeals' supervisory power over District Courts in that Circuit. The court expressed its reluctance to exercise its supervisory authority because the Fifth Circuit Judicial Council was at that time reviewing the local Rules of the District Courts in the Circuit.

We granted certiorari, and now reverse. Pursuant to our supervisory authority, we hold that the District Court was not empowered to adopt its local Rules to require members of the Louisiana Bar who apply for admission to its bar to live in, or maintain an office in, Louisiana where that court sits. We therefore need not address the constitutional questions presented.

We begin our analysis by recognizing that a district court has discretion to adopt local rules that are necessary to carry out the conduct of its business. *See* 28 U.S.C. §§ 1654, 2071; Fed.Rule Civ. Proc. 83. This authority includes the regulation of admissions to its own bar. A district court's discretion in promulgating local rules is not, however, without limits. This Court may exercise its inherent supervisory power to ensure that these local rules are consistent with " 'the principles of right and justice.' " ... Section 2071 requires that local rules of a district court "shall be consistent with" the "rules of practice and procedure prescribed by the Supreme Court." Today we invoke our supervisory authority to prohibit arbitrary discrimination against members of the Louisiana Bar, residing and having their office out-of-state, who are otherwise qualified to join the Bar of the Eastern District.

In the present case, our attention is focused on the requirements imposed by Rule 21.2 of the Eastern District of Louisiana, namely that, to be admitted to the bar, an attorney must reside or maintain an office in Louisiana. Respondents assert that these requirements facilitate the efficient administration of justice, because nonresident attorneys allegedly are less competent and less available to the court than resident attorneys. We disagree. We find both requirements to be unnecessary and irrational. . . .

Notes and Questions

1. The *Horn* case notes that, unlike the power to issue extraordinary writs which is expressly authorized by a statute and implemented by court rules, the supervisory power of the United States Supreme Court is considered to be either incidental to the grant of judicial power in Article III or implicit in the separation of powers. The same doctrine applies by analogy to the highest courts in each state.

2. In *Horn*, it is also noted that inherent supervisory power must be exercised with restraint and circumspection "only when there is no effective alternative provided by rule, statute, or constitutional clause." Why was the

doctrine invoked in *Marshall* and *Frazier*? What other circumstances might give rise to the use of inherent supervisory power?

3. Unlike extraordinary writs, inherent supervisory power is not a basis for invoking the jurisdiction of the United States Supreme Court or a state's highest court. Rather, it is a basis for seeking relief after the jurisdiction of the court has been properly invoked.

Index

References are to Pages

†